SPAIN

KT-194-442

Tom Burns

Series Editor
Erica Witschey

Assistant Editor
Hawys Pritchard

Everything Under the Sun Travel Guide Series
Other Titles in the Series: Barcelona, Benidorm, Cáceres, Calvià (Majorca),
Córdoba, Granada, Ibiza, Las Palmas (Canary Islands), Lloret de Mar
(Costa Brava), Madrid, Marbella, Maspalomas (Canary Islands), Palma
(Majorca), Puerto de la Cruz (Canary Islands), Salamanca, Salou (Costa
Dorada), Santiago de Compostela, Seville, Sitges (Costa Dorada), Toledo
and Torremolinos

First published in Great Britain 1988
by HARRAP COLUMBUS
19-23 Ludgate Hill, London EC4M 7PD

First published in Spain 1988
by NOVATEX EDICIONES S.A.
Explanada, 16, 28040 Madrid

First published in the United States 1988
by NATIONAL TEXTBOOK COMPANY
4255 West Touhy Avenue, Lincolnwood, IL 60646

Assistant Editor: Hawys Pritchard
Cartography: Instituto Nacional de Promoción del Turismo
Collaborator: Lettice Small
Cover Design: Jill Raphaeline
Cover Logo: Joan Miró
Field Research: Novatex research team, with the collaboration of Evelyn
Ezra, Paul Harsh, Victoria Hughes, Carlos Pascual, María Perpiñá, Llum
Quiñonero, Lettice Small and María Unceta
Layout: Novatex layout team
Maps: Luis Miguel Pulgar
Photographs: Archives of the Instituto Nacional de Promoción del Turismo, P.
Aparisi, A. Camoyán, L. Carré, J. Dieuzaide, J.L.G. Grande, R.G. López
Alonso, F. Ontañón, C. Pérez Siquier and A. Schommer
Senior Series Writer: Tom Burns
Series Editor: Erica Witschey

Colour Separation and Reproduction: Progreso Gráfico, S.A., Madrid
Electronic Editing: Begoña Cano, Ana de Dompablo and José Luis Medina,
software and interface by Protec, S.A., Madrid
Printed by: Gráficas Enar, S.A., Madrid
Typeset at: Pérez Díaz, S.A., Madrid

ISBN 0-7471-0077-2
D.L. M-26654-88

Printed in Spain

Some 53 million people visit Spain every year according to the latest count. If you form part of the nearly 40 million of these who come to spend their holidays, then this book is for you, for it aims to give as much information about Spain as can be bound between the covers of a pocket book.

For millions who annually arrive in the country, Spain remains, in many ways, an unknown entity. Familiarity may not breed contempt but it can induce a certain degree of ignorance especially among those who rapidly assume they know it all. In addition Spain has traditionally been packaged with stereotype images and, consequently, is prey to preconceived notions.

The essential point about Spain is a very simple one: it is more varied than you could imagine, for there is not one Spain, there are many. In part this is because it is a large country but more importantly it is because Spain's rugged mountain ranges have preserved the distinctiveness of its separate communities. Andalusia is one aspect of Spain and Catalonia is another. If you trace a straight line from the NW to the SE you pass from the humid, Celtic Galicia to the arid, austere central tableland and end up immersed in the Mediterranean culture of Levante.

You will find contrasts at every turn. It is not just the climate and the vegetation that change. It is the regional accents and the local languages that Spaniards speak and their bearing and approach to life. It is the houses they live in, the way they organize their *fiestas*, sing and dance, their artisan tradition, how they prepare their food and the wine they produce.

Spain suggests clichés like a patchwork and a melting pot of cultures and they are no less true for being hackneyed. Spain is, after all, a crossroads. It embraces the Mediterranean and the Atlantic and it is the meeting point of Europe, Africa and the New World.

From the earliest inhabitants who painted bison on the cold rock faces of the Altamira Caves, Spaniards have been shaping a rich tableau of culture and of history. There are more Roman remains in Spain than anywhere else outside Italy for Spain was for 500 years a jewel of the Roman empire. Islam left more traces in Spain than anywhere else in Europe for the Arab presence on the Peninsula lasted 800 years.

Old Spain, an empire that once was, is innumerable castles and great cathedrals and monasteries. It is the indomitable spirit of the conquistadors and it is mysticism and spirituality. Don Quixote had a mix of the two. His companion, Sancho Panza, had the call-a-spade-a-spade wisdom of an ancient people that is solidly rooted to the earth and he, also, is Spain.

The Spanish tableau has cultural climaxes that run from El Greco and Velázquez to Picasso and Miró by way of the towering genius of Goya. Spaniards have always been able to paint. In poetry and theatre, the creativity of García Lorca's genius mirrored a Golden Age of drama and lyricism. Historically Spain has more than its fair share of triumphs and disasters.

Now, particularly now, Spain is at peace with itself; courteous and hospitable, proud and caring about its past and confident about its future. Spain is as diverse and as vibrant as it ever was. It is also, emphatically, a young society, easy-going, fun-loving and tolerant.

It is said, truthfully, that Spain is a country in which no man is a stranger. But Spain can appear strange to many who cross its frontiers, armed with curiosity, and begin to explore its highways and byways. This book is especially for those who, venturing beyond their chosen resorts, are willing to cross the sound barrier of the stereotype.

Puerto Banús... a symphony in blue and white.

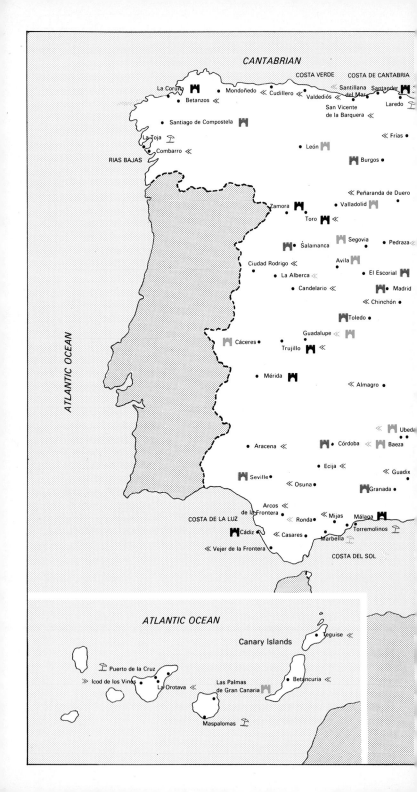

BAY OF BISCAY
COSTA VASCA

Fuenterrabía
San Sebastián
Vitoria • Pamplona
Estella • Puente la Reina
Olite • • Sos del Rey Católico Tahúll
La Seo de Urgel Cadaqués
COSTA BRAVA
Huesca S'Agaro
Gerona Tossa de Mar
Lloret de Mar
Soria • Zaragoza • Lérida
Montblanc • Barcelona
Sigüenza • Daroca Sitges
Salou • Tarragona
Morella •
Albarracín • Peñiscola
Teruel COSTA DEL AZAHAR Puerto
Cuenca de Pollensa Ciudadela
Deia Formentor
Belmonte Peguera Palma de Mallorca
Santa Ponsa Cala d'Or
Valencia •
Ibiza Balearic Islands
Guadalest •
Benidorm •
Alicante
Elche • COSTA BLANCA
Murcia • MEDITERRANEAN
Cazorla COSTA CALIDA
Almería • Mojácar

A SELECTION OF SPAIN'S HISTORIC CITIES,
BEACH RESORTS AND PICTURESQUE VILLAGES

Picturesque village
≪ Rating

≪ Rating

≪ Rating

Historic cities
Rating

Rating

Rating

Beach resort
Rating

Rating

Rating

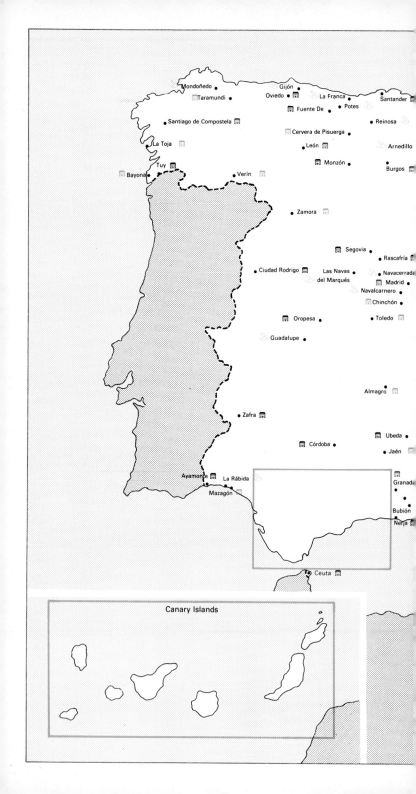

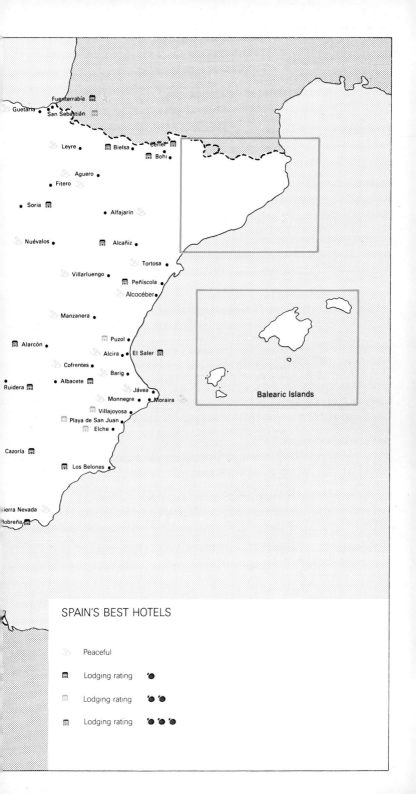

SPAIN'S BEST HOTELS

🌿 Peaceful

🏨 Lodging rating '●

🏨 Lodging rating '● '●

🏨 Lodging rating '● '● '●

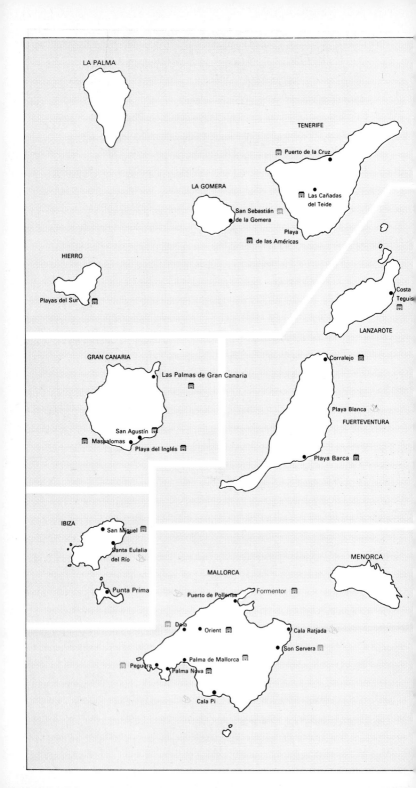

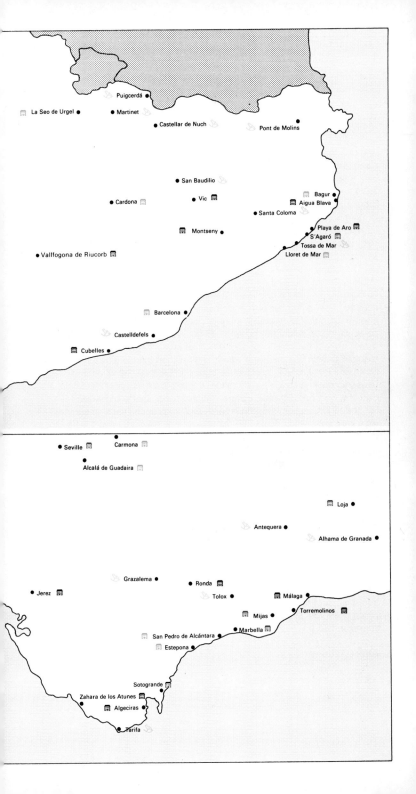

HOW TO USE THIS GUIDE

This guidebook offers you **everything** that is **under the sun** in Spain and everything that is under its moon and stars as well because it is a several guidebooks-in-one guide. Our aim has been to tell you just about everything you can possibly need to know or want to know about the most interesting places in Spain, be they historic towns, holiday resorts or national parks. We list places to stay and also itineraries; we suggest places at which to eat and describe the local cuisine; we detail monuments and museums and fill you in on Spain's history, art and culture; we inform you about local *fiestas* and where to be when. From *tapa* bars to sports clubs, from discos to hidden away artisan workshops this book, with its maps and city plans, tells you more about Spain than any other single guidebook to the country.

We have organized the guide into five separate parts: following the introduction there is a section covering basic facts about Spain; the second part consists of maps and the third is a bird's eye view of Spain; the fourth part is a guide to towns and places and the fifth is a general index.

The **Maps** section has the detailed information you require for travelling through Spain. The **Bird's Eye View of Spain** section is a novelty in the guidebook genre because what it does is give you a complete picture of the country under a number of specific headings. Conventional guidebooks take it for granted that the traveller already knows what interests him about a particular place and where he wants to go. We decided, however, that an overall view of the country and a number of broad suggestions are also required to help you plan your travels. This section therefore treats aspects of Spain at a general level in order, as it were, to separate the wood from the trees. We deal here with a wide range of topics such as accommodation, art, beaches, best buys, cuisine, culture, national parks, sports and wines.

The fourth section is **Spain from A to Z**, a guide to towns and places. Here we have divided Spain into regions such as Andalusia and the Balearics; this generally, though not invariably, follows the administrative framework of Spain's Autonomous Communities. Each region has an introduction and then its cities, towns and areas, such as national parks or stretches of coast, are listed in alphabetical order framed by a blue band like the one which opens this page. After each particular place name you will see the name of the province to which it belongs. Each entry heading then gives certain basic data in the following order: ☎ = the provincial telephone code (if you are dialling from outside Spain omit the initial 9); the population; ℹ = the local tourism office; ☏ = the local telephone exchange; ✉ = the local post office; ✚ = the local red cross station; **P** = the local police station; ✈ = the nearest airport; ⛴ = boat services; 🚂 = the railway station; 🚌 = the local bus station; and distances to other towns and cities. Each entry contains detailed information about the particular place under a number of headings that range from best buys to sports. Finally, the fifth section is the **Alphabetical Index** which gives you all the relevant page references to places, national parks, coasts and so on.

Abbreviations

The guide uses common abbreviations for compass directions, weights and measures. When addresses are given, the abbreviation *c/* means *calle*, or street; avenue, *avenida*, is *Av*; highway, *carretera*, is *Ctra*; housing development, urbanización, is *Urb*; square, *plaza*, is *Pl* and building, *edificio*, is *Edif*. When an address does not have a street number, it is usually marked *s/n* for *sin número*.

Highlighted Text and Classifications

Throughout this book you will find words, complete sentences and names of famous local personalities which are highlighted. The guide has four grades of highlighting. The first, in **black**, indicates anything that is interesting for one reason or another. The second, third, and fourth levels are designated by one, two and three **Miró suns**, which appear alongside the text beside an item highlighted in black. The three grades indicate: ✹ : Noteworthy; ✹✹ : Outstanding; and ✹✹✹ : Excellent.

Prices and Symbols

Generally speaking, this guide does not give prices since they become outdated so quickly. Instead guidelines are given using price symbols that range from $ to $$$$$$.

Hotel guidelines:
$: up to 2,200 pesetas
$$: from 2,250 to 4,500 pesetas
$$$: from 4,550 to 6,950 pesetas
$$$$: from 7,000 to 10,000 pesetas
$$$$$: from 10,050 to 15,000 pesetas
$$$$$$: more than 15,050 pesetas

Restaurant guidelines:
$: up to 850 pesetas
$$: from 900 to 1,650 pesetas
$$$: from 1,700 to 3,450 pesetas
$$$$: from 3,500 to 5,250 pesetas
$$$$$: more than 5,300 pesetas

Symbols are also used to represent the grading and facilities of hotels and restaurants.

★	category	≪	view
✹	rating	🐎	children's playground
☎	telephone	⇄	waterskiing
⊨	number of rooms	⬧	sailing
✕	hotel restaurant	▲	windsurfing
Ⴘ	hotel bar	ⵕ	tennis
⚕	access and facilities for the handicapped	⁄	golf
[TV]	television	🐴	horseback riding
(	room phone	⌐	fishing
P	parking	⊠	hunting
✦	gardens or terrace	AE	American Express
⬚	meeting rooms	CB	Carte Blanche
⬎	quiet/peaceful place	DC	Diners Club
⚓	swimming pool	EC	Euro Card
⚑	beach	MC	Mastercard
♫	discotheque	V	Visa
▦	sauna/workout facilities	$	cost of a double room or a three-course meal

Up-dating the Guide

The book that you are holding in your hands contains more information than any other of its type. It is the work of a team of professionals and is as up-to-date and accurate as possible at the time of going to press. Should you come across any erroneous or outdated information, or should you wish to contribute additional information, **help us to help you** in the next edition. Please send any information or suggestions you have to: Novatex ediciones, s.a., c/ Explanada, 16, 28040 Madrid, Spain.

Spain occupies the greater part of the Iberian Peninsula in the **SW of Europe**. It has an Atlantic coastline on the N, NW and SW, a Mediterranean one on the E and SE, and land frontiers with France in the N and Portugal in the W. The southernmost tip of peninsular Spain faces Morocco and looks onto the Straits of Gibraltar that link the Atlantic Ocean with the Mediterranean Sea. In addition to the Peninsula, the Kingdom of Spain comprises the Balearic Islands in the Mediterranean, which lie between 80 and 250km E of the coast of Valencia; the Canary Islands in the Atlantic, which lie near the Tropic of Cancer 1,100km SW of the Peninsula and 115km, at their nearest point, from the African mainland; and the enclave towns of Ceuta, on the Straits of Gibraltar, and Melilla, which are situated on Morocco's Mediterranean shore. There are in addition a large number of small islands scattered about the western end of the Mediterranean.

The paramount feature of Spain is that it is a land of **contrasts**. Rather more than half the wild flowers to be found in Europe grow naturally in Spain, which gives you an idea of the extreme variety and **diversity** of the country. It is the second largest European nation in terms of space (Spain's **504,782km²** put it immediately after France) and it is the most **mountainous** after Switzerland. Its **climate** and vegetation range widely; the NW corner of peninsular Spain resembles Ireland and parts of the SE are semi-desert. With **39,000,000 inhabitants**, Spain is the fifth most populous country in Europe after West Germany, Great Britain, France and Italy. But Spain comes well down the list in terms of population density for it has just 77 inhabitants per square kilometre —great tracts of the inland Peninsula are barely inhabited.

Spain joined the European Economic Community (**EEC**) in 1986 and it is also a member of the Organization for Economic Co-operation and Development (**OECD**). Its gross national product, mixing industry, agriculture and services, ranks tenth in the world economy. It became a member of the North Atlantic Treaty Organization (**NATO**) in 1982 and was invited to join the Western European Union in 1988.

Under the terms of its 1978 constitution Spain is a constitutional monarchy. **King Juan Carlos I** is Head of State and **Parliament,** the *Cortes,* has two chambers, a congress and a senate, which are elected every four years under a system of proportional representation.

MADRID is the capital of Spain but the state administration is organized according to a quasi-federal framework of 17 Autonomous Communities, known as the ***Comunidades Autónomas***. Each community has its own executive and legislature which is likewise elected every four years. Spain is a **non-confessional state** and freedom of religion is enshrined in the constitution. Catholicism is, at least nominally, the national religion.

Climate

Climatically speaking, Spain is one of the most privileged areas in the world. The general rule, although not a very exact one, is that the N is wetter and the S sunnier, and that the climate is more extreme in the interior and more benign on the coast. The Cantabrian coastline, in the N, is the most humid and the SE province of Almería is the driest. On the whole the climate in Spain is **temperate** but it can vary enormously and it is this that accounts for the great contrasts that are to be found in the country.

Broadly speaking there is a **humid Spain**, a continental Spain and a Mediterranean Spain. The first of these stretches from Galicia, in the NW corner of the Peninsula, along the Cantabrian coastline of Asturias, Cantabria and the Basque Country, and then along the Pyrenees that separate Spain from France, through the regions of Navarre, Aragón and Catalonia. The land is green here and the rainfall, brought in by the Atlantic, ranges between 900-2,000mm a year. Temperatures are not extreme although in winter there are heavy snowfalls where the mountain ranges rise above 1,200m.

The plateau area of central Spain, called the Meseta, and the Ebro river valley enjoy a **continental climate**. The annual rainfall is around 500mm rising to 600mm in Extremadura, along the Portuguese border, and dropping to 300mm in the very dry Ebro area. The temperature is very extreme as the winters are long and severe in provinces such as Avila, Burgos, León, Soria and Zamora and yet the thermometer soars up to the 40°C (104°F) mark and even higher in the summer. In Extremadura, Atlantic winds ensure a more temperate winter.

More than a third of Spain enjoys a **Mediterranean climate**. This area runs along the coastline of Catalonia, Valencia, Murcia and Andalusia and embraces, too, the S Atlantic coast and the valley of the Guadalquivir river. Protected by mountain ranges and the Meseta, this third part has mild winters, lots of sunshine and an average yearly rainfall of some 500mm. Catalonia, with 600-700mm of rain a year is the wettest part while Cabo de Gata, in the SE, has barely 130mm, making it the driest spot in Europe. Parts of the provinces of Murcia and Almería are **semi-desert** with 200-250mm of rain while the Costa del Sol area has a **sub-tropical** vegetation. There are searingly high summer temperatures along the Guadalquivir valley in the cities of Córdoba and Seville, and the town of Ecija, which is between them, is known as the *Frying Pan of Spain* because the temperature here has exceeded 47°C (117°F). The **Balearic Islands** on the whole share the Mediterranean climate. Temperatures in Majorca are generally equable although July and August can be hot. The island is usually rainy in the autumn and it is famed for its magnificently calm month of January. Menorca is more humid and also windier as it receives gusts of the N wind called the *Tramontana* and Ibiza, which in contrast receives the hot winds from the Sahara, is by far the driest of the islands.

The **Canary Islands** form an archipelago of eternal spring. Average rainfall is scarce and the mild warm temperatures are equable throughout the year. But there are also extreme contrasts for the so-called *Fortunate Isles* form a mini-continent of their own —the islands of Lanzarote and Fuerteventura are very dry with less than 100mm of rainfall at their S ends, while inland in Gran Canaria and Tenerife there is a lush tropical vegetation thanks to the 750mm of rain a year that these areas receive.

Most visitors to Spain come looking for the **sun** and they will not be disappointed. Spain is the sunniest nation in Europe. The cloudiest part of the country is a narrow N strip that goes from Galicia's border with Asturias, continues along the coast and then goes roughly E along the Pyrenees. But even this strip is only relatively overcast for it has an average 1,700-1,900 hours of sunshine a year, which is a great deal by the standards of N Europe. Galicia's SW Atlantic coast, on the border with Portugal, enjoys some 2,400 annual hours of sunshine, which is more or less what the Costa Brava on Catalonia's N Mediterranean coast enjoys. Going S along the Mediterranean the yearly average of clear skies increases. The Costa Dorada has 2,600 hours, the Costa del Azahar as far as Gandía and the N part of the Costa Blanca have 2,800 hours, and the coast from Alicante down to La Manga del Mar Menor in the region of Murcia has 3,000 hours, which is the average also for the coast of Almería and for the appropriately named Costa del Sol. At the southern tip of the Peninsula, on the Straits of Gibraltar, the sun hours

	January				March				May				July				September				November			
	Temp. °C/°F		Rain		Temp. °C/°F		Rain		Temp. °C/°F		Rain		Temp. °C/°F		Rain		Temp. °C/°F		Rain		Temp. °C/°F		Rain	
	max.	min.	mm	days	max.	min.	mm	days	max.	min.	mm	days	max.	min.	mm	days	max.	min.	mm	days	max.	min.	mm	days
La Coruña	13/55	7/45	118	18	15/59	8/47	95	16	18/64	11/51	60	13	22/71	15/59	29	8	22/71	14/58	71	12	16/60	9/49	125	17
Lugo	10/50	2/35	151	18	13/55	3/37	113	17	17/63	6/43	97	15	23/73	11/52	28	7	22/71	10/50	88	12	13/55	4/39	132	18
Santiago	11/51	4/40	203	17	15/59	6/42	175	16	18/65	8/47	107	13	24/75	13/55	38	6	22/71	12/54	51	10	14/58	7/45	191	16
Vigo	14/57	7/45	171	16	16/61	9/49	158	15	19/67	12/53	101	14	24/76	16/60	26	6	23/73	15/59	65	10	17/62	10/50	188	16
Oviedo	11/52	3/38	85	12	13/56	5/41	91	14	18/64	9/49	78	13	22/71	14/57	44	7	21/70	13/55	75	10	14/57	6/43	106	14
Santander	12/53	7/44	114	17	15/59	8/47	73	13	17/63	11/52	89	15	21/70	16/61	59	12	21/70	15/59	114	13	15/59	10/50	134	16
Bilbao	12/54	5/41	140	15	17/62	7/44	82	12	20/68	9/49	84	14	25/77	14/58	47	10	23/74	13/56	131	13	16/60	8/47	125	15
San Sebastián	10/50	5/41	145	16	10/50	8/46	92	15	17/63	11/51	126	16	21/70	15/59	93	14	21/70	15/59	154	14	13/56	8/47	148	17
León	7/44	-1/30	57	10	13/56	2/36	57	11	19/66	6/43	52	10	28/82	12/53	18	3	23/74	10/50	40	5	12/53	2/36	57	10
Burgos	6/42	-1/31	46	11	12/54	2/36	54	13	18/64	7/44	61	13	26/79	12/54	28	5	22/71	10/50	43	7	10/50	3/37	53	12
Soria	7/44	-2/28	46	10	12/54	1/34	50	12	18/65	6/42	63	12	27/81	12/53	32	5	23/74	9/49	49	8	11/52	1/34	50	10
Valladolid	7/45	-0/32	31	11	14/58	3/38	43	12	20/68	8/47	37	11	29/84	14/57	14	4	24/76	12/53	27	6	12/54	3/37	42	11
Avila	6/43	-2/29	23	10	11/52	2/35	32	12	18/64	7/44	55	13	27/81	13/55	11	4	22/72	10/50	32	6	10/50	2/36	36	10
Madrid	9/48	1/34	38	8	15/59	5/41	46	10	21/70	10/50	44	9	31/88	18/64	11	3	26/78	14/58	31	6	13/55	5/41	47	9
Toledo	10/50	2/35	31	8	16/61	5/41	41	10	23/73	11/52	42	9	33/92	19/66	9	2	28/82	15/59	25	5	15/59	5/41	38	9
Cuenca	8/47	-2/28	43	8	13/56	1/34	71	11	20/68	7/44	72	10	30/88	14/57	19	3	25/77	11/52	43	10	13/55	2/35	50	7
Ciudad Real	10/50	1/33	36	7	17/62	4/40	50	8	23/73	9/48	48	7	34/94	17/62	2	1	28/83	13/56	23	4	15/59	4/40	38	7
Albacete	9/49	-1/31	26	5	16/60	2/36	32	8	22/72	8/47	50	8	33/91	16/60	8	2	27/81	13/55	35	6	14/58	3/38	22	5
Cáceres	11/52	4/40	57	9	16/61	7/45	71	11	23/74	12/53	44	8	34/93	19/66	3	1	29/84	16/61	24	4	16/60	8/46	59	9
Badajoz	13/56	4/40	61	10	18/64	8/46	68	11	24/76	12/53	37	7	34/93	18/64	3	1	29/85	16/61	25	4	17/63	8/47	62	9
Logroño	9/48	2/35	35	11	15/59	4/40	29	10	21/70	10/50	53	11	29/84	15/59	24	6	25/77	13/55	39	9	13/56	5/41	33	11
Pamplona	9/48	1/33	110	12	14/57	4/39	79	12	20/68	9/48	91	14	27/80	14/57	48	8	24/76	12/54	78	8	12/54	4/39	111	12
La Molina	2/36	-6/22	67	8	5/41	-4/24	80	11	12/53	2/36	147	14	19/66	8/47	98	10	16/61	6/42	130	9	6/43	-3/27	132	9
Zaragoza	10/50	2/36	16	7	17/62	6/43	30	7	23/73	11/52	47	8	31/87	17/63	18	4	26/79	15/59	31	6	14/58	6/43	28	6
Teruel	9/48	-3/27	16	3	13/55	0/32	28	6	21/69	7/44	55	9	30/86	13/55	23	5	24/76	10/50	50	8	12/54	2/35	32	5

	January Temp. max	min.	Rain mm	days	March Temp. max	min.	Rain mm	days	May Temp. max	min.	Rain mm	days	July Temp. max	min.	Rain mm	days	September Temp. max	min.	Rain mm	days	November Temp. max	min.	Rain mm	days
Lérida	9/49	1/34	23	6	17/62	5/41	33	7	24/76	11/52	48	8	32/89	18/64	48	4	25/77	15/59	38	5	14/57	5/41	27	6
Gerona	13/55	2/35	35	5	17/62	5/41	86	9	23/73	11/52	73	10	30/86	17/63	45	6	26/79	15/59	92	9	17/62	6/43	60	7
Barcelona	13/55	6/43	30	5	16/60	9/49	53	8	21/70	14/57	54	8	28/82	21/69	30	4	25/77	19/66	82	8	16/61	11/51	54	7
Tarragona	14/57	6/42	22	4	16/60	7/45	31	6	20/68	12/54	45	6	27/81	19/66	18	3	25/77	17/63	75	6	17/63	9/48	40	6
Castellón	15/59	6/42	26	4	18/64	9/48	30	6	22/72	13/56	43	6	28/83	19/66	14	2	27/80	19/66	61	5	19/67	10/50	46	5
Valencia	15/59	6/42	33	5	18/65	8/46	25	7	23/73	13/55	31	6	29/84	20/68	8	2	27/81	18/64	54	5	19/67	9/49	36	6
Alicante	16/61	6/43	33	5	20/68	8/47	18	6	25/77	13/56	29	6	32/89	19/67	4	2	30/86	18/64	47	6	21/69	10/50	33	6
Murcia	16/61	5/41	16	4	20/68	7/45	25	4	26/78	13/55	31	7	33/91	19/67	3	1	29/85	17/62	36	4	20/68	9/48	50	4
Mahón	13/56	7/45	60	10	16/60	9/48	48	8	21/70	14/57	30	6	28/83	20/68	4	1	26/79	19/66	63	6	18/64	11/52	92	10
Pollensa	15/59	6/43	81	8	16/61	7/45	71	8	22/72	12/54	54	6	29/84	19/66	6	2	27/80	18/64	72	6	18/65	10/50	112	9
Palma	14/58	6/42	39	8	17/62	8/46	36	8	22/72	13/55	27	5	29/84	19/67	4	1	27/80	18/65	56	6	18/65	10/50	54	8
Ibiza	15/59	8/47	38	7	17/62	9/48	35	7	22/71	14/57	20	4	29/84	20/68	5	1	27/81	19/67	43	4	19/66	12/53	62	7
Almería	16/60	8/46	31	6	18/64	10/50	20	6	22/72	15/59	17	3	29/84	21/69	1	◁	27/81	20/68	15	3	19/67	12/54	27	5
Granada	12/53	1/34	44	8	18/64	5/41	53	11	24/75	9/49	38	7	34/93	17/62	3	1	29/85	14/57	20	4	17/62	5/41	41	8
Málaga	17/62	9/48	59	6	19/66	11/52	62	8	23/74	15/59	25	4	29/85	21/70	1	◁	28/82	20/68	28	2	20/68	12/53	63	7
Cádiz	17/63	4/40	75	8	24/76	9/49	81	9	28/83	14/57	26	5	29/84	20/68	1	◁	32/89	17/63	25	2	29/84	10/50	77	8
Córdoba	14/57	5/41	88	8	19/66	8/47	110	9	26/79	14/57	50	5	36/97	20/68	3	1	31/88	17/63	23	3	19/66	8/47	76	8
Seville	16/60	5/41	72	7	20/68	8/47	90	9	26/79	12/54	35	5	35/95	17/63	1	◁	31/88	16/61	25	3	20/68	9/49	70	8
Huelva	16/61	6/43	62	8	20/68	9/49	73	10	25/77	13/56	28	5	32/89	18/65	1	◁	29/85	17/62	19	2	21/69	10/50	64	8
Santa Cruz de Tenerife	20/68	14/58	36	8	22/71	15/59	28	5	24/75	17/62	6	2	28/83	20/68	0	1	28/82	21/69	3	1	24/75	17/63	45	9
Las Palmas	21/69	16/60	19	7	22/71	16/61	13	5	23/74	18/65	2	2	25/77	21/69	1	1	26/79	22/71	3	1	24/76	19/66	31	7
Lanzarote	21/69	13/56	28	5	22/72	14/57	13	3	24/75	15/59	3	1	28/82	18/65	0	0	28/83	19/66	4	2	24/76	16/61	21	3
Fuerteventura	19/66	12/54	18	4	20/68	13/55	6	2	23/73	15/59	2	1	26/79	18/65	0	0	26/79	18/65	4	1	22/71	15/59	32	4

can drop to 2,600 but from Cádiz to Huelva, on the Costa de la Luz, you find yourself once more in the 3,000 per annum league. In the Balearics there is an average of 2,750 hours of sunlight (2,600 in Majorca's mountainous interior and in Menorca and 2,900 in Ibiza and Formentera). In the Canaries the sunshine hours can vary annually between 2,000 (in the inland regions) and 3,000 (in the southern coasts of Tenerife and Gran Canaria, Lanzarote and Fuerteventura).

Geography and Landscapes

Playing with the Castles in Spain image, you could describe peninsular Spain as one giant fortress in which the central plateau or meseta is the keep and the mountain ranges that surround it and criss-cross it are the battlements. The average altitude in Spain is 650m above sea level, which is an extraordinary statistic when you consider that it has some 6,000km of coastline. The highest peak on the Peninsula is the perpetually snow-capped 3,482m-high **Mulhacén** in Granada's Sierra Nevada mountain range, while on the Canary Island of Tenerife **Mount Teide** rises to 3,718m. Uniformly high, the Peninsula has two great depressions which are formed by the Ebro river in the NE and the Guadalquivir river in the SW.

Green Galicia, Spain's NW corner, is a land of gentle hills and very small farmsteads. Roads can be tortuous here linking tiny hamlets and isolated farms. A backward area, the agricultural pattern consists in the main of small maize plots and meadows with each family possessing a couple of cows, the odd pig and not very much more. Going W along the Cantabrian coast, the landscape becomes wilder as it reaches the area called the **Picos de Europa**, a range of mountains that rise to more than 2,000m. The N flank of these peaks drops down to the coast through beech, chestnut and oak woods that give way to orchards and to the best dairy cattle pastures in Spain. Again this is a farmstead area, although with bigger plots than in Galicia, and villages are mostly isolated from each other. This pattern of 'How Green is my Valley' continues through into the Basque Country.

The N foothills of the **Pyrenees** begin in the Basque Country. These are the most alpine of Spain's mountain ranges and they stretch for 435km right across to the Mediterranean forming a natural border with France. The highest summit here is the majestic **Aneto Peak** which rises to 3,404m and the central area of the mountain range receives heavy snowfalls from December to April. The valleys run N-S and the rivers on the Spanish side of the Pyrenees flow down among the pine forests into the mighty Ebro, the biggest of Spain's flowing rivers and the only major one to run its course into the Mediterranean.

The **Ebro depression** is a vast triangular segment that is just 200-300m above sea level between the Pyrenees and the **Sistema Ibérico** mountain range that rises up to more that 2,000m and forms the NE border of the central plateau, the Meseta. If you travel downstream through the valley you will be passing the wine growing La Rioja area, expanses of wheat fields, intensive fruit cultivation in Lérida province, the lunar landscapes of the Los Monegros area and, eventually, the rice paddies of the Ebro Delta on the Mediterranean.

The **Meseta**, a uniformly high plateau within the 600-1,000m range, is the heart of Spain, the keep of the Spanish Castle, and it has Madrid right in the middle of it. The backbone of these plains is the **Cordillera Central** mountain range that scores through the plateau from the SW to the NE starting with the Peña de Francia Peak (1,732m), and continuing on through the Sierra of Gredos (2,592m), the Sierra of Guadarrama (2,430m), on

Madrid's doorstep, and, finally, the Sierra of Somosierra (2,127m). The area N of the backbone is the region called Castile and León, also known as Old Castile, and it is the granary of Spain, the vast wheat producing area. The **River Duero**, which has its source in the 2,000m high Sierra of Urbión of the Sistema Ibérico range, meanders through this N part of the Meseta on its way to meet the Atlantic at Oporto in Portugal. The S part of the Meseta is called Castile-La Mancha or New Castile. It was the stamping ground of Don Quixote and his impossible dreams and it stretches down to yet another mountain range, the Sierra Morena, that forms the border between Castile and Andalusia. A low-lying sierra called the Montes de Toledo runs E-W across part of this Castile-La Mancha section and N of these hills lies the 1,000km long **River Tagus** (Spain's longest), which makes a stately progress towards its Atlantic *rendez-vous* at Lisbon, capital of Portugal. S of the Montes the **Guadiana river** runs a course which includes chunks of the Spanish-Portuguese border and eventually flows out into the Atlantic at the frontier formed by the Portuguese town of San Antonio and by Ayamonte in the province of Huelva.

The Meseta, with its endless landscapes and climatic extremes, is hard, austere, tough and arid. It is a distinct contrast to the lush N of the Peninsula. Stock-raising country, it was the home of massive flocks of wandering merino sheep in the Middle Ages. Nowadays highly specialized breeding of fighting bulls is conducted in the province of Salamanca and a more diversified agriculture includes sugar beet in Valladolid province and tobacco along the southern flanks of the Gredos mountain range. The all encompassing crops are however wheat in the N section of Castile-León, an area that has been known as the *Granary of Spain* since Roman times, and vines in the Castile-La Mancha S section, a region that is one of the biggest wine-producing areas in the world.

You can trace the cultivation of wine right along the Mediterranean third of Spain, down from the Catalonian coastline to the Straits of Gibraltar and across, W, to the province of Huelva and the border with Portugal. Together with the grape you will find here, and also in the Balearics, the alpha and omega of Mediterranean products, the almond and the olive and, of course, a wide variety of citrus fruits. This shoreline section of Spain is the nation's great agricultural reservoir for it grows virtually everything for the European shopping basket. The Valencia coast is a patchwork of orange groves and rice paddies, Murcia is Spain's giant market garden, Almería has successfully experimented with early seasonal produce cultivated under plastic, Granada harvests subtropical fruits and vegetables and Huelva has discovered it can produce strawberries virtually year round.

S of the Meseta, and on the other side of the barren **Sierra Morena** mountains, lies Andalusia and, specifically, the rolling **Guadalquivir valley**. Fertilizing and draining the province of Jaén, which is Spain's olive oil producing centre, and those of Córdoba and Seville where vines and cotton are grown all along its banks, the Guadalquivir meets the Atlantic in the marshlands of the **Coto de Doñana** wildlife reserve. Andalusia is undeniably picturesque with its whitewashed villages and its springtime blaze of colour when its wildflowers are in full bloom. Cádiz is the home of **sherry** at Jerez and, together with the province of Seville, of fighting bulls. In the E, in the province of Granada, the snow-capped peaks of the **Sierra Nevada** which form part of the **Cordillera Bética** range shelter the area's Mediterranean coastline.

In the **Canary Islands** there is a bit of everything: snowy peaks, sand dunes, volcanic lava landscapes and tropical forests. The archipelago is a world of its own and a world apart.

Language

The official language throughout Spain is what the world knows as Spanish and what in Spain is called *castellano*, or Castilian Spanish. In addition, Catalan is spoken in Catalonia, Valencia and the Balearics, Basque, or *euskera*, in the Basque Country and Galician, or *gallego*, in Galicia.

Society and Economy

The majority of Spaniards live in large cities, in Madrid and Barcelona, which alone account for one in six of the population, and in the cities of Valencia, Seville, Zaragoza, Málaga, Bilbao and Murcia, which have each more than half a million inhabitants. Although inland Spain accounts for two thirds of the land space, three out of four Spaniards live either along the country's periphery, including the Canaries and the Balearics, or in land-locked Madrid. The current demographic trend is one of no-growth for its birth rate is as low as the lowest in Europe. Life expectancy, on the other hand, is higher than in Great Britain and West Germany.

Spain underwent a profound and lasting **change** during the 1960s when it ceased to be a rural, backward society dependent on a primitive agriculture. Today it has a diversified economy with a strong **manufacturing** base, a well developed **services** sector and an increasingly important **high-tech** industry. With its growth rate currently doubling that of the European Community average and its inflation rate now comparable to that of its major trading partners, Spain is attracting record inflows of **foreign investment**. **Tourism** is a key component of the Spanish economy and income from tourism exceeds Spain's imported oil bill.

More than 700 of Spain's top 2,000 companies are headquartered in Madrid, Spain's financial and business as well as political capital, and a further 500 have their main offices in Barcelona. The two provinces account for 30 per cent of Spain's national wealth although the Balearics, followed by Madrid and Barcelona, enjoy the highest per capita income in the nation. Heavy industry has traditionally been located in the N (Asturias is Spain's chief coal belt and Vizcaya is the most important steel manufacturing area) and also in Barcelona (textiles, chemicals and light engineering). The automobile industry is an important one: Spain is the sixth biggest car manufacturer in the world, with plants in Zaragoza, Valencia, Barcelona, Vigo and Valladolid, while the shoe industry, another solid export sector, is concentrated in Alicante, Valencia and the Balearics. Valencia disputes the leadership of the furniture manufacturing industry with Barcelona, and Barcelona vies with Madrid as the leader of the book publishing business.

The dual scourges of contemporary Spain are unemployment which is in part the consequence of the former baby boom (Spain has the unenviable record of the highest jobless rate in Europe) and political terrorism in the shape of the Basque separatist organization ETA. At a more general level Spain is in the throes of an accelerated growth cycle and is fast outstripping its existing infrastructure in essential areas such as telecommunications, education and domestic transport.

Tourism Organizations

The nationwide authority is the *Secretaría General de Turismo*, c/ Castelló, 117 ✉ 28006 Madrid ☎ 411 40 14. Each Autonomous Community in Spain has its own tourism organization which is normally in the capital of the community (consult your local tourist office).

Maps

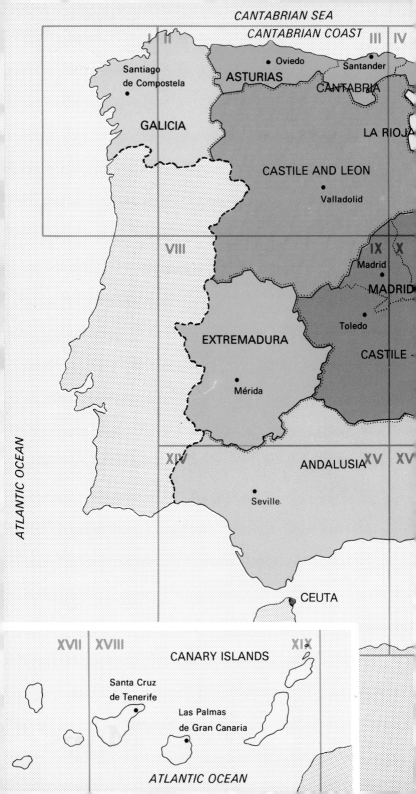

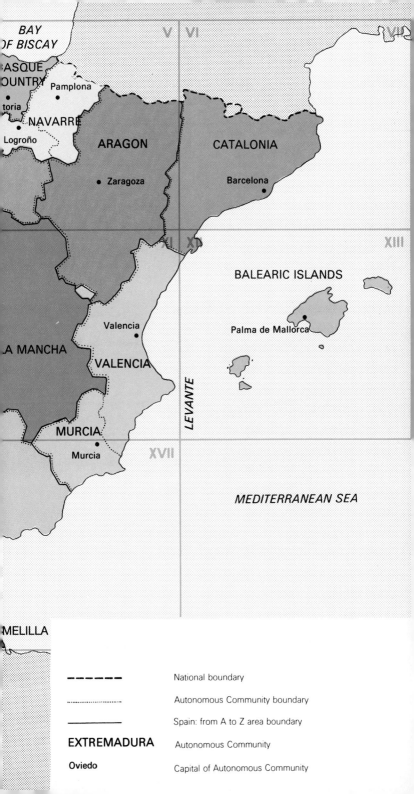

BAY OF BISCAY

BASQUE COUNTRY

Vitoria

Pamplona

NAVARRE

Logroño

ARAGON

• Zaragoza

CATALONIA

Barcelona

V | VI

VII

XI | XII

XIII

BALEARIC ISLANDS

Palma de Mallorca

LA MANCHA

Valencia

VALENCIA

LEVANTE

MURCIA

Murcia

XVII

MEDITERRANEAN SEA

MELILLA

— — — — — National boundary

.... Autonomous Community boundary

———— Spain: from A to Z area boundary

EXTREMADURA Autonomous Community

Oviedo Capital of Autonomous Community

═══════	Motorway	♜	Castle, walls
═══════	Dual carriageway	⌂	Civic building
▬▬▬▬▬	National highway	⌂	Cathedral, church, monastery
═══════	Minor road	Ⓜ	Museum
─+─+─+─	Railway	ⅲ	Archaeological site
✈	Airport	↶	Cave paintings
⛴	Commercial port	⚭	Gardens of historic and artistic interest
⌂ ⌂	Customs	⚲	Holy place, shrine
SORIA	Provincial capital	⛏	Scenic view
●	Town of more than 5.000 inhabitants	≋	Health resort
●	Town of fewer than 5.000 inhabitants	✪	Winter resort
▬▬▬▬	National boundary	⚓	Water sports
▬▬▬▬	Autonomous Community boundary	⛳	Golf club
─ ─ ─ ─	Provincial boundary	▲	Camping site
℗	Parador	▬▬▬	St James' Pilgrimage Route to Santiago
★ *Mezquita*	Cultural Heritage of Mankind	P. N.	National Parks
● MIÑO	A site of historic and artistic interest	P. Nat.	Nature Parks
● HERVAS	A site of historic and artistic interest with fewer than 5.000 inhabitants	R.N.C.	National Hunting Preserves and Reserves
● Padrón	Other places of interest to tourists	C.N.C.	National Hunting Preserves and Reserves

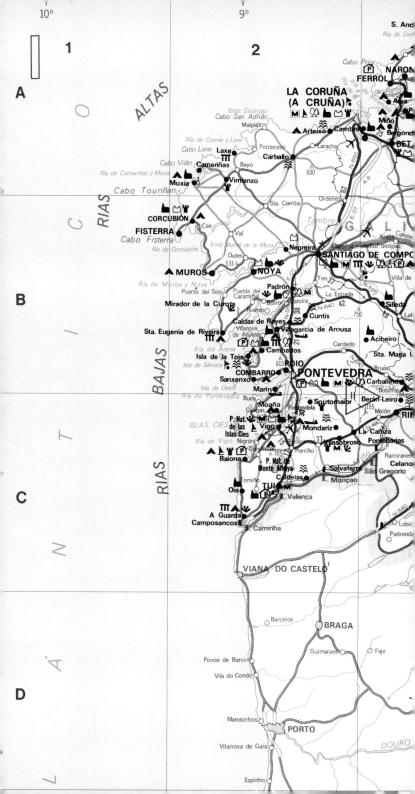

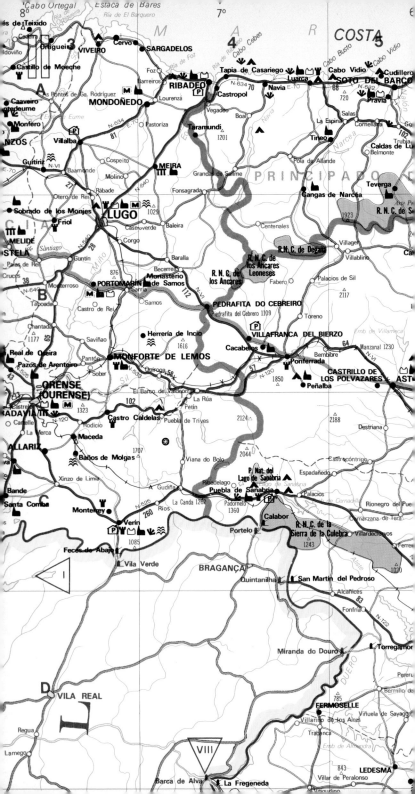

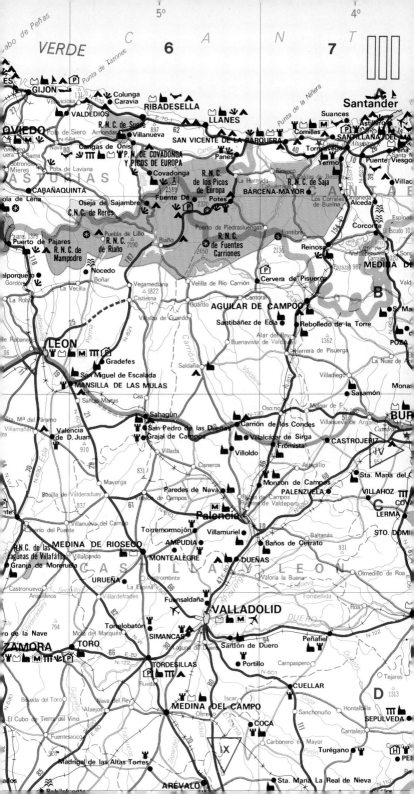

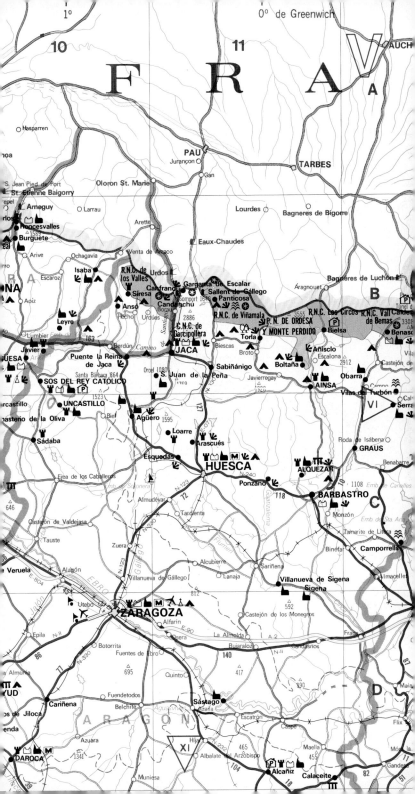

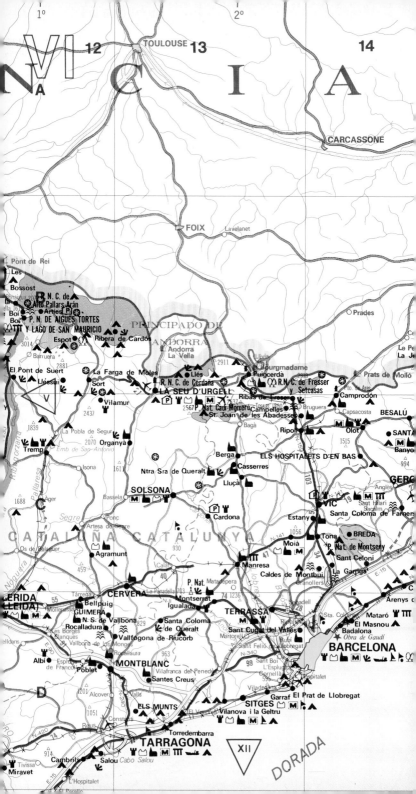

43

asaltés
ERPIGNAN

Elne

Cerbère
Portbou
Colera
Llançà ⚓▲
Peralada   *Cabo de Creus*
▲⚓ ㎡▲▲ ● St. Pere de Rodes ▲⚓
ROSES ● Cadaqués ▲
● Castelló d'Empúries ⌂ ▲ ⚓▲
TORROELLA DE FLUVIÀ
         Golfo de Rosas
Empúries ㎡
La Escala ㎡ ⚓▲
▲▲ L' Estartit
   ● Torroella de Montgrí P. Nat. Islas Medas
PALS ▲
LADA   ● Aiguablava P▲
RONA La Bisbal
⌂ M ● Palafrugell ⚓ ⌂▲
órnélls de ▲ Palamós ▲
a Selva ● Castell-Platja- D'Aro
es de M.
gostera ● S'Agaró ⚓▲
     ● Sant Feliu de Guixols ▲
● Tossa de Mar ♈⌂▲▲
Lloret de Mar ▲
es
▲
▲▲

BRAVA

42

E

COSTA

N

A

▽XIII

41

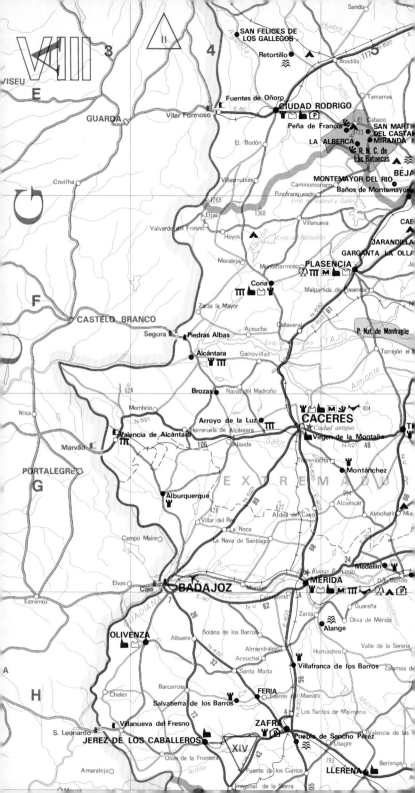

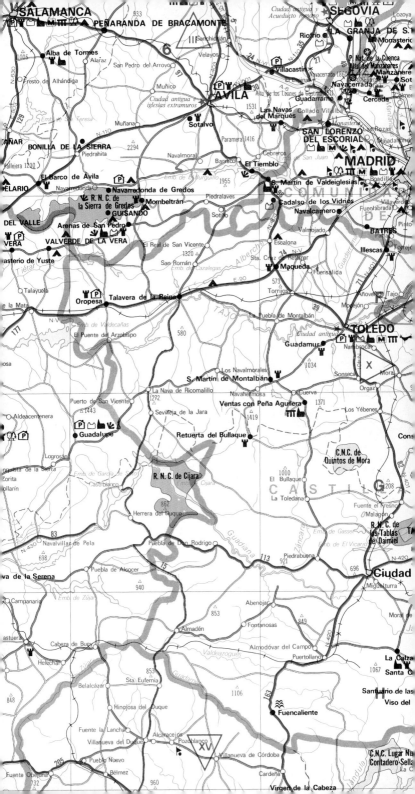

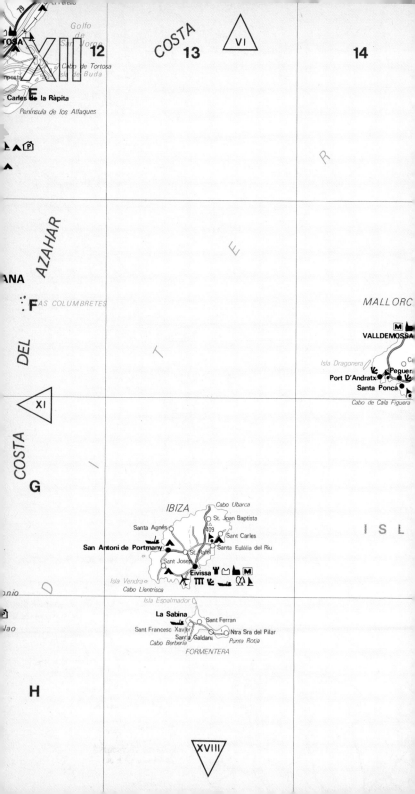

El Perelló

Golfo de Sant Jordi

COSTA 13

△ VI

14

XII **12**

el Cabo de Tortosa

Isla de Buda

Imposta

Carles **E** la Ràpita

Península de los Alfaques

▲ ⓟ
▲

AZAHAR

ANA

∴ **F** AS COLUMBRETES

DEL

△ XI

COSTA

G

MALLORC

M
VALLDEMOSSA

Isla Dragonera

Port D'Andratx

Santa Ponça

Peguer

Cabo de Cala Figuera

I S L

IBIZA

Cabo Ubarca

St. Joan Baptista

Santa Agnés

409

Sant Carles

San Antoni de Portmany

St. Rafel

Santa Eulália del Riu

Sant Josep

Isla Vendra

Eivissa ☗ ⌂ ⛴ M

Cabo Llentrisca

☗ 𝍫 ⚓ ♒

onio

D

Isla Espalmador

La Sabina

Sant Ferran

Jao

Sant Francesc Xavier

Santa Galdana

Cabo Berbería

Ntra Sra del Pilar

Punta Rotja

FORMENTERA

H

▽ XVIII

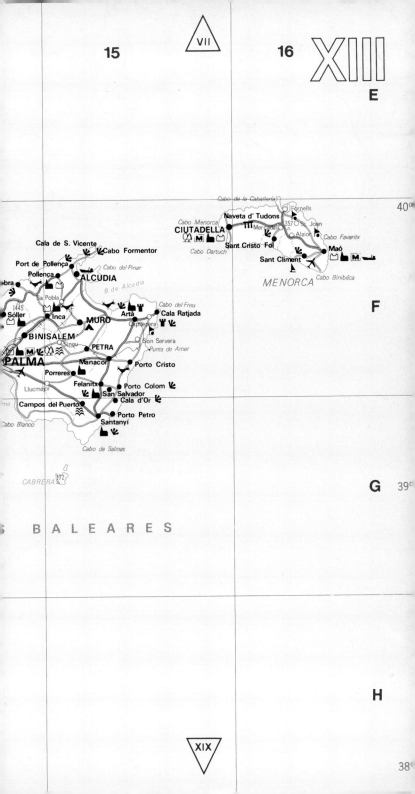

40°

Cabo de la Caballería
Fornells
Naveta d' Tudons
Cabo Menorca
CIUTADELLA　　357　St. Joan
Mercadal
Alaior
Sant Cristo Fol　　　　　Cabo Favaritx
Cabo Dartuch　　　Sant Climent　　Maó

Cabo Binibéca

MENORCA

F

Cala de S. Vicente　　Cabo Formentor
Port de Pollença　　Cabo del Pinar
Pollença
ALCUDIA　　B. de Alcudia
Sa Pobla
1445
Sóller　　Inca　　Artá　　Cabo del Freu
MURO　　　Cala Ratjada
BINISALEM　　Capdepera
Sineu　　　Son Servera
PALMA　　PETRA　　Punta de Amer
Manacor　　Porto Cristo
Porreres
Llucmajor　　Felanitx　　Porto Colom
San Salvador　　Cala d'Or
Campos del Puerto　　Cala d'Or
Cabo Blanco　　Santanyí　　Porto Petro

Cabo de Salinas

CABRERA　　172

G　　39°

BALEARES

H

XIX

38°

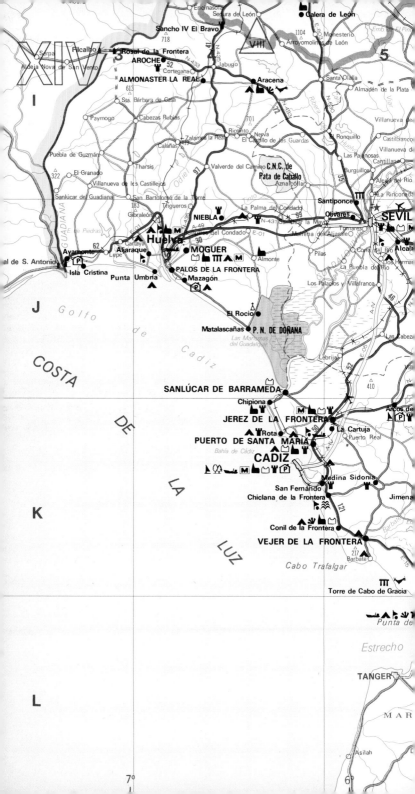

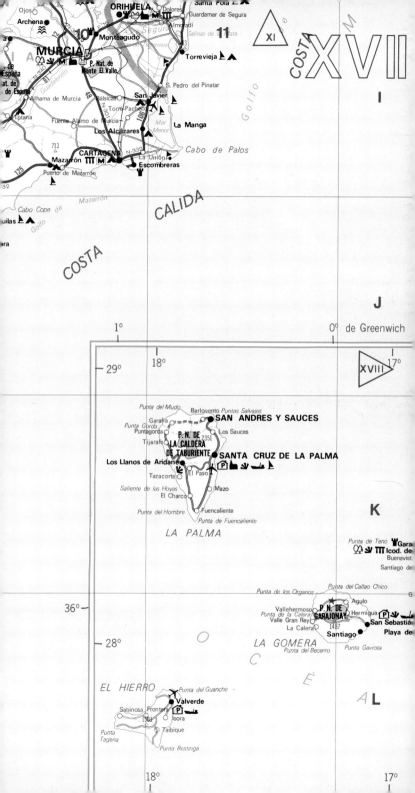

Ojos
Archena
a
de
España
at. de
de España
Alhama de Murcia
Aptana
713
△
125
32

ORIHUELA
Dolores
Guardamar de Segura
Almoradí
Segura
Salinas de
11
Santa Pola
XI
COSTA
XVII
I

10°
Montéagudo
Torrevieja
MURCIA
P. Nat. de
Monte El Valle.
Guadalentín
S. Pedro del Pinatar
Bálsicas
San Javier
Torre-Pacheco
Fuente Álamo de Murcia
Los Alcázares
La Manga
Mar Menor
Cabo de Palos
Mazarrón
CARTAGENA
La Unión
Escombreras
Puerto de Mazarrón
Mazarrón

Golfo

Cabo Cope
uilas
Golfo
ra

CALIDA

COSTA

J

1°
18°
0° de Greenwich

— 29°
XVIII
17°

Punta del Mudo
Barlovento
Puntas Salvajes
Garafía
SAN ANDRES Y SAUCES
Punta Gorda
Puntagorda
Los Sauces
P. N. DE
Tijarafe
LA CALDERA
2351
DE TABURIENTE
Los Llanos de Aridane
SANTA CRUZ DE LA PALMA
El Paso
Tazacorte
Saliente de las Hoyas
Mazo
El Charco
Punta del Hombre
Fuencaliente
Punta de Fuencaliente
LA PALMA

K

Punta de Teno
Gara
Icod. de
Buenavist
Santiago de

Punta de los Organos
Punta del Callao Chico
36°
Agulo
Vallehermoso
P. N. DE
Hermigua
Punta de la Calera
GARAJONAY
Valle Gran Rey
San Sebastiá
La Calera
1487
Playa de
— 28°
Santiago
LA GOMERA
Punta del Becerro
Punta Gaviota

AL

EL HIERRO
Punta del Guanche
Valverde
Sabinosa
Frontera
Isora
Punta
Tagena
Taibique
Punta Restinga

18°
17°

Scale   1:1.500.000

0   50   100

0   30   :   60

Proyección conforme de Lambert
Consejo Superior Geográfico. Registro General de Cartograf

1°   2°

16°

◁XVII

I S L A S   C A N A

Punta Hidalgo   *Punta de Anaga*
Bajamar   *Tejina*
TENERIFE   **La Laguna**
TACORONTE   1024   **S. Andrés**
El Rosario
La Matanza de Acentejo   **STA. CRUZ DE TENERIFE**
K
Pto. de la Cruz   *Santa Ursula*
Vinos   **LA OROTAVA**
Los Realejos
1003   *Punta de Guadamojete*
P. N. DE LAS   2387   **Candelaria**
CAÑADAS DEL TEIDE
Fasnia
Las Cañadas 2300
Isora   3718   *Arico*

Punta de Sardina   *Bahía del Confital*   289
Granadilla de Arona   1003   **ARUCAS**   **Las Palmas**
Américas   *San Miguel*   **Agaete**   **Tafira Alta**
Adeje   171   *Punta Roja*   *Los Berrazales*   **TEROR**
s Cristianos   **El Abrigo**   **Cruz de Tejeda**
nta de la Rasca   **Artenara**   **Santa Brígida**
Punta de la Aldea   1949   **TELDE**   *La Garita*
San Nicolás   *Valsequillo*   *Ingenio*   *Punta de Gando*
San Bartolomé   *Agüimes*   *Arinaga*
de Tarajana
Playa de Veneguera   *Mogán*   **Sta. Lucía**
San Agustín   *GRAN CA*
L   *Arguineguín*   *Juan Grande*
O   **Maspalomas**
Punta Maspalomas   *A*

I

150 Km.

100 ml.

.140 Año 1.987

37° — 14°

3°

4°

ALEGRANZA ㉙
P. Nat. de los Islotes del Norte
de Lanzarote y riscos de Famara

LA GRACIOSA

Orzola

Jameos del

LANZAROTE

Haría

J

La Caleta

Cueva de los Ve
Arrieta

Tinajo

171

Cabo Rosso

**Montaña
de Fuego**

**P. N. DE
TIMANFAYA**

368

671

Teguise

S. Bartolomé

29°

Tiñosa

595

Arrecife

Yaiza

608

Femés

Playa Blanca

Cabo Ginés

Punta Papagayo

Isla de Lobos

Punta de la Vera Gorda

P. Nat. de las
Dunas de Corralejo
e Isla de Lobos

A   S

Punta de la Ballena

Corralejo

Tostón

Lajares

572

Tindaya

La Oliva

669

Casillas del Angel

PUERTO DEL ROSARIO

K

Valle de Sta. Inés

593

P

FUERTEVENTURA

Betancuria

Pájara

Punta del Peñón Blanco

Tuineje

Pozo Negro

Punta de las Borriquillas

Playa de Barlovento

462

Gran Tarajal

Matas Blancas

O

Península de Jandía

Tarajalejo

28°

Punta de Jandía

807

Punta del Morro Jable

C

L

Á   N   T   I

L

5°

14°

28°

L

Spain
A Photo Album

Sunshine and showers ..

...ntiago de Compostela under a typical Galician sky.

The charms of northern Spain ...

Asturian Romanesque: San Miguel de Lillo

Santander's uncrowded beaches

Alpine scenery in the Basque Country: Monte Txindor

La Rioja's famous vineyards

Machismo observed from

Away from it all in Ordesa National Park

ife distance in Pampeona

The 13C miracle of Léon Cathedral

Spain's answer to Buckingham Palace

Trujillo - cradle of conquistadors

e Palacio Real in Madrid

Wayside philosophers in La Alberca

To think that El Greco painted Toled

from where I'm standing now!

Like an inspired sandcastle - Gaudí's Sagrada Família

Cadaqnés. Hello Dalí!

Island paradise — Menorca's Santa Galdana

This picture conjures up for me th

This was like a trip back to the Midd[le]

A timeless sight:
the Rocío pilgrimage in Huelva

...ges — Holy Week in Granada

The night we discovered what 'fiesta' really means
— Valencia's fallas

Our first night in Granada ... W

Awestruck man in the thousand

uld have stayed a thousand more

ar-old setting of Córdoba's Mosque

Orson Welles' favourite place

Everything under the sunset in the Canary Islands

Spain
A Bird's Eye View

BEACHES AND COASTS

Spain has some 2,000km of beaches, so varied in character that whatever you have in mind —solitary sunbathing, a family holiday, learning to water-ski or exploring the sea bed— you are guaranteed to find what you are looking for. If **climate** is your main concern, then here are a few pointers.

CLIMATE

The northern and northwest coasts of Spain are green, cool and rainy and are at their best from late spring to early autumn. The N-facing **Cantabrian corniche**, embracing northern Galicia, Asturias' Costa Verde (Green Coast), the Costa de Cantabria (Cantabrian Coast) and the Costa Vasca (Basque Coast) enjoys a cool climate which makes July and August the perfect months for seaside holidays for those who don't enjoy too much heat. The average temperatures in these months ranges from 16-20°C (61-68°F), with a maximum of 20-27°C (68-81°F) on average, although there are days when the temperature rises above 33-35°C (91-95°F). The nights are somewhat cool, however, with temperatures around 10-14°C (50-57°F) in Santander and San Sebastián, and even lower in Galicia, Asturias and Vizcaya. Humidity is high (nearly 80%) and rainy days are frequent (about 10-15 per month —more in the Basque Country and fewer in Asturias). The daily average for hours of sunshine is low (6-8 hours) in comparison with the Mediterranean, southern Cádiz, Huelva and the Canaries, where the daily average is about double, and the sea water is usually bracing.

Galicia's Atlantic beaches are, like northern Cantabria's, strictly for summer use although the climate is milder, especially in the W-facing Rías Bajas which are protected from the cold northerly winds. This part of the country is also slightly less rainy, with an average of 8-10 wet days per

Maspalomas... sun, sea, sand and eternal spring.

month in July and August, and more hours of sunshine (8-9 per day in the same months).

The coast along the **Mediterranean** —the Costa Brava, Costa Dorada, Costa del Azahar and Costa Blanca— cradle of civilization, is completely different in character. The mild, dry climate and caressing sunshine make Levante and the Balearic islands ideal holiday spots from spring to autumn. The average temperatures along the E coast range from 5-14°C (41-57°F) in January and 20-25°C (68-77°F) in August. Murcia and particularly Almería are very dry, with an annual rainfall of less than 300mm. Winters are very mild, with temperatures rarely going below 10-12°C (50-54°F), and summers are torrid, with average temperatures of 20-28°C (68-83°F). During July and August, the temperature in Almería never drops below 15°C (59°F) at night which is hardly surprising since it enjoys up to 13 hours of glorious sunshine during the day.

In the **Balearic Islands**, Majorca combines Mediterranean landscape with surprisingly lush green vegetation, especially along the steep, pine-clad coasts. The average temperature in Majorca is 17°C (63°F), with a summer average of 30°C (86°F) and winter averages ranging from 5 to 10°C (41 to 50°F). Rainfall, some 500mm a year, is concentrated in autumn and spring —in July and August it rains, on average, three days a month, amply compensated for by the monthly average of 340 hours of sunshine. Menorca, to the N, has a more varied climate, cool and windy, with a N wind known locally as the *Tramontana* really making its presence felt at times. Ibiza, to the S, is drier and hotter, with warm winds sometimes blowing in from Africa.

The **Costa del Sol**, in the southern Mediterranean, stretches along Almería, Granada and Málaga as far as Gibraltar. It enjoys the warmest climate of all Europe, with mild winters —winter averages in Marbella and Torremolinos are 15-19°C (59-66°F), seldom falling below 12°C (54°F)— and warm summers —average 22-29°C (72-84°F), though maximum temperatures can reach 40°C (104°F). It is wonderfully sunny (320 days of sunshine per year), with rainfall, often heavy, concentrated in winter and spring. The climate is essentially subtropical as the rich local vegetation reflects. This makes it an ideal holiday spot for about 11 months of the year, though if you enjoy the social whirl you should try to come here at Easter or in high summer.

The **Costa de la Luz** stretches from the southernmost point of Spain, the Punta de Tarifa, on the Straits of Gibraltar, to the mouth of the river Guadiana in Ayamonte (Huelva) on the border with Portugal. Its magnificent beaches are bathed by the Atlantic and by the brilliant light which gives the *costa* its name. The climate of this stretch of coast is more extreme: cold in winter —8-15°C (47-59°F) average— and hot in summer, with high maximum temperatures rising above 40°C (104°F), although the summer average tends to be around 20-30°C (68-86°F). Frequent changes of temperature can occur throughout the day due to fresh winds from the SW, and a less frequent, and less welcome, hot wind from the E.

A thousand kilometres away to the SW of mainland Spain, near the Tropic of Cancer, in the Atlantic and 115km off the African coast, lies the volcanic archipelago of the **Canaries**. In ancient times, the mythical *Garden of the Hesperides* was located here, later to be called the *Fortunate Islands* because of the eternal spring-like climate of the archipelago. There is little difference between minimum and maximum temperatures and they remain consistent all year long. The average yearly temperature in Gran Canaria is 20°C (68°F), rarely rising above a maximum of 30°C (86°F) in summer in the sunny S (nearly 3,000 hours of sunshine per year), and there are barely 15 rainy days a year. In Tenerife, the yearly average is slightly lower and it is slightly more humid too (75%, with 75 days of rain per year); it enjoys some 2,000 hours of sunshine per year. People therefore visit these islands all year round, although the high season is between December and February.

The parts of Spain where the beaches can be **visited all year round** are, therefore, those in the Canaries —Las Canteras in Las Palmas de Gran Canaria, Maspalomas and all the beaches in the S of the island; Puerto de la Cruz, Las Teresitas and Playa de las Américas in Tenerife. Benidorm, thanks to its microclimate, is also busy in **winter**, as are Marbella and Nerja (Málaga), Mojácar and Roquetas (Almería) and Motril (Granada), not forgetting Santa Ponsa (Majorca), Sitges (Barcelona), Salou (Tarragona), Benicassim (Castellón) and Denia (Alicante). In brief, then, if you can take your holidays in **spring, summer** or early **autumn**, take your choice of the Mediterranean resorts (the season is even longer down towards the SE corner of Spain). The Costa de la Luz enjoys a good long summer while Galicia and the Cantabrian Coast can only really depend on July and August for beach-going weather. Given these basic weather conditions, your choice will now depend on whether you like resort beaches with every facility close at hand or natural beaches, feeling closer to Nature in some less-developed part of the coast.

NATURAL BEACHES

If you like big beaches with limitless sands open to the sea, then you will enjoy La Lanzada (La Toja-El Grove) and the Islas Cíes, in Galicia; the lovely beaches of Catalonia's Bahía de Rosas, N of Ampurias (Gerona), and the ones along the Ebro Delta (Tarragona). On the Costa del Azahar, there are the beaches of **EL SALER** (Valencia), and on the Costa Blanca, the dunes of **GUARDAMAR** (Alicante) and the beaches along the **La Manga del Mar Menor** area and in Aguilas (Murcia). The beaches for you in the Balearics are

Es Trenc (S Majorca) and **Las Salinas** (S Ibiza), and in Andalusia, the duned beach near the salt flats of Cabo de Gata (Almería), on the Mediterranean. On the Atlantic coast, the best natural beaches are those of **Bolonia** (Cádiz), **Zahara de los Atunes** (Zahara de los Atunes, Cádiz), **La Barrosa** (Chiclana, Cádiz), and practically all those in Huelva, particularly **Playa de Castilla** (near the Coto de Doñana, see 'Wide Open Spaces'), **Matalascañas, Mazagón, Punta Umbría, El Portil** and the vast **La Antilla** in Lepe, which stretches for kilometres from **ISLA CRISTINA** to the mouth of the River Piedras, much of it totally virgin. In the Canaries, head for the dunes of **MASPALOMAS** (in the S of Gran Canaria), and in the N of the island of Fuerteventura, the **Dunas de Corralejo** which stretch for 15km. To the S, the **Dunas de Jandía** stretch for 40km and the capital, Puerto del Rosario, also has the vast **Playa Blanca**.

While some enjoy far horizons, others prefer secluded **coves**, protected from the open sea by rocky promontories. The Costa Verde (Green Coast) has some lovely sandy coves accessible from villages such as Celorio and Colunga, though the Costa Brava (Wild Coast) and the Balearics are the best sources of idyllic hideaways. Along the Costa Brava, some of them, like the **Puerto de la Selva**, lapped by crystalline waters, are accessible only by sea. You will find beaches of outstanding beauty between **Aiguafreda** and **Aiguablava**, while further S, between San Feliú and Tossa de Mar, there are marvellous **coves** nestling between awe-inspiring cliffs. Better still are the little coves of the Balearic Islands. Beaches with pine trees and warm transparent waters, such as **Santa Ponsa, Paguera, Cala Fornells, Es Caló d'En Monjó** and **Camp de Mar** in the SW of Majorca are a foretaste of paradise. You also have **Torrent de Pareis** in the N, the various beaches which make up the magnificent **Cala San Vicente** in the NW, and in the E, the lovely, sandy **Cala Figuera** and **Cala Santanyí**. Among Menorca's gems are **Cala'n Porter, Cala Santandria** and the beautiful cliff-sheltered **Cala Santa Galdana**. Ibiza, the southernmost island of the Balearics, has some magnificent places such as **Cala Gració**, the sandy **Cala Vedella** and **Cala Portinatx**, which is actually a series of tiny coves tucked into the cliffs and shaded by pines.

URBAN BEACHES

The above-mentioned natural beaches are largely unspoiled, though they do have the odd hotel or housing development nearby. Urban beaches where you can be in the sea within minutes of the city centre have quite a different charm, whether they be in traditional resorts like Santander, San Sebastián, Barcelona, Cádiz and Las Palmas de Gran Canaria, or the new cities like Benidorm, Salou or Maspalomas which have sprung into being with the tourist boom. The town of **SANGENJO** (Pontevedra) has a very popular beach which is said to enjoy the best climate in Galicia, though **Riazor**, the city of La Coruña's beach, boasts the lowest rainfall in the region. **San Lorenzo** in Gijón (Asturias) is another good example, while Santander has five magnificent beaches in the stretch known as **El Sardinero** and the 5km-long beach of **Laredo**, with dunes. San Sebastián, on the Basque Coast, is a city of turn of the century charm, and the urban setting of the beaches that make up **La Concha** qualify as a masterpiece of 19C town planning.

On the Costa Brava (Gerona), **PALAMOS, TOSSA DE MAR**, with its medieval towers, and nearby **LLORET DE MAR** all have their beaches a stone's throw away from the town centre, while in **SITGES**, S of Barcelona, the pretty esplanade makes it possible to take a seaside walk in town clothes without feeling out of place. Heading S, you come to **SALOU** (Tarragona) on the Costa Dorada, **PEÑISCOLA** (Castellón) in the region of Valencia, the long stretch of fine sands in **GANDIA** (Valencia), and **DENIA** (Alicante), where the beach has all sorts of facilities at hand. Most famous of all, of course, is

BENIDORM (Alicante), nerve-centre of the Costa Blanca (White Coast), while Alicante itself has easy access to the **Playa de San Juan**, a resort popular for Spanish family holidays. **LA MANGA DEL MAR MENOR** (Murcia) almost qualifies as an urban beach in that it has undergone a lot of tourist development. The Balearics, though best known for their seaside retreats, also have their sophisticated tourist complexes, particularly at **El Arenal**, the beach which serves the town of Palma de Mallorca (Majorca), and **Palma Nova** and **Magaluf**, W of the Bay of Palma.

Back on the Peninsula, the S Mediterranean Coast has a string of beaches for people who like to have every facility within walking distance: **MOJACAR** (Almería), El Palo near Málaga city, **TORREMOLINOS**, **FUENGIROLA** and **ESTEPONA**, all in the province of Málaga.

On the Costa de la Luz (Coast of Light), W Andalusia, are the Atlantic-facing beaches of **La Victoria** in the city of Cádiz, **Regla** in Chipiona (Cádiz), and **Bajo de Guía** in Sanlúcar de Barrameda (Cádiz), a town famous for its *manzanilla* sherry, whose distinctive salty tang is attributed to the fact that the grapes grown here absorb the sea air. Jutting out into the Gulf of Cádiz is the **Punta Umbría** headland, whose sun-baked beaches are a foretaste of nearby Portugal.

The city of Las Palmas de Gran Canaria, in the Canaries, has its own beach in **Las Canteras**, while the famous big beaches in the S of the island are Maspalomas' **Playa del Inglés**, and further NE, the **Playa de San Agustín**. Tenerife's Puerto de la Cruz has a marvellous natural swimming pool complex known as the Lago de Martiánez, futuristically designed by Lanzarote-born architect César Manrique, while Santa Cruz de Tenerife's local beach is **Las Teresitas**, artificially created with sand from the Sahara. The **Playa de las Américas** is arguably the island's best stretch of beach and is consequently backed up by plenty of tourist facilities.

SPECIAL BEACHES

Then there are beaches which come into the special-beach category for one reason or another. Here are some that qualify. **Ampuria Brava** is huge, with a tasteful tourist development and marvellous facilities. **Tamariu** (Palafrugell) would qualify on grounds of landscape alone, though it also has very luxurious facilities, as does the Playa de Aro in **S'Agaró**. All these are on the Costa Brava. In Alicante, **CALPE'S** beach is outstandingly good for water sports and is surrounded by wonderful scenery, while **La Zenia** has a beautiful sandy beach and has been tastefully developed. Majorca's special beaches are **Illetas,** **Son Servera,** **Cala Ratjada, Ca'n Picafort, Alcudia, Formentor,** set on a pretty bay with a magnificent hotel, and the luxury resort around **Cala D'Or** with white houses, green pines and crystal clear waters. On the lively Costa del Sol some of the beaches along the 28km of **MARBELLA'S** coast, playground of the beautiful people, are Puente Romano, Río Verde, Los Monteros, Don Carlos, Cabopino and Calahonda and, near Estepona, the **Costa Natura**, a self-sufficient microcosm for nudists. The Costa de la Luz's gems are **Fuentebravía** and **Valdelagrana** in Puerto de Santa María (Cádiz).

ATMOSPHERE

Further clues which may be useful in deciding which seaside area of Spain to spend your holidays at are that Galicia and the Cantabrian coast in the N and Andalusia's Costa de la Luz in the S are favourites for Spanish family holidays, while Santander, Zarauz and San Sebastián are the traditional summer retreats of the middle classes and the upper crust. Foreign tourists tend to head *en masse* for the Costa Brava, Sitges and Salou (which is also popular with Spaniards) on the Costa Dorada, Benidorm, Majorca, Ibiza, Mojácar, the Costa del Sol (especially Torremolinos) and the Canary Islands.

BEST BUYS

No jumble sale is without its share of discarded tourist souvenirs. Amusing and evocative in their place of origin, they just never seem to find their niche back home. Yet shopping abroad can be a tremendous success. You just need to know what the country you are visiting is particularly good at and where to find it at a reasonable price.

Some of Spain's specialities have been world-famous for centuries —its noble **Arab horses** (contact the *Asociación de Cuidadores de Caballos Arabes*, c/ Hermosilla, 20, Madrid ☎ (91) 275 90 65), **sherry** from Jerez, **swords and armour** from Toledo, **guitars** from Madrid and Seville, **wine** from La Rioja and Penedés (and especially that from the *Vega Sicilia* winery in Valbuena del Duero, Valladolid ☎ (983) 68 01 47), **olive oil** from Jaén, **cigars** from the Canary Islands...— while others, like young **designer fashion** (see 'Design') are just starting to make an impact abroad.

Despite its booming tourist trade, Spain is one of the countries of Europe whose traditional **arts and crafts** have survived best. Armed with a few basic guidelines, the discerning shopper can find excellent bargains in this area. Anyone interested in investing in **works of art**, particularly **paintings**, should head for Madrid or Barcelona where there is a huge range of commercial galleries as well as reputable auction houses. Both cities are also good for **antiques**, as are Bilbao, San Sebastián, Seville, Zaragoza, Orense, Vigo, Pontevedra, Valencia, Oropesa del Mar (Castellón) and the whole of Castile and León, particularly Palencia. Modern **furniture** can also be a good buy, like the *avant garde* designs you will find in Barcelona or the stylish wicker pieces made in Gata de Gorgos (Alicante). On a smaller scale there is **wrought iron** work from Logroño, Seville and the Balearic Islands; beaten **copper** pots from Guadalupe and Granada; hand-made **lace** from Camariñas, Majorca, Almagro and Arenys de Mar; **openwork** from Ingenio and La Guancha in Gran Canaria; **embroidered silk** from the Canary Island of La Palma; **ceramics** from Talavera de la Reina, Puente del Arzobispo, Manises, Paterna, Alcora, Muel and the lovely dishes and porcelain from *Sargadelos* and *La Cartuja de Sevilla* (see 'Design'), and **blown glass** from Barcelona and Majorca. The price of **gold** and **silver** jewelry and ornaments is relatively reasonable and the choice ranges from traditional designs from Santiago de Compostela, Córdoba and Valencia to *avant garde* pieces by young designers in Madrid, Barcelona and Valencia. Spain is also good at flamboyant **costume jewelry** and has scored a huge international success with its **cultured pearls** from Majorca, which are even exported to Japan.

Apart from the exciting young **fashion** generated by designers based in Madrid, Barcelona and Galicia and, to a lesser extent, Seville and Ibiza (see 'Design' for the big names), Spain's **leather** clothes and accessories are instantly seductive to visitors from abroad for their stylish cut, high quality and very reasonable prices. *Loewe*, known the world over, leads the field, but you will also find excellent buys with less exclusive labels. Spanish **furs** are also interesting buys, especially for their innovative cut —**Elena Benarroch** is a leading designer in this field. **Boots and shoes** are another bargain, from traditional **espadrilles** (now glamorously updated) and sturdy hunting boots (from Salamanca and Huelva) to imaginative fashion designs from famous firms based in the Balearics and Alicante.

Visiting gastronomes will have to enjoy some of the best food buys, like Jabugo **cured ham** and Spain's many **artisan cheeses** (Cabrales from Asturias, Mahón from Menorca, Picón and Aliva from Cantabria, Manchego from Castile-La Mancha, Roncal from Navarre, Idiazábal from the Basque Country, Tetilla from Galicia, Garrotxa from Gerona...) on the spot because of import regulations, but top quality **virgin olive oil** (much cheaper in Spain than in Britain or the United States), traditional Christmas *turrón* (an almond and honey nougat) and **marzipan** (both part of Spain's enduring Moorish legacy) travel well and make excellent presents.

If you are only on a flying visit, take note of the following national chains with shops throughout the country: *Artespaña*, an excellent source of crafts, fabrics and furniture from all over Spain (branches in Madrid, Barcelona, Santander, Alicante, Bilbao, Seville, Granada, Marbella, Oviedo, Santa Cruz de Tenerife, Murcia, Cáceres and Palma de Mallorca); *El Corte Inglés*, Spain's leading department store which sells just about everything, including good delicatessen in its bigger shops, and where tax concessions are available on purchases for export to certain countries —make enquiries at the central cash desk, where interpreters are provided (branches in Madrid, Barcelona, Seville, La Coruña, Vigo, Valencia, Bilbao, Valladolid, Málaga, Zaragoza, Las Palmas de Gran Canaria and Murcia); *Galerías Preciados*, a smaller department store (branches in Madrid, Barcelona, Alicante, Valencia, Vitoria, Bilbao, Seville, Oviedo, Zaragoza, Las Palmas, Santa Cruz de Tenerife, Murcia and Palma de Mallorca); *Cortefiel*, for middle-of-the-road fashion at reasonable prices (branches in some 25 cities); *Don Algodón*, for fun casual clothes for children and teenagers (about 70 branches); *Zara*, for cheap and cheerful fashion for men, women and children (some 35 branches) and *Tokio*, for gloves, socks, swimwear and so on (branches in Madrid, Barcelona, Valencia, San Sebastián, Vitoria, Zaragoza, Orense, Pamplona, Santa Cruz de Tenerife, La Coruña and Palma de Mallorca).

Now for a brief guide to other local specialities starting, geographically speaking, at the top:

In **Galicia**, look out for traditional Carnival masks from Ginzo de Limia, Ribeiro and Albariño wine (see 'Wines'), ceramics from Buño and Nuñodaguía, jet jewelry from Santiago de Compostela and fashion from Santiago de Compostela, Orense (birthplace and launching pad of Adolfo Domínguez), Vigo and La Coruña.

Asturias is the place to buy dry cider, jet crafts, ceramics from Llamas de Mouro and fashion from Oviedo and Gijón, which have good boutiques.

Visitors to **Cantabria** should look out for traditional musical instruments, *sobaos* (buttery sponge cakes), and fashion and presents sold in Santander, whereas those visiting the **Basque Country** should take note of its typical Basque berets, wines from the Alava region of La Rioja, *txacolís* (the local green wines) from Guetaria, and the excellent selection of stylish baby clothes on offer in San Sebastián.

In **Navarre's** capital, Pamplona, you will come across good fashion shops; the region as a whole, however, is best known for its *pacharán* herb liqueur and its typical wineskins. Wineskins also figure prominently in the list of things to buy while visiting **La Rioja**, as do its exquisite wines and its wide range of bottled local fruit and vegetables.

In **Aragón**, best buys include ceramics from Teruel and Alhama de Aragón, cowbells from Mora de Rubielos, drums from Calanda, wine from Cariñena and local cheeses from the Ansó valley. The region's capital, Zaragoza, offers good shopping possibilities in general.

Catalonia as a whole is a wonderful shopping emporium. Keep your eyes open for fashion, gifts and perfume from the Costa Brava, pottery from La Bisbal and Olot, anchovies from La Escala, charcuterie (*salchichón, fuet* and *butifarra* sausages) from Vich and the Ampurdán and wine from El Priorato and the Ampurdán region. Barcelona, needless to say, is a shoppers' paradise —here you will find all sorts of shops selling fashion, interior design, books, collectors' stamps, or whatever it is that your heart desires.

The **Balearic Islands** also have a wide gamut of typical local products on offer —ceramics from Felanitx, *ensaimada* pastries, *sobrasada* spicy paté, cultured pearls and ceramic whistles from Majorca, Mahón cheeses from Menorca, and *Ad-lib* fashion, leather goods and herbs from Ibiza, among others.

Back on the peninsula, **Valencia** is well known for its gorgeous fans, local wines, citrus fruits and toys from Ibi and Onil. Valencia city, the third largest in Spain, has as many shops and boutiques as you could wish for. **Murcia**, Valencia's neighbour to the S, is a good place to buy wine from Jumilla and Yecla, gold and silver crucifixes from Caravaca de la Cruz, and canned and bottled local fruit and vegetables.

Visitors to **Castile and León** should look out for the traditional silver jewelry and ornaments from Salamanca and Mogarraz, wine from Rueda and Ribera del Duero, wrought-iron and ceramics from Alba de Tormes, cured ham and other charcuterie from Guijelo, fresh cheese from Villalón and Burgos and country boots from Salamanca.

Extremadura's specialities include cured ham from Montánchez and pottery from Arroyo de la Luz. **Castile-La Mancha**, on the other hand, is best known for honey from the La Alcarria region and wine from Valdepeñas. And as for **Madrid**... well, it has everything under the sun!

Andalusia's sherry and other fortified wines from Sanlúcar de Barrameda, Puerto de Santa María, Montilla and Moriles need no introduction. Other good buys in the area include leather luggage and purses from Ubrique, blankets and rugs from Berja (Almería) and Grazalema (Cádiz), ceramics from Granada and Ubeda, guitars from Seville and Córdoba, fabrics from Níjar (Almería), country boots from Valverde del Camino (Huelva), gypsy dresses from Seville and Antequera, and fashion from Seville and Marbella.

When visiting the **Canary Islands** keep in mind that, besides local crafts and products —open-work embroidery, traditional pottery from Santa Cruz de Tenerife and, above all, cigars— this duty-free haven is the ideal place to buy photographic and hi-fi equipment, watches, silk and so on from the local bazaars.

Just remember to leave room in your suitcase for your Spanish bargains. Of course, you'll have to make other arrangements for the Arab stallion...

BULLFIGHTING

Ask any foreigner to say the first thing that comes into his head when you mention Spain, and the chances are that it will be bullfighting. Few realize that it also goes on in France, Portugal and many Latin American countries. While not all Spaniards are bullfighting fans —there is an anti-blood sports league in Spain— huge numbers, from the man in the street to leading intellectuals, are captivated by the aesthetics of this ritual which dates back to the sports of ancient Greece and Rome. The fact that 4,000 bulls a year are killed in bullrings all over Spain, attracting over 40 million spectators, gives you some idea of its enduring popularity.

The confrontation between man and bull is always a fight to the death, generally, though not invariably, the bull's. Matadors killed in the ring are elevated to the realm of legend, and the names of José Cándido (18C), *Espartero* (19C) and, in our century, *Manolete* and *Paquirri* are never likely to be forgotten. Of course, many big-name matadors live to tell the tale, like the great Pedro Romero (18C), who killed 5,800 bulls during his 28-year career without suffering serious injury.

Experts say that the secret of bullfighting lies with the bull and not the bullfighter. However skilled or brave the *torero* may be, unless the bull is *bravo* (spirited), the magic just does not happen.

In other countries and cultures, the fighting qualities of bulls have gradually been bred out, but in Spain they are still cultivated. Nowadays, fighting bulls are bred in Seville, Cádiz and Jaén in Andalusia, in southern Spain, in the uplands of Salamanca near Madrid in Castile, and in Extremadura in the south-west.

There are some 250 stock farms, though they are not the sort of places you can drop into casually. If you are genuinely interested in visiting one, contact the *Unión de Criadores de Toros de Lidia* (Fighting Bull Breeders' Association), c/ Eduardo Dato, 7, 28010 Madrid ☎ 447 57 81; Av República Argentina, 27, 41011 Seville ☎ 27 79 64; and c/ Pozo Amarillo, 22, 37002 Salamanca ☎ 21 32 84. For a thoroughly Andalusian experience —horse-riding, a visit to one of the most famous stock farms, Alvaro Domecq's *Torrestrella*, or to the *bodegas* where sherry has been made for centuries, a hunting expedition, or an overnight stay in a *cortijo*, a typical local farmhouse— contact Urb El Paquete, Portal 1, Jérez de la Frontera (Cádiz) ☎ 30 41 68.

In the stock farms —such as the Sevillian Miura and the Extremaduran Victorino Martín— fighting bulls are bred and reared from the day they are born to highlight the qualities which will make for a good performance in the ring. The breeders watch their every move during a fight and plan their breeding strategy accordingly.

There are several sorts of *corridas*, or bullfights. **Novilladas** are fights between inexperienced *toreros* and bulls just three years old (*utreros*) or younger (two year-old *erales*). Since the animals are not as strong as fully developed bulls, the fights do not usually involve *picadores*, riders armed with pikes, who stab the bull to weaken it. Fully fledged *matadores* are pitched against bulls at least four years old (*cuatreños*) —at five (*cinqueños*), they have reached the peak of their strength and fighting spirit. Then there is bullfighting on horseback, when the **rejoneador**, as the *torero* is known in this genre, shows off his skills as a rider as well as all the rest.

But bullfighting in its present form has evolved gradually over its 600-year history. Festivals involving bullfighting were held in 14C Navarre, Rioja and Vizcaya in northern Spain. In the 16-17C, it was the aristocratic sport, and it was not until the 18C, under the Bourbons, that it captured popular attention. At this time, official bodies in Seville and Córdoba laid down the official rules of bullfighting. The first *torero* to emerge as a popular personality was Miguel Canelo in 1733, and by 1761, bullfighting was being advertised on posters. During this period, the Sevillian bullfighter *Costillares* introduced patterns of modern bullfighting which are still standard, such as the *verónica*, the use of the cape to demonstrate the bull's qualities, and the use of the *muleta*, the stick draped with a red cloth, as an instrument of manipulation rather than defence.

The Golden Age of the sport reached its climax with Seville's José Gómez, popularly known as *Joselito*, and Juan Belmonte, both folk heroes and great rivals until *Joselito* was killed in the Talavera de la Reina bullring in 1920. His style was classical, while Belmonte was more of a showman and improviser. The major figures who followed them included Ignacio Sánchez Mejías, whose tragic death in the ring inspired a poem by his friend Federico García Lorca. With Córdoba's *Manolete*, the *torero* became the undisputed star of the show, and with Antonio Bienvenida, Luis Miguel Dominguín and, especially, Antonio Ordóñez, Ernest Hemingway's favourite, who combined the best of the Seville and Ronda schools, bullfighting became more popular than ever. But larger audiences also meant a less discerning public, and spectacle tended to triumph over subtlety. It was during this period that *El Cordobés* shot to international fame. Nevertheless, the finer points have survived in figures like Curro Romero and Rafael de Paula, and in the younger generation, *Espartaco* and *El Niño de la Capea*, although new names are likely to appear from one day to the next.

Everyone in bullfighting circles knows that no two bulls are the same. The bulls which appear in important fights have never experienced the cape or *muleta*, and their reactions are therefore highly unpredictable. This, in combination with the *torero's* artistic temperament, is what provides the excitement of a *corrida*.

A **corrida** is a complex and clearly defined ritual, and a board of experts ensures that it is followed to the letter. Parts of the ritual, like the dressing of the matador, the ceremonial entry of the bullfighters and the toast are pure ceremony, and in a sense optional, while the rules of the fight itself are essential to its artistic integrity and authenticity.

Connoisseurs of bullfighting require a lot more than cheap thrills. What they enjoy is not the sight of blood but the spectacle of brute force being manipulated and dominated by skill and wit (it is interesting that bullfighters are often popularly known by diminutive names which, as well as expressing affection, seem to stress their youth and fragility), the bull being made to dance to the *torero's* tune.

The bullfight is divided into three parts or **tercios**. During the first of these, the *torero* wields his cape in certain formal moves, revealing something of the bull's character to the crowd and preparing it for the **picadores**, riders armed with pikes, who stab the bull three times at particular points to weaken it and test its character —the true *toro bravo* will react ferociously.

The next stage is the planting of the *banderillas*, darts trailing coloured streamers, in the back of the bull's neck, in spectacularly daring and athletic moves, by the **banderilleros**. Again this goading reveals the spirit and character of the bull which, if sufficiently *bravo*, will charge furiously at its attackers.

During the third stage, the *torero* manipulates the movements of the bull with the *muleta*, the stick draped in red cloth. If properly judged, the previous stages will have left the bull with enough strength and spirit to make this the part of the fight where the beauty of the *torero's* moves can be appreciated to the full as he builds up to the climax of the whole event.

The **suerte suprema**, or art of the kill, lies in doing it quickly. The moves leading up to it and the position of the death thrust are preordained, and however well the **matador** has performed, he loses all glory unless the final blow is properly delivered. Even the degree of public enthusiasm is ritualized, and a *torero's* performance will be acclaimed with simple applause, an ovation, a triumphal circuit of the ring, one or both of the ears of the bull he has killed, both ears and the tail or, the ultimate accolade, his being carried out of the plaza on the shoulders of the crowd.

Different bullrings are famous for different reasons, be it the quality of the *corridas* or the knowledgeability of the audience. The bullfighting meccas are Seville's *La Maestranza*, Pamplona's bullring during the famous San Fermín festival when bulls are run through the streets, and Madrid's *Las Ventas*, though the rings in Barcelona, Bilbao and Valencia are also great crowd-pullers.

As might be expected, the Spanish calendar is full of bullfighting *fiestas* and no true *aficionado* will miss the April Fair in Seville, San Isidro in Madrid (May), San Fermín in Pamplona (July), Valencia's *fiesta* in July or Bilbao's in August.

Tourists to the package Costa resorts could be forgiven for thinking that Spaniards live on indifferent ***paella*** washed down by quantities of ***sangría***. Little do they know that no self-respecting Spaniard would dream of ordering *paella* unless he had a good three-quarters of an hour to spare while it was being made (from scratch) nor would he be entirely convinced about drinking wine which needed mixing with fizzy pop and bits of fruit to make it palatable.

Better informed foreigners will know that there is nothing better than a chilled ***gazpacho*** vegetable soup on a hot day, that the ***tortilla de patata*** (potato omelette) is an invention on a par with the snack which to this day bears the name of its 18C inventor, the 4th Earl of Sandwich, and that the **wines of Rioja** can hold their own against the French any day. Connoisseurs will be familiar with the exquisite dryness of a pale **fino** sherry (experts swear that its flavour changes subtly during shipment and that you have to taste it on its home ground to know it at its best), the silken texture of a wafer-thin slice of **Jabugo** cured ham, and the incomparable flavour of the freshly caught **fish** and **seafood** than can be enjoyed not only on the coast but even in land-locked Madrid, to which it is whisked daily straight from the quays of Galicia. Even so, the chances are that most visitors will come to Spain expecting to do battle with foreign food or, put another way, too much oil and too much garlic.

It isn't like that. Spain is a nation where food is taken seriously and cooking is an art form (the current genre is *nouvelle cuisine*). You have only to watch a woman choosing her fish in the market or the consultations which go on in restaurants before ordering to see how the Spaniards feel about food. It is a country of all-male gastronomical fraternities, of gastronomical academies, of restaurateurs who dip into ancient recipe books to keep traditional dishes alive... And furthermore, it is a country of contrasts which are reflected in its very different regional styles of cooking.

Andalusia

Bullfighting, sherry, flamenco, Carmen... It is interesting that the foreigner's stereotypical impression of Spain should be composed of such quintessentially Andalusian ingredients. Andalusia is one of the most extensive and varied regions in Spain, bounded by hundreds of kilometres of coastline, both Mediterranean and Atlantic, separated from the rest of the peninsula to the N by the Sierra Morena and just a stone's throw from N Africa at its southernmost point. Its strategic location, its wealth of natural resources —copper, olive oil, wine— and nowadays its seaside resorts and historic cities, have made Andalusia a magnet for foreign invaders for over 3,000 years. Geographically it embraces mountains and valleys, fertile farmland and arid desert, while culturally it bears the imprint of the Phoenicians, Romans and, above all, the Moors. It is an area which, under Muslim domination during the Middle Ages enjoyed a cultural Golden Age and which, after the historic events of 1492 played a key role in trade and interchange on all levels with the New World. Despite its subsequent decline, Andalusia's past glories are still to be discerned in its vivid and individual character, an amalgam of both the tangible and the more ephemeral elements of this rich heritage.

In culinary terms, Andalusia's outstanding contribution to Spain's overall panorama is ***gazpacho***, Semitic in origin, which appears in many guises even within Andalusia itself. In its classic form, it is a bright red cold tomato, onion, garlic and cucumber soup made with the excellent local olive oil. Variants include *salmorejo* (a less diluted version used as a sauce for meat and fish) and *ajoblanco* (a cold soup of crushed almonds and garlic served with peeled moscatel grapes). Another classic makes full use of the plentiful seafood of the coast and the region's olive oil: *pescaíto frito* is a fried fish mixture which, thanks to the freshness of the fish and the cook's knack of timing so that it is crisp and golden on the outside yet still succulent within, is a far cry from Britain's famous fish and chips. Andalusia is also credited with the invention of *tapas*, little aperitif snacks which put the unimaginative peanut and potato crisp to shame. Emblematic of a way of life where the heat of the day is avoided by taking one's time over glasses of chilled *fino* sherry and conversation, *tapas* are an art form in Andalusia and, as you move from bar to bar, can make a meal in themselves.

Andalusia's varied geography is reflected in its cuisine. **Almería** at its eastern extreme, forms the tail end of the 'rice belt', and *arroz a la banda* (see 'Catalonia' below) and similar dishes are common along the coast, while inland ancient recipes for game stews and the like still survive.

Granada is a special case. This last stronghold of the Moors whose privileged geographical situation enabled the self-sufficient Nasrid kingdom to thrive until it was finally ousted in 1492 still bears its imprint. Some of the best cured ham in Spain, *Jamón de Trévelez*, comes from the mountainous Alpujarra, and in combination with tender broad beans from the fertile plain below produces the Granada classic *habas con jamón*. *Tortilla sacromonte*, a dish traditional to the Monastery of Sacromonte, has now become a feature of tourist menus though in a form that bears little relation to the original recipe for this extraordinary omelette of poached brains sautéed in bread crumbs, bull or lamb's testicles, potatoes, red peppers and peas. Granada's fertile *vega* also produces tropical fruits, while the Costa del Sol is rich in fish and seafood. In both Granada and neighbouring Córdoba, there are local gastronomical academies which, in co-operation with enterprising restaurateurs, are making efforts to save traditional local recipes from extinction.

The gastronomy of **Córdoba**, best known for its *salmorejos* (see above) and *estofado de rabo de toro* (stew of ox or bull's tail), shows a clear division between the N and SW area (whose cuisine owes much to the traditional dishes of the shepherds who brought their flocks to graze annually in the Guadalquivir basin) and the more vegetable oriented *vega*, or fertile plain, and farmlands. Some clearly Moorish dishes have been reinstated —among them *alboronía* (an aubergine-rich ratatouille) and *cordero a la miel* (lamb with honey)— in this area where tourism does a great deal to keep restaurateurs on their toes.

Jaén's individual contributions to Andalusian cuisine include *ajilimójili* sauce, *pipirrana* (a tomato, tuna and black olive salad) and various *bacalao* (salt-cod) dishes.

Seville is the capital of Andalusia and its many good restaurants are very much in tune with modern movements in gastronomy while sharing the region's overall concern for keeping ancient traditions alive. Among Seville's own particular specialities are *pescaíto frito* (succulent crisp fried fish), *pavías de pescado* (crisply fried chunks of cod or hake in batter), *huevos a la flamenca* (baked eggs with *chorizo* sausage and asparagus), *flamenquines* (pork and ham croquettes —a typical *tapa*) and the classic *pato con aceitunas*, also known as *pato a la sevillana* (duck with olives in a sherry sauce).

Málaga's stretch of the Costa del Sol around Marbella, haven of the international jet set, has countless restaurants, many of them excellent, to cater for a demanding cosmopolitan clientele. But traditional favourites survive in parallel —*ajoblanco* (a milky almond and garlic soup served with sweet grapes found elsewhere in Andalusia), *chanquetes* (tiny transparent anchovy-like fish usually served fried), *gambas* (prawns), *coquinas* (bean clams), the ubiquitous *pescaíto frito* (see above), barbecued sardines... all supremely simple but delicious.

Upmarket tourism has also made its mark on the cuisine of **Cádiz**. Here, too, seafood reigns supreme —look out particularly for Sanlúcar *langostinos* (king prawns)— and it features in many traditional dishes like **urta a la roteña** (seabream baked with green peppers and brandy), *chocos con habas* (cuttlefish with broad beans) and *caldillo de perro* (fish broth given a sharp tang by the juice of a Seville orange). Others, like *riñones al jerez* (kidneys in sherry sauce), have gone on to become international classics.

The coast of **Huelva** also excels for its seafood, particularly its splendid *cigalas* (Norway lobsters), *coquinas* (bean clams), and *gambas* (prawns), and fish dishes like *pargo encebollado* (seabream with onion), *raya en pimentón* (ray cooked with sweet paprika) and *pez espada* (swordfish), but it is from the mountainous interior that its star contribution comes. *Jamón de Jabugo*, a silky-textured cured ham often served in thin slices as an aperitif or first course, is a delicacy prized throughout Spain.

Andalusia's Moorish past is particularly evident in its traditional confectionery. As the region was gradually reconquered from the 13C on, Moorish sweets were adopted and 'Christianized', though in name only, by the nuns of the many convents which were founded at that time. They still make the sweets to this day and sell to the public direct from the convents where, secluded from the outside world, ancient recipes survive unchanged. Typical specialities include *alfajores* (almond, walnut and honey cakes), *turrón* (a type of nougat), *polvorones* (crumbly shortcakes), *mantecados* (cinnamon cup cakes), *arropes* (fruit syrups), *pestiños* (crisp honey-soaked pancakes), *buñuelos* (fritters with various fillings) and *yemas de San Leandro* (candied egg yolks). Some of them are produced all the year round and others, despite their unmistakably Muslim provenance, are now inextricably associated with the big Christian festivals.

Aragón, Navarre and La Rioja

The food of Navarre and La Rioja is similar to what you will find in the mainland areas of the Basque Country, though with its own particular nuances. In the Middle Ages, hordes of pilgrims passed through Navarre after crossing the Pyrenees on their way to the shrine of Saint James in Santiago de Compostela in Galicia. The area had to learn to cater for what were, in effect, foreign tourists and its cuisine absorbed influences from France, its immediate neighbour to the N —some elaborate meat stews using chocolate still survive from those times. The fertile local soil is excellent for growing vegetables —asparagus, beans, peppers— so it is hardly surprising that *menestra de verduras* (a mixture of boiled and fried fresh vegetables) should be one of Navarre's classic dishes. *Trucha a la navarra* (trout sautéed with a slice of cured ham inside it) is another, as are game stews, particularly made with snipe and pigeon.

La Rioja, best known for its excellent wine, also produces the delicious fruit and vegetables typical of the fertile Ebro basin. Local specialities include *menestra* (see 'Levante' below), *pisto riojano* (a sort of ratatouille), *pimientos rellenos* (stuffed peppers) and, providing a delightful viticultural touch, *chuletas al sarmiento* (chops cooked with young vine-shoots).

The most characteristic recipes of Aragón are its *chilindrón* dishes. This means that red peppers feature as an important ingredient of rich stews of lamb, rabbit or, particularly, chicken. Others, like *cabrito en espedo* (spit-roasted kid) and hearty meat stews reflect the culture of the herdsmen of the Pyrenean foothills, while the prized *trufas* (truffles) of El Maestrazgo and the delicious vegetables grown in the alluvial soil alongside the Ebro provide a delicate counterbalance. As in so many other parts of Spain, the desserts in this area are a survival from the period of Muslim occupation: *frutas de Aragón* (crystallized fruit filled with chocolate), Maraschino cherries and *guirlache* (almond nougat) bear the unmistakable stamp of a Moorish pedigree.

Asturias and Cantabria

Although Asturias and Cantabria are closely linked geographically, their traditional dishes are as different from each other as from those of neighbouring Galicia and the Basque Country. Nevertheless, they all share the common bond of climate, close proximity to the sea and centuries of isolation which have accentuated their regional allegiance.

Both Asturian and Cantabrian cooking reflect their situation between sea and mountain. Classic Asturian dishes like *merluza a la sidra* (hake in cider sauce) and *caldereta* (a rich fish and seafood stew) reflect Asturias' maritime links, whereas its most famous dish of all, *fabada*, which has become a favourite throughout Spain, is a clear product of the interior. *Fabada* is a stew made of dried white beans which take on a delicious buttery consistency as they absorb the juices of the pork, bacon and spicy sausages with which they are cooked. *Chosco* and other locally made sausages are a basic ingredient in various hearty Asturian dishes, while the more delicate salmon, which makes its way upriver from the sea, is another great favourite.

Asturias' best desserts are *casadielles* (walnut-filled puff pastry turnovers), *arroz con leche* (rice pudding) made with creamy local milk and topped with a crisp layer of caramelized sugar, and *frixueles* (pancakes). As one would expect of an area of such rich pastureland, this is also a cheese-making region. Few Spanish cheeses are exported, so make a point of sampling them on the spot —Afuega'l pitu, Gamoeu and, most famous of all, **Cabrales**, a pungent blue cheese wrapped in vine leaves.

Asturias is not a wine-growing area, but produces quantities of excellent **dry cider**, ritually served by pouring small quantities from a great height into large tumblers to let it 'breathe' on the way.

Neighbouring Cantabria has particularly good **sardines**, always cooked as simply as possible, and **anchovies** which are delicious fried in batter or marinated in oil and vinegar, as well as the more elegant tuna and salmon.

The mountainous interior produces excellent meat and dairy products, including some outstanding **cheeses**. Among the region's most famous culinary inventions are *quesada*, a kind of cheesecake, and *sobaos pasiegos*, light buttery spongecakes from Vega de Pas.

Balearic Islands

Anyone who goes island-hopping in the Balearics will find surprising differences in the cuisine of one island and another, although they all share the common bond of being essentially Mediterranean. In this respect, Balearic cuisine is similar to Catalonia's —Menorca's answer to *alioli* is *mahonesa*, known the world over as mayonnaise. They also share the same predilection for mixing savoury and sweet, and nuts and dried fruit play an important role in many local recipes which, despite the islands' having been discovered by tourism, still retain their traditional character.

There is a curious approach to soup here —*sopa mallorquina* is more solid than liquid in that it incorporates a hearty chunk of country bread. Charcuterie of all sorts is very popular, particularly *sobrasada* (a spicy sausage spread) and *botifarrons* (sausages similar to Catalonia's *butifarras*). Pork lard is used to make *ensaimadas*, delicious sweet spiral rolls eaten for breakfast or *merienda* (see 'Spanish Way of Life') which never taste as good elsewhere as in their native Majorca. Pastries and pies, like *empanadillas* and *cocas*, can have either savoury (anchovies, spinach, tomato) or sweet (peach, candied pumpkin, custard) fillings and make excellent light snacks on a hot day.

As one would expect of island cuisine, fish and seafood are a staple. You will find *caldereta de peix* (a fish and seafood stew) in Majorca, *caldereta de langosta* (lobster and tomato stew) in Menorca, various rice and seafood dishes common to both of them and, in Ibiza, *langosta al estilo de Ibiza* (the local lobster speciality), *burrida de ratjada* (poached ray served with a sauce of chopped almonds) and its famous *flaó*, a mint and cinnamon flavoured cheesecake mentioned in Ruperto de Nola's 16C cookery book.

Basque Country

The cuisine of the Basque Country is arguably the most stylish in Spain. The Basques love to eat well, in terms of both quality and quantity, and this is the part of Spain where gastronomical societies flourish. These are men-only gourmet clubs whose members prepare, consume and criticize gargantuan meals and hold cooking competitions whose winners often go on to fame and fortune. Small wonder, then, that many of the best restaurants in the country are concentrated here, open to the latest innovations and the spearhead of Spain's *nouvelle cuisine* movement.

Traditional Basque food is hearty and full-flavoured. Although its best known classics are fish dishes, vast beef steaks and rich meat stews are equally popular. *Bacalao* (cod, either fresh or salt) is plentiful in these parts, and *bacalao a la vizcaína* (a casserole of cod with sweet peppers, cured ham and egg yolk), *bacalao a la bilbaína* (a more piquant version) and *bacalao al pil-pil* (*pil-pil* is the sound of the fish simmering gently in its own juices, oil and garlic) have become favourites all over Spain.

Merluza (hake) is another favourite fish, and is classically cooked in *salsa verde* (a rich green parsley sauce), *al pil-pil* (in its own juices, oil and garlic), or in combination with *angulas* (baby eels) and *almejas* (clams). The little fleshy part around the gills of the fish is considered a particular delicacy —you will see it on menus as *kokotxas* or *cocochas*. Look out, too, for *besugo* (sea bream); *chipirones* (squid), often served in a sinister looking but delicious black sauce made with their own ink; *sardinas* (sardines), at their best in August; *bonito* (tuna), which features in the Basque Country's *marmitako*, a casserole of tuna, tomatoes and potatoes; *mero* (grouper); *txangurro* (spider crab) and delicately flavoured *angulas* (tiny baby eels), usually cooked in a little oil and garlic and served piping hot. For dessert, try *mamiya* (home-made junket prepared in a little earthenware pot and served topped with honey) or fragile *canutillos de crema* (puff-pastry custard horns dusted with icing sugar and cinnamon).

Canary Islands

Canary Island cooking, the most exotic in Spain, bears vestigial traces of the island's original Guanche culture but the outstanding influence on it has been the islands' role as the link between Europe and the Americas. The *tomate* (tomato), unknown before the discovery of the New World, was introduced into the Canaries at an early stage and has flourished there ever since as has its successor, the *plátano* (banana).

One of the most characteristic features of Canary Island food is *gofio*, little balls of toasted maize meal which serve as a substitute for bread. The staple everyday dish, the equivalent of the *cocido* stew which crops up in various guises all over Spain, is *puchero canario*, which incorporates local ingredients like pumpkin, sweet corn, yams, pears, sweet potatoes and potatoes. The classic special occasion dish is *sancocho*, poached fish, usually *sama* (dentex) served with a *mojo* sauce. These cold sauces are another typical feature of local cuisine: basically made with water, oil, vinegar, garlic and salt, various additions are made according to the dish in question —*mojo verde* adds fresh coriander to the basic sauce and is served with fried and salt fish; *cherne salado* (salt wreck-fish) is usually served with a piquant sauce. *Papas arrugadas* (literally 'wrinkled potatoes' —potatoes boiled in their skins with lots of salt) will appear on every menu alongside a vast variety of local fish and seafood. Only those with an incurably sweet tooth will bother to look at the dessert section in these islands where all sorts of **tropical fruits**, like mangoes, papayas and pineapples, are so cheap, fresh and delicious.

Castile

Castilian cuisine is the most widespread in the whole of Spain yet it varies little from area to area with the exception of León, which offers a foretaste of its northern neighbours Galicia and Asturias and, to a lesser degree, Salamanca and Zamora which have certain individual gastronomic characteristics.

In the main, the predominant style of cooking throughout the various provinces which make up present-day Castile and León has a certain austerity about it, reflecting its extreme, continental climate and the character of the local people who are famed for their determination and endurance rather than their lively imagination. This is an important cereal, pulse and meat producing area and these are the mainstays of its cuisine, though there are also plenty of fruit and vegetables from its greener pockets and game from the mountains.

Castile is known in Spanish as *'la tierra de pan'* (the land of bread) and its long wheat-growing tradition shows not only in the presence of bread in many everyday dishes like *migas* (savoury fried bread), *sopa castellana* and *sopa de ajo* (paprika and garlic flavoured broth poured over a slice of fried bread, with an egg added just before serving) but also in its wide range of buns and cakes. The unirrigated land produces excellent pulses —*garbanzos* (chickpeas), *lentejas* (lentils) and *alubias* (beans)— which, in combination with various parts of the pig and spicy cured sausage once nourished a race of empire builders and today are often to be found on the menus of the smartest restaurants in Madrid. The region is also famous for its roasts, eaten for Sunday lunch or on special occasions. Both suckling pig and baby lamb, simply roasted with a little water, salt and perhaps a sprig of thyme are eaten very young which, in combination with perfect timing in the oven, gives the meat a supremely delicate flavour and texture. Roasts are usually cut into pieces and brought to the table in the earthenware dish in which they were cooked, and served with their own juices and a simple salad.

The best roast lamb is to be found within the Burgos - Soria - Segovia triangle (particularly around Segovia), while *tostón* or *cochinillo* (suckling pig) is said to be at its best from Segovia up to Arévalo and Zamora.

In **León**, especially in the northern areas of El Bierzo and Los Ancares, the food takes on an increasing similarity to what is to be found in neighbouring Galicia and Asturias with dishes like *lacón con grelos* (ham hock with turnip greens), *botillo* (sausage cooked with potatoes and other vegetables) and *empanadas* (large flat savoury pies). León was the home of the *arrieros*, or muleteers who, in times gone by, transported provisions from the N of Spain to the S and one of their typical recipes, *ajoarriero* made with salt cod, crops up all along their route. In **Salamanca**, a bull-breeding area, it is hardly surprising that the local dishes should be predominantly meaty —*rabos de buey estofados* (ox-tail stew), ragouts, steaks and chops are all very typical. There are also very good cured sausages in the area, particularly from Candelario, and you are also likely to be offered *farinato*, a seasoned sausage made basically of pork fat and bread which you should be warned is something of an acquired taste.

Catalonia

Catalan food is held by many to be the most varied and sophisticated in Spain. It is certainly the best documented —Spain's first cookery book, by Ruperto de Nola, chef to Alfonso V, was published in Barcelona in 1520. Its privileged geographical situation and its eventful history have subjected Catalonia to many varied influences over the centuries, a fact clearly reflected in its cuisine. The waters off its extensive coastline are rich in fish and seafood, while inland fruit and vegetable orchards and vineyards flourish. Unsurprisingly, over 2,000 years ago Phoenicians, Greeks and Romans were attracted to this area of the peninsula and implanted elements of their Mediterranean cultures whose gastronomic influence, among others, is felt to this day (*alioli*, a typical Catalan sauce of crushed garlic and olive oil, is believed to date from those times). Later, in the 13-14C, Catalonia flourished as a base from which Spain extended her dominion over the Mediterranean and, in the 19C, saw the emergence of a prosperous middle class with the arrival of the Industrial Revolution. All these elements had their effect on local cuisine in which the peasant and the bourgeois are still clearly discernible in an approach to food which, like the Basque's, is essentially open-minded and imaginative —some of the best *nouvelle cuisine* in Europe is to be found in the restaurants of Catalonia.

Within Catalonia, various distinct styles of cooking are clearly identifiable —in Gerona, for example, the traditional food along the Costa Brava is quite different from what you will find in inland Ampurdán. **Ampurdán** attracts quite as many tourists for its gastronomy as for its lovely medieval architecture. It is known for its excellent country, which is not to say rustic, cooking. Surprising combinations of sweet and savoury (a characteristic of Catalan cooking as a whole) produce dishes like *oca con peras* (baby goose with pine nuts, raisins and pears), *pato con manzanas e higos* (duck with apples and figs) and *liebre con castañas* (hare with chestnuts). Even the more hearty dishes of the Ampurdán, like *sopa de menta* (mint soup), *bon estofat* (beef stew) and *escudella de pagés* (a bean, rice and noodle stew with spicy sausage and vegetables) have a certain finesse about them. The excellent local sausages —both black and white *butifarras*, *bisbe* blood sausage, the thinner spicy *fuet*, particularly good *salchichón* from Vic— crop up again and again in the region's originally peasant dishes, now elevated to gourmet status.

Fish is, of course, the main staple of the cuisine of the **Costa Brava**, and many ancient simple fishermen's recipes, like *suquet de peix* (a fish stew whose contents vary according to the catch) have now become classics to be found in the smartest restaurants. *Zarzuela de mariscos* is a more sophisticated medley of seafood which features one of the star local ingredients, *langosta* (lobster). You will be offered lobster grilled, stuffed, and in the surprising combination of the Catalan classic *llagosta i pollastre* (lobster with chicken in a hazelnut sauce).

The cosmopolitan city of **BARCELONA** is, understandably, where the cuisine enjoyed by the prosperous Catalan bourgeoisie has flourished, and it has been famous for its superb restaurants since the 19C. Favourite dishes range from the supremely simple and delicious *pan con tomate* (fresh bread rubbed with a cut tomato and sprinkled with salt and olive oil), the everyday *escudella i carn d'olla* (a stew of rice and noodles cooked with meat and local sausages, now elevated to the rank of a regional classic), to adopted foreign dishes, like *canelones* (cannelloni) which are eaten on special occasions. Others, like *fideos en cazuela* (a noodle hot-pot), *mongetes amb botifarra* (bean stew with *butifarra* sausage) and *xamfaina de bacallá* (ratatouille with cod) make full use of the traditional local ingredients from the coast and inland.

Barcelonans are great bakers of *cocas*, pizza-like pies made with a vast variety of sweet or savoury ingredients; they also make famous Easter versions called *monas*, topped with chocolate, which you must be sure to try if you are there around the right time. The most popular desserts are *menjar blanc* (an almond flavoured custard similar in both name and texture to England's blancmange), *mel i mató* (curd cheese with honey) and *crema catalana* (crème brulée).

The food in the mountainous region of Lérida is sturdier and simpler altogether and meat, game and trout play an important role in local dishes, the best known of which include *manos de cerdo con nabos* (pig's feet with turnips), *arroz con conejo* (rice cooked with rabbit in a rich stock —there are also fish versions), *conejo al alioli* (rabbit with garlic and olive oil sauce) and more elaborate *civets* (casseroles of game cooked in red wine). The local olive oil is excellent (and would make a good buy to take home with you), as is the fruit, particularly pears. The area of the Pyrenees which is within Lérida is famous for its hand-made cheese, a gourmet's delight and hard to come by even in Spain.

Tarragona's cuisine offers a foretaste of things to come further down the coast with rice dishes like *arroz negro* (rice with squid called 'black rice' because of the colour the rice absorbs from the squid's ink) and *arroz a la banda* (rice cooked in a rich fish and seafood stock) which often look quite unprepossessing but whose subtle combination of flavours accompanied by a crisp salad and a light local wine exemplify perfectly the principle that simple is beautiful. This is the area, too, of *romesco*, a sauce made of dried sweet peppers, almonds, garlic and olive oil, which is believed to date back a thousand years or more. It appears in many guises and is particularly good as a dressing for grilled shellfish, though it also crops up in some meat dishes. The maritime tradition is particularly clear in local favourites like *bull de tonya* (underside of tuna with beans and snails), *pataco* (a tuna casserole similar to the Basque's *marmitako*), *langostinos* (king prawns —the best ones come from San Carlos de la Rápita) and *parrillada de pescado* (a platter of mixed grilled seafood).

Extremadura

Extremadura formed part of the route from León to the banks of the Guadalquivir followed by the shepherds of the famous Castilian *Mesta* (see 'Castile and León') in search of fresh pasture for their flocks. In compensation for stripping the landscape of its greenery, these wandering shepherds left behind them an enduring gastronomic legacy of hearty one-pot dishes like *caldereta* (a piquant kid or lamb stew), *rabos de cordero* (a stew of lamb's tails), *gazpacho extremeño* (similar to Andalusia's) and *migas de pastor* (literally 'shepherd's crumbs' —a way of making stale bread palatable by frying it with bacon, garlic, onion and paprika). But most everyday dishes in this landlocked region are pork-based —its **Montánchez hams** and **sausages** are particularly good— backed up by *tenca* (tench), *ancas de rana* (frogs' legs) and *bacalao* (salt cod) which features in many local recipes.

Surprisingly, given the general aridity of Extremadura, the microclimate enjoyed by the Jerte and La Vera valleys produces excellent **fruit** —cherries, strawberries, peaches, figs, apples, pears, oranges and lemons, while melons and watermelons grow well in the irrigated land around Badajoz. The region's traditional honey-soaked pastries are a clear legacy of its sybaritic Moorish-Jewish past.

Galicia

Ask any Spaniard what's best to eat in Galicia and he is sure to say **fish** and **seafood**, though he is also likely to mention *lacón con grelos* (ham hock with turnip greens), *empanadas* (large flat savoury pies) and recommend the light local wines, **Ribeiro** and, more expensive and exquisite, **Albariño**.

Even in this nation of food lovers, *gallegos* stand out for their reverential attitude to food. This rainy, mountainous region's natural resources are essentially its green pastureland and the sea. Small wonder, then, that it should produce excellent meat, cheese, game and, above all, a vast variety of fish and seafood which flourish in its rivers and in the chilly waters off the northern coasts. Galicia's Celtic mists and the constant possibility of rain, even at the height of summer, produce 'green' wines, low in alcohol and with an attractive acidic edge, similar to those of nearby Portugal, which perfectly complement the delicate flavours of seafood. The essential feature of Galician food is simplicity. Anything prepared *a la gallega* has a touch of oil, garlic and paprika, perhaps, but little else so that all the freshness of the ingredients shows through.

Galicia even goes so far as to hold *fiestas* in honour of fish and *mariscos* (seafood) which, given that fishing has been its main source of employment for centuries, is hardly surprising. *Ostras* (oysters, especially ones from Arcade), *percebes* (goose-barnacles), *santiaguiños* (little locust lobsters), *mejillones* (mussels) and *vieiras* (scallops), whose shell became the badge worn by pilgrims who followed Saint James' Way to Santiago de Compostela, are all Galician classics. You will also find that *pulpo* (octopus) is on the menu at even the tiniest quay-side bar —don't be put off by the look of it: the white flesh is delicate and delicious. One of the lasting impressions you are sure to take away with you from Galicia is the appetizing smell of *sardinas* (sardines) being grilled in the open air on the pavement or even on the beach —you will often see them being delivered fresh off the boat. Upmarket fish, like *lenguado* (sole), *merluza* (hake), *rodaballo* (turbot) and *salmón* (salmon) are always cooked as simply as possible, though salmon, along with *lamprea* (lamprey eel), also features as one of many fillings for Galicia's famous *empanada* pies.

Galicia has two famous desserts: *filloas* (pancakes) and *tarta de Santiago*, a ground almond tart traditionally decorated with icing sugar sprinkled around a cross-shape, now all too often a dull commercial imitation of the moist, spicy delicacy it should be.

La Mancha

La Mancha, the barren elevated plateau of central Spain immortalized by Cervantes as the scenario for the adventures of *Don Quixote*, embraces part of several modern-day provinces. The cuisine of the entire area is fairly consistent throughout with the obvious exception of Madrid and, to a lesser extent, the region of La Alcarria where the food resembles that of neighbouring Aragón.

The traditional everyday dishes of La Mancha are stews made of various pulses cooked with pork and sausages, while special occasions are celebrated with roasts of suckling pig or baby lamb. Some local specialities date back many centuries: *gazpacho manchego* bears no relation to Andalusia's famous soups but is a rich stew of rabbit, lamb, chicken and pork believed to be Roman in origin, while the Moorish touch is obvious in *pisto manchego*, a sort of ratatouille. *Mojete, ajoarriero* and *tiznao* are all based on *bacalao* (salt cod) and are relics of the time when fresh fish was not easy to come by in the interior. More specifically local dishes include *perdices escabechadas* (soused partridge), particularly associated with Toledo, and *monteruelo* (a paté of pig's liver and game) typical of Cuenca.

MADRID, though it does have its own classics like *cocido madrileño* (a stew of chickpeas with meat, sausage and vegetables served in separate stages) and *callos a la madrileña* (tripe in a piquant red sauce), like all capitals has come to cater for all tastes. Its range of restaurants is vast and the top ones are among the best in Europe. The fact that fresh fish and seafood are whisked within hours from the coast of Galicia to the restaurants and markets of Madrid, hundreds of miles from the sea, just goes to show what foodies Spaniards are.

La Alcarria (Guadalajara) is best known in gastronomic terms for its excellent lamb eaten very young and roasted with the wild thyme and other herbs which also lend their flavour to the local honey, famous throughout Spain.

Levante

Valencia and Murcia were occupied by the Moors in the 8C. With their customary skill in matters of irrigation, they exploited to the full the potential of the green tidal flatlands between coast and mountains, adding rice to the local crops of fruit and vegetables thus giving rise to a culinary tradition which flourishes to this day. This is an area of rice connoisseurs (Spanish rice is short grained with a nutty flavour) and the different areas of this long stretch of coast have their own local specialities.

Castellón's local rice dish is *arroz empedrado*, made with beans, and it also has excellent seafood, particularly the *langostinos* (king prawns) from Vinaroz. The wild picturesque hill country of the Maestrazgo, thanks to its relative inaccessibility, has retained its traditional way of life very much intact. This is true of local customs, architecture and food. The locals still love hearty food, full of calories, with plenty of meat, both fresh and cured. *Flaon*, a traditional version of cheese cake, is still made hereabouts as described in Ruperto de Nola's 16C cookery book (see 'Catalonia' above).

Valencia is the heart of the rice country and is the home of *paella*. Pedants will enjoy the information that the *paella* is actually the large flat pan in which the rice is cooked, and that the dish is really called *arroz en paella*. There are literally hundreds of Valencian rice recipes, some cooked in a *paella* pan, like *paella marinera* (rice with seafood), *paella de anguilas* (rice with eel), *paella de montaña* (rice with meat and game) and others in earthenware casseroles, like ***arros amb fesols y naps*** (the Catalan name for a rice dish with pork, dried beans and turnips) and ***arroz negro*** (see 'Catalonia' above). But the classic ***paella a la valenciana***, saffron-tinted rice with chicken, *chorizo* sausage, lobster, clams and mussels among its many ingredients is the local star. A true *paella* is a thing of beauty and therefore worth waiting for. The golden rule is not to eat anywhere that offers you a quick *paella*: be prepared to wait a good 40 minutes and you will be rewarded not only with a delicious meal but also with the satisfaction of knowing that you are a cut above the average tourist.

Around **La Albufera** there is a local version of *alioli* known as ***all-i-pebre***, which includes locally produced paprika and serves as the cooking liquid in the eel dish known as ***all-i-pebre de anguilas***. As well as simple fishermen's recipes like ***sepia a la plancha*** (grilled cuttlefish), there are more complex ones which combine the many local varieties of seafood —***salmonete*** (red mullet), ***mujol*** (grey mullet), ***dentón*** (dentex), ***lubina*** (sea bass)— with the produce of the fertile plain.

The coastal cuisine of **Alicante** is very much a continuation of the Valencian, though it does have a rice dish all its own called ***arroz con costra*** (rice with a crust, the crust in question being a topping of beaten egg). The mountainous area inland has a more distinctive culinary personality. Here you will find ***bajoques farcides*** (stuffed peppers), ***olleta de music*** (a sweet-corn stew traditionally eaten at *fiesta* time), the famous Jijona ***giraboix*** (cod with *alioli* sauce) and a local version of the Andalusian ***gazpacho*** (a cold tomato and cucumber soup).

As in many other parts of Spain which absorbed the culture of their Muslim overlords during centuries of domination, the confectionery of this area is unmistakably Moorish in origin. The most famous are the different types of ***turrón*** (a sort of nougat made of honey and almonds) made in Jijona and Alicante, but there are masses of sweets and cakes, like ***buñuelos*** (little doughnuts with a variety of fillings), ***carquinyols*** (crushed almond cookies), ***arrope*** (fruit cooked in wine must), ***monas*** and ***cocas*** (sweet or savoury pizza-like pies which tend to make an appearance at *fiesta* time). Then, of course, there are Valencia's famous ***naranjas*** (oranges) —a freshly picked orange is hard to beat— and excellent hot weather antidotes like ***horchata de chufas*** (a chilled milky drink made from tiger nuts) and the ***helados*** (ice creams) for which both Valencia and Alicante are well known.

Murcia is still within the 'rice belt', but here the rice is most frequently combined with the vegetables from the fertile plain. Vegetarians will be spoiled for choice in this area of ***arroz con habas tiernas*** (rice with baby broad beans), ***arroz y pava*** (rice with cauliflower), ***paella huertana*** (vegetable *paella*), ***pisto murciano*** (the local version of ratatouille), ***menestra de verduras*** (a medley of boiled and fried fresh vegetables), ***alcachofas*** (artichokes) and ***berenjenas*** (aubergines, another Moorish legacy), ***pipirrana*** (a tomato, green pepper and tuna salad with an egg dressing) and various ***revueltos*** (scrambled egg dishes) mixed with, for example, garlic shoots, beans or asparagus. ***Pastel murciano*** (a puff pastry veal pie), which also makes use of Murcia's famous tomatoes and peppers, is easy to come by and is excellent for picnics. Around the Mar Menor, the lagoon-like stretch of sea in the SE corner of the province, and the Costa Cálida stretch of Murcia's coastline the accent is more on fish. ***Caldero murciano*** (rice with dried red peppers and seafood) is traditionally cooked in an iron pot, or *caldero*, suspended over the fire, and served with *alioli* garlic sauce. Simpler, but equally delicious, are dishes like ***dorada a la sal*** (salt-baked sea bream), ***mujol*** (grey mullet) and tiny, full-flavoured ***langostinos*** (prawns) from the Mar Menor.

Here let the antiquarian pore over the stirring memorials of many thousand years, the vestiges of Phoenician enterprise, of Roman magnificence, of Moorish elegance, in that storehouse of ancient customs, that repository of all elsewhere long forgotten and passed by; here let him gaze upon those classical monuments, unequalled almost in Greece or Italy, and on those fairy Aladdin palaces, the creatures of Oriental gorgeousness and imagination, with which Spain alone can enchant the dull European; here let the man of feeling dwell on the poetry of her envy-disarming decay...; here let the lover of art feed his eyes with the mighty masterpieces of Italian art... or with the living nature of Velázquez and Murillo...; here let the artist sketch the lowly mosque of the Moor, the lofty cathedral of the Christian...; art and nature here offer subjects, from the feudal castle, the vast Escorial, the rock-built alcazar of imperial Toledo (to) the sunny towers of stately Seville...; let the botanist cull from the wild hothouse of nature plants unknown, unnumbered, matchless in colour, and breathing the aroma of the sweet south; let all, learned or unlearned, listen to the song, the guitar, the castanet; ...(For here,) as Don Quixote said, there are opportunities for what are called adventures elbow-deep .

RICHARD FORD   *Hand-book for Spain*

Thus wrote one Romantic English traveller in 1845. A century and a half later Spain remains that and much more. Spain's contribution to culture continues to be rich and diverse. Among the highlights are the works of major 19C novelists, Benito Pérez Galdos and Leopoldo Alas, better known as Clarín; two famous groups of writers —the Generation of '98 and the Generation of '27— that included among its members Nobel Prize winners Vicente Aleixandre and Juan Ramón Jiménez, and other names of international renown like Ramón María del Valle-Inclán, Miguel de Unamuno, Federico García Lorca, Antonio Machado, Rafael Alberti, Camilo José Cela and Miguel Delibes; the philosophy of José Ortega y Gasset and the scientific research of Santiago Ramón y Cajal and Severo Ochoa, both of them Nobel Prize winners; the artistic genius of Francisco Goya and Pablo Picasso, of Salvador Dalí, Joan Miró, and the more recent work of Antonio Tàpies and Antonio López; the sculpture of Mariano Benlliure, Pablo Gargallo and Eduardo Chillida; the architecture of Antonio Gaudí, José Luis Sert, Rafael Moneo, and Ricardo Bofill; the town planning of Arturo Soria, precursor of Le Corbusier; the audacious engineering and the innovative technology of submarine designer Narciso Monturiol and Juan de la Cierva, creator of the autogiro; the music of figures of the stature of Pablo Casals and Andrés Segovia, Plácido Domingo and Montserrat Caballé, Manuel de Falla and Luis de Pablo; the movie-making of Luis Buñuel, Luis Berlanga and Oscar winner José Luis Garci; the fashion of Pedro Morago and Adolfo Domínguez; the youngest and hardest rock in Europe and the post-modern *movida* —the contemporary culture of Spain's artistic in-crowd...

Architecture and Town Planning

The successive civilizations and empires that swept across Spain left an exceptional architectural heritage, harvest of the cross-fertilization that occurred down the centuries which, in cultural terms, enriched both the victors and the vanquished. Stop for a moment and see how all this has its roots in a rich and varied cultural legacy built up over Spain's 3,000 years of history and civilization.

PREHISTORIC REMAINS

Prehistoric remains in Spain include Megalithic structures, more than 4,000 years old, such as the **dolmens** of Antequera (Málaga), the **talayot** watchtowers and **naveta** tombs of Menorca (Balearic Islands), and the **cave-dwellings** of Guádix (Granada). Samples of Greek, Carthaginian and Phoenician architectural legacies are scarce, although traces survive of the Greek foundation of Ampurias in the 4C BC and ruins of the walls of Ullastret (Gerona) from the Iberian period.

ROMAN (2C BC-4C AD) AND VISIGOTHIC (5-7C AD) HERITAGE

Roman engineering and architectural legacies include the great **aqueducts** of Segovia, Tarragona and Mérida (Badajoz); **theatres** in Sagunto (Valencia), Mérida (Badajoz) and Tarragona; **bridges** such as the one at Alcántara (Cáceres); innumerable **city walls**, like Lugo's, triumphal **arches** as in Borà (Tarragona) and Medinaceli (Soria), **mosaics** from Itálica (Seville) and Ampurias (Gerona) and countless other relics of the Roman era now exhibited at the outstanding Museo de Arte Romano (Museum of Roman Art) in Mérida (Badajoz).

The Visigothic heritage is more discernible in ideas than in architecture, though some **churches** have survived. The 7C **Santa Comba** in Bande (Orense) and **San Pedro de la Nave** in El Campillo (Zamora) are tiny rectangular stone-built churches, their horseshoe arches and stylized decorative motifs redolent of Byzantine influence and dating from the most fruitful period of Visigothic culture.

MUSLIM AND CHRISTIAN ARCHITECTURAL STYLES (8-15C)

After the Muslim invasion of 711, the architecture of northern, Christian Spain and southern, Muslim Spain were to follow their own separate development for the next 800 years. While in the Moorish kingdom of *Al Andalus* the architectural styles of the Caliphate (8-11C), the Almohads (12-13C) and the Nasrids (14-15C) impressed the indelible imprint of the aesthetics of Islam on southern Spain, the Christian kingdoms of northern Spain were leaving their own, very different, stamp with the Pre-Romanesque (8-10C), the Romanesque (9-13C) and the Gothic (13-15C). But in architecture, as in so many areas of culture, there was cross-fertilization between Christians and Muslims (see 'History') to the extent that two important inter-cultural architectural styles emerged, the **Mudéjar** (11-15C), product of Arab artists and craftsmen living and working in Christian territory, and the **Mozarabic** (9-11C), engendered by their Christian counterparts in Muslim territory.

HISPANO-ARABIC ARCHITECTURE OF THE CALIPHATE OF CORDOBA (8-11C)

The most impressive example of early Muslim architecture is Córdoba's **Mosque** with its 850 columns supporting horseshoe arches alternating creamy stone with red brick and its dense, stylized decoration featuring caligraphic inscriptions, geometric drawings and plant motifs. Córdoba's **Alcázar**, or palace, is organized in typically Moorish style around rectangular patios where gardens, fountains and the play of light and shade are deployed as integral architectural elements.

PRE-ROMANESQUE ARCHITECTURE (8-10C)

Various architectural styles emerged in politically divided northern Spain. Using Visigothic architecture as a basis, Christian **Asturias** developed a style of building that was a precursor of the Romanesque: it consisted of simple, austere, unornamented churches built of solid stone with semicircular arches. **Santa María del Naranco** and **San Miguel de Lillo** (Oviedo) are two examples. Meanwhile, in León **San Miguel de la Escalada** combines the Visigothic with the Caliphal while in **Catalonia** there is a combination of the Caliphal with the Carolingian.

Hispano-Arabic Architecture of the Almohads of Seville (11-13C)

After an initial period of rampage and destruction, the Almoravids and Almohads built mosques and minarets of austere brick, replacing the Moorish horseshoe arch with a more oriental, pointed arch and introducing wooden coffered ceilings and the use of *azulejos* (glazed pottery tiles), as in Seville's **Giralda** and Zaragoza's **Alfajería** palace.

Romanesque Architecture (11-13C)

With the fall of the Córdoban Caliphate in the 11C, the Christian kingdoms of the N saw the blossoming of the Romanesque style —solid stone-built architecture in almost symbolic contrast to the more delicate Moorish approach to form and materials, typically brick, wood and plaster. The earliest Romanesque, in the Pyrenean valleys of Catalonia, is represented by sober little churches with rounded apses and tall steeples, as in **San Clemente de Tahúll** (Lérida). The religious fervour of the medieval world, together with the flood of European pilgrims who travelled the route to Santiago de Compostela, later engendered a succession of churches characterized by softer lines and greater ornamentation, with capitals, arches and bas-reliefs sculpted with a considerable degree of artistic licence. The **Cathedral of Santiago de Compostela** —fronted by a later, Baroque façade— is generally regarded as the culminating work of this architectural period, though there are other major gems, among them the **churches** of Frómista (Palencia), Segovia and Zamora. In the early 12C, the austere **Cistercian** order paved the way for the transition to the Gothic: severe lines, pointed arches, barrel and ribbed vaulting instead of wooden ceilings, smooth walls and long, narrow windows are all typical features and may be seen in the monasteries of **Ripoll**, **Santes Creus**, **La Oliva** and **Santa María de Huerta**. The Romanesque period's major contributions to civic architecture include the **city walls** of Avila and Zamora, **castles**, like Turégano's (Segovia), and palaces like the **Palacio de los Gelmírez** in Santiago de Compostela and the **Palace of the Dukes of Granada** in Estella (Navarre).

Mudejar Architecture (11-15C)

The Mudéjars —Arabs who lived and worked under the Christians after the Reconquest— perpetuated the typically Moorish use of brick and of sophisticated **coffered and tiled ceilings** creating a quintessentially Spanish style which survives in many parts of Spain to this day. Courtly and ecclesiastical examples of the Mudéjar include Seville's **Alcázar** and the **synagogues** in Toledo, while on a popular level the style developed regional variants: in **Castile**, as in Arévalo (Avila) and Toledo, blind arches are a typical feature, while in **Aragón**, the 13-16C **towers** of Zaragoza and Teruel are typified by their decorative geometric tiles.

Hispano-Arabic Architecture of the Nasrids of Granada (14-15C)

Built during the Nasrid period (14C-15C), the **Alhambra** in Granada is *the* great monument to Muslim architecture. Its sophisticated design, intricate lacework carving, ceramic and stucco decoration, stalactitic ceilings, arrangement of open spaces, delicate columns, sculpture and water all speak of an elegant and sybaritic culture. Stone was reserved for defensive buildings, while wood, brick, plaster and tiles were used for royal palaces intended for comfort rather than protection, which mercifully, despite their fragility, have survived to this day.

Gothic Architecture (13-16C)

In the 13C, Gothic architecture was imported from France, and the foreign influence is clearly discernible in Spain's first truly Gothic buildings, like the **cathedrals** of Cuenca and Sigüenza, though the style was soon to take on its own Spanish stamp. Greater technical skill now permitted the use of flying buttresses supporting lofty barrel vaults; ogival arches and fine stone carvings with filigree details became apparent; tall, stylized columns stretched upwards to the ceilings and enormous rose and stained-glass windows lit church interiors and gave buildings a hitherto unknown delicate quality. The **cathedrals** of Burgos, Toledo and León are three Gothic jewels. **Catalonia, Valencia** and **Majorca** evolved their own local variant of the Gothic church, with one single high nave, no transept, pointed or wood-covered vaulting and bare smooth walls, like **Santa María del Mar** in Barcelona. In 14-15C **Castile**, great Flemish architects like **Juan de Colonia** (d. 1481) developed the **flamboyant Gothic** style so characteristic of Spain, as seen in the Cathedral of Segovia and Salamanca's New Cathedral. Later Gothic **cathedrals**, like Seville's, strove for immensity and returned to a strict cruciform floor plan that contrasted with the richer ornamentation absorbed from the Arabs. The **Castle of Coca** (Segovia) and the Palace of the Generalitat (Barcelona) and various middle-class **mansions** in Barcelona and Palma de Mallorca are examples, generally well preserved, of Gothic civic architecture.

ISABELLINE ARCHITECTURE (15-16C)

The Isabelline style of the Catholic Monarchs linked the Gothic with the Renaissance and embraced elements of the flamboyant and Mozarabic styles, covering façades with exuberant sculptural decoration. The major exponents of the style included **Juan Guas** (d. 1496, **Church of San Juan de los Reyes** in Toledo), **Simon de Colonia** (1450-1511, **Church of San Pablo** in Valladolid) and **Enrique Egas** (d. 1534, **Capilla Real** in Granada).

RENAISSANCE AND CLASSICAL ARCHITECTURE (16C)

Golden Age Spain was quick to absorb the effects of the Italian Renaissance and emerged with its own unmistakably **Plateresque** style which had much in common with the Isabelline. The Plateresque, which took its name from the silversmiths whose work it so closely resembled, featured finely chiselled and profusely ornamented stonework surfaces, as in the **University of Salamanca**.

Another, more **Classical**, tendency was seen in the works of **Rodrigo Gil de Hontañón** (1500-1577), architect of the **University** of Alcalá de Henares (Madrid) and of **Pedro Machuca** (1490-1550), designer of the **Palace of Charles V** in Granada. **Diego de Siloé** (1495-1563, University of Granada) and particularly **Andrés de Vandelvira** (1509-1575, Jaén Cathedral) express the austerity of the Hapsburg dynasty. Yet another important style was the **Herreriano**, named after **Juan de Herrera** (1530-1597). He was the architect of **El Escorial**, built for Philip II with the austerity of a monastery and the functionality of a royal residence. This monument of rectilineal severity reflects the spirit of Spanish religious orthodoxy during the Counter-reformation and is emblematic of the imperial psychology of Spain.

CLASSICIST ARCHITECTURE (17-18C)

The Classicism of Herrera was perpetuated to co-exist with the Baroque by **Juan Gómez de Mora** (1580-1647) who, taking as his model the Escorial with its strong horizontal lines and corner turrets, contributed enduring features to the urban landscape of Madrid (Plaza Mayor, Casa de la Villa, Palace of Santa Cruz). With **Herrera the Younger** (1622-1685, **Basilica del Pilar** in Zaragoza), a more relaxed approach saw the absorption of elements of the Italianate Baroque.

BAROQUE ARCHITECTURE (17-18C)

At the height of Spain's Golden Age, there was an exuberant explosion of voluptuous lines and curves, of exaggerated reliefs and motifs drawn from nature. Architecture, sculpture and painting blended together to decorate façades, altarpieces, retrochoirs and niches. The style may be seen at its most sumptuous in the wreathed columns of the ornate **Churrigueresque** fashion initiated by the **Churriguera** brothers (Alberto 1676-1750 and Joaquín 1674-1724), architects of Salamanca's **Plaza Mayor**. But Baroque architecture in Spain differed from province to province. In Celtic **Galicia**, its characteristic features are grandeur of scale, sweeping lines and the granite so typical of the region, best exemplified by **Fernando Casa y Novoa's** (d. 1749) **Obradoiro** façade of Santiago de Compostela's Cathedral; in austere **Castile**, **Pedro de Ribera** (1683-1742) superimposed elaborate decoration on basically Herrerian lines in various buildings around Madrid. In flamboyant **Andalusia**, the Baroque found sumptuous expression in palaces (Ecija and Seville), cathedrals (Guádix) and the elaborate façades of churches and mansions (Jerez). Andalusia had been prepared for the Baroque by the work of **Alonso Cano** (1601-1667, façade of Granada's Cathedral), and found the best exponent of the period in **Vicente Acero** (c. 1700), designer of the cathedrals of Guádix and Cádiz while, in **Levante**, the style often verges on the Rococo, as in the façade of the **Palace of the Marquis of Dos Aguas** by **Ignacio Vergara** (1715-1776). Under the Bourbons, the Baroque was chastened by Classicism as seen in the palaces of Aranjuez, La Granja, Riofrío and Madrid's **Palacio Real**.

NEOCLASSICAL ARCHITECTURE (18-19C)

As a reaction to the excesses of the Baroque period, there was a return to the Greco-Roman classical world of columns and cupolas. Charles III promoted the new style and Neoclassical landmarks in Madrid such as the **Prado Museum**, the **Botanical Gardens**, the **Cibeles Fountain** and the **Alcalá Arch** were built during his reign. The Neoclassical style was to survive well into the 19C (Madrid's National Library and Barcelona's Plaza Real), coexisting with an eclecticism born of the availability of new building materials like **cast iron** (Madrid's Delicias Railway Station and the Crystal Palace in the Retiro Park).

MODERNIST AND NEOMUDEJAR ARCHITECTURE (19-20C)

With the Restoration (see 'History') came a new appreciation of the intrinsically Spanish which gave rise to a wave of **Neomudéjar** brick-built buildings, among them churches, bullrings and railway stations. Meanwhile, the Romantic movement's enthusiasm for the medieval and the Gothic paved the way for the triumph of **Modernism**, especially in Catalonia. **Antonio Gaudí** (1852-1926), its leading figure, conceived a new architectural style that went deeper than superficial decoration and owed much to the precepts of John Ruskin and the pre-Raphaelites. Gaudí used curved forms, plant motifs, and earth colours. His lintels appeared to flow over doors and windows, and towers and balconies melted into heavy curves, as seen in the Batlló and Milá houses, Güell Park and Neighbourhood, and the **Sagrada Familia**, or Church of the Holy Family (Barcelona).

20C ARCHITECTURE

During the first decades of this century, buildings in the Classical style with clearly European influences were being put up in Madrid and other big Spanish cities. Monumental office buildings, like the **Bank of Spain** offices in Madrid, are especially good examples of this style, with their impressive façades and classical solidity.

Rationalism, inspired by Le Corbusier and preached by the GATEPAC group, became popular toward the end of the 1920s. GATEPAC was an architectural and design group, headed by **Fernando García Mercadal** in Madrid and by **José Luis Sert** (who designed the **Miró Foundation** building in Barcelona and later in 1958 became Dean of the Harvard Faculty of Architecture) in Barcelona. The most ambitious Spanish Rationalist project was the residential area of Madrid known as **El Viso**, designed by Rafael Bergamín and the architect and poet Luis Felipe Vivanco. At the same time, engineer **Eduardo Torroja** was designing audacious concrete structures, such as the roof of the Zarzuela Race Course in Madrid, whose innovative quality met with international acclaim.

After the Civil War, the nationalist ideas propagated under Franco encouraged a return to the Neoclassical, grandiose styles of the past, as can be seen in the Air Force Ministry building and the church in the **Valle de los Caídos** outside Madrid on the way to El Escorial (see 'San Lorenzo del Escorial' in 'Madrid and Castile-La Mancha'). There was general stagnation in terms of original ideas until the 1960s, when the economic boom was accompanied by a rejection of Classical pretensions and a new kind of Realism began to be propounded by **Oriol Bohigas**, **Federico Correa** and **Alfonso Milá** in Barcelona and **Rafael de la Hoz** and **Fernández Alba** in Madrid. The latest works springing from the Spanish *avant garde* are **Ricardo Bofill's Les Halles** in Paris, several buildings in Barcelona and the Barrio Gaudí in Reus. The current Dean of Harvard is the Madrid-born **Rafael Moneo** whose most recent building, the **Museum of Roman Art** in Mérida (Badajoz), integrates Classicism with the most modern tendencies of this century. The ideas of **Sainz de Oíza** are reflected in unique modern buildings, such as the futuristic Torres Blancas building and the high-tech glass and steel offices of the **Banco de Bilbao** in Madrid.

POPULAR AND TRADITIONAL ARCHITECTURE

A country with as long and as varied a history as Spain, and as large and as varied a geography (not to mention its diverse climate) will obviously be rich in different vernacular architectural styles, each adapted to the specific needs and traditions of the region. The type of popular Spanish architecture best known abroad is probably the traditional **whitewashed house** of **Andalusia**, with flowers blooming in its window boxes, and the simple white cubes of **Ibiza**, whose eternal qualities have inspired contemporary architects throughout the world, among them José Luis Sert. The **courtyard**, usually decorated with plants and flowers, is the main focus of domestic architecture in the S (Seville, Córdoba), where most houses continue to open inwards, as did Roman and Moorish houses. The tradition also survives in the **Canary Islands**, where the courtyards are filled with exotic flowers whose glorious colours spill over the typical wooden **balconies**.

In the countryside, the **Andalusian farmstead** or *cortijo* is like a village in itself. Usually shaped like a big, white rectangle, it is composed of the main house, stables, outhouses, staff quarters and so on, all grouped around an enormous courtyard. But as one goes further N and NE, the rural home becomes more compact, a smaller social unit of more humble design and usually built of stone, such as the *masía*, the typical **Catalan farmhouse**. One could say that in the S the accent is on life outside the home, and the architecture reflects this with its more open style, its porches, large windows and elegant Mediterranean style galleries, whereas inland, the typical farmhouses are more self-sufficient and solid, rectangular, with two storeys (the ground floor being used to house livestock in the past, as a form of central heating), sloping roofs with eaves and attics.

Although used to different effect, whitewash is favoured in some places in the N as well. The **Basque farmhouse** is usually whitewashed, although its style is quite different from the Andalusian, with enormous **eaves** sloping over the house to keep away the rain, **support beams** of dark wood holding up the building as well as forming part of the façade (in the style the British call Tudor) and window shutters, often painted in bright colours, to close against inclement weather. There are also whitewashed houses in the highlands of the interior (where the white is set against the sturdy dark wood of the porticoes, galleries and balconies as in La Alberca) or in the fishermen's houses in Galicia. In **Galicia** and **Asturias**, the *hórreo* is a typical adornment to the landscape: a rectangular granary or store-house, supported by stone pillars, with a tiled roof. In the NW corner of the Peninsula, in **Los Ancares**, you can still see *pallozas*, round dry-stone houses with primitive thatched roofs, one-room houses of the sort used in Celtic settlements before the advent of the Romans. Further NW, the Galician countryside is populated with *pazos*, large, stone mansions, built in the Baroque style of the 18C and 19C and set in lush gardens though now often in a state of picturesque decay.

Town planning

The town has a long history in Spain, reaching back at least 3,000 years to the first Iberian settlements. In Roman times, towns were built on a grand scale, with important civic and religious buildings around which the houses were built, sometimes enclosed within a protective wall. The towns founded by the Christians and Visigoths were smaller and generally walled. Their defensive walls were reinforced by the Arabs when they took them over, for the Arabs preferred their towns to be like fortresses, and the Islamic **Medina** (town) is typically surrounded by at least one thick wall. The Arabs built their houses in a rather higgledy-piggledy fashion along narrow, winding alleys, usually around the **Alcázar** or palace, often on a hillock or steep hillside. Córdoba and other big towns were equipped with sophisticated facilities such as sewers, lighting, public baths and the like that were not to be equalled in Europe until the 19C.

The Christian reconquest did not make any immediate impact on the face of the typical medieval towns, parts of which still exist today. The walls and defences were perhaps fortified even more, especially on the coasts and in the castle towns of the central plateau. The Islamic mosques, when they were not demolished, were simply consecrated as churches, Muslim palaces were occupied by Christian nobles, monasteries, convents and churches were built and the towns divided into parishes. Most important of all, most towns were given a new **Plaza Mayor**, or main square (often with arcades along its four sides), which became the focus of the town's trade as well as its political and social life. The towns remained within the boundaries of the walls until the 14C, when population growth and the greater security of peacetime led to houses being built beyond the walls, clustered around churches or monasteries. The best ports on the Spanish coasts were built in the 16C, when Spain's fame as a seafaring nation was at its height. However, it was not until the 18C that any real town planning took place as, for example, in the Barceloneta area of Barcelona. Philip V, the first of the Spanish Bourbon kings, took a personal interest in urban planning. Then, under **Charles III**, entire **new towns** were built, influenced by the ideas of the Enlightenment, their streets laid down in parallel lines (El Ferrol, San Carlos de la Rápita), ports were built, sewage systems installed, and so forth. Finally, at the end of the 19C, population growth, industrialization and the emergence of a thriving middle class meant rapid expansion of nearly all towns, such that the old walled cities, up till then the nucleus of many towns' life, were closed in by modern towns, remaining as their old quarter, while business and other activities were set up outside, where the necessary modern facilities could be installed.

The big old towns were expanded in a relatively ordered manner (Madrid's **Ensanche** under the **Castro plan** and Barcelona's under the **Cerdá plan**). The streets were laid down in parallel lines, within a quadrilateral space, with long façades along blocks of houses and apartments, and wide avenues between them, leading on to a few main arterial roads.

As this enlightened town planning advanced, it became known as Rationalism. At the beginning of the 20C, **Arturo Soria** was one of the first to take account of the environmental aspects of inner-city life in his **Ciudad Lineal**, or Linear City, plans for Madrid. Le Corbusier, influenced by Soria's ideas, used them in building Stalingrad in 1930. These ideas also made their mark on Seville and Barcelona, but the most important impact on the physiognomy of these two cities was made by the two big **world fairs** which took place in 1929, creating brand new urban spaces. In the 1930s, the GATEPAC group propagated the advantages of Rationalism and modernity in Madrid and Barcelona. However, the movement was interrupted by the Civil War, which destroyed vast areas of towns and villages.

It took several years before the Spanish economy was able to even begin to cope with its housing problems. And when it did, during the 1950s and 1960s, its approach led to rampant speculation and chaotic development which were not corrected until the advent of democracy in the 1970s. The non-existence of ordered town planning was most obvious on the Mediterranean coast, where skyscrapers and hotels were thrown up willy nilly to cater for the tourist boom so that, in a mere twenty years, tiny fishing villages, such as Torremolinos and Benidorm, were transformed beyond recognition and some completely new **beach towns**, like Salou and Maspalomas, were built from scratch.

Nowadays, Spain is trying to correct the mistakes of its past while retaining its triumphs. Adventurous modern architectural plans are being carried out, but no longer at the cost of the old. Planning permission is now far more stringent, and listed buildings must be respected. The old city centres are being cleaned up and renovated, and city space is being reallocated for more efficient, more ecological use. Meanwhile, attempts are being made to anticipate the demands of modern society, rather than letting them take town planners by surprise. This can be seen in the planning put into the facilities for the Olympics in **BARCELONA** and the Universal Exhibition in **SEVILLE**, both planned for 1992. Events such as these require planning that looks ahead to the 21C and alters the very face of the host city.

Design, Crafts and Fashion

The domestic objects of everyday life are a testimony to the habits and culture of a people. Spain has always been rich in arts and crafts and many centuries-old traditional skills still thrive today. That quintessentially Spanish accessory, the **fan**, is a little work of art in itself. It must surely be one of the most popular souvenirs of Spain but is also still very much an object of everyday use among Spanish women during the hot months of the year. Both Seville and Valencia are famous for their beautiful traditional fans. Less well known outside Spain is the **jet jewelry**, known to date back to the Middle Ages as a craft, still made in the N, particularly in Santiago de Compostela, Gijón, Villaviciosa and Oviedo. Equally ancient is the artisan **glass work** so typical of Catalonia and Majorca, where it is kept alive today by *Gordiola*, established in 1719 (km19 on the Manacor road at Algaida), *Lafiore* (km11 on the Valdemosa road at L'Espalyera) and *Menestralia* (km36 on the Alcudia road at Campanet) and given a new lease of life by the innovative approach of **Pere Ignasi Bisquera** (c/ Puig des Teix, 22, at S'Hostalot). You can also find traditional glass at *J. del Río* in Pamplona and *Pertegaz Hernández* in Valencia. The **Spanish saddle** is another classic item to have survived unscathed, and saddlers still make them by hand in Segovia (*F. Abad* in Maderuelo) and, particularly, in the cities of Seville, Talavera de la Reina and Salamanca.

Spain has always been famous for its magnificent **earthenware** and **glazed tiles** or *mosaicos* and other handmade ceramics. Catalonia's vitality and prolific productivity allowed it a virtual monopoly of the European ceramics trade during the 14-15C which was sustained until the arrival of Modernism at the turn of this century. The history of glazed tiles goes back to the cups, plates, pitchers and flower vases decorated with metallic glazes and relief patterns dating from the 10C in Elvira (Granada) and the 11-12C in Málaga, and to the *azulejo* —an ornamental tile quintessentially Spanish in style— that appeared in the 12C with the Almohads in **Triana** (Seville) where they are still made today.

The principal ceramic workshops of the Middle Ages were also Arabic: **Paterna** (Valencia) —green and white, and later blue and white, ware— and **Manises** (Valencia) —famous since the 14C for its ceramics decorated with shimmering metallic glazes and botanical motifs and characters (fine examples are exhibited in Valencia's National Ceramics Museum). With the rise to prominence of the ceramics centre of **Talavera de la Reina** (Toledo) in the 15C, Arabic themes were replaced with Christian ones, bringing a Renaissance spirit to the work and blue and yellow colours to the kiln. The factory of **Alcora** (Castellón), founded by Philip V in 1727, originally produced Rococo *azulejos* in shades of blue and yellow; later it concentrated on **porcelain** and today produces the hugely successful *Lladró* work, known the world over. In the 18C, the **Buen Retiro Factory** (Madrid), founded by Charles III, became the leading porcelain producer, while in the 19C, *Sargadelos* (Galicia) ceramics and later the British-style glazed earthenware of Pickman (*La Cartuja de Sevilla*), decorated with vivid colours and designs, achieved world fame which has lasted to the present day. Today, the Cartuja, or Charterhouse, is being restored to serve as the Royal Pavilion in Seville's 1992 Universal Exhibition, Expo'92, while thanks to the efforts of painter and potter **José Díaz Pardo**, Sargadelos has become a cultural centre as well as a modern and efficient factory. At the start of the 20C, the tile factories of Triana (Seville) were still working in the Arab-Andalusian tradition while the Catalans to the north experimented with tiling in a more Modernist style.

This long tradition was carried into the modern day with the ceramic work of **Pablo Picasso** (1881-1973), **Joan Miró** (1893-1983), **José María Sert** (1876-1945), **José Llorens Artigas** (1892-1980) and **Modesto Cuixart** (b. 1925). **Durán-Lóriga**, **Arcadio Blanco** and many other young artists and craftsmen still work in the medium. There are interesting workshops in Lorca (*I. Larios*) and all over Murcia province (famous for its **nativity scenes**), Puente del Arzobispo (*G. de la Cal*), Toledo (*J. Aguado*) and Zaragoza (*Taller Escuela de Muel*).

Spain's **metal crafts** are deeply rooted in the Muslim tradition —clearly evident in the copper vases that are popular to this day in Andalusia. Hispano-Arab genius in this field was brilliantly exemplified in the clocks, instruments and automats made for the court of Alfonso X, the Wise. The craft reached its zenith in the 16C **monstrances**, enormous silver-embossed conical towers replete with columns and statues that are still used today to display the host during Holy Week processions all over Spain. Iron was used with as much stylized delicacy as silver in **wrought ironwork** —the iron gates of the gardens and courtyards of Seville and the balconies of Ronda (Málaga) are today's humble successors to the grating or grillework found in the chapels and choirs of the churches and cathedrals of Toledo, Avila, Jaén and Granada. Despite working on a massive scale, master craftsmen like **Francisco de Salamanca**, **Juan Francés**, **Francisco de Villalpando**, **Maestro Bartolomé** and **Domingo de Céspedes** achieved effects of extraordinary delicacy. The tradition lives on in crafts like **knife-making** in Albacete, Taramundi and Santa María de Guía (Gran Canaria), **armour** and the damascene-decorated **swords** typical of Toledo, and the gold and silver filigree ornamentation which features in the local costumes of Ciudad Rodrigo, Mogarraz and Tamames in the province of Salamanca.

Spain also has a long tradition of **furniture-making** with a flourishing modern industry which it is tempting to trace back to the **Mudéjar hip chair**, decorated with classical Moorish geometric designs; the **friar's armchair**, of a typically Castilian austerity, with leather seat and back fastened together by bronze or brass nails; and, above all, the universal contribution of the *bargueño*, the lovely decorated wooden trunk with drawers, which opens up into a desk decorated with wooden inlays encrusted with ivory and ebony, all recognized as Spain's great contributions in this field. The other classic Spanish craft using wood is, of course, **guitar-making**. World-famous guitarists buy their instruments from *F. Manzano* and *Ramírez* in Madrid and there are also respected craftsmen still working in the cities of Seville and Córdoba.

Contemporary Spanish **basket-weaving** is another survival of an ancient craft. Along the Mediterranean and in the Canaries the pieces are generally more delicate than the stout, angular forms of Galician basketwork and the simpler, linear styles of Castile and Extremadura.

Spanish **fashion** is in fashion. It is competing vigorously with Europe's most important fashion centres —Dusseldorf, Paris and Milan— in the area of *prêt-à-porter* and casual wear, very expensive *couture* clothes, shoes (**Teresa Ramallal, Sara Navarro, Farrutx, Yanko, Lotusse, Gorg Blau and Camper**), bags, belts, jewelry and costume jewelry (**Joaquín Berao, Chus Burés, Puig Doria, Chelo Sastre, Sardá, Oriol, Montse Guardiola and Balcarsa** are the trend setters) and leather goods (**Elena Benarroch** is a leading fur designer, while **Loewe's** superb quality leather goods need no introduction).

The Spanish fashion industry has built on the solid foundations of *haute couture* names like Balenciaga and **Pertegaz** and has found its place in the contemporary designer clothes market. **Pedro Morago, Adolfo Domínguez** —with shops in Paris, London and Japan—, **Sybilla, Jesús del Pozo, Toni Miró, Purificación García, Margarita Nuez, Teresa Ramallal, Agatha Ruiz de la Prada, Antonio Alvarado, Juanjo Rocafort, Pedro del Hierro, María Moreira, Caramelo, Cabaleiro, Vitorio & Lucchino, Meye Maier, Roser Marcé, Nacho Ruiz, Roberto Verinno, Francis Montesinos** and **Manuel Piña** are some of the designers who have made their names during the burst of creativity in the Spanish fashion industry.

Behind the current fashion boom lies a Spanish **textile** tradition that stretches back to prehistory. The rugs to be found today in Crevillente and La Alpujarra show Hispano-Arabic influence that can be traced back to the 9C court of Abd ar-Rahman II in Córdoba; Hispano-Muslim fabrics with geometric designs still survive from the 10-15C; the technique of the Spanish knot is known to have existed in the 12C; richly coloured fabrics were manufactured in 14-15C Granada in the style favoured by the aesthetically inclined Nasrid dynasty; **tapestry** factories like Madrid's Santa Isabel factory —masterfully portrayed by Velázquez in *Las Hilanderas*— date back to the 17C, and its Real Fábrica de Santa Bárbara —founded by Philip V, and for which Goya created tapestry designs— to the 18C; 3,600 Catalan factories and 9,000 mechanical looms made Spain an important competitor in the 19C international textile trade... a rich tradition indeed. Today, **modern tapestries** are a thriving art form in Barcelona (*M. A. Raventós*, c/ Ganduxer, 5, *J. Royo*, c/ Montcada, 25), Madrid (*L. Garrido*, c/ A. Marcé,

3, and ***Ana Roquero***, c/ Arias Montano, 18), Seville (***J. Ruesga***, c/ San Diego, 8), San Fernando (***Sagra Ibáñez***, Pl Neptuno, 15) and in Bubión, in La Alpujarra (***Nade Fabreau***). In Pradena de la Sierra (Segovia), the young craftsmen at the ***Talleres de San Pablo*** tint their woollen tapestries with natural dyes, ***María Fernández Feijó*** in Val de San Lorenzo (León) and ***C. Valgañón*** in Ezcaray (La Rioja) work with ancient looms, while in Villoslada de Cameros (La Rioja), ***Lola Barásoain*** creates tapestries out of odd pieces of cloth. Along more general lines, take note of the Canary Island's famous **openwork embroidery**, Seville's *mantilla* shawls, Camariñas' **bobbin lace**, Toledo's hand-made embroidery and La Palma's **silk** products.

Spaniards have always shown aesthetic flair in the field of **design**. Some of the outstanding figures since the middle of last century have been **Narciso Monturiol** (1819-1895), the submarine engineer; the Modernist **Antonio Gaudí** (1852-1926) who, in addition to his architectural achievements, created wonderful furniture and iron fittings in the tradition established by architects **Juan de Herrera** (1530-1597) and **Juan de Villanueva** (1739-1811); painters **Ramón Casas** (1866-1932) and **Santiago Rusiñol** (1861-1931), who produced genuine works of art in their posters for *Anís del Mono* and *Codorniú*; graphic artists like **Apel.les Mestres** (1854-1936) and **Ricardo Opisso** (1880-1966); and, from the 1920s up to the Civil War, architects **Luis Feduchi** and **José Luis Sert** (1902-1983), designers of modern furniture, and the aeronautical engineer **Juan de la Cierva** (1895-1936), inventor of the autogiro. Spain is rapidly becoming a post-industrial society whose latest designs combine the artistic with the functional: **Goicoechea's** high-speed train, the *Talgo* —now in use in the United States; **Oscar Tusquets'** chairs; the lamps and other objects designed by **André Ricard, Milá, José Antonio Coderch, Carvajal, Pep Cortés** and **Cirici**; **Daniel Gil's** book-cover designs; the general graphic design of **Alberto Corazón, Enric Satué, Cruz Novillo** and **Javier Mariscal**, designer of the logo for Barcelona's '92 Olympics; and the industrial design of **Moneo, Riart** and **Miralles**.

These are just a few of the many names whose work reflects the way in which Spain has gradually evolved into the dynamic member of the European Community, both economic and artistic, that it is today.

Literature

Spain, the nation universally accredited with having provided Europe with the first modern novel in Cervantes' *Don Quixote*, has a literary tradition which spans the two thousand years which separate Seneca the Rhetorician from the prolific contemporary novelists. The whole of its culture reflects the fact that Spain was for many centuries the jewel in the crown of successive conquerors and as such produced or attracted many of the outstanding polymaths of the Roman, Muslim and Jewish worlds. Spanish literature could therefore be said to embrace works in Latin, Arabic and Hebrew as well as the indigenous Castilian, Catalan and Galician languages.

Before the emergence of the Romance languages, major works were written in Latin by **Seneca the Elder** (54 BC-AD 39), known as the Rhetorician, **Seneca the Stoic** (4 BC-AD 65), the epic poet **Lucan** (AD 39-65), one-time favourite of the Emperor Nero, and the epigrammist **Martial** (AD 42-104), all of whom were great Roman authors born in Spain. Christian literature, coming with the Roman adoption of Christianity, proved to be rather less creative. One major intellectual of the era, however, was **Isidore of Seville** (AD 570-636), compiler of the *Etymologies*, an encyclopedic work summarizing the wisdom of the western world.

In contrast to the Christian kingdoms of the early medieval period, the Muslim kingdoms within the Iberian peninsula were powerhouses of literature and scholarship. Arab writers and scholars preserved the heritage of antiquity for the western world and produced a wealth of poetry, scientific treatises, historical documents and religious tracts. Most prominent among these was the Córdoba-born Jewish intellectual **Maimonides** (1135-1204), a controversial figure during his lifetime, subsequently recognized as the greatest of the Jewish philosophers and whose work, translated into Latin, influenced not only the great medieval thinkers but also made a major contribution to the history of medical science. The influence of the Muslim religious philosopher **Averroës** (1126-1198), also born in Córdoba, best known for his summaries and commentaries on the works of Aristotle and Plato which merged Muslim traditions with Greek philosophy, was to have an enduring effect on Christian thought throughout Europe. The poetic forms used by the outstanding and multi-faceted Arabic poets of the period also penetrated into Christian literature, and Dante's *Divine Comedy* is said to have been influenced by the works of Córdoba's **Ibn Suhayd** (992-1035). Today, the most-read Arabic poet of Moorish Spain's Golden Age is **Ibn Hazm** (994-1063), author of *El Collar de la Paloma* (The Dove's Collar).

Castilian began to achieve predominance in literature with the development of epic poetry in the 12C —the *Song of My Cid* (c. 1140), which recounts the deeds of the hero of the Reconquest, Rodrigo Díaz de Vivar, is the greatest work to survive. The early poetry of the troubadours began to be recorded in writing in the 13C. At first it was mainly concerned with Christian religious themes —like the poems of **Gonzalo de Berceo** (c. 1195-1268) about the life of the Virgin—, though subjects taken from antiquity and Spanish history soon began to figure prominently. The collections of troubadour poetry (which found its best expression in *gallego*, the language of Galicia), the *Cantigas de Amigo* and the 13-14C *Cancioneiros* are evidence of the heights of lyricism reached during this medieval period. The erudite **Alfonso X, the Wise** (1252-1284) suppressed Latin and made Castilian the language of the court and of scholarship. Himself a poet, translator, historian, and compiler calling on Classical, Oriental, Hebrew, and Christian sources, he fostered an atmosphere of flourishing intellectual activity. The period of compilation was succeeded by one of brilliant creation in the 14C. The **Infante Juan Manuel** (1283-1348), nephew of Alfonso X, introduced the use of narrative prose in an original collection of moral tales of great stylistic perfection, while Juan Ruiz (c. 1300), the **Archpriest of Hita**, wrote his brilliant satirical verse work, *The Book of Good Love*, which mingles the secular with the mystical.

Meanwhile, Catalan literature developed in parallel. Although the earliest surviving literary text in Catalan, the *Homilies d'Organyà*, dates from the late 12C, Catalan literature is generally said to have been launched with the 13C prose chronicles of **James I** (1208-1273) and **Ramón Muntaner** (1265-1336), the treatises of **Arnau de Vilanova** (1238-1311), doctor to popes and kings, and by the outstanding contribution of Majorca's **Ramón Llull** (1233-1314), mystic, philosopher, scientific encyclopaedist, poet and novelist who was indisputably one of the leading intellectuals of 13C Europe. Catalonia enjoyed its own literary Golden Age during the 15C with the rationalism of **Anselm Turmeda** (1352-1432) and **Bernat Metge** (1340-1413), the poetry of **Ausias March** (1397-1459) and the great chivalric novel *Tirant lo Blanch* by **Joanot Martorell** (1413-1468), a source of inspiration to Cervantes and now translated into English. The early 16C saw a decline in Catalonia's literary output which was not to revive until the 19C.

One of the outstanding figures of 15C Castilian literature was the **Marquis of Santillana** (1398-1458), aristocrat, statesman, scholar and poet regarded as the father of formal literary criticism in Spain. He also introduced the use of the sonnet form into Spanish poetry, a reflection of the far-reaching influence of the Italian Renaissance in that his experiements in the genre are clearly imitative of Petrarch.

In the 16C, at the dawn of imperial Spain's Golden Age —an outstanding period in the history of world literature— writing reflected the vivid new experience of overseas adventure. One of the earliest Spanish humanists of the time was **Bartolomé de las Casas** (1474-1566), chronicler of the conquest and literary champion of the Indians of the New World (*The Tears of the Indians*).

Early Spanish drama, written in verse, developed out of religious presentations like the 15C Assumption play, *Misteri d'Elch* (see 'Fiestas'). The masterpiece of the early Renaissance was **Fernando de Rojas'** (1465-1541) dialogue novel *La Celestina*. Renaissance drama reached its zenith with **Félix Lope de Vega** (1562-1635), one of the world's most prolific playwrights, with more than 1800 plays to his credit, and a lyrical poet who blended comedy and tragedy. The greatest of his successors were **Tirso de Molina** (1584-1648), creator of the legendary lover Don Juan in *The Trickster of Seville*, and **Pedro Calderón de la Barca** (1600-1681), author of *Life is a Dream*.

In the field of poetry, **Friar Luis de León** (1527-1591) typified the Salamanca School with his emphasis on content rather than form, while **Luis de Góngora** (1561-1627) rose to prominence as a leading representative of a school of writers working in a high-flown Latinate style. The Golden Age also produced the mystical works of **Saint Teresa of Avila** (1515-1582) and her disciple, **Saint John of the Cross** (1542-1591). In sharp contrast to their mysticism were the realism of the picaresque novel —exemplified in the anonymous *Blind Man's Boy*— and the satirical nature of the works of **Francisco de Quevedo** (1580-1645), essayist and master of language, whose trenchant attacks were directed against the decadent society and literature of his day.

Spanish literature reached its pinnacle in the Golden Age with **Miguel de Cervantes** (1547-1616), author of *Don Quixote*, unquestionably Spain's greatest contribution to world literature. Hailed as the first modern novel and anticipating literary forms by several centuries, it is a work of immense sophistication and profound human significance which has influenced authors from Cervantes' contemporary, Shakespeare, to modern writers like Joyce and Nabokov.

Decadence and a loss of energy in the arts marked the end of the Golden Age, at the close of the 17C. This uninspired era lasted from the death of Calderón until the advent of Romanticism, a movement to which poet **Gustavo Adolfo Bécquer** (1836-1870) and novelist **José de Espronceda** (1810-1842) belonged. Simultaneously, the *Costumbrismo* movement of realistic prose, descriptive and often critical of the manners of the time, flourished. The sceptical journalist **Mariano José de Larra** (1809-1837) was one of the most outstanding writers and social commentators of this movement.

Toward the end of the 19C the realistic novel, chronological in structure and acidly critical in tone, made its appearance in Spain. It was mainly concerned with the contrast between the customs and traditions of the past and the demands of modern progress and culture. The genre is best exemplified by the works of **Leopoldo Alas** (alias *Clarín*, 1852-1901, author of *La Regenta*), and **Countess Emilia Pardo-Bazán** (1852-1921). Still within the realistic movement, **Benito Pérez Galdós** (1843-1920) in his vast sequence of novels, *National Episodes*, interpreted contemporary life in terms of the effect of the past and, like many of his contemporaries, condemned in his writing the social injustice he saw around him.

The 19C saw a resurgence of literary activity in the languages of both Catalonia and Galicia. In Galicia, the period produced the outstanding Romantic poet **Rosalía de Castro** (1837-1885) while in Catalonia, flourishing thanks to the Industrial Revolution, there was a veritable renaissance. **Jacint Verdaguer** (1845-1902), with his epic poems *L'Atlàntida* and *Canigó*, was the leading poet of the Romantic movement while **Manuel Milà i Fontanals** (1818-1884) was an intellectual of international stature.

The group of intellectuals known as the Generation of '98 was deeply analytical of Spain's decadence —especially after its defeat in the Spanish-American War of 1898 and the loss of its last colonies— and sought to reawaken the nation from its apathy. The most famous member of this group was **Miguel de Unamuno** (1864-1936), whose copious output included philosophical works, essays, novels and poetry. Other members included the innovative playwright **Ramón María del Valle Inclán** (1869-1936), **José Martínez Ruiz** (1873-1967), critic, novelist, and essayist who wrote under the pen name *Azorín*, and the novelist **Pío Baroja** (1872-1956), whose works are characterized by an intense social realism.

In line with contemporary currents in Europe, the social novel was complemented by an upsurge of modern Spanish thinking. The existentialist **Miguel de Unamuno** (see above), philosopher and humanist **José Ortega y Gasset** (1883-1955) —a key intellectual whose *Revolt of the Masses* made an impact throughout Europe— and **Salvador de Madariaga** (1886-1978) —critic and essayist— were the most influential thinkers of the time. Spanish poetry blossomed during this period, with the works of **Antonio Machado** (1875-1939) and **Juan Ramón Jiménez** (1881-1958) —1956 Nobel Prize winner— laying the foundations for a new, modern, lyrical approach.

At the start of the 20C in Catalonia, the middle class was the moving force behind the intense cultural activity which generated literature characterized by its cosmopolitanism and its concern with form. The founder of this *Noucentisme* movement was **Eugeni D'Ors** (1881-1954), and the poetry of the time contributed figures like **Carles Riba** (1893-1959) and **Josep Vicenç Foix** (b. 1894).

The group of outstanding poets known as the Poetic Generation of '27 followed the lead of Machado and Jiménez. **Jorge Guillén** (1893-1984), **Luis Cernuda** (1902-1963), **Dámaso Alonso** (b. 1898), **Rafael Alberti** (b. 1902) and **Vicente Aleixandre** (b. 1898) were leading members of the group, though its best known figure is probably **Federico García Lorca** (1898-1936), who combined the folk atmosphere of his native Andalusia with sophisticated symbolic imagery. His works include *Gypsy Ballads*, *The Poet in New York*, and the plays *Blood Wedding* and *The House of Bernarda Alba*. Set outside this intellectual group, authors concerned with Catholicism or the Republic were **Miguel Hernández** (1910-1942) and **José Bergamín** (1895-1983). In the novel, the Generation of '98 was succeeded by **Francisco Ayala** (b. 1906), **Ramón José Sender** (1902-1982), **Rosa Chacel** (b. 1898) and **León Felipe** (1884-1968), among others, most of whom fled Spain after the Civil War ended in 1939. The following generation of new novelists and the many poets belonging to the Generation of '36 who began writing then —**Leopoldo Panero** (1909-1962), **Luis Rosales** (b. 1910), and **Luis Vivanco** (1907-1975)— were fashionable and approved of by the regime, while others, such as the communist **Blas de Otero** (1916-1979), attacked the Franco regime and dealt with themes of human rights and oppression. Social, ethical, political and human preoccupations were later vividly expressed, in a move away from traditional use of language, by the young poets of the decade of the 1950s: **José Angel Valente** (b. 1929) and **Claudio Rodríguez** (b. 1934) among them.

During the 1950s, many novelists, like **Luis Martín Santos** (1924-1964) and **Juan Benet** (b. 1927), were influenced by James Joyce, Franz Kafka, and Marcel Proust, while others, like **Juan Marsé** (b. 1933) and **Juan Goytisolo** (b. 1931), absorbed the aesthetics and techniques of the *nouveau roman* and North American literature in their writing. Other well known novelists who came to prominence at that time include **Miguel Delibes** (b. 1920), **Camilo José Cela** (b. 1916), **Rafael Sánchez Ferlosio** (b. 1927), Catalans **Llorenç Villalonga** (1897-1980) and **Mercè Rodoreda** (1909-1983), and Galicians **Rafael Dieste** (1899-1981) and **Eduardo Blanco Amor** (1897-1979). **Alvaro Cunqueiro** (1911-1981) and **Gonzalo Torrente Ballester** (b. 1910) led a trend of surrealistic fantasy that is still current in the literature of both Spain and Latin America.

In the theatre, the beginning of this century produced the comedy of social satirist **Jacinto Benavente** (1866-1954), winner of the 1922 Nobel Prize for Literature, and the satirical pieces of **Carlos Arniches** (1866-1943). Contemporary playwrights **Antonio Buero Vallejo** (b. 1916) and **Antonio Gala** (b. 1936) share their popularity with the revivals of the plays of **Lorca**, currently receiving international attention, while the *avant garde* **Fura dels Baus** and **Els Joglars** fringe groups bring a satirical note to the contemporary stage.

Finally, essayists **Pedro Laín Entralgo** (b. 1908), **José Luis López Aranguren** (b. 1909), and **María Zambrano** (b. 1907) have become national institutions, while a group of younger philosophers, spearheaded by **Fernando Savater** (b. 1947) and **Javier Sádaba**, has started to emerge over the last few years.

Music

Spain is a musical country whose people like to sing and dance. There is music to suit every style and temperament —from classical music, regional folk song and dance to pop and rock. Reflecting the nation's vitality, Spanish music is characterized by a joy of living.

CLASSICAL MUSIC

Early Spanish music is not well known outside Spain itself, with the exception of the *Cantigas*, written by **Alfonso X, the Wise** (1221-1284), which constitute an impressive legacy from the Middle Ages whose cultural wealth was due in great part to the far-reaching influence of the Hispano-Muslim Caliphate of Córdoba. Catalonia, meanwhile, absorbed European influences from N of the Pyrenees and two liturgical gems from this period, the *Cant de la Sibil.la* and the *Misteri d'Elx* (see 'Fiestas') are still performed to this day. During the Golden Age of the 16C the **guitar**, instrument of the people, began to displace its ancestor the more courtly *vihuela*. This was a period of great religious composers like **Cristóbal de Morales** (1500-1553) and, most outstanding of all, **Tomás Luis de Victoria** (1548-1611). By the 18C, the Bourbon Monarchs had made Madrid one of the focal points of musical creativity in Europe and their court attracted composers of the calibre of **Domenico Scarlatti** (1685-1757) and **Luigi Boccherini** (1743-1805).

In the 19C, as Romanticism laid down roots in Spain, the guitar, by now the quintessentially Spanish instrument, spread its influence. Modern guitar-playing is largely based on the work of **Francisco Tárrega**

(1852-1909). As the Romantic writers and painters of Europe 'discovered' Spain, so too did its composers turn S for inspiration: Lalo's *Symphonie Espagnole*, Bizet's *Carmen*, Rimsky Korsakov's *Capriccio Espagnol*, Ravel's *Bolero*, Rossini's *Barber of Seville*... Romanticism within Spain developed into what critics term 'musical nationalism' through the work of Joaquín Turina (1882-1949), Isaac Albéniz (1860-1909) and Manuel de Falla (1876-1946). In *La Procesión del Rocío, Mujeres Españolas* and *Danzas Gitanas*, perceptible French influences are balanced by **Turina's** pronounced Spanishness. In **Albéniz's** *Iberia Suite*, a collection of twelve highly original piano pieces, nationalism in Spanish music reaches its zenith. The influence of Albéniz, together with that of French impressionism, is discernible in the refined and vivid work of the Andalusian **Falla**, composer of *El Amor Brujo*, the *Concerto for Harpsichord and Five Instruments* and *Atlantida*, which was completed by his disciple, **Ernesto Halffter** (b. 1905).

The musical renewal of the 20C has been a mixture of classicism and newer movements. The synthesis is apparent in the work of **Frederic Mompou** (1893-1987), a fine pianist and composer of works for a range of instruments —*Suburbios* (piano), *Becquerianas* (voice) and *Suite Compostelana* (guitar). **Joaquín Rodrigo** (b. 1902), composer of the popular *Aranjuez Concerto*, and **Xavier Montsalvatge** (b. 1912) are the best-known postwar composers. The new generation of Spanish composers, among them **Luis de Pablo** (b. 1930), **Cristóbal Halffter** (b. 1930), **Carmelo Bernaola** (b. 1929) and **Tomás Marco** (b. 1942) have embraced the *avant garde* tendencies like electroacoustics which characterize contemporary Western music.

In the field of musical performance, guitarists **Andrés Segovia** (1894-1987) and **Narciso Yepes** (b. 1927) are known the world over, while the late **Pablo Casals** (1878-1973), cellist, conductor, and composer (*Cantata for the United Nations*) in the course of a career that spanned the first half of this century became an international musical institution. Spain has also produced brilliant virtuoso singers, like **Teresa Berganza, Alfredo Kraus, Victoria de los Angeles**, and **José Carreras**, and its leading conductor, **Jesús López-Cobos**, has directed some of the world's finest orchestras.

CONCERTS IN SPAIN

Madrid, Barcelona and Valencia all have regular **classical music** seasons. **MADRID'S** resident orchestras and choirs include the **Spanish National Orchestra and Chorus**, the **Orchestra and Chorus of RTVE** (Spanish National Radio and Television), and the **Arbós Orchestra**, and its main concert halls are the **Teatro Real** (in the process of being converted back to its original function as an Opera House), the **Teatro de la Zarzuela** and the new **Auditorio Nacional de Música**, said to be one of the best in Europe. **BARCELONA**, a city of music lovers, boasts a Modernist **Palau de la Música**, seat of the Barcelona City Orchestra, and the **Teatro del Liceo**, something of a cultural institution, which is where the opera season takes place. **VALENCIA** is an area of Spain where **brass bands** are hugely popular and standards are high. The city also has its own **Orchestra**, based in the new **Palau de la Música**.

Conveniently for many visiting music lovers, Spain's **classical music** and **ballet** seasons tend to be held in the summer. Among the tops are **SANTANDER'S** International Music Festival, held in a lovely porticoed square, in August; **GRANADA'S** International Music and Dance Festival, whose events are staged in the marvellous setting of the Alhambra and the brand-new **Auditorio Manuel de Falla**, in June and July, and **CUENCA'S** Religious Music Week, held around Easter-time.

The **flamenco festivals** of **Andalusia** are a marvellous opportunity to experience the genuine article. Again they are concentrated in the summer months, and take place throughout Seville, Málaga, Granada and Cádiz. The best are Seville's *Bienal de Arte Flamenco*, in September, and the triennial *Concurso Nacional de Arte Flamenco* in Córdoba (the next will be in May 1989 and May 1992), and Madrid also holds its own *Cumbre Flamenca*.

LYRICAL MUSIC

In the world of opera, **Montserrat Caballé, Plácido Domingo** and **José Carreras** have gained international fame and prestige for Spain. Nevertheless, the great popular tradition of Spanish music tends more toward the *zarzuela*, a form of operetta that is genuinely Spanish, than toward opera as such. In the 17C the Spanish court was much taken with hunting. Hunting parties camped in tents out in the countryside, and in clearings surrounded by brambles (*zarza* in Spanish, hence *zarzuela*) the evening's entertainment took the form of theatrical presentations accompanied by music and song: thus the *zarzuela* was born. It remained very popular up to the 19C, but subsequently waned in favour of the great German operas. The *zarzuela* returned to prominence, however, with the work of **Tomas Bretón** (1850-1923), *La Verbena de la Paloma* (1894), which was purely Spanish and Goyaesque in its aesthetics, and the genre made its influence felt throughout Europe. **Francisco Barbieri** (1823-1894, prolific composer of some 70 *zarzuelas*), **Federico Chueca** (1846-1908, whose *Gran Vía* was said to have been admired by both Nietzsche and Verdi) and **Ruperto Chapi** (1851-1909, best known for *La Revoltosa*, which favourably impressed Saint-Saëns) are enduringly the big names among Spain's *zarzuela* composers.

SPANISH POPULAR MUSIC, ROCK AND POP

Spain produces some of the wildest, most aggressive and sometimes even sinister rock and roll in Europe. Young groups are constantly being born, breaking up, reforming —**Hombres G, Radio Futura, Gabinete Caligari, Nacha Pop** and the hugely successful **Mecano** and **Orquesta Mondragón** have been the chart-toppers of the mid-1980s. More enduring stars include **Miguel Ríos**, a Spanish equivalent of Cliff Richard; the multi-faceted **Ana Belén** and **Victor Manuel**; urbanites and social commentators **Joan Manuel Serrat, Luis Eduardo Aute** and **Joaquín Sabina; María del Mar Bonet**, her lyrical style clearly based on the Mediterranean folk tradition, and **Julio Iglesias**, the international crooner who needs no introduction.

In parallel to this contemporary music, which is very much on a par with what is going on in the rest of Europe and the US, Spain has a genre of popular singing all its own (albeit shared with a huge following in Latin America) perhaps best described as the tear-jerking romantic ballad with a strong Andalusian flavour. Tales of passion, loss and despair are sung with voluptuous flamboyance by **Isabel Pantoja** and **Rocío Jurado** (undisputed star in this field), in Spain's equivalent of North America's country and western music.

TRADITIONAL FOLK SONG AND DANCE

The origins of Andalusia's **flamenco** musical tradition are little known and much debated —as early as Roman times writers such as Martial mention the dancers of Cádiz—, especially since truly flamenco folk songs (*cante*) and dances (*baile*) have blended with Andalusian popular singing to the point where it is difficult to mark out the precise boundaries of this exotic and picturesque art form. Whatever flamenco's origins, the genre has come to be the archetypal music of Spain, the heart-rending quality of the *cante* and the rhythms and gestures of the *baile* combining the primitive with the sophisticated in a way that never fails to stir the deeper reaches of the onlooker, whatever his native culture. Flamenco experts will know that the genre embraces countless clearly-defined song and dance forms. Suffice it here to say that flamenco, its roots traceable to Byzantine, Moorish and Jewish origins, survives as a flourishing art form, as susceptible to the star system as any other. The legendary figures of **Antonio Chacón, Antonio Mairena** and **La Niña de Los Peines** have been followed by **Camarón de la Isla** and **Morente** as the big names of flamenco singing, **Antonio Gades, Matilde Coral, Farruco** and **Manuela Vargas** are the best known dancers, while **Paco de Lucía, Manolo Sanlúcar** and **El Habichuela** are today's top flamenco guitarists. You will have no trouble tracking down a flamenco show in most parts of Spain, but do remember that the more commercially orientated they are, the less authentic they are likely to be. Go informed.

A foreigner could be forgiven for thinking that flamenco is *the* Spanish genre of folk song and dance. Yet, like so many of the archetypal notions of Spain, flamenco is an Andalusian phenomenon quite strange to other regions of the country which have their own ancient local traditions.

Catalonia's *sardana*, a communal dance performed by men and women linking hands in a closed circle, has come to be emblematic of the Catalans' feeling of regional identity. In its present form it dates back no further than the 19C, though it is based on the ancient *contrapás* which lacked the symbolic circular formation. Nowadays, no Catalan *fiesta* is complete without a performance of this gentle, rhythmic dance to the sound of the *cobla* group of wind instruments and small drums.

In Celtic Galicia, the wail of the *gaita*, the local version of the bagpipe, accompanies the sprightly *muñeira*, or dance of the miller's wife, and is also heard in neighbouring Asturias on festive occasions.

The songs, dances and musical instruments of the Basque Country, Navarre and La Rioja are quite different from those of the rest of Spain. The typical instruments are the flute, small drum and large tambourine and the dances include various versions of a stick dance, another unique dance performed on stilts by young men in swirling skirts, and the vigorous *jota*, a leaping dance which does occur in other parts of the country, including Extremadura and Aragón.

Bagpipes crop up again in Majorca in the Balearics where they accompany dances like the *bolero mallorquín*, the *jota mallorquina* and the *parado*. Menorca has its own version of the *jota* and the *fandango*, danced to the sound of guitars and castanets, while the wooden flute, drum and giant castanets are more typical of Ibiza.

The music and dances of the Canary Islands clearly betray their links with Andalusia, Portugal and Latin America. The typical musical instrument of the islands is the guitar-like *timple* whose sharp-edged, lively sound in combination with drums, tambourines, castanets and flutes accompany traditional dances like the *isa* and the *folía*.

Painting and Sculpture

Spanish painting and sculpture spans the period from the Paleolithic cave-paintings of **Altamira** to the 20C genius of **Pablo Picasso**, and has produced such outstanding figures as the master carver **Maestro Mateo** (12C), **El Greco** (16C), **Velázquez** (17C), **Goya** (18-19C)... From the old masters to Picasso's contemporaries, **Salvador Dalí** and **Joan Miró**, Spanish painters and sculptors have always been in the front rank. It is not surprising, then, that the country's most impressive contribution to world culture has been in the realm of the plastic arts.

PREHISTORIC LEGACIES

The bison, deer and wild boar of the **Altamira Cave** (Cantabria) —dubbed the *Sistine Chapel* of rupestrian art— are Spain's most impressive cave paintings, executed with great realism in several shades of yellow and red and outlined in black. Thousands of years later, along the Mediterranean coast in SE Spain, an Iberian culture evolved with the coming of the Iron Age. Cultural interchange with the seafaring Greeks and Phoenicians resulted in the beginning of a rich gold-working and sculptural tradition: the famous *Lady of Elche* (Archaeological Museum, Madrid), with her seashell-like headdress, dates from this period.

ROMAN, VISIGOTHIC AND ROMANESQUE HERITAGE (3C BC-13C AD)

The main features of Roman and Visigothic sculpture —their cultural output was rich in statues, capitals and sarcophagi— survived in the art forms of the Christian kingdoms in Asturias and Catalonia. It was not until after the Moorish invasion in 711, when the Muslim culture began to mix with pure Catalan Romanesque —as seen in **TAHULL** (Lérida) and in the painted panels of **VIC** (Barcelona) and **RIPOLL** (Gerona)— that strong new influences on Spanish art came into play. Romanesque sculpture in Spain reached its zenith in the Cathedral of Santiago de Compostela, with Master Mateo's 12C **Pórtico de la Gloria** (Doorway to Glory).

GOTHIC ART (13-15C)

Gothic painting in Spain was influenced by three major sources: France during the 13C; Siena and Florence, especially in Catalonia (**Ferrer Bassa, Destorrents**, the **Serra** brothers), during the 14C; and Flanders in the courts of Aragón and Castile (**Martorell, Huguet, Dalmau, Bermejo, Fernando Gallego** and **John of Flanders**) during the 15C. Nonetheless, the naturalism and picturesque details of works of this period were entirely Spanish. Gothic sculpture adorned cathedrals with great **reredos** (altarpieces incorporating elaborate carvings and paintings), densely decorated **porticoes**, carved **choir stalls** and exquisite **sepulchres**, like the tomb of the *Doncel*, or young nobleman, in Sigüenza (Guadalajara). Many of its master craftsmen are unidentified, though some outstanding names are known, among them **Pere Johan** (Barcelona's Generalitat building and Tarragona Cathedral), **Juan** and **Rodrigo Alemán** (Toledo Cathedral), **Juan Guas** (San Juan de los Reyes Church in Toledo) and the prolific **Gil de Siloé** (works in Burgos).

RENAISSANCE ART (16C)

Lured by the patronage of the Spanish kings, several Italian sculptors and painters came to work in Spain during the 16C, among them **Leoni the Elder** and **Leoni the Younger**, commissioned by Philip II to work on the Escorial. Meanwhile, many Spanish sculptors learned their art in Italy, among them **Diego de Siloé** (Burgos and Granada Cathedrals), **Bartolomé Ordóñez** (works in Granada, Barcelona and Alcalá de Henares), **Alonso Berruguete** (works in Toledo and Valladolid), a sculptor of the Valladolid School whose work is characterized by lyricism and the use of tormented human forms, and **Juan de Juni** (works in Valladolid), of the same school, known for his theatrical approach.

The Renaissance brought with it mastery of perspective, the glorification of the human body and clarity of composition. The Extremaduran painter **Luis de Morales**, known as *El Divino* (works throughout Spain), and painters of the Valencian School, **Yáñez de la Almedina** and **Fernando de Llanos** adopted the style of Leonardo, while **Vicente Macip** followed the style of Raphael, which evolved into Mannerism in the work of his son, **Juan de Juanes**, nicknamed *The Spanish Raphael*. In Castile, the outstanding figure of the late 15C was **Pedro Berruguete**, while the 16C produced the great portrait painters **Sánchez Coello** and **Pantoja de la Cruz**.

Towering above the rest, however, was **Domenico Teotocopuli**, better known as **El Greco**, the Greek immigrant whose unique style defies easy definition. El Greco settled in Toledo in 1577, and it was there that he painted his best works: *The Burial of the Count of Orgaz* and *Disrobing of Christ* among others. The lengthening of human figures and the original use of vibrant colours and geometric composition so characteristic of his paintings somehow combine to convey a mystical quality (works in Madrid's Prado Museum and Toledo).

BAROQUE ART (17-18C)

The Baroque era, a period that unfolded during the Golden Age, produced an extraordinary wealth of artists in what was undeniably one of the high points in world art. The sculpture of the period was naturalistic and emotive, with two main focuses of activity, Andalusia and Castile. A rich heritage of polychromed images has come down to us from the Schools of Valladolid (**Gregorio Fernández**), Seville (**Martínez Montañés** and **Juan de Mesa** —sculptor of Seville's famous figure of the *Cristo del Gran Poder*) and Granada (**Alonso Cano**, creator of delicate *Inmaculadas*, and his disciple, the realistic sculptor **Pedro de Mena**) and many feature in Holy Week processions to this day.

The exceptional Spanish painting of the 17C was stimulated by Italian influences that are obvious in the assimilation of Caravaggio by **Francisco Ribalta** (works in the Prado Museum, Madrid). **José de Ribera**, known as *The Spagnoletto*, headed the Valencian School of realist painting which can be seen as a reaction against the excessive idealism of the Renaissance. The Sevillian School produced several great masters: **Zurbarán**, the stark simplicity of whose paintings of monastic figures and still lifes look surprisingly modern even to 20C eyes (works in Seville, Guadalupe and Madrid), **Murillo**, especially famous for his *Inmaculadas*, and **Valdés Leal**, painter of grandiloquent allegorical and sacred compositions (works in Seville). In Granada, the painter, sculptor and architect **Alonso Cano** was renowned for the delicacy of his work, particularly his figures of the Virgin. In Castile, **Claudio Coello, Juan Carreño** and **Vicenzo Carducci** were the outstanding figures of the period, again with realism as their outstanding characteristic.

The greatest painter of the epoch, however, was the Sevillian **Diego Velázquez**, court painter to Philip IV (works in the Prado Museum, Madrid). Unlike the spiritual El Greco, Velázquez painted few religious pictures. His mastery of space, light, and shade are evident in his shrewd and detailed portraits (*Philip IV, The Count Duke of Olivares, Innocent X*), historical canvases (*Surrender at Breda*), mythological paintings (*The Drunkards*), and landscapes (*Villa Medicis*). An innovative artist, he was the first Spanish painter to portray a female nude —the *Rokeby Venus*, exhibited at the London National Gallery. His masterpiece, *Las Meninas*, shows such consummate style and technique that it places him on a par with other giants of Spanish painting, Goya and Picasso.

NEOCLASSICAL ART (18C)

As a reaction against the Baroque, classical forms were revived. During this period, the Bourbon monarchs founded the San Fernando Academy in Madrid and brought foreign painters, such as **Mengs** and **Tiepolo**, to teach there. But head and shoulders above these and others was a man of complete genius who was to lead the way into the Romanticism of the 19C. **Francisco de Goya**, a multi-faceted, dynamic and sarcastic man, broke with all the academic principles of painting and anticipated artistic trends of more than a century later. Working in various media, the scope of his work was enormous, ranging from the chilling *Executions of the Spaniards on the Third* *of May 1808*, the series of engravings *The Horrors of War*, the suggestive and erotic *Clothed Maja* and *Naked Maja*, the terrifying *Lunatic Asylum*, and the bright tenderness of *Children Playing* to his macabre so-called *Black Paintings* (works in the Prado Museum, Madrid). His work is a vivid reflection of the dramatic period of Spanish history through which he lived, and the *Goyesca* School which followed him, dominated by **Eugenio Lucas**, perpetuates his concentration on quintessentially Spanish themes.

The outstanding sculptor of the 18C was the Murcian **Francisco Salzillo** whose spectacular Baroque style inspired a vast following of disciples and imitators (works in Murcia).

ART IN THE 19C

The influence of the great 18C painters lasted well into the 19C and had a marked effect on the character and attitudes of its painters. The academic approach is evident in the work of **José de Madrazo** and his son **Federico**, while **Eduardo Rosales** tended toward historical, monumental themes. Some, like **Mariano Fortuny**, developed a lighter touch and a more cosmopolitan and almost frivolous approach, while others, like **Isidro Nonell, Santiago Rusiñol** and **Joaquín Sorolla** (works in Madrid's Sorolla Museum), were clearly attuned to contemporary currents in European art. In sculpture, naturalism and an impressionist cast also feature in the work of **Mariano Benlliure**, particularly famous for his bullfight scenes.

ART IN THE 20C

The genius of **Pablo Picasso** is undisputed. Although he left Spain as a very young man, the influence of his native country is discernible throughout the vast body of his multi-faceted work —encompassing his early Blue, Pink, and Cubist periods, his depiction of the horror of the bombing of *Guernica* (the Prado Museum, Madrid), and experiments in various media, all executed with consummate skill in the course of a long and indefatigably productive life. Along with Picasso, the 20C also produced the great Spanish Surrealist painters **Salvador Dalí** (*The Burning Giraffe*) and **Joan Miró** —also a skilled muralist (works in Cincinatti, Harvard, and Barcelona), ceramicist and sculptor— and the analytical Cubist **Juan Gris**. Gutiérrez Solana and **Ignacio Zuloaga** were contemporary realistic painters of everyday life, **José María Sert** was known for his vast decorative religious and secular murals, and **Angel Ferrant** and **Alberto Sánchez** were admired for their Surrealist sculptures.

After the Civil War, several schools of painting developed. They included the Catalan group *Dau al Set* formed by **Juan José Tharrats, Antonio Tàpies, Modesto Cuixart** and **Joan Ponç**; the Neo-figurative group which brought together **Daniel Vázquez Díaz, Pancho Cossío** and **Antonio Clavé**; the informal work of **Luis Feito** and **José Guinovart**; and Madrid's *El Paso* group which included **Manuel Viola, Manuel Millares, Antonio Saura** and **Rafael Canogar**. The best-known modern sculptors include **José Llimona, Julio González, José Clará, Pablo Gargallo, Pablo Picasso, Angel Ferrant, Pablo Serrano, Eduardo Chillida** and **José María Subirachs**.

More recently, the stylized painting of **Eusebio Sempere**, the highly individual work of **Juan Genovés**, the colourful canvases of **Manuel Mompó**, and the masterly hyperrealist pictures of **Antonio López** have gained international recognition. New values are also making their appearance in present-day Spain: new Expressionists **Guillermo Pérez Villalta** and **Ferrán García-Sevilla**, **Chema Cobo, José María Sicilia** and post-Modernist **Miquel Barceló** already have firmly-established reputations despite their youth. In the field of sculpture, **Evaristo Bellotti, Francisco Leiro, Juan Muñoz** and **Susana Solano** are names to look out for.

FIESTAS AND FESTIVALS

Contrary to their archetypal image —what foreigner doesn't know what *mañana* and *siesta* mean?— the Spanish are an extremely hardworking people and proud of the fact. Where they differ from the rest of us is that they are equally energetic about having a good time and grasp every opportunity to do so. This must be why their traditional *fiestas* still thrive, keeping the ancient, the tribal, the undeniably Spanish, very much alive while the nation forges a place for itself in modern Europe.

Spain is a country of geographical contrasts with a vast extent of coastline, arid inland areas, gently rolling fertile countryside, soaring snow-topped mountain peaks —features which have played a decisive role in its history in serving either as magnets or natural barriers to successive waves of invaders. The resulting cultural patchwork finds vivid expression in thousands of local *fiestas*. Some of these have become national institutions and tourist attractions in their own right, like the quintessentially Andalusian **April Fair** and **Holy Week** celebrations in Seville, Valencia's ***Fallas***, Huelva's **Rocío Pilgrimage** and, best known of all beyond Spain, Pamplona's bull-running on the day of **San Fermín**, a show of macho bravado to gladden the heart of Hemingway.

Yet these major crowd pullers form only a tiny proportion of similar events going on in some part of the country all year round. The Spanish are inveterate celebrators and commemorate religious festivals (often superimposed on earlier pagan ones), historic battles (many dating back to the Middle Ages) and give thanks for traditional sources of livelihood (the land, the sea) with a characteristic mixture of solemn zeal and frivolity. The element that all *fiestas* have in common is that everyone joins in. People take to the streets and dance, sing, drink, form human towers, flagellate themselves or festoon themselves with cow-bells, as the occasion demands, with an enviable enthusiasm and abandon. Does today's hooded penitent, scourging himself in public until his back bleeds, revert to bank managerdom tomorrow with no feeling of incongruity? Those of us from more inhibited parts of the world find it hard to imagine. The folk memory seems to flourish in the fertile soil of the Spanish temperament.

Winter

Christmas Eve, December 24, receives more attention in its own right than in Britain or the States, and dinner that night is a major family reunion followed, in church-going families, by Midnight Mass and perhaps carol-singing in the streets. In some parts of Spain, ancient plays, songs or dances are performed during the midnight service, as in **CALLOSA DE SEGURA** (Alicante), **LABASTIDA** (Alava) and **PALMA** (Majorca, where in a mixture of pagan and Christian ritual the *Cant de la Sibil.la*, or Song of the Sybil, forms an integral part of the service). In Catalonia, Nativity tableaux known as *pesebres* or *pastorets* are performed by the locals, particularly in **CORBERA DE LLOBREGAT**. December 28 in Spain is a sort of April Fools' Day, a time for practical jokes which is probably a survival of the Roman Saturnalia amalgamated into a celebration of the Day of the Holy Innocents, as suggested by the cry of *Inocente!* that goes up when the butt of the joke sees the light. On the same day in La Venta del Túnel, an inn 8km from **MALAGA**, there is a 'confrontation' of rival bands of singers and dancers known as the *Pandas de Verdiales*, while in **IBI** (Alicante), elaborately disguised figures called *Els Enfarinats* swoop on the town's shops and banks declaiming satirical commentaries on local life and demanding 'fines'. On December 30

in **CENTELLES** (Barcelona), the *Festa del Pí* (Feast of the Pine)
commemorates the martyrdom of Santa Coloma (who was burned to death
on a fire of pine branches) in a lively, noisy *fiesta* during which a pine tree is
paraded through the streets, to the accompaniment of fireworks, eating and
drinking, before being decorated and displayed in the local church.

New Year's Eve celebrations on December 31 reach their climax as
midnight strikes, and every Spaniard pops a grape into his mouth with each
chime of the clock (it is easy to spot a foreigner on these occasions —he's
the one who goes purple and coughs). But there is more to come. While the
rest of us regard Epiphany as little more that the deadline for taking down
Christmas cards and decorations, for Spain, January 6 is the Day of the
Three Kings, *Los Reyes Magos*, and since it is they on their camels, rather
than Santa Claus drawn by reindeer, who distribute presents to children, the
night of the 5 is a time of tremendous excitement. The Kings and their
retinue, in full regalia and often accompanied by local public figures, form
part of extravagant **processions** of floats, bands and dancers through the
major towns and cities. The children of Majorca in the Balearics and Tenerife
in the Canaries get the added thrill of seeing the Kings arrive by sea. These
processions are a relatively recent phenomenon —**SEVILLE'S**, the oldest, dates
back only as far as 1916— but they are very popular. Much older are the
plays featuring the Three Kings performed in Aledo (Murcia), **CAÑADA**
(Alicante), **SANTILLANA DEL MAR** (Cantabria) and Sangüesa (Navarre).

Though January 6 marks the end of the Christmas season, there are more
fiestas just around the corner. The day of **San Antonio Abad** (Saint Anthony
of Egypt, 4C founder of organized Christian monasticism) is celebrated all
over Spain, and particularly in Majorca, with processions and bonfires. In
Navalvillar de Pela (Badajoz), there are elaborate *Encamisada* cavalcades
whose horsemen ride round and round the town, which is lit up by bonfires.

San Sebastián's day, on January 20, is celebrated to the full, as one
might expect, with the *Tamborada* of **SAN SEBASTIAN** (Guipuzcoa). In
ACEHUCHE (Cáceres), the *Carantoñas* consist of men curiously disguised in
animal hides and grotesque masks, who bow down before the image of the
saint as it is paraded through the town. On the same day, the **Pilgrim of
Tossa** makes his way from Tossa de Mar to Santa Coloma de Farnés
(Gerona), thus fulfilling a popular vow made in the 14C.

February 5 is the day of Saint Agueda, patron saint of married women,
celebrated on the following weekend in **ZAMARRAMALA** (Segovia) with the
election of *Las Alcaldesas* (the Mayoresses), two married women dressed in
16C local costume, who enjoy the heady experience of running the village, if
only for a day.

The end of February and the beginning of March see the arrival of
Carnival time. Long suppressed during the dictatorship for being pagan and
'conducive to immodesty', the carnivals hung on by, suitably enough, by
disguising themselves as winter or spring festivals. Now they are back in
unashamedly full force, and nowhere more spectacularly than in **SANTA CRUZ
DE TENERIFE** in the Canary Islands, gateway to the Americas, where a
Brazilian-style explosion of colour, flamboyance and abandon engulfs not only
the city but the whole island and much of the rest of the archipelago.
CADIZ'S processions and stunts at carnival time are often masterpieces of the
mocking irony said to be typical of Andalusians, who are equally famous for
knowing how to have a good time. Further N, the carnivals take on a more
medieval, European and Christian tone and provide a brief respite from the
rigours of Lent, finding their most elaborate expression in Galicia, particularly
in **LAZA** and Xinzo de Limia (Orense). In some places, like Lanz (Navarre),
gigantic effigies representing the devil are paraded through the streets: in the

case of **VILLANUEVA DE LA VERA** (Cáceres), he is a huge wooden figure, dressed in sober black suit and hat, known as the ***Pero Palo***, who is beaten, beheaded and buried in an ancient traditional ritual. There are some forty more major traditional carnivals, some ancient, some relative newcomers, held at this time throughout Spain —Lalín (Pontevedra), **SITGES** (Barcelona), San Sebastián (Guipúzcoa)...— all with their own local flavour.

VALENCIA'S famous *Fallas*, which begin on March 12, reach their climax a week later on the night of San José, with the burning of the *ninots*, huge elaborate *papier maché* tableaux, which have been on display around the city since the *fiesta* began. The bonfires light up the night sky and provide the Valencians with the perfect excuse for the fireworks and music which accompany all their festivities.

Spring

The first big event of the spring *fiesta* calendar is the ***Fiestas de la Magdalena*** in **CASTELLON DE LA PLANA** (Castellón), around the third Sunday in Lent, celebrated with bullfights and a parade. But the unchallenged star of the season is **Holy Week** celebrated in Spain with unrivalled pageantry in which Christian fervour and, particularly in the S, more exotic elements combine in a heady mix. Easter Sunday was fixed by the Council of Nicea, in the year 325, to fall on the Sunday following the first full moon after the Spring Equinox (March 21), so the date can vary by over a month. Palm Sunday can therefore fall any time between March 15 and April 18.

Palm Sunday marks the beginning of this week-long *fiesta* with the traditional blessing of the palms, a ceremony which in **ELCHE** (Alicante), where palm trees flourish, is particularly flamboyant. The elements which make up the week to follow vary considerably all over Spain and are often a clear reflection of how history has treated the area in question. In **SEVILLE**, whose *Semana Santa* celebrations are perhaps the most famous in Spain, over 50 religious brotherhoods parade through the streets, with floats bearing life-sized figures carried on the shoulders of *costaleros*, or bearers, concealed beneath. They are preceded by long lines of hooded penitents bearing candles, though their slow, shuffling, rhythmic progress in time to the music, bearing a mighty weight through densely-packed crowds is a penitential act in itself. The most famous images, the Virgin known as ***La Macarena*** and the ***Jesús del Gran Poder***, generate a frenzy of enthusiasm from the vast crowds that gather to watch them being carried shoulder-high through the streets. The cries of *'Guapa, Guapa!'* (Pretty! Pretty!) that greet *La Macarena*, the Moorish cadences of the spontaneous *saeta* laments that soar above the noise of the crowd, the smells of spring, the whiff of incense give some idea of the disparate elements —carnal and spiritual, Christian and Pagan, penitential and celebratory— that combine in this moving and unforgettable event.

The other great Andalusian Holy Week celebrations are **MALAGA'S**. Here the floats are even bigger and heavier and are carried on the shoulders of visible bearers moving to a more rigid and insistent rhythm. The star turn is the figure of Christ known as *Nuestro Padre Jesús El Rico*, to which Charles III in the 18C granted the royal privilege of releasing a prisoner on the day of the procession, a privilege exercised to this day.

While the hedonistic abandon of Andalusia may seem typically Spanish to foreigners, the sober austerity of Castile is no less typical. The solemn **processions** in **VALLADOLID** of hooded penitents and floats bearing veritable artistic treasures in the form of polychromed wooden figures, often many centuries old, and the impressive 'Sermon of the Seven Words' in the Plaza

Mayor move the spectator in quite a different way from Andalusia's. In **ZAMORA**, the solemnity of the event is underlined by the mercilessly insistent sound of drums and discordant trumpets. Somewhere between these two extremes, **LORCA** (Murcia) stages flamboyant lively processions for which the two rival brotherhoods, the *Paso Blanco* and the *Paso Azul* spare no expense on costumes, draperies and hiring the finest of horses from Andalusia and Galicia.

CARTAGENA (whose processions date back to the 16C), **CUENCA**, **MURCIA** (with outstanding processional figures by 18C sculptor, Francisco Salzillo) and Puente Genil (Córdoba) all hold Holy Week celebrations that you should make every effort to see if you are within striking distance at the right time of year.

Drumming, or *Tamboradas*, forms an inseparable part of the *Semana Santa* experience, and in some parts of Aragón, like **CALANDA**, **ALCAÑIZ**, **HIJAR** and **ANDORRA**, marathons of monotonous rhythmic drumming contribute to the theme of mortification of the flesh in that the drummers play on despite bleeding hands, as they charge the atmosphere with a sense of impending doom and drama.

Passion Plays are a common feature of Holy Week celebrations all over Spain, but particularly in Catalonia. They are usually performed by local amateurs and are based on ancient traditional texts; they are all the more moving for the resultant ingenuity and spontaneity and for the frequently picturesque surroundings in which they are staged. Among the best are the plays in Benetúser (Valencia), Callosa de Segura (Alicante), **CERVERA** (Lérida), Chinchón (Madrid), **ESPARRAGUERA** (Barcelona), **OLESA DE MONTSERRAT** (Barcelona), **ULLDECONA** (Tarragona), Valmaseda (Vizcaya) and **VERGES** (Gerona).

During *Semana Santa* in Spain, you often feel you have been whisked back in time to the Middle Ages, and never more so than if you witness the scenes of mortification of the flesh which, incredibly to many foreigners, have by no means been reduced to mere symbolic gestures with the passage of time. In **SAN VICENTE DE LA SONSIERRA** (La Rioja), hooded penitents —the *Picaos*— with their backs exposed flagellate themselves with knotted ropes then pierce their inflamed flesh with broken glass embedded in wax until it bleeds. In **VALVERDE DE LA VERA** (Cáceres), penitents known as *Empalaos* endure the agony of parading for hours with their outstretched arms lashed by ropes to the beams of a plough in imitation of Christ's suffering.

The atmosphere of suffering and doom lifts on Easter Sunday. Throughout Catalonia, the sound of *caramelles*, traditional Easter songs, is heard in the streets, while in **MURCIA**, the *Fiestas de Primavera* (Spring Festival) celebrates the Resurrection with a carnival.

Spain's outstanding April *fiesta* is **SEVILLE'S** *Feria de Abril*, an event which encapsulates every foreigner's travel-poster image of Spain. The area of the city reserved for the fair fills up with brightly coloured canvas booths, some private, some commercial, for eating and drinking in, and people flock in their thousands to enjoy and be part of the spectacle. At midday, hundreds of horsemen in high-waisted suits and flat-crowned *sombreros* ride elegantly by on superbly groomed Andalusian horses, dusky beauties in vivid, flounced gypsy dresses riding sidesaddle behind them. In an unflagging explosion of *joie de vivre*, the *fiesta*, originally a simple horse fair, has become a week of non-stop parading, eating, drinking, flamenco singing and dancing, and is a high point of Spain's bullfighting calendar (see 'Bullfighting'). The fun goes on all night, when the sky is lit up by thousands of lanterns and fairy lights, and only those with an Hispanic upbringing can hope to stand the pace. A similar event, though less of a crowd puller, and where horses (marvellous

Arab-Andalusian creatures) play an even more important role, is the *Feria del Caballo* in **JEREZ DE LA FRONTERA** (Cádiz) in early May.

April is also an important month for Catalonia, Valencia and Majorca, the territories which made up the kingdom of James I, the Conqueror, in the 13C, the day of whose patron saint, **Sant Jordi** (Saint George) falls on April 23. In **ALCOY** (Alicante), the day is celebrated with a symbolic confrontation of **Christians and Moors** (a feature of *fiestas* in many parts of Spain throughout the year), as well as the usual ingredients of fireworks, music and general hilarity. The sophisticated Barcelonans celebrate the occasion by presenting a book and a rose to their loved ones. The last Sunday in April sees the *Romería de la Virgen de la Cabeza* in **ANDUJAR** (Jaén), a three-day celebration which starts with displays of horsemanship and culminates in a pilgrimage, whose participants from all over Andalusia travel in their thousands on horseback or in horse-drawn carriages, to the shrine of their Virgin high up in the Sierra Morena.

By May, sunshine bathes most of Spain, and its *fiestas* are celebrations of love and fertility, many of them originally homages to pagan goddesses, now translated into the Christian Mother Figure, the Virgin Mary. One exception are the *Fiestas de Mayo* in Santa Cruz de Tenerife in commemoration of the founding of the capital of the Canary Islands. But the month's classic *fiestas* are centred around the *Cruces de Mayo*, crosses of flowers which are set up in towns all over Spain and in which *Mayos*, essentially love songs offered up to the Virgin, are sung and unmarried girls are serenaded. This is particularly typical in **Castile-La Mancha**. The conical structures and crosses decked with flowers and foliage known as *maios* in Galicia, around which people dance and sing satirical songs, bear more than a passing resemblance to England's traditional maypoles. These have become competitive events in **PONTEVEDRA**, Villagarcía de Arosa and Orense, as has the *Cruces de Mayo* fiesta in **CORDOBA**; here the inspired introduction of a parallel *Festival de los Patios* during which a prize is awarded for the city's most beautiful patio has saved from extinction these plant and flower-decked inner sanctuaries, so typical a feature of Córdoba's popular architecture.

For **MADRID**, May means the celebrations in honour of its patron saint, the *Feria de San Isidro*, a classic example of a once flagging *fiesta* successfully resuscitated. Its high point is May 15, but a whole season of **drama, music** and other open-air events has grown up around it, not to mention some of the top attractions of the Spanish **bullfighting** calendar.

Ascension Day, however, seems to have lost its traditional *fiestas*. Whitsun, on the other hand, ten days later, is the day of one of the most massively attended events in the world, the pilgrimage to the shrine of the little figure of *Nuestra Señora del Rocío* (Our Lady of the Dew) in **ALMONTE** (Huelva), in the heart of the sparsely populated marshlands near the Doñana Reserve (see 'Wide Open Spaces'). The origins of this pilgrimage are believed to be ancient and pagan, and it seems more than likely that the Virgin Mary took over the role previously occupied by Tanit or Astarté. The whole event is a heady mixture of the sacred and profane, and up to a million pilgrims from quite far afield, dressed in Andalusian costume and riding on horseback or in ox-drawn carts, wend their way towards their destination, eating, drinking, singing, dancing and sleeping in the open air. A night-time celebration charged with religious fervour marks their arrival at the shrine and the figure of the Virgin is paraded on the shoulders of the young men while other candle-carrying pilgrims sing age-old *sevillanas*.

The *Caballada de Atienza* in Guadalajara is an ancient ritual in commemoration of an historic event in 1162 when local muleteers rode to the defence of the boy king Alfonso VIII, against attempts to dethrone him by his uncle, Ferdinand II. Meanwhile, *romerías*, or festive pilgrimages, are going on all over **Catalonia**, in **PEÑAS DE SAN PEDRO** (Albacete) and in **LUMBIER** (Navarre), where a more sombre note is struck by the black-clad pilgrims who make their way to the shrine of the Virgin bare-footed and weighed down by heavy crosses.

The next major *fiesta*, also a moveable feast, is **Corpus Christi**, whose widespread celebration as a Christian festival dates back to the 14C. Traditionally, the Host is carried in procession, and huge elaborate monstrances in precious metals made for this purpose feature among the Spanish Church's artistic heritage (see 'Design'). Outstanding Corpus Christi processions take place in **TOLEDO**, **VALENCIA**, **MORELLA** (Castellón) and **SEVILLE**, where the traditional ritual includes a performance by the Cathedral's *Seises*, young boys in 16C costume who dance and sing before the Host to 18C music. In many parts of Spain the procession's route is strewn with aromatic herbs, elaborate **carpets of flowers** —as in **SITGES** (Barcelona) and Las Palmas de Gran Canaria—, coloured sand as in **LA OROTAVA** (Tenerife), or salt, as in the island of Lanzarote. The procession is often accompanied by symbolic plays or interludes generally representative of the struggle between Good and Evil, many dating back to the Middle Ages. In **BERGA** (Barcelona), history and morality, mime and dance, combine in the traditional Corpus Christi play known as *La Patum*: Moors and Christians do battle, devils let off rockets and firecrackers, a huge dragon-like monster breathes fire, and a crowned eagle representing royal power commemorates the town's liberation from its feudal overlords. In **CAMUÑAS** (Toledo), two brotherhoods dressed in spectacular costumes perform medieval dances symbolic of the triumph of Good over Evil.

From May to July, it is *curro* time in Galicia. These traditional round-ups of wild horses which are herded into pens (*curros*) for branding have evolved into full-scale *fiestas* that attract huge crowds in **BAYONA-OYA** (Pontevedra), **CEDEIRA** (La Coruña), **SAN LORENZO DE SABUCEDO-LA ESTRADA** (Pontevedra), **SAN ANDRES DE BOIMENTE-VIVERO** (Lugo) and **AMIL-MORAÑA** (Pontevedra).

Summer

The summer *fiestas* could be said to begin on June 24, the longest day or Summer Solstice. In celebration of the triumph of Light over Darkness, bonfires light up the night sky and fire and water play a key role in the clearly pagan rites, albeit amalgamated with the Christian *Festival de San Juan*, which characterize these *fiestas*. In **SAN PEDRO MANRIQUE** (Soria), barefooted **fire walkers**, sometimes carrying another person on their backs, tread a path of glowing coals in a rite that dates back to time immemorial, while in **ALICANTE** and **BARCELONA**, huge elaborate tableaux of wood and *papier maché* are burned in what are known as the *Hogueras de San Juan* (the Bonfires of Saint John). The *fiesta* in **CIUDADELA** (Menorca) is quite different in character: in a vivid spectacle, horses and their riders prance to ancient music and play games which clearly date from medieval times.

June 29 is the saint's day of **San Pedro** (Saint Peter), patron saint of fishermen, celebrated with sea-borne processions in many coastal areas. But he is feted inland too. In **HARO** (La Rioja), the annual **Battle of Wine** —a bacchanalian event during which everyone gets drenched in wine— does its best to reduce the EEC wine lake. In **SEGOVIA**, Saint John and Saint Peter share a joint celebration featuring folk dancing and bullfights. The following day in **IRUN** (Guipúzcoa), the historic **Battle of San Marcial** is commemorated with a lively *fiesta* during which a parade of cavalry and infantry makes its way to the shrine of the saint.

What is probably Spain's best known *fiesta*, thanks to Hemingway, is 🐂🐂🐂 **PAMPLONA'S** (Navarre) *San Fermín*, known to date back at least as far as 1591. Though the saint's day actually falls on July 7, the *fiesta* lasts from the 6 to the 14 —a whole week of uninterrupted drinking and general casting off of inhibitions— the best known feature of which are the morning bull runs when the bulls are released from their pens and run through the crowded narrow streets, goaded on by red and white clad youths, to the *plaza de toros* where they will take part in the afternoon bullfights. Pamplona's world-wide fame has somewhat overshadowed the similar *Sanfermines* in Lesaca (Navarre) and Pasajes (Guipúzcoa).

The patron saint of the sea, the *Virgen del Carmen*, is feted in coastal towns all over Spain, on July 16, from **CANGAS DE NARCEA** (Asturias) to **PUERTO DE LA CRUZ** (Tenerife) in quayside celebrations, and the figure of the Virgin heads a sea-borne procession of boats, flower-decked in her honour. The following day sees the start of the *Fiestas de San Jaime* in **VALENCIA**, with battles of flowers, and bullfights which last until the end of the month. In **ANGUIANO**, a lovely village in La Rioja, the festival of Saint Mary Magdalene is celebrated with street processions and, in an age-old custom, the *Danza de* 🐂 *los Zancos*, young men in swirling skirts dance on wooden stilts to the accompaniment of bagpipes, drums and castanets. Dancing is also the outstanding feature of the *fiesta* in honour of Saint Anne, patron saint of **LLORET DE MAR** (Gerona) on June 24.

The following day, June 25, is the saint's day of **Santiago** (Saint James), patron saint of all Spain, celebrated throughout the country but most 🐂 particularly in **SANTIAGO DE COMPOSTELA** in Galicia, whose shrine, believed to contain the remains of the Apostle Saint James, attracted droves of pilgrims from all over Europe throughout the Middle Ages. Galicia is fond of 🐂 *romerías*, festive pilgrimages, to this day, among them the Santiago celebrations in **A CANIZA** (Pontevedra) and **PADRON** (La Coruña). One of the most curious ones is the *Romería de Santa Marta de Ribarteme* in **LAS NIEVES** (Pontevedra), on June 29, during which, in a typically Celtic mixture of gloom and whimsy, a procession of coffins, some of them occupied by people who believe themselves to be dying, is carried to the shrine of the saint to plead for her intervention. The Virgin of the Snows is particularly venerated in the Canary Island of **La Palma**: every five years since 1680 (the next will be 1990 and 1995), thousands of islanders dressed in vivid regional 🐂 costumes make the pilgrimage to the shrine of the Virgin, the *Bajada de la Virgen*, though the traditional plays and dances performed during the *fiesta* strike a more secular note.

Countless towns and villages celebrate their patronal festivals during August which, fortunately for interested visitors, coincides with the peak tourist season. One huge attraction of the first Saturday of the month is the 🐂🐂 **Descent of the River Sella**, an 18km international canoeing race between Arriondas and Ribadesella in Asturias, said to be one of the toughest in the world. That same weekend sees the patronal festivity of **ESTELLA** (Navarre) with traditional events, including the famous parade of *papier maché* giants dating back to the Middle Ages. August 15, the feastday of the *Virgen de la Asunción*, is the most *fiesta*-packed day of the Spanish year. One of the 🐂 most outstanding of these is the *Misteri* of **ELCHE** (Alicante), a 13C mystery play fascinating for its musical and dramatic content. It is performed in two parts, one on the 14 and one on the 15, and represents the Dormition, or falling asleep, of Mary and her Ascension, body and soul, into heaven. The cast is entirely male, the female roles being played by children, and the sung text is in *Lemosín*, an old Valencian variant of Catalan (attendance is free on the 14 and 15, but you will need to buy tickets from the Municipal Tourist

Office for the performances on the 11, 12 and 13). August 15 also sees the beginning of the *Semana Grande* (Big Week) in **SAN SEBASTIAN**, celebrated a week later in **BILBAO**, with good bullfighting, but the 15 and 16 are reserved for the Virgin Mary in the picturesque town of **LA ALBERCA** (Salamanca), where an Offertory ceremony, the *Ofertorio*, is held in the Plaza Mayor and a traditional religious play, the *Loa*, is performed in front of the church the following day. Around the 18 in the lovely town of **BETANZOS** (La Coruña), another of Galicia's *romerías*, *Os Caneiros*, features a procession of vividly decorated boats along the river. On the 28, the *fiestas* in **FELANITX** (Majorca) feature dancing cavaliers and demons, while rounding off the month on the 30, **VILLAFRANCA DEL PANADES** (Barcelona) holds one of Catalonia's most typical *fiestas*, the high point of which are the competitions among *castellers* who form incredibly tall human towers.

September 1 sees the *Fiestas de la Vendimia*, the grape harvest festival, in the wine-growing area of Valdepeñas (Ciudad Real), and in **TEROR** (Gran Canaria) the pilgrimage to the shrine of the *Virgen del Pino*. Around the 24, the *Fiestas de la Merced* in **BARCELONA** are a heady mixture of religious services, sporting events, music, drama and cinema festivals and a riotous parade of *gigantes y cabezudos* (figures disguised as giants or wearing huge *papier maché* heads) in the Pl de San Jaime. Saint Tecla's Day, September 23, is celebrated in **TARRAGONA** with a *Fiesta Mayor*, with traditional *sardana* folk dancing and human towers of *castellers*. The **Grape Harvest Festival** in **JEREZ DE LA FRONTERA** (Cádiz), the home of sherry, is understandably an affair of some importance. Newly-pressed grapes are offered up before the image of the patron saint of wine-growers, San Ginés de la Jara, followed by typically Andalusian events like a cavalcade of splendid horses, a flamenco festival and bullfighting.

Autumn

October 12 is a **national holiday**, celebrated in **ZARAGOZA** with the *Fiestas del Pilar*, a festival whose high point is the offering of flowers to the figure of the Virgin in the Basilica del Pilar by women in regional costume. November is ushered in with All Saints' Day celebrations, and the *Día de los Difuntos* (Day of the Dead) is, suitably enough, the start of the traditional pig-slaughtering time in rural areas, advantage being taken of the chillier weather to prepare the sausages and hams which will last throughout the winter. In Molló (Gerona), the slaughtering is carried out in the Plaza Mayor and the meat is subsequently auctioned. In typically Spanish fashion, this grisly event has been embellished into a *fiesta*, accompanied by traditional *coca* pies and flambé rum. The *fiesta* of *As San Lucas* in **MONDOÑEDO** (Lugo) around November 18 is one of the biggest horse fairs in Galicia and still retains much of its original medieval character. It also provides a marvellous opportunity for buying local craftwork. Another of Galicia's famous *romerías*, to the shrine of *San Andrés de Teixido*, takes place on the 30. Popular belief has it that unless you make this pilgrimage during your lifetime, you will do so as some lower form of life after your death. Consequently, animals and insects encountered along the pilgrimage route are treated with the greatest respect just in case.

The *fiesta* year draws to a close with the celebration of Saint Lucia's Day on December 13. In Barcelona, the *Fira de Santa Llucía* marks the start of the Christmas season. Meanwhile in Santa Lucía (Gran Canaria), then at the height of the Canary Islands' tourist season, the saint is honoured with gifts of exotic fruit and flowers presented by youngsters in vivid regional costume. Who can deny it? Spain has everything under the sun.

HEALTH AND BEAUTY

Mens sana in corpore sano: one can see it now writ in gold upon the school crest. Small wonder that the generations of schoolboys who endured compulsory cross-country running under a fine drizzle twice a week tended to settle down happily to a plump middle age. The beauty aspect was, of course, for women (generally rich and idle). The only way a man could concern himself with the aesthetics of the body without doubts being cast on his manhood was to go in for body building, striking gleaming poses to his heart's content since it was macho and therefore quite above suspicion.

Thank goodness, then, for women's lib and the men's lib it has brought in its wake. We can all, now, go in for the sports we like (and there are masses of opportunities in Spain, see 'Holidays in Action') and make the best of our bodies without worrying about subliminal messages. Today's sports clubs and gyms with their saunas, jacuzzis and return-to-the-womb isolation bubbles are surely far nearer to what the Ancient Romans had in mind than shivering in shorts on a hockey pitch on a winter's morning. Indeed, here in Spain there are still remains of Roman baths and later Moorish ones with facilities for steaming, cleaning and· massage, and the spirit of these sybaritic cultures lives on in up-to-the-minute health farms set in superb locations throughout Spain, making full use of the country's enviable natural resources —sunshine, sea and fresh mountain air. Here are a few pointers for people interested in spending their holiday getting fit and beautiful and enjoying it. (A word of warning here about signs or advertisements offering *saunas, relaxation* or *massages*: these are the standard code words in Spain for 'personal services' if not outright prostitution, so do make full enquiries before turning up in your track suit.)

Health and Beauty Farms and Clinics

The use of sea-water for its curative properties, or thalassotherapy, also dates back many centuries. The clumsily-named but attractive **Centro de Termalismo Helio-Marino y Recuperación Funcional** ☎ (964) 30 04 50 is a thalassotherapy centre marvellously situated at sea level in **BENICASIM** (Castellón) on the shores of the Mediterranean and sheltered by a backdrop of mountains. Geographical accident provides it with a privileged microclimate, with very low humidity and mild temperatures all year round, averaging 12°C (54°F) in winter and 26°C (79°F) in summer. The centre has 156 rooms, sun terraces, swimming pools, saunas, a gymnasium and medical services (minigolf, television and other amusements are also provided). It provides therapy for injuries, neurological problems, rheumatism and orthopaedic treatment. It is right by the beach, and just 35km from Valencia.

On Andalusia's Costa del Sol, just 5km from the beach and 4km from the ancient whitewashed village of **MIJAS** stands the beautiful white hotel complex of *Byblos Andaluz* which incorporates three restaurants, another health-food restaurant, swimming pools, two golf courses, tennis courts and the *Louison Bobet Thalassotherapy Centre* ☎ (952) 47 30 50, telex 79713 byane, fax (952) 47 67 83. Named after the legendary French cycling champion, the centre is an oasis of calm, open throughout the year, and ideal for people suffering from stress, rheumatism, or who simply want to get in shape and attack their cellulitis and surplus weight. There is medical service on hand and the treatments combine advanced technology with long-recognized curative properties of sea water, sea weed and other natural substances.

In nearby **MARBELLA** (Málaga), favourite playground of the international jet set, the *Incosol Clinic*, Urb Río Real ☎ (952) 77 37 00 is extremely well known, not least for the rich and famous who make up its clientele. Neither clinic nor hotel in any usual sense, this little microcosm provides accommodation, leisure facilities, medical and beauty treatments and general cossetting, and is an ideal retreat for well-off stress sufferers. Treatments include acupuncture, dietary advice and control, physiotherapy, slimming, and facials. Also in Marbella, the *Buchinger Clinic*, Rocío de Nagüeles ☎ (952) 77 27 00, telex 77835 bukle, applies the principles of the German Doctor Buchinger in its fasting and liquid diet-based treatments, which usually last two weeks.

The *Curhotel Hipócrates* in **SAN FELIU DE GUIXOLS** (Gerona) is an hotel, clinic and spa all in one. Scenically and peacefully situated, the treatments provided include physiotherapy, physical rehabilitation, dietary advice and control, hydrotherapy, massage, mud and sauna baths and psychotherapy.

The *Hacienda del Sol* in **VILLAJOYOSA** (Alicante) ☎ (965) 589 20 00, originally a Norwegian foundation, is a holiday centre for mentally handicapped young people. It has accommodation for 125 guests plus a gymnasium and facilities for physiotherapy, manual exercises, and so on.

Another little microcosm, though in a category all its own, is the **naturist** complex known as *Costa Natura* ☎ (952) 80 15 00 in **ESTEPONA** (Málaga), at km151 on the N-340 from Cádiz to Málaga, with apartments, shops and so on for people for whom casting off their clothes is a therapy in itself.

Spas

Two thousand years ago the Romans had already discovered the benefits of many of Spain's 2,000 medicinal and thermal springs, an enthusiasm shared by the Moors who occupied the peninsula throughout the Middle Ages. Spas became the height of fashion throughout Europe and the United States in the 19C, and just as the *beau monde* of England flocked to Bath, celebrities like the Empress Eugénie of France (Granada's own Eugenia de Montijo) and the Romantic poet, Lord Byron, took the waters at Carratraca (Málaga). At that time there were over 160 flourishing spas in Spain. Today there are about 90, some 25 of them well-equipped and now coming back into favour among the fashionable set, though the news has not yet filtered through to foreign tourists. The *belle époque* atmosphere of their heyday is still in evidence and, in combination with the complete relaxation and contact with nature they offer, constitutes much of their charm.

Except for one in Palma de Mallorca (Majorca), Spain's spas are all on the mainland, mainly concentrated in Catalonia, Upper Aragón, Galicia, and Andalusia. About a quarter of them are open all year round, but they are all in operation for the high season of July and August. Many of them are in idyllic situations: in lush green valleys, on mountain tops (like Benasque in Huesca, 1,720m ☎ 55 10 11) and by the sea (La Toja, Galicia). Gone are the days when the spas were for the elderly. Today their clients include children, young executives and show-business personalities. The atmosphere tends to be simple and friendly, their privileged location makes them a good base from which to explore the surroundings which, in combination with their giving very good value for money makes the spas of Spain an attractive holiday proposition.

The Spanish Tourism Promotion Office (*INPROTUR*), c/ Castello, 117, 28006 Madrid ☎ 411 40 14 publishes a guide to spas and thermal spring resorts which gives full details of their facilities, treatments provided, properties of the water and so on. Here is a brief selection.

Place	Spa	Altitude	Accommodation
Alhama de Granada (Granada)	Alhama de Granada	850m	★★★Hotel, very peaceful
Tolox (Málaga)	**Tolox**	360m	★★ Hotel, very peaceful
Alhama de Aragón (Zaragoza)	Termas Pallarés	660m	★★★ Hotel
Panticosa (Huesca)	**Panticosa** ☉	1,636m	★★★ Hotel, very peaceful ★★ Hotel, very peaceful 7 ★ Hotels ★ Hostal
Campos del Puerto (Majorca)	**San Juan de la Font Santa**	5m	★★ Hotel, very peaceful
Cestona (Guipúzcoa)	**Cestona**	60m	★★★ Hotel ★★★ Hotel ★ Hotel
Bohí (Lérida)	**Estación Termal y de Montaña Caldas de Bohí**	1,500m	★★★★ Hotel, very peaceful ★ Hotel, very peaceful
Caldas de Montbuy (Barcelona)	**Broquetas**	210m	★★★ Hotel, peaceful
Caldas de Malavella (Gerona)	**Prats**	90m	★★★ Hotel, peaceful
Caldas de Malavella (Gerona)	**Vichy Catalán**	95m	★★★ Hotel, peaceful
Vallfogona de Riucorb (Tarragona)	**Vallfogona de Ruicorb**	560m	★★★ Hotel, very peaceful
La Toja (Pontevedra)	**La Toja**	sea level	★★★★★ Hotel ☉☉ ★★★★ Hotel ★ Hotel R
Arnedillo (La Rioja)	Arnedillo	651m	★★★ Hotel ★★ Hotel, both very peaceful
Fitero (Navarre)	Baños de Fitero	425m	★ Hotel, very peaceful ★ Hotel, very quiet

Setting	Water temp ° C (° F)	Ailments Treated	Added Attractions
Large park	47-49° (117-120°)	Rheumatic and respiratory	Beautifully **situated** village 🐦🐦 3 km away.
	21° (70°)	Asthmatic, respiratory and urinary	Whitewashed village in a mountain setting.
Large park	34° (93°)	Rheumatic, respiratory and otorhinological	Lovely natural **hot water pool.**
Beautiful mountain-top **location** 🐦	50° (122°)	Dermatological, digestive and rheumatic	Impressive range of services. **Mountain surroundings** 🐦🐦 offer scope for excursions.
	38-39° (100-102°)	Rheumatic, dermatological and respiratory	Young, fun atmosphere. Near unspoiled beach of **Es Trenc.** 🐦
Wooded hillsides.	27-31° (81-88°)	Hepatic and biliary	Various services. 14km from **Zarauz.**
Splendid park	from cold to warm	Rheumatic, neuralgic, dermatological and respiratory	Wide range of services. Near **Romanesque churches** and 🐦 **Aigües Tortes.** 🐦🐦
Lovely wooded garden	69. 9° (158°)	Rheumatic, obesity and traumatological	Various services. 28 km from **Barcelona.** 🐦🐦🐦
Tree-shaded terrace	60° (140°)	Rheumatic, circulatory and respiratory	Less than half an hour from the **Costa Brava.** 🐦🐦
Park	60° (140°)	Rheumatic, circulatory and respiratory	As above.
Pleasant park	14° (57°)	Dermatological, hepatic and biliary	Various services. Buses to Tarragona and **Barcelona.** 🐦🐦🐦
Beautiful green 🐦🐦 **landscape** with views.	37-60° (99-140°)	Dermatological, rheumatic and physical rehabilitation	Wide range of services. In the heart of the **Rías Bajas.** 🐦🐦
Pine-clad hills on the banks of a river	52.5° (126°)	Rheumatic, neuralgic, and post-injury rehabilitation.	
	47.5° (118°)	Rheumatic, neuralgic and post-injury rehabilitation	Various services. 4 km from the historic town of **Fitero.** 🐦

Spain is an old country, with a history stretching back 3,000 years, yet its outlook is young, democratic and modern. It is an open country which has seen different peoples coexist on its soil since time immemorial and has, throughout its history, been the cradle of explorers and emigrants to all parts of the globe. Occupying the greater part of the Iberian Peninsula, Spain is closely linked with the sea, and from across the sea it has attracted visitors down the ages. Bounded by both the Atlantic and the Mediterranean, Spain has been profoundly influenced by its close bond with America and by its links with Europe which date far back into antiquity. Understandably, Spaniards are proud of their rich past.

ORIGINS AND PREHISTORY

In the beginning was myth. It is said that, in the mists of time immemorial, somewhere on the westernmost point of the European continent Geryon tended the cattle that Hercules stole as his tenth labour and the columns on either side of the Straits of Gibraltar held up the sky. Later, a more scientific approach was taken to history and myth became legend: Herodotus located the *Garden of the Hesperides* in the Canary Islands, which Homer later declared to have been the site of the *Elysian Fields*. Even today, there are some who will argue that Atlantis must have been somewhere between Cádiz, Huelva and the Canary Islands.

For those who prefer tangible evidence of their forebears, scientists have found pre-Acheulean remains in the S and SE of Spain (Andalusia and Levante), dating back to 1.5 million years BC, as well as remains of Neanderthal man (Middle Paleolithic, 100,000-30,000 BC) in Gibraltar and Bañolas. *Homo Sapiens* (Late Paleolithic, 25,000 BC) has left his mark in the marvellous **Altamira cave** drawings (Cantabria), sometimes acclaimed as the *Sistine Chapel* of ancient history. Around 4000 BC, Neolithic man brought agriculture to the Mediterranean coasts, and the first fixed human settlements were established (Levante and burial ditches in the NE). Roughly 2000 years later, the **Los Millares** culture was flourishing in Almería, and Spain could be said to have made its first contribution to European culture: the bell-shaped vase that may have first been made here, and was subsequently to spread throughout Europe.

Around 1000 BC, the **Phoenicians** founded *Gadir* (Cádiz), *Malaka* (Málaga) and other trading posts along the Spanish coasts; the **Greeks** settled in *Mainaké* (neighbouring on Málaga), *Lucentum* (Alicante) and other coastal enclaves. Inland, civilization had not advanced so far and was still in the Iron Age. Several **Iberian** tribes inhabited the Spanish central plateau and from 900 BC, **Celts** coming from the European mainland settled first in the N of the Peninsula and then gradually moved further towards the centre where they mixed with the original **Iberians** thus founding the **Celtiberian** tribes. However, in the NW (namely Galicia, Asturias and the N of Portugal) the Celts' beliefs, language, architecture and crafts predominated over rather than being absorbed by the native culture they encountered, and left an eduring legacy.

Around the 8C BC, the **Greeks** colonized the eastern Mediterranean coasts (lands that they called *Iberia*, after the River Iber, now the Ebro River), and Ampurias, while in the W, the **Tartessian Kingdom** flourished, its centre in Seville. This kingdom finally fell to the **Carthaginians** when they crossed the Straits in about 500 BC and took over southern Spain. Thus the basis of Iberian civilization was laid, with strong Greek and Punic (N African) influences. This constant intermingling of European and African cultures was to be repeated in Spain for the next two and a half thousand years.

ROMAN AND VISIGOTHIC SPAIN

After its defeat by Rome in the First Punic War, Carthage attempted to establish an empire in *Iberia*. The systematic conquest of the Peninsula was initiated by **Hamilcar Barca** in 237 BC and culminated in the conquest of Sagunto by **Hannibal** in 219 BC. In 218 BC, the **Roman** troops of **Publius Cornelius Scipio** disembarked in Ampurias, thus beginning the Second Punic War. After expelling the Carthaginians, the victorious Romans had political dominion over the entire peninsula that they called *Hispania*, albeit in the face of constant resistance, such as the uprisings led by Viriathus (154-138 BC) and the heroic resistance of Numancia from 143-133 BC. Such unrest continued for some time —take, for example, the civil war that ended with **Julius Caesar's** famous defeat of Pompey at *Baetica* (Andalusia) in 45 BC— but finally, the conquest of Asturias and Cantabria in 19 BC led to centuries of peace, although the mountain Basques were never fully pacified. Roman influence was strong and lasting. Spaniards not only adopted the Roman currency (the *denarium*), but also its language (Latin), its architecture, its culture and its laws. *Hispania*, made up of three provinces, was an important economic and cultural power within the Roman Empire, giving birth to philosophers, writers and even Emperors (Trajan, 98-117 and Hadrian, 117-138, both from *Itálica*). Impressive monuments were erected, equalled only in Rome itself. Christianity came to Spain at the same time as it did to Rome, spread by Roman soldiers returning from Africa in the 1C, and became widely accepted by the 2C.

In the 5C, the decline and fall of the Roman Empire created a crisis in Spain. Germanic tribes (Suebi, Alans, Vandals and Visigoths) had been making constant incursions ever since the 3C, sacking the country and destroying its administrative system. The **Visigoths** finally allied themselves with Rome against the other barbarian invasions and, after the fall of Rome (476), when there must have been roughly 100,000 Visigoths in Spain, they set up their capital in **TOLEDO** and proclaimed themselves heirs to Roman legitimacy as rulers of the entire country. Following the conversion of **Recared** (586-601) to Christianity, the Visigoth kingdom, although a fragile military unit, was backed by the cultural power of the Catholic church and its rule over a largely rural society was consolidated. Complete political unification of the peninsula, however, did not take place until Suintila (621-631) expelled the last Byzantines from the southern coasts and finally made subject the Basques. Culture flourished as Spanish bishops, saints and writers made Spain famous worldwide, and a full body of laws was drawn up, a testimony to the persistence of the influence of Roman civilization over Visigothic Spain.

ISLAMIC SPAIN AND THE CHRISTIAN RECONQUEST

At the beginning of the 8C, the strength of the Visigothic rule was undermined by factionalism among leading Visigothic families. After the death of Witiza, his sons, in an attempt to overthrow his successor, Roderick, appealed for help to the N African Muslims, who crossed the Straits of Gibraltar in **711**, headed by **Tariq**, to defeat King Roderick's forces near Guadalete. Realizing how weak and divided the country was, they began fighting their way N, making pacts with those who surrendered, and took only seven more years to conquer nearly the entire country, which they called *Al Andalus*. They were to remain on Spanish soil for nearly 800 years. The Asturians, Cantabrians and other Christians who had fled to the mountains of the N chose **Pelayo** as their king; he led them on to win the **Battle of Covadonga** in 722, thus initiating the Christian **Reconquest** and founding the kingdom of **Asturias**. In 756, **Abd ar-Rahman I** (756-788) declared the Spanish Emirate independent of Damascus; its capital at Córdoba became the centre of a flourishing economy and culture. In 801 Charlemagne seized Barcelona, extending the border of Christian Europe to Catalonia where he established the Spanish March, the frontier between Christian and Muslim Spain. And in **813** pilgrims from all over Europe began to flock to Galicia, in northern Spain, to pray at what was claimed to be the tomb of the apostle, Saint James or Santiago. A defence line of castles was built along the northern Meseta, thus giving the area its name: Castile (first found in written form in the 9C). Iñigo Arista became the first king of Navarre; and Basque fishermen reached Greenland. *Al Andalus* extended its influence all over the Mediterranean under the reign of Abd ar-Rahman II (822-852). However, Alfonso III, the Great (866-910) pushed the southern frontier of the kingdom of Asturias forward, down to the River Duero, and established the royal line of kings of **León**, while, to the E, Count Wilfred (879-897) reunited several counties and established the **Royal House of Barcelona**, going down in history as Wilfredo el Velloso, or Wilfred the Hairy.

Abd ar-Rahman III (912-961) proclaimed the independence of the Western Caliphate in 929. Its capital, **CORDOBA**, was the biggest city in Europe, with 250,000 inhabitants, an advanced sewage system, public lighting and the biggest mosque in the Islamic world. Muslim Spain saved the cultural heritage of Greece for Europe during the Dark Ages through its superb translation schools and contributed a new body of ideas and wisdom. It was roughly at this time that the Castilian language (later known as Spanish) took on its own identity, as did Galician and Catalan. This linguistic separation was consolidated by Count Fernán González's struggle for Castile's independence from the kingdom of León.

In the 11C, **al-Mansur** ravaged the Christian territories, but after his death, the Caliphate of Córdoba disintegrated into several lesser kingdoms, known as *taifas*, of which Seville, under the poet king al-Motamid, was perhaps the most splendid. The **GRANADA** *taifa* lasted 482 years. In the N, Count Borrell II of Barcelona declared his independence from the vassalage to the French monarchy in 988. The kingdom of **Castile** was constituted in 1037, with Ferdinand I (son of Sancho III of Navarre) as its first king. In 1085-1086, it conquered Toledo, and the *taifas* were forced to turn to the Almoravids (a fanatical Muslim sect from N Africa) for help, as the wars hotted up, and the legendary Castilian knight, **El Cid** (meaning 'Lord' in Arabic) conquered Valencia.

Although usually dated in the 12C, the so-called Reconquest was not so much an event as a changing relationship between Muslims and Christians, which fluctuated between war and peace, mutual influence, vassalage, exchange, Christian kings helping Muslims against other Christian kings, and vice versa... Another N African sect, the austere Almohads, came to Spain to restore Muslim authority in *Al Andalus*, and made Seville the most important city in the country. Ramón Berenguer III (1097-1131) turned the County of Barcelona into a Mediterranean power and the name 'Catalan' began to be used. Alfonso VII was crowned Emperor of Castile and León in 1135. Portugal emerged as an independent kingdom in 1143, and Aragón and Catalonia were united under the **Crown of Aragón** during the reign of Alfonso II.

By the 13C half the peninsula was under Christian rule, with Castile, León, Asturias and Aragón becoming increasingly powerful. The popularity of the Santiago pilgrimage route had reached its apogee. In 1212, the Christians, led by Alfonso VIII, won the decisive Battle of **Las Navas de Tolosa**. Later, Castile and León were united under **Ferdinand III, the Saint** (1217-52), and became increasingly important as a producer and exporter of wool. The Christian forces moved S, conquering Córdoba (1236), Seville

(1248), Murcia (1243) and Jaén (1246) and **James I of Aragón** conquered
Majorca, Ibiza and Valencia (1245). But then the momentum slowed down
and the Muslim kingdom of Granada was left to enjoy a further 250 years of
prosperity. Meanwhile, in Castile and León, literature and learning blossomed
during the reign of **Alfonso X, the Wise**, while the energies of the
burgeoning middle class in Catalonia were directed toward economic
development, under King James I of Aragón, conqueror of Majorca and
Valencia, who concluded Catalonia's separation from France in the Corbeil
Treaty (1258).

Having conquered Sicily in the 13C, the Aragonese and Catalans went on
expanding their dominions during the 14C to include Sardinia and parts of
Greece, thus consolidating their Mediterranean empire. However, the wars
between Catalonia (during the reign of Peter the Ceremonious of Aragón) and
Castile (under Peter I, the Just) from 1356-1375 had a negative effect on
Catalonia's economy, while Castile's, more dependent on wool and wheat
production than trade, prospered. At the beginning of the 15C, Jean de
Bethencourt, in the name of **Henry III** of Castile, began to take possession of
the **Canary Islands**, whose native population was still living in the Iron Age.
When Martin the Humane (1396-1410) died without heir, the Church and
the Catalan bourgeoisie voted for Aragón's candidate, the Castilian Fernando
de Tratámara in the so-called Caspe Compromise (1412), initiating a new
dynasty, which was to conquer Naples in 1442, and also opening the path to
unification of the Catalan-Aragonese kingdom with Castile.

THE CATHOLIC MONARCHS AND THE MODERN STATE

In 1469, the marriage between **Ferdinand V** of Aragón (the model for
Machiavelli's *The Prince*) and **Isabella I** of Castile united the two largest
kingdoms in Spain. At the beginning of their reign, King Ferdinand made
many efforts to reverse the economic decline of Catalonia. With the
Guadalupe Ruling, he solved the old question of feudal obligations by
effectively freeing the serfs in return for monetary payments to their lords,
thus establishing the foundations for the later agricultural efficiency of
Catalonia. He also continued to uphold Spanish supremacy in the
Mediterranean while the Queen pushed this supremacy towards the Atlantic.
Together, they fought for the religious unity of Spain with campaigns against
the Nasrid kingdom of Granada, for which they went down in history as 'the
Catholic Monarchs'. They also managed to put a stop to the factional fights
between the nobles of Extremadura and Galicia, subjecting them to
obedience to the Castilian-Aragonese crown.

1492 was a watershed in Spanish history. Not only did **Columbus** sail
the ocean blue to discover **America**, but it was also the year in which the
kingdom of Granada was finally conquered, concluding the **Christian
unification** of Spain. At the same time, a member of the Valencian Borja, or
Borgia, family, **Alexander VI** was elected pope. It was also the year in which
the **Inquisition** was especially active and 400,000 **Jews** were expelled from
Spain.

SPAIN'S GOLDEN CENTURY

The 16C began with the conquest of the kingdom of Naples (by the
'Great Captain', Gonzalo Fernández of Córdoba), the final conquest of the
Canary Islands (1500) and the consolidation of Spanish dominions in N
Africa. The American trading monopoly was granted to Seville, which thus
became the gateway to America and the commercial and financial centre of
Europe. Its port was the starting point of the journey made by **Americo
Vespucci**, who was to give his name to the new continent, and Magellan, to
name but two of the daring seafarers who set out to sail where no European
had ever sailed before. The **Burgos Laws** were passed protecting the

indigenous Indians of America. Following Isabella's death in 1504, the kingdom was ruled for a short while by her daughter, Joan the Mad, under the regency of Ferdinand (1506-1516) and Cardinal Cisneros, until Charles I, grandson of the Catholic Monarchs, came to the throne. In 1512, the annexation of Navarre completed Spain's **political unity** in the same year as Núñez de Balboa discovered the Pacific. The Catholic Monarchs had established one of the first modern civil states, and prepared the way for two centuries of Spanish glory and influence which were to redound throughout the world.

Charles I of Spain was also ruler of the Netherlands, and, as heir to the Hapsburg dominions, **Charles V**, Emperor of the Holy Roman Empire. During his reign, the Spanish empire stretched from Naples and Sicily, in the Mediterranean, across the Atlantic to America, and also included Germany, Austria, the Franche-Comté and the Low Countries. The world seemed to be Spain's oyster: Cortés conquered Mexico (1519), Elcano first circumnavigated the globe (1519-1522), Pizarro conquered Peru (1532) and Almagro arrived in Chile (1536). Ships reached Seville laden with gold, silver and precious gems. Considering himself God's standard-bearer, Charles I actively involved Spain in the fight against Luther's Protestant movement in Germany. Although initially eyed with suspicion by Spaniards, who considered him a foreigner, Charles became accepted as a strong king after he had put down the rebellion of the Castilian communards and the Germanias brotherhoods in Valencia and Majorca. Spain was reaching the heights of its glory and, despite emigration to America, there was a sharp increase in its population, which reached 7.5 million.

Philip II (1556-1598), husband of Mary Tudor of England, had dominions in four continents. After defeating the French at San Quintin (1557), he established his court in **MADRID** (1561), then just an unimportant village, and began the construction of the monastery-palace of El Escorial. In 1571 the victory at Lepanto put an end to the threat of Turkish power in the Mediterranean, and in 1580, Spain and Portugal were locked in temporary union. It seemed that the Spanish **Golden Age** of literature and art was at its height, but there were also some underlying problems. The Inquisition and the fight against Protestantism crushed the country's creative energies in the grip of a conservative Counter-Reformation, and Spain's coffers were being emptied to fund European wars in the crusade against Protestantism, while its riches from America were merely leading to a spiralling inflation of its currency and there was a marked reluctance among Spaniards to become actively involved in the productive process. In 1588, Spain suffered the disastrous defeat of its 'Invincible' Armada, sent against Elizabeth I's England. British naval power began to prevail and Protestantism became increasingly unassailable.

THE DECLINE OF SPAIN

Under **Philip III** (1598-1621), Spain's international hegemony came to an end. *Don Quixote* (1605, see 'Literature') gives a perfect parody of the transition between the two eras. While on the outside the Baroque generation and the glory of the 'Golden Century' dazzled the eye, the reality behind this superficial peace and splendour was quite different. There was a structural economic crisis, and the expulsion of the Jews and later the Grenadine Moors (the Moriscos) marked the end of the fertile cultural diversity and tolerance of the past, as well as removing the most active financial, commercial and industrial agents who could be considered as Spain's middle class. Nor was a governing class built up, effective power being passed to the Duke of Lerma, who proved to be incapable of holding on to Spanish possessions in the Low Countries.

Under **Philip IV** (1621-1665), and his favourite, the **Count-Duke of Olivares**, the situation worsened yet further. Portugal became independent in 1640, and Spain was forced to accept the independence of the Low Countries in 1648. The Catalan region of Roussillon was ceded to France in 1659 (thus establishing the present-day border), and Catalonia itself rebelled against the Castilian crown, transferring its allegiance to France for a few years (1641-1652).

The last of Spain's Hapsburg kings, **Charles II** (1665-1700), was physically and mentally handicapped and died without issue. The War of Succession between Philippe of Anjou (backed by France) and Archduke Charles of Austria (supported by Aragón, Catalonia and England), finally ended with the victory of Philippe who, as **Philip V**, was the first Bourbon king of Spain (1700-1746). Under the Treaty of Utrecht (1714), Spain lost the Low Countries, Menorca and Gibraltar, its Italian possessions, Sicily and Sardinia. But undeterred by loss of power abroad, Philip fought to strengthen his grip on Spain itself, and in 1716, the Nueva Planta Decree replaced local laws with Castilian law, a decisive step in centralizing government. This put an end to autonomous regional politics, although Navarre, Catalonia and the Basque Country were allowed to retain parts of their own legal codes under special charter from Castile. The new Bourbon dynasty soon consolidated its power and, from 1724 onwards, Philip V made a serious effort to reconstruct the country.

The **Enlightenment** spread immediately to Spain, when **Charles III** (1759-1788), known as the 'reformer king', introduced a series of reforms with the help of his competent ministers Floridablanca, Aranda and Campomanes. The Inquisition was called off; the Jesuits were expelled (1767); Spain backed the future United States' independence from Britain, and was given back Sacramento, the two Floridas and Menorca for supporting the Treaty of Versailles (1783). The monarchy encouraged economic and agricultural reform, rescinding the Sevillian trade monopoly (1765), thereby opening the market to free trade. New crops (potatoes, maize, tobacco), were introduced from America, and industrialization began, with the first tobacco factory being set up in Seville in 1771 and the installation of British industrial weaving machinery in Barcelona. Science and literature also flourished in this more liberal atmosphere.

Under **Charles IV** (1788-1808), the government was run by his wife's favourite, **Godoy**. After the French Revolution (1789) and Napoleon's coronation as Emperor (1804), Spain allied itself with France against Britain. Nelson's victory at the **Battle of Trafalgar** marked the end of Spain as a maritime power.

ROMANTICISM AND TURBULENCE IN THE 19C

In 1808, public insurgence against Godoy and Charles IV led to their resignation, and Murat led Napoleon's forces into Madrid. The Spaniards were not pleased when Napoleon placed his brother, Joseph Bonaparte on the throne. On the second of May, Madrid rose up against the French and the **War of Independence**, or Peninsular War, began, with enormous losses to the country in terms of lives and material riches.

In 1812, the Cádiz Cortes, or parliament, proclaimed a liberal constitution. In 1814, Buenos Aires, Colombia, Chile, Uruguay and Paraguay broke away from Spanish rule. The Spanish forces fought alongside the British (commanded by the Duke of Wellington) to expel Napoleon's troops in 1813, and the Spanish throne was handed back to the Bourbon king, **Ferdinand VII**. A virulent antiliberal, he repealed the constitution and brutally suppressed liberal ideas. His absolutist beliefs resulted in a period of insurrection and the loss of the American colonies, with Mexico, Venezuela and Peru becoming independent from 1821-1824. Attempts to **industrialize** the S (blast furnaces in Marbella, 1815), failed dismally, and heavy industry became focused in the N, around the Basque and Asturian coalfields, while lighter industry (textiles and the like) was established in Barcelona. In 1833, Isabella II came to the throne, under the regency of Ferdinand VII's wife, Queen María Cristina. Her claim was contested by her uncle, Charles (Ferdinand's brother), thus triggering the Carlist Wars, which were fought between the Carlist (traditionalists) and the liberals, and discrediting civil politics. Against a background of constant insecurity and war, many changes took place. In 1835, the prime minister, Mendizabal, forced the sale of Church lands (known as the Disentailment), suppressing religious orders and confiscating their assets. Other laws, such as the suppression of the old-fashioned guilds, dismantled the old regime. The army began to play a strong role in politics, and finally ousted the regent, María Cristina, in favour of Espartero, a military man and a convinced liberal. Usually uninterested in politics, the English, French and German Romantics 'discovered' Spain around this time, writing novels, poems and operas about it.

The reign of **Isabella II** (1843-1868) saw the end of the economic crisis, and as the big cities began to expand beyond their medieval walls, a new urban **middle class** was consolidated, active in industry and business. The first **railway** was built from Barcelona to Mataró to handle the greater volume of trade. Isabella II's reign ended with her dethronement and exile by General Prim, and in 1870, after the declaration of a liberal democratic constitution, Amadeo de Saboya was voted king. He remained on the throne for three years, after which the Cortes (parliament) proclaimed the **First Republic**. However, in 1874, General Pavía dissolved the Cortes, and following a year of peasant and worker unrest, the middle class supported the **restoration** of the monarchy. In 1875, following a military coup in Sagunto, Cánovas del Castillo proclaimed **Alfonso XII** (1875-1885) as king. The middle class revolution had failed. Although the industrialized N and Catalonia prospered during the peaceful period following the restoration, the economic vitality seeped away in the rest of the country and the colonies. The government was alternately led by Cánovas' conservatives and Sagasta's liberals, while a new political **nationalism** grew in Catalonia, Galicia and the Basque Country, accompanied by a parallel movement in art and literature. On the death of Alfonso XII, his wife, **María Cristina** (1885-1902), became regent and presided over the demise of Spain as a colonial power, with the loss of Cuba, Puerto Rico and the Philippines in the Spanish-American War. The accompanying crisis in Spain was reflected in the literature of the period (see 'Literature').

THE 20C

Under the rule of **Alfonso XIII** (1902-1931), new political forces such as socialism, republicanism and organized worker's movements sprang up. The worldwide depression and the specific Spanish economic and political conditions were met with protest by the workers in the industrialized areas and the peasants in the rural S. In 1910, Pablo Iglesias was the first Socialist deputy to be voted into the Spanish parliament. Although Spain reaped certain economic advantages from its neutrality during the First World War (1914-1918), in 1917 a wave of strikes began, followed by mass confrontations between workers and their employers, the rebellion of Catalan members of parliament, and military disaster at Annual in Morocco (1921).

In 1923, the Captain General of Catalonia, **Primo de Rivera**, supported by the Catalonian middle classes, became dictator of Spain. His dictatorship ushered in seven years of prosperity, peace in Morocco and a far-reaching plan for public expenditure on infrastructure. However, he failed to address the underlying problems in Spain, and had instead resorted to the oppression of workers and intellectuals. When the worldwide economic crisis occurred, the peseta began to fall in value despite desperate rescue attempts. Furthermore Primo de Rivera lost the support of the King and the army and on January 28, 1930, he was forced to resign. The public debt was enormous, as was unemployment. Yet in spite of all this, in cultural terms, Spain was flourishing.

In 1931, the Republicans won the municipal elections. Alfonso XIII went into exile and the **Second Republic** was proclaimed on April 14. The social situation continued to worsen, and the Republic was torn between different revolutionary pressures from the masses, while being subjected to sabotage by the conservative forces. There were right-wing uprisings, a majority victory for the centre-right in the 1934 elections and revolts in Asturias and Catalonia. The triumph of the Popular Front (the left-wing coalition) in 1936 gave Manuel Azaña a clear mandate as head of the Spanish government, but the military uprising led by Generals Franco and Mola on July 18 that year began the **Civil War**, which lasted until April 1, 1939, leaving behind it a country shattered by bloodshed and destruction.

The first years of **General Franco's** dictatorship were especially hard. Many Spaniards were forced into exile in the face of economic depression and harsh political repression. Spain remained neutral in the Second World War, but sent military divisions of volunteers to fight alongside Hitler and Mussolini's troops. The installation of American military bases in Spain (1953), Spain's membership of the UN (1955), the granting of independence to Morocco (1956) and the economic stability plan (1959) were milestones along the road toward a progressive opening up of Spain to the outside world. The tourist boom and increased economic prosperity of the 1960s were accompanied by radical changes in Spanish society. Many rural workers left the countryside for the towns or went abroad to work in other European countries, becoming more open-minded in the process.

Franco's death in 1975 was followed by the proclamation of **Juan Carlos I** as king and the transition of Spain from a republic and dictatorship to a constitutional monarchy and democracy. Adolfo Suárez led the centre-right government that oversaw this transition.

SPAIN TODAY

The **Spanish Constitution** came into force in **1978**. It proclaimed the democratic rights of individuals and organizations and made it possible for the country to be divided into Autonomous Communities. In 1980, the first Autonomy Charters became operative for the Basque Country and Catalonia. An attempted military coup in 1981 was crushed with the personal intervention of the king, after which the future of democracy in Spain seemed to be fully guaranteed. In **1982**, the **Socialist Party** won the general elections with an absolute majority, and Felipe González became Prime Minister. On January 1, **1986**, Spain joined the **EEC**, and that same year, the Socialists were voted in for another term in government. The economy is gradually becoming more modern and more efficient, as it is increasingly liberalized. Its services sector has undergone spectacular growth over the last few years and tourism still plays an important role in this sector, with more than 53 million tourists travelling to Spain each year.

1992 is a key date. Not only will Spain form part of the united European market, but it will also host the summer **Olympic Games** in **BARCELONA** and the **EXPO '92** universal exhibition in **SEVILLE**, while **MADRID** will be the **European Capital of Culture** —a fitting way to celebrate the **quincentenary** of Columbus' discovery of **America** and the beginning of contacts with the New World.

The Spanish love sports. Their abiding passion is, of course, football. But their ancient regional sports are more likely to have you reaching for your camera than offering to join in: in the Basque Country and Navarre, he-men compete against each other chopping tree trunks or lifting boulders, while skill and strength combine more subtly in traditional Canary Island wrestling.

The picturesque apart, Spain has masses to offer those who enjoy an energetic holiday. The Spaniards' own enthusiasm and the tourist boom have equipped the nation with countless sports facilities which, in combination with the natural attributes of its coasts, mountains, rivers and climate make it a sportman's paradise. Here are some of the favourite sporting possibilities around which you could have a holiday in action.

Fishing

For those who like peaceful holidays and enjoy the mysterious art form of waiting quietly, rod in hand, Spain has over 75,000km of river and 6,000km of coast. *ICONA*, Av Gran Vía de San Francisco, 35, Madrid ☎ (91) 266 82 00, with branches in every provincial capital in the country, provincial Departments of Agriculture and the *Federación Española de Pesca y Casting* (Spanish Fishing and Casting Federation), c/ Navas de Tolosa, 3, Madrid ☎ (91) 232 83 52, will give you all the information you need.

In **freshwater fishing**, the most sought after species is the **Atlantic salmon**, found exclusively in Galicia (in the River Ulla and, particularly, the Eo), Asturias (in the Sella and Narcea), Cantabria and Guipúzcoa-Navarre (in the Bidasoa). **Trout** is found in nearly all river headwaters, the common species being, despite its name, the scarcest and the best for eating. There are vast reserves of trout in the **rivers of León** (the Orbigo, Esla and Porma), and in the Arga and Erro in Navarre. That great predator, the **pike**, is abundant in the River Tagus, the Entrepeñas, Buendía and Balarque reservoirs, the River Guadiana, and in the Cijara, García Sola and Orellana reservoirs near Cáceres and Badajoz. **Black bass**, best fished in the summer, abounds in the Tagus and artificial lakes of its basin (El Burquillo in Avila and Azután in Toledo), in the reservoirs of Cijara, García Sala and Orellana in Extremadura and in the Bañolas lake in Gerona. The best two fishing spots for **eel** are La Albufera in Valencia and the Ebro Delta in Catalonia, although eel are also found in the salmon-fishing rivers in the N. **Carp** and **bogue** can be caught in nearly all rivers day or night, while **river cray-fish** can only be caught during the daytime —presumably to prevent overfishing.

Lapped by the waters of the Bay of Biscay, the Mediterranean and the Atlantic, the coasts of Spain offer a huge variety of marine species to **sea-fishermen** whether they fish from shore, boat, or underwater (see 'Scuba Diving'). In Galicia and the Basque Country, both traditional fishing areas, **bream, bass**, conger eel and dentex are very common, and out to sea, off the Island of La Toja (Pontevedra), you can catch **baby shark**. Off the Costa Brava, besides white sea-bream, bass and conger eel, you can catch **gilthead, common sea-bream, tunny fish** and **scorpion fish**. Further down the Mediterranean coast, the Costa Dorada is also rich in bass, tunny fish, gilthead and bream, but you can also get **weever, bonito, red sea-bream** and, in deeper waters, **blue shark**. The Costa del Azahar has bream, gilthead, tuna, bass, dentex, and white and black sea-bream. The Costa Blanca has sea-bream, scorpion fish, **wreckfish, bullet tuna** and **mackerel shark**, while off the Costa del Sol among the varieties common to the Mediterranean coast you will also come across **swordfish, pandora** and **meagre**. The waters around the Balearics are full of grouper, bream, **grey mullet** and **meagre**. In the Atlantic off Andalusia, in the S, there is **turbot, striped sea-bream** and meagre, while around the Canaries there are all sorts of local species, though the star of them all for sports fishermen is the **shark**, out at sea.

Golf

Its marvellous climate and over 90 courses make Spain —homeland of the great Severiano Ballesteros— ideal for golfing holidays. There are 11 courses in Madrid alone, some of them (*Golf La Moraleja* and the *Real Club Puerta de Hierro*) among the best in the country. Barcelona's best is the *Real Club de Golf El Prat* and Seve's home town, Santander, has another top course, the *Real Golf de Pedreña*.

But most visiting golfers head for the Costa del Sol, better known among the fraternity as the *Costa del Golf*, or Golf Coast, whose 15 courses are the busiest in Europe. They are of an extremely high standard, designed by world experts in a setting of sub-tropical vegetation, excellent hotels and restaurants, marinas, entertainment galore and, surely most attractive of all for those who spend the rest of the year playing in a heavy drizzle, superb weather. Predictably, **MARBELLA'S** courses, the *Golf Río Real* and four others, are the tops, closely followed by those at **SOTOGRANDE** (Cádiz), **ESTEPONA**, **BENALMADENA** and **TORREMOLINOS** (Málaga), and the courses at **EL EJIDO** and **ROQUETAS DE MAR** (Almería).

Of the nine courses in Catalonia, the best are Barcelona's *El Prat* and the *Club de Golf de Pals* in Pals (Gerona), while in Galicia the unbeatable setting of the course in **LA TOJA** (Pontevedra), an island joined to the mainland by a sound, makes up in scenic beauty for the unreliability of the weather. You can be surer of sunshine along the Levante coast: note the course at **EL SALER**, adjacent to the parador just outside Valencia, and the courses at **TORREVIEJA** (Alicante) and **LA MANGA DEL MAR MENOR** in Los Belones (Murcia).

The Balearic Islands are also favourites among golfers and have eight courses in all, the best of which are in **PALMA DE MALLORCA, SANTA PONSA** and **MAGALUF** (Majorca), while in the Canaries, land of eternal spring, the course in **MASPALOMAS** (Gran Canaria) is just the place for a winter golfing break.

For further information contact the *Real Federación Española de Golf* (Royal Spanish Golf Federation), c/ Capitán Haya, 9, Madrid ☎ (91) 455 26 82.

Hunting

Spain's varied geography means that many game species which have become rare or even extinct elsewhere in Europe still thrive, or at least survive, in various parts of the country, and hunting is still a hugely popular sport here among locals and foreigners alike. Some companies (see list below) organize hunting and shooting trips, but travel agencies and National Tourist Offices will tell you where, when and how to hunt. The *Secretaría General de Turismo* (National Tourist Board), c/ Castelló, 117, 28004 Madrid ☎ (91) 411 40 14 can give you detailed information.

The small game hunting season is generally from mid October to early February, the most sought after bird being the **red partridge** (the grey partridge is much more common), though the open season for **quail** and **turtle-dove** is very short, from the end of September to the beginning of October. **Rabbit** and **hare** are the most popular small game animals, while

133

wild boar, hunted or stalked from the middle of October to the middle of February, is one of the most prized larger animals. The famous *capra hispanica*, or Spanish goat, is stalked between November and January, especially in the sierras of Cazorla (Andalusia) and Segura (Murcia); the **moufflon**, or wild mountain sheep, is stalked; and the **deer** is either hunted or stalked. Other popular game in the Pyrenees and Cantabrian mountains are the **chamois**, a wild antelope the size of a goat, and the ibex. A word of warning: should you be lucky enough to spot a bear, don't even think of shooting it... you could end up behind bars!

Spain has some 36 million hectares of hunting territory. You can either hunt on occupied land, which only requires your own documentation, or otherwise, choose from nine Natural Parks, 36 National Hunting Reserves, 13 National Preserves, 4,000 private big game reserves, and 22,000 private small game reserves. Spanish citizens and foreign residents alike need hunting licences, compulsory insurance and the relevant firearms permit. A non-resident foreigner in Spain also needs a hunting licence (you will have to show your passport when you apply for it), compulsory insurance, proof that you have complied with customs requirements for bringing firearms into the country and a special police permit obtained at the point of entry.

For more general information, contact the *Federación Española de Caza* (Spanish Hunting Federation), Av Reina Victoria, 72, Madrid ☎ (91) 253 90 17. Some of the companies that organize trips, normally of one or two weeks, are: *Cazatur*, c/ Velázquez, 22 ☎ (91) 275 96 99, and *Servicios y Cacerías*, c/ Claudio Coello, 46 ☎ (91) 435 43 10, for big game hunting, and *Espacaza*, c/ Núñez de Balboa, 31 ☎ (91) 275 76 22, and *Trophy Hunt Ibérica*, c/ María de Molina, 60 ☎ (91) 262 58 82, for big and small game hunting, all in Madrid. In Cáceres, contact *Sierra de San Pedro*, c/ Virgen de la Montaña, 5 ☎ (927) 22 99 50, and in Córdoba, *Catur*, Av Conde de Vallellano, 19 ☎ (957) 29 44 44.

Sailing and Windsurfing

Spain is among the leaders in international competitive sailing, as one might expect of a country with such an ancestral sea-faring tradition whose weather and facilities have allowed sailing to develop into a sport that can be enjoyed all the year round off much of the coast. The area you choose will depend on the type of sailing you prefer.

Medium winds, just right for sailing and cruising, blow in the **Ría de Arosa**, between La Coruña and Pontevedra (Galicia); light to strong winds in the **Santander and Laredo bays** (Cantabria) for light craft sailing and cruising; and strong winds, sometimes exceeding 4 knots, in the Costa Brava's **Golfo de Rosas** and off **PALAMOS** (Gerona), also for light craft sailing and cruising. In the **Barcelona to Sitges** stretch of coast (Barcelona), the medium winds are ideal for light craft sailing and cruising, while in the **Bay of Palma** (Majorca) there are light and constant winds practically all year round, except on occasional winter days, making it a perfect site for international regattas. Windwise, there are far better places than the waters off **BENALMADENA**, **MARBELLA** and **ESTEPONA** (Málaga), but their climate, port facilities and general atmosphere attract a lot of tourist craft, while the **Bay of Cádiz**, with winds usually around 3 knots and good temperatures, is good for light craft sailing and cruising. The **Canary Islands**, just off the African coast and the Tropic of Cancer, are the point of departure for transatlantic voyages, both historically and to this day.

For more information contact the *Federación Española de Vela* (Spanish Sailing Federation), c/ Juan Vigón, 23, Madrid ☎ (91) 233 53 05.

As well as the places mentioned for sailing in general, there are also parts of the coast that are particularly good for **windsurfing** like the **Golfo de Rosas** (Costa Brava) and **Sopelana beach** in Vizcaya, but the two most famous places are **Tarifa** (Cádiz), near the Straits of Gibraltar, and **El Médano** (S Tenerife), where the wind conditions are so ideal —4 to 9 knots— that they have become favourites with the top windsurfers in Europe.

Scuba Diving

The variety of its coasts and its benevolent climate attract many scuba diving enthusiasts to Spain both for the simple pleasure of underwater exploring and for underwater fishing (be warned that fishing with an aqualung is illegal). Favourite areas for underwater exploration include the **Cíes Islands** off the coast of Vigo (Pontevedra), in Galicia, and the waters off **LLANES** and **VIDIAGO** in Asturias. The Costa Brava (Gerona) has the advantage of warmer sea temperatures, and the **Medas Islands** are surrounded by fascinating marine life, but for real warmth and crystal clearness you will find the sea around the **Balearic Islands** hard to beat. The best underwater beauty spots in Majorca are found near the islands of **El Toro**, **Cape Figuera**, the **Malgrats** islands, **Cape Andritxol**, the neighbouring **Es Caló d'En Monjó**, **Peñasco de S'Aguillot**, the island of **Dragonera**, **Cape Enderrocat**, and off the coast of **SAN TELMO**, **SOLLER**, **SA CALOBRA**, **FORMENTOR** and **CALA RATJADA**. Menorca, Ibiza and Formentera are also a scuba diver's delight, and the sea bed around the island of **Cabrera** is said to be particularly fascinating.

The Costa Blanca's rocky coastline is one of the best areas of the peninsula for scuba diving, particularly the natural marine reserve of **Tabarca** (Alicante), the stretch from **La Manga del Mar Menor** to Cabo de Palos, and further S still, the warm waters off the **coast of Almería**.

The subtropical waters off the **Canary Islands**, with temperatures of around 17°C (63°F) in winter and 22°C (72°F) in summer, are very rich in all types of marine life. Some exceptional places are the islands of **Lobos**, **Graciosa**, **Montaña Clara** and **Alegranza**; the **rocks** to the E and W of Lanzarote; off **ANAGA** and **GARACHICO** in Tenerife, and **Punta de Salmor** in Hierro. You can get more information from the *Federación Española de Actividades Subacuáticas* (Spanish Federation of Subaquatic Activities), c/ Santaló, 15, Barcelona ☎ (93) 200 67 69.

Skiing

When people think of Spain, they automatically think of the sun and beach, and tend to forget that this is the second most mountainous country in Europe after Switzerland. Because the climate is milder than in central Europe, more and more skiers are coming to Spanish slopes every year. There are some 30 ski stations throughout Spain, from *Baqueira-Beret* in the N to *Solynieve* in the S, which makes it possible to ski from Christmas to May, but do always remember to make reservations beforehand.

Even though all the stations are equipped with modern facilities, there are three outstanding ones: *Baqueira-Beret* (Lérida), in the Pyrenees, where the Royal Family and entourage go, has the largest number of runs and hotels —excellent food and a sophisticated après-ski atmosphere complete the scene. *Candanchú* (Huesca, in Pyrenean Aragón) is one of Spain's most traditional resorts —national team skiers are trained here, and competitions are held frequently. Down S, in the Sierra Nevada (Granada), *Solynieve* is the resort where you can ski under radiant sunshine and luminous blue skies. It is the highest station in Europe (with slopes up to 3,472m high) and just over

135

an hour from the Costa del Sol, which means that on a good spring day you can go skiing in the morning and swimming in the afternoon.

All stations have Spanish Ski School monitors who teach skiers of all ages and levels, and equipment can be hired on the spot. For information, contact the *Federación Española de Deportes de Invierno* (Spanish Winter Sports Federation), c/ Claudio Coello, 32, Madrid ☎ (91) 275 89 43.

Yacht Clubs and Marinas

To meet the demands of the tourist boom, Spain's coasts are dotted with modern marinas —there are even some on rivers like **SEVILLE'S**— mainly concentrated in the tourist resorts of the Mediterranean coast and the Balearics. The *Secretaría General de Turismo* (National Tourist Board), c/ Castelló, 117, Madrid ☎ 411 40 14, publishes a book with useful information on dock specifications and facilities.

On the N Coast, there are marinas in **VIGO** and **BAYONA** in Galicia, **GIJON** in Asturias, and **LAREDO** and the well-equipped *Marina del Cantábrico* in **SANTANDER**, Cantabria. On the E coast, the Costa Brava (Gerona) has marinas in **AMPURIA BRAVA** (Castelló de Ampurias), **LA ESCALA** (with nearly 500 berths) and, further S, **ARENYS DE MAR**. **BARCELONA** has several excellent yacht clubs which provide very good services and are always full, and the *Aiguadolç marina* in nearby **SITGES** is very modern, with moorings for boats up to 35m long.

Thousands of boats from all parts of the world, but particularly the rest of Europe, converge on the Balearics every year. The port of **PALMA DE MALLORCA** (Majorca), the busiest in the islands, has two local long-established yacht clubs, both with an excellent reputation and both always full. To the N of the bay is the modern marina of *Portals Nous* (in Calvià), on the island's W coast the yacht club of **SANTA PONSA** is in a beautiful natural inlet, and to the S **PUERTO DE ANDRAITX'S** marina is also very safe and sheltered. **MAHON**, in Menorca, has one of the most sheltered natural ports in the world, while Ibiza also has its own busy marina.

Back on the mainland, the Levante coast has a marina at **PUEBLA DE FARNALS** (Valencia) with moorings for boats up to 25m long; yacht clubs in **VALENCIA** and **DENIA** with good facilities; a modern marina, the *Luis Campomanes*, in **ALTEA**, and a yacht club in **ALICANTE**. Murcia's Costa Cálida has yacht clubs in **LA MANGA DEL MAR MENOR** and **SANTIAGO DE LA RIBERA**.

Further S in Andalusia is the *Almerimar* marina in **EL EJIDO** (Almería) with some 1,000 berths, and the *Marina del Este* in **ALMUÑECAR** (Granada), which is pleasant. Málaga's Costa del Sol attracts fleets of luxury vessels from Europe, the Arab countries and N America, and has facilities to match...

Puerto de la Duquesa in **MANILVA**; the marina in **ESTEPONA**, which manages to cater for both tourist and serious fishing craft; *Puerto Banús* in **MARBELLA** where, against a background of picturesque whitewashed houses, the rich and famous moor nearly 1,000 luxury yachts up to 50m long; the more run-of-the-mill marina of **BENALMADENA**, for boats up to 30m long and, in Cádiz, *Sotogrande*, with 500 berths for boats up to 50m long.

On the Atlantic coast, near Jerez, **PUERTO DE SANTA MARIA** is developing into one of the great sea-borne tourist magnets with its curiously named *Puerto Sherry*, one of the best equipped marinas in Europe. In the Canaries, gateway to the Americas, *Puerto de la Luz* in **LAS PALMAS DE GRAN CANARIA** is almost at the source of the African Trade Winds, and there is also a smaller marina in **PUERTO RICO** in the S of the island. The **SANTA CRUZ DE TENERIFE** yacht club, on the island of Tenerife, is for anchoring only.

Spaniards are given to boasting proudly that their country has everything, a claim which it is tempting to dismiss with a patronizing smile. But penetrate beyond the tourist clichés of packed sun-baked beaches, bullfights and *sangría* and you will discover that this is indeed a country of infinite variety.

In Spain, you can just follow your nose and be sure of finding something interesting, but there are some basic itineraries which may be useful as a basis for your own explorations. You may choose to tour the historic cities of its areas of outstanding natural beauty (see 'Wide Open-Spaces'), follow the multi-faceted coastal route or enjoy the smaller-scale charms of its little towns and villages.

Some of the routes through Spain date back hundreds, even thousands, of years. Along the *Camino de Santiago*, or **Way of Saint James**, the pilgrimage route to Santiago de Compostela in Galicia, medieval pilgrims from all over Europe flocked in their thousands to what was to become the third Holy City in Christendom. This was Spain's first experience of mass tourism, and splendid religious and civic buildings sprang up all along the route, which you can still follow today. It will take you through the stunning green, mountainous countryside of northern Spain, punctuated by beautiful Romanesque buildings and famous for its excellent food and hospitality.

Two thousand years ago, the Roman trade route known as the *Vía de Plata*, the **Silver Route**, linked northern and southern Spain, and you can still trace its course from Salamanca to Mérida or opt for an extended version stretching from Gijón to Seville. This is a marvellous route for revealing the

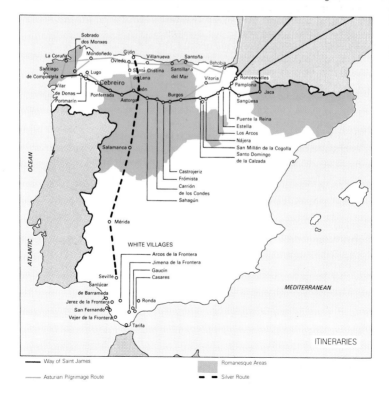

137

many faces of Spain in that it takes you from the green mountains of Asturias through the rural landscape of Salamanca (fighting-bull breeding territory) and Extremadura (homeland of the conquistadors), past some of the best-preserved Roman architecture in Europe to land you finally in Seville, capital city of Andalusia where Jews, Moors and Christians combined to leave an incomparable cultural legacy.

The *Pueblos Blancos* or **White Villages** Route takes you worlds away from the tourist hurly-burly of the nearby Costa del Sol. It leads you into the heart of Andalusia in whose little villages of whitewashed houses, on the slopes of the Sierra de Cádiz and the Serranía de Ronda, a different rhythm of life holds sway. It is a route evocative of Christian warriors, Muslim princesses, 19C bandits... this is the Spain with which the Romantic writers like Rilke fell in love.

The vast, bare horizons of **La Mancha** evoke quite different images. This is where **Don Quixote** jousted with windmills, a characteristic feature of the landscape to this day. It is also a land of good wine and even better Manchego cheese.

Then there is the **Romanesque Route** (see 'Architecture') tracing a period beginning in the late 11C which saw the emergence of the phenomenon of the pilgrimage route to Compostela, fostered by the monks of Cluny and the fall of the Caliphate of Córdoba and the subsequent decline of Muslim dominion in Spain. This route can be subdivided into styles and areas: the early Romanesque in Catalonia; the 'European' Romanesque of the Way of Saint James which begins in the Pyrenees of Aragón, passing through Navarre on its way to Santiago de Compostela in Galicia; and, further south, the route through Castile, exploring the Romanesque buildings of Zamora, Valladolid, Salamanca and Segovia. Less well known, but no less fascinating, are two other routes of artistic and architectural interest which explore the **Mudéjar** and Asturian **pre-Romanesque**. The architecture of the Mudéjars, Muslims who remained in Spain after the Christian Reconquest, flourished in various parts of the country —Andalusia, Aragón, Toledo and Castile and León— while the best examples of the pre-Romanesque are concentrated in Asturias where the stolid churches scattered over the green hillsides seem symbols of the Christian determination to rout the infidel even though it was to take several centuries.

Although the Christians finally emerged triumphant from their long period of coexistence with the Jews and Arabs, the defeated cultures have left rich evidence of their presence. **Muslim Spain** and **Jewish Spain** would be fascinating routes to plan and explore.

There is so much to be said for the car and plane in terms of independence and speed that you tend to think of other forms of transport as somewhat outmoded nowadays. **Spanish railways** offer two particularly attractive tourist routes that might make you think again: the **Transcantábrico** along northern Spain's Cantabrian Coast and the **Al-Andalus** through Andalusia in the south. Any travel agency or RENFE (Spanish National Railways) office will provide further information.

For those who really want to get away from it all and back to nature, with perhaps a little culture and history thrown in for good measure, what could be better than exploring Spain **on horseback**? Depending on your skills and inclinations, you can spend anything from a day to a fortnight riding in the Sierra de Gredos, the Sierra de Madrid, the Tiétar Valley (Extremadura), El Escorial (Madrid), or following the White Villages Route (Málaga and Cádiz), the Route of the Conquistadors (Extremadura)... Ask at your travel agency or contact *Caminos a Caballo*, c/ Duque de Liria, 3 ☎ 242 31 25, or *Rutas a Caballo*, c/ Agustina de Aragón, 84 ☎ 402 95 00, both in Madrid.

You may be taking a well-earned vacation from news of industrial unrest and fluctuating stock markets, but however much you claim to enjoy getting away from it all, you are probably loath to lose touch completely. Whether you wish to gloat over the inclement weather your compatriots are suffering as you bask in Spanish sunshine or whether you want to keep an eye on the political situation or simply find out what's on locally, you are sure to be able to find the source of information you need at a nearby news-stand, or on the radio or TV. If your Spanish is good enough to tackle the newspapers, you will need to know that the major national dailies are *El País, Diario 16* (both relatively Liberal), *ABC* (Conservative) and *Ya* (Catholic). Spanish radio is lively and imaginative with lots of music, both pop (like *Radio Ochenta*, 89.0 MHz, in Madrid) and classical *(Radio Nacional 2*, 96.5 MHz, in Madrid) and news on the hour. TV is State-run, and its two Channels, *TVE 1* and *2*, both carry commercial advertising. The Daily news broadcasts are at 3.00 pm on *TVE 1* and *2* and at 8.30 pm on *TVE1*, with a final summary just before close-down. If you prefer your news in English, note the following:

Press

Most of the international newspapers in English are available at the bigger local news-stands (or *quioscos* as they are called in Spain). British dailies, quality and tabloid, are usually on sale in the afternoon of the day of issue. American ones (*Miami Herald* and *New York Times*) appear a day or two late as a general rule, though the *International Herald Tribune* and the European edition of *The Wall Street Journal*, both printed in Paris, are available on the morning of issue in major cities and resorts. Heavy transport costs tend to double the original price of newspapers. Most stands also carry English-language magazines and periodicals, such as *Time, The Economist, Newsweek* and others, as well as women's magazines such as *Cosmopolitan* (US edition) and *House and Garden* among others. If you have a special favourite, find an amenable news-seller who will order it and keep it especially for you. Or, if you are staying in Spain for a while, it may be worth your while to subscribe to the *Guardian Weekly*, which can be sent to you direct and includes a digest of the main international news of the week from *The Guardian, The Washington Post* and *Le Monde*.

For local news, you can find several English-language publications published in Spain. Here are some of them which you will find on many, though not all, news-stands.

The **Madrid** area is served by the glossy monthly *In Spain*, which gives general information plus useful advertising and tips on restaurants, entertainment and so forth (a year's subscription costs 2,500 pesetas —write to c/ Dr. Esquerdo, 35, 1F, 28028 Madrid); the weekly *Guidepost*, which gives general information plus extra gossip on the American Club community (a one-year subscription costs 3,800 pesetas —contact c/ Gran Vía, 88, 28013 Madrid ☎ (91) 248 01 07); the daily newspaper *Iberian Daily Sun* (write to c/ Zurbano, 74, 28010 Madrid ☎ (91) 442 77 00); *Madrid Visitor*, an informative fortnightly publication on what to see in Madrid, available from the Madrid Town Hall and many hotels (otherwise phone ☎ (91) 242 25 56); and the fortnightly *The English Press*, a general information paper intended for Spaniards wanting to read news in English with explanatory vocabulary notes, but equally useful for English-speakers wanting information and a few key Spanish words (contact the publishers at c/ Huesca, 21, 28020 Madrid ☎ (91) 270 51 09).

English-language bookshops in Madrid also carry magazines and periodicals. Head for *Booksellers*, c/ José Abascal, 48, 28003 Madrid ☎ (91) 442 79 59, for magazines and books; *English Editions*, Pl San Amaro, 5, 28020 Madrid ☎ (91) 571 03 21, for magazines, newspapers, videos, second-hand and new novels, and a selection of English and American food products, games and the like; and *Turner's Bookshop*, c/ Génova, 3, 28004 Madrid ☎ (91) 410 29 15, for a very wide selection of books.

In **Barcelona**, the monthly Spanish 'what's on' guide *Vivir en Barcelona* contains a couple of pages in English at the end to give English-speaking visitors an idea of what is going on.

The **Balearic Islands** are served by the *Majorca Daily Bulletin*, a daily newspaper published in Palma de Mallorca (Majorca) and addressed specifically to the English-speaking community and tourists. The news-stands on Paseo del Born and S'Aigo Dolça specialize in foreign press, but English and American papers can also be found in almost all bookshops.

In the **Canary Islands**, the Tenerife-based *Diario de Avisos* is published twice weekly in English (Santa Cruz ☎ (922) 27 23 50), while the *Island Gazette* is a monthly providing general information for the Canaries, but mainly concerned with the island of Tenerife. In the island of Gran Canaria you will find *Holiday Time*, a quarterly supplement of the daily papers *La Provincia* and *Diario de Las Palmas* offering information on the island of Gran Canaria, and *Canarias Tourist*, published in English, Spanish, German and Swedish, which is full of information and maps of Gran Canaria.

The **Mediterranean Coast** also has plenty of English-language papers and magazines. Among the monthly general information magazines, *Lookout* covers all of Spain but with special reference to the South, and quite a lot of real estate advertisements (write to Puebla Lucía, 29640 Fuengirola, Málaga ☎ (952) 46 09 16) and *Marbella Times* makes specific references to the cosmopolitan resort of Marbella (write to c/ Ionso de Ojeda, 2, P.O. Box 153, 29600 Marbella). The weeklies include *The Entertainer* (published in Mojácar, P.O. Box 414, 04630 Garrucha, Almería ☎ (951) 47 87 89) and *Costa Blanca News* (published in Benidorm, P.O. Box 95, 03500 Benidorm, Alicante ☎ (965) 585 52 86).

Radio

If you have a short-wave radio, you can tune in to 24-hour English broadcasts on the *BBC World Service* at frequencies between 13m and 49m (tuning down the dial as night falls). In some places, you may also be lucky enough to pick up the *World Service* and *BBC Radio 2* on medium wave. And if you are near an American airbase, you can get their FM broadcasts (*Radio Torrejón*, 100.2 MHz).

There are also broadcasts in English by some Spanish stations on the tourist coasts, as well as by the Spanish Foreign News Service (*Radio Exterior*) at night on short wave. In Majorca, tune to 103.2 FM to hear *Antena 3* international broadcasting in English and German.

Television

Some late-night films on the State-run channels *TVE1* and *TVE2* are broadcast in the original version, and some classics, although dubbed on TV, have the original soundtrack broadcast simultaneously on radio. Many hotels and upmarket housing developments are equipped with parabolic aerials to pick up satellite TV broadcasts, among them *Channel 10* (broadcasting in English and Spanish from the U.K.), *Sky Channel, Super, CNN, Children Channel* and others in French, Italian and German.

Spain is in many ways the most easygoing country in the western hemisphere. Its extraordinary youthfulness reflects, in part, the fact that Spain is demographically young. Many are surprised by the extent to which the country's key professional, business and political posts are held by people who are barely 45 years old. As an open-minded, young society, Spain is hospitable to strangers. Pride in the recent recognition of his country as both newly democratic and European —and the determination to keep it that way— have given the Spaniard a special respect for the differences and peculiarities of foreigners.

Freedom Spanish-style extends to shopping hours and to ways and rhythms of living. This unhurried life, together with the ingrained youthfulness of its contemporary society, makes Spain a particularly pleasant place to visit.

Bars, *Bodegas, Tabernas* and Cafeterias

Alcoholic drinks can be bought in virtually any grocery store, and can be consumed legally almost anywhere, including in the street. *Bodegas, tabernas,* bars and cafeterias all serve alcoholic drinks, but are all subtly different. *Bodegas* are essentially liquor shops, but some also serve drinks on the premises —wine from the barrel, more often than not from local vineyards; draught beer served as a *caña,* a fifth of a litre serving that takes its name from the cane-shaped glasses it usually comes in; and spirits and liqueurs. *Tabernas* serve cheap bottled wine, beers and soft drinks, often accompanied by a little snack of tinned mussels or something similar on a piece of bread. *Bares* serve a variety of alcoholic and soft drinks, coffee and tea, *bocadillos* ('French' loaf sandwiches), and specialize in the *tapa* (see below). The *cafetería* is more modern in conception and is, as its name suggests, essentially a coffee-shop though alcoholic drinks, snacks and cakes are also served.

Tapas, a wonderful Spanish creation, are little snacks served with drinks, and the range is immense: sausages, tuna, nuts, olives, cheese, salami, cured ham, clams in red sauce, grilled prawns, *tortilla* (Spanish potato omelette), *boquerones* (fried or marinated anchovies), kebabs, octopus, snails.... You may also come across stewed chick-peas, offal and *paella,* the saffron-flavoured rice and seafood dish for which Spain is justly famous. *Raciones* are simply somewhat larger orders of *tapas.* A very Spanish way of eating lightly and informally is to order *raciones;* better yet, if you are in a group, the best thing to do is order an assortment of them and share them around.

The *tapa* as a gastronomic institution is explained by the lightness of the typical Spanish breakfast, generally eaten mid-morning: usually a simple *café con leche* with a croissant or bun, or the traditional fried dough *churros* which are sometimes served with thick drinking chocolate. The *tapa* also sustains the Spanish habit of drinking before lunch, the day's first major meal, which is eaten as late as 3.00 pm. A tradition of socializing has grown up around the *tapa,* and the name *tapeo* has been given to bar hopping around town, drinking and eating snacks.

The Spanish eating and drinking schedule is full of surprises for the foreigner. Bars and cafeterias usually serve breakfast until about midday, when they begin offering *tapas* and aperitifs: wine, beer, vermouth, *vino fino* and other varieties of sherry. This continues until lunch-time, which can be any time between 2.00 pm and 4.00 pm, although midday meals are served as of noon in many tourist resorts. After lunch, you usually have coffee, and men often have a liqueur and a cigar. Theoretically the traditional *siesta* time is round about 4.30 pm, but this is now pretty much a relic of the past except during vacations and weekends. Towards 6.30 or 7.00 pm many Spaniards have a snack, or *merienda*. This is usually *café con leche* or a chocolate drink. Women often arrange to meet their friends for *merienda* after work or after picking up the children from school. After about 8 o'clock, the bars and cafeterias begin to fill up again with a mixed crowd, who will continue drinking and eating until 10.00 or 10.30, when dinner time —finally— arrives (again, dinner is served earlier in most tourist resorts). Dinner can last until midnight or later, although most restaurants close around that time. Specialized restaurants such as hamburger bars and pizza parlours, however, often remain open after midnight, particularly in the big cities.

Currency

The peseta is available in coins of 1, 5, 10, 25, 50, 100, 200 and 500 pesetas and in notes of 100, 200, 500, 1,000, 2,000, 5,000 and 10,000 pesetas. Visitors are allowed to bring into Spain any amount of foreign currency in notes or traveller's cheques.

Customs and Courtesy

Spanish men normally greet one another with a handshake (and a hug if they are good friends); women normally kiss each other once on either cheek. It is general practice in Spain to heap courtesies on women, opening doors for them and so on, and the same also applies to the elderly and to guests. Queuing, on the other hand, is not a Spanish virtue and is not widely practised. The best thing is to accept this as a national characteristic and step forward determinedly when it is your turn to be served.

The Spanish have an apparently ambivalent attitude to their country: they are invariably immensely fond and proud of it yet they criticize it fiercely. As might be expected, Spaniards appreciate strong interest in their country and an informed discussion; criticism from outside, however, does not go down too well.

Spaniards are very dress-conscious and are particularly good at stylish casual dressing. Spain is rightly proud of its thriving fashion industry. But the spirit of living together that characterizes the country means that conventional dress takes its place alongside the more bizarre styles known among Spaniards as 'new-look postmodern' and 'punkie', especially in the cities and popular summer resorts. Establishments that require formal dress are few, most of them casinos and very expensive restaurants. These latter often stock a whole range of ties to lend the improperly attired customer.

Drinks

Apart from its excellent wines or *vinos* (see 'Wines'), Spain also produces soft drinks and a great deal of **beer** (*cerveza*), both draught and bottled. Some of the better-known bottled brands include *Aguila, San Miguel, Mahou* and *Cruzcampo*. Typical **soft drinks** (*refrescos*) include *Trinaranjus, Kas* and *Coca-Cola* and *Pepsi-Cola* made under licence in Spain. An enormously popular brand of *gaseosa* —a sweetened bubbly water— is *La Casera*, so much so that its name has become synonymous with *gaseosa* as a generic term. *Gaseosa* mixed with beer (ask for *una clara*) or wine (*vino con gaseosa*) is increasingly popular.

Spanish **coffee** (*café*) is very good, and is normally served espresso-style. It comes *solo* (black), *con leche* (with hot milk) or *cortado* (with a dash of hot milk). Irish coffee (*café irlandés*) is very popular, especially among the middle and upper classes; another variant, *carajillo*, or black coffee with brandy, is its working-class equivalent. **Tea** (*té*) —remember to ask for milk if you want it— and herbal infusions are usually made with tea-bags.

Sangría, the summer drink made with red wine, lemon, brandy, slices of orange and peach, sugar and cinnamon, must be one of Spain's best-known inventions. There are also lots of **fresh, non-alcoholic drinks**, like *horchata*, made from tiger nuts, *granizados*, sherbet drinks and *agua de cebada* and *agua de arroz*, barley and rice water.

Electricity

Electricity in Spain is normally alternating current at 220v-225v, although many hotels have a special 110-125v plug so that travellers may use electric razors without danger to the appliance. The plugs are generally of the universal two-pronged, round-shaped variety.

Gambling

The Spanish are great enthusiasts of games of chance. These include the *Lotería Nacional*, or National Lottery and the popular *Loto*, or *Lotería Primitiva*, which have weekly draws, and the *Cupón de los Ciegos*, a lottery run by the organization for the blind, ONCE, which has daily draws. There are also football pools and horse racing punts both known as *quinielas*. Big cities and tourist resorts generally have a casino, and the humblest of bars inevitably has its one-armed bandit.

Pharmacies

Pharmacies or chemist's shops (*farmacias* in Spanish) in most towns have a rota system so that one is always open round the clock; you will find a list outside every chemist's and in the local newspaper. Pharmacies in Spain sell many medicines, including antibiotics, over the counter that require prescriptions elsewhere. Contraceptives are available without much difficulty.

Public Washrooms

Do not be alarmed by the apparent scarcity of public washrooms. There is an informal network of public services in bars, cafeterias and other eating and drinking establishments. Most owners do not mind non-customers walking in off the street to use their washroom facilities. Some of the washrooms in bars, restaurants and railway stations, however, are not models of cleanliness, so you would do well to stick to better eating and drinking places, hotels, museums and so on. If there is an attendant, a small tip is customary.

The Spaniards' Schedule

Although it might take the foreigner a few days to get used to it, the Spaniards' schedule is a very sensible adaptation to their climate, designed to provide refuge from the heat of the day and to take full advantage of the cool night hours. Although factories start work at 8.00 am and offices at 9.00 am (often earlier in summer), just as in any industrialized country, lunch-time is not until about 3.00 pm and is a leisurely affair so that you avoid being out and about at the hottest time of day. Dinner is usually at 10.00 pm or later. It is usual to go out in the evenings, even if only to take the air, have a drink, socialize, indulge in a little flirtation and generally take advantage of the cool hours. Not for nothing is Spain known for its tradition of night life.

Generally, shops of all kinds are open from 10.00 am until 1.30 pm or 2.00 pm, and again from 4.00 pm or 5.00 pm until 8.00 pm. Department stores do not usually close during the lunch hour and many are open all day Saturday and even Sunday. Of course, there are also many shops of all types that remain open longer hours in cities and tourist centres.

Taxis

A taxi is usually identified by a horizontal or diagonal stripe on the body and a sign marking it as a taxi on the roof or behind the windshield. As a general rule, the rates charged are set by local authorities. In cities, at least, the rate schedule is posted where the traveller can easily read it. There are many taxi ranks, marked by signs in blue that carry the letter T or the word 'taxi'. There are also a good many radio-dispatched taxi companies that you can reach by telephone, and of course you can hail one in the street. Unoccupied taxis carry a card in their windshield marked *libre* during the day; at night, they are marked by a green roof light.

Telephone

Spain has a good telephone communications system that has a fully automatic national and international network. International telephone calls to most countries can be dialled directly (see the instructions and list of codes below). Apart from the many telephone booths along the streets, equipped with instructions in several languages, most restaurants, bars and cafeterias have coin-operated public telephones. You insert 5, 25, or 50 peseta coins, wait for the dial tone and then dial. You can make local, national and international calls on these phones. It is generally advisable to use these rather than hotel phones —hotels often charge more than 25% extra. If you are planning a longer international call you should either provide yourself with a good supply of coins or find a phone marked 'international'. Better yet, go to the local public office of the CTNE, (*Compañía Telefónica Nacional de España*), better known as *Telefónica*, where you can pay after making your call without the bother of having to find the right change. Rates are substantially lower at night and on holidays.

When you dial a number, the sound of the ringing phone will be long intermittent tones. A busy signal is more rapid.

All Spanish provincial codes begin with 9, followed by the number in the province. These prefixes must always be used when calling from another Spanish province. Within a province they are dropped. When calling Spain from another country the provincial 9 prefix is also dropped.

To make automatic calls from Spain to another country —calls without the assistance of the operator— you need to dial 07, wait for a high-pitched tone and then dial the code for the country you are calling (see the list of international prefixes below), the area code (dropping the initial zero if there is one), and finally, the number of the party you wish to reach. If you do not know the area code, want to make a collect call or need the help of an operator for another reason, dial 008 (Europe) and 005 (the rest of the world) if you are calling from Madrid; dial 9198 (Europe) or 9191 (the rest of the world) if you are in any other province of Spain. Remember that Spanish time usually runs an hour ahead of Greenwich Mean Time (GMT).

International Prefixes

Algeria: 213
Argentina: 54
Australia: 61
Austria: 43
Bahrein: 973
Belgium: 32
Bolivia: 591
Brazil: 55
Cameroon: 237
Canada: 1
Chile: 56
Colombia: 57
Costa Rica: 506
Cyprus: 357
Czechoslovakia: 42
Denmark: 45
Dominican Republic: 508
Ecuador: 593
Egypt: 20
El Salvador: 503
Federal Republic of Germany: 49
Finland: 358
Formosa: 886
France: 33
Gabon: 241
German Democratic Republic: 37
Greece: 30
Guatemala: 502
Haiti: 509
Honduras: 504
Hong Kong: 852
Hungary: 36
India: 91
Indonesia: 62
Iran: 98
Ireland: 353
Israel: 972
Italy: 39
Ivory Coast: 225

Japan: 81
Jordan: 962
Kenya: 254
Kuwait: 965
Liechtenstein: 4175
Luxemburg: 352
Mexico: 52
Monaco: 3393
Morocco: 212
Netherlands: 31
New Zealand: 64
Nicaragua: 505
Nigeria: 234
Norway: 47
Panama: 507
Paraguay: 595
Peru: 51
Philippines: 63
Poland: 48
Portugal: 351
Puerto Rico (USA): 80
Rumania: 40
San Marino: 39541
Saudi Arabia: 966
Senegal: 221
Singapore: 65
South Africa: 27
South Korea: 82
Sweden: 46
Switzerland: 41
Thailand: 66
Tunisia: 216
Turkey: 90
United Arab Emirates: 971
United Kingdom: 44
United States of America: 1
Uruguay: 598
Venezuela: 58
Yugoslavia: 38

Tipping

Tips should generally be between 5% and 10%, depending on the size of the bill: the larger the bill, the smaller the percentage. Bills for many services already include a service charge of 5%. Some establishments do not permit individual tipping, and instead pool all tips. For those cases where a service charge is not included in your bill, here is a general guide to some key services: a hotel porter should normally get a tip of between 100 and 150 pesetas; a taxi driver about 5% over what shows on the meter; parking lot attendants, 15 to 25 pesetas above the cost of the ticket; 25 to 100 pesetas to a cloakroom attendant and 20 to 25 pesetas to a shoeshine boy. Of course the size of the tip depends on the type of place and how expensive it is. And it is always up to the customer to decide how well he has been served and what he wants to leave.

Spaniards have a long history of hospitality, stretching back to the Middle Ages when the first wave of 'tourists' (pilgrims to Santiago de Compostela) created a huge demand for accommodation all along their route through northern Spain. There can be few other countries in the world with such a range of choice in places to stay: from sumptuous 15C palaces to what Spaniards call *campings* (camp sites to native English speakers). Whether you are visiting busy resorts where the fun never stops or seeking fresh air and solitude in mountain top paradises, you can be sure of a wide selection.

At the top end of the scale, you can choose between historic buildings now converted into hotels or any of the many international and Spanish luxury hotel chains, with all mod. cons., at a price of up to 60,000 pesetas a night (even more for a suite). Less extravagant are the more functional hotels in the big cities and tourist resorts. Or, if you prefer to keep your pesetas for other pleasures, you may opt for a low-cost, but spick-and-span room in a family-run *hostal* or *pensión* (Spanish equivalent to Britain's Bed-and-Breakfast) at a cost of as little as 2,000 pesetas for a double room. For holiday makers who do not want to tie themselves down to hotel schedules, there are villas (*chalés*) and bungalows for rent at various prices, not to mention the thousands of camp sites and caravan sites throughout Spain. And for something completely different, you might opt for a 13C monastery (see below) or perhaps a spa or hotel-clinic (see 'Health and Beauty'), where loving care will be lavished on your spiritual or corporal health and beauty, soothing away the stress of your everyday life.

You can get bargain discounts by travelling under the auspices of travel agencies, but even the independent-minded tourist can be sure of excellent value for money from any sort of lodging in Spain.

But be warned: despite this enormous supply of accommodation, there is sometimes an equally enormous demand from travellers, businessmen, conference members and tourists. Madrid and Barcelona tend to be full the whole year round. And nobody seems to know when the high season in the Canaries finishes and when the low season begins (if there even is one any more). Moreover, if you fail to check beforehand, your stay could turn out to coincide with a local *fiesta* in almost any town in Spain, in which case you could well end up pawning your diamonds for a space on the floor. Famous and even not so famous beach resorts attract foreign and Spanish holiday makers, and are usually fully booked during July and August. First come, first served. So do yourself a favour and **book in advance**.

Apartments

Apartments can be rented in the big cities (Madrid and Barcelona) or on the coasts, especially in those seaside towns that particularly attract young people or general large-scale tourism (Salou, Benidorm, Torremolinos and the like). Again, play it safe and consult your travel agency to make sure they reserve you one in advance, stating your preference as to size, style, location and price. You can be pretty sure of good value for money. Obviously, if you want an apartment directly overlooking the beach during July and August or in big towns during trade fairs, conferences, *fiestas* and similar events you will have to pay a bit extra. However, the longer you stay, the lower the rates.

As a general rule, apartment prices include contract costs as well as water, electricity, bed and table linen, rubbish collection and use of common facilities. The preliminary legal work is quite straightforward: the tenant signs a standard contract, usually accompanied by an inventory of furniture, household appliances and linen. Check carefully that everything on the list is there and in good working order before you sign anything. You will be asked for a deposit, which should not exceed 25% of the total rental fee.

Tourist apartments are rated on a scale ranging from one to four keys. The minimum requirements for the different ratings are as follows:

Luxury (Four keys). A well-located, high-quality building. Air conditioning. Lifts in buildings higher than two floors. Service lift. Private parking. Reception and advice desk. Lobby. Telephone. Rubbish disposal on every floor. Bar service. Restaurant/cafeteria. 24-hour hot water. Independent kitchen.

First class (Three keys). A well-built structure. Lifts in buildings of more than three floors. Heating. Hot water. Reception and advice desk. Small lobby. Telephone communication to reception from every room.

Second class (Two keys). A well-built structure. Lifts in buildings of more than three floors. Heating. Hot water. House telephone at the reception desk and on every floor.

Third class (One key). Lift in buildings of more than four floors. Hot water and at least a shower.

One last word of warning. Many holiday makers have so loved their apartments that they have decided **to buy** them —usually time sharing— on what appeared to be bargain terms. Some have lived to regret it. Do not get carried away by smooth-talking salesmen. If you want to invest in real estate in Spain (and Spain is full of opportunities in this field), always check with a reputable lawyer first. Time sharing is covered by neither British nor Spanish law at present, and too many foreigners (and Spaniards) have blown their hard-earned pennies with companies that turned out never to have existed or buying time that had already been bought by six other would-be part-owners. The same holds true of buying straight out. If the seller cannot show you the title deed (the *escritura*), duly registered, then there is something fishy going on. Take the same precautions as you would if buying property in less exotic places. Make sure you have comprehensive information on taxes, legal fees, registration expenses, exchange control, and so forth, and ensure that the seller is the *bona fide* owner before putting down a deposit.

Camp Sites

There are more than 600 good camp sites in Spain. During peak season, you would be well advised to book in advance. You can write direct —the National Tourist Office (c/ Castelló, 117, 28006 Madrid) publishes a handy, low-priced guide, the *Guía Oficial de Campings*, which provides comprehensive information on existing sites— or to the central camping reservation service of the *Federación Española de Empresarios de Campings*, c/ Gran Vía, 88, Grupo 3, 10-8, 28013 Madrid ☎(91) 242 31 68.

Off-site camping is permitted in Spain, except on mountains, beaches and river banks, or at less than 1km from towns or villages, 100m from a national monument or 150m from a drinking water supply. **Fire precautions** are extremely important, as fires spread dangerously fast in Spain.

Hotels and Boarding Houses

Spain's selection of hotels is spectacular, in terms of number, modernity (most have been opened since the mid-1960s), variety of categories, styles and location... and, above all, for the marvellous value for money that they usually represent. This is especially true of ★★★ hotels, whose facilities and services are of much higher quality than could be expected at the same price in other countries. There are also about twenty hotels which belong to the fantasy category and form part of the *crème de la crème* of the best in the world.

Hotels are officially classified on a scale ranging from ★ to ★★★★★ according to facilities and services. The symbols appear on a blue sign under the letter H, displayed on the front of the building. Prices are regulated by the Spanish tourist authorities. If you have any queries about the price, ask at the reception desk. There is a mandatory rates card in the lobby, and individual sheets showing the rate usually hang on the back of the door to each room. Hotels are legally required to stick to these prices, but there are some variations, such as when the Value Added Tax, VAT, in Spain *IVA*, is added (not applicable in the Canary Islands). If you ask for a single room and only a double one is available, you should not be charged more than 80% of the price of a double. For a room with an extra bed, you should not be charged more than 60% the price of a single or 35% the price of a double. There are usually discounts for children, according to their age. Do not be surprised at any differences between official prices and those paid by organized groups or package tours that include hotels and other services; tour prices are sometimes much lower and at others about the same.

HOTELS

The statutory minimum requirements for the different categories of hotel are the following:

★★★★★ Air conditioning in all lounges and bedrooms. Central heating. Two or more lifts. Several lobbies. Bar. Garage (in cities). Hairdressers. Bathroom with bath in all rooms. Some suites with reception rooms. Laundry service. Telephone in every room.

★★★★ Air conditioning in lounges and bedrooms, unless the local climate requires central heating instead. Lift. At least two lobbies. Bar. Garage (in cities). Bathroom with bath in 75% of rooms; shower, washbasin and toilet in 25% of rooms. Laundry service available. Telephone in every room.

★★★ Heating appliances provided. Lift. Lobby. Bar. Bathroom with bath in 50% of rooms; shower, washbasin and toilet in 50% of them. Laundry service available. Telephone in every room.

★★ Heating appliances provided. Lift when there are more than three floors. Lobby. Bar. Bathroom with bath in 15% of the rooms; shower, washbasin and toilet in 45% of them; washbasin in 40% of the rooms; common bath for every six rooms. Laundry service. Telephone in every room.

★ Heating appliances provided. Lift when there are more than four floors. Lobby. Shower, washbasin and toilet in 25% of the rooms; shower and washbasin in 25%; washbasin in 50% of them; common bath for every seven rooms. Laundry service available. Telephone on every floor.

BOARDING HOUSES

Like hotels, boarding houses are officially classified according to facilities and functions, the scale being from ★ to ★★★. This rating will appear on a blue sign under the letters Hs for a *hostal* —modest hotel with or without meals— and HsR for a *hostal residencia* —bed and breakfast. The minimum requirements for boarding houses, or *hostales*, are:

★★★ Heating appliances provided. Lift in buildings of more than three floors. Lobby. Bathroom in 5% of rooms; shower, washbasin and toilet in 10%; shower and washbasin in 85% of them; common bath for every eight rooms. Laundry service. Telephone in every room.

★★ Heating appliances provided. Lift in buildings of more than four floors. Reception area. Washbasin in all rooms; common bath for every 10 rooms. Public telephone.

★ Washbasin in all rooms, with cold water; common bath for every 12 rooms. Public telephone.

The *pensión* —indicated on a sign under the letter P— provides a very cheap way to stay in Spain; meals are usually eaten with the family that runs the establishment and a laundry service is provided. Inns —*fondas*, under the letter F— and guest houses —*casas de huéspedes*, under the letters CH— are another alternative: they usually offer simple accommodation in central parts of town.

Monasteries

There is a side to Spain that the tourist posters do not show. Although famous for being fun-loving and extrovert, the Spaniards are also a deeply religious people. The roots of their monastic culture stretch back far into Spanish history and are closely linked to it. Travellers who want to dig deeper into this facet of the Spanish character or who simply want to enjoy a total rest from the hustle and bustle of modern-day life will find a welcome in the monastic communities listed below.

Although many of the monastery and convent buildings are imposing and house works of art of enormous value, the visitor should not expect luxury. They are not hotels, and their orders are inspired by values of extreme simplicity: silence, prayer and seclusion. The austerity of their Romanesque architecture and sculpture and the pure beauty of the Gregorian chant provide aesthetic pleasure on quite a different level.

Many of these communities (mainly Benedictine and Cistercian) offer lodging to visitors. They are usually single-sex and the visitor is expected to respect the ways of the Order while under its roof. Several will refuse to charge a price for their hospitality, preferring to suggest a voluntary donation. Here are a few ideas:

- *Abadía de Leyre*, Yesa (Navarre) ☎ (948) 88 40 11. A Benedictine abbey in beautiful surroundings lodging male guests in cells. Roughly 1,200 pesetas a day. Both men and women can stay at the annexed guest house, where they can enjoy a more independent lifestyle.
- *Abadía de Montserrat*, Montserrat (Barcelona) ☎ (93) 835 02 51. A Benedictine abbey with a small guest house in a stunning mountain setting. Roughly 1,500 pesetas a day.
- *Abadía de San Pedro de Cardeña*, Burgos (Burgos) ☎ (947) 29 00 03. A Cistercian abbey providing accommodation for male guests for a maximum of eight days. Lodging is within the abbey in 24 rooms (with bathrooms), in an atmosphere of silence and meditation. Roughly 1,400 pesetas a day.
- *Abadía de Santa María de Poblet*, Espluga de Francolí (Tarragona) ☎ (977) 87 00 89. A Cistercian abbey providing accommodation for men inside the abbey itself. Although no obligations are imposed, visitors are expected to keep to the community's timetable. Meals are eaten with the monks in the communal refectory. Voluntary donation.
- *Abadía de Santo Domingo de Silos*, Santo Domingo de Silos (Burgos) ☎ (947) 38 07 68. A Benedictine abbey providing accommodation for men (21 rooms, with individual bathrooms, hot water and central heating) within the abbey, in a studious, peaceful atmosphere. Although there is no obligation to join in prayers and study, guests are expected to be punctual for meals. The monks' prayers and services are sung in magnificent **Gregorian chant**, the Holy Week services being especially impressive. Roughly 1,200 pesetas a day.
- *Abadía de Viaceli*, Cobreces (Cantabria) ☎ (942) 72 50 17. A Cistercian abbey providing accommodation for men only for a maximum of one week. The atmosphere is strictly religious. Voluntary donation.

🏛 *Convento de Carmelitas Descalzos* in Las Mestas, La Alberca (Salamanca), in the Las Batuecas Valley ☎ (923) 43 71 33. At the entranceway, on the small façade with its niche and bell gable, there is a sign warning visitors not to disturb, since the monastery *'is intended to be the Spiritual Desert for the contemplative life of prayer (...) there is no church, public mass, or community leader. It is a closed order, ordained by the Pope, forbidding the entrance of women. It is not open to tourists.'* Only men may go there for spiritual retreat, by prior request. King Alfonso XIII stayed in the old building on his trip to Las Hurdes in 1922. Later, Luis Buñuel stayed here, while shooting his film *Land Without Bread* in the area, and fell in love with the valley, which he called *'one of the few paradises I have known on this Earth'.* Roughly 800 pesetas a day.

🏛 *Monasterio de Carrizo*, Carrizo (León) ☎ (987) 35 70 55. This Cistercian convent provides accommodation (four rooms) for members of both sexes for a maximum of eight days. Although under no spiritual obligations, guests are expected to keep within the nuns' timetable —to be punctual for meals and be in when the convent closes in the evening. Voluntary donation.

🏛 *Monasterio de El Paular*, Rascafría (Madrid) ☎ (91) 869 14 25. A Benedictine monastery accommodating men for a maximum of ten days. Roughly 1,200 pesetas a day.

🏛 *Monasterio de Las Huelgas Reales*, Burgos (Burgos) ☎ (947) 20 16 30. A Cistercian nunnery housing women (five rooms) in an annex building. Voluntary donation.

🏛 *Monasterio de la Oliva*, Cascastillo (Navarre) ☎ (948) 72 50 06. Lodging for members of both sexes in this superb example of Cistercian architecture. The atmosphere is of hard work and seclusion. Roughly 1,200 pesetas a day.

🏛 *Monasterio de Palacios de Benaver*, Palacios de Benaver (Burgos) ☎ (947) 45 10 09. A Benedictine nunnery with four guest rooms for members of both sexes. Gregorian chant at services. Roughly 1,400 pesetas a day.

🏛 *Monasterio de San Isidro de Dueñas*, Venta de Baños (Palencia) ☎ (988) 77 07 01. A Trappist monastery providing accommodation for men or married couples seeking spiritual retreat. Gregorian chant features in some parts of the mass and in some services. Roughly 1,100 pesetas a day.

🏛 *Monasterio de San Pedro de las Dueñas*, Sahagún (León) ☎ (987) 78 01 50. A Benedictine nunnery providing lodging for members of both sexes in an annex to the convent. There is no obligation to join in convent life. Visitors seeking rest, roughly 1,800 pesetas a day; visitors going to study or for spiritual retreat, roughly 1,300 pesetas a day.

🏛 *Monasterio de Santa María de Huerta*, Santa María de Huerta (Soria) ☎ (975) 32 70 02. A Cistercian monastery accommodating men (eight rooms). It is best to write in advance. Roughly 1,000 pesetas a day.

🏛 *Monasterio de Santa María de El Parral*, Segovia (Segovia) ☎ (911) 43 12 98. A Hieronymite monastery offering lodging (three bedrooms with bathrooms) for a week maximum to men seeking spiritual retreat. Although meals are shared with the monks, guests can either lead an independent or monastic life. Voluntary donation.

🏛 *Monasterio de Sobrado de los Monjes*, in Sobrado, 72km from La Coruña ☎ (981) 78 90 09. A Cistercian monastery accommodating male guests only. Roughly 1,200 pesetas a day.

🏛 *Monasterio de Yuste*, Cuacos (Cáceres) ☎ (927) 46 05 30. The Hieronymite order provides lodging for men for a maximum of a week.

The rooms are inside the monastery with communal showers and toilets. Guests can lead an independent or monastic life, although meals are shared with the monks. Voluntary donation.

▥ *Real Santuario de Montesclaros*, Santander (Cantabria) ☎ (942) 75 13 83. An annexed guest house offers lodging to members of both sexes. The rooms have communal bathrooms. Guests lead independent lives except during meal times. Roughly 1,800 pesetas daily.

▥ *Santuario de El Miracle*, Solsona (Lérida) ☎ (973) 48 00 02. This Benedictine order will accommodate men in monks' cells. There is a communal kitchen for preparing meals. Nearby, nuns run a spiritual retreat for members of both sexes ☎ 48 00 45. Roughly 1,800 pesetas a day.

▥ *Santuario de la Peña de Francia* (Salamanca) see 'Francia, Sierra de' in 'Castile and León'. To arrange a stay in this Dominican retreat, contact the San Esteban Monastery in Salamanca ☎ (923) 21 50 00. It only accommodates men and women seeking voluntary retreat, for study or meditation, during July and August. Roughly 1,800 pesetas a day.

Paradors

The Parador chain is an exceptional hotel network **unique to Spain**. It was set up during the reign of Alfonso XIII, who inaugurated the first one, in the Sierra de Gredos, in 1928 (see 'Gredos, Sierra de' in 'Castile and León'). Since then, especially during the boom in the 1960s, the State-run network has grown to 86 establishments. Paradors (literally 'stopping places'), usually of ★★★ and ★★★★ category, have been established in spots of recognized interest for tourists, or of particular beauty all over Spain, except for the Balearics. Thirteen are in medieval **castles**, nine in Baroque or Gothic **palaces**, six in ancient **monasteries** or **convents**. The buildings have all been renovated with the greatest respect for their original structure, but also with an eye to meeting the needs of the modern-day tourist for up-to-date, efficient services. All the other paradors are new purpose-built buildings, located on prime sites for views and tourism.

They range in size from the tiny (six rooms in a medieval tower in Villalba, for example) to the grandiose (258 rooms in León). Some are in buildings whose noble history and beauty set them apart —León's and Santiago de Compostela's are the outstanding ones in this category, though Granada's, in the Alhambra itself, is not far behind— while others are set in landscapes of breathtaking natural beauty. In all cases, the service is of a consistently high professional standard and their restaurants serve good Spanish food.

Advance bookings are necessary, especially in the high season and resort areas. They may be made direct or at the *Central de Reservas de Paradores*, c/ Velázquez, 25, 28001 Madrid ☎ (91) 435 97 00.

Villas and Bungalows

Renting your own accommodation is an interesting alternative to hotel rooms, especially for a long stay, and it is relatively easy to find the sort of housing one requires. It is best to make the arrangements before setting off, either through a reputable travel agency or specialist villa-rental services. Some camp sites also offer small bungalows. Obviously prices vary according to the size, quality and location of the accommodation, but they are usually very reasonable. The lease contract usually includes a deposit, a downpayment of at least one month's rent or, if the stay is less than a month, for however long you are staying, and an inventory of furniture and household goods.

WIDE OPEN SPACES

Spain is a country of impressive historic cities, remote picturesque villages and immensely varied landscapes. All too often, the countryside is something the visitor appreciates incidentally as he drives through it from one point of his holiday itinerary to another wondering, perhaps, about an unfamiliar crop or bird that might happen to catch his eye. But there are some marvellous areas of natural beauty, often with flora and fauna all their own, which are well worth exploration and where close contact with the wonders of nature can help place the historic achievements of Man in their proper perspective.

. . Spain's officially designated **National Parks** are protected areas. There are nine of them altogether, five on the mainland and four in the Canary Islands. Legislation for the protection of areas of natural beauty in Spain has been in effect since 1916, and Covadonga and Ordesa were the first to be declared National Parks.

Spain's National Parks include mountainous areas (Ordesa, Covadonga, Aigües Tortes and Lago de San Mauricio), wetland bird sanctuaries (Tablas de Daimiel and the Doñana Reserve), and the areas of unique landscape and vegetation in the Canary Islands.

Covadonga National Park (see 'Cantabrian Coast') is in the western Picos de Europa mountains (between León, Asturias and Cantabria), and lies mostly within Asturias although it overlaps slightly into León. The most direct way of getting there is to take the road 4km out of Cangas de Onís which leads to the Santuario de Covadonga shrine and the glacier-formed lakes of **Enol** and **La Ercina** beyond, in the very heart of the park. There are various hotels in Covadonga, Cangas de Onís, Soto de Sajambre and Posada de Valdeón, and a lakeside hostel at La Ercina. There are also several campsites and mountaineers' refuge huts.

Ordesa National Park lies within Aragón's area of the Pyrenees in the province of Huesca (see 'Aragón'). The best route is the N-330 from Huesca to Sabiñánigo, turning off on the C-136 towards Biescas and there taking the C-140 to Torla. Accommodation is plentiful nearby and includes the Monte Perdido parador in Bielsa, hotels and boarding houses in Torla, Boltaña, Ainsa, Broto and Biescas, and several camp sites. There are quite a few mountaineers' refuges within the park itself. The best time to visit is from April to early October, and there are several well-signposted routes through the park of varying degrees of difficulty.

The **National Park of Aigües Tortes and Lago de San Mauricio** lies in the Catalan Pyrenees (see 'Catalonia'), an area of breathtaking scenic beauty. Nearby is the Bohí Valley, site of some of Catalonia's finest Romanesque churches. If you are approaching from the W, take the N-230 which leads from Lérida to the French border, turning off in Pont de Suert for Caldas de Bohí. Coming from the E, take the C-147 which leads from Balaguer to the Pyrenees, turning off 25km from Sort towards Lake San Mauricio. There is ample hotel accommodation in the area, including paradors in Viella and Arties, several hotels in the Arán valley, and others in Rialp, Sort, Llavorsí, Espot, Llesuy, Pont de Suert, Tahúll, Caldas de Bohí and more. There are also plenty of camp sites. The proximity of the Arán Valley and other ski-resorts makes this a marvellous area for a winter holiday.

In a marshy area of La Mancha into which the rivers of Guadiana and Cigüela overflow, the **Tablas de Daimiel National Park** (see 'Madrid and Castile-La Mancha') is a vast lake-strewn area with a huge bird population, some permanent residents and others migratory. There are marked routes through the park with observation platforms for bird-watchers and photographers. There is an access road to the park from the nearby town of

Daimiel, 21km from Manzanares (see 'Madrid and Castile-La Mancha') which is on the N-IV, 29km from Ciudad Real. As far as accommodation is concerned, there are paradors in Manzanares and in the historic town of Almagro, and several hotels in Ciudad Real and Daimiel.

Another wetland park, which extends into the two provinces of Seville and Huelva in the marshy area around the mouth of the Guadalquivir, is the **Doñana Reserve** (see 'Andalusia'). This park incorporates several ecosystems —dunes, marshland and areas of vegetation which provide cover for game. The game in question consists of wild boar, deer, roe deer and foxes, but this park's true wealth lies in the bird-life concentrated in its marshlands. Many migratory birds spend the winter here, but there are also large colonies of resident birds —there are up to 60 different species in the park at times. Winter is the ideal time to see the migratory birds on their way to Africa, while spring offers the opportunity to see new birds coming to life. There are guided tours through the park by land-rover; these have to be arranged in advance ☎ (955) 43 04 32. The quickest route to the Doñana Reserve is by the Seville-Huelva motorway, the A-49, as far as La Palma del Condado and Bollullos Par del Condado, turning off southwards onto the El Rocío road. The Cristobal Colón parador near Mazagón beach is a delightful place to stay.

Cañadas del Teide National Park (see 'Canary Islands') in the centre of the Canary Island of Tenerife is an area of volcanic, rocky landscape around the **Teide** volcano, at 3,710m the highest mountain in Spain. The vast crater of Las Cañadas is full of rare plants which flourish in the fertile lava-based soil —white broom, red *tajinaste*, wallflowers, violets. There are various routes you can take through the park —ask at the information office near El Portillo— and there is also a cable car which takes you almost to the summit of the Teide. The park is easy to get to from any point in the island which, being one of Europe's major tourist magnets, has ample accommodation. The Las Cañadas del Teide parador, right in the heart of the park, is in an incomparably beautiful setting.

The **Timanfaya National Park** (see 'Arrecife' in 'Canary Islands') in the island of Lanzarote is in a volcanic area, the product of various eruptions which occurred during the 18C and 19C. The landscape of craters and strata of lava has a curious lunar beauty all its own. Vegetation is sparse but fascinating in that very rare plants, some of them unique to the island, grow here. There are also curious indigenous Haria lizards, though the bird-life, mainly pigeons, cormorants and seagulls, is less extraordinary. Most people choose to explore the park via the **Volcano Route**, a 14km guided bus tour, and you can also join a camel train, an irresistible sight for photographers in this visually thrilling setting. The main route to the park is along the Tinajo to Yaiza road, turning off onto the road which leads to the Islote de Hilario at the foot of the Timanfaya mountain. Arrecife, the island's capital, has numerous four- and three-star hotels, and there is also accommodation in Yaiza and an excellent luxury hotel in the tourist complex of Costa Teguise.

The **Caldera de Taburiente National Park** (see 'Santa Cruz de La Palma' in 'Canary Islands') takes its name from the gigantic volcanic crater in the centre of the island of La Palma. The crater has a radius of 7km and is 1,800m deep, and within it grow pines, beeches, heather and many other species of shrubs and plants, some of them vividly colourful. There is little wild life, but it includes various kinds of lizard, kestrels, cormorants and rooks. The surrounding landscape is characterized by spectacular rock formations. One of these, the 2,423m high Roque de los Muchachos, serves as the base for the Canary Island's Astrophysical Observatory, the most important in Europe. There are various routes around the park. For spectacular views, head up to the look-outs of **Lomo de las Chozas** and **La Cumbrecita** (1,833m high), from where you can walk to Las Caldas de Taburiente. There are land-rovers available to take you on a route starting at Llanos de Ariadne, and through various ravines to the look-out point known as Mirador de Farola, from which point you explore La Caldera on foot. The park can be entered from several points —a road leads from El Paso to La Cumbrecita, and there are other access roads from Los Llanos de Ariadne and Mirca. In the island's capital, Santa Cruz de La Palma, there is a parador, and accommodation is also available in Los Llanos de Ariadne.

The fourth of the Canary Islands' National Parks is **Garajonay** (see 'San Sebastián de La Gomera' in 'Canary Islands') in La Gomera. It is a vast and surprisingly green area of some 4,000ha crowned by the 1,487m high peak of Garajonay. The woodlands within the park include the only surviving colony of *laurisilva*, a species of tree which, millions of years ago, populated the entire Mediterranean area. In combination with bay, lime trees, heather, mosses and lichens, these form a dense jungle barely penetrable by sunlight so that the park is enveloped in a heavy, moist atmosphere. In the upper region of the park is a ***tagoror***, a Megalithic monument which served as a congregation point for the Guanches, the island's original inhabitants. Again the wildlife is scarce but interesting, and includes various reptiles, pigeons, finches and blackbirds among many other species of birds, and a huge and varied insect population. To explore this park properly you should plunge into the jungle, suitably equipped with waterproof clothes and boots. Various winding roads from all over the island lead to the park. Accommodation is concentrated almost entirely in the island's capital, San Sebastián de La Gomera, where there is a parador and several hotels and boarding houses.

WINES

Spain is a country with an age-old wine-making tradition, a fact which is vividly reflected in its history and culture. The Greeks and Phoenicians who settled along the Mediterranean coast of Spain traded in its wines; wine looms large in the works of countless Spanish painters and writers; and wine must surely have made a contribution to the extrovert Hispanic character.

Spain could be described as a vivid mosaic of different wines, as varied as the nation's many regions: here you find fresh 'green' wines reminiscent of Portugal; young fruity wines made from the same varieties of grape grown in the Rhine and Moselle valleys; noble, aged Riojas which rank alongside the finest Burgundies and Bordeaux; light Galician Ribeiros and young Catalan wines to rival the freshest of Beaujolais; the unique and incomparable *claretes*, or light reds, of Cigales and Jumilla; Priorato reds as dense and rich as bull's blood, feather light Txacolís and Alellas; sparkling cavas so fine that French champagne is having to look to its laurels on the international market. Then there are the rich wines of Andalusia —sherry, manzanilla Moriles-Montilla— full of southern sunshine and the perfect accompaniment to *tapas* and conversation, two time-honoured Spanish institutions (see 'Spanish Way of Life' and 'Cuisine').

The excellent quality of the wines of Spain is controlled by the *Instituto Nacional de Denominaciones de Origen* (National Institute of Denominations of Origin) whose label appears on the back of the bottle. Spanish wines are at last beginning to achieve the recognition they deserve outside Spain, not least because of the excellent value for money they represent compared with other European and American wines.

The most famous and prestigious of all Spanish wines is, of course, **sherry**, whose English name is a corruption of Jerez, the town in Andalusia from which sherry has been exported for centuries. Sherry is full-flavoured and high in alcohol, as one might expect of a product of the hot climate of southern Spain. The more temperate north produces a variety of wines: **Riojas** which compete in quality with the best French table wines; Catalonia's excellent table wines and **cavas**, sparkling wines made by the *méthode champenoise*; **Albariños** and **Ribeiros**, fresh young whites from rainy Galicia which go beautifully with the seafood for which the Galician coasts are famous. Central Spain is a prolific producer of robust everyday wines, among them the well-made, full-bodied wines of **Ribera del Duero** and the immensely popular all-purpose **Valdepeñas**.

Catalonia

Catalonia is the region with the widest range of wines, both still and sparkling. **Alella** is primarily a producer of white wines, pale, fresh and fruity and with a very distinctive flavour and nose which go well with seafood, fish and uncured cheeses. *Marqués de Alella* is a good example. The area of **Ampurdán-Costa Brava** is better known for its rosés —cherry-coloured, fruity and highly aromatic— which are an excellent accompaniment to light fish and meat dishes and pasta. It also produces some good, fresh whites, like *Blanc Pescador*. Its robust, full-bodied reds are not for the uninitiated. **Priorato** is known for its rich, dark, potent reds, while **Tarragona's** are somewhat lighter in weight.

The Denomination of Origin of **Penedés** is the best-known of Catalonia for its sparkling wines, especially the cavas, and the outstanding wines, especially the whites, of the Torres bodega. The best of the sparkling wines are the cavas, wines with a natural sparkle made by the classic Champagne method and fermented and aged in the same bottle. Their superb quality and the good value for money they represent have met with tremendous success in foreign markets. *Brut* (extra-dry) and *seco* (dry) cavas can be drunk on any occasion, while the *dulce* (sweet) and *semiseco* (semi-dry) ones are best with desserts. Bear in mind when making your choice that they all tend to be very slightly sweeter than their French equivalents. The cava bodegas are concentrated around San Sadurní de Noya: Codorniú, Freixenet (the two biggest), Castellblanch, Conde Caralt, Juve & Camps, Segura Viudas and Marqués de Monistrol are all labels which guarantee outstanding quality and can be bought anywhere in Spain.

The bodega of Miguel Torres, in Villafranca del Panedés —the capital of the region, with a fascinating **Wine Museum**— is one of the most prestigious in Spain. Among its excellent wines are the white *Gran Viña Sol* and *Viña Sol*, and the red *Gran Coronas Etiqueta Negra*. René Barbier produces excellent whites —*Kraliner* is a good example.

Central Spain and Extremadura

La Mancha is the biggest wine-growing area in Europe, and embraces the Denominations of Origin of **Mancha, Manchuela, Méntrida, Almansa** and **Valdepeñas**. The Valdepeñas are immensely popular everyday wines drunk throughout Spain. The most typical Valdepeñas is *clarete*, an all-purpose light-weight and light-coloured red, relatively low in alcohol, a carafe wine served in bars and *tabernas*. The whites and reds are equally light-weight. Among the reds, *Viña Albali* and *Los Molinos* are interesting for their good colour and body.

Castile and León produces a wide range of wines, from the rather harsh, robust reds of **Toro** and **Cebreros** to the *claretes* of **Cigales** and the delicate whites of **Rueda** —like La Seca's excellent *Cuatro Rayas*. The Denomination of Origin of **Ribero del Duero** covers Spain's legendary Vega-Sicilia bodega, with its superb reds like the excellent *Valbuena*.

León's best-known wines are from **Cacabelos**, which are similar to the wines of neighbouring Galicia in having a slightly acidic edge.

Extremadura is a big wine producer, especially La Serena and Tierra de Barros, though its products are little known outside the area, except for the rather robust **Cañamero**.

Galicia and the Basque Country

Albariños, made with grapes from pergola-trained vines, are exquisitely delicate whites, straw-coloured, acidic and fresh and with a slight natural petillance. They are low in alcohol and go beautifully with fish and seafood in general. White **Ribeiros** are also a classic accompaniment to seafood while the reds are particularly good with the octopus and hake dishes so typical of Galician cuisine.

The Basque Country, home of some of the best restaurants in Spain and very much in the forefront of *nouvelle cuisine*, produces the perfect accompaniment in the form of its light fruity **txacolís**, slightly petillant 'green' wines, drunk young and cold.

Jerez and Andalusia

The wines of Jerez and Andalusia are in a category all their own. Known the world over for centuries, even mentioned in the Bible, some claim, a favourite of Shakespeare's... **Jerez-Xerès-Sherry**, as it is officially designated, is not a wine with which to lubricate a meal, but one to be savoured slowly for its own intrinsic qualities. It is blended and matured over a period of years by the elaborate *solera* system, tiered rows of casks containing progressively younger vintages from which the casks of older vintages are topped up when wine has been drawn from them for final blending and bottling.

Many of today's sherry-making bodegas date back to the 18C —Terry, Duff Gordon, Garvey, Agustín Blázquez, Osborne, Domecq, Sandeman— and some to the 19C —González Byass and Williams/Humbert. The generic name sherry covers various different types, the most important of which are the **finos**. Light and dry, they are a pale straw-gold with a characteristically pungent yet delicate aroma and an alcoholic strength of between 15.5° and 17°. The leading brand names are *Tío Pepe, La Ina, Carta Blanca, San Patricio, Perla, Quinta* and *Tío Mateo*. **Manzanilla** sherries come from Sanlúcar de Barrameda and are similar to finos, though with a subtle difference generally described as a salty tang and attributed to the effects of the sea air. *La Guita* is one of many popular brands. **Amontillados** are amber-coloured, smooth and fuller-bodied with a nutty aroma and between 16° and 18° of alcohol. The best-known brands are *Coquinero, Don Zoilo* and *Etiqueta Blanca*. **Olorosos** are dark in colour and very aromatic, as their name implies, full-bodied and dry, with between 18° and 20° of alcohol. *Río Viejo* and *Dry Sack* are typical brands. **Palo Cortado** is a type of sherry somewhere between oloroso and amontillado. Then there are the **sweet wines** like Moscatel, Pedro Ximénez and Cream.

Finos are drunk chilled and make the perfect aperitif, as do amontillados; they are both excellent with *tapas* of fried or grilled fish and cured ham. Olorosos and palo cortados are good with nuts, cured ham and charcuterie.

The sweet wines are classically drunk with desserts. Experts advise that sherry is at its best drunk from the classic stemmed glass which narrows at the top.

Córdoba is famous for its sherry-like **Montilla-Moriles** wines, from the famous bodegas of Alvear, Crismona and Navarro. The most popular brands of fino are *C.B.*, *Moriles* and *Montilla*, and *Oloroso Viejo* is the label to look out for if you prefer olorosos. **Málaga's** sweet wines, made from *Moscatel* and *Pedro Ximénez* grapes are perfect with desserts. Both Montilla and Cádiz have recently started producing an attractive new line in deliciously fruity white table wines which may also succeed in attracting attention to the table wines traditionally made in **Condado de Huelva**, hitherto little known outside the area of Huelva and Seville.

La Rioja and Navarre

The wines of La Rioja have long been recognized for their fine quality, surpassed only by Bordeaux and Burgundy in reputation. Although it is known to have been a wine-producing area since pre-Roman times, La Rioja's present-day bodegas mainly date back to the 19C: names like Bodegas Bilbaínas, Martínez Lacuesta, Muga, CVNE, Paternina, López de Heredia, Berberana, Marqués de Cáceres, AGE, Franco-Española, Lan, Marqués de Murrieta and so on all guarantee high quality, with the best wines coming from the area known as Rioja Alta. La Rioja is best known for its reds, light-bodied and with a characteristic hint of oak in both aroma and flavour developed during long periods in oak casks, though fresh, fruity whites have also come into production over the last few years. 1964, 1970, 1978, 1981, 1983 were **excellent** years, while the wines of 1972, 1977 and 1980 are best avoided.

Going back no further than 1970, *Marqués Villamagna*, *Viña Cumbrero*, *Prado Enea*, *Viña Albina*, *Imperial Gran Reserva*, *Viña Vial*, *Viña Ardanza*, *Marqués de Murrieta Reserva* and *Viña Tondonia* are some of the outstanding reds from among an excellent range. *Cerro Añón* stands out among the rosés and *Monopole* and *Marqués de Cáceres* among the whites.

The young whites are good with grilled fish and seafood while the matured ones suit more elaborate fish dishes. The rosés go well with egg, pasta and rice dishes, and current year reds with oily fish and light meat. Matured reds are very versatile and, according to their age, are drunk with anything from chicken and fish to game.

From **Navarre** come very distinctive, full-bodied reds, luscious, aromatic rosés and adaptable *claretes*. Its best wines resemble those of neighbouring La Rioja. Among the reds, the excellent *Gran Vino Señorío de Sarriá*, *Castillo de Irache* and *Cirbonero* and the rosé *Gran Feudo* are all good examples of the high quality of Navarre wines.

Levante and Aragón

Spain's other great supplier of everyday wine is the area made up by Valencia and Utiel (fresh, dry whites), Yecla, Jumilla (*claretes* and reds) and Alicante (potent reds and rosés, and *mistelas* —partly fermented sweet must).

The wines of Aragón are sturdy, full of flavour and aroma and highly alcoholic, and are well-matched to the region's hearty traditional cuisine. That being said, however, local wine-producers are now complementing their traditional wines with lighter, more delicate ones— a general tendency throughout Spain to meet the changing demands of the modern market-place. The local Denominations of Origin are **Cariñena** and **Campo de Borja**.

Spain
From A to Z

ANDALUSIA

Andalusia fits everyone's romantic image of tourist brochure Spain. This is the southern belt, stretching down from the high and forbidding plateau of Castile to the shores of the Mediterranean and the Atlantic. Here, one expects every woman to be a 'Carmen' in gypsy dress, a carnation behind her ear or, better still, clenched between her teeth and a smouldering temperament to match, and every man a swaggering 'Don Juan', proud and quick to take offence, valiant and incorrigibly amorous. These type-cast images act out passion and intrigue to the rhythm of castanets, footstamping and the flamenco guitar, they drink in the heavy scents of jasmine, orange blossom and geraniums and they are never far from the terrifying shadow of the jet black fighting bull.

There is an element of truth in every cliché and in Andalusia there is so much colour and contrast, vivaciousness, variety and imagination that fact and fiction are constantly blurred. There is a special beauty about such images for Andalusia is spellbinding with its perfumes and its music. It is the home of gyspy lore, of flamenco, and of bullfighting. Bandits did once infest the rocky crags of its mountain ranges, and the majestic valley of the Guadalquivir river was a land of milk and honey to conquering Muslims and Christians in turn. As the traveller passes through isolated, whitewashed *pueblos* and explores the old quarters of Andalusia's ancient cities he will come across places and situations that should be in a tourist brochure but which mercifully remain a shared secret so far.

As befits a land that bewitches its visitors, Andalusia traces its ancestry to a mythical kingdom called *Tartessos* which is said to have exerted considerable power and to have been the height of refinement and culture. Greeks and Phoenicians made sporadic appearances in the region's distant past and then the Romans arrived and stayed. Andalusia was a jewel in the Roman imperial crown and much the same was to occur when the Muslim invaders established a glittering court first in Córdoba and then in Granada. When Granada, the last Muslim possession in Spain, finally fell to the Catholic Monarchs at the end of the 15C, it was the turn of the Castilian nobles to become ensnared by Andalusia's charms. Seville was marked out for glory as the base camp for the discovery, conquest and administration of the New World. Other favours fell elsewhere such as in Jerez where sun, soil and twisted vines combined to produce the authentic sherry wine.

ALGECIRAS Cádiz ☎ (956), pop. 97,213, *i* Av de la Marina ☎ 60 09 11, ✉ c/ José Antonio, s/n ☎ 66 31 76, ✚ 60 31 44, P 66 01 55, ⚓ Trasmediterránea (ferries to Tangiers, Ceuta and the Canaries) ☎ 65 11 59. Cádiz 121km, Málaga 133km, Madrid 712km.

Ferries depart regularly from here to North Africa across the 14km-wide Straits of Gibraltar making Algeciras, with 4 million passengers a year, Spain's busiest passenger port. At the beginning of the holiday season there is considerable congestion as Moroccan emigrants working in Northern Europe return home for their vacation. The town was conquered by the Muslims in 711 at the very start of the Arab invasion of Spain and named *Al-Djezirah*. It was not retaken by the Christians until 1344. Today, Algeciras has all the bustle of a major transit zone and shipping centre. An oil refinery and other industrial plants have disfigured its large **bay**, which has the British Crown Colony of Gibraltar at its northern end, but the *pueblos* and hills behind Algeciras are among Spain's loveliest.

- 🏨 **★★★★** *Octavio*, c/ San Bernardo, 1 ☎ 65 24 61 🛏 80 **AE, DC, V** $$$ to $$$$. Central.
- 🌑 🏨 **★★★★** *Reina Cristina*, Paseo de la Conferencia, s/n ☎ 60 26 22 🛏 135 ♿ 📺 ♦ 🏊 🚬 ≪ ९ **AE, DC, MC, V** $$$$ to $$$$$. A restful hotel in its own gardens outside the town.
- 🏨 **★★★** *Alarde*, c/ Alfonso XI, 4 ☎ 66 04 08 🛏 68 **P** **AE, DC, MC, V** $$$. Central.
- 🏨 **★★★** *Al-Mar*, Av de la Marina, 2 ☎ 65 46 61 🛏 192 ♿ **P** ≪ **AE, DC, MC, V** $$$. Andalusian decor.
- 🍴 *Marea Baja* (closed: Sundays), c/ Trafalgar, 2 ☎ 66 36 54 **AE, DC, MC, V** $$$.
- 🍴 *Mesón El Copo* (closed: Sundays), 8km from town in Palmones ☎ 65 27 10 **P** ❋ **AE, DC, MC, V** $$$. Excellent fish.

Best buys: Hand crafted textiles are sold at *T. Moya*, c/ Maestro Miguel Picazo, s/n.

Cultural highlights: One of Algeciras' few architectural ornaments is the Baroque chapel of Nuestra Señora de Europa which was built in 1704. On the town's outskirts there are remains of an aqueduct and kilns built by the Romans in an area called El Rinconcillo.

Local sights: There are Roman ruins in the ancient settlement of *Carteya*, 8km, and an archaeological museum in **SAN ROQUE**, 13km NE. Seven kilometres SE of San Roque, **GIBRALTAR** is a duty-free shopping zone with plenty of tourist attractions. A passport is required to enter the colony and
🌑🌑 there can be queues at the border during peak hours. The **Costa del Sol** (see separate entry) is little more than half an hour away.

- 🌑 **On the town:** *El Cigarrón Club*, km110 on the N-340, is a popular disco.
Sports: Golf can be played at the *Club de Golf La Cañada*, in Guadiaro, 30km NE from Algeciras along the N-340.

ALHAMA DE GRANADA **Granada** ☎ (958), pop. 5,839. Granada 54km, Córdoba 158km, Madrid 483km.
🌑🌑   This is a **beautifully situated** spa village whose medicinal waters were popular among the Romans and the Moors. Alhama's conquest by the army of the Catholic Monarchs paved the way for the 1492 fall of the kingdom of Granada and the completion of the Christian Reconquest of Spain.

- 🏨 **★★★** *Balneario Alhama de Granada* (closed: 10/11-9/6), 3km from town ☎ 35 00 11 🛏 116 **P** ♦ 🏊 🚬 🎞 ≪ ९ $$. An ideal place to rest.

Cultural highlights: The parish church was founded by the Catholic Monarchs who commissioned their outstanding architect and sculptor, Gil de Siloé, to design the tower. The monarchs also left their mark on the Casa de la Inquisición (Inquisition House) which was built in the Isabelline-Gothic style. The Hospital de la Reina shows the impact of the incoming Renaissance taste. The village preserves its Roman bridge and the ancient Moorish baths form part of the present day spa.

🌑 ALMERIA **Almería** ☎ (951), pop. 156,838, 🛈 c/ Hermanos Machado, 1 ☎ 23 47 05, ✉ Pl de Ecuador, s/n ☎ 23 72 07 and 22 20 00, ✚ 22 09 00 and 22 50 00, **P** 23 46 33, ✈ Almería, 8km ☎ 22 19 45 (Iberia, Paseo de Almería, 42 ☎ 23 09 33 and 23 84 11), ⛴ Trasmediterránea, c/ Parque Nicolás Salmerón, 26 ☎ 23 61 55 and 22 63 56, 🚌 Pl de Barcelona, s/n ☎ 22 10 11, 🚂 25 11 35. Motril 112km, Granada 171km, Jaén 232km, Cartagena 240km, Madrid 550km.

The city and its province are one of the fastest growing development areas in Spain thanks to the introduction of new agricultural techniques that have prompted a boom in fruit and vegetable exports. There is evidence that Almería was a prosperous trading centre in antiquity when Greek, Phoenician and Carthaginian traders were regular visitors to its coast. The city, which takes its name from the Arab *Al-Maryya*, meaning Mirror of the Sea, lived a golden age much later, in the 11C, when its local Muslim ruler **Motacín** encouraged poets, musicians and scientists to stay at his court. The sovereign's enlightened patronage allowed the geographer **Ibn Obeid-Bekri** to write an encyclopedia of geographical knowledge that became a milestone of learning and culture in Muslim Spain. A dependency later of the Moorish kingdom of Granada, Almería was finally conquered by the Christians in 1484.

In recent years, the use of drip irrigation and the development of cultivation under plastic has transformed Almería's economy and scenery. The area is able to produce a wide range of horticultural products throughout the year and it has been labelled the **greenhouse of Europe**. While great areas of the province are covered by what is called a sea of plastic, other parts remain the abrupt, desert land they always have been. Before the agricultural boom, Almería put its dramatic and forbidding landscape to use as a location for the European cowboy films that came to be known as spaghetti westerns.

- ★★★★ *Gran Hotel Almería*, Av Reina Regente, 8 ☎ 23 80 11 ⊨ 124 TV ⚓ ≪ AE, DC, MC, V $$$$.
- ★★★★ *Playaluz*, 6km W from town at Bahía el Palmer ☎ 34 05 04 ⊨ 156 ✦ ⚓ ≪ ✚ ♘ Ҷ AE, DC, MC, V $$$$ to $$$$$. Very quiet.
- ★★★★ *Torreluz IV*, Pl Flores, 5 ☎ 23 47 99 ⊨ 56 TV ✦ ⚓ AE, DC, MC, V $$$$. Central.
- ★★★ *Guitar Club Alborán*, c/ Alquián Retamar, s/n ☎ 22 58 00 ⊨ 103 ✦ ⚓ ♘ Ҷ $$$.
- ❘❘ *Anfora* (closed: Sundays and 17/7-31/7), c/ González Garbín, 25 ☎ 23 13 74 ✳ AE, V $$ to $$$. Seasonal cooking.
- ❘❘ *Rincón de Juan Pedro 2* (closed: Sunday nights), c/ Federico Castro, 2 ☎ 23 58 19 ✳ AE, DC, MC, V $$ to $$$. A well-established classic.

Beaches: Alternatives to the local one are the beaches of La Garrota, El Palmer and Cerrillos going W and, going E, Alquián beach and the magnificently solitary area of **Cabo de Gata**.

Best buys: Locally crafted *jarapas*, or rag rugs, and tropical fruits are a definite must —they are sold in several shops around town. For wicker and esparto crafts, go to *Cordelería Casado*, c/ General Saliquet, 4; for hams, to *J. Andalucía*, c/ Puerta Purchena, 11; for local cakes and pastries to *La Dulce Alianza*, Paseo Almería, 18, and for Spanish fashion to *Adolfo Domínguez*, c/ Reyes Católicos, 12.

Cultural highlights: Almería's main landmark is its **Alcazaba** which was built in the 8C by Abd ar-Rahman III and enlarged by Al-Mansur in the 10C. The fortress has the typical **gardens** of Hispano-Arab architecture and a keep that was added during the reign of the Catholic Monarchs. The battlements offer fine views of the city and beyond. The **Cathedral** was built in the 16C, on the site of a former mosque, to plans drawn up by the period's great builder Diego de Siloé, son of Gil, the master carver. Its fortified aspect and severity, set as it is by the old walls and near the sea, are relieved by delicate Renaissance façades designed by Juan de Orea who was responsible also for the Plateresque choir stalls in the interior. High points include the vaulting, the 18C **main altarpiece**, the marble and jasper pulpits and the magnificent sepulchre of Bishop Villarín, the Cathedral's founder. The Diocesan Museum, alongside the Renaissance cloister, exhibits paintings by Murillo and Alonso

Cano. There are more exhibits, chiefly archaeological, at the Museo de Almería, Ctra de Ronda, 91 (open: 10.00-2.00; closed: Sundays and Mondays ☎ 22 50 58).

For strolls around the town you can choose between the busy shopping area around the **Paseo de Almería**, the area called **La Almedina**, at the foot of the Alcazaba and the Castle of San Cristóbal, the gardens of the **Parque de Nicolás Salmerón** and the picturesque fisherman's quarter called **La Chanca**.

Fiestas and festivals: Almería stages a summer fair in the last week of August and a winter one in the first week of January. There is also a Flamenco *Cante Jondo* festival in the second half of July.

Local sights: The province of Almería rewards the traveller with very spectacular scenery. Taking the N-340 and then the N-324 towards Guádix, you pass through alternating barren highlands and intensely cultivated valleys.

☼ The **N-340 going NE** towards Tabernas and **SORBAS** (a ceramics centre ☼ whose products are sold at *S. Alpañés*, Barrio de San Roque, s/n), takes you through typical cowboy film scenery. The village of **NIJAR**, 34km from Almería on the N-332, once poor and arid, has been transformed by the 'sea of plastic' cultivation of fruit and vegetables. However, the village has not lost its artisan traditions of glazed pottery and *jarapa* blanket weaving. A **drive W** along the N-340 leads along clifftops overlooking the Mediterranean to **AGUADULCE** (See 'Costa de Almería').

On the town: The Paseo de Almería and especially the *El Alcázar* form the ☼ city's *tapa rendez-vous* point. The *Club Fennea*, c/ General Tamago, s/n, is a popular disco and the ice-creams at the *Heladería Italiana*, c/ Marcos, 1, are a well-established favourite.

Sports: Most water sports are practised at the yacht club, the *Club Mar de Almería*, Muelle, 1 ☎ 23 07 80, and underwater fishing at Cabo de Gata ☎ 25 32 30. Tennis fans can play at the *Club de Tenis Almería* ☎ 30 01 04.

ALMUÑECAR **Granada** ☎ (958), pop. 17,606, *i* c/ Puerta del Mar, s/n ☎ 63 11 25, ✚ 63 33 34, **P** 63 24 12, ▤ Alsina ☎ 25 13 58. Málaga 85km, Granada 89km, Almería 136km, Madrid 521km.

☼☼ This is now a cosmopolitan and fun resort on the **Costa del Sol** so its ancient name of *Sexi*, as it was known when it was a Phoenician colony, sounds plausible to modern ears. A Roman colony later and subsequently a Moorish stronghold, Almuñécar has also become a flourishing tropical fruit-growing centre.

▦ ★★★ *La Najarra*, Av General Galindo, s/n ☎ 63 08 73 ⊨ 30 **P** ✦ ⬥ ≈ ⚲ DC, MC, V $$.

▦ ★ *La Tartana*, in San Nicolás de la Herradura ☎ 64 05 35 ⊨ 6 ✕ ✦ $ to $$. It has a pleasant **restaurant** with a terrace for open-air eating.

❙❙ *Los Geranios* (closed: Wednesdays and 10/11-10/12), Pl Rosa, 4 ☎ 63 07 24 **AE, DC, MC, V** $$ to $$$. Regional cooking.

❙❙ *Vecchia Firenze*, Pl de la Fabriquilla, s/n ☎ 63 19 04 ✦ **AE, DC, EC, V** $$$. French and Italian cooking.

Beaches: Alternatives to the local one, which is pebbly, are the beaches of La Herradura and San Cristóbal.

Cultural highlights: The town's Roman remains are mostly displayed in the Archaeological Museum housed in what is called the Cueva de los Siete Palacios, the Seven Palace Cave, which were possibly stables in Roman times (open: Mondays, Wednesdays and Fridays 6.00-8.00). Parts of an aqueduct and a tower, the Torre del Monje, also survive from that period. On the slopes of the Cerro de San Cristóbal, outside the town, you can visit a Phoenician burial ground.

Fiestas: The penitential processions in Holy Week are picturesque as is the sea-borne procession on Assumption Day, August 15.

Local sights: There is a splendid 60km drive N along a local road to the **Suspiro del Moro** (see 'Granada') in the Sierra del Chaparral. After Otívar, there is a 20km **cliff-top stretch** that is particularly impressive. Taking the **coastal road W**, the road between Nerja and La Herradura gives beautiful **sea views**. See also the entry for the **Costa del Sol**.

On the town: *El Corral*, on the road to Motril, is a popular garden disco.

Sports: Water sports are practised at the local yacht club, the *Marina del Este* ☎ 64 03 50.

ANDÚJAR **Jaén** ☎ (953), pop. 34,640, ✢ 50 00 34, **P** 50 12 50. Jaén 61km, Córdoba 77km, Madrid 321km.

An important centre for the olive oil industry, set as it is among the rolling olive-covered hills of Jaén in the fertile Guadalquivir valley, Andújar has a number of 15-16C Renaissance churches and fine houses that indicate its traditional olive-based importance.

🍴 *Don Pedro*, c/ Gabriel Zamora, 5 ☎ 50 12 74 **P** ✦ ❈ AE, DC, MC, V $$ to $$$. The restaurant serves home cooking. It also has ★★★ accommodation $$.

Best buys: Basket-work is sold at *Molero*, c/ B. Martínez, 1.

Cultural highlights: The chief feature of the **Church of Santa María** is its **El Greco** painting of *The Garden of Gethsemane* which hangs in a side chapel behind a splendid wrought iron **grille** fashioned by the master craftsman Bartolomé. The church itself was built in the Gothic period and enlarged in the 18C and has a good Renaissance façade. The **Church of San Miguel**, altered in the 16C, has a distinctive ochre stone façade, an interesting 17C carved wooden **retrochoir** and another example of master Bartolomé's wrought iron grilles. The town has a number of other high points such as the 16C **Church of San Bartolomé**, the 18C Town Hall and the Palace of the Marquis of la Montilla.

Fiestas: An important and popular *romería*, a picnic and religious procession combined, takes place on the last Sunday in April, culminating at the shrine of La Virgen de la Cabeza, 32km N of town.

Local sights: The 32km drive N to the **Santuario de la Virgen de la Cabeza** goes deep into the spectacular wilderness of the Sierra Morena and offers good **views** of the area. The shrine itself was the scene of a long siege and bitter fighting during the 1936-1939 Spanish Civil War.

ANTEQUERA **Málaga** ☎ (952), pop. 40,156, *i* c/ Coso Viejo, s/n ☎ 84 21 80, ✢ 84 22 83, **P** 84 11 91, ⚑ 84 40 68. Málaga 57km, Granada 99km, Madrid 529km.

A dazzlingly white town of cobblestoned streets and old houses whose windows are well protected by typically Moorish wrought iron grilles, Antequera lies in a fertile valley and is the market town for a flourishing agricultural area.

🏨 ★★★ *Parador de Antequera*, Paseo García del Olmo, s/n ☎ 84 02 61 ⌕ 55 ✕ **P** ✦ ⅀ ⚓ ≪ AE, DC, EC, V $$$ to $$$$. A quiet, modern parador built in the style of the *cortijo*, the traditional Andalusian farmhouse.

🍴 *Lozano* (closed: Tuesdays), c/ Trassierras, 1 ☎ 84 10 93 **P** V $$$. Local cooking.

Best buys: Women's flamenco dresses can be bought at *Ríos Quintana*, c/ Lucena, 45, and cakes and sweets made by nuns, at the *Convento de Santa Clara*.

❍ **Cultural highlights:** For a bird's eye **view** of the town climb to the top of the **Alcazaba**, the Moorish fortress. This was the first important Muslim garrison to fall to the Catholic Monarchs during their campaign to conquer Granada. Among the churches, the 16C **Colegiata de Santa María la Mayor** has an ornate Plateresque façade, a fine Mudéjar coffered ceiling and a Gothic main altarpiece. The **Iglesia del Carmen**, which also has the

❍ Mudéjar coffered touch, has an excellent **altarpiece** in the 18C Churrigueresque style. The Puerta de Málaga was built by the Arabs in the 13C as the town's main gate and the Arco de los Gigantes, which is adorned with Roman inscriptions found in nearby sites, was raised in honour of Philip II in the 16C. The **Museo Arqueológico Municipal** (Municipal Archaeological Museum) is in the Nájera Palace (open: 10.00-1.30; Saturdays: 10.00-1.00; Sundays: 11.00-1.00; closed: Mondays ☎ 84 21 80), and its showpiece is the 1C Roman bronze figure called the

❍ *Efebo de Antequera*.

Local sights: Leaving town by the N-342 and turning off to the left you

❍❍ reach the so-called **dolmens** which are a series of funeral chambers dating back to 2500 BC. The chambers in the **Menga** and **Viera** caves are reached through galleries and the nearby **Dólmen del Romeral** has a chamber for offerings as well as a funeral chamber.

❍   The limestone rocks in the natural park of **El Torcal**, 16km S, have been whipped by wind into fascinating formations which you can explore along the two marked routes, one lasting 90 minutes and the other about three hours. In the Ardales area you can visit a cave setllement known as Bobastro which was used by one Omar ben Hafsun who headed a doomed rebellion of Christian and Mozarabic rebels against the Caliphate of Córdoba. Nearby, **CARRATRACA** still maintains a spa that has seen better days: it once counted among its clients Lord Byron, Alexandre Dumas and the Spanish beauty, Eugenia de Montijo, who married Napoleon III of France. The **Parque Natural del Chorro** has an impressive gorge and a series of blue lakes that mark the early stages of the Guadalhorce river.

   ARCHIDONA, 20km NE, has an especially picturesque 18C square, the Pl

❍❍ Ochavada. To make a round trip that will include good **views** of the port of Málaga and the Mediterranean from the Puerto de León mountain pass, take

❍ the **Antequera to Málaga** 62km route along the N-342, N-331, C-340 and C-345.

   ARACENA **Huelva** ☎ (955), pop. 6,664, **P** 11 02 32. Seville 72km, Huelva 108km, Madrid 504km.
   This extremely pleasant mountain village is set in the bracing Sierra de Huelva. A Templar castle lends an historic touch and caves and grottoes draw the tourists.
   ▥ ★★ *Sierra de Aracena*, Gran Vía, 21 ☎ 11 07 75 ⇢ 30 **P** V $$. Modern and comfortable.

❍ ¶¶ *Casas*, Pl San Pedro ☎ 11 00 44 **P** V $$ to $$$. Local cooking and Andalusian decor.

Cultural highlights: The castle's church, built on the site of a former mosque, has a tower decorated with typical diamond patterns, and the church of the Convento del Carmen and the Iglesia de la Asunción have

❍❍ altarpieces that are worth inspecting. The caves, called the **Gruta de las Maravillas** (open in summer: 11.00-7.00; winter: 10.00-6.00) are rich in ore deposits which have coloured the stalactites green, blue and pink.

❍ **Local sights:** Driving S, the **Sierra de Aracena** becomes very wild country. The roads wind their way through sometimes dense holm oak and eucalyptus forests and past isolated villages. It comes as a surprise to hit civilization again at **MINAS DE RIO TINTO** where there are houses that would not look out of place in suburban England. These buildings were put up for the British engineers who developed the local open cast copper mines in the 19C. Ore has been extracted from the Río Tinto area since before the Romans and the place, peppered with craters, looks as if it has survived salvoes of meteorites down the centuries. The most prized inhabitant of this sierra is the local semi-wild, acorn-eating pig of the *pata negra*, or black leg, variety which provides what are generally considered to be the best **hams** in Spain. The village of **JABUGO**, W of Aracena, is the centre of the ham industry and provides the trade mark for this delicacy. *Jamón de Jabugo* can be bought at *Romero Delgado*, c/ Toledo, 3 and at *Sánchez Romero Carvajal* just outside the village.

ARCOS DE LA FRONTERA Cádiz ☎(956), pop. 26,095, ✉ 70 15 60, ♁ 70 03 55, **P** 70 16 52, 🚌 Transportes Generales Comes ☎ 70 20 15. Cádiz 66km, Ronda 86km, Seville 91km, Madrid 584km.

The town is a landmark on the *Ruta de los Pueblos Blancos*, the itinerary that takes the traveller through a succession of glittering white villages, and it is as **picturesque** as any of its peers. It used to be a frontier town on the border of the old Muslim kingdom of Granada and was defended as much by its castle as by its **position** atop a rock overlooking the Guadalete river.

🛏 **★★★** *Parador Casa del Corregidor*, Pl de España, s/n ☎ 70 05 00 🛏 24 **P** ❖ 🏊 « AE, DC, EC, V $$$$. A fine old building magnificently situated on the cliff top.

🍽 *Mesón del Brigadier* (closed: June), on the shore of the Arcos lake ☎ 70 10 03 **P** ❖ AE, DC, V $$$. Home cooking.

Cultural highlights: As in so many small Andalusian towns, there is pleasure enough in just seeing Arcos from a distance, such as from the road to El Bosque that borders the reservoir, and in walking around its old streets when the sun begins to set. The 16C **Church of Santa María** has a good **Plateresque W door** and an 18C tower, and houses a number of Baroque paintings. The remains of the castle are near the Plaza Mayor and the Gothic **Church of San Pedro**, with its interesting Renaissance altarpiece, is hidden among a labyrinth of whitewashed alleyways and stands on the edge of the precipice.

Fiestas: The solemn **Holy Week** processions are followed by an extremely festive Easter Sunday celebration, the high point of which is the release of a fully grown fighting bull, called the *Toro del Aleluya*, that careers dangerously around the town.

Sports: There is hunting in the nearby **Parque Natural Macizo de Grazalema** and the **Reserva Nacional de Caza Cortes de la Frontera** game reserves, and water sports are practised in the Arcos lake.

AYAMONTE Huelva ☎ (955), pop. 16,775, ♁ 32 15 40, **P** 32 09 50, ⚓ Ayamonte Vila Real (Portugal). Huelva 60km, Madrid 684km.

Ayamonte is an old frontier town on the estuary of the Guadiana river that marks the border with Portugal. A bridge just N of Ayamonte linking Spain and Portugal is due to open in 1991 but the frontier crossing at present is cumbersome and by way of ferry boats. Ayamonte's old quarter, called **La Villa**, away from the crowded ferry jetties, has a distinct *pueblo* charm and boasts a couple of old churches, the 13C Church of El Salvador and the 16C Church of San Francisco. The light here, typically of Huelva's Costa de la Luz, is dazzling and the sunsets over the estuary are a wonderful sight from the garden of the parador. Splash insect repellent on yourself at nightfall because the mosquitoes come out in force in summer.

◐ ▥ ★★★ *Parador Costa de la Luz,* El Castillito ☎ 32 07 00 ⇌ 20 **P** ✦
 ⚲ « AE, DC, EC, V $$$ to $$$$. There are splendid **views** towards
 Portugal and across to the Atlantic from the hotel's gardens. The
 restaurant specializes in seafood and regional cooking.

◐ **Beaches:** Isla Canela is spacious and not yet blighted by developers.
 Best buys: Leather chaps and harnesses are sold at *J. Romero,* c/ Arrecife,
 13.
 Fiestas: The *Feria de las Angustias* is celebrated on September 7.
 Local sights: A trip along the **Costa de la Luz** and its beaches (see
 separate entry) is rewarding. The ferry trip to Portugal takes just 10 minutes
 but in summer you can wait for hours before being waved onto the boat.

◐◐ ▨BAEZA Jaén ☎ (953), pop. 14,503, [i] Pl del Pópulo, s/n ☎ 74 04 44.
 Jaén 48km, Madrid 321km.

 Hidden away among the endless **olive groves** of the province of Jaén,
 Baeza is an old cathedral town that boasts more monuments and a richer
 past than many places four times its size. The Romans called it *Baetia* and
 later, as the Caliphate of Córdoba began to disintegrate, it became the capital
 of one of the several Moorish mini-kingdoms that were called *taifas*. As the
 Castilian troops began to press down on Andalusia in the 13C, Baeza
 became, in 1227, the first important southern town to be reconquered by the
 Christians from the Muslims. By the 16C the town was important and
 prosperous. It had a university, which survived until the 19C, and a printing
 works and its nobles and church leaders competed with each other in
 building the fine Renaissance palaces and churches that occupy its present
 day old quarter. For students of literature, Baeza is associated with the poet
 Antonio Machado (1875-1939). This outstanding figure of Spain's
 Generation of '98 (see 'Literature') spent some time in the town teaching at its
 school and he reflected Baeza's serenity, its time-tempered stones and its
 gnarled olive trunks in his verse.

 ¶ *Casa Juanito* (closed: Sundays and 1/10-15/10), Paseo Arca del Agua,
 s/n ☎ 74 00 40 **P** ✦ ❋ AE, V $$$. Excellent local cooking. It also offers
 ★★ ⇌ 21 $$ accommodation.

◐◐◐ **Cultural highlights:** A starting point for an itinerary around the **old quarter**
 ◐ can be the **Pl del Pópulo** which is entered through the **Puerta de Jaén** that
 formed part of the old walls and the **Arco de Villalar**, a triumphal arch
 rather than a gate which was built during the reign of Charles V, grandson of
 the Catholic Monarchs and the Holy Roman Emperor who founded the
 Hapsburg dynasty in Spain. The arch is named after the Castilian town where
 Charles' imperial troops defeated the rebels who formed the so-called
 comuneros baronial revolt in 1521. The gate was installed here to put Baeza
 in its place for the town was one of the very few in Andalusia that backed the
 rebellion against the new monarch and his northern European officials. On
 the square stands the building called the **Antigua Carnicería**, the old
 butcher's shop, which first opened its doors for business in 1550 and finally
 closed them in 1962, and the Plateresque façade of the courthouse, the
 Casa del Pópulo. The square's fountain was built with remains from the
 nearby Roman site of Cástulo. The **Pl de Santa María** is the Cathedral
 square: the walls of the old Seminary (1660) are on its left, as you enter by
 the Cuesta de San Gil, and the arch and **fountain** in its centre were built in
 the reign of Philip II, son of Charles V. Adjoining the cathedral is the building
 called the **Casas Consistoriales Altas**, adorned with the coats of arms of
 Joan the Mad and Philip of Burgundy, the Handsome, Charles's parents. The
 ◐ **Cathedral** is outstandingly beautiful: the interior was almost entirely
 reconstructed in the late 16C in the Renaissance style and has lovely

chapels and a Gothic cloister. Leaving the square by the Cuesta de San Felipe, you reach the **Palacio de Jabalquinto** which has a splendid **façade** in the Isabelline style of the Catholic Queen that is attributed to Juan Guas. Nearby stands the 16C **University** which has an elegant patio and good Mudéjar panelling in its Assembly Hall. Be sure to explore the web of well-restored small streets behind the cathedral and the clutch of historic buildings, convents and palaces around the **Town Hall** and Baeza's agreeable little park. The town offers a wide range of examples of Spanish architectural styles of the 16C and the 17C —the enthusiast can trace the impact of the Renaissance and the development of the so-called Plateresque. The **Church of San Andrés**, which stands a bit back from the town centre, has, for example, a fine **S door** in the Plateresque style and it also contains a good collection of **Gothic panels**, while the 16C **Palacio de Montemar** has fine Gothic windows and a Plateresque patio.

Fiestas and festivals: A feature of the Holy Week processions of penitents is the theatrical embrace of the articulated images of Jesus and the Virgin. In August the town hosts a **Flamenco Festival**.

Local sights: **IBROS**, 5km NW, is a picturesque walled town with several churches and a castle in ruins. For **UBEDA**, 9km NE, see separate entry.

CABRA **Córdoba** ☎ (957), pop. 20,134. Córdoba 71km, Madrid 430km.

A mountain town, called *Egabrum* by the Romans, this was the birthplace of the 19C author **Juan Valera** and provided the setting for his rural novels of Andalusian life. In June a famous *romería*, or pilgrimage, attracts gypsies from all over Spain to the shrine of the Virgin of La Sierra.

Best buys: The things to buy here are sweets and cakes made by the nuns of the *Agustinas Recoletas* convent, in the Pl San Agustín.

Local sights: The town of **LUCENA**, 9km SW, once the centre of an important Jewish colony, has several fine churches, particularly the 16C Church of San Mateo, and a long established artisan tradition. You can buy local pottery from *J. Pascual*, c/ Puente Córdoba, 14, and bronze and tin work from *L. Durán*, c/ Calrada, 51.

CADIZ **Cádiz** ☎ (956), pop. 154,051, *i* c/ Calderón de la Barca, 1 ☎ 21 13 13, ℂ c/ Duque de Tetuán, 24, ✉ 21 39 45, ✛ 25 42 70, **P** 22 81 06, ✈ Jerez, 43km ☎ 33 43 00 (Iberia ☎ 34 66 54), ⚓ Trasmediterránea, Av Ramón de Carranza, 26 ☎ 28 44 50, 🚃 Av Ramón de Carranza, 31 ☎ 22 42 71, 🚌 25 43 01. Seville 123km, Algeciras 124km, Córdoba 239km, Huelva 243km, Málaga 260km, Madrid 633km.

Founded by the Phoenicians in 1100 BC, Cádiz lays claim to being the oldest continually inhabited city in Europe. The Carthaginians turned what was known as *Gadir* into an important seaport and the town was later to be a key ally of Rome. The city's origins stretch, however, far back into the realm of myth for Cádiz is said to have been the spot where the labouring Hercules raised his pillars as he opened up the Mediterranean to the Atlantic. In the 8C the invading Muslims poured in from Africa through Cádiz to conquer Spain and the city was finally recovered by the Christians during the 13C reign of Alfonso X, the Wise.

Cádiz played a major role in the discovery of the New World and was a natural target for seamen like Sir Francis Drake who sacked the port in 1587 and thereafter boasted that he had singed the King of Spain's beard. In the 18C the city prospered greatly when it replaced Seville as the centre for the monopoly trade with Spain's American empire. At the beginning of the 19C, Cádiz was rarely out of the headlines. A Franco-Spanish fleet sailed from its harbour in 1805 and met its fate off **Cape Trafalgar** when it encountered

Admiral Nelson and the Royal Navy. The city was then gallantly to resist Napoleon and it hosted a sitting **parliament** of Spanish patriots that guided the fortunes of what Britons call the Peninsular War and what Spaniards know as the War of Independence. In 1812 the parliament promulgated Spain's first constitution, a liberal document that enshrined the principle of the sovereignty of the people. The absolute monarch Ferdinand VII, who returned to Spain from exile in France in 1814, gave the idealistic Cádiz legislators short shrift but their constitution was to remain a landmark in Spanish history.

Cádiz, today, is an industrial and commercial city whose old quarter, standing on a rocky promontory, shows signs of wear and tear. Its deep water **bay** remains an important fishing and shipbuilding centre and its Atlantic beaches have become established tourist resorts. Its famous sons this century have included the musician **Manuel de Falla** and the poet **Rafael Alberti**.

- ★★★ *Atlántico* (linked to the Parador network), c/ Parque Genovés, 9 ☎ 21 23 01 ⊨ 153 ✕ � 🅿 ✦ ⚓ « AE, DC, EC, V $$$$. Excellent sea views and a good restaurant.
- ★★★ *Francia y París*, Pl San Francisco, 2 ☎ 22 23 48 ⊨ 69 **AE, DC, EC, V** $$ to $$$.
- ★★★ *Isecotel*, Paseo Marítimo, s/n ☎ 25 54 01 ⊨ 30 ✕ « **AE, DC, EC, V** $$$.
- ¶ *El Anteojo*, c/ Alameda Apodaca, 22 ☎ 21 36 39 ✦ ❄ « **AE, V** $$$.
- ¶ *El Faro*, c/ San Félix, 15 ☎ 21 10 68 ❄ **AE, DC, EC, V** $$$. Regional cooking and *nouvelle cuisine*.

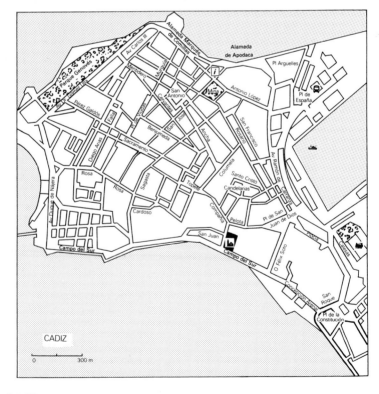

CADIZ

0   300 m

❅ *Mesón del Duque*, Paseo Marítimo, 12 ☎ 28 10 87 ✳ AE, DC, MC, V $$$.

❅ *Ventorrillo del Chato* (closed: Sunday nights), km647 on the N-IV ☎ 25 00 25 🅿 AE, DC, V $$$. An 18C tavern, mercifully unspoilt.

Best buys: Antiques can be bought from *Belle Epoque*, c/ Antonio López, 2; cakes and sweets from the convent of the *Carmelitas Descalzas*, c/ Costa Rica, 4, and *La Camelia*, Av Ana de Villa, 7.

Cultural highlights: The gate called the Puerta de Tierra used to form part of the city walls and marks the entrance to the old quarter. Cádiz's ancient past is best appreciated in its recently renovated museum, the **Museo de Cádiz**, c/ Antonio López, s/n (open: 10.00-2.00 and 5.00-8.00; closed: Saturday afternoons and Sundays ☎ 21 43 00) which, in addition to **Phoenician**, Greek and Roman remains, has an **art gallery** with paintings by Murillo, Zurbarán and Ribera and a section devoted to local customs and folklore. C/ Zorrilla leads to the city's showpiece **garden promenades** that look out on the bay, the **Alameda de Apodaca**, the **Alameda Marqués de Comillas** and the **Parque Genovés**. C/ San José leads to the 17C **Oratorio de San Felipe Neri**, a hallowed spot for many Spaniards for it was here that the Cádiz parliament met to draw up the liberal constitution of 1812. The city's history museum, the **Museo Histórico Municipal**, alongside the Church of San Felipe Neri, c/ Santa Inés, 9 (open: 9.00-1.00 and 4.00-7.00; weekends: 9.00-1.00; closed: Mondays ☎ 22 17 88), includes among its exhibits a **model** of the city as it was in its boom 18C years. C/ Sacramento leads to the **Cathedral** with its domes and imposing 18C façade. The cathedral's museum (open in summer: 10.00-1.00 and 5.00-7.00; winter: 10.00-1.00 and 4.00-6.00; Sundays: 10.00-1.00) has an impressive display of rich **church ornaments** which include a giant monstrance called the *Custodia del Millón*, so called because it is said to have a million precious stones adorning it. The Iglesia de la Santa Cueva houses Goya frecoes and the Mudéjar Iglesia de San Francisco, heavily restored in the 18C, has interesting Baroque altarpieces and carvings by Pedro Roldán.

Fiestas and festivals: Carnival time in Cádiz is non-stop music, noise and fun. There is a **Flamenco Festival** in August and a film festival, the *Muestra Cinematográfica del Atlántico*, in September ☎ 23 38 13.

Local sights: The town of **MEDINA SIDONIA**, 44km E, in addition to its general picturesqueness, has several fine Mudéjar buildings such as the Church of Santiago and the Torre de Doña Blanca, as well as a particularly good church, the Iglesia de Santa María, which has a noteworthy Renaissance altarpiece.

On the town: The star *tapa* snack in Cádiz, as in the rest of Andalusia, is *pescaíto frito*, an assortment of crisply fried fish. The local classic can be sampled all over town at places such as *Cervecería El Puerto*, c/ Zorrilla, 4, *El Candil*, c/ Javier de Burgos, 19, *El Maestrito*, c/ La Paz, 8, and *El Recreo Chico*, c/ San José, 21. Much of Cádiz's evening entertainment goes on in Puerto de Santa María (see separate entry) and the city's best dicos are on the beach promenade along the Playa de la Victoria —*La Boîte*, *Las Pérgolas* and *Sao Borja*.

Sports: Water sports are practised at the yacht club, the *Club Náutico* ☎ 21 29 91, and golf at the 9-hole, par 36 *Golf San Andrés* ☎ 85 56 67.

CARMONA Seville ☎ (954), pop. 22,765. Seville 33km, Córdoba 105km, Madrid 505km.

Carmona is perched on a high cliff and dominates a huge valley. It can be seen from miles away and looks even more impregnable close up thanks to its massive walls erected by the Romans and later rebuilt by the Muslims.

⚫️⚫️ ▦ ★★★★ *Parador Alcázar del Rey Don Pedro* ☎ 14 10 10 🛏 59 ✕ ✦ 🐟 ≈ « AE, DC, EC, V $$$$. A magnificent Moorish castle on the edge of the town with grand **views** of the valley.

Cultural highlights: A stroll through Carmona takes you through a typical network of old Andalusian streets in which noble houses with grand stonework façades jostle for space with humbler whitewashed dwellings. Carmona has more than its fair share of interesting churches: the 16C

⚫️ **Church of Santa María**, which has a Plateresque altarpiece and good

⚫️ **vaulting**, was built over an old mosque and preserves the original Muslim patio; the Church of San Felipe is a good example of Mudéjar religious architecture; the Church of Santiago was altered in the 18C but retains the 16C decorative tiles in its interior; the **Convento de Santa Clara**, another Mudéjar building, has two good cloisters; the churches of El Salvador and San Pedro are both in the Baroque style, the latter with a fine tower. A glimpse of Carmona's ancient past can be had from the archaeological exhibits on show at the Town Hall. The old quarter itself is walled and is entered through the double arched **Puerta de Sevilla** or, at its N end, the 17C **Puerta de Córdoba**. The dominant features of this enclosed part of the town are the two Moorish **Alcázares**, or castles, one of them now a parador. They were both Roman in origin and were rebuilt by the Muslims.

⚫️ **Local sights**: Well signposted on the Seville road, the **Roman burial ground** has a number of important funerary monuments dating from the 4C-2C BC and a small museum (open: 10.00-1.00 and 4.00-6.00; closed: Sunday afternoons and Mondays). A Roman amphitheatre is being excavated nearby.

The village of **MARCHENA**, 27km SE on the C-339, was an important Muslim settlement and achieved a certain grandeur as the seat of the Duchy of Arcos. The Church of San Juan Bautista, built in the Mudéjar style, has the typical coffered ceilings and panelling of that period and boasts canvases attributed to Zurbarán. The Church of San Agustín has stucco work that lends it a distinctly Mexican air. The Muslim legacy is discernible in the village's remaining walls and gateways. Marchena's flamenco festival held in July is

⚫️ known as the *Fiesta de la Guitarra* and draws the stars of the genre.

⚫️⚫️ ▨ CAZORLA AND SEGURA, SIERRAS OF Jaén ☎ (953), 🛈 c/ José Antonio, 1, Cazorla ☎ 72 01 08. Access from Ubeda along the national or the local roads to Peal de Becerro, and then along a local road to Cazorla; from the N, take the N-322 and the C-321 or C-3210.

Situated at the eastern end of the province of Jaén these mountains form

⚫️⚫️ one of Spain's top **Nature Parks**. The area is well watered and is the source of the rivers Guadalquivir and Segura which flow on to create fertile swathes across the provinces of Seville and Murcia respectively. The park is a mix of extremely rocky and inaccessible peaks, the highest of which, the Pico de las Empanadas, rises to 2,107m, and of dense valley woodlands mostly of pines that are typical of what is called the Mediterranean forest. The flora is varied and the mountains and valleys are the natural habitat of a great deal of wildlife. You should be on the lookout for golden and imperial eagles, mouflons and the Spanish wild goat known as the *capra hispanica*. The park has also a good population of deer and wild boar and fine trout streams.

The park is well served by its network of roads and forestry tracks and a number of beauty spots are conveniently signposted. Popular excursions include visits to the summit of the Yelmo mountain, 1,805m, and the sources of the Guadalquivir and the Segura rivers. Some 9km N of Villacarrillo the

⚫️ road enters a **gorge** formed by the Guadalquivir and leads to the Tranco de Beas reservoir which has facilities for sailing and canoeing. The village of

HORNOS is scenically located and if you take the road bordering the
reservoir at dusk there is a fair chance you will see the deer which come
down to the water to drink. Other beauty spots include the canyons formed
by the rivers Tus and Zumeta and their numerous cascades.

Here and there in the park traces have been found of Bronze Age
settlements. There are cave drawings in the Cueva de Parolis by the Segura
river. Nowadays the inhabitants of the sierra live in very agreeable villages
among which LA IRUELA is particularly famous for its picturesqueness. The
forestry track from this village leads to a number of panoramic lookout spots
that afford excellent views of the upland sierra's rocky circus.

The best introduction to the sierra and its park is the castle town of
CAZORLA which has a first-class parador. The town itself has two pretty
plazas and is very unspoilt. It is geared to catering for hunters and trekkers
visiting the park. A steep road leads up through the pine trees to the parador
which commands a staggering view of the Guadalquivir valley.

- ★★★ *Parador El Adelantado,*Sierra de Cazorla ☎ 72 10 75 ⇔ 33 ✕
  P ✦ ⅏ ≪ 🐎 ♪ 🅧 AE, DC, MC, V $$$$. Extraordinarily well situated and
  blissfully quiet. The restaurant, as is increasingly the vogue among
  paradors, specializes in regional cooking and serves Andalusian cuisine.
- ★★ *Sierra de Cazorla*, Ctra de la Sierra, 2km from La Iruela ☎ 72 00 15
  ⇔ 60 **P** ⅏ ≈ ≪ V $$. Peaceful, with good views.
- ★ *Mirasierra*, km20 on the Cazorla-Pantano del Tranco road ☎
  72 04 42 ⇔ 16 **P** ✦ ⅏ EC, V $. Very quiet.

Local sights: The medieval towers at PEAL DE BECERRO lend a distinctive
flavour to the village. At Toya, 7km away, evidence, including a burial
chamber, has been uncovered of a 4C BC Iberian settlement. The villages of
QUESADA and TISCAR are also worth visiting.

CORDOBA Córdoba ☎ (957), pop. 304,826, *i* Pl de Juda Leví, 3 ☎
29 07 40, **(** Pl de las Tendillas, ✉ c/ Conde, 21 ☎ 47 82 67 and 47 20 09,
⚘ 29 34 11, **P** 25 14 14, ✈ 7km ☎ 23 23 00 (Iberia, c/ Ronda de los
Tejares, 3 ☎ 47 26 95), ⇒ Av de América, s/n ☎ 22 29 88. Seville 138km,
Granada 172km, Málaga 175km, Madrid 400km.

Córdoba belongs by birthright to Spain's premier division of historic
towns and its cathedral-mosque, the **Mezquita**, rivals Granada's Alhambra as
the most important artistic legacy of Muslim civilization in Spain. The city was
already important in Roman times as the capital of the province known as
Hispania Ulterior which occupied much of the southern belt of the Iberian
Peninsula. The philosopher **Seneca** was born here and Córdobans are said
to be especially imbued with the stoicism that he taught. Other illustrious
sons were the poet **Lucan** and **Bishop Hosius**, who was to play a key role in
the early Christian Council of Nicea.

Córdoba's real zenith came in the 10C when its caliphs established their
independence from their titular overlords in Damascus and turned the city
into the glittering capital of the Muslim Spanish kingdom of *Al Andalus*. One
of the features of this period was the tolerance that existed in Córdoba
between Muslims, Jews and Mozarabs, or conquered Christians. Poets and
scientists, jurists and philosophers thronged the Caliphate's court but the
heroes of the hour were its translators, for they were responsible for the
detailed compilation and distribution of all the learning of Antiquity. The great
men of this period included the Jewish doctor **Maimonides**, the philosopher
Averroës and the poet **Ibn Hazm**, but Córdoba's real contribution was the
manner in which it became a centre of learning and culture at a time when
much of Europe was groping its way through the Dark Ages. The Caliphate
died a sudden death when the Christian armies of Ferdinand III, the Saint,

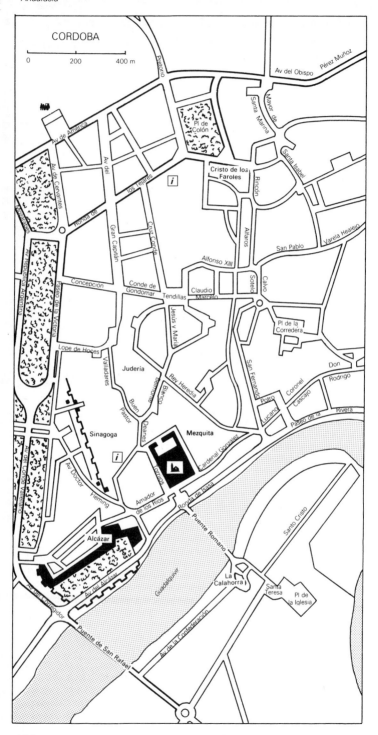

CORDOBA

0   200   400 m

conquered the city in 1236. The new monarchs built a new Alcázar, or palace, in Córdoba and reinforced the city walls but the days of glory were over and would never fully return. Occasionally Córdoba was to re-enter the limelight as when **Christopher Columbus** had a series of key meetings there with his patron Isabella of Castile, the Catholic Queen, prior to his journey of discovery. But the city gradually decayed while others, like Seville, prospered and Córdoba remained for a long time a shared secret among Romantic travellers who were seduced by the poignant beauty of its decaying heritage. Thanks largely to their recognition of its value, this heritage is now carefully preserved though much of it just in the nick of time.

▦ ★★★★ *Adarve*, c/ Magistral González Francés, 15 ☎ 48 11 02 ⋿ 103 ⅗ TV P ✦ ⅋ 📺 AE, DC, EC, MC, V $$$$$. Very central.

▦ ★★★★ *Meliá Córdoba*, Jardines de la Victoria, s/n ☎ 29 80 66 ⋿ 106 TV P ✦ ⅋ ⚭ ≪ AE, DC, EC, MC, V $$$$$. Good views of the Judería quarter.

▦ ★★★★ *Parador La Arruzafa,* Av de la Arruzafa, s/n, 3.5km from town ☎ 27 59 00 ⋿ 83 ⤬ TV P ✦ ⅋ ⅖ ⚭ ≪ ⚘ AE, DC, EC, MC, V $$$$. Good gardens and views as well as peace and quiet.

▦ ★★★ *El Califa*, c/ Lope de Hoces, 14 ☎ 29 94 00 ⋿ 46 P ⅋ V $$$$.

▦ ★★★ *Los Gallos Sol*, Av Medina Azahara, 7 ☎ 23 55 00 ⋿ 105 ⅗ TV ⚭ AE, DC, EC, MC, V $$$$.

▦ ★★★ *Maimónides*, c/ Torrijos, 4 ☎ 47 15 00 ⋿ 61 ⅗ P ✦ ⅋ AE, DC, MC, EC, V $$$$ to $$$$$. Right by the Mosque.

▦ ★★ *Marisa*, c/ Cardenal Herrero, 6 ☎ 47 31 42 ⋿ 28 ≪ DC, EC, V $$. Modern and quiet.

🍴 *Ciro's*, Paseo de la Victoria, 19 ☎ 29 04 64 ✳ AE, DC, EC, V $$$. Modern international cooking.

🍴 *El Blasón*, c/ José Zorrilla, s/n ☎ 48 06 25 P ✦ ✳ AE, DC, MC, V $$$$. Regional favourites and *nouvelle cuisine* in a rather select atmosphere.

🍴 *El Caballo Rojo*, c/ Cardenal Herrero, 28 ☎ 47 53 75 ✳ AE, DC, EC, V $$$ to $$$$. A place to go for classic Córdoba food.

🍴 *El Churrasco* (closed: Thursdays and August), c/ Romero, 16 ☎ 29 08 19 ✦ ✳ AE, DC, EC, MC, V $$$. Regional cooking served in a lovely patio.

🍴 *Oscar* (closed: Sundays and August), Pl de Chirinos, 6 ☎ 47 75 17 ✦ ✳ AE, DC, EC, MC V $$$. Fish and seafood.

🍴 *Séneca*, Av de la Confederación, s/n ☎ 20 40 20 ✳ AE, DC, EC, V $$$. Good international cooking and also local fare.

Best buys: Hand-crafted silver filigree jewelry can be bought from *J. Villar*, c/ Muro de la Misericordia, 3, and typical Córdoban embossed leather work from *C. López*, Calleja de las Flores, 2. If you are feeling peckish, try the local cakes and pastries sold at *San Rafael*, c/ Cardenal Portocarrero, 23, or those made at the **Convento Santa Isabel**, c/ Santa Isabel, 13. Local crafts hunters can buy ceramics in the Caliphate style from the cloister of the Episcopal Palace, and all sorts of arts and crafts are sold at the **Zoco Municipal**, c/ Judíos, s/n (open: 10.00-2.00 and 5.00-8.30; closed: Sunday afternoons and Mondays). Music lovers can buy guitars from *M. Reyes*, c/ Armas, 4, while antiques, copper and wrought iron work are sold at *Aguilera Punta*, c/ Encarnación, 7, and *Studio 52*, Ronda de los Tejares, 15. Spanish fashion is available at **Adolfo Domínguez**, c/ Cabrera, 4, *C. Durán*, c/ Concepción, 2, and *T. Granados*, Pl Los Carriles, 5.

Cultural highlights: The **Mezquita-Catedral**, or Mosque-Cathedral, ranks by any standard as a truly astonishing building. Nobody can ever become quite used to the sensation on entering it of finding himself among an endless forest of columns and archways. The fact that a Renaissance cathedral should have been plonked into the middle of it seems outrageous, though one grudgingly recognizes its symbolic importance for the Christian conquerors.

The Mosque was built on the site of an old Visigothic church and was enlarged and beautified by stages. Abd ar-Rahman I had the initial naves built in 785 and in the following century Abd ar-Rahman II extended the wall known as the *quibla* that faces Mecca and added a minaret. In 951, Abd ar-Rahman III had another minaret built and his successor al-Hakam II extended the naves still further, this time towards the river. The Mosque was the greatest ornament in the jewel-rich Caliphate when the Christians arrived in the 13C and set about changing it into a church. Alfonso X, the Wise, built the Christian Capilla Mayor which is alongside the later **Royal Chapel** (1260). In 1523 the city authorities, embarrassed by the fact that their town had a mosque instead of the grand Gothic edifice that graced every other place of importance in Golden Age Spain, decided to build a cathedral among the forest of columns. Things could have been worse for few then would have turned a hair had Córdoba's notables decided that the Mosque should have been reduced to rubble to make way for the new Christian building.

Built at different periods, the Mosque has richer and more dazzling ornamentation in some areas than in others. The part called the *mihrab* is probably the most memorable and the horseshoe arched doorway now called the **Puerta de San Esteban** is the oldest entrance to the Mosque and arguably the most beautiful. The Mosque, the forest of columns, is however a whole and should be viewed as such. The **Christian Cathedral** for its part should not be dismissed as an outrageous intrusion for it has its good points. Hernán Ruiz and his son, the chief architects of the project, clearly strove to create something of value amidst so much existing beauty and, men of their age as they were, they combined a basically Gothic structure with rich Renaissance ornamentation. Note particularly the 18C **choir stalls** by Duque Cornejo and the two **pulpits** in mahogany, jasper and marble. It is ironic, but fitting, that the best chapel in the Christian Cathedral within the Mosque is the **Capilla de Villaviciosa**, which was in fact built in the 13C and was created by the Mudéjar artisans who had lived so peacefully and unmolested under the Caliphate. There is a small Cathedral Museum (open: 10.30-1.30 and 4.00-7.00) where some of its historical treasures are on show.

The **Alcázar de los Reyes Cristianos** (open: 9.00-1.30 and 5.00-8.00; garden night-time visits: 10.00-12.00) was built during the 14C reign of Alfonso XI alongside the Muslim Alcázar Omeya, the site of which is now occupied by the Episcopal Palace. The high points of this Christian castle include its tower, the **Torre de los Leones**, which has a Gothic chapel imbued with the severity and simplicity of the Cistercian order, and its great hall which has fine Baroque vaulting and now displays splendid 1C **Roman mosaics** and an important-looking **Roman sarcophagus** dating from the 3C. After passing through a Morisco **patio** you enter the Alcázar's **gardens** which are among its most pleasant features. Like all the gardens created during the Hispano-Muslim period these are cool and refreshing for, through a skilful combination of shade and water, they bring down the temperature by several degrees. Here you have ponds and fountains, cypresses, orange trees and myrtles.

The **Judería**, or Jewish quarter, is the labyrinth of secret looking streets that extend from the NW corner of the Mosque. It is nowadays crammed with souvenir shops but if you persevere and reach the **Puerta de Almodóvar** you will be rewarded with a great view of the city walls that used to enclose

this area. In the centre of the Judería there is a 14C **synagogue**, the only
surviving one in Andalusia (open: 10.00-2.00 and 6.00-8.00; Sundays:
10.00-1.30).

The **Museo Arqueológico Provincial** (Provincial Archaeological
Museum), c/ Jerónimo Páez, 7 (open: 10.00-2.00 and 5.00-8.00; Sundays:
10.00-1.30; closed: Mondays ☎ 22 40 11), is in a Renaissance palace the
main façade of which was designed by Hernán Ruiz, who built the Cathedral
inside the Mosque. Its collection includes examples of Iberian carvings,
Roman mosaics, a Roman **patio** and a few Visigothic ornaments but its real
strength is its collection of Moorish art. The **Museo Provincial de Bellas
Artes** (Provincial Fine Arts Museum), Pl del Potro (open: 10.00-2.00 and
6.00-8.00; Sundays: 10.00-2.00; closed: Mondays ☎ 22 13 14), is in the
Charity Hospital building founded by the Catholic Monarchs and its collection
includes works by Córdoba painters and old masters including Zurbarán,
Murillo, Ribera and Goya. Next door stands the **Museo Julio Romero de
Torres** (open: 10.00-1.15 and 5.00-6.45; Sundays: 10.00-1.45; closed:
Mondays ☎ 22 13 14) which is devoted to the work of a local artist, highly
successful between the wars, who specialized in painting sensuous *señoritas*
and did it very skilfully. The **Museo Municipal de Artes Cordobeses y
Taurino**, installed in a 16C town house on Pl de las Bulas (open: 9.30-1.30
and 5.00-8.00; closed Mondays and afternoons at weekends ☎ 22 51 03),
is a fascinating collection of bullfighting bric-à-brac. The multi-media
happening at the **Torre de la Calahorra** (open: 9.30-2.00 and 5.00-7.30;
closed: Sunday afternoons and Mondays) is an attempt through videos and
special effects to recreate for visitors the cultural and spiritual climate of
Muslim Córdoba between the 9-13C.

Córdoba has a good number of 13C churches built in the
Gothic-Mudéjar style immediately after the Christian conquest of the city.
These *fernandine* churches, so-called after the conquering monarch,
Ferdinand III, the Saint, include **San Miguel, San Lorenzo, San Pedro,
Santa Marina** and **San Pablo**. The church of **San Nicolás de la Villa**,
which has a Renaissance baptismal font, and the **Colegiata de San Hipólito**
also date from that initial period but were added to later. The Neoclassical
Iglesia de Santa Victoria is something of a stylistic rarity in Córdoba and
the former **Convento de la Merced**, which is now the County Hall or
Diputación Provincial, is spectacularly colourful and Baroque and more in
keeping with local tastes.

The best of Córdoba's **noble houses** is the **Palace of the Marquises of
Viana**, c/ Reja de Don Gome, 2 (open: 10.00-2.00 and 5.00-8.00; closed:
Wednesdays ☎ 25 04 14), which has no fewer than 14 patios. The **Roman
bridge** has been much restored but it remains a Córdoba landmark. From the
river you get the best view of the city walls, their lookout towers and grand
gates such as the **Puerta de Almodóvar**. For strolling around it is hard to
beat areas like the **Pl del Potro** which has a pleasant fountain, the 17C
porticoed **Pl de la Corredera** and the **Pl de los Capuchinos** which is made
memorable by its central crucifix, the *Cristo de los Faroles*. Strolling around
the city you will come across several Baroque monuments, known as
triunfos, in honour of the archangel Raphael, the patron saint of Córdoba.
Fiestas and festivals: May is the merrymaking month of the year with a
Cruces de Mayo fiesta that has all the usual ingredients and a very charming
competition, the *Festival de los Patios Cordobeses*, among inhabitants of
the old quarter in which prizes are awarded for the best adorned patios. The
major religious festivals, such as **Holy Week** and **Corpus Christi**, are
solemnly observed in Córdoba, and the city also hosts a biennial **National
Flamenco Festival**.

177

Local sights: The ruins of what was an imposing 10C summer residence built by Abd ar-Rahman III, **Medina Azahara**, are 12km out of town on the road to the airport. The sumptuous palace was destroyed 70 years after it was built by feuding princelings and some of its building materials were reused in the 15C **Monasterio de San Jerónimo** which is close by. Taking the road to El Brillante you reach, after 13km, **Las Ermitas**, or The Shrines, a retreat for hermits and ascetics since the 4C. The castle of **ALMODOVAR DEL RIO** stands 20km SW of the city on the old road to Seville by a picturesque whitewashed village. A further 20km along the C-431 road, the town of **PALMA DEL RIO** has some notable old buildings but is chiefly famous for being the birthplace of *El Cordobés*, the mythical Beatle of the Bullring. Taking the N-432 SE from Córdoba, **ESPEJO**, 40km away, is distinguished by a 15C castle with a particularly fine keep that was built by the Dukes of Osuna. Continuing on that road, **BAENA** is famed for its local custom of having competing bands of drummers making a deafening noise during Holy Week. The village has a 16C Gothic style church, Santa María, a convent from the same period, the Convento de la Madre de Dios, which possesses canvases by Bassano, and a third church, the Iglesia de Guadalupe, that has notable coffered ceilings. **ZUHEROS**, 8km on along a local road, is perched on a rocky hillside in the shadow of its castle and is undeniably picturesque. There is an important **prehistoric cave** called the **Cueva de los Murciélagos** 4km away (visits by prior arrangement ☎ 47 80 18).

On the town: The best *tapa* area is the Judería quarter, and favourite halting places along the route are *Casa Rubio*, c/ Puerta de Almodóvar, 5, *Casa Salinas*, across the street at No. 2, *La Mezquita*, c/ Cardenal Herrero, s/n, and, most popular of all, the *Taberna de Pepe el de la Judería*, c/ Romero, 1. There are concerts at the *Auditorio del Conservatorio de Música* and music of a different kind at discos such as *Disco 3*, km3 on the Trassierra road, *Saint Cyr*, c/ Eduardo Lucena, 4, and, for the younger crowd, *Contactos*, c/ Eduardo Dato, 8. For typical Spanish entertainment, go to a **bullfight** in season.

Sports: There is excellent hunting in the area; for information contact the *Federación de Caza* (Hunting Federation) ☎ 60 25 08 in Puente Genil or at ☎ 29 44 44 in Córdoba. Golfers can play at the 18-hole course at the *Los Villares Golf Club*, 9km from town on the road to Obejo ☎ 35 02 08.

COSTA DE ALMERIA (ALMERIA COAST) Almería ☎ (951).

This 200km stretch of coastline between Murcia's Costa Cálida to the NE and the all too well-known Costa del Sol which runs alongside the provinces of Granada and Málaga to the W is one of the less crowded and developed parts of Spain's Mediterranean shoreline. One cannot expect this state of affairs to last because the Costa de Almería has considerable potential as a resort area. The desert-like landscapes that are so characteristic of the province of Almería lend this coast a peculiar and highly original beauty and the water temperature is as high as anywhere else on the Mediterranean. Running from the fishing port and beach of Adra, a one time Phoenician settlement by the border with the province of Granada, to the **Cabo de Gata** in the W which is rubbing shoulders with the Levante shoreline, the Costa de Almería is basically flat except for the stretch where the Sierra de Gádor meets the sea.

EL EJIDO, 31km W of Almería city, is the centre of the intensive cultivation under plastic of horticultural produce for export to northern Europe and the whole of this area is, for obvious reasons, known as the 'sea of plastic'. The local tourist and leisure facilities are centred on the **Almerimar** development, 10km S, which includes a yacht club, the *Almerimar*, 35km from El Ejido ☎

48 01 34, and an 18-hole, par 72 golf club, the *Golf Playa Serena*, 25km from El Ejido by Roquetas de Mar ☎ 32 20 55. The ★★★★ *Golf Hotel*, Urb Almerimar ☎ 48 09 50 ⊨ 38 ♦ ⅏ ≈ ☂ « ٩ ┘ AE, DC, EC, V $$$$, is quiet, overlooks the golf course and has tennis courts. *El Segoviano* (closed: Wednesdays and December), Urb Almerimar ☎ 48 00 84 Ⓟ ✳ EC, V $$$, is recommended for its Castilian cooking.

ROQUETAS DE MAR, 18km SW from Almería, was until quite recently a small village of little whitewashed houses; it is now packed with apartments, hotels, bars and discos. Its **beach** has facilities for windsurfing and underwater fishing and there is golf at the nearby 18-hole, par 72 *Golf Playa Serena* ☎ 32 20 55. Hotel options include the ★★★★ *Playalinda*, Urb Playa Serena ☎ 32 31 11 ⊨ 127 ⅃ TV ♦ ≈ ☂ ▦ ♞ ▲ ٩ AE, DC, MC, V $$$$ to $$$$$, a modern hotel near the beach, and the ★★★ *Playasol* (closed: November), Urb Playa Serena ☎ 32 08 25 ⊨ 270 ⅃ ♦ ≈ ☂ ▦ ♞ ٩ AE, DC, MC, V $$$ to $$$$, also near the beach and set in its own gardens. The next resort, AGUADULCE, just 9km SW of Almería, was the pioneering tourist centre on this coast and nowadays plays host to more than 20,000 holidaymakers, the vast majority of them Spaniards, in the peak season. Hotels include the ★★★★ *Playadulce*, Av del Palmeral, s/n, Urb Playadulce ☎ 34 12 74 ⊨ 86 TV ♦ ◉ ≈ ☂ ٩, which looks onto the beach, and the ★★★ *Satélites Park*, Urb Aguadulce ☎ 34 06 00 ⊨ 300 ♦ ≈ ☂ « ♞ ٩ AE, DC, EC, V $$$, by the beach and with good views. Good fish and seafood are served at *Mesón Los Mariscos* (closed: Mondays), Urb Las Terrazas ☎ 34 00 06 ✳ $$$. From here ALMERIA (see separate entry) is approached along a **clifftop road** that gives good views of the city, its harbour and bay.

The salt flats of Cabo de Gata are home to flocks of flamingoes and other aquatic birds and are marvellous bird-watching territory. The Isleta del Moro, rocky and guarded by reefs, is a charming fishing village. SAN JOSE, 40km SE of Almería, marks the start of what is called Almería's Levante coast. It has a lovely beach and offers first class conditions for underwater fishing. Quiet, scenic accommodation is available at the ★ *San José*, Barriada San José ⊨ 8 Ⓟ ⅏ ☂ « EC, V $$$. From here on the landscape and terrain are wild, barren and arid, punctuated only by the odd cactus. A break in this oddly romantic monotony comes with the abandoned gold mines of **Rodalquilar**. From Las Negras onwards the shore is a succession of small coves, the deep blue of the sea dotted with little islands. Further N, CARBONERAS is a quiet and mostly unspoilt fishing village. It has a grey sandy beach, and bathing is better in the La Puntica and the El Ancón areas. Accommodation is available at the ★★ *El Dorado* ☎ 45 40 50 ⊨ 17 ✗ ♦ ≈ AE, DC, MC, V $$, which suits the mood of most travellers through this area for, just like the surrounding wilderness, its decor fits into the Wild West mould.

MOJACAR, 2km from the coast, is a typical Andalusian *pueblo* of whitewashed houses clinging to a hillside (see separate entry). Nearby, GARRUCHA is a fishing village that has learnt to tap the new prosperity of suntan enthusiasts and nautical sports fans. A trip inland to Vera will be rewarded by a close acquaintance with the village's curiously oriental ceramic tradition and a detour to Cuevas de Almazora is made worthwhile by its 16C castle.

COSTA DE LA LUZ (COAST OF LIGHT) Huelva and Cádiz

Running between the Guadiana river estuary in the W, which forms the border with Portugal's Algarve, and the southern tip of Europe at Tarifa in the Straits of Gibraltar, the Costa de la Luz is Andalusia's Atlantic stretch of coastline. This coast claims to have the best **natural beaches** in the whole of

Spain and it owes its name to its dazzling light. It is an area of sand dunes and eucalyptus and pine trees. The Costa is shared by the provinces of Huelva and Cádiz and its two sections are divided by the majestic Guadalquivir river which flows into the Atlantic by Sanlúcar de Barrameda. On the Huelva side of the Guadalquivir estuary lies the Doñana National Park (see 'Wide Open Spaces' and separate entry), one of the world's key wildlife reserves for it is a huge and vital rest and recreation centre for birds on their annual N-S migrations. The Costa as a whole has all the warmth and vivacity so typical of S Spain with the added ingredient of the bracing Atlantic with its ozone and tides and its summer holidaymakers are nearly all Spanish.

Lately new agricultural techniques have transformed parts of the Costa in Cádiz and especially in Huelva by introducing strawberry, asparagus and also citrus cultivation. Formerly the staple crops were olives and grapes. Inland from the Costa fighting bulls and fine horses have been bred since time immemorial. The area's original settlers are lost in the proverbial mists of antiquity. Much nearer our own day, half a millennium ago, Costa de la Luz fishermen sailed Christopher Columbus to the New World. Local wits have it he made the voyage (from the village of Palos de la Frontera) to escape from the mosquitos. These insects used to be the virtual sole drawback to the Costa but in recent years the problem has mostly disappeared. Just in case, explore this Costa with your own repellent handy.

At its W extreme, the Costa's first town is **AYAMONTE** (see separate entry) on the border with Portugal. Nearby **ISLA CRISTINA** is on a 3km-long isthmus and has an important fishing fleet. The magnificent **beach** here, in common with the majority of those on this Costa, is fairly wild and has few facilities. Best buys here include fish and shellfish from the **quayside market** and delicacies such as tuna roe and *mojama* (strongly salted dried fish), which are available from *Usisa*, Muelle de la Ribera, s/n. If you could choose the time to visit the town, you should do so on July 16, the feast day of the *Virgen del Carmen*, which is celebrated in style with boat processions and religious ceremonies. The town also celebrates a typically Andalusian fair with flamenco singing and dancing until the early hours of the morning. At other times, you can have good local seafood *tapas* at *Europa*, c/ José Antonio, 5, *Gran Vía*, Gran Vía, 16, *Marinero*, on the quayside, and *El Nido de Rodri*, c/ José Antonio 2. For a full fish-based meal the choice includes *Acosta* (closed: Mondays except in summer), Pl Caudillo, 13 ☎ (955) 33 14 20 ✳ V $$, and *Casa Rufino* (closed: Mondays except in summer), Camino de la Playa, s/n ☎ (955) 33 05 65 **AE, DC** $$$. Quiet and simple lodging is available at the ★★ *Los Geranios*, on the Isla Cristina seaside road ☎ (955) 33 18 00 ⊨ 24 **P** ✚ ⌘ ⌂ V $$, and at the ★ *El Paraíso*, Camino de la Playa, s/n ☎ (955) 33 18 73 ⊨ 35 ⌘ ⌂ EC, V $$.

LEPE, 6km inland, was founded as *Leptis* to serve as a military camp for Rome's XII legion. Its most famous son is **Rodrigo de Triana**, the local fisherman who, doing crow's nest duty on Columbus' fleet, first cast eyes on the New World. In 1515 a fleet sailed from here under the command of **Díaz de Solís** and discovered the River Plate. There is good fruit in Lepe —figs, water melons, grapes and strawberries— and a magnificent and endless natural beach called **La Antilla**. At the W end of the beach there is a morning auction of freshly caught fish on the sand. There are a number of apartments and summer villas here but accommodation is not easy to find in the holiday season unless you have made arrangements months ahead. The modest, beachside ★ *Miramar*, c/ Atlántico, 1 ☎ (955) 48 00 08 ⊨ 16 **P** ⌂ ≪ $$ is also usually fully booked for summer.

CARTAYA, an agricultural village on the banks of the River Piedras, was founded by the Phoenicians. Here, *Consolación*, on the outskirts of the village

☎ (955) 39 02 08 $$, serves fresh fish without any frills and simple stews.
EL ROMPIDO, 6km on, is a fishing village on the river's estuary which is a
natural breeding ground for various species of shellfish. As in La Antilla, and
all along this coast, there is a cluster of apartments and villas here among the
pine trees and an unspoilt and uncrowded **beach**. Again, as is the norm
along much of the Costa de la Luz, accommodation is scarce and there are
few facilities but the upside is that you can have a long stretch of sandy
beach entirely to yourself. The road continues, skirting the endless **beach**,
towards Huelva passing through the El Portil area, where the occasional
group of holiday houses breaks the wild solitude of sand dunes and pine
trees. **PUNTA UMBRIA**, the next port of call, is more developed since it has
been used as a holiday resort, principally by families from Huelva and Seville,
for generations. It has a lovely natural **beach** which borders the open sea,
and another part which gives onto the large Huelva estuary that is formed by
the Tinto and the Odiel rivers. It also has a yacht club, anchorage in the
estuary, and fishing and water skiing facilities, as well as a 9-hole golf course,
the *Golf Bellavista* ☎ (955) 31 80 83, at Aljarque. Accommodation consists
of villas and apartments, the ★★ *Ayamontino*, Av Andalucía, s/n ☎ (955)
31 14 50 ⌿ 40 ✕ ▣ ✦ ☂ ✍ AE, DC, EC, V $$, which has a good
restaurant $$$, and the ★★ *Ayamontino Ría*, Pl Pérez Pastor, 25 ☎ (955)
31 14 58 ⌿ 20 ✕ AE, DC, EC, V $$, which likewise serves simple fresh fish
and seafood. Eating alternatives include *Don Diego* (closed: 1/10-1/7), Av
Océano, s/n ▣ ✳ $$, *La Esperanza*, c/ Pérez Pastor, 7 ☎ (955) 31 10 45
✦ $$, and *Los Conductores*, Barriada de San Sebastián ☎ (955) 31 08 11
$$ to $$$. Good *tapa* bars include *Cofradía*, c/ Ancha, s/n, *Las Tinajas*, Pl
Pérez Pastor, s/n, and *Los Tarantos*, c/ M. Auxiliadora, s/n. There are
excellent ice-creams at *La Ibense* and *Los Valencianos*.

To continue the coastal drive you have to cross the Tinto and Odiel
estuaries by a series of bridges and skirt **HUELVA** (see separate entry). This
will put you back on the coast alongside the very picturesque villages of
MOGUER and **PALOS DE LA FRONTERA** which are intimately linked to
Columbus' voyage of discovery (see 'Huelva'). As before, kilometres of **sand
dunes**, pine trees and eucalyptus forests typify the whole character of this
coast. Don't expect many facilities but don't expect many people either.
MAZAGON, 23km SE from Huelva, is a Spanish family beach resort with a
good **beach** set against a backdrop of pinewoods. *Casa Hilaria* at the
entrance to the resort and *Las Dunas*, down by the beach, serve wholesome
food, and in summer *El Faro*, on Av Fuentepiña, 61 ☎ (955) 37 61 77 $$, is
the centre of a lively *tapa* bar area. The best accommodation in the area is at
the ★★★ *Parador Cristóbal Colón*, on the road from Mazagón to Moguer
☎ (955) 37 60 00 ⌿ 23 ✕ ▣ ✦ ☃ ☂ ≪ ♀ AE, DC, MC, V $$$$
—modern and tasteful, it is on a cliff top in its own gardens and has a
swimming pool and tennis courts.

A leisurely half-hour drive through more **dunes** and pines takes you to
the edges of the Parque Nacional de Doñana wild life reserve and bird
sanctuary and to **MATALASCAÑAS**, which unlike so much of this part of the
coast has been developed extensively as a tourist resort in recent years. In
contrast to the other places here there are hotels and apartments for rent and
a certain number of foreign holiday-makers, chiefly West Germans. Here you
can actually choose among the ★★★ *El Rocío* (closed: 1/10-1/5), Sector L
☎ (955) 43 03 50 ⌿ 270 ✦ ☂ ☂ $$ to $$$, the ★★★ *Flamero* (closed:
1/10-1/5), Ronda Maestro Alonso ☎ (955) 43 00 00 ⌿ 484 ▣ ✦ ☂ ☂ ♀
$$ to $$$, and the ★★★ *Tierramar* (closed: 1/10-1/5), Parcela 12 U-3 ☎
(955) 43 02 75 ⌿ 253 ✕ ✦ ☂ ☂ ♀ $$$ to $$$$. For a full meal or a
succession of *tapas* there are bars and restaurants such as *Los Galanes*,

Edif Las Begoñas ♣ $$, **Manolo Vázquez**, Edif Los Mimbrales $$, and **Da Pino** (closed: Mondays lunchtime in summer and 15/12-15/1), Av Adelfas, 1 ☎ (955) 43 02 03 ♣ DC, MC, V $$$. **El Cortijo** (closed: 1/9-30/6), aimed at the tourist market, serves meals, has horses for hire and stages

🐚🐚🐚 good flamenco in the evenings. The **Parque Nacional Coto de Doñana** (see 'Doñana National Park') seals off the costal route here and extends to the Guadalquivir estuary, thus effectively breaking the Costa de la Luz into two. To pick up the coast again you have to double back to Seville and then drive S to Cádiz.

On the E, or Cádiz side, of the Gualdalquivir, the first towns are **SANLUCAR DE BARRAMEDA** (see separate entry) and **CHIPIONA** (see 'Sanlúcar de Barrameda'). Eighteen kilometres on, **ROTA**, a sea-faring town, now serves as the Spanish-US naval base on the W edge of the Bay of Cádiz and is the main depot for the American Sixth Fleet. Its old quarter is picturesque and, thanks to the US personnel, cosmopolitan and there are a number of agreeable **beaches** in the vicinity. Nearby, 2km on the road to Chipiona, the ★★★ **Playa de la Luz**, Arroyo Hondo, s/n ☎ (956) 81 05 00 ✕ よ ♣ ⅋ ⚓ ⌖ ℂ AE, DC, EC, V $$$ to $$$$ is a quiet and well-designed Andalusian style hotel. The **Bodegón La Almadraba,** Av Diputación, 150 ☎ (956) 81 18 82 ♣ ❋ AE, DC, EC, V $$ to $$$, is a recommended restaurant. Further on, the sparkling town of **PUERTO DE SANTA MARIA** serves as a sort of

🐚 antechamber to **CADIZ** (see separate entries).

Beyond Cádiz, **CHICLANA DE LA FRONTERA** forms part of the succession of dazzlingly whitewashed small Andalusian *pueblos* that dot the shore and the countryside of Cádiz province and form what is called the *Ruta de los Pueblos Blancos*, or route of the **White Towns of Andalusia**. Chiclana lives off its fishing, its wineries and its farming. Best buys here are the almond cakes made by the nuns of the *Convento de las Agustinas Recoletas*, c/ P. Félix, 31, the egg and sugar based desserts called *tocinos de cielo* sold at the *Pastelería España* and the hand crafted dolls from *Marín*, c/ M. Herrero, s/n. Golfers take note that there is a 9-hole, par 36, golf club here, the *Golf San Andrés* ☎ (956) 85 56 67. For meals, try **El Santuario de las Carnes** (closed: Mondays and May), c/ San Antonio, 7 ☎ (956) 40 02 15 **AE, DC,**

🐚 **V** $$$. The **beach** called **La Barrosa**, 8km from town, is set against a backdrop of pines and has been spared the excesses of development. It has very fine sand and clear, clean water. Fresh fish and shellfish form the staple offerings at **Popeye**, km4 on the Chiclana to Barrosa road ☎ (956) 40 04 24 🅿 ♣ AE, DC, MC, V $$ to $$$.

CONIL DE LA FRONTERA is a picturesque old fishing village that is fast becoming a leisure centre as tourist developments spring up along its adjoining **beaches**. The village stages an annual **Flamenco Festival** towards the end of July. The place to eat fresh fish by the shore is **La Fontanilla** (closed: 1/1-15/2), c/ La Fontanilla, s/n ☎ (956) 44 07 79 🅿 ♣ $$ to $$$, and there is international cuisine at *La Gaviota* (closed: Tuesdays and 1/11-31/1), Pl Nuestra Señora de las Virtudes ☎ (956) 44 08 36 🅿 $$$. Accommodation possibilities include the ★★ **Don Pelayo**, Ctra del Punto, 19 ☎ (956) 44 02 32 ⇌ 30 ♣ AE, DC, V $$ to $$$, the ★ **La Gaviota** (closed: 1/11-31/1), Pl Nuestra Señora de las Virtudes ☎ (956) 44 08 36 ⇌ apartments DC, EC, V $$$. and, on Fuente del Gallo beach, the ★★★ **Flamenco** (closed: 1/11-31/3) ☎ (956) 44 07 11 ⇌ 84 🅿 ♣ ⅋ ⚓ ⌖ ≪ 🥅 ℂ ⌁ AE, V $$$$. It is well worth driving inland up to the **scenically**

🐚 situated hillside castle village of **VEJER DE LA FRONTERA** for this is one of the most beautiful and picturesque of the *pueblos blancos*. A stroll through its narrow, brilliantly whitewashed streets is, especially at nightfall, a delicious aesthetic experience. The Mudéjar parish church, altered and enlarged in the

16C, has a fine altarpiece and a tiled dado. **Cape Trafalgar**, the scene of Nelson's greatest and last naval victory is 14km away. Nelson's triumph spelt the end of all Spain's pretensions to becoming a major naval power. Nearby there are a couple of fairly wild beaches known as El Palmar and Los Caños de Meca.

BARBATE DE FRANCO is a flourishing fishing village and canning centre where, unsurprisingly, the fish is excellent. You can have a good meal at *Torres* (closed: Tuesdays and October), c/ Ruiz de Alda, 1 ☎ (956) 43 09 85 🅿 ✦ ❄ ≪ AE, DC, EC, V $$$, or you can buy tuna roe and sun-dried salted tuna at *El Rey de Oros*. If possible, visit the town during its *fiestas*: the day of the *Virgen del Carmen*, patroness of fishermen, is celebrated on July 16, and a popular sardine eating event takes place in August. A bit further S, 70km from Cádiz and 62km from Algeciras, **ZAHARA DE LOS ATUNES** is a small fishing village with an excellent unspoiled local beach that is served by two attractive hotels —the ★★ *Antonio* (closed: 24/11-22/12), 1km SE of the village in Urb Quebrante-Micho ☎ (956) 43 12 14 ⇌ 18 ✕ ✦ ⅖ ≪ AE, DC, EC, V $$ to $$$, a small and simple hotel with scenic views and a good **restaurant** specializing, naturally, in fish $$$, and the ★★★★ *Atlanterra*, 4km S of the village in Bahía de la Plata ☎ (956) 43 26 08 ⇌ 284 ✕ ⅄ ✦ ⅖ ⩰ ⅏ 🐎 Q 🐾 AE, DC, EC, V $$$$$ to $$$$$$, which is a large though hospitable German-designed attempt at creating an Arab-Andalusian palace. Continuing along the coast and just 10km short of Tarifa, at km68 on the N-340, comes the surprising apparition of a group of **Roman ruins**, the remains of the 1C town of *Baelo Claudia*. The site has walls, an aqueduct, a theatre, a burial ground and also evidence of prehistoric settlements (open: 9.00-2.00 and 4.00-6.00; closed: Sunday afternoons and Mondays). Alongside there is a very fine, virtually wild **beach**. The Costa de la Luz comes to an end at the entrance to the Straits of Gibraltar by the old town of **TARIFA**. Nowadays its beach is a world mecca for **windsurfers** who come from all over with their backpacks, tents and boards. The winds sweeping through the Straits require great windsurfing expertise and guarantee the best possible sport, though it can also be dangerous for children. For the more sedentary, Tarifa offers extremely good **views** of the Straits and of the coast of Africa which is plainly visible being just 13.4km away. The town has a very important place in Spain's history books for it was here that the first Muslim units landed at the start of what was to be the rapid conquest of the Iberian Peninsula in the 8C. Tarifa's **castle**, built in the 10C, was the scene of one of the most famous gestures of the long Christian crusade to reconquer Spain for it was here that a local baron, who is remembered as **Guzmán el Bueno**, refused to surrender the fortress to the Muslims even when the besiegers captured his son and threatened to kill him' at the foot of the castle's walls if the Christian resistance continued. Guzmán, so the chroniclers record, threw down his dagger from the battlements commanding his son's captors to use his blade to kill the unfortunate youth. As in other fishing towns along this coast, the best buys are canned tuna fish, tuna roe and *mojama*, sun-dried salted tuna, a delicacy which dates back to Moorish times. For a good meal, go to *Mesón de Sancho*, 11km on the road to Málaga ☎ (956) 68 49 00 🅿 ⩰ ≪ AE, DC, EC, V $$$, which also offers ★★ accommodation $$ to $$$. The windsurfing community stays, suitably enough, at the ★★ *Hurricane*, km77 on the road to Cádiz ☎ (956) 68 49 19 ⇌ 28 ✦ ⩰ AE, MC, V $$$$. The ★★★ *Balcón de España* (closed: 1/11-31/3), km76 on the Cádiz-Málaga road ☎ (956) 68 43 26 ⇌ 40 ⅙ 🅿 ✦ ⅖ ⩰ ⅏ Q 🐾 AE $$$, and the ★★ *Dos Mares* (closed: 1/11-31/3), km78 on the road to Cádiz ☎ (956) 68 40 35 ⇌ 17 🅿 ⅖ ⩰ ≪ Q 🐾 AE, EC, V $$$, are both extremely peaceful.

🐦🐦 **COSTA DEL SOL (SUN COAST)** Málaga, Granada and **Cádiz**.

This 300km stretch of Mediterranean coastline from Punta Negra in the province of Almería down to Tarifa on the Straits of Gibraltar is the most famous of all Spain's *costas*. It currently attracts some five million non-Spanish holidaymakers a year and the number is growing. The tourist invasion is not surprising. Protected by the Ronda and the Sierra Nevada mountain ranges, this part of the coast has a magnificently benign climate in winter, when temperatures remain at an average 12°C (54°F), and there is just sufficient rainfall to nourish the area's lush, sub-tropical vegetation. In summer the coast is uniformly sunny, hence its name, and hot. But the tourists also come because the Costa del Sol is supremely well equipped to cater for everyone. There are very luxurious hotels, built for the super wealthy and celebrities, and there are down market zones which aim to give package tour visitors value for money. Exclusive golf courses and yacht clubs attract one class of visitor and fun fairs and aquaparks attract another. There are top restaurants and cocktail bars and fast food places and pubs of the *paella* and chips variety. With its different appeals and attractions, the Costa del Sol has built up a huge and intensely loyal following that would not dream of spending leisure time anywhere else. The real specialists of this area also know that just a little back from the crowded coast there is an inland, timeless Andalusia of picturesque *pueblos* that is as lovely and as unspoilt as anywhere in S Spain.

At the **eastern** end of the **Costa del Sol**, **LA RABITA** is a quiet old fishing village with good accommodation at the ★ *Las Conchas*, c/ Generalísimo, 55 ☎ (958) 60 25 58 ⊨ 25 🅿 ⌾ « DC, EC, V $$ to $$$. **CASTELL DE FERRO**, 131km from Málaga, is likewise for those who prefer peace and tranquillity —★ *Paredes*, km24 on the Motril-Almería road ☎ (958)

🐦🐦 64 61 59 ⊨ 27 ✕ 🅿 ♣ ≋ ⌾ EC, V $$. The **cliff-top** road from here, with good views, leads to the equally quiet village of **CALAHONDA**, where you can stay at the ★ *Las Palmeras* (closed: 15/10-15/6), c/ Acera del Mar, s/n ☎ 62 30 11 ⊨ 30 🅿 ♣ ⌂ ⌾ DC, V $$. Continuing W, **MOTRIL** is now quite a large town (pop. 44,000) with a well developed leisure infrastructure but which is essentially the centre of a booming agricultural area which specializes in the cultivation of tropical fruits. Motril was first settled by the Phoenicians and was subsequently an important town in the Muslim kingdom of Granada. Modern Motril has a yacht club in its port area and there are a cluster of *tapa* bars and restaurants along the quayside. It has three local beaches, Las Azucenas, Poniente and Granada, which has a 9-hole, par 36 golf course, the *Golf Playa Granada* ☎ (958) 60 04 12. For accommodation in the town centre, try the ★★ *Tropical*, Av Rodríguez Acosta, 23 ☎ (958) 60 04 50 ⊨ 21 AE, DC, EC, V $$, which has a $$ to $$$ restaurant. In Torrenueva, 5.5km SE, you can stay at the ★ *Sacratif* (closed: 1/11-31/3) ☎ (958) 65 50 11 ⊨ 68 ✕ ⌾ AE, EC, V $$, and in Gualchos, 17km, you can eat at *La Posada* (closed: Mondays), Pl Constitución, 9 ☎ (958) 64 60 34 ♣ ≋ $$$, which also offers accommodation.

SALOBREÑA is extremely **picturesque** for it is a whitewashed group of houses clinging to a rock amidst a patchwork of subtropical fruit orchards. If you pant your way up its narrow streets and alleyways you will eventually emerge at its Arab castle on the crest of the hill and your exertions will be rewarded by the superb **views**. The local beach is not excessively attractive for it is of the coarse black sand type. There are two interesting hotels which are somewhat old fashioned but agreeable and comfortable, quiet and well situated —some 4km out of town and heading W on the N-340, the ★★★ *Salobreña* ☎ (958) 61 02 61 ⊨ 80 🅿 ♣ ⌂ ≋ ⌾ « ⌘ ⌗ AE, DC, EC, V $$ to $$$, and nearby but closer to town, the ★ *Salambina* ☎ (958)

61 00 37 ⌷ 13 ⅄ 🅿 ✦ ⚓ « AE, DC, EC, V $ to $$. In August Motril becomes quite a lively arts centre and its castle, which looks wonderful when illuminated at night, hosts a variety of concerts and shows. There are also a number of flamenco festivals during July and August. **ALMUÑECAR** (see separate entry), an ancient and fascinating town which has become a busy holiday centre, is the next port of call, and if you feel like making a scenically spectacular detour, try the **clifftop road** that leads to Granada by way of Jete, Otívar, Cabra Montes (from where there are splendid views), Prados de Lopera and the wooded hunting territory of El Franco before joining the N-323 at the Suspiro del Moro, the pass where Boabdil is said to have wept as he took his last, backward look at Granada.

The next stretch of the N-340 that leads into the province of Málaga and to **NERJA** (see separate entry) is particularly **scenic**. It is worth swinging inland to drop in on the unspoiled and charming *pueblo* of **TORROX**. In contrast Torrox Costa, on the coastal highway, is a jungle of highrise apartment blocks that stand cheek by jowl on the grey-black sandy beach and much the same can be said for Torre del Mar. A feature along much of the Costa del Sol is that there is a lovely village called X just back from the coast and a high density eyesore of a resort called X Costa which has sprung up alongside the crowded beach. **VELEZ-MALAGA**, slightly inland, is the capital of a district called **La Axarquía**, that has good farming, mostly olives and vines, and picturesque *pueblos* that have a distinctly Moorish air to them and are usually graced by the remains of the old Arab watchtowers. Vélez itself, known as *Menoba* in Roman times, preserves part of its old Arab castle and its Town Hall is a good looking Renaissance palace that was built for the Marquises of Vendel. The Gothic Church of San Juan has several wooden statues carved by Pedro de Mena who was probably the best and most spiritual of the army of religious sculptors that Spain produced in the 17C. The Mudéjar style church of Santa María la Mayor, built in 1487 by the conquering king, Ferdinand the Catholic, on the site of a former mosque, has a 16C main altarpiece. *Los Mayorales* (closed: September), Pasaje Pintor Antonio de Vélez ☎ (952) 50 11 84 **V** $$, is a recommended restaurant.

In the **western** stretch of the **Costa del Sol**, and after **MALAGA** (see separate entry), the notorious N-340, although technically a highway, becomes a high street and a highly dangerous one at that. It is terribly congested in the summer months and has more accidents per kilometre than anywhere else in Spain. Unless you have a helicopter, which is the Costa's celebrity status symbol, you will inevitably get caught in a traffic jam. When you do get stuck take things philosophically and think about this same stretch of road 2,000 years ago when it was a Roman Via Augusta and had chariots charging up and down it. As you drive S you will have the Mediterranean on your left and less often than you think you will catch a glimpse of the sea between the hotels and apartments. There are more hotels and apartments and villas on your right and behind them you will occasionally see the mountains that form the characteristic backdrop of the Costa del Sol. One resort follows another forming an almost continuous urban area in which speculators have often done their worst. This is Spain's concrete wall on the Mediterranean and though parts of it are a complete eyesore, others are quite appealing and even pleasant. Some developments, marinas and hotels are of course the last word in what some call taste and others term ostentation but the luxury goes without saying.

TORREMOLINOS, 14km out of Málaga (see separate entry) is like a honey pot to hordes of European, mostly British, youths who are often more interested in the discos and cheap drinks than in the undeniably well equipped beaches. It is followed, almost immediately, by **BENALMADENA** (see

'Torremolinos') which also serves the charter flight, value-for-money market. The next stop is **FUENGIROLA**, which is a halfway house between the Torremolinos youth emporium and upmarket Marbella and is also geographically halfway between the two resorts. Nearby and inland, perched 475m high, is the very **picturesque white village** of **MIJAS** (see separate entries).

Before you know it you are in luxurious, sophisticated, celebrity-conscious **MARBELLA**, the flagship of the Costa del Sol (see separate entry). The tone is set by the limousines and custom-made sports cars that cruise around and by the multi-million dollar yachts that are moored in the *Puerto Banús* marina. This is a place where the very beautiful and very talented try to rub shoulders with the very rich. Marbella, the *pueblo*, is beautifully manicured and pretty and they certainly won't turn you away from the open-air terraces when you order a drink and wait for the movie stars to show up. Gawping is the name of the game. Pushing on now along the so-called Golden Mile, past marinas and mansions and golf greens in the distance, you come to **ESTEPONA** (see separate entry) the last of the mega tourist resorts on the Costa del Sol. Just beyond it, a right turn takes you away from it all to one of the loveliest of the white villages, **scenically situated CASARES**, 16km from Estepona. This *pueblo*, clinging to a hillside, is the genuine picture postcard article and it has a ruined castle on the crest of the hill to complete the effect. It was the birthplace of **Blas Infante**, the writer and politician who is known as the father of modern Andalusian regionalism and self-awareness and was executed by Franco's forces during the 1936-1939 Spanish Civil War.

The Punta de la Chullera marks the start of the province of Cádiz's section of the Costa del Sol. The most outstanding resort and leisure complex here is **SOTOGRANDE**, one of the best in Europe with its fine beach, three golf courses —the 18-hole and 9-hole courses at the *Sotogrande* club ☎ (956) 79 20 50, and the 18-hole course at *Las Aves* ☎ (956) 79 27 75— extensive horseback riding facilities which include a polo ground, tennis courts and a luxurious marina. For accommodation, try the ★★★★ *Sotogrande*, km132 on the Cádiz-Málaga road ☎ (956) 79 21 00 ⇌ 46 ✕ ✦ ⅏ ⇌ 🎠 ♉ ⅃/ⅺ, AE, DC, EC, V $$$$$ to $$$$$$, which is an extremely peaceful base camp for golfers, polo and tennis players and those who simply like to lounge in the sun.

Going inland now, and skirting the Rock of Gibraltar, you reach **SAN ROQUE** which was a town founded by the Spaniards who fled from Gibraltar when it was conquered by Britain in 1704. There are several gourmet restaurants in this area, including *Los Remos* (closed: Sunday nights), Playa de Guadarranque ☎ (956) 76 08 12 🅿 ✦ AE, DC, EC, V $$$ to $$$$, which serves excellent fish and seafood, and *Don Benito* (closed: Tuesday), Pl de Armas, 10 ☎ (956) 78 07 78 ✦ V $$$, where the cooking is French inspired although the setting is an 18C Andalusian mansion.

From San Roque you can go up into the hills to the white *pueblo* of **CASTELLAR DE LA FRONTERA**, which was fortified by the Arabs because they rightly saw that it was a ready-made watchtower over the Straits of Gibraltar. On a clear day you have **views** of Africa and the Ronda Sierra within sight. Nearby is the vast estate of La Almoraima, said to be the biggest hunting estate in Europe. It used to belong to the Dukes of Medinaceli, one of the oldest noble houses in Spain and is now owned by the government. The one-time hunting lodge, formerly a 17C convent, has been turned into a guest house. You can stay at the ★ *Almoraima*, La Almoraima ☎ (956) 69 30 02 ⇌ 17 ✕ ✦ ⬥ ⅏ ⇌ ⅺ ⋗ 🅧 AE, V $$$$, whose facilities include the hire of four-wheel drive vehicles for exploring the estate, riding, tennis and, of course, hunting and fishing.

DOÑANA NATIONAL PARK AND WILDLIFE RESERVE Huelva and 🐚🐚🐚
Seville. Access along the Seville-Huelva A-49 highway, turning off in
Bollullos Par del Condado and taking the local road to Almonte and El Rocío.

This is one of Europe's key biological stations and bird sanctuaries for it is
the vital link for migratory birds who use it as a rest and recreation stopping
post on their N-S travels. It occupies the swampy estuary of the Guadalquivir
river and forms the border between the provinces of Huelva and Seville. You
can either make a limited visit to part of the park and its museum a few
kilometres from El Rocío ☎ (955) 40 61 40, or join one of the groups
accompanied by an official guide who are taken on a four-hour 'safari' in
jeeps. These visits are strictly controlled for the well-being of the birds is
paramount. In order to join a guided tour you should book well ahead by
phoning ☎ (955) 43 04 32. There are two tours a day (except Mondays and
during the weekend at the end of May when the *romería* to the shrine of El
Rocío takes place) and they leave at 8.30 in the morning and at 3.00 in the
afternoon (5.00 in summer) from El Acebuche, 5km from Matalascañas (see
'Costa de la Luz'). The tour consists of an 80km, often bumpy, overland round
trip that passes through the swamps, the sand dune area and the dry ground.
The swamps are the home of flamingoes and many species of water birds,
particularly geese and ducks. The **sand dunes** are an interesting natural 🐚🐚🐚
phenomenon because they are in practice moveable dunes in that they
advance inland from the beach to the dry ground. The latter area is home to
deer, wild boar, foxes and even the odd lynx. Birds of prey, including golden
eagles and vultures, are well established in this area. The tour makes periodic
stops to observe the **wildlife** and on a good day you should see a wide
range of species. This cannot, of course, be guaranteed. The nearest available
lodging is at **MATALASCAÑAS** and **MAZAGON** (see 'Costa de la Luz').

ECIJA Seville ☎ (954), pop. 34,748. Córdoba 51km, Seville 87km, Ronda 🐚
141km, Madrid 451km.

If you are passing through the town at the height of summer, be warned
that it is known as the *frying pan of Andalusia* because it is reputed to be the
hottest place in S Spain. The temperature can top 45°C (113°F) in the shade.
That said, this very old town is an extremely pleasant sight as you approach
it for it is graced by a succession of church towers that look like the minarets
that once towered over the town. As you enter it you realize that Ecija has
more fine churches and buildings than many an old city three times its size.
🏛 ★★ *Ciudad del Sol*, c/ Miguel de Cervantes, 42 ☎ 83 03 00 🛏 30 ✕
🅿 ✦ AE, DC, MC, V $$. With a **restaurant**.

Cultural highlights: The towers of Santa Cruz and Santa María are as
agreeable close up as they are from a distance. The **Church of Santiago** is a 🐚
very fine example of the Mudéjar-Gothic mix that was in vogue during the
early 15C in this part of Spain. It has a good 16C **altarpiece** and a stylish 🐚
18C tower. There seems to have been an 18C rush to build towers in Ecija
for the 15C Church of San Gil acquired one then as did the Church of San
Juan Bautista, which has arguably the most outstanding **tower** in the town.
The best among the several fine civic buildings are the 16C Renaissance-style
Palace of the Counts of Vallehermoso, the 17C **Palace of the Counts of
Benamejí**, which has a monumental Baroque façade and, dating from the
same period, the **Palace of the Marquises of Peñaflor**, which has a long
façade adorned with frescoes. Roman remains dot the city and its outskirts
and there are a number of lesser 16C buildings that have withstood the test
of time.

Fiestas and festivals: **Flamenco recitals** are staged during the second half
of August, late at night when it is cooler.

ESTEPONA **Málaga** ☎ (952), pop. 31,399, *i* Paseo Marítimo, s/n ☎ 80 09 13, ✉ Paseo Marítimo, Edif Castillo ☎ 80 05 37, ✚ 80 39 98, **P** 80 10 86, 🚌 c/ Ceuta, s/n ☎ 80 10 95. Algeciras 51km, Málaga 85km, Madrid 661km.

You would hardly know it given the high rise apartments and hotels that have taken over so much of Estepona, but it is one of the oldest towns in Spain. It was an Iberian settlement and was later colonized by the Romans, who named it *Salduba*, and then the Muslims, who held the town until 1456 and knew it as *Estebbuna*. Like so many other places on the **Costa del Sol**, Estepona changed in almost a blink of the eye from a quiet fishing village into a major tourist resort for northern Europeans. There are still little backstreets that preserve the old flavour but Estepona has been pitched well and truly into the 20C. One of its latest facilities is an all-year nudist colony on the outskirts of the town. It is a tastefully designed Andalusian *pueblo*-style complex on the sea front and is called *Costa Natura*, km157 on the N-340 ☎ 80 15 00.

🏨 ★★★★ *Atalaya Park*, km168 on the Cádiz road, 13km in the direction of Málaga ☎ 78 13 00 🛏 239 ✕ **P** ✦ 🎤 🏊 ♨ ☂ 🖼 ≪ 🐎 ♀ 🚴 🎿 AE, DC, V $$$$. Very quiet, set in its own gardens and golf course and conveniently close to Puerto Banús.

🏨 ★★★★ *Stakis Paraíso*, km167 on the Cádiz road, 3km from Estepona ☎ 78 30 00 🛏 201 **P** ✦ 🎤 🏊 ♨ 🖼 ≪ 🐎 ♀ 🚴 AE, DC, MC, V $$$$. Quiet, with good views and facilities for golf and tennis.

🏨 ★★★ *Santa Marta*, km173 on the Cádiz road ☎ 78 07 16 🛏 37 **P** ✦ 🏊 ♨ 🐎 AE, MC, V $$$. Quiet, little bungalows set in a tropical garden.

🏨 ★★ *Buenavista*, Av España, 180 ☎ 80 01 37 🛏 38 **TV P** 🍽 V $$.

🏨 ★★ *Dobar* (closed: 24/12-8/1), Av España, 117 ☎ 80 06 00 🛏 39 AE, DC, EC, V $$.

🍴 *El Molino* (closed: Tuesdays and February), km166 on the Cádiz-Málaga road ☎ 78 23 37 **P** ✦ ❉ AE, DC, EC, V $$$. French cuisine.

🍴 *The Yellow Book* (closed: Sundays and 1/1-15/2), km161 on the Cádiz-Málaga road ☎ 80 04 84 **P** ✦ AE, MC, V $$$ to $$$$. A *costa* classic serving international cuisine.

Beaches: The local beach has grey sand.

Cultural highlights: The 17C parish church has a good looking Baroque tower and the Convento de los Dominicos has an ornate façade of the same period and style.

Fiestas: An Andalusian-style fair with horsemen and flamenco dancers is held at the begining of July, and in the middle of that month there are more festivities to mark the feastday of the patroness of fishermen, the *Virgen del Carmen*.

Local sights: There are Roman baths in Manilva, 20km SW, and the remains of a Roman aqueduct at *Salduba*. In the mountains, to the W, is the beautiful white village of **CASARES** (see 'Costa del Sol').

Sports: The local marina is the *Puerto Deportivo de Estepona* ☎ 80 09 54, and there is an alternative, newer, one, *Puerto de la Duquesa* ☎ 89 01 00, 13km S on the N-340 at Manilva. Golfers are spoiled for choice —they can play at the 18-hole, par 72 *Golf El Paraíso*, km173 on the Cádiz-Málaga road ☎ 78 30 00, at the 18-hole *Atalaya Park* ☎ 78 18 94, and at the 18-hole, par 72 *Golf La Duquesa*, Urb El Hacho, Sabanillas-Manilva ☎ 89 03 00.

FUENGIROLA **Málaga** ☎ (952), pop 42,758, *i* Pl España Park ☎ 47 95 00, ✉ c/ Daoiz y Velarde, 20 ☎ 47 43 84, **P** 47 31 57, 🚌 Portillo ☎ 47 40 86. Málaga 29km, Algeciras 104km, Madrid 587km.

Founded by the Phoenicians 3,000 years ago and as *Sohail*, Fuengirola later became an Arab town of some importance and the birthplace of a noted medieval Muslim philosopher, Abd ar-Rahman Ben Sohail. Up to the late 18C it was a busy coastal trading port. However, few vestiges of such a long past remain in today's resort city. Fuengirola is in the dead centre of the **Costa del Sol's** leisure heartland for it is halfway between Torremolinos and Marbella. In atmosphere, it is a mixture between package-tour crowded Torremolinos and the more select Marbella scene and has less hype and is more family orientated than either. Along its long seaside promenade high rises and open-air terraces reign supreme.

★★★★ *Las Palmeras Sol*, Paseo Marítimo, s/n ☎ 47 27 00 ⇔ 398 ✦ 🎤 ⚲ ☂ ♃ ✓ AE, DC, MC, V $$$ to $$$$. A huge complex.

★★★★ *Las Pirámides*, Paseo Marítimo, s/n ☎ 47 06 00 ⇔ 320 P ✦ 🎤 ⚲ ☂ ≪ 🎠 ♃ 📧 AE, DC, MC, V $$$$. By the beach with good sea views.

★★★ *Angela*, Paseo Príncipe de España, s/n, in Los Boliches ☎ 47 52 00 ⇔ 260 P ✦ ⚲ ☂ ≪ 🎠 ♃ AE, DC, V $$$ to $$$$. Sea views.

★★★ *Florida*, Paseo Marítimo, s/n ☎ 47 61 00 ⇔ 116 ✦ ⚲ ☂ ≪ 🎠 AE, DC, V $$ to $$$. Set in its own pretty gardens with a swimming pool right by the sea.

★★★ *Pyr Fuengirola*, c/ Lamo de Espinosa, 6 ☎ 47 17 00 ⇔ 399 ♿ P ✦ 🎤 ⚲ ☂ ≪ 🎠 ♃ AE, DC, EC, MC, V $$$ to $$$$. By the marina, its rooms are functional apartments.

🍴 *Don José* (closed: Wednesdays), c/ Moncayo, s/n ☎ 47 90 52 ✦ ❄ AE, V $$ to $$$. International cuisine.

🍴 *Don Pedro* (closed: Mondays, August and September), Pl Picasso, 1 ☎ 47 30 43 P V $$$. Basque cooking.

🍴 *El Abuelo* (closed: Sundays, November and December), Av Boliches, 11 ☎ 47 46 72 ✦ MC, V $$$. Home cooking.

🍴 *Los Marinos I* (closed: Mondays and November), Paseo Marítimo, s/n ☎ 47 62 91 ✦ ❄ AE, MC, V $$$. Fish and seafood.

🍴 *Monopole* (closed: Thursdays and July; dinners only in summer), c/ Palangreros, 7 ☎ 47 44 48 P AE, V $$$. French cuisine.

🍴 *Oscar* (closed: Tuesdays), c/ Cruz, 15 ☎ 47 35 70 AE, DC, MC, V $$$. International cuisine.

Beaches: There are 6km of sandy beaches, the best ones being **Santa Amalia**, **Las Gaviotas** and **Los Boliches**.

Cultural highlights: The **Castle of Sohail** was built by Abd ar-Rahman III in the 10C and was refortified and enlarged by Charles V in the 16C. To catch the fast vanishing flavour of old Fuengirola stroll around the quarter of Santa Fe de los Boliches.

Fiestas: The day of the *Virgen del Carmen*, July 16, is celebrated in style particularly by the fishing community, and the October *Feria del Rosario* involves street parties, flamenco and bull runnings.

On the town: Children will enjoy the *Parque Acuático*, the local aquapark at km209 on the ring road, and the small *zoo* at c/ Camilo José Cela. Adults take note that the best area for *tapas* is around the Callejón Moncayo, and the fried fish served by *Moreno* is very popular.

Sports: There is golf 3km N at the 18-hole, par 72 *Club de Golf de Mijas* and also at the heavily booked and challenging 18-hole, par 72 course of *Golf Torrequebrada*, 7km ☎ 44 27 42. Tennis players will enjoy Australian champion Lew Hoad's tennis complex, the *Campo de Tenis Lew Hoad*, 3.5km ☎ 47 48 58, which has a number of facilities including a swimming pool and a restaurant. Water sports are practised at the small marina and yacht club ☎ 47 50 84.

ꝏ ꝏ ꝏ GRANADA **Granada** ☎ (958), pop. 280,592, ⓘ Pl del Padre Suárez, s/n
☎ 22 10 22, (c/ Reyes Católicos, 29 ✉ Puerta Real, s/n ☎ 22 48 35, ✚
22 20 24, **P** 20 94 61, ✈ 15km ☎ 44 64 11 (Iberia, Pl Isabel la Católica, 2
☎ 22 14 52), ⚌ Av Andaluces, 12 ☎ 27 12 72. Málaga 126km, Seville
256km, Murcia 284km, Madrid 432km.

Granada is one of the very finest of Spain's historic cities and its
ꝏ ꝏ ꝏ **Alhambra** is one of the greatest buildings in the world. But Granada is much
more than a museum honouring Hispanic-Muslim genius and the Catholic
Monarchs' conquest of the Islamic stronghold. It is a city that has a loveliness
and a mystery all of its own. The first-time traveller to Granada will be struck
ꝏ ꝏ by the city's extraordinary **location** for it lies in the fertile vale of the Genil
ꝏ ꝏ river and has the towering backdrop of the snow-capped **Sierra Nevada**
mountains. This awesome emplacement never fails to sharpen the sensibilities
every time the traveller returns to Granada. Getting to know Granada,
however, awakens sensations of a more complex kind for it is a bewitching
city, dream-like, poetic and musical, that provokes a personal, different
response in every visitor. Some will lose themselves in the swan-song of
refinement and culture that the last Muslim sovereigns of Spain created here
for themselves. Others will hear the sound of the ancient gypsy ballads that
Federico García Lorca shaped into contemporary lyricism or the echo of the
rhythms that **Manuel de Falla** rescued and turned into musical scores.

Granada was first settled by the Phoenicians and then the Romans but it
was the Moors who marked out its destiny. When the Caliphate of Córdoba
was at its zenith in the 10C, Granada was the leisure capital and summer
residence of that sophisticated and arts-loving dynasty. When Córdoba fell to
the Christian armies in 1236, Granada was the natural refuge for Islamic
civilization in Spain. This enchanting city was to remain Muslim for more than
250 years. It bought time for itself through a series of pacts and alliances
with the Christian monarchs and Granada's rulers even went as far as helping
the Christians take fellow Muslim cities such as Seville and Jaén. The
kingdom of Granada became a court of the Thousand and One Nights,
ensnared by its own beauty.

Decadence usually accompanies an Arcadian lifestyle and so it was with
Granada. Its ruler Muley Hacén repudiated his wife Aisha when he fell in love
with the Christian maiden Zorayda. The scorned Aisha pushed her son
Boabdil into raising the standard of revolt against her errant husband and his
father. The **Catholic Monarchs**, Isabella of Castile and Ferdinand of Aragón,
were obsessed with unifying Spain under the Christian banner and they were
not the sort of people to let slip the opportunity that presented itself. Muslim
Granada's die was cast and on January 2, 1492, when Boabdil himself
handed over the keys of the city to the conquering monarchs. Isabella and
Ferdinand were thoroughly businesslike and did nothing by halves. They
called in the best masons and craftsmen in the land to build a cathedral on
the site of Granada's main mosque and decided that they would be buried in
the new cathedral's Royal Chapel. All over Granada they left their personal
stamp in the form of churches and convents, hospitals and other public
buildings. Granada thus became a monument to the extraordinary Muslim
legacy to the Peninsula and to the drive and energy of the monarchs that
created modern Spain.

ꝏ ꝏ 🏨 ★★★★ *Alhambra Palace*, c/ Peña Partida, 2 ☎ 22 14 68 ⇌ 121 ♿ ✦
♨ ⚒ « AE, DC, EC, V $$$$$. Well situated near the Alhambra.
🏨 ★★★★ *Carmen*, c/ Acera del Darro, 62 ☎ 25 83 00 ⇌ 205 📺 ♨ AE,
DC, EC, V $$$$$.
🏨 ★★★★ *Luz Granada*, Av Constitución, 18 ☎ 20 40 61 ⇌ 174 ♿ 📺 ♨
AE, DC, EC, V $$$$$.

🏨 ★★★★ *Meliá Granada*, c/ Angel Ganivet, 7 ☎ 22 74 00 🛏 221 🎤 AE, DC, EC, V $$$$$. Very central.

🏨 ★★★★ *Parador San Francisco*, in the Alhambra ☎ 22 14 40 🛏 39 ✕ ➿➿➿ ♣ ⅏ ≪ AE, DC, EC, V $$$$$. This 15C convent in the Alhambra complex is the most magical of all Spain's paradors. Booking, weeks or even months ahead, is essential.

🏨 ★★★ *América*, c/ Real de la Alhambra, 53 ☎ 22 74 71 🛏 14 ♣ ⅏ ≪ $$$. In the Alhambra, this quiet little hotel is nearly always booked up.

🏨 ★★★ *Guadalupe*, Av Alixares del Generalife, s/n ☎ 22 34 23 🛏 43 ✕ ♣ ⅏ ≪ AE, DC, EC, V $$$. Pleasantly situated behind the Generalife.

🏨 ★★★ *Juan Miguel*, c/ Acera del Darro, 24 ☎ 25 89 12 🛏 66 ✕ TV P 🎤 ➿ ⅏ AE, DC, EC $$$$. With a pleasing 19C air to it.

🏨 ★★★ *Los Alixares*, Av Alixares del Generalife, s/n ☎ 22 55 06 🛏 148 P ♣ 🎤 ≈ ≪ AE, DC, EC, V $$$.

🏨 ★★★ *Victoria*, c/ Puerta Real, 3 ☎ 25 77 00 🛏 69 TV 🎤 AE, DC, EC, V $$$.

🏨 ★★★ *Washington Irving*, Paseo del Generalife, 2 ☎ 22 75 50 🛏 68 ✕ ♣ ≪ $$$. As romantic as it ought to be.

🏨 ★ *Doña Lupe*, Av de los Alixares, 51 ☎ 22 14 73 🛏 27 Υ TV ⅏ ≈ ≪ AE, DC, EC, V $$. Well situated, with good services and facilities a cut above its official category.

🍴 *Aldebarán* (closed: Saturday nights and Sundays), c/ San Antón, 10 ☎ 25 46 87 AE, MC, V $$$. Modern cooking.

🍴 *Baroca* (closed: Sundays and August), c/ Pedro Antonio de Alarcón, 34 ➿ ☎ 26 50 61 ✳ AE, DC, EC, V $$$$. International cooking.

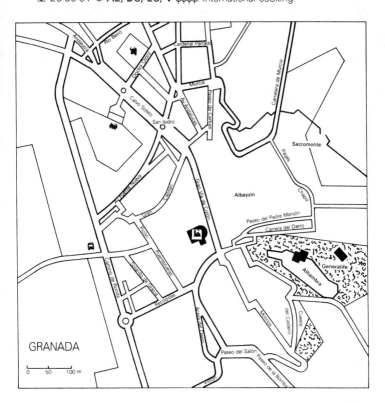

GRANADA

0   50   100 m

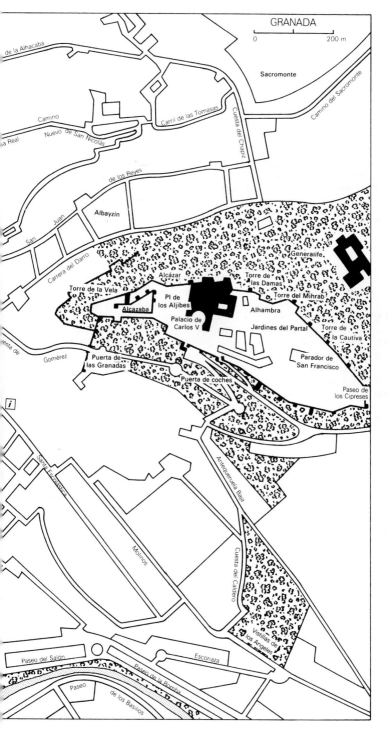

¶ **Carmen de San Miguel** (closed: Sundays), c/ Torres Bermejas, 3 ☎ 22 67 23 **AE, V** $$$. In a typical *carmen* country house.

¶ **Cunini** (closed: Sunday nights), c/ Capuchina, 14 ☎ 26 37 01 ✳ **AE, DC, EC, V** $$$. Fish and seafood.

¶ **Los Manueles**, c/ Zaragoza, 2 ☎ 22 34 15 **V** $$$. Opened as a tavern in 1917, it has not changed much, still serving good *tapas* and regional cooking.

¶ **Ruta del Veleta**, at Cenes de la Vega, km5 on the road to Sierra Nevada ☎ 48 61 34 **P AE, DC, EC, V** $$$. Charcoal grilled steaks.

¶ **Sevilla**, c/ Oficios, 12 ☎ 22 12 23 ✳ **AE, DC, EC, V** $$$. Opened by the bullfighter Lagartijo Chico in 1930..

Best buys: Arts and crafts produced in Granada and its province abound in the Albaicín quarter —you can buy typical *fajalauza* ceramics from **Cerámica M. Yedra**, Ctra Murcia, s/n; marquetry furniture and ornaments from **A. González**, c/ Cuesta de Gomérez, 16, and **V. Molero**, c/ Santa Rosalía, 8; woollen goods and textiles typical of the Alpujarra region in several shops, and guitars from *G. Pérez*, c/ Camino Nuevo de San Nicolás, 10. **Artespaña**, one of a prestigious national chain of shops, in the Corral del Carbón, also sells top quality arts and crafts. Antiques are best bought along c/ Elvira, while souvenirs and gifts abound in the Alcaicería, by the Cathedral. Cakes and local delicacies made by nuns can be bought from the **Convent of las Comendadoras**, c/ Santiago, 20, and good cured hams are sold at **Sierra Nevada**, c/ Carrera de la Virgen, 7. Spanish fashion is sold at **Adolfo Domínguez**, c/ Mesones, 57, and at **Avance**, c/ Conde Alcalá, 4.

Cultural highlights: The first stop for the visitor is, of course, the **Alhambra**. When that has been digested the cultural tour moves on to the **Cathedral** quarter. Next comes the **Albaicín** district and finally interest homes in on **Sacromonte** which belongs, more properly, to the 'On the Town' section.

The name **Alhambra** is a corruption of the Arabic *Qalat Alhamrá* meaning the Red Castle. It is more than a fortress for it was conceived and used as a complex of palaces and residences, a self-sustaining city, that was a seat of government and pleasure, labour and leisure, for the two were virtually indistinguishable. The first buildings were put up by al-Ahmar who transferred his court from the Albaicín district to the hill known as *Sabika* in 1238 in the wake of the fall of Córdoba. However, the major part of the complex was built in the 14C reigns of Yusuf I and his son **Muhammad V**. The Holy Roman Emperor, Charles V, grandson of the Catholic Monarchs and founder of the Hapsburg dynasty in Spain, shamefully knocked down part of the Alhambra to build his own residence, the **Palacio de Carlos V**, and thereupon seldom used it. A whole new appreciation of the Alhambra that rescued it from neglect and oblivion came with the sensibility of the 19C Romantic movement, and in particular of authors such as **Washington Irving** whose *Tales of the Alhambra* became an international bestseller.

The tour of the Alhambra, approached by the 16C tree-lined walk, the **Alameda**, starts at the Puerta de las Granadas doorway which was designed by Pedro Machuca in 1536, guarded on its right by the **Torres Bermejas** towers. From here you enter the older part of the complex through the 14C **Puerta de la Justicia** which leads to the 9C **Alcazaba** built by al-Ahmar and the adjoining garden called the Jardín de los Adarves which was added in the 17C. The bell tower here, the Torre de la Vela, used to ring out to signal when irrigation was permitted in the Genil vale or *vega*; nowadays it is an excellent **lookout** point. Nearby stands what used to be one of the main entrances, the Puerta de Armas. Following along the barbican the tour reaches the buildings that formed the **royal household** of Granada.

The network of palaces and residences here includes the hall of justice called the **Mexuar**, the official seat of government known as the **Palacio de Comares** and the monarch's own private apartments, the **Cuarto de los Leones**. Each building has its own patio and gardens —the **Patio del Mexuar** has a beautiful S façade, while the **Patio de los Arrayanes** is best known for its pond surrounded by myrtles— in which, according to the principles of Islamic ingenuity, flowering shrubs, fountains and artificial streams play an essential role. The most stunning patio of all is the **Patio de los Leones** which best embodies the aesthetic principles deployed throughout the Alhambra. The tour continues through a series of apartments which include the grandiose **Salón de Embajadores** where visiting delegations were received, the **Sala de los Abencerrajes** which has a domed ceiling representing a starry sky, and the smaller **Sala de los Reyes**, decorated with court and hunting scenes. This part of the tour ends at the **Lindaraja Garden** and the **Baths** which lead to another section of gardens called the **Jardines de Partal** that in turn descend, through terraced levels, to the **Torre de las Damas**, built in the reign of Yusuf I.

The tour now continues around the Alhambra's **walls and gardens** and leads to the post-Moorish part of the Alhambra. Its dual centrepiece is the 17C Convent of San Francisco, which is now a parador (book months ahead if you want to spend a night there), and the Renaissance palace that Pedro Machuca built for Charles V. The **Palacio de Carlos V**, with its circular, double-galleried patio, is as good an example as one can find of 16C civic architecture and it would be splendid anywhere else but in the Alhambra. Face to face, the swan-song sensitivity of Boabdil's forebears wins hands down against the tastes of the Renaissance new learning. The palace houses a Fine Arts Museum, the **Museo Provincial de Bellas Artes** (open: 10.00-2.00; closed: Mondays) which exhibits works of the 17C Granada school that embraced artists of the calibre of Alonso Cano and Pedro de Mena, and the **Museo de Arte Hispano-Musulmán** (open: 10.00-2.00; closed: Sundays), a museum of Hispano-Muslim art. The **Generalife** was used as a leisure garden (open in summer: 9.30-7.45; winter: 9.30-5.15; night visits by prior arrangement ☎ 22 75 27) and by the Muslim monarchs and incoporates the fountains and irrigation techniques typical of their culture. From its pavilions and terraces there are wonderful views of the Alhambra and the city.

The building of the **Cathedral**, in the centre of the town, designed by the Catholic Monarchs' architect, Enrique Egas, began almost as soon as Boabdil handed over Granada's keys but it acquired its definitive shape when the ubiquitous and highly skilled Diego de Siloé took over the design in 1528. Siloé, son of Gil the last of Spain's great Gothic carvers, was a man of the Renaissance and was determined to build in the confident, grand style of the new age. By a fortunate coincidence, another great artist, Granada-born Alonso Cano, was commissioned to add an exceptional **main façade** in 1667 as well as a series of canvases (for he was first and foremost a magnificent painter) that adorn the cathedral's chancel and sacristy. The **chancel**, highly original and richly decorated with 16C stained glass and with works by Juan de Sevilla, Bocanegra and Pedro de Mena, in addition to Alonso Cano's contributions, is the highlight of Siloé's Cathedral. The **Museum** (open: 10.30-1.00 and 4.00-7.00) contains ornaments, vestments and various works of art.

The chief interest of the Cathedral, however, lies in its annex, the **Royal Chapel**, or Capilla Real, where the Catholic Monarchs are buried together with their adored son, Prince John, who died when he was a student at Salamanca University, and their ill-fated daughter Joan the Mad and her husband Philip the Fair, the parents of Charles V. The Chapel was founded by the monarchs specifically to serve as their final resting place and the design was entrusted to Egas who built it between 1506-1517. The crypt, in its mix of simplicity (the **tombs** themselves) and grandeur (the religious artwork), is a very moving and expressive illustration of what the Catholic Monarchs were all about. Diego de Siloé and Philippe de Vigarni, who had worked together on major projects such as Burgos Cathedral, joined forces again here with Siloé carving the praying figures of the monarchs and Vigarni executing the magnificent **main altarpiece**. The **Sacristy** (open: 11.00-1.00 and 4.00-7.00) houses Isabella's **private collection of paintings** and shows what a discerning collector she was for it includes works by Memling, Van der Weyden, Boticelli and Berruguete.

Granada's **Cartuja**, or Charterhouse, Paseo de la Cartuja, on the Alfacar road (open: 10.00-1.00 and 3.00-7.00 ☎ 23 19 32) is a deceptive building for the severe Herrera-style exterior encases an explosion of Baroque exuberance within. The **church** is richly decorated with 17C Baroque stucco work and an elaborately inlaid interior, and the **Sagrario** and the sacristy, which were designed and decorated early in the 18C, are quintessentially Baroque in their almost dizzying ornamentation. The 16C **Monasterio de San Jerónimo**, c/ Rector López Argüeta, 9 (open: 10.00-1.30 and 2.00-9.30 ☎ 27 93 37), in contrast, was designed by Diego de Siloé, who would probably have disapproved of Baroque excesses had he lived 200 years later. The **church**, which has sober Gothic vaulting, houses the tomb of Gonzalo Fernández de Córdoba, who was one of the greatest of the Catholic Monarchs' officers and was known in his lifetime as *El Gran Capitán*. His tomb, in the style of his masters', is simplicity itself, but the altarpiece that faces it is an impressive Renaissance work of art.

A number of the town's churches, such as **San Juan de Dios** and **Nuestra Señora de las Angustias**, are important examples of the Baroque style but there are other earlier ones, such as the **Church of Santa Ana**, which are decorated in the Plateresque style that the Catholic Monarchs favoured and incorporate the Mudéjar artistry that was developed by the Christian master masons who lived in Muslim territory.

Moorish architectural highlights in the city include the 10C **baths**, known as the **Bañuelo**, at Carrera del Darro, and a number of buildings in the Albaicín district where part of the old walls and doorways, such as the **Elvira** and **Monaita** gates, remain. There is a one-time Nasrid leisure palace called **Dar al-Horra**, and the **Corral del Carbón** which is a unique building in Spain for it was a 14C Arab inn. The **Alcaicería** is a reconstructed Arab market place on the site of the one that burnt down last century. The high point of Christian civic architecture is the **Hospital Real**, c/ Real de Cartuja, s/n (open: 11.00-1.00), founded by the Catholic Monarchs and built by the trusty Enrique Egas. The **Casa de Castril**, c/ Carrera del Darro, 41, is a pleasing Renaissance palace that currently houses the **Archaeological Museum** (open: 10.00-2.00 ☎ 22 55 90). The **Casa de los Tiros**, Pl del Padre Suárez, is another example of the Renaissance architecture of 16C Granada, while the **Casa de los Girones** is 13C Moorish, though subsequently altered. The **Real Cancillería**, at Pl Nueva, was the government building erected soon after the Christian takeover of the city and it has a fine patio. On a different scale, the **Fundación Rodríguez Acosta**, c/ del Aire, is a typical *carmen*, the name given to the out of town country houses overlooking Granada, and it exhibits works of the 20C painter after whom the foundation is named (visits by prior arrangement ☎ 22 21 44).

Fiestas and festivals: Granada's crowded calendar starts off on January 2, when the 1492 conquest of the city by the Catholic Monarchs is

commemorated, and **Holy Week** and **Corpus Christi** are celebrated with
due solemnity. On the cultural front the highlight is the international music
and dance festival, the *Festival Internacional de Música y Danza*, in June
and July, which is part of the well established Festivals of Spain circuit ☎
22 52 01 and 22 54 41. There is also a series of classical concerts known as
the *Conciertos Románticos de Granada* that are staged in the Alhambra
from April to October and a theatre festival, the *Festival Internacional de
Teatro*, between May and June ☎ 22 84 03 and 22 36 15.

Local sights: Taking the N-323 towards the coast and then the turn off
towards Lanjarón you enter the magnificent natural scenery and hidden
valleys of **La Alpujarra** (see separate entry). Just 32km out of the city,
reached via the highest surfaced road in Europe, lies the **Sierra Nevada** (see
separate entry). An alternative **scenic route** is to head off from the N-323 on
the minor roads to Ojívar and Almuñécar which again pass through wild
mountain terrain. Any one of these trips passes close by the charming little
hotel ★★ *Mundo Nuevo*, c/ Mundo Nuevo, s/n ☎ 50 06 11 🛏 12 🅿 ✦ ⚓
🐎 ♀ $$$. When you pass by what is called the **Suspiro del Moro**, the Sigh
of the Moor, on the N-323 spare a thought for Boabdil, the last dethroned
Muslim monarch of Granada. Legend has it that it was here that he looked
back for a last glance at his beloved city and burst into tears. His bossy and
clearly insufferable mother berated him saying: *'You weep like a woman for
what you could not defend as a man.'* **MONTEFRIO**, picturesquely situated,
has a ruined Arab castle, an old church designed by Diego de Siloé and a
more modern one, the Church of La Encarnación, built by the 18C
pacemaker of Spanish Neoclassical architecture Ventura Rodríguez.

On the town: There are a number of flamenco shows called *tablaos* —a
reliable one is the *Peña Platerías*, c/ Patio de los Aljibes, 13— and there
are also flamenco parties called *zambras* that can go on all night —these are
the speciality of the gypsies living in the Caves of Sacromonte. The *tapa* bars
and drinks *rendez-vous* are concentrated around c/ Pedro A. de Alarcón and
c/ Martínez de la Rosa. Popular places include *Aben Humeya* and *Casa
Yanguas* in the Albaicín, *Casa Enrique*, c/ Acera del Darro, 8, and
Castañeda, c/ Elvira, 6. The *Auditorio de Manuel de Falla*, Paseo de los
Mártires in the Alhambra ☎ 22 82 88, is a very good concert hall and, at the
opposite pole, *Granada 10*, c/ Cárcel Baja, 13, is a popular disco.

Sports: Skiers enjoy the slopes of the *Solynieve* ski resort, 32km E of
Granada (see 'Sierra Nevada'), as do mountain climbers —for information call
☎ 25 27 55. Hunters call ☎ 25 10 04. City sports facilities include tennis
courts and swimming pools at the *Piscina Zaidín*, c/ Prolongación Padre
Damián, s/n ☎ 12 11 65.

GUADIX **Granada** ☎ (958), pop. 19,785, ✚ 66 05 66, 🚍 66 06 25.
Granada 59km, Almería 112km, Jaén 117km, Madrid 438km.

The tourist attraction here is the upper part of the town where there are a
number of cave dwellings inhabited mostly by gypsies. It was originally a
prehistoric settlement. Later the Romans arrived and called it *Acci* and later
still it was an Arab town of some importance.

Cultural higlights: Diego de Siloé had a hand in the design of the town's
Cathedral, but the towers were built in the 17C and the Baroque **façade**
was added in 1713. The **choir stalls** are particularly good and were
acquired by the Cathedral in the 18C. There is a fine 16C palace that
belonged to the Marquises of Peñaflor near the ancient walls and the
Moorish fortress. The Plaza Mayor took on its present shape in the 17C. The
cave dwellings, in the upper part of the town, are certainly picturesque with
their whitewashed walls and conical chimneys.

Fiestas: On September 6 there is a very typical *fiesta* that involves a fun-filled mock battle between the neighbours of Guadix and those of the village of Baza. Traditionally, the Guadix townspeople attempt to borrow the statue of the Virgin Mary that is revered in Baza, and inhabitants of the latter town make quite certain this does not happen.

🌑 **Local sights:** There are more **troglodyte**, and less well-known, dwellings
🌑 6km NW in the village of **PURULLENA**. Taking the N-324, **LACALAHORRA**,   🌑
🌑 17km SE, is graced by a very beautiful hilltop **castle** which is more of a palace than a fortress and was built by Italian architects in the 16C according to the Renaissance norms with a splendid **patio**. **BAZA**, also on the N-324, is an old Roman and Arab town which preserves its **Moorish baths**, the Collegiate Church of Santa María la Mayor, built in a late Gothic style, and a good 16C palace, the Palacio de los Enríquez (visits by prior arrangement ☎ 70 03 95 ext. 4). An archaeological museum is to be opened soon in the Plaza Mayor for the area is rich in ancient treasures. An Iberian bust, the *Dama de Baza*, which has pride of place today in Madrid's National Archaeological Museum, was found by chance during excavations of the Roman settlement of *Basti* on the hill known as the Cerro de Cepero. Close to Baza, in the village of **ORCE**, the remains of the oldest Stone Age man in the Iberian Peninsula were discovered recently. For accommodation, try the ★★★ *Baza*, on the road to Granada ☎ 70 07 50 ⇌ 26 $$.

HUELVA **Huelva** ☎ (955), pop. 135,427, *i* c/ Vázquez López, 5 ☎ 25 74 03, (c/ General Mola, s/n, ✉ Av Italia, s/n ☎ 24 91 84, ⊕ 26 14 15, P 24 51 35, 🚌 Damas ☎ 25 69 00, 🚍 Av Italia, s/n ☎ 24 89 02. Seville 92km, Badajoz 248km, Mérida 282km, Madrid 629km.

This unpretentious capital of Andalusia's SW province of Huelva has lost a lot of its sleepy charm and acquired a fair deal of pollution with the growth of industrial plants, particularly in the chemical and petrochemical sector. Situated on a peninsula formed by the estuaries of the Odiel and Tinto rivers, Huelva is essentially a fishing port serving a large home town fleet and lately it has also become a centre for the booming agriculture of Huelva province. In the 8-6C BC Huelva is said to have been the capital of a kingdom called *Tartessos* of which no trace remains but which some identify with the mythical Atlantis. The Phoenicians are known to have established themselves here. They named their settlement *Onuba* and began to exploit the copper and silver mines in the Sierra of Huelva, close to the source of the Río Tinto, the Red River, so called because of the hue lent to its waters by the copper. Last century, British engineers reopened the Río Tinto mines and left the dual legacy of a railway to the pitheads and a sports club, the Huelva football club, which is the oldest in the Spanish league. The Atlantis myth turned full circle when Christopher Columbus sailed from these shores on his first voyage of discovery.

🏨 ★★★★ *Luz Huelva*, c/ Alameda Sundheim, 26 ☎ 25 00 11 ⇌ 105 ⅃ TV P 🎤 ⚓ ℚ AE, DC, MC, V $$$$.

🏨 ★★★ *Tartessos*, Av Martín Alonso Pinzón, 13 ☎ 24 56 11 ⇌ 112 🎤 AE, DC, MC, V $$$.

🍴 *Doñana* (closed: Sundays), Gran Vía, 13 ☎ 24 27 73 ✳ V $$$. Fish.

🍴 *La Muralla*, c/ San Salvador, 17 ☎ 25 50 77 ✳ $$ to $$$. Refined and imaginative cuisine.

🌑 🍴 *Las Candelas* (closed: Sundays), at the Aljarque intersection on the Punta Umbría road ☎ 31 83 01 P ✳ $$$. Always crowded because of its high quality seafood.

🍴 *Las Meigas* (closed: Sundays in July and August), Pl América, s/n ☎ 23 00 98 P ♣ ✳ DC, MC, V $$ to $$$.

Best buys: The famed Jabugo hams from the acorn-eating pigs of Huelva's sierra are sold at *E. Castaño*, c/ Tendaleras, 18, and at *Los Angeles*, c/ Concepción, 17, while fresh fish, seafood and a huge variety of vegetables are available from the *Mercado Central*, c/ del Carmen.

Cultural highlights: Few, if any, provincial capitals in Spain have fewer historic monuments than Huelva. This is in part because the town was virtually levelled by an earthquake in 1755. Its two main churches, both 18C, the Iglesia-Catedral de la Merced and the Iglesia de la Concepción are of little architectural interest. The town's museum, the Museo Provincial Arqueológico y de Bellas Artes, c/ Alameda Sundheim, 13 (open: 10.00-2.00 and 4.00-7.00; Sundays: 10.00-2.00; closed: Mondays ☎ 25 93 00) exhibits Roman amphorae fished up from Huelva's estuary and other archaeological specimens as well as a collection of paintings by the 20C Spanish muralist **Vázquez Díaz**. To get a taste of Huelva's atmosphere, stroll around the pedestrian street c/ Concepción and its main square, the Pl de las Monjas.

Fiestas and festivals: The *Colombinas* festivities commemorating Columbus' departure on August 3, 1492, for the New World are a typical Andalusian fair. In December there is a Latin American cinema festival, the *Semana Internacional de Cine Iberoamericano*.

Local sights: The **Monastery of La Rábida**, 8km on the other bank of the Tinto river (open: 10.00-1.00 and 4.00-8.15; closed: Mondays ☎ 35 04 11), is the Cape Kennedy and NASA space centre of the discovery of the New World. **Columbus**, with his young son, arrived here penniless from Portugal and was given lodging and sympathy by the kindly Franciscan monks. Most important of all the prior, Juan Pérez, listened enthusiastically to Columbus' theories about a western route to the Indies and, through the Franciscan circuit, put him in touch with Isabella of Castile, the Catholic Queen. The discoverer returned to La Rábida to recruit a crew and fit out his ships in Huelva's estuary and to receive a final blessing from the monastery's fathers. And the rest is history. The monastery, founded towards the end of the 14C, is whitewashed and simple, surprisingly unpretentious about its extraordinary participation in the New World epic. There is a somewhat run-down small museum showing models of Columbus' caravelles and caskets of earth from the different nations of the American continent, and a Gothic chapel with a good coffered ceiling, but what you will most remeber from a visit here is the peace and serenity of its charming little Mudéjar cloister with its geranium pots and bougainvillea creepers. Alongside the monastery the ★★★ *Hostería La Rábida* ☎ 35 03 12 ✕ **P** ✢ 🍴 🐾 ≪ V $$, is peaceful and scenic, and has a good **restaurant** $$. La Rábida's local village, **PALOS DE LA FRONTERA**, used to have its own harbour until the Tinto river silted up. It was from here that Columbus' fleet actually sailed on August 3, 1492, having first drawn water from the well which still stands at the bottom of the hill near the 15C Mudéjar parish church, the **Iglesia de San Jorge**. Columbus' crew were mostly men from Palos and his two captains were the local seadogs, the Pinzón brothers. Today Palos has become suddenly prosperous thanks to the success of strawberry cultivation in its outlying fields. **MOGUER**, 11km NE, is an extremely pretty whitewashed village which, like its neighbour Palos, has grown forever rich thanks to its strawberry fields and is likewise well kept and hospitable. It has a very good monastery in the centre of the village, the Convento de Santa Clara, which has been restored to its Gothic-Mudéjar grandeur but it is chiefly famous for being the birth-place of the poet **Juan Ramón Jiménez**, a member of the Generation of '27 (see 'Literature') and the Nobel Literature Prize winner in 1956. The poet's house, the Casa-Museo de Juan Ramón Jiménez, at No. 10 of the street named after him (open: 10.00-2.00 and 4.00-8.00), contains part of his library and memorabilia.

The town of **NIEBLA**, 29km out of Huelva on the N-341, is spectacularly encased in **Arab walls** and you enter it through massive gateways. Continuing on towards Seville, **LA PALMA DEL CONDADO** has a pleasant Plateresque-style church dedicated to San Juan and it is the centre of the Condado wine-growing area that produces very agreeable young white wines. Beyond the wine producing village of **BOLLULLOS PAR DEL CONDADO**, having turned S at La Palma on a minor road towards the coast, you reach the very rustic *pueblo* of **ALMONTE** where good home cooking can be sampled at *El Tamborilero*, c/ Unamuno, 15 (closed: Sundays and 7/8-15/8) **V** $ to $$. The *Casino*, c/ Cepeda, 2, has an authentic Andalusian feel to it and serves good *tapas*. Almonte's proud boast is that it is the village closest to the hamlet of **El Rocío**, 11km S, with its shrine of the much revered *Virgen del Rocío*. The hamlet is virtually deserted all year round except during the week in May when an astonishing *romería*, or festive pilgrimage, brings an invasion of literally hundreds of thousands of the *Virgen del Rocío's* fanatical followers for several days of prayer, flamenco and drinking.

On the town: Top *tapa* bars specializing in seafood include *Amario*, c/ General Primo de Rivera, 18, and *Bajamar*, c/ M. Redondo, 4. *El Nido*, c/ Cardenal Albornoz, 4, serves excellent cooked *tapas* such as *rabo de toro* (oxtail), and *Las Tinajas*, c/ Alfonso XII, 5, is very popular. *Génesis*, Gran Vía, 26 and *Piranchelo*, c/ Legión Española, 2, are popular discos and *La Ibense*, c/ Concepción, 7, is Huelva's top ice-cream parlour.

Sports: Golf can be played at the *Club de Golf Bellavista*, 6km ☎ 31 80 83, and the *Golf Rústico El Higueral* ☎ 24 93 18. Water sports are practised at the *Club Marítimo de Huelva* ☎ 24 76 27.

JAÉN **Jaén** ☎ (953), pop. 102,826, *i* c/ Arquitecto Bergés, 1 ☎ 22 27 37, (c/ Roldán y Marín, 3, ✉ Pl de los Jardinillos ☎ 22 40 07 and 22 20 00, ✚ 25 15 40, **P** 25 80 11, 🚌 Pl Coca de la Piñera, s/n ☎ 25 01 06, 🚆 Av del Generalísimo ☎ 25 56 07. Úbeda 57km, Granada 87km, Córdoba 108km, Madrid 335km.

Nestling under the brow of a hill and at the foot of the Jabalcruz Sierra, Jaén is somewhat off the beaten track and is one of the least visited of Andalusia's provincial capitals. Those who do make the trip out to the town are immediately rewarded by the magnificent **vistas** of rolling expanses of olive groves. It is the most important olive producing area in Spain and its olive oil has a well deserved reputation. Occupied by the Carthaginians and the Romans it earned a measure of prosperity later as a crossroads of Arab caravan trails. It was ceded to Ferdinand III, the Saint, the Christian conqueror of Seville in 1246 and was an important base camp in the campaigns that led to the capture, more than 200 years later, of the kingdom of Granada. Briefly a silk producing centre, it slipped into a gracious decadence from the 16C onwards.

🏨 ★★★★ *Parador Castillo de Santa Catalina*, Santa Catalina Castle, 4.5km from town ☎ 26 44 11 🛏 43 ♣ 🏊 ≈ ≪ DC, MC, V $$$$. Beautiful views and typical parador comforts in a medieval castle.

🏨 ★★★ *Condestable Iranzo*, Paseo de la Estación, 32 ☎ 22 28 00 🛏 147 📺 **P** 🔔 $$$. Modern and central.

🏨 ★★★ *Reyes Católicos* (closed: 22/12-9/1), Av de Granada, 1 ☎ 22 22 50 🛏 28 $$.

🏨 ★★★ *Xauen*, Pl de Deán Mazas, 3 ☎ 26 40 11 🛏 35 **P** $$. Central.

🍴 *Casa Vicente* (closed: Sunday nights), c/ Arco del Consuelo, 1 ☎ 26 28 16 ✳ $$$. Local cooking.

🍴 *Nelson* (closed: Sundays), Paseo de la Estación, 33 ☎ 22 92 01 ✳ AE, V $$$. Classic and innovative dishes.

Best buys: Local olives and olive oil are sold at the **weekly market** held on Thursdays in the Real de la Feria. Spanish fashion is sold at *Marisa*, Av Granada, 12.

Cultural highlights: The **Cathedral**, built between 1540-1573, was the major commission undertaken by the architect Andrés de Vandelvira. He was succeeded by Juan Aranda, who designed the S door, and Pedro Roldán, one of the major carvers of the Baroque period, who completed the building's exterior by sculpting the eye-catching W door. Vandelvira's skills and tastes can best be seen in the Cathedral's sacristy which, together with the late 15C **choir stalls**, is the highlight of the church's interior. The Cathedral's most precious relic is the cloth believed to have been used by Veronica to wipe the face of Christ. Known as the *Santo Rostro*, the Holy Face, it is kept in the chapel and displayed to the public after mass on Fridays. The **Museum** has a fine collection of church ornaments. The **Church of San Andrés**, built on Mudéjar lines in the 15C, has an extremely fine and intricate **wrought iron grille** screening off the **Chapel of La Purísima**. It was fashioned by the 16C acknowledged expert of this art form, **maestro Bartolomé de Jaén**, one of whose many works adorns the crypt of the Catholic Monarchs in Granada. The Gothic **Church of San Ildefonso** has a Neoclassical façade which was added by **Ventura Rodriguéz**, a prolific 18C architect and Spain's high priest of straight lines and Doric columns.

The **Museo Provincial**, c/ Camino de la Estación, 27 (open: 10.00-2.00 and 4.00-7.00; closed: Sunday afternoons and Mondays ☎ 25 03 20), exhibits a number of rare **Iberian sculptures** and an interesting **Roman mosaic**. It also has a picture collection which includes works by Alonso Cano. The **old quarter** of the town is mostly unspoiled and a stroll through it takes you past remains of the original walls and old churches and mansions which mix Mudéjar horseshoe arches with Renaissance ornamentation. Scenically situated outside the town, the **Castle of Santa Catalina**, now a parador, was built by Granada's King al-Ahmar and restored after Jaén's capture by Ferdinand III.

On the town: The *tapa* bar area is in the c/ Nueva and around the Cathedral, while the young people's discos are around **Paseo de la Estación**.

JEREZ DE LA FRONTERA Cádiz ☎ (956), pop. 180,444, *i* c/ Alameda Cristina, 7 ☎ 33 11 50, (Pl General Primo de Rivera, 4, ✉ c/ Cerrón, 1 ☎ 34 22 95, ✛ 30 74 54, P 34 21 97, ✈ Jerez, 11km on the N-IV ☎ 33 43 00 (Iberia ☎ 33 99 08, Aviaco ☎ 33 22 10), ⬛ 34 06 37. Cádiz 35km, Seville 90km, Ronda 116km, Madrid 613km.

The wineries on the outskirts of Jerez leave the traveller in no doubt that he is entering the capital of the sherry-producing district. This is a prosperous, aristocratic and fun-loving town. With its sherry, its great landed families, its fine horses (shows at the Royal Andalusian School of Equestrian Arts every Thursday at midday ☎ 31 11 11), fighting bulls, flamenco and *fiestas* it is quintessentially Andalusian. Early in the last century a number of British and French merchants settled in the town to develop the sherry and brandy trade; they were rapidly absorbed into the wealthy Andalusian landed class and their oddly un-Spanish names —Harvey, Osborne, Williams, Terry, Sandeman, Domecq and the rest— are now international trade marks.

- ★★★★★ *Jerez*, Av Alvaro Domecq, 35 ☎ 30 06 00 ⬛ 121 TV ✦ ⬕ ⬟ ⬔ ⬕ AE, DC, MC, V $$$$$. It has an attractive garden with a swimming pool.
- ★★★ *Capele*, c/ Correredera, 58 ☎ 34 64 00 ⬛ 30 TV P AE, DC, EC, V $$$ to $$$$.

▥ ★★ *Avila*, c/ Avila, 3 ☎ 33 48 08 ⇥ 30 EC, V $$.

▥ ★★ *Joma*, c/ Fermín Aranda, 28 ☎ 34 96 89 ⇥ 29 AE, DC, EC, V $$$.

▥ ★★ *Mica*, c/ Higueras, 7 ☎ 34 07 00 ⇥ 38 AE, DC, V $$$.

❙❙ *Gaitán* (closed: Sunday nights), c/ Gaitán, 3 ☎ 34 58 59 **P** ✳ AE, V $$$. Seasonal cuisine.

❙❙ *Mesón la Cueva* (closed: Mondays), km10 on the road to Arcos ☎ 32 16 20 **P** ✦ ⛄ AE, DC, EC, V $$$. Home cooking.

❙❙ *Tendido 6* (closed: Sundays), c/ Circo, 10 ☎ 34 48 35 **P** ✦ ✳ AE, MC, V $$$. A very popular tavern by the bullring.

🕭 ❙❙ *Venta Antonio* (closed: Mondays from 1/10-31/3), km5 on the road to Sanlúcar ☎ 33 05 35 **P** ✦ ✳ AE, DC, MC, V $$$. Excellent fish and seafood.

Best buys: You can buy the sherry you liked best during your visit to the *bodegas* at source. Other best buys include distinctive sherry vinegar from *Garvey*, c/ Guadalete, 14, and *J. Pemartín*, c/ Pizarro, 17, and cakes and sweets made by nuns from the convents of the *Agustinas*, c/ Santa María de Gracia, 2, the *Clarisas*, c/ Borja, 2, and the *Dominicas*, c/ Espíritu Santo, 9.

Cultural highlights: The 11C **Alcázar** and the remains of the old walls form the vestiges of the town's Arab legacy. The buildings have been restored and embellished by gardens (open: 10.30-1.30). The town's churches include the 16-18C Cathedral, which has a fine art collection, the **Church of Santiago**, whose **W door** is a good example of the Isabelline style of the Catholic Monarchs, the **Church of San Miguel**, which has interesting sculptures by Martínez Montañés and José de Arce in its high altarpiece, and the Mudéjar Church of San Dionisio, which has good Gothic vaulting.

As befits a town associated with the landed rich, Jerez has a good number of mansions and palaces. A selection includes the **Casa del Cabildo**, with a beautiful Renaissance façade, the **Palacio del Marqués de Bertematí**, with a Baroque façade, the **Palacio de los Pérez Luna**, the Renaissance **Casa de los Ponce de León** and the 18C **Casa de los Domecq**. An interesting watch museum, the Museo de Relojes, c/ Cervantes 3 (open: 9.30-1.30; closed: weekends ☎ 33 21 00), is in the Neoclassical Palacio de La Atalaya. But the highlight of a trip to Jerez is a tour of the *bodegas*, or wineries, which are open on weekday mornings and close for a month, usually July, in summer. Drinks, during these tours, are on the house.

Fiestas and festivals: At the begining of May, Jerez stages its colourful horse festival, the *Feria del Caballo* (see 'Fiestas') and in September the town lets rip with its sherry harvest festival, the *Fiesta de la Vendimia*. There is also an annual **Flamenco Festival** and a **National Flamenco Guitar Festival**.

Local sights: The **Cartuja de Santa María** charterhouse, 5km out of town (open: 4.30-6.30, men only ☎ 34 11 03), was founded in 1467. It has a very rich 16C Baroque façade, a Gothic **patio** and a pleasant Gothic cloister.

On the town: Popular central bars in this town where *tapas* are so typical of the local lifestyle include *Bodega La Andana*, *El Colmado*, *Taberna Inglesa*, *La Tasca*, *Tío Diego* and *La Venancia*. On the outskirts the list extends to *Camino del Rocío*, c/ Nuestra Señora de la Paz, 21, in the España district, and *La Brasa*, on the Arcos de la Frontera road, in the Asunción district. You can buy rations of assorted fried fish, *pescaíto frito*, at take-aways like the *El Boquerón de Plata*, Pl Santiago, and the *Nuevo Jerezano*, c/ Arcos, 5 and then eat them at the nearest bar.

Sports: There is flying at the *Aero Club Jerez* ☎ 33 38 80, and car and motorcycle racing at the *Circuito de Jerez*, km10 on the road to Arcos ☎ 34 98 12.

LA ALPUJARRA **Granada-Almería**. Access from Granada, turning off the N-323 towards Lanjarón and continuing NE along the local road, and also by taking the C-332 to Ugíjar; from Almería, along the N-324 and then the C-332 to Canjáyar.

A sort of forgotten, hidden land between the snow-capped peaks of the **Sierra Nevada** and the Mediterranean, La Alpujarra has always been and still remains a magnet for rebels and romantics. The 19C traveller Richard Ford was enchanted by its isolation and the late hispanist Gerald Brenan was so taken by the area that he lived in one of its sparkling villages for the greater part of the interwar years. It is a world of its own, packed with the curious customs and crafts that have survived thanks to its tenuous links with the outside and set in dramatic scenery that is characterized by peaks, ravines and canyons.

The Muslims ousted from Granada by the conquering Catholic Monarchs took refuge in this wild terrain and in the late 16C they staged a fearsome revolt against Philip II that was finally put down by the king's half brother, John of Austria. The legacy of the Moriscos, as the nominally Christianized Muslims were known, remains to this day in the distinctive folklore, **popular architecture** and the cuisine of the Alpujarra.

▥ ★★★ *Villa Turística de Bubión*, Barrio Alto, in Bubión ☎ 76 31 11 ⊨ 43 **P** ⅏ ≪ **AE, DC, V $$$**. In the heart of the Alpujarra.

Best buys: Local textiles can be bought from the *Cooperativa de Tejidos Alpujarreños*, Ctra de Murcia, s/n, in Ugíjar ☎ 76 70 48.

LANJARON **Granada** ☎ (958), pop. 4,233, ▤ c/ Queipo de Llano, 43 ☎ 77 00 03. Granada 47km, Málaga 140km, Almería 157km, Madrid 475km.

Nicely situated at the entrance to the wild valleys of the **La Alpujarra** region (see separate entry), this **picturesque** little town is one of Spain's top spas and an important mineral producing centre. It has a ruined Arab castle and an agreeably cool summer climate.

▥ ★★★ *Miramar*, c/ Generalísimo Franco, 10 ☎ 77 01 61 ⊨ 60 **P** ✦ ⚓ **$$**.

Local sights: A tour of the **Valley of Lecrín**, centred on Lecrín, in whose castle the Muslim kings of Granada are buried, takes you through a number of picturesque villages such as Saleres, Albuñuelas, Pinos del Valle, Guájar Faragüit, Guájar Alto, and Guájar Fondón. In the N of this district and 25km from Granada, the village of **DURCAL** boasts an excellent restaurant in a lovely old mill, *El Molino* ☎ 78 02 47 **P** **AE $$$**, that specializes in resurrecting old Granada recipes.

LOJA **Granada** ☎ (958), pop. 19,669. Granada 55km, Málaga 71km, Madrid 484km.

Loja is an old, white-washed Arab town in the fertile Genil valley.

▥ ★★★★★ *La Bobadilla*, Finca la Bobadilla ☎ 32 18 61 ⊨ 35 ✕ ⵏ **TV** ✦ ⏚ ⅏ ⚓ ▦ ≪ ⚞ �’ ⅏ ⊠ **$$$$$$**. This is an extremely luxurious hotel and leisure centre, built in the style of an Andalusian country house and set in the extensive grounds of its own private estate. It has riding, shooting and tennis facilities, and its **restaurant** has earned a gourmet reputation.

Cultural highlights: There are good views of the town and valley from the 9C Alcazaba, or castle. The Church of San Gabriel was designed by Diego de Siloé, designer of Granada's cathedral. It has a good W door and an outstanding coffered ceiling within. Ventura Rodríguez left his Neoclassical stamp on the Gothic Church of la Encarnación by adding towers to it in the 18C.

◐ MALAGA **Málaga** ☎ (952), pop. 595,264, *i* c/ Larios, 5 ☎ 21 34 45, *i* at the airport ☎ 31 20 44, (c/ Molina Larios, s/n, ✉ Paseo del Parque ☎ 21 89 32 and 21 39 78, ✚ 25 04 50, **P** 21 24 14, ✈ Málaga, 9km ☎ 35 17 25 (Iberia ☎ 32 20 00, Aviaco ☎ 31 39 92), ⛴ 22 21 17, ⛴ Trasmediterránea, c/ Juan Díaz, 4 ☎ 22 43 93 and 22 78 81, 🚂 Pl Queipo de Llano, s/n ☎ 21 25 35, 🚌 c/ Cuarteles, s/n ☎ 31 25 00 (information and tickets, c/ Strachan, 2 ☎ 21 31 22). Algeciras 139km, Córdoba 176km, Seville 207km, Madrid 576km, Valencia 651km.

The biggest city in Andalusia after Seville, Málaga is the busy capital of
◐◐ the **Costa del Sol**. In peak periods tourists arrive by the thousands every hour at the city's airport and then fan out along the coast to their chosen resort. Outside the high season rush, Málaga remains a pleasant, happy-go-lucky Mediterranean seaport.

The city was the main harbour of the Moorish kingdom of Granada and it fell to the Catholic Monarchs in 1487, just five years before they conquered the city of Granada itself. Málaga was founded by the Phoenicians and was a well established Carthaginian colony before coming under the aegis of Rome. Like Granada it grew in importance under the Muslims after the 13C fall of the Caliphate of Córdoba.

▦ ★★★★ *Guadalmar*, km238 on the Cádiz road, 10km W of Málaga at the Urb Guadalmar ☎ 31 90 00 🛏 195 TV ✦ 🎤 🏊 ⛱ ⅏ 🏊 ≪ 🎿 ९ ⤵ **AE, DC, MC, V $$$ to $$$$$**. Near the sea in a quiet estate with good views.

▦ ★★★ *Casa Curro*, c/ Sancha de Lara, 7 ☎ 22 72 00 🛏 105 TV **AE, DC, MC, V $$$**. Traditional and central.

▦ ★★★ *Las Vegas*, Paseo de Sancha, 22 ☎ 21 77 12 🛏 73 ✦ 🎤 🏊 ⅏ 1km ≪ **AE, DC, V $$$**. Near the town centre and the Paseo Marítimo, it is set in its own gardens and has a swimming pool.

▦ ★★★ *Los Naranjos*, Paseo de Sancha, 35 ☎ 22 43 17 🛏 41 TV **P** ✦ 🏊 1km **AE, DC, MC, V $$$$**. In a residential area.

◐ ▦ ★★★ *Parador de Gibralfaro*, Paseo García del Olmo, s/n ☎ 22 19 02 🛏 12 ✦ 🏊 ≪ **AE, DC, MC, V $$$$**. Very quiet and with great views of Málaga and its bay.

🍴 *Antonio Martín* (closed: Sunday nights in winter), Paseo Marítimo, 4 ☎ 22 21 13 **P** ✦ ✳ ≪ **AE, DC, MC, V $$$**. Málaga cuisine served on a fine seafront terrace.

🍴 *Café de París* (closed: Tuesdays and 15/10-30/10), Malagueta district ☎ 22 50 43 ✳ **AE, DC, MC, V $$$ to $$$$**. Imaginative international cooking.

🍴 *El Figón de Bonilla* (closed: Sundays and 15/2-28/2), c/ Cervantes, Edif Horizonte ☎ 22 32 23 ✳ **V $$ to $$$**. Also a popular *tapa* bar.

🍴 *La Alegría* (closed: Saturdays except holidays), c/ Marín García, 10 ☎ 22 41 43 ✳ **AE, DC, EC, V $$$**. A well established classic.

🍴 *Refectorio II* (closed: Sundays), c/ Fernando de Lesseps, 7 ☎ 22 23 97 ✳ **AE, MC, V $$$**. Simple home cooking.

Best buys: Spanish fashion is sold at *C. Suárez*, Pasaje Chinitas, 10, and shoes and accessories at *A. Parriego*, c/ Bolsa, 14 or c/ Marqués de Larios, 2, *Sublime*, c/ Nueva, 22 or c/ Granada, 33, *Dover* c/ Angel, 1, *Roselli*, c/ Molina Larios, 10, *Nicolás*, c/ Larios, 3, and *Venia*, c/ Granada, 7. You can get antiques at *Los Remedios*, c/ Alamos, s/n, *Trianon*, c/ Madre de Dios, 22, and *El Vendaval*, c/ Granada, 61. Ceramics are sold at the *Morillo* workshop, c/ M. Rivadeneira, s/n, in the Santa Inés district. A wide range of hunting and fishing equipment is available at *Aguirre*, c/ Carretería, 1, and of nautical accessories at *A. de la Peña*, Paseo de la Farola, 37. For those with a sweet tooth, *Lepanto*, c/ Larios, 7, sells good cakes and

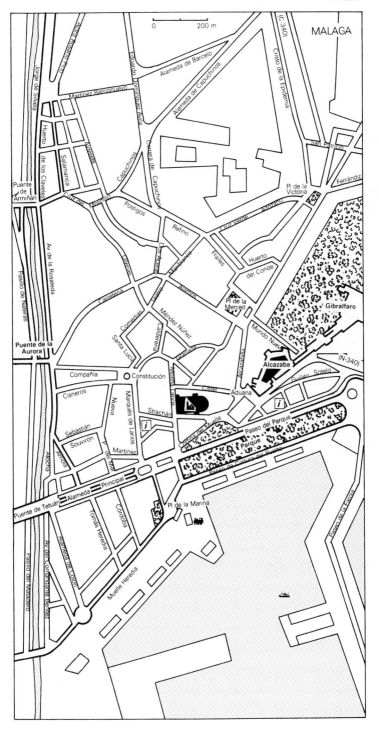

MALAGA

desserts, and the nuns of the *Convento de Clarisas*, c/ Zumaya, s/n, bake and sell delicious traditional cookies. The town's large department store is *El Corte Inglés*, Av Andalucía, 4.

◐ **Cultural highlights:** Málaga's main Muslim legacy is the **Alcazaba** and the castle of **Gibralfaro**. You arrive at the 11C Alcazaba by way of a series of zigzag ramps that lead through a succession of fortified gates. One of the area's highlights is the typical Hispano-Muslim gardens and the other is the

◐ **Archaeological Museum**, housed in the palace, which has a very good collection of Mediterranean antiquities and an excellent collection of the ceramics produced during the Muslim period. The castle (open in summer: 10.00-1.00 and 5.00-8.00; in winter: 10.00-1.00 and 4.00-7.00; Sundays: 10.00-2.00; closed: Mondays ☎ 21 60 05) was originally Phoenician and was rebuilt in the 14C by Yusuf I. Like every good castle it has excellent

◐◐ panoramic views.

◐ With a characteristic twist of Andalusian humour, the **Cathedral** is known as *La Manquita*, or 'The One-handed One', because its second tower was never built. It was founded by the Catholic Monarchs immediately after they conquered the city but the building process proved to be both costly and prolonged. The Cathedral was pronounced finished in the 18C when the W door and the elegant staircase leading up to it were completed. Inside the church the high points are the choir stalls with their 40 statues of saints sculpted by Pedro de Mena, the rose marble pulpits and the very fine 18C organ. The cathedral's **museum** (open: 10.00-1.00 and 4.00-5.30; closed: Sundays) is located in the Chapter House which has a good coffered ceiling. Exhibits include works by Ribera and Morales. More works of art, and particularly church ornaments, are exhibited across from the cathedral in the **Palacio Episcopal** (open: 10.00-1.00 and 4.00-7.00; closed: Saturday afternoons and Sundays ☎ 22 25 52). This building has a good Baroque façade and pleasant patios. Nearby the **Iglesia del Sagrario**, built at the end of the 15C, has an interesting **N door** sculpted in the Isabelline style of the Catholic Queen and a Plateresque altarpiece created by Juan de Valmaseda.

◐ In the same Cathedral area, the **Museo de Bellas Artes**, c/ San Agustín, 6 (open in summer: 10.30-1.30 and 5.00-8.00; in winter: 10.30-1.30 and 4.00-7.00; Sundays: 10.00-1.00; closed: Mondays ☎ 21 83 82) is housed in a 16C palace and has works by Alonso Cano, Zurbarán, Murillo and other old masters as well as canvases by **Picasso**, who was Málaga-born although his family later moved to Barcelona, which is the Spanish town most clearly associated with him. A third city musuem, the **Museo de Tradiciones y Artes Populares**, c/ Pasillo de Santa Isabel, 10 (open in summer: 10.00-1.00 and 5.00-8.00; winter: 10.00-1.00 and 4.00-7.00; Sundays: 10.00-1.00; closed: Mondays ☎ 21 71 37), housed in a 17C building that used to be an inn, deals with the traditions and the crafts of Málaga province.

◐ For a change of scene, stroll around the local 19C **Botanical Gardens** and along c/ Larios, the nerve-centre of Málaga.

◐◐ **Fiestas and festivals:** Religious occasions such as **Holy Week**, Corpus Christi, Saint John's day (June 24) and the feast day of the *Virgen del Carmen* (July 16) are celebrated with the inimitable Andalusian mix of solemnity and gaiety. The city's big annual *feria* is in August. There is also a theatre festival, the *Festival Internacional de Teatro* ☎ 22 86 00, in June-July, a flamenco festival in the summer, a cinema festival, the *Muestra de Cine Ciudad de Málaga*, in October, and another flamenco festival, the **Pandas de Verdiales**, in the nearby Venta del Túnel, in December.

◐ **Local sights:** The **Jardín de la Concepción**, 5km on the N-321, is a wonderfully exuberant tropical private garden which can be visited on weekdays. It was created by the daughters of a British consul in Seville.

On the town: Málaga is a great place for *tapa* enthusiasts. Two very popular *tapa* areas are El Palo, the old fishermen's quarter which now has a pleasant promenade, and the area called El Rincón de la Victoria, 12km away on the N-340. In Málaga proper, a selection of bars would have to include the *Antigua Casa Guardia*, c/ Alameda, 16, *Casa Vicente*, Callejón Comisario, s/n, and the host of bars along c/ Marín García. A conscientious *tapa* bar hop along c/ Marín García involves stopping off at *El Boquerón de Plata*, *La Manchega*, *La Tasca*, and ⚪ *Lo Güeno*. The *Café Teatro*, c/ Císter, s/n, is somewhat different for it organizes music recitals and exhibitions and its rarefied atmosphere is in keeping with the building which used to be the home of the sculptor Pedro de Mena. For discos and late night drinking, the Pedregalejo area is best and the **flamenco** haunts —*Gloria Bendita*, *Rincón Andaluz* and *Rincón de Panta*— are along c/ Cánovas del Castillo. For a bit of jazz, go to *El Cantor de Jazz*, c/ Lazcano, 7.

Sports: Málaga has two yacht clubs, the *Real Club Mediterráneo*, Paseo de la Farola, 18 ☎ 22 63 00, and the *Club Náutico El Candado*, 5km from town at El Palo ☎ 29 05 47. Golfers can play at the 18-hole, par 72 *Club de Campo*, 9km from Málaga ☎ 38 11 21, and at the 9-hole, par 68 *Club El Candado*, 5km from Málaga ☎ 29 46 66. Tennis players also have an option between the *Club de Tenis Málaga* ☎ 29 10 92, and the *Club de Tenis El Candado* ☎ 29 00 45.

MARBELLA **Málaga** ☎ (952), pop. 82,696, *i* Av Miguel Cano, 1 ☎ 77 14 42, ✉ c/ Alonso Bazán, 1 ☎ 77 28 98, ✚ 77 45 34 and 77 36 76, **P** 77 31 94, ✈ Málaga, 52km on the N-340 ☎ 35 17 25 (Iberia ☎ 32 20 00, Aviaco ☎ 31 39 92), ⛴ Trasmediterránea, c/ Juan Díaz, 4, Alay beach ☎ 22 43 93, 🚌 Portillo, Av Ricardo Soriano, 21 ☎ 77 21 92. Málaga 59km, Ronda 64km, Algeciras 83km, Madrid 617km.

The glitter and the hype of the Costa del Sol are concentrated along Marbella's 28km of beaches, luxury hotels, marinas, country clubs and exclusive discos. There is even a **Golden Mile** where the super wealthy, mostly sheiks, have set up massive holiday homes. It is a place where tourists come to gawp and where celebrities of one kind or another come to be gawped at. There are limos and custom-made sports cars in the parking lots and amazing yachts moored by the quayside. If razzmatazz is the name of the game, then Marbella is a first division player in the international league. In the heart of Marbella town itself, for the municipality is strung out along the coast, there is an old quarter that shows off its old Muslim ancestry. Once upon a time, Marbella was a quiet agricultural hamlet and the Iberians, the Carthaginians, the Romans and the Muslims in turn established little settlements in this area.

🏨 ★★★★★ *Del Golf Plaza*, Urb Nueva Andalucía ☎ 81 17 50 🛏 65 **P** ✱ 🏊 ⛱ 🍴 🖾 ✒ $$$$$ to $$$$$$. Peace and tranquillity with a golf course close at hand.

🏨 ★★★★★ *Don Carlos*, Urb Jardines de la Golondrina, km198 on the Cádiz road ☎ 83 11 40 🛏 236 ✕ **P** ✱ 🎤 ⛱ 🍴 🖾 🐴 ♀ ✒ 🐶 AE, DC, EC, V $$$$$$. Quiet and well situated on a lovely beach, with a good **restaurant** and a pool-side buffet in summer.

🏨 ★★★★★ *Los Monteros*, Urb Los Monteros ☎ 77 17 00 🛏 171 ✕ ♿ TV **P** ✱ 🎤 ⛱ 🍴 🖾 ♀ ✒ 🐶 AE, DC, EC, MC, V $$$$$$. Unbeatable with just about every facility that a de luxe client expects, including a good **restaurant**.

🏨 ★★★★★ *Meliá Don Pepe*, Finca Las Merinas ☎ 77 03 00 🛏 218 TV **P** ✱ 🎤 ⛱ 🍴 🖾 ≪ 🐴 ⛵ ♀ ✒ AE, DC, EC, MC, V $$$$$$. Good views and a sub-tropical garden.

🖙🖙 ▦ ★★★★★ *Puente Romano*, km184 on the Cádiz road ☎ 77 01 00 🛏 198 TV P ✦ ♀ ∽ ♨ ⚘ ⚲ ✦/ AE, DC, EC, MC, V $$$$$$. A very successfully custom-made Andalusian *pueblo* with a host of facilities.

▦ ★★★★ *Andalucía Plaza*, km180 on the Cádiz road ☎ 78 20 00 🛏 418 P ✦ ♀ ♀ ∽ ♨ ⚘ ⚲ ✦/ ⚘ AE, DC, EC, V $$$$$. Tennis courts, a covered swimming pool and Marbella's casino.

▦ ★★★★ *El Fuerte*, Av El Fuerte, s/n ☎ 77 15 00 🛏 146 P ✦ ∽ ♨ ⚘ ⚲ ✦/ AE, DC, V $$$$$. Good views and a pleasant palm-shaded garden.

🖙🖙 ▦ ★★★★ *Golf Hotel Gualdalmina*, Urb Guadalmina, San Pedro de Alcántara ☎ 78 14 00 🛏 80 P ✦ ⚲ ∽ ♨ ≪ ⚲ ✦/ ⚘ AE, DC, EC, V $$$$ to $$$$$. For golfers, tennis players and classy people (Glenda Jackson's *A Touch of Class* was filmed here).

🖙🖙🖙 ▦ ★★★★ *Marbella Club*, km184 on the Cádiz road ☎ 77 13 00 🛏 76 ✗ TV P ✦ ∽ ♨ ▦ ⚘ ◬ ✦/ AE, DC, EC, V $$$$$$. A sophisticated
🖙 pace-setter on the Golden Mile. Its tropical garden restaurant ($$$$) is a celebrity *rendez-vous*.

▦ ★★★★ *Marbella Dinamar Club-24*, km181 on the Cádiz road ☎ 81 05 00 🛏 117 P ✦ ♀ ∽ ≪ ⚘ AE, DC, EC, V $$$$ to $$$$$. Good views, tennis and year-round swimming.

▦ ★★★ *Guadalpín*, km186 on the Cádiz road ☎ 77 11 00 🛏 103 ✦ ∽ ♨ AE, V $$$. Functional.

▦ ★★★ *Las Fuentes del Rodeo*, km180 on the Cádiz road ☎ 78 10 00 🛏 85 ✦ ∽ ♨ ⚲ AE, DC, V $$$ to $$$$. Pleasant gardens and tennis courts.

▦ ★★★ *San Cristóbal*, c/ Ramón y Cajal, 3 ☎ 77 12 50 🛏 100 ♨ EC, V $$ to $$$.

▦ ★★ *Lima*, Av Antonio Belón, 2 ☎ 77 05 00 🛏 64 AE, DC, EC, V $$ to $$$.

▦ ★ *Nagüeles*, km184 on the Cádiz road ☎ 77 16 88 🛏 17 ✦ ∽ AE, DC, V $ to $$.

🍴 *Antonio*, Muelle Ribera, Puerto Banús ☎ 81 10 91 ✦ ❉ ≪ AE, DC, EC, V $$$. Nice terrace.

🍴 *Don Leone* (closed: 21/11-20/12), Muelle Ribera, 45, Puerto Banús ☎ 81 17 16 ✦ ❉ $$$. Pastas and steaks served on its open-air terrace.

🖙 🍴 *El Corzo*, Hotel Los Monteros, km186 on the Cádiz road ☎ 77 17 00 P ✦ ❉ ≪ AE, DC, EC, V $$$$ to $$$$$. Upmarket international cuisine.

🍴 *El Refugio* (closed: Mondays), km25 on the C-337 Ojén road ☎ 77 18 48 P ✦ ❉ ≪ AE, DC, EC, V $$$. Dinners only, served on the terrace in summer.

🍴 *Gran Marisquería Santiago*, Paseo Marítimo, s/n ☎ 77 00 78 P ✦ ❉ ≪ AE, DC, EC, V $$$. Specializes in seafood.

🖙🖙 🍴 *La Fonda* (closed: Sundays), Pl Santo Cristo, 9 ☎ 77 25 12 P ✦ ❉ AE, DC, V $$$$. Quality-conscious regional dinners in an attractive 18C Andalusian house.

🖙🖙 🍴 *La Hacienda* (closed: Mondays, Tuesdays and 1/11-31/12), km200 on the Cádiz road ☎ 83 11 16 P ✦ ❉ ≪ $$$$ to $$$$$. A *Relais et Gourmands* restaurant serving memorable dinners in an agreeable garden.

🖙🖙 🍴 *La Meridiana* (closed: 22/11-20/12), Camino de la Cruz, s/n, behind the Mosque in Las Lomas ☎ 77 61 90 P ✦ ❉ ≪ AE, DC, EC, V $$$$ to $$$$$. A fashionable and luxurious restaurant serving Andalusian cuisine with a creative touch (dinners only in summer).

🖙 🍴 *La Taberna del Alabardero* (closed: Sundays and 15/11-15/12), Muelle Benabola, Puerto Banús ☎ 78 27 94 ✦ ❉ ≪ AE, DC, EC, V $$$. Basque and Andalusian dishes served on a quayside *terraza*.

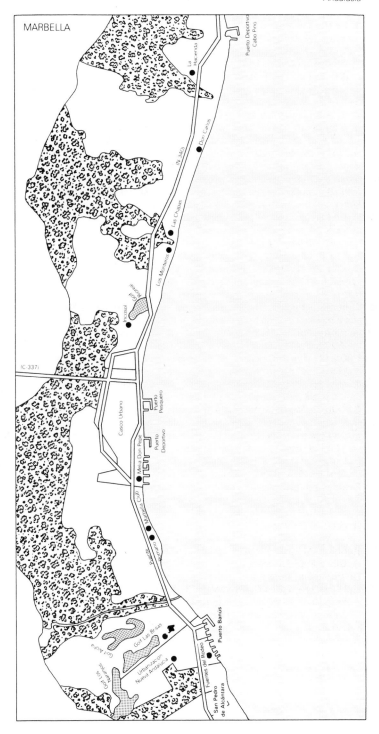

- ⚫ ¶ *Le Restaurant* (closed: Sundays), km173 on the Cádiz road, Camino de Edgar Neville, at the Rodeo Beach Club ☎ 78 11 12 **P** ✦ ❋ AE, DC, V $$$$$. French cuisine dinners served on an elegant seaside terrace.
- ⚫ ¶ *Marbella Club*, km185 on the Cádiz road ☎ 77 13 00 **P** ✦ ❋ ≪ AE, DC, EC, V $$$$. Traditional and modern cuisine.

⚫⚫ **Beaches**: Of Marbella's 28km of beaches, the best ones are the Marbella Club beach (good for celebrity spotting) and, alongside it, Nagüeles, Río Verde, Las Chapas and the ones at the Los Monteros and Don Carlos hotels.

⚫ **Best buys**: Jet set big-name fashion is sold at the **boutiques** and stores around the Pl de los Naranjos and the Av Ricardo Soriano in Marbella town, and along the Puerto Banús marina. In Marbella, the boutique list includes *S. Vega*, c/ Valdés, 2, and, at No. 8, *Gucci*; and on Av Ramón y Cajal, *Giorgio*, *Stéphane Kélian* for shoes, and *Gómez Molina* for jewelry. In Puerto Banús keep an eye open for *Ted Lapidus*, *Mic Mac*, *Exseption*, *Trussardi*, and *Fancy*. For the horse lover, riding equipment is sold at *El Caballo*, Av

⚫ Ricardo Soriano, 49. Arts and crafts are sold at *Artespaña*, Av Ricardo Soriano, 54, and modern art can be bought from *Isa's* in Puerto Banús and from *M. Vilches* in Torre Real (along the Cádiz road). Antique bargains can be had from the Saturday morning flea market by the Nueva Andalucía bullring. On the extremes, gourmet food is sold at *Semon*, c/ G. Marañón,

⚫ s/n (also a small **restaurant**), and boats at *Marina Marbella*, in the fishing port.

⚫ **Cultural highlights**: The **old quarter** lies around the **Pl de los Naranjos** and it makes a change from the hustle of modern Marbella. The 16C **Casa del Correjidor** houses the contemporary art and archaeological exhibits of the **Municipal Museum** (open weekdays in summer: 6.00-9.00; winter: 5.00-8.00). The 16C Hospital de Bazán is in the Renaissance style and other buildings from the same period are the Church of the Encarnación, which has an interesting altarpiece, and the late Gothic chapel of the Hospital de San Juan de Dios. Marbella's earlier inhabitants, in the 10C period of the Córdoba Caliphate, built a **castle and walls** and some of the towers, which

⚫ were rebuilt in the 16C, remain. In the outlying district of **SAN PEDRO DE ALCANTARA** there are remains of a very **early Christian church** in the Vega del Mar site (visits by prior arrangement ☎ 77 46 38) and there is also evidence of Roman baths that could have been part of the elusive town of *Cilniana* for there are no other traces of it.

Fiestas and festivals: As elsewhere in Andalusia, Holy Week is a religious and festive mix, and like most fishing ports, Marbella celebrates the *fiesta* of the *Virgen del Carmen* on July 16. There is also a **Flamenco Festival** in the second half of June.

⚫⚫ **Local sights**: The scenic mountain **route** from San Pedro de Alcántara to
⚫⚫ **RONDA** (see separate entry) is full of twists and turns but it is worth every bend of the road.

On the town: Popular bars in the old quarter include *Los Cazadores*, c/ San Francisco, 7, and *Guerra*, Av Ramón y Cajal, s/n, but the big crowd-pullers are the **open-air terraces** along the Paseo Marítimo and along

⚫ the beach —*Menchu's Bar* at the Rodeo Beach Club is a favourite. Marbella
⚫⚫⚫ really comes into its own at **night**, when the action centres on a series of clubs that include *Old Joy's Pub* in Puerto Banús, *Jimmy's Club* at the ⚫ Hotel Marbella Club, *Puente Romano* at the hotel of the same name, *Olivia*, ⚫ *Ipanema Palace*, *Menchu* at the Rodeo Beach Club and *Pepe Moreno* out ⚫ of town at km186 on the Cádiz road. There is a fringe theatre at Puerto Banús' *Comedia* and flamenco at *Ana María*, Pl del Santo Cristo, and

⚫⚫ gamblers go to the *Casino Nueva Andalucía*, km188 on the Cádiz road ☎ 78 08 00.

Sports: Marbella is served by three yacht clubs —the *Puerto Deportivo Cabopino*, km202 on the Cádiz road ☎ 83 19 75, the **Club Marítimo de Marbella** ☎ 77 25 04 and the **Puerto José Banús**, Urb Nueva Andalucía ☎ 78 33 50. Golfers here are spoilt for choice, since they can play at the 18-hole, par 72 **Aloha Club**, 8km from town at Urb Nueva Andalucía ☎ 78 23 88 and 78 23 89, the 18-hole, par 72 **Golf Río Real**, km152 on the Cádiz road ☎ 77 37 76, the 18-hole, par 72 **Club de Golf Las Brisas**, km181 on the Cádiz road ☎ 78 03 00, the 18-hole, par 72 **Golf Guadalmina**, in San Pedro de Alcántara ☎ 78 13 17, or the 18-hole, par 72 **Los Naranjos**, at Urb Nueva Andalucía ☎ 78 72 00. Tennis players, too, have plenty of options —choose between the courts at the **Club de Tenis Puente Romano**, on the Cádiz road ☎ 77 01 00, the **Hotel Don Carlos**, Urb Elviria ☎ 83 11 40, the **Hotel Los Monteros**, on the Cádiz road, and the **Club de Tenis Aloha**, Urb Nueva Andalucía ☎ 78 09 90. Other racket sports include squash at the *Puente Romano* and *Los Monteros* hotels and paddle tennis at the *Marbella Club* hotel. There is hunting in the **Ronda National Reserve** and the **Cortes de la Frontera Reserve** ☎ 32 82 00 and in the Refugio de Juanar area in Ojén, 9km away.

MIJAS **Málaga** ☎ (952), pop. 25,573. Málaga 30km, Madrid 585km.
Just back from the Costa del Sol and overlooking it, this is a bijou Andalusian *pueblo* with carefully manicured whitewashed walls and narrow streets. It is so 'typical' that half its residents are non-Spanish.

★★★★★ *Byblos Andaluz*, Urb Mijas-Golf ☎ 47 30 50 ⊨ 135 ♦ ⊕ ⇌ ▦ ⛵ ♞ ✓ AE, DC, EC, V $$$$$. A luxurious, quiet and relaxing health therapy centre with many facilities and a good **restaurant**.

★★★★ *Mijas*, Urb Tamisa ☎ 48 58 00 ⊨ 100 ✕ ♦ ⌂ ⇌ ▦ ♞ ⛵ ⛳ AE, DC, EC, V $$$$$. Scenically located and typically Andalusian in architecture.

Best buys: Local ceramics, wickerwork and woven esparto craftwork are typical buys.

Cultural highlights: This is a pleasant village to stroll about in. The church of the Immaculate Conception was founded by the Catholic Monarchs and altered in the 18C to suit the Baroque tastes of that period. Its tower is all that remains of the original mosque that stood on the site and it formerly served as a minaret. There are very good **panoramic views** from the shrine of la Virgen de la Peña.

Local sights: A drive through the mountain *pueblos* takes you through **ALHAURIN EL GRANDE**, which has a good **flamenco festival** in mid-August, Cártama and the ceramic producing village of **COIN**.

Sports: Golfers can play at the *Mijas Golf* club, 5km S of town ☎ 47 29 12, and tennis players at the courts of most hotels.

MOJACAR **Almería** ☎ (951), pop. 6,656, ✚ 47 89 52. Almería 91km, Murcia 141km, Madrid 527km.
A **picturesque** white village clinging to a rocky promontory 2km from the sea, Mojácar has become a popular tourist resort and an expatriate residential centre. The new buildings have tried, with varying degrees of success, to reproduce the traditional local architecture.

★★★★ *Parador Reyes Católicos*, 2.5km on the Carboneras road ☎ 47 82 50 ⊨ 98 ♦ ⇌ ✓ AE, DC, MC, V $$$ to $$$$. Looking out onto the Mediterranean, this peaceful parador has a swimming pool and tennis courts.

★★★ *El Moresco*, Av Horizón, s/n ☎ 47 80 25 ⊨ 147 ♦ ⇌ ⛵ ⛳ AE, DC, V $$$ to $$$$. Quiet, with good views and a year-round pool.

▦ ★★★ *Indalo*, 6.5km on the Carboneras road ☎ 47 80 01 ⛴ 308 ✦ ⚓
☂ 🏄 ⚲ 🎣 AE, DC, MC, V $$$ to $$$$. By the beach, with tennis courts
and a pool.

❙❙ *El Palacio* (closed: Thursdays, November and February), Pl del Caño, s/n
☎ 47 82 79 AE, MC, V $$ to $$$.

❙❙ *La Lubina*, Urb Pueblo Indalo ☎ 45 83 76 🅿 ✦ ❄ AE, DC, MC, V $$$.

Beaches: The local grey sand beaches are extensive and the climate is hot
and dry.

Best buys: Arts and crafts are sold at *El Alfar*, Multicentro, 15, and you can
buy fresh fish from the quayside auctions in the village of **GARRUCHA**, 2km N.

Local sights: The 22km **coastal route** S to **CARBONERAS** passes through
strange rock formations and offers attractive views.

On the town: The atmosphere is extremely lively in summer when people
crowd beachside locales such as the *Budú* disco bar and the *Ninfas y
Faunos* terrace on the road to the beach.

Sports: There is good underwater fishing in the area, and golf can be played
at the *Club Cortijo Grande*, in Turre, 10km SW ☎ 47 91 76.

▥ MONTILLA Córdoba ☎ (957), pop. 21,263, ▟▙ 47 93 02. Córdoba 46km,
Jaén 117km, Madrid 443km.

Montilla is of interest to lovers of architecture for it is a good example of
a small town that has survived almost unspoiled since its 17C heyday, to
lovers of history because it was the birthplace of the creator of Spanish
military power in the late 15C, **Gonzálo Fernández de Córdoba**, whose
exploits earned him the title of the *Gran Capitán*, and to lovers of wine for
the Montilla trademark rivals that of Jerez except that it does not travel as well
and is therefore best drunk here, chilled and preferably accompanied by the
local olives.

▦ ★★★ *Don Gonzalo*, km447 on the Madrid-Málaga road ☎ 65 06 58 ⛴
28 ✕ 🅿 ✦ ⚓ ⚲ AE, DC, EC, V $$ to $$$.

Best buys: Montilla wines are sold in the local bodegas and cakes lovingly
made by the nuns in the *Convento de las Clarisas*, c/ Benedicto XIII, 4.

Cultural highlights: Architectural interest centres here on the Convent of
Santa Clara, where the Mudéjar style is clearly evident, and on the 17C
Baroque Convent of Santa Ana, which has a fine altarpiece by the always
skilful Pedro Roldán. The Casa-Museo del Inca Garcilaso, c/ Capitán Alonso
Vargas, 3, is a museum which honours the memory of the 16C writer
Garcilaso de la Vega who was known as *El Inca* because he was born in
Cuzco and was of Peruvian blood. In an interesting counterpoint to the black
legend that had Spain's conquistadors slaughtering every Amerindian in sight,
Garcilaso rose to become an acknowledged master of Castilian prose. The
museum, in reality a library and archive, was for a time his home in Spain.

Fiestas: Towards the end of August the town celebrates the wine harvest
with the *Fiestas de la Vendimia Montilla Moriles* and a flamenco
🔊🔊 symposium known as the *Cata Flamenca*.

Local sights: There are a number of authentic and little-visited Andalusian
pueblos in the vicinity. **MONTEMAYOR**, to the NW, is a picturesque village
defended by a 14C castle that was once the seat of the Duchy of Frías. In **LA
RAMBLA**, SW of Montemayor, there were some 40 potters at the last count.
AGUILAR DE LA FRONTERA, to the S of Montilla, is another picture postcard
pretty *pueblo* and **PUENTE GENIL**, a further 18km SW along the C-329, is
famed for its quince paste, or *dulce de membrillo*. It also stages dramatic
🔊 *Semana Santa* celebrations in Holy Week and a **Flamenco Festival** in
mid-August. Local best buys include craftsman-made wooden chests
(*bargueños*) and trunks (*arcones*) from *A. Márquez*, c/ Castejón, 33.

NERJA **Málaga** ☎ (952), pop. 13,833, *i* c/ Puerta del Mar, 4 ☎
52 15 31, ✉ c/ Almirante Ferrandis, 6 ☎ 52 17 49, ✚ 52 14 09, **P**
52 15 45. Málaga 52km, Granada 120km, Madrid 549km.

Scenically located, Nerja strives hard to maintain the balance between
the fishing village that it once was and the tourist centre that it has become.
Its El Salón beach was one of the main departure points to North Africa of
the large population of Moriscos, the Christians of Muslim descent, who were
expelled from Spain in the 16C.

▦ ★★★★ *Parador de Nerja*, c/ El Tablazo, s/n ☎ 52 00 50 🛏 73 ❖ ☗
⅋ ⚲ « ⚲ AE, DC, MC, V $$$$. Marvellous views of the Mediterranean.

▦ ★★★ *Balcón de Europa*, Paseo Balcón de Europa, 1 ☎ 52 08 00 🛏
105 TV P ❖ ☗ ▦ « ⚲/ DC, EC, V $$$. Alongside the Balcón and sharing
the famous views.

❙❙ *Casa Luque* (closed: Thursdays), Pl Mártires, 2 ☎ 52 10 04 MC, V $$.

❙❙ *Casa Paco y Eva* (closed: Thursdays), c/ Alemania, 50 ☎ 52 15 24. P ✱
$$$. Spanish cooking.

❙❙ *Rey Alfonso* (closed: Wednesdays), Paseo Balcón de Europa, s/n ☎
52 01 95 ✱ « $$$.

Best buys: Crafts are sold at *Artesanía Popular* on the Balcón de Europa.
Cultural highlights: The promontory jutting out into the Mediterranean
called the **Balcón de Europa** is one of the Costa's beauty spots.
Local sights: The **Cuevas de Nerja**, 4km E on the road to Motril (open in
summer: 9.00-9.00; winter: 10.00-1.30 and 4.00-7.00 ☎ 52 00 76), are an
impressive limestone cave network where evidence of Stone Age dwellings
has been discovered. In August the caves serve as a concert hall for the
Festivales de Música y Danza. **FRIGILIANA**, deep in the Almijara sierra, 7km
NE via the **scenic road** to La Herradura, is a picturesque *pueblo* closely
associated with the Morisco population.
Sports: This is a good area for underwater fishing. Golf can be played at the
9-hole *Club de Golf Nerja* ☎ 52 02 08.

OSUNA **Seville** ☎ (954), pop. 16,148, *i* Plaza Mayor, s/n ☎ 81 16 17,
P 81 00 50, ➤ 81 03 08. Córdoba 85km, Seville 86km, Granada 169km,
Madrid 489km.

Like so many small Spanish towns with a long history behind them,
Osuna reverberates with past glories and grandeur. The town is the nominal
seat of the **Dukes of Osuna**, one of the great Spanish aristocratic houses
which traces its lineage back to the Middle Ages. In Roman times, when it
was known as *Urso*, it had the privilege of minting its own money.
Cultural highlights: A stroll through Osuna's **old streets** —c/ San Pedro,
c/ Sevilla, c/ Gordillos and those adjoining them— takes you past a
succession of stately mansions with fading Renaissance and Baroque façades
and clusters of humbler old dwellings. The collegiate church, the **Colegiata**,
is a classic Spanish Renaissance building and it lists canvases by Ribera
among its treasures. It also houses the **Pantheon of the Dukes of Osuna**,
which is a good example of the Plateresque style of the 16C, and an
interesting collection of religious art objects in its Museo de Arte Sacro (open
in summer: 10.00-1.30 and 4.30-7.30; winter: 10.00-1.30 and 3.30-6.30
☎ 81 04 44). The building alongside it was a **university** in the 16C. The
Torre del Agua tower, c/ Cuesta de San Agustín, 2, owes its present
structure to a 14C facelift but it dates right back to Roman times. It is now
home to the town's **Archaeological Museum** (open: same times as the Arte
Sacro museum ☎ 81 12 07). The **Monasterio de la Encarnación**, founded
in the 16C at the height of Saint Teresa of Avila's reform of the Carmelite
Order, has a charming patio decorated with 18C Sevillian glazed tiles.

Local sights: The village of ESTEPA, 24km NE along the N-334, is worth visiting for its **historic buildings** and its famous short-cake biscuits known as *polvorones*. SW of Osuna, MORON DE LA FRONTERA is yet another unspoiled old town where fine historic buildings rear their heraldic façades among modest but dazzlingly whitewashed houses. Morón stages a flamenco festival in mid-July that is memorably entitled *Gazpacho Andaluz*.

❧ PUERTO DE SANTA MARIA **Cádiz** ☎ (956), pop. 63,327, *i* c/ Guadalete, 1 ☎ 85 75 45, ✉ Pl General Varela, s/n ☎ 85 53 22, ✢ 86 39 07, **P** 87 15 44, → Jerez, 25km ☎ 33 43 00, ⛟ 86 25 85. Cádiz 19km, Seville 102km, Madrid 610km.

The eternal rival to its neighbour Jerez, Puerto de Santa María also prides itself on being a sherry and brandy producing centre and a home to bull-breeders, matadors and flamenco artists. It has been a fishing town since Roman times and was an important dockyard for the galleons of Spain's 16C age of discovery and conquest. Nowadays El Puerto is a growing holiday resort that is highly popular with people from Seville and Jerez.

🏨 ★★★★ *Meliá Caballo Blanco*, km658 on the N-IV ☎ 86 37 45 ⛱ 94 ✦ ⚓ ♨ AE, DC, MC, V $$$$ to $$$$$. With a pleasant garden.

🏨 ★★★ *Los Cántaros*, c/ Curva, 6 ☎ 86 42 42 ⛱ 39 **P** $$$ to $$$$.

🍴 *Alboronia* (closed: Saturday evenings, Sundays and May), c/ Santo Domingo, 24 ☎ 85 16 09 ✦ ❄ AE, DC, MC, V $$$. Traditional local recipes served in a stylish 18C mansion.

🍴 *Casa Flores*, c/ Ribera del Río, 27 ☎ 86 35 12 **P** ❄ DC, EC, V $$$. Good fish.

❧ 🍴 *Don Peppone* (closed: Sundays and holidays), c/ Cáceres, 1, in Valdelagrana ☎ 86 10 99 **P** ✦ ❄ AE, V $$$. Home cooking; stews and fish.

🍴 *El Patio*, Pl de la Herrería ☎ 86 45 06 ❄ AE, DC, EC, V $$ to $$$. Andalusian cuisine served in an 18C patio.

🍴 *La Goleta* (closed: Mondays and 1/11-15/11), Ctra de Rota, s/n ☎ 85 42 32 **P** ✦ ❄ AE, DC, EC, V $$$. Good fried and salt-baked fish.

Beaches: Fuentebravía and **Valdegrana** are the local beaches.

Best buys: Wines from the local *bodegas*, which can be sampled on the spot, make good buys.

Cultural highlights: A very agreeable palm-lined walk leads to the **Castillo de San Marcos**. It was built in the 11C on the site of a mosque and acquired its present fortified church structure in the 13C. The Iglesia Mayor Prioral has a splendid Baroque façade which was added to the original late Gothic building. The town has an archaeological museum, the Museo Arqueológico Municipal, c/ Pagador, 1 (open: 10.00-2.00; closed: Sundays ☎ 85 27 11) but the real crowd pullers are the Osborne and Terry *bodegas*

❧ or **wineries**.

On the town: The custom here, as elsewhere along the Cádiz coast, is to buy seafood at takeaways called *cocederos* and then eat it at the neighbouring bars. This *tapa* custom is practised along the banks of the

❧ Guadalete river, the area known as the **Ribera del Río** —*Salvador*, Ribera del Puerto, is a popular *cocedero*. On the N-IV, there are a couple of well-established roadside inns, known as *ventas* —*Maka* at km658 and *El Corneta* at km659— which specialize in fish and seafood. *El Sitio*, c/ Santo Domingo, 30, has long been a very popular evening *tapa* bar and *La Ribera*, Ribera del Marisco, 1, is currently the fashionable disco. For gamblers there are full facilities at the *Casino Bahía de Cádiz*, km650 on the Madrid-Cádiz road, which also has a discotheque, a swimming pool, a shopping mall and a restaurant complex.

Sports: There are extensive yachting facilities at the newly-built *Puerto Sherry* ☎ 87 03 03 and at the established club, the *Club Náutico del Puerto de Santa María* ☎ 85 25 27.

RONDA **Málaga** ☎ (952), pop. 35,504, *i* Pl España, 1 ☎ 87 12 72, **P** 87 13 69, **⬛** Av de la Estación, s/n ☎ 87 16 73, **⬛** Pl de Concepción García Redondo, s/n ☎ 87 26 57. Málaga 96km, Seville 147km, Cádiz 149km, Madrid 612km.

Set high on a ridge and divided in two by a dramatic **gorge**, Ronda is immediately arresting and appealing. It lies in the middle of the wild hills of the Serranía de Ronda which were the stamping ground for rebels and ruffians throughout Spanish history. The Iberian chieftain Viriato fought against the Romans here and much later the same crags formed the redoubts of the Muslim revolt led by Omar ben Hafsun. In the 19C, the Romantic travellers from Britain, France and Germany who inquisitively explored Spain were fascinated by the bandits and highwaymen who turned every trip to Ronda into an adventure of totally unforeseen consequences. As does Granada, Ronda shows off the decadent splendour of Muslim Spain's dying days and asserts, in an impressive style, the new order of the conquering Catholic Monarchs. The Castilian nobles who led the Christian troops into the town were quick to reflect the tastes of the Renaissance age into which they had been born. A final point about Ronda that excites the imagination is the status that it holds as the **cradle of bullfighting**, or rather, of the art of tauromachy. **Pedro Romero**, the matador who at the begining of last century redefined what the *corrida* was all about, was born in Ronda and left such an impression on succeeding generations that the so-called school of Ronda is held to be the purest form of bullfighting. The matador Antonio Ordóñez, hero of **Ernest Hemingway** and one of the greatest post-war bullfighters was also born in Ronda. **Orson Welles**, another devoted Ordóñez fan, took his love of Ronda and admiration of his friend to such a degree that before his death he requested that his ashes be interred in the *matador's* estate outside the town.

▦ **★★★★ *Reina Victoria***, c/ Jerez, 25 ☎ 87 12 40 ⇌ 89 ♣ ≈ « ♞ DC, V $$$ to $$$$. A place of pilgrimage for admirers of the Austro-German poet Rainer Maria Rilke who once stayed here. Others come for the magnificent views and Victorian atmosphere.

▦ **★★★ *Polo***, c/ Mariano Soubirón, 8 ☎ 87 24 47 ⇌ 33 AE, DC, EC, V $$$.

▦ **★ *El Tajo***, c/ Cruz Verde, 7 ☎ 87 62 36 ⇌ 37 **P** $$.

⑪ *Don Miguel* (closed: Tuesday nights, Wednesdays, 20/1-20/2 and Sundays in summer), c/ Villanueva, 4 ☎ 87 10 90 **P** ♣ ❋ AE, DC, EC, V $$$. A pleasant *terraza* by the gorge, where you can sample good home-made dishes while enjoying the views.

Best buys: You can buy antiques from *Muñoz*, c/ Armiñán, 24; cakes made by the nuns of the Carmelite Convent from the *Carmelitas Descalzas*, Pl de la Merced, 2; and local *chorizos* and other artisan sausages from the outlying *pueblos* of Arriate (4km), Benaoján (17km) and Montejaque (20km).

Cultural highlights: Probably the first thing that every visitor does as he arrives in Ronda is to make for the **Puente Nuevo** (it was *nuevo*, or new, in the 18C) that spans the **gorge**, a sheer drop of 90m. Once Ronda's fantastic **setting** is digested, the next stage is to stroll around old, or Arab, Ronda which is where the conquering barons staked their claim to the town in the late 15C. The **Palacio de Mondragón** is a fine Renaissance building that was the temporary residence of the Catholic Monarchs and stands on the site of what was a royal court during a brief period when Ronda formed an independent Moorish kingdom. The patios are particularly good. The Casa del Rey Moro, from the earlier Muslim period, has pleasant gardens and a long stairway with unpleasant associations to it for it was along there that Christian slaves used to drag pitchers of water to the royal household. The **Palacio del Marqués de Salvatierra**, another outstanding example of what the Renaissance meant to 16C Ronda, leads to a magnificent network of Andalusian **streets** and alleyways lined with dazzling whitewashed houses graced by **wrought iron balconies**. The route leads on to the **Arab Baths** which are by the Puente Viejo that was thrown across the gorge in the 17C, 100 years before the 'new' one. By the Pl de la Duquesa de Parcent there is a cluster of interesting buildings. The collegiate church, the **Colegiata de Santa María la Mayor**, shows the impact of the Plateresque ornamentation that superimposed itself on Gothic structures during the reign of the Catholic Monarchs. The church preserves the archway of the old mosque that originally occupied the site, and has a Baroque balcony, presumably added to allow noble spectators to view events staged in the plaza. The square is completed by the 17C Town Hall and by the 16C Church of la Caridad. Nearby there are unmistakable Muslim traces in the 14C **Casa del Gigante** and in the 13C gateway, the **Puerta de Almocábar**. On the other side of the Puente Nuevo, on the modern side of the gorge the **Mercadillo**, or market, district stands on the site where traders and merchants used to gather outside the town's walls. The Posada de las Animas here is a 16C house where Cervantes is reputed to have stayed for bed and breakfast. The bullring, the **Plaza de Toros**, a staple ingredient of every Spanish town, deserves special mention in Ronda for, built in 1784, it is one of the oldest in Spain and it is also architecturally beautiful. In this district one should take the opportunity of strolling around the tree-lined walk, the **Alameda**, to capture, once more, the magic of Ronda's towering position.

Fiestas: In August the celebrations in honour of Pedro Romero, the grandfather of all matadors, include flamenco recitals and the so-called *Corridas Goyescas* in which the bullfighters wear period costumes that make them look as if they have sprung out of a Goya lithograph.

Local sights: The ruins of the Roman city of *Acinipo*, popularly known as Ronda la Vieja, lie 20km out of town. Near Benaoján (27km), the cave called the **Cueva de la Pileta** (open in summer: 9.00-2.00 and 4.00-7.00; winter: 4.00-6.00) has Stone Age paintings and is where some of the oldest pottery in Europe was found. You should not miss, once in Ronda, a tour of the nearby **Serranía**, or hills, where botanical curiosities include the *pinsapo*, or indigenous Spanish fir, and a drive along the white villages route, or the *Ruta de los Pueblos Blancos*. Taking this route W on the N-344, you reach **GRAZALEMA**, where its all too evident picturesque attractions are increased by a charming little hotel, the ★★ *Grazalema*, on a local road turning off at km344 ☎ 11 13 46 (ext. 101) 🛏 12 ⵏ 🅿 🌊 ≪, and by the *San José* handwoven textile workshop. Continuing SW you reach **UBRIQUE**, which is an excellent place to buy leather goods (purses, wallets and so on) —try *J. Batista*, c/ Guadalete, 1. The C-341, heading S, leads to Atajate, Jimena de Líbar, Benadalid, Algatocín, **GAUCIN** and to the Moorish castle town of **JIMENA DE LA FRONTERA**. From there the picturesque **clifftop road**, the C-339 which links Ronda and San Pedro de Alcántara, leads through barren, wild hills with no sign of human habitation to the all-too populated **Costa del Sol**.

On the town: The *Jerez*, opposite the bullring, is typical of Ronda's *tapa* bars.

Sports: There is good hunting in the **Coto Nacional de la Serranía de Ronda** game reserve.

SANLÚCAR DE BARRAMEDA **Cádiz** ☎ (956), pop. 52,832, ✚ 36 00 57, **P** 36 01 02. Cádiz 63km, Seville 99km, Madrid 625km.

On the estuary of the Guadalquivir river, Sanlúcar de Barrameda has a lot of things to boast about. Great discoverers, including **Columbus**, **Magellan** and **Elcano**, used the port of Sanlúcar de Barrameda for it was one of the most important in Spain in the late 15C. Somewhat less in the public eye now, the town is home to a delicious local type of sherry called **manzanilla** and is the centre of good horse, bull and flamenco country. Sanlúcar looks across the river to the **Doñana National Park**. The estuary has fine sandy   ⓑⓑⓒ **beaches** and is famous for its *langostinos* (king prawns).

- 🏨 ★★★ *Guadalquivir*, c/ Calzada del Ejército, s/n ☎ 36 07 42 🛏 85 **AE, DC, MC, V** $$ to $$$.
- 🏨 *Palacio de los Duques de Medina Sidonia*, c/ Conde de Niebla, 1 ☎ 36 01 61 🛏 3 ♣ $$. Lodging in a Renaissance style palace.
- 🍴 *Casa Bigote* (closed: Sundays), Bajo de Guía ☎ 36 26 96 **P** V $$ to $$$. ⓒ A modest tavern serving excellent fresh fish and seafood.

Best buys: Wines from the local *bodegas* and antiques from *Quirós*, c/ Santo Domingo, 13, are good buys.

Cultural highlights: The **Church of Santa María de la O**, with its ⓒ interesting Gothic-Mudéjar **W door**, and the 16C **Church of Santo Domingo** ⓒ are worth visiting. The Palace of the Dukes of Medina Sidonia is in the Renaissance style. There are good views from the ramparts of Santiago castle.

Fiestas: August events include a flamenco festival and horse racing along the beach. At Corpus Christi, solemnly celebrated here as elswhere in Spain, the custom is to carpet the streets with flowers. In May there is a wine festival, the *Feria de la Manzanilla* and later that month huge parties set off from the town, on horseback and with waggons rolling, to take part in the El Rocío pilgrimage (see 'Fiestas'). This involves a continual ferry service, and a very colourful one, across the Guadalquivir for the Shrine of El Rocío lies in Huelva province, just beyond the Doñana National Park.

Local sights: A visit to the **Doñana National Park** is a must.   ⓑⓑⓒ

SEVILLE **Seville** ☎ (954), pop. 668,356, [*i*] Av de la Constitución, 9 ☎   ⓑⓑⓒ 22 14 04, (Pl Nueva, 3, ✉ Av Constitución, s/n ☎ 22 88 80, ✚ 35 12 42, **P** Pl de la Gadivia, s/n ☎ 22 88 40, ✈ San Pablo, 12km ☎ 51 06 77 (Iberia, c/ Almirante Lobo, 2 ☎ 22 89 01), 🚌 c/ José María Osborne, s/n ☎ 23 22 10, 🚲 c/ Zaragoza, 29 ☎ 23 19 18. Huelva 94km, Cádiz 154km, Córdoba 155km, Málaga 207km, Madrid 538km.

There are a host of sensations surrounding Seville. First and foremost it is a joyous town which has an infectious gaiety about it. The Sevillians are famed for their wit and sparkle, gifts which are called *gracia*, a mix of humour and graciousness that is unknown outside Seville. The city itself is synonymous with *alegría*, another local concept which means sheer *joie de vivre*. If the vitality of the place is the most striking aspect about Seville, the next is its sensuality. There are special scents associated with Seville such as the pungent aroma of jasmine and orange blossom and then there are the rhythms of the *sevillanas*, dances which are charged with both *alegría* and *gracia* and an indefinable allure that just stops short of provocation.

The colourfulness of Seville comes next on most people's list and this is associated with the city's sense of show, of theatricality and of drama. The Sevillians are great actors and they put on an extraordinary performance in their annual *Feria* which is a gigantic street party that allows them to parade on their fine horses and in their tight-fitting costumes. Holy Week, *Semana Santa*, in Seville comes immediately before the *fiesta* blowout and is characterized by high drama and collective catharsis. Finally there is in Seville the sensation of beauty —parts of the city are insuperably beautiful and this seems to have instilled an instinctive feel for beauty in its inhabitants. The **Barrio de Santa Cruz** quarter, a sort of village within the city, is in its way as aesthetically satisfying as the more obvious twin architectural splendours of the city, the **Cathedral** and the royal palace and castle known as the **Alcázar**.

Suitably for such a fantasy city, Seville traces its past back to 2500 BC and a myth-shrouded kingdom called *Tartessos*. Known as *Hispalis* by the Carthaginians and capital of the province of *Baetica* during the Roman period, Seville was for a time the seat of the Visigothic court which succeeded the Romans and which eventually moved to Toledo. Though Córdoba was the capital of Muslim Spain, Seville, like Granada, was showered with favours. When Seville fell to the Christian troops of **Ferdinand III, the Saint**, in 1248, a decade after the conquest of Córdoba, the city became the southern capital of the Castilian monarchs. **Peter I, the Cruel**, who provoked a civil war during the 14C and was eventually murdered, to everyone's relief, by his half brother, adored Seville and rebuilt the Muslim Alcázar to serve as his palace.

Seville really came into its own with the discovery of the New World when the city became the clearing house for all the transatlantic trade and prospered immensely. Virtually every name associated with Spain's Golden Age —writers **Tirso de Molina, Lope de Vega** and **Cervantes**, painters **Velázquez, Murillo** and **Zurbarán**— was linked to Seville by birth or by extended stays in the city. Seville became the living, bustling and imaginative

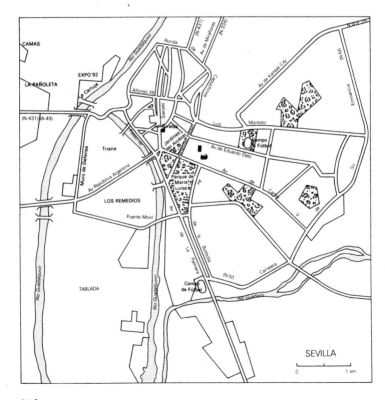

expression of Baroque Spain. Inevitably it declined and in its receding and fading glory it became emblematic of the collapse of Spanish might during the 17C. The city was buffeted by plagues, by an earthquake, by successive floods as the Guadalquivir (meaning 'Great River' in Arabic) broke its banks and, worst of all by the decision to switch the American trade centre from Seville to Cádiz.

Yet the effervescence that characterizes Seville kept bubbling during the bad times for the city had its heroes in its dancers, poets, artists and bullfighters. In 1929 things did begin to look up when a major fair, the **Ibero-American Exposition**, was staged in the city in honour of Seville's Latin American connection and did much to modernize parts of it and beautify others. Seville will receive another boost in 1992 when the **EXPO '92** Universal Exposition is held to commemorate the quincentenary of the discovery of the New World. Expo '92 will draw, on initial estimates, up to 40 million visitors over a six-month period and Seville is smartening itself up to receive them. This is something that it is adept at doing.

- ★★★★★ *Alfonso XIII*, c/ San Fernando, 2 ☎ 22 28 50 ⇌ 149 ᕯ TV ♣ ♗ ♗ ♗ ♨ ঌ ≈ AE, DC, EC, MC, V $$$$$ to $$$$$$. Gracious living in a palatial building.
- ★★★★ *Doña María*, c/ Don Remondo, 19 ☎ 22 49 90 ⇌ 61 ঌ ≈ ≪ ♗ ♗ AE, DC, V $$$$ to $$$$$. A bit like an elegant private home, it is near the Cathedral and has good views of the Giralda from its terrace.
- ★★★★ *Inglaterra*, Pl Nueva, 7 ☎ 22 49 70 ⇌ 120 TV ♨ AE, DC, EC, V $$$$ to $$$$$. A recently refurbished, central hotel, opposite the Town Hall.
- ★★★★ *Los Lebreros Sol*, c/ Luis de Morales, 2 ☎ 57 94 00 ⇌ 439 ᕯ TV ♣ ♨ ≈ 🖳 AE, DC, EC, MC, V $$$$$ to $$$$$$. A modern and functional hotel, with a popular restaurant, discotheque and cafeteria, near the Seville football stadium.
- ★★★★ *Macarena Sol*, c/ San Juan de Rivera, 2 ☎ 37 57 00 ⇌ 305 ᕯ TV ♨ ≈ AE, DC, V $$$$ to $$$$$$. Opposite the basilica of the Macarena, it has a typically Sevillian air to it.
- ★★★★ *Nuevo Lar*, Pl de Carmen Benítez, 3 ☎ 41 03 61 ⇌ 137 TV ♨ 🖳 AE, DC, EC, V $$$$ to $$$$$$. Popular with the business community.
- ★★★★ *Pasarela*, Av Borbolla, 11 ☎ 41 55 11 ⇌ 82 TV ♨ ঌ 🖳 AE, DC, EC, V $$$$$ to $$$$$$. Modern and agreeable.
- ★★★★ *Porta Coeli*, Av Eduardo Dato, 49 ☎ 57 00 40 ⇌ 246 TV ♣ ≈ AE, DC, V $$$$$ to $$$$$$. A modern hotel in the Nervión residential area.
- ★★★ *Alcázar*, c/ Menéndez Pelayo, 10 ☎ 41 20 11 ⇌ 96 P ♣ AE, DC, EC, MC, V $$$ to $$$$.
- ★★★ *América*, c/ Jesús del Gran Poder, 2 ☎ 22 09 51 ⇌ 100 TV ♣ ≪ AE, DC, MC, V $$$$ to $$$$$.
- ★★★ *Bécquer*, c/ Reyes Católicos, 4 ☎ 22 89 00 ⇌ 126 P AE, DC, EC, V $$$ to $$$$.
- ★★★ *Corregidor*, c/ Morgado, 17 ☎ 38 51 11 ⇌ 69 TV ♣ AE, DC, V $$$ to $$$$.
- ★★★ *Fernando III*, c/ San José, 21 ☎ 21 73 07 ⇌ 156 P ♨ ≈ AE, DC, EC, MC, V $$$ to $$$$. Pleasantly located near the picturesque Barrio de Santa Cruz.
- ★★★ *Monte Carmelo*, c/ Turia, 7 ☎ 27 90 00 ⇌ 68 P $$$ to $$$$. In the Remedios area, near the *Feria* zone, with a bullfighting atmosphere.
- ★★★ *Reyes Católicos*, c/ Gravina, 57 ☎ 21 12 00 ⇌ 26 TV AE, DC, EC, V $$$ to $$$$.
- ★★ *La Rábida*, c/ Castelar, 24 ☎ 22 09 60 ⇌ 87 ✕ ♣ $$ to $$$.

SEVILLA

Triana

0   100   200 m

- ▣ **★★ *Murillo***, c/ Lope de Rueda, 7 ☎ 21 60 95 ⛼ 61 **AE, DC, EC, V** $$ to $$$$.
- ▣ **★★ *Sevilla***, c/ Daoiz, 6 ☎ 38 41 61 ⛼ 32 $$ to $$$.
- 🍴 **Bodegón el Riojano** (closed: Sundays), c/ Virgen de las Montañas, 12, Los Remedios ☎ 45 06 82 ❋ **AE, DC, EC, MC, V** $$$. Andalusian cooking and a great array of *tapas* in the bar.
- 🍴 **Don Raimundo** (closed: Sunday nights), c/ Argote de Molina, 26 ☎ 22 33 55 ❋ **AE, DC, EC, MC, V** $$$. Seasonal cooking.
- 🍴 **Enrique Becerra** (closed: Sundays lunchtime), c/ Gamazo, 2 ☎ 21 30 49 ❋ **AE, V** $$$. Andalusian cooking and a good *tapa* selection.
- 🍴 **Figón del Cabildo** (closed: Sunday nights), Pl Cabildo, s/n ☎ 22 01 17 ❋ **AE, DC, MC, V** $$$ to $$$$. In a lovely square, it serves particularly good desserts.
- 🍴 **Jamaica**, c/ Jamaica, 16, Heliópolis ☎ 61 12 44 ❋ **AE, DC, EC, V** $$$ to $$$$. Simple and off the tourist beat.
- 🍴 **La Albahaca** (closed: Sundays), Pl Santa Cruz, 12 ☎ 22 07 14 ♣ ❋ **AE, DC, EC, MC, V** $$$. Seasonal cooking in a lovely old mansion.
- 🍴 **La Dorada** (closed: Sunday nights and 15/7-15/8), c/ Virgen de Aguasantas, 6, Los Remedios ☎ 45 51 00 and c/ J.L. de Caso, 18, Nervión ☎ 65 27 20 ❋ **AE, V** $$$. Specializes in fried fish and seafood.
- 🍴 **La Taberna del Alabardero** (closed: weekends), c/ Genaro Parladé, s/n ☎ 62 75 51 ❋ **AE, DC, V** $$$ to $$$$. Basque cuisine.
- 🍴 **Maîtres** (closed: Sundays), Av República Argentina, 54, Los Remedios ☎ 45 68 80 ❋ **AE, DC, V** $$$. Spanish cooking.
- 🍴 **Or-Iza** (closed: Sundays and August), c/ San Fernando, 41 ☎ 22 72 11 ❋ **AE, DC, EC, V** $$$. Basque cuisine.
- 🍴 **Ox's** (closed: Sundays and August), c/ Betis, 61, Triana ☎ 27 95 85 **P** ❋ **AE, DC, EC, V** $$$. Basque cuisine.
- 🍴 **Rincón de Curro**, c/ Virgen de Luján, 45, Los Remedios ☎ 45 02 38 ❋ **AE, DC, MC, V** $$$. A very popular restaurant serving Andalusian cooking.
- 🍴 **Río Grande**, c/ Betis, s/n, Triana ☎ 27 83 71 ♣ ❋ ≪ **AE, DC, EC, V** $$$. By the river, with good views of the Torre del Oro.
- 🍴 **San Marco** (closed: Sundays and August), c/ Cuna, 6 ☎ 21 24 40 ❋ **AE, DC, EC, MC, V** $$$ to $$$$. Creative cooking in a fashionable setting.

🍴 **Best buys:** Ceramics bearing the **Cartuja de Sevilla** trademark can be bought from various shops or from the factory itself, just outside town at km529 on the Mérida road, close to the *Itálica* Roman ruins, and other ceramics from the workshops in the Triana quarter such as **Cerámica Santa Ana**, c/ San Jorge, 31, **Montalbán**, c/ Alfarería, 23, and the **Taller de Reproducciones del s. XVIII**, c/ Aguilas, 25. Other local buys would have to include saddlery from **San Pablo**, c/ San Pablo, 8, and **El Caballo**, c/ Antonio Díaz, 7; wrought iron from **J. Contreras**, c/ Obispo Zumárraga, 45; castanets from **Hernández**, c/ Purgatorio, 6; flamenco guitars from **A. Pantoja**, c/ Pozo, 20; fans from **Rubio**, c/ Sierpes, 56; wide-brimmed Andalusian hats from **A. García**, c/ Alcaicería, 29; flamenco dresses from **Maricruz**, c/ Cuna, 74, and **Lina**, c/ Lineros, 15; lace and shawls from various shops including **Foronda**, c/ Alvarez Quintero, 52; religious embroidery crafted by nuns from the **Convento Santa Isabel**, c/ Iníesta, 2; local delicacies, cakes and pastries from **La Campana**, c/ Sierpes, 1, **Nova Roma**, c/ Virgen de Luján, 16, **Ochoa**, c/ Sierpes, 45, and **Horno de San Buenaventura**, c/ C. Cañal, 28; egg-yolk sweets known as *yemas* from the **Convento de San Leandro**, Pl San Ildefonso, 1; home-made jam from the **Convento de Santa Paula**, c/ Santa Paula, 11; wines from **La Casa de los**

Licores, c/ Virgen de Luján, 35; works of art from *Juana de Aizpuru*, c/ Zaragoza, 26, *La Máquina Española*, c/ Pastor y Landero, 22, and *Rafael Ortiz*, c/ Mármoles, 12; arts and crafts from the *Lonja de Artesanía del Postigo* workshop, c/ Arfe, s/n, and from *Artespaña*, Pl de la Concordia, 2; and antiques from *Almoneda Santa Teresa*, c/ Santa Teresa, 17, *Altamira*, c/ Rodrigo Cano, 7, *A. Plata*, c/ Placentines, 41, *Segundo*, c/ Sierpes, 81, and from the important antiques fair staged in April ☎ 21 65 58. All sorts of general bargains can be had at the Thursday morning flea market called *El Jueves*, in c/ Feria, and at the Sunday morning one in the Alhameda de Hércules, while coins and stamps are best bought at the Sunday morning mart in the Pl del Cabildo. For Spanish fashion, go to *Adolfo Domínguez*, c/ Rioja, 1, *Boutique 78*, c/ Asunción, 78, *Vitorio y Lucchino*, c/ Sierpes, 87, and *Meye Maier*, Pasaje Vilas, 12, selling original blouses and lingerie. Leatherwear is best at *Loewe*, Pl Nueva, 12, while shoes are ideal at *P. Burgos*, c/ San Vicente Paul, 20, and *Ruster*, c/ Asunción, 40. The city's large department stores are *El Corte Inglés*, Pl del Duque, 10 and Av Luis Montoto, 122, and *Galerías Preciados*, c/ San Pablo, 1.

Cultural highlights: Walking around Seville, there are certain obvious landmarks and essential itineraries. The Cathedral is a clear starting point and if you are feeling fit, treat yourself to the **best view of the city** by walking up the ramps to the top of the Giralda tower. The Reales Alcázares, nearby, are the next most important item on every city tour and the magical *pueblo* world of the **Barrio de Santa Cruz** with its intimate little plazas and **patios** comes next and is also in the immediate vicinity. Streets and alleyways like the Callejón del Agua and the c/ Pimienta and squares like the **Pl Doña Elvira** and the **Pl Santa Cruz** are in the heart of the *barrio* and the best time to visit the quarter is as evening falls. The Ayuntamiento, or Town Hall, is another landmark and this is the starting point for an exploration of the pedestrianized **c/ Sierpes** which is a perpetual human thoroughfare and is perfect for window shopping and bar hopping. A third starting point is the Archivo de Indias which serves for walks along the banks of the Guadalquivir. Going down river and away from the town centre, you reach the extremely pleasant gardens of the **María Luisa Park** through which you can ride in a horse-drawn carriage. Going up river, you reach the bullring, the **Plaza de Toros de la Maestranza**, from where you can cut back to the Town Hall and the Cathedral or continue on to the **Puente de Triana** to cross the river and enter **Triana**, the extremely popular fishermen's quarter of Seville that is not spectacular in any way but is very authentic. A proper cultural tour of the city must necessarily include a call on the religious images that are kept in their respective shrines all year round but are brought out for Holy Week's penitential processions and paraded around the streets accompanied by a fervent devotion that borders on fanaticism. The image of Mary, the *Virgen de la Macarena*, in the basilica of the same name, is deeply revered throughout the city as is the image of Christ called the *Jesús del Gran Poder* which was sculpted by Juan de Mesa in 1620 and stands in its basilica on the Pl de San Lorenzo. Two further indisputable stars of Sevillian religious imagery and of the Holy Week processions are in Triana. The Virgin known as the *Esperanza de Triana* is in a chapel on c/ Pureza and the striking 17C *Cristo del Cachorro* is in the Patrocinio chapel in c/ Castilla.

The **Cathedral** is so massive and so embedded in the middle of the city that it is difficult to obtain a proper perspective of its size and shape from ground level. It is the third largest cathedral in Christendom after Saint Peter's in Rome and Saint Paul's in London. As is so often the case in Spain's cathedrals it is built on the site of what was first a Visigothic church and then an important mosque. When Seville's authorities decided to build a major cathedral on this site in 1402 they fortunately preserved the tower, the Giralda, from the original mosque and also the spacious courtyard called the Patio de los Naranjos. Work on the cathedral's structure was not completed until 1519 and mishaps included the collapse of the cimborium which was replaced in 1511 by Juan Gil de Hontañón, the master builder responsible for the cathedrals of Salamanca and Segovia. Diego de Siloé, another frontline 16C artist, collaborated on the Chapter House. The outstanding portal is the Puerta del Perdón, whose stucco work dates from 1522, and the Patio de los Naranjos courtyard, which contains a Visigothic baptismal font, is another exceptional architectural feature. Inside the cathedral the vastness, the pervading gloom and the wealth of chapels and works of art produce a confusing first impression. Memorable features include the gigantic altarpiece in the chancel, or Capilla Mayor, the huge 16C wrought iron screen that closes off the chapel from the public, the Gothic choir stalls, and the richly decorated Capilla Real. The statue of the *Virgen de los Reyes*, a 13C image revered as the patroness of Seville, occupies pride of place on the high altar and just as memorable are the silver urn said to contain the allegedly uncorrupted remains of Ferdinand III, the Saint, who conquered Seville, and the tomb of his wife, Beatrice, and of his son and successor, Alfonso X, the Wise. Another magnificent 16C wrought iron screen closes off the choir, and the 18C organs look splendid and sound even better. The other chapels, although less grand, are full of surprises such as paintings by Murillo in the one dedicated to San Antonio and by Zurbarán in the San Pedro Chapel. Just as startling, but out of place, is the 19C funeral monument to Christopher Columbus in the transept. You might expect a good museum in a cathedral as big, old and wealthy as Seville's and you are not disappointed in that there are religious pictures, including works by Zurbarán and Goya, in the Sacristía de los Cálices, and there are more Zurbaráns in a larger picture collection which includes works by Murillo, Van Dyck and Morales in the Sacristía Mayor. One high point of what the cathedral rightly calls its Treasure is the huge golden monstrance, or *custodia*, which is used in Corpus Christi processions, and another is the Murillo *Inmaculada* which dominates the Chapter House (open in summer: 10.30-1.30 and 4.30-6.30; winter: 10.30-1.30 and 4.00-6.00; closed: Sunday afternoons). The 98m high Giralda, the cathedral's Arab tower and Seville's best known landmark, was built in the 12C. It had a belfry added to it in 1568 and also an allegorical sculpture known as the *Giraldillo* which purports to show the triumph of the True Faith but which is in reality a weather vane.

The Reales Alcázares (open: 9.00-12.00 and 3.00-5.00 ☎ 22 71 63) is a complex of buildings, gardens and patios that has served as a royal residence from the 8C to the present day. It has been used in turn by the early emirs who began to build it in 712, by the Almohad dynasty of the 12C who enlarged it, and from which period the Patio del Yeso survives, and then by the kings and queens of Spain who added buildings and carried out alterations down the centuries. Alfonso X, the Wise, added three Gothic halls to the Almohad palace in the 13C but it was Peter I, the Cruel, 100 years later who built a whole Alcázar castle here and ensured that his residence would stand the test of time as one of the great examples of Christian-Muslim cultural cross-fertilization that is called Mudéjar art. The Catholic Monarchs later added their refurbishings, as did their grandson, Emperor Charles V, who married Isabella of Portugal here. More gardens and the courtyard called the Patio de la Montería were added in the 17C by the Count Duke of Olivares, the strongman who virtually ruled Spain during the reign of the feeble Hapsburg Philip IV. The interior of the complex revolves around the **Patio de las Doncellas**, site of official functions, which was unfortunately altered in the 16C, and the delightful **Patio de las Muñecas** which had apartments added in the 19C for royal visitors. The main hall is the Salón de Embajadores where visiting dignitaries were received under the finely carved 15C wooden cupola. The most historical rooms are the stucco decorated ones that were used by Isabella the Catholic Queen, Philip II and the earlier Muslim monarchs. One of the most pleasurable aspects of a visit to the Reales Alcázares is, of course, the complex's magnificent **pleasure gardens**.

The **Casa de Pilatos**, Pl Pilatos, 1 (open in summer: 10.00-8.00; winter: 10.00-6.00 ☎ 22 52 98), is arguably Seville's top aristocratic town mansion and it is the only one open to the general public. Built in 1521, it is an admirable architectural mix, and an essentially Spanish one, which combines Mudéjar, Gothic and Renaissance elements. In addition it exhibits old master canvases, Roman and Renaissance statues and also exemplifies beautifully the typically Andalusian use of **glazed tiles** for decorative effect.

The **Hospital de la Caridad**, c/ Temprado, s/n (open: 10.00-1.00 and 4.00-7.00 ☎ 22 32 32 and 21 77 38), occupies a special place in the Sevillian imagination for it was founded by a dissolute 17C gentleman called Miguel de Mañara who, in repentance for his wayward life, endowed the hospital just before his death. Local lore has it that Mañara was the model for the legendary Don Juan but this is wishful thinking for the play by Tirso de Molina that first put Don Juan, the repentant reprobate, on the literary map was already being staged when Mañara was a child. What is important here is the church's art collection which includes paintings by Murillo and Valdés Leal and a fine carving of the Holy Sepulchre by Pedro Roldán.

A visitor who really wants to discover the essence of Seville will soon find that this involves becoming acquainted with an incredible number of **churches** and convents for these are the guardians of the explosion of art work that occurred in the city during its 17C Golden Age. A short list of what are called the *fernandine* churches, those built in the aftermath of the city's Christian conquest by Ferdinand III, the Saint, in the Gothic-Mudéjar style, includes **San Isidoro**, **San Marcos**, **Omnium Sanctorum**, **San Pedro** and **San Esteban**. The top Renaissance period churches are the **Anunciación** and **Santa Ana** in Triana. Baroque, in a place like Seville, is best and the selection here must include the very beautiful **Church of La Magdalena**, the **Hospital de los Venerables** on Pl de los Venerables (open: 10.00-2.00 and 4.00-8.00; closed: Sunday afternoons), with a good art collection, the **Church of San Luis** and the grandiose, cathedral-like **Church of El Salvador** which preserves the orange-tree courtyard of the original mosque on whose site it stands.

To complete Seville's cultural tour, there are a number of secular buildings that deserve closer scrutiny. The **Ayuntamiento**, or Town Hall, was designed in the florid Plateresque style in 1527 by Diego de Riaño and it provides an interesting contrast to the **Archivo de Indias** (open: 10.00-1.00; researchers: 8.00-3.00; closed: weekends) which was designed by Juan de Herrera, the influential architect patronized by Philip II 50 years later, who introduced severe forms and austerity into Spanish design. The building used to be the main exchange in the days when Seville held the New World trade monopoly and when the privilege moved to Cádiz it was turned into a records office. Anybody who seriously wants to study the age of discoveries, and in particular the colonization of Latin America, must sooner rather than later consult the manuscripts housed in its archives. In the same neighbourhood, the riverside round tower called the **Torre del Oro** was built during the Almohad dynasty in the 13C and contains a maritime museum, the **Museo Náutico** (open: 10.00-2.00; Sundays: 10.00-1.00; closed: Mondays ☎ 22 24 19). The old Tobacco Factory, or **Fábrica de Tabacos**, now part of Seville's University, was the first of its kind in Europe, and in the 18C employed 6,000 cigar-rolling girls, one of whom was **Carmen** of opera fame. Among the elegant private houses in Seville are the mansion of the Countess of Lebrija, c/ Cuna, 18 (visits by prior arrangement ☎ 22 78 02), which contains many antiquities from the Roman town of *Itálica*, and the very impressive **Palacio de las Dueñas**, c/ Dueñas, s/n (visits by prior arrangement ☎ 22 09 56), which is unspoilt Mudéjar-Renaissance.

🜂 The **Archaeological Museum**, Pl de América, s/n (open: 10.00-2.00; closed: Sundays and Mondays ☎ 23 24 01 and 23 53 89), has a very
🜂 important **Roman art collection** drawn from *Itálica* and other sites in
🜂🜂 Andalusia, and fascinating pieces from the **kingdom of *Tartessos***. The Fine
🜂🜂 Arts Museum, or **Museo de Bellas Artes**, Pl Museo, 9 (open: 10.00-2.00; weekends: 10.00-1.00 and 4.00-7.00; closed: Mondays ☎ 22 18 29 and 22 07 90), is magnificently housed in a Baroque convent and has a fine collection including works by members of the 17C Seville School (Pacheco and his son-in-law Velázquez), Murillo, Zurbarán, Valdés Leal, El Greco, Ribera, Morales and others. The **Museo de Arte Contemporáneo**, c/ Santo Tomás, 5 (open: 10.00-2.00 and 5.00-8.00; closed: weekend afternoons and Mondays ☎ 21 58 30), housed in an 18C mansion, exhibits 20C works
🜂 emphasizing those of Sevillian artists, and the **Museo-Casa Murillo**, c/ Santa Teresa, s/n (open: 10.00-2.00 and 4.00-7.00; closed: weekend afternoons and Mondays), is a collection of paintings by the master, his pupils and his imitators in a charming setting of period furniture and objects.
Fiestas and festivals: The Holy Week penitential processions of Seville's
🜂🜂🜂 *Semana Santa* draw enormous crowds and, just as in the *Feria* week, it is 🜂🜂 very difficult to find a hotel bed in Seville if you have not booked well in advance. An extraordinary atmosphere of popular religious fervour is created during Holy Week as images of the Virgin and Christ are paraded around the streets at night by brotherhoods of hooded penitents. The local press and, better still, the Sevillians themselves will tell you where to be and at what time to watch the floats pass by. One of the most moving moments of this indescribable Holy Week happening comes when the procession stops and the crowd is silenced as individual spectators spontaneously break into a piercing wail of flamenco song called a *saeta* in tribute to the passing
🜂🜂🜂 religious figure. The *Feria* in April is the city's other major outdoor show. It consists of an extraordinarily colourful week during which horsemen and carriages parade up and down the fair's grounds and there is non-stop eating, drinking and flamenco dancing until dawn and some of the top events
🜂🜂🜂 of the **bullfighting** calendar. Originally a cattle fair, it has become a gigantic city party in which Sevillians flaunt themselves before each other and the
🜂 world. The June **Corpus Christi** procession in Seville is very ceremoniously celebrated as the giant **monstrance** is rolled out of the Cathedral to wind its way through the city. In the Cathedral itself a unique liturgical event is staged which consists of a minuet that is danced before the High Altar by a troupe
🜂 of young boys called the *seises* who are dressed up as Renaissance pageboys. From April to June there is a varied programme of theatrical productions, art exhibitions, classical concerts and flamenco and rock shows that is called *Cita en Sevilla*. There are also **bullfights** every Sunday during the season as well as every day during the April *Feria* and during a second
🜂🜂 bullfight fair in September. Other cultural events include the *Bienal de Arte Flamenco* flamenco festival in September, the *Festival Internacional de Cine* cinema festival in October, and the *Festival Internacional de Títeres* puppet festival in December.

Local sights: Taking the Huelva road and crossing the Guadalquivir river just out of town you pass by the Isla de la Cartuja which is the site of the **1992 Seville Universal Exposition - EXPO'92**. The **Cartuja de Santa María de las Cuevas**, or Charterhouse, was the only building on these grounds before work began in preparation for the Expo '92 and it will be the royal pavilion during the Expo. It was founded in 1440 and was, for a time, Pickman's ceramics factory (producing the *La Cartuja de Sevilla* glazed earthenware and tiles) in the 19C after the friars left.

The **Roman ruins** of the 3C town of *Itálica* are just out of the village of **Santiponce**, 8km along the N-630. Originally a military camp created by Scipio for his legions, *Itálica* grew into a town of some consequence and was the birthplace of the emperors Trajan and Hadrian. Today the visitor sees the remains of an **amphitheatre**, a forum, baths and of several villas and town buildings. There is a small **museum** (open: 9.00-5.30; weekends: 10.00-4.00) exhibiting some of the site's antiquities but the main treasures are in Seville's Archaeological Museum and in the Palace of the Countess of Lebrija. Leaving Santiponce, the 15C **Monastery of San Isidoro del Campo** is worth visiting for its excellent altarpiece executed by Martínez Montañés in 1613.

On the town: You will find that people rarely sit down to eat in Seville for they prefer wandering from bar to bar eating *tapas*. On summer evenings the taverns in the villages just outside the city, known as the *ventas sevillanas*, are very popular and people make trips out to places like *Vázquez Gaviño* in La Pañoleta, 2km from Seville taking the Huelva exit, *Manolo* in La Algaba, 5km away, and the *Ventorrillo Canario* in Santiponce, 9km from town. A short list of Seville's *tapa* bars would have to include *Alicantina*, Pl del Salvador, 2, *Caimán*, c/ Virgen de las Montañas, 16, *Casa Alonso*, c/ Pagés del Corro, 96, *Casa Morales*, c/ García de Vinuesa, 11 (you can buy fried fish in the takeaway across the road), *Casa Román*, Pl de los Venerables, 1, *El Joven Costalero*, c/ Torneo, s/n, *El Morapio*, c/ Pelay Correa, s/n, *Sopa de Ganso*, c/ Pérez Galdós, 8, *El Tenorio*, c/ Mateos Gago, 11, and *Giralda* at No. 3 and, perhaps the most typical of the lot, *El Rinconcillo*, which is in a 17C house at c/ Gerona, 42. *Abades*, c/ Abades, 13, is a beautiful old mansion turned into a sophisticated, spacious and gracious cocktail bar and *Bai Bai*, Av Blas Infante, 6, is different again for it serves Polynesian concoctions and stages fringe theatre shows. Young people gather at the *Patio de San Laureano*, c/ Alfonso XII, s/n, and the arts crowd at *La Carbonería*, c/ Levíes, 18. Discos include *El Coto*, c/ Luis Montoto, 118 (all-comers), *Holiday*, c/ Jesús del Gran Poder, 7 (more sedate), *Piruetas*, c/ Asunción, 3, and *Tukán*, Av República Argentina, 66 (wilder). For **flamenco shows** try 🝊 *Los Gallos*, Pl Santa Cruz, 11, *Tablao de Curro Vélez*, c/ Rodó, 7, and *La Trocha*, Ronda de Capuchinos, 23. If you prefer all your entertainment in one area, try c/ Betis in the Triana district, which is full of riverside terraces like the *Río Grande*, discos like *Dragón Rojo* and bars like *La Albariza*.

Sports: Flying and parachuting fans can go to the *Aeroclub de Sevilla* ☎ 43 34 79. Land sports include good fishing and hunting throughout the province —hunters contact the *Sociedad Deportiva de Caza* ☎ 22 86 89; riding and horse racing at the *Club Pineda* country club ☎ 61 14 00, which also has a 9-hole, par 70 golf course and tennis courts; tennis at the *Betis Tenis Club* ☎ 23 10 28, the *Club de Tenis El Pino* ☎ 25 36 50, and the *Real Automóvil Club de Andalucía* ☎ 63 13 50; squash at the *Antares Squash Raquet Club* ☎ 21 78 89; and clay-pigeon shooting at the *Club El Carambolo* ☎ 33 04 01. Finally, water sports fans can go sailing at the *Club Náutico de Sevilla* ☎ 45 03 10.

◐◑ **SIERRA NEVADA** **Granada** ☎ (958). Granada 32km, Madrid 461km.
Just 32km from Granada and 80km from the Costa del Sol reached via
the highest surfaced **highway** in Europe —from which **panoramic views** are ◐◑
commonplace— the Sierra Nevada mountain range is home to the highest
mountain peaks in the peninsula, the 3,478m high **Mulhacén** and the
3,392m high **Veleta**. Along with Alcazaba, Vacores, and El Caballo, these
peaks are excellent mountain climbing territory and even better skiing ground.

◐ The **Solynieve** ski resort (see 'Holidays in Action') enjoys an average of 250
days of sunshine a year, easy access to the slopes and so much snow that
the skiing season lasts from December to late April. The slopes are between
2,100 and 3,470m above sea level, and the resort has all sorts of facilities,
including 18 lifts which give access to a total of 25 marked ski runs. For
information, call *CETURSA* ☎ 48 05 00 or the *Escuela Española de Esquí*
(Spanish Skiing School) ☎ 48 01 68. But there is more to *Solynieve* than
sun and snow... there are good hotels and restaurants catering to all tastes
and pockets, and there is also a lively *après ski* scene at the **Babel** disco, in
the *Meliá Sierra Nevada* hotel, and at *Gunila's* disco pub.

▦ ★★★★ *Meliá Sierra Nevada* (closed: 1/5-30/11), c/ Pradollano, s/n
☎ 48 04 00 ⇌ 221 ✕ ☲ ▣ ♪ ▦ AE, DC, EC, V $$$$$. Near the
lifts and with a heated swimming pool.

▦ ★★★ *Meliá Solynieve* (closed: 1/5-30/11), c/ Pradollano, s/n ☎
48 03 00 ⇌ 178 ☲ ▣ ♦ ≪ ◆ AE, DC, EC, V $$$$. Near the lifts, with
good service and a pleasant atmosphere.

▦ ★★★ *Nevasur* (closed: 1/6-30/11), c/ Pradollano, s/n ☎ 48 03 50 ⇌
50 ≪ AE, V $$$. 1km from the lifts, with a pleasant atmosphere and
good views.

▦ ★★★ *Parador Sierra Nevada*, km36 on the Sierra Nevada road, in
Monachil ☎ 48 02 00 ⇌ 32 ✕ ☲ ▣ ♦ ⅏ ≪ ◔ AE, DC, EC, V $$$ to
$$$$. Outside the *Solynieve* ski resort, this alpine chalet has a good
restaurant with an open fire, and large picture windows offering
panoramic views.

▯ *Cunini* (closed: 1/6-30/11), Edif Bulgaria, 2 ☎ 48 01 70 AE, DC, V
$$$. Fish and seafood from the nearby Costa del Sol.

▯ *Pourquoi Pas* (closed: 1/6-30/11), Pl Pradollano, s/n ☎ 48 03 07 $$$.
French cuisine in an intimate atmosphere. Advance bookings are
necessary.

◐ **TORREMOLINOS** **Málaga** ☎ (952), pop. 25,000, *i* c/ Guetaria, s/n ☎
38 15 78, *i* at the airport ☎ 31 20 44, ℭ Pl de la Estación, s/n, ✉ Av
Palma de Mallorca, s/n ☎ 38 45 18, ✛ 25 04 50, **P** 38 14 22, ✈ Málaga,
4km ☎ 35 17 25 (Iberia ☎ 32 20 00, Aviaco ☎ 31 39 92), ▭ c/ Hoyo, s/n
☎ 38 09 65, ▥ Av de la Estación, s/n ☎ 38 57 64. Málaga 14km,
Algeciras 124km, Madrid 572km.

Torremolinos is a product of the **costa tourist boom** in all its glory and
you either love it or loathe it. It seems an unbelievable cliché to say that this
was a quiet little fishing village not so long ago but it really was and one
keeps bumping into people who knew it as it used to be. Nowadays it has the
highest number of apartment blocks on the coast and one of the highest in
Europe. It is a visitor's paradise —the perfect place for young, fun-loving
people in summer, for elderly folk in winter, and for businessmen all year
round (it has one of the best **congress halls** in Spain).

◐ ▦ ★★★★★ *Castillo de Santa Clara*, c/ Suecia, 1 ☎ 38 31 55 ⇌ 191
and 97 apartments ✕ ▣ ♦ ♦ ⅏ ▦ ☲ ▥ ≪ ◔ AE, DC, EC, MC, V
$$$$$. Ideally located on a promontory overlooking the sea, with
Bajondillo beach on one side and La Carihuela beach on the other.

▥ ★★★★★ *Meliá Torremolinos* (closed: 1/11-1/3), Av Carlota Alessandri, ✆
109 ☎ 38 05 00 ➤ 283 TV ✦ ♦ ⅗ ≈ ⌁ 200m ≪ ⅋ ⚲ AE, DC, EC, MC,
V $$$$ to $$$$$. Set 200m from the beach, it has lush tropical gardens
and a pleasant swimming pool.

▥ ★★★★ *Al-Andalus*, Av Montemar, s/n ☎ 38 12 00 ➤ 164 Υ ✦ ≈ ⌁
300m ≪ ⚲ AE, DC, EC, V $$ to $$$$. Set 300m from the beach, with
good views and a pleasant garden.

▥ ★★★★ *Aloha Puerto-Sol*, Vía Imperial, 55 ☎ 38 70 66 ➤ 418 ⅙ ✦ ♦
⅗ ≈ ⌁ 100m ▦ ≪ ⅋ ⥅ ▲ ⚲ AE, DC, V $$$ to $$$$$. Quiet, with
good views of the sea and the port of Benalmádena.

▥ ★★★★ *Cervantes*, c/ Las Mercedes, s/n ☎ 38 40 33 ➤ 393 TV ✦ ❊ ♦
⅗ ≈ ⌁ 700m ▦ ≪ ⅋ AE, DC, EC, MC, V $$$ to $$$$. Located in the
centre of Torremolinos near most of the shops and nightlife, it has a lively
atmosphere and a heated swimming pool.

▥ ★★★★ *Don Pablo*, Paseo Marítimo, s/n ☎ 38 38 88 ➤ 443 ⅙ ✦ ❊ ♦
≈ ⌁ ▦ ≪ ⅋ ⥅ ▲ ⚲ AE, DC, EC, MC, V $$$ to $$$$. Set on
Bajondillo beach facing the sea, it has good views, a heated swimming
pool and a disco.

▥ ★★★★ *Meliá Costa del Sol*, Paseo Marítimo s/n ☎ 38 66 77 ➤ 540
🅿 ✦ ♦ ⅗ ≈ ⌁ 50m ≪ ⅋ ⥅ ▲ AE, DC, EC, MC, V $$$ to $$$$.
Ideally situated on Bajondillo beach, it has good views.

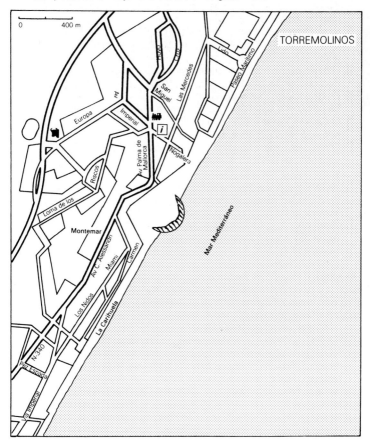

○ ▦ ★★★★ *Parador del Golf*, 4km on the Málaga road ☎ 38 12 55 ⇤ 40 TV
▪ ▪ ▪ ▪ ▪ « ▪ ▪ AE, DC, V $$$$. Quiet, set amidst leafy gardens and next to the golf course and a semi private beach.

▦ ★★★★ *Pez Espada*, Vía Imperial ☎ 38 03 00 ⇤ 149 ▪ ▪ ▪ ▪ ▪ ▪
« ▪ ▪ AE, DC, EC, V $$$ to $$$$. One of the pioneers of the coastal hotels, it has large tropical gardens extending to the beach.

▦ ★★★★ *Tropicana*, c/ Trópico, 6 ☎ 38 66 00 ⇤ 86 TV ▪ ▪ ▪ 100m «
▪ AE, DC, V $$$ to $$$$. Set in an exotic garden bordering La Carihuela beach.

▦ ★★★ *Amaragua*, c/ Los Nidos, s/n ☎ 38 47 00 ⇤ 198 P ▪ ▪ ▪ ▪
▪ ▪ « ▪ ▪ ▪ ▪ AE, DC, EC, MC, V $$$. On La Carihuela beach, it has good views of the bay.

▦ ★★★ *Don Pedro*, Av de Lido, s/n ☎ 38 68 44 ⇤ 290 Y ▪ ▪ ▪ ▪
200m ▪ ▪ AE, DC, EC, V $$ to $$$. Near the beach, with good facilities.

▦ ★★★ *Las Palomas Sol*, c/ Carmen Montes, 1 ☎ 38 50 00 ⇤ 294 ▪
▪ ▪ ▪ 350m ▪ ▪ ▪ $$ to $$$. Set on the motorway next to the exit for La Carihuela, it is 350m from the beach.

▦ ★★★ *Sidi Lago Rojo*, c/ Miami, 1 ☎ 38 76 66 ⇤ 144 ▪ ▪ ▪ $$$.

▦ ★★ *Miami*, c/ Aladino, 14 ☎ 38 52 55 ⇤ 26 P ▪ ▪ ▪ ▪ 100m «
$$. Originally an Andalusian residence belonging to a cousin of Picasso's, it has been turned into a hotel with a lot of character, pleasant banana tree-shaded gardens and a swimming pool.

○ ⑪ *Casa Guaquín* (closed: Thursdays and December), c/ Carmen, 37, La Carihuela ☎ 38 45 30 ▪ « AE, DC, V $$$. Excellent fried fish and grilled pepper salad served on a typical open-air terrace.

⑪ *Casa Prudencio* (closed: Wednesdays and Christmas), c/ Carmen, 43, La Carihuela ☎ 38 14 52 ▪ « AE, EC, V $$$. Also offers ★ lodging $$.

⑪ *El Atrio* (closed: Sundays), Casablanca, Pueblo Blanco, La Nogalera ☎ 38 88 50 ▪ V $$$. French cuisine served in a pleasant terrace.

⑪ *El Caballo Vasco* (closed: Mondays and November), Casablanca, La Nogalera ☎ 38 23 36 ▪ ※ ▪ ▪ AE, DC, EC, V $$$. Basque cuisine.

⑪ *El Roqueo* (closed: Tuesdays and November), c/ Carmen, 35, La Carihuela ☎ 38 49 46 ▪ « AE, V $$$. Good fish and seafood served on a pleasant terrace with good views.

⑪ *Frutos* (closed: Sunday nights from 1/10-1/6), km235 on the Cádiz road, Urb Los Alamos ☎ 38 14 50 P ▪ ※ AE, V $$$. Popular with the locals, it serves simple home cooking on a pleasant terrace.

⑪ *Juan* (closed: 1/11-15/12), c/ Mar, 9, La Carihuela ☎ 38 56 56 ▪ «
AE, V $$$. Fresh fish served on an outdoor terrace.

⑪ *La Jábega*, c/ Mar, 17, La Carihuela ☎ 38 63 75 ▪ « V $$ to $$$. Local fish dishes.

Beaches: The beaches are sandy and clean but crowded. To the E of the
○ promontory marking the *Castillo de Santa Clara* hotel, **Bajondillo** beach is followed by the very pleasant sandy stretch of **El Lido** (also called **Playamar**), while **La Carihuela** and Montemar beaches are to the W. There is a nudist zone between Bajondillo and El Lido.

Best buys: Andalusian crafts like leather goods made in Ubrique, ceramics from Coín and carpets woven in the Alpujarras region are sold in the many local bazaars. Spanish fashion is available from *Don Miguel*, Ctra de Cádiz, 5; suede and leather goods are best at *Zerimar*, c/ San Miguel, 22, and, on the same street at Nos. 13 and 40, *Saco* and *Candy* sell *avant garde* costume jewelry.

Local sights: In Churriana there are two extremely attractive gardens close to each other which can make a good break from the sea and sand hurly

burly. The **Finca de El Retiro**, created in the 18C, has a perfect romantic air
to it with its fountains and marble statues and a similar atmosphere is created
by the **Finca de la Cónsula**, which was set up in the last century by the
Russian consul stationed in Málaga. Also inland, **BENALMADENA** (*i* Castillo
del Bil-Bil ☎ 44 13 63), originally a Phoenician colony which was later
settled by the Romans and the Moors, still retains its network of typically
Moorish narrow streets. While here you can visit the town's Archaeological
Museum, Av Luis Peralta, 43 (open: 10.00-2.00 and 4.00-7.00; Sundays:
10.00-4.00; closed: Mondays ☎ 44 84 00), with a number of pre-Colombian
Amerindian exhibits, and then head for the village church, which provides
magnificent views of the Sierra de Mijas mountains, of the azure sea below
and of the exotic surrounding landscape with its luxuriant and vivid
vegetation. For a completely different scene, wend your way down to the
modern tourist complex of **BENALMADENA COSTA**, which is virtually a
continuation of Torremolinos' seaside wall of concrete. Here there are good
water sports and **golf** facilities (see 'Sports' below) for daytime entertainment,
and lots of bars, open-air terraces and a casino (see 'On the town' below)
make for a very lively nightlife. For accommodation in Benalmádena Costa, try
the ★★★★★ *Tritón*, Av Antonio Machado, 29 ☎ 44 32 40 ☎ 196 TV ✦ ☘
☮ ☂ ▦ ≪ ☙ ♃ AE, DC, MC, V $$$$$, set in lovely tropical gardens and
with good views, the ★★★★ *Riviera*, Av Antonio Machado, 49 ☎ 44 12 40
☎ 189 P ✦ ☘ ☮ ☂ ▦ ≪ ♃ AE, DC, MC, V $$$ to $$$$$, which has
pleasant garden terraces and good views, the ★★★ *La Roca*, Santa Ana
beach, km221.5 on the Cádiz-Málaga road ☎ 44 17 40 ☎ 53 ☖ P ✦ ☮ ☂
≪ AE, DC, EC, V $$$, with good views, the ★★★ *Los Patos Sol*, km227
on the Cádiz Malaga road ☎ 44 19 90 ☎ 270 P ✦ ☙ ☮ ☂ ≪ ☙ ♃ AE,
DC, MC, V $$$, with a lovely garden and heated swimming pool, or the
★★★ *Siroco*, km228 on the Cádiz Málaga road ☎ 44 30 40 ☎ 256 P ✦
☮ ≪ ☙ ♃ ☙ AE, DC, EC, V $$ to $$$, set in an attractive garden with
good views. And for meals, try *La Rueda* (closed: Tuesdays and November),
c/ San Miguel, 2 ☎ 44 82 21 P ✦ AE, DC, MC $$$, serving international
cuisine, *Mesón del Virrey* (closed: Wednesdays), c/ Constitución, 87, in
Arroyo de la Miel ☎ 44 35 99 ✦ AE, V $$$, serving Malaguenian inland
cuisine in a typical Andalusian inn, or *Ventorrillo de la Perra* (closed: two
weeks in November), Av Constitución, s/n, in Arroyo de la Miel ☎ 44 19 66
P ✦ DC, MC, V $$$, an 18C Andalusian inn serving Malaguenian, Spanish
and international cuisine.

On the town: Children will love the *Aquapark* (open: April-October from
10.00-8.00 ☎ 38 88 88), an enormous swimming pool funfair, and the
Tívoli World, the Costa's major amusement park (in Benalmádena ☎
44 18 99). Adults will no doubt prefer Torremolinos' hundreds of bars and
pubs and close to 50 discos at the latest count. The best fish and seafood
tapa bars —such as *Pasaje Begoña*, *Vip's* and *Viña P*— are on c/ San
Miguel and along La Carihuela, although the most authentic are in the
Calvario district. *A La Reine Astrid*, Paseo Marítimo, and *Lepanto*, c/ San
Miguel, 52, in La Nogalera, cater to those prefering coffee and tea to beer
and wine. Late at **night**, the action shifts to the discos in the Montemar
district —*Borsalino*, *Number One*, *Why Not* and *Gatsby* being the best.
There is flamenco at *El Jaleo*, Pl de la Gamba Alegre, and gambling and
floor shows nearby at the *Casino Torrequebrada*, km226 on the Cádiz road
in Benalmádena ☎ 44 25 45.
Sports: Water sports are practised at the nearby yacht club, the *Puerto
Deportivo y Club Náutico de Benalmádena* ☎ 44 13 44 and 44 42 34,
and golf at the *Club de Campo*, 5.5km from Málaga ☎ 38 11 20 and at the
Golf Torrequebrada in Benalmádena-Costa.

🌑🌑 UBEDA **Jaén** ☎ (953), pop. 30,938, *i* Pl de los Caídos, s/n ☎
75 08 97, ✉ c/ Trinidad, 4 ☎ 75 00 31, ✚ 75 00 88, **P** 75 04 40, 🚌 Av
Ramón y Cajal ☎ 75 00 26. Jaén 57km, Granada 141km, Madrid 319km.

🌑🌑🌑   This is a very interesting and unspoiled **historic town** that provides a
good sample of Spanish Renaissance architecture and of the talents of the
16C architect **Andrés de Vandelvira**. By a fortunate coincidence both the
Emperor Charles V and his son Philip II employed Ubeda men, Francisco de
los Cobos and Juan Vázquez de Molina, as their secretaries and the two were
loyal to their birthplace and showered the town with grace and favour. Ubeda
was reconquered from the Muslims by the troops of Ferdinand III, the Saint,
in 1234 as they drove down towards Córdoba and Seville and a number of
Castilian nobles took a break from campaigning to build themselves
mansions in the town. In recognition of its historic and architectural merits,
Ubeda has been awarded the title of **Heritage of Mankind** by UNESCO.

🌑   ▦ **★★★** *Parador Condestable Dávalos*, Pl Vázquez de Molina, 1 ☎
75 03 45 ⇄ 26 ✕ **P** ✚ 🎤 🍸 AE, DC, MC, V $$$$. In a lovely palace.
Best buys: You can buy artisan pottery from *F. Martínez*, c/ Valencia, 22;
wrought iron pieces from the long established *Santa María* workshop, c/
Jurado Gómez, 1; esparto crafts from *P. Blanco*, c/ Real, 47; cakes made by
the nuns from the *Convento de las Clarisas*, Pl Santa Clara, s/n, and local
pastries from *Don Lope*, Pl Doctor Quesada, 4.

🌑🌑 **Cultural highlights:** The town's showpiece is the **Pl de Vázquez de
Molina** and the grand buildings that surround it. The Town Hall occupies the
Palacio de las Cadenas which bears the stamp of Vandelvira in the majestic
Classical façade that he created for it in 1562. Opposite stands the **Iglesia
de Santa María** with its agreeable Gothic cloister, fine **wrought iron grilles**   🌑🌕
🌑 enclosing its **chapels** and 17C Baroque portals. The Cárcel del Obispo, or
Bishop's Prison, used to serve as a reformatory for 'fallen women' and behind
it is the Palacio de Mancera, also 16C. Opposite stands the present day
parador which is an especially sober-looking former palace and illustrates the
🌑🌑 restraint and austerity favoured by the court of Philip II. The **Sacra Capilla
del Salvador**, which was designed by Diego de Siloé and built by Vandelvira
between 1540-1556 is, in contrast, quite sumptuous and its ornate façade
🌑 reflects the grandeur and optimism of the early part of the 16C. The **interior**
🌑 is extremely rich and its high points are the huge **grille** created by
Villalpando and the 18C altarpiece featuring a *Christ* sculpted by Berruguete.

🌑🌑   The **Iglesia de San Pablo** has an interesting **S door** which shows how   🌑
the Isabelline floridness that the Catholic Queen favoured overtook the more
🌑🌑 sober Gothic style and the church's **chapels** have good **grilles** separating   🌑🌕
them from the nave. The W door of the **Church of Santo Domingo** shows
the development of the Isabelline into the even more ornate Plateresque style
and the interior of the **Church of San Isidoro** shows a firm commitment to
the Renaissance. A 14C Mudéjar building houses an Archaeological
Museum, c/ Cervantes, 6 (open: 10.00-2.00 and 4.00-7.00; Sundays:
10.00-12.30; closed: Mondays ☎ 75 37 02). A further half a dozen major
buildings such as the **Palacio de la Calle Montiel**, the **Casa del Obispo
Canastero**, the **Casa de las Torres**, the **Palacio del Marqués de
Contadero**, the **Palacio de la Rambla**, the **Palacio de Vela de los Cobos**
and the **Casa de los Salvajes** together with several other period houses are
examples of Ubeda's particular interpretation of Renaissance architecture.
Fiestas: *Semana Santa* and the *Feria de San Miguel*, September 29, are
noteworthy local *fiestas*.
Local sights: **LINARES**, 29km NW from Ubeda, is a mining town that stages
🌑🌑 a national flamenco competition, the *Concurso Nacional de Tarantos*,
in the second half of August.

ARAGON

The Aragonese have a reputation in Spain for being straightforward people who call a spade a spade. Theirs is an open land, harsh and abrupt in places, hard and stark. **Francisco Goya**, born in the village of Fuendetodos, was, with his mental toughness and firm principles, quintessentially Aragonese and so was the sardonic film maker **Luis Buñuel**. Both grew up in a region whose geography makes few concessions and where very little can be taken for granted. In the N, Aragón is bordered by the **Pyrenees** and in the S the **Sistema Ibérico** mountain range separates it from Castile and the orchard lands of Valencia. The **Ebro**, Spain's mightiest river, flows through Aragón's centre and past its capital, Zaragoza, forming a vast depression and creating a measure of fertility in an area racked by the scarcity of water.

In the 13C, Aragón was very much a power to be reckoned with in the Mediterranean. Its progression to imperial strength had started in the 9C, in the foothills of the Pyrenees or what is known as the Alto Aragón (Upper Aragón). There a local baron count, **Aznar Galindo**, led a successful revolt against the occupying Muslims and carved out a Christian fiefdom for himself. In 1035 **Ramiro I**, the bastard son of Sancho III, the Mayor of Navarre, turned Galindo's county into a kingdom and established its capital at Jaca. The following century the Aragonese, under Alfonso I, broke out of the Pyrenees, pushed their way onto the plain and took Zaragoza, which in 1134 became their new capital. The growing Christian kingdom intelligently maintained the large and industrious Muslim population and was becoming steadily prosperous by 1154 when the marriage of Ramón de Berenguer, Count of Barcelona, and Petronila, daughter of Ramiro II of Aragón, took place. The wedding was a watershed event for it fused the crown of Aragón with the aggressive mercantile Catalan dynasty, with spectacular results quickly following. By the 13C, under **James I, the Conqueror**, the Catalan-Aragonese crown had expanded into Valencia, occupied the Balearic Islands and taken Roussillon in what is modern-day France. By 1296 the kingdom had acquired more dominions and was making its influence felt.

A second major turning point in Aragón's history was also the result of a dynastic marriage alliance. The wedding in 1476 of **Ferdinand II of Aragón** and Isabella of Castile, known to history as the Catholic Monarchs, united the two crowns, marked the start of Spain's modern history and signalled the beginning of Aragón's decline. The first casualties of this keynote development were Aragón's several regional and municipal representative institutions. Their powers and privileges were gradually whittled away by the all-encompassing drive for centralism in the newly united Spain. The second casualties were the Moriscos, the converted Muslim population which accounted for 16 per cent of Aragón's inhabitants. The obsession with religious orthodoxy and pure Christian ancestry led to their expulsion and their departure dealt a terrible blow to Aragón's economy. The industrious Moriscos had created a complex irrigation system and when they left, the fertile lands they had farmed returned to being semi-desert areas. In the War of the Spanish Succession, Aragón, like Catalonia, backed the losing Hapsburg claimant and the incoming Bourbon dynasty under Philip V, following the 1713 Treaty of Utrecht, took its revenge by ending Aragón's few outstanding autonomous prerogatives.

Art lovers will find in Aragón fine examples of the **Mudéjar culture** of the converted Muslims, which flourished thanks to the region's tolerant policy between the 13C and the 16C. In contrast to the ornamentation of the Muslim style there are, in the Pyrenean valleys of Upper Aragón, magnificent **Romanesque** churches, monasteries and cathedrals such as Jaca's. These owe their existence to the medieval pilgrim route to Santiago de Compostela which entered Aragón from France at the mountain pass of Somport. The Way of Saint James brought in its wake the best of Europe's art forms. The Renaissance left its mark in Aragón through the carvings of local artists such as **Damián Forment** and **Gil Morlanes**, father and son, but above all through the personality of Ferdinand, the Catholic King who was a monarch worthy of the age of the New Learning. The Tudor court of Henry VII who mistrusted him called him 'Foxy Ferdinand' but Machiavelli, who was more perceptive, made him the model for *The Prince*.

One expects folklore, old customs and traditions to lie close to the surface in Spain and Aragón is true to the norm. The region's singular contribution to Spanish folk dancing and singing is the *jota*. Danced by pairs who leap and kick high into the air and sung with terrific power, the *jota* is as spirited a display as can be found anywhere. The region's top *fiesta* is the one in honour of the *Virgen del Pilar* in Zaragoza on October 12. Others, like the one in the village of Calandra which consists of all night demented drumming during Holy Week, rank among Spain's strangest.

There is, naturally, much more to Aragón. It is good territory for **hunters** and **fishermen, skiers, mountain climbers** and **hill trekkers**. The **Parque Nacional de Ordesa** nature reserve is one of Spain's great open spaces. The region's cuisine has its memorable peculiarities such as the *chilindrón* method of stewing chicken and lamb with red peppers. The local wine from Cariñena has that honest, no-holds-barred quality that one soon learns to appreciate in Aragón.

● ALBARRACIN **Teruel** ☎ (974), pop. 1,023. Teruel 37km, Cuenca 105km, Zaragoza 191km, Madrid 268km.

This is an exceptionally picturesque and unspoiled, walled medieval village, hidden away in the sierra of the same name. It was briefly the capital of an independent Moorish kingdom in the 11C under the Beni Razin dynasty and then a Christian one ruled by the Navarrese Azagra family before coming under the crown of Aragón in 1300.

▥ ★★★ *Albarracín*, c/ Azagra, s/n ☎ 71 00 11 ✦ ⅌ ♒ ≪ ⚘ AE, DC, EC, V $$$. Quiet and with good views.

▥ ★ *Mesón del Gallo*, c/ Los Puentes, 1 ☎ 71 00 32 ✕ $$. The restaurant serves excellent home cooking.

Cultural highlights: The best overall aesthetic impression is gained by simply strolling around its silent, narrow **cobbled streets**. The Renaissance **Cathedral** was built in the 16C and has a couple of interesting Renaissance altarpieces and a collection of 15C Flemish **tapestries**. The Church of Santa María dates from the same period. The Episcopal Palace has a showy Baroque façade, and one of its best features is its location which affords a fine view over the town and the **walls**.

Fiestas: On April 30, the *Noche de los Mayos* (see 'Fiestas') takes place. September 8-17 marks the celebration of *Santa María de Albarracín*.

Local sights: Some 4km out of the town there are a number of prehistoric sites. The most accessible are the ones known as Doña Clotilde, La Cocinilla del Obispo, El Callejón del Plou and La Cueva de Navazo. Exploring further into the Albarracín sierra, you reach the source of the Tagus river.

Sports: This area is popular with mountaineers, fishermen and hunters.

ALCAÑIZ **Teruel** ☎ (974), pop. 12,051. Tortosa 102km, Zaragoza 103km, Teruel 156km, Madrid 397km.

The capital of Bajo Aragón (Lower Aragón), Alcañiz is the centre of a prosperous agricultural and industrial district. It was reconquered from the Muslims in 1119 and remained in the possession of the Military Order of Calatrava until the 16C.

▦ ★★★ *Parador de la Concordia*, Castillo de los Calatravos ☎ 83 04 00 🛏 12 ✕ ✦ ♨ ≪ AE, DC, EC, V $$$$. Located in the medieval castle, the parador is quiet and has good views over the valley.

▦ ★ *Senate* Ctra de Zaragoza, s/n ☎ 83 05 50 🛏 29 ⊻ TV P ✦ V $$. A central hotel.

❙❙ *Calpe* (closed: Sunday nights), c/ Comunidad General de Aragón, 1 ☎ 87 07 32 DC, V $$. Aragonese cooking.

❙❙ *Meseguer* (closed: Sunday and holiday nights and 14/9-30/9), Av Maestrazgo, 9 ☎ 83 01 41 DC, V $$$. Regional cuisine. ★★ accommodation is also available $$.

Cultural highlights: The **castle**, now a parador, served in the 12C as a headquarters for the Calatrava order. The main façade and the structure of the church are Romanesque in style and the cloister belongs to the Gothic period. There are 14C frescoes in the keep but the fortress complex dates mostly from the 18C. The **Collegiate Church of Santa María**, apart from its sumptuous Baroque **façade** and Gothic tower, also belongs to the 18C. The town's architectural centrepoint is its old square, the **Pl de España**, which is graced by a 14C Gothic Exchange and a 16C Renaissance Town Hall. The gallery feature in both buildings is typical of this part of Aragón.

Fiestas: **Holy Week** is marked here by a *Tamborada*, incessant drumming that starts at midnight on Maundy Thursday and continues until Easter Sunday (see 'Fiestas').

Local sights: The village of **HIJAR**, 45km along the N-232 in the direction of Zaragoza, celebrates Holy Week with a *Tamborada* or marathon drumming session (see 'Fiestas') and is also noted for its lovely Plaza Mayor. ★★ *Casa del Hijarano*, Parque Calvario, s/n ☎ 82 02 80 🛏 15 $$, is the town's boarding house, while *Arse*, on the Alcañiz road ☎ 82 01 11, serves regional cooking $$ to $$$. **CALACEITE**, 25km along the N-420, is a very picturesque village with a fine Baroque parish church and a number of noble houses around its porticoed main square. *Fonda Alcalá*, Av Cataluña, 49 ☎ 85 10 28, serving regional cooking, is a recommended restaurant. Just outside the village, on the Monte de San Antonio, there are the remains of a 3C BC Iberian settlement.

VALDERROBRES, a few kilometres on from Calaceite, has a 14C **castle**, a former Moorish fortress looming over its red roofed village houses and a church, **Santa María**, which has a very beautiful Gothic W door. **BECEITE**, nearby, is in a beautiful mountain setting and is a good base for hunters; for meals, try *La Fonda de la Tía Cinta*, c/ Villanueva, 19 $$.

The village of **CALANDA**, S of Alcañiz on the N-420, is the home of the region's most famous drumming marathon, or *Tamborada*. The infernal racket is supposed to ward off the dead but it virtually kills the drummers who end up with bleeding hands. Local man Luis Buñuel, who was fascinated by the spectacle's pagan barbarism, filmed it superbly. You can stay at ★★ *Balfagón* ☎ 84 63 12 🛏 34 ⊻ ℂ P DC, MC, V $$, and buy one of those noisy drums at *T. Gascen*, c/ San Miguel, 1.

Sports: Hunting and fishing in the river Guadalope are popular sports. There is also motor racing at the local track, site of an annual national championship (variable date) and a local championship held on the first Sunday in September.

BARBASTRO **Huesca** ☎ (974), pop. 15,538, *i* Town Hall, ✣ 31 20 20. Huesca 52km, Lérida 68km, Madrid 442km.

Already an important crossroads in Roman times and later a Muslim market town, Barbastro was the setting for the marriage alliance that united the houses of Aragón and Catalonia in the 12C.

▥ ★★ *Rey Sancho Ramírez*, Ctra N-240, km162.7 ☎ 31 00 50 ⊨ 78 **P**
♣ ≈ ≪ 🐎 ♘ AE, DC, V $$$. Lovely views.

🍴 *El Chopo*, km8 on the Barbastro-France road ☎ 31 01 64 ❊ DC, EC $$$.

🍴 *Flor*, c/ Goya, 3 ☎ 31 10 56 ♣ ❊ AE, DC, V $$$. Seasonal cuisine .

Best buys: Antiques are sold in the old quarter; pastries at *Confitería Guerri*, c/ Argensola, 16, and wicker work at *R. Lecina*, c/ Ainsa, 4.

Cultural highlights: The 16C Gothic **Cathedral** has slender columns along its three naves supporting a lovely vault, and also it has a good **altarpiece** by Damián Forment. The Argenosal Palace and the 15C Town Hall are examples of the Aragonese Renaissance civic architecture which is a notable feature of Barbastro.

Local sights: A drive along the road parallel to the River Vero takes you to the very **picturesque** medieval mountain town of **ALQUEZAR** which has an interesting 11C **collegiate church** (rebuilt in the 16C). Continuing towards Lecina you reach the **Vero canyon** which is challenging but beautiful exploring territory. A 60km drive on the C-138 takes you to the castle town of **AINSA**, capital of the 11C Kingdom of Sobrarbe and a Morisco centre for many centuries. Set well into the Aragonese section of the Pyrenees, this is a timeless cluster of old houses and its Plaza Mayor is particularly appealing —*Bodegas del Sobrarbe*, Pl Mayor, 2 ☎ 50 02 37 $$$, picturesquely set in the cellars of 12C buildings, is a good restaurant. Taking the C-139 off the C-138 for 38km, **GRAUS** has fine stone houses and celebrates with traditional processions and folk dancing when it holds its *fiestas* on September 14.

Taking the N-240 S from Barbastro, **MONZON**, 18km, was the birthplace of Joaquín Costa, an influential and polemical engineer and politician at the turn of the century. Its castle, built in the 10C and restored in the 12C and the 18C, was used by James I, the Conqueror, as a royal residence. The Collegiate Church of Nuestra Señora del Romeral was built in the 12C in the Romanesque style and has a Mudéjar tower reflecting the impact of the local Morisco community. *Mesón del Carpintero*, c/ San Antonio, 15 ☎ 40 10 66 $$, is a recommended restaurant serving fish and seafood.

BENASQUE **Huesca** ☎ (974), pop. 1,638. Lérida 148km, Huesca 150km, Madrid 538km.

A Pyrenean village, 1,138m high, Benasque is scenically located on the banks of the River Esera in the verdant **Benasque Valley** close to the 3,404m Pico Aneto mountain, the highest peak in the Pyrenees. With its steep narrow streets and medieval houses, Benasque is undeniably picturesque.

▥ ★★★ *Monte Alba* (closed: 1/5-15/6 and 15/9-15/12), Cerler ski station ☎ 55 11 36 ⊨ 134 ♣ ⅏ ≈ ▦ ≪ $$$ to $$$$$. Very quiet, 1,540m high and with excellent mountain views.

▥ ★★ *Aneto*, Ctra Ancilles, 2, Benasque (closed: 1/5-20/6 and 1/10-20/12) ☎ 55 10 61 ⊨ 38 ♣ ⅏ ≈ 🐎 ♘ $$. Quiet. Good value for money.

▥ ★★ *Cerler*, Cerler ski station ☎ 55 12 61 ⊨ 107 $$ to $$$.

▥ ★★ *El Puente*, c/ San Pedro, s/n, Benasque ☎ 55 12 79 ❊ ⅏ ≪ V $$$. Quiet, with good views.

🍴 *La Parrilla* (closed: 15/9-30/9), Ctra de Francia ☎ 54 11 34 ♣ ❊ V $$$.

Cultural highlights: The 13C Church of San Marcial and the Palace of the Counts of Ribagorza are interesting.

Fiestas: On June 30 a traditional dance called the *Ball de Benás* is staged in honour of San Marcial.

Local sights: The town is the starting point for numerous excursions along the Benasque Valley. There are very fine **views** heading W on the road to Coll de Fadas.

Sports: Mountaineering, **hunting** in the National Game Reserve, and skiing at *Cerler*, 6km ☎ 55 10 12, which has 19 ski runs, 10 lifts, a ski school, equipment for hire and other facilities, are all popular.

CALATAYUD **Zaragoza** ☎ (976), pop. 18,975, ✛ 88 15 13. Zaragoza 139km, Teruel 139km, Madrid 235km.

Its name, redolent of the Muslim occupation, comes from *Kalat Ayub* or Ayub's castle, although there is no record of either the building or its owner. It is recorded, however, that Ferdinand, the Catholic King, who with Queen Isabella ended Arab rule in Spain, was baptised here in 1461.

▦ ★★★ *Calatayud*, 2km out of town at km237 of the N-II ☎ 88 13 23 ⇌ 63 **P** ✦ 🐂 AE, V $$$.

❚❙ *Lisboa* (closed: Sunday nights), Paseo de Calvo Sotelo, 10 ☎ 88 25 35 AE, DC, EC, V $$ to $$$.

Cultural highlights: The old quarter features a Jewish and a Moorish district (the *judería* and *morería* respectively). The 13C **Collegiate Church of Santa María la Mayor** is typically Aragonese in its Gothic and Mudéjar style and its use of bricks. The **tower** shows a clear Arab influence, but the **W front's** alabaster ornamentation is in the ornate Plateresque style of the Spanish Renaissance. The **Church of San Andrés** also has a fine Mudéjar **tower**.

Fiestas: The town's celebrations from September 3-12 are in honour of the *Virgen de la Peña*. A *romería*, or religious cross country procession marked by picnicking and folk dancing, winds its way to the shrine of San Roque on August 16.

Local sights: E of the town lie the ruins of the old Roman settlement of **Bilbilis**, birthplace of the poet **Martial** (see 'Literature'). The old quarter of **ATECA**, 15km towards Madrid on the N-II, shows off Mudéjar architecture at its best. Continuing for a further 14km you reach the spa of **ALHAMA DE ARAGON**, famous since the time of the Romans. The ★★★ *Balneario Termas Pallarés* (closed: 1/10-30/5), c/ General Franco, 20 ☎ 84 00 11 ⇌ 35 ✕ TV **P** ✦ ⇌ ▦ 🐂 ℚ AE, DC, EC, V $$ to $$$, is small, agreeably old fashioned and olde worlde, and attracts a generally elderly clientele. The thermal baths are set in spacious grounds. **Ceramics** and glassware, including recreations of 18C Aragonese designs, are sold at *M. Palacín Muela*, km205 of the N-II.

NUEVALOS, 24km S of Calatayud on the C-202, is a picturesque village on the banks of the Tranquera reservoir. A bit further on you reach the **Monasterio de Piedra**, which was founded in the 12C as a Cistercian community but has now been converted into an hotel —★★★ *Monasterio de Piedra* ☎ 84 90 11 ⇌ 61 ✦ ⅏ ⇌ ℚ AE, DC $$ to $$$, located in the former abbey, it preserves a monastic tranquillity. What makes this place really astonishing is its **park** which is a true oasis of water and luxurious vegetation in the midst of the arid plain. Open from 9.00 until sunset, the park is very Romantic with its grottoes, **cascades** —look out for the **Cola de Caballo**, a lovely 53m cascade, and the **Cueva Iris** grotto behind it, with wonderful views— and lakes —the **Baño de Diana** and **Lago del Espejo** are particularly lovely— and has marvellous trees, which is something you see all too little of in this part of Spain.

❦ ▌DAROCA▐ **Zaragoza** ☎ (976), pop. 2,859, ✚ 80 03 36. Zaragoza 83km, Madrid 276km.

This totally walled town was a very prosperous crafts centre in the Middle Ages. The **walls**, 3km long, are studded with more than 100 turrets and, within them, the town houses with their characteristic medieval eaves are extremely picturesque.

¶ *Legido*, Ctra N-234, km217 ☎ 80 02 28 $$$. Regional cuisine.

Cultural highlights: The **Collegiate Church of Santa María** was built to a Romanesque design but underwent a major overhaul in the 15-16C when a Gothic nave substituted the previous one. The **side chapels**, decorated with

❦ 16C glazed tiles, are interesting and the 15C alabaster **altarpiece** in the first
❦ chapel on the right is very beautiful. The **Parish Museum** exhibits panels, altarpieces, a valuable **monstrance** and a number of old chasubles, some woven in Daroca and others in 17C Mexico. The **Church of San Miguel** has a very pure Romanesque W door and chancel dating from the 12C.

Fiestas: Corpus Christi is celebrated here with special zeal in commemoration of a miracle said to have occurred in 1239. Communion bread concealed from the infidel during a Muslim attack left bloodstains on the clothes in which they were concealed, and they are preserved as relics to this day.

▌EL MAESTRAZGO▐ **Teruel** ☎ (974).

The name Maestrazgo, given to this harsh mountainland in the SE corner of Teruel province, is derived from its original owners, the grand *maestres* or masters first of the crusading order of the Templar and then of the Spanish-based Military Order of Montesa. At the time of the medieval Christian Reconquest of Spain from the Muslims this was a raw frontier land for battle-hardened men. The landscape, desolate and forbidding, has not changed at all and the villages —for somehow a receding population still manages to find subsistence here— remain fortified and as medieval looking as any you are likely to find in Europe. Driving through this area you are setting your watch back several centuries.

The entry point, from the N, to the Maestrazgo is the village of La Puebla de Valverde, 23km SE of Teruel along the N-234. From here you take the C-232 to **MORA DE RUBIELOS** where you are met by an imposing 13C castle, a Gothic collegiate church and a number of fine houses huddled around these two village focal points. A further 13km lead to a village named like the first but back to front, **RUBIELOS DE MORA**, where the stone heraldic shields emblazoning the houses tell the visitor that noble men once occupied the dwellings. The 17C parish church has a good 15C altarpiece. If you ever wanted big, clanging, hand-crafted cow bells you can buy them here at *A. San Martín*, c/ Vallado, 10. The next stage is to take the road from here heading N to **GÚDAR** which appears on the descent from the mountain pass of the same name. In this village, surrounded by pine and ilex trees, *El Rancho Grande*, Pl Iglesia ☎ 80 10 76, serves good roasts.

From Gúdar, the road continues to **CANTAVIEJA** but not before crossing first the mountain passes of Sollavientos, Villarroya and Cuarto Pelado. Cantavieja is already in the Alto, or High, Maestrazgo and it is an undeniably historic village that preserves the remains of the old Templar fortifications. The centrepiece of its attractive porticoed Plaza Mayor is its 13C Romanesque Town Hall. The 17C parish church has a late Renaissance flair to it for architectural styles arrived tardily in this isolated part of the world.

★★ *Balfagón Alto Maestrazgo*, Av del Maestrazgo, 20 ☎ 18 50 76 ⇌ 22 **P** $$, is adequate for an overnight stop and *Buj*, Ctra Iglesuela, s/n ☎ 18 50 33 $$, serves hearty home cooking.

IGLESUELA DEL CID lies next on this road. Again the houses have noble heraldic adornments, the Gothic Town Hall looks important and the parish church shows off Plateresque ornamentation. The village is associated with El Cid, Spain's top Reconquest hero, because tradition has it that he prayed at the nearby shrine of Nuestra Señora del Cid. It is better, however, to branch off N from Cantavieja to go to **MIRAMBEL**, which is one of the most unspoiled old villages in Europe. Strolling around its old walled quarter you would not be surprised if El Cid and his knights rode clattering down the cobblestones to challenge you. The bar *Las Tejas* serves a fortifying wine and good *tapas*. The itinerary ends in **MORELLA**, in the province of Castellón (see 'Morella' in 'Levante and Murcia').

HUESCA **Huesca** ☎ (974), pop. 45,068, *i* c/ Coso Alto, 23 ☎ 🖬
22 57 78, ✝ 22 11 86. Zaragoza 71km, Pamplona 164km, Madrid 395km.
  Known as *Osca* by the Iberians, this was the refuge of the resistance chieftain **Sertorius** during the Roman occupation. He declared it an independent state in 83 BC and, aping his cultured enemies, he organized his own senate and founded a school for the sons of his nobles and officers. Today this pleasant town is capital of the Pyrenean province of Huesca, an area of great natural beauty and of unexpected artistic splendour.
- ★★★ *Pedro I de Aragón*, Av del Parque, 34 ☎ 22 03 00 🖬 52 **P** ✦ **DC, EC, V $$$**.
- ★★ *Montearagón*, km208 on Ctra N-204, 2km from Huesca ☎ 22 23 50 🖬 27 ✕ **P** ≋ **$$$**.
- ¶ *La Bodega de Gratal*, 14km from Huesca on the Tarragona-San Sebastián highway, in Lierta ☎ 27 02 90 ✦ **V $$$**. Charcoal grills in an old farmhouse in the heart of the country.
- ¶ *Monrepos*, 12km from Huesca on Ctra N-330 ☎ 27 10 64 **MC, V $$$**. Good roasts.
- ¶ *Navas*, c/ San Lorenzo, 15 ☎ 22 47 38 **AE, DC, MC, V $$$ to $$$$**. 🖬 *Nouvelle cuisine* and the odd regional dish.
- ¶ *Sauras* (closed: Sunday nights and 1/10-16/10), c/ Zaragoza, 2 ☎ 24 46 60 **$$$**. *Paella* dishes.
- ¶ *Venta El Sotón* (closed: Mondays), 14km from Huesca along Ctra 🖬 N-240, in Esquedas ☎ 27 02 41 **P** ✳ **AE, MC, V $$$**. Wholesome food with particularly good desserts and a well stocked wine cellar.

Best buys: Local cakes and desserts are sold at *Confitería Vilas*, c/ Coso Bajo, 23, and *Pastelería Ascaso*, c/ Coso Alto, 9. Wrought iron products can be found at *E. Cajal Marzal*, c/ Sariñena, s/n.

Cultural highlights: The 13-16C Gothic **Cathedral** occupies, as do many 🖬 ecclesiastical buildings in Spain, the site of a demolished mosque. Its main artistic features are the **choir stalls** and the embossed silver high altar which has an alabaster **altarpiece** carved by Damián Forment, the ubiquitous 🖬🖬 Renaissance artist whose work crops up in virtually all important buildings of the period in Aragón. We get to know him better here for he portrayed himself in one of the medallions in the lower part of the chancel. The Cathedral Museum exhibits beautiful enamelled chests, masterpieces of medieval craftsmanship in precious metals. The 16C Town Hall, opposite the Cathedral, is a good example of Aragonese Renaissance civic architecture.

The **Provincial Museum** (open: 10.00-2.00; closed: Mondays) is mostly 🖬 devoted to local archaeological exhibits and **Gothic panels** painted by Aragonese masters. The **Church of San Pedro El Viejo** is worth visiting for its very beautiful Romanesque **cloister**. 🖬

Fiestas: There are celebrations marking the saints' days of Saint Vincent on January 22 and Saint George on April 23, but the big ones, and the most solemn, are in honour of **Saint Lawrence** (August 10), who was born in Huesca and was martyred in 258.

Local sights: The ruins of the **Monastery-Fortress of Montearagón** lie 6km out of town on the N-240. A further 8km on, the village of **BARLUENGA** has a church, San Miguel, with a very good coffered ceiling and beautiful 13C Romanesque frescoes. To reach the magnificent **Loarre Castle**, continue on the N-240 towards Jaca and turn right after passing Ayerbe. The castle, built by Sancho Ramírez, King of Aragón and Navarre in the 11C, is one of the most perfect early medieval fortresses in Spain and it is superbly situated 1,100m high on a rocky promontory with wonderful **views** overlooking a wide area of the Ebro river valley. Continuing on the N-240, beyond Loarre, there are strange cylindrical rock formations, called the **Mallos de Riglos**, which rise to some 200m on either side of the road. There are similar, although smaller, formations near the village of **AGÜERO** where there is also an interesting 12C church dedicated to Santiago. ★★ *La Costera* (open: 15/6-15/9), c/ San Jaime, 1 ☎ 38 03 30 🛏 12 ⛏ ⚲ ≈ ≪ $, is a small hotel with a swimming pool where peace and spectacular views are assured.

Forking right now off the C-134, which links the N-240 and Jaca, you reach the 10C **Monastery of Santa Cruz de la Serós**. The church dates from the 11C and has a single nave with a barrel vault and a lovely octagonal tower. This abbey is a sort of antechamber for the truly amazing surprise of the **Monastery of San Juan de la Peña** which you reach from here along a forestry track. San Juan is almost impossibly **situated** under a crag which forms its roof and hangs, inaccessibly, over an incredible view. It was founded by Benedictine monks in the 9C and was for centuries the pantheon for members of the Navarrese and Aragonese royal families. The older sections, which are in part underground, are an astounding example of Mozarabic art (namely, art produced by Christians living under Muslim rule) while the columns and **capitals** in the 12C **cloister** are among the best Romanesque carvings in Spain. Legend has it that the first occupant of San Juan de la Peña was a hunter who cornered a stag in this spot and was so overcome by the beauty of the grotto that he instantly decided to stay where he was and become a hermit.

The **route** from Huesca to Sabiñánigo is also extremely **scenic**.

On the town: *Ricocu*, c/ Huesca, 12, is a good place for *tapas*, and the terrace of *Rugaca*, c/ Porches de Galicia, 1, is recommended for summer drinks. *Manhattan*, c/ San Jorge, 43, is good for a nightcap.

Sports: The Aragonese section of the Pyrenees is excellent for winter sports and mountaineering. There are five ski stations in the province: *Cerler, Panticosa, Formigal, Candanchú* and *Astún*. Tennis players head for *C.T. Osca* ☎ 21 19 03, the city's tennis club.

JACA **Huesca** ☎ (974), pop. 13,335, ⃞*i* Paseo Calvo Sotelo ☎ 36 00 98, ✉ 36 00 85, ✚ 36 11 01, 🚌 36 13 32. French border 18km, Huesca 90km, Madrid 486km.

There were two routes over the Pyrenees and into Spain for the medieval pilgrims who undertook the arduous **Route to the Shrine of Saint James the Apostle** in Compostela. One was over the Roncesvalles mountain pass in Navarre and the other was over the pass at Somport which allowed the weary traveller to reach Jaca well before nightfall. The presence of hundreds of thousands of pilgrims right through the Middle Ages explains the historical and artistic importance of this mountain town and its surrounding villages and monasteries. Nowadays mountaineering and winter sports draw a different kind of visitor.

▦ ★★★ *Aparthotel Oroel*, Av de Francia, 37 ☎ 36 24 11 ⋐ 124 ✖ P ♦
⌕ ⌖ ⋜ AE, DC, MC, V $$$. Service apartments. It has a **restaurant**.

▦ ★★★ *Gran Hotel*, Paseo del General Franco, 1 ☎ 36 09 00 ⋐ 98 ✖ P
♦ ⌕ AE, DC, V $$$.

▦ ★★ *Conde Aznar*, c/ General Franco, 3 ☎ 36 10 50 ⋐ 23 MC, V $$.
Friendly. Mountaineering decor.

❙❙ *Gastón* (closed: 21/9-30/9), Av Primo de Rivera, 14 ☎ 36 29 09 ♦ ❋
AE, MC, V $$$ to $$$$. Home cooking.

❙❙ *La Cocina Aragonesa* (closed: Tuesdays out of season), c/ Cervantes, 5
☎ 36 10 50 ❋ MC, V $$$ to $$$$. Classic cooking.

Best buys: Skiing and mountaineering equipment is sold at *Chus*, c/ Unión
Taguesa, 3, and *Piedrafita*, c/ Primo de Rivera, 1. Local cakes can be bought
from *Echeto*, Pl Catedrales, and *Imperial*, c/ Mayor, 14.

Cultural highlights: Jaca's 11C **Cathedral** is among the oldest
Romanesque ones in Spain. The dome over the crossing, the lateral apses
and the decorations of the **capitals** were to serve as models that were
repeated and refined in religious architecture all along the pilgrim route. Here
at Jaca's cathedral the Compostela travellers were left in no doubt that they
were on the right track for they met the symbols and emblems that were to
accompany them all the way to their destination: the statue of Saint James
the pilgrim with his wide-brimmed hat and cape, and his cockleshell, staff
and gourd and the cockleshell on its own which seems to beckon those who
view it to the distant, wild Atlantic coastline of Galicia. The **Diocesan
Museum** (open: 11.30-1.30 and 4.30-6.30) has interesting exhibits that
trace the development from the Romanesque architecture that the pilgrim
route introduced through Jaca into the Gothic style. The 16C Town Hall is a
particularly good example of Aragonese Plateresque. The Castle of San Pedro
(open: 11.00-12.00 and 5.00-6.00) was built towards the end of that
century by Philip II who was wary of French attacks.

Fiestas: On the first Sunday in May the Christian reconquest of the town is
celebrated in style as are the *fiestas* in honour of Santa Orosia on June 25.
The *Festival Folklórico de los Pirineos* (Pyrenean Folk Festival), consisting
of regional dancing and singing is held in July and August every other year.

Local sights: There are a number of fine Romanesque churches in the
immediate vicinity of Jaca such as **Santa María de Iguacel**. The trip along
the **high valleys of the Pyrenees** is an interesting one; take the C-134 and
then, after reaching the N-240, follow the directions to Ansó and Hecho. The
forests and meadows, criss-crossed by gurgling trout streams, are delightful
and the people here speak a curious Aragonese dialect called *Cheso*. The
village of **Hecho** is the area's main centre of population, and its popular
architecture and narrow streets are appealing. The village was the birthplace
of Alfonso I, the Battler, and it boasts a monastery, the Abbey of San Pedro
de Siresa, built in 833 and an **11C church** which contains interesting 15C
altarpieces. In this picturesque location, a symposium on modern painting
and sculpture is held every summer with open-air exhibitions. For meals, try
the restaurant *Casa Blasquico*, Pl Palacio, 1 ☎ 37 50 07 $$ to $$$.

On the town: *Tomás*, c/ Terrenal, 8, serves good *tapas*, while *Equiza*, c/
Primo de Rivera, 3, and *Doña Taberna*, Pl Calvo Sotelo, 6, are popular beer
halls. *Ciros* and *Copos* are respectively a disco and a disco-pub, and both
are noisy. *Chapeau*, c/ Terrenal, 17, is a quieter place for a nightcap.

Sports: Jaca has a *Mountaineering School* ☎ 36 08 50, and an ice skating
rink, the *Club de Hielo Jaca* ☎ 36 06 66, where national and international
ice-hockey and skating competitions are staged. The town is the base camp
for mountaineering and ski enthusiasts (see the ski stations listed under
'Benasque' and 'Pirineos Aragoneses').

ᗷᗷᗷ ORDESA NATIONAL PARK **Huesca** ☎ (974), *i* c/ General las Heras, 8, Huesca ☎ 22 04 62 and 22 11 80.

The National Park of Ordesa is the heart of the Aragonese section of the Pyrenees and it is essentially a huge, 15,000ha canyon encircled by ridges that tower 1,000m above it. The Arazas river (excellent for trout fishing) runs through the valley picking up the waters that cascade down from the peaks. The park has magnificent forests of pines, birch, giant poplars and fir trees that grow to a height of more than 25m.

May to September are the best months to visit the park. You enter it from the village of **TORLA** and you should come equipped with good trekking footwear. The initial path runs alongside the most spectacular waterfall, the 70m **Cola de Caballo**, or Horse's Tail, and continues along the circuit of the **Soaso Circus**. An alternative trek, around the **Cotatuero Circus**, also passes cascades, some of them falling for 250m, but they tend to dry up in high summer. The nearest accommodation to the park is in Torla, 8km from the entrance.

🏨 ★★ *Ordesa* (closed: 15/10 until Easter), Ctra Ordesa, s/n, 1km from Torla ☎ 48 61 25 ⇌ 69 ✦ ♨ ⚊ ≪ 🐴 V $$. Peaceful and with wonderful mountain views.

🏨 ★ *Bujaruelo* (closed: 10/1-1/3), Ctra Ordesa, s/n, Torla ☎ 48 61 74 ⇌ 27 ✕ ⅄ 🅿 ✦ ♨ ≪ MC, V $$. Peaceful, with excellent views and facilities. The restaurant serves home cooking.

🏨 ★ *Edelweiss* (closed: 15/11-15/3), Av de Ordesa, 1 ☎ 48 61 73 ⇌ 30 🛍 ✦ ♨ ≪ EC, V $$. Quiet and scenic.

Sports: Rock climbing and trekking are excellent here.

ᗷᗷ PIRINEOS ARAGONESES (THE ARAGON PYRENEES) **Huesca** ☎ (974), 🚌 Canfranc ☎ 37 30 44. See also 'Wide Open Spaces'. Access from Huesca on the N-330 as far as the French border or on the C-136, C-138, C-139, C-140 and C-144; from Barbastro, 51km from Huesca, on the C-138 or C-139.

Also called the Central Pyrenees, this Aragonese section is the most abrupt and highest of the whole range. The kings of the crest are Pico de Aneto (3,404m), Posets (3,371m) and Monte Perdido (3,355m). An extremely beautiful area, it features peaks with challenging rock faces, lush forest vegetation in the valleys, narrow gorges and majestic circuses formed by ancient glaciers. The area is dotted with little towns, ski stations and spas, ᗷᗷᗷ and is well equipped for catering for tourists. The **Ordesa National Park** forms the heart of this region and there are two hunting reserves, one at **BENASQUE**, at the foot of the Aneto peak, and a second one in the W formed by the valley of the Cinca river called the **Reserva Nacional de los Circos**.

Going from W to E you have a choice of the following areas. Taking the N-330 from Jaca up the valley of the River Aragón you reach **CANFRANC**, which is a popular summer mountain resort. For stopovers, ★★ *Villa Anayet*, Pl José Antonio, 8 ☎ 37 31 46 ⇌ 67 ✦ ⚊ 🖥 ≪ $$, is an agreeable wood and stone building patronized by skiers and rock climbers.

ᗷ Nearby, 31km from Jaca, *Candanchú* ☎ 37 31 92, is a well equipped ski station on the border with France. It has 37 ski runs between 1,450-2,320m for skiers of all levels, 24 lifts, a ski school and full services. The following three hotels are all at the foot of the ski lifts and they share good views and peace and quiet: ★★★ *Edelweiss*, km189.4 on the Zaragoza to France road ☎ 37 32 00 ⇌ 76 ♨ ≪ AE, V $$$; ★★ *Tobazo*, km184 on the road to France ☎ 37 31 25 ⇌ 52 🅿 ♨ ≪ $$$; and ★★ *Candanchú*, on the road to France ☎ 37 30 25 ⇌ 48 ✕ 🅿 ♨ ≪ AE, DC, V $$ to $$$, with an acceptable **restaurant**.

Nearby is the *Astún* ski station ☎ 37 30 34, with 22 ski pistes at 1,420-2,394m, 11 lifts, a ski school and other facilities. For accommodation, try the apartments and hotels at Jaca, Candanchú and Canfranc. Apart from the ones listed above and under 'Jaca', take note of ★★ *La Paz*, c/ Mayor, 41, in Jaca ☎ 36 07 00 ⇌ 34 ⵏ AE, DC, EC, V $$, and the apartments of ★★ *Mallo Blanco*, Av Juan XXIII, 30 ☎ 36 33 61 ⇌ 50 🅿 ☽ « ⵟ AE, DC, EC, V $$$ to $$$$ (depending on the number of people occupying the apartment). Finally, on the French frontier and still on the N-330, the **Somport mountain pass** (1,632m) offers panoramic views of the Central Pyrenees. This is the only border crossing in the region that stays open all year round although exceptional snow falls can occasionally close it.

A second itinerary starts at **SABIÑANIGO**, the chief town of the El Serrablo district, notable for its **Mozarabic churches** such as the ones at Lárrede (10C), Lasiego (10-12C), Susín (11C) and Satúe (11C). In the town itself there is an interesting museum, the Museo A. Orensanz y Artes del Serralbo, created by the New York based artist Angel Orensanz who was born here. It oddly but successfully combines his own conceptual sculptures and the works of his Greenwich Village friends with primitive, rustic exhibits that trace the folk culture of the area. For overnight stays, try ★★★ *La Pardina*, c/ Santa Orosia, 36 ☎ 48 09 75 ⇌ 64 🅿 ✦ ⵏ ☽ ☽ ⵟ V $$$, a quiet hotel situated among gardens and woods.

Heading N, the C-136 follows the course of the River Gállego and after Biescas enters the **Tena Valley**. By Sandiniés, a **local road** which passes through the **Escalar Gorge** (it is so deep and narrow that the sun hardly filters through) leads to the **Balneario de Panticosa** spa. This is magnificently set at a height of 1,535m and surrounded by a circus of high mountain peaks. There is good trout fishing here and also a nearby ski station ☎ 48 71 12, at 1,185-1,986m, with 11 ski runs and seven lifts. The spa itself is served by six sulphurous springs which were known to the Romans and which have earned Panticosa an enduring reputation. The hotels are set in a wooded, verdant and quiet area and share the facilities of the thermal baths. For accommodation, try ★★★ *Gran Hotel* (closed: 15/9-15/6), Balneario de Panticosa ☎ 48 71 61 ⇌ 54 🅿 ✦ ⵟ V $$ and ★★★ *Mediodía*, Balneario de Panticosa ☎ 48 71 61 ⇌ 52 ✕ 🅿 ✦ ☽ ⵟ DC, V $$.

If you keep on the C-136 instead of turning off for the Panticosa spa, you will reach the picturesque mountain village of **SALLENT DE GALLEGO**, at 1,305m, which is popular among mountaineers, trout fishermen and skiers. Just 4km from the village the ski station of *Formigal* ☎ 48 81 25, at 1,500-2,245m, has 24 pistes, 19 lifts, a ski school and full services. For accommodation, you might try ★★★★ *Formigal* ☎ 48 80 00 ⇌ 125 ✕ ☽ ▦ « AE, DC, MC, V $$$ to $$$$, which is quiet and scenically located; or ★★★ *Eguzki-Lore* ☎ 48 80 75 ⇌ 30 ✕ ☽ ☽ « AE, DC, MC, V $$$ to $$$$, a peaceful and well situated hotel built in the style of a Basque country mansion and decorated like an alpine lodge.

From Barbastro you reach Aínsa (see 'Barbastro') along the C-138 and there take a local road N to the hamlet of **BIELSA** which you reach via a 2,000m high pass, the Desfiladero de las Devotas. A further 14km NW, after passing Espierba, you enter the Pineta Valley and reach the small, scenically situated ★★★ *Parador del Monte Perdido* ☎ 50 10 11 ⇌ 24 🅿 ✦ ☽ « ⵟ AE, DC, MC, V $$$ to $$$$. Peace is assured here and, at 1,320m, so are the views.

The basin of the Esera river is on the eastern edge of Aragón's Pyrenees, close to the border with Catalonia, and it winds up to the **Benasque Valley**, at the foot of the towering Pico Aneto and *Cerler* ski station.

🅑 SOS DEL REY CATOLICO **Zaragoza** ☎ (948), pop. 1,025. Zaragoza 143km, Madrid 421km.

As its name indicates, this was the birthplace, in 1452, of Ferdinand of Aragón, the future husband of Isabella of Castile, who was to become known as the Catholic King. Parts of the village, by the walls and around the parish church, have not changed that much since the 15C.

🏨 ★★★ *Cinco Villas*, Paseo del Muro, 12, in Ejea de los Caballeros ☎ 66 03 00 🛏 30 **DC, MC, V** $$.

🏨 ★★★ *Parador Fernando de Aragón*, c/ Sáinz de Vicuña, 1, in Sos del Rey Católico ☎ 88 80 11 🛏 66 **P** ﹩ ≪ **AE, MC, V** $$$. Set in an Aragonese style building, it is quiet and has good views over the town.

Best buys: Ceramics and wrought iron are sold in the Las Delicias quarter of the town of Ejea de los Caballeros.

🅑 **Cultural highlights:** The Romanesque-Gothic **Church of San Esteban** is
🅑 worth visiting for its Renaissance **choir stalls**, expertly carved by Juan de Moreto in 1556, and its 11C **crypt**.

Local sights: Visits should be made to the district of the Cinco Villas, or Five Towns. In Tᴀᴜsᴛᴇ the chief feature is the octagonal tower of the parish church and in Eᴊᴇᴀ ᴅᴇ ʟᴏs ᴄᴀʙᴀʟʟᴇʀᴏs, an important wheat growing centre, there are several noble houses of the Renaissance period. The village of Sábada lies under the shadow of a very impressive castle and close by, 22km from Sos, the village of Uɴᴄᴀsᴛɪʟʟᴏ has, in addition to its fortress, the very interesting **Church of Santa María**. The **S façade** of this building shows off 🅑🅑 wonderful Romanesque workmanship and later additions, such as the 16C
🅑 **choir** and the Plateresque ornamented **cloister**, kept up the church's high 🅑 artistic standards.

🅑 TARAZONA **Zaragoza** ☎ (976), pop. 11,255, 🇮 Town Hall ☎ 64 01 00. Soria 68km, Zaragoza 85km, Pamplona 107km, Madrid 294km.

Somewhat come down in the world for it used to be second only to Zaragoza among Aragón's towns 200 years ago, Tarazona has an agreeable old quarter which recalls its old Mudéjar colony.

🏨 ★★ *Brujas de Bécquer*, 1km along the N-122 to Zaragoza ☎ 64 04 04 🛏 60 **P** ✦ **DC, V** $$.

Cultural highlights: The 16C Town Hall has a typically grand, ostentatious
🅑 Plateresque façade. The Gothic-Mudéjar **Cathedral** (12-14C) incorporates Plateresque and Baroque elements. Its outstanding features are the two Gothic tombs in the **Clavillos Chapel** and a beautiful **cloister** with 16C 🅑 Mudéjar latticework. The town also has an interesting 18C building.

Local sights: The local national park, the **Parque Natural del Moncayo**, 15km, occupies the highest peak of the Sistema Ibérico mountain range. The start of the park, in the foothills, is covered by dense forests. Only trek-hardened hill walkers should attempt the climb to the top but the **views**, once there, are worth the exhaustion. On a clear day you can take in the plain of northern Castile and the Ebro basin. There are pleasant villages in the district, such as Borja, but the main attraction is the 12C Cistercian abbey, 🅑🅑 the **Monasterio de Veruela**. Its **church** is grand in size but simple to the 🅑 point of austerity in its decoration as is the norm in foundations of this 🅑 monastic order. The **cloister** is rather more flamboyant and veers towards the Plateresque in its upper gallery. Literature lovers should note that **Gustavo Adolfo Bécquer**, the leading figure of Spain's 19C Romantic movement, spent some time writing and convalescing in the monastery. The splendid 🅑 **Chapter House** contains 15C tombs of former abbots, and other rooms are occupied by the **Museo Contemporáneo de Pintores Aragoneses**, a museum of paintings by contemporary local artists.

TERUEL **Teruel** ☎ (974), pop. 28,156, *i* 'c/ Tomás Nougués, 1 ☎ 60 22 79, ✚ 60 26 09, ⬛ 60 22 79. Valencia 145km, Madrid 300km.

Capital of Aragón's SE province of the same name, Teruel lies at a height of 916m among mountains and ravines in an area that saw some of the bitterest fighting of the 1936-1939 Spanish Civil War. Its distinguishing feature is the extent and the excellence of its Mudéjar architecture which it owes to the large number of Muslims who took refuge in the town when Alfonso I conquered Zaragoza and its surrounding plain. In recognition of its **Mudéjar treasures**, UNESCO has declared Teruel part of the **Heritage of Mankind**. The town's emblem is a bull, recalling an episode in the Muslims' resistance to the conquering Alfonso during which the Christian monarch was stopped in his tracks and put to flight by stampeding bulls. Bulls, or *toros*, also stampede around the town during its *fiestas*.

- ▥ ★★★ *Parador de Teruel*, 2km from the town centre on the N-234 to Calatayud ☎ 60 18 00 ⬛ 60 🅿 ✚ ⬱ ℭ AE, DC, EC, V $$$ to $$$$. Regional cooking in its **restaurant**.
- ▥ ★★★ *Reina Cristina*, Paseo de Ovalo, 1 ☎ 60 68 60 ⬛ 62 DC, MC, V $$$$.
- ▥ ★ *Oriente*, Av de Sagunto, 5 ☎ 60 15 50 ⬛ 31 ⏀ $ to $$. Centrally located.
- ▥ *Civera* (closed: 14/12-6/1), Av de Sagunto, 37 ☎ 60 23 00 $$$. This restaurant serves regional dishes such as local ham with tomatoes and garlic.
- ▥ *El Milagro*, km123 on the Zaragoza-Valencia road, 2km from Teruel ☎ 60 30 95 AE, DC, EC, V $$$.
- ▥ *Kalanchoe*, Av de Sagunto, 39 ☎ 60 01 03 AE, DC, MC, V $$$.
- ▥ *La Menta* (closed: Mondays and September), c/ Bartolomé Esteban, 10 ☎ 60 75 32 V $$$.

Best buys: Curious ceramics, reproductions of 16C designs with Mudéjar ornamentation and green and manganese glaze, are sold at *Artesanía de la Catedral*, c/ Joaquín Costa, 7. First-class local cured hams are available at *Rokelín*, c/ Comandante Fortea, 8, and *Lapuente*, c/ Carlos Castel, 5. Home-made local cakes are sold at *Albarracín*, c/ Joaquín Costa, 41 and *Muñoz*, c/ Carlos Castel, 23.

Cultural highlights: The town's **five Mudéjar towers**, built in three sections and decorated with inserts of brick and multi-coloured tiles, are very much Teruel's show stoppers. The two most beautiful ones, known as the **San Martín** and the **Salvador** towers, were built, according to tradition, by the brothers Omar and Abdala, who were rival suitors for the hand of a lovely lady known as Zoraida. The **Cathedral** was originally Romanesque (13C) but was rebuilt in the 16C and 17C and then again this century after it was badly damaged in the Civil War. Gabriel Joli was responsible for the fine **high altarpiece** and there is another good **retable**, on the theme of the Coronation of the Virgin Mary, in the left arm of the transept. The splendid **coffered ceiling** of the central nave (13C) depicts scenes of medieval life.

The most visited church in Teruel is, however, **San Pedro** near the *judería* or old Jewish quarter. Visitors are drawn by the church's Mudéjar **tower** and Romanesque apse, but most of all by the **mausoleum** in the church which contains the bodies of the **Lovers of Teruel** (*Los Amantes de Teruel*) who are more celebrated in Spain than Romeo and Juliet. The mausoleum, sculpted by Juan de Avalos, is somewhat morbid for you can spy the mummies of the loving pair through a lattice. Legend has it that young Diego Marcilla loved Isabel Segura and she loved him but they were forbidden to marry because he had no fortune. Off the young man therefore went to earn the necessary and when he returned, duly enriched, he discovered that Isabel was marrying someone else that very same day. Diego died of sadness within a matter of hours and she, stricken by the same sickness, followed him to the same grave shortly afterwards.

The focal point of Teruel is the **Pl del Torico**, and it also has an interesting Diocesan Museum in the 15-16C Episcopal Palace and a fine Mudéjar influenced building which houses the local *Casino*.

Fiestas: On the Sunday nearest to July 10 the *fiesta* called the *Vaquilla del Angel*, or the Angel's Calf, has a bull as the guest of honour. In September there is a ham fair.

On the town: Young people hang about c/ San Esteban in disco-pubs and bars such as *York, Nebraska, Mambo* and *Pachá*. *La Parrillada* is a good place to try cold cut aperitifs. *Tapas* are ideal at *Los Juncos*, c/ San Juan, and *Plata*, c/ Amantes, 7. Cocktails are served at *Marx*, c/ San Esteban, 20 and people tend to go discoing at *Láser*, Pl Torico.

Sports: Teruel province is renowned for its hunting and fishing reserves. A very limited number of mouflons and Spanish mountain goats, the *Capra Hispánica*, can be stalked by holders of the necessary and extremely scarce and expensive licences in the **Beceite Reserve**, and the same is true of deerstalking in the **Albarracín Reserve**. Wild boar is fairly common in the sierras of Formiche, Valderrobres, Cantavieja and Mora de Rubielos. The rivers Guadalaviar, Guadalope Alto and Apelluz can be fished for trout, again by holders of the required permits, and duck shoots are organized in the Estaca de Alcañiz. There are winter sports at the *Sierra de Gúdar Station*, 1,600-2,024m, which has two ski runs and a ski school.

ZARAGOZA (SARAGOSSA) **Zaragoza** ☎ (976), pop. 596,080 [i] Glorieta de Pío XII ☎ 23 00 27, ✚ 44 07 49, ✈ 9km ☎ 34 90 50 (Iberia, c/ Canfranc, 22 ☎ 21 82 50), ⛴ c/ San Clemente, 13 ☎ 22 65 98. Lérida 150km, Barcelona 307km, Madrid 322km, Valencia 330km.

Capital of Aragón, this is a busy commercial and industrial town, the fifth largest city in Spain. Zaragoza looks essentially modern although it was important to the early Iberian settlers who knew it as *Salduba*, to the Romans who named it *Cesaraugusta*, and to the Muslims who called it *Sarakusta*. The succeeding civilizations cherished the city's strategic location on the banks of the Ebro and in the midst of the river's fertile valley for elsewhere Aragón is arid and inhospitable. Zaragoza stands at the crossroads of the routes linking Madrid with Barcelona and the Basque Country with the Mediterranean.

Zaragoza, for all its modern and busy looks, is a proud city with a soul and a romantic heart. It is very much under the spell of the Virgin of the Pillar, whose huge Basilica is the city's most recognizable landmark and Spain's most important Marian shrine. Every Spaniard will plump for his own local version of the Virgin Mary, but that of the Pillar is almost inevitably second on his list. Tradition has it that in the year AD 40 the Virgin appeared atop a pillar to the Apostle James in the spot where her shrine now stands. Zaragoza, which is also the home of Spain's military academy, has that Aragonese no-nonsense directness about it and, when called upon, it is stout hearted beyond the limits of human endurance. During the Peninsular War it resisted Napoleon's armies for many bitter months between 1808 and 1809 and at the cost of 54,000 dead through battle, famine and plague. The hero of that hour was a very gallant woman who went down in history as **Agustina de Aragón**. She and the rest of the population were clearly sustained by the spiritual support of the Virgin whom every Aragonese refers to fondly as *La Pilarica*.

▦ ★★★★★ *Corona de Aragón,* Av César Augusto, 13 ☎ 43 01 00 ⛽ 249 ✗ ⛲ ▣ AE, DC, EC, V $$$$$. A big, modern and central hotel.

▣ ★★★★★ *Gran Hotel*, c/ Joaquín Costa, 5 ☎ 22 19 01 ⚲ 138 ✕ **AE, DC, EC, V $$$$ to $$$$$**. It has a quality restaurant.

▣ ★★★★★ *Palafox*, c/ Casa Jiménez, s/n ☎ 23 77 00 ⚲ 184 ✕ ⚴ ▦ **AE, DC, MC, V $$$$ to $$$$$**.

▣ ★★★★ *Casino Montesblancos*, km343.45 on the N-II, 20km from Zaragoza, in Alfajarín ☎ 10 00 04 ⚲ 37 ✕ ✦ ⚲ ⚴ ▦ ⚭ **AE, DC, MC, V $$$$**. A quiet and comfortable hotel on top of a hill. The restaurant serves an excellent buffet.

▣ ★★★★ *Don Yo*, c/ Bruil, 4 ☎ 22 67 41 ⚲ 181 ✕ ⚘ **AE, DC, MC, V $$$$**.

▣ ★★★★ *Rey Alfonso I*, c/ Coso, 17 ☎ 21 82 90 ⚲ 117 ✕ **AE, DC, MC, V $$$$**. Very central.

▣ ★★★ *Ramiro I*, c/ Coso, 123 ☎ 29 82 00 ⚲ 105 ✕ **P** **AE, DC, MC, V $$$**. In the old quarter.

▣ ★★★ *Zaragoza Royal*, c/ Arzobispo Domenech, 4 ☎ 21 46 00 ⚲ 92 ✕ ⚵ **P** ⚘ ⛉ **AE, DC, MC, V $$$$**. Modern facilities.

🍴 *Costa Vasca*, c/ Teniente Coronel Valenzuela, 13 ☎ 21 73 39 ✳ **AE, DC, MC, V $$$ to $$$$**. Imaginative dishes and a good wine cellar.

🍴 *El Cachirulo* (closed: Sunday nights), 4.5km out of town on the N-232 to Huesca ☎ 45 74 75 **P** ✦ ✳ **AE, DC, MC, V $$$**. A fine building decorated in the Aragonese style. It has a good *tapa* bar.

🍴 *Gurrea* (closed: Sundays and August), c/ San Ignacio de Loyola, 14 ☎ 23 31 61 **P** ✳ **AE, DC, MC, V $$$ to $$$$**. International cuisine.

🍴 *Horno Asador Goyesco* (closed: Sundays and 5/8-20/8), c/ Manuel Lasala, 44 ✳ **AE, DC, EC, V $$$**.

🍴 *La Aldaba* (closed: Wednesdays), c/ Santa Teresa, 26 ☎ 35 63 79 ✳ **AE, DC, MC, V $$$**. Innovative cuisine. Game in season.

🍴 *La Casa del Ventero* (open: dinners; closed: Sunday nights, Mondays and August), Paseo 18 de Julio, 24, 14km out of town on the Huesca road, in Villanueva de Gállego ☎ 11 51 87 ✳ **DC, MC $$$**.

🍴 *La Matilde* (closed: Sundays, holidays, Christmas, Holy Week and August), c/ Casta Alvarez, 10 ☎ 44 10 08 ✳ **AE, DC, MC, V $$$**. Imaginative cooking, good wine-list and friendly service.

🍴 *La Rinconada de Lorenzo* (closed: Mondays, Holy Week and August), c/ La Salle, 3 ☎ 45 51 08 ✳ **AE, DC, MC, V $$$**. Regional cooking.

🍴 *Los Borrachos*, Paseo Sagasta, 64 ☎ 27 50 36 **P** ✳ **AE, DC, MC, V $$$**. Ostentatious decor, but good international cuisine, with excellent game in season.

Best buys: For arts and crafts try *Arte y Artesanos*, c/ León XIII, 18, *J. Beltrán*, c/ Don Jaime, 18 (embroidery and lace), *Sigilata*, Pl de Sos, *Tlaloc*, c/ Temple, 10, and the *Escuela de Cerámica de Muel*, Ctra Valencia, km28, which maintains the traditions of 15C **Muel pottery**. Antiques are sold at *Aroya*, c/ Tomás Castellano, 1, *El Arca de Noé*, c/ San Braulio, 9, *El Quinqué*, c/ Molino, 6, *Maturen*, c/ Santa Isabel, 14, *P. Echevarría*, c/ Costamina, 2, and *Yasmina*, Paseo Sagasta, 29. For modern design go to *B.D. Ediciones de Diseño*, c/ San Jorge, 3. The best fashion shops are around the Paseo de la Independencia —the *Centro Independencia*, at No. 24, is a mall with over 100 varied shops—, c/ Alfonso I and near the *El Corte Inglés* department store on Paseo de Sagasta, 1. Exceptional leather clothes and accessories are sold at *Loewe*, c/ Costa, 3. Spanish fashion can be found at *Adolfo Domínguez*, c/ San Ignacio de Loyola, 9, *María Valdenebro*, c/ Marcelino Isabal, 2, *Carrión*, c/ Zurita, 6, *Las Cinco Eles*, c/ Isaac Peral, 14, and shoes at *Molinos*, c/ Valenzuela, 2, and Paseo Sagasta, 2. Jewelry lovers head for *Sucesores de Aladren*, c/ Alfonso I, 25, and *Nueva Joyería*, at No. 34.

◐◐ **Cultural highlights:** The **Cathedral**, known here as **La Seo**, is a hotch potch of every style in the Spanish architectural gamut. You will come across bits and pieces of Romanesque, Mudéjar, Aragonese Gothic, Churrigueresque and transitions between them. The whole lot is topped by an interesting octagonal tower that was erected in the 17C. The Cathedral's chief features

◐ are the 16C Gothic **high altarpiece** by Pere Johan, Juan de Suabia and Gil

◐ de Morlanes the elder, the stalactitic Mudéjar **dome** over the **Parroquieta Chapel**, the Gothic arch linking the cathedral to the Episcopal Palace, the Romanesque apse, the Renaissance sepulchre of Archbishop Ferdinand of Aragón and his mother in the Chapel of San Bernardo and the sculptures, in the same Renaissance style, in the **retrochoir** by Arnaud of Brussels. The

◐ museum in the sacristy, the **Museo Capitular**, exhibits a huge processional **monstrance** which is used during Corpus Christi celebrations and an extensive collection of religious ornaments. The cathedral's **Museo de**

◐◐ **Tapices** (Tapestry Museum) has a very rich collection of Flemish and French tapestries from the 14-17C.

◐ The extremely distinctive **Basílica de Nuestra Señora del Pilar** with its 11 domes casting their shadows onto the Ebro is the third church to Spain's number one Virgin to be built on this riverside site. Underneath lie the remains of a more modest Gothic church and beneath that, the remains of a Romanesque shrine said to have been the first dedicated to Mary in the Christian world. The present church was mostly built in the 17C and was substantially modified in the following century by Ventura Rodríguez, the architect responsible for most of Madrid's Neoclassical landmarks. The influential Rodríguez added the emblematic domes (some of which are decorated with frescoes by Goya), and redesigned the all-important chapel of the Virgin. The basilica has three naves and, aside from the venerated image itself in the **Chapel of the Virgin**, its highlights are the impressive **main altarpiece** sculpted in alabaster by the local Renaissance artist Damián Forment and the **choir**, closed off by a gigantic grille, which has stalls

◐ decorated in the flamboyant Plateresque style. The **Museo Pilarista** exhibits designs and models that trace the construction of the basilica and, fascinatingly, the awesomely rich jewelry and vestments that are used to adorn the venerated figure of the Virgin.

◐ The **Lonja**, or Commercial Exchange, which stands in the Pl de la Seo opposite the Cathedral was built in the 16C and illustrates, as do similar buildings in Barcelona, Palma (Majorca) and Valencia, the mercantile wealth and sophistication of the Catalan-Aragonese empire. The **Aljafería Palace** was the residence of the Muslim emirs during the 9C and subsequently the home of the Beni-Hud dynasty who declared *Sarakusta* an independent kingdom in the 11C. Remodelled in the 14C, it became the palace of the Christian kings of Aragón and was used subsequently by the Catholic Monarchs before becoming a local headquarters for the Inquisition. There is a Muslim prayer room or ***musallah*** on the ground floor and the throne

◐ room, which has a splendid Mudéjar **coffered ceiling**, is on the first floor. The panelling is also interesting in the room where **Saint Isabel**, queen of Portugal, was born in 1271.

Zaragoza's artistic highpoints include the remains of the 3C Roman walls in the Pl Lanuza and the 10C Zuda tower which is all that is left of what used to be the Muslim governors' residence. At the other end of the scale the covered market, called the Mercado Lanuza, built in 1903, is an interesting example of the Modernist tendencies that took Barcelona by storm. The Aula Dei Charterhouse in the Montañana district is an interesting monastery which has Goya frescoes in its refectory. However, it is open only to men, since it is occupied by a closed order of monks.

The Museo de Camón Aznar, c/ Espoz y Mina, 23 (open: 10.00-2.00; closed: Mondays and February), exhibits paintings, ceramics, sculptures and drawings that were collected by the noted Goya expert after whom the museum is named. The Museo Pablo Gargallo, Pl de San Felipe, s/n (open: 10.00-1.00 and 5.00-7.00; holidays: 11.00-2.00; closed: Tuesdays), is in the Arguillo Palace and exhibits contemporary sculpture. The Museo Provincial, Pl de los Sitios, 6 (open: 10.00-2.00; closed: Mondays and holidays), houses some works by Goya and important prehistoric and archaeological exhibits.
Fiestas: On October 12 all eyes in Spain are on the city's *fiestas* in honour of the **Virgen del Pilar**. There are processions, displays of *jota* singing and dancing, fireworks, bullfights and more.
Local sights: Taking the N-330 S, you pass the important pottery centre of **Muel** on the way to the wine-growing district of **Cariñena**. The local brew here is a full-bodied, rough, red which has a high alcoholic content and should be drunk with caution. As you knock it back spare a thought for **Francisco Goya** who grew up on this beverage for he was born in 1746 in the nearby village of **Fuendetodos** where you can visit his house, the **Casa Museo de Goya**. Heading for **Caspe**, an historic village in its own right, you are near the **deep canyons** at Sástago where the Ebro meanders aimlessly as if it too had drunk a couple of bottles of Cariñena wine.
On the town: The *Casino Montesblancos* ☎ 10 00 04 (open: 5.00 pm-4.00 am), is at Alfajarín, km343 on the N-II. Gambling possibilities include American and French roulette, baccarat and black jack. You don't need a jacket and tie to get in, but jeans are not permitted.

There are good *tapa* bars in the Coso Bajo area, such as *Alta Taberna Pedro Saputo, Roman* and the *Antigua Venta de la Cepa Dorada*. More fashionable cocktail bars are in the La Paz area, while the Mercado Central district passes for a pick up zone (*Adonis*, c/ Almagro, 5, is a gay bar). Student *tapa* bars are in the university quarter and include *Casa Paco*, c/ C. Arenal, 24, *El Serón*, c/ Lorente, 54, *El Trujalico*, c/ B. Gracián, 21, and *Tirol*, at No. 29. There are similar bars in the Don Jaime I area. For something different there are places like *El Monaguillo*, c/ Refugio, 8, for drinks to the sound of classical music and Gregorian chant, *El Plata*, c/ 4 de Agosto, 23, where ageing professionals and amateurs from the crowd sing *tangos* and, another popular relic, *El Oasis*, c/ Boggiero, 28, a music-hall that opened during World War I and is ever so innocently naughty and has showgirls swapping ribald stories with the audience. *Heildelberg*, c/ Santa Catalina, 3, is a usually crowded beer hall, *Sala M-tro*, c/ Casa Jiménez, 8, has live music and *Torreluna*, Ctra de Castellón, 53, is a fashionable disco with a restaurant, garden and swimming pool. *Al-Andalus*, c/ León XIII, 12, and *Casa Amadico*, c/ Jordán de Uríes, 3, are wine bars serving seafood snacks, *El Granuja*, c/ La Ripa, 3, is a disco bar and *Chaston*, Pl Ariño, 4 is a jazz club with a pleasant summer terrace. *Iguana*, c/ Madre Vedruna, 11, is Zaragoza's evergreen disco, and *Scratch*, c/ Casa Jiménez, 8, is the city's aggressively modern one. Finally, *Espumosos*, Paseo Sagasta, 5, has been a classic *rendez-vous* at aperitif time for generations.
Sports: The *Aeroclub de Zaragoza*, 12km out of town on the N-232 ☎ 21 43 78, has facilities for gliding and skydiving and a nine hole golf course. There is an 18-hole, par 72 course at *Club de Golf de la Peñaza*, 15km ☎ 34 28 00, which also has tennis courts, jai alai and a swimming pool. City pools include *Club Natación Helios* ☎ 23 04 55 and *Club Deportivo Paraíso*. The *Stadium Casablanca* ☎ 31 10 51, has 13 top class tennis courts. There is a very fast go-kart track at the *Kartódromo de Aragón* and riding stables at the *Centro Ecuestre Ruiseñores*, c/ Puente Virrey, 53 ☎ 49 52 99. Football and basketball are the favourite local spectator sports.

BALEARIC ISLANDS

Commonly lumped together as if they were uniform, the islands are in fact different in geography and climate, and they tend to attract different types of people. Strictly speaking the **Balearics** are the islands of **Majorca** and **Menorca** together with their uninhabited satellites like the island of Cabrera and other rocky accidents. **Ibiza** and its neighbour, the island of **Formentera**, are properly called the **Pitiusas** Islands. All four major islands, even when modern day land speculation has done its worst, indisputably form a string of proverbial pearls set in the turquoise **Mediterranean**, 80 km to 250 km from the coast of Levante in mainland Spain.

There are a number of impressive prehistoric monuments in Majorca and Menorca such as the burial chambers called **navetas**, the **talayots** or lookout towers and the **taulas**, the sacrificial altars, which indicate that there was a flourishing population in these parts back in the Bronze Age. Later the islands were to become a crossroads for successive Mediterranean travellers and superpowers. The Phoenicians and the Greeks left their mark and so did the Carthaginians who turned Ibiza into their personal stronghold. The Romans settled more than their predecessors for they came to stay. With the Muslim invasion of the 8C a new civilization struck roots in the islands. The Arabs brought with them their irrigation and windmill techniques and they turned Palma de Mallorca into one of the principal cities in their flourishing peninsular kingdom of *Al Andalus*.

The modern history of the Balearics really starts in 1229, when they were conquered by **James I, the Conqueror**, King of Aragón, Count of Barcelona and lord and master of the NE of Spain. As the islands came under the axis of Barcelona, they acquired the Catalan culture and language, although they did develop their own personality, distinct from the mainland and from each other. The islands then entered their commercial and cultural golden age —by the 14C the Balearics had a merchant navy that numbered some 900 vessels and some 30,000 sailors and the island's **cartographers** were highly respected. One Majorcan in particular, the learned **Ramón Llull** (see 'Literature'), criss-crossed the Mediterranean, writing, teaching and advising the high and mighty.

By the late 15C times were changing. The Aragón dynasty was absorbed into the united Spanish monarchy, political power passed to Castile and the Atlantic and the New World became national obsessions as Spain became the pacemaker of the Age of Discoveries. The Mediterranean was mostly neglected and the Balearics became the favoured prey of legendary pirates such as Barbarossa.

At the beginning of the 18C Menorca had a hundred year interlude of British rule. The island was ceded to the British crown, as was Gibraltar, but, unlike the Rock, Menorca was returned to Spain at the beginning of the 19C. Majorca, during this period, produced another larger than life figure in **Fray Junípero Serra** who evangelized California and founded the missions of San Francisco and San Diego along the Pacific.

By the mid-19C the Balearics were coming close to finding their real role and purpose in life. A whole new different invasion was in the making. The precursor was the Austrian **Archduke Louis Salvador**, a romantic, an intellectual and a lover of beauty. He bought a large estate in Majorca, wrote a learned treatise on the Balearics and lived happily ever after among sea views and pine trees. Later, the poet **Robert Graves** was another who said *'Goodbye to All That'*, as he entitled his memoir of First World War England, and also settled in Majorca. The dice was cast for the islands: they would become a place of refuge from northern Europe.

Majorca, holiday home of the King of Spain amongst others, is big enough to embrace all sorts of climes and resorts; **Menorca**, rather smaller, is basically humid and leads a more sedate lifestyle; **Ibiza** is dry, whitewashed and can be wild and outrageous, and **Formentera**, also dry, is the least spoilt of the lot. Together the Balearics offer the full range of leisure resorts.

FORMENTERA

FORMENTERA ISLAND **Baleares** ☎ (971), pop. 4,725, *i* Town Hall in San Francisco Javier ☎ 32 00 32, **P** 32 02 10, ⛴ Cargua (ferry to Ibiza) ☎ 31 31 55, ⛴ Umafisa (ferry to Ibiza) ☎ 31 45 13.

Formentera, three miles from Ibiza, is the fourth largest of the Balearic Islands (82km²). The *Wheat Island*, as it was called by the Romans (wheat in Latin being *frumentum*), was abandoned from the Middle Ages up to the end of the 17C when the crown ceded lands to native Ibizans to encourage its resettlement. Over the next century, five fortified watch-towers —S'Espalmador, Gavina, d'Es Cap Barbaria, d'Es Pi d'Es Catala and Punta Prima— were built to protect the settlers from the harassment of pirates.

Today, with its cereal fields, almond groves, vineyards and fig trees, Formentera, though somewhat less beautiful than the other islands is the most unspoilt, a miniature paradise for lovers of peace and quiet and of simple, natural beauty. The island's four town centres are administered from the municipality of **SAN FRANCISCO JAVIER**; a road that begins at the port of **L A SABINA** in the NE and ends at **La Mola** in the SW connects them. To the N, the Estany Pudent and Estany d'Es Peix lakes and saltflats attract migratory birds, particularly flamingoes.

- ▦ **★★★ *La Mola*** (closed: 1/11-1/4), Mitjorn beach ☎ 32 00 75 ⇛ 328 ✕ ✦ ☻ ⛱ ⚓ ≪ ⚑ ⚲ DC, V $$$ to $$$$$. A quiet beachside hotel with good views.
- ▦ **★★★ *Punta Prima Club***, Punta Prima, 2km E of Es Pujols ☎ 32 03 68 ⇛ 120 **P** ✦ ☻ ⛱ ≪ ⚲ $$$$. Very quiet garden bungalows, with splendid views of the sea and the neighbouring island of Ibiza. Half board is compulsory.
- ▦ **★★ *Cala Sahona*** (closed: 1/11-1/4), Cala Sahona ☎ 32 00 30 ⇛ 69 **TV** ✦ ☻ ⛱ ⚓ ≪ ⚑ AE, DC, EC, V $$$. Quiet accommodation with good views, on the beach of the same name.

Beaches: The quality of the beaches varies from N to S. **Mitjorn** in the S is long and pebbly, while the fine-sanded **Es Pujols**, in the N, is protected by the Punta Prima headland. Westwards, Cala Sahona is a popular tourist spot.

Best buys: The La Mola Sunday market is good for bargain hunting.

Cultural highlights: Although Formentera's best assets are its undeveloped beaches, the beautiful countryside of the **Ses Salinas** saltflats with its varied flora and fauna, its impressive cliffs, as in **LA MOLA**, and its lighthouse, Formentera's Land's End —whose **balcony** commands spectacular **views** of the area— there are also other man-made sights worthy of note, among them the Megalithic monument of **Ca Na Costa** near San Ferrán, that pre-dates the Carthaginians, and the 18C churches of San Francisco Javier and of **Our Lady of Pilar** in La Mola.

Sports: There are facilities for all water sports at the *Puerto Deportivo Cala Sabina* yacht club.

IBIZA

Ibiza, at 572km² the biggest of the *Pitiusas*, as the western Balearics are known, is a tiny twinkling gem set in the azure of the Mediterranean, just 80km off the coast of Alicante. Its gentle rural landscape dotted with olive and carob trees, simple **whitewashed houses** and **fortified churches** has a **timeless** quality and is inhabited by small farmers and fishermen who live their lives at a suitably timeless pace. Sounds like an unspoiled paradise, the perfect retreat for those who like to get away from it all? It is. Yet at the same time, Ibiza has come to be a **mecca for the uninhibited**, a little microcosm where anything goes. In summer, the European young set and the international jet set converge on the island avid for sensation revelling in sun and sea by day and scenes of **unimaginable extravagance by night**. The tone varies according to where you are: **SANTA EULALIA DEL RIO** is quiet, unpretentious and restful; **SAN MIGUEL**, in its rural setting, is quieter still and attracts the smart set to its splendid *Na Xamena* hotel; **SAN ANTONIO ABAD** is a built-up area and has masses of discos and entertainment catering for the young German and English tourists it attracts; while **IBIZA** is for the 'in' crowd, where people go to be seen and where both in dress and behaviour, anything goes.

But the eternal qualities of Ibiza have miraculously survived unscattered... Even at the height of summer there are still hidden corners where you can forget that we live in the 20C, while out of season although the sun continues to shine the discos and fast-food bars close down and life resumes its perennial pace.

🏍🏍 IBIZA-EIVISSA **Baleares** ☎ (971), pop. 25,489, *i* Paseo Vara de Rey, 13 ☎ 30 19 00, ✉ c/ Madrid, 25 ☎ 33 00 95, ✚ 30 12 14, **P** 31 58 61, ✈ Es Codolar, 9km ☎ 31 20 00 (Iberia ☎ 30 09 54) ⚓ Trasmediterránea, Av Bartolomé Vicente Ramón, 2 ☎ 30 16 50, ⚓ Isnasa (ferry to Denia), Estación Marítima ☎ 30 40 96, 🚗 Av Isidoro Macabich, 42 ☎ 31 56 11.

The visitor to Ibiza is following in a long tradition. Since its settlement in the 8C BC, the island has attracted a lot of visitors: Phoenicians, Romans, Muslims —under whom Ibiza attained its greatest splendour from the 10C to the early 13C— and Christian conquerors... Some were not so welcome, and in the 16C defensive walls were built around Ibiza as a protection against continual pirate attacks. Some four centuries later, the walls are still there but they no longer fend off foreigners. Hippies and film stars made their assault on Ibiza in the 1960s, and tourists of all shapes, sizes and tastes have been arriving in large numbers over the last decade. Today, Ibiza's power to ensnare visitors has brought it world-wide fame, making it one of the main tourist resorts in the world. Whether it is the ancient and timeless that attracts you or the brash and futuristic, Ibiza has it all.

🏨 ★★★★ *Los Molinos* c/ Ramón Muntaner, 60, Ses Figueretes beach ☎ 30 22 50 ⇆ 147 ✦ 🎤 🏊 ⚓ ☂ ≪ AE, DC, EC, MC, V $$$ to $$$$$. A quiet hotel with good views and a pleasant garden with a seaside swimming pool.

🏨 ★★★★ *Royal Plaza*, c/ Pedro Francés, 27 ☎ 31 00 00 ⇆ 117 TV 🎤 ⚓ AE, DC, EC, MC, V $$$$ to $$$$$. A modern hotel with excellent facilities including, unusually for Ibiza, a good telephone service.

🏨 ★★★★ *Torre del Mar* (closed: 1/11-31/3), Av Pedro Matute Noguera, s/n, d'En Bossa beach, Es Viver ☎ 30 30 50 ⇆ 217 ✦ 🎤 ⚓ ☂ 🖼 ≪ 🐎 ⚘ AE, EC, DC, MC, V $$$$ to $$$$$. A well-equipped hotel, with good views and a pleasant garden with a seaside swimming pool, frequented by celebrities.

▩ ★★★ *Argos* (closed: 1/11-31/3), Talamanca beach ☎ 31 21 62 🛏 106 🅿 ⅃ ⚓ ⌇ ≪ AE, EC, MC, V $$$ to $$$$. A quiet hotel with good views.

▩ ★★★ *Ibiza Playa* (closed: 1/11-31/3), Ses Figueretes beach ☎ 30 48 00 🛏 157 ⚓ ⌇ ≪ EC, MC, V $$$ to $$$$. A mere stone's throw from the beach, it has good views and even better service.

▩ ★★ *El Corsario*, c/ Ponent, 5 ☎ 30 12 48 ♣⅃ ⌇ ≪ AE, DC, MC, V $$$. In traditional Ibizan style, this Dalt Vila hotel still retains its old-world atmosphere from the time when it was frequented by people who wanted something more than just to get a tan and live it up. A quiet hotel, it has wonderful views of the city.

▩ ★ *La Colina* (closed: 1/11-31/3), km10 on the road to Santa Eulalia ☎ 33 08 90 🛏 12 ✗ ⅄ 📺 🅿 ⅃ ⚓ AE, EC, V $$$

▩ ★ *Ses Figueres* (closed: 1/11-31/3), Ses Figueretes beach ☎ 31 43 13 🛏 39 ⅃ ⚓ ⌇ ≪ EC, MC, V $$. A quiet, charming, family-run hotel.

🍴 *Alfredo* (closed: Sundays in summer), Paseo Vara del Rey, 6 ☎ 31 42 70 ✳ AE, DC, EC, MC, V $$. A veritable institution in Ibiza, it serves the traditional Ibizan dishes whose recipes have been handed down from generation to generation.

🍴 *Ama-Lur*, km2.3 on the San Miguel road, Santa Gertrudis ☎ 31 45 54 🅿 ♣ ✳ AE, DC, MC, V $$$ to $$$$. Basque *nouvelle cuisine* and a good wine list.

🍴 *Grill San Rafael* (closed: Sunday nights and Mondays from 1/10-1/5), Pl de la Iglesia, s/n, San Rafael ☎ 31 44 75 ♣ ≪ AE, DC, EC, MC, V $$$ to $$$$. Professional and imaginative Catalan-French cuisine served in a pleasant restaurant, with good views.

🍴 *La Masía d'En Sord* (closed: 1/11-31/3), km6.5 on the road to San Miguel ☎ 31 02 28 🅿 ♣ AE, DC, EC, V $$$$. A beautiful restaurant in an old Ibizan farmhouse with a pleasant terrace.

🍴 *Mesón de Paco* (closed: Wednesdays), c/ Bertomeu de Roselló, 17 ☎ 31 42 24 ✳ DC, EC, MC, V $$$. Home cooking, specializing in fish and seafood.

🍴 *Sa Gavina* (closed: Wednesdays), c/ Pedro Matute Noguera, s/n ☎ 30 51 64 ♣ EC, MC, V $$$. This large yet cosy restaurant serves international cuisine and especially delicious home-made pastries.

Beaches: The most popular beaches are Talamanca, in the N, and **Ses Figueretes**, in the S. Incorrigible sophisticates will enjoy the nearby d'En Bossa beach, home of the *Ku Beach* bar, which even has a gym.

Best buys: Gastronomes in search of local specialities should go to *Casa Vadell*, c/ Aníbal, 3, and *Los Andenes del Puerto*, Av Andenes, s/n, for *ensaimada* pastries, and to *Mari-Mayans*, Puig d'En Valls, s/n, for Ibizan herb liqueurs. If you are interested in arts and crafts, then head for the excellent potteries of *Daifa* and *Frígoles* in the Can Bufi district. *Avant garde* jewelry can be bought at *Joaquín Berao*, c/ Antoni Mari Ribas, 6 and *Torres*, Pl Sa Font, 12, and pearls at *Perlas Orquídea*, on the Ibiza to Santa Eulalia road. Leatherwear and shoes are good buys at *Lucky Lizard*, c/ Mestre Joan Mayans, 2, *Salambó*, c/ José Verdera, 4, and *Stéphane Kélian*, c/ Guillem de Montgrí, 22, and colourful espadrilles at *S'Espardenya*, c/ Ignací de Riquer, 19, in the Dalt Vila. But Ibiza is best known for its *Ad-lib* fashion, which is sold at *Aubergine and Co.*, c/ de la Virgen, 36, *Cantonada*, c/ Conde de Rosellón, 10, *Dora Herbst*, c/ Mayor, 12, *Francis Montesinos*, c/ Bisbe Cardona, 6, *María M*, c/ de la Virgen, 29, *Paula's*, c/ de la Virgen, 4, *Pink Fly*, c/ Riambau, 4, and *The End*, c/ Sa Creu, 26. For the final touch, go to *Campos de Ibiza*, c/ Azara, 2, for perfumes and toiletries.

◑ **Cultural highlights:** The thing to do in Ibiza is to walk up to the quiet **Dalt Vila**, or up-town area, which is entered through the 16C **Puerta de las Tablas**. Here Renaissance walls stand guard over a combination of stately mansions and humbler dwellings. You will find that from the balcony of the **Cathedral**, with its Gothic belfry and Baroque nave, there are **panoramic**
◑ **views** of the port and the city. Opposite the Cathedral, the **Museo**
◑ **Arqueológico** (Archaeological Museum), in the old university (open: 10.00-1.00; closed: Sundays), has a fine collection of Punic art. Relics from Phoenician-Punic times may also be seen at the **Necropolis of Puig des Molins**, Vía Romana, 31 (open: 4.00-7.00; closed: Sundays ☎ 30 17 71), where more than 2,000 tombs, ceramic pieces, tools and so on are exhibited. For a taste of popular life, visit the old fishermen's quarters of **La**
◑ **Marina**, an area of noisy bustling streets and lively cafés and taverns by the
◑ port, and **Sa Penya**, a rocky promontory on which white houses huddle.
  Local sights: Heading NE along the road to Santa Eulalia, after 3km you will come to **Jesús**, a little village built around a 16C church with a beautiful Gothic **altarpiece**. For a different sort of beauty drive S along the road to San Carlos and La Canal. After 8km you will arrive at **Las Salinas**. It is believed that the Carthaginians were the first to exploit these saltflats. Today, not only are they a profitable private venture but they are also an important natural reserve from an ecological point of view —the varied vegetation and
◑ water attract large flocks of migratory birds. The nearby **beach**, lapped by turquoise waters, is largely favoured by nudists; lack of inhibition has spread to the *Malibu* beach bar, where meals and drinks are served by topless waitresses.
◑◑◑ **On the town:** In Ibiza, **night-time** is when things really come alive. If you
◑ like flirting with Lady Luck, your best bet is to go to the *Casino de Eivissa*, Paseo Marítimo, s/n ☎ 30 55 25, where there are French and American roulette, black jack, baccarat and *chemin de fer* tables as well as a night club. If, on the other hand, what you like is to see and be seen, then the **open-air**
◑ **terraces** near Av de los Andenes, parallel to the port, are your scene —*El Mono Desnudo*, c/ Garijo, 16, is for the young set, *La Tierra*, Callejón Trinidad, 4, serves good pre-disco cocktails at reasonable prices, *Zoo*, c/
◑ Pou, 1, is a leftover from the hippy era, *La Maravilla*, Pl de la Constitución, 1, is a good place to stop for a ham and tomato sandwich on your way to bed (they start serving at 6.00 am), *Los Valencianos*, c/ Antoní Riquer, 5,
◑ serves cool local drinks, and *Mar y Sol*, c/ Ramón Tur, s/n, is perhaps the
◑ most popular, and exhibitionist, terrace around. *Montesol*, Paseo Vara del
◑ Rey, 2, and *Ku Beach*, d'En Bossa beach, are excellent places to have an aperitif in an international atmosphere. Later in the evening, the action shifts to the town discos —don't go before 1.00 am, or you might be taken for one
◑ of the staff—, among the best of which are *Amnesia* (closed: 1/11-1/5),
◑ km5 on the road to San Antonio, in San Rafael, *Pachá* (closed: weekdays in winter), Paseo Marítimo, s/n, which has a swimming pool and a decent
◑◑ restaurant, and *Ku* (closed: 1/10-1/5), Urb San Rafael, 6km from Ibiza, which is a luxurious microcosm (bars, restaurant, swimming pool, boutique, disco, gym...) peopled by the rich and famous.
  Sports: The marinas along the Paseo Marítimo seaside promenade —*Club Náutico de Ibiza* ☎ 30 11 35, *Club de Vela Pitiusas* ☎ 31 35 24, *Puerto de Eivissa Nova* ☎ 31 20 62 and *Marina de Botafoch* ☎ 31 33 31— are all well-equipped for water sports. Scuba diving enthusiasts should contact the *Club Acuático Pitiusas*, c/ Felipe II, 18, while those who prefer to sweat it out on a squash or tennis court, or in a gym or sauna should head for *Ahmara*, km2.7 on the road to San José ☎ 30 77 62. Golfers can play at the Santa Eulalia golf course ☎ 30 40 60.

SAN ANTONIO ABAD-SANT ANTONI ABAT Baleares ☎ (971), pop.
12,379, *i* Paseo les Fonts, s/n ☎ 34 31 19, ✉ c/ San Rafael, s/n ☎
34 07 79, **P** 34 08 30, ⚓Flebasa (ferry to Denia), Edif Faro ☎ 34 28 71, ⚓
Isnasa (ferry to Denia), San Antonio port ☎ 34 30 21, 🚌 Paseo Marítimo,
s/n ☎ 31 20 75. Ibiza 18km.

Originally a Bronze Age settlement, this town began attracting visitors
early on in our era, when the Romans established *Portus Magnus* on its
🕭 delightful **bay**. Today, it is synonymous with **mega-mass tourism**.

🏨 ★★★★ *Palmyra* (closed: 1/11-31/3), Av Doctor Fleming, s/n ☎
  34 03 54 🛏 160 ♦ 🎤 ⚲ ⚲ ≪ 🐎 **AE, DC, MC, V** $$$$$. With a
  palm-lined terrace and swimming pool overlooking the bay.

🏨 ★★★ *Bahía* (closed: 1/11-31/3), c/ Bellavista, 1 ☎ 34 10 51 🛏 85 **P**
  ♦ 🏊 ⚲ ≪ $$$. Tastefully decorated in Ibizan-style.

🏨 ★★★ *Bergantín* (closed: 1/11-31/3), S'Estanyol beach ☎ 34 09 50 🛏
  205 **P** ♦ ⚲ ⚲≪ 🐎 ⛳ **DC, EC, V** $$$. About 2.5km from the town
  centre, with a heated swimming pool.

🏨 ★★★ *Cala Gració* (closed: 1/11-31/3), Cala Gració cove ☎ 34 08 62
  🛏 50 🏊 ⚲ ⚲ ⛳ **V** $$$. An excellently located Ibiza-style hotel.

🏨 ★★★ *San Diego* (closed: 1/11-31/3), Es Caló de S'Oli ☎ 34 08 50 🛏
  132 ♦ 🏊 ⚲ ⚲ ≪ $$$. Quiet, with good views of the bay.

🏨 ★★★ *Tropical* (closed: 1/11-31/3), c/ Cervantes, s/n ☎ 34 05 50 🛏
  142 ♦ 🏊 ⚲ **AE, DC, EC, MC, V** $$$.

🏨 ★★ *Pikes*, Camí de Sa Vorera, s/n ☎ 34 22 22 🛏 17 **P** ♦ ⚲ ⛳ **AE,**   🕭
  MC, V $$$$$. Rumour has it that Pikes is used for one-night stands,
  while others claim that it is a haven for publicity-shy celebrities...
  whichever is the case, it is ideal for visitors seeking a quiet holiday.

🏨 ★★ *Tagomago* (closed: 1/11-31/3), S'Estanyol beach ☎ 34 09 62 **P** ⚲
  ⚲ $$. Well located, with good views, but noisy rooms at the back.

🍽 *Rías Baixas* (closed: 15/12-7/3), c/ Ignacio Riquer, 4 ☎ 34 04 80 ❄
  AE, DC, MC, V $$$. Galician cuisine.

🍽 *Sa Capella* (closed: winter), km 0.5 on the road to Santa Inés ☎
  34 00 57 **P** ♦ $$$. International cuisine in a pretty, never-completed
  chapel outside the town.

Beaches: The bay's narrow sandy strip can hardly be called a beach,
although it has all sorts of facilities to enhance a day's outing. If you want real
beaches, head 2km N to **Cala Gració**, which has fine sand surrounded by   🕭
pine trees, or 5km SW to **Port des Torrent** and the popular **Cala Bassa**.

Best buys: Spanish fashion is sold at *Pandora*, c/ Santa Agnes, 1.

Cultural highlights: If you walk around town you will discover that, amidst
the high-rise jungle, there is a quaint old quarter with charming, narrow
streets and a fortified 16-18C parish church.

Fiestas: On June 24, the spirit of **San Juan** invades the town as the
summer solstice is celebrated with typical bonfires.

Local sights: The most beautiful boat trip the island has to offer explores
the Es Amuts **coastline** NW of San Antonio to Portinatx, taking in the Ses
Fontanelles cave, Cap Negret, the Ses Margalides islands, **Aubarca** and the
quiet little bay of **Cala Portinatx**.   🕭

On the town: San Antonio has masses of bars and open-air terraces
catering to the young, especially around Av Doctor Fleming, where *Café*
Melody serves good cocktails. Night-time here is disco-time, and the best
places to be seen at are *Es Paradis Terrenal* (closed: 1/11-1/5), Pasaje de   🕭
Can Mañá, s/n, and *Estudio 7*, Av Doctor Fleming, s/n.

Sports: There are water sports facilities at the *Club Náutico* and the marina
☎ 34 06 45. Horse lovers can go to the *Club Hípico*, Camí de Sa Vorera,
s/n ☎ 34 19 32, for riding trips.

SAN JOSE-SANT JOSEP **Baleares** ☎ (971), pop. 8,535, 🚌 Pl de la Església, s/n ☎ 34 07 03. Ibiza 19km.

The inland town of San José stands next to the highest mountain in Ibiza, **Sa Talaiassa** (475m), from which there are magnificent **views** of the entire island as far as the coast of Valencia in mainland Spain.

🏨 ★★★ *Don Toni* (closed: 1/11-31/3), c/ Ronda de la Pleta, s/n ☎ 30 29 50 ⊨ 328 ✦ ▱ ♀ $$$.

🍴 *Ca Na Joana* (closed: lunchtime in summer), km10 on the road from San José to Ibiza ☎ 34 23 44 🅿 ✦ AE, V $$$. It has a pleasant terrace.

Beaches: Going from N to S, the local beaches are: Cala Tarida, which has 300m of clean sand and all sorts of facilities; Cala Molí, which is smaller, pebbly, and well-equipped; **Cala Vedella**, which is fairly clean and very popular, and Cala d'Hort, which has the most impressive view of all, standing as it does in front of the twin rock islands of **Es Vedrá** and Es Vedranell.

Cultural highlights: Make sure to visit the town's 18C fortified church.

Local sights: Inland sights include the ascent along a rocky dirt road to the peak of **Sa Talaiassa** mountain, from which there are magnificent **views**. On the coast along the Ibiza road, **Cova Santa** is a 25m deep cave which served as a hiding place during pirate raids, and which rose to fame in the 18C, when therapeutic qualities were ascribed to its waters.

Sports: San José has two sports clubs, the *Ibiza Club de Campo*, km3 on the road to San José, and *Sport Center*, on nearby d'En Bossa beach. On the coast, **scuba divers** will enjoy searching the depths around Es Vedrá and Es Vedranell islands.

SAN JUAN BAUTISTA-SANT JOAN BAPTISTA **Baleares** ☎ (971), pop. 3,520. Ibiza 22km.

In the middle of a valley surrounded by mountains, San Juan has a timeless air about it that makes it an ideal place for a relaxing visit.

Beaches: From San Juan you can go to nearby **Cala Portinatx**, a cove formed by two sandy beaches lapped by shallow, clear waters, Cala Xarraca and **Cala Sant Vicenç**, perhaps the best cared-for beach in all Ibiza.

Cultural highlights: The town's 18C parish church is an interesting example of fortified religious architecture.

Local sights: S of San Juan, a dirt road leads to the fortified village of **BALAFI**, a magnificent example of Ibizan popular architecture.

SAN MIGUEL-SANT MIQUEL **Baleares** ☎ (971), pop. 1,817. Ibiza 19km.

San Miguel is really a small group of farmhouses gathered around a 15C parish church from whose roof-terrace there are wonderful views of the surrounding countryside.

🏨 ★★★★ *Hacienda Na Xamena* (closed: 1/11-31/3), Urb Na Xamena ☎ 33 30 46 ⊨ 60 ♿ 🎣 ✦🏊 ▱🖼 ≪ ▱ ♀ AE, DC, EC, MC, V $$$$$ to $$$$$$. An extremely quiet hotel ideal for people who are seeking style and relaxation. Its Ibizan architecture blends in well with its surroundings, and from the promontory on which it stands there are wonderful views. It has good facilities and an even better **restaurant**; the only problem is that you have to book months in advance.

Beaches: Cala Beniarraix, 3km along a track off the road to San Juan, is a pleasant beach.

Local sights: Heading S towards Ibiza you will come to **SANTA GERTRUDIS**, an enchanting rural village with several shops selling hand-made accessories, antiques, second-hand books and decorative objects. While here, you can eat at *Ca'n Pau* 🅿 ✦ $$$, where Catalan cooking is served in an old country house with a charming tree-lined patio.

SANTA EULALIA DEL RIO-SANTA EULARIA DEL RIU | **Baleares** ☎
(971), pop. 14,027, *i* c/ Mariano Riquer, s/n ☎ 33 07 28, **P** 33 08 41, ▉
c/ Mariano Riquer, s/n. Ibiza 14km.

Santa Eulalia is situated on the estuary of the island's only river, at the
mouth of which are remains of a Roman necropolis.

▦ ★★★★ *Fenicia* (closed: 1/11-31/3), Urb Siesta, Ca'n Fita ☎ 33 01 01
▭ 191 ✕ ♦ ♨ ▦ ℚ **AE, DC, EC, V** $$$$$. Quiet, with good views and
a large terrace with a swimming pool.

▦ ★★★ *S'Argamasa Sol* (closed: 1/11-30/4), Urb S'Argamasa ☎
33 00 51 ▭ 217 **P** ♦ ◈ ♨ ⚓ ≪ ◪ ℚ **AE, DC, MC, V** $$$$. Very
quiet, with good views.

▦ ★★★ *Tres Torres* (closed: 1/11-31/3), Ses Estaques ☎ 33 03 26 ▭
112 **P** ♦ ◈ ♨ ⚓ ≪ ◪ **AE, DC, EC, MC, V** $$$. Quiet, with good views
of the sea.

▦ ★ *La Colina* (closed: 1/11-31/3), km5.5 on the road to Ibiza ☎
33 08 90 ▭ 12 **P** ♦ ◈ ♨ **AE, DC, EC, V** $$$$. A quiet little hotel.

▦ ★ *Ses Roques* (closed: 1/11-30/4), c/ del Mar, s/n ☎ 33 01 00 ▭
34 ⚐ ♦ $$. Next to the harbour in Santa Eulalia, it is centrally located,
simple and clean.

⚞ *Chiringuito de Joan Ferrer* (open: summer only), Cala Mastella, San
Carlos ♦ ≪ $$. Owner Joan Ferrer prepares the best *bullit de peix* (fish
stew) on the island with fish he catches himself.

⚞ *Donya Margarita* (closed: December), Paseo Marítimo, s/n ☎ 33 06 55
♦ **AE, DC, EC, MC, V** $$$. This pleasant restaurant features a nice
outdoor terrace with a splendid view of the bay.

⚞ *El Naranjo* (closed: all year lunchtime, Mondays and 1/12-1/4), c/ Sant
Josep, 31 ☎ 33 03 24 ♦ **AE, DC, EC, MC, V** $$$. International cuisine
and clientele.

⚞ *Sa Punta* (closed: Sunday nights, Mondays and 15/1-15/2), c/ Isidoro
Macabich, 36 ☎ 33 00 33 **P** ♦ ✳ ≪ **AE, DC, EC, MC, V** $$$. Basque
cuisine served on a pretty garden terrace which overlooks the sea.

Beaches: The nearby beaches of Cala Pada, Niu Blau, Santa Eulalia del Río
and Caló de S'Alga all have good facilities.

Best buys: The town has several good shops where you can buy works of
art, antiques, perfumes, fashion, shoes and boots.

Cultural highlights: Puig de Missa is a small group of white houses
clustered around a 16C fortified church, all perched on top of a hill, or *puig*.

On the town: *Mozart*, c/ San José, 33, is a noisy, fun bar to visit in
summer, while *Top Hat*, Av Isidoro Macabich, 4, is a classic open all year
round. *Studio 64* is the town's only disco.

Sports: Golfers can play at the 9-hole *Club de Golf Roca Llisa*, km7 on the
road to Cala Llonga ☎ 30 40 60, horseback riders can hire mounts at *Club
Mayans*, 3km from the town, and water sports fans will soon be able to
practise their favourite sport at the brand-new marina, the *Puerto Deportivo
Santa Eulalia del Río*, c/ San Juan, 16 ☎ 33 20 20.

MAJORCA

The island of Majorca is a classic example of the principle of small is
beautiful. Although the largest of the Balearics at 3,640m², it measures just
75km from N to S and 100km from E to W, yet its typically Mediterranean
landscape varies from the fertile central lowland where cereals, figs, almonds
and oranges flourish to the precipitous cliffs of the NW coast, from the
Sierra Tramontana which provides protection from the chilly N wind to the
sheltered arc of the natural haven formed by the **Bay of Palma**.

A magnet for explorers of the Mediterranean for thousands of years, Majorca's aesthetic appeal was given the stamp of artistic approval when it was 'discovered' by Chopin and Georges Sand in the 19C. Scores of writers and painters, among them Gustave Doré, Rubén Darío, D.H. Lawrence, Gertrude Stein, Joan Miró and Robert Graves, who said *'Goodbye to All That'* and made his permanent home in Deyá, have since been seduced by its charms and since the 1950s it has also been a favourite Mediterranean hideaway of film stars and pop musicians.

Nowadays, tourism, while hugely important to Majorca's economy, has by no means taken over the island. Its agriculture still flourishes, the terraced hillsides making their own contribution to the island's visual appeal and there is a thriving footwear industry. Don't be content with the usual haunts: exploring the coasts by boat, or taking the narrow gauge train from Palma to Sóller, you could almost believe that the tourist boom never happened.

ALCUDIA, PUERTO DE (PORT OF ALCUDIA) **Baleares** ☎ (971), *i* c/ Vicealmirante Moreno, 2 ☎ 54 63 71. Alcudia 2km, Palma 27km.

The Port of Alcudia, on **Alcudia Bay**, forms part of a wide arc of white-sand beaches lapped by emerald waters against a background of pine groves and tasteful housing developments. There are boat connections from here with Menorca and Barcelona.

- ★★★★ *Princesa* (closed: 1/11-31/3), Av Minerva, s/n ☎ 54 69 50 🛏 102 ✗ ♣ 👤 ♨ 🏊 🖥 🛥 Q AE, DC, EC, V $$$$$.
- ★★★ *Condesa de la Bahía* (closed: 1/12-31/3), Urb Lago Esperanza ☎ 54 53 24 🛏 491 ♿ ♣ ♨ 🏊 🛥 Q AE, DC, EC, V $$$$.
- ★★★ *Golf* (closed: 1/11-31/3), Alcudia Beach ☎ 54 52 98 🛏 12 P ♣ 🏊 ≪ $$$$. Right on the beach, with good views of the bay.
- ⑪ *Es Segay*, Muro Beach ☎ 54 44 35 AE, DC, EC, V $$$.

Beaches: There is a **15km stretch of beach** that gives onto the bay from Puerto de Alcudia to Cabo Ferrutx.

Cultural highlights: The 13-17C Ermita de la Victoria rises out of the sloping cliff to the N. There are wonderful views of the bay from the top of Sa Talaia, 444m up.

Local sights: The port actually belongs to the municipality of **ALCUDIA**, 2km NW, a town that stands on the isthmus that separates the bays of Pollensa and Alcudia, close to the 2C BC Roman settlement of *Pollentia*. Alcudia wears its heritage proudly —notice the stately 16-17C mansions and the two majestic **gates** on the 14C **city walls** originally built during the reign of James II and extended by Philip II. In the town, you can visit the parish church, which has a very interesting 17C Chapel of the Holy Sacrament and several fine altarpieces, and the Museo Monográfico de Pollentia, c/ General Goded, 7 (visits by prior arrangement ☎ 56 64 13), which exhibits remains found in the Roman city of *Pollentia*. Archaeologists may care to potter round the **ruins** themselves, 1.5km SE of Alcudia, which include the remains of a Roman **theatre** and a Palaeochristian necropolis on the site of the old Roman forum.

Heading SE along the C-712, **CA'N PICAFORT** is a tourist enclave at the apex of the bay set in a verdant landscape. It has an excellent **beach** and good housing developments. From here, you can visit the talayotic settlement at Son Real and the 16m talayot at Morell. A trip to the area of **La Albufera** is also worthwhile. Partially dried up in the 19C, this beautiful landscape of sand dunes and woods bordering the sea and, further inland, saltflats, is a bird sanctuary that stretches over Alcudia, La Puebla and Muro. You may also like to drive 12km along the C-713 in the direction of Palma to the **Cuevas de Campanet** underground caves (open in summer: 10.00-1.00 and

2.00-7.30; winter: 10.00-1.00 and 2.00-6.00), which cover a total area of some 1300m² and offer an impressive display of slender stalactites.

On the town: The *Disco Pub Menta*, a popular summer haunt, is usually full of German tourists until the early morning hours.

Sports: Water sports fans will find that the two sports clubs, *Puerto de Alcudia*, c/ Vicealmirante Moreno, s/n ☎ 54 60 00, and *Puerto Deportivo de Bonaire*, near Mal Pas ☎ 54 69 55, are well equipped. The best hotels have their own tennis courts.

ANDRAITX, PUERTO DE (PORT OF ANDRAITX) **Baleares** ☎ (971), **P** 67 14 62. Palma 25km, Sóller 58km.

This delightful little port, situated at the end of a narrow bay, has retained its fishing village charm despite the intrusion of tourism. Today it is used by all types of pleasure craft.

- 🏨 **★★★★** *Gran Hotel Camp de Mar* (closed: 1/11-31/3), Camp de Mar beach ☎ 67 10 00 🛏 75 ✕ ♦ ≈ ♉ AE, DC, EC, V $$$$.
- 🏨 **★★★** *Villa Real* (closed: 1/11-31/3), Ctra del Puerto, 14, in Camp de Mar ☎ 67 10 50 🛏 52 ⅏ ≈ ☂ ♉ $$$. Quiet.
- 🏨 **★★** *Brismar*, Av Almirante Riera Alemany, s/n ☎ 67 16 00 🛏 56 ♦ ☂ ≪ AE, DC, V $$. Good views.
- 🍴 *Miramar* (closed: Mondays in winter and November), Av Mateo Bosch, 22 ☎ 67 16 17 **P** ♦ ≪ AE, DC, MC, V $$$. Good fish and typical Majorcan dishes served on an attractive terrace.
- 🍴 *Mola Club* (closed: 1/11-31/5), Urb La Mola ☎ 67 17 23 AE, EC, V $$$. Freshly-caught fish served in a pleasant setting.

Beaches: Five kilometres E, **Camp de Mar** cove has a beautiful, fine-sanded beach against a backdrop of pine trees. Closely rivalling it, the beach of San Telmo is protected by the Sa Dragonera island.

Best buys: On Wednesdays you can pick up good bargains at the street market in the Son Mas housing development.

Cultural highlights: From the 18C watchtower which stands on the Cape of Sa Mola you get a panoramic view of the bay and the island of **Sa Dragonera**, 1km across the channel.

Local sights: Nestling in a valley of almond groves, **ANDRAITX** is one of the most beautiful spots in the island. Up to the 18C it lived with its back to the sea, surrounded by watchtowers and fortifications which protected it from the constant raids by pirates and privateers. Son Mas, nearby, is a beautiful example of noble architecture. In S'Arracó, 3km SW, the estate of La Trapa, where there was once a Trappist monastery (with a good sculpture of the Virgin), belongs to the Balearic Ornithological Society. Continuing W, from San Telmo (a good area for walks through the woods) there are boat excursions to the island of Sa Dragonera. Back in Puerto de Andraitx, the coastal **road** to Camp de Mar offers good views of the bay.

Sports: Water sports are practised at the *Club de Vela del Puerto de Andraitx* ☎ 67 17 21, and there is excellent **scuba diving** off the coast of Camp de Mar and Sa Dragonera island.

BAÑALBUFAR-BANYALBUFAR **Baleares** ☎ (971), pop. 459. Palma 26km.

At Bañalbufar, the cliffs dominated by watchtowers which bring to mind the far off days of Turkish assaults and the **terraced hillsides** of grapevines and tomatoes provide an unforgettable picture of the Mediterranean countryside adapted to meet the needs of man.

- 🏨 **★★★** *Mar i Vent* (closed: 1/12-1/2), c/ José Antonio, 49 ☎ 61 00 25 🛏 19 ✕ **P** ♦ ⅏ ≈ ≪ ♉ $$. Quiet, with lovely views of the sea.

Beaches: S'Arenal is a small, pebbly cove with a cascade of cold spring water. The coves of Sa Galera and Sa Pedra de S'Ase are lovely but not easy to get to.

Cultural highlights: The 18C church is worth seeing, as are the stately Son Bunyola mansion with its twin towers, the coastal watchtowers, and the steep flight of steps leading down to the sea.

Local sights: There are beautiful seascapes from the **corniche road** that hugs the coast as well as from the **Ses Animes** lookout point built in the 17C. SE along the C-710, **ESTELLENCHS**, surrounded by almond trees, is a pretty little village sitting at the foot of the Galatzó mountain with its own lovely cove. For accommodation, try the ★★ *Maristel* (closed: November), c/ Eusebio Pascual, 10 ☎ 61 02 82 ⊨ 53 ✕ ✦ ⅋ ⩘ ≪ ℺ $$, which is quiet and has good views.

Sports: This coast is ideal for scuba diving.

BENDINAT COAST Baleares ☎ (971).

See the 'Calvià' entry for general information on the area.

▣ ★★★ *Bendinat*, Urb Bendinat ☎ 67 52 54 ⊨ 31 ⅄ **P** ✦ ⅋ ⅀ ℺ V $$$. An attractive complex of garden bungalows by the seaside.

Local sights: The town of **PORTALS NOUS**, 2km S, borders a sheltered cove of golden sand and clear, blue waters, where the winters are extremely mild. The town is a water sportsman's haven —the islet of d'En Sales is ideal for **scuba diving**, while the port area, *Puerto de Portals*, besides its shops and apartments, has moorings for hundreds of vessels. Racket players will find tennis and squash courts at the *Club Tenis Nous*, c/ California, 28 ☎ 67 58 77. The port also has many good restaurants, including *Tristán* (closed: Mondays and 10/1-10/2) ☎ 68 25 00 ✦ ❋ ≪ AE, EC, V $$$$$, which serves excellent modern European cooking, and the *Bar del Puerto*, on the road to Palma ☎ 68 25 00 **P** ✦ AE, MC, V $$$$. A good place to stay in the area is the nearby ★★★★ *Punta Negra*, km12 on the road to Andraitx ☎ 68 07 62 ⊨ 61 ✕ ✦ ⅋ ⩘ ⅀ ≪ AE, DC, EC, V $$$$. Set on an isolated rocky outcrop which has access to two lovely, semi-private coves, this very peaceful hotel has very good views of the bay.

CALA D'OR Baleares ☎ (971). Palma 69km.

Cala d'Or, or Cove of Gold, is an opulent sort of resort that draws pretty wealthy visitors, though the buildings are traditionally whitewashed rather than golden. The lush, green pine groves, the clear water and the fine sandy beach at the **cove**, tucked in between looming rocks, make Cala d'Or one of the most attractive little coves on the eastern coast of Majorca. Several art galleries, pricey leather shops, tasteful boutiques and other stylish establishments live side by side with hamburger bars, bazaars and cheaper open-air stalls. The town also has a lively nightlife which attracts a young and cosmopolitan, predominantly Scandinavian, crowd.

▣ ★★★★ *Cala Esmeralda* (closed: 1/11-31/3), Urb Cala Esmeralda ☎ 65 71 11 ⊨ 151 ⅄ ✦ ⬥ ⅋ ⩘ ⅀ AE, DC, EC, V $$$$ to $$$$$. Very quiet.

▣ ★★★ *Cala d'Or* (closed: 1/11-31/3), Av Bélgica, s/n ☎ 65 72 49 ⊨ 27 ✦ ⅋ ⩘ ⅀ AE, V $$$$. Quiet, with spacious terraces set among pine trees.

▣ ★★★ *Rocador* (closed: 1/11-31/3), c/ Marqués de Comillas, 3 ☎ 65 70 76 ⊨ 95 ✕ ✦ ⩘ ⅀ ≪ V $$$. Good views.

▣ ★★★ *Rocador Playa* (closed: 1/11-31/3), c/ Marqués de Comillas, 1 ☎ 65 77 25 ⊨ 105 ✕ ✦ ⬥ ⩘ ⅀ ≪ V $$$. With a pretty garden set among pine trees; good views.

▦ **★★★ *Rocamarina*** (closed: 1/11-31/3), Urb Es Fortí, 1.5km S of town ☎ 65 78 32 ⇥ 207 ✕ 🄿 ✤ ⅏ ≈ ⌖ ⌕ $$$. Quiet, with tennis courts and a swimming pool.

🍴 *Es Clos* (closed: Sundays and in winter), c/ Convento, 17, in Alquería Blanca ☎ 65 34 04 🄿 ✤ **AE, DC, EC, V** $$$. Set in a grand country house with a very pleasant garden, this restaurant serves excellent desserts.

🍴 *La Cala* (closed: 15/11-15/4), Av Bélgica, s/n ☎ 65 70 04 **AE, V** $$$. Traditional Majorcan cuisine.

🍴 *Yate d'Or* (closed: January), Av Bélgica, s/n ☎ 65 79 78 ✤ **AE, EC, V** $$$. A combination of international cooking and typical Majorcan dishes served on a pleasant terrace.

Sports: Sailing, windsurfing, scuba diving... you name it —everything at the *Puerto Marina de Cala d'Or* ☎ 65 70 70.

CALA RATJADA **Baleares** ☎ (971), 🛈 Town Hall ☎ 56 30 52. Palma 80km. ☗

Cala Ratjada, once a fishing village and today a tourist magnet, has a small fishing port and marina in its bay and some of the most spectacular beaches in Majorca close at hand.

▦ **★★★ *Aguait*** (closed: 2/10-31/2), Av de los Pinos, s/n ☎ 56 34 08 ⇥ 188 ✕ ✤ ⅏ ≈ ≪ ⌕ $$$. Quiet, with good views.

▦ **★★★ *Son Moll*** (closed: 2/10-31/2), c/ Tritón, s/n ☎ 56 31 00 ⇥ 125 ✕ ≈ **DC, V** $$$.

▦ **★★ *Ses Rotges*** (closed: 1/12-1/4), c/ Alcedo, s/n ☎ 56 31 08 ✤ **AE, DC, MC, V** $$$. With a pretty terrace and a good **restaurant** serving ☗ French cuisine $$$.

🍴 *Lorenzo* (closed: Mondays and 26/10-28/12), c/ Leonor Servera, s/n ☎ 56 39 39 **AE, EC, V** $$$. Excellent grilled fish platters.

Beaches: Besides the local **Cala Ratjada** beach, there are several others in ☗ the neighbourhood such as the Cala Mesquida, Son Moll, Cala Sa Font and, 2km to the N, **Cala Agulla**, which is beautifully sandy.

Best buys: Bargain hunters will enjoy the Saturday market in Cala Ratjada and the Wednesday market in Capdepera.

Cultural highlights: The **Casa March** mansion, surrounded by beautiful gardens, houses an outstanding private collection of modern art.

Local sights: Driving W for 2km, there are pretty views of the area from Cabo de Capdepera. The agricultural town of **CAPDEPERA**, 2.5km W, can be approached either on foot, up a flight of steps, or by car through tiny, narrow back streets. Here you can visit the 13C Almudaina castle and walk around the ancient walls, from which there are beautiful **views** of the area. If you visit ☗ on August 24, you will also be able to witness the traditional trotting race that takes place in the Es Camp Roig estate. If, instead, you drive S from Cala Ratjada, after 11km you will come to the **Cuevas de Artá** caves, formed by ☗☗☗ seawater erosion and magnificently situated some 35m above sea level. Inside, the vast arcade unfolds to reveal caves known as the **Vestibule**, the **Queen of the Columns**, the **Hall of the Flags** and the Dantesque lower room aptly called **Hell**. In the neighbouring village of **ARTA** take a stroll through the narrow streets to visit the Museo Histórico de Artá, with interesting prehistoric statues, and the picturesque Santuario de San Salvador, a shrine built within the walled enclosure of the 13C Almunia castle and refurbished in the 19C. The area is rich in **Megalithic** ruins, especially **talayots**, the ancient fortified lookout towers so typical of Majorca.

Sports: The *Puerto Deportivo de Cala Ratjada* sports club ☎ 56 30 67 stages an International Windsurfing Marathon in July.

CALVIA **Baleares** ☎ (971), pop. 37,126, **P** 67 01 04, ✈ Son San Juan ☎ 26 46 24. Andraitx 11km, Palma 18km.

The old city centre of Calvià is some 10km from the coast of Santa Ponsa where, in 1229, the troops of **James I of Aragón** disembarked to set about conquering the island. Up to the 1950s Calvià was just an agricultural area, but in the last 30 years it has been transformed into a tourist centre with more than 100,000 tourist beds in some of the most important resorts in Majorca —the urban areas of **Magaluf** and **Palma Nova**, full of blocks of flats and with a young, lively nightlife, are the heartland of British charter flight holidaymaker territory; **Paguera**, dotted with small and medium sized family hotels frequented by Germans and Scandinavians, is the historic site where Peter IV of Aragón disembarked in the 14C to snatch back his kingdom from James III of Majorca; **Illetas** and **Cas' Catalá**, full of four-star hotels, have been traditional tourist resorts since the 1960s; **Santa Ponsa**, a glorious mix of young people, families with children, medium size hotels and some luxury developments, all with a lively nightlife, is another favourite British haunt; **Costa d'En Blanes**, **Bendinat** and the **Sol de Mallorca** and **Costa de la Calma** developments are distinctly up-market; **Portals Nous**, the newest of the marina-centred developments, is lively and luxurious; while **Cala Fornells** is the retreat of the famous, the aristocratic and the artistic.

🍴 *Can'a Cucò* (closed: Mondays, Tuesdays, 22/12-1/2 and at lunchtime during August), Av de Palma, 14 ☎ 67 00 83 **P** ✿ V $$$. Traditional Majorcan cooking.

🍴 *Vista del Rey*, Bellavista-Paguera ☎ 68 62 70 ✿ ✱ ≪ AE, MC, V $$$.

Beaches: The coast of Calvià embraces some 38km of beaches and small coves, some of them quite delightful like, for example, **Santa Ponsa**, **Cala Fornells**, **Cala Vinyes** and **Camp de Mar**...

Best buys: The Monday morning street market on c/ Moncada, in Calvià proper, is good for fruit, vegetables, pastries and savouries. There are also many shops and **boutiques** along this stretch of coast.

Cultural highlights: In the town proper, visit the parish church, which dates from the 13C but has undergone numerous subsequent modifications. Notice how in the interests of symmetry, each of the towers has been adorned with a clock —neither of them works. In the area of Calvià, be sure to explore the unspoiled beauty spots and **coves** along the coast.

Local sights: Besides exploring the entire coast of Calvià, your sightseeing should take you inland to the typical rural towns of Andraitx and Capdellá. At **Cabo Andritxol**, next to the Fornells cove and accessible only on foot, there is an ancient watchtower with splendid views, similar to those seen from Cape Negret, which stands between the Fornells cove and Santa Ponsa.

On the town: There is no shortage of fun in the Calvià district —here you will find everything from a casino, the *Casino de Mallorca* in the Sol de Mallorca housing development ☎ 68 00 00, to aquaparks, the *Aquapark* in Magaluf and the *Marineland* on the Costa d'En Blanes, not to mention the hundreds of bars and **discos** all along the coast.

Sports: There is a horseback riding school in Magaluf, a golf course in Santa Ponsa ☎ 69 02 11, and ultralight flying ☎ 67 00 00 and all kinds of water sports facilities all along the coast.

DEYA-DEIA **Baleares** ☎ (971), pop. 531. Palma 27km.

The **setting** of this enchanting, old-fashioned village, bathed by the Mediterranean below and crowned by hillsides of pine, olive and almond trees from above, is extraordinarily beautiful. Unsurprisingly, Deyá has always attracted foreign painters, musicians and writers and counts English poet and critic **Robert Graves** among those who succumbed to its charms.

▦ ★★★★ *Es Moli* (closed: 1/11-28/2), on the road from Valdemosa to Deyá ☎ 63 90 00 ⊨ 73 ✕ ✦ ☒ ⩲ ≪ ⸦ DC, MC, V $$$$$. A very peaceful hotel set in beautiful terraced gardens and with fine views of the valley and the sea.

▦ ★★★★ *La Residencia* (closed: 1/1-31/3), c/ Son Canals, s/n ☎ 63 90 11 ⊨ 31 ✕ ✦ ⩲ ⸦ AE, DC, MC, V $$$$$. A quiet hotel in a Majorca-style mansion with a good **restaurant** $$$.

Beaches: The sunsets seen from the small and usually crowded Deyá cove, 2km from the town centre, are breathtaking.

Cultural highlights: A stroll through the narrow streeted village of pink houses is an aesthetic experience in itself. In Deyá everything captures the imagination, including the small **cemetery** where Graves is buried, and from which there is a splendid view of the Mediterranean and the surrounding countryside, and the 16C parish church. The town is also home to the d'Es Clot Archaeological Museum, which has interesting island exhibits.

Local sights: The stately **Son Marroig** mansion, once the estate of the Archduke Louis Salvador of Austria, is today a museum of Majorcan ceramics and furniture. Surrounded by beautiful gardens, from the white marble lookout there are wonderful **views** of the sea and the **Na Foradada** rock.

FELANITX **Baleares** ☎ (971), pop. 14,330, ✉ 58 02 52, ✚ 75 14 45, **P** 58 00 51. Palma 48km.

Founded in 1300, Felanitx —which has been said to mean 'Faithful to the Night' or 'Faithful by Night'— has been something of an *avant garde* cultural centre since its foundation, cradle of the 15C architect and sculptor Guillem Sagrera and of the most representative and commercially successful of Spain's young contemporary painters, Miquel Barceló.

Local sights: Approximately 7km from Felanitx on the road to Porto Colom, the 14C **Monastery of San Salvador**, a centre of mystical and magical attraction steeped in history, is set in a perfect landscape 500m above sea level, from where there are wonderful **views** of the eastern part of the island. Inside the Monastery's chapel there is an interesting 17C wood carving of *The Last Supper*, a statue of the *Virgin and Child* behind the Baroque high altar, three *Nativity* scenes and a beautiful 14C Gothic **altarpiece** of polychromatic stone depicting scenes of the Passion. Next door, a century-old tavern serves the best soufflé omelettes in the island. Further E, the coast is dotted with beautiful villages like **CALA D'OR** (see separate entry). Six kilometres from Felanitx on the road to Porto Colom, the restaurant *Vista Hermosa* (closed: February) ☎ 57 59 00 ✦ ≪ $$$$, looks out on beautiful views of the mountain, the valley and the sea. Another 6km take you to **PORTO COLOM**, an enchanting little port, with good beaches nearby and one of the best closed harbours in the island. You will also find here one of the very best restaurants in Majorca, the *Celler Sa Sinia* (closed: Mondays, except in July and August), c/ Pescadores, s/n ☎ 57 53 23 **P** ✳ AE, DC, MC, V $$$$. Farther S **PORTO PETRO** retains the charm of a small fishing village, which is what it was before becoming a residential centre. Nearby you will find some of the most beautiful coves in Majorca —**Cala Santanyi**, a sandy beach in a rugged rocky setting, and **CALA FIGUERA**, a fine sandy beach dotted with fishing boats against a backdrop of white houses set among pine trees. The waters off this fishing town are excellent scuba diving territory, and other water sports are practised at the town's marina ☎ 65 37 05 and at the *Club Náutico* ☎ 65 76 57. Accommodation is available at the ★★ *Cala Figuera* (closed: 1/11-30/4), c/ San Pedro, 30 ☎ 65 36 95 ⊨ 103 **P** ✦ ☒ ⩲ ⚘ ≪ ⸦ $$, which is quiet and has good views.

● ● ● FORMENTOR, PENINSULA OF **Baleares** ☎ (971). Puerto de Pollensa 20km, Palma 78km.

In the N of the island, Formentor is a peninsula of high cliffs formed by the foothills of the Sierra de Tramontana as they stretch out into the sea closing in the Bay of Pollensa. Four kilometres N of Pollensa you will get to
● ● the scenically set **CALA SAN VICENTE** —the towering cliffs to the E provide a dramatic contrast to the green pine groves and the white sand of its beaches to the S. Accommodation is available at the ★★★★ *Molins* (closed: 6/11-31/3), Cala Molins ☎ 53 02 00 ⇌ 90 ● ⅍ ⚓ ⅀ ≪ ⚲ AE, DC, V $$$ to $$$$, a quiet hotel with large terraces offering good views of the area.

● ● ● Returning to the main road, wind your way along the spectacular **route** that leads into the Formentor peninsula, an impressive natural sight of dramatic cliffs, dense pine forests and fine sandy beaches lapped by crystal-clear waters. From the **d'Es Calomer** lookout point, reached by the steps carved
● ● ● into the rock face on the edge of the precipice, there are impressive **views** of
● ● blue sea and the dramatic coastline. **Cala Pi**, set back against the mountains, surrounded by pine trees and looking out over turquoise water, is the most
● ● ● sheltered cove in the island. Here, the famous ★★★★★ *Formentor*, Formentor beach ☎ 53 13 00 ⇌ 127 ✕ **P** ● ⅍ ⚓ ⅀ ≪ ⚲ 🐎 AE, DC, MC, V $$$$$, draws celebrities who are attracted as much by its cuisine as its beach and its magnificent setting. A quiet, stately hotel, it has excellent views and facilities, including a heated swimming pool, a good **restaurant** and a beach-side buffet in summer. Advance bookings are necessary. The trip
● ● ● to the lighthouse at **Cabo Formentor**, some 13km from the hotel, is well worth it. A wall of stone drops a sheer 200m to the blue sea below. All along the way there are places to stop and admire the view but it is best to go right on to the lighthouse itself, from where you get a panoramic view of the Mediterranean and the northern coastline.

● ILLETAS-ILLETES **Baleares** ☎ (971). Palma 8km.

Illetas gets its name from the two islets that face its three fine-sanded
● **coves**, lapped by clear, shallow waters and bounded by rocky promontories. Unfortunately, indiscriminate building has rather spoiled the beauty of the natural landscape which, in the past, attracted international figures such as King Saud of Saudi Arabia, ex-President Nixon and actor Errol Flynn among others.

● ▥ ★★★★★ *Meliá De Mar*, Paseo del Mar, s/n ☎ 40 25 11 ⇌ 136 ♿ **TV** ●
♨ ⅀ ≪ 🐎 ⚲ AE, DC, EC, MC, V $$$$$$. With a pretty, tree-shaded garden and lovely views of the bay and the mountains.

▥ ★★★★ *Gran Hotel Albatros*, Paseo de Illetas, 13 ☎ 40 22 11 ⇌ 119
♨ ⅍ ⚓ ⅀ ▦ ≪ ⚲ $$$$. Magnificent views of the sea and coast.

▥ ★★★★ *Gran Hotel Bonanza Playa*, on the Illetas road ☎ 40 11 12 ⇌ 294 ♿ ● ♨ ⅍ ⚓ ⅀ ▦ 🐎 ≪ ⚲ AE, DC, EC, V $$$$ to $$$$$. Quiet, with a beachside swimming pool and terrace, and good views of the sea.

● ▥ ★★★★ *Iberotel Bonanza Park*, on the Illetas road ☎ 40 11 12 ⇌ 138 ⅀ ● ⚓ ≪ ▦ 🐎 ⚲ AE, DC, EC, V $$$ to $$$$$.

▥ ★★★ *Playa Marina Sol* (closed: 1/11-30/11), Paseo de Illetas, s/n ☎ 40 26 11 ⇌ 172 ✕ 🍸 ● ⅍ ⚓ ⅀ 30m ≪ DC, MC, V $$.

🍴 *Bon Aire* (closed: Sunday nights), c/ Adelfas, s/n ☎ 40 00 48 ● ❊ AE, EC, MC, V $$$. Fish and seafood *nouvelle cuisine* served on a pleasant terrace with wonderful views of the Bay of Palma.

On the town: Late-night drinkers will find the *Sorrento*, which faces the *Bonanza Playa* hotel, open at all hours; for earlier drinking, music while you eat and late-night chatting, the place to see and be seen is the very pleasant
● terrace (with swimming pool) of the *Anchorage Club* restaurant, Paseo de

Illetas, s/n ☎ 40 52 12 ♣ ❋ ⚓ AE, DC, EC, V $$$ to $$$$$. And, of course, you are within easy reach of the lively nightlife bars and discos that Palma de Mallorca and the Calvià coast have to offer.

Sports: The area is ideal for scuba diving, swimming and tennis —try the *La Solana* recreational complex.

INCA **Baleares** ☎ (971), pop. 21,720, ✉ Pl del Angel, 12 ☎ 50 04 23, **P** 50 01 50, 🚍 Palma-Inca ☎ 25 22 45. Alcudia 24km, Palma 29km.

In the Middle Ages this little town played a significant part in the wars between the *Ciutat* and the *Part Forana* —that is, between the city and the other towns in the island. It was here that the peasants assembled for their march on the capital in 1450 to air their agrarian grievances. Today, Inca is the centre of a flourishing **footwear** industry and its **markets** have a reputation well outside its borders.

¶ *Ca'n Amer* (closed: Saturdays and Sundays), c/ Miguel Durán, 39 ☎ 50 12 61 **P** ❋ MC $$$. Typical Majorcan dishes served in an old wine cellar or *bodega*.

Best buys: Markets have been held in Inca since the 13C, and they are the most popular in the entire island. If you enjoy bargain hunting, visit the town on a Thursday to catch the market on the Plaza Mayor. Other good buys would have to include the cakes made by the nuns at the *Convento de las Jerónimas*, and footwear and leatherwear from any of several stores in town.

Cultural highlights: The outstanding sight here is the Gothic Church of Santa María, which was built in the 13C and renovated in the Baroque style in the 17C, with its fine belltower. The convents of Santo Domingo and San Francisco, both 18C, have attractive Baroque cloisters.

Local sights: After visiting the shrine of the Magdalene, some 4km from Inca at the summit of the Puig de Inca, move on NW to **SELVA**, where a flight of steps flanked by cypress trees leads to the majestic Gothic façade of the **Church of San Lorenzo**. Inside, the first chapel on the left has a
marvellously realistic *Calvary* altarpiece. To the NE, visit Muro's **Museo Etnológico de Mallorca** folk museum, c/ Mayor, 15 (open: 9.00-1.30 and 4.30-7.30; closed: Mondays).

LLUCHMAYOR-LLUCMAJOR **Baleares** ☎ (971), pop. 24,468, **P** 66 17 63. Palma 23km.

Founded by James II in 1300, Lluchmayor nowadays is an agricultural and shoe manufacturing centre set in a landscape still punctuated by old **windmills** used for pumping water.

Cultural highlights: The 18C parish church and the 17C Convent of San Buenaventura are two outstanding architectural sights.

Local sights: Between Cape Enderrocat and the Beltrán Cove, the Marina de Lluchmayor is one of the most interesting areas, from a naturalist's point of view, in the island. Bird watchers will have a field day spotting the species that swoop up and down its wind-swept cliffs. In the S, you can visit **CALA PI** —4km E, there is accommodation at the ★★ *Es Pas* (closed: 1/11-31/3), in Es Pas de Vallgornera ☎ 66 17 18 🛏 39 **P** ♣ ⚘ ⚓ ⚲ EC, V $$$, a quiet hotel scenically situated in a pine grove— and the large, virgin beach of **Es Trenc**. S of Lluchmayor, on the road to the impressive Cabo Blanco headland, you will come upon the well preserved talayot settlement of **Capocorb Vell**. If, instead, you drive SE on the road to Campos, you will find the 19C Molí d'En Gaspar, a mill turned museum which exhibits tools and other equipment. Continuing SE along the C-717, **CAMPOS DEL PUERTO**, famous for its pastries and capers, has several interesting buildings: the 16C Town Hall, the 13C Chapel of San Bui and the 17-18C Convent of San

Francisco de Paula. Here, too, is the only spa in Majorca, the ★★ *Balneario San Juan de la Font Santa* (closed: 1/10-31/5), on the road to Campos del Puerto ☎ 65 50 16 🛏 19 ⅙ 🅿 ✦ ⅍ $$, a very relaxing hotel with a youthful atmosphere. To the N of Lluchmayor, the lovely hamlet of **RANDA** is followed by the **Monasterio del Cura**, where tradition has it Ramón Llull retired to meditate, and in whose library there are original Llull manuscripts. From the W side of the monastery's terrace there is a lovely **panoramic view** of the island from Cape Formentor in the N to the Bay of Palma in the W.

MANACOR Baleares ☎ (971), pop. 26,360, **P** 55 00 63. Palma 48km.
      This is an important manufacturing centre which brings together coastal tourism, farming, thriving furniture manufacturing and, best of all, a highly profitable **cultured pearls** industry.

Best buys: Cultured pearls can be bought from the *Perlas Majórica* factory, Vía Roma, 22, and handmade articles fashioned from olive wood from the *F. Ortiz* workshop, c/ Muntaner, 10.

Cultural highlights: The Municipal Archaeological Museum (visits by prior arrangement ☎ 55 33 12 ext. 45) is a veritable storehouse of mosaics and Palaeochristian sarcophagi. The town also boasts a neo-Gothic parish church and the beautiful 17C Cloister of San Vicente. The **Palau tower**, which is all that remains of the one-time summer residence of James II, and the Ses Puntes and Els Eginastes Gothic military towers are among Manacor's other interesting buildings.

Local sights: S'Hospitalet is an interesting talayot village some 15km away. **PETRA**, 10km NW of Manacor, was the birthplace of **Fray Junípero Serra**, the 18C evangelist who in the course of missionary work in California founded San Francisco and San Diego; the house where he was born is now a museum. Thirteen kilometres E of Manacor, **PORTO CRISTO** is a fishing port on a narrow cove side by side with a modern marina, the *Club Náutico* ☎ 57 01 23. Here you can stay at the ★ *Perelló*, c/ San Jorge, 30 ☎ 57 00 04 🛏 95 🅿 ✦ ⬥ ⌾ V $$$. Recommended restaurants include *El Patio* (closed: 1/11-15/12), c/ Burdils, 54 ☎ 57 00 33 ✦ $$$, and *Ses Comes* (closed: Mondays and 1/11-31/12), Av de los Pinos, 50 ☎ 57 04 57 AE, EC, V $$$ to $$$$. One kilometre S, the **Cuevas del Drac** caves, nicknamed the 'Underground Alhambra' (open: times vary, call ☎ 57 07 74), consist of spectacular limestone formations produced by seawater erosion. The **domes** of these caves are immediately impressive, as is the 177m long crystal-clear **Martel lake**, which can be explored by boat or admired from the shore. The lighting, designed by engineer Bohigas, accentuates the natural beauty of the place, and background music adds to the theatrical effect. Also close by, the **Cuevas dels Hams** caves, route of an old underground river, are spectacular for their fine white stalactites, the most impressive of which hang in the **Sala de los Anzuelos**. If you continue further S, you will reach the **coves** of Magraner, Domingo, and Murada.

ORIENT Baleares ☎ (971). Palma 27km.
      This charming farming hamlet lies in a valley in the foothills of the Alfábia mountains. Much of its charm lies in its traditional cooking; local dishes include such delights as a rice stew called *arros brut*, literally crude rice, and a stew of thrush with cabbage.

🖽 ★★★★ *L'Hermitage*, km8 on the Sollerich road, 1km out of Orient ☎ 61 33 00 🛏 20 📺 ✦ ⬥ ⅍ ⩰ 🖽 ≪ ⌾ AE, EC, V $$$$. A peaceful hotel in a pretty country mansion, with pleasant views of the area.

Local sights: There are fine examples of stately homes in the area, and a scenic route which leads SE to the medieval castle town of **ALARO**.

PAGUERA-PEGUERA **Baleares** ☎ (971), 🛈 68 70 83, ✚ 68 11 22, **P** 🐾
67 01 04. Palma 22km.

Paguera, once a nobleman's estate and now a tourist resort, stands on a beautiful sandy **inlet** of historical significance —it was here that Peter IV of 🐾 Aragón disembarked in the 14C to reconquer Majorca from James III. Today, Paguera attracts thousands of Germans and Scandinavians to its small and medium-sized hotels. (See 'Calvià' for general information on the area).

▦ ★★★★ *Club Galatzó*, km20 on the road from Palma to Andraitx ☎ 🐾🐾
68 62 70 🛏 198 ⅙ ♣ 🖾 « 🐴 ⅄ ⬧ 🛦 ⚲ ⚲ 🛦, 🖾, **AE, DC, EC, MC, V**
$$$$. A peaceful hotel perched atop a hill and commanding lovely views of the sea and the surrounding hillsides. Its restaurant, the *Vista de Rey*, is quite good.

▦ ★★★★ *Gran Hotel Sunna Park*, c/ Gaviotas, 25 ☎ 68 67 50 🛏 75 ✕
⬱ ⌁ « **AE, DC, EC, V** $$$$$.

▦ ★★★★ *Villamil*, km22 on the Andraitx road ☎ 68 60 50 🛏 106 ♣ ⬱ 🐾
🖾 ⚲ **AE, DC, V** $$$$ to $$$$$$. With a pretty swimming pool set in a pine-shaded terrace.

▦ ★★★ *Bahía Club*, Av de Paguera, 81 ☎ 68 61 00 🛏 55 **P** ♣ ⬱ ⌁ $$.

🍽 *La Gran Tortuga* (closed: Mondays and 11/1-11/2), on the road to Cala Fornells ☎ 68 60 23 ♣ ❋ ⬱ ⌁ **AE, EC, V** $$$ to $$$$. With pleasant terraces and a swimming pool overlooking the cove and the sea.

🍽 *Vista de Rey* (open: summer only), Club Galatzó, Urb Ses Rotes Velles ☎ 🐾
68 62 70 ♣ ❋ « **AE, DC, MC, V, CB** $$$$. *Nouvelle cuisine*.

Best buys: Go to *Jordá Oliva*, on the road to Andraitx, for typical Majorcan embroidery.

Local sights: The beautiful, sandy **CALA FORNELLS** cove, 2km SW, is a 🐾
haven of peace where the famous, the aristocratic and the artistic hide from the crowds... One of the best places to stay here is the ★★★★ *Coronado* 🐾
(closed: 1/11-31/3), Cala Fornells beach ☎ 68 68 00 🛏 139 ♣ ⬦ ⬱ ⌁
🖾 « 🐴 ⚲ $$$$, a pleasant hotel in a setting of pine woods with beautiful views of the sea and the cove.

PALMA DE MALLORCA **Baleares** ☎ (971), pop. 321,112, 🛈 Av Jaume 🐾🐾
III, 8 ☎ 71 22 16, ☏ c/ Jaime III, 18, ✉ c/ Constitució, 6 ☎ 72 18 67 and
71 66 25, ✚ 75 14 45, **P** 28 16 00, ✈ Son San Juan, 11km ☎ 26 46 24
(Iberia ☎ 26 26 47 and 46 34 00, Aviaco ☎ 26 02 73), ⛴
Trasmediterránea, Paseo Muelle Viejo ☎ 72 67 40 ⛴ Transbalear, c/ 16 de
Julio, s/n ☎ 29 60 00, 🚌 Pl España, s/n ☎ 75 22 24 🚌 Mallorca, Pl de
España, 1 ☎ 75 22 45, 🚃 Palma-Inca Line ☎ 25 22 45, 🚃 Palma-Sóller
Line ☎ 25 20 51. Sóller 25km, Manacor 48km, Alcudia 53km.

Blessed with an almost perfect climate and protected from the sometimes fierce N winds, Palma —or the *Ciutat* (from the *Ciutat de Mayorques*, translation of the Arabic *Medina Mayurka*), as the natives like to call it— stands on the beautiful **Bay of Palma**, on the SW coast of the island. 🐾🐾🐾
Founded by the Romans in the 1C BC, the city was already prosperous when the Muslims conquered it in 903, and it continued to expand at a steady pace until the 13C when, after its Reconquest on December 31, 1229, it began to grow even more rapidly during the reign of James II. During the island's medieval period of splendour under the Christians, the Jewish community prospered, the Genoese introduced a banking system, Gothic painting and cartography flourished, its merchant fleet sailed the seven seas in pursuit of trade and stately mansions sprang up in profusion. Later still, both Ferdinand the Catholic Monarch and Charles I realized the strategic importance of the city and fortified it. During the 15C and 16C, the bourgeoisie and the aristocracy both adopted and adapted Italianate

aesthetics in the island's architecture, giving rise in the 18C to the typical Majorcan **courtyard**. At the beginning of the present century the city was further developed when the walls around the Cathedral were demolished to make way for streets and avenues. Today, Palma has the heaviest passenger traffic in Spain. Its **port**, flanked by the long, palm-lined boulevard called the **Paseo Marítimo**, is a veritable forest of the masts of pleasure craft that dock below the cathedral and of the larger boats stationed at the Estación Marítima and the Gran Dique to the SW. The heart of the city is the **Paseo del Born** (until the 16C the riverbed of the La Riera), which gently slopes down to the sea. The old quarter, including the **La Portella** Jewish area, extends N of La Lonja on Paseo Sagrera and E of the Paseo del Born, the Almudaina castle and the cathedral, while the residential districts of **Terreno** and **Bonanova** stand below the outer walls of the Bellver Castle. The tourist centres of **Cala Mayor** and **San Agustín** are at the SW end of the bay, while on the opposite side, to the E, the city is bordered by the Portixol and Molinar neighbourhoods and by the **beaches** of **Ca'n Pastilla**, **Ciudad Jardín** and **El Arenal** (a large beach with hundreds of bars, pizza parlours, stalls and a lively and international atmosphere) which together form an uninterrupted sequence of resorts known collectively as *Playa de Palma*.

🏨 ★★★★★ *Meliá Victoria*, Av Joan Miró, 21 ☎ 23 43 42 🛏 167 ✕ TV ✦ 🍴 ⚓ « AE, DC, EC, V $$$$$$.

🏨 ★★★★★ *Son Vida Sheraton*, Urb Son Vida, 13, 6km to the NW of Palma ☎ 45 10 11 🛏 170 ✕ ✦ 🏊 ⚓ 🖼 « ♀ ✦ AE, DC, EC, MC, V $$$$$ to $$$$$$. In a reconstructed castle, this quiet hotel is set among pine trees near the golf course, and it has magnificent views.

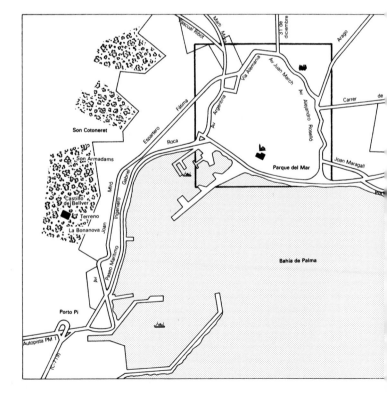

🏨 ★★★★★ *Valparaíso Palace*, c/ Francisco Vidal, s/n, in La Bonanova ☎ 🛥️🛥️🛥️
40 04 11 🛏️ 138 ✕ ✚ ⚓ 🖼️ « ♀ AE, DC, EC, MC, V $$$$$ to
$$$$$$. A quiet, modern and luxurious hotel with lovely views of the city,
the port and the bay... it lives up to its name.

🏨 ★★★★ *Alexandra-Sol*, c/ Pineda, 15, in Ca'n Pastilla ☎ 26 23 50 🛏️
164 ⚓ ⚖️ « 🐕 AE, DC, EC, V $$$$.

🏨 ★★★★ *Bellver-Sol*, Paseo Marítimo, 11 ☎ 23 80 08 🛏️ 393 ✕ & 📺 🎤
⚓ « AE, DC, EC, V $$$$$.

🏨 ★★★★ *Delta*, on the road to Cabo Blanco, 6km from town in Playa de 🛥️
Palma ☎ 26 47 54 🛏️ 288 ✕ ✚ 🖼️ « ♀ $$$$. Quiet, with pleasant views
and surrounded by beautiful pine woods.

🏨 ★★★★ *Garonda* (closed: 1/11-31/3), Ctra El Arenal, 28 ☎ 26 22 00
🛏️ 112 🎤 ⚓ ⚖️ « ♀ AE, DC, V $$$$$.

🏨 ★★★★ *Maricel*, on the road to Andraitx, 7km from town in Ca's Catalá 🛥️
☎ 40 27 12 🛏️ 56 ✚ 🖼️ ⚖️ « ⅀ ⚠ ♀ 🐕 AE, DC, EC, MC, V $$$ to
$$$$. A typical Majorca-style building with stepped terraces and lovely
views of a cove and the sea.

🏨 ★★★★ *Nixe Palace*, Av Joan Miró, 269, in Cala Mayor ☎ 40 38 11 🛏️ 🛥️
130 ✕ ✚ ⚓ ⚖️ « ⚠ ⚐ ♀ AE, DC, EC, MC, V $$$$$. A good hotel with
large, palm-shaded terraces, lovely views, a heated swimming pool and a
good restaurant.

🏨 ★★★★ *Palas Atenea-Sol*, Paseo Marítimo, 29 ☎ 28 14 00 🛏️ 370 ✕
& 📺 🎤 ⚓ 🖼️ « AE, DC, EC, V $$$$$$.

🏨 ★★★★ *Playa Cala Mayor*, c/ Gaviota, s/n, in Cala Mayor ☎ 40 32 13
🛏️ 143 ⚓ « V $$$.

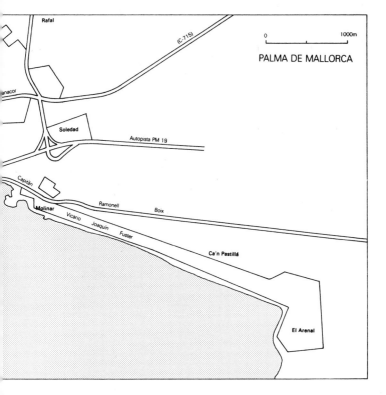

PALMA DE MALLORCA

🔌 🏨 ★★★★ *Racquet Club Son Vida*, in Son Vida, 6km NW of Palma ☎ 28 00 50 🛏 51 ✦ 🎬 ≪ ♀ ⌣ 🐾 AE, DC, EC, MC, V $$$$. Extremely quiet with a pleasant atmosphere, ideal for sportsmen, particularly **tennis** and **golf** enthusiasts.

🏨 ★★★★★ *Río Bravo*, c/ Misión de San Diego, s/n, in El Arenal ☎ 26 63 00 🛏 200 ✕ ✦ ♠ ≈ 🏊 🐎 $$$ to $$$$.

🏨 ★★★ *Boreal*, c/ Mar Jónico, 11, between Ca'n Pastilla and El Arenal ☎ 26 21 12 🛏 64 ✦ ≈ 🏊 ♀ $$$.

🏨 ★★★ *Constelación*, c/ Corp Mari, 27 ☎ 40 05 01 🛏 42 ✕ 🐾 ≈ ≪ $$$$.

🏨 ★★★ *Cristóbal Colón*, c/ Parcelas, 13, in El Arenal ☎ 26 27 50 🛏 158 ✦ 🐾 ≈ 🏊 $$ to $$$.

🏨 ★★★ *Jaime III-Sol*, Paseo Mallorca, 14 ☎ 72 59 43 🛏 88 AE, DC, EC, V $$$.

🏨 ★★★ *Las Arenas*, c/ Tito Livio, 14, in Ca'n Pastilla ☎ 26 07 50 🛏 152 ≈ 🏊 ≪ $$.

🏨 ★★★ *Majórica*, c/ Garita, 3 ☎ 40 02 61 🛏 153 ✦ 🐾 ≈ ≪ $$$.

🏨 ★★★ *Reina Constanza*, Paseo Marítimo, s/n ☎ 40 07 11 🛏 97 ♠ ≈ ≪ DC, EC, V $$$ to $$$$.

🏨 ★★★ *Royal Cupido*, c/ Marbella, 32 ☎ 26 43 00 🛏 197 🅿 ♠ ≈ 🏊 ≪ 🐎 AE, V $$ to $$$$.

🏨 ★★★ *San Francisco*, in El Arenal, c/ Laud, 24 ☎ 26 46 50 🛏 138 ♠ ≈ 🏊 ≪ $$$.

🏨 ★★★ *Santa Ana*, c/ Gaviota, 9, in Cala Mayor ☎ 40 15 12 🛏 190 🅿 ✦ ≈ 🏊 ≪ AE, DC, V $$$.

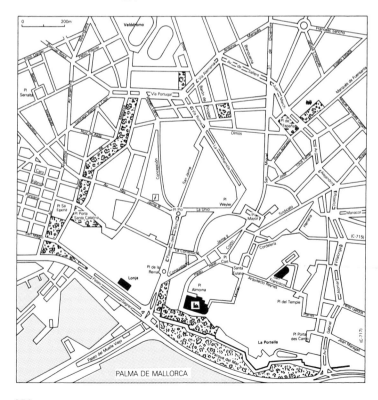

PALMA DE MALLORCA

▥ ★★★ *Saratoga*, Paseo Mallorca, 6 ☎ 72 72 40 ⊨ 187 🅿 ✦ ⩱ V $$$.

▥ ★★ *Rex* (closed: 1/10-31/3), c/ Luis Fábregas, 4 ☎ 23 03 65 ⊨ 81 ✦ ⩱ ▦ $$.

❙❙ *Caballito de Mar* (closed: Sundays), Paseo de Sagrera, 5 ☎ 72 10 74 **AE, DC, EC, V** $$$. Fish and seafood in a restaurant facing the fishing port.

❙❙ *Ca'n Nofre* (closed: Wednesday nights, Thursdays and February), c/ Manacor, 27 ☎ 46 23 59 ✳ **AE, DC, EC, V** $$$. Traditional Majorcan cooking.

❙❙ *Ca's Cotxer* (closed: Wednesdays from November to May, and January and February), Ctra Arenal, 31 (exit 5), in Playa de Palma ☎ 26 20 49 ✳ **AE, DC, EC, V** $$$. Specializes in fish, seafood and typical Majorcan cooking.

❙❙ *Club de Mar* (closed: winter), Pelaires Wharf on the Paseo Marítimo ☎ 40 36 11 🅿 ✦ ✳ $$$. Exclusive, sailing and jet set atmosphere.

❙❙ *Club Náutico Cala Gamba* (closed: Mondays, except on holidays), Paseo Cala Gamba, in Call d'En Rabassa, 6km E of Palma ☎ 26 10 45 🅿 ✦ ≪ **AE, DC, MC, V** $$$$. Fish and seafood served on an open-air terrace with good views of the sea.

❙❙ *El Gallo* (closed: Saturdays lunchtime, Sunday nights and August), c/ Teniente Torres, 17 ☎ 23 74 11 ✳ **AE, MC, V** $$$$. Majorcan *nouvelle cuisine*.

❙❙ *Es Parlament* (closed: Sundays), c/ Conquistador, 11 ☎ 72 60 26 ✳ $$$. Simple cooking and typical Majorcan desserts.

❙❙ *Honoris* (closed: Sundays, holidays, Holy Week and 1/8-15/8), Ctra Vieja de Buñola, 76 ☎ 28 83 32 🅿 ✳ **AE, DC, MC, V** $$$. Set in a typical Majorcan house on the outskirts of town.

❙❙ *Le Bistrot* (closed: Sundays and July), c/ Teodoro Llorente, 4 ☎ 28 71 75 🅿 ✳ $$$. French cuisine served in a typically French bistro.

❙❙ *Porto Pi* (closed: Saturdays lunchtime and Sundays), Av Joan Miró, 174 ☎ 40 00 87 **AE, DC, V** $$$. Basque cooking in a century-old summer house.

❙❙ *Rififí* (closed: Tuesdays and February), Av Joan Miró, 186 ☎ 40 20 35 🅿 ✳ V $$$. Fish and seafood, simply prepared. Take note that reservations are necessary.

❙❙ *Xoriguer* (closed: Holy Week and August), c/ Fábrica, 60 ☎ 28 83 32 ✳ **MC, V** $$$. Basque and international dishes with a touch of French cuisine and a good wine list.

Beaches: Heading E, the beaches of Ca'n Pastilla are 10km away, and the golden-sand, well-equipped beaches of **El Arenal** are 14km from town. In the opposite direction, to the SW, you will find **Cala Mayor**. In summer they are all densely packed, but if you drive farther, some 30km from town you can find solitary coves lapped by an emerald sea.

Best buys: Palma is a city where you can find almost anything your heart desires, from the most typical handmade articles to international designer items. Look out for cultured pearls, best bought at *Majórica*, Av Jaime III, 11, and gold and silver jewelry sold at *Joyería Mallorca*, Pl del Rosario, 4 (designs by **Carrera and Carrera)**, along c/ Platería and at *Gregory*, along the Paseo del Born. Good Spanish and international fashion boutiques include *Lollipop*, c/ Brondo, 2 (for women), *Girone di Vento*, c/ Fátima, 20 (for men), *Adolfo Domínguez*, c/ Bonaire with c/ Aragonés, 2 (for men and women), *Es Portal*, c/ La Ravaleta, 23, *Trazos*, c/ Isidoro Macabich, 20, and *Zavella,* Pl Santa Catalina Thornas, 17. Along the Paseo del Born there is excellent fashion and leather accessories at *Loewe*, No. 22, and more accessories at *L'Ofre*, No. 28. The Av Jaime III is Palma's main commercial street —along it you will find large department stores like *Galerías Preciados*, antique shops like **Persépolis**, Spanish fashion boutiques like **Timoteo**, and shoe shops like **Stéphane Kélian** and **Camper**. Other good shoe shops include **Patricia**, c/ San Miguel, 11, and **Yanko**, c/ Unió, 3. Closing the fashion scene, furs and leather clothes are good value for money at **Pink**, Pl Pío XII, 3, and **Reus**, c/ Barrera, 15, in the Son Españolet area. Gastronomes take note that spicy *sobrasada* patés and Majorca cheeses are sold at *La Montaña*, c/ Jaime II, 29, wines and liqueurs at *Colmado Colón*, c/ Santo Domingo, 5, and typical island sweets at *Fresquet*, c/ Orfila, 4. Local crafts include embroidered table linen from **Casa Bonet**, c/ Puigdorfila, 3, hand-made pottery from **Amengual**, c/ Trinidad, 37, and blown glass from **Casa Gordiola**, c/ Conquistador, 2 and c/ Jaime II, 26. Spanish decorative items and hand-made gifts are also sold at **Artespaña**, Paseo Mallorca, 17. The city has several open-air markets —try the **Baratillo**, Polígono de Levante, 7 (open: 7.00-2.00), for a little bit of everything; the stalls along the Rambla for flowers and plants; the Tuesday, Thursday and Saturday flea-market at Pl Pedro Grau for ceramics and art objects, and the street market on the Plaza Mayor for handicrafts in general.

Cultural highlights: The **Arab Baths**, c/ Serra, 3 (open: 10.00-1.30 and 4.00-6.00; closed: Saturday afternoons and Sundays), constitute the best preserved example of the architecture of the Muslim era in Palma. Nearby, off c/ Sol, the 13-14C Gothic **Church of San Francisco** is one of the city's loveliest buildings. With its Baroque high altarpiece and 15C choir stalls, its cloister is now the resting place of 13C mystic and poet Ramón Llull. Also nearby, down c/ Arquitecto Reynes, is the austere 13-15C Gothic **Church of Santa Eulalia**. The **Cathedral** is a fine 13-16C building with a nave of unorthodox design, outstanding façades (the S one dating from the 14C and the N one, designed by Francesc Sagrera, from the 15C), windows sculpted by Guillem Sagrera in the San Antonio de Padua side chapel, and an 18C Baroque altarpiece by Francisco de Herrera in the Chapel of San Sebastián. From 1904 to 1914, Modernist architect **Gaudí** did some renovation work here —the wrought iron baldachin for the high altar, the sculptural decoration of the royal chapel and the canopy of the E pulpit were his major contributions. The pulpits themselves are excellent 16C Plateresque pieces by Juan de Salas. The two chapter houses are used as the **Cathedral Museum**. Near the **Consulado del Mar** building, with a beautiful 17C Plateresque gallery, you will come to the 15C **Lonja**, or Exchange building, designed by Guillem Sagrera, a simple, practical building of Gothic outline where symmetry is the key to its otherwise rather sober beauty. Walk W along the Paseo Sagrera to get to the **Almudaina Palace**, an originally Moorish fortress (the **Arco de la Almudaina** dates from those times) that was substantially altered in the 14-15C (open: 10.00-1.00 and 3.00-6.00; closed: Saturday afternoons, Sundays and holidays ☎ 22 71 45 and 21 43 68). Art and archaeological exhibits can be viewed at the Majorca Museum, c/ Portella, 5 (open: 10.00-2.00 and 4.00-7.00; weekends: 10.00-2.00; closed: Mondays ☎ 71 75 40). Palma's 16-18C mansions are stately and charming —outstanding examples would have to include the Gothic and Renaissance **Oleza House**, c/ Morey, 33, with a lovely 17C courtyard; the austere Gothic 16C **Palmer House**, c/ Sol, 17; and the 18C **Morell House**, also known as the house of the **Marquises of Sollerich**, c/ San Cayetano, 22, with an elegant gallery and a beautiful Majorcan-style **patio**, which houses the City Museum of Modern Art (open: 11.00-1.30 and 5.00-8.30; Saturdays: 11.00-1.30; closed: Sundays and Mondays ☎ 72 20 92).

Fiestas and festivals: **San Sebastián**, patron saint of the city, is celebrated on January 20. More international events include the theatre festival held in

June and July, the **International Music Festival** (the *Gener a Mallorca* ☎ 72 77 44) in August, and the Jazz Festival in September.

Local sights: Perched on a hill 2.5km W of central Palma, **Bellver Castle** is one of the best kept 14C medieval fortresses in the Mediterranean. *Bellver* means 'Beautiful View' in Catalan, a term which understates the breathtaking **panorama** of the town and the bay that can be enjoyed from the castle's esplanade. The ochre-coloured castle is also quite stunning, given its circular shape —in fact, everything in the castle is round: its turrets, courts and main towers. Its history has been quite eventful: for a time the seat of the kings of Majorca, it then became the prison of the widow and heirs of King James III. Centuries later, in 1801, controversial statesman and writer Gaspar Melchor Jovellanos was also imprisoned here, and his cell is one of the chilling attractions of the castle. Bellver's present role as the **Municipal Art and History Museum** is rather more pleasant.

Other places to visit include the old fishing port of Es Portixol, E of the Bay, and the stately country houses —such as the 18C **Son Berga**— in Establisments, now become a dormitory town. The **Cuevas de Génova** caves in the Génova district, 5km SW of town (open: 10.00-1.15 and 3.00-9.00), are also interesting.

On the road to Manacor, **ALGAIDA** is a good place for souvenir shopping —at km19, the factory of **Gordiola**, built in 1719, still makes blown glassware according to the 14C traditional Majorca process (you can watch it being made), while at the **Alorda** factory, leather and suede clothes and accessories are good value for money.

On the town: During the daytime, the **Bosch** bar, Pl Pío XII, 6, is as good a place to meet as any. As the evening approaches, people move to **Granja Royal**, c/ San Felio, 6, for a good *merienda* of *ensaimada* pastry and thick drinking chocolate, or to **Ca'n Joan de S'Aigo**, c/ Sans, 10, where people have been gathering since 1700 to drink *horchata* or chocolate with typical Majorcan pastries. At nightfall, the action moves to the terraces along the Paseo del Born and the Pl de la Lonja. Later at night you might want to try your luck at the **Casino de Mallorca**, Urb Sol de Mallorca ☎ 68 00 00. Or you might prefer to sample the international **nightlife** atmosphere in the Pl Gomila, crowded with discos, pubs and bars for people of all types and ages —**Moncloa** is the place to meet for a chat against a background of soft music, **Nagual** is the area's international pub, while **Tito's** is Gomila's famous discotheque. The area of El Arenal, where English rules over Spanish, is also crowded with discos —**Bel Air**, **Río Palace** and **Zorba's**, Av Son Rigo, s/n, are the best. The other great, and stylish, nightlife area centres around the Paseo Marítimo's open-air terraces and discos —the exclusive **Club de Mar** is frequented by the jet set, the international **Victoria** (in the hotel of the same name) attracts a slightly older clientele, and the terrace of the **Jazz Piano Bar** caters to jazz lovers. Dilettantes will love **Abaco**, c/ San Juan, 1, which serves good drinks against a background of classical music, candlelight and flowers.

Sports: **Palma Bay** is famous for sailing, having staged numerous international regattas; its many sailing clubs include the **Club Náutico de Palma de Mallorca** ☎ 22 68 48, the *Puerto de Palma de Mallorca* ☎ 21 51 00, the **C.N. El Arenal** ☎ 26 40 19, the **Club de Mar** ☎ 40 36 11, and the **Escuela de Vela de Cala Nova** (Cala Nova Sailing School) ☎ 40 25 12, in San Agustín. For scuba diving, contact the *Centro de Actividades Subacuáticas Tritón*, Pl Weyler, 2, and the *Centro de Investigaciones y Actividades Subacuáticas* (Centre for Underwater Research Activities), c/ Obispo Cabanellas, 29-A. Horseback riders can rent horses at the **Club Escuela de Equitación de Mallorca** (Majorca Riding School),

km12 on the road to Sóller ☎ 61 31 57, while **golfers** can play at the
18-hole, par 72 ***Son Vida Club de Golf***, Urb Son Vida ☎ 23 76 20, 5km
NW of town. Energetic players might enjoy a game of squash at the ***Squash
Mallorca***, c/ R. Servera, 43 ☎ 45 41 41, while more sedate sportsmen who
prefer watching to doing might like to visit the trotting races staged at the
Hipódromo Son Pardo, km13 on the road to Sóller ☎ 25 40 31.

PALMA NOVA and MAGALUF **Baleares** ☎ (971). Palma 14km.
    Palma Nova and Magaluf together form the largest tourist complex on
this part of the coast of Calvià which juts out into the Bay of Palma. They are
popular resorts, teeming with apartment blocks, hamburger bars and pizza
parlours, pubs and bars, supermarkets and shops of all types that make for a
lively, neon-light nightlife and cater to the young, mostly British, charter flight
brigade. In winter, the pace of life in Magaluf changes to suit the senior
citizens who take advantage of its mild climate and out-of-season prices.

▦ ★★★★ ***Atlantic*** (closed: 1/11-31/3), Punta Ballena, s/n, in Magaluf ☎
68 02 08 ⇔ 80 ✕ ✦ ⚓ ⌘ ≪ V $$$. With a large terrace set among
pine trees.

▦ ★★★★ ***Comodoro*** (closed: 1/11-31/3), Paseo Calablanca, s/n, in
Palma Nova ☎ 68 02 00 ⇔ 83 ✕ ✦ ⚓ ⌘ ≪ AE, DC, EC, V $$$$.
Lovely views of the bay.

▦ ★★★★ ***Coral Playa***, c/ Torrenova, s/n, in Magaluf ☎ 68 05 62 ⇔ 184
✕ ▮ ⚓ ⚓ ⌘ ≪ AE, DC, EC, V $$$$. Overlooking the bay.

▦ ★★★★ ***Delfín Playa***, c/ Hermanos Moncada, 32, in Palma Nova ☎
68 01 00 ⇔ 144 ✕ ⚬ ✦ ⚓ ⌘ ▦ ≪ $$$$. A pretty terrace with a
swimming pool.

▦ ★★★★ ***Meliá Magaluf***, in Magaluf ☎ 68 10 50 ⇔ 300 ✕ TV ✦ ▮ ⚓ ⌘
⚲ AE, DC, V $$$$.

▦ ★★★ ***Pax***, Av Notario Alemany, 12, in Magaluf ☎ 68 03 12 ⇔ 161 ⚬ P
✦ ▮ ⚓ ⌘ ≪ ⚱ ⚲ V $$$. Very good views.

▯▮ *Ciro's*, Paseo del Mar, 3, in Palma Nova ☎ 68 10 52 ✦ ❈ ≪ AE, EC, V
$$$. A large and very pleasant beachside terrace with lovely views at
night.

▯▮ *Gran Dragón II*, Paseo del Mar, 2, in Palma Nova ☎ 68 13 38 ✦ ❈ ≪
AE, DC, EC, V $$$. Chinese cuisine.

Beaches: Palma Nova I, the pleasant, golden-sanded stretch of **Palma Nova
II** and Son Matiés are all local beaches. In Magaluf, **Magaluf** beach is the
longest on this stretch of the Calvià coast.

Best buys: You can buy reasonably priced leather goods at *Ca'n Joan*, in
Magaluf.

Cultural highlights: Some distance inland, the Capella de Sa Pedra
Sagrada is believed to be the site where the first mass was said after James I
took the island in 1229; a Neo-Romantic Oratory was built there earlier this
century. Also inland, you can visit the **navetiforme Alemany**, an important
pre-talayot settlement dating from 3000-1300 BC.

Local sights: N of Palma Nova, **COSTA D'EN BLANES** is a more relaxed
tourist resort. Here you can get a speedy suntan at the appropriately named
San Calíu Cove —*calíu* means hot coal—, enjoy a good dolphin show at
Marineland, or, for the energetic, play racket sports at the *Sporting Tenis
Playa*. S of Magaluf, people who prefer the simple life and whose idea of a
seaside holiday is good swimming, sunbathing and quiet evenings lulled by
the sound of the sea go to the well equipped beach of **Cala Vinyes**.
Accommodation is available at the ★★★★ ***Forte Cala Vinyes*** (closed:
1/11-31/3), c/ Las Sirenas, s/n ☎ 68 11 00 ⇔ 245 ✕ ⚬ ✦ ▮ ⚓ ⚓ ⌘
≪ ⚲ $$$$ to $$$$$. Further S and set in a pine wood, **Cap Falcó** is a

beautiful solitary cove; you have to climb down steps in the rock face to get to it. Access to the nudist beach of **Bella Dona** is easier. Facing this is the **El Sec** islet, whose waters are great scuba diving territory. Still further S, the luxurious **Sol de Mallorca** development has a small marina. And next to the Cala Axada cove you will find the ***Casino de Mallorca*** ☎ 68 00 00, which has a vast range of entertainments under its roof —table and machine games, a restaurant, bars, a discotheque, dance halls, plus squash and paddle tennis courts. At the end of this stretch, you will come upon some ancient caves with enigmatic drawings and a 16C watchtower at **PORTALS VELLS**. You can dine on the beach at the delightful *chiringuito* of ***Ca'n Pau Perdiueta*** (closed: Sunday nights, Mondays and 25/12-31/1), c/ Ibiza, 222 ♣ ≪ $$$, which serves excellent fish and seafood caught by the owners whose boat is moored alongside.

On the town: Fun daytime places in the area include the *Aquapark*, with exciting water toboggans and so on, and the very popular go-kart circuit at the *Karting Magaluf*, both in Magaluf. In the evening, Britishers will feel at home playing English billiards at the *Snooker Club*, Av Magaluf, s/n, in Magaluf, or, if it's discos you want, head for the good music and strobe lights of *Barrabás* and *Borsalino* in Palma Nova.

Sports: Inland, golfers can play at the 18-hole, par 72 *Golf Poniente*, Km16 on the Palma-Andraitx road, in Magaluf ☎ 22 36 15. On the coast, sailing, windsurfing and water skiing facilities abound —go to the *Puerto deportivo Palma Nova* ☎ 68 10 55 and, for skiing, to the *Club de Ski Náutico* on Son Matíes beach.

POLLENSA-POLLENÇA **Baleares** ☎ (971), pop. 12,456, ✉ c/ San José, 5 ☎ 53 11 25, **P** 53 04 37. Sóller 60km, Palma 85km.

Set between the 320m high **Puig de Pollença** hill to the E and the **Puig del Calvari** hill to the W, Pollensa is a charming town of quaint little streets lined with small houses of rose-coloured stone with arched doorways, its Moorish heritage evident in the form of its many water-wheels, wells and fountains. This quiet town, set 6km back from the coast, has always attracted painters and writers of all nationalities and consequently enjoys a lively cultural scene.

🍽 *Ca'n Pacienci* (closed: Sundays and 1/11-31/3), km4 on the road to Puerto de Pollensa ☎ 53 07 87 **P** ♣ **EC, V** $$$. International cuisine in a British atmosphere. Dinner only.

Beaches: **Cala de San Vicente**, 7km N, is a lovely beach bordered by a pine grove to the S and by towering cliffs to the E. The beach of Puerto de Pollensa, 6km NE, is less attractive, but if you continue further NE you will soon reach the sandy stretches of **Cala Pi** and Cala Murta in Formentor.

Best buys: Head for the Plaza Mayor, where there is a good art dealer, *Bennassar*, and an open-air Sunday market for general bargains.

Cultural highlights: The Baroque Cloister of Santo Domingo in the 16-17C Monastery of Our Lady of Calvario is an interesting building where the international painting and music festivals staged by the town are held. Outside the town, there is a 14C fortified Gothic sanctuary at Puig de María and, nearby, at **Puig del Calvari**, 365 stone steps, flanked by rows of cypress trees, lead to a high, white-walled 14-18C chapel at the very top. Back in town, the Museo de Pollensa, c/ Santo Domingo (open: 10.00-12.00; closed: Mondays, Wednesdays, Fridays and Saturdays), has interesting zoological and medieval art exhibits. Another museum, the **Casa Museo Anglada Camarasa**, Paseo Anglada Camarasa, 87 (closed: Wednesdays and Sundays), includes numerous works by the painter of the same name, as well as embroidery, furniture, and Chinese porcelain dating from the 16C to the 18C. There are interesting Roman remains of an aqueduct and a bridge very close to the town.

Fiestas: Every Good Friday, the ***Devallament*** (lowering Christ from the Cross) is celebrated with a torchlight procession that begins at Puig del Calvari and ends in the valley below. Corpus Christi is also festively celebrated with a procession and a series of typical dances. Later in the year, a mock battle against invading pirates is staged on August 2 and, in the same month, the town holds a **Music Festival**.

Local sights: Heading inland along the C-710 in a southerly direction, the **Shrine of Our Lady of Lluc** is the spiritual centre of the island. It dates from 1239, although most of what you see today was built during the 17C and 18C. The monastery's highlights include a beautiful 14C alabaster sculpture of the black Virgin and the midday chants sung by the *Escolanía de Blauets* choir in her honour. A 6km drive NE of Pollensa leads to **PUERTO DE POLLENSA** (see separate entry).

● | POLLENSA, PUERTO DE (PORT OF POLLENSA) | **Baleares** ☎ (971). Pollensa 6km, Palma 91km.

Once a quiet fisherman's village, Puerto de Pollensa was discovered by the painter Anglada Camarasa at the beginning of this century, when it became an artists' colony. Today, it is a residential area and up-market resort in a particularly beautiful **setting**.

- ▦ ★★★ *Daina* (closed: 1/11-31/3), c/ Atilio Boveri, 2 ☎ 53 12 50 ⊨ 60 ⑤ ✦ ⚓ ⌧ « AE, V $$$$. Good views.
- ▦ ★★★ *Illa D'Or* (closed: 1/11-31/3), c/ Colón, s/n ☎ 53 11 00 ⊨ 119 ✦ ⚓ ⌧ « ⚲ V $$$$. Quiet, with a pleasant, tree-shaded terrace and good views of the bay.
- ▦ ★★★ *Miramar* (closed: 1/11-31/3), Paseo Anglada Camarasa, 39 ☎ 53 14 00 ⊨ 69 **P** ⌧ « ⚲ AE, EC, V $$ to $$$. Good views.
- ▦ ★★★ *Pollentia* (closed: 1/11-31/3), on the road from Puerto de Pollensa to Alcudia ☎ 53 12 00 ⊨ 70 **P** ✦ ⌧ « $$$. Good views and a pleasant, plant-filled terrace.
- ▦ ★★★ *Sis Pins* (closed: 1/11-31/3), Paseo Anglada Camarasa, 229 ☎ 53 10 50 ⊨ 55 ⌧ « $$$ to $$$$.
- ▦ ★★★ *Uyal* (closed: 1/11-31/3), Paseo de Londres, s/n ☎ 53 15 00 ⊨ 105 **P** ✦ ⚓ ⌧ ⚲ $$$ to $$$$. Good views and a tree-shaded terrace.
- ▦ ★ *Panorama* (closed: 1/11-31/3), Urb Gomar, 5 ☎ 53 11 92 ⊨ 20 ✦ ⚓ ⌧ $$$.
- ❡ *Club Náutico* (closed: Tuesdays), Muelle Viejo ☎ 53 10 10 ✦ « AE, DC, EC, V $$$. Fish and seafood served on an open-air terrace with good views of the bay.
- ❡ *Lonja del Pescado* (closed: Wednesdays except in July and August, and January), Muelle Viejo ☎ 53 00 23 ✦ ❊ « EC, V $$$. Seafood dishes and Majorcan wines served in a restaurant with good views of the sea.

Local sights: The SE drive along the coastal route to Alcudia has very good views of the Bay of Pollensa. In the opposite direction, the spectacular 20km road leading into the Formentor Peninsula takes you through some of the most marvellous scenery in the whole of this unforgettable island (see 'Formentor').

On the town: *Marcha Fresca* and *El Garrito* serve good drinks to pleasant background music.

Sports: Given its ideal location in a well protected bay, with Cape Formentor to the N and Cape Pinar to the S, Puerto de Pollensa is perfect for sailing, water skiing, windsurfing and scuba diving, and a good harbour for pleasure boats.

SANTA PONSA-SANTA PONÇA **Baleares** ☎ (971). Palma 20km.

It was in this beautiful **bay** that James I disembarked in 1229 to take
possession of the island. Several centuries later, its wonderfully mild winter
temperatures and its sparkling, golden, sandy **beach** have contributed to
making it a cosmopolitan holiday resort for German, British, Swiss and
Belgian visitors who enjoy its lively nightlife.

- ▥ ★★★★ *Golf Santa Ponsa*, Urb Santa Ponsa ☎ 69 02 11 ⊨ 18 ✕ ⍊ ♣
  ⇔ ⚲ ↙ AE, MC, V $$$$.
- ▥ ★★★ *Bahía del Sol*, c/ Jaime I, s/n ☎ 69 11 50 ⊨ 161 ✕ 🅿 ⇔ ⚲ ▦
  ≪ ⛴ AE, DC, EC, V $$ to $$$$. Good views.
- ▥ ★★★ *Rey Don Jaime*, Vía del Puig Mayor, 4 ☎ 69 00 11 ⊨ 417 ✕ ⅄
  ♣ ♫ ⇔ ⚲ ⛺ ⛴ $$.
- ▥ ★★ *Casablanca* (closed: 1/11-30/4), Vía Rey Sancho, 6 ☎ 69 03 61
  ⊨ 87 ✕ ♣ ⇔ ⚲ ≪ $$ to $$$. Lovely views of the bay.
- ▯ *Las Velas* (closed: 1/11-27/3), c/ Puig de Galatzó, 4 ☎ 69 03 28 ♣ ≪
  AE, DC, EC, V $$ to $$$.
- ▯ *Nick's* (closed: 26/12-28/2), Vía Jaime I, 97 ☎ 69 02 67 ♣ ≪ AE, EC,
  V $$ to $$$$. An open-air terrace with beautiful views of the bay.

Cultural highlights: In Santa Ponsa you will find a beautiful 14C Gothic
tower and an interesting monument, the Sa Creu del Rei En Jaume, from
which there is a pretty view of the bay.
Sports: Scuba divers will find that the Bufador marine grotto, at the foot of
the Sa Creu monument, invites underwater exploration. Golfing enthusiasts
can tee off at the 18-hole, par 72 course of the *Santa Ponsa* golf club ☎
69 02 11. The *Club Náutico Santa Ponsa*, which attracts pleasure craft
from all over Europe, has moorings for 500 vessels.

SOLLER **Baleares** ☎ (971), pop. 11,026, *i* Pl Calvo Sotelo, 1 ☎
63 02 00, ✚ 63 08 45, ⇌ Palma-Sóller ☎ 25 20 51. Palma 30km, Pollensa
60km.

Set in a lovely valley flanked by purple-tinged mountains which have long
been the inspiration of painters like Catalan Santiago Rusiñol and Joaquín
Mir, Sóller, now a sleepy agricultural village, reached its zenith in the 19C
when it boasted its own hospital and thriving textile industry. Even if you have
a car, the best way to go from Palma to Sóller is by the **narrow gauge
railway** which has the double attraction of being a relic from the past and
providing an enjoyable little jaunt through a lovely landscape of fields and
valleys.
▯ *El Guía*, c/ Castañer, 3 ☎ 63 02 27 🅿 V $$$. Simple home-cooking.
Best buys: Bargains can be had from the open-air market held in the Pl de
A Maura on Saturdays.
Cultural highlights: The Baroque 18C Convent of San Francisco and the
16-17C parish church are worth visiting. Sóller also has an interesting
museum, the Museo Casa de Cultura, c/ Mar, 11 (open: 11.00-1.00 and
4.00-7.00; closed: Wednesdays and Sundays), with folk art exhibits.
Local sights: Some 5km N along the C-711 or on the charming **streetcar**,
PUERTO DE SOLLER, standing on a small, almost completely circular bay, is
one of the best natural havens along the northern Majorcan coast. Among
other facilities, the bay boasts an underwater diving school, a sandy **beach**,
and a small pleasure harbour from which excursion boats depart on their
cruises around Majorca's northern coast, the so-called *costa rocosa* or **rocky
coast**. Shorter excursions include one to the curious rock formations in the
gorge of **Torrent de Pareis**. In Puerto de Sóller you can stay at the ★★★
Edén, c/ Es través, s/n ☎ 63 16 00 ⊨ 152 🅿 ♣ ⇔ ⚲ AE, EC, V $$, the
★★★ *Eden Park* (closed: 1/11-31/3), c/ Lepanto, s/n ☎ 63 12 00 ⊨ 64

P ✦ ≈ ⚲ AE, EC, V $$, or the ★★★ *Espléndido* (closed 1/11-31/3), c/ Marina, 23 ☎ 63 18 50 ⇌ 104 ✦ ⚲ ≪ V $$$, which is ideally situated next to the sea and has good views of the area. If all you want is a meal, try the fish and seafood served at *Es Canys* (closed: Mondays and from 30/11-28/2), d'En Repic beach ☎ 63 14 06 ✦ ≪ AE, DC, EC, V $$$, which has good views of the port.

Heading S of Sóller along the C-711 **road** that climbs up the verdant N slope of the Sierra de Alfàbia mountain range, after 14km you will reach the romantic **Gardens of Alfàbia**, a combination of the Hispano-Arabic style of gardening with Italian aesthetics that produces an oriental paradise heavy with scents, the sound of water and subtropical vegetation. Further S and 2km before reaching Bunyola, the **Finca Raixa** estate was once the property of the Despuig family, who built the Italian-style house and nostalgic gardens you see today.

NE of Sóller you can head for **BINIARRAIX**, a charming cluster of medieval streets and houses with a timeless air to them, and then on to **FORNALUTX**, a picturesque village with steep streets and houses with roofs of Moorish tiles. Continuing your drive NE along the C-710, you will pass through a tunnel and emerge with the 1,445m-high **Puig Mayor** mountain on your left. Turn left off the C-710 at the **Gorg Blau** dam onto the **road to Sa Calobra**, a narrow and incredibly winding route through a strangely attractive landscape of green olive trees and unexpected rock formations, which suddenly slopes steeply towards the blue sea below. **SA CALOBRA**, a tiny village situated at the foot of the mountain descent and right on the coast, is also connected by cruising boats with Puerto de Sóller. If you are so enchanted with the village that you want to stay, there is accommodation at the ★★ *La Calobra* (closed: 1/11-31/3), Sa Calobra beach ☎ 51 70 16 ⇌ 51 **P** ✦ 🦀 ⚲ ≪ $$, which is very peaceful and has good views of the cove.

SON SERVERA **Baleares** ☎ (971), pop. 5,867. Palma 64km.

Son Servera, which owes its name to its first feudal master, was once prey to pirate attacks and consequently has a defensive watchtower and a fortified church to guard its **bay**. The privateer raids are now long forgotten and instead, the bay of Son Servera has become a first-rate tourist area with upmarket villas in the developments of **Costa de los Pinos**, 7km NE, **Cala Millor**, 3km SE and **Cala Bona**, 3km E.

▦ ★★★★ *Eurotel Golf Punta Rotja*, in Costa de los Pinos ☎ 56 76 00 ⇌ 244 ✦ 🍴 🦀 ≈ ▦ ⚲ ≪ ۹ ⚞ 🦅 $$$$$. Set in a lovely pine wood near the golf course, this extremely peaceful hotel has marvellous views of the sea and mountains.

▦ ★★ *Osiris*, c/ Na Peñal, s/n, in Cala Millor ☎ 56 73 25 ⇌ 207 ✦ ≈ ⚲ ≪ $$ to $$$. Good views.

🍴 *Ca's Patro* (closed: Sundays), 2km from Son Servera in Cala Bona ☎ 58 57 15 AE, V $$$. Majorcan fish and seafood cuisine.

🍴 *S'Era de Pula* (closed: Mondays and 8/1-15/3), km3 on the road to Capdepera ☎ 56 79 40 **P** ✦ ≈ AE, DC, MC, V $$$$.

🍴 *Son Floriana* (closed: Sundays and 15/12-15/1), Urb Son Floriana, in Cala Bona ☎ 58 60 75 **P** $$$. Good fish and rice dishes.

Beaches: The beaches of **Cala Bona** are 3km E, and those of **Cala Millor** are 3km SE.

On the town: The nightlife here centres around the pubs and discos in **Cala Millor**.

Sports: There are water sports facilities at the *Puerto Deportivo Cala Bona* ☎ 57 20 73, and a 9-hole golf course at the *Club de Golf Son Servera* ☎ 56 78 02, in Costa de los Pinos.

Baleares
☎ (971), pop. 1,262. Palma 19km.

Set in a valley covered with olive and almond groves, Valdemosa is a charming little village whose houses today look much the same as they did in the 18C.

❙❙ *Ca'n Pedro* (closed: Sunday nights and Mondays), c/ Archiduque Luis Salvador, s/n ☎ 61 21 70 $$ to $$$. Local cuisine served in a Majorcan house.

Beaches: There is a little cove in Puerto de Valdemosa tucked in between steep cliffs, a little quay and old fishermen's cottages.

Cultural highlights: **La Cartuja**, or the Charterhouse (open: 9.30-1.30 and 3.00-6.30; closed Sundays ☎ 61 21 48 and 61 21 06), the most famous historic building in the village, was built during the reign of James II of Majorca. It was used as the court palace until 1399, when the Catalonian-Aragonese king, Martin the Humane, bequeathed it to the Carthusians who, down through the centuries, carried out various architectural modifications. In 1835, following the expropriation of church property, La Cartuja was bought by private individuals who opened its cells to anyone who wished to spend time there. Chopin, George Sand, Nicaragua's national poet Rubén Darío, Argentinian writer Jorge Luis Borges, and Spanish literary giants Miguel de Unamuno and Azorín are just a few of the big names who took the opportunity of a sojourn in the magnificent monastery. While here, visit the monastery's 18C church, which has interesting frescoes painted by Goya's father-in-law, Bayeu, the library, which has many incunabulae and a valuable 15C triptych, and the 18C **pharmacy**, where the sign on the wall still reads 'God is the only true medicine'.

Local sights: Interesting sights N of Valdemosa include the Trinidad Hermitage and the **Ses Pites** lookout point, both with beautiful views.

Menorca, at 669km², is the second largest of the Balearic Islands. Although it is only 48km long, it is quite varied geographically. Its northern face is a series of open valleys and treeless landscape, with an indented, rocky coastline; the NW is greener, with luxuriant vegetation, while the rocky S, protected from the N and NW *tramontana* winds, is one long, straight cliff with a few beautiful coves lapped by crystal clear waters. The S is also an important centre of Bronze Age culture (2000 BC) —remains of more than 200 conically shaped **talayot** fortified dwellings and **naveta** tombs exist along this shore. Much closer to our times, in the 18C Menorca was a British possession, a fact immediately evident in its architecture. Today, the island owes its prosperity largely to its excellent Mahón **cheese**, leather goods, particularly **footwear**, and **costume jewelry**. Tourism helps, too. Menorcan chefs have a reputation for being imaginative, so do not miss the local *langosta* (lobster) dishes, and when on the town the potent local *ginebra* (gin) is guaranteed to bring a twinkle to the eye.

Baleares ☎ (971), pop. 5,917. Mahón 12km.

Although Alayor is known to have been inhabited since ancient times, the town as such was not founded until 1304 during the reign of **James II**. Over the years it has become a little white town of beautiful 17-18C balconied mansions, in striking contrast to the houses in the rest of the island, where the English-style sash windows predominate.

▦ ★★★ *Los Milanos-Sol* (closed: 20/10-1/4), Son Bou beach ☎ 37 11 75 ⛱ 300 ✕ ✦ ⚓ ♨ ♞ ♞ $$$ to $$$$.

¶¶ *Club San Jaime* (closed: lunchtime except on feast days), Urb San Jaime, on the Son Bou beach ☎ 37 27 87 **P ♣ ≈ ℚ AE, DC, EC, V $$$**. With an open-air terrace, a swimming pool and tennis courts.

Beaches: Between Son Bou and Es Canutells beaches there is a series of charming little coves and creeks, many of them accessible only by dirt tracks and consequently semi-deserted. The most popular are Son Bou itself, 8.5km to the SW of Alayor, and the fine-sanded **Cala'n Porter**, which is on a narrow estuary.

Best buys: Footwear may be bought direct from the factories.

Local sights: In an island teeming with Megalithic remains, those in Toralba d'En Salort and Torre d'En Gaumes are outstanding. Enthusiasts of ancient architecture will also enjoy a visit to the ruins of a 4-5C Palaeochristian basilica near Son Bou and the ancient troglodyte houses carved out of the rocks of Cala Coves and the Cala'n Porter cliff.

On the town: *Sa Cova d'En Xeroi* (closed: 11/11-30/4), in a natural cave under the Cala'n Porter cliff, is a very lively disco.

CIUDADELA-CIUTADELLA DE MENORCA Baleares ☎ (971), pop. 19,945, ✚ 38 07 87, **P** 38 10 50. Mahón 42km.

An episcopal see in the 4C and capital of the island during the Muslim era, the *Civitella*, as it was known under James I, was completely walled in during the 13C to protect it against pirate incursions. The transfer of the capital to Mahón in 1732 checked urban development in the city, so that today its beautiful Gothic and Renaissance mansions, such as those in the **Pl de España** and **Pl del Born**, and its Gothic **Cathedral** (with a later Neoclassical façade) lend it a stately, old-world atmosphere. For a good view of the city and its walls, go to the **port**.

★★★ *Cala Blanca* (closed: 1/11-1/5), Urb Cala Blanca ☎ 38 04 50 ⇌ 147 **P ♣ ≈ ♞ $$** to **$$$**. Well situated in a charming cove, with very good service.

★★★ *Esmeralda* (closed: 1/11-1/4), Paseo de San Nicolás, 171 ☎ 38 02 50 ⇌ 135 ✗ ♣ ≈ ☲ ♞ ℚ **$$** to **$$$$**. Centrally located.

★★★ *Iberotel Almirante Farragut* (closed: 1/11-1/5), Av Los Delfines, s/n, in Cala Forcat ⇌ 472 ✗ ♣ ♨ ≈ ☲ ♞ ℚ V **$$** to **$$$$**. A large and luxurious hotel facing the sea.

¶¶ *Casa Manolo* (closed: Sundays in winter and 10/12-10/1), c/ Marina, 117 ☎ 38 00 03 ♣ ✳ **AE, DC, EC, V $$$** to **$$$$**. Fish and seafood.

¶¶ *Es Pou* (closed: 1/10-30/5), c/ San Rafael, 10 ☎ 38 42 51 ♣ ✳ **MC, V $$$**. Seasonal cuisine.

Beaches: The coves of En Forcat, Brut and Blanes are near the town. Heading S, you can drive to the sandy beaches of **Cala Santandria**, Son Sauyra, En Turqueta and Macarella, while to the N, there are more rugged beaches like Algairens cove, Fontanelles and Morell.

Best buys: *Patricia*, Pl Dalt Els Panyals, 13, sells leather footwear and accessories.

Fiestas: The ancient sport of jousting, which dates back to the 14C, is revived during the feast of **San Juan** on June 23 and 24.

Local sights: While in Ciudadela, visit some of the Megalithic monuments that abound in the area —the **Es Tudons** naveta tomb and the rupestrian art at Santa Ana de Tourraulbet, near the Macarella cove, are especially worthwhile.

On the town: In Ciudadela, people tend to meet in the Pl de Alfonso III, either at the *Ca's Quintu*, a typical café, or at *Es Moli*, a bar with a lively atmosphere. As for the disco scene, *Adagio's*, at c/ Son Oleo, is the town's best.

Sports: There are water sports facilities at the *Club Náutico* ☎ 38 39 18. For those less energetically inclined, spectator sports include trotting races at the *Hipódromo*, Urb Torre del Ram ☎ 38 41 32.

FERRERIAS-FERRERIES **Baleares** ☎ (971), pop. 3,253. Mahón 22km.
Traditionally an agricultural town, Ferrerías is best known today for its footwear and costume jewelry industries. The village itself is quite picturesque, with red and white houses and a 14-18C church founded by James III.

▦ ★★ *Cala Galdana* (closed: 1/11-1/4), in Cala Galdana ☎ 37 30 00 ⇌ 259 ✕ ⅃ ♦ ⅍ ⅍ ⅏ ▦ « AE, DC, EC, V $$ to $$$$. A quiet hotel with a pleasant swimming pool.

Beaches: Santa Galdana cove, 7km S, is an ideal sandy spot, with very clear water against a typically Mediterranean backdrop of pine trees. Mitjana and Trebelútger coves are also to the S. In the N, Calderer, Moragues and Pilar beaches are in a sheltered area, well out of sight of peering eyes.

Local sights: Energetic visitors who enjoy nature and don't mind walking should trek from Cala Galdana or Ferrerías to the spectacular, 6km long Algendar ravine —good views are guaranteed. Other sights in the area include the ruins of the Arab castle of Sent Agayz, at the top of Santa Agueda mountain, and the prehistoric remains at Benimassó, Binicossitx, Santa Ponsa and Son Bell Llot.

On the town: For lively night life, head for the complex of bars and night-clubs in the Cala Galdana district.

MAHON-MAO **Baleares** ☎ (971), pop. 22,159, [i] Pl de la Constitución, 13 ☎ 36 37 90, ☾ c/ de Calvo Sotelo, 4, ✉ c/ del Buen Aire, 15 ☎ 36 38 92, ✚ 36 11 80, P 36 39 61, ✈ San Clemente, 5km ☎ 36 01 50 (Iberia, c/ Doctor Orfila, 9 ☎ 36 41 50, Aviaco, at the airport ☎ 36 56 73), ⛴ Trasmediterránea, Nuevo Muelle Comercial ☎ 36 29 50. Alayor 12km, Mercadal 22km, Ciudadela 42km.

Mahón's 5km long bay is one of the world's best and most sheltered **natural harbours**. First settled by the Romans in the 2C BC, the town's privileged location later attracted waves of Vandal, Byzantine and Muslim invaders. Colonizing invasions were followed by frequent raids during the 15-16C, when the port had to fight off pirates of the calibre of the infamous Barbarossa. Two centuries later, when the British occupied Menorca, they moved the capital to Mahón and established a period of free trade. But the island's eventful history did not end there —Menorca then passed in succession from the French to the British until 1802, when it was finally returned to the Spanish crown. Today, peaceful Mahón is a prosperous town with a flourishing mayonnaise and cheese industry.

▦ ★★★★ *Port Mahón*, Av Fort de l'Eau, s/n ☎ 36 26 00 ⇌ 74 ✕ ♦ ♪ ⅍ « AE $$$$. In the port area, with good views.
▦ ★★★ *Capri*, c/ San Esteban, 8 ☎ 36 14 00 ⇌ 75 ✕ TV P MC, V $$ to $$$. Centrally located.
▦ ★★ *Miramar* (closed: 1/11-1/5), in Cala Fonduco, 1km E of Mahón ☎ 36 29 00 ⇌ 30 ⅍ ⅍ « AE, DC, EC, V $$. Quiet, with good views.
¶ *Chez Gastón* (closed: Sundays and 1/12-15/1), c/ Conde de Cifuentes, 13 ☎ 36 00 44 $$$. French cuisine.
¶ *Club Marítimo* (closed: Sunday nights in winter), c/ Mártires del Atlante, 27 ☎ 36 42 26 P ♦ « AE, DC, EC, V $$$. Good fish and seafood served on its open-air terrace.
¶ *El Greco* (closed: Sundays and 1/12-15/1), c/ Conde de Cifuentes, 13 ☎ 36 00 44 $$$. Fish and seafood.

¶ *Gregal*, c/ Mártires de Atlante, 43 ☎ 36 66 06 **AE, DC, MC, V** $$. Fish and seafood.

¶ *Pilar* (closed: Mondays and November), c/ Forn, 61 ☎ 36 68 17 **V** $$$. Authentic Menorcan cuisine.

☼ ¶ *Rocamar* (closed: Mondays in winter and November), c/ Fonduco, 32 ☎ 36 56 01 **P** ✦ ❋ ☙ ≪ **AE, DC, MC, V** $$$. It also offers accommodation with wonderful daytime views of the port.

Beaches: Cala Mesquida, Sa Albuferas d'Es Grau and Cabo de Favaritx beaches are in the N, while **Cala'n Porter** (see 'Alayor'), Cala Canutells, Cala Biniali and the very pretty Cala Benisafúa are in the S.

Best buys: In Mahón, you can buy leather shoes and accessories at *Patricia*, c/ Ses Morenes, 31, costume jewelry at the *Catisa* factory, c/ San Sebastián, 75, and hand-made silverware and alpaca items at *Pérez Oliver*, c/ Isabel, 32.

Cultural highlights: The Ateneo, or Athenaeum, c/ Conde de Cifuentes, 25 (open: 9.00-2.00 and 3.00-10.00 ☎ 36 05 53) houses a large collection of pottery, maps and fossils. The 13-18C Church of Santa María, with a splendid 19C pipe organ, is also interesting. Best of all, just drink in the general atmosphere as you stroll through the tiny streets with their many Victorian buildings, and along the **port**, from which there is an unforgettable view of the city on the cliff above and the quay below.

Fiestas: On September 8, the feast day of Mahón's patron saint is celebrated with a medieval cavalcade and much general merrymaking.

Local sights: The Megalithic monuments at Trepucó, 1km away, are worth a trip. You can visit more recent historical sites at **VILLACARLOS**, 4km SE of Mahón, where the remains of the old fort of San Felipe, built in 1554 to keep out pirates, still stand. The town, formerly occupied by the English in 1763 —when it was named Georgetown after George III— also has a lovely British colonial style Town Hall and a picturesque old fishing port, where you can have a drink at the taverns opened in the caves the fishermen once used to store their gear. For a change of scene you might try *Bananas*, c/ Fort de l'Eau, s/n, where all sorts of refreshing fruit juices are served on a large open-air terrace. For accommodation, try the ★★★ *Agamenón* (closed: 1/11-1/4), Pasaje Fontanillas, s/n ☎ 36 21 50 ⊨ 75 **P** ✦ ☙ ≈ ☲ ≪ **AE, DC, EC, V** $$ to $$$, a quiet hotel with good views, the ★★★ *Rey Carlos III* (closed: 1/11-1/4), c/ Miranda de Cala Corp, s/n ☎ 36 31 00 ⊨ 87 ✕ ✦ ☙ ≈ ☲ ≪ **V** $$$, a quiet, beachside hotel with good views and terraces, and the ★ *Del Almirante* (closed: 1/11-30/4), c/ Fonduco, s/n, Puerto de Mahón, on the road to Villacarlos ☎ 36 27 00 ⊨ 38 ✕ **P** ✦ ≈ ◔ $$.

On the town: Mahón's traditional meeting place is the *American Bar* in the Pl Real, which has a pleasant terrace. For a more lively nightlife, head for any of the town's three disco bars —*Chocolate*, c/ Carrer Alayor, 14, *Lui*, on the road to Villacarlos, or the original *Tonic*, set in a natural cave on the outskirts of town. And for a completely different scene, during the daytime you can visit the *Aquarium*, next to the Estación Marítima, which features Mediterranean flora and fauna.

Sports: There are excellent water sports facilities at the *Club Marítimo de Mahón*, c/ Mártires de Atlanta, s/n ☎ 35 07 46, and at the *Club Naútico Villacarlos*, c/ Miranda de Cala Fons, s/n, in Villacarlos ☎ 36 58 84, which organizes an annual international **scuba diving** competition. Golfers have a choice between the 18-hole course at the *Real Club de Golf de Menorca*, 7km from the city centre at the Sangri-La development ☎ 36 39 00, or the 18-hole course at the *Club de Golf Son Parc*, 18km N of Mahón ☎ 35 38 40. Those who prefer spectator sports will enjoy the trotting races at the *Hipódromo* (Race Track).

MERCADAL-ES MERCADAL **Baleares** ☎ (971), pop. 2,983. Mahón 22km.

In the centre of the island, Mercadal stands in a valley beneath the 357m high **Mount Toro**, the highest point in Menorca, from whose shrine there are wonderful views of the whole island. The medieval *Pobla de Mercadal* is attractive not only for its well preserved examples of popular island architecture but also for its local gastronomic speciality, an exquisite *caldereta de langosta* (lobster stew).

🍽 *Ca N'Aguedet*, c/ Lepanto, 23 ☎ 37 53 91 **AE, DC, EC, V $$ to $$$.** Menorcan dishes.

🍽 *Moli des Raco*, c/ Vicario Fuxá, 53 ☎ 37 53 92 **P ✦ AE, MC, V $$$.** Typically Menorcan cuisine.

Beaches: From Mercadal, you can drive N to the beaches of Pregonda, Barril, Tirant, Arenal de Son Saura (adjoining Cabo Gros) and the popular Arenal d'En Castell, or S to the sandy cove of Excorsada and Benigagus.

Local sights: **FORNELLS**, 8km N along the C-723, is a pleasant little fishing village on Fornells Bay. The area is ideal for water sports and, for the less energetically inclined, it has two fine-sanded coves, Cala Rotja and Cala Blanca. While here, be sure to visit the Na Polida sea cave, with its sculpturesque stalactites and stalagmites, and indulge in the island's typical lobster stew served at *Es Plá*, in the d'Es Pla arcade ☎ 37 51 55 **P ✦ ≪ EC, MC, V $$$**, or feast on *tapas* and fish dishes at the *La Palma* bar. Shoppers looking for leatherwear accessories will find excellent buys at *Patricia*, c/ Poeta G. Roca, 1.

SAN CRISTOBAL **Baleares** ☎ (971). Mercadal 6km, Mahón 21km.

The agricultural hamlet of San Cristobal is a splendid example of Menorcan popular architecture —many of its households still have open air kitchens with ovens for baking bread, fireplaces and indigenous systems for collecting rain water.

🏨 ★★★★ *Santo Tomás*, Santo Tomás beach ☎ 37 00 25 ⌷ 80 ✗ Υ TV P ✦ 🐾 ⚓ ☂ ≪ **AE, EC, MC, V $$$$.**

🏨 ★★★ *Los Cóndores Sol* (closed: 1/11-31/3), Santo Tomás beach ☎ 37 00 50 ⌷ 188 ✗ P ✦ 🐾 ⚓ ☂ ≪ 🛥 **AE, DC, V $$$ to $$$$.** Quiet, with good views and a garden beside the sea.

Beaches: The beaches of San Adeodat and **Santo Tomás** are 4,5 km S of San Cristobal.

Local sights: Nearby, the ancient village of Son Agustí has a magnificent talayot conical fortified dwelling featuring a very large chamber and a roof of two mighty wooden beams.

SAN LUIS-SANT LLUIS **Baleares** ☎ (971), pop. 3,425. Mahón 4km.

Founded by the French in the 18C —the parish church still bears the coat of arms of Louis XV— this village is a showpiece of picturesque narrow streets and whitewashed houses.

🏨 ★★★ *Biniali*, c/ Suestra, 50, on the road from the Binibeca Vell beach, 2km to the SW of San Luis ☎ 36 17 24 ⌷ 9 ✗ P ✦ 🐾 ⚓ ≪ **DC, MC, V $$$$.** A very quiet hotel with a pretty swimming pool in the garden, charming staff and a good **restaurant**. It is, in fact, much more like a private home than an hotel.

Beaches: S of town, there are fine beaches at the **Alcaufar, Punta Prima**, Binibeca and Binisafuller coves.

Local sights: S of San Luis, **BINIBECA** is a white, modern complex whose architecture is reminiscent of a typical fishing village. To the N, Caló d'es Rafalet, a cove in a narrow cleft between two cliffs, is rather pretty.

CANARY ISLANDS

The Canary Islands are Spain's tropical paradise and for Spaniards living in mainland Spain they are synonymous with holidays, as they are for the hundreds and thousands of foreign tourists who pack the islands' resorts all year round. Colonized and populated by Spaniards, they lie 1,150km SW of the Iberian Peninsula, close to the Tropic of Cancer, and just 115km off the coast of Africa. They are politically and administratively Spanish and yet culturally and geographically they have very much their own personality.

The Canaries today consist of seven islands divided, for administrative purposes, into two areas. The province of Las Palmas brings together the major island of Gran Canaria and the lesser ones of Lanzarote and Fuerteventura. The province of Santa Cruz de Tenerife encompasses Tenerife and its satellite islands of La Gomera, La Palma and Hierro. Within the archipelago there is a variety so extreme that it is easiest to refer to it as a mini-continent. The isles share an eternal spring climate but they differ dramatically amongst each other. Exploring the Canaries you move from sub-tropical vegetation to volcanic semi-deserts, from verdant cliffs and gorges to sand dunes by the sea shore.

One wonders to this day when and how the ancients learnt about this little paradise which Herodotus called the *Garden of Hesperides*, Homer the *Elysian Fields* and Pliny the *Fortunate Isles*. Modern contact with the Canaries began to develop in the Middle Ages as sailors from peninsular Spain arrived to plunder the isles of their orchids, which were used to make dye, and of their inhabitants, who were enslaved. Conquest in earnest only began with the Norman adventurer **Jean de Bethencourt** who, in 1402, claimed Lanzarote on behalf of his feudal lord, Henry III of Castile. In 1483, during the reign of the Catholic Monarchs, **Pedro de Vera** established a base in Gran Canaria and in 1496 **Alonso Fernández de Lugo** won control of Tenerife. From then on colonization started in earnest.

The original inhabitants of the Canaries were a race known as the **Guanches**, a name derived from *guan*, meaning man or people, and *achinch*, meaning white mountain in an obvious reference to Tenerife's snow-capped Mount Teide. The natives lived a **Stone Age** existence of shepherding and very rudimentary agriculture. They buried their dead and, in the case of chieftains, mummified them, much like the ancient Egyptians. In Tenerife, **Bencomo**, the *mencey* or leader of the tribe, fiercely resisted the conquistadors with his flint axes and slings, while in Gran Canaria the ruling *guanarteme*, **Semidán**, welcomed the European strangers and established truces.

The isles began to realize their potential for the Crown of Castile as the links developed with the New World. Right at the beginning of that awesome period **Christopher Columbus**, on his first voyage, rested at La Gomera before venturing into the unknown, westwards in search of the Indies. Before long the Canaries were to become the vital link in transatlantic crossings, a stepping stone between Europe, Africa and the American continent. Last century, as trade and travel increased, the first hotels began to open in Tenerife. Since then commerce and leisure have spread and never ceased developing throughout the archipelago which still retains the paradisiacal qualities that earned it such poetic appellations so many centuries ago.

FUERTEVENTURA

One of the first islands to be discovered by Western civilization, Fuerteventura was conquered by Jean de Bethencourt in the early 15C. Although historically it has always been the runt of the litter, Fuerteventura shows real promise for the future as a haven for tourists who like to get away from it all. It is the closest island to Africa and has arid, barren landscapes, little urban development, unending white-sand **beaches**, rocky coasts good for **scuba diving**, large sea banks for **deep sea fishing**, and plenty of **sun**.

CORRALEJO **Las Palmas** ☎ (928), pop. 1,001, **P** 86 61 07, ✈ Fuerteventura, 44km ☎ 85 12 50. Puerto del Rosario 38km.

In the northern part of the island, the small fishing village of Corralejo has 15km of lovely, virgin white-sand **beaches** and **sand dunes**. It is also an excellent place to eat fresh *vieja* (horned blenny), a fish typical of the Canaries.

- ★★★★ *Iberotel Tres Islas*, Corralejo beach ☎ 86 60 00 ⮠ 356 ✦ ⚲ ⌘ ≈ ⛴ ⊞ ≪ ⚞ ⚲ $$$$$. A very quiet hotel with good sea views and a heated swimming pool.
- ★★★ *Iberotel Oliva Beach*, Corralejo beach ☎ 86 61 00 ⮠ 410 Ⴘ ✦ ≈ ⛴ ≪ ⚞ ⚲ $$$. An hotel with good views of the area and a heated swimming pool.

Local sights: From the fishing port you can make a day trip to the **Isla de los Lobos** (Island of the Sea Lions) —in this tiny island (5.4km²) the legendary Antoñito of *Casa Antonio*, the lighthouse keeper, will be happy to rustle up a *paella* made with freshly caught seafood.

GRAN TARAJAL **Las Palmas** ☎ (928), ✉ Pl de la Candelaria, s/n ☎ 87 03 34, ✚ 87 08 28. Puerto del Rosario 52km.

Gran Tarajal, the second largest town in the island, is the port from which tomatoes are exported to mainland Spain and the rest of the world.

- ★★★ *Tosio*, 15km from Gran Tarajal along the Tarajalejo-Fuerteventura road ☎ 87 00 50 ⮠ 61 Ⴘ **P** ✦ ≈ ⛴150m ⚞ ⚲ AE, V $$$. Room or apartment (3-4 people) accommodation.

Local sights: To the S, El Jable is a sand isthmus that links the N of the island to the Jandía Peninsula in the SW. It has miles of unending white sand beaches, undeveloped until very recently when new tourist complexes such as the **Costa Calma** began to appear on the horizon. However, the area is still largely deserted, so if you wish to spend the day on one of the golden beaches of the **Jandía Dunes** (mostly accessible along dirt tracks) bring along food and drink, as there are no bars or restaurants in the vicinity. The closest place to the dunes is Morro de Jable, a small fishing village on the outskirts of Jandía's tourist complex. For accommodation, you could try the ★★★★ *Casa Atlántica*, 2km from Morro Jable, in Matorral beach ☎ 87 60 17 ⮠ 80 Ⴘ ✦ ≈ ≪ ⚲ AE, DC, V $$$$ which is quiet and has good views, the ★★★ *Los Gorriones Sol*, Barca beach ☎ 87 08 50 ⮠ 321 ✕ Ⅳ **P** ✦ ⚲ ⌘ ≈ ⛴ ⊞ ≪ ⚞ ⚲ ⚑ AE, DC, V $$$, also quiet with good views of the sea as well as a garden terrace with a heated swimming pool, the ★★★ *Taro Beach*, Urb Cañada del Río, in Costa Calma ☎ 87 07 76 ⮠ 128 **P** ✦ ⌘ ≈ ⛴ ≪ ⚲ AE, DC, V $$$$$$, which offers quiet apartment and bungalow accommodation near the sea, with good seaviews, or the ★★★ *Robinson Club Jandía Playa*, 1km from Morro Jable ☎ 87 60 25 ⮠ 360 ✕ Ⴘ ≈ ⛴ ♫ ⊞ ≪ $$$, which has pleasant tropical gardens and excellent facilities. Off the Playa de Jandía, a 6km-long beach mostly frequented by nudists, the coast offers good **scuba diving** possibilities.

PUERTO DEL ROSARIO **Las Palmas** ☎ (928), pop. 13,878, *i* Av Primero de Mayo, 33 ☎ 85 10 24, ✉ c/ León y Castillo, 15 ☎ 85 04 12, ⚕ 85 13 76, P 85 06 35, ✈ Fuerteventura, 6km ☎ 85 12 50 (Iberia, c/ 23 de Mayo, 7 ☎ 85 12 50), ⚓ Trasmediterránea (ferries to Lanzarote, Gran Canaria and Tenerife), c/ León y Castillo, 46 ☎ 85 08 77, ⊞ c/ Alfonso XIII, 25 ☎ 85 09 51.

Puerto del Rosario is the island's capital. The town's lovely beach, **Playa Blanca**, is 3km N of the town centre.

▦ ★★★ *Parador de Fuerteventura*, Playa Blanca ☎ 85 11 50 ⇔ 50 ✕ P ♦ ⚒ ⚓ ⌂ ≪ ⚘ AE, DC, EC, V $$$$. A quiet parador with good views.

Local sights: In the town of **LA OLIVA**, 23km N, you will come across the **Casa de los Coroneles** (The Colonels' House), an 18C building which was the official residence of the island's governors for over a century. This two-storey building, with its patio and six Canary pine balconies, is flanked by two towers. A curious feature of the house is that the total number of windows and doors adds up to 365, one for each day of the year. Nearby is the **Casa del Capellán** (The Clergyman's House), whose doors and windows are decorated with Aztec motifs.

Twenty-seven kilometres SW of the capital, the most interesting place of historical-artistic merit is **BETANCURIA**, the original capital of Fuerteventura founded in the 14C in a sheltered mountain valley by the Norman conqueror Bethencourt. The white **Cathedral**, built in 1410 and reconstructed in 1691, has a beautiful coffered ceiling in its sacristy. The town's Archaeological Museum has an interesting collection of pre-historic tools and implements and ancient local pottery. A 15km drive SW will bring you to the town of **PAJARA**, where the local church is decorated with Aztec motifs.

GRAN CANARIA

A bird's eye view of the island (1,532km²) shows that Gran Canaria is shaped rather like a large, upturned cone with steep, water eroded slopes running down from its highest point, the Pozo de las Nieves, or Snow Pond (1,980m). Because of its varying climatic conditions and constantly changing landscapes, the island is often described as a miniature continent in itself. The N part is humid with large pine forests in the upper areas and lush banana plantations below, whereas the S is arid with crops (like tomatoes) and flora which are typical of dry regions with sunny weather. Again in contrast, the sheer cliffs along the N and W coasts are interrupted by rocky coves, while the S coast is made up of miles of sandy beaches and dunes. If you want to enjoy the contrasts to the full, your best bet is to rent a car, or better still a roofless jeep, at the cheap island rates, fill it with low-tax petrol, and tour around on your own.

CRUZ DE TEJEDA **Las Palmas** ☎ (928), pop. 2,115, ✆ 65 80 10, ✉ c/ Ezequiel Sánchez, 18 ☎ 65 80 67, ⚕ 65 82 20, P 65 80 27, ⊞ c/ Cruz Blanca, s/n ☎ 65 80 61. Las Palmas de Gran Canaria 42km.

From this 1,450m high pass you can look out over the wide valley where the village of **TEJEDA** stands in a volcanic landscape which Spanish philosopher and author Unamuno justly described as a *'petrified storm'*. Notice how the two imposing masses of volcanic rock that you can see from here, the **Nublo Rock** and the **Bentayga Rock**, jut out from the landscape as if they were gigantic sculptures. If the airy heights build up your appetite, have a meal at the parador restaurant or a quick snack of the local *bienmesabe* (literally 'tastes good to me'), Tejeda's typical sweet made from almonds and honey.

¶¶ *Hostería Cruz de Tejeda* c/ Hernández Guerra, 9 ☎ 65 80 50 **P**
♣ ≪ AE, DC, MC, V $$. Designed by the Canary Island artist Néstor de la
Torre in the early 1900s, this former parador was recently turned into a
restaurant where you can sample the local cuisine while enjoying the view
of the volcanic basin.

Local sights: NW of Tejeda, the Cueva Corcho road takes you to
ARTENARA, the highest village in Gran Canaria (1,219m), where many
families live in cave dwellings and sell reddish-brown reproductions of the
tools and utensils originally used by the Guanches. Still heading NW, after
30km you will reach the **Pinar de Tamadaba**, a beautiful Canary pine forest.
If instead you drive SW from Artenara, you will eventually hit **SAN NICOLAS DE
TOLENTINO**, a flourishing agricultural town with a small fishing harbour and a
quiet beach. Heading SE along a road that will give you splendid views of
colourful volcanic cliffs and ravines you will reach the town of **MOGAN**, in the
middle of a valley carpeted with fruit orchards and inhabited by exotic birds.
The C-810 then drops steeply into the **Puerto de Mogán**, a modern
development of well-kept hotels and houses. Adventurous lovers of unspoiled
nature will enjoy following the coast NW along the geographical
smorgasbord of wild, abrupt landscapes and idyllic beaches like **Veneguera**
and **Güi-Güi** that characterize the landscape here.

LAS PALMAS DE GRAN CANARIA **Las Palmas** ☎ (928), pop. 366,454,
[i] Pl Ramón Franco, s/n, Santa Catalina Park ☎ 26 46 23, **(** c/ Diderot, 26
and c/ León y Castillo, 327, ✉ Av Primero de Mayo, 62 ☎ 37 39 28, ✚
23 00 00, **P** 20 22 77, ✈ Gando, 30km ☎ 25 41 40 (Iberia, c/ Alcalde
Ramírez Bethencourt, 49 ☎ 36 01 11, 25 46 40 and 25 59 66, Aviaco ☎
25 56 01 and 70 01 75), ⚓ Trasmediterránea (ferries to Tenerife, La Palma
and mainland Spain), Santa Catalina dock ☎ 26 00 70 and 26 56 50, 🚗 c/
General Franco, 142 ☎ 75 04 66.

On June 24, 1478, **Juan Rejón** established the Royal Citadel of Las
Palmas, winning the island back from Islam and declaring it to be under the
rule of the Kingdom of Castile. Still under Spanish rule, it is now a genuinely
cosmopolitan town, a booming tourist resort, the capital of the province of Las
Palmas and the seat of the autonomous government of the Canary Islands, as
well as one of the most important **ports** in the world, a chief stop-over for
Spanish, Russian, Japanese, Korean, Chinese and many other fishing fleets.
The town stretches along the sea from the S, where the **Triana** and **Vegueta**
areas date back to the times of the Christian reconquest, to the N, where you
can visit **Puerto de la Luz**, built in the 19C by León y Castillo, and the beach
of **Las Canteras**, a modern tourist development. The **Av Marítima** runs
along the seafront to the E, while the land to the W banks up steeply,
covered by houses built into its rocky cliffs.

🏨 ★★★★★ *Meliá Cristina,* c/ Gomera, 6 ☎ 26 76 00 ⛵ 316 ♿ TV 📞 ♨
♒ ⚓ ≪ AE, DC, EC, MC, V $$$$$. In Las Canteras.

🏨 ★★★★★ *Reina Isabel,* c/ Alfredo L. Jones, 40 ☎ 26 01 00 ⛵ 234 ♿
TV ♣ 📞 ♨ ♒ ♒ 🖼 ≪ AE, DC, EC, MC, V $$$$$. A modern hotel on
the promenade bordering Las Canteras beach.

🏨 ★★★★★ *Santa Catalina,* c/ León y Castillo, 227 ☎ 24 30 40 ⛵ 208
♿ ♣ 📞 ♨ ♒ ≪ ⚲ ⚑/AE, DC, EC, MC, V $$$$$. In Doramas Park and
surrounded by lush palm trees, this hotel is a real oasis of peace and
quiet amid the hustle and bustle of the city centre.

🏨 ★★★★ *Concorde,* c/ Tomás Miller, 85 ☎ 26 27 50 ⛵ 127 ✗ ♒ ♒ AE,
DC, EC, V $$$.

🏨 ★★★★ *Iberia Sol,* Av Marítima del Norte, s/n ☎ 36 11 33 ⛵ 298 ♿ TV
📞 ♨ ♒ 🖼 ≪ AE, DC, EC, MC, V $$$$. Functional.

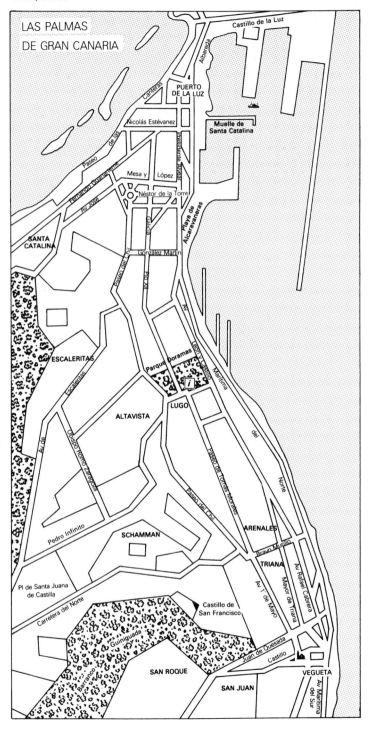

LAS PALMAS
DE GRAN CANARIA

▥ ★★★★ *Imperial Playa*, c/ Ferreras, 1 ☎ 26 48 54 ⇌ 173 ⅙ TV ⌂ ≪ AE, MC, V $$$$. In Las Canteras.

▥ ★★★★ *Los Bardinos Sol*, c/ Eduardo Benot, 3 ☎ 26 61 00 ⇌ 215 TV ♨ ≈ ≪ AE, DC, EC, V $$$$. Next to the Santa Catalina Park.

▥ ★★★★ *Rocamar*, c/ Lanzarote, 10 ☎ 26 56 00 ⇌ 87 TV ⌂ ≪ $$$.

▥ ★★★ *Fataga*, c/ Néstor de la Torre, 21 ☎ 24 04 08 ⇌ 92 ✕ TV P AE, MC, V $$$.

▥ ★★★ *Olympia*, c/ Dr. Grau Bassas, 1 ☎ 26 17 20 ⇌ 41 $$.

▥ ★★★ *Nautilus*, Paseo de las Canteras, 5 ☎ 26 32 74 ⇌ 49 TV ⌂ $$$.

▥ ★★★ *Gran Canaria*, Paseo de las Canteras, 38 ☎ 27 50 78 ⇌ 90 ⅙ TV ♨ ⌂ ≪ AE, DC, EC, V $$$.

▥ ★★★ *Miraflor*, c/ Dr. Grau Bassas, 21 ☎ 26 16 00 ⇌ 78 ✕ P $$.

▥ ★★ *Pujol*, c/ Salvador Puyás, 5 ☎ 27 44 33 ⇌ 48 TV ⌂ $$.

▥ ★★ *Syria*, c/ Luis Morote, 27 ☎ 27 06 00 ⇌ 26 TV $$.

🍴 *Acuario* (closed: Sundays), Pl de España, 3 ☎ 27 34 32 ✳ AE, DC, EC, MC, V $$$ to $$$$. Local and French cuisine served in this pleasantly decorated restaurant.

🍴 *El Novillo Precoz*, c/ Portugal, 9 ☎ 22 16 59 ✳ V $$$. Typical Argentinian grills cooked over wood fires.

🍴 *El Pote* (closed: Sundays), c/ José María Durán, 41 ☎ 27 80 85 ✳ V $$ to $$$. Galician cuisine in a pleasantly decorated restaurant.

🍴 *El Timple* (closed: Sundays and August), c/ Dr. Miguel Rosas, 10 ✳ $$$. Asturian home-cooking.

🍴 *Fuji* (closed: Sundays and August), c/ Fernando Guanarteme, 56 ☎ 26 13 93 ✳ $$$. Japanese food.

🍴 *Hamburgo* (closed: Wednesdays, Sunday nights and September), c/ General Orgaz, 54 ☎ 22 27 45 ✳ AE, DC, EC, V $$$ to $$$$. International food and a pleasant atmosphere.

🍴 *House of Ming*, Paseo de las Canteras, 30 ☎ 27 45 73 ✳ ♨ MC, V $. Chinese food.

🍴 *Julio* (closed: Sundays), c/ La Naval, 132 ☎ 27 10 39 ✳ AE, DC, MC, V $$$. This restaurant serves excellent fish and seafood. It also has a bar where clients can enjoy smaller portions of seafood *tapas*.

🍴 *La Cabaña Criolla*, c/ Los Martínez de Escobar, 37 ☎ 27 02 16 ✳ AE, DC, MC, V $$ to $$$. Grilled steaks Argentinian-style.

🍴 *La Masía de Canarias*, c/ Murillo, 36, in Tafira Alta ☎ 35 01 20 ◆ $$$.

🍴 *Mesón La Paella* (closed: Saturday nights, Sundays and 15/8-15/9), c/ José María Durán, 47 ☎ 27 16 40 ✳ AE, V $$$. Excellent *paellas* and other rice dishes.

🍴 *Parrilla Reina Isabel*, c/ Alfredo L. Jones, 40 ☎ 26 01 00 ◆ ✳ ≪ AE, DC, MC, V $$$$. The most luxurious restaurant in the city, serving international cuisine.

🍴 *Tenderete*, c/ León y Castillo, 91 ☎ 24 63 50 ✳ V $$$. This cheerful restaurant serves *nouvelle* Canary Island cuisine.

Beaches: To the W of Puerto de la Luz, and in the very heart of the city, **Las Canteras** is a 3km-long sandy beach protected by a volcanic barrier reef about 150m from the shore.

Best buys: Las Palmas de Gran Canaria is a duty free shopping emporium where you can buy almost anything your heart desires at very **attractive prices**. Specially interesting buys would have to include cigarettes, leather goods, flowers and plants, shoes, clothing, jewelry, crafts, furniture, basketwork, electronic goods, video equipment, household appliances, wines and liqueurs... Most famous of all are the hundreds of **bazaars**, or *Indian shops*, that make the city a shopper's paradise. They are mainly concentrated on c/ Juan Rejón, c/ Alvareda and c/ Triana —*Maya*, c/ Triana, 105, is the most prestigious. Tobacco, and especially the island's hand-crafted cigars, can be bought at *J. Márquez*, c/ Ripoche, 1. As far as local products are concerned, you can buy Ingenio's famous embroidery and open-work at *A. Linares*, Pueblo Canario, in Doramas Park; knives at *R. Torre*, c/ Párroco Segundo Vega, 9; and ceramics at *Artesanía Canaria Taguguy*, c/ Armas, 1. Turning to clothes, you will find good furriers here —try *N. Chelala*, c/ Arena, 15, *Peridis*, Paseo Las Canteras, 6, and *V. Mitsakou*, c/ Luis Morote, 28. Stylish fashion, leather goods and gifts are sold at *Loewe*, c/ San Bernardo, 6. Spanish fashion is also available at *Adolfo Domínguez*, Av Mesa y López, 2, *J. Botter*, c/ Peregrina, 8, *Polo Difusion*, c/ Peregrina, 6, *Gamma*, c/ Travieso, 11, and *Kif Kif*, c/ Cano, 41. The city's large department stores are on Av Mesa y López, El Corte Inglés at No. 18 and *Galerías Preciados* at No. 15. Local handicrafts and products, antiques and trendy fashion are sold in the flea market of *El Rastro*, open every Sunday from 10.00-2.00 in the Vegueta district. Jewelry and cultured pearls are sold at *Las Perlas*, c/ Luis Morote, 32.

Cultural highlights: Walk along **Las Canteras beach** and through **Santa Catalina Park**, enjoying the cosmopolitan atmosphere in the neighbouring streets full of bars and open-air cafés, or enjoy the superb **views** of the sea along the **Av Marítima**. In **Doramas Park** you will find the **Pueblo Canario**, which stages folk dancing and singing exhibitions (performances: Sundays 11.45-1.15 and Thursdays 5.30-7.00), and the house of the Pueblo's founder, Modernist painter Néstor de la Torre, which has now been turned into a **museum** (open: 10.00-12.00 and 4.00-7.00; Sundays: 10.30-1.30; closed: Saturday afternoons, Wednesdays and holidays ☎ 24 51 35). **San Telmo Park**, with palm trees and other local flora (such as the famed *dragos*, or 'dragon trees' indigenous to the Canary Islands), and the Baroque **San Telmo Church** are just off the ancient **Triana** street, now a bustling pedestrian shopping precinct, leading into the **Vegueta** area. Here, in the **Pl de Santa Ana**, stop to look at the Town Hall's beautiful façade and visit the 15-19C **Cathedral**, with a Neoclassical façade and a Plateresque interior, in whose transept you will find interesting statues carved by the Canary-born sculptor **José Luján Pérez** (1756-1815). The old palace of the island's governors, where Christopher Columbus stayed in 1502, has been converted into the **Casa de Colón** museum (open: 9.00-1.30; Saturdays: 9.00-1.00; closed: Sundays and holidays ☎ 31 58 68). Nearby, you can visit the **Church of San Antonio Abad**, or wander around the charming squares of **Espíritu Santo** and **Santo Domingo**. If you want to find out more about the history of the islands and their native inhabitants, the Guanches, visit the **Museo Canario** (open: 10.00-1.00 and 3.00-7.30; Saturdays: 10.00-12.00; closed: Sundays and holidays ☎ 31 56 00).

To the N, the 15C **Castillo de la Luz** is worth a visit —the first fortress to be built on the Canary Islands, it is now a cultural centre. More recent culture is commemorated in the **Pérez Galdós Museum**, c/ Cano, 6, the novelist's house and birthplace. To round it all off, from the **La Cornisa** lookout in the Escaleritas district you can enjoy a wonderful **view** of Puerto de la Luz and La Isleta.

Fiestas and festivals: In January the city celebrates the **Canary Islands' Music Festival**, one of the best in Spain, followed in February or March by the **Las Palmas Opera Festival**, which has gained international recognition; more popular, however, are the crowd-pulling **carnivals** that take place during the same months.

Local sights: **Southern Routes**. Some 13km S of the city, TELDE is the second biggest town in the province and one of the two most important centres of Guanche culture prior to the arrival of the Spaniards. As you walk through the old **San Francisco quarter** you are stepping back four centuries in time. While here, visit the 15C Church of San Juan Bautista, with an interesting Flemish **altarpiece** in the high Gothic style and, on the main altar, a beautiful sculpture of *Christ*, believed to have been made by the Tabasco Indians of Mexico from roots and leaves of maize. On the black-sand beach in nearby Melenara, you can have a superb fish luncheon at *Casa Perico*.

Heading out of Telde on the southbound C-816, turn right at the first crossroads and follow the minor road to the **Montaña Sagrada de Cuatro Puertas** (literally 'Holy Mountain of the Four Gates'), an impressive Megalithic monument used by the native Guanches in ancient times to perform their sacred rites. Back on the C-816 and before reaching Ingenio you will arrive at Las Mejías, where you can visit the **Museo de Piedra's** (Museum of Stone ☎ 78 11 24) collection of volcanic rocks, crystals and quartz, and then move on to *C. Gil*, next door, a crafts shop that makes and sells embroidered goods, especially the openwork embroidery so typical of the Canary Islands. If you like crafts, once in **INGENIO** look out for the hand-made basketwork in *J. Vega*, c/ A. Benítez Galindo, 7. Continue S past Agüimes to **TEMISAS**, where the adobe houses built amidst the olive groves have given the town the nickname of the '*Jerusalem of the Canaries*'. For wonderful volcanic settings continue along the C-816 and take a left turn before reaching Santa Lucía —you will come to an unusual formation of volcanic rocks in the shape of a castle known as the **Fortaleza de Ansite**. Drive now to **SANTA LUCIA**, a village at the foot of the enormous **Caldera de Tirajana** crater, where visitors driving no further can try the local *guindilla* (sour cherry) liqueur, which is very strong but has a pleasing flavour. But first, take a look around the **Museo de la Fortaleza's** (Fortress Museum) archaeological, cartographical and folk exhibits, walk around its small botanical garden and grab a bite to eat at its restaurant, which serves typical local cuisine. The final stop on this route, **SAN BARTOLOME DE TIRAJANA** (see 'Maspalomas'), is 7km NW along the C-815.

Central Inland Routes. SW of Las Palmas de Gran Canaria, the residential town of **TAFIRA** is set in lush vegetation, and its **Jardín Canario Viera y Clavijo** is one of the best tropical botanical gardens in this part of the world. You can see it from above, from the *Jardín Canario* restaurant ☎ 35 16 45, especially placed for its view but also known for its Canary Island home cooking. For accommodation, you could try the ★ *Los Frailes*, on the road to Tafira Alta ☎ 35 12 06 ⊨ 26 ⏂ ✦ $, established by the British at the end of the 19C and built in the local style, which has been renovated for travellers who like to do their own thing with a certain degree of exclusivity and spaciousness. In winter, it is full of escapees from the British climate who revel in its family atmosphere and good food. Three kilometres from Tafira, the **Pico de Bandama** peak, 596m above sea level on the edge of an enormous crater, has panoramic **views** of the eastern coast of Gran Canaria and the city of Las Palmas. Golf enthusiasts can visit it on their way to the 18-hole *Club de Golf de Bandama* ☎ 35 01 08.

SANTA BRIGIDA is another 3km SW along the road, set in the midst of lush woods and palm groves. Here you can visit *Manohierro* (closed: Mondays and summer), c/ El Pino, 45 ☎ 64 03 88 $$, where even the Germans who eat here are pleasantly surprised to find sausages made in the old German style, an art which is rapidly being lost back home. But if you prefer a rather more typical meal in fantastic surroundings, then you had better head for *Grutas de Artiles* ☎ 64 05 75 DC, V $$, set in a grotto.

Continuing SW you will come to **VEGA DE SAN MATEO**, especially picturesque on Sundays when its fruit and vegetable market, overflowing with exotic local produce, is held. On other days you can visit the Casa-Museo de

Cho Zacarías, an old house turned museum with traditional Canarian furniture, kitchenware and pottery, as well as a wine cellar where you can taste some local wines. Going on from here to the Los Chorros crossroads, turn right (NW) on to the C-814 and drive through lush, green countryside until you reach **TEROR**, a well-preserved old town with aristocratic houses and wooden balconies. Do not miss the magnificent 18C Church of Nuestra Señora del Pino (Our Lady of the Pine Tree), patron saint of Gran Canaria, whose sumptuous wardrobe of richly embroidered clothes is a treasure trove in itself. Even better, try to visit on September 8, when the traditional *Fiesta de la Virgen del Pino* takes place. The nuns of the town's convent make such delicious sweets and nougats that they make a trip here a finger-licking experience. For a light snack, you could try the delicious *tapas* served at the *Bar Americano*, opposite the church, and for a fuller meal the *Balcón de Zamora*, Ctra General, 36 ☎ 63 10 42 $$$, or *San Matías*, 1km along the road to Arucas ☎ 63 07 65 🅿 ✦ ≪ $$.

Twenty-two kilometres NW, **ARUCAS** is located in the middle of the banana and sugar cane plantations that cover the broad valley. Here you can visit the *Arehucas Rum Factory* to sample the local rum. You can also pay a more cultural visit to the **Church of San Juan Bautista** that looms imposingly over the valley. Neo-Gothic in style, though only recently finished, its painstakingly detailed stonework is impressive, as is the recumbent figure of *Christ*, sculpted by Manuel Ramos, in the interior. For a good meal and a good view after your sightseeing, try the nearby restaurant on **Montaña de Arucas** mountain.

Northern Routes. Driving N of Las Palmas along the El Rincón road you will come across the **Monument to Atlas**, carved from volcanic lava by local sculptor Tony Gallardo. Continuing along the road and going past **SAN FELIPE**, a small fishing village with several simple little restaurants serving fresh fish, you will cross the modern **Puente de Silva**, the highest bridge in Europe and a feat of advanced engineering. Very close by are the **Cenobio de Valerón** caves (open: 10.00-1.00 and 3.00-5.00; closed: Mondays), an archaeological site impressively set against a deep ravine which used to be where the young noblemen's daughters were schooled to become *harimaguadas*, or vestal virgins, in pre-Hispanic times. At its peak you will find a *Tagoror*, where the ancient government moots were held.

In **SANTA MARIA DE GUIA** you can buy pottery and knives with carved bone handles in various village shops and if you get peckish as you look around, try some of the local *queso de flor* cheese. Sculptor Luján Pérez was born here, and some of his carvings can be admired in the parish church, where the traditional *Romería de las Marías* —one of the most authentic and popular *fiestas* of the island— is held during the last week of September. Three kilometres further on, **GALDAR** was an important settlement in ancient times, with two reminders of its Guanche past: the **Cueva Pintada** (Painted Cave), with its cryptic geometrical **mural paintings** dating from 2000 BC, and the **Guancha necropolis**, 1.5km from Gáldar on the coast, with ruins of houses built with enormous stones. You can also visit the **Casa-Museo de Antonio Padrón**, a museum exhibiting the work of this highly individualistic Expressionist painter.

Nine kilometres SW of Gáldar along the C-810 you will come to **AGAETE**, a whitewashed fishing village on the most rugged point of the island's coastline. From the neighbouring **Puerto de las Nieves**, another fishing village, you will get a wonderful panoramic **view** of the cliffs to the NW, especially of a strange volcanic rock that thrusts up out of the sea and is commonly known as *El Dedo de Dios* (The Finger of God). Extrovert by nature, the natives of Agaete cherish their traditions, one of which is the

Bajada de la Rama, celebrated every August 4, when spirited locals go up to the Tamadaba pine wood in the early hours, cut pine branches and bring them down to the beach, dancing all the way. It is believed that the Guanches used to do this in times of drought to persuade their god, *Alcorac*, to send rain. Now the locals do it for fun, and perhaps to show off their strength, for the entire route takes a good six to eight hours.

If you want to stay in the extraordinarily fertile, beautiful and peaceful **Agaete Valley**, try the ★★ *Princesa Guayarmina* ☎ 89 80 09, set in an old spa right next to the **Los Berrazales** mineral water spring and serving delicious home-made food in a homely atmosphere. A bit further along the Berrazales road, at km35, *Casa Romántica* serves Swiss food and also provides accommodation. If, on the other hand, you want to prolong the excursion, you can drive SW from Agaete along the C-810 road that winds its way down a spectacular craggy coastline all the way to San Nicolás de Tolentino (see 'Cruz de Tejeda').

On the town: Those starting their evening on the town usually go to the *Bar Carabela*, *Santa Catalina* hotel, for tea or coffee, *La Posada*, c/ Naval, 8, for coffee prepared 16 different ways, and to the open-air terrace of the *Derby*, Santa Catalina Park, for a quiet drink. Later in the evening, the action shifts to the town's discos —*Cupé*, c/ Nicolás Estévanez, *Dinos*, on the top floor of the *Los Bardinos* hotel, or *Toca-Toca*, c/ Secretario Artiles, 53. At the approach of the wee hours, everybody who is anybody (politicians, intellectuals...) can be found at the *Utopía* pub, c/ Tomás Miller. Those looking for a different kind of entertainment can go to *Xayo*, c/ Joaquín Costa, s/n, where quick-change artist Xayo gives nightly performances, or to the *Casino* at the *Santa Catalina* hotel ☎ 24 30 40, where roulette, black jack and poker are played in a friendly atmosphere.

Sports: Canary wrestling and Canary lateen sailing (you can watch the Sunday morning regattas from the seaside promenade) are sports native to these islands. More international water sports include surfing and windsurfing in El Confital Bay and sailing from the town's two **marinas**, the *Puerto Deportivo*, c/ León y Castillo, 308 ☎ 24 45 66, and the *Real Club Náutico de Gran Canaria*, Puerto de la Luz ☎ 24 52 02. Golfers can head for the 18-hole, par 71 course at the *Campo de Golf de Bandama*, 14km ☎ 35 10 50, tennis players for the courts at the *Club de Tenis Gran Canaria*, c/ Beethoven, 1 ☎ 24 34 13, and squash players for those at the *Club Metropole*, Paseo A. Quesada, s/n ☎ 24 43 46.

MASPALOMAS **Las Palmas** ☎ (928), *i* Urb Campo Internacional, s/n ☎ 26 46 23, ✉ Av de Tirajana, s/n, Edif Mercurio ☎ 76 23 41, ✛ 76 28 81, P 76 24 12, ✈ Gando ☎ 25 46 40, 25 60 04 and 20 81 11 (Iberia ☎ 25 46 40 and 25 59 66, Aviaco ☎ 25 56 01), 🚌 Salcai, c/ Viera y Clavijo, 34 ☎ 37 21 33. Las Palmas de Gran Canaria 40km.

In the 1960s, plans were set in motion to turn this oasis of palm trees, set amidst extensive sand dunes, into one of the most important year-round **beach resorts** in Europe. With more than 350 sunny days —a total of 3,000 hours of sunshine per year— to recommend it, the plans have succeeded. The resort now stretches along 10km of coast and is split up into three separate developments: Maspalomas, Playa del Inglés and San Agustín. Next to the **lighthouse**, nudists and non-nudists (if you count tiny bikinis as clothing) bathe and sun themselves side by side on the marvellous **Maspalomas beach**, at the southern tip of the island. **Maspalomas** is the most elegant of the three developments, known for its magnificent hotels, its palm-shaded oasis and its wonderful **sand dunes**. To the N, the trendy, busy **Playa del Inglés** (literally 'Englishman's Beach') offers the widest range of attractions —lively night life, hotels, apartments, restaurants and bars galore, good shops... and another excellent **beach** of powdery, almost white sand. Further NE, **San Agustín**, the oldest development, is more residential, with luxury hotels, landscape gardens and a fine, black volcanic sand **beach** lapped by clean waters. You can move around this part of the island on the *Maspalomas Express*, a small electric train which travels a route through the main streets. Nine kilometres from Maspalomas by bus you can visit **Palmitos Park**, a subtropical garden with a thriving bird life. Nearby, in Montaña la Data, is the **Monte León** private estate of luxurious houses, where famous people such as Leonard Bernstein, Ivo Pogorelich, Helmut Schmidt and many others spend their holidays.

★★★★★ *Meliá Tamarindos*, c/ Retama, 3, San Agustín beach ☎ 76 26 00 ⊨ 318 ✕ TV ✦ 🎤 ⚓ ☂ « 🛥 ♀ AE, DC, EC, MC $$$$$. Surrounded by tropical gardens and shopping arcades, this modern hotel looks out over the Morro Besudo beach and has a **casino**.

★★★★★ *Royal Maspalomas Oasis*, Maspalomas beach, next to the lighthouse ☎ 76 01 70 ⊨ 342 ✕ ✕ TV ✦ 🎤 🏊 ⚓ ☂ 🖼 « 🐎 ♀ AE, DC, EC, MC, V $$$$$ to $$$$$$. Surrounded by lush exotic flora and only a few metres from the beach, this quiet, modern hotel combines luxury with first-class tourist facilities.

★★★★ *Apolo*, Av de Estados Unidos, 28, Playa del Inglés ☎ 76 00 78 ⊨ 115 TV ✦ 🎤 ⚓ 🖼 « ♀ AE, DC, EC, V $$$$ to $$$$$. A quiet hotel with good views that stands close to the beach.

★★★★ *Bahía Feliz*, Tarajalillo beach, 7km NE ☎ 76 46 00 ⊨ 255 ✦ 🎤 🏊 ⚓ « AE, DC, EC, V $$$$ to $$$$$. A quiet hotel, decorated in African-style, with good views.

★★★★ *Catarina Playa*, Av de Tirajana, 1, Playa del Inglés ☎ 76 28 12 ⊨ 402 ✕ TV ✦ 🎤 ⚓ ☂ 🖼 « 🐎 ♀ AE, DC, EC, MC, V $$$$ to $$$$$$. This modern hotel offers its guests a wide range of entertainment including sports facilities and an art gallery.

★★★★ *Corona Caserío*, Av de Italia, 8, Playa del Inglés ☎ 76 10 50 ⊨ 106 TV ⚓ ☂ « ♀ AE, DC, EC, MC, V $$$ to $$$$. This hotel looks out over one of the busiest and most colourful areas of the centre.

★★★★ *Costa Canaria*, Ctra General del Sur, km61, San Agustín beach ☎ 76 02 04 ⊨ 162 ✕ TV ✦ 🎤 ⚓ 🖼 « 🐎 ♀ AE, DC, EC, MC, V $$$ to $$$$. This hotel's distance from the beach is compensated for by its excellent service, tasteful decor, large terrace, pleasant garden with swimming pool and good views.

★★★★ *Don Gregory*, c/ Las Dalias, 11, San Agustín beach ☎ 76 26 58 ⊨ 241 TV ✦ 🎤 ⚓ 🐎 ♀ AE, DC, EC, MC, V $$$$$$. Magnificent sea views.

★★★★ *IFA Dunamar*, c/ Helsinki, 8, Playa del Inglés ☎ 76 12 00 ⊨ 184 TV ✦ 🎤 ⚓ ☂ 🖼 ♀ AE, DC, EC, MC, V $$$$$. This hotel has a pleasant terrace.

★★★★ *IFA Faro Maspalomas*, Maspalomas beach, near the lighthouse ☎ 76 04 62 ⊨ 188 ✕ TV ✦ 🎤 🏊 ⚓ ☂ « AE, DC, EC, MC, V $$$$$ to $$$$$$. Surrounded by gardens and shopping arcades, this quiet hotel has lovely views of the sea and the lighthouse and excellent service.

★★★★ *Lucana*, Pl del Sol, s/n, Playa del Inglés ☎ 76 27 00 ⊨ 167 TV ✦ ⚓ ☂ « ♀ AE, DC, EC, MC, V $$$ to $$$$. Good views and a heated swimming pool.

★★★★ *Maspalomas Palm Beach*, Av Oasis, s/n, Maspalomas ☎ 76 29 20 ⊨ 358 TV ✦ 🏊 ⚓ ☂ 🖼 « AE, DC, EC, MC, V ♀ $$$$$$. This is a quiet hotel with a well-kept lawn shaded by a lush palm grove surrounding its terraces and swimming pool. It has good sea views.

🏨 ★★★ *Buenaventura Playa*, Pl de Ansite, 1, Playa del Inglés ☎ 76 16 50 ⬚ 716 ♿ ✦ ≈ ⛱ 🖼 ≪ 🛌 ♉ AE, DC, EC, MC, V $$$ to $$$$$. This hotel has good views of the beach and many facilities, including tennis courts, a heated swimming pool and a scuba diving club.

🏨 ★★★ *Don Miguel*, Av de Tirajana, 36, Playa del Inglés ☎ 76 15 08 ⬚ 251 ✦ 🎙 ≈ 🖼 🛌 ♉ AE, DC, EC, V $$$ to $$$$.

🏨 ★★★ *Ifa Beach*, c/ Los Jazmines, 25, San Agustín beach ☎ 76 51 00 ⬚ 200 🅿 ≈ ≪ AE, DC, EC, V $$$$.

🏨 ★★★ *Parque Tropical*, Av de Italia, 2, Playa del Inglés ☎ 76 07 12 ⬚ 235 📺 ✦ ≈ ⛱ 🖼 ≪ 🛌 ♉ AE, DC, EC, MC, V $$$ to $$$$$. The Canary-style architecture of this hotel, its pleasant gardens, good views and heated swimming pool make it rather attractive.

🏨 ★★★ *Waikiki*, Av de Gran Canaria, 20, Playa del Inglés ☎ 76 23 00 ⬚ 508 ♿ 📺 ✦ 🎙 ⬥ ≈ ⛱ 200m 🖼 🛌 ▲ ♉ AE, DC, EC, MC, V $$ to $$$$. A modern hotel, this one has everything: garden, heated swimming pool, tennis court and night entertainment, with the San Fernando shopping centre close at hand.

🍴 *Buganvilla*, San Agustín beach (closed: May and September), c/ Morro Besudo, 17 ☎ 76 30 10 ✱ AE, DC, EC, V $$ to $$$. European cuisine in a small, pleasant restaurant.

🍴 *Chez Mario* (closed: June), c/ Los Pinos, 15, Urb Nueva Europa, San Agustín beach ☎ 76 18 17 AE, DC, EC, V $$$. Italian cuisine.

🍴 *La Choza*, Av Tirajana, s/n, Playa del Inglés ✱ ≪ AE, DC, EC, V $$$. Fish and seafood.

🍴 *La Toja* (closed: 20/6-25/7) Av Tirajana, s/n, Playa del Inglés ☎ 76 11 96 ✦ ✱ ≪ AE, DC, EC, V $$$ to $$$$. Galician fish and seafood.

🍴 *San Agustín Beach Club*, Pl Los Cocoteros, 1, San Agustín beach ☎ 76 04 00 ✦ ✱ ≈ ≪ AE, DC, EC, V $$$ to $$$$. Architecturally eye-catching, this restaurant has terraces and swimming pools which make it possible to spend the whole day here. The restaurant serves international cuisine, specializing in fish and seafood.

🍴 *Tenderete II*, Av Tirajana, s/n, Playa del Inglés ☎ 76 14 60 ✦ ✱ AE, DC $$$. New Canary Island cuisine of both coastal and inland regions.

Best buys: Maspalomas is a permanent market —there are shops, street markets (Tuesdays in the San Fernando district) and, above all, supermarkets everywhere.

Local sights: To the N, the road to San Bartolomé de Tirajana climbs up the spectacularly beautiful **Barranco de Fataga** gorge to the town of **FATAGA**. Continuing N you will finally come to **SAN BARTOLOME DE TIRAJANA**, which stands in a verdant setting surrounded by grey rocks.

On the town: The climate of Maspalomas is so mild that day and night there are hundreds of places where you can have fun and enjoy yourself, whatever your age or inclination. At night the area of **Playa del Inglés** becomes a hive of activity, bright neon lights along Av Italia beckoning visitors to *Big Apple*, a bar, disco and restaurant, or to the *Spider* disco, which plays good music, while *Banana*, Av Tenerife, s/n, attracts an international clientele. The *Terraza El Metro*, in the El Metro shopping centre, stages local folk singing and dancing performances on Sunday mornings, turning to live international music in the evenings. For a first-class night show go to *Scala*, c/ Las Retamas, 3 ☎ 76 68 28. In the area of **San Agustín**, the *Beach Club* complex has a disco where live shows and *fiestas* are often staged in the summer, while the *Casino Gran Canaria*, c/ Retama, 3 ☎ 76 27 24, provides gamblers with all sorts of gaming tables. In **Maspalomas**, you can enjoy good cocktails and music at the *Maspalomas Oasis* hotel.

Sports: You can hire light aircraft, fly an ultra-light or go parachuting at the *Aeroclub Maspalomas* ☎ 76 24 47. Water sports fans take note that 🐚🐚 **deep-sea fishing** and shark fishing boats leave from Puerto Rico ☎ 76 26 96 and 76 00 76, and that **sailing,** 🐚 **windsurfing** and **scuba** 🐚🐚 **diving** facilities are widely available: ask at hotels like *Catarina Playa, IFA Dunamar, IFA Faro, Buenaventera* and clubs like *Sun Club*, Playa del Inglés ☎ 76 31 32, or *Inter Club Atlantic*, San Agustín ☎ 76 09 50. Horse lovers can ride at the *Picadero Oasis Maspalomas* ☎ 76 23 78, most good hotels have tennis courts, and golfers can have a game at the 18-hole, par 72 *Campo de Golf de Maspalomas*, Av Africa, s/n ☎ 76 25 81. There is also a go-kart track next to the airfield.

PUERTO RICO **Las Palmas** ☎ (928), ✚ 76 10 22, **P** 76 12 87, ✈ Gando ☎ 25 41 40. Las Palmas de Gran Canaria 90km.

You may be content to bask in the sun in the place that boasts the record for hours of sunshine in Spain, and perhaps in Europe, but if you want a change from the toils of rubbing oil into your skin, the beach offers all sorts 🐚🐚 of services for more energetic activities. You can go **sailing** or **windsurfing,** 🐚 moor your yacht at the 600-berth **marina** (☎ 74 57 57), or take a boat from 🐚🐚🐚 the port to go **deep sea fishing**. And don't worry about not being a pro 🐚🐚 —Puerto Rico is a learner's paradise. The *Escuela Territorial de Vela de Puerto Rico* (Puerto Rico Sailing School), c/ Doreste, s/n ☎ 74 53 31, has trained Olympic champions, and it is known as one of the best in Europe, with more than 3,000 pupils passing through it each year. Or you might simply want to move on to another beach, in which case you could try the fine, golden sand of **Playa de Patalavaca**.

🏨 ★★★ *Aquamarina*, Patalavaca beach ☎ 73 52 00 ⛱ 360 **P** ✚ ⚓ 🌴 **AE, DC, V** \$\$\$\$\$. This bungalow and apartment complex has a fine restaurant, the *Aquarela* \$\$\$\$ to \$\$\$\$\$.

🍴 *Puerto Rico*, Paseo de la Playa, s/n ☎ 74 51 81 ✚ \$\$ to \$\$\$. Fresh fish and seafood.

HIERRO

Hierro is the most westerly and the smallest of the major Canary Islands. Measuring only 278km², its terrain is far from flat (with elevations of up to 🐚 1,500m) and is rather varied, with rocky coasts excellent for **scuba diving**. It is sparsely populated and as yet attracts few tourists, and its inhabitants —mostly farmers and shepherds— live a fairly isolated existence with little to interfere with their day to day routine. They speak a pure form of Castilian Spanish, a real oddity in the Canary Islands.

Some of the indigenous mysteries of Hierro —unknown to most tourists— are its ancient **sabine trees** with twisted trunks, unique in the world, and the **lajiales**, peculiar volcanic rock formations with human and animal shapes. Local products made here are *quesadillas*, exquisite almond-flavoured cheesecakes, and Hierro cheese, famous even outside the island.

VALVERDE **Santa Cruz de Tenerife** ☎ (922), pop. 3,474, *i* c/ Real, s/n ☎ 41 21 06, ✉ c/ General Franco, 10 ☎ 55 02 91, **P** 55 00 25, ✈ Hierro, 10km ☎ 55 01 81 (Iberia, c/ Doctor Quintero, 6 ☎ 55 02 78), ⛴ Trasmediterránea (ferries to Tenerife, Gran Canaria, Fuerteventura, Lanzarote and mainland Spain), Estaca Port ☎ 55 01 29.

The capital city of Valverde, 571m above sea level, often appears to have a misty, nordic air about it.

📠 ★★ *Boomerang*, c/ Doctor Gost, 1 ☎ 55 02 00 📠 17 ▼ (☕ AE, DC, V $$.

📠 ★ *Casañas*, c/ San Francisco, 9 ☎ 55 02 54 📠 11 $.

Local sights: Heading NE of Valverde, you will come to **TAMADUSTE**, where a picturesque lagoon has been formed by a sandy reef which closes off the cove. If you drive NW instead, you will reach **El Golfo**, an enormous depression marking the bottom of an old crater surrounded by *laurisilva* trees and broom. Splendid **views** of this crater can be had from the lookout point 1km from Guarazoca. Nearby you can contemplate the famous **Salmor Rocks**, natural habitat of the island's huge primeval lizards, the only survivors of the species on earth today. From **La Dehesa**, an immense expanse of desert, you have a magnificent **view** of sloping cliffs pitted with craters which gradually blend into the calm sea to the S. To the W, the **Orchilla lighthouse** marks the last European farewell to ships bound for America. The zero meridian was actually fixed at Orchilla Point before being changed to Greenwich. In contrast to La Dehesa, in the E **El Pinar** offers a verdant region of Canary pines. For accommodation, try the recently-built and scenically located ★★★ *Parador Isla de Hierro*, Las Playas, 20km S of Valverde ☎ 55 01 00 📠 47 🅿 🎤 ☕ ♒ ⚓ ≪ AE, DC, EC, V $$$$, which is quiet and has good views of the area.

LA GOMERA

La Gomera, still largely unknown to tourists, is an almost round island crowned by the 1,480m Alto de Garajonay peak, and characterized by coastal cliffs and fertile, rich farmlands where bananas, grapes, tomatoes and date palms grow in abundance. Its landscape of mountains and deep valleys forced the natives to evolve a whistling language for communicating from one mountain top to the next, which still survives today.

SAN SEBASTIAN DE LA GOMERA Santa Cruz de Tenerife ☎ (922), pop. 5,732, ✉ c/ del Medio, 68 ☎ 87 10 81, ✚ 87 00 00, P 87 00 62 (ext. 6), ⛴ Trasmediterránea (ferries to Tenerife), c/ General Franco, 35 ☎ 87 13 00.

History tells us that **Christopher Columbus** stopped off here in 1492 for repairs and supplies before sailing to the Americas; legend, however, claims that his real reason for visiting the island was a wild desire to see the Countess of Gomera who, despite her promises to see him off, never appeared. Be that as it may, the island still evokes his presence: the well of the corner house on the main street provisioned him with water, the **Iglesia de la Asunción** provided succour for his soul and a white house near the post office gave him shelter.

📠 ★★★★ *Parador Conde de La Gomera*, Balcón de la Villa y Puerto ☎ 87 11 00 📠 42 📺 ✚ 🎤 ☕ ♒ ≪ AE, DC, EC, V $$$$. One of the most picturesque in Spain, this beautifully re-decorated parador would certainly have pleased someone like Somerset Maugham, a great enthusiast of Spanish paradors. Its restaurant serves exquisite Canary Island dishes using ingredients typical of La Gomera such as mackerel roe, mangoes, dates and so on. This extremely peaceful hotel also has a tropical garden and marvellous views. Though on an island with little tourism, it is always very busy, so make your reservation well beforehand.

📠 ★★ *Garajonay*, c/ Ruiz de Padrón, 15 ☎ 87 05 50 📠 30 $$.

🍴 *Casa del Mar*, c/ Fred Olsen, 2 ☎ 87 12 19 ≪ $$ to $$$.

Beaches: San Sebastián has two impeccable beaches, one next to the sailing club (☎ 87 10 02) and the other alongside the town itself.

Local sights: A pleasant excursion takes you along the southern coastal road to **Playa de Santiago**. Those in the know agree that this pebbly beach is the cleanest on the island and the fish served there is the best in the archipelago. Following the coastal road past Playa de Santiago you come to two recently-built vantage points where you can take in **splendid panoramic views** of the area. You will next come to the very typical village of **ARURE** and, beyond, to the lovely **panorama** of Taguluche. Further E, **CHIPUDE** is the quintessential village of La Gomera. Traditional Gomera pottery is sold here at the *Cueva de María*. S of Arure, **VALLE GRAN REY** is spectacularly located in a deep ravine; 1km away, the soft, fine sand beach of **Playa del Inglés** is frequented by nudists.

Heading NW from San Sebastián you can visit the **Hermigua Valley**, where the white of the houses stands out against the intense green of the banana and palm trees. Further N, in the picturesque coastal village of **AGULO** you can indulge in products typical of La Gomera, particularly sweets and *traperas*, colourful Mexican-style blankets, sold at *C. Placencia*. Driving W, **VALLEHERMOSO** stands in a beautiful valley overshadowed by one of the largest volcanic **rocks** on the island.

In the centre of the island, the **Parque de Garajonay** is steeped in legend. The laurisilva woods that form part of this National Park are a relic of the Tertiary Age. Walk among its trees and ferns, and discover the pleasure of feeling unspoiled nature all around you.

LA PALMA

La Palma is often described in travel guides as *'la isla bonita'* or the pretty island —stereotyped, perhaps, but a well-deserved description. The greenest island in the archipelago, it is also said to be the highest on earth (2,432m). Its incredibly varied landscapes, sometimes shrouded in mist, make it a geographical wonder. La Palma is a peaceful island and for the most part self-sufficient. Traditions have survived unchanged the wave of tourism —one example is the production of **hand-made cigars**, acclaimed by experts as being superior to their Cuban counterpart; another is the annual celebration of its ancient **festivals** which are ethnically and artistically fascinating. Natives of this island have a long-standing liberal and cultural tradition.

SANTA CRUZ DE LA PALMA **Santa Cruz de Tenerife** ☎ (922), pop. 16,629, *i* c/ O'Daly, 8 ☎ 41 21 06, ✉ Paseo de la Constitución, 2 ☎ 41 17 02, ✚ 41 64 00, P 41 11 50, ✈ La Palma, 8km ☎ 41 35 44 (Iberia, c/ Apurón, 1 ☎ 41 41 45), ⚓ Trasmediterránea (ferries to Tenerife, Gran Canaria, Fuerteventura, Lanzarote and mainland Spain), Av Pérez de Brito, 2 ☎ 41 11 21, 🚌 Transportes del Norte de La Palma ☎ 41 19 24.

Founded in 1493 by Alonso Fernández de Lugo at the foot of an old volcanic crater, by the 16C Santa Cruz de La Palma was one of the main ship-building and sugar cane exporting ports in Spain. Today it is a charming, peaceful city whose promenade is characterized by its elegant façades and Canary style balconies. The 16C **Church of El Salvador**, opposite the Town Hall in the Pl de España, has beautiful **coffered ceilings**. Nearby is a charming little square, the **Pl de Santo Domingo**.

🏨 ★★★ *Parador de Santa Cruz de La Palma*, Av Marítima, 34 ☎ 41 23 40 ⊨ 32 Υ ♦ AE, DC, EC, V $$$. This parador is in a Canary-style building.

🏨 ★★★ *San Miguel*, Av El Puente, 33 ☎ 41 12 43 ⊨ 72 Υ ♦ DC, EC, V $$$.

🍴 *El Parral*, c/ Castillete, 7 ☎ 41 39 15 EC, V $$.

Local sights: Heading N along the C-830 corniche road, you will get wonderful views of the coast all the way to **LA GALGA**. After passing through the tunnel and a luxuriant **ravine**, the winding road will take you to the enchanting village of **SAN ANDRES**, the **Charco Azul** salt-water lagoon and the fishing village of **ESPINDOLA**, where colourful barges are moored along its pebbly beach. At **Punta Cumplida** the waves crashing furiously against the rocks are a stirring sight. Continuing along the road, in **BARLOVENTO** you will find accommodation at the peaceful ★★ *La Palma Romántica*, Las Llanadas ☎ 45 08 21 🛏 12 🅿 ⚑ ≪ **EC, V $$ to $$$**, from where there are wonderful views of the area. On the way back, you could stop at **Los Tilos**, a wood that covers the Barranco del Agua ravine.

Not far from the city to the W stands the **Santuario de Nuestra Señora de las Nieves** (Shrine of Our Lady of the Snows), patron saint of the island. Going S, the **Mirador de la Concepción** provides an excellent **vantage point** for taking in the splendour of the countryside. Continuing S you will come to **MAZO**, where at *Finca El Molino*, Ctra Hoyo de Mazo ☎ 44 02 13, the craftsmen echo the methods used by the Guanches by building their black earthenware pots layer upon layer without using a potters' wheel.

FUENCALIENTE and, next to it, the **San Antonio Volcano** are on the southern tip of the island. Fuencaliente used to be a spa whose hot water springs were destroyed by the eruption of the neighbouring volcano in 1677. Another nearby volcano, Teneguía, caused a more recent stir among the islanders when it suddenly erupted in 1971. Turning N you will drive along the beautiful, pine-clad coast to **SAN NICOLAS**, a town split in two by the lava spurted out by the Nambroque volcano in 1949. The road then winds its way along volcanic fields dotted with banana groves to **PUERTO DE NAOS**. Further N you can visit **PUERTO DE TAZACORTE**, in 1492 the landing place of Fernández de Lugo's crew and today a popular beach resort. Also on the W coast, **LOS LLANOS DE ARIDANE**, the second largest city in the island, stands in a banana-tree covered plain. You can get a wonderful view of it from the summit of the **El Time** mountain.

Heading E towards Santa Cruz de la Palma you will come to **EL PASO**, a town famous for its hand-made **silks**, unique in Spain —you can visit any of the following workshops in town: *S. Morante*, *A. Bermúdez* or *B. Pérez González*. In the centre of the island, the pine-covered Taburiente crater, the largest in the world, forms part of the **Caldera de Taburiente National Park**. Excellent vantage points for getting a bird's eye **view** of the island and the volcano's peaks —such as the Roque de los Muchachos (2,423m)— are **La Cumbrecita** (1,833m) and **Lomas de las Chozas** (1,000m).

LANZAROTE

Early in the 14C, the Genoese sailor **Lancellotto Mallocello** rediscovered the Canary Islands, giving Lanzarote its name. The island was subsequently conquered in 1402 by Jean de Bethencourt in the name of Henry III of Castile. Two volcanic eruptions (1730 and 1824) have altered Lanzarote's physiognomy since, covering it with craters, fields of lava —known as *malpaís*— and ashes, and forcing the natives to use new methods of cultivation for survival. Thanks to its mixture of lunar-like landscapes and exotic plants, this island is perhaps the most magical and mysterious in the entire archipelago. Famous in the past for its malmsey wine, today the island is best known for the camels that slowly make their way across its black sands. Spring is the best time of year to visit, when the vegetation is at its luxuriant best. Except for its capital, Lanzarote is a model of architectural planning thanks to native ecology-conscious architect **César Manrique**.

▊ARRECIFE▊ **Las Palmas** ☎ (928), pop. 29,500, ⓘ Parque Municipal ☎ 81 18 60, ✉ Av Generalísimo, 8 ☎ 81 19 17, ✚ 81 20 62, **P** 81 13 17, ✈ Lanzarote, 6km ☎ 81 14 50 (Iberia, Av Rafael González, 2 ☎ 81 03 50 and 81 53 75), ⛴ Trasmediterránea (ferries to Gran Canaria, Tenerife, La Palma and mainland Spain), c/ José Antonio, 90 ☎ 81 10 19, 🚌 Transportes Lanzarote ☎ 81 15 22.

Though the capital city of Arrecife is a confused jumble of modern buildings, it still preserves some of its historical ones, such as the 16C fortified **Castle of San Gabriel**.

▦ ★★★★ *Arrecife Gran Hotel*, Av Mancomunidad, 11 ☎ 81 12 50 ⊨ 148 ⵙ ✦ ✉ ⚲ ▦ ≪ ⛵ ⚲ AE, DC, EC, V $$$$. Good views and a pleasant garden terrace with a swimming pool.

▦ ★★★ *Cardona*, c/ 18 de Julio, 11 ☎ 81 10 08 ⊨ 62 $$.

▦ ★★★ *Miramar*, c/ Coll, 2 ☎ 81 04 38 ⊨ 90 ⵙ AE, DC, EC, V $$.

🍴 *Castillo de San José*, 2km NE along the road to Puerto de Naos ☎ 81 23 21 **P** ❈ ≪ $$$. Set in an 18C fortress, it commands good views.

Local sights: Heading NW and after passing through San Bartolomé you will come to **MOZAGA** and its Monument to Fertility in honour of Lanzarote's hardworking peasants. Turning SW, the road crosses **LA GERIA**, a curious area of black earth foreshadowing what is to come. Five kilometres N of Yaiza you finally arrive at Lanzarote's spectacular attraction, the **Timanfaya National Park** with its breath-taking **Fire Mountains** which can be seen even before you enter the park. You can tour the park either astride a camel or, to the accompaniment of phantasmagorical music, in one of the hourly tours in the buses known as *guaguas*. Even though the craters are not active, the fire still burns beneath the surface, and water poured through certain holes is expelled in jets of steam. For lunch, try the Fire Mountains' *El Diablo* restaurant where meat is grilled by the heat given off by these volcanoes.

After touring Timanfaya, return to Yaiza and head 8km W to **EL GOLFO**, a beautiful site where an emerald lagoon in an old crater is barely separated from the dark blue sea by a thin strip of sand. Nearby, to the S, **Los Hervideros** offers a different spectacle: here the sea flows in and out of volcanic formations. For further unusual seascapes, you can go to the **Salinas del Janubio**, where a crater has been invaded by the sea.

To the S, **PLAYA BLANCA** is a small fishing village where you can stop for a swim and a tasty meal in the open air at one of the *chiringuitos*, or open-air bars, along the beach. For accommodation, try the ★★★ *Lanzarote Princess*, in Yaiza ☎ 83 00 00 ⊨ 407 **P** ✉ 🏊 ⛵ ≪ ⚲ AE, EC, V $$$ to $$$$, a quiet hotel with good views and a pleasant terrace with a heated swimming pool, and for lunch, try the open-air terrace of *Casa Salvador*, where you can eat fish and seafood while enjoying the view. From here, 5km W along an asphalted road brings you to **Punta del Papagayo**, from where there are views across the ocean all the way to Fuerteventura, and below you the best beach on the island: white sand, clear blue water and hardly a soul in sight. On the way back, 15km before arriving at Arrecife, you will hit **PUERTO DEL CARMEN**, where you can have lunch at *La Romántica*, Atlántico shopping mall ≪ AE, DC, V $$$, or stay at the ★★★★ *Los Fariones*, Urb Playa Blanca, in Puerto del Carmen-Tías ☎ 82 51 75 ⊨ 237 ✦ ✉ 🏊 ⛵ ⚲ ▦ ≪ ⚲ AE, DC, EC, V $$$$, which has lovely tropical gardens, a heated pool, and terraces with sea views. In the neighbouring beach resort of Pocillos, the thing to do is to eat at the pool-side buffet served at *La Gaviota* (closed: Sundays), Marina Bay centre ☎ 82 50 50 **P** ✦ ❈ ≪ AE, DC, EC, V $$$ and to stay at the ★★★★ *San Antonio*, Pocillos beach ☎ 82 50 50 ⊨ 331 ✗ ♿ ✦ ✉ 🏊 ⛵ ⚲ ▦ ≪ ⛵ ⚲ AE, DC, EC, V $$$$, a quiet hotel with a lovely botanical garden and good views of the sea.

COSTA TEGUISE **Las Palmas** ☎ (928), **P** 84 52 52. Arrecife 10km.

Costa Teguise, 10km N of Arrecife, is an international tourist resort that comes complete with hotels, housing developments, restaurants, supermarkets, bars and open-air terraces.

▦ ★★★★★ *Meliá Las Salinas*, Las Cucharas beach ☎ 81 30 40 ⇌ 310 TV ✦ ⏣ ⏦ ⚓ ⏚ ♫ ▦ « ⏏ ⌣ AE, DC, EC, V $$$$$$. This modern luxury hotel offers excellent views of the sea, a heated swimming pool, a semi-private black-sand beach and beautifully landscaped gardens. The rooms, each with a terrace looking out to sea, are very pleasant.

▦ ★★★ *Los Zocos*, Las Cucharas beach ☎ 81 58 17 ⇌ 244 **P** ✦ ⏣ ⚓ ⏚ ⌣ AE, DC, EC, V $$$$ to $$$$$. A very quiet hotel with good views.

🍴 *La Chimenea* (closed: Sundays and July), Cucharas beach ☎ 81 47 00 ✦ ❋ AE, EC, V $$$ to $$$$. A classic on the island.

🍴 *La Tabaiba* (closed: Sundays and 15/5-15/6), Av Islas Canarias, s/n, Pueblo Comercial, Cucharas beach ☎ 81 17 07 ✦ AE, DC, EC, V $$$ to $$$$. Dinners only.

🍴 *Los Molinos* (closed: Tuesdays), Los Molinos apartments ☎ 81 20 08 ⚓ AE, DC, V $$$. Seafood.

Local sights: You should plan a trip to the ancient capital of **TEGUISE**, where you can visit the 16C **Castle of Guanapay** at the top of an extinct volcano and enjoy the spectacular **views** of the area. Nearby to the NE are the windmills of **GUATIZA**, a village where cochineal insects are raised in immense fields of prickly pears. Going N you will pass Arrieta and then encounter the **Jameos del Agua**, a beautiful volcanic grotto with a seawater lagoon which is the only natural habitat in the world for a species of tiny, blind, white crabs. Part of the grotto has been stunningly converted by César Manrique into an auditorium, with seating for 1,000 people: the British singer Brian Eno gave a very successful concert here in 1986. The nearby swimming pool, also by Manrique, is open to all visitors. The impressive **Cueva de Los Verdes** caverns (open: 11.00-6.00) are definitely worth a visit. Once used by the Guanches as a hideout from invading pirates, there are countless caverns at varying levels, all lit up to show a rainbow of colours and curious rock formations. If you are feeling hungry, you can have a meal at *Típico Canario*, Punta Mujeres **MC, V** $$$, which serves fresh fish. From here you can travel N to the **Riscos de Famora** escarpment and to another Manrique site: the **Mirador del Río** which, carved into the rock, offers a **splendid view** of La Graciosa island across the **El Río** inlet. La Graciosa is the perfect place to spend a pleasant day and try one of the tasty local dishes. On the way back to Arrecife, 5km S of **HARIA** there is a lookout point offering panoramic **views** of the verdant *Valle de las Diez Mil Palmeras* (Valley of the Ten Thousand Palms).

Sports: Golfers can play at the 9-hole course of the *Golf Costa Teguise* ☎ 81 35 12.

TENERIFE

The largest of the Canary Islands, Tenerife (2,053km²) —or the 'snowy mountain' island in the language of the Guanches, its original inhabitants— is dominated by Spain's highest mountain, the 3,718m-high snow-capped **Teide**. The Teide is one of a chain of mountains that splits the triangular island in two very different geographical and climatic areas —the southern part of the island is dry with desertlike scenery, while the N blooms in tropical splendour, with lush vegetation, palm trees, enormous pines up to 60m tall, **dragon trees** (the sacred tree of the Guanches) and a glorious array of the most varied species Nature can offer.

During the time of the crusades, the island was divided up among nine clans, each governed by a *mencey*, or tribal king. Due to their ferocious opposition, Tenerife was the last island to be captured by Christian forces, when **Alonso Fernández de Lugo** defeated the last *mencey*, **Bencomo**, in 1495. Although incorporated into Europe by force, the island has been dedicatedly European ever since. Its tradition for hospitality embraced European (and even some American) political and religious refugees as far back as the 17C, and with them, the revolutionary ideas of the Enlightenment. In the 19C, it gave an equally warm welcome to the chill-ridden Britishers who had followed the British Medical Society's recommendation to spend the winter months basking in its healthy warmth. Thus, the island has gradually built up a long experience of dealing with tourists and taken on a totally cosmopolitan flavour —more than 20,000 foreigners of some 70 different nationalities have fallen in love with the place and decided to settle here for good.

🕭🕭 CAÑADAS DEL TEIDE NATIONAL PARK **Santa Cruz de Tenerife** ☎ (922), *i* in Portillo de la Villa. Santa Cruz de Tenerife 67km.

🕭🕭🕭 This park is full of extraordinary geological phenomena, including the famous volcano itself, the now extinct **Teide**. In **EL PORTILLO** where the C-821 (the Vilaflor to Orotava road) and the C-824 (the La Laguna road) meet, there is a tourist bureau where you can get information on the park. About 3km further on, the turn-off to Montaña Blanca leads to the Refugio de Altavista (closed: 15/12-31/3), a welcome resting place for hikers on the long haul up to the top of the Teide. The alternative route to the top is via a **cable car** (open in summer: 9.00-5.00; winter: 10.00-4.00) which will carry less energetic visitors from 2,356m to 3,555m. The final 163m to the summit of this magnificent, sulphurous crater have to be climbed on foot —this takes about 40 minutes for it is no easy stroll. It is extremely high and there are people for whom walking under these conditions is not advisable.

🕭 The 2,200m high **★★ *Parador de Las Cañadas del Teide*,** 5km from the cable car and 43km from La Orotava ☎ 33 23 04 ⊨ 23 🅿 ♦ ⅍ ⊶ ≪ ⚲ **AE, DC, EC, V** $$$, set in an intriguing volcanic landscape that has inspired many a futuristic film and documentary on the origins of the earth, is extremely peaceful and has good views of the valley and the Teide. Here you can just sit back and enjoy the beauty of the surroundings, the clean air, the limpid skies, the sunsets and the occasional soft drizzle, so fine that it is barely more than a mist.

LA LAGUNA **Santa Cruz de Tenerife** ☎ (922), pop. 112,635, *i* Av del Gran Poder, 3 ☎ 54 08 10, ✉ c/ Santo Domingo, 3 ☎ 25 96 05, ✚ 25 96 26, **P** 25 10 80, ✈ Los Rodeos/Tenerife Norte, 3km ☎ 25 79 40 (Iberia ☎ 25 77 45), 🚍 Pl San Cristóbal, s/n ☎ 25 94 12. Santa Cruz de Tenerife 9km.

The oldest town in the island and the former capital of Tenerife, La Laguna was founded by Alonso Fernández de Lugo in 1496 on the shores of a lake that has since dried up. Today it is essentially a university town where the *avant garde* and the traditional live happily side by side.

🍴 *Bodegón Campestre* (closed: Mondays except holidays), on the Las Cañadas-El Rosario road ☎ 54 80 57 $$.

🍴 *Mesón El Cordero Segoviano* (closed: 15/8-30/8), km14.8 on the Ctra General del Norte ☎ 25 22 39 **AE, V** $$$.

Best buys: *M. Lázaro*, c/ Numancia, 24, sells Canary Island contemporary works of art. If you are interested in flowers, plants and birds, then your best bet is the market on the Pl del Adelantado.

Cultural highlights: Flanking the **Pl del Adelantado**, the oldest square in town, are the 17C **Nava Palace**, the 18C **Town Hall** and the **Convent of Santa Catalina**, with a typical Canary Island wooden gallery. Besides these buildings, the whole of the historic quarter is dotted with stately homes and mansions dating from the 17C and 18C. Don't miss the Neoclassical **Cathedral**, where you can see the tomb of the conquistador Fernández de Lugo, or the 16C **Church of La Concepción**, a classic example of a Canary Island shrine of the conquest period with a beautifully carved wooden choir and pulpit and sculptures by Pérez Luján. The **Convento de San Francisco** is home to the venerated 15C figure of the *Cristo de la Laguna*.

Fiestas: During **Corpus Christi**, Laguna covers its streets with multicoloured **carpets of flowers** which qualify as genuine works of art. The first Sunday in July gives the locals another excuse to celebrate: on this occasion, the **Pilgrimage of San Benito** is followed by much wine drinking and fish eating. Yet another procession, that of the *Cristo de La Laguna*, takes place on September 14, when authentic **Canary wrestling** competitions are staged among other entertainments.

Local sights: To the N, the C-822 climbs upwards for 11km towards the **Monte de las Mercedes**, where plants from the Tertiary period, like the *laurisilva*, still abound. Stop at the **Mirador de Cruz de Carmen** for a marvellous view of the valley and the Teide, and then go on to the **Mirador del Pico del Inglés**, from where you will get impressive panoramic views of the Anaga Massif and its sheer cliffs which drop straight down into deep waters, making this part of the coast ideal for **scuba diving**. Further on, the **Bailadero** mountain pass also offers beautiful views. If you decide to head N, follow the picturesque **road** that descends to the charming town of **TAGANANA**. The entire place is steeped in mysterious beauty, far from the madding crowd, set between the wide open sea and the mountains. Its few, unpretentious bars serve excellent fish, and for a touch of culture, ·the Hispano-Flemish altarpiece in the church there is well worth a visit. If you want a swim, manoeuvre your way down the steep road to the Las Gaviotas beach, a favourite spot for nudists and people who want to get away from it all and lie on the fine, black sand, undisturbed by civilization.

Sports: Golfers can play at the *Club de Golf de Tenerife*, 7km W of the town ☎ 25 02 40, while flying enthusiasts can cruise the skies from the *Aero Club Tenerife-La Laguna* ☎ 22 25 16.

PLAYA DE LAS AMERICAS **Santa Cruz de Tenerife** ☎ (922), *i* San Eugenio, Pueblo Canario ☎ 79 33 12, ✉ San Eugenio, Pueblo Canario ☎ 79 10 56, ✛ 79 05 05, **P** 79 21 31, ✈ Reina Sofía/ Tenerife Sur, 17km ☎ 77 13 00 (Iberia ☎ 77 05 61 and 77 11 87, Aviaco ☎ 77 12 00), ⛴ San Eugenio, Pueblo Canario ☎ 79 33 12 and 79 33 90. Santa Cruz de Tenerife 75km.

After Puerto de la Cruz, Playa de las Américas is the largest **tourist resort** on the island, where you can be sure to meet up with the European in-crowd who flock here to live it up and revel in the greatest nightlife Tenerife has to offer. Although some of the hotels are so enormous as to be a blot on the landscape, they never seem to have enough rooms to fit in all the tourists who want to enjoy the town's leisure facilities and magnificent **beach**.

🏨 ★★★★ *Bitacora*, Playa de las Américas ☎ 79 15 40 🛏 314 ✦ ⛱ ♿
   AE, DC, EC, V \$\$\$ to \$\$\$\$. It has a heated swimming pool.
🏨 ★★★★ *Bouganville Playa*, Urb San Eugenio ☎ 79 02 00 🛏 481 ✦ 🎤
   ⛱ 🎱 🖼 « ♿ AE, DC, V \$\$\$ to \$\$\$\$. Good views and a heated pool.
🏨 ★★★★ *Conquistador*, Av Litoral, s/n ☎ 79 23 99 🛏 485 ⛱ 🎱 « ♿
   AE, DC, EC, V \$\$\$\$. Good views and a heated swimming pool.

▥ **★★★★ *Europe Tenerife***, Av Litoral, s/n ☎ 79 13 08 🛏 244 ♦ 🎙 ≈
🏊 📺 « 🐎 Q̓ AE, DC, EC, V $$$$. Right on the coast, this hotel has a
semi-private beach, lovely tropical gardens and a wide range of facilities,
including a heated swimming pool.

🗇 ▥ **★★★★ *Gran Tinerfe***, Av Marítima, s/n ☎ 79 12 00 🛏 357 ♿ 📺 ♦ 🎙 ≈
🏊 📺 « Q̓ AE, DC, EC, V $$$$. One of the most traditional of all, this
seaside hotel has good views and a pleasant terrace with a heated
swimming pool.

▥ **★★★★ *Las Palmeras***, Playa de las Américas ☎ 79 09 91 🛏 531 ♦ ≈
🏊 « Q̓ AE, V $$$$. Good views and a heated swimming pool.

▥ **★★★★ *La Siesta***, Av Marítima, s/n ☎ 79 23 00 🛏 280 ♿ ♦ ≈ 🏊 🐎
Q̓ $$$$. Heated swimming pool.

▥ **★★★★ *Tenerife Princess***, Av Litoral, s/n ☎ 79 27 51 🛏 386 ♿ ♦ 🎙
≈ 🏊 🐎 Q̓ AE, DC, V $$$$. Heated swimming pool.

▥ **★★★★ *Tenerife Sol***, Playa de las Américas ☎ 79 10 62 🛏 523 ♦ 🎙
≈ 🏊 Q̓ AE, DC, EC, V $$$$ to $$$$$. Heated swimming pool.

▥ **★★★ *Park Hotel Troya***, Playa de las Américas ☎ 79 01 00 🛏 318 ♿ ♦
🎙 ≈ 🏊 📺 Q̓ AE, DC, V $$$$. Heated swimming pool.

🍴 *Costa Brava* (closed: Sundays and 16/5-16/6), Centro Comercial
Verónica 4 ☎ 79 06 55 « AE, EC, V $$$ to $$$$. Pleasant views.

🍴 *Folías*, Pueblo Canario ☎ 79 22 69 ♦ « AE, EC, V $$$ to $$$$. You
can eat fish, seafood or roast lamb on the terrace of this restaurant while
enjoying the views of the area.

🍴 *Mesón de Orgaz*, Pueblo Canario ☎ 79 31 69 ♦ AE, DC, EC, V $$$.
This restaurant specializes in Castilian roasts and fish and seafood from
the mainland.

Best buys: You will find lovely open-work embroidery at *La Casa de los
Balcones*, American shopping centre.

Local sights: Nearby, to the S, **LOS CRISTIANOS** was one of the first small
fishing villages to be 'discovered' by the international travel agencies of the
sixties. Although in the initial euphoria of the tourist boom the development
hardly deserved such a name, later more far-sighted building projects have
given this **tourist resort** some very tasteful and well-kept tourist estates and
hotels. The town has a small but very pretty **beach**, a marina, a port from
which the ferry to the island of La Gomera sets out, and a couple of good
pottery shops, the best of which is *Pepe's*, c/ R. Pino, 52. For
accommodation, you can try the **★★★ *Oasis Moreque***, Av Penetración, s/n
☎ 79 03 66 🛏 175 🅿 ≈ 🏊 « Q̓ AE, V $$$, with pleasant views and a
heated swimming pool, the **★★★ *Tryp Princesa Dacil***, Av Penetración, s/n ☎
79 08 00 🛏 366 🅿 ♦ 🎙 ≈ 🏊 📺 🐎 Q̓ AE, DC, MC, V $$$$, right on the
beach, or **★★ *Andrea's***, Av Valle Menéndez, s/n ☎ 79 00 12 🛏 49 🅿 🎙
🏊 AE, DC, EC, V $$ to $$$. Local and international dishes are served at
L'Escala, c/ Paloma, 7 ☎ 79 10 15 ♦ $$$, which has a terrace where you
can dine in the open-air to live music.

Heading NE along the C-822, after 12km you will come to the **Mirador
de la Centinela** lookout point, from where there are superb **views** of the
area, and, 9km further, to **GRANADILLA DE ABONA**, a charming village that
grows the best oranges in the islands —for something more substantial, you
could try the home cooking at *Los Hermanos*. For a different kind of setting,
head S along the San Isidro road to the unspoilt fishing village of **EL MEDANO**
and take a dip from its scenically set golden-sand **beach**, bordered on the N
by the steep Montaña Roja (Red Mountain) which seems to absorb the red
hues of the sunset over the sea. **Windsurfers** should take special note of this
beach —the strong winds here have turned El Médano, into a windsurfers'
mecca. For accommodation, try the **★★★ *Médano***, El Médano beach ☎

70 40 00 ⊨ 65 ⚲ ≪ **AE, DC, EC, V** $$$, situated right on the beach, and enjoy its views. **VILAFLOR**, the highest village in the island at 1,450m, is known not only for its good wine and delicious cheese, but also for the purity of its water and air. The road then winds on around the **Montaña Colorada** mountain, with its deep red stone, through a beautiful pinewood and then, behind the spectacular **Boca de Tauce** ravine (2,055m), the **Cañadas del Teide** appear (see separate entry).

Driving N along the C-822 from Playa de las Américas you will get to **ADEJE**. From there, you will have to walk for 2km to get to the **Barranco del Infierno** (Hell's Gully), a gaping ravine whose sheer walls, covered in vegetation, reach down so deep that even the sun's rays cannot penetrate to the bottom. Apart from its visual impact and geological interest, it has also attracted the attention of archaeologists who have found, to everyone's amazement, several Guanche funerary caves in its inaccessible walls.

PUERTO DE LA CRUZ Santa Cruz de Tenerife ☎ (922), pop. 39,241, *i* Pl de la Iglesia, 3 ☎ 38 60 00, (c/ Quintana, s/n, ✉ c/ del Pozo, s/n ☎ 38 58 05, 38 57 16 and 38 27 14, ♔ 38 38 12, **P** 38 04 58, ✈ La Laguna/Tenerife Norte ☎ 25 01 08, ✈ Reina Sofía/Tenerife Sur ☎ 77 00 50 (Iberia, c/ Blanco, 20 ☎ 38 00 00, and Av Generalísimo, s/n ☎ 38 00 50, 38 36 50 and 38 36 35), ▯ Tenerife Bus, c/ Virtud, 3 ☎ 38 54 08. Santa Cruz de Tenerife 36km.

This 400-year old port has built up a long tradition as a **tourist resort**. The British began holidaying here over a century ago... and Puerto de la Cruz can boast such important visitors as Winston Churchill and Bertrand Russell among the many thousands of tourists who have visited from all over the world —it has attracted some 900,000 a year during the 1980s, not to mention the resident international community. As early as the 16C, the port was known for its liberal, enlightened atmosphere, always open to British and German traders and the ideas they brought with them. Surrounded by miles of banana plantations, with an exceptional **climate** all of its own, it is a healthy place, with temperatures that never get unbearably hot or unbearably cold at any time of the year. Its brand of tourism has always been definitely upmarket, and its tourist facilities are efficient and well established —more than half of its more than 90 hotels are in the four or five star category, some of them dating back to the 1880s.

Variety is the spice of life, and you will find it here. Choose between the tiny beaches that look out towards the untameable, often choppy open sea, or bathing in the man-made rock pools of the splendid **Lago de Martiánez** swimming pool complex, designed by Canary Island artist César Manrique, where Man has more than compensated for Nature's limitations and unruliness. Look at the architecture, which offers a cross-section of old and new: high concrete blocks along the **Paseo Marítimo** seaside promenade and other brightly lit modern streets stand side by side with the picturesque fishermen's houses in old areas such as La Ranilla and typically Spanish squares, like the one in front of the church; modern structures rub shoulders with typical Canary Island buildings, like the Miranda, Iriarte, Lavaggi and Nieves Ravelo houses... You will probably enjoy the modern comforts and the entertainments offered by the town's trendy bars and nightclubs, but will be equally able to revel in the peace of the old San Felipe Castle or the Hermitage of San Telmo, or delight in the sunsets from the palm groves of the 19C **Taoro Park**.

▤ ★★★★★ *Meliá Botánico*, c/ Richard J. Yeoward, s/n ☎ 38 14 00 ⊨ 282 **TV** ♦ ⓔ ⯑ ⯑ ⚲ ▦ ≪ ⯑ ⯑ **AE, DC, MC, V** $$$$$$. A quiet hotel with pleasant views and beautiful tropical gardens.

🏢 ★★★★★ *Meliá San Felipe*, Av de Colón, 13, Playa de Martiánez ☎ 38 33 11 🛏 260 ⅙ TV ✦ 🎤 ⅍ ⇌ 🌡 ▦ ≪ 🐎 ℚ AE, DC, EC, V $$$$$ to $$$$$$. This functional hotel is situated on one of the town's main roads, close to the focal point of its lively night-life. The rooms overlook the Playa de Martiánez complex and its adjacent walkways.

🏢 ★★★★★ *Semiramis*, c/ Leopoldo Cologán, 12 ☎ 38 55 51 🛏 275 TV ✦ 🎤 ⇌ 🌡 ▦ ℚ AE, DC, EC, MC $$$$ to $$$$$$. A lift in the hotel takes you 16 floors down to a natural swimming pool.

🏢 ★★★★ *Atalaya Gran Hotel*, c/ Parque de Taoro, s/n ☎ 38 46 00 🛏 183 ⅙ ✦ 🎤 ⇌ ▦ ≪ 🐎 ℚ AE, DC, EC, MC $$$ to $$$$. A quiet hotel with good views and a pleasant garden with a heated swimming pool.

🏢 ★★★★ *Florida*, Av Blas Pérez González, s/n ☎ 38 12 50 🛏 335 ✦ 🎤 ⇌ 🌡 ≪ AE, DC, EC, MC $$$ to $$$$. This hotel has good views and a heated swimming pool.

🏢 ★★★★ *Gran Hotel Concordia Playa*, Av del Generalísimo, 3 ☎ 38 54 11 🛏 236 ⅙ TV ✦ ⇌ 🌡 ≪ 🐎 AE, DC, EC, MC $$$$. This hotel has good views over the Martiánez complex and the sea.

🏢 ★★★★ *Gran Hotel Los Dogos-Sol*, Urb El Durazno ☎ 38 51 51 🛏 237 ⅙ TV ✦ ⇌ 🌡 ▦ ≪ 🐎 ℚ AE, DC, EC, MC, V $$$ to $$$$. Set slightly away from the town centre, its design and surrounding palms give this quiet hotel a typically Canary atmosphere.

🏢 ★★★★ *La Paz*, Urb La Paz, s/n ☎ 38 50 11 🛏 167 TV ✦ 🎤 ⇌ ≪ AE, DC, MC $$$ to $$$$. A typical Canary style building with a heated pool.

🏢 ★★★★ *Las Vegas-Sol* (closed: December), Av de Colón, 2 ☎ 38 34 51 🛏 223 ⅙ TV ✦ ⇌ 🌡 ≪ 🐎 ℚ AE, DC, EC, $$$ to $$$$. This functional hotel has rooms overlooking the Lago Martiánez complex, a heated swimming pool and a popular bar.

🏢 ★★★★ *Meliá Puerto de la Cruz*, Av Marqués Villanueva del Prado, s/n ☎ 38 40 11 🛏 300 TV ✦ ⅍ ⇌ 🌡 ▦ ≪ ℚ AE, DC, MC, V $$$$ to $$$$$. Set 300m from the sea, it has pleasant views and a pool.

🌺🌺 🏢 ★★★★ *Parque San Antonio Sol*, Ctra de las Arenas, s/n ☎ 38 49 08 🛏 211 ✦ ⇌ 🌡 ≪ AE, DC, EC $$$$. Situated near the Taoro Park, it has lovely tropical gardens and a heated swimming pool, as well as good sporting facilities.

🌺 🏢 ★★★ *Las Aguilas Sol*, 3km from town in Las Arenas ☎ 38 32 00 🛏 500 ✦ ⇌ 🌡 ≪ 🐎 ℚ AE, DC, EC, MC, V $$$ to $$$$. A very quiet hotel with good views over the valley to the town, sea and mountains.

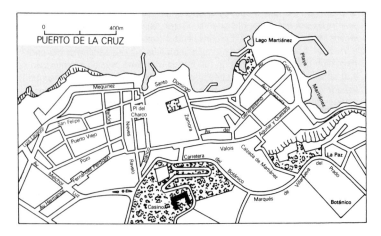

▦ ★★★ *Monopol*, c/ Quintana, 15 ☎ 38 46 11 ⊨ 92 ✦ ⚓ ☂ « AE, DC, MC $$$. A traditional style building with a beautiful Canary Island patio filled with flowering plants, and a heated swimming pool.

▦ ★★★ *San Telmo*, c/ San Telmo, 18 ☎ 38 58 53 ⊨ 91 ⚓ ☂ « AE, DC, EC $$$. This hotel has good views and a heated swimming pool.

❛❜ *Castillo de San Felipe*, Av Luis Lavaggi, s/n ☎ 38 21 13 ✦ ❉ AE, DC, EC, V $$ to $$$. You can eat good fish and meat in this 17C castle.

❛❜ *El Gordo Otto* (closed: Sundays), Av del Generalísimo, 3 ☎ 38 26 96 ✦ ❉ « $$$. Best known for its grilled fish and meat.

❛❜ *Magnolia* (closed: Mondays and 1/5-1/6), Ctra del Botánico, 5 ☎ 38 56 14 🅿 ✦ ❉ « AE, DC, EC, V $$$ to $$$$$. This restaurant specializes in Catalan cuisine, although it also serves seafood dishes.

❛❜ *Mi Vaca y Yo* (closed: 25/6-25/7), c/ Cruz Verde, 3 ☎ 38 52 47 AE, DC, EC, V $$$ to $$$$. A very popular restaurant set in a large house.

❛❜ *Patio Canario*, c/ Cruz Verde, 4 ☎ 38 04 51 AE, EC, V $$$. Canary Island cuisine and wines.

Best buys: You can buy typical embroidery and open-work at *La Casa de los Balcones*, c/ San Telmo, 22, and local pottery at *La Calesa*, c/ La Asomada, s/n. Typical crafts and clothes are also sold at the open-air markets along Paseo Colón, La Ermita de San Telmo and Camino de las Cabras. Shop around for duty free goods at the town's **bazaars** along c/ Valois, c/ San Telmo, c/ Santo Domingo and c/ La Hoya, where there are excellent bargains to be had. **Flowers** and **plants** are sold at florists all over town and in the nurseries on the outskirts, and tropical and subtropical **fruits** are found in the big markets. If all you need is a well-stocked supermarket then your best bet is to go to *S.M. 2.000*, in the La Paz development.

Cultural highlights: The **Botanical Gardens** (open 1/10-31/3: 9.00-6.00; 1/4-30/9: 9.00-7.00), Puerto de la Cruz's most interesting cultural and natural feature, are a product of the Spanish Enlightenment of the 18C, when agricultural development and a spirit of scientific enquiry were the passion of the day. Today, the park's 2ha are home to a collection of 4,000 species of plants from all over the world, as well as to parrots, pigeons, turtledoves, geese and other local birds. If parrots are your passion, take one of the free buses from Martiánez to **Loro Park**, which is said to have one of the two largest collections of these birds in the world.

Fiestas: **Carnival** time is one big *fiesta* all over the island. On July 16, the more religious celebration of the *Virgen del Carmen*, patron saint of fishermen, takes place as locals carry her effigy shoulder-high over land and sea.

Local sights: Eight kilometres from town, the **Mirador Humboldt** vantage point takes its name from German naturalist Alexander Humboldt, who was enthusiastic about the view of the valley seen from here. The **Orotava Valley** runs from the foot of the Teide to the ocean in an unending stretch of green banana groves, interrupted only by the elegant white town of **LA OROTAVA**. Here, the 18C **Church of La Concepción**, with a Baroque façade and two towers, has a secular beauty despite its function. Walking along the cobble-stoned **c/ San Francisco** you will come to another architectural gem, the **Casa de los Balcones** (House of Balconies), which takes its name from its beautiful Canary Island balconies —today, it houses the local crafts centre where you can see ladies at work on the famous local open-work embroidery. If you can, visit La Orotava during its Corpus Christi celebrations, when the town's streets are covered with vast multicoloured **carpets of flowers and earth** from the Teide or, two Sundays later, when the traditional and colourful **pilgrimage of San Isidro** takes place. After strolling around town, you can take the C-821 **road** that winds its way up to the **Cañadas del Teide**

National Park (see separate entry), or you can drive W for 9km to **Los realejos**, the valley's second major attraction. Art lovers will enjoy visiting the upper part of town and the Church of Santiago, as well as the nearby Church of La Concepción, with its magnificent Baroque altarpiece and fine jasper font. If you have grown hungry by now, pop into *La Finca* (closed: Sundays and 15/6-15/7), c/ El Monturio, 5 ☎ 34 01 43 ♣ V $$$, which serves good German food and beer, or *Las Chozas* (closed: Sunday nights), Ctra El Jardín ☎ 34 20 54 **EC, V** $$$, which serves both German and Spanish dishes. Leaving the town and continuing W for another 9km along the C-820 you will get to **San Juan de la Rambla**, a picturesque town of 17-18C aristocratic houses and lively, colourful squares such as the **Pl de la Iglesia**. The neighbouring town of **La guancha** is best known for its hand-made open-work embroidery, made and sold at the *Cooperativa de Calados La Guancha*, Av H. Sinforiano, 31. From here, continue driving W to the seaside town of **Icod de los vinos**, set against a backdrop of mountains and in the heart of a wine-growing area. Icod owes its spiritual tranquillity to the **Church of San Marcos** and its mysterious quality to the 2,500 year old **drago** tree that was once revered by the Guanches. The town is at its mysterious best on Saint John's day, when great balls of fire are rolled down the mountain, striking awe into visitors and locals alike. Still further W you will get to the seaside port of **Garachico**, another of Tenerife's legendary towns. Partially destroyed in 1716 by an eruption of the Teide, the town still has a pleasant old quarter and an interesting Castle of San Miguel, and its coast is excellent for **scuba diving**. If you enjoy good views, drive 5km S towards San Juan del Reparo, from where there are panoramic **views** of the town and the field of volcanic lava surrounding it. Further W, you can drive on to the **El Palmar Valley**.

An alternative drive takes you 15km N of Puerto de la Cruz to **Tacoronte**, set in an important wine-producing area and birthplace of the Surrealist painter Oscar Domínguez. Here you can stroll around the historic quarter —whose churches and old houses are among the best preserved examples of local architecture in the island— and visit the *Bodegas Alfaro* wine museum. Tacoronte's situation between sea and mountain and its fine wines have produced a concentration of 'typical' restaurants, most of which are found along the road to Los Rodeos. There is also accommodation at the modern ★★★ *Club Parque Mesa del Mar*, Urb Mesa del Mar ☎ 56 13 00 ⊨ 82 **P** ♣ ≈ ♿ AE, DC, MC, V $$$ to $$$$, scenically set amidst lush gardens, with good facilities and a heated swimming pool.

On the town: Puerto de la Cruz has a first-rate **night life** with something for everybody —choose from the party atmosphere at La Ranilla, the elegant urbanity of the sophisticated night clubs of La Paz and the Lago de Martiánez, or the more strident tones of the discos in the tourist quarter of town. Best discos include *Atlantis* in the *Atlantis* hotel, *El Coto* in the *Meliá Botánico* hotel, and *Joy*, Av Generalísimo, s/n. If you prefer a riskier evening, you can always flirt with Lady Luck at the *Casino Taoro* in the *Taoro* hotel. Daytime entertainment can centre around tea or coffee at the open-air terrace of *Calypso*, Av Colón, 9, or at the *Café de París*, Av Colón, 2, in the gardens of the *Valle Mar* hotel.

Sports: If you enjoy spectator sports, head for the *Hotel Tigaiga* ☎ 37 11 90 on Sunday mornings for spectacular Canary wrestling matches. Sports for those who prefer to do rather than watch include **rod fishing** at Punta de la Laja, La Vinagrera (in the Punta Brava district), El Beril and Punta de la Salena, and tennis at any of the hotel courts or at those of the *Oceánico Tennis Club*, Ctra Fuerteventura ☎ 38 00 18, and the *Club Británico de Juegos*, on the Taoro road ☎ 38 48 23.

PUERTO DE SANTIAGO **Santa Cruz de Tenerife** ☎ (922). Santa Cruz de Tenerife 101km.

What used to be a tiny fishing port is now a popular tourist resort with luxury hotels and a marina (☎ 86 71 79, with more than 300 moorings) alongside the fine black sand of its beaches. In general, it is an ideal place for **deep sea fishing** (tunny and suchlike) and **scuba diving** enthusiasts. Those less inclined towards being active on holiday can enjoy the town's **La Arena** beach which, although surrounded by examples of somewhat disordered town planning, is well protected from the wind —the waves still have to be looked out for, though. Two kilometres further N, **Los Gigantes** is a curious formation of black, craggy rocks.

▥ ★★★★ *Los Gigantes-Sol*, on the Los Gigantes cliffs ☎ 86 71 25 ⇥ 225 ♿ ♣ ♨ ≈ ☂ ▦ ≪ ♞ � $$$$. Beautiful views of the cliffs and sea.

▥ ★★★★ *Santiago* ☎ 86 73 75 ⇥ 406 ♣ ♨ ♨ ≈ ☂ ≪ � AE, MC, V $$$ to $$$$. Quiet, with good sea views and a heated swimming pool.

SANTA CRUZ DE TENERIFE **Santa Cruz de Tenerife** ☎ (922), pop. 211,389, *i* Av José Antonio, 2 ☎ 24 25 92, (c/ Villalba Hervás, 1, ✉ Pl España, 2 ☎ 24 51 16, ✛ 28 18 00, P 21 51 00, ✈ Rodeos/Tenerife Norte, 13km ☎ 25 79 40 (Iberia ☎ 25 77 45), ✈ Reina Sofía/Tenerife Sur, 60km ☎ 77 13 00 (Iberia ☎ 77 05 61 and 77 11 87, Aviaco ☎ 77 12 00), ⚓ Trasmediterránea, c/ Marina, 59 ☎ 28 78 50, ☐ Av 3 de Mayo, s/n ☎ 21 93 99.

Thanks to a special **free port** charter granted in 1852, what used to be the port of La Laguna (see separate entry) has expanded into one of the largest towns in the archipelago, rivalled only by Las Palmas de Gran Canaria. Nowadays it has its own refinery and a flourishing tobacco industry, and its enormous trans-Atlantic port handles shipping from all over the world. Visit the busy docks and look back inland to get a fascinating **view** of the entire town, which has been the seat of the Canary Islands' Autonomous Parliament since the devolution of various governmental powers from the mainland.

▥ ★★★★★ *Mencey*, c/ Doctor José Naveiras, 38 ☎ 27 16 59 ⇥ 298 ♿ TV ♣ ♨ ≈ ▦ ♞ � AE, DC, EC, V $$$$$. It has a pleasant tropical garden.

▥ ★★★ *Colón Rambla*, c/ Viera y Clavijo, 49 ☎ 27 25 50 ⇥ 40 TV P ♣ ♨ ≈ AE, V $$$$. With a heated swimming pool.

▥ ★★ *Tamaide*, Rambla General Franco, 118 ☎ 27 71 00 ⇥ 65 ≈ AE, DC, EC, V $$.

❙❙ *Andrea's II* (closed: Sundays and August), c/ García Morato, 9 ☎ 27 77 22 ✳ AE, DC, V $$$. Basque cuisine.

❙❙ *El Coto de Antonio* (closed: Sunday nights), c/ General Goded, 13 ☎ 27 21 05 ✳ AE, DC, EC, V $$$. This restaurant specializes in seasonal home cooking and also serves good fish dishes.

❙❙ *La Caseta de Madera* (closed: Saturday nights and Sundays), c/ Los Llanos, s/n, Regla district ☎ 21 00 23 $$$. A popular restaurant.

❙❙ *La Fragua* (closed: Sundays), c/ General Antequera, 17 ☎ 27 74 69 ✳ AE, V $$$. European and Basque cuisine.

Beaches: Ten kilometres N and next to the fishing village of **SAN ANDRES**, the Sahara-sand beach of **Las Teresitas** is safe, clean and full of facilities.

Best buys: You will find just about everything here, from tobacco to shoes, leather goods, flowers and plants, clothes, jewelry, crafts, furniture, electronic goods and video equipment... and all at **very attractive prices** given the islands' duty free status. Most famous of all are the **bazaars** —around Pl de La Candelaria, Pl de España, c/ Castillo and c/ Bethencourt Alfonso— that make Santa Cruz a shopping emporium. If you already know exactly what you want, take note of the following addresses. Canary Island embroidery and

🕭 open-work is sold at *La Casa de los Balcones*, Pl de la Candelaria. Shoes and accessories are best bought at *Lucky*, c/ Castillo, s/n, and *Lurueña*, c/ Bethencourt Alfonso, 28. For jewelry, go to *Cíes y Gutiérrez*, c/ Méndez Núñez, 38, and *Sergio*, c/ Pilar, 20, and for Spanish fashion, to *Adolfo*

🕭 *Domínguez*, c/ Pilar, 6. For a wide assortment of everything, head for the town's department stores, *Galerías Preciados*, c/ Pilar, 3, and *Maya*, Pl de la Candelaria, 31. There is an excellent range of gifts, arts and crafts at

🕭 *Artespaña*, Pl de la Candelaria, 8, and modern art at *Leyendecker*, c/ San Clemente, 3. For more typical crafts like Guanche-style pottery, go to *Centro S. José Obrero*, c/ M. Marín, 5, and for Canary Island musical instruments to *Musicanarias*, Rambla de Pulido, 60. On the spot gifts like flowers, plants, fruit and local cheeses are sold at the picturesque *Nuestra Señora de Africa* market, open from 6.00-2.00, and there is a little bit of everything at the Sunday open-air market on Av de Anaya.

Cultural highlights: The 17C **Iglesia de la Concepción** is a treasure trove of interesting items —in it you will find 18C sculptures by **Luján Pérez**, the crucifix from Fernández de Lugo's encampment and banners captured from Nelson. Nearby secular sights include the 18C **Palacio de los Carta** (with a beautiful patio) which stands on the **Pl de la Candelaria**, with an 18C Carrara marble monument; the popular Pl Weyler square, adorned with flower beds and a lovely Genoese fountain; and the neighbouring tropical gardens of the **García Sanabria Park**. You can also visit the **Paso Alto Castle** where, in 1797, England's Admiral Nelson failed in his attempt to take Santa Cruz de Tenerife, losing his right arm in the process. The *El Tigre* cannon on exhibition inflicted the damage. If you want to learn more about the island's history, tour the **Museo Arqueológico** (Archaeological Museum), c/ Bravo Murillo, 5 (open: 9.00-1.00 and 4.00-6.00; closed: Sundays and holidays, and Saturday afternoons in July and August), which has an interesting collection of mummies and other remains of the native Guanche culture. And for a selection of Canary Island art and weaponry, visit the **Museo de Bellas Artes**, c/ J. Murphy, 1 (open: 2.00-7.00; closed: Sundays and Mondays).

🕭🕭 **Fiestas:** Santa Cruz's famous **Carnivals**, held in February or March, are among the most colourful and lively in the world.

Local sights: La laguna (see separate entry), the oldest town in Tenerife, is a must. Heading SW, the fishing village and tourist resort of CANDELARIA is the spiritual focus of the island, since this is where homage is paid to the patron saint of the archipelago as a whole. According to legend, the much venerated figure of the *Virgen de la Candelaria*, now in the town's 20C basilica, was found by Guanche shepherds before the arrival of the Spanish in the 15C —the pagan cult that grew up around it was later rechannelled into Marian worship by the conquistadors. The ideal date for visiting the town is August 14, when the local young people, dressed in an approximation of the Guanche costume, re-enact the discovery of the Virgin —the performance is followed by a pilgrimage and festive celebrations during which typical local

🕭🕭 food and drink are served to one and all. For some of the best **views** on the island, continue SW beyond Güimar to the **mirador de Don Martín**, from where you will be able to see the contrasting landscapes of the dry valley and its surprising vineyards and the Güimar volcano.

Sports: Golfers should head for the *Club de Golf de Tenerife* course 16km from town ☎ 25 02 40, and horseback riders for the *Club Hípico La Atalaya*, 11km along the Ctra del Norte ☎ 25 14 10. Water sports lovers will find the *Club Neptuno*, c/ Pérez Galdós, 19 ☎ 28 13 21 ideal for fishing, and the *Real Club Náutico Santa Cruz de Tenerife* ☎ 27 31 17 and 25 75 03, best for sailing and motorboating, although it also has tennis courts as does the *Club de Tenis Tenerife* ☎ 21 00 14.

CANTABRIAN COAST

Asturias, Cantabria and the **Basque Country** are three very different areas of Spain and each has its own different historical and cultural characteristics. However they are grouped together here because they do have a number of geographical and touristic common denominators for the traveller along the northern Spanish coast.

As you travel along this coastline you will be as likely to come across grassy meadows and contentedly munching cattle as slag heaps and billowing factory chimneys. Parts of the sea shore are rocky and parts form wide open beaches; cliffs suddenly rise up and then disappear. This is a wet part of Spain. Short, swiftly flowing rivers gush down from the highlands and a not unpleasant drizzle, called *chirimiri* in the Basque Country and *orbayu* in Asturias, can fall for hours on end. Inevitably, this is also a green part of Spain. Seasoned travellers along the Cantabrian Coast claim they can tell which of the three regions they are in by the shades of green of its valleys.

The backdrop to the coastal strip is the imposing **Cordillera Cantábrica** mountain range which blocks off the tableland of Castile from the sea. Spain is by no means short of dramatic sierras and these mountains in Cantabria rank high in the listings for their beauty. They are called the **Picos de Europa**, or the European Peaks, and this is no misnomer for they tower up to 2,500m and present a daunting challenge to skilled mountaineers. Asturias and Cantabria share this range and each region has its national parks and trekking trails for the visitor. If you are lucky you might catch sight of a mouflon goat, of a capercaillie and, even, of a brown bear for the thick woods of the **Picos** form a natural sanctuary for threatened species.

The actual coastal strip itself, hemmed in close to the sea by the mountain range, is no more than 50km wide. The Cantabrian sea itself is a sight to behold as it tirelessly breaks and breaks on the grey rocks. Milennia of battering have produced the abruptness and variety of this **beautiful coast**. Here cliffs, promontories and fiords are the order of the day as are, in total contrast, sudden calm bays with fine sandy beaches. There are a number of major industrial ports along this coast such as Avilés, Bilbao, Gijón and Santander. There are also numberless small fishing villages which are picture postcard pretty and unspoiled.

In many ways the Cantabrian coast is the shrine of the Spanish national heritage. Extremely early settlers of the Paleolithic age have left in their cave drawings numerous souvenirs of their passing. The **Altamira caves** have earned for themselves the grand title of the **Sistine chapel of rupestrian art** but they are nothing more than a pointer, albeit a magnificent one, to the richness of literally dozens of caves, scattered around the area, that were adorned between 20,000 and 8,000 BC. It is perhaps the proprietorial sense of a people who had been a long time in the area that made inhabitants of the Cantabrian valleys utterly hostile to foreign invaders. They fiercely resisted the Roman penetration of Spain and they were to show their mettle again in the 8C when they rose up against the Moorish invaders. The national shrine *par excellence* is the valley of **Covadonga**, in the heart of the Picos de Europa, where a legendary local chieftain named **Don Pelayo** inflicted a singular defeat on the Saracens and went on to found the first Christian kingdom in the Iberian peninsula. The Covadonga victory was the starting pistol for that long period of Spanish history called the Reconquest which was to culminate 800 years later in the capture of Moorish Granada by the Catholic Monarchs. The Christian Kingdom of Asturias was, in its early days, to develop peacefully and prosperously. It was also to emerge as something of a cultural power for its rulers encouraged a style of local architecture known as Asturian pre-Romanesque which today seems striking for its technical accomplishment.

As befits every arresting strip of coastline, Cantabria's is famed for its seamen. There is evidence that as early as the 9C Basque whaling boats were to be found plying their trade off the coast of Greenland. A native of these shores, **Juan Sebastián Elcano**, took over when Magellan was killed in the Philippines and was the first captain to sail his vessel right round the globe. It was natural that men from this coastline should have left to seek glory and fortune in the New World. Many returned wealthy and influential. They were dubbed *Indianos* and the houses, follies more often than not, that they built in their home villages are a singular feature of the area. As you travel along this coastline you will pass one fishing village after another. Together their fleets form one of the largest in the world.

Fishing and farming formed the twin pillars of the economy of all three regions right up to the last century. Then, in rapid succession, coal mines and iron ore seams were opened up, and a steel industry and a ship building industry developed. The face of one green valley after another was changed forever. Asturias with its coal and steel and the Basque Country with mines and also with plants manufacturing a whole range of capital goods became the powerhouses of Spain's Industrial Revolution. Nowadays much of what was built up a century ago is in need of drastic restructuring and scaling down. The proud industrial centres that were have now, in most cases, become decaying milestones along a rust belt.

The curious and inquisitive traveller to this coastline will soon become aware that he is passing through areas that have preserved ancient, ancestral customs and traditions. The most remarkable are the survival of ethnic languages and, in particular, the continued and growing use of the Basque language or *Euskera*. This is a language that baffles experts who disagree sharply over its roots and origins though they all coincide over its linguistic complexity. In Asturias there are a few areas where another obscure language called *Bable* is spoken. As you would expect the folklore of the different regions is deeply rooted in their rural and fishing background. In Asturias the cowboy-type cattle herders have their highly original ***fiestas*** towards the end of June near the town of Luarca and the shepherds have theirs a month later up in the highlands by lake Enol. The Basques are experts at turning rural jobs into sporting events and thus they compete against each other in skills such as chopping logs and lifting stones. All along the coast there are fine oarsmen, a reflection of the seamanship here, and regattas between teams from neighbouring villages involving heavy long boats are a popular summer event. **Dancing**, mostly by men, is also taken seriously and the Basque people have a wide repertoire of different steps, almost invariably highly athletic, which mark a variety of ceremonial occasions.

Well established peoples, like the Asturians, the Cantabrians and the Basques must, almost by definition, eat and drink well and the inhabitants of the Cantabrian Coast are no exception to this rule. They are fortunate in having top quality products from the valleys and from the coast and they have a long tradition behind them in the culinary arts. The local **cheeses** are always interesting and sometimes exceptionally good. The freshness and variety of the **fish and shellfish** is outstanding and there is an addiction in these parts to eating outsize red steaks. In the drinks division regional highlights include the Asturian **cider** which packs a very powerful punch and the Basque **txacolí** white wines which are also deceptively innocuous when drunk. Perhaps the most exciting feature of the area's cuisine is the manner in which traditional recipes are being renovated and utterly new formulae like *nouvelle cuisine* are being discovered for the age-old ingredients. San Sebastián is right now the home of all that is best in Spain's cooking and it has for some time been spreading its good influence westwards along the Cantabrian Coast.

AVILES **Asturias** ☎ (985), pop. 80,057, [i] c/ Ruiz Gómez, 21 ☎ 54 43 35, ✚ c/ Jovellanos, 1 ☎ 54 62 99, ✈ Larón-Avilés ☎ 56 17 09 and 56 51 46, 🚍 56 33 56. Gijón 25km, Oviedo 31km, Madrid 466km.

Avilés is a medieval town side by side with an industrial city. 'Dark Satanic Mills', in fact the smelters of the **ENSIDESA** steel plant, Spain's biggest, have risen up among the green hills and meadows.

🏨 **★★★ *Luzana***, c/ Fruta, 9 ☎ 56 58 40 🛏 73 **AE, DC, MC, V** $$$. Central.

🏨 **★★ *San Félix***, Av de Lugo, 48 ☎ 56 51 46 🛏 18 ✕ **P V** $$ to $$$. The **restaurant** serves excellent fish, seafood and *fabada*.

Beaches: Salinas, 5km away.

Best buys: Asturian cheeses, copper pots known as *calderillas*, ceramics from Miranda de Avilés and the typical wooden clogs called *madreñas* are all local classics. Local confectionery can be bought at *Galé*, c/ La Camora, 9.

Cultural highlights: The old quarter has arcaded streets and fine town houses —c/ de Galiana, c/ del Rivero, c/ de Bances Candamo (Sabugo). The Romanesque Church of San Nicolás, with its 14C Gothic chapel, is dedicated to the Alas family. The fountains known as the *Fuente de los Caños de San Francisco* and the *Fuente de Rivero* are also attractive. The Ceramics Museum-school, at Pl de Camposagrado, exhibits regional pottery.

Fiestas: The *Fiesta del Bollu* takes place on Easter Sunday and Monday.

Local sights: The **western coast** is exceedingly beautiful, with summer resorts like **SALINAS**, only 5km NW from Avilés (see 'Costa Verde'), offering fine **views**. The village of **PRAVIA**, 22km inland, was once the capital of the kingdom of Asturias. It stands on high ground and offers magnificent **views** from the Mirador de Monteagudo beauty spot. The *Hostal Sagrario*, c/ Valdés Bazán, 10 ☎ 82 00 38, serving fine Asturian food, is recommended.

On the town: The classic wine and **cider**-tasting and bar-hopping route follows c/ Bances Candamo, c/ Galiana, c/ Los Alas —the *Casa Alvarín* cider house is at No. 2— and Pl Carlos Lobo. *Casa Lin*, serving cider and seafood, is at Av Telares, 5. *Real Compañía Sonora y Electrónica*, at c/ González Abarca, 6, is the 'in' disco.

Sports: You can play tennis at the *Club de Tenis Avilés* ☎ 56 59 17.

BILBAO-BILBO **Vizcaya** ☎ (94), pop. 378,221, [i] Alameda de Mazarredo, s/n ☎ 424 48 19, ✉ 318 38 31, ✚ c/ General Concha, 34 ☎ 444 05 00, ✈ Sondica ☎ 453 13 50 (Iberia, c/ Ercilla, 20 ☎ 424 43 00), ⚓ Trasmediterránea, c/ Buenos Aires, 2 ☎ 442 18 50, 🚍 Abando station, c/ Hurtado de Amézaga, s/n ☎ 423 85 23 (RENFE ☎ 423 86 34/5/6). Santander 116km, San Sebastián 100km, Madrid 395km, Barcelona 607km.

A sort of Hispanic Glasgow, this city forms the industrial hub of northern Spain. Eleven kilometres inland, it straddles the Nervión river along whose banks a succession of factories and housing estates have sprung up to form **Greater Bilbao**.

Bilbao was founded in 1300 by **Diego López de Haro** and its **old quarter** is situated on the right bank of the Nervión. The left bank, with its

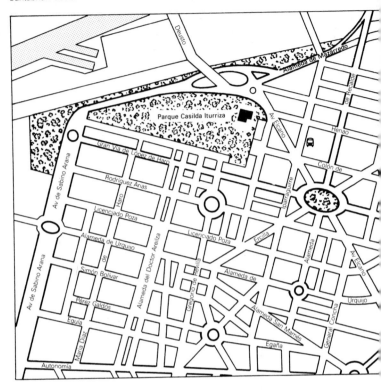

wide avenues and civic buildings (**El Ensanche**), developed rapidly in the
19C as Bilbao became a prosperous manufacturing and financial centre. The
Nervión's extremely polluted banks, upriver and down to the sea, are cluttered
with **port** docks, steel mills, factories and oil refineries. Bilbao was the
birthplace of **Miguel de Unamuno** among other literary figures (see
'Literature').

★★★★★ *Villa de Bilbao*, Gran Vía, 87 ☎ 441 60 00 🛏 142 🎤 ≈ ᛩ
AE, DC, MC, V $$$$$. Very modern.

★★★★ *Aranzazu*, c/ Rodríguez Arias, 66 ☎ 441 32 00 🛏 173 ≈ 🖼
⚓/ AE, DC, MC, V $$$$$.

★★★★ *Ercilla*, c/ Ercilla, 37 ☎ 443 88 00 🛏 350 🎤 AE, DC, V
$$$$$. The meeting point of all Bilbao's movers and shakers.

★★★★ *Husa Carlton*, Pl de Federico Moyúa, 2 ☎ 416 22 00 🛏 142 📺
🎤 AE, DC, MC, V $$$ to $$$$.

★★★ *Avenida*, Av Zumalacárregui, 40 ☎ 412 43 00 🛏 116 ♿ 🅿 ✦ MC,
V $$$ to $$$$.

★★★ *Conde Duque*, c/ Campo Volatín, 22 ☎ 445 60 00 🛏 67 🅿 ✦
🎤 $$$$.

🍴 *Begoña* (closed: Sundays and August), c/ Virgen de Begoña, s/n ☎
412 72 57 AE, DC, MC, V $$$.

🍴 *Bermeo* (closed: Sundays and holiday evenings), c/ Ercilla, 37 ☎
443 88 00 🅿 ✳ AE, DC, MC, V $$$ to $$$$. Traditional cuisine.

🍴 *Goizeko Kabi* (closed: Sundays), c/ Particular de Estraunza, 4 ☎
442 11 29 🅿 ✳ AE, DC, MC, V $$$$ to $$$$$. Always full, its bill of fare
ranges from the traditional to the revolutionary.

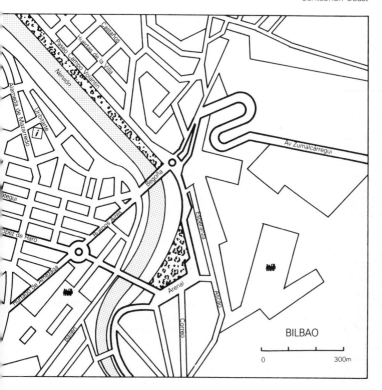

🍴 *Gredos*, c/ Alameda de Urquijo, 50 ☎ 443 50 01 **AE, DC, MC, V** $$$.
Traditional cuisine.

🍴 *Guría* (closed: Sundays), Gran Vía, 66 ☎ 441 90 13 and 441 05 43 ✳ 🌣🌣
AE, DC, MC, V $$$$ to $$$$$. A classic restaurant devoted to traditional
Basque cooking.

🍴 *Iturriaga* (closed: Sundays and August), c/ Alameda Mazarredo, 20 ☎ 🌣
423 83 90 **AE, DC, EC, V** $$$$. Luxurious, classic and sophisticated
cuisine.

🍴 *Kirol* (closed: Sundays, holidays and August), c/ Ercilla, 28 ☎ 443 70 11
$$$. Excellent hake.

🍴 *Lepanto* (closed: Sundays and holidays), Pl Egüillor, 2 ☎ 415 04 26 ♣ ✳
AE, DC, MC, V $$$.

🍴 *Machimbenta* (closed: Sundays), c/ Ledesma, 26 ☎ 424 84 95 **AE,
DC, V** $$$$. Another classic.

🍴 *Rogelio* (closed: Sundays, holiday evenings and 15/8-15/9), Ctra
Basurto-Castrejana, 7 ☎ 431 30 21 **AE, DC, MC, V** $$$. Authentic
Basque cuisine.

🍴 *Señor* (closed: Sunday evenings and 22/7-15/8) c/ General Eguía, 50
☎ 441 21 01 **AE, DC, MC, V** $$$ to $$$$. Fish, seafood and good
wines.

🍴 *Víctor* (closed: Sundays, except in May, and 1/8-15/9, except during the
fiestas week), Pl Nueva, 2 ☎ 415 16 78 **AE, DC, EC, V** $$$. Excellent
game and a good wine list.

🍴 *Zortziko* (closed: Sundays and 24/8-7/9), c/ Licenciado Poza, 54 ☎ 🌣
441 50 33 ✳ **AE, DC, MC, V** $$$ to $$$$.

Best buys: Shopping is excellent in general as befits Bilbao's solidly prosperous status. The best shops are in and around the Gran Vía and c/ Ercilla in the modern part of the city and there are also boutiques in the old quarter's pedestrian zone. Spanish fashion is available at *J. de Juana*, c/ Doctor Achúcarro, 7, *J. Bilbao*, c/ Ercilla, 29, *Tarte*, c/ Bidebarrieta, 6, *Veritas*, c/ Rodríguez Arias, 46, and *Yedra*, c/ Rodríguez Arias, 8. Splendid leather goods and clothes are sold at *Loewe*, Gran Vía, 39. The city's two important department stores are *El Corte Inglés*, Gran Vía 7-8, and *Galerías Preciados*, c/ Ercilla, 22. For furniture, typical arts and crafts go to *Artespaña*, c/ Colón de Larreategui, 45. Antiques hunters head for *C. Laucirica*, Pl San José, 3, *Crisos*, c/ Colón de Larreategui, 50, and *Don Braulio*, c/ Ledesma, 32. There are several first-class pastry shops around town; for gourmet food, go to *Au Bon Vivant*, c/ Rodríguez Arias, 59. There are also good shops in Las Arenas, and a very popular open-air market, the *mercadillo de los gitanos*, is held on Mondays and Saturdays in Algorta.

Cultural highlights: The **Museo de Bellas Artes** (Fine Arts Museum), **Parque de Doña Casilda Iturriza** (open: 10.00-1.30 and 4.30-7.30; Sundays, 11.00-2.00; closed: Mondays and holidays), has a fine **Spanish Romanesque and Gothic art** section and also a collection of 15-18C Flemish and Italian paintings. It exhibits works by El Greco, Velázquez, Ribalta, Ribera, Zurbarán and Goya in its **Spanish Old Masters** collection, and by Francis Bacon, Chillida, Gargallo, Tàpies, Vasarely, Gaugin and Picasso among others in its **Contemporary Art** section. **20C Basque artists** are well represented with works by Regoyos, Zuloaga and Iturrino among others. The **Museo Arqueológico, Etnográfico e Histórico Vasco** (Basque Archaeology, Anthropology and History Museum), c/ Cruz Conde, 4 (open: 10.30-1.30 and 4.00-7.00; closed: Sunday afternoons, Mondays and holidays) has a collection that ranges from prehistoric exhibits to items illustrating Basque folklore and craftsmanship. The Cathedral dates from the 15C but its façade was rebuilt last century. The cloister is Gothic. The Church of San Nicolás, Pl del Arenal, is a better bet for religious architecture: it is early Gothic and contains superb sculptures by Juan de Mena. The **old quarter** is a picturesque pedestrian zone that contains some interesting civic architecture such as the 19C Arriaga Theatre, the houses of the Cortázar and Salceda families and the La Ribera market.

Fiestas: Bilbao's annual blowout, known as the *Aste Nagusia* or the *Semana Grande*, takes place in the third week of August. A lot of street dancing, drinking, eating and general merrymaking goes on and there are also very good bullfights.

Local sights: Take the road along the right bank of the Nervión river and drive 17km to meet the sea at the very popular beach near the village of **Las Arenas**. The stately homes of Bilbao's super wealthy are close by in **Neguri**. From Las Arenas you can take the **hanging bridge**, built by a disciple of Eiffel and the first of its kind in the world, to cross the broadening estuary and reach the docks and harbour of **Portugalete**. From here head up to the village of **La Reineta** where you will be rewarded with an extraordinary **view** of the estuary, the smoke-belching chimney tops flanking the Nervión and Bilbao itself.

On the town: Bilbao, on the whole, goes to bed early, by Spanish standards that is. *Chiquiteo*, derived from *chiquito*, a small glass of wine, is the local term for bar-hopping and is a Basque national pastime. The old quarter is a succession of pubs and taverns which are crowded for pre-lunch aperitifs and in the evenings. There is a first-class *chiquiteo* route in the modern part of the town centre between c/ **Licenciado Poza** and c/ **Rodríguez Arias**, where top bars include *Busterri, Ganeko, Joserra, Juantxu* and *Or-Kompon*.

The best nightspots are around c/ Lersundi, c/ Heros and the Alameda de Mazarredo. *Iruña*, c/ J.F. Leguerica, 5, and the *Chaflán* pub, Jardines de Albia, 5, are very popular. Jazz and drinks are available at *Bluesville*, c/ Telesforo Aranzadi, 1. *Yoko-Lennon's*, at c/ Nicolás Alcorta, 2, is an 'in' disco. All-night ravers and early risers meet at the *Café Nervión*, by the Merced bridge, which opens at 5.00 am.

Sports: The *Athletic de Bilbao* football club, founded by Englishmen last century, is a civic institution and is passionately supported. Its ground, the San Mamés stadium, is alongside Av Sabino Arana. For golfers, the 18-hole, par 72 *Club de Campo La Bilbaína* is 14km out of town on the Bermeo road ☎ 674 08 58 and 674 04 62 (also tennis), whereas the *Real Sociedad de Golf de Neguri*, also 18 holes and par 72, is in Algorta ☎ 469 02 00/8. Sailing and water sports can be practised at the *Club Marítimo del Abra/Real Sporting Club*, Av Zugazarte, 11, El Abra, Las Arenas ☎ 463 76 00. Tennis players go to *Real Club Jolaseta*, at Guecho ☎ 460 06 00. Rowing regattas, in whaleboat-type vessels called *traineras*, take place in August and September. For jai alai go to *F.C. Deportivo*, Alameda Recalde, 28 ☎ 424 28 30.

COSTA CANTÁBRICA (CANTABRIAN COAST) ☎ (942)

This 210km-long stretch of stunningly green and pleasantly hilly coast packs a powerful ozone punch. There are a number of long, wide open and fine, sandy **beaches**. The sea can be gloriously calm for bathing and also muscular and rough. Some resorts, like Comillas, have a long-standing and family holiday tradition while others, like Laredo, are more recent but no less elegant.

SAN VICENTE DE LA BARQUERA, *i* c/ A. Garelly, 9 ☎ 71 07 97 (Santander 63km), is extremely picturesque. The village is in two parts. The upper part is the old quarter and it comes complete with a medieval castle, a colonnaded main square and the mixed Romanesque and Gothic **Church of Nuestra Señora de los Angeles**. The lower part, along the seafront, contains the more modern holiday facilities. The **beach** can be rough but is always clean. An interesting *fiesta* called *La Folía* takes place in April, on the Sunday following Easter. *Maruja*, Av Generalísimo, s/n ☎ 71 00 77 $$$ is a good place to eat. Recommended hotels are ★★ *Miramar*, Ctra del Faro, s/n ☎ 71 00 75 ⇤ 15 ♦ ⅏ ⅉ ≪ $$, peaceful and with fine views of the sea and mountains, and *Boga-Boga*, Pl José Antonio, 9 ☎ 71 01 35 ⇤ 18 $$, with a good **restaurant**.

COMILLAS, *i* c/ Aldea, 6 ☎ 72 07 68, is a beach resort with a difference and not just because it was the summer residence of King Alfonso XII. Thanks to the enthusiastic artistic patronage of the Marquis of Comillas, the town contains a number of Modernist buildings designed by turn of the century Catalan architects. They include the **Capricho** or Folly in the **Marquis' Palace** which was designed by the genius **Gaudí** himself and the cemetery that was built by his contemporary **Domènech i Montaner**. Aside from such architectural eccentricities, the town, with its lovely main square and small fishing harbour, is of picture postcard prettiness. It has a fine, clean **beach** and there is a second sandy stretch 5km away at Oyambre. *Fonda Colasa*, at c/ Antonio López, 9 ☎ 72 00 01 $$$, has good food and is set in a lovely typical building. Good hotels include ★★ *Josein*, c/ Santa Lucía, 27 ☎ 72 02 25 ⇤ 23 ⅉ ≪ $$, with first-class views of the beach and sea, and ★★★ *Casal de Castro*, c/ San Jerónimo, s/n ☎ 72 00 36 ⇤ 45 ♦ $$$, in a peaceful setting surrounded by trees.

The intimate little hamlet of Cobreces and the agreeable fishing village of SUANCES are equidistant from the superlative town of SANTILLANA DEL MAR (see separate entry). This is a fine part of the coastline that leads to the two promontories, the Cabo Mayor and the Cabo Menor, which protect the bay of **SANTANDER** (see separate entry). Beyond the Cubas estuary you can explore small secondary roads that take you through huge meadowlands that run right down to the sea shore. At **SOMO** the beach, which is very long, stretches out to sea in a long spit that is known as **El Puntal**. Three kilometres inland, at **BAREYO** there is a charming, though much restored, Romanesque church. The **beaches** of Ris (with two peaceful hotels, ★ *Montemar* ☎ 63 03 20 ⮯ 57 $ to $$, and ★ *La Encina* ☎ 63 01 41 ⮯ 50 $$) and **NOJA** are cosily protected by the small bay of Quejo and they foreshadow the much grander bay of **SANTOÑA**. After passing Colindres, which has a small fishing port, you reach **LAREDO** (see separate entry).

CASTRO URDIALES, [*i*] Town Hall ☎ 86 02 54 (Bilbao 34km, Santander 73km), known in Roman times as *Flaviobriga*, is a first-class town by any standards. It is **spectacularly situated**, has a good Gothic church and a castle in its old quarter, a fine **beach** and a superb beachfront promenade and, perhaps best of all, it has a very lively fishing port and marina, the *Club Náutico Castro Urdiales* ☎ 86 09 98. The *fiestas* known as the *Coso Blanco* (first Friday in July) include a night-time parade of floats, fireworks and a flower battle. Recommended restaurants include *Mesón El Marinero*, c/ La Correría, 23 ☎ 86 00 05 $$$ and *El Segoviano*, at No. 19, ☎ 86 18 59 $$$. For lodging, try ★★★ *Las Rocas*, Ctra Playa, s/n ☎ 86 04 04 ⮯ 621 **P** ⌕ $$$ to $$$$ and ★★ *Miramar*, on the beach ☎ 86 02 00 ⮯ 33 $$$ ⌕ ≪. The bars and discos along c/ de la Rúa are popular, as are the cafeterías *Harvey* and *Ostende*.

COSTA VASCA (BASQUE COAST) Vizcaya and Guipúzcoa.

This jagged stretch of coast, bordered on the W by the Nervión river and on the E by the Bidasoa and the frontier with France, alternates between high cliffs and peaceful bays. It is dotted all along with lovely fishing villages and is the cradle of great seamen, not least among whom was **Juan Sebastián Elcano**, the local sea dog who sailed Magellan's ships round the world.

ALGORTA, by Bilbao's estuary, has its own little fishing harbour which has friendly quayside taverns that are very lively in the evenings —★★★ *Los Tamarises*, alongside the Ereaga beach (which is as pretty as it is polluted) ☎ (94) 469 00 50 ⮯ 42 ⌕ ≪ $$$$, is a peaceful hotel with good views; it also has a fine **restaurant**. **GUECHO**, 15km from Bilbao, has a golf course (see 'Bilbao') and there are great views of the estuary from the road, especially at night when the whole sky is lit up by the red glow of the blast furnaces. The **promenade** which is almost hanging over the coast is a good place to work up an appetite with a stroll, and *Jolastoky*, Av Chopos, s/n ☎ (94) 469 30 31 $$$ to $$$$, is an elegant villa with a summer open-air terrace serving imaginative cuisine to satisfy any gourmet's hunger. In summer the people of Bilbao flock to the **beach** of **SOPELANA**, which is very beautiful but has extremely wild waves (good for surfing), and to the one at **PLENCIA**, which is altogether more peaceful, is large and well tended.

Some of the most beautiful **panoramas** of the Basque Coast are to be found along the **road** that joins the fishing and resort villages of **ARMINZA** and **BAKIO**, where the local **beach** is well cared for though bathing is somewhat dangerous at both ends. From Bakio the road climbs to present a splendid **view** of the rock known as **San Juan de Gaztelugache** and of its hermitage where a *fiesta* is held every year on Saint John's Day (June 24). The promontory known as **Cabo Machichaco** is a splendid sight and marks the western boundary of the gigantic arc of the Bay of Biscay. You are now close to the grand old fishing town of **BERMEO** which prides itself on its trawler fleet. It is very much a historical town for in its **early Gothic church**, Santa Eufemia, the medieval kings of Castile used to swear to uphold the ancient Basque privileges. But Bermeo's real claim to fame has to do with fishing and it does, in fact, have the largest trawler fleet of the whole Cantabrian coastline. Quite properly, Bermeo boasts a fishing museum, the **Museo del Arrantxale** (*arrantxale* is the Basque word for fisherman). It is located in the **Torre de Ercilla**, c/ Toorrontero Emparaza, 1 (open: 10.00-2.00 and 5.00-7.00; closed: Mondays). The fishermen's quarter along the harbour looks, feels, sounds and smells exactly as it is supposed to and it hasn't changed very much for many generations. The return of the fishing boats to port is a colourful spectacle, as is the early morning fish auction on the quayside. A hotly contested **regatta** is staged every June 22 to commemorate a historic dispute between Bermeo and the neighbouring village of Mundaca for ownership of the Isle of Izaro. Recommended restaurants include *Artxanda*, c/ Santa Eufemia, 14 ☎ (94) 688 09 30, and *Casa Pili*, Parque de Ercilla, 1 ☎ (94) 688 18 50 $$$.

Continuing E, the beach of **Mundaca**, 3km away, is good for windsurfing as long as you don't fall in near its estuary end. Much the same is true of the beaches at Pedernales and Laida by the **Guernica estuary** (see 'Guernica') a further 5km E. The next landmark is a **15C castle** at **Arteaga** which was refurbished last century to serve as a residence for the Spanish-born Empress Eugenie, the wife of Napoleon III. **Elanchove**, a sleepy little village and **Ea**, a fishing port as minuscule as its name, are the next points on the route followed by the more important town of **Lequeitio** (see separate entry). **Ondarroa**, with its steep, narrow streets, its gaily-painted wooden balconies and its busy fishing harbour belongs to the picture postcard prettiness division. Ask for *merluza a la plancha* (grilled hake) at *Penalty*, c/ Eribera, 32 ☎ (94) 683 00 00. **Motrico**, no less picturesque with its wild **Santurrarán beach** and also proud of its seafaring tradition, lies close by —for lunch, try *Mendixa*, Pl de Churruca, 13 ☎ (943) 60 34 93 $$$.

The road continues now along some spectacular **scenery** as it hugs the cliffs overlooking the sea and approaches the estuary of the Deva river. The small fishing village of **Deva** has long been favoured as a family holiday resort. Its **beach** is well tended, which compensates for the rather poor quality of the sand, and it does have a very agreeable promenade. Two architectural landmarks are Deva's church, the **Iglesia de la Asunción**, which has a Gothic façade and cloister, and the nearby **Santuario de Nuestra Señora de Iciar**, a shrine containing a 13C Romanesque figure of the Virgin. You now reach **Zumaya**, straddling the Urola estuary and hemmed in against the sea by green mountains. Like Deva, this is a fishing village that is popular with summer visitors. Its 15C church, the **Iglesia de San Pedro**, contains two beautiful triptychs. The **Villa Zuloaga**, at the entrance to the village and near the **San Sebastián beach**, is a museum dedicated to the painter **Ignacio Zuloaga**, an influential realist artist during the first half of this century, whose house it once was. The museum contains works by Zuloaga as well as pictures from his own collection including an El Greco, a Zurbarán and a Goya.

The **road** from Guetaria to Zarauz is like a balcony over the sea. When the weather is rough take care for the waves can and do come crashing onto the road. **Guetaria** is special because it was the birthplace of **Juan Sebastián Elcano**, the first man to circumnavigate the world, and it is also famous because of its *chipirones* (baby squid) and its **Txacolí**, the slightly fizzy and very dry white wine which is produced here. The town has picturesque houses, a 13C church, the **Iglesia del Salvador**, and a number of open-air fish barbecues which are very popular in the evenings. Recommended fish

🛏 grills include *Elkano*, c/ Herrerieta, 2 ☎ (943) 83 16 14 $$$$; *Kaia-Kaipe*, c/ General Arnao, 10 ☎ (943) 83 24 14 $$$ to $$$$, with good views of the port, and *Talai-Pe*, at the end of the harbour ☎ (943) 83 16 13 $$$$.

ZARAUZ (Bilbao 85km, San Sebastián 22km), i c/ Nafarroa, s/n ☎ (943) 83 90 09, is an ancient fishing village that suddenly became an aristocratic watering hole when Queen Isabella II decided to make it her summer residence last century. Today it is a cosmpolitan and well-equipped resort. The old quarter of the town boasts several **palaces** such as the 16C Marqués de Narros Palace and the 15C building known as the Torre Luzea. Its church, Santa María La Real, has a 14C belltower. It is a distinguished town, for it has numerous grand family homes and a good **beach**, although the sea can be rough and is not for the inexperienced. Facilities include a nine-hole golf course, the *Real Club de Golf de Zarauz* ☎ 83 01 45, which also has tennis courts and swimming pools.

You can stay at ★★★ *La Perla*, c/ Bizkonde, 21 ☎ (943) 83 08 00 🛏 72 AE, DC, MC, V $$$ and ★★★ *Zarauz*, Av Navarra, 4 ☎ (943) 83 02 00 🛏 82 占 **P** ♦ ☲ AE, DC, V $$$. Recommended restaurants include *Aiten*

🛏 *Etxe*, on the Guetaria road ☎ (943) 83 18 25 ≪ $$$ to $$$$ with fine views
🛏🛏 of the beach; *Karlos Arguiñano*, c/ Mendilauta, 13 ☎ (943) 83 01 78 $$$$, serving *nouvelle cuisine*, and *Otzarreta*, c/ Santa Clara, 5 ☎ (943) 85 16 19 $$$. Most of the action takes place in the bars along the c/ Mariñel, such as *Fany*. *Mimo's*, at Lonja Zaharra, is a popular disco.

ORIO (San Sebastián 20km) is particularly famous thanks to its local rowing team. The **regattas**, a local passion, involve long boats called *traineras*. Before moving on, visit Orio's old quarter and try the town's *besugo* (sea bream) at *Joshe Mari*, c/ Herriko Emparantza, s/n ☎ (943) 83 00 32
🛏🛏🛏 $$$. The road now swings inland to enter SAN SEBASTIAN (see separate
🛏 entry). If you want to visit PASAJES DE SAN JUAN and PASAJES DE SAN PEDRO, two picturesque fishing villages with an abundance of good fish restaurants, turn off the A-8 motorway following the signposts. By doing this you will
🛏 reach FUENTERRABIA (see separate entry) along the secondary road that links it to Pasajes de San Juan. This road takes you through LEZO and onto a steep climb over mount Jaizkibel, from which you can look down over the cliffs on which stand the Virgin of Guadalupe and the Higuer lighthouse that casts its beams out over the sea.

🛏🛏🛏 COSTA VERDE (GREEN COAST) Asturias ☎ (985).

This extensive stretch of rocky coastline is clearly marked into two sections, E and W, by the Cabo de Peñas headland, and it has the towering mountain range of the Cordillera Cantábrica looming over it throughout. With its deep, narrow estuaries and its small beaches, this is an astonishingly
🛏 scenic area. The **W Coast** starts at the Eo estuary and at the typical fishing village of CASTROPOL —★★★ *Palacete Peñalba*, El Muelle, s/n ☎ 62 37 60 ☲ $$$, is a good place to eat and to spend the night; ★★ *Casa Vicente*, on Ctra N-643, km362 ☎ 62 30 51 $$, offers fresh fish and seafood, as well as accommodation, at very good prices. TAPIA DE CASARIEGO is a solitary beach and small fishing harbour, where a good meal can be had at *Palermo*, c/ B. Amado, 1 ☎ 62 83 70 ≪ $$. In ORTIGUEIRA, another picturesque fishing village, you will come across the so-called *Indiano* houses which are a constant feature right across northern Spain. *Indiano*, derived from the Spanish word for the Indies, was the name given last century to emigrants returning from South America who flaunted their wealth in their home villages by building large mansions. These houses usually have tropical gardens for their owners liked to be reminded of the source of their wealth. From here the road swings inland, and then returns to the coast to reach

🌢 **LUARCA**, a very beautiful town that is **scenically set** on the estuary of the river Negro. Be sure not to bathe near the river. The whitewashed houses with their black slate roofs give Luarca a distinctive air. A special treat awaits you if you visit on August 15, when all the boats are finely decked in honour of the Virgin's *fiesta*. For lodging, try ★★★ *Gayoso*, Paseo Gómez, 4 ☎ 64 00 54 🛏 26 $$$; for eating, *Leonés*, Pl Alfonso X, s/n ☎ 64 09 95 $$$, and *Casa Consuelo*, km317 on the Santander to La Coruña road ☎ 64 08 44 $$$. Continuing on to Cudillero you pass **Cabo Vidio**, from where there are wonderful **views**, and the magnificent **Concha de Artedo beach**.

CUDILLERO is an extraordinary sight, for the village's houses cling to the sides of a gorge as if they were mussels on the rocks below. Every June 29 the fishermen and their wives perform a series of curious traditional dances, accompanied by a sing-song narrative of the main events of the past year. Try the excellent sardines in the port-side bars. Once past **SAN ESTEBAN DE PRAVIA**, a one time coaling station, the coast opens up to form **SALINAS**, the largest **beach** in Asturias. This is a stylish and well maintained resort surrounded by pine groves —a lovely **setting** indeed. *Piemonte*, at c/ Príncipe de Asturias, 74 ☎ 51 00 25 $$$, is a good restaurant; for lodging try ★ *Esperanza*, c/ Príncipe de Asturias, 31 ☎ 51 02 00 🛏 43 $$. People get together after dinner along the Paseo Marítimo at places such as *Cherry Lane*. There are very fine **views** from the crag that encloses the bay.

The **E Coast** of Asturias is less mountainous and much more accessible. In its first stretch there are numerous **beaches** such as the small one in **LUANCO**. This is a small seafaring village which boasts its own little maritime museum, the Museo Marítimo, exhibiting model ships. Recommended restaurants include *Casa Néstor*, c/ Conde del Real Agrado, 6 ☎ 88 03 15 $$$ and *Guernica*, c/ de la Riva, 20 ☎ 88 04 10 $$$. The village is well known for the knitwear hand-made by local women. **CANDAS**, the next stopping point, is very picturesque and is famous for its sardines, its seafood and fish stews and its **bullfight** held on the beach on September 14. ★★★ *Marsol*, c/ Rufo Rendueles, 1 ☎ 87 01 00 🛏 64 🅿 « AE, DC, MC, V $$$ to $$$$, is a good place to stay and enjoy the good views. If you want to taste an unforgettable *fabada* and a delicious rice pudding, head for Prendes and lunch at *Casa Gerardo* (closed: Mondays and September), on Ctra N-632, km79 ☎ 87 02 29 $$. **PERLORA**, a summer resort, **GIJON** (see separate entry) and **TAZONES** are next on the coast. You will find that there is a succession of small beaches and coves between **VILLAVICIOSA** and **RIBADESELLA** (see separate entries). A bit further on, from the village of Nueva, you can reach the **Cuevas del Mar** caves at low tide. On the way to **LLANES** (see separate entry) you pass by Barro beach and another very beautiful beach called **Playa de Celorio**. The bay of **LA FRANCA** boasts a charming beach and a relaxing hotel, the ★★ *Mirador de La Franca* ☎ 41 21 45 🛏 52 ✦ 🏖 ⚓ « 🐴 $$$. Alongside the Tina Mayor estuary, 2km from Pimiango and on the border with Cantabria, there are prehistoric cave paintings in the **Cueva del Pindal**.

COVADONGA, NATIONAL PARK OF Asturias ☎ (985), *i* Pl de la Basílica, s/n ☎ 84 60 35. Oviedo 84km, Santander 157km, Madrid 429km.

This is a gorgeous green valley in the Picos de Europa mountains, covered with oak, beech and chestnut woods. Its 16,925ha are home to ibex, deer and rare species such as the capercaillie.

The **scenically situated** national shrine called the **Basílica de Covadonga** (see 'History'), together with a monument to national hero Pelayo, was built in the last century on the spot where the Asturian warrior is said to have claimed the first Christian victory over the Moorish invaders. From

November to March, the shrine is only open at weekends and on public holidays.

🐚🐚   The **Mirador de la Reina**, 8km from the Basilica, is a magnificent spot for panoramic views of the park, but go in the morning for there can be mists in the afternoons. Four kilometres further on you reach the glacier-formed
🐚 **lakes** of Enol and **La Ercina**.

🏨 ★★★ *Pelayo* ☎ 84 60 00 ⇌ 43 **P** ✿ ≪ V $$$ to $$$$. Next to the basilica, it is the ideal place for relaxing in this bucolic setting.

Fiestas: The annual pilgrimage to the basilica takes place on September 8.

Sports: Hunting is allowed with licences. The area is great for hiking, but keep to the trekking trails because the terrain is difficult and there can be sudden mists. In the lake there is good trout fishing.

DURANGO **Vizcaya** ☎ (94), pop. 26,665. Bilbao 32km, San Sebastián 71km, Vitoria 40km, Madrid 425km.

This is the chief town of the area known as the Duranguesado, one of the most beautiful inland regions in the province of Vizcaya.

Cultural highlights: The Iglesia de Santa Ana is the church that stands beside the gateway of the same name in the old town walls, which were rebuilt in the 17C.

Local sights : Abadiano, 3km away, boasts the tower of Muntxarat dating from the Middle Ages. There are fine 18C mansions in **ELORRIO**, 9km away. The parish church here, the Iglesia de la Concepción, has a high Gothic tower and an excellent Churrigueresque altarpiece. There is a fine drive,
🐚 11km S of Durango, up to the 700m high **Urquiola mountain pass** —*Mendi Goika*, at Axpe, 9km away via Apatamonasterio ☎ 682 08 33, set in a beautiful country house but open only at weekends, is a good restaurant.

Sports: The traditional Basque game of jai alai is played at the *Ezkurdi* court, Pl Ezkurdi ☎ 681 24 41.

🐚 **FUENTERRABIA-HONDARRIBIA** **Guipúzcoa** ☎ (943), pop. 13,173, *i* Town Hall ☎ 64 23 40, ✈ 64 22 40. San Sebastián 20km, Irún-Hendaye frontier 9km, Madrid 490km.

This charming old fishing village is a busy summer resort. Its dominating feature is the castle built by the Emperor Charles V to command the frontier with France formed by the Bidasoa river. The well preserved **old quarter**, with its steep narrow streets and its fine town houses, clusters around the castle. The lower part of the town, known as **La Marina**, once the bustling fisherman's neighbourhood, has now given way to restaurants and bars, antique shops and art galleries.

🏨 ★★★ *Pampinot*, c/ Mayor, 3 ☎ 64 06 00 ⇌ 8 ⌚ ⚓ AE, DC, V $$$$$. A stunning building dating from the 17C.

🐚 🏨 ★★★ *Parador El Emperador*, Pl de Armas ☎ 64 21 40 ⇌ 16 ⌚ ≪ AE, DC, MC, V $$$$. Part of the medieval castle, where kings and queens once stayed. It has superb views from the terrace.

🍴 *Arraunlari* (closed: Sunday nights and Mondays in winter), Casa Etxealay, Paseo Butrón, 6 ☎ 64 15 81 **P** ✿ ≪ AE, MC, V $$$. Modern Basque cooking.

🍴 *Beko-Errota* (closed: at Christmas), Jauzibia district ☎ 64 31 94 **P** ✿ AE, MC, V $$$. Fish and seafood in an idyllic old farmhouse.

🐚🐚 🍴 *Roteta* (closed: Sunday nights and Thursdays except in July and August), Villa Ainara, c/ Irún, s/n ☎ 64 16 93 **P** ✿ AE, MC, V $$$ to $$$$. Modern cooking in a stylish old villa.

Beaches: Fuenterrabía's **beach** is clean and safe.

Cultural highlights: Note the wrought-iron balconies and carved wooden eaves of the town mansions in the old quarter along c/ **Mayor**, c/ Tiendas y Pampinot and c/ Obispo. The Gothic **Church of Santa María** underwent restoration in the 18C. The castle, **Castillo de Carlos V**, Pl de las Armas, was built by the emperor in the 16C using the remains of fortifications that dated from at least the 10C. It now houses a hotel belonging to the state-run Parador chain. The walls flanking the **Puerta de Santa María** gate were built in the 15C.

Fiestas: The *Alarde*, on September 8, commemorates the population's successful resistance of a French siege in 1638. People dress in historical costumes and parade around amidst much drinking, feasting and general merrymaking.

❍ **Local sights:** Cabo Higuer, a promontory with **magnificent views**, is 4km N taking the road by the harbour and the beach. Heading W out of the town along the **Jaizkíbel road**, you reach the shrine of the Virgin of Guadalupe, halfway up the Jaizkíbel mountain. There are panoramic **views** from here and there are still better ones if you push further up to the *Hostal Jaizkíbel*. If you keep on that road you will reach **PASAJES DE SAN JUAN**, 18km away. This charming fishing town had Victor Hugo as a distinguished resident during a spell of exile. He lived at No. 63 of the village's only street.

On the town: In summer this is one of the liveliest resorts on the entire Basque coast. There are a great number of bars and pubs in the marina area and along the beach. There are places along c/ Almirante Alonso, such as *Kaizar*, which attract a more select clientele; *Tapikua*, at No. 8, has a lovely terrace with good views out to sea.

Sports: Sailing and water sports are practised at the *Club Náutico de Fuenterrabía* ☎ 64 10 41. There is fishing in the Bidasoa river and golf at the 18 hole, par 72 *Real Golf Club de San Sebastián* ☎ 61 68 45.

GIJÓN **Asturias** ☎ (985), pop. 259,226, *i* c/ Marqués de San Esteban, 1 ☎ 34 60 46, ✚ 36 25 22, P 33 11 11, ✈ Larón-Avilés, 36km away ☎ 56 52 46 and 56 17 09, ⊞ RENFE ☎ 32 12 59. Oviedo 29km, Bilbao 296km, Madrid 474km.

The fourth Roman legion camped here, on the Santa Catalina peninsula, and thus founded the town. The same strip of land is now occupied by the fishermen's quarter called **Cimadevilla** and it is packed with fantastic taverns. **San Lorenzo beach** was just as lovely then as it is now albeit with no facilities. Everything else has changed. Gijón is a steel and shipbuilding centre and a major **industrial port** as well as a lively, recreational town. Over the years it has built up great leisure assets such as the *chigres* or cider bars that populate its steep narrow streets.

In summer, Gijón becomes the principal holiday centre of the Green Coast. All year round it is a busy, fairly happy-go-lucky commercial town. Modern Gijón, extending along the San Lorenzo beach is an aesthetic disaster but elsewhere the town has a good feel to it and a definite charm. Its most outstanding son was **Gaspar Melchor de Jovellanos**, the towering figure of Spain's 18C Enlightenment (see 'Literature').

▥ ★★★★ *Hernán Cortés*, c/ Fernández Vallín, 5 ☎ 34 60 00 ⇌ 109 ⅂ ⏚ AE, DC, MC, V $$$ to $$$$. Near the beach.

▥ ★★★★ *Parador El Molino Viejo*, Parque de Isabel la Católica ☎ 37 05 11 ⇌ 40 ✦ AE, DC, MC, V $$$$. Peaceful and set in a nice park.

▥ ★★★★ *Príncipe de Asturias*, c/ Manso, 2 ☎ 36 71 11 ⇌ 80 ⏚ ⚲ ≪ AE, DC, V $$$$. In San Lorenzo beach, with good views of the sea.

▥ ★★★ *Agüera*, c/ Hermanos Felgueroso, 28 ☎ 14 05 00 ⇌ 32 P AE, DC, EC, V $$$.

▥ ★★★ *Robledo*, c/ A. Truán, 2 ☎ 35 59 40 ⇌ 138 AE, DC, EC, V $$$.

❀ ❙❙ *Casa Gerardo* (closed: Mondays, except in August, and 1/9-30/9), Ctra Aviles, km10, Prendes ☎ 87 02 29 $$. This restaurant is known as the 'cathedral of the *fabada*' because it has been dishing up magnificent *fabadas*, the region's totemic bean stew, for more than 100 years.

❙❙ *Casa Tino* (closed: Thursdays and 15/6-20/7), c/ Alfredo Truán, 9 ☎ 34 13 87 **AE, V** $$$. Very popular and always crowded.

❀ ❙❙ *Casa Víctor* (closed: Thursdays, Sunday nights and 15/10-15/11), c/ Carmen, 11 ☎ 35 00 93 **AE, DC, MC, V** $$$. Fish and seafood.

❙❙ *El Retiro*, c/ Enrique Cangas, 28 ☎ 35 00 30 ✳ **AE, MC, V** $$$. Simple. There is also a bar serving cider and seafood.

❙❙ *Las Delicias* (closed: Tuesdays and August), in Somió, Barrio Fuejo, s/n 🅿 ♣ **AE, DC, MC, V** $$$ to $$$$. Elegantly furnished.

❀ ❙❙ *Los Hórreos* (closed: Mondays), in La Providencia, 5km along Av García Bernardo ☎ 33 08 98 🅿 **AE, DC, EC, V** $$$. Very good fish and seafood.

❙❙ *Zagal* (closed: Sundays and February), c/ Trinidad, 6 ☎ 35 13 98 **AE, DC, MC, V** $$$.

❀ **Beaches: San Lorenzo** is a first-class city beach. Two kilometres long, it is very sandy and has excellent facilities. It is best to avoid being close to the River Piles estuary.

Best buys: Most of the best shops are in and around c/ Corrida, c/ Moros and c/ Menéndez Valdés. The town sells good nautical gear, and handmade Asturian bagpipes are a favourite souvenir. Costume jewelry is available at *Azabache*, c/ San Antonio, 1; Spanish fashion at *M. Sol*, c/ Alfredo Truán, 8; and sportswear at *Tablas*, c/ Jovellanos, 11. The region's typical black pottery can be bought at *L. Avilés*, c/ Los Angeles, 22. Gourmet foods are available at *La Argentina*, c/ Munuza, 7 and c/ Domínguez Gil, 2.

Cultural highlights: The **old quarter**, adjoining the fishing port, has been declared an historic and artistic zone which means that its buildings and its character are protected. There are a number of fine buildings such as the 16C Valdés Palace and the 18C Nava Palace. The Plaza Mayor, though unfinished, has its charm. The home of Jovellanos, now a museum, is a key cultural outpost in the town and has a good collection of paintings and sculptures by local artists in addition to archaeological exhibits —**Casa Museo de Jovellanos**, Pl de Jovellanos, s/n (open: 10.00-1.00 and 4.00-8.00; holidays: 10.00-1.30; closed: Sundays and Mondays). The **Revillagigedo Palace**, standing on the Pl del Marqués alongside the 15C **Collegiate Church of Saint John**, has a fine Renaissance-Baroque façade built in the 17C. When strolling around the town, don't miss the impressive ❀ port of **El Musel**.

Fiestas: Asturias Day, the first Sunday in August, is celebrated with parades of floats and bands and a lot of regional dancing. There is also a well-attended International Trade Fair in August.

Local sights: Outings to the picnic areas and cider taverns among the woods and meadows of **SOMIO**, **LA PROVIDENCIA** and **CABUEÑES** are very popular. There are great trips E and W of Gijón along the Costa Verde (see separate entry). Along the old Gijón-Avilés road there are several raised wooden granaries, some dating from the 18C. Known in Spanish as *paneras* or *hórreos*, they are emblematic of Asturias and neighbouring Galicia.

On the town: In Gijón few things beat drinking and eating sardines and joining in the sing-songs in the taverns along the port. The *chigres*, cider bars, are in a different category and they, like the cider they serve, are ❀ exclusive to Asturias. Recommended *chigres* are *La Zamorana*, c/ Hermanos Felgueroso, 40, *Casa Rubiera*, c/ Asturias, 7, and *El Cartero*, c/ Cienfuegos, 30. The wine bars form a 'route' or perhaps 'crawl' of their own:

go up and down c/ Santa Lucía, c/ Santa Rosa and c/ Buen Suceso. In summer, c/ Corrida is shaded by canopies stretched over the street and it becomes a very popular **terrace**, packed with people from dusk to dawn. C/ Capua has several of the best pubs, as opposed to cider and wine taverns, in the town. The *Café Gijón*, c/ Marqués de San Esteban, 26, and the *Sed de Mal*, c/ Dindurra, 21, attract intellectuals and artists, pseudo or real, *poseurs* and watchers. *Don Giovanni*, c/ Magnus Blikstad, 13 and *Tik*, at La Guía, Ctra de Villaviciosa, are the most popular discos.

Sports: This is a sailing and fishing town, and watersport fans will be in their element —*Real Club Astur de Regatas* ☎ 34 42 02, **Club Marítimo Astur** ☎ 34 23 30, and *Federación de Submarinismo* (Scuba Diving Federation), c/ Dindurra, 20 ☎ 36 99 33. Golfers go to the 18 hole, par 68 *Club de Golf de Castiello*, at Castiello, 4km SE ☎ 36 63 13. Horseback riders head for the *Club Hípico Astur* in Gijón ☎ 37 46 11, or *El Forcon* in Castiello ☎ 54 89 16.

GUERNICA AND LUNO **Vizcaya** ☎ (94), pop. 17,936, *i* c/ Goyencalle, 8 ☎ 685 35 58, **P** 685 05 54, 🚍 Pl de la Encarnación, 7 ☎ 433 12 79, 🚃 Eusko-Trenbideala narrow gauge train service, c/ Aihuri, 8 ☎ 433 00 88. Vitoria 69km, San Sebastián 84km, Madrid 429km.

The town barely needs an introduction for it was immortalized by Picasso's *Guernica* masterpiece which currently hangs in Madrid's Casón del Buen Retiro (Prado Museum). The giant canvas is an allegorical anti-war protest that was inspired by the April 26, 1937 bombing of Guernica by the Nazi Condor Legion which fought for General Franco in the 1936-1939 Spanish Civil War. More than 2,000 died in what was the world's first experience of a blitz, a trial run for World War II. Guernica was a psychological rather than a military target for the town, founded in 1336, was the home of the old Basque assemblies which met around the ancient oak **Guernica tree**. It was there that from the 15C onwards the Kings of Spain swore to respect local Basque laws and privileges. The remains of the sacred oak tree are now covered by a small shrine alongside the reconstructed **Casa de Juntas**, the traditional Basque Assembly Hall, where there is a museum and library. The town has been rebuilt since the horror of more than half a century ago.

🍴 *El Faisán de Oro* (closed: Tuesday nights, Wednesdays and November), c/ Adolfo Urioste, 4 ☎ 685 10 01 **AE, DC, V** $$$ to $$$$. Basque-French *nouvelle cuisine*.

Beaches: Pedernales (9km away) and Laida (12km away) are spacious and clean. Laida is especially good for windsurfing.

Best buys: Wooden handicrafts are the town's speciality.

Fiestas: A regional crafts fair involving jai alai and other rural Basque sports competitions is held on the last Monday of October.

Local sights: Guernica's surroundings are really very beautiful. Villages such as Mundaca, Pedernales —recommended restaurant: *Zaldúa*, c/ Sabino Arana, 10— and Busturia are stunningly set amidst the meadows and the sea. Taking the road to Elanchove on the other side of the estuary, you reach the **Cuevas de Santimamiñe** caves (open: 10.00-12.00 and 4.00-7.00; closed: weekends and Mondays) containing Stone Age cave paintings and splendid **stalagmites**. An 18km drive S of Guernica takes you to the so-called **Biscay Balcony**. There is a marvellous **panoramic view** from here of the patchwork of fields and forests that are so characteristic of the region. It is a mosaic in green.

Sports: *Pelota* or jai alai, the Basque national sport, is played at the *Frontón Jai Alai*, c/ Janioti, 14 ☎ 685 02 00.

IRUN **Guipúzcoa** ☎ (943), pop. 54,524, *i* Puente de Santiago ☎ 62 22 39 and at the Estación del Norte ☎ 61 15 24, 🚌 RENFE ☎ 61 67 08 and 61 12 56 (Autoexpreso). San Sebastián 20km, Bayonne (France) 34km, Madrid 509km.

Almost wholly reconstructed after the Spanish Civil War when it was badly shelled, Irún has had its ups and downs thanks to its border location. The **Isla de Los Faisanes** in the middle of the Bidasoa river that forms the frontier between Spain and France has a well deserved place in history books. A keynote peace agreement, the Treaty of the Pyrenees, was signed on it in 1659, putting an end to a period of constant warfare between the two nations.

🏨 ★★★ *Alcázar*, Av Iparralde, 11 ☎ 62 09 00 🛏 48 **P** ✦ **AE** $$$. Just off the town centre.

🍴 *Jaizubía* (closed: Mondays and February) Urdanibia, on the Fuenterrabía to San Sebastián road ☎ 61 80 66 **P** ✦ **AE, DC, MC, V** $$$ to $$$$. *Nouvelle cuisine.*

🍴 *Mertxe* (closed: Sunday nights, Wednesdays and 20/3-20/4), c/ Francisco Gainza, 7 ☎ 62 46 82 **P** ✦ **AE, DC, MC, V** $$$. French cuisine.

Beaches: Fuenterrabía beach is 8km away.

Best buys: The Paseo de Colón is the main shopping street. Look out for the addictive local chocolates, and if you are after hand-crafted wooden objects, head for *Alberti*, c/ Descarga, 6.

Cultural highlights: The **Ermita de Santa Elena** is the oldest shrine in the Basque Country and was built over a pre-Roman burial ground. Remains unearthed there have identified the spot as the Roman border settlement of *Oiarso*. It has a small archaeological museum.

Fiestas: The Duke of Wellington's victory at the Battle of San Marcial, fought close by, put an end to the Peninsular War. The *Alarde de San Marcial* is suitably celebrated every June 30 with cannon salvos, fireworks, street dancing and parades.

Local sights: The **Ermita de San Marcial**, 3km in the direction of Behobia, is not every Frenchman's favourite picnic spot. From the shrine you have a fine **view** of the battlefield where the French were beaten in 1521 and again in 1813 at the end of the Peninsular War.

Sports: Jai alai is played at the *Frontón Uranzu*, Pl de Urdanibia, and golf at the 18 hole, par 72 *Club de Golf de Urdanibia* ☎ 61 68 45.

LAREDO **Cantabria** ☎ (942), pop. 12,963, *i* c/ López Sena, s/n ☎ 60 54 92, ✚ 60 51 04. Santander 49km, Bilbao 58km, Madrid 427km.

The population of this resort town, scenically located on the Bay of Santoña, almost tenfolds to 120,000 in summer. The holidaymakers take up residence among the apartment blocks and the neon lights of the modern part of Laredo, along the **beach**. The old quarter, bunched around the fishing harbour and banked up against the hillside, dates from the Middle Ages.

🏨 ★★★ *Cosmopol* (open: 15/6-15/9 and Easter), Av de la Victoria, s/n ☎ 60 54 00 🛏 60 **P** ✦ ⟰ ⊼ ≪ **AE, DC, EC, V** $$$. Good views.

🏨 ★★★ *El Ancla*, c/ González Gallego, 10 ☎ 60 55 00 🛏 25 **P** ✦ 🎤 🐌 ⊼ ⊲ **AE, V** $$$. A peaceful hotel with a large garden, near the beach.

🏨 ★★★ *Risco*, c/ La Arenosa, 2 ☎ 60 50 30 🛏 25 **P** ✦ 🐌 ≪ **AE, DC, MC, V** $$$. Magnificent views of the town and bay from up here. The **restaurant** serves regional cuisine. The town's local cheese fair is held here in April.

🍴 *Mesón del Marinero*, c/ Eguilior, s/n ☎ 60 60 08 ✦ **AE, V** $$$. Fish and seafood.

❙❙ *Risco*, c/ La Arenosa, 2 ☎ 60 50 30 **P ♣ AE, MC, V** $$$ to $$$$.

Beaches: There is no trouble in locating the **beach** here; it is huge and also very well kept.

Best buys: People go for the local Cantabrian cheeses, like **Picón, Lebeña** or **Aliva**, which are often difficult to find elsewhere, and Laredo stages a regional cheese fair to make things easier in March and April.

Cultural highlights: The 13C church, the **Iglesia de la Asunción**, has very beautiful capitals, a Flemish altarpiece and massive bronze lecterns that were a gift to the parish from the Emperor Charles V. The oldest part of the town, called **Puebla Vieja**, has narrow cobblestone streets that have remained pretty much unchanged for at least 500 years.

Fiestas and festivals: There are sea-borne religious processions on June 16 in honour of the Virgin of Mount Carmel, who is revered by fishermen. A popular **flower battle** takes place on the last Friday of August, and there are classical music concerts and ballet productions during the summer months of July and August.

Local sights: SANTOÑA, on the other side of the bay, is an important fishing port and it has an interesting Romanesque-Gothic **church**, Santa María del Puerto, which was last reformed in the 18C. **COLINDRES** is a peaceful fishing port which has not been spoilt by the holiday houses that have been built there. Going inland, along the Asón river, you reach **LIMPIAS**. A figure of Christ, *El Cristo de las Lágrimas*, attributed to Juan de Mena and said to be miraculous, is venerated in the village's Renaissance church. Continuing a further 4km along a sinuous road you reach a shrine, the **Santuario de la Bien Aparecida**, where the Baroque image of the Virgin has been venerated since 1605. The **views** from here over the Ansó valley are particularly good.

On the town: The Puebla Vieja and modern Laredo have as many bars, pubs and restaurants as one could wish for. *Oliver*, at c/ Gutiérrez Rada, s/n, and *Garras* in Colindes are popular discos.

Sports: There are three marinas —Colindres, Santoña and Laredo— and also a yacht club, the *Club Náutico de Laredo* ☎ 60 58 12, where sailing —the stretch of coast between Laredo and Santander is especially good for **light sailing** and **cruising**— and windsurfing classes are given. There is also salmon fishing along the Ansó for those equipped with the necessary permits and licences.

LEQUEITIO-LEKEITIO Vizcaya ☎ (94), pop. 7,314, ⚓ Port ☎ 684 05 00. Bilbao 59km, San Sebastián 61km, Madrid 452km.

Queen Isabella II put the town on the resort map when she spent a few summer sojourns here in the 19C. But Lequeitio has been very much a seaman's town from time immemorial: the island of San Nicolás turns the bay into a naturally protected harbour and Lequeitio is home to a considerable number of the coast's trawler vessels.

▦ ★★ *Beitia*, Av Pascual Abaroa, 25 ☎ 684 01 11 ⇤ 30 ✕ ♣ **AE, V** $$$. Unfussy.

Beaches: There is a **beach** opposite the harbour, but the **Carraspio** beach, along the bay, is safer. There is good swimming at Ondárroa, 12km E, at the well kept Arringorri and the **Saturrarán** beaches.

Cultural highlights: The 15C **Church of Santa María** is an example of Basque Gothic and it boasts a fine flamboyant Gothic **altarpiece** in the third chapel of the right nave.

Fiestas: On June 29, the feastday of Saints Peter and Paul, a curious folk dance called the *Kaxarranca* takes place which involves a highly skilled dancer leaping about on top of a sort of trunk carried shoulder-high by eight hefty local lads. The town's better known bash is the controversial goose *fiesta* that takes place during the first week of September. A goose is hung up over the harbour and youths leap from rowing boats to grab its neck. Goose and youth are then dunked into the water by a system of pulleys until the youth lets go or until the goose's neck comes off. It is not for the squeamish.

☉☉ **Local sights:** There are fine scenic views all around here of the **Basque Coast**. Going W to **ISPASTER** you arrive at a good restaurant, *Arropain* (closed: Wednesdays and 15/12-15/1), Barrio Arropain ☎ 684 03 13 **P** ✦ **AE, DC, MC, V** $$$, which has a very good wine list.

Sports: Deep-sea fishing boats dock at the quayside and enthusiasts belong to the *Club de Pesca de Atún*, a tuna fishing society ☎ 684 05 00.

LLANES **Asturias** ☎ (985), pop. 13,801, *i* c/ N. Sobrino, 11 ☎ 40 01 64. Santander 96km, Oviedo 113km, Madrid 453km.

Llanes is a very peaceful, and scenic, resort-cum-fishing village. The **Paseo de San Pedro** promenade along the clifftop offers good views of the area. There are a number of houses here built by the so-called *Indianos*, the returning emigrants who had made their fortunes in Latin America.

▦ ★★★ *Don Paco* (open: 1/4-31/11), Parque de Posada Herrera, s/n ☎ 40 01 50 ⇌ 42 **P** ✦ ⌟ **AE, DC, EC, V** $$$.

▦ ★★★ *Montemar*, c/ Jenaro Riestra, s/n ☎ 40 01 00 ⇌ 41 **P** ⌟ « **AE, DC, EC, V** $$ to $$$. Next to the beach.

🍴 *La Bolera* (closed: Wednesdays except at Easter and in summer), Muelle, s/n ☎ 40 13 36 **P** ✳ **V** $$$. Eat good fish and seafood while enjoying the views of the port.

Beaches: There are a number of beaches, among them the tiny **El Sablón**, surrounded by greenery.

Cultural highlights: The 14C **Church of Santa María** and the remains of the town's 13C **walls** are interesting. The *Indiano* houses are in all styles, from the tasteful folly to the ostentatious kitsch.

Fiestas: On July 16 the feastday of San Roque is celebrated with ancient dances (like the ***Pericote*** and the ***Peregrina***) whose origins are unclear and which are unique to the village.

☉☉☉ **Local sights:** The **Costa Verde** (see separate entry).

Sports: Underwater sports activities can be practised off the Llanes and the Cabo Vidiago coasts.

OÑATE-OÑATI **Guipúzcoa** ☎ (943), pop. 10,440. Vitoria 45km, San Sebastián 74km, Madrid 401km.

The town of Oñate is redolent with memories of the 19C civil wars in Spain that were known as the Carlist wars after their chief instigator, Carlos the pretender to the throne. The town was his headquarters until he surrendered in 1839 to troops loyal to Queen Isabella II. Set now in a heavily industralized area, Oñate was already prosperous in the 16C and as a result it boasts arguably the best collection of fine buildings in the province of Guipuzcoa.

🍴 *Txopekúa* (closed: Wednesday evenings, 1/2-15/2 and 1/8-15/8), Ctra Aránzazu, km2 ☎ 78 05 71 **V** $$$.

Cultural highlights: The old **University** was founded in 1522 but was finally closed down at the turn of the present century. It has a fine Renaissance façade and a **quadrangle** in the Plateresque style. Ask at the Town Hall for permission to visit it. The 15C Gothic **Church of San Miguel** has later Baroque additions. Its lovely Plateresque cloister and its Renaissance Piedad Chapel are worth visiting. The **Town Hall** is a good example of 18C Baroque civic architecture and the **old quarter** of the town is full of noble houses and churches.

Fiestas: The **Corpus Christi** day processions, celebrated all over Spain, here have the special characteristic of incorporating dances that date from the 16C.

🌣 **Local sights:** The modern shrine of **Arantzazu**, 9km S, is surrounded by high peaks in a wonderful **setting**. You reach it by driving along a **road** that leads up narrow gorges, and if you arrive in time for the 11.00 Sunday High Mass you will be able to hear the magnificent choir of the Franciscan friars. The shrine boasts a set of sculptures of the *Apostles* by the contemporary Basque artist Jorge de Oteiza.

OVIEDO **Asturias** ☎ (985), pop. 195,651, *i* c/ Cabo Noval, 5 ☎ 21 33 85 and c/ Hermanos Pidal, 32 ☎ 23 05 33, ✉ c/ Alonso Quintanilla, s/n ☎ 21 26 72 and 21 41 86, ✚ c/ Martínez Vigil, 36 ☎ 21 54 47, **P** 22 26 40, ✈ Larón-Avilés, 47km ☎ 56 17 09 (Iberia, c/ Uría, 21 ☎ 24 02 50), 🚌 Pl de Rivera, 1 ☎ 28 12 00, 🚂 RENFE, c/ Uría, s/n ☎ 24 33 64 (Narrow Gauge Train Service ☎ 21 90 26). Gijón 27km, Bilbao 306km, Santander 203km, Madrid 451km.

Oviedo is essentially a modern town with wide avenues and well-appointed parks. It is the capital of the Asturias region which is a major coal mining and steel manufacturing centre, and it has an immediate look of solid prosperity about it. The first appearance is however deceptive for Oviedo is an extremely old town. It was the seat of the first Christian kings of Spain who began slowly to push back the Moorish invaders in what was to be that long chapter of Spanish history, from the 8-15C, known as the *Reconquista* or Reconquest. Hidden inside Oviedo, around the cathedral and deep inside the old quarter, there are historical buildings aplenty. If you really want to penetrate Oviedo's façade you could do worse than to read *La Regenta* (Penguin Books), the outstanding Spanish 19C novel by Leopoldo Alas, who wrote under the pen name of *Clarín*. The novel is set in what Clarín calls the town of Vetusta but which was recognizable then, and remains so now, as Oviedo. All life and humanity are in that novel.

Oviedo was much visited by the medieval pilgrims on their way to the shrine of Santiago de Compostela in Galicia, and its treasures were, as a result, well known in Medieval Europe. What you have now are the vestiges of the Asturian pre-Romanesque that so impressed them then and a collection of art and architecture which has accrued since those early days.

🏨 ★★★★★ *Reconquista*, c/ Gil de Jaz, 16 ☎ 24 11 00 🛏 142 ♨ 🖥 AE, DC, MC, V $$$$$. A very central, beautiful 18C building.

🏨 ★★★★ *Gran Hotel España*, c/ Jovellanos, 2 ☎ 22 05 96 🛏 89 AE, DC, EC, V $$$$.

🏨 ★★★★ *La Jirafa*, c/ Pelayo, 6 ☎ 22 22 44 🛏 89 ♨ AE, MC, V $$$$. Central.

🏨 ★★★★ *Ramiro I*, Av Calvo Sotelo, 13 ☎ 23 28 50 🛏 83 ♨ AE, DC, MC, V $$$ to $$$$. Modern.

🏨 ★★★★ *Regente*, c/ Jovellanos, 31 ☎ 22 23 43 🛏 88 **P** ♨ AE, DC, MC, V $$$$. Central.

🏨 ★★★ *La Gruta*, c/ Alto de Buenavista, s/n ☎ 23 24 50 🛏 55 **P** ≪ AE, DC, MC, V $$$. On the exit road to Galicia, with nice views and a very good **restaurant** that has become a classic $$$.

🏨 ★★★ *Principado*, c/ San Francisco, 6 ☎ 21 77 92 🛏 66 AE, DC, MC, V $$$.

🍴 *Casa Conrado* (closed: Sundays and August), c/ Argüelles, 1 ☎ 22 39 10 ✳ AE, DC, MC, V $$$. Traditional.

🍴 *Casa Fermín* (closed: Sunday nights), c/ San Francisco, 8 ☎ 21 64 52 ✳ MC, V $$$ to $$$$. *Nouvelle cuisine* Asturian-style.

¶ *Del Arco* (closed: Sundays and August), Pl de América, 1 ☎ 25 55 22 **AE, DC, MC, V** $$$$. Innovative cuisine.

☻ **¶ *La Goleta*** (closed: Sundays and July), c/ Covadonga, 32 ☎ 22 07 73 **AE, DC, MC, V** $$$$.

¶ *La Máquina* (closed: Sundays and 23/7-15/8), in Lugones, 6km on the old Avilés road ☎ 26 00 19 **P** $$$. Splendid helpings of *fabada*, the rich, local bean stew, and excellent rice pudding.

¶ *Marchica*, c/ Doctor Casal, 8 ☎ 21 30 27 **AE, DC, MC, V** $$$. Specializes in fish.

☻☻ **¶ *Trascorrales*** (closed: 15/8-31/8), Pl de Trascorrales, 19 ☎ 22 24 41 **AE, MC, V** $$$$. A pleasantly rustic setting for a mix of traditional and modern food.

☻ **Beaches: San Lorenzo,** in Gijón, 27km away, and **Salinas,** 38km away.

☻ **Best buys:** The top shops —**Artespaña** (lovely traditional crafts), *Galerias Preciados* (department store), **Veneto** (shoes), *Zara* (cheap and cheerful clothes) and the rest— are on c/ Uria and in the *Hotel Reconquista* area. As you might expect, art galleries and arts and crafts shops are to be found in

☻ the old quarter. **F. Prieto,** c/ Jovellanos, 5, is an excellent leather craftsman; for more of the same, go to **M. Blanco,** c/ M. Pedregal, 5. The objects made of jet are especially interesting and you can learn more about them at the **F. Escandón García** workshop in Av Galicia, 3, 4°. The Fontán market is a good place to acquire the wooden clogs locally known as *madrueñas,* and cider lovers shop at *Vetusta,* c/ Magdalena, 15. Spanish fashion is available at **Fortunata,** c/ Marqués de Teverga, 4, and **Valtueña,** c/ General Yagüe, 4, and c/ Gil Jaz, 3; costume jewelry at **Cabala,** c/ Palacio Valdés, 1.

Cultural highlights: Allow at least two hours to visit the **old quarter**. The starting point is, quite obviously, the **Cathedral** which was begun in 1388 in the flamboyant Gothic style and was finally triumphantly completed with a tower nearly 200 years later in 1565. Its major features include the huge **reredos** in polychromed wood behind the high altar, the beautiful ogival vaults in the **cloister** and the **Chapel of Alfonso II**, the Chaste, which is the royal pantheon of the kings of Asturias of a millennium ago. The oldest part of the cathedral is the **Cámara Santa** or Holy Chamber which is a pre-Romanesque building that was restored in the 12C. Unfortunately it was blown up during a 1934 insurrection by the region's miners and it was later rebuilt after the Spanish Civil War. The **Treasure chamber** contains valuable exhibits of relics and church ornaments which certainly amazed the medieval pilgrims to Compostela (open: 10.15-1.00 and 4.00-7.00; closed: Sunday mornings and holidays). At the entrance to the chamber there is a set of remarkable 12C **statues** of the Twelve Apostles that were sculpted to serve as columns.

The **Church of San Tirso** in the cathedral square dates from the 9C but subsequent restorations and additions have meant that little is left of the orginal pre-Romanesque edifice save the apse window. The **Casa de la Rúa**, built in the 15C, is the oldest civic building in the town. The learned cleric, **Padre Feijoo**, who was one of the key figures of Spain's 18C Enlightenment, wrote a good deal of his extensive work in his cell in the nearby Monastery of San Vicente (16-17C). He would no doubt have approved of the building's present use as an Archaeological Museum, the **Museo Arqueológico**, c/ San Vicente, 3 (open: 11.30-1.30 and 4.00-6.00; Sundays and holidays: 11.00-1.00; closed: Mondays). The museum has prehistoric exhibits and is a good introduction to the anthropology of the region. Its real strength is, however, its collection of pre-Romanesque Asturian art. Alongside the museum stands another religious building, the **Convent of San Pelayo**, built in the 17C, and from here you should start wandering towards the Plaza Mayor to gain the feel of the old and historic quarter. You will be walking along c/ Canónigo, c/ San Antonio and c/ Cimadevilla. On your way you will pass the severe-looking **old University** —building began on it in the 15C and continued until the 17C. The building's chief feature is its Neoclassical, and later restored, cloister. You will cross the **Pl de Porlier** which is graced by two fine palaces, the Palacio de Toreno, built in the 17C, which today serves as a library, and the 18C Camposagrado Palace, distinguished by enormous eaves, and presently used as the home of the region's High Court.

The **Pl del Fontán** is delightful. Its porches are busy and crowded on Thursdays and on Sundays when market stalls are set up between the colonnades. On its S front stands the 18C Baroque Palace of the Marqués de San Feliz.

Landmarks in the modern part of the city include the 9-10C **Foncalda Fountain** in the street of the same name and the very fine building that was, 200 years ago, the **Royal Hospice**, a hospital and home for down and outs and is now the very luxurious *Hotel Reconquista*. The large Baroque **shield** on the main façade survived the metamorphosis and is very lovely. The **Parque de San Francisco**, with its trees and fountains, is as good a piece of green real estate as any city could wish for. Its lushness could owe something to the fact that it was originally the large and carefully tended kitchen garden of a Franciscan monastery, hence the park's name. One of the sights in today's ornamental gardens is the **Romanesque archway** that was once the entrance to a church dedicated to Saint Isidore, that has long since disappeared. One old church that does remain is the 9C pre-Romanesque **San Julián de los Prados** on the edge of the city. It is only just still with us for its extremely interesting frescoes, for example, were badly damaged by construction work on the Gijón-Oviedo motorway. The local Fine Arts Museum, the Museo de Bellas Artes de Asturias, c/ Santa Ana, 1 (open: 11.30-1.30 and 5.00-8.00; Sundays and holidays: 12.00-2.00; closed: Mondays), stands in what was once the Velarde Palace, built in the 18C. The gallery concentrates on local painters and sculptors from the last century to the present.

Fiestas and festivals: The celebrations in honour of **San Mateo**, on or around September 21, include bullfights, funfairs and concerts. On September 19, there is a special *fiesta* dedicated to **Latin America** which involves a sort of Columbus Day parade. An **opera season** opens at the end of September and a regional music and dance festival is staged in May-June.

Local sights: Just 4km along the Ctra de los Monumentos take you 600m up to the peak of **Monte Naranco** and to a **great view** of Oviedo and of the towering Picos de Europa mountain range. NW of here stand two extraordinary remnants of the pre-Romanesque hour of Asturian glory. The 9C **Santa María del Naranco** was built as a summer residence for King Ramiro I, and he had every reason to be pleased with it for it is a charmingly harmonious construction with delightful balconies, blind arches and lovely reliefs in the interior (open in winter: 10.00-1.00; from 1/4-30/9: 10.00-1.00 and 4.00-7.00). **San Miguel de Lillo** is interesting for its stone framed windows, its Classical decoration and Mozarabic-style paintings.

On the town: The typical taverns and cider halls, called *chigres*, are mostly to be found in the old quarter, and while everyone has his favourite, a list of the most popular over the years would have to include *El Ferroviario*, c/ Gascona, 5, *El Cantábrico*, c/ Río San Pedro, 11, and *Ovetense*, c/ San Juan, 8. The tavern hopping crowds also congregate around c/ Mon, c/ de la Rúa, c/ Altamirano, Pl del Paraguas, and Pl del Fontán. C/ Rosal is also favoured for its wine cellars and its *tapas*, and *Cabo Peñas*, c/ Melquíades Alvarez, 24 has earned a following with the originality of its snacks. Later into the night the drinkers and chatters of café society move on to places such as *El Paraguas*, Pl del Paraguas, and *Xuantipa*, Callejón de San Tirso. *Factory*, Pl Riego, is more modern and elegant. There are a number of disco-bars and video-pubs, and a short list would include *Chaquetón*, c/ Gonzalo Besada, 8, *New York, New York*, c/ 19 de julio, 6, and *Nero* at No. 10. *La Real* c/ Cervantes, and *Pasarela*, Viaducto Marquina, are popular discos.

Sports: The local football team plays at the Carlos Tartiere stadium and the town's indoor sports centre is in the Barrio de Ventanielles. There are tennis courts at the *Centro Asturiano de Oviedo* ☎ 29 52 06. The nearest golf course is in Siero, 1km away, at the *Centro Deportivo La Barganiza* ☎ 25 63 61 (18 holes, par 72), while the closest ski resort is *Valgrande-Pajares* (1,366-2,100m), 60km on the N-630 ☎ (985) 49 61 23, with 13 lifts, 18 ski runs and good facilities. Oviedo, close as it is to the Picos de Europa mountain range, has enthusiastic trekkers and climbers who mostly belong to the *Federación Asturiana de Montañismo* (Asturian Mountaineering Federation), c/ Melquíades Alvarez, 16 ☎ 21 10 99. Gliding, hang-gliding and ultra-light aircraft facilities are available at the Llanera aerodrome, 9km N.

PICOS DE EUROPA Asturias, Cantabria, León. *i* c/ Emilio Laria, 2 (Cangas de Onís) ☎ (985) 84 80 43 and c/ Mayor, s/n (Panes) ☎ (985) 41 40 48.

This magnificent stretch of high mountain, with peaks that top the 2,500m ceiling, offers the visitor one of the most unique landscapes in Europe. This massive slab of grey limestone forms, both geologically and botanically, quite a separate entity within the mountain range, known as the

Cordillera Cantábrica, that runs along the N of Spain. It starts in the W with the valley of the Sella river and it tapers off in the E into what is called the Liébana trough. Glaciers, thousands of years ago, did an extraordinary job here shaping gigantic walls and summits that are inaccessible to all but the truly expert and carving out huge gorges and canyons. There are three distinct parts to the Peaks of Europe. The western area lies almost totally within Asturias between the Sella and the Obra rivers in the W and the Cares river in the E. Its highest mountain is the Peña Santa de Castilla, meaning the Holy Peak of Castile, which rises up to 2,596m and virtually all of this area forms part of the **Covadonga National Park** (see separate entry). The central part of the Picos is the most abrupt, barren and rough of all. One sheer rock face here, a really huge one, is called the **Naranjo de Bulnes** and it is one of the most seductive and feared climbs for Spain's top rock climbers. The easier and less intimidating part of the Picos is its easternmost sector bordered to the E by the Deva river. This part lies within Cantabria and it forms the **Saja National Reserve**.

The vegetation is mostly shrubs, gorse and brushwood with alpine meadowlands that explode with colour in spring further down the slopes below the 1,500m line. The contrasts between the green and grey where the flora thins out is always pleasing.

Summer is certainly the ideal time to visit these mountains. Take a map and work out your own route. A four wheel drive car can take you well into them and bring you near the mountain huts that dot the range far from human habitation. You can hire rough-country vehicles at Arenas de Cabrales, Espinama, La Hermida, Potes and Sotres.

Taking **PANES** (Asturias), [i] ☎ (985) 41 40 78, as your starting point, going S, pass through the **Desfiladero de la Hermida**, a 20km gorge formed by the Deva river, to reach the cherry and almond trees and vines of the area called **La Liébana**. The architecural landmark here is the **10C Mozarabic monastery** of Santa María de Lebeña. **POTES** is a delightful village of old farmhouses along the banks of the Deva, surrounded by stunning **scenery**. There is an eye-catching 15C defence tower in the village square. You can spend the night in ★★ ***La Cabaña***, c/ La Molina, s/n ☎ (942) 73 03 15 🛏 24 ≪ **V** $$, which is peaceful and has good views, and *Martín*, c/ Roscabao, s/n ☎ (942) 73 00 25 $$, provides a wholesome meal. Local cheeses called Aliva and Picón can be bought in the village. The **Monastery of Santo Toribio de Liébana**, originally 7C but rebuilt in the Gothic style, is 5km away. It is a special place for it was there that a near contemporary of the Venerable Bede, the **Beato de Liébana**, wrote an illuminated and celebrated ***Commentary on the Apocalypse*** in 786. It is quite proper to think that he was inspired by the vistas that surrounded him.

The tiny and charming hamlet of **COSGAYA** is the stuff of legends. It is supposed to have been the birthplace of the Christian warrior King Pelayo, and also the place where the 8C king of Asturias, Favila, was killed by a bear while hunting. You will hear about it if you dine and sleep at the Bear's Tavern, the ***Mesón del Oso*** ☎ (942) 73 04 18, a peaceful mountain inn. From Espinama, you can drive in a jeep up to the Aliva mountain shelter and on as far as Poncebos. **FUENTE DE** is 1,070m high and on the edge of a glacial ring. A **cable car** takes you up a further 800m where the **view** is everything and more than you imagined it to be. The ★★★ ***Parador del Río Deva*** ☎ (942) 73 00 01 🛏 78 ≪ **P** $$$ to $$$$, is superbly located and is a haven of calm and quiet. It has magnificent views of the area.

Approaching the Picos from the S the first stop is probably the **Mirador de Llesba**, a lookout point which you reach by turning off at the mountain pass of **San Glorio** which is 1,609m high. There are more great views from the **Puerto de Pandetrave** pass (1,562m) and, continuing in the same vein, even more stunning scenery awaits you if you turn off at the **Puerto de Panderruedas** (1,450m) to reach the **Mirador de Piedrafitas**. From this lookout you can see the highest peak of the range, the 2,648m-high Torre de Carredo. After crossing the **Puerto del Pontón** (1,290m) you descend into the Sajambre valley.

You will be able to take in the breathtaking beauty of this valley from the **Mirador de Oseja de Sajambre** before entering a 10km gorge, the **Desfiladero de los Beyos**, that the Sella river has created. There are really **wild ravines** at the point where the Sella meets the Ponga river. With the Picos now behind you, you have reached the endearing town of **CANGAS DE ONIS**, *i* c/ Emilio Laria, 2 ☎ (985) 84 80 45, which was actually the capital of Asturias in the 8C. You can cross the raging Sella by a Gothic bridge, cast your eyes over the typical raised granaries called *hórreos*, see the dolmen of Santa Cruz, and sleep or eat or do both at ★★ *Casa Ventura*, Av Covadonga, s/n ☎ (985) 84 82 00 $$$.

Paleolithic caves, the **Cueva del Buxu**, with cave paintings within, form the local attraction just 2km away following the Cares river towards Panes. Covadonga (see separate entry) lies to the SE. The awesome **scenery** does not let up as you pass through Estazas and there is a definite bonus awaiting you at **ARENAS DE CABRALES** if you happen to be a lover of strong blue cheese: this is the home of Cabrales cheese, pungently delicious and wrapped in vine leaves —the Cabrales Cheese Fair is held during the last week of August. A scenic **gorge** takes you from here to Poncebos where an 11km path —hire a jeep if you are not up to trekking— takes you to Caín at the foot of the central section of the Picos by way of the **Cares canyon**.
Sports: In the Picos de Europa National Reserve, holders of sparingly and expensively distributed licences can hunt the ibex mountain goat, deer and wild boar. The same applies to the salmon and trout fishing, especially along the Cares river ☎ (985) 22 27 48. There are endless possibilities for trekking and climbing, and there is skiing at the *Alto Campoo* ski resort (see 'Reinosa'). Horseback riders take note that there are organized one-day and weekend riding tours from Potes ☎ (942) 73 04 72 and from Arenas de Cabrales, *Camping Naranjo de Bulnes* ☎ (985) 85 51 78.

REINOSA **Cantabria** ☎ (942), pop. 13,151, *i* Pl de España, 5 ☎ 75 02 62. Santander 74km, Burgos 116km, Madrid 355km.

Here you meet the Ebro river, Spain's longest, in its infancy, for its source is just 5km away in Fontibres. Reinosa is the chief town of the region known as Campoo and although its old stone houses, with their heraldic shields, lend a Cantabrian feel to Reinosa it is set in what is quite clearly Castilian countryside. Reinosa has seen better times, even splendid ones in the 18C for it was a vital communications link between Castile and the Cantabrian sea. Today it is industrialized but saddled with loss-making plants and uncertain about its future development.

▦ ★★★ *Vejo*, Av de Cantabria, 15 ☎ 75 17 00 ⊨ 71 **P** ✦ ⬤ ≪ AE, DC, V $$ to $$$. Modern and popular with skiers. The **restaurant** serves excellent meat.
Best buys: Good local pastries are available from *Casa Vejo*, c/ Generalísimo, 32.
Cultural highlights: The 18C Church of San Esteban with its Baroque altarpieces, the porticoed main square and the Convent of San Francisco, with its severe façade in the style that came to be known as Herreriano after the architect Juan de Herrera, are interesting.
Fiestas: Campoo Day is celebrated on the last Sunday of September and is a

good opportunity to witness local folk customs. On Saint Sebastian's feastday, January 20, part of the fun consists of receiving free wine and pastries.

Local sights : The **Alto Campoo** (High Campoo), going W, is well named for the mountains here are above the 2,000m level. From the village of **FONTIBRE**, several paths lead to the source of the Ebro river. In winter you can take a ski lift up to the top of the **Pico de Tres Mares** (2,175m). The name means the Peak of the Three Seas which is apt for three rivers are born here, which eventually flow into the Cantabrian sea, the Atlantic and the Mediterranean. It is a 360° **view**.

Taking the C-625 from Reinosa for 20km, you will come to the **Bosque del Saja**, a magnificent park populated with birch, beech and oak trees. Just 3km from Reinosa, a Roman settlement has been excavated and identified as *Julióbriga*, the capital of Roman Cantabria.

Five kilometres S of Reinosa on the N-611, you will come to the **Collegiate Church of Cervatos**, which is a very good example of pure Romanesque. There are interesting **reliefs** on the capitals but just about everything in the building, from the apse windows to the 14C fan vaulting in the nave, is pleasing.

Sports: The *Alto Campoo* ski station ☎ 75 10 99, 25km away, has ten lifts, ten good runs and facilities including a ski school —the *Corza Blanca* ☎ 75 10 99, is a very quiet hotel with good views, as you would expect from a place that is 1,660m high, and with a swimming pool. Various water sports, including sailing and water skiing, are practised on the Ebro reservoir.

RIBADESELLA **Asturias** ☎ (985), pop. 6,456, *i* Ctra Piconera, s/n ☎ 86 00 38. Oviedo 84km, Santander 128km, Madrid 485km.

Astride the Sella river as it flows into the sea, this is an enchanting fishing town with a fine old quarter.

- ★★★★ *Gran Hotel del Sella* (open: 1/4-30/9), La Playa, s/n ☎ 86 01 50 ⚲ 74 ♣ 🍴 ⚓ 🏊 ⚖ ≪ ♀ **AE, DC, MC, V** $$$ to $$$$. This used to be a palace owned by local aristocrats. It is on the beach.
- ★★ *La Playa* (open: 1/4-30/9), Paseo de la Playa, 42 ☎ 86 01 00 ⚲ 12 ♣ 🏊 ⚖ ≪ ♀ $$$.
- 🍴 *El Repollu*, c/ Santa Marina, 2 ☎ 86 07 34 $$$. Fish and stews.

Beaches: The local stretch of shore has no facilities so the choice is between La Vega (10km away), **LA ISLA** (22km away) —where ★ *Beni-Mar*, Barrio de Quejo, 131 ☎ 63 03 47 ⚲ 26 **P** 🏊 ⚖ ≪ ♣ $ to $$ is a peaceful hotel with good views— and Lastres going W, and Nueva (12km away), San Antolín and Barro going E.

Best buys: The traditional local craft is boat-building, both full size and model, but latterly craftsmen have branched out into ceramics and leatherwork.

Cultural highlights: The **old quarter** is worth a stroll. The 13C Romanesque Church of Santa María de Junco has later Gothic additions. The star attractions are the impressive prehistoric **cave paintings** in the **Caves of Tito Bustillo** (open 1/4-30/9: 10.00-1.00 and 3.30-6.30; closed: Mondays, and Sundays during July and August). Using ochres and red pigments, primitive man recorded horses, deer and reindeer for posterity.

Fiestas: The **International Descent of the River Sella** is a genuine competitive trial at one level and a huge party at another. It takes place on the first Saturday in August and it draws thousands to the town and to the river's banks all the way up to Arriondas where the canoeists start. For a ringside view try getting a place aboard the special, and very crowded, train that chugs along parallel to the river keeping up with the leading canoeists. At the end of the event, drinking, dancing and feasting take over.

🕭🕭🕭 **Local sights**: From Ribadesella you can explore the **Costa Verde** (see separate entry), E and W, at your leisure. On the Colunga-Arriondas road,
🕭🕭 stop at the **Mirador de El Fito**, a vantage point from which there are marvellous views.

Sports: There are a number of salmon, trout and crayfish reserves along the Sella (☎ 22 27 48) and there are hunting reserves in the local park, the *Reserva Nacional del Sueve* ☎ 22 27 48, in the mountains SW of Ribadesella. Water sports are popular as are climbing and hill trekking. The top sporting activity is, however, **canoeing**, which is understandable since the town plays host to the Descent of the Sella, an extremely popular event in the international canoeing calendar.

🕭🕭🕭 SAN SEBASTIAN-DONOSTIA **Guipúzcoa** ☎ (943), pop. 180,043, $\boxed{i}$ c/ Miramar, s/n ☎ 42 62 82 and c/ Reina Regente, s/n ☎ 42 10 02 and 42 31 80, (Av de la Libertad, 26 ☎ 003, ✉ c/ Urdaneta, s/n ☎ 46 49 14, ✚ Emergencies ☎ 27 22 22, ✈ Fuenterrabía, 20km away ☎ 64 22 40 (Iberia and Aviaco, Hotel Londres, c/ Zubieta, 2 ☎ 42 36 07/8/9), 🚍 c/ Sancho el Sabio, s/n, 🚌 RENFE, c/ Camino, 1 ☎ 42 48 23 and 42 77 76. Bilbao 100km, Santander 207km, Madrid 488km, Barcelona 565km.

🕭🕭🕭 The first thing that strikes the visitor about San Sebastián is its **perfect location**. The city's natural **elegance** is a second impression. San Sebastián
🕭🕭 is built around the almost perfect semicircle of the **Bahía de la Concha** (Bay of the Shell). The Island of Santa Cristina, in the centre of the bay, helps hold off the strong sea and inland, the city is protected by three small mountain peaks —the **Urgull**, the **Ulía** and the **Igueldo**— which augment the agreeable symmetry of the city.

The 19C air to San Sebastián is real enough for the city was almost entirely rebuilt in the last century after the Duke of Wellington's troops, having expelled Napoleon's troops in 1813, set fire to the garrison in the closing stages of the Pensinular War. The little that was left of what used to be a walled city is now known, aptly, as the **Parte Vieja** or old part. With its narrow little streets and rickety looking houses this surviving rectangle of the city by the fishing port is a distinct contrast to the tree-lined boulevards and graceful buildings that characterize the rest of San Sebastián. The old part is the scene of a local ritual called ***poteo*** which is the term used in many areas of the Basque country for hopping from one wine and *tapa* bar to the next. Groups of friends carry out the ritual regularly before lunch and in the evening. They have an astonishing number of bars in the old quarter to choose from.

San Sebastián is a wonderful city for walking around. The stroll from one end of the bay, by the fishing port, to the other is about 2km long and fills your lungs with **bracing sea air**. At the farthest point of the bay, tucked into the Igueldo mountain, there is an impressive modern sculpture called *El Peine de los Vientos* (the Winds' Comb) by Eduardo Chillida, a local man and one of the foremost 20C Spanish sculptors. The walk takes you along the promenade looking over the city's two **beaches**, the **Playa de la**
🕭🕭 **Concha**, which is the one nearest the port, and the **Playa de Ondarreta**. The 🕭🕭 two are separated by a small promontory called *El Pico del Loro* (the Parrot's Beak) which is where the **Palace of Miramar** is located. The palace was donated by the city council to Queen María Cristina, who was regent at the turn of the century during the infancy of her son the future King Alfonso XIII, and it played a key part in the development of San Sebastián as an **aristocratic resort**. The royal family took up summer residence in Miramar and the court followed. For a really bracing walk take the **Paseo Nuevo** which goes from the estuary of the Urumea river, round the corniche of the

Urgull hill and ends up at the fishing port. If it is rough be careful for the waves come crashing over the road as it juts out to sea on the corniche. If you have had enough ozone, good walking alternatives include the boulevard alongside the river Urumea, where the *Hotel María Cristina* stands, and the **Av de la Libertad**, the city's main artery; you won't catch sight of the sea but you will see a lot of **good shops**.

Walking and sea breezes build up appetites and this is just as well for San Sebastián believes in **good eating**. The bars have huge arrays of outsize *tapas* which most people would take for a meal but which for the locals are merely appetizers. The city is justifiably extremely proud of its **quality restaurants** for some of the finest in Spain are here. San Sebastián's gourmet reputation is no mere accident for the city boasts a great number of gastronomic societies. The point of these eating clubs, which are common all over the Basque Country but do not exist anywhere else in Spain, is that the members cook huge and expert meals for each other on a regular basis. They are men-only clubs and women are only allowed into their gourmet sanctuaries twice a year, on January 19 and August 14, which are both *fiesta* days in the city.

San Sebastián is an all year round city and as capital of the province of Guipúzcoa, an important one. But it swells out in summer and becomes especially lively for it is very much a resort as well. Less fashionable now than it was in the 1920s when it was the hub of high society on vacation, San Sebastián has neverthless kept up its **casino** and a succession of **arts festivals** that take place from July through to September. The night life has not ebbed either.

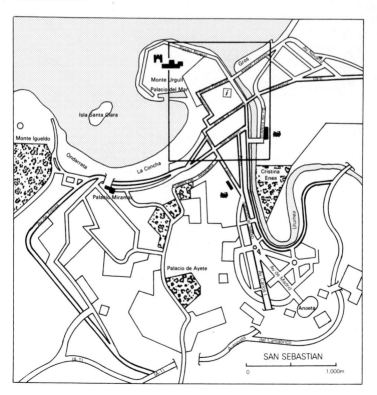

◐◐ ▦ ★★★★★ *María Cristina*, Paseo República Argentina, s/n ☎ 29 33 00 ⇌ 139 ✕ TV ♦ ≪ ▦ AE, DC, MC, V \$\$\$\$\$ to \$\$\$\$\$\$. This hotel has regained its super-luxury *belle époque* atmosphere.

▦ ★★★★ *Costa Vasca*, Av Pío Baroja, 9 ☎ 21 10 11 ⇌ 203 ♦ ♦ ♨ ⇌ ♝ AE, DC, MC, V \$\$\$\$ to \$\$\$\$\$.

▦ ★★★★ *De Londres y de Inglaterra*, c/ Zubieta, 2 ☎ 42 69 89 ⇌ 120 ♦ ♒ ≪ AE, DC, MC, V \$\$\$\$ to \$\$\$\$\$. Strategically placed on La Concha beach, it has good views of the bay.

◐◐ ▦ ★★★★ *Monte Igueldo*, Monte Igueldo, s/n ☎ 21 02 11 ⇌ 125 ♦ ♦ ⇌ ⚲ AE, DC, MC, V \$\$\$\$. This hotel offers **fantastic views** of the bay. It has an amusement park at its doorstep.

▦ ★★★★ *Orly*, Pl Zaragoza, s/n ☎ 46 32 00 ⇌ 60 ♦ ≪ AE, DC, V \$\$\$\$ to \$\$\$\$\$. Centrally located.

▦ ★★★★ *San Sebastián*, Av Zumalacárregui, 20 ☎ 21 44 00 ⇌ 94 ♦ ♦ ⇌ ≪ AE, DC, MC, V \$\$\$\$.

▦ ★★★ *Avenida*, on the Igueldo ☎ 21 20 22 ⇌ 47 P ♦ ⇌ V \$\$\$.

▦ ★★★ *Gudamendi*, Ctra de Igueldo, s/n ☎ 21 41 11 ⇌ 17 ♦ ♦ ⇌ AE, V \$\$\$\$. It has three clay pigeon shooting courts.

▦ ★★★ *Niza*, c/ Zubieta, 56 ☎ 42 66 63 ⇌ 41 AE, DC, MC, V \$\$\$. Opened in the 1920s, it has good views.

◐◐◐ ¶¶ *Akelarre*, Paseo de Orkolada, s/n ☎ 21 20 52 P ✳ ≪ AE, DC, MC, V \$\$\$\$ to \$\$\$\$\$. Run by Pedro Subijana, Arzak's rival and colleague.

◐◐◐ ¶¶ *Arzak*, c/ Alto de Miracruz, 21 ☎ 27 84 65 P ✳ AE, DC, MC, V \$\$\$\$ to \$\$\$\$\$. Owner-chef Juan Mari Arzak is the undisputed pace-setter of Spain's *nouvelle cuisine*.

¶ *Bretxa*, c/ General Echagüe, 5 ☎ 42 05 49 ✳ $$$. Reputed to serve the best sea bream in the N of Spain.

¶ *Casa Nicolasa*, c/ Aldamar, 4 ☎ 42 17 62 **AE, DC, MC, V** $$$$. A classic restaurant patronized by generations of gourmets.

¶ *Chomin*, Av Infanta Beatriz, 14 ☎ 21 07 05 **P** ✦ **AE, DC, MC, V** $$$ to $$$$. French-Basque cuisine.

¶ *Kokotxa*, c/ Campanario, 11 ☎ 42 01 73 ✳ **AE, MC, V** $$$ to $$$$.

¶ *La Oka*, c/ San Martín, 43 ☎ 46 38 84 ✳ $$. Top rate self-service.

¶ *Panier Fleuri*, Paseo de Salamanca, 1 ☎ 42 42 05 ✳ $$$$. Traditional Basque cooking and exquisite French cuisine.

¶ *Patxiku Quintana*, c/ San Jerónimo, 22 ☎ 42 63 99 ✳ **AE, V** $$$ to $$$$. An old restaurant full of new ideas.

¶ *Rekondo*, on the way up the Igueldo ☎ 21 29 07 **P** ✳ **AE, DC, EC, V** $$$. Roast meats and the best wine cellar in Spain.

¶ *Salduba*, c/ Pescadería, 6 ☎ 42 56 27 ✳ **MC, V** $$$ to $$$$.

¶ *Urbano*, c/ 31 de Agosto, s/n ☎ 42 04 34 ✳ $$$. First-class fish.

¶ *Urepel*, Paseo de Salamanca, 3 ☎ 42 40 40 ✳ **AE, DC, MC, V** $$$ to $$$$. Very popular.

Best buys: There are stylish shops along the Av de la Libertad and its side streets in the centre of town. Children's clothes and shoes are good buys but there is also plenty of fashion to suit all tastes. Leather clothing and accessories are available at *Loewe*, c/ Miramar, 2, and at *Fancy*, c/ Andía, 4. For Spanish fashion, visit *J.B.*, c/ San Martín, 9, *Brown's*, c/ Urbieta, 25, *Casual*, c/ Hernani 27, and *Mayffred*, c/ San Martín, 15. Children's clothes are sold at *Dang-Dang*, c/ Guetaria, 10, and at *Friky*, Av Zumalcárregui, 6, and Av Libertad, 6. In the old part there are a number of shops specializing in nautical and fishing gear. If you are interested in antiques, head for *Ayete*, Villa Ochanda-Ayete, *Emily's Nook*, Pl Buen Pastor, 12, and *Pimplico*, c/ San Bartolomé, 2. In the market in the old quarter, the **Mercado de la Brecha**, look out for local foodstuffs such as **Txacolí** —the white, slightly bubbly Basque wine— local cider, red beans from Tolosa and the somewhat smoky mature cheese called **Idiazabal**. Wines and liquors are also available at *Eceiza*, c/ Prim, 51; chocolates at *Juncal*, Av Libertad, 32, and delicious confectionery at *Labeak*, c/ Legazpi, 5, and *Otaegui*, c/ Garibay, 23.

Cultural highlights: The 18C **Church of Santa María** which has a Baroque façade in the style known as Churrigueresque after the Spanish architect who developed it, and the 16C Church of San Vicente with an ornate reredos in the style known as Plateresque which evolved during Spain's Golden Age are both in the old part of the city. The **Museo de San Telmo**, Pl Ignacio Zuloaga (open: 10.00-1.30 and 3.30-5.30; closed: Sunday afternoons and Monday mornings) was built in the 16C as a convent and has an interesting Renaissance cloister. The art collection includes works by El Greco, Ribera and Goya and there are some very fine **frescoes** by Catalan painter José María Sert in the chapel. There are fine **views** of the bay and the city from the top of **Mount Urgull**, where a **Military Museum** is to be found inside the **Castle of La Mota**, and from the top of **Mount Igueldo** (take the cable car) where an amusement park exists.

Fiestas and festivals : Saint Sebastian's day is on January 20, and festivities begin the night before with the traditional *Tamborada*, literally the beating of the drums, which is as noisy as its name suggests. The general feasting and parades led around the city by neighbourhood bands last for 24 hours. San Sebastián's big *fiesta*, though, is the *Semana Grande* (Great Week) which takes place in the middle of August and features sporting competitions, concerts, funfairs and magnificent fireworks over the bay. The prestigious *Jazzaldía* jazz festival is held in the second half of July and a classical music festival in the second half of August. Rowing regattas in the bay, using heavy boats called *traineras*, take place on the first two Sundays of September. The

🔂 **International Film Festival** also takes place in September.

🔂 **Local sights:** See 'Costa Vasca'.

🔂 **On the town:** There are more than 100 *tapa* bars, known as *txokos* locally. Recommended ones are **Casa Alcalde**, c/ Mayor, 19; **La Cepa**, c/ 31 de Agosto, 9, and **Martínez** on No. 13 of the same street; **La Espiga**, c/ San Marcial, 48; **Tamboril**, c/ Pescadería, 2, and **Negresco**, c/ Zubieta, 5. At night the action shifts to the bars along the boulevard and the old part such as *Bee-Bop*, at the start of the Paseo de Salamanca, **Dioni's**, c/ Igentea, 2, **Dickens**, Bulevar, 1, and *Etxe-Kalte*, by the port. Another popular area for music, drinks and *tapas* lies between c/ Urbieta and c/ Reyes Católicos: the most popular bars and pubs are **Casa Vallés**, *Nido*, *Pokara* and *Uda-Berri*. The Paseo de Miraconcha, by the beach, is for the really late night crowd and

🔂 for the gay community. Popular discotheques include **Bataplán**, at Paseo de
🔂 La Coruña, **Kabutzia** (excellent cocktails) in the yacht club by the port, **Ku** in
the Igueldo neighbourhood which is loud and stays open late, and **Don**
🔂 **Surio**, c/ Manterola, 5. Gamblers can flirt with Lady Luck at the **Casino Gran Kursaal**, c/ Zubieta, 2 ☎ 42 92 14, where French and American roulette, baccarat, *punto y banca* and black jack tables are always open.

Sports: The local football team is always in the front line of the first division and plays at the Atocha stadium. The **Lasarte** horse-racing track seasons run from December to February and during the summer. There is clay pigeon shooting at the *Hotel Gudamendi*, Ctra de Igueldo, s/n, tennis at the *Real Club de Tenis San Sebastián*, Paseo de Ondarreta, s/n ☎ 21 51 61, and golf at Zarauz (15km away) and Fuenterrabía (20km away), where there is also a flying club, the *Aero Club San Sebastián*, for all sorts of flying sports. The yacht club, the *R.C. Náutico San Sebastián* ☎ 42 35 74/5, organizes sailing and windsurfing courses. Jai alai is played at the *Frontón Galarreta Jai Alai* in Hernani (11km away) and at San Sebastián's indoor sports stadium **Anoeta** which is also the venue for a number of sporting competitions. Ice skaters head for the *Palacio del Hielo* in Anoeta ☎ 46 03 37; horseback riders for the *Real Sociedad Hípica de San Sebastián* ☎ 45 05 37; and squash players for **Mundaiz**, c/ Raimundo de Mundaiz, 6 ☎ 28 34 89.

🔂 SANTANDER **Cantabria** ☎ (942), pop. 188,539, *i* Pl de Velarde, 1 (Porticada) ☎ 21 14 17, ✚ c/ León Felipe, 8 ☎ 27 10 22, ✈ 25 09 00 (Iberia, Paseo de Pereda, 18 ☎ 22 97 00), ⚓ Marítima Aucona (Santander Plymouth Ferry), Paseo de Pereda, 13 ☎ 22 72 88, 🚆 RENFE, Paseo de Pereda, 25 ☎ 21 23 87. Bilbao 116km, Burgos 154km, Madrid 393km.

Santander is at least three things: it is a solid, busy commercial city, it is a stylish summer resort and it is an arts and intellectual centre. It is the political capital of the Cantabrian region and has been prosperous since the Middle Ages when it was already a major **port** exporting Castile's wheat and wool. Heavy industry, expanding docks and an important fishing fleet have this century underscored Santander's role as the financial hub of a wide area of northern Spain. The city developed as a resort towards the end of the last

🔂 century when fashionable villas began to spring up along the **Sardinero beaches**. It became extremely fashionable, as was so often the case, when the Spanish Royal Family began to spend their summer holidays in Santander. This was the result of an enterprising move by the city authorities who presented King Alfonso XIII and his English-born Queen Ena, Victoria Eugenia, a great grand-daughter of Queen Victoria, with the peninsula called **La Magdalena** which borders Sardinero beach on the W. Queen Ena had a palace built there and had it designed to look like Osborne House in the Isle of Wight where she had lived as a child. Santander's bracing northern climate and the English country mansion style palace were more than enough to turn the city into **Queen Ena's favourite resort** and high society naturally followed. The Magdalena Palace is today the headquarters of Santander's **International University**. From June to September a succession of seminars, lectures and courses are delivered there by academics of all disciplines from far and wide. The city, during the summer months, also plays host to a prestigious **International Piano Competition** and to a no-less important **Classical Music and Ballet Festival**.

▥ ★★★★★ *Real*, Paseo Pérez Galdós, 28 ☎ 27 25 50 ⇌ 124 ✦ ❦ ≪ **AE, DC, MC, V** $$$$$ to $$$$$$. Classic in style, beautifully situated and peaceful, it has splendid views of the bay.

▥ ★★★★ *Bahía*, c/ Alfonso XIII, 6 ☎ 22 17 00 ⇌ 181 🎤 **AE, DC, MC, V** $$$ to $$$$. Centrally situated.

▥ ★★★★ *Santemar*, c/ Joaquín Costa, 28 ☎ 27 29 00 ⇌ 350 ✦ 🎤 ⚓ ⌕ **AE, DC, MC, V** $$$$ to $$$$$. Modern, situated 150m from the beach.

▥ ★★★ *Sardinero*, Pl de Italia, 1 ☎ 27 11 00 ⇌ 113 ℗ 🎤 ⚓ ≪ **AE, DC, MC, V** $$$ to $$$$. Next to the beach and the Casino, it has good views.

▥ ★★ *Rhin*, Av Reina Victoria, 55 ☎ 27 43 00 ⇌ 95 ⓨ ⚓ ≪ **AE, DC, EC, V** $$$. Good views.

▥ ★★ *Roma*, Av de los Hoteles, 5 ☎ 27 27 00 ⇌ 52 ✦ ⚓ ⌕ **AE, DC, EC, V** $$$ to $$$$.

❙❙ *Bar del Puerto*, c/ Hernán Cortés, 63 ☎ 21 30 01 ✳ **AE, MC, DC, V** $$$ to $$$$. A well-established classic restaurant and **bar** serving fish and seafood.

❙❙ *Bodega Cigaleña* (closed: Sundays in summer, Wednesdays and Sunday nights in winter, 20/10-20/11 and 20/6-1/7), c/ Daoiz y Velarde, 19 ☎ 21 30 62 **AE, DC, V** $$$. Unfussy cuisine and a wine museum.

❙❙ *Cañadío* (closed: Mondays and 15/11-30/11), c/ Gómez Oreña, 15 ☎ 31 41 49 ✳ **AE, DC, MC** $$$$. A classic serving meat and fish. It has a very popular **bar**, ideal for a cider or beer aperitif.

❙❙ *El Molino* (closed: Mondays and 15/1-15/2), in Puente Arce, Ctra N-611, km13 ☎ 57 40 52 ℗ ✦ **AE, V** $$$. Set in an old windmill with a sophisticated atmosphere, it serves trendsetting, imaginative cuisine.

❙❙ *Il Giardinetto* (closed: Sunday nights and Mondays), c/ Joaquín Costa, 18 ☎ 27 62 36 **DC, EC, V** $$$. Pastas, pizzas and good cod dishes.

❙❙ *Iris*, c/ Castelar, 5 ☎ 21 52 25 **AE, DC, MC, V** $$$. Specializes in fish.

❙❙ *La Barca* (closed: Sunday nights), c/ Hernán Cortés, 40 ☎ 31 47 69 ✳ **AE, MC, V** $$$. Seafood.

❙❙ *La Concha*, Av Reina Victoria, s/n ☎ 27 37 37 ✦ ✳ ⚓ **AE, EC, V** $$$. On the beach. In summer it serves a buffet lunch and stays open until 6.00 am for drinks, dinner, shows and finally a dawn breakfast.

❙❙ *La Sardina* (closed: Mondays and 15/1-15/2), c/ Doctor Fleming, 3 ☎ 27 10 35 ℗ **AE, V** $$$. Regional cooking with *nouvelle cuisine* leanings.

❙❙ *Posada del Mar*, c/ Juan de la Cosa, 3 ☎ 21 30 23 ✳ **AE, DC, MC** $$$. A typical inn serving excellent hake.

❙❙ *Rhin*, Pl Italia, s/n ☎ 27 30 34 ✦ ✳ ⚓ **AE, V** $$$. On the beach, it has good views.

Beaches: Sardinero beach, which is actually divided into two by the tamarinds and palms of the El Piquío gardens, is a really splendid beach full of facilities and above all spacious at low tide. There are three little **beaches** around the Promontory and La Magdalena and then there are a number of others right on the other side of the bay. These, like the beaches W of the city (see 'Villaviciosa'), cannot compete with the Sardinero's facilities but they are much less crowded in the high season.

Best buys: Santander and its surrounding Cantabrian region is famous for its delicious **Picón** and **Aliva** cheeses and there is also good regional confectionery like *sobaos* and others: ***Sonderklas***, Paseo de Pereda, 24, has a good selection. For wines and liquors, try *Finca Tablanca*, c/ Castilla, 53. The area around the Pl Porticada has stylish fashion shops. Spanish fashion is available at ***Carot***, c/ Daoiz y Velarde, 29, ***Perchas***, c/ Isabel II, 11, and ***Rossi***, c/ E. Pino, 2. Decadent hats designed by Queen Victoria Eugenia's modistes, who were also related to Coco Chanel, are good buys at ***La Cotera***, Av Calvo Sotelo, 23. For shoes, try *Carell y Stella*, Av Calvo Sotelo, 16, and *Charlotte*, c/ San Francisco, 24. ***Estudio***, Av Calvo Sotelo, 21, is a

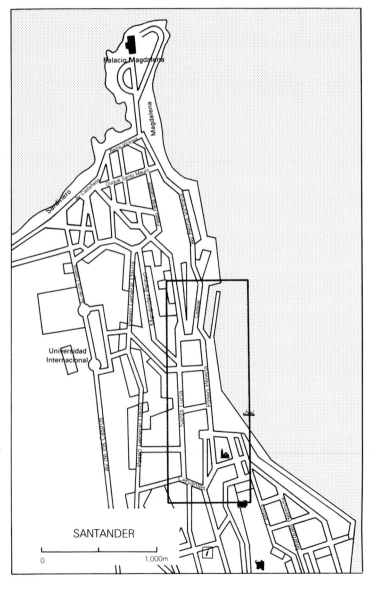

SANTANDER

0   1,000m

very good bookstore. Antiques hunters go to *Camus*, c/ Isabel la Católica, 15. Traditional regional jewelry is available at *F. Venero*, c/ General Alonso Vega, 5. Good sports shops are *Arriola*, Av Calvo Sotelo, 6, *Godofredo*, Paseo Pereda, 31 (fishing and diving gear) and *Yates y Cosas*, c/ Hernán Cortés, 40 (yachting). Furniture, crafts and gifts are ideal at *Artespaña*, c/ Cádiz, 20. Music lovers should pay a visit to *Real Musical*, c/ Rualasal, 21.

Cultural highlights: Santander is an extremely pleasant city to walk around, up and down the **Paseo de Pereda**, a seaside promenade, into the Magdalena's **grounds** and around the main square, the **Pl Porticada**. Specific city landmarks include the Gothic **Cathedral**, c/ Somorrostro, s/n (largely reconstructed for, in common with much of the city's buildings, it was severely damaged by a fire that followed the gigantic explosion of an arms ship on the quayside in 1941), and the Iglesia del Santísimo Cristo which has a **12C crypt**. The **Biblioteca Menéndez Pelayo**, c/ Rubio, 4 (open: 9.30-1.00; closed: Sundays and public holidays) has a very valuable book collection, numbering more than 45,000 volumes, that belonged to Santander-born Marcelino Menéndez Pelayo, a towering scholar whose conservatism and religious principles had a profound effect on Spanish ideas at the end of the last century. The city's museum, in the same street, the **Museo Municipal de Bellas Artes** (open: 10.00-1.00 and 5.00-8.00; Saturdays: 10.00-1.00) includes works by Goya, Zurbarán and Mengs in addition to those of local artists. The Archaeological Museum, the **Museo Provincial de Prehistoria y Arqueología**, c/ Juan de la Cosa, 1 (open: 9.00-2.00; closed: Mondays) exhibits the finds from prehistoric and Roman sites in Cantabria.

Fiestas and festivals: Santander's patronal festival falls on July 25; then during July and August the **Santander International Festival** attracts top international orchestras and ballet and theatre companies. Many of the performances take place in the lovely setting of the Pl Porticada.

Local sights: PEDREÑA, a summer resort on the other side of the bay, has fine beaches and is famous for being the home village of Severiano Ballesteros whose family used to farm the land where the golf course now stands.

The lovely village of LIÉRGANES, 29km away, with its noble old family mansions is unspoilt and peaceful despite the fact that it is a popular spa that specializes in treating respiratory ailments. Try the good local cream cheese.

Travellers interested in cave paintings should make a note of **PUENTE VIESGO**, 28km along the N-623. There are a number of caves there, La Pasiega, Las Chimeneas and **Castillo** (open: 10.00-12.00 and 3.00-6.00; closed: Mondays and afternoons from 1/11-31/3) which are packed with rupestrian art dating from the Paleolithic period (40,000 BC).

For a gentle valley with old farmhouses, meadows, oaks and chestnut trees head for the **Valle del Pas. VEGA DE PAS**, the valley's main centre of population, is famed for its *sobaos* (buttery sponge cakes) and *quesadas* (cheese cakes) —*México*, on the junction with the road to Entrambasmestas, is a good restaurant. If you drive 7km N, you will be rewarded with panoramic views of the coast from the **Cabo Mayor** lighthouse. The same distance to the S along the Burgos highway brings you to **MURIEDAS**, where there is an interesting Ethnographic Museum, the **Museo Etnográfico de Cantabria** (open: 11.00-1.00 and 4.00-7.00; Sundays and holidays: 11.00-2.00).

On the town: In winter, Santander mostly stays at home but in summer, the city breaks out into the terraces along the Sardinero's promenade and most of the day and night seems to be spent in the open air. Open-air **terraces** like *Lisboa*, alongside the Casino on the Sardinero, become crowded *rendez-vous* for people in the afternoon as they work out their plans for the evening's entertainment. Most of the action, as far as the young crowd is

🕭 concerned, takes place in the **bars** and taverns around c/ Peñas Herbosa, c/ Bonifaz and c/ Lope de Vega, and especially **c/ Río de la Pila**. Students gather mostly around c/ Vargas, and the Perines area is popular for drinks in the late evening. A lot of really late night partying goes on in the Sardinero in the Panamá area. Two elegant spots to drink and hear music are *Castelar-5*,

🕭 c/ Castelar, 5, and the *El Emboque* pub, c/ Pedruéca, 8. *La Bohemia*, c/   🕭
🕭 Daoíz y Velarde, 25, and *La Conveniente*, c/ Gómez Oreña, 19, have live music. Recommended discos are *La Real Compañía Sonora y Electrónica*, Pl Rubén Darío, s/n, which sometimes has live bands, and *Pentágono*, c/

🕭 General Mola, 45. The *Gran Casino del Sardinero*, Pl de Italia, in the middle of the Sardinero ☎ 27 60 54 (open: 7.00 pm-4.00 am) has French and American roulette tables, black jack, *chemin de fer*, one-armed bandits and also bars, restaurants and a show.

Sports: The *Real Club Marítimo de Santander* yacht club, Dársena de Molnedo, s/n ☎ 21 40 50/54/58, and the *Marina del Cantábrico*, Av Parayas, s/n ☎ 33 80 00/03 (that provides all kinds of facilities), organize sailing and windsurfing courses. The official sailing school *Isla de la Torre*, run by the Cantabrian Sailing Federation, c/ San Fernando, 48 ☎ 37 00 50, is one of the best in Spain. There is also rowing and fishing. Golfers should

🕭🕭 need no introduction to the beautiful 18 hole, par 70 *Real Golf de Pedreña*, 24km away ☎ 50 00 01 and 50 02 66, for it is the home of Seve Ballesteros, where he used to caddy and learnt to swing. There are golf classes for children at the *Campo de Golf Municipal de Mataleñas*, on the road from the Sardinero to the Cabo Mayor lighthouse. There are tennis courts at *Club Parayas S.D.*, at Maliaño ☎ 25 02 50, and at the *R.S.T. de La Magdalena* ☎ 27 30 16; squash courts at *Floranes*, c/ Floranes, 10 ☎ 37 22 58. Horseback riding can be practised at the *Sociedad Hípica de Santander* ☎ 21 56 68.

🕭🕭 ⬛SANTILLANA DEL MAR⬛ Cantabria ☎ (942), pop. 3,840, [*i*] Pl Ramón Pelayo ☎ 81 82 51. Santander 30km, Bilbao 130km, Madrid 393km.

This is a jewel of a medieval town. During the Middle Ages it became popular with the local nobility because it was near a famed monastery that at the time drew a lot of pilgrims. Their patronage caused a number of fine palaces to be built in the village but life carried on as normal with the local folk tending to their cattle and their fields. Nothing has really changed very much since then and Santillana is, as a result, one of the most atmospheric villages in the whole of Spain. If you can visit it out of season count yourself lucky, for in summer tourists arrive by the busload.

🏨 ★★★ *Los Infantes*, Av Le Dorat, 1 ☎ 81 81 00 ⇌ 30 🅿 ✦ AE, DC, MC, V $$ to $$$. In an old mansion.

🏨 ★★★ *Parador Gil Blas*, Pl Ramón Pelayo, 11 ☎ 81 80 00 ⇌ 28 📺 🅿 ✦ ⚓ ⅖ AE, DC, MC, V $$$$. A peaceful hotel in an old stately mansion.

🍽 *Altamira*, c/ Cantón, 1 ☎ 81 80 25 🅿 ✦ ⅖ AE, DC, MC, V $$$. Good roasts served in this 17C mansion, which also offers accommodation.

Best buys: Take the opportunity to sample the home-made sponge cakes sold in the village and the fresh milk provided by Santillana's amiable cows.

Cultural highlights: The best thing to do is to just walk about taking the place in. There is something extraordinary about a place that is on the whole as hidden away as Santillana is and that has such a succession of fine stone buildings, each with its proud heraldic shield, standing side by side with much humbler dwellings where cattle are kept. There are virtually no buildings less than 300 years old in this picturesque village with its cobbled streets and wooden balconies vivid with flowers and, inevitably, the visitor keeps thinking the place is a film set. The **Collegiate Church of Santa Juliana** has a magnificent 12C pure Romanesque apse and **cloister** with beautiful **capitals**. Inside the church is a 17C embossed altar frontal, four figures of the *Apostles* carved in stone and a **reredos** also dating from the 17C. In the irregularly shaped **main square**, one of the old palaces is currently a Parador, belonging to the state-run hotel chain. On the same square stands the **Torre de Don Borja**, a 15-16C building now occupied by the Santillana Foundation which stages art exhibitions and other cultural events. The **Palace of the Marquis of Santillana**, on c/ del Cantón, was the home of the 15C writer, politician and warrior Iñigo López de Mendoza who was made Marquis of Santillana by King John II of Castile in return for his services in battle. See, too, the **Casa de los Hombrones** on c/ de las **Lindas** and the 16C **Convent of Regina Coeli** (Diocesan Museum). **Fiestas:** On January 6 there is a representation of the Three Magi.

<u>Local sights:</u> The famed **Altamira Caves**, discovered in 1879 and reckoned to contain the best examples of Paleolithic cave paintings in the world, are now highly restricted to visitors. You have to request permission a long time ahead from the Town Hall in Santillana ☎ 81 80 75. This is just as well because the caves were in danger of being irreparably damaged by the crowds who used to mass into the underground chambers.

SOMIEDO NATIONAL RESERVE Asturias ☎ (985)

Of all Spain's Nature Parks, Somiedo's is among the most precious. This is because its principal purpose is zealously to save from extinction the reserve's 30-odd **brown bears**, which once roamed all over this area, and its 110 beautiful, and once plentiful, **capercaillies**. You can count yourself very lucky if you catch sight of either of these rare species but grand views of high mountains are guaranteed —Peña Ubiña, the highest peak, rises to 2,417m— as are thick forests of beech, oak and chestnut. The park, which extends over 87,900ha is bounded by the Pajares and the Pigüeña rivers and there are glacier-formed lakes, the **Lagos de Somiedo**, near the source of the Pigüeña. You will also come across the stumpy and endearingly primitive little pre-Romanesque 9C **Church of Santa Cristina de Lena**, built in a style typical of northern Spain. From here there are fine **views** of the green and industrialized Caudal valley. The whole area is so wild and away from it all that it even has its own strange indigenous inhabitants, the **vaqueiros de alzada** —small pockets of migrant shepherds whose origins are as disputed as their folklore is curious.

TARAMUNDI Asturias ☎ (985), pop. 1,125. Oviedo 195km, Madrid 571km.

This village, or hamlet, is wonderfully situated among the mountains and woods of a little known area called **Los Oscos**. This is ideal, intensely rural, trekking country and there are numerous trails to explore. In addition to the great outdoors, Taramundi is especially interesting for it has preserved its ancient tradition of wrought-iron craftmanship —knives and penknives with decorated boxwood handles— and there are no fewer than 24 forges in and around the village, among them *A. Calvin*, Monsende. The surprises do not end there. Explore the **forestry tracks** or take the road to Grandas de Salime via Villanueva de Oscos and San Martín de Oscos and you are likely to come across evidence of Celtic settlements and of mines that were worked before and during the Roman occupation. The villages in the area are unspoiled and unselfconscious about their splendid popular architecture and their fascinating ancestral folklore.

🅾️🅾️ 🏨 ★★★★ *La Rectoral* ☎ 63 40 60 🛏 12 ✕ ✦ 🎤 🖼 🦪 ≪ ♟ 🐾 EC, V
$$$ to $$$$. Fabulously situated and extremely peaceful, with wonderful views of the valley and mountains. It is tastefully decorated with rustic artifacts that go back to the 18C and the staff in the **restaurant** ($$$) is attentive and courteous.
Best buys: Local knives and penknives with boxwood handles.

VILLAVICIOSA **Asturias** ☎ (985), pop. 15,351. Gijón 32km, Oviedo 44km, Madrid 447km.
On the banks of the Villaviciosa estuary, this is an agreeable resort town that styles itself as the capital of the region's **cider industry**. In Asturias, the local cider, which is quite unlike that anywhere else, has a cult following. It is poured into large glasses at arm's length so that it can 'breathe' and you toss the dregs away onto the floor of the bar. It is very slightly fizzy and pretty potent.

🍴 *El Cantábrico* (closed: Thursday evenings and October), Venta de las Ranas, Ctra N-632, km52 ☎ 89 90 86 $$$.

Cultural highlights: The old quarter is interesting. The 13C **Church of Santa María** has a Romanesque doorway and a Gothic rose window.
Fiestas: There is a representation of the Passion during Holy Week.
Local sights: In the village of **AMANDI**, 1km S, the 12C **Church of San Juan** has a Romanesque main door and chancel and magnificent capitals. 🅾️
🅾️ There is an interesting 9C pre-Romanesque church, **San Salvador** in **VALDEDIOS**, 9km away on the road to Oviedo, that stands appealingly on its own in the middle of the meadow. The pretty fishing village of **TAZONES**, 12km in the direction of Gijón, has a place in Spanish history books: it was here that Emperor **Charles V** landed in 1517 to inherit the Spanish throne as Charles I and establish the Hapsburg dynasty in Spain. Try the fresh fish and seafood in the fisherman's taverns, or take a swim off the nearby beaches of **El Puntal** and **Rodiles**.
Sports: You can dock your boat at the *Club Náutico Albatros*, at El Puntal ☎ 39 17 02.

VITORIA-GASTEIZ **Alava** ☎ (945), pop. 207,501, [i] Parque de la Florida, s/n ☎ 13 13 21, ☏ 003, ✉ c/ Postas, 17 ☎ 23 21 13 (telegrams ☎ 22 20 00), ✚ c/ Castilla, 13 ☎ 24 74 26, P 24 16 16 (emergencies ☎ 091), ✈ Forondona, 8km ☎ 27 33 00 and 27 40 00 (Iberia, Av Gasteiz, 50 bis ☎ 22 82 50/4), 🚗 c/ Francia, 34 ☎ 25 84 00, 🚂 RENFE, c/ Dato, s/n. Bilbao 66km, San Sebastián 114km, Madrid 351km.
The capital of the province of Alava, Vitoria used to be something of a backwater but it grew rapidly in importance at the start of the 1980s when it became the seat of the Basque Country's autonomous government. The regional executive resurrected the Visigothic name of *Gasteiz* which was how Vitoria was known when it was founded in 1181 by King Sancho the Wise of Navarre. It is Vitoria, however, that rings a bell for Anglo-Saxons, for it is the name of a key **battle** during the Peninsular War, won by Wellington; it was fought in 1813 on the city's outskirts. The Iron Duke is duly honoured in the central Pl de la Virgen Blanca with a fine monument, the only big one erected to him in Spain.
The old quarter of Vitoria is a spider's web of little streets that go up and down a small hill. The **medieval Gothic quarter** around the old Cathedral has lots of steps because it is on different levels, and its streets are named after the old artisan guilds. The later **Pl de la Virgen Blanca**, nearby, and its surrounding area are only broadly Neoclassical for the palaces and churches are in a variety of styles from different periods. Modern Vitoria is generally

attractive, with pleasant gardens such as the Florida park, buildings with glazed balconies, and a busy atmosphere which provides a marked contrast to the sobriety of the old quarter.

- ★★★★ *Canciller Ayala*, Av Ramón y Cajal, 5 ☎ 22 08 00 ⇌ 185 TV 🎤 AE, DC, MC, V $$$$.
- ★★★★ *El Caserón*, Camino de Armentia, 5 ☎ 23 00 48 ⇌ 5 ✦ ⌘ ≈ ≪ ⌘ AE, V $$$$$.
- ★★★★ *Gasteiz*, Av Gasteiz, 19 ☎ 22 81 00 ⇌ 150 🎤 AE, DC, MC, V $$$$.
- ★★★ *General Alava*, Av Gasteiz, 53 ☎ 22 22 00 ⇌ 105 TV P 🎤 AE, DC, MC, V $$$. An established classic.
- ★★★ *Parador de Argómaniz*, in Argómaniz, 13km ☎ 28 22 00 ⇌ 54 ✕ P ✦ 🎤 ⌘ ≪ AE, DC, MC, V $$$. A very peaceful hotel located in a 17C palace with good views.
- 🍴 *Don Carlos* (closed: Sunday evenings, Mondays and 10/8-31/8) c/ 12 de Octubre, 8 ☎ 28 24 78 AE, EC, MC, V $$$. Good game dishes.
- 🍴 *Dos Hermanas* (closed: Sundays and three weeks in August), c/ Madre Vedruna, 10 ☎ 24 36 96 AE, DC, EC, MC, V $$$$. It has been serving regional Alava recipes for more than a century.
- 🍴 *El Caserón*, Camino de Armentia, 5, 2km from Vitoria ☎ 23 00 48 ⌘ ≪ AE, V $$$.
- 🍴 *El Portalón* (closed: Sundays, at Christmas and three weeks in August), c/ Correría, 151 ☎ 22 49 89 AE, DC, MC, V $$$$. Basque cooking is what was once an old medieval shop.
- 🍴 *Elguea* (closed: Sunday evenings, Tuesdays and three weeks in August) c/ Cruz Blanca, 8 ☎ 22 50 50 ✳ AE, MC, V $$$.
- 🍴 *Ikea* (closed: Sunday evenings, Mondays, Easter week and three weeks in August), c/ Paraguay, 8 ☎ 22 41 99 P ✳ AE, DC, MC, V $$$. Good fish.
- 🍴 *Mesa* (closed: Wednesdays and 10/8-10/9), c/ Chile, 1 ☎ 22 84 94 V $$$. Unfussy.
- 🍴 *Olarizu* (closed: Sunday evenings and Mondays), c/ Beato Tomás de Zumárraga, 54 ☎ 22 88 46 P AE, DC, MC, V $$$. Basque cuisine.
- 🍴 *Zabala* (closed: Sundays and 11/8-11/9), c/ Mateo Moraza, 9 ☎ 23 00 09 $$ to $$$. Very popular.
- 🍴 *Zaldiarán* (closed: Sundays), Av de Gasteiz, 21 ☎ 24 81 12 ✳ AE, DC, MC, V $$$. Basque *nouvelle cuisine*.

Best buys: Works of art and antiques, especially furniture, are available from shops along c/ Correría (Nos. 54, 59 and 151). There are cake shops selling local specialities all over town, but especially on c/ Postas and c/ Eduardo Dato —try *Goya* at Nos. 6 and 20— and the best place to purchase Rioja wines produced in Alava province is at the *Unión de Cosecheros de la Rioja Alavesa*, c/ Sancho el Sabio, 20. Wines and gourmet foods are also available at the splendid *Rekondo*, Pl General Loma, 2. Spanish fashion is available at *Chomi Rodrigo*, c/ M. Iradier, 21, *Globo*, c/ Fueros, 24, *Dani*, c/ Eduardo Dato, 10, and *Kendal*, c/ Postas, 23.

Cultural highlights: The Cathedral of Santa María is 14C Gothic, with a broad portico and beautiful façade. It has an unusually good art collection with works by Van Dyck, Rubens and Caravaggio and several tombs that are representative of Spain's ornate Plateresque style. The Church of San Miguel proudly shows off the Gothic statue of Vitoria's patron, *La Virgen Blanca* (The White Virgin), in its portico. Inside it has a fine altarpiece by Gregorio Hernández, a Baroque artist famed for the shock tactic realism he injected into his carvings. The Church of San Pedro is distinguished by its outstanding Gothic portal and by two bronze Plateresque tombs within.

The **Pl de la Virgen Blanca**, surrounded by buildings whose balconies look down on Wellington, is Vitoria's best known landmark. The porticoed, Neoclassical **Pl Nueva** is nearby. To get the feel of Vitoria's historical civic architecture note the 15C **Casa del Cordón** and the 16C **Palacio de Bendaña**, which stand at Nos. 24 and 48 respectively of c/ Cuchillería.

The Archaeological Museum, **Museo de Arqueología**, c/ Correría 116 (open: 10.00-2.00 and 5.00-7.00; Saturdays and holidays: 11.00-2.00; closed: Mondays) exhibits treasures unearthed during digs in Alava province. Vitoria also has a modest Fine Arts Gallery, the **Museo Provincial de Bellas Artes**, Paseo de Fray Francisco, 8 (open: 11.00-2.00 and 5.00-7.00; Saturdays and holidays: 11.00-2.00; closed: Mondays), showing an excellent *Christ* by Ribera, and a Weapons Museum, the **Museo Provincial de la Armería** (housed in the Ajuria Enea Palace, seat of the Basque regional government) whose exhibits range from a prehistoric axe to 19C duelling pistols.

Fiestas: The *fiesta* in honour of the city's patron, *La Virgen Blanca*, lasts the week starting on August 4, and involves unique rituals such as every onlooker lighting a cigar as the chimes of San Miguel church signal the start of the *fiesta* and other more common ones like nonstop street dancing, drinking and afternoon bullfights. There is also a **Jazz Festival** in mid-July and an International Theatre Festival in October.

Local sights: The village of Mendoza, 7km W, has an interesting fortified mansion known as the **Torre del Infantado**, which used to be the home of the once powerful Marquis of Santillana. Nearby there is a well-preserved Roman bridge in **TRESPUENTES**, and on a hill overlooking it are the remains of a Roman settlement called *Iruña*. Vitoria was sufficiently close to the famed pilgrimage route to Santiago de Compostela to have received its share of Romanesque influence. A good example is the church in **GACEO**, reached via the N-I to Irún, which has some exceedingly good **Romanesque frescoes**. The village of **SALVATIERRA**, 25km out of town, has a noble feel to it thanks to well-preserved solid old houses —*José Mari*, c/ Mayor, 3 ☎ 30 00 42, is a recommended restaurant. The Aizkomendi **cromlech** near the village of **EGUILAZ** is the biggest in the Basque country.

Alava province's section of the **Rioja** is as pleasing to the eye as its produce is to the palate. This is rolling, **vine-packed countryside** and it is delightful to explore. **LAGUARDIA**, 45km from Vitoria, founded in the 12C by the omnipresent Sancho the Wise of Navarre, preserves its medieval walls and turrets. Its church, Santa María de los Reyes, has a 14C late Gothic portal and a polychromed Baroque altarpiece —*Marisa*, c/ Sancho Abarca, 8 ☎ 10 01 65, serves the regional cuisine of Alava and the dining room has good views. In the area, the **best buy** is wine. Wine lovers should head straight for *Bodegas Alavesas*, Ctra Elciego, s/n, and then press on from there to **ELCIEGO** itself, home of the famous *Marqués de Riscal* winery (c/ Torres, 1).

On the town: *Chiquiteo* drinking is a classic at *Felipe*, c/ Fueros, 2. There are a great number of popular places along Av de Gasteiz where mostly young people meet to drink, chat and listen to music. At c/ Urbina, 15, you will find *Bogart*, the 'in' disco; later on at night, people gather at *Studio 48*, c/ Beato Tomás de Zumárraga, and at *Borsalino*, c/ M. Barandiarán. In the city centre, along c/ San Antonio and c/ Dato, there are more conventional bars and pubs and fashionable places such as *Río*.

Sports: Fishing, sailing, water-skiing and other nautical sports are pactised at the nearby reservoirs of Urrunaga and Ullivarri, where the *C.N. Vitoria* ☎ 20 00 08, is stationed. Ice-skating can be practised at *C.H. Gasteiz*, c/ Hortaleza, 8 ☎ 25 07 01.

CASTILE
AND LEÓN

Castile and León (Castilla y León) is the **heart of Spain**, historically, aesthetically and culturally. The cliché images of Spain focus on flamenco singers and olive-skinned girls with jet black hair and flouncy gypsy dresses, clicking castanets —but that is the romantic image and belongs to the south of the country. The part of Spain which has really shaped the nation's history is the lofty central plain with its open skies, frontier land where **castles** and **walled towns** mark the slow progress south against the Muslim invader in the long medieval struggle to forge the nation's unity. Castile's vernacular emerged as the literary language of the nation, and epic poems, the foundation of Spanish literature, were penned to celebrate Spain's heroes in an age of chivalry. In the age of discovery, soldiers and priests set forth with the banner of the Castle and Lion to create a Spanish empire overseas. It is a mystical land where there are as many churches as there are fortified ramparts. *'Castile',* **Saint Teresa of Avila** used to say, *'is where you are closer to God.'* Teresa, who was quintessentially Castilian, combined mysticism with sound common sense and her countrymen have not changed that much. The men and women of Castile and León have been shaped by harsh winters and baking summers into forbearance and fortitude, and are known for their austerity and an innate sense of pride. Hospitable, with a touch of gravity, to strangers, they are economical with their words and judicious in their opinions.

Castile and León stands on a high plateau with mountain ranges on the N, E and S and is drained by the majestic River **Duero** as it meanders W towards Portugal. The mountains in the N, the **Cordillera Cantábrica**, shield the region from the coast and the range known as the **Sistema Ibérico** in the NE separates it from the basin of the River Ebro. In the S, the Gredos and the Guadarrama ranges, which together form the **Cordillera Central**, sever the plateau into two, separating Castile and León from Madrid and from the region known as Castile-La Mancha. Looked at on a relief map, Castile and León's 94,147km² seem perfectly defended on three sides. It has its own giant, geographical ramparts, much like its own emblematic castles. Once divided into separate kingdoms, Castile and León today forms an autonomous community within the quasi-federal administrative framework of modern Spain and is composed of nine provinces: Avila, Burgos, León, Palencia, Salamanca, Segovia, Soria, Valladolid and Zamora. Each province has its own very marked identity but they share an extremely rich heritage as well as the grandeur of the sparsely-populated plateau's sense of infinite space.

The story of Castile and León really starts in the 8C when the first of Spain's Christian kingdoms was established in the city of León. Gradually the Muslims were pushed back but it was far from being a linear progress. Castile broke away from León to form its own feudal kingdom and there were as many skirmishes and battles among the Christians as there were against the common enemy. It was not until the 13C that the two monarchies united. The Christian capital had, by that stage, moved from León to the stronghold city of Toledo, in today's Castile-La Mancha region, and Christian armies were driving deep down into the Islamic territory of Al-Andalus, today's Andalusia, and advancing on the cities of Córdoba and Seville. The plateau was by that time making the best use of its resources. Its wheat production turned it into the granary of Spain and the wool from its merino sheep created a brisk trade with medieval England. The capitals of today's nine provinces were all well established cities in the early Middle Ages and each boasted its cathedral and its scores of monasteries and convents. The pilgrim route to Santiago de Compostela, which passed through the provinces of Burgos, Palencia and León, introduced Romanesque and then Gothic architecture and art forms into the region, and a magnificent **cultural legacy** was built up as the new aesthetic ideas combined with its own innate spirituality.

Castile and León reached its zenith in the late 15C when that extraordinary woman **Queen Isabella** married King Ferdinand of Aragón and thus united Christian Spain. If today's traveller feels intimidated by the expanse of Castile and León he ought to be encouraged by Isabella's example. With her mobile court hurrying in her wake, she visited just about every corner of her kingdom, giving birth to a child here, fighting a battle there and stamping her personality everywhere. It is not at all difficult to bring her to life here for Castile and León has not changed that much physically. The region's spirit has hardly altered at all.

AGREDA **Soria** ☎ (976), pop. 3,726. Soria 50km, Zaragoza 107km, Pamplona 118km, Madrid 276km.

This was a fortified frontier town between the kingdoms of Castile and Aragón before they were united under Isabella and Ferdinand, the Catholic Monarchs, in the 15C. Today only the gate of its castle remains of the former battlements but fine churches have survived. A quiet agricultural village now, it is close to the 2,313m high **Moncayo** mountain, the highest in the Sistema Ibérico range.

🏨 ★★ *Hostal Doña Juana*, Av de Soria, 2 ☎ 64 72 17 🛏 38 ✗ $ to $$.
There is a restaurant as well as accommodation.
Best buys: Good home-made *chorizos* (spicy sausages) are available from *A. Ruiz*, c/ Venerable, 22, and first-class cheeses are made in the town of **Olvega**, a few kilometres S.
Cultural highlights: The Church of the Virgen de la Peña is Romanesque, and the Gothic and Plateresque **Church of San Miguel** has an earlier Romanesque fortified tower and a good 16C altarpiece. The Convent of la Concepción was founded by one of the most interesting figures of Spain's Baroque age: **Sister María de Agreda**, a mystical nun much given to visions who maintained an extensive correspondence with King Philip IV, the sad-faced Hapsburg so frequently portrayed by Velázquez.
Local sights: The mountain peak of Moncayo is irresistible hiking territory.

AGUILAR DE CAMPOO **Palencia** ☎ (988), pop. 7,699, [i] Plaza Mayor, 31 ☎ 12 20 24, ✚ 12 27 48. Palencia 97km, Santander 104km, Madrid 325km.

On the N edge of the plateau, Aguilar de Campoo is within striking distance of the green valleys of the Cordillera Cantábrica mountains and the Castilian wheatfields that form the granary of Spain. Quite properly it has mixed the dairy products of the former with the cereals of the latter to establish itself as one of Spain's top **biscuit** producing centres. An intoxicating smell of baking cookies wafts around its old buildings.

🏨 ★★★ *Valentín*, Av Generalísimo, 21 ☎ 12 21 25 🛏 50 ✗ 🅿 ✚ 🎤 🐎
AE, DC, MC, V $$ to $$$. The restaurant serves regional cooking $$.
Best buys: You can buy biscuits direct from the factories or, if you shun the mass-produced, try the cakes made by the nuns at the *Convento de las Clarisas*.

Cultural highlights: The **Collegiate Church of San Miguel** in the Plaza Mayor dates from the Gothic period and has impressive 16C tombs of members of the Marquis of Aguilar family. The Puerta de Reinosa archway bears a Hebrew inscription indicating that Aguilar had an important Jewish community before their summary expulsion at the end of the 15C. Outside the town, the **Monasterio de Santa María La Real** has a pleasing cloister in the Cistercian style which has well carved capitals depicting biblical scenes. A 12C shrine honouring Santa Cecilia stands at the foot of the town's castle.

Local sights: By common consent, the province of Palencia has many of the finest Romanesque buildings in Spain. There is something to thrill lovers of the Romanesque in virtually every village. Just follow the signposts that bear the legend *'Rutas del Románico Palentino'* (Palencian Romanesque Itineraries). Such villages in Aguilar's immediate vicinty include Mave (8km), Frontada (7km) and **OLLEROS** (6km), where the local Romanesque church has been carved into a rock face. The N-611, following the course of the Pisuerga river, leads to the old fortified village of **HERRERA DE PISUERGA**.

Sports: Hunting, fishing (the River Pisuerga is rich in crayfish), river canoeing and various water-sports on the Aguilar lake are all popular. In winter, skiing can be practised at the Picos de Europa (see 'Picos de Europa' in 'Cantabrian Coast').

ALBA DE TORMES **Salamanca** ☎ (923), pop. 4,383. Salamanca 19km, Avila 85km, Madrid 193km.

This medieval village on the banks of the River Tormes is much visited as **Saint Teresa of Avila**, the enormously influential mystic who reformed the Carmelite order, is buried here in the Carmelite convent that she founded in 1571.

🏨 ★★ *Benedictino*, c/ Benitas, 6 ☎ 30 00 25 ⮌ 40 DC $$. It has a restaurant $$.

Best buys: Local ceramics, which are profusely decorated, are available from *B. Pérez Correas*, c/ Matadero, 17, and good home-made confectionery can be bought at *La Madrileña*, Pl General, 18. Antiques hunters head for *E. Navarro*, c/ Espolón, 12, specializing in Castilian furniture and with a wide selection of 17-18C *bargueños*.

Cultural highlights: Saint Teresa's **Convento de M.M. Carmelitas** (open: 9.30-1.30 and 4.00-7.30 ☎ 30 02 11) contains relics of the saint and interesting paintings. Other convents in the town include the 15C **Convento de Santa Isabel** and Santa María de las Dueñas, easily recognizable by its Renaissance main façade. The most interesting churches in the town are in the Romanesque-Mudéjar style, that is to say that they bear evidence, such as horseshoe arches, of the influence of the skilled Muslim craftsmen who remained in the area after the Christian reconquest. The **Church of San Juan** has a fine **sculptural group** dating from the 11C and the Church of Santiago has a good coffered ceiling. The village is dominated by a medieval tower that is all that remains of an imposing castle that belonged, as the village's name indicates, to the Duke of Alba.

Sports: This is good hunting and fishing territory.

ALMAZAN **Soria** ☎ (975), pop. 5,776, Soria 35km, Madrid 194km.

Too close to the strategic Duero river for its own good, the town was the scene of numerous battles between Christians and Moors during the see-saw reconquest period. Three gateways remain of the old defensive walls. The Romanesque **Church of San Miguel** has a splendid **dome** showing clear Muslim influence and a carving in the N transept of the murder of Thomas

Becket by Henry II's knights in Canterbury Cathedral. The cult of Becket spread rapidly in Spain due to the influence of Henry's daughter, Eleanor, who married Alfonso VIII of Castile and loathed her father for the rest of her life.

🏨 ★★ *Antonio*, Av Soria, 13 ☎ 30 07 11 🛏 28 **AE, EC, V** $$. The restaurant serves regional cooking $$.

Best buys: Almazán is one of several Spanish towns that claims to make the best *yemas*, very rich, sticky sweets made from sugar and egg yolks. They are sold at *Casa de las Yemas*, Arco de la Villa, 4.

Fiestas: Ancient country dances called *Danzas de Zarrón y del Milanazo* are the high point of the local celebrations held in May.

Local sights: The 15C castle of **BERLANGA DE DUERO**, 26km W, is one of the most spectacular in Spain. Berlanga also has a Gothic **Collegiate Church** and an interesting Jewish quarter. The 11C Mozarabic **Chapel of San Baudelio de Berlanga** is in Casillas, 8km SE. In 1922, when the chapel had already been declared a national monument, an unscrupulous international art dealer stripped the walls of its frescoes. They are now, shamefully, in New York's Metropolitan Museum save for six which eventually returned to Spain but are, absurdly, in Madrid's Prado Museum instead of in the chapel they once adorned.

ARANDA DE DUERO **Burgos** ☎ (947), pop. 28,242, ✛ 22 15 00, **P** 50 01 00, 🚌 26 55 65, 🚍 20 35 60. Burgos 82km, Madrid 160km.

The market town and the chief industrial centre for miles around, it claims to be the home of the best roast lamb in the whole of Castile and León, but this title is hotly disputed by a number of other towns, notably Sepúlveda.

🏨 ★★★ *Los Bronces*, Ctra N-1, km160 ☎ 50 08 50 🛏 29 ✕ **P** ♦ 🐾 **AE, DC, MC, V** $$$. The restaurant is quite good $$$.

🏨 ★★★ *Montehermoso*, Ctra N-1, km163 ☎ 50 15 50 🛏 54 **P** ♦ 🎵 **AE, DC, EC, V** $$.

🏨 ★★★ *Motel Tudanca*, in Fuentespina, 8km along the Ctra N-1 ☎ 50 60 11 🛏 20 ♿ **P** ♦ 🎵 **AE, DC, V** $$. It has a shopping centre and a restaurant $$$.

🏨 ★★★ *Tres Condes*, Av Castilla, 66 ☎ 50 24 00 🛏 35 **P** 🎵 **V** $$.

🍴 *Casa Florencio*, c/ Arias de Miranda, 14 ☎ 50 02 30 **P** $$$. Well established, a classic restaurant serving regional cuisine.

🍴 *Mesón El Roble*, Pl Primo de Rivera, 7 ☎ 50 29 02 ❄ **V** $$$. Good roasts.

◐ 🍴 *Mesón de la Villa* (closed: Mondays and 12/10-31/10), c/ Alejandro Rodríguez de Valcárcel, 3 ☎ 50 10 25 ❄ **AE, V** $$$. Regional cuisine.

🍴 *Rafael Corrales*, c/ Obispo Velasco, 2 ☎ 50 02 77 $$$. Excellent roasts cooked in a wood-fired oven.

Best buys: Typical pine-nut coated cakes called *empiñonados* are sold at *Tudanca*, Av Castilla, 8, and *Cebas*, c/ San Gregorio, is locally famous for its flat, dry cakes called *tortas*. Local pottery is available at *M. Martín*, c/ La Prensa, 1.

Cultural highlights: The **Iglesia de Santa María** was ordered to be built by Isabella and Ferdinand and its main **façade** is suitably in the late Gothic Isabelline style which was fostered in the late 15C by the Catholic Monarchs. The Church of San Juan is Romanesque.

Fiestas: The town lets itself go with street parties, country picnics and bullfights in September and also has traditional Easter celebrations.

◐ **Local sights:** **PEÑARANDA DE DUERO**, 18km NE along the C-111, has a main square, complete with porticoes and wooden beams, that is so picture postcard pretty that it has been used as a film set on numerous occasions.

The cameras pan up to the castle, high on a crag, that dominates Peñaranda and its square and then explore the village's narrow medieval streets. Peñaranda's main building is its Renaissance **Miranda Palace** which has an elegant patio and main staircase and rooms with coffered ceilings and elaborate friezes. Note, too, the 15-16C pillory and the fascinating 17C pharmacy, the **Botica Ximénez**.

Continuing on the C-111 and turning left after Coruña del Conde, you reach the Roman city of **Clunia**. The remains of the theatre and of a number of mosaic-decorated villas are in an above average state of preservation (open: 10.00-2.00 and 4.00-7.00; closed: Mondays).

The old village of Roa de Duero, 22km W, has a Romanesque church, the Collegiate Church of Santa María, and a good antique shop selling Castilian furniture, *Z. Sierra del Campo*, c/ P. Manjón, 15. *El Nazareno*, c/ El Fresno, s/n ☎ 54 02 14 $$$, serves good local roasts.

Madéruelo, SE along the C-114, is a medieval village with more than its fair share of Romanesque churches.

AREVALO **Avila** ☎ (918), pop. 7,279. Avila 55km, Valladolid 78km, Salamanca 95km, Madrid 121km.

Isabella of Castile, who with Ferdinand of Aragón reigned as the Catholic Monarchs, spent her childhood in Arévalo's castle. The town, on the main NW highway, is also famous in Spain as being a first-rate place to eat one's fill of roast suckling pig, known here as *tostón*.

¶¶ *Goya* (closed: Thursday evenings and September), Av Emilio Romero, 33 ☎ 30 03 62 ✳ **AE, EC, V** $$$. Roast suckling pig.

¶¶ *La Pinilla* (closed: Mondays and 15/7-31/7), c/ García Fanjul, 1 ☎ 30 00 63 ✳ **AE, DC, EC, V** $$$. Roast lamb and suckling pig.

Best buys: Castilian antiques, mostly furniture, are sold at c/ San Miguel, 4, and c/ Descalzos, 67.

Cultural highlights: From a distance what you see is the 14C **castle**, which has undergone considerable reconstruction, and the Mudéjar towers of the churches of San Martín and **Santa María** which are more or less the same as they were in the 13-14C. Once in the town, the main square, the **Pl de la Villa**, and the smaller Pl de Arrabal and Pl Real are all porticoed. The **Alcocer Gate** gives some idea of the old town walls for it is virtually all that remains of them, and the bridges over the Arevalillo and the Adaja rivers are in the Mudéjar style that was practised by the Muslim craftsmen living under Christian rule.

Fiestas: Local celebrations starting on the first Sunday of July include a cattle fair, bullfights and Pamplona-style bull running.

Local sights: Isabella was actually born in the village of **MADRIGAL DE LAS ALTAS TORRES**, 30km along the C-605, in a palace that is today an Augustine convent. Little has changed in the village and the 23 **watchtowers** that existed when the remarkable Catholic queen was born are still standing. On the Nava road, 2km S of Arévalo, are the remains of the 13C Mudéjar **Church of La Lugareja**.

ASTORGA **León** ☎ (987), pop. 13,298, *i* Pl España, s/n ☎ 61 68 38, ✉ c/ Alferez Provisional, 3 ☎ 61 54 42, P 61 60 91, ⚎ Paseo de la Estación, s/n ☎ 61 51 63. León 45km, Ponferrada 62km, Madrid 322km.

This town has always been a busy thoroughfare. The Roman **Silver Route**, the *Vía de la Plata*, which brought the precious metal up from Extremadura passed through Astorga (it was then known as *Astúrica Agusta*) and in the Middle Ages it was an important stopping point on the pilgrimage route to the shrine of Saint James in Compostela. It was also the chief town of an area peopled by an ancient tribe of uncertain origin called **Maragatos**. Their descendants, who have preserved an ethnic folklore all their own, showed a peculiar ability as mule drivers and they distributed goods throughout Spain before the arrival of the steam engine.

🏨 ★★★ *Gaudí*, Pl Eduardo de Castro, 6 ☎ 61 56 54 ⛟ 35 ✕ TV P ♣ 🎙 AE, V $$$. The restaurant is imaginative $$ to $$$.

🏨 ★★★ *Pradorrey*, Ctra N-IV, km331 ☎ 61 57 29 ⛟ 64 ⛫ TV P ♣ 🐎 AE, DC, MC, V $$$. Good facilities in a medieval setting.

🍴 *La Peseta* (closed: 15/10-30/10), Pl San Bartolomé, 10 ☎ 61 72 75 $$ to $$$. Home cooking.

Best buys: Artisan crafted carpets and tapestries are woven at *M. Nistal*, Ctra N-IV, km326 ☎ 16 55 95. **Benavides**, c/ Prieto de Castro, 3, sells curious costume jewelry based on Maragato designs.

Cultural highlights: The **Bishop's Palace** was designed by the turn-of-the-century Modernist architect Antonio Gaudí and is a colossal extravagant folly in the midst of the wilds of NW León province. Fortunately it has been put to good use for it is now a museum, the **Museo de los Caminos** (open in summer: 10.00-2.00 and 3.00-8.00; winter: 11.00-2.00 and 3.00-6.00; closed: December through February), which exhibits works of art related to the Way of Saint James pilgrimage route to Compostela.

🕯 **Cathedral** was built over a period of time, between the 15C and the 17C, and inevitably is a mix of styles. The main façade and the cloister are Baroque
🕯 while the interior is Gothic. The magnificent **high altarpiece** by **Gaspar Becerra** (1520-1570) is clearly influenced by Michelangelo. The 16C choir stalls were subsequently added to by Nicholas of Cologne and others. The
🕯 **Diocesan Museum** (open: same times as the Museo de los Caminos) has a particularly rich collection of Romanesque wooden statues of the Virgin Mary. Elsewhere in Astorga there are remains of the 13C town walls, an imposing 17C Town Hall and a number of churches, the most curious of which is Santa Marta which incorporates a cell for women of ill repute.

Fiestas: The Good Friday penitential processions are particularly moving.

Local sights: The 13C Monastery of Santa María de Carrizo, 2km away, and the typical Maragato village of Castrillo de Polvazares, 5km away, with its thatched stone houses are interesting. The bridge at Hospital de Orbigo, 15km along the N-120, was the scene of an extraordinary series of exploits by a demented 15C knight who refused to let anyone pass until they had admitted that his damsel was the fairest in the land. Scores of jousts took place here as a result and it became something of a tourist attraction for the pilgrims making their slow way to Compostela.

🕯🕯 AVILA **Avila** ☎ (918), pop. 44,618, *i* Pl de la Catedral, 4 ☎ 21 13 87, ℂ Pl de la Catedral, s/n, ✉ Pl de la Catedral, s/n ☎ 21 13 54, ⛫ 22 48 48, P 21 11 88, 🚌 Av de Madrid, s/n ☎ 22 01 54, 🚄 Av José Antonio ☎ 22 65 79. Segovia 65km, Salamanca 100km, Madrid 108km, Valladolid 116km.

Every provincial capital in Castile and León has its well-defined characteristics that set it apart from the others. Avila's are its town walls and its association with Saint Teresa of Avila. The two represent the essence of the city: it is a mix of warriors and mystics. The combination is central to the national psyche for the sword and the cross go hand in hand right down through Spanish history. Avila, with its battlements and its convents, expresses this duality with a greater impact than anywhere else in Spain. You could add that Avila's climate reflects the extremes of the Spanish temper. Standing 1,131m above sea level it is the highest city in Spain. It is bitterly cold in winter, while in summer the heat is unrelenting.

The **walls** came first. When Alfonso VI of Castile re-took the city from the Muslims in the 11C, he ordered his son-in-law, Raymond of Burgundy, to fortify this latest Christian outpost. Raymond complied with alacrity and also repopulated the city with knights who had accompanied him down from N Spain in the crusading battle against Islam. The warriors that installed themselves in Avila were to show their mettle in the ensuing push S by the Christian armies. They came into their own during the 16C when men from Avila led regiments right across the extensive possessions of King Philip II, from the fields of Flanders to the unknown territories of the New World. The palaces and town houses in the city were built by this class of haughty, battle-hardened gentlemen who naturally thought business and trade to be demeaning. It was inevitable that Avila should decline in the 17C as Spain's military power, exhausted by so much warfare, went into a tailspin.

Saint Teresa (1513-1582) was very much a child of her age and of Avila. In her youth she voraciously read epic accounts of knightly valour and imagined herself as a crusader. As a teenager she joined the Carmelite order and entered Avila's Convento de la Encarnación. Twenty years later this exceptional woman broke out of the cosy atmosphere of what was essentially a nunnery for women of gentle birth, and spearheaded the drive for stricter adherence to the rules of poverty and piety. Teresa's reforming zeal turned conventional Catholicism upside down. In Avila she founded her first convent of the Discalced, or reformed, Carmelite order and from there she crisscrossed Spain tirelessly, injecting a new spirit and a new purpose into the religion of her time. An immensely courageous, practical and intelligent woman, she was at the same time utterly unworldy and raised mysticism to new heights. Her spirit pervades all of Avila.

▥ ★★★★ *Palacio de Valderrábanos*, Pl de la Catedral, 9 ☎ 21 10 23 ⇌ 73 ♨ **AE, DC, MC, V** $$$ to $$$$. An old Gothic palace.

▥ ★★★ *Parador Raimundo de Borgoña*, c/ Marqués de Canales y Chozas, 16 ☎ 21 13 40 ⇌ 62 ✕ **P** ♦ ♨ ⅍ **AE, DC, MC, V** $$$ to $$$$. The restaurant specializes in Castilian food.

❙❙ *Mesón del Rastro*, Pl del Rastro, 1 ☎ 21 12 18 ✳ **AE, DC, EC, V** $$$. Also a ★★ boarding house ⇌ 16 ♦ $$. Local fare such as beans, steaks and fortifying red wine from Cebreros.

❙❙ *Piquio*, c/ Estrada, 4 ☎ 21 14 18 ✳ **AE, DC, EC, V** $$$. Local cuisine.

Best buys: The candied egg-yolks known as the *yemas de Santa Teresa* are sold at *La Flor de Castilla*, Pl Santo Tomé, 4, and *Muñoz Iselma*, Pl Santa Teresa, 6. Antiques are stocked at *I. González Rey*, c/ San Segundo, 22.

Cultural highlights: The finest views of the best-preserved medieval **walled** town in Europe are from the approach road to Avila from Salamanca and from the spot known as the Cuatro Postes. The walls extend for 2.5km, and were built between 1090 and 1099 by some 2,000 imported labourers. Completely encircling the city, the walls are fortified by 88 turrets. Nine gates lead into the city, of which the most beautiful are the **Puerta de San Vicente** and the **Puerta del Alcázar.**

The **Cathedral** looks a bit like a castle and its huge semi-circular **apse** forms part of the walls at one of its more vulnerable points. The fact that it is built of granite and the general absence of decorative features on the façades add to its somewhat grim appearance. Work started on the cathedral in the 12C, making it one of the earliest big Gothic churches in Spain, but the 13C portal, the **Puerta de los Apóstoles**, which is its best exterior feature, was not placed in its present position at the N door until midway through the 15C when Juan Guas designed major alterations. In 1779, an attempt to beautify the plain W door, which was also erected by Guas, led to the incorporation of some unfortunate floral motifs. The interior of the cathedral is less severe and the red and white brick work and the high ogival naves lend a transparent air to it. The most notable work of art is the Gothic **high altarpiece**, which was started by **Pedro Berruguete** and completed by Juan de Borgoña. The area behind the altar is decorated with four panels by the Renaissance artist Vasco de la Zarza, who also carved the **tomb of Bishop Alfonso de Madrigal**, known as *El Tostado* (The Swarthy). The **retrochoir** facing the W door is in the Plateresque style. Further notable features are the **choir stalls**, designed by Cornelius of Holland, two 15-16C gilt iron **pulpits** and a number of Renaissance side chapels. The **Cathedral Museum** (open in winter: 10.00-1.00 and 3.00-5.30; in summer: until 7.00), is beyond the 13C **sacristy** and contains works by El Greco and Luis Morales.

The impressive **Church of San Vicente** (open: 10.00-1.00 and 4.00-6.00), outside the walls and opposite the gate of the same name, with its fine **W door** was built where Saint Vincent and his sisters Sabina and Cristeta were martyred together in 306. All three are buried inside in a **magnificent tomb** under a curious, 15C Gothic canopy. The church, which has three naves and a triforium, dates from the second half of the 12C though the vaults are 14C Gothic.

Santo Tomás Monastery was built in or around 1492 when Granada was finally conquered by the Catholic Monarchs. The pomegranate, *granada* in Spanish, is symbolic of the captured Muslim kingdom and it appears in the frieze above the doorway. The Isabelline façades are decorated with the ball motifs so typical of Avila. The Catholic Monarchs often used the monastery as a summer residence, and the grandest of the monastery's three cloisters is known as the **Claustro de los Reyes** (The Royal Cloister) —the **Claustro del**

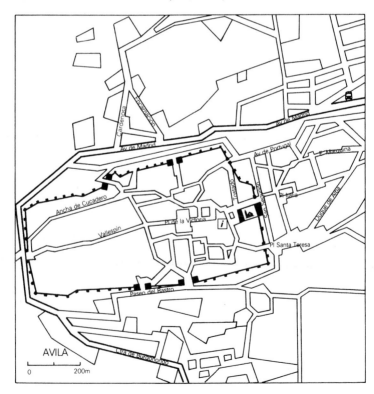

Silencio (Cloister of Silence) preceding it is noteworthy. The single-naved church contains the tomb of their adored son, Prince John, who died when he was a student at Salamanca. His **tomb** (1512) was delicately sculpted in ◐ alabaster by Domenico Fancelli who represented him very simply as a page boy. The **high altarpiece** dedicated to Saint Thomas Aquinas is considered ◐◐ to be one of the masterpieces of 15C artist Pedro Berruguete. The monastery has an interesting Oriental Art Museum, the Museo de Arte Oriental (open: 10.00-1.00 and 4.00-7.00) which exhibits objects collected by Dominican missionaries during their far eastern travels.

The Romanesque **Church of San Pedro**, outside the walls and opposite the Alcázar gateway, has fine ogival vaults and a splendid rose window. The Romanesque **shrine of San Segundo**, on the banks of the River Adaja, contains a magnificently extravagant **monument** (1572) to Saint Segundo by ◐ the magical Renaissance artist Juan de Juni. The good saint is supposed to have brought Christianity to Avila in the 1C.

Turning to civic architecture the chief Gothic buildings are the **Valderrábanos Palace**, with a lovely 15C façade, and the **Oñate Palace**. The outstanding Renaissance palaces are the **Palacio de Polentinos** (1535), the **Palacio de los Verdugos** and the **Palacio de los Núñez Vela**. The 16C **Casa de los Deanes** houses the **Provincial Museum** (open: 10.00-2.00 and 5.00-7.00; closed: Mondays and certain holidays ☎ 21 10 03) which exhibits collections of Spanish furniture, ceramics and paintings.

Saint Teresa is more or less everywhere in the city but her memory is particularly venerated in the **Encarnación Convent** (open: 9.30-1.30 and 3.30-6.00) where she took the veil and spent her first 20 years as a nun, and the **Convent of Santa Teresa** (open: 8.00-1.00 and 3.30-9.00), where a Baroque chapel now occupies what used to be her cell. In the first of her many foundations, the **Convent of San José**, which is also known as the *Convento de las Madres*, there is a museum dedicated to her life and works (open: 9.30-1.30 and 3.30-9.00).

Fiestas and festivals: The town has interesting Corpus Christi processions yearly. A choral singing and organ music week, the *Semana de Polifonía y Organo*, is held in July. Saint Teresa's feast day on October 15 is celebrated with processions, bullfights and fireworks.

Local sights: LAS NAVAS DEL MARQUES, 30km along the C-505, is a quiet summer vacation centre for heat-weary city people —*Magalia*, Paseo Damas, s/n ☎ (91) 897 02 10 $$, is a good restaurant serving Castilian cuisine. A second mountain resort, 4.5km S of Las Navas, Ciudad Ducal, has a peaceful little hotel set among pine trees, the ★★★ *San Marcos* ☎ (91) 897 01 01 ⇌ 16 ✦ ॐ $$. Also see the entry for 'Gredos, Sierra de.'

BEJAR **Salamanca** ☎ (923), pop. 17,151, *i* Paseo Cervantes, 6 ☎ 40 30 05, ✉ c/ Colón, 42 ☎ 40 11 59, ✛ 40 28 28, P 40 01 15, ⬛ 40 01 11. Plasencia 63km, Salamanca 70km, Avila 105km, Madrid 216km.

Picturesquely **situated** among the foothills of the Sierra de Béjar mountains, the town was a prosperous textile centre last century and today maintains a number of artisan looms that manufacture blankets and cloth.

▦ ★★★ *Colón*, c/ Colón, 42 ☎ 40 06 50 ⇌ 54 **P** ✦ AE, DC, V $$. Central, with a popular disco and a restaurant.

¶ *Argentino*, Ctra Salamanca, km70 ☎ 40 26 92 **P** ✦ ❊ AE, DC, EC, V $$ to $$$.

Best buys: Cloth, blankets and sausages are local products. Ceramics are sold at c/ Marsilla, 31.

Cultural highlights: Industrial archaeology enthusiasts are fascinated by the long dormant **19C factory chimneys** of the town. The more conventional architecture found in the area is well represented by the remains of the town walls with two surviving Gothic gateways, the 13C Church of San Juan and the 16C Palace of the Dukes of Béjar which nowadays houses a small museum. There is a fine 16C garden called **El Bosque**.

Local sights: The village of **CANDELARIO**, 4km S, is extremely pretty and is reputed to be one of the best preserved in the whole of Spain. It is also famed for its **sausages** and general pork products which are sold at *Hijos de Trinidad García*, c/ Enrique Fraile, 22.

Sports: This is good hunting territory.

BENAVENTE **Zamora** ☎ (988), pop. 13,523, ✉ c/ Gonzalo Silvela, s/n ☎ 63 03 97, ✛ 63 11 66, 🚍 63 18 40. Zamora 65km, León 71km, Valladolid 99km, Orense 242km, Madrid 258km.

An old market town, this was a stopping point on the Roman Silver Route, the *Vía de la Plata*, which traced a N-S line the length of Spain.

🏨 ★★★★ *Parador Rey Fernando II de León*, Paseo Ramón y Cajal, s/n ☎ 63 03 00 🛏 30 ✕ ✦ 🎙 🐾 ≪ AE, DC, MC, V $$$$. A peaceful hotel set in a 16C castle with very good views of the valley. The restaurant serves regional Zamora cuisine.

Best buys: Leather hunting accessories are good buys.

Cultural highlights : The **Church of San Juan del Mercado**, founded by the Knights of Saint John, has an early Gothic vault in the presbytery and three pure Romanesque portals. Note the 12C Crucifixion in the interior. **Santa María del Azogue** (12-14C) has a five-apsed chancel and two lovely Romanesque portals. There are fine 13C reliefs on the S portal and an Annunciation, also 13C, in the transept. The 16C tower of the local **castle** which survives is now part of the parador, which has magnificent views over the surrounding plain.

Fiestas: The town has picturesque Corpus Christi celebrations, including peculiar bull games called *Toro Enmaromado*.

Local sights: For an endearingly primitive Romanesque chapel there is little to beat **Santa Marta de Tera**, 28km along the C-620, in the Tera valley along which the Roman road once passed.

BIERZO, EL AND LOS ANCARES **León** ☎ (987). Access from Astorga via the N-VI and via the C-631 from Ponferrada.

Try to imagine the medieval **pilgrims to Compostela** footslogging their way through this mostly desolate, wild country; fortunately it is teeming with monasteries and abbeys which could put them up for the night. Old crafts, such as basket-weaving, are still practised in this region and its traditional *fiestas* are very much alive. Ponferrada (see separate entry) is its chief town.

VILLAFRANCA DEL BIERZO is an extremely pleasant village with good local wine and market produce that was much patronized by the pilgrims before they embarked on the daunting next stage of their journey, which took them over the mountains and into Galicia. The Iglesia de Santiago, dedicated to the apostle James, is a typical old pilgrim church and is liberally decorated with the pilgrimage's cockleshell emblem. For accommodation, try the ★★★ *Parador Villafranca del Bierzo*, c/ Calvo Sotelo, s/n ☎ 54 01 75 🛏 40 ✕ 🅿 ✦ ≪ AE, DC, MC, V $$$, a modern hotel with good views of the town. For lunch, try *La Charola*, c/ Doctor Arén, 19 ☎ 54 00 95 **V** $$, serving simple home cooking.

Los Ancares, N of the Bierzo region, is an extremely wild part of the country. There are a number of hamlets (Tejedo de Ancares, Balouta, Suarbol) where the thatched stone houses, called *pallozas*, look as if they are straight out of the Stone Age. The whole area is a **National Hunting Reserve**.

BRIVIESCA **Burgos** ☎ (947), pop. 5,002, ✛ 59 08 28, **P** 59 00 10.
Burgos 42km, Vitoria 78km, Madrid 285km.

The chief town of a cattle-rearing district, Briviesca has its place in the
Spanish history books because it was here that nobles gathered in 1388 to
create the title of Prince of Asturias for the heir to the Spanish throne, the
equivalent of Britain's Prince of Wales.

▦ ★★ *El Vallés* (closed: 24/12-22/1; restaurant closed: Wednesdays) Ctra
N-I, km280 ☎ 59 00 25 ☕ 22 ✕ **P** ✦ $$. The hotel **restaurant** serves
game in season $$$.

▦ ★★ *Hostería del Santuario*, Santa Casilda, km16 ☎ 59 01 52 ☕ 14 $$.

Cultural highlights: There is a particularly impressive **main altarpiece** in
the 16C **church** of the Convent of Santa Clara. It was created by the Basque
artist Juan de Archeta in 1568. But the most striking religious building is the
little **shrine of Santa Casilda** outside the village where the collection of
votive objects almost constitutes a museum of popular art.

Local sights: The gorge called the **Desfiladero de Pancorbo**, 27km along
the N-I, makes for a memorable car trip. Miranda del Ebro, 16km further on,
is a good place to relax with a hearty meal in local restaurants such as
Achuri, Paseo de la Estación, 86 ☎ 31 00 40 **AE, DC, MC, V** $$ to $$$,
serving home cooking and also offering accommodation, and *La Vasca*, c/
Olmo, 3 ☎ 31 13 01 **V** $$ to $$$, serving simple cuisine.

BURGO DE OSMA, EL **Soria** ☎ (975), pop. 4,964, ✛ 34 01 51, **P**
34 01 07. Soria 56km, Madrid 183km.

This immensely agreeable small town has been a bishopric since the 6C.
The Cathedral is well worth visiting and there is an added pleasure of a
different kind for the town happens to have one of the best restaurants for
miles around.

❙❙ *Virrey Palafox* (closed: Sunday nights and 16/12-16/1), c/ Universidad,
7 ☎ 34 02 92 **P** **AE, DC, V** $$$. A very interesting and imaginative
restaurant. In February and March, the pig slaughtering season, it
organizes massive fixed-price banquets at weekends during which the
entire animal is consumed in a variety of amazing dishes. Rooms are
available.

Best buys: Regional arts and crafts are available at the fair held at weekends.
Local confectionery is sold at *Paeneva*, Pl Santo Domingo.

Cultural highlights: Building on the **Cathedral** started in 1232 and was
completed by 1300. It is pure Gothic in its conception but it incorporates a
number of Romanesque features in the chancel and the transept and boasts
the exceptional Romanesque **tomb of San Pedro de Osma**. Later additions
came in the 16C with the typically extravagant **high altarpiece** by Juan de
Juni who was aided on this occasion by Juan Picardo and Pedro Andrés; the
wrought iron **screen** before the high altar and the retrochoir likewise show
Renaissance influence. The Palafox chapel was designed in the 18C by Juan
de Villanueva, the architect who introduced Neoclassicism into Madrid. Other
notable features of the cathedral are the luxurious marble **pulpit**, the Baroque
organs and the 16C stained glass. The **Cathedral Museum** (open:
10.00-12.30 and 5.00-8.00; closed: Sunday afternoons and holidays), in
addition to the ornaments that are exhibited in so many Spanish churches,
has a truly interesting collection of manuscripts and **codices**. It is the best
collection in Spain outside the Escorial.

Local sights: The almost abandoned medieval village of Calatañazor, nearby,
is utterly atmospheric and beautiful. It dominates a valley where a key battle
was fought in 1002 in which the Muslim chieftain, Al-Mansur, was mortally
wounded. The **Río Lobos Canyon**, to the N, is spectacular, while to the S is

the Arab **castle** of **GORMAZ** (10C). To the W, in the village of San Esteban de Gormaz on the banks of the Duero river, there are remains of the old town walls and the castle, and several Romanesque churches. Heading S from San Esteban, you will come to the ruins and museum of **Termancia**, a partially excavated Iberian town.

🐞🐞🐞 BURGOS **Burgos** ☎ (947), pop. 163,910, *i* Pl Alonso Martínez, 7 ☎ 20 31 25 and Paseo del Espolón, 1 ☎ 20 18 46, **(** c/ San Lesmes, s/n ☎ 20 18 36, ⊠ Pl Conde de Castro, 1 ☎ 20 11 02, ⊹ 22 15 00, **P** c/ Cardenal Benlloch, 2 ☎ 20 16 10, 🚍 c/ Miranda, 4 ☎ 20 55 75, 🚌 c/ Conde Guadalhorce, s/n ☎ 20 35 60. Vitoria 111km, Santander 154km, Madrid 239km.

There is a solid feel to Burgos and the city has every reason to feel self-important. It was the capital of the Kingdom of Castile for more than 400 years, it was the headquarters of the extremely powerful association of sheep farmers who moved their flocks around the central plateau and, for good measure, it was the stamping ground of Spain's epic hero **El Cid**. This rich background has produced a wealth of historic buildings. In addition, Burgos is strategically placed on Madrid's route to the French border at Hendaye and to the traditional Castilian export port of Santander. The city has had travellers and traders passing through it down the centuries and has built up good services as a result.

The royal court moved to Burgos in 1037 during the reign of Ferdinand I of León who inherited the crown of Castile. The city thereafter remained the kingdom's chief administrative centre until the Catholic Monarchs moved to the rival city of Valladolid in the awesome year of 1492 that marked the discovery of the New World and the conquest of Granada. Burgos' early years as the kingdom's capital were to be marked by the fluctuating fortunes of the valiant romance hero Rodrigo Díaz de Vivar (1026-1099) whose nickname El Cid is derived from the Arabic *Sidi*, meaning 'master.' The warrior's real or imagined exploits were written up in the following century in the **Cantar del Mio Cid** (1180) which is the cornerstone of Spain's epic poetry (see 'Literature') and enthralled a medieval audience. By the time Valladolid found favour with the Catholic Monarchs, Burgos was already well entrenched as a powerful city in its own right. This owed much to the sheep farmers' association called the **Mesta** that had built up a lucrative wool trade during the Middle Ages. The gigantic migrant flocks of merino sheep that grazed all over Castile and León filled the pockets of the *Mesta* members who were based in Burgos, but they were an ecological disaster for Spain for they turned the plateau into a semi-desert.

By the end of the 16C Burgos, like the rest of Spain, was entering a period of decline and decadence. The golden days of the *Mesta* were over, wars were exhausting the royal coffers and the treasures arriving from the New World had created an inflationary process that nobody at the time could understand, still less check. Burgos at least had its Gothic monuments to maintain its civic pride and it was, and continues to be, well located on the main Spanish highway.

🐞🐞🐞 🏨 ★★★★★ *Landa Palace*, Ctra N-I, km236 ☎ 20 63 43 ⇌ 39 ✦ 🎤 🏊
🐞 ⚓ V $$$$$. Three kilometres out of town on the highway to Madrid, this is a well-established and elegant roadside hotel which incorporates a 14C castle tower. Its **restaurant** is well above average $$$.
🏨 ★★★★ *Almirante Bonifaz*, c/ Vitoria, 22 ☎ 20 69 43 ⇌ 79 📺 ♠ AE, DC, MC, V $$$$. Centrally located.
🏨 ★★★★ *Condestable*, c/ Vitoria, 8 ☎ 26 71 25 ⇌ 78 ♿ 📺 🎤 AE, DC, MC, V $$$$.

🏨 ★★★ *Cordón*, c/ La Puebla, 6 ☎ 26 50 00 🛏 35 TV AE, MC, V $$ to $$$.

🏨 ★★★ *Corona de Castilla*, c/ Madrid, 15 ☎ 26 21 42 🛏 52 P AE, DC, V $$ to $$$.

🏨 ★★★ *Fernán González*, c/ Calera, 17 ☎ 20 94 41 🛏 66 P 🎤 V $$ to $$$.

🍴 *Casa Ojeda* (closed: Mondays and Sunday nights in summer), c/ Vitoria, 5 ☎ 20 90 52 ✳ AE, DC, MC, V $$$.

🍴 *Los Chapiteles* (closed: Sundays and Wednesday nights) c/ General Santocildés, 7 ☎ 20 59 98 ✳ AE, DC, MC, V $$$. Castilian cuisine.

🍴 *Mesón del Cid* (closed: Sunday nights), Pl Santa María, 8 ☎ 20 59 71 AE, DC, MC, V $$$. The restaurant, in a 15C building, serves typical cuisine; its adjoining ★★★ hotel is agreeable and modern $$ to $$$$.

Best buys: Local specialities like the fresh soft cheese called *queso de Burgos* and the black puddings called *morcillas* are available from *Cuevas*, c/ Santander, 11, *Regia*, c/ San Lorenzo, 18, and *La Selecta*, c/ Laín Calvo. Antiques can be acquired at *Los Porches*, c/ Paloma, 12. Spanish fashion is available at *Dorothy y Peter*, Pl España, 13, *You*, c/ Vitoria, 15, *Adolfo Domínguez*, c/ Vitoria, 19, and *El Zoco*, Pl Calvo Sotelo, 9. The town's department store is *El Corte Inglés*, c/ Vitoria, 48.

Cultural highlights: The **Cathedral** is, together with the cathedrals of León, 🔯🔯🔯 Seville and Toledo, in the top division of Spain's huge Gothic church edifices. Work started on it in 1221 under the direction of the master builder Enrique, also responsible for León's Cathedral, and mass was first said in the cathedral nine years later although the building was not finally completed until the 15C This period was indeed Burgos' golden period. King Ferdinand III, the Saint, who ordered the cathedral's construction, was the powerful monarch who spearheaded the Christian drive down to the Muslim cities of Córdoba and Seville. European artists flocked to the capital of this successful crusader leader to add their talents to the great Gothic building that was being erected there. As the cathedral was nearing completion, **Hans of Cologne**, Juan de Colonia as he was known in Burgos, was at work adding French Gothic touches to its towers, **Gil de Siloé**, the last of the really great Gothic masters, was sculpting tombs and archivolts and schooling his son Diego in his art to carry on the family tradition, and Philippe de Vigarni was teaching a local man, Andrés de Nájera, the intricacies of carving choir stalls.

Walking around the exterior you will encounter on the W front, or **main façade**, the balustrade called the Galería de los Reyes, created by Juan de Colonia, which portrays the first eight kings of Castile, from Ferdinand I to Ferdinand III. The **Puerta de la Coronería** gate, on the N transept face after going up a ramp, has rich carvings of saints with Christ and of sinners in cauldrons. The **Puerta de la Pellejería**, on the E face of the N transept, was carved by Francisco de Colonia, Juan's grandson, and shows the mannerist influence of the 16C Plateresque style. The **Puerta del Sarmental**, the S transept entrance, is probably the finest and has just about everyone represented, from Moses and Aaron to Peter and Paul.

The interior of the cathedral is just as rich. Making a striking contrast, the remains of El Cid and his wife Doña Jimena lie under a plain marble tombstone beneath the central **cimborium**, 55m high. The **choir** is of inlaid 🔯🔯 walnut and was designed by Philippe de Vigarni (1512), who also designed the reredos in the **ambulatory**. Vigarni also worked on the decoration of the 🔯🔯 🔯 opulent **Capilla del Condestable**, at the E end, this time with **Diego de Siloé**. The chapel itself was built by Simón de Colonia. The chapel's collection of works of art includes outstanding gold and silver pieces and a panel of *Mary Magdalene* attributed to Leonardo da Vinci. You will take some time to work your way around the cathedral but it is a continuous source of delight for anyone remotely interested in Gothic and Renaissance art —take special note of the **Chapel of Santa Ana** with an altarpiece by Gil de Siloé. There are also some surprises: the Christ figure in the **Capilla del Santo Cristo** made of animal skins is popularly believed by the locals who venerate it to grow real hair and is considered fairly unsavoury by most outside visitors. There is also an ugly, gnome-like automaton called the *Papamoscas* that moves its right hand on the hour and sets the clock tower bell chiming.

The 14C **cloister** and adjacent chapels contain the **Cathedral Museum**, with religious objects, Flemish tapestries from the 15C and 16C, carvings by Vigarni and Siloé the Elder and the Younger, and ancient manuscripts.

In the city's old quarter four towers still survive from the original castle. Some stretches of the 13C city walls still stand and five out of the eight city gateways have remained. The main one, the 14C **Arco de Santa María** was added to in the 16C, and now features the figures of the Emperor Charles V in the centre flanked by Fernán González, the first independent count of Castile, and by the stocky El Cid on his right.

After the Cathedral the most important church in Burgos is the Gothic **San Nicolás** where Simón de Colonia produced an excellent **high altarpiece** in polychromed alabaster. The church of Santa Agueda is the site of a celebrated incident between King Alfonso VI and El Cid. The powerful and high-minded vassal forced the monarch to swear that he had played no part in the murder of his elder brother Sancho II. Alfonso complied under duress and later avenged the affront by exiling El Cid. The 15C **Casa del Cordón**, with its Gothic façade, was where the Catholic Monarchs received **Columbus** when he returned from his second voyage to the New World and it was also the palace where Isabella and Ferdinand's son-in-law, Philip the Fair, father of the future Emperor Charles V, died suddenly. This inopportune death sent his wife, Joan, the Catholic Monarch's daughter, off her head and she earned the title Joan the Mad as she subsequently travelled around Spain with Philip's rotting corpse. The local museum, the **Museo Provincial** (open: 10.00-1.00 and 4.45-7.15; Saturdays: 11.00-1.00; closed: Sundays and holidays ☎ 26 58 75), whose exhibits include a **sepulchre** by Gil de Siloé and a 12C **altar frontal** in enamelled copper from the Monastery of Santo Domingo de Silos (see separate entry) is in the Renaissance Miranda Palace. **Fiestas and festivals:** There is a **Festival of Religious Music** in Holy Week, the week before Easter (☎ 26 33 92), and another **Ancient Music Festival** in August. The **Corpus Christi procession** is picturesque.

Local sights: The **Monasterio de las Huelgas Reales**, just W of the city, was founded by Alfonso VIII and his English wife Eleanor (the daughter of the Plantagenet Henry II) in 1180, and they are both buried here along with several other members of the Castilian royal family. It is an extraordinarily rich convent for it was founded specifically as a Cistercian retreat for women of noble birth who opted for the veil and it enjoyed considerable royal patronage. Although predominantly Cistercian in style, it also features Romanesque, Mudéjar, Gothic and Plateresque elements. The **church**, with a separate section for use by the nuns of the closed order, contains 16-17C **tapestries** and an interesting 16C **pulpit**. The Gothic **cloister** still preserves fragments of its original Mudéjar stuccoed ceilings. The founder, Alfonso VIII, defeated the Moors at the battle of Las Navas de Tolosa in 1212, thus opening up the route into Andalusia. The enemy standard taken at this decisive engagement is on display in the **Chapter House** (open: 11.00-1.00 and 4.00-6.00; closed: Sunday afternoons and Holy Week). The room also exhibits a wooden statue of Santiago, the apostle James who is the patron saint of Spain, that has a mechanical right hand gripping a sword. This arm was ceremoniously lowered to touch the shoulders of kneeling future kings of Castile in dubbing them knights. The **Museo de Ricas Telas** exhibits fascinating ancient garments and accessories discovered in the sepulchres. Alfonso VIII, who was very much a Santiago knight, also founded a hospital for sick pilgrims travelling to the saint's shrine in Compostela. The **Hospital del Rey** is 3km W, outside the city and on the old pilgrimage route.

Burgos' other great monastic institution is the Charterhouse, 4km E of the city, the **Cartuja de Miraflores**. Juan de Colonia took time off from his supervision of the cathedral to build here a pantheon for King John II and his wife Isabella of Portugal, the parents of Isabella of Castile, the Catholic Queen. Gil de Siloé, who was at the height of his extraordinary artistic powers, was also called away from his patient work on the cathedral to create really magnificent **sculptures** such as the retable and the Gothic sepulchre for the monarchs. In a recess on the left is the tomb of Prince Alfonso, brother of the Catholic Queen. His death as a teenager proved to be a turning point in Spanish history for it paved the way for Isabella's accession to the throne.

The **Monastery of San Pedro de Cardeña**, in Fesdelval, 11km away, was founded in the 9C and has a place in El Cid lore. Its community of Trappist monks protected El Cid's wife Doña Jimena and their daughters when he was forced into exile by the treacherous Alfonso VI. Spain's number one hero was originally buried here before being moved to Burgos cathedral.

Castrojeriz, W of Burgos on the N-120, was much admired by the Compostela pilgrims; its main street, through which they passed, was lined with churches and it still is. The Collegiate Church of Santa María del Manzano has paintings by Mengs and a notable 18C choir and organ.

On the town: Good *tapa* bars in the Las Bernardas quarter include *Don Jamón*, c/ Alvor García, 2, *Rimbombín*, c/ Sombrería, 6, and *Puerto Chico*, c/ Reyes Católicos, 24. *Pentágono*, c/ Conde de Jordana, 2, is a good disco.

Sports: Flying (*Aero Club Burgos* ☎ 20 16 24), hunting in the nearby **National Reserves** and fishing (☎ (983) 23 46 72) are all local sports.

CARRIÓN DE LOS CONDES Palencia ☎ (988), pop. 2,850, ✚ 88 01 06. Palencia 39km, Burgos 86km, Madrid 257km.

Today an agricultural centre in the heart of the cereal growing area known as the Tierra de Campos which served as the granary of Spain, Carrión was an important halt on the Way of Saint James for the Compostela pilgrims. They must have arrived exhausted after trekking over the plateau from Burgos and they doubtless found succour at the village's 11C Monastery of San Zoilo.

⑪ *Mesón Pisarrosas* (closed: weekends and 1/7-20/9), c/ Piña Blasco, 27 ☎ 88 00 58 $$$. Home cooking.

Best buys: Old silver jewelry from *I. García*, Ctra N-120, and antiques from *Luis Andrés*, c/ Peña Brasco.

Cultural highlights: Carrión's best church is, like every second one on the pilgrim route, dedicated to **Santiago** and it has a pleasing late-12C **façade**. See, too, the 12C **Church of Santa María** and the originally 11C **Monastery of San Zoilo** with 16C additions including a fine Renaissance cloister.

Local sights: The village of **VILLALCAZAR DE SIRGA**, 7km SE, has a remarkable early Gothic church built in the 13C, the **Iglesia de Santa María la Blanca**, which has a particularly fine S façade and contains splendid tombs.

CERVERA DE PISUERGA **Palencia** ☎ (988), pop. 3,158, 🚂 3km away ☎ 87 00 42. Palencia 122km, Madrid 350km.

Set among mountains and lakes, this village is a *rendez-vous* for nature lovers and for art *aficionados* alike. The former take their backpacks up into the Fuentes Carrionas reserve and the latter explore the shrines and monasteries that lie along Palencia's Romanesque route which runs northwards and southwards along the C-627.

🍴🍴 🏨 **★★★ *Parador de Fuentes Carrionas*** ☎ 87 00 75 🛏 80 ✗ 🅿 ✦ 🎤 🐾
≪ **AE, DC, MC, V** $$$ to $$$$. Quiet and scenically situated.
Sports: The **Fuentes Carrionas National Hunting Reserve** is good hunting ground.

🍴 CIUDAD RODRIGO **Salamanca** ☎ (923), pop. 14,862, *i* c/ Arco de Amayuelos, 6 ☎ 46 05 61, (Pl del Caudillo, 20, ✉ c/ Castillejo, 14 ☎ 46 01 17, ✚ 46 12 28, **P** 46 00 54, 🚗 46 10 09, 🚂 46 11 13. Salamanca 90km, Plasencia 124km, Madrid 296km.

This is a wonderfully unspoiled medieval town on the banks of the River Agueda where you can walk right round the 12C walls that encircle it. In 1812 Wellington captured it from the French in a singularly bold assault during the Peninsular War; the cost after a 12-day siege was heavy: 1,300 casualties including two of his generals. The Iron Duke was granted the courtesy title of Duke of Ciudad Rodrigo by the grateful Spaniards and the tower over the Cathedral's W door still bears the scars of the British cannon fire.

🍴 🏨 **★★★ *Parador Enrique II*,** Pl del Castillo, 1 ☎ 46 01 50 🛏 27 ✗ ✦ 🐾
AE, DC, MC, V $$$ to $$$$. This impressive 15C castle has an extremely agreeable garden.

🏨 **★★ *Conde Rodrigo*,** Pl del Salvador, 9 ☎ 46 14 04 🛏 35 **TV** 🅿 🎤 **V** $$.
🍴 *Estoril*, Travesía Talavera, 1 ☎ 46 05 50 ✳ **DC, V** $$$.
Best buys: Filigree metal work is the local craft. Traditional local pastries are sold at *Gregorio Etreros*, c/ D. Ledesma, 6.

🍴 **Cultural highlights:** The **Cathedral** was built between the 12C and the 14C and had its central apse rebuilt in the 16C by the prolific Renaissance master builder **Rodrigo Gil de Hontañón**, whose major works include the cathedrals of Segovia and Valladolid and the University at Alcalá de Henares.
🍴 Note the delicate ornamentation of the 13C portal, the **Portada de la Virgen**.
🍴 The Renaissance **altarpiece** in the left nave is interesting. The Isabelline choir stalls are by Rodrigo Alemán, the master woodcarver who was responsible for the choir stalls in Avila Cathedral and for the truly astonishing series of
🍴 carvings in Toledo Cathedral's choir. The **cloister** (open: 8.00-12.00 and 4.00-8.00) is very peaceful and has Romanesque columns and capitals on the S and W sides and more ornamented Plateresque ones added in the 16C on the N and E flanks. Near the cathedral is the **Capilla de Cerralbo** (1588-1685) built in the Herreriano style, which contains a good Ribera. On the **Plaza Mayor** stand two Renaissance palaces, the **Casa de los Cueto** and another currently used as the **Town Hall**. The square is admirably picturesque and is the ideal place for a drink and a rest after touring the **walls** and the cathedral. The old medieval fort with its fine keep is a parador nowadays.
Fiestas: A yearly pilgrimage to La Caridad takes place on February 3. Carnival is celebrated here with considerable style and there is another excuse for merrymaking in May during the *Feria del Botijero*.
Local sights: San Felices de los Gallegos, 39km NW, is a beautiful fortified village. It is also the starting point for trips into the **Arribes del Duero**. The C-515 takes you to the **Sierra de Francia** (see 'Francia, Sierra de').

COVARRUBIAS **Burgos** ☎ (947), pop. 741. Burgos 40km, Madrid 227km.

This delightful walled village in the bucolic valley of the Arlanza river was the 10C home of **Fernán González**, a hero of several Romance epics, who prised himself free from the Kingdom of León to become the first independent count of Castile.

▥ ★★★ *Parador Colaborador Arlanza*, Pl Mayor, 11 ☎ 40 30 25 ⇌ 38 ⚏ AE, DC, MC, V $$$. Medieval banquets are held here on Saturdays in an old Castilian setting.

Cultural highlights: The whole medieval village is magnificently atmospheric but the Gothic **collegiate church**, where Fernán González is buried, deserves closer and more serious attention. Juan de Colonia and Gil de Siloé, the dynamic duo that beautified Burgos Cathedral and so many other places in Castile and León, worked closely together on this church. Gil was responsible for the superb *Triptych of the Adoration* which is the most eye-catching feature of the church's interior. The **organ** dates from the 17C and, now restored, is reckoned to be one of the best in Spain. The church's **museum** (open: 10.30-1.30 and 4.30-7.30; closed: Tuesdays) has panels by Pedro Berruguete and interesting 15C and 16C ornaments and sculptures. The village is dominated by the 10C tower named after Doña Urraca, Fernán González's grand-daughter, and one of its more modern buildings is the **Archivo del Adelantamiento de Castilla**, an archive tracing the history of Castile, which has a Renaissance main façade designed by Juan de Herrera, architect of the Escorial monastery for Philip II.

Festivals: Organ concerts are held in the summer.

Local sights: In Hortigüela, the ruins of the **Monastery of San Pedro de Arlanza**, founded by Fernán González, are very impressive. Students of Spanish Romance literature can spend a very satisfying holiday around these parts visiting the places and following the routes mentioned in the epic *Poema de Fernán González*. Some 23km away on the N-234, just outside **QUINTANILLA DE LAS VIÑAS**, stands the ancient Visigothic **shrine of Santa María**, with interesting Byzantine-influenced reliefs. The C-113 local road leads to the source of the Arlanza river through fantastic pine-clad mountains and picturesque villages. See separate entries for **LERMA** and **SANTO DOMINGO DE SILOS**.

FRANCIA, SIERRA DE **Salamanca** ☎ (923). Access from Salamanca along the C-512 and from Ciudad Rodrigo or Béjar along the C-515.

This is the isolated SW corner of the province of Salamanca bordering the Extremadura region. The Sierra de Francia, together with the Sierra de Gredos and the Sierra de Gata, forms the westernmost edge of the Sistema Central mountain range which cuts right across the tableland of Spain's inner plateau. Sierra de Francia's highest point is the 1,732m high **Peña de Francia** where there is a monastery which takes in guests —men only, though. The area's most visited spot is **LA ALBERCA**, an extremely pretty little mountain village with an arcaded main square, now in danger of becoming rather touristy. Its former isolation has meant that old customs and regional dress have been especially well preserved —*El Ofertorio* and *La Loa* are ancient liturgical ceremonies held on August 15 and 16. Best buys in La Alberca include hams and sausages from *F. Martín* and *Hermanos Becerra*, and hand-crafted embroideries from *Natividad Hoyos*. ★★ *Las Batuecas*, Ctra Las Batuecas, s/n ☎ 43 70 30 ⇌ 24 ✕ ℙ ✦ ⚏ $$, provides lodging and meals. Other scenic villages which have the advantage of being off the tour bus route are **MIRANDA DEL CASTAÑAR** —with an interesting festival called *Las Mayordomas* on February 5, when the men surrender their authority to the women, and traditional dances on September 8—, San Martín del Castañar and Sequeros.

The **Valle de las Batuecas**, S of La Alberca, is a gorgeously green and peaceful little valley —its **National Hunting Reserve** is good hunting territory. Continuing S you reach the even more isolated region of **Las Hurdes** (see 'Hurdes, Las' in 'Extremadura').

FROMISTA **Palencia** ☎ (988), pop. 1,133. Palencia 31km, Burgos 78km, Madrid 257km.

Right on the pilgrim route to Compostela, Frómista boasts what most critics claim to be Spain's **perfect Romanesque church**.

♯ *Hostería de los Palmeros* (closed: September, and Tuesdays in winter), Pl Mayor ☎ 81 00 67 **DC, V $$$**. A very pleasant inn with a pilgrim flavour to it.

Best buys: Local cheese, one of the best in Spain, is sold at *Quesería Campera* ☎ 81 00 40 (mornings).

Cultural highlights: Medieval travellers must have marvelled at the beauty of the **Church of San Martín** (it was built in 1066, the year of the battle of Hastings and of the introduction of Norman architecture to Britain) every bit as much as visitors do today. Few can fail to be impressed by the painstaking carvings of the capitals and corbels, at the lightness and balance of the vaults over the church's three naves and at the use of space in the three rounded apses. The church was zealously restored at the turn of this century, some would say over-restored, and it is in reality a museum now for no church services are held in it. Critics who claim that San Martín lacks spirituality nowadays have a point but it is indisputably a jewel of a building which set a standard by which all Romanesque architecture in Spain has to be measured.

The **Church of Santa María**, dating from the early 14C, has an imposing Hispano-Flemish altarpiece.

GREDOS, SIERRA DE **Avila** ☎ (918). Access from Hoyos del Espino (SW of Avila along the C-500) and from Arenas de San Pedro.

Gredos is one of the finest of Spain's many sierras. The philosopher and essayist Miguel de Unamuno (1864-1936) who, like virtually every sensitive Spaniard, loved Gredos, called these massive granite mountains the spinal column of Spain. They form the highest part of the Sistema Central range and the highest of its summits, **Pico Almanzor**, rises to 2,592m. The sierra is at its most rugged, windswept and barren along its N face where glaciers have formed circuses and lakes. The S flank acts as a protective shield for the fruit-laden valley of the gurgling Tietar river (see 'Vera, La' in 'Extremadura'). All over the sierra there are hiking trails that draw outdoor enthusiasts in the summer months, for Gredos is a national park that is well-stocked with wild life as well as scenically stunning. You can even catch sight of the mouflon type of wild goat, the *Capra Hispanica*, as it leaps from one impossibly narrow craggy ledge to another.

The main town on the southern slopes is the agreeably hospitable **ARENAS DE SAN PEDRO** and it is a favourite starting point for the drive up and into the mountains. The complex of underground caverns called the **Cuevas del Aguila**, close to the village of Ramacastañas, is a nearby tourist attraction. The caves have as many stalactites and stalagmites as you could wish for. The **road** up to the **Puerto del Pico** mountain pass, 1,352m, goes first through the village of **MOMBELTRAN**, which has a very conspicuous 14C castle built by the Duke of Alburquerque, and then starts a steep ascent. The modern day road clings to the side of the slope and winds its way up but the Romans, in an astonishing feat of engineering, contrived to build a **road**, parts of which run parallel to the one used today and almost perfectly preserved, which zigzags up to the pass at its most perpendicular point. Once you have taken in the **view** from the pass, looking down towards the valley and Arenas and across to the vista of mountain peaks, follow the signs to the Parador de Gredos. Shortly after passing the parador, a surfaced forestry road from the village of Hoyos del Espino takes you right into the heart of the Sierra. There comes a point where you have to park your car and from then on it's a question of strong boots, a backpack and a pair of field glasses as you hit the trails that lead up to the glacial formations. Continuing from Hoyos del Espino you eventually come down the N flank of Gredos to reach the no less agreeably hospitable village of **BARCO DE AVILA** on the River Tormes, which is the starting point for penetrating Gredos from the N. This particular village is very famous for its beans and like all the settlements in the sierra it has picturesque wooden balconies and is imbued with the welcoming aroma of log fires.

▦ ★★★ *Parador de Gredos*, Navarredonda de Gredos ☎ 34 80 48 ⊨ 77 ✕ �a �ⓟ ✦ ⓓ ⓢ ≪ ⓠ ⓡ, AE, DC, MC, V $$$ to $$$$. Built in the 1920s this was the first of Spain's prestigious parador chain to be opened to the public. It is wonderfully **situated**, is utterly peaceful and has a fantastic terrace that looks across to the Almanzor peak. It also has a pleasant restaurant.

Sports: The **Gredos National Hunting Reserve** is exceptional hunting territory, while there is good trout fishing in the area's many rivers.

LEÓN **León** ☎ (987), pop. 137,414, *i* Pl de la Catedral, 4 ☎ 23 70 82, ℂ Av del Padre Isla, 26, ✉ Jardines de San Francisco, s/n ☎ 23 42 90 and 22 20 00, ☧ 22 71 00, **P** Villa Benavente ☎ 25 26 08, ▣ c/ Cardenal Lorenzana, 4 ☎ 22 62 00, ⚅ c/ Roa de la Vega, 26 ☎ 22 26 25 (North Station: c/ Astorga ☎ 22 37 04). Oviedo 119km, Valladolid 135km, Burgos 192km, Madrid 319km.

León is a delight to visit, particularly if you can stay at the Renaissance **Monastery of San Marcos** which has now been turned into a luxury hotel. From these lodgings, which must be among the architecturally most beautiful in the world, or from wherever you happen to be staying, you can saunter forth to visit artistic musts: a Romanesque royal pantheon which has quite extraordinary murals and a glorious Gothic **cathedral** which, by general consensus, is the best of its kind in Spain.

The town itself dates its foundation to a Roman legion's 1C camp. It was occupied by the Arabs in 717 but it was back in Christian hands by the 10C when it became the capital of the Visigothic Kingdom of Astur-León, comprising the present day region of Asturias as well as León province. The kingdom's fortunes soon became inextricably linked with those of Castile and by the 13C the capital had moved over to Burgos. Today León is a prosperous provincial city, a well established agricultural centre and a developed focal point for local industries.

▦ ★★★★★ *San Marcos*, Pl San Marcos, 7 ☎ 23 73 00 ⊨ 253 �a TV ✦ ⓓ AE, DC, MC, V $$$$ to $$$$$. Luxurious lodging in a magnificent 16C monastery —an unbeatable setting.

▦ ★★★★ *Conde Luna*, c/ Independencia, 7 ☎ 20 65 12 ⊨ 154 ⓓ ⚲ ▣ AE, DC, MC, V $$$ to $$$$.

▦ ★★ *Quindós*, Av José Antonio, 24 ☎ 23 62 00 ⊨ 96 MC, V $$ to $$$. Central.

▯ *Adonías* (closed: Sundays and 10/7-25/7), c/ Santa Nonia, 16 ☎ 20 67 68 ✳ AE, DC, MC, V $$ to $$$. Typical León cuisine with a touch of class.

¶ *Casa Pozo* (closed: Sundays and at Christmas), Pl San Marcelo, 15 ☎ 22 30 39 ✳ **AE, DC, V** $$$. It has been serving local cuisine for the past 50 years.

¶ *Patricio* (closed: Sunday evenings and Mondays), c/ Condesa de Sagasta, 24 ☎ 24 16 51 ✳ **AE, DC, V** $$$. Imaginative local cuisine.

Best buys: Sausages and local delicacies are available from ***Guerra de Paz***, c/ Platerías, 3, and sweets and cakes from ***C. de Blas***, c/ Generalísimo, 13. Tin ornaments are sold at ***V. Monroy***, c/ Santa Cruz, 16, and Castilian antiques at ***A. Alonso***, c/ Los Cubos, 32. Spanish fashion is available at ***Adams***, c/ San Agustín, 4.

Cultural highlights: Unlike Burgos Cathedral, which was built slowly over the centuries, Leon's **Cathedral** was built within 100 years and precisely at the moment (13-14C) when the medieval master builders felt utterly confident about their ability to raise higher and higher vaults and to let in more and more light. This means that Leon's Cathedral has a unity of style and a finished and completed look about it that you do not find easily elsewhere, and it also reflects perfectly the ambition of reaching up to the heavens and becoming part of them that so obsessed the big church designers of the Middle Ages. León has the great advantage of being set high on the Spanish plateau and beneath normally cloudless skies, so the visitor to the cathedral receives the full effect of the stained glass windows. You do not step inside the usual old church gloominess when you enter León's cathedral: shafts of multi-coloured light beam down from above and you feel as if you are inside a diamond.

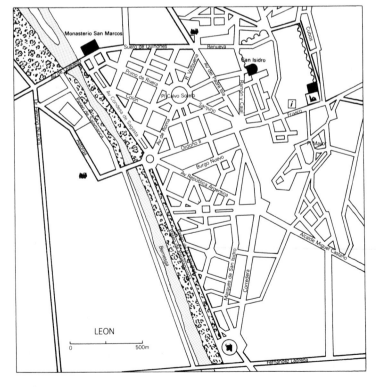

At the **W façade**, the triple portico beneath the rose window features an intricate series of carvings of the Last Judgment, the Coronation of the Virgin Mary and of the Infancy of Jesus. Medieval man understood the images as instantly as his descendants today follow a cartoon film. Going round the Cathedral what you notice more than anything else is the huge effort that went into shaping stone into something of spiritual beauty that might serve to elevate mortal man's thoughts. Inside, the chief effect comes from the height of the vaults and the delicacy of the columns supporting them, as well as from the dazzling light introduced by the 125 **windows**. The high altarpiece is composed of a 15C triptych by Nicolás Francés who also painted the frescoes in the cloister. The choir was installed in the 15C, making it one of the earliest in Spain, and Esteban Jordán, who was the son-in-law of the celebrated Spanish Renaissance decorator Alonso Berruguete, demonstrated that he was an artist in his own right with the reliefs he added to the **retrochoir**. From the Gothic and Renaissance **cloister** a Renaissance stairway leads to the **Cathedral Museum** (open: 10.00-1.00 and 4.00-7.00) with a collection of early sculptures, works by Pedro de Mena, Juan de Juni and, best of all, interesting **codices**.

The Romanesque **Colegiata de San Isidoro** is at once the **pantheon of the ancient kings** of the Astur-León kingdom and a unique insight into the medieval world at its most creative. Inside the church, the **capitals** are eye-catching but it is the 12C Romanesque **frescoes** decorating the walls and vaults which are the most moving. They deal not only with New Testament themes but also with the daily life of people in the 12C in an unforgettable series that depicts scenes from each month of the year. Returning to the outside you have a number of firsts. The lateral portico was the first in the Romanesque style to be used in a Spanish church, and the **Puerta del Perdón**, the Door of Forgiveness, which was a staple element in churches of the period, is the first in Spain to depict scenes from the gospels. The effect of the latter must have been at the time like the invention of moving pictures a century ago. The author of this innovation was the master-builder Esteban who worked initially on the building of Burgos Cathedral. In the interior, the **retable** with 24 Flemish panels is suitably magnificent. From the cloister you pass to the Library and **Treasury** (open in summer: 9.00-2.30 and 3.00-7.00; winter: 10.00-1.00 and 4.00-7.00; closed: Sunday afternoons and holidays) which have a rich manuscript collection and a number of important medieval religious objects including a **chalice** that belonged to Doña Urraca, the founder of the church and the grand-daughter of Fernán González, the first independent count of Castile. Urraca was married to Ordoño III of León in the hope of reuniting the two regions but unfortunately her husband spurned her and sent her packing back to Covarrubias in 978.

The **Monastery of San Marcos** is one of Spain's Renaissance masterpieces. A hotel today, it was founded by Ferdinand of Aragón, the Catholic King, to serve as a hospital for the pilgrims travelling to Compostela and it was entrusted for safekeeping to the military order of the Knights of Santiago. The **main façade** is an excellent example of the style known as Plateresque, derived from the Spanish word for silversmith because the carvers sculpted the stone as if they were imitating the filigree craft of those who worked with precious metals. The style is sufficiently mannerist to be the antechamber of the Baroque and the central Baroque door on this façade proves the point by not upsetting the harmony of the building. Inside the monastery-hospital turned luxury hotel, the church, which was completed in 1531, has beautiful choir stalls, Juan de Badajoz's (1549) **sacristy** is a true work of art, and the **Chapter House** has a fine Mudéjar coffered ceiling. The

🕭 16C **cloister** (open: 10.00-2.00 and 4.00-7.00) is an **Archaeological Museum** showing archaeological exhibits and a collection of Romanesque
🕭🕭🕭 figures that includes an exceptional ivory crucifixion, the *Cristo de Carrizo*.

Except for the Cathedral, the Collegiate Church of San Isidoro and the San Marcos Monastery there is little of great interest in León bar the odd picturesque corner between the **Plaza Mayor** and the porticoed market square, the **Pl del Mercado**, and in the new part of town, the 19C **Casa de Botines**, by Gaudí, built in the Neo-gothic style.

Fiestas and Festivals: Street parties and fairs mark the week between the feast days of Saint John and Saint Peter (21-30 June) and there is an **Organ Festival** in the Cathedral in September and October.

Local sights: There are a couple of villages S of León which have a fine medieval air to them and underline the importance that the old kingdom once
🕭 exerted. **San Miguel de la Escalada**, 28km from León, is an interesting Mozarabic church (built in 913 by Christians living under Muslim rule) with an 11C **portico**. The **Cuevas de Valporquero**, 47km N, have beautiful stalactites in different shades of red, grey and black.

On the town: The bars around the Pl de San Martín and its adjoining sreets are full of people in the evenings and *tapa* bars such as *La Bicha, La Bodega Regia, Caño Valdillo* and *La Mazmorra* are popular. The *Café Victoria*, c/ Generalísimo 25, which opened its doors more than a century ago, is rather more sedate. If you feel like dancing, head for *Branco*.

🕭🕭🕭 **Sports:** This is good large game hunting and excellent **trout fishing** territory ☎ (987) 39 52 67 (see 'Holidays in Action'), In winter, skiing can be practised at *Valgrande-Pajares* ☎ (985) 49 61 23 and *San Isidro* ☎ (987) 73 50 66, 1,500-1,955m, with 12 ski lifts and 12 runs.

LERMA **Burgos** ☎ (947), pop. 2,583, ✚ 17 00 60, 🚑 17 02 69. Burgos 37km, Palencia 76km, Madrid 200km.

You cannot miss this village for it is perched on high ground dominating the highway between Madrid and Burgos. It is interesting for its connection with the avaricious, scheming and temporarily powerful **Duke of Lerma** who built the palace and virtually everything else in the place. He was the favourite of King Philip III in the early 17C, was replaced as number one vassal by his son, the Duke of Uceda, and was finally disgraced by the new king, Philip IV, and forced to spend the last years of his life in Tordesillas castle.

🖾 ★★ *Alisa*, Ctra N-I, km202 ☎ 17 02 75 🛏 26 ✕ ✦ V $$. It has a restaurant $$$.

Cultural highlights: The lower part of the village is prettily medieval with its **Arco de la Cárcel** archway, old houses and steep, narrow streets. The upper part is a monument to the Duke of Lerma's megalomania. Unfortunately he was lacking in taste and his gigantic palace, currently showing signs of wear and tear, could not have been particularly attractive even in its prime. The adjoining collegiate church that the duke had built in 1605 shows the influence of Classical lines which here and there, in this period, formed a counterpoint to the Baroque exuberance. The church contains the substantial bronze tomb, in the style of Pompeo Leoni, of Cristóbal de Rojas, who was Lerma's uncle and Archbishop of Seville.

MEDINACELI **Soria** ☎ (975), pop. 940. Soria 76km, Madrid 154km.

This mountain-top village, 3km uphill from its modern part beside the N-II, has a 2C Roman **arch** which will look very familiar for it is used on all official signposts to denote an historical building. It also has a foreign population of artists who have very sensibly elected to live surrounded by old buildings, spectacular views and very bracing fresh air.

¶ *Duque de Medinaceli* (closed: 14/2-14/3), Ctra N-II, km150 ☎ 32 61 11 **AE, DC, MC, V** $$$. It has a good wine cellar and an even better collection of antique clocks. ★ Rooms are available ⌷ 12 ⌷ $$.

Cultural highlights: The **Roman arch** and walls and the remains of an Arab ⌷ castle and restored Moorish arch are particularly interesting. Many of the buildings have been lovingly restored, stone on stone, by the new cosmopolitan community and the whole place has a timeless feel to it which is exactly what these enterprising residents intend. The main edifices are a 16C Gothic collegiate church and the 17C Palace of the Dukes of Medinaceli, which stands on the charmingly porticoed **Plaza Mayor**.

Fiestas and festivals: A series of ancient music recitals, the *Noches Musicales de Medinaceli*, are staged in the second half of August. An old rite, called the *Toro Júbilo* takes place on the Saturday nearest to September 13. This particular *fiesta*, in which a bull with blazing torches attached to its horns runs through the village, has clear pagan connotations and is not for the squeamish.

Local sights: Not far from the nearby village of Ambrona is a Palaeontological Museum in the form of a barn covering an excavated site revealing the remains of elephants which roamed the area many thousands of years ago. The **Monastery of Santa María de Huerta**, a 12C Cistercian ⌷ abbey founded by Alfonso VIII, which now has a parador attached to it —★★★ *Parador Santa María de Huerta*, Ctra N-II, km180 ☎ 32 70 11 ⌷ 40 ✕ **P** ✦ **AE, DC, MC, V** $$$— lies some 30km further on towards Zaragoza on the N-II. The first of its cloisters, the **Claustro del Caballero**, ⌷ was added in the late 16C and clearly bears the severe stamp of Juan de Herrera, the builder of the Escorial. You will find austerity of a much more pleasing and certainly impressive kind in the vast 13C Gothic **monks** ⌷⌷ **refectory** with its rose window and its pointed archways. The **church** has a high altar that is richly decorated in the style that the Churriguera family of Baroque decorators and carvers made famous throughout Spain in the 18C. The **upper choir** has fine Renaissance stalls but, best of all, it has an ornamented floor made up of very old glazed tiles. *A. Sánchez*, in the monastery, carves polychromed wooden figures.

MEDINA DEL CAMPO **Valladolid** ☎ (985), pop. 19,597, 80 00 75, ⌷ 80 00 99. Valladolid 43km, Salamanca 81km, Madrid 156km.

This was already an important wool town in the Middle Ages and it still holds the most important sheep fairs in Spain. Its main historical and architectural feature is the **Castillo de la Mota** which is near the top of the Castles in Spain league.

¶ *Madrid*, c/ Claudio Moyano, 2 ☎ 80 01 34 ✳ **P** V $$$.

Best buys: Furniture from *Rembrandt*, Ctra N-IV.

Cultural highlights: The 15C Gothic-Mudéjar **Castillo de la Mota** is where ⌷ Isabella of Castile, the Catholic Queen, died in 1504. Her daughter, the mad Queen Joan, spent a considerable time locked up in the castle's dungeon, raving and mourning her husband, Philip the Fair. See, too, the 16C Palacio de las Dueñas and the grandiose houses around the splendid **Pl de España**, which illustrate the town's long standing prosperity.

Local sights: A 21km drive along the C-112 leads to **OLMEDO**, a village with Gothic and Romanesque-Mudéjar churches which is redolent of former splendour and echoes with the poetry of one of Golden Age playwright Lope de Vega's greatest plays, *The Knight of Olmedo*. The play involves the dastardly murder on the road between Olmedo and Medina of the Knight, the play's hero, who loves and is loved by the wretched murderer's future wife.

This area produces extremely good Rueda **white wines** which are much appreciated in Spain but little known beyond its frontiers. A selection of villages and their wineries includes: Nava del Rey (*Alvarez y Díez*, c/ J.A. Carmona, 16); **RUEDA** (*A. Maldonado*, c/ Primo de Rivera, 12, *A. Rodríguez Vidal*, c/ Torcida, s/n, *Bodegas Castilla La Vieja*, Ctra N-VI, km170, *F. Sanz Revuelta*, c/ Santísimo Cristo, 30); **LA SECA** (***Bodega Cooperativa Agrícola Castellana***, Ctra Rodilana, s/n, *S. Sanz*, c/ Cuatro Calles, s/n) and Pozaldez (*F. Lorenzo Cachazo*, c/ Mauro García, 2).

A 20km drive takes you to **MATAPOZUELOS** and its **Castile and León Zoo** ☎ 35 56 00.

MEDINA DE RIOSECO Valladolid ☎ (983), pop. 5,037. Valladolid 41km, Palencia 48km, Madrid 225km.

A medieval wool trade town, it was rich enough to bring in top artists to decorate its churches in the 16C. Nowadays farming has shifted to cereals and Medina de Rioseco is a key centre in the Tierra de Campos (Land of the Fields), poetically known as the 'Granary of Castile'.

▥ ★★★ *Los Almirantes*, Paseo de San Francisco, 2 ☎ 70 01 25 ⊨ 30 ✕ ✦ 🖢 ⚬ 🐎 AE, DC, V $$ to $$$. The restaurant is acceptable.

❙❙ *Mesón La Rúa* (closed: Thursday evenings and September), c/ San Juan, 34 ☎ 70 07 83 🅿 ✳ DC, V $$$.

Best buys: Antiques, mostly ecclesiastical, can be bought at *Arte Castellano*; cakes at *El Cubero*, *La Espiga* and *Castilviejo*.

Cultural highlights: The ubiquitous Esteban Jordán created one of his several main retables for the 16C **Church of Santa María**. The altarpiece in the **Benavente Chapel** is by the irrepressible Juan de Juni whose showiness earned him fame and fortune in the High Renaissance. The master builder Rodrigo Gil de Hontañón, whose time was fully booked for most of the 16C, helped design the **Church of Santiago** and the Churriguera family, who was as successful and busy two centuries later, worked on the retable. The picturesque main street, **La Rúa**, is porticoed and has ancient wooden supporting columns.

Fiestas: The Holy Week penitential processions, when floats bearing life-sized figures, many dating from the 16C, are carried through the streets by hooded penitents, are movingly austere events.

Local sights: **VILLALON DE CAMPOS**, 28km N along the Ctra N-610, is as famous for its **fresh cheese** as it is for its monuments, among them the 15C **pillory**.

OÑA Burgos ☎ (947), pop. 2,039. Burgos 73km, Logroño 99km.

This very ancient town, on a **gorge** formed by the River Oca, was a seat of the counts of Castile and the burial place of many of the descendants of the legendary Fernán González. The little town was sacked in 1367 by the troops of England's Black Prince who spent a spell in Spain earning some mercenary money from King Peter the Cruel.

Cultural highlights: The three-tiered **Plaza Mayor**, flanked by the church of the 11C Monastery of San Salvador is interesting. Several of those involved in the Burgos Cathedral project, including Simón de Colonia and Philippe de Vigarni, were brought in later to restore and beautify the **church**. Note the beautiful 16C **cloister**.

Local sights: **FRIAS**, to the NE, is one of the most picturesque villages in Castile. Its chief feature is its castle which looks as if it is literally hanging on to its craggy location. The village's bridge over the Ebro river was built by the Romans and restored in the 13C; from here you have a lovely **view** of the valley. A treat awaits you if you visit on the Sunday closest to Saint John's Day (June 24), for the *Baile del Capitán* dances are performed then.

PALENCIA **Palencia** ☎ (988), pop. 76,707, 🅸 c/ Mayor, 105 ☎ 74 00 68, ☎ c/ Felipe Prieto, s/n, ✉ Pl de León, 1, ✚ 72 41 00, **P** 74 76 77, 🚌 74 32 22, 🚄 74 30 19. Valladolid 44km, Burgos 84km, León 128km, Santander 203km, Madrid 228km.

Palencia is a pleasant market town and it appears quietly satisfied about its status as the capital of a province that justifiably boasts the best Romanesque architecture in Spain. You should not be put off by the standard ugliness of Palencia's outskirts. This is something that the traveller in Spain encounters in one town after another. It is worth penetrating this outer shell.

🏨 **★★★ *Castilla la Vieja*,** c/ Casado del Alisal, 26 ☎ 74 90 44 🛏 87 📺 **P** 🎙 **AE, DC, V $$ to $$$.**

🏨 **★★★ *Rey Sancho de Castilla*,** Av Ponce de León, s/n ☎ 72 53 00 🛏 100 **P** ✦ 🎙 ⚓ 🐎 ✕ **MC, V $$ to $$$.**

🏨 **★★ *Castillo de Monzón*,** in Monzón de Campos, 12km out of town ☎ 80 80 75 **P** 🎙 🦮 **AE, DC, MC, V $$ to $$$.** Set in a medieval castle, this is a very peaceful hotel with a panoramic view of the grain lands that are known as the Tierra de Campos. Good value for money.

🍴 *Casa Damián* (closed: Mondays and 25/7-25/8), c/ Martínez de Azcoitia, 9 ☎ 74 38 70 ✳ **AE, DC, V $$$.** Home-cooking.

🍴 *Lorenzo* (closed: Sundays and 15/9-5/10), Av Casado del Alisal, 10 ☎ 74 35 45 **AE, DC, V $$$.**

Best buys: Woollen blankets from *L. Casañé*, c/ Casañé, 2; local pastries from *Portillo*, c/ Regimiento de Villarobledo and *El Pastelero de Madrigal*, c/ Mayor, 106; antiques from *Marugán*, Av Casado del Alisal, 10; regional arts and crafts are exhibited and sold at a fair that is held in the Plaza Mayor at the beginning of September. Spanish fashion is available at *Bess Bess*, c/ Mayor, 52.

Cultural highlights: Palencia's Gothic **Cathedral** was built between the 14-15C which, compared with the cathedrals of León and Burgos, makes it a fairly late one. The cathedral occupies the site of an earlier Romanesque church which in turn was built over a Visigothic shrine, vestiges of which remain in the crypt. The tour de force of the richly ornamented **interior** is the very large retable behind the high altar in the chancel. This is a five-tier Renaissance **altarpiece** that was for the most part carved by Philippe de Vigarni after he had completed his commissions in Burgos cathedral. The outstanding contribution to the retable is, however, the series of 12 panels painted by Juan de Flandes. The whole structure is capped by a Crucifixion sculpted by Juan de Valmaseda. Valmaseda was also responsible for the impressive Plateresque style retable in the **Capilla del Sagrario** which houses the simple 12C tomb of Doña Urraca, the wife of King Sancho VI of Navarre. Plateresque ornamentation also makes its impact in the retrochoir area. The cathedral's **cloister** was designed by Juan Gil de Hontañón, who was the architect of the cathedrals in Salamanca and Segovia and the father of the equally talented Renaissance master builder, Rodrigo Gil de Hontañón. The **Cathedral Museum**, in the Chapter House (open: 10.00-1.00 and 4.00-6.00; closed: Sundays in winter), offers an opportunity to gain a closer look at Valmaseda's and Vigarni's carvings. It also contains four splendid 16C **Flemish tapestries** and a number of paintings by El Greco, Valdés Leal, Nicolás Francés and Pedro Berruguete among others.

Those interested in Rodrigo Díaz de Vivar, better known as El Cid, should visit the Romanesque **Church of San Miguel** because that is where he married Doña Jimena. The 14C Monastery of Santa Clara contains an image of the Dead Christ which inspired Miguel de Unamuno (see 'Literature') to write a poem, *El Cristo de las Claras de Palencia*, in which he gave full rein to his pessimism about the abject state of Spain at the turn of this century.

Fiestas and festivals: Traditional celebrations take place on January 1, when an ancient carol, the *Ea*, is sung. The town's *fiesta* in honour of its patron San Antolín takes place between August 28 and September 3. A music festival is held in March (☎ 74 97 00).

Local sights: What is allegedly the oldest church in Spain, a 7C Visigothic

☉ chapel dedicated to John the Baptist, is in the village of **BAÑOS DE CERRATO**, 12km SE and close to the railway junction of Venta de Baños. The Trappist **Monastery of San Isidoro**, whose founding dates back to the 10C, stands just short of Dueñas, 12km out of Palencia. Vistors can attend the plain-chant services, buy chocolates manufactured by the monks, and even spend a night at the monastery (see 'Where to Stay').

The village of **PAREDES DE NAVA**, to the NW on the C-613, was the birthplace of the soldier-poet **Jorge Manrique** who wrote a moving existentialist elegy on the death of his father and himself died when storming the gates of a castle in La Mancha in the service of Isabella of Castile, the Catholic Queen. The remarkable father and son team of Renaissance sculptors, **Pedro and Alonso Berruguete** (see 'Painting and Sculpture'), whose works are scattered around Castile and León, were also born here.

☉ You can see the **retable** they jointly carved and decorated in their local parish church, the village's **Iglesia de Santa Eulalia**.

☉☉ PEDRAZA DE LA SIERRA **Segovia** ☎ (911), pop. 467. Segovia 35km, Madrid 125km.

This **walled medieval village** is probably too pretty for its own good. It has become very popular with Madrid city dwellers who have restored its old houses to use as weekend homes and it has a bijou flavour to it as a result. But pretty it undeniably remains. As a plus it has a first-class antique shop which remains open on Sundays, lots of welcoming *tapa* bars and several restaurants with wood-fired roasting ovens.

🍴 *Bodegón Manrique*, c/ Procuradores, 6 ☎ 50 40 79 $$$. Only weekend lunches. Roast lamb.

🍴 *Hostería Pintor Zuloaga* (closed: Tuesdays), c/ Matadero, 1 ☎ 50 40 88 ♣ ≪ AE, DC, EC, V $$$. The restaurant used to be the local headquarters of the Inquisition. Typical Pedraza roasts.

🍴 *El Yantar de Pedraza* (closed: Mondays), Plaza Mayor ☎ 50 41 07 ♣ AE, DC, EC, V $$$. Try to get a table on the balcony overlooking the main square. Classic roasts.

Best buys: You will find antiques, Castilian furniture, rural bric-à-brac and several surprises at *De Natura*, which is owned by one of Spain's most successful interior decorators. Pewter art objects, a well-established local craft, are available at *Estaños de Pedraza*, c/ Procuradores.

Cultural highlights: The porticoed **Plaza Mayor** with its 15C columns is delightful. The castle was in ruins at the turn of the century when it was bought for a song and lovingly restored by the Spanish painter **Ignacio Zuloaga**. In its 16C prime the castle served as a prison for the sons of Francis I of France after they had been taken hostage by the Emperor Charles V. Most visitors to Pedraza walk around its imposing **walls** in order to work up an appetite or to digest the gargantuan roasts served in the hostelries.

Fiestas and festivals: As in many villages in this area the local celebrations, held in September in Pedraza's case, are accompanied by bull running thrills and spills that are called *encierros*. In early summer, classical music concerts are frequently staged in the castle.

On the town: Wine and cheese beside a log-burning stove in the 15-year old *Taberna de Mariano* on the Plaza Mayor is a classic. Try the cider at *Sidreía El Yantar*.

PEÑAFIEL **Valladolid** ☎ (983), pop. 5,284, ✚ 88 07 69, ⚕ 88 14 63.   ◐
Valladolid 55km, Madrid 180km.

The walls of Peñafiel's ruined castle are one of the best sights in Castile.
They run along the length of the ridge and are more than 200m long. The
castle was built by the Infante, or royal prince, **Juan Manuel** (see 'Literature'),
a grandson of Ferdinand III, the Saint, who conquered Córdoba and Seville.
Despite the 14C castle's forbidding appearance, the Infante was not really
warlike: he preferred writing books, one of which, a romance called the
Conde Lucanor, has survived. Peñafiel is nowadays the commercial centre of
the highly recommendable **Ribera del Duero** wines.

🍴 *Asador Mauro* (closed: Sunday nights), c/ Atarazanas, s/n ☎ 88 08 16
V $$$. Roast lamb.

Best buys: The **wines** of the Ribera del Duero can be exceptional and the
Peñafiel *clarete*, or light red, is very pleasing. Tipplers should stock up at the
Cooperativa, Camino del Cementerio, s/n. Serious wine buffs after the real
stuff know exactly where to go: the ***Vega-Sicilia winery*** at Valbuena del   ◐◐◐
Duero, 10km from the town. For rustic furniture, go to *Chambalo*, c/ O.
Redondo, 16.

◐ **Cultural highlights:** Aside from the **castle**, the town's old **Pl del Coso** is
very typically Castilian. Knights used to charge at each other across the plaza
in medieval tournaments and fair damsels would watch from the shuttered
windows that look on to it. Today the plaza is used for bullfights which is why
it remains sandy. The **Church of San Pablo**, founded by the Infante in the
14C, has interesting Mudéjar ornamentation and a bold Renaissance vault in
the Infante Juan Manuel chapel.

Fiestas: In common with many Castilian villages, the September *fiestas* in
Peñafiel are marked by *encierros* or bull running. There are also picturesque
celebrations on Easter Sunday.

PONFERRADA **León** ☎ (987), pop. 58,544, [*i*] Av de la Puebla, 1 ☎
41 22 50 ext. 226, ✉ c/ General Vives, 1 ☎ 41 18 24, ✚ 41 45 55, **P**
41 55 65, 🚍 Av Libertad, 15 ☎ 40 10 65, ⚕ 41 00 67. León 109km,
Orense 159km, Madrid 385km.

The town owes its name to the 11C iron bridge, *Pons Ferrata* in Latin,
that was built across the Sil river to help the thousands of medieval pilgrims
on their way to Compostela. The capital of the **Bierzo** region (see 'Bierzo, El'),
Ponferrada has always been a centre for iron-ore mining and today it is very
much an industrial town.

🏨 ★★★ *Del Temple*, Av Portugal, 2 ☎ 41 00 58 ⇄ 114 📺 **P** ≈ AE, DC,
MC, V $$$. Original decor reminiscent of the age of the Templar Knights.

🍴 *Virgen de la Peña*, at Congosto, 10km from the town ☎ 46 71 02 ✦ ≈
≪ V $$$. By the shrine of the same name and scenically located.

Cultural highlights: The heavily restored Romanesque and Gothic **castle**
(open: 10.00-1.00 and 5.00-7.00; closed: Mondays) used to belong to the
Knights Templar. The dilapidated Plaza Mayor's sole redeeming feature is the
splendid Baroque Town Hall.

Fiestas and festivals: The castle stages a theatre season in August. In
September an agricultural and food produce fair is a great opportunity to
sample the best results of the Bierzo area's longstanding farming tradition.

Local sights: The 10C Mozarabic **Church of Santo Tomás de las Ollas** is
1.5km E. Going W, the village of **CACABELOS** was an important stopping
point on the pilrimage route to the shrine of Saint James. In the Middle Ages,
when Compostela attracted pilgrims in their thousands, Cacabelos had no
fewer than five hospitals that provided them with care and succour. Perhaps
in those days the local *clarete* wine was as comforting as it is today.

Driving S from Ponferrada on a local road, head for the village of San Esteban de Valdueza. Just beyond, the road peters out and you find yourself in the so-called **Valley of Silence**. This was a favoured haunt of medieval hermits who hid themselves away among the chestnut, walnut and oak trees. The Monastery of San Pedro still stands in the Valdueza hills. Taking the N-120 from Carucedo, you can approach the open worked Roman gold mines, **Las Médulas**. Spades full of stones were extracted from galleries in the rock face and then panned in canals that drew their water from the Cabrera river. These must have been important mines in their time, for they permanently altered the surrounding landscape.

PUEBLA DE SANABRIA **Zamora** ☎ (988), pop. 1,826. Zamora 110km, León 126km, Madrid 341km.

This is one of Spain's idyllic spots. It is beautifully surrounded by mountains and valleys, meadows and woods but its number one attraction is its **lake**. Extremely popular with fishermen, yachtsmen and bathers, the lake is 1,028m above sea level and is 90m deep. Regattas are held here in summer. Hunting is practised at the **Sierra de la Culebra Hunting Reserve**.

▦ ★★★ *Parador Puebla de Sanabria*, Ctra Zamora, km0.3 ☎ 62 00 01 ⇌ 44 ✕ **P** ⅏ ≪ AE, DC, MC, V $$$ to $$$$. A quiet and relaxing hotel.
Cultural highlights: The village's 15C castle and 12C parish church are interesting.
Local sights: There are good walks in a NW direction through the woods and meadows of the **Sanabria Valley**, which also has good fishing streams. In **SAN MARTIN DE CASTAÑEDA**, 20km away along a scenic road, a 12C monastery is still standing. It was built over a Visigothic shrine that was flattened in the Muslim invasion.

◐ ◑ ◑ SALAMANCA **Salamanca** ☎ (923), pop. 166,615, *i* Av España, 31 ☎ 24 37 30 and at the Town Hall, Pl Mayor ☎ 21 83 42, **C** c/ Peña Primera, 1, ✉ Av España, 3 ☎ 24 30 11 and 22 20 00, ✛ 21 43 83, **P** Av Lasalle, 114 ☎ 21 23 10, ✈ Matacán, 14km on the N-501 ☎ 21 48 73, 🚌 Av Filiberto Villalobos, 79 ☎ 23 67 17, 🚆 Av de la Estación, s/n ☎ 22 57 42. Zamora 62km, Avila 98km, Valladolid 115km, Madrid 205km.

Salamanca is Spain's answer to Oxford and Bologna. Like those two cities it has been a home for university students since the 13C. Like all ancient places of higher learning it has dreaming spires aplenty; in Salamanca's case these are timeless sand-stone buildings that trace architectural development from the Gothic to the Baroque style. As you would expect from a centuries-old scholarly *rendez-vous*, Salamanca has made a habit of swimming against the tide and setting the pace of Spain's intellectual life. When the conquistadors were busily, and, so often, viciously, carving up the New World, Salamanca's theologians and law professors were speaking up for the rights of the Indians; when people were still stupefied by romantic epics, Salamanca was spearheading a wholly new literary genre, packed with realism and sardonic wit, that came to be known as the *picaresca*, or picaresque novel.

Out of the galaxy of intellectual stars that shone in Salamanca, two deserve special mention: **Fray Luis de León**, a brilliant Renaissance theologian and poet, and **Miguel de Unamuno**, the towering man of letters who profoundly influenced what came to be known as Spain's Generation of '98 (see 'Literature'). Both suffered political repression and temporarily lost their professorships. Luis de León was imprisoned by the Inquistion after he translated the *Song of Songs* and Unamuno was exiled when, as the university's rector, he opposed the Primo de Rivera dictatorship in the 1920s.

When Unamuno eventually returned to his classes, he opened his first lecture with exactly the same words that Luis de León had used to address his students again on his release from prison: *'As I was saying yesterday...'*

Salamanca's Roman bridge underlines its early importance as a communications centre on the all-important Silver Route that stretched the length of what is today western Spain. The flourishing Roman, and later Visigothic, town had a hard time during the Muslim invasion. Al-Mansur, the most successful of the Arab military leaders, twice razed the city to the ground. Life improved after Alfonso VI conquered Toledo in 1085 and ensured a Christian hold on all land north of the River Tagus. Alfonso's son-in-law, Raymond of Burgundy, was put in charge of repopulating Salamanca which was a task he was particularly good at: he built walls and an Alcázar, or castle, much the same as he was to do in Avila. However, disaster was to strike the city in 1812 when Napoleon's troops descended on it in an orgy of destructive pillaging after they had been defeated by Wellington's allied troops at the battle of Salamanca some 12km outside the city centre. The Iron Duke withdrew to Madrid after the engagement, which is something that the people of Salamanca have not forgiven him for to this day.

- ★★★★ *Gran Hotel*, Pl Poeta Iglesias, 5 ☎ 21 35 00 ⇌ 100 ♠ AE, DC, MC, V $$$$.
- ★★★★ *Monterrey*, c/ Azafranal, 21 ☎ 21 44 00 ⇌ 89 ⚲ AE, DC, MC, V $$$$.
- ★★★★ *Parador de Salamanca*, Teso de la Feria, 2 ☎ 22 87 00 ⇌ 108 ✦ ⚲ ⅋ ⇌ ≪ AE, DC, MC, V $$$$. A quiet and modern hotel on the outskirts of town, with good views of the city.

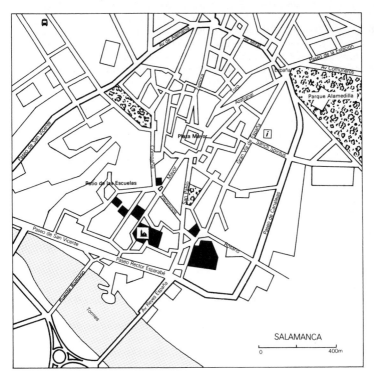

SALAMANCA

0   400m

▦ ★★★★ *Regio*, Ctra N-501, km4 ☎ 20 02 50 ⇌ 121 ✗ TV ✦ ⚲ ⚍ ⚞ A DC, MC, V $$$. The **restaurant** is good.

▦ ★★★ *Alfonso X*, c/ Toro, 64 ☎ 21 44 01 ⇌ 66 AE, DC, MC, V $$$.

◐ ¶¶ *Chez Victor* (closed: Sunday nights, Mondays and August), c/ Espoz y Mina, 26 ☎ 21 31 23 ✳ AE, DC, EC, V $$$. French cuisine.

¶¶ *El Candil Nuevo*, Pl de la Reina, 2 ☎ 21 90 27 AE, DC, EC, V $$$. Castilian cuisine.

¶¶ *Río de la Plata* (closed: Mondays and July), Pl del Peso, 1 ☎ 21 90 05 ✳ $$. Home-cooking Salamanca style.

¶¶ *Venecia* (closed: Sunday nights and Mondays), Pl del Mercado, 5 ☎ 21 67 44 ✳ AE, DC, MC, V $$$.

◐ **Best buys:** Spain's cowboy **boots** are sold at *Castaño*, c/ Iscar Peyra, 2, and *Esterra*, c/ Consuelo, 16, specializes in hunting equipment. Typical *charra* gold and silver jewelry and ornaments can be bought at *Roberto Cordón*, Centro Multiplaza, Plaza Mayor. Local delicacies, mostly hams and sausages, are available at *Iglésias*, Pl del Mercado, 6, while local cakes made to classic recipes are sold at the *Convento de las Dueñas*, opposite the Church of San Esteban. Spanish fashion is available at *Escarlata*, c/ Padilleros, 9, *Adolfo Domínguez*, Pl Libertad, 12, and *Yules*, c/ Prior, 13, and footwear at *Zapattoni*, c/ Zamora, 48.

Cultural highlights: In most Castilian cities the old Romanesque cathedral was knocked down to make way for the Gothic one, as occurred in Burgos. Palencia is one exception because there the old and the new cathedrals are mixed together since the finance ran out during the building of the latter. Salamanca is a second exception because the city fathers here opted for building a new cathedral alongside the old one. The first stone of

◑◐ Salamanca's **New Cathedral** was laid in 1513 and for the next 200 years just about every carver, decorator and artist of note was involved in the project. Thus the work of Gil de Hontañón, father and son, in the 16C was carried on in the 18C by the Churriguera family. The cathedral's exterior is richly decorated but, following the norm, the most intricate carvings are

◑◐ concentrated on the **W façade's** archivolts. So much money was spent on the façades and on the towers that economy set in when it came to ornamenting the interior and the cathedral within is sober and restrained as a result. The earliest chapels are the first two on the right and the first three on the left which were designed and decorated by Juan Gil de Hontañón and by Juan de Alava respectively. Joaquín Churriguera designed the octagonal lantern which illuminates the transept and the retrochoir, where he incorporated sculptures by Juan de Juni. Alberto and José Churriguera were the authors of the choir itself, where there are two fine organs, one Baroque and one Plateresque (1558), and José de Lara of the choir stalls.

◐ The **Old Cathedral** is entered from the right hand nave of the new one. What you find here is a very lovely 12C Romanesque building. The early Gothic fan vaults are supported by capitals in the purest Romanesque style.

◐ The **cimborium**, called the **Torre del Gallo** or Tower of the Cock, shows very obvious Byzantine influence. The old cathedral's showstopper is the **high**

◑◐ **altarpiece**. Its tempera paintings of scenes from the life of Christ and the Virgin Mary are by the 14C artist Dello Delli, and the surrounding Last Judgment is by Nicolás Florentino. The **cloister**, which has some fine capitals, retains its Romanesque atmosphere despite considerable later additions. There are four chapels around the cloister. The Talavera Chapel, with its early Gothic ribbed vault, is where Mozarabic rites were held. The Gothic Chapel of Santa Barbara used to be the meeting place of the University doctors prior to the construction of the University. The 16C Chapel of Santa Catalina houses an outstanding painting attributed to Sánchez

Coello, and the Chapel of San Bartolomé contains the 15C **sepulchre of**   🦋🦋
Diego de Anaya. The **Diocesan Museum** in the Chapter House (open
October-May: 9.30-1.15 and 3.30-5.45; summer: 10.00-1.00 and
3.30-6.00) has works by Fernando Gallego and Juan de Flandes.

A visit to the **University** should begin in the courtyard known as the   🦋🦋
Patio de las Escuelas, where you rapidly understand what Salamanca   🦋🦋
University at its high point was all about. The **façade** is quintessentially   🦋🦋🦋
Plateresque and it is obvious just why this style of ornamentation so typical
of the Spanish Renaissance took its name from the silversmith's art. The
stonemasons seem to have defied the limitations of their medium, as if
underlining the high confidence of a nation that in the 16C knew itself to be
united, strong and opening up an entire New World. Here in the patio you
are led into the lecture hall where Fray Luis de León taught theology to the
generations that sat on those same insufferably hard benches you see today.
Then there is the **library** with its collection of 40,000 volumes amassed   🦋
between the 16C and the 18C and its treasure house of codices and
incunabula that goes back to the 11C. In the **Escuelas Menores**, which is
where the students who were not noblemen lived, there is a gigantic 15C
fresco of the zodiac, the *Cielo de Salamanca*, painted by Fernando Gallego.   🦋
The mural seems to symbolize the way that Salamanca felt it had the universe
in its grasp.

Salamanca's highlights include watching the reflection of the Cathedrals'
towers on the waters of the River Tormes from the **Roman bridge**. If you are
a serious student of Spanish literature they include recalling events and
passages from the anonymous picaresque novel *El Lazarillo de Tormes*
(*Blind Man's Boy*) set in Salamanca, as was the boisterous contemporary
comedy of *La Celestina* (*The Procuress*) which was a glorious send-up of
romantic love. Continuing on the literary note they include, also, drawing
closer to the tortured soul of Miguel de Unamuno whose house, now the
Casa-Museo Umanumo museum, is on the Cuesta de Tentencio. The
Museo de Salamanca (open: 10.00-2.00; closed: Mondays and holidays)
and the **Clerecía** Jesuit college are on c/ Serranos. Returning to what is
purely visual, they include sights such as the amazing façade of the c/
Serranos' **Casa de las Conchas** (The House of Shells), so called because its   🦋
15C proprietor was a devout enthusiast of Santiago, Saint James, and he
therefore adorned his house with 400 stone cockleshells, the emblem of the
pilgrimage to the Compostela tomb of Saint James. C/ de la Compañía will
take you to the 15C **Church of San Benito**, with an Isabelline façade and,
further along, the **Palace of Monterrey**, a prototypical palace of the Spanish   🦋
Renaissance period. Opposite stands the 17C **Church of La Purísima**
Concepción which contains an *Inmaculada* by Ribera.

There is an embarrassment of architectural and artistic riches in
Salamanca. The 16C **Colegio de Fonseca**, founded by the powerful
Archbishop Fonseca who moved from the see of Santiago de Compostela to
the one of Toledo, was designed by Diego de Siloé and its Gothic chapel has
a fine retable by Alonso Berruguete. Diego de Siloé was later to show his
appreciation for his patron with the **tomb** he carved for Fonseca in the   🦋
Convento de las Ursulas. The **Convent of las Dueñas** is another must on
account of its Renaissance **cloister**. If your visit is a short one then, after the   🦋🦋
Cathedrals, every effort should be made to see the **Convent of San Esteban**   🦋
which stands as the enduring monument to the artistry of Juan de Alava, one
of the élite decorators of the 16C Spanish Golden Age and the architect
responsible for the magnificent vaults of Palencia cathedral. Alava's
Plateresque façade at San Esteban should be seen, if possible, in the evening
when the dying sunshine turns the sandstone the colour of old gold and

brings to life the intricate carvings that cover it like patchwork. The scene of the Martyrdom of Saint Stephen is by Ceroni (1610) and the Royal Cloister, the **Claustro de los Reyes**, is by Sardiña. The altarpiece inside the church was created in 1693 by José de Churriguera, the founder of a dynasty of Churrigueras that was as prolific as it was industrious and successful. The retable's main canvas is one of Claudio Coello's last major works.

Salamanca's superlative **Plaza Mayor**, built in the early 18C by García de Quiñones, is the focus of city life. An architectural gem in itself, it provides the perfect setting, with its many bars and open-air terraces, for recovering from intensive tourism with a drink in your hand, watching the world go by.

Fiestas: In September the town celebrates in style the feast day of the Virgin of La Vega; the festivities include good bullfights for Salamanca is an important bull-breeding area.

Local sights: The **Castillo del Buen Amor**, 21km away, literally the Castle of the Good Love, underwent an all too human metamorphosis. It was a forbidding fortress when the Catholic Monarchs used to stay there but Alonso Fonseca, a munificent arts patron, an administrator on the grand scale and, as archbishop first of Santiago and then of Toledo, the most powerful cleric of his age, transformed it into a Renaissance palace so that it could serve as a home for the beautiful María de Ulloa.

On the town: As befits a Spanish city with a large student population there is an enormous choice of *tapa* bars for one to indulge in the time honoured custom of *tapeo* or bar hopping. The route generally goes along c/ Bermejos, c/ de la Reina, c/ Obispo Jarrón, c/ Clavel, Pl Amarillo, Pl San Julián and Pl Zamora. In the Plaza Mayor the most classic bar opened its doors at the turn of the century, was patronized by Unamuno, and is charmingly called *Novelty*; in a similar vein is *Las Torres* at No. 26, patronized by the upper strata of Salamanca society. Open air **terraces**, particularly on the Plaza Mayor, are an ideal place to sip your favourite drink while watching the world go by. *Number One*, Pl España, and *Limón y Menta*, c/ Bermejeros, are popular discos.

Sports: Football, fishing —**crayfish**, pike, carp and trout— and hunting ☎ 23 36 00 are all local pastimes. Water sports are common in the Santa Teresa reservoir ☎ 38 11 46. Skating, swimming and other sports can be practised at the *Pabellon Deportivo* sports pavillion ☎ 23 40 69. Finally, squash players head for *Kata*, Av Alemania, 79 ☎ 25 96 89.

SANTO DOMINGO DE SILOS **Burgos** ☎ (947), pop. 368. Burgos 58km, Madrid 203km.

This small town grew up around the **monastery** that was founded by Fernán González in 919 and rebuilt in 1042 by the monk **Domingo** —who was to become its patron saint— after it had been sacked, like so much of Castile and León, by the marauding Arab chieftain Al-Mansur. A community of **Benedictine** monks currently occupies the monastery, rebuilt in the 18C, and it is famed for its school of **Gregorian chant**. The monks show vistors round the cloister and also offer accommodation (see 'Where to Stay').

🏨 ★★★ *Tres Coronas*, Pl Mayor, 6 ☎ 38 07 27 ⇌ 16 ⑤ MC, V $$ to $$$. Lodging in a Castilian setting.

Best buys: Honey and Gregorian chant recordings are typical buys.

Cultural highlights: The 12C **cloister** is an oustanding illustration of the Romanesque art of decorating **capitals**. This particular cloister is especially interesting because three different sculptors were at work on it and their different styles and themes are clearly discernible. The corner piers are magnificently intricate in their loving execution. Santo Domingo de Silos himself is buried in the N Gallery. The visit to the monastery includes a visit to its old **pharmacy** which is a fascinating insight into the poisons and potions of yesteryear and to its **museum** (open: 10.00-1.00 and 4.15-6.40; holidays: 12.15-1.00 and 4.15-6.40 ☎ 38 07 68) which contains very valuable incunabula that include missals of the medieval Mozarabic rite.

As you emerge from the cloister, you will see a doorway and other remains of the Romanesque church. The present church was built midway through the 18C by the extremely academic Ventura Rodríguez, one of the chief architects of the Spanish Enlightenment, and it is typically Neoclassical. Vespers, sung by the community, are very moving for those sensitive to Gregorian chant.

Local sights: The gorge called the **Desfiladero de la Yecla**, 3km SW, is   ◐
scenically spectacular.

SEGOVIA **Segovia** ☎ (911), pop. 55,496, *i* Plaza Mayor, 10 ☎   ◐◐
43 03 28, **(** Pl de los Huertos, s/n, ✉ Pl Doctor Laguna, 5 ☎ 43 16 11, ✚
43 03 11, **P** 43 12 12, 🚍 42 77 25, 🚃 Pl Estación, s/n ☎ 42 07 74. Avila
67km, Madrid 87km, Valladolid 110km, Burgos 198km.

Some of Segovia's landmarks, such as its awesome Roman **aqueduct**   ◐◐◐
and its dramatic **Alcázar** (it looks like something out of Disneyland but is the ◐
real stuff) are among the most well known in Spain. The **scenically set** city,   ◐◐
despite these tourist magnets and many, many more artistic and architectural
treasures, is not, however, overwhelming in the way that Toledo, for example,
is. Segovia has a charm all its own that prompts visitors to stay as long as
possible and to return time and again. Most people soon conclude that
Segovia is an especially romantic city and they are right. It has constantly
inspired poets and painters.

Its history, like that of every big Castilian cathedral city, is a rich one.
Isabella, the Catholic Queen, was proclaimed Queen of Castile here in 1474.
Nearly 50 years later the ringleaders of a revolt by Castilian barons against
her grandson, the Emperor Charles V, were beheaded near today's Pl San
Martín. The suppression of the *Mesta*, the powerful Castilian sheep farmers
association, accelerated Segovia's decline as Spain entered its 17C period of
decadence. The decision by the incoming Bourbon dynasty in the 18C to
build a country palace in La Granja, close to Segovia and in the foothills of
the Guadarrama sierra, did little to inject new life into the city. Segovia
remained pleasantly sleepy and to a great extent it still does. But then the city
has a lot of former glories to dream about and its fresh mountain air is,
proverbially, like champagne.

▦ ★★★★ *Parador de Segovia*, Ctra Valladolid, s/n ☎ 43 04 62 ⨺ 80 ✕ TV ◐
  ✦ 🎤 🕭 ⛱ ▦ « 🐾 AE, DC, MC, V $$$$. Modern, well equipped and
  quiet. Its strongpoints are its restaurant and its views of Segovia and the
  Guadarrama Sierra.

▦ ★★★ *Acueducto*, c/ Padre Claret, 10 ☎ 42 48 00 ⨺ 78 **P** 🕭 MC, V
  $$$.

▦ ★★★ *Los Linajes*, Doctor Velasco, 9 ☎ 43 12 01 ⨺ 55 TV ✦ 🐾 AE, DC,
  MC, V $$$ to $$$$.

▦ ★★★ *Puerta de Segovia*, Ctra Soria, s/n ☎ 43 71 61 ⨺ 118 ♿ ✦ 🕭 🐾
  ⛱ 🐾 ⛳ $$$. In the outskirts of town.

🍴 *Casa Amado* (closed: Wednesdays and October), c/ Fernández Ladreda,
  9 ☎ 43 20 77 $$. Good roast suckling pig.

🍴 *César* (closed: Wednesdays and November), c/ Ruiz de Alda, 10 ☎
  42 81 01 AE, DC, V $$$.

🍴 *Mesón de Cándido*, Pl Azoguejo, 5 ☎ 42 59 11 ✳ AE, DC, MC, V $$$.   ◐
  Just about everyone who has been to Segovia has eaten at Cándido's,
  famous for the tenderness of its roast suckling pig.

¶ *Mesón Duque*, c/ Cervantes, 12 ☎ 43 05 37 🅿 ✳ AE, DC, V $$$.
Cándido's eternal rival.

¶ *Mesón José María* (closed: November), c/ Cronista Lecea, 11 ☎
43 44 84 AE, DC, V $$$. It has a good bar.

Best buys: Antiques are sold at *Daoiz*, c/ Daoiz, 13, and *El Anticuario*, c/
San Martín, 4; wrought iron and copper at *J. Morales*, c/ Progreso, 4;
polychromed wooden statues at *M.M. Dominicas*, c/ Capuchinas Altas, 2;
Spanish fashion at *Antaviana*, Pl de la Merced, 1, and *Don Braulio*, c/ Juan
Bravo, 18.

👁👁👁 Cultural highlights: The Roman Aqueduct meets you head on at the
entrance to the old city as you arrive from Madrid. With its 167 arches and
its 728m length it is immediately impressive. It was built late in the 1C and it

👁 sits stone on stone without a spot of cement in the seams. The 14C Alcázar
was a royal household until the reign of the Catholic Monarchs (though
crowned in Segovia, Isabella showed no particular affection for the city) and it
was destroyed by fire and faithfully rebuilt late last century. The climb to the
top of the ramparts is worth every exhausting step for the view from there
over the plain of Castile stretches to infinity. The Alcázar houses an armoury
and weapons museum (open: 10.00-2.00 and 4.00-6.00; summer:
10.00-7.00).

👁👁 The Cathedral, which replaced the 12C cathedral destroyed during an
insurrection in 1520, was one of the last great Gothic cathedrals to be built
in Spain. The indomitable father and son team, Juan and Rodrigo Gil de
Hontañón, took on the task in 1525 after working on Salamanca's cathedral.

👁 They are both buried in the cloister that was designed by the great Flemish
master builder Juan Guas and originally formed part of the earlier cathedral.

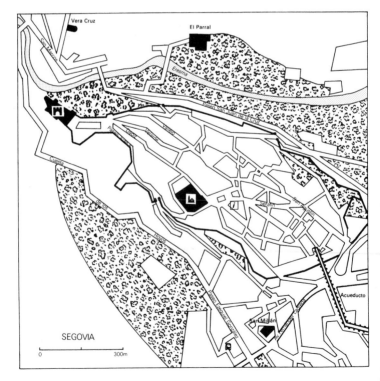

SEGOVIA

0   300m

Guas, who taught his contemporaries to embrace Gothic grandeur, and the younger Gil de Hontañón, who perfected the Renaissance innovations, span between them the period of great Spanish architecture; Juan Gil de Hontañón, who laid Segovia cathedral's first stone, acted as the link between them. Juan de Juni, a permanent fixture when it came to decorating Castilian cathedrals, makes his guest appearance here with the **retable** of the first chapel on the right. The **Cathedral Museum** (open: 10.00-1.00 and 3.30-6.00; summer: 10.00-6.00) exhibits works by Berruguete, Morales and other artists who were much patronized by bishops and canons up and down the country and has a fine collection of **early printed books**. The Chapter House contains magnificent 17C **Flemish tapestries** which is again a feature common to all Castile's better churches.

Segovia has magnificent **Romanesque churches** which share the arcaded portico characteristic that one imagines helped shield the faithful from the icy winter winds of the Guadarrama mountains. **San Millán**, at the entrance to Segovia along the old road to Madrid, is one of the earliest (12C) and sets the tone for the rest: porches along the S and N sides, a single nave with aisles on either side leading to two semi-circular apses and splendid carvings on archivolts and capitals that despite their intricacy never detract from the essential simplicity of the building. Within the city's walls the key churches are **San Esteban** (13C) which has really beautiful Romanesque towers, **San Lorenzo** which shows Mudéjar influence, **San Martín** (12C) and **San Juan de los Caballeros** which has arguably the best decorated portico. The porch here now forms the Zuloaga Museum exhibiting works by the successful ceramist and potter of the 1920s, Daniel de Zuloaga, who at one point acquired the whole church and installed his workshop in it.

Just outside the city walls there are a number of undoubted attractions. The **Church of the Vera Cruz**, with its 12-sided nave, was founded by the Knights Templar at the begining of the 13C. It contains a sort of church within a church consisting of a two storeyed walled chamber, the upper part of which was allegedly used for initiation rites. The **Monastery of El Parral** which was allowed to fall into ruin last century and has now been mostly restored by public funds (and even provides accommodation, see 'Lodging') was endowed by Isabella of Castile's brother, King Henry IV, known as the Impotent. A magnificent alabaster retable has survived its changing fortunes. The Carmelite convent, the **Convento de las Carmelitas Descalzas**, is especially important because Saint John of the Cross, Saint Teresa of Avila's contemporary and fellow mystic, is buried here. John of the Cross, a man of extraordinary humility and one of the greatest lyric poets in the Spanish language is unfortunately buried in a monstrously vulgar and ostentatious pantheon that was built in the 1920s. He was formerly buried under a far more fitting simple slab.

In addition to churches, Segovia has a number of important civic buildings. The **Casa de los Picos** is an imaginatively decorated 14C fortified palace that takes its name from the faceted stones which stud its façade. It has been attributed to Juan Guas. The 15C **Casa del Marqués de Lozoya** with its tower on the beautiful **Pl de San Martín** is a good example of the mini urban castle or fortified town house. The views of Segovia are in themselves outstanding highlights. The one of the Alcázar from the banks of the Eresma river is astonishing and the one of the whole city seen from the NE (say from the Parador) is unforgettable, particularly at dusk.

Fiestas and festivals: From July 24-29, the festivities of **Saint John** and **Saint Peter** take place. August's International Festival of Segovia consists of exhibitions, film shows and theatrical productions and there is also a **Chamber Music Festival** in September.

🔖 **Local sights:** The **La Granja Royal Palace and Gardens**, built in the early 18C by Philip V at the village of San Ildefonso de la Granja, lie 11km from the city along the N-601 that climbs up to the Guadarrama Sierra's Navacerrada mountain pass and ski station. French-born Philip was the first of the Bourbon dynasty which replaced the Hapsburgs and he lost little time in having this complex built to remind him of the splendours of Versailles. The **palace** (open: 10.00-1.00 and 2.00-6.00; summer: until 7.00) has a 🔖🔖 good collection of furniture, 16C **Flemish tapestries** and objets d'art, but 🔖🔖 the **gardens**, in the midst of the majestic sierra, are La Granja's real crowd 🔖🔖 puller. This is because their chief feature are 26 extravagant **fountains** that spurt and splash with great enthusiasm (the best one shoots up a full 40m). The gardens and the fountains (which are switched on at 5.30 in summer) are almost as good as the Sierra's own natural forests and fast-flowing streams.

Taking the N-110, which is the alternative route to Madrid via the Guadarrama tunnel and the A-6 motorway, you pass close to the **Riofrío**
🔖 **Royal Hunting Lodge** (open: 10.00-6.00; summer: until 7.00) which was built by Philip V's widow, Isabella de Farnese. The **palace** is designed in the Baroque style of her native Italy and it houses a **hunting museum** that exhibits stuffed trophies. The living deer in the surrounding **park** are more pleasant to watch.

The best carved capitals of Segovia province are reputedly to be found in the Convent of Santo Domingo's 14C **cloister** in the village of **SANTA MARIA LA REAL DE NIEVA**, 30km from Segovia on the N-605. The convent was founded by Henry III and his wife Catherine of Lancaster, who was a daughter of John of Gaunt. In the cloister there are heraldic quarterings showing the
🔖🔖 three lions of England and the castle of Castile. The **castle** in the village of **COCA**, a further 17km NW along a local road, does not look as if it would withstand an enemy cannon ball but it forms a very pretty backdrop for a contemporary photographer. Built in the late 15C by the powerful Fonseca family that numbered archbishops amongst its clan, it is a Mudéjar-Gothic folly more than anything else and all the more agreeable for it. The village of **CARBONERO EL MAYOR**, 28km on the N-601 going N, has a good Gothic church with a fine Renaissance retable but it is especially interesting because craftsman-made old musical instruments like the Castilian *dulzaina*, a primitive clarinet, and the Baroque oboe are sold at **L. Sánchez**, c/ Calvo Sotelo, 31.

On the town: The *Tasca La Posada*, c/ Judería Vieja, 1, and *La Concepción*, Plaza Mayor, 15, are top *tapa* bars, and *Poetas*, c/ Escuderos, 22, *Lennon*, c/ Fernández Ladreda, 25, and *Café Cantante La Escuela* in San Millán are for the late night crowd. *Oky*, c/ Carmen, 1, is a popular disco.

Sports: In winter, skiing can be practised in *La Pinilla* (Riaza), reached via the N-I ☎ 56 03 04, at 1,500-2,273m, with 12 ski lifts and 12 runs.

SEPULVEDA **Segovia** ☎ (911), pop. 1,528. Segovia 59km, Madrid 123km.

🔖 A genuinely picturesque village **set** on a rocky promontory, Sepúlveda has a number of restaurants (locally called *figones*) that are equipped with large wood-fired roasting ovens and serve the traditional huge platters of suckling pig and lamb.

🍴 *Casa Paulino* (closed: Mondays and November), c/ Calvo Sotelo, 2 ☎ 54 00 16 ♦ ❋ **AE, DC, V** $$ to $$$. Roast lamb.
🍴 *Cristóbal* (closed: Tuesdays, 1/7-10/7 and 1/12-20/12), c/ Conde de Sepúlveda, 9 ☎ 54 01 00 ❋ **AE, DC, EC, V** $$$. Roast lamb and Ribera del Duero *clarete* wine.

Best buys: Pottery, antiques and delicious local cakes are good buys here. There is a regional arts and crafts fair in July.

Cultural highlights: You are unlikely to miss the charming Plaza Mayor because that is where most of the *figones* are. The **Church of El Salvador** has a typical 11C Romanesque portico to feed the soul.

Local sights: Ask for directions to the **Hoces del Duratón**, 20km away along local roads —you will have to walk the last bit. It is a spectacular gorge and a shared secret among bird watchers. Hermits used to like this place too, as the Romanesque shrine of San Frutos proves. Cutting down to the N-110 and taking the Soria direction, you cross the N-I highway and reach the lovely *pueblos* of **RIAZA** and **AYLLÓN** with their fine stone houses and porticoed **plazas**, and in the case of Ayllón, with the 15C **Palace of Contreras** and its beautiful Plateresque **façade**. Move onto the C-114 and you will be driving through magnificent beech forests.

SORIA **Soria** ☎ (975), pop. 32,490, *i* Pl Ramón y Cajal, 2 ☎ 21 20 52, **(** Pl San Clemente, s/n, ✉ Paseo del Espolón, 4 ☎ 22 13 99 and 22 11 15, ✝ 21 26 40, **P** 21 18 62, ᗕ Av Valladolid, 40 ☎ 22 51 60, ⚕ 22 28 67. Burgos 142km, Pamplona 167km, Guadalajara 169km, Madrid 225km.

Girded by the Duero river, Soria was once a good deal lovelier than it is today, now that modern speculators have done their best to disfigure it. This should not however put off the traveller. The city has an old history that is very much its own, a number of architectural highlights have, mercifully, survived and Soria has a special place in 20C Spanish literature in so far as it was the spiritual home of the great poet **Antonio Machado**.

Prehistoric man settled near here, along the Duero's banks, and the old Iberians made heroic stands against the Romans just outside the city. In the 10C, Soria, by virtue of being on the Duero, was on the frontier line between Castile and the Muslim warlords who owed allegiance to the Caliphate of Córdoba. The Duero frontier was to push southwards gradually and the great fortresses of Almazán, Berlanga, Gormaz, Peñaranda and Peñafiel marked each advance and held the line. In the 13C, Soria was living its moment of glory as the headquarters of the *Mesta* association of sheep breeders who in summer moved their flocks from the exhausted pasturelands of Extremadura to the juicy meadows of Soria's Sistema Ibérico. At the time it had a thriving Jewish community and another of Moriscos, Muslims converted to Christianity, who made important contributions to local trade and crafts. For several centuries now Soria has grown more remote as befits the capital of the least populated province in Spain. It took the intelligence and beauty of Machado's verse to put Soria back on the map.

🏨 ★★★ *Alfonso VIII*, c/ Alfonso VIII, 10 ☎ 22 62 11 🛏 103 **P** ⚕ DC, MC, V $$ to $$$.

🏨 ★★★ *Caballero*, c/ Eduardo Saavedra, 4 ☎ 22 01 00 🛏 84 ⚷ **P** ⚕ AE, DC, V $$ to $$$. On the outskirts of town.

🏨 ★★★ *Mesón Leonor*, Paseo del Mirón, s/n ☎ 22 02 50 🛏 32 **P** ⚕ ⚘ ≪ DC, MC, V $$ to $$$. Very quiet, with good views.

🏨 ★★★ *Parador Antonio Machado*, Parque del Castillo, s/n ☎ 21 34 45 🛏 34 **P** ✿ ⚕ ⚘ ≪ AE, DC, EC, V $$$$. Very quiet, with beautiful views.

🍽 *Maroto*, Paseo del Espolón, 20 ☎ 22 40 86 ✿ ❋ AE, DC, EC, V $$$. New, imaginative cuisine and decor to match.

🍽 *Mesón Castellano*, Plaza Mayor, 2 ☎ 21 30 45 ❋ DC, MC, V $$$. Regional cooking and a good **bar**.

Best buys: Soria's excellent cheese and butter are sold at *Mantequerías York*, c/ Marqués de Vadillo, 6.

Cultural highlights: The 12C **Church of San Juan de Rabanera** has discernible Byzantine and generally oriental influences on its basic Romanesque style which must have been a product of the multi-racial Soria of its post-frontier days. Though the church is dedicated to a local Saint John, the tympanum above the W door shows scenes of the life of Saint Nicholas. This is because the **portico** did in fact belong to a church honouring Nicholas; it was rescued when that church collapsed and was installed in its present site in 1908. The **Church of Santo Domingo**, also dating from the 12C, has a beautiful **façade** and a very richly carved tympanum which told illiterate medieval man virtually everything he needed to know about the life of Christ. The **Co-Cathedral of San Pedro** (which shares the honours with the one at Burgo de Osma) has a very fine 16C Plateresque façade. All that remains of the original Romanesque church is the serene 12C **cloister**. The **Church of San Juan de Duero** (open: 10.00-2.00 and 4.00-7.00; closed: Mondays, Sunday afternoons and holidays) across the river is, thanks to its fascinating 12-13C **cloister**, in the top league of Spanish architectural highlights. Its arcading is in four different styles, each quite different from the other, yet everything is perfectly balanced and in harmony. There is a very obvious Mudéjar influence and it would appear that Muslim master builders were allowed to give their artistry and their imagination free rein.

Unlike most Castilian towns which have their clearly defined old quarter, in Soria the old civic buildings are spread around and you have to look for them. The **Palace of the Counts of Gómara** is one landmark that is hard to miss for it has a long and impressive Renaissance façade and a fine tower. There are some stately houses along the c/ **Real**, the c/ **Aduana Vieja** and the c/ **Caballeros**. The **Provincial Museum** (Paseo del Espolón, 8 ☎ 22 13 97) is undergoing extensive alterations and will open soon to show off the result of extensive digs in prehistoric and Roman settlements in the province such as Numancia, Torralba and Clunia.

Fiestas: The city's celebrations in honour of **San Juan** on July 24 are very traditional and colourful.

Local sights: The **ruins of Numancia**, 7km NE along the N-III, are part of Spain's national heritage. They lie on a desolate, windswept hill near the village of Garay overlooking the confluence of the Tera and Duero rivers. It was here in AD 133-134 that 10,000 Numantines resisted for months the siege of 60,000 Romans led by the conqueror of Carthage, **Publius Scipio Emilianus**. Eventually the beseiged fell to killing themselves and burning their houses rather than surrender. What you see today is basically the remains of the Roman city that was built after the carnage (open: 10.00-2.00 and 4.00-7.00; closed: Sunday afternoons and Mondays).

The mountains that form the **Sierra de Urbión**, reached via the N-234, where the source of the Duero river lies, are covered with forests and rise to more than 2,200m. The scenery along this **road** is magnificent. The village of Vinuesa, which is very unspoilt, has surprisingly luxurious old stone houses because it was an important cart building centre and as such a sort of Detroit of the Middle Ages. From there forestry roads take you up to a large tarn called the **Laguna Negra de Urbión** (Soria), the Black Lagoon, which is said to be bottomless and to flow out to the Cantabrian Sea. It is a favourite stop for serious campers and hikers.

Taking the C-115 for 46km and then branching off on local roads you reach the village of **SAN PEDRO MANRIQUE** which is the site of a celebrated **fire walking** exercise on Saint John's Night in July. The local lads have kept up a probably pagan custom that involves skipping across a bed of glowing embers. In the morning of this strange ancestral *fiesta*, local girls carry out a series of rituals called *Las Móndidas* that have more than a passing resemblance to the pagan offerings to Ceres, the ancient Roman goddess of fertility.

On the town: The best *tapa* bars are in the alleyway popularly called *El Tubo* (The Tube) that joins c/ El Collado with Pl San Clemente. In summer café terraces crowd the plaza. Try the excellent *gambas* (prawns) and beer at *Torcuato*, c/ El Collado, 34. During the evening, the action shifts to the *Neón* disco, Ctra Valladolid, five minutes from the town centre.

Sports: The area is hunting, shooting and fishing country. With the required permits sportsmen can hunt in the **Urbión National Hunting Reserve** and the **Cameros National Hunting Reserve**. The rivers Abión, Ucero and the Laguna Negra are rich in crayfish and trout. Water sports are practised on the Cuerda del Pozo lake.

TORDESILLAS **Valladolid** ☎ (983), pop. 7,224, [i] Plaza Mayor, 1 ☎ 77 00 61, ✚ 77 09 77. Valladolid 30km, Zamora 67km, León 142km, Madrid 179km.

The name of this medieval town, high up on a promontory and overlooking the Duero river, was immortalized by the **Treaty of Tordesillas** between the crowns of Spain and Portugal in 1494 which drew a line down the Atlantic to separate the New World discoveries of either nation. The line, from pole to pole, was drawn 370 leagues W of the Cape Verde Islands and the Spaniards were short-changed by their deficient cartographers for Portugal obtained a chunk of South America that is modern day Brazil. Tordesillas is also linked to the sad figure of **Joan the Mad**, the daughter of the Catholic Monarchs and the mother of the Emperor Charles V, who was locked up here for some 40 years after the death of her husband, Philip of Hapsburg, the Fair, left her mentally deranged.

🏨 ★★★ *Parador de Tordesillas*, Ctra N-620, km153 ☎ 77 00 51 🛏 73 [P] ✦ ⅍ ∾ ⬦ ⚑ AE, DC, EC, V $$$ to $$$$. Modern, quiet and 2km outside the town in a pine grove.

🏨 ★★★ *El Montico*, Ctra Burgos-Salamanca, km145 ☎ 77 07 51 🛏 34 [P] ⬦ ⅍ ∾ ⚑ ⚲ AE, DC, EC, V $$ to $$$. Set in a quiet pine grove 5km outside the town.

🍴 *Mesón Valderrey*, Ctra N-VI ☎ 77 11 72 $$ to $$$. Good roasts and local wines.

Best buys: Santa Clara cakes are sold at the convent; cowboy boots and leather chaps at *J. Rodríguez*, c/ José Antonio, 8.

Cultural highlights: The **Convent of Santa Clara** was built as a palace by Alfonso XI in 1340 in the Sevillian Mudéjar style that is reminiscent of Seville's Alcázar; Peter the Cruel, Alfonso's son, turned it into a convent for his illegitimate daughters by the Sevillian **María Padilla**. It was here that poor mad **Joan** spent most of her time between her husband's death in 1507 and her own in 1555. There is an enclosed order of nuns in the convent but visitors are shown the classic Mudéjar **patio** with the horseshoe arches and the glazed tiles that were the trademark of these Muslim artisans and the church, formerly the throne room, which has the characteristic **Mudéjar coffered ceiling**. The 15C Church of San Antolín has a retable by Juan de Juni and a museum that exhibits more of his works and some by Gregorio Fernández and Alonso Berruguete who, with Juni, formed the great trio that peppered Castile with wooden religious carvings (see 'Valladolid'). See, too, the attractive porticoed **Plaza Mayor**.

Fiestas: A particularly violent and bloodthirsty medieval ritual called the *Toro de la Vega*, that involves the lancing of a wild bull on the banks of the Duero, is the main event of the town's September celebrations.

TORO **Zamora** ☎ (988), pop. 10,079 ✚ 69 01 85, **P** 69 00 12, ⚑ 69 02 67. Zamora 33km, Madrid 217km.

Toro is an agreeable old town whose name crops up again and again in Spanish history. Ferdinand III of Castile, the Saint, who conquered Córdoba and Seville, was crowned king of León here in 1230 thus uniting the two kingdoms for evermore. It was here that Peter the Cruel locked up his wife María of Portugal and in the 17C the disgraced and once totally powerful minister of Philip IV, the Duke of Olivares, was another forced resident of the town. Isabella of Castile fought a decisive battle in Toro to gain the throne against the supporters of Juana, the alleged daughter of her brother Henry IV, the Impotent. Juana was known as *La Beltraneja* because her real father was reckoned to be the Queen's favourite, Beltrán de la Cueva.

▦ ★★★ *Juan II*, Pl del Espolón, 1 ☎ 69 03 00 ⇞ 42 ✕ ♠ ♬ ⚏ ⅁ AE, **DC, MC, V** $$. A hotel with beautiful views of the Duero valley. The **restaurant** is quite good $$$.

Best buys: Traditional ceramics can be bought at *F. Rodríguez*, c/ Negrillo, s/n; local Toro wines at *Bodegas Luis Mateos*, c/ Eras de Santa Catalina, s/n; home-made biscuits at the *Convento Mn. Dominicas*, c/ Canto, 27.

Cultural highlights: The **Colegiata**, or collegiate church, was built between 1160 and 1240 during the transitional period from the Romanesque to the Gothic style —the **W façade** is definitely Gothic. Certain features such as the corner turrets, the S face corbels and the capitals of the exterior apse columns bear great similarities to those of the cathedral at Zamora which was built at the same time. Toro's church and Zamora's cathedral, together with the old cathedral at Salamanca, are very interesting to students of architecture because they mark the first daring steps towards the soaring vaults of the Gothic style. Here at Toro, the quadripartite vaults of the Romanesque style have been replaced by slightly pointed barrel vaults. The church's Pórtico de la Gloria used to be its main entrance but it was closed off to serve as the retable of a church, now ruined, that was added on to the collegiate church. Framed by scenes of the Last Judgment, with the crowning of the Virgin on the tympanum and scores of assorted figures on the archivolts, this is a magnificent door which has the added bonus of being well preserved thanks to its temporary role as an altarpiece (visits by prior arrangement ☎ 69 03 88). There are several fine Romanesque Mudéjar churches, the best of which is the 13C **San Lorenzo**, with a good coffered ceiling and a Gothic altarpiece by Fernando Gallego. Besides the castle, civic architecture is seen at its best in c/ Santo Domingo and c/ Tablarredonda.

TUREGANO **Segovia** ☎ (911), pop. 1,202. Segovia 34km, Madrid 123km.

Most Castilian towns and villages have a good church and a castle but Turégano has the two in one. Its church was so fortified that it eventually became a **castle**, and a very impressive **sight** it is too as you look up at it from the village's very pleasant **Plaza Mayor**. Madrilenians like to gather here at weekends to nose about the **antique shops** and to eat suckling pig and lamb, roasted Castilian-style, at restaurants such as *Casa Holgueras* (open: weekends and holidays, reservations advisable), Plaza Mayor, 11 ☎ 50 00 28 $$$.

Best buys: Antiques are good value for money here.

Local sights: The tiny village of **SOTOSALBOS**, S of Turégano, has a stumpy, porched church, San Miguel, that is everything a Romanesque religious building should be, and includes a museum of Romanesque and Gothic paintings and statuary. It also has a restaurant that is equally intense and artistic about its lamb roasts: *Las Casillas* (open: weekends and holidays) ☎ 40 11 70 **AE, V** $$ to $$$.

VALLADOLID **Valladolid** ☎ (983), pop. 341,194, [*i*] Pl Zorrilla, 3 ☎ 🕭🕭
35 18 01, **(** c/ Ramón Pradera, s/n, ✉ Pl de Rinconada, s/n ☎ 33 06 60
and 34 20 00, **P** c/ Felipe II, s/n ☎ 35 70 66, ✈ Villanubla, 14km away ☎
25 92 12 (Iberia, c/ Gamazo, 17 ☎ 30 07 88), 🚌 c/ Puente Colgante, 2 ☎
23 63 08, 🚍 30 35 18. Zamora 95km, Salamanca 111km, Burgos 121km,
León 135km, Madrid 184km.

Valladolid has more than its fair share of historical associations. The city
can name drop as much as it likes and mention in passing that it was here
that the Catholic Monarchs were married, that Columbus died and that Philip
II was born. It took over from Burgos as the administrative centre for Castile
and León and was the capital of Spain when a whole new Empire was being
opened up in Mexico and Peru. Philip II, a somewhat ungrateful son of
Valladolid, eventually transferred his court to Madrid. It briefly became Spain's
political centre again at the start of the 16C in the subsequent reign of Philip
III but his son, the sad-faced Philip IV who employed Velázquez as his court
painter and repeatedly posed for him, lost little time in moving everyone back
to Madrid, which was to remain Spain's fixed capital. Curiously this monarch,
like his grandfather Philip II, was also born in Valladolid. Today the city has
recovered something of its administrative clout for it is the home of Castile
and León's regional government and parliament. It has also become a very
important industrial centre. You will see engineering works, car plants and
food factories as you approach the city long before you glimpse an historical
building.

🏨 ★★★★ *Felipe IV*, c/ Gamazo, 16 ☎ 30 70 00 🛏 130 ♦ 🎤 **AE, DC,**
   MC, V $$$ to $$$$.
🏨 ★★★★ *Olid Meliá*, Pl San Miguel, 10 ☎ 35 72 00 🛏 238 [TV] 🎤 **AE, DC,**
   MC, V $$$ to $$$$. One of the best in the city.
🏨 ★★★ *Meliá Parque*, c/ García Morato, 17 ☎ 47 01 00 🛏 306 **P** 🎤
   $$$ to $$$$. In the outskirts of town.
🏨 ★★ *Imperial*, c/ Peso, 4 ☎ 33 03 00 🛏 81 Ⴤ ढ **AE, MC V** $$ to $$$.
   In the 16C Palace of the Gallo family.
🍴 *La Fragua* (closed: Sunday nights), Paseo Zorrilla, 10 ☎ 33 71 02 ♦ ❈   🕭
   AE, DC, EC, V $$$. Castilian cuisine in a luxurious setting.
🍴 *La Goya* (closed: Sunday nights, Mondays and August), c/ Puente
   Colgante, 79 ☎ 23 12 59 $$$. It has been a popular restaurant for more
   than 100 years.
🍴 *Mesón Cervantes* (closed: Mondays and November), c/ El Rastro, 6 ☎
   30 85 53 **P** ❈ **AE, DC, EC, V** $$$.
🍴 *Mesón Panero* (closed: Sunday nights), c/ Marina Escobar, 1 ☎   🕭
   30 16 73 ❈ **AE, DC, EC, V** $$$. Old recipes with a modern touch.

Best buys: *Dubicentro*, c/ Duque de la Victoria, 13, is a mall with 40
shops; another mall, *Multicentro Las Francesas*, c/ María de Molina, 3,
consists of 30 shops gathered around the 16C cloister of the French
Dominican Nuns —for Spanish fashion, take note of *Cocco*. Leather fashion
🕭🕭 is available at *Loewe*, c/ Ferrari, 20, and leather footwear at *Yanko*, c/
María de Molina. The *El Corte Inglés* department store is at c/ General Ruiz,
10. Antiques can be bought at c/ Colmenares, 2, and c/ Campanas, 1; art
at the *C. Durango* gallery, c/ Fray Luis de León, 2; gourmet food at *La Gloria*,
Pl de Madrid, 6, Paseo Zorrilla, 4, and c/ Conde Ansúrez, 1; and ceramics at
the *Tiendas de Valid* workshop and school, c/ Duque de Lerma, 14.

Cultural highlights: Philip II did his home town one good turn when he
ordered his favourite architect, Juan de Herrera, to start designing Valladolid's
Cathedral as soon as he was through with the job of building the royal   🕭
palace and monastery of El Escorial. After working on the massive Escorial for
such a long time, size and grandeur were obviously second nature to Herrera

and he planned a Cathedral for Valladolid that would have been bigger than Seville's and probably the longest in the world. Herrera died in 1597 before completing the Cathedral and his original project was considerably scaled down in size. But the Cathedral, nevertheless, captures magnificently Herrera's essential gravity and sobriety and his very special sensitivity to space and proportion. Though his name is intimately linked with the Escorial, it could be that Herrera's greatest work is Valladolid's cathedral. The lower part of the W front and the tower were built during Herrera's life time and it was left to Alberto Churriguera in 1735 to complete the upper reaches of the façade.

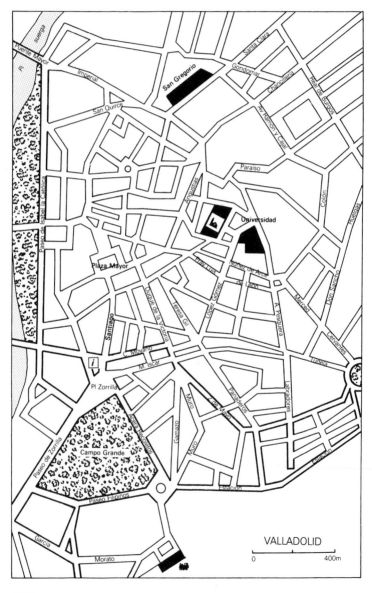

VALLADOLID

0   400m

The very distinct artistic personalities of these two men, each of whom was to lend his name to define the style of a specific period (Herreriano and Churrigueresque) somehow blends together very successfully. Inside the cathedral, Juan de Juni steals the show with a typically flamboyant **main retable** he carved in 1572. The **Diocesan Museum** (open: 10.00-2.00 and 5.30-8.00; closed: Sunday afternoons) is a good one and it is housed in what remains of the old collegiate church that was knocked down bit by bit to make way for the Cathedral. Had Herrera's original plans been carried out, nothing would have been left of this adjoining Gothic church. The **Church of Santa María la Antigua**, originally Romanesque and rebuilt to conform with Gothic tastes, stands alongside the ruins of the collegiate church and the **Church of las Angustias** is also nearby. The latter houses a statue of the Virgin that is reckoned to be one of Juni's masterpieces. The carving is so arrogantly mannerist that Valladolid's townspeople know it by the punchier name of *La Virgen de los Siete Cuchillos*, the Virgin of the Seven Daggers.

Just as the main reason for visiting Madrid is to walk around the Prado Museum, the chief excuse for travelling to Valladolid is to visit its **Museo Nacional de Escultura Policromada** (open: 10.00-1.30 and 4.00-7.00; closed: Sunday afternoons, Mondays and holidays ☎ 25 03 75), the museum devoted to the religious imagery in polychromed wood that a visitor to Spain sees in one church after another. This is an exceptional collection that is very well exhibited and it is fittingly housed in the extravagant building called the **Colegio de San Gregorio**. The college was founded by Fray Alonso de Burgos, who was Isabella of Castile's confessor, and it was conceived in the grand style. Juan Guas designed the **chapel** and Gil de Siloé and Simón de Colonia, who worked tirelessly on the **main façade**, were clearly determined to say the last word on the Isabelline-Gothic style. The museum is in the rooms that lead off from the beautiful main **patio** with its carefully decorated columns and royal emblems along the frieze. The stars of the exhibition are Alonso de Berruguete (1480-1561), Juan de Juni (d. 1586) and Gregorio Fernández (1556-1636) who between them formed the Valladolid school of religious imagery. These men were never short of commissions and were as popular as a David Hockney or an Andy Warhol might be today. They put their skills wholeheartedly into bringing religion to life and they were the beneficiaries of all the Renaissance excitement about rediscovering the human form. Berruguete was strongly influenced by the mannerism of his day and Juni (who was born Jean de Joigny in Champagne, France and arrived in Valladolid around 1540) went one stage further into the style that is called illusionism, which today's tastes might find overdone and cartoon-like. Fernández, whose life spans the Baroque period, was quite unconscious of any restraints and he was purposely out to shock. His much admired *Cristo Yacente*, the Recumbent Christ, in the museum, has human teeth, leather nails, glass eyes and leaves nothing to the imagination. He was to repeat this composition several times because he knew his public and gave it exactly what it wanted.

The **Church of San Pablo**, alongside the college and museum, has a very rich **façade**, the bottom half of which was carved by Simón de Colonia in the Gothic style leaving later artists to complete the upper decorations in a pronounced Plateresque manner. Opposite stand the Royal Palace that Philip III used and the adjoining Palacio de los Pimenteles where his son, the future Philip IV, was born. Other top Valladolid buildings include the **University** which is in the Churriguresque style, the 15C Gothic **Church of San Benito** which had a fine Herrera style **patio** added to it, and the **Colegio de Santa Cruz** that was founded by Cardinal Mendoza, Isabella of Castile's favourite cleric. The college was begun in the late Gothic style in 1479 but by the time it was completed, 12 years later, the Renaissance was very much in evidence. Valladolid boasts a number of other museums though they are small beer in comparison to the sculpture one. The Museo Colombino (open: 11.00-1.30 and 4.00-6.00; Sundays: 10.00-1.00; closed: Mondays and holidays ☎ 29 13 53) is only really interesting because it stands on the site where Christopher Columbus died. The **Archaeology Museum** (open: 10.30-1.30 and 4.00-6.30; Sundays: 10.00-2.00; closed: Mondays and holidays ☎ 35 04 22) is grandly housed in the 16C palace of royal courtier Fabio Nelli and has some interesting Roman mosaics. The **Museo Oriental** (open: 4.00-7.00; Sundays and holidays: 10.00-2.00 ☎ 30 68 00) is in an 18C building designed by the Neoclassical architect Ventura Rodríguez and exhibits mainly Chinese art and has a section dedicated to the Philippines. The **Museo del Monasterio de Santa Ana** has canvases by Goya and by his father-in-law Bayeu as well as carvings including another Gregorio Fernández Recumbent Christ. The **Casa de Cervantes** (open: 10.00-6.00; Sundays and holidays: 10.00-2.00; closed: Mondays ☎ 30 88 10), which is where Don Quixote's author lived between 1603 and 1606, has a small museum of Man of la Mancha memorabilia as well as a library. Literary seminars are held here on Sunday mornings.

Fiestas and festivals: Holy Week or *Semana Santa* is marked by very sober and moving religious processions. There is an **International Film Week** in October ☎ 33 95 81.

Local sights: SIMANCAS, 11km away along the N-620, is the second home of every researcher into Spanish history. Its castle has been storing the **National Archives** (open: 9.00-1.30 and 4.00-7.30; closed: November to February and afternoons in July and August ☎ 59 00 03), one of the largest (over eight million documents) and most valuable **collections of documents** in the world, since the 14C. CUELLAR (Segovia), 52km away on the N-601 and in the province of Segovia, has several Mudéjar buildings and is especially proud of its highly dangerous **bull running** *fiesta* on the last Sunday in August, reputed to be the oldest *fiesta* of this kind in Spain.

On the town: *Tapa* bar enthusiasts hang around the Santa María la Antigua and c/ Padre Francisco Suárez areas. At night the action shifts to *Bogui*, c/ Recoletos, 11, while dancers head for *Pentágono*. Live jazz and folk music can be heard at *El Moscardón*, c/ San José, 7. Gamblers willing to flirt with Lady Luck should head for the *Casino de Castilla y León*, 14km away in Boecillo ☎ 55 44 11.

Sports: Football, flying at *Aero Club Valladolid* ☎ 22 43 58, and hunting ☎ 39 52 67 are all local pastimes.

ZAMORA **Zamora** ☎ (988), pop. 63,051, [*i*] c/ Santa Clara, 20 ☎ 51 18 45, (c/ Travesía, 7, ✉ c/ Santa Clara, 15 ☎ 51 53 71, ⊹ 52 33 00, **P** c/ General Sanjurjo, 2 ☎ 51 14 34, 🚌 c/ Monsalve, 1 ☎ 51 25 88, 🚂 52 19 56. Salamanca 61km, Valladolid 95km, Madrid 248km, Orense 266km.

Like Soria, Zamora is on the banks of the Duero river which soon becomes the Douro as it crosses the frontier and enters Portugal. Duero towns and villages have been blighted by battles since the river was taken to be a border zone by Christians and Muslims as much as by Christian barons among themselves, and Zamora is no exception to the norm. Like so many of the trouble spots of León and Castile, Zamora was also El Cid country and the gallant hero actually received his knightly arms in the city's Church of Santiago. Like the neighbouring town of Toro, it was fully involved in the civil war that followed the death of Henry IV, the Impotent, and backed Isabella of Castile's winning side.

🏨 ★★★★ *Parador Condes de Alba y Aliste*, Pl Cánovas, 1 ☎ 51 44 97   🌣🌣
🛏 27 ✕ ✦ 🎤 🐾 ⚱ AE, DC, MC, V $$$$. Quiet, in a **15C palace**.

🏨 ★★★ *Dos Infantas*, c/ Cortinas de San Miguel, 3 ☎ 51 28 75 🛏 68 TV
AE, DC, MC, V $$$.

🍴 *París*, Av Portugal, 14 ☎ 51 43 25 ✳ AE, DC, MC, V $$$. Despite the
name, the cooking is Spanish.

🍴 *Rey Don Sancho II*, Parque de la Marina, s/n ☎ 52 60 54 ✦ ✳ AE, DC,
MC, V $$$.

🍴 *Serafín*, Pl Maestro Haedo, 10 ☎ 51 43 16 P ✳ AE, DC, EC, V $$ to
$$$. Fish and seafood.

Best buys: There are good cakes and pastries made by the nuns of the
Monasterio de Santa María la Real de las Dueñas (on the road to
Fuentesaúco); local wines can be bought at *Bodegas J.M. Fermoselle*, Av
Galicia, 147, and cheeses at ***Riespri***, c/ Santa Clara, 12. Spanish fashion is
sold at ***C. Mayado***, c/ Lope de Vega, 8, and at ***Galo***, c/ Braza, 1.

Cultural highlights: The 12C **Cathedral** introduced pointed vaulting and   🌣
thereby marked a milestone in the development of Gothic church building
(see 'Toro'). It has three naves, a Gothic apse and a **cupola** at the crossing   🌣
where the daring innovation is used to full effect. The S front is the only
remaining Romanesque one (the N front is Neoclassical and much later) and
the cloister, housing the **Cathedral Museum** (open: 11.00-2.00 and   🌣
4.00-8.00) was built in the Herrera style that Philip II's architect popularized
in the 16C. The chief interior features, in addition to the Byzantine-influenced
lantern, are the **wrought iron grilles** and the 16C **choir stalls**.   🌣🌣

🌣   Zamora's **Romanesque churches** like **Santo Tomé**, **La Magdalena**,
Santa María de la Orta and **Santiago del Burgo** typically have lobed
arches and carved archivolts around the main doors which do not feature a
tympanum. If you arrive in the town coming from Palencia or Segovia you will
find their simplicty disappointing, though Santiago del Burgo has a lovely S
façade and Santa María has a charmingly squat tower.

Very little is left of Zamora's medieval walls which were once extremely
sturdy but received a constant battering. You can get an idea of them from
the **Doña Urraca Gateway** which is named after the daughter of Ferdinand
I. She was given the feudal lordship of Zamora by her father only to be
attacked by one brother, Sancho II of León, who besieged Zamora, and to
finally lose the city to another, Alfonso VI of Castile, after Sancho was
treacherously murdered near this gate. El Cid, who was fighting for Alfonso
against Sancho, was very upset by this development and in a famous episode
he made his feudal lord, Alfonso, swear that he had had no part in Sancho's
death (see 'Burgos'). Among the civic buildings, note the 16C **Casa de los
Momos**, now used as the Court House, and the **Casa del Cordón**, the
Provincial Fine Arts Museum. The **Museo de la Semana Santa** or Holy
Week Museum, Pl Canovas, 10 (open: 11.00-2.00 and 4.00-7.00; Sundays:
10.30-2.00) is interesting.

Fiestas: The **Holy Week** religious processions are very impressive.   🌣
Local sights: The village of Campillo, 20km NW, is good for a peep at what
was happening in church architecture before the Romanesque artists took
over. Its 7C Visigothic church, **San Pedro de la Nave**, has three naves and   🌣
very primitive, stylized friezes and capitals. The C-527 takes you to the village
of **FERMOSELLE** which has a good castle and is the starting point for the
picturesque route called the **Arribes del Duero**. A series of geological
accidents here have made the river course down wide canyons that plunge
down a full 400m. The route can start by the Almendra reservoir on the River
Tormes and continue through Trabanca, Villarino and Pereña before
descending to Aldeávila de la Ribera and Vilvestre.

CATALONIA

In Catalonia you are in Spain and yet not. Of all the regions that make up the ethnic, cultural and historical patchwork that is Spain, Catalonia is the most distinctly different from all others. You will notice immediately that people, in their vast majority, speak **Catalan** and not Castilian Spanish (the two languages are co-official) and you will soon learn that this is a community that is intensely proud of its own identity and separate heritage. The rivalry between Madrid and Barcelona, or Castile and Catalonia, is a constant theme of the Spanish story, sometimes controversial and occasionally violent. The distinct differences were shaped by a geographical accident and were underlined by a historical development. Castile, and the rest of Spain, opened out to the Atlantic and the New World; Catalonia, whose possessions used to extend much farther than its present-day borders, directed all its energies to the Mediterranean.

Ask the Catalans themselves and they will tell you that their NE corner of Spain is not a region but a nation. As far as climate and landscapes are concerned they have sufficient variety to claim they live in a mini-continent. Bordered on the N by the ski stations of the Pyrenees and on the E by the international holiday playgrounds that form the **Costa Brava** and the **Costa Dorada**, Catalonia embraces gentle, fertile valleys and, in the S, utterly different arid lands.

Catalonia's destiny was shaped by the Mediterranean and its first important settlers arrived by way of this wine-dark sea of antiquity. The **Greeks** established stable colonies in the 6C AD in what are today Rosas and Ampurias. The **Carthaginians** founded Barcelona three centuries later. The **Romans**, who were to have a lasting impact, created the province of *Tarraconia*, what was to become modern-day Tarragona. Unlike the rest of Spain, the Visigoths, who took advantage of the crumbling Roman Empire, never struck lasting roots in Catalonia and much the same was true of the Muslim invaders. Whereas elsewhere on the Peninsula Christians and Moors battled it out for centuries, Catalonia was protected by the frontier that Charlemagne established, which came to be known as the **Spanish March**.

By the 9C, when the local chieftain **Wilfredo el Velloso**, Wilfred the Hairy, proclaimed himself Count of Barcelona, Catalonia was very much a compact political entity. Purposefully the **County of Barcelona** began to move towards its medieval splendour. The union of the County with the Kingdom of Aragón in the reign of Ramón Berenguer IV was a giant fillip to Catalan expansion and by the 13C and 14C what one had was a powerful nation state in every sense of the word. Catalonia's possessions stretched out as far as Sicily and Catalan seamen and traders, retracing the routes of the original Greek settlers, went far beyond to the eastern Mediterranean. At home the great **monasteries** of Santa Creus and Poblet were built under royal patronage to enable Catalonia to hold its own on the medieval cultural circuit. Most impressively of all civic institutions, an assembly of notables called the *Consell de Cent*, a *Cortes* to act as a legislature and an executive body called the *Generalitat*, were created. These rudimentary democratic institutions pre-date the Magna Carta and Simon de Montfort's parliaments.

The epoch-making marriage between Isabella of Castile and Ferdinand of Aragón in 1479 —as the Catholic Monarchs they ushered in Spain's modern era— put a stop to Catalonia's separate development. From then on monarchs centred in Madrid called the shots and successive uprisings in Catalonia were able to do little about it. The Hapsburg Philip IV cut short Catalonia's European ambitions by ceding Roussillon to France in 1649 and the French-born Philip V, the first king of the new Bourbon dynasty, suppressed the Catalan *fueros*, or local laws and privileges, in 1714. Catalonia knew very well what it could expect from the absolute rule-minded Bourbon and had opposed him during the War of Spanish Succession.

But Catalonia is nothing if not resilient. Adversity only served to affirm the Catalan identity. By the 19C Catalonia was bouncing back as the powerhouse of Spain's industrial revolution and Barcelona became a sort of Manchester on the Mediterranean with the advantage that it had a genius like **Antonio Gaudí** designing the huge houses of its increasingly prosperous bourgeoisie. Catalonia came to mean progress, Europeanism and commercial acumen. The Catalan national identity was further strengthened by the repression that General Franco's regime meted out. With the return of democracy Catalonia recovered its historical institutions and prerogatives. The wheel of fortune had turned in its favour once more.

AIGÜES TORTES NATIONAL PARK **Lérida** ☎ (973), *i* Sort ☎
62 00 00. Access from the Bohí valley via the turn-off to the right off the local valley road to the W, and from Espot in the NE via the turn-off to the left off the C-147.

In terms of flora, fauna and panoramic views Aigües Tortes, in the Pyrenees, can hold its own with any Mediterranean forest in Europe. The park's name means 'tortuous waters' in Catalan and refers to the meandering flow of its rivers as they fill up and flow out of a number of lakes. Separated by the Potarró peaks, Potarró d'Espot (2,423m) and Agulla del Potarró, to the W lie the foothills of the Fonguera (2,881m), **Els Encantats** (2,747m) and the Escrita Valley which has a fair-sized lake called **San Mauricio**, while to the E lies the valley of San Nicolás, also dotted with lakes and overlooked by the mass of La Muntanyeta. Birches, poplars and willows crowd the river banks giving way to pines as one climbs up through the meadows to the grey Pyrenean rock faces. The rivers and lakes are well stocked with trout, there is a considerable wild boar population, squirrels, martinets and the rest are fairly plentiful and so are eagles and other birds of prey. Sportsmen with the right permits can hunt at the **Alto Pallars-Arán National Reserve**.

The forestry tracks are not ideal but you can normally use your own car to drive along them. If in doubt, hire a fourwheeler at Bohí or Espot.

In **ESPOT**, ★★ *Saurat*, c/ San Martín, s/n, ☎ 63 50 63 ⊨ 52 **P** ♦ ⅍ ≪ **DC, V $$** is a recommended hotel. In the Bohí Valley, there are several early churches which enchant enthusiasts of Romanesque architecture: Barruera (13C), Cardet (14C), **Erill-La Vall** (11C), Coll (11C), Bohí itself (12C) and, above all, **Sant Climent de Taüll**, which is just 2km SE of Bohí. For lodging in Bohí, see 'Valle del Bohí'.

AMPURDÁN, EL-L'EMPORDÁ **Gerona** ☎ (972).

Of all Catalonia's counties, the Ampurdán is the most visited by non-Spaniards for it embraces the **Costa Brava**, the holiday playground that does not really require much of an introduction. Few tourists might, however, be aware that, as far as Catalans are concerned, one of the essential characteristics of this NW belt of the province of Gerona is its local wind which is called the *Tramontana*. A second key feature is its first-class cuisine and a third is not so much its summer resorts but its inland medieval **villages** and country houses.

The *Tramontana* is a cold N wind that whistles down from the Pyrenees from mid autumn to early spring. It is feared by farmers who for generations have planted hedges and cypress trees to act as wind breaks and protect their crops and it is reckoned to send people slightly crazy much like the no less legendary gusts of the mistral wind across the border in France. The eccentricities of a **Salvador Dalí**, for example, who is an Ampurdán man through and through, are blamed on the *Tramontana*. Food and local wines are very much part of the area's culture. Special pride is taken in the preparation of fish and seafood dishes and in the quality of Ampurdán vegetables. One of the most agreeable features of the area is the way in which a lot of loving energy has gone into restoring and preserving **medieval villages** and **country houses**, a reflection of the fact that the Ampurdán has produced and attracted many artists and enjoys a very lively **cultural scene**. Many of the old houses have been converted into inns and restaurants and inland Ampurdán is a pleasure to explore as a result.

The towns of **CASTELLO DE AMPURIAS**, **FIGUERAS**, **PALAFRUGELL**, **PERATALLADA** and **PERELADA** (see separate entries) all form part of the Ampurdán region.

ARENYS DE MAR **Barcelona** ☎ (93), pop. 10,204, *i* Paseo Xifré, 25 ☎ 792 15 37. Barcelona 37km, Gerona 60km, Madrid 672km.

The tourist invasion every summer has not totally swept away the indigenous charms of this originally Roman settlement. The late Catalan poet Salvador Espriú inspired contemporary nationalists with the lyrical and committed verse which he wrote in this village. Timeless features that transcend the holiday hubbub are the tall **cemetery** cypresses that overlook the sea and the arrival of the fishermen with their catch at the quayside.

- 🏨 ★★ *Carlos I* (closed: 1/11-15/5), Paseo de Cataluña, 8 ☎ 792 03 83 🛏 100 TV P ✦ 🦢 ⚓ $$. Quiet atmosphere.
- 🏨 ★ *Carlos V* (closed: 1/8-31/5), Paseo de Cataluña, 4 ☎ 792 08 99 🛏 59 ✚ TV P 🦢 $$. Quiet.
- 🍴 *Hispania* (closed: Tuesdays, Sunday nights, Holy Week and October), c/ Real, 54 ☎ 791 04 57 P ✳ AE, MC, V $$$ to $$$$. Excellent regional food imaginatively treated.
- 🍴 *Portinyol*, at the port ☎ 792 00 09 P ✦ ✳ AE, DC, MC, V $$$$ to $$$$$. Fish and seafood.

Beaches: As well as the local beach, there is Canet de Mar, 3km N on the N-II, and San Pol de Mar, 6km along the same road.

Best buys: Handmade lace and embroidery from the *Taller-Escuela*, Carrer de l'Esglesia, 5 ☎ 792 34 89 is the local speciality.

Cultural highlights: Arenys' renovated 13C tower, the Torre del Encantats, and the parish church with its Baroque altarpiece give an idea of the pre-concrete village. There is an interesting permanent exhibition of local handmade lace at the Museo de la Punta Frederic Marès, Carrer de l'Esglesia, 41 (open in summer: 6.00-8.00; Saturdays: 11.00-1.00; Sundays: 11.00-2.00; closed: Mondays, and Wednesdays and Fridays in winter ☎ 792 17 84).

Fiestas: The night of Saint John's Day (June 23) is celebrated in style as in many places in Spain and a sea-borne procession marks the feast day of Our Lady of Mount Carmel, patron of fishermen, on July 16.

Sports: Arenys is an important sailing centre that hosts several national and international competitions every year. The *Club Náutico de Arenys de Mar* ☎ 792 08 96 is one of the most active marinas in Spain. Golfers head for the 9-hole, par 68 *Club de Golf Llavaneras*, 6km towards Mataró ☎ 792 60 50.

ARGENTONA **Barcelona** ☎ (93), pop. 7,163. Mataró 4km, Barcelona 27km, Madrid 657km.

The ceramics tradition here has been strong for centuries.

🍴 *Racó d'En Binu* (closed: Sunday nights, Mondays, 1/6-18/6 and 1/11-18/11), c/ Puig i Cadafalch, 14 ☎ 797 01 01 ✳ AE, DC, EC, MC, V $$$$ to $$$$$. French-inspired top cuisine.

Cultural highlights: There is a permanent exhibition of pitchers from all over Spain at the Museo Municipal del Cantir, Pl de l'Esglesia, 3 ☎ 797 07 11. The town is graced by some turn of the century **Modernist houses** built by Barcelona families who came here to take the waters.

Fiestas and fairs: Every August 4 there is a pottery fair, the *Fira del Cantir*, with particular attention paid to pitchers.

BAGUR-BEGUR **Gerona** ☎ (972), pop. 2,513, *i* Pl de l'Esglesia, 1 ☎ 62 24 00. Gerona 46km, Barcelona 146km, Madrid 739km.

Beaches and coves surround Bagur and, naturally, so do large, though scenically set, tourism complexes like **Aiguablava** and Cap-Sa-Sal. In the heart of the **Costa Brava**, Bagur proper has still managed to preserve five large towers that were once part of its defensive wall.

🏨 ★★★★ *Aiguablava* (closed: 24/10-24/3), Fornells beach, 3.5km SE of Bagur ☎ 62 20 58 🛏 85 ♦ 🎙 🦌 ≈ ⚓ ≪ ♀ V $$$. Quiet and extremely well equipped, it is set in gardens and has fine sea views.

🏨 ★★★★ *Parador de la Costa Brava*, Aiguablava beach, 3.5km SE of Bagur ☎ 62 21 62 🛏 87 TV ♦ 🎙 🦌 ≈ ⚓ 🖼 ≪ 🎱 AE, DC, MC, V $$$$. Quiet and relaxing, it is well situated for panoramic seascapes.

🍴 *La Lluna* (closed: November, February and weekdays in winter), c/ Comar i Ros, 7 ☎ 62 20 23 ♦ $$ to $$$. Simple, good cooking in a pretty village house.

🍴 *Sa Punta* (closed: Mondays in winter and 15/1-15/2), Pals beach ☎ 63 64 10 P ✳ ≈ ♀ AE, EC, V $$$$. Unfussy imaginative cooking and excellent desserts.

Beaches: The beach at **Pals**, 8km N, is large and a surprising change from the Costa's small coves. Beyond it lie the more typical beaches of Sa Riera and **Aiguafreda**. Heading S there is **Fornells** (3km) and **Aiguablava** (5km). All along this coastline there are numerous beautiful, mostly rocky, **inlets**, some of them almost inaccessible by land.

Cultural highlights: The 18C parish church is interesting.

Fiestas: *Sardana* dancing is typical at the end of August. Concerts and plays are staged during the Summer Festival in July.

Local sights: The stretch of coastline between Sa Riera and Aiguablava, explored either by land or by sea, is reckoned to be one of the most beautiful on the **Costa Brava**; the Costa's cocktail of blue sea, rocky cliffs and pine trees is arguably more potent here than elsewhere. **PALS**, 7km W, has a well restored and agreeable medieval old quarter —note the tower of the old castle, the town walls, the Gothic Church of San Pedro, the Town Hall and the fortified *masías*, or farmhouses, in the surrounding area— and also a Marine Archaeology Museum, Museo de Arqueología Submarina, at Carrer de la Creu, 7 (open in summer: 10.00-9.00; Saturdays and holidays: 10.00-1.00 and 4.00-8.00 ☎ 30 17 00).

On the town: *Rivelino's*, Ctra Satuna, s/n, is an up-market and seductive disco; *Cleopatra*, Av del Mediterráneo, packs in crowds of young boppers, tourists and Spaniards alike.

Sports: This part of the coast is ideal for sailing, water skiing and windsurfing —for information, contact the *Club Náutico de Aiguablava* ☎ 62 31 61. For golf, the 18-hole *Club de Golf de Pals* is 7km inland ☎ 62 30 06.

BAÑOLAS-BANYOLES LAKE **Gerona** ☎ (972). Gerona 20km, Barcelona 120km, Madrid 729km.

Top national and international water skiing, speedboat racing and rowing competitions are held on this scenically situated **lake**, which will host rowing events in the **1992 Barcelona Olympics**. You can try your hand at any of these sports ☎ 57 00 50, or just lazily paddle away an afternoon.

Cultural highlights: The 12C church on the W side of the lake, the **Iglesia de Porqueres**, has an interesting, Byzantine influenced, Romanesque portico. There is a good 15C Gothic altarpiece in the Monastery of Sant Esteve and the local museum, the Museo Arqueológico Comarcal, has an eclectic collection that runs from prehistoric remains to 17C ceramics. A curious collection of prehistoric human skulls and stuffed animals is on display at the Museo Municipal Darder.

▦ ★ *L'Ast* (closed: 1/11-30/11), Passeig Dalmau, 63 ☎ 57 04 14 ⇌ 34 **P** ✦ ♿ ⚓ $$. A quiet hotel on the shores of the lake.

Local sights: BESALÚ (i Pl de la Llibertat, 1 ☎ 59 02 25), 14km NW on the C-150, is a charming medieval village that grew up around the local abbey, the Romanesque Monastery of Sant Pere (12C). Its Romanesque bridge over the River Fluviá dates from the Middle Ages when the village had an important Jewish community.

BARCELONA **Barcelona** ☎ (93), pop. 1,694,064, i El Prat airport ☎ 325 58 29 (open weekdays: 8.00-8.00; weekends 8.00-3.00); i Town Hall, Pl Sant Jaume ☎ 318 25 25 (open weekdays: 9.00-9.00; Saturdays: 9.00-2.00); i Estación de Francia railway station ☎ 319 27 91 (open Monday-Saturday: 8.00-8.00); i Generalitat de Catalunya, Gran Vía de les Corts Catalanes, 658 ☎ 301 74 43 (open weekdays: 9.00-1.30 and 4.30-8.30); i Pl Pablo Neruda (Diagonal-Aragó) ☎ 245 76 21 (open 15/3-15/10: 8.30-8.30); i Port, Porta de la Pau (open daily, except Mondays: 10.00-8.00); i Patronato Municipal de Turismo, Sants Central Station ☎ 250 25 94 (open daily: 7.30-10.30); i Pueblo Español, Montjuïc ☎ 223 24 20, **Lost Property Office** ☎ 301 39 23, ✚ 235 93 00 (Emergency medical service ☎ 212 85 85), **P** 092, ✈ El Prat, 14km ☎ 370 10 11, 325 43 04, and 317 87 08 (train to the airport ☎ 379 00 24; Iberia, Pl España, s/n ☎ 325 12 02 and 325 69 00; Iberia reservations ☎ 325 15 15), ⚓ Port of Barcelona ☎ 318 87 50 (International Maritime Station ☎ 301 25 98), 🚆 RENFE ☎ 322 41 42 (Catalan railway ☎ 205 15 15), **Radio-Taxi** ☎ 330 08 50. Perpignan 187km, Valencia 316km, Bilbao 607km, Madrid 627km.

Barcelona, the site of the **1992 Olympics**, is something vital and memorable to everybody that visits it. It is new and it is old and it is incredibly alive. It wins you over almost immediately and you don't forget it. People seem to walk faster in the streets than they do anywhere else in Spain; there is a special pace to Barcelona for like New York it is a place in a hurry, always on the front edge of what is valuable or at least innovative. Back in the 12C the city was experimenting with democracy and at the end of the 19C libertarian anarchism was in vogue. It is no coincidence that **Modernism** struck roots and flourished in Barcelona or that Picasso set out here on his self-chosen path to alter permanently the way people looked at a picture. But Barcelona, restless and vibrant, is also one of Europe's great medieval cities. It has a cultural heritage and an historical background to rival that of Paris or Florence. You are acutely and constantly aware here of a long tradition and of a people intensely proud and reverent about its past. The sense of life about Barcelona is in great measure shaped by its **seaport**. Barcelona revels in its status as a big, boisterous Mediterranean city. Its seaport meant, and still means, a constant traffic of ideas and influences. If the Mediterranean is the cradle of western humanity then Barcelona is one of those ornaments or mobiles that is put over a creche to amuse and stimulate the child.

If you want to go back right to the beginning of Barcelona's story, you should know that there were settlements here, in the folds of the Mountjuïc mountain, 4,000 years ago. The story really begins with the occasional visits by Phoenician, Greek and Carthaginian seamen and traders and it starts in earnest with the decision by the Carthaginian chieftain **Hamilcar Barca**, Hannibal's father, to found a settlement here, called *Barcino* after himself, in AD 236. In the ensuing Punic wars, Rome wrested control of the Mediterranean from Carthage and by AD 201 Hamilcar's encampment had been grandly renamed *Julia Faventia Augusta Pia Barcino*. By the 5C the Visigoths were firmly installed here and the Barcelona place name had acquired currency. The Muslim impact, unlike in the rest of Spain, was limited here. The Berber invaders arrived in 717, were generally tolerant about most things and were forced out in 798 by Charlemagne himself. The founder of the Holy Roman Empire set down the frontier between Muslim Spain and Christian Europe in Catalonia known as the **Spanish March**.

By the following century Barcelona was a town of nearly 20,000 that was growing steadily prosperous as a shipbuilding centre. **Wifredo el Velloso**, Wilfred the Hairy, felt politically strong enough to create what he called the County of Barcelona and his dynasty of Counts of Barcelona survived until the 12C when Ramón Berenguer IV, through marriage alliances, merged his kingdom with the County. This was a clear turning point in the history of Catalonia and of Barcelona. Under the crown of Aragón the NE corner of Spain entered a period of expansion in every field, especially during the reign of **James I of Aragón**. In Barcelona itself the creation of representative institutions, the *Consell de Cent* which was an assembly of 100 notables and the *Corts*, a forerunner of the modern parliament, underlined the sophistication of the medieval town.

The union of the crowns of Castile and Aragón under Ferdinand and Isabella, the Catholic Monarchs, in 1479 cut short the separate development of Barcelona and Catalonia. The opening up of the New World was a Castilian enterprise and the port of Seville obtained the monopoly of the transatlantic trade to the detriment of Barcelona. The decline of the Catalan capital was accelerated by a secessionist attempt in 1640 and the city's decision to back what was to be the losing Hapsburg side during the War of Spanish Succession (1700-1713) spelt disaster. The new French Bourbon dynasty assumed the Spanish throne and took its revenge on its disloyal Catalan subjects by suppressing Barcelona's medieval autonomy.

It was not till the mid 19C that the city recovered its flair and vitality but when it did so it progressed rapidly and in style. Its new prosperity was symbolised by the demolition of the old medieval walls in 1858 and the creation of a whole new city, properly planned on a grid system, that was known then as it is now as the **Ensanche**, the Broadening. Barcelona had become the trail blazer, and in fact almost the sole exponent, of Spain's Industrial Revolution. Fortunes were made in the textile and allied industries and the city's increasingly prosperous **middle classes** turned out to be tasteful arts patrons who bankrolled a multi-discipline cultural movement called the *Renaixença*, which is Catalan for Renaissance. The new-found confidence was expressed in literature and in music and, most visually, in the Modernist art forms that had the genius designer and architect **Antonio Gaudí** as their high priest and prophet. The *Renaixença* movement also had strong political overtones for it was linked to nationalist ambitions to recover Catalonia's former autonomy.

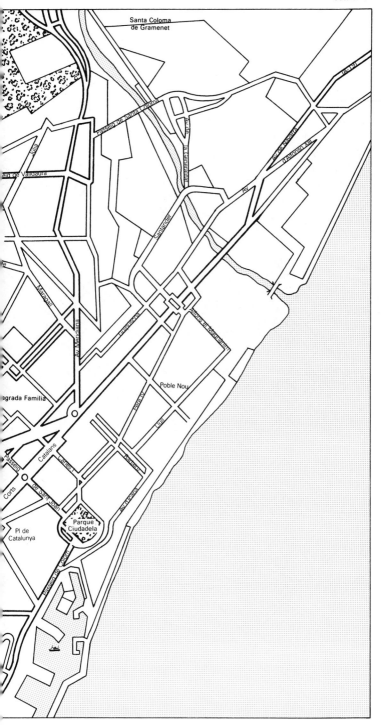

Santa Coloma
de Gramenet

Poble Nou

Parque
Ciudadela

Pl de
Catalunya

Sagrada Familia

Catalans

Corts

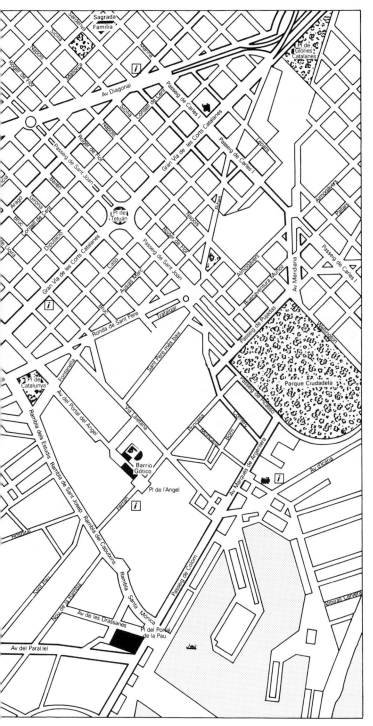

Today, Barcelona has satisfied many of its last-century ambitions on the economic, cultural and political fronts. It is a solid commercial and artistic centre and it is also, since 1980, the capital of the Autonomous Community of Catalonia, the seat of its regional executive, the Generalitat, and of the Parliament of Catalonia.

▥ ★★★★★ *Avenida Palace*, c/ Gran Vía, 605 ☎ 301 96 00 ⊨ 211 TV ♪
▦ AE, CB, DC, EC, MC, V $$$$$$. Central, with good service.

▥ ★★★★★ *Diplomatic*, c/ Pau Claris, 122 ☎ 317 31 00 ⊨ 213 Υ TV ♪
≈ ℳ AE, CB, DC, EC, MC, V $$$$$$. Well situated, with good bars.

▥ ★★★★★ *Gran Hotel Sarriá*, Av Sarriá, 50 ☎ 410 60 60 ⊨ 314 TV P
♪ ▦ ≪ ℳ AE, CB, DC, EC, MC, V $$$$$$. In a residential area, it was recently renovated.

▥ ★★★★★ *Presidente*, Av Diagonal, 570 ☎ 200 21 11 ⊨ 161 Υ TV P ♪
≈ ℳ AE, CB, DC, EC, MC, V $$$$$. Central, with a good bar.

◐ ▥ ★★★★★ *Princesa Sofía*, Pl Pío XII, s/n ☎ 330 71 11 ⊨ 505 TV P ♦ ♪
≈ ♫ ▦ ≪ AE, CB, DC, EC, MC, V $$$$$$. In the premier division, with a good disco.

▥ ★★★★★ *Ritz*, c/ Gran Vía, 668 ☎ 318 52 00 ⊨ 161 TV ♦ ♪ ♨ AE,
CB, DC, EC, MC, V $$$$$$. Classic old world grandeur.

🏨 ★★★★ *Arenas*, c/ Capitán Arenas, 20 ☎ 204 03 00 🛏 59 📺 🎤 🐎 🐴
AE, CB, DC, EC, MC, V $$$$$. Quiet, in the upper part of the city.

🏨 ★★★★ *Balmoral*, Vía Augusta, 5 ☎ 217 87 00 🛏 94 📺 🅿 🎤 🐎 🐴 AE,
CB, DC, EC, MC, V $$$$$. Good service.

🏨 ★★★★ *Calderón*, Rambla de Cataluña, 26 ☎ 301 00 00 🛏 244 ✕ 𝖄 📺
🎤 🐎 🌊 🎏 🐴 AE, CB, DC, EC, MC, V $$$$$. Central, with a
reasonable restaurant and a good bar.

🏨 ★★★★ *Colón*, Av Catedral, 7 ☎ 301 14 04 🛏 161 📺 🎤 🐎 ≪ 🐴 AE,
CB, DC, EC, MC, V $$$$$. Across the square from the Cathedral.

🏨 ★★★★ *Condes de Barcelona*, Paseo de Gracia, 75 ☎ 215 06 16 🛏
100 📺 ✦ 🎤 🐎 ≪ 🐴 AE, CB, DC, EC, MC, V $$$$$. Set in a Modernist
building, it is always full.

🏨 ★★★★ *Cóndor*, Vía Augusta, 127 ☎ 209 45 11 🛏 78 📺 🅿 🎤 🐴 AE,
CB, DC, EC, MC, V $$$$$. Central.

🏨 ★★★★ *Cristal*, c/ Diputación, 257 ☎ 301 66 00 🛏 148 📺 🅿 🎤 $$$$$.

🏨 ★★★★ *Dante*, c/ Mallorca, 181 ☎ 323 22 54 🛏 81 🅿 🎤 $$$$.

🏨 ★★★★ *Derby*, c/ Loreto, 21 ☎ 322 32 15 🛏 116 𝖄 📺 🅿 🎤 🐎 🐴 AE,
CB, DC, EC, MC, V $$$$$. Quiet, with a good cocktail bar.

🏨 ★★★★ *Europark*, c/ Aragón, 325 ☎ 257 92 05 🛏 66 🅿 $$$$.

🏨 ★★★★ *Gran Derby*, c/ Loreto, 28 ☎ 322 32 15 🛏 38 📺 🅿 ✦ 🎤 🐎 📹   ◉
🐴 AE, CB, DC, EC, MC, V $$$$$. Good, modern service flat facilities.

🏨 ★★★★ *Hesperia*, c/ Los Vergos, 20 ☎ 204 55 51 🛏 144 📺 🅿 🎤
$$$$$.

🏨 ★★★★ *Majestic*, Paseo de Gracia, 70 ☎ 215 45 12 🛏 336 📺 🅿 ✦ 🎤 🌊
≪ 🐴 AE, CB, DC, EC, MC, V $$$$$. Classic.

🏨 ★★★★ *Putxet*, c/ Putxet, 68 ☎ 212 51 58 🛏 125 📺 🅿 ✦ 🎤 🐎 🎏 ≪
🐴 AE, V $$$$$. Not central, but it has good service flat facilities.

🏨 ★★★★ *Ramada Renaissance Barcelona*, Ramblas, 111 ☎ 318 62 00
🛏 210 📺 🅿 🎤 AE, CB, DC, MC $$$$$.

🏨 ★★★★ *Regente*, Rambla de Cataluña, 76 ☎ 215 25 70 🛏 78 📺 🅿 🎤 🌊
$$$$$.

🏨 ★★★★ *Victoria*, Av Pedralbes, 16 ☎ 204 27 54 🛏 79 📺 🅿 🎤 🌊 $$$$$.
In the upper part of the city.

🏨 ★★★ *Astoria*, c/ París, 203 ☎ 209 83 11 🛏 114 🎤 🐎 ≪ 🐴 AE, CB,
DC, EC, MC, V $$$$. A classic, central hotel.

🏨 ★★★ *Augusta*, c/ Lincoln, 32 ☎ 218 33 55 🛏 30 📺 🅿 $$$$$. It
deserves a better rating.

🏨 ★★★ *Gran Vía*, c/ Gran Vía, 642 ☎ 318 19 00 🛏 48 🅿 ✦ 🎤 AE, CB,
DC, EC, MC, V $$$. Set in a 19C palace, with good service.

🏨 ★★★ *Mikado*, Paseo de la Bonanova, 58 ☎ 211 41 66 🛏 66 📺 🅿 ✦ 🎤
🐎 🎏 ≪ 🐴 AE, CB, DC, EC, MC, V $$$$$. Good views from the rooftop
solarium.

🏨 ★★★ *Mitre*, c/ Bertran, 9 ☎ 212 11 04 🛏 57 📺 🅿 🎤 🐎 🐴 AE, CB,
DC, EC, MC, V $$$$. A quiet hotel in the upper part of the city.

🏨 ★★★ *Regina*, c/ Vergara, 2 ☎ 301 32 32 🛏 102 🎤 🐎 🐴 AE, V $$$.
Family run, near the Ramblas.

🏨 ★★★ *Rubens*, c/ Nuestra Señora del Coll, 10 ☎ 219 12 04 🛏 136 📺 🅿
✦ 🎤 🐎 ≪ 🐴 AE, CB, DC, EC, MC, V $$$$. In a residential area, with
good views from the solarium.

🏨 ★★★ *Urbis*, Paseo de Gracia, 23 ☎ 317 27 66 🛏 61 📺 🌙 🎤 🐴 AE, DC,   ◉
EC, MC, V $$$. A family-run pension in a 19C house, with good service.

🍴 *Agut* (closed: Sunday nights, Mondays and July), c/ Cignàs, 16 ☎
315 17 09 ✳ $$$. Catalan cuisine and an informal atmosphere.

🍴 *Agut d'Avignon*, c/ Trinidad, 3 ☎ 302 60 34 ✳ AE, DC, V $$$ to $$$$.   ◉
A classic of Catalan cuisine.

🐂 ❙❙ *Ara-Cata* (closed: Saturday and holiday nights, Holy Week and August), c/ Doctor Ferrán, 33 ☎ 204 10 53 ✳ **AE, DC, EC, V** $$$$. Catalan cuisine.

🐂🐂 ❙❙ *Azulete* (closed: Saturday lunchtime, Sundays, Christmas and August), Vía Augusta, 281 ☎ 203 59 43 ♣ ✳ **AE, DC, EC, V** $$$ to $$$$. It has a fashionable and pleasant terrace.

🐂🐂 ❙❙ *Botafumeiro* (closed: Sunday nights and Mondays), c/ Mayor de Gracia, 81 ☎ 218 42 30 **P** ♣ ✳ **AE, DC, EC, V** $$$$ to $$$$$. Very good seafood.

🐂 ❙❙ *Casa Isidre* (closed: Sundays and August), c/ Flores, 12 ☎ 241 11 39 **P** ✳ **AE, V** $$$. Catalan-French *nouvelle cuisine*.

🐂 ❙❙ *Casa Leopoldo* (closed: Sunday nights, Mondays, Holy Week and August), c/ San Rafael, 24 ☎ 241 30 14 **P** ✳ **AE, MC, V** $$$. Excellent, simple Catalan cooking.

🐂 ❙❙ *Chicoa* (closed: Saturday nights, Sundays and August), c/ Aribau, 71 ☎ 253 11 23 **P** ✳ **AE, DC, EC, V** $$$. Catalan cuisine.

❙❙ *Del Teatre* (closed: Sundays, Mondays and 14/7-14/8), c/ Montseny, 47 ☎ 218 67 38 ♣ ✳ $$. Imaginative Catalan cuisine.

🐂 ❙❙ *El Túnel* (closed: Sunday nights, Mondays and 15/7-15/8), c/ Ample, 33 ☎ 315 27 59 $$$. Excellent cannelloni.

🐂🐂 ❙❙ *Eldorado Petit* (closed: Sundays and August), c/ Dolors Monserdá, 51 ☎ 204 51 53 ✳ **AE, DC, EC, MC, V** $$$$ to $$$$$. *Nouvelle cuisine*. A pleasant terrace.

🐂 ❙❙ *Els Perols de l'Empordá* (closed: Saturday nights and 15/8-31/8), c/ Villaroel, 88 ☎ 323 10 33 ✳ **AE, DC, EC, MC, V** $$$ to $$$$. Cuisine from the Ampurdán region.

❙❙ *Flash Flash*, c/ La Granada, 25 ☎ 237 09 90 ✳ **AE, DC, MC, V** $$. A very informal omelette parlour open until 1.30 am.

🐂🐂 ❙❙ *Florián* (closed: Sundays and August), c/ Bertrand i Serra, 20 ☎ 212 46 27 ✳ **DC, EC, MC, V** $$$$. Imaginative cuisine.

❙❙ *Giardinetto Notte* (closed: Sundays), c/ La Granada, 22 ☎ 218 75 36 ✳ **AE, DC, EC, V** $$$ to $$$$. Sophisticated, it stays open until very late for drinks and meals.

🐂🐂 ❙❙ *Gorría* (closed: Sundays and August), c/ Diputación, 421 ☎ 232 78 57 ✳ **AE, DC, MC, V** $$$ to $$$$. Basque-Navarrese cuisine.

🐂 ❙❙ *Guría* (closed: 2 weeks in August), c/ Casanova 97 ☎ 253 63 25 ✳ **AE, DC, MC, V** $$$$. Basque cuisine.

🐂 ❙❙ *Hostal Sant Jordi* (closed: Sunday nights and August), Travesera del Dalt, 123 ☎ 213 10 37 ✳ **AE, DC, EC, V** $$$. Modern and traditional Catalan cuisine.

🐂🐂 ❙❙ *Jaume de Provença* (closed: Sunday nights, Mondays and August), c/ Provença, 88 ☎ 230 00 29 ✳ **AE, DC, EC, V** $$$ to $$$$. Imaginative cuisine.

🐂 ❙❙ *La Balsa* (closed: Sunday nights), c/ Infanta Isabel, 4 ☎ 211 50 48 ♣ ✳ **AE, DC, EC, V** $$$ to $$$$. Slightly pretentious but the terrace is very agreeable.

🐂 ❙❙ *La Ciboulette* (closed: Sundays and August), c/ Camp, 63 ☎ 417 21 22 ✳ **AE, DC, EC, V** $$$ to $$$$. French cuisine.

🐂 ❙❙ *La Dorada* (closed: Sundays), Travesera de Gracia, 44 ☎ 200 63 22 **P** ✳ **AE, DC, EC, V** $$$. Fish, seafood and Andalusian specialities.

🐂 ❙❙ *La Odisea* (closed: Sundays, Holy Week and August), c/ Copons, 7 ☎ 302 32 92 ✳ **AE, DC, EC, V** $$$ to $$$$. A very varied menu.

🐂 ❙❙ *L'Indret-Semon* (closed: Sundays and 15/7-15/9), c/ Ganduxer, 31 ☎ 201 69 31 ✳ $$$. Next to the *Semon* delicatessen, it is open from 10.00-8.00.

¶¶ *L'Olivé*, c/ Muntaner, 171 ☎ 230 90 27 ♣ ❋ EC, V $$$. A small, usually crowded, bistro serving Catalan cuisine.

¶¶ *Neichel* (closed: Sundays, holidays, August and Christmas), c/ Pedralbes, 16 bis ☎ 203 84 08 ❋ AE, DC, EC, MC, V $$$$. French cuisine.

¶¶ *Orotava* (closed: Sundays lunchtime), c/ Consejo de Ciento, 335 ☎ 302 31 28 ■ AE, DC, MC, V $$$$. Classic French cuisine in a luxurious, Baroque setting.

¶¶ *Petit Paris*, c/ Paris, 196 ☎ 218 26 78 ❋ MC, V $$$ to $$$$. Good cod dishes.

¶¶ *Reno*, c/ Tuset, 27 ☎ 200 91 29 ❋ AE, DC, MC, V $$$$. Elegant, Spanish cooking.

¶¶ *Roig Robí* (closed: Sundays and holidays), c/ Séneca, 20 ☎ 218 92 22 ♣ ❋ AE, DC, MC, V $$$ to $$$$. Catalan cuisine.

¶¶ *Vía Veneto*, c/ Ganduxer, 10 ☎ 200 70 24 ■ ♣ ❋ AE, DC, MC, V $$$$. Elegant setting and imaginative cooking.

¶¶ *Vips*, Rambla de Cataluña, 7 AE, DC, MC, V $ to $$$. A drugstore and soda fountain with restaurant service from 10.00 am-3.00 am.

Beaches: Barcelona has two city beaches, Barceloneta beach and Mar Bella beach, which are exactly as you might expect them to be: crowded. They do have a lot of snack bars and waterside restaurants and Mar Bella has a sailing, **windsurfing** and canoeing school. Outside the city, **Castelldefels**, 20km along the motorway, is big, sandy and has been a favourite with Barcelonans for generations. Sɪᴛɢᴇs, 42km on Ctra C-245, has good beaches and a fun atmosphere.

Best buys: What makes shopping in Barcelona particularly pleasurable is the undisputed style that the city possesses. Barcelona as a whole is design conscious and this rubs off on its commerce. To describe the city as a shopper's paradise sounds trite but that is exactly what it is. The following listings can only serve to point you in the right direction.

The area around the Cathedral and the Ramblas and the Gothic Quarter as a whole is the best place for **souvenirs** and traditional haberdashers, milliners and so on. There are several **antique shops** in this area including *A. Grasas*, c/ Palla, 10 and c/ Banys Nous, 14, *Anamórfosis*, c/ Bajada de Santa Eulalia, 4, and *Noirjean*, c/ Sant Sever, 9. *Austerlitz*, c/ Palla, 3, specializes in antique weapons and *Violan*, Pl del Rey, 1, in rare books. The Pl del Rey is the scene of a **coin and stamp market** every Sunday morning.

If you are looking for **fashion** and designer names you will need to explore the Ensanche area and in particular the Paseo de Gracia, Av Diagonal and the streets that lead off them. A check list of shops and boutiques would have to include the following: *Pertegaz*, Av Diagonal, 423, *Galon Glace*, c/ Lauria, 87, *A. Villalba*, Rambla Cataluña, 88, *Pedro Morago*, Av Diagonal, 518, *Christian Dior Monsieur*, c/ Pau Casals, 7, *Fancy Men*, Av Diagonal, 463, *Adolfo Domínguez*, Paseo de Gracia, 89 and c/ Valencia, 245, *Loewe*, Paseo de Gracia, 35 and 95, *Giorgio Armani*, Av Diagonal, 624, *Jean Pierre Bua*, Av Diagonal, 469, *Trecce*, c/ Escuelas Pías, 2, *Teresa Ramallal*, c/ M. Nicolau, 17, *Matrícula*, c/ Pau Casals, 24, *Next Door*, Av Diagonal, 461, and *Groc*, Rambla de Cataluña, 100 (**Toni Miró** designs). Turning to accessories, the **shoes** check list includes *Christiane*, c/ Muntaner, 239, *Patricia*, Av Diagonal, 466, *Stéphane Kelian*, c/ Rosellón, 218, *Vermont*, Pl Françesc Maciá, 8, and *Xinel.la*, Travesera de Gracia, 10. The **jewelry**, classic, modern and costume, list includes *Diamantissimo*, c/ Provenza, 233 and c/ Muntaner, 337, *Puig Doria*, Av Diagonal, 580, *Cubic*, Paseo de Gracia, 49, *Joaquín Berao*, c/ Rosellón, 277, *Vasari*, Paseo de Gracia, 33, *R. Oriol*, c/ Bori i Fontestá, 11, and *Hipotesi*, Rambla Cataluña, 105.

If what you are interested in is **design** then you should look in on **Vinçon**, Paseo de Gracia, 96, and **B.D. Ediciones de Diseño**, c/ Mallorca, 291. The **art gallery** list includes **Dau al Set** and **Sala Gaspar**, at c/ Consell de Cent, 333 and 323 respectively, and **Joan Prats**, Rambla de Cataluña, 54. **Antiques** are available at **Gothsland**, c/ Consell de Cent, 331 (specializing in Modernism), and the **Centro de Anticuarios**, Paseo de Gracia, 55, which has some 70 shops buying, evaluating and selling. This same shopping mall has a wide range of gift shops and clothes stores on its **Boulevard Rosa**, and its ground floor area includes a craft centre which exhibits the work of local craftsmen. For top quality crafts you can also go to **Artespaña**, Rambla Cataluña, 75.

Spain's leading department store chain, *El Corte Inglés*, has a number of branches in Barcelona: Pl de Cataluña, 14, Ausías March, 38 and 40, Bolivia, 234, Av Catedral, 17, Av Diagonal, 617 and Gran Vía de les Corts Catalanes, 613. The rival big store company, *Galerías Jorba Preciados*, has branches at Av Diagonal, 471, Av Mare de Deu de Montserrat, 39, Av Meridiana, 352, Av Portal de l'Angel, 19 and c/ Valencia, 527.

If you feel peckish, you can always visit the excellent **Semon** delicatessen, c/ Ganduxer, 31, the pastry shops **Baixas**, c/ Calaf, 9, and **Vilaplana**, Pl San Gregorio Taumaturgo, 4 (with its own sandwich shop and restaurant), or any of the many general food stores selling charcuterie, cheeses, wines and cavas such as **Quílez**, Rambla Cataluña, 63, **Lafuente**, c/ J.S. Bach, 20, and **Gran Colmado**, c/ Consell de Cent, 318.

Of course if all you need is a show stopping bouquet, an obscure periodical or a talking parrot you had better wander down the Ramblas where you'll find them all.

Cultural highlights: Barcelona is a big city in every way. You will need at least three days to come to grips with it, see the essentials and be confident about your bearings. Each of the following itineraries can be covered on foot once you have reached the starting point.

The **Barrio Gótico (Gothic Quarter) and the Ramblas**. As you would expect the **Cathedral** is the focal point of medieval Barcelona. The first stone of this Gothic cathedral was laid in 1298 and building and additions of one sort or another continued right through to the 19C. The loftiness of the Cathedral is immediately striking on entering it. The **side chapels** are on the whole interesting with their alabaster tombs, and the second on the right has a Gothic altarpiece of the **Transfiguration** which is especially good. The **choir stalls**, a key feature of every medieval cathedral, are distinguished and the **trascoro**, or the space behind the high altar, has fine marble reliefs. The **cloister** is big and very attractive. Its ogival arches date from the 15C and they look out on to an extremely pleasant garden which is shaded and populated by gurgling fountains and placid looking geese. The **Cathedral Museum** (open: 9.00-1.00) has a collection of paintings and religious imagery, with a 15C retable of Saint Bernard by Jaume Huguet as its main exhibit.

The very charming **Pl del Rey** alongside the Cathedral has two museums worth visiting. The **Museo Frederic Marès**, housed in the historic building called the Palacio de los Condes de Barcelona, the residence of the Counts of Barcelona (open: 9.00-2.00 and 4.00-7.00 ☎ 315 58 00), has a very rich and fascinating collection of polychromed wood medieval religious imagery. The plaza's Casa Padellas is the home of the **City Museum**, Museo de la Historia de la Ciudad (open: 9.00-2.00 and 3.30-8.30 ☎ 315 11 11 and 315 00 08). The **Palacio Real Mayor**, in the same plaza, was the site where the Catholic Monarchs received **Christopher Columbus** on his return from his first voyage to the New World.

The **Pl de Sant Jaume**, close by, has been the political heart of Barcelona for centuries. Its W flank is taken up by the 15-17C **Generalitat building**, the palace of the chief minister of Catalonia's regional government. This is a fine example of Catalan Gothic civic architecture and its façade is graced by a carving of Saint George, Barcelona's patron saint, purposefully slaying a dragon. Inside, the palace's notable features include its great stairway, Saint George's chapel and a lovely interior patio graced by orange trees. The E flank is taken up by the no less imposing façade of the **Town Hall** which was where the assembly of notables used to meet in the Middle Ages. One of the major halls within, the **Salón de las Crónicas**, is decorated by the powerful frescoes of 20C Catalan muralist José María Sert.

Moving N out of this square you are walking in the direction of **Santa María del Mar** (open: 5.00-7.00), a really magnificent 14C Gothic church whose Virgin was the object of enormous devotion among Barcelona's medieval sailors. The district around here, close to the port, is a mix of tenements which are being turned into lofts by the city's artistic movers and shakers, and of palaces and large town houses that are being converted into exhibition halls. Along **c/ Montcada**, the **Picasso Museum** occupies the Berenguer-Aguilar palace (open: 9.00-2.00 and 4.00-8.30; closed: Monday mornings ☎ 319 69 02), which is particularly rich in Picasso's very early work, produced when he lived in Barcelona. In the same street, the **Dalmases Palace**, now the Institute of Catalan Studies, is an interesting Baroque building; the Llió Palace is the home of a **Textile and Costume Museum** (open: 9.00-2.00 ☎ 310 45 16 and 319 76 03); and the Cervelló Palace is now the *Galería Maeght* exhibition hall. The concert hall, the **Palacio de la Música Catalana**, on c/ Amadeo Vives, 1, is a typically Modernist building by Gaudí's contemporary, Domènech i Montaner; it was built between 1905 and 1908.

The **Ramblas**, Barcelona's famed boulevard, are on the other side of the Pl de San Jaume, if you are walking in a S direction. On the way down towards the port from the massive Pl de Cataluña, there is a wonderful covered market, the **Mercado de la Boquería** on your right that dates from the last century and is a delight to wander through. Spain's premier opera house, the 19C **Gran Teatro del Liceo**, is on the left. The Decorative Arts Museum, **Museo de Artes Decorativas** (open: 9.00-2.00 and 4.30-9.00 ☎ 301 77 75 and 302 77 52) is also on the left in the 18C **Palacio de la Virreina**. At the end of the Ramblas, by the statue in honour of Columbus and the port, you can visit the Maritime museum, the **Museo Marítimo** (open: 10.00-2.00 and 4.00-7.00; Sundays: 10.00-2.00 ☎ 301 18 71) which is housed in the **Reales Atarazanas**, the 14C dockyards. Other Ramblas landmarks are the Modernist extravaganza that Baron Güell, a 19C financier, had built for himself, the **Palacio Güell**, and the porticoed **Pl Real**, which lies just off the boulevard, where a coin and stamp market is held in the square on Sunday mornings. The Barrio Chino (red light district) is on the other side of the Ramblas and beyond, the 12C **Church of San Pablo del Campo**, with a beautiful **cloister**.

El Ensanche. This is the grid pattern residential and business area that was built up half way through last century to accommodate the needs of the prosperous middle classes when Barcelona, literally bursting at the seams, knocked down the walls that used to enclose the Gothic Quarter. The Ensanche —Paseo de Gracia, Gran Vía, Vía Layetana, Rambla de Cataluña, **Av Diagonal**— is the location of the city's best **shops** and art galleries and of most of its top hotels and restaurants. It is also the best place to view the Modernist architecture that Gaudí and others created at the turn of the century. The unfinished Cathedral, the **Sagrada Familia**, which is Gaudí's masterpiece and Barcelona's most recognizable emblem, is on the plaza of the same name. You can watch the work in progress for the astonishing temple is still being built according to Gaudí's ideas (he left no written plans) under the direction of local artist and sculptor Josep María Subirachs. Gaudí's most famous town houses are on the **Paseo de Gracia**. You should take special note of the **Batlló** and the **Milá** houses which are at No. 43 and No. 92 of this boulevard. Two parks, very different from each other and both rather unique, border the Ensanche. The **Parque Güell**, designed by Gaudí for his extremely wealthy patron, the Baron Güell, can best be described as a folly and is typically *avant garde*. N of the port, the **Parque de la Ciudadela** occupies the site of a former fortress built by the first Bourbon king, Philip V, to keep the Barcelona populace in check. In 1888 its grounds were used for a Universal Exposition staged to show off Barcelona's industrial progress. The park now houses the city's prestigious **Zoo**, the **Geology Museum** (open: 9.00-2.00 ☎ 319 93 12) and the **Zoology Museum** (open: 9.00-2.00; ☎ 319 68 93), and the Modern Art Museum, the **Museo de Arte Moderno** (open Tuesdays to Saturdays: 9.00-7.30; Sundays: 9.30-2.00; Mondays: 1.00-7.30 ☎ 319 57 28).

Montjuïc and Tibidabo. Barcelona has two hills overlooking the city, Montjuïc the on S by the sea and Tibidabo, the higher of the two, which is behind the city, as it were, and keeps Barcelona hemmed in against the Mediterranean. **Montjuïc** will be the centre of world attention come 1992 for it is the site of the **Olympic Stadium** which will host that year's summer games. It is a very well landscaped **park** with excellent **panoramic views** that rises up to 213m and there is plenty to see and do there once you enter it. Montjuïc boasts no fewer than four museums: the **Museo de Arte de Cataluña**, Museum of Catalan Art, has an extremely important collection of **Romanesque and Gothic sculptures** (open: 9.30-2.00; closed: Mondays ☎ 223 18 24 and 325 58 24); the **Museo de Cerámica**, Ceramics Museum, exhibits ceramics from the 12C to the present day (open: 9.00-2.00 ☎ 325 32 44); the **Fundación Joan Miró**, a very impressive building designed by Catalan architect José Luis Sert, houses the extensive artistic legacy of the incomparable Miró, and the **Museo Arqueológico**, Archaeological Museum, exhibits antique remains uncovered mostly in Catalonia (open: 9.30-1.00 and 4.00-7.00; Sundays: 10.00-2.00; closed: Mondays ☎ 223 21 49 and 223 56 01). Other attractions on Montjuïc include a fascinating and very faithful life sized reconstruction of popular architecture from all over Spain in the area called the **Pueblo Español**, interesting pavilions like the **Mies van der Rohe** pavilion, delightful **fountains** and a Greek Theatre where cultural events are staged.

The **Tibidabo**, 532m high, towers over Barcelona to give a superb **view** of the whole city and of the Mediterranean, particularly spectacular at night. A funicular railway takes you to the top, where there is an amusement park, if you want to avoid the steeply winding but picturesque road. At the foot of the mountain, in the area called Pedralbes, there is a 14C abbey, the **Monasterio de Santa María de Pedralbes**, which has fine murals in its Gothic church. Nearby the **Palacio Nacional de Pedralbes** was built in the 1920s to serve as an official residence for the Spanish Royal Family when visiting Barcelona.

Fiestas: Barcelona's big *fiesta* week is the ***Setmana Gran*** that takes place around September 24 which is the feast day of the *Virgen de la Merced*, the city's patron saint. The city indulges in street parties, concerts, firework displays, bullfights, *sardana* dancing and general merrymaking. A high point of the *fiesta* is the concentration in the Pl Sant Jaume of the ***gigantes***, or giants, enormous *papier-maché* carnival figures, from all over Catalonia. The day of ***Sant Jordi*** (Saint George) on April 23 is another excuse to have a holiday. This *fiesta* has a typical Catalan civilized feel to it for it is traditional to celebrate the day by handing out roses and books to friends and relatives. As in many other parts of Spain, the feast day of **San Juan** (Saint John) on June 24 involves a special midsummer ritual of bonfires and parties. Catalonia's national day, known as *La Diada*, a public holiday, is on September 11.

In addition to the annual *fiesta* calendar there are a number of cultural and **musical** cycles and it is best to check in the local press for details of what is on where and when. The **opera** season at the Liceo Theatre runs from November to June. A cycle of concerts called the *Semana de Música* takes place in March at the Palau de la Música and the same concert hall stages a **Festival of Ancient Music** in May. Other musical cycles include the **Festival of Romantic Music** in January, the **Cycle of Polyphonic Music** in April and the *Serenatas d'Estiu* summer serenades in July and August. A theatre season which takes over several city playhouses and venues and is known as the *Grec* takes place from late June to mid August. An international film week, the *Semana Internacional de Cine*, is held in either June or July. Top cultural events in September and October include an **International Jazz Festival** and a series of orchestral concerts under the umbrella of the **International Music Festival**.

Local sights: The N-II stretches for 64km NE along the coast before swinging inland, passing through a series of resorts interspersed with industrial towns that form an area known as the **Maresme**. Badalona, 6km outside Barcelona, is an important manufacturing centre while **El masnou**, a further 10km on, is quieter and residential and has a good beach and a marina. **Mataro**, continuing along the N-II, is a busy commercial town and the historical capital of the Maresme zone. The first railway in Spain, built in 1848, linked Barcelona to Mataró. Its main church, the 16C Basílica de Santa María, is worth visiting for it has a splendid Baroque altar, and *Can Dimas* (closed: December), Pasaje Callao, s/n 🅿 ☎ 790 32 09 AE, DC, MC, V $$$, is an above average restaurant. Though still in the Maresme district, the **Costa Brava** is reckoned to start, as far as the tour operators are concerned, at **Arenys de mar** (see separate entry), 10km from Mataró and 34km from Barcelona. Camping sites, hotels and the rest of the holiday infrastructure now begin in earnest as the N-II continues through one time small villages such as **Canet de mar**, Sant Pol de Mar and **Calella**.

Heading SW and leaving Barcelona along the A-7 motorway or along the C-245 you reach **Castelldefels** (see separate entry), which has become a busy suburb of Barcelona and a pleasant one at that thanks to its **beach**. Continuing on from here the stretch of coastline is known as the **Costa de Garraf** after the mountains of the same name that lie behind it. The cliff-top route is sometimes tortuous but it is very picturesque. It leads to the cosmopolitan resort of **Sitges** (see separate entry), 43km from Barcelona.

The Romanesque-Gothic **Monastery of San Cugat de Vallés** is interesting both for its artistic merits and because it is the starting point for the whole Vallés area, a traditional and graceful residential district which is now heralded as a Silicon Valley or rather a *Silicona Vallés* in the vernacular. You reach the abbey, 12km from Barcelona, by taking the local road to Tarrasa and you cannot miss it for its massive bell tower is a local landmark. The **monastery** was rebuilt in the 11C after the Muslim invasion and its **church** dates from the 12C. One highlight is the All Saints altarpiece in the church painted in tempora, very much in the Catalan Gothic style. The other is the 13C **cloister** which has more than 100 expertly carved capitals. The chief town of this area is the manufacturing centre of Granollers, 28km from Barcelona. Just 8km from here along the N-152 lies a wholly different world of leisure and gracious living in and around the village of **LA GARRIGA**. A typical Barcelona mix of wealthy business people, politicians and poets built a whole series of summer houses here attracted by the waters of the local spa. The spa itself, the ★★★ *Balneario Blancafort*, c/ Baños, 55 ☎ 871 46 00 ⊨ 52 ◻ ✦ ⬤ ⟐ ⚏ ▦ ℚ AE, DC, V \$\$ to \$\$\$, is quiet and comfortable.

On the town: Barcelona has a wealth of bars and drinking holes, night spots and day spots. It is a city that takes leisure very seriously and there is fun and amusement to suit every taste and age group.

Cafés and Cocktail Bars. A short list is fairly long for it would have to include *Amarcord*, c/ Provença, 265, and *Marcel*, c/ Santaló, 44, which are straight coffee bars that stay open until the early hours; *Maison Dorée*, Rambla Cataluña, 104, which is a well-known café with a pleasant open-air terrace in the summer; *KGB*, c/ Alegre de Dalt, 55, *Otto Zutz*, c/ Lincoln, 15, *Bar-Librería Cristal-City*, c/ Balmes, 294, *Café de Las Artes*, c/ Valencia, 234, and *Berimbau*, Paseo del Born, 17, which are pub-type drinking bars with music (Brazilian in the case of *Berimbau*); and *Dry Martini Bar*, c/ Aribau, 162, *Network*, Av Diagonal, 616, *Boadas*, c/ Tallers, 1, *Gimlet*, c/ Rech, 24 and c/ Santaló, 46, *Merbeyé*, Pl del Funicular (at the foot of the Tibidabo mountain and with good views), *Ricos y Bellas*, c/ Aribau, 242, *Nick Havanna*, c/ Roselló, 208, and *Snooker*, c/ Roger de Lluria, 42, which are top cocktail bars each creating a special atmosphere. In a slightly different category are the **champagne bars**, a typical feature of Barcelona: *La Xampanyería*, c/ Provença, 236, *La Cava del Palau*, c/ Verdaguer i Callís, 10 (opposite the Palau de la Musica concert hall), and *Casablanca*, c/ Buenavista, 6, which is very popular.

Daytime Snacks and Drinks. These run into the hundreds but keep in mind *Jamón-Jamón*, c/ Maestro Nicolau, 4, which, as its name indicates, is strong on ham, *Mundial*, Pl San Agustín el Viejo, 1, for shellfish and *tapas*, and *Piscolabis*, Rambla de Cataluña, 49, for sandwiches.

Discotheques. These form a very competitive market in Barcelona and you will find the latest in sounds and lights and every gimmick imaginable, from swimming pools to mobile stages. Favourites among younger disco fanatics are *Studio 54*, Av Paralelo, 54, and *Zeleste*, c/ Almogàvers, 122. The more sophisticated and elegant boppers go to *Regine's*, Pl Pío XII, and *Up and Down*, c/ Numancia, 179.

Gambling. The *Gran Casino de Barcelona* ☎ 893 36 36, at Sant Pere de Ribes, 40km from the city centre, has a disco, shows and a restaurant as well as roulette and black jack tables and the rest.

Music Halls. Some of them are survivors of the days when the stage was lit by gaslights and others are in line with the big shows that you will find in every big city. The ones in the district called the Paralelo, *Arnau*, Av Paralelo, 60, *El Molino*, c/ Vila, 99, *Bodega Apolo*, Av Paralelo, 59, and *Belle Epoque*, c/ Muntaner, 246, belong to the first category and provide a magnificent mix of innocence and sauciness; *Scala*, Paseo de San Juan, 47, belongs to the second category and is very grand.

Other Entertainments. Barcelona has two mountain-high **amusement parks**, one atop Montjuïc, Ctra de Montjuïc, s/n ☎ 241 70 42, and the other on the Tibidabo peak ☎ 417 03 38. The city's **zoo** is in the Ciudadela Park (open: 9.30-7.30 ☎ 309 25 00). An alternative recreation is provided by the *Sports Center*, Ctra N-150, km14.700, which has a go-kart track and a variety of circuits for mini-motor bikes, bicycles and electric cars ☎ 726 66 44. Typical Spanish entertainment is to be had during the **bullfighting** season in Barcelona.

Other Sounds. A number of **dance halls** cater for people who have a yen for the rhythms and steps of the 1940s and 1950s. If there are two of you to tango head for places like *La Paloma*, c/ Tigre, 27, *Cibeles*, c/ Córcega, 363 and *Sutton*, c/ Tusset, 13. There is jazz at the *Cova del Drac*, c/ Tusset, 30, and flamenco in *El Patio Andaluz*, c/ Aribau, 242, and in *Los Tarantos*, Pl Real, 17.

Sports: People in Barcelona are very sport and fitness conscious, even more so now that they are going to host the 1992 Olympics. The following list will give you some idea of the athletic possibilities.

Golf. The closest golf club to the city centre is the *Real Club de Golf del Prat*, Prat de Llobregat, 16km, which has an 18 and a 9-hole course ☎ 379 02 78. The 18-hole *Club de Golf de San Cugat* is at San Cugat del Vallés, 20km ☎ 674 39 08. The *Club de Golf de Llavaneras* is 34km out of town, and the 18-hole *Club de Golf Vallromanas* is at Montornes de Vallés, 25km ☎ 568 03 62.

Gymnasia and Squash Clubs. Well equipped clubs for the keep fit crowd include *Llars Mundet*, Paseo de la Vall d'Hebrón, s/n ☎ 229 16 00, *Squash Club Barcelona*, Av Roma, 2 ☎ 325 81 00, and *Can Melich Club*, Av 11 de Septiembre, s/n, in Sant Just Desvern ☎ 372 82 11.

Horseback Riding. Stables and pony clubs include the *Real Club de Polo de Barcelona*, Av Diagonal, s/n ☎ 249 29 70 and Av Doctor Marañón, 17 ☎ 334 92 11, the *Club Hípico Llavaneras*, in San Andrés de Llavaneras ☎ 792 73 61, and the *Campo de Hípica*, Av Montanys, in Montjuic ☎ 301 16 18.

Sailing. Barcelona's marina has 278 berths and all the necessary facilities. The city has two yacht clubs, the *Real Club Marítimo de Barcelona* ☎ 315 00 07, and the *Real Club Náutico de Barcelona* ☎ 315 11 61.

Skiing. The winter sports stations in the Pyrenees (*Baqueira-Beret, La Molina, Llesui, Port del Comte* and *Vallter 2.000*) are more than 150km out of town but have good roads connecting them (see 'Holidays in Action').

Swimming Pools. Barcelona has numerous open air and indoor pools. Top ones include those at the *Club Hispano-Francés*, Camí Sant Cebrián, s/n ☎ 229 10 29, and at the *Club Natación Barcelona*, c/ Escullera Llevant, s/n ☎ 319 46 00.

Tennis. Inner city clubs include the *Real Club de Tenis Barcelona*, Av Diagonal, s/n ☎ 240 92 44 and c/ Bosch i Gimpera, s/n ☎ 203 77 58, the *Club de Tenis Barcino*, Pasaje Forasté, 33 ☎ 417 08 05, the *Club de Tenis La Salud*, c/ Mare de Deu de la Salut, 75 ☎ 213 56 98, and the *Real Club de Tenis del Turó*, Av Diagonal, 673 ☎ 203 80 12.

BLANES Gerona ☎ (972), pop. 22,372, *i* Paseo de Dintre ☎ 33 03 48. Gerona 43km, Barcelona 61km, Madrid 691km.

This is the southernmost resort of the Costa Brava. Its fishing port and marina are very popular with tourists in the summer holiday season.

★★★ *Horitzó* (closed: 26/10-25/3), Paseo Marítimo S'Abanell, 11 ☎ 33 04 00 ⇌ 122 ⚲ ⚓ ≪ AE, V $$.

★★★ *Park Hotel Blanes* (closed: 1/10-30/4), S'Abanell beach ☎ 33 02 50 ⇌ 131 P ✦ ≈ ⚓ ≪ ⚐ ⚲ ⚒ $$$ to $$$$. By a pine wood.

❙❙ *Patacano* (closed: Mondays in winter, 1/11-25/11 and 7/1-25/1), Paseo del Mar, 12 ☎ 33 00 02 P ✦ AE, DC, MC, V $$ to $$$. Open since the beginning of the century, it specializes in lobster dishes.

Beaches: In addition to its local beach you can opt for San Francisco, Sa Forcanera or Santa Cristina, en route to Lloret de Mar. S'Abanell beach is by the Tordera river estuary.

Best buys: You may find a bargain at the second-hand boat show which is held in the first week of May.

Cultural highlights: Holding their own against the concrete high-rise invasion are the Gothic Church of Santa María, the ruined Palace of the Viscounts of Cabrera and the 10C Castle of San Juan. There is an **Aquarium** at c/ Explanada del Puerto, 12 (open: 10.00-8.00) and a very fine botanical garden, the **Jardín Botánico Mar i Murtra**, along the Ctra de San Juan, which has more than 4,000 species of exotic plants and lovely views over the Mediterranean (open: 9.00-6.00 ☎ 33 16 14).

Fiestas and festivals: The highpoint of the town *fiesta* on July 26 is the spectacular **International Firework Competition**. A theatre festival is staged in summer ☎ 33 02 62.

Local sights: The **Costa Brava** extends N. Turning inland from Blanes, you reach the **Montseny** mountain range (see separate entries).

On the town: Bars and discos are everywhere here. Popular ones include *Big-Ben*, Paseo del Mar, *Kramer*, c/ Anselmo Clavé, and *Cleopatra*, Av Mediterráneo, in Els Pins.

Sports: Water sports at the *Club de Vela de Blanes* ☎ 33 05 52.

CADAQUES Gerona ☎ (972), pop. 1,639, *i* c/ Cotche, 2 ☎ 25 83 15. Gerona 69km, Barcelona 169km, Madrid 776km.

The artistic shadow of **Salvador Dalí**, who built an extravagant home for himself in the nearby cove of Port Lligat, falls across Cadaqués and this lovely Costa Brava fishing village is a sort of Greenwich Village on the Mediterranean as a result. The list of visitors to Cadaqués reads like a Who's Who of 20C culture for it includes Albert Einstein, Federico García Lorca, Thomas Mann and Pablo Picasso. Chock-a-block with art galleries and studios, craft shops and antique boutiques, Cadaqués is also picturesque.

▦ ★★★ *Playa Sol* (closed: 1/1-1/3), Playa Pianch, 5 ☎ 25 81 00 ⫞ 49 **P** ✦ ⩙ ⌖ ⌕ **DC, V $$$$**. Good views.

▦ ★★★ *Rocamar*, c/ Doctor Bartomeu, s/n ☎ 25 81 50 ⫞ 70 **P** ✦ ⩙ 🎠 ⌕ **$$$$**.

▦ ★★★ *S'Aguarda* (closed: 1/11-30/11), Ctra Port Lligat, 28 ☎ 25 80 82 ⫞ 27 **P** ✦ **AE, DC, EC, V $$**.

❚❙ *La Galiota* (closed: weekdays in winter), c/ Narcís Monturiol, 9 ☎ 25 81 87 **AE, V $$$ to $$$$**.

Beaches: Cadaqués itself has a tiny patch of sand but most people head for the Bay of Rosas (25km) where there is a big beach or stop off at the numerous, isolated and beautiful **coves** in between.

Best buys: *Avant garde* paintings can be acquired at *Galería Cadaqués*, c/ Hort d'en Sanes, 9 ☎ 25 82 44, and at *C. Lozano*, c/ Carrer les Voltes, 9.

Cultural highlights: The parish church has a good Baroque altarpiece. There are two public art galleries, the Museo Municipal de Arte Contemporáneo, c/ Narcís Monturiol, 15 (open in summer: 11.00-1.00 and 4.00-8.00) and the **Museo Perrot Moore de Arte Gráfico Europeo**, Pl Frederic Rahola, s/n (open: 4.00-9.00 ☎ 25 83 12).

Fiestas and festivals: An annual International Music Festival is held in late July-early August.

Local sights: Cabo Creus is an 8km trek for there is no road, but the views from the headland are spectacular. **PORT DE LA SELVA**, 15km NW, is a very picturesque beach resort and fishing village. There is a 10C Romanesque abbey nearby, the **Monasterio de San Pedro de Roda**, at the foot of the San Cristóbal mountain.

On the town: The evergreen *Maritim* still pulls in regulars. Good music and a relaxed atmosphere are provided at *Bistrot*, in Es Portal, there is live jazz at *L'Hostal*, on the Paseo Marítimo, and energetic disco swingers go to *Es Porro*, Portal de la Font, 1.

CALDAS DE MONTBUY-CALDES DE MONTBUI Barcelona ☎ (93), pop.
10,256. Barcelona 29km, Madrid 636km.

The Romans were the first to take the waters here and the resort became
very fashionable last century. Currently there are five spas with thermal
springs, open all the year round.

▦ ★★★ *Balneario Broquetas*, Pl Font de Lleó, 1 ☎ 865 01 00 ⊨ 89 🔲 ▯
◆ ⬥ ⚲ ⇌ ▨ ♒ AE, DC, EC, V $$ to $$$. Set in beautiful gardens, it is
very quiet and has a swimming pool open all year round.

CAMBRILS Tarragona ☎ (977), pop. 13,907. [*i*] Pl Creu de la Missió, s/n
☎ 36 11 59. Reus Airport, 20km ☎ 30 35 04. Tarragona 18km, Barcelona
116km, Madrid 554km.

This is a top resort on the **Costa Dorada**. It has one of the highest annual
ratios of sun hours on the coast and it is a favourite spot among **gourmets**
for the fame of its restaurants has spread far and wide. Its fishing port is
extremely busy.

▦ ★★★ *Princep*, Pl Iglesia, 2 ☎ 36 11 27 ⊨ 27 🔲 ▯ ⬥ AE, DC, MC, V $$
to $$$.

▦ ★★★ *Rovira* (closed: 1/11-28/2), Av Diputación, 6 ☎ 36 09 00 ⊨ 58
◆ ⚲ AE, DC, EC, V $$.

▦ ★★ *Mónica* (closed: 1/10-31/3), c/ Galceván Marquet, 3 ☎ 36 01 16
⊨ 56 ▯ ◆ AE, DC, EC, V $$.

❙❙ *Bandert* (closed: Tuesdays and 15/12-15/1), Rambla Jaume I with c/
Ancora ☎ 36 10 63 ◆ ❋ AE, DC, MC, V $$$. Intimate and romantic.

❙❙ *Can Bosch* (closed: Sunday nights, Mondays and 15/12-25/1), Rambla
Jaime I, 19 ☎ 36 00 19 ◆ ❋ AE, DC, EC, V $$$ to $$$$. Once a
fisherman's bar, it is now a very popular fish and seafood restaurant.

❙❙ *Ca'n Gatell* (closed: Monday nights, Tuesdays in winter, lunchtime
Tuesdays and Wednesday in summer, 1/10-31/10 and 1/2-15/2),
Paseo Miramar, 27 ☎ 36 01 06 ▯ ◆ ❋ ⇌ ≪ AE, DC, MC, V $$$$.
Looks onto the fishing port, the source of its excellent fish and seafood.

❙❙ *Casa Gatell* (closed: Sunday nights, Mondays, Christmas and January),
Paseo Miramar, 26 ☎ 36 00 57 ◆ ❋ ≪ AE, DC, MC, V $$$$. Its
splendid terrace overlooking the fishing port is matched by its fish and
rice dishes.

❙❙ *Eugènia* (closed: lunchtime Wednesdays and Thursdays in summer,
Tuesday nights and Wednesdays in winter, and 15/11-2/1), c/ Consolat
de Mar, 80 ☎ 36 01 68 ▯ ◆ AE, DC, MC, V $$$ to $$$$. Imaginative
fish cuisine and a lovely terrace for outside eating at night.

❙❙ *La Caseta del Rellotge* (closed: 15/11-30/11), 4.5km SW along the
N-340 ☎ 83 78 44 ▯ ◆ EC, V $$$. An old inn with rustic decor.

Beaches: The **Ardiaca** beach in town is good; furthermore, the 6km of coast
as far as Salou are a practically uninterrupted stretch of **sand**.

Cultural highlights: The fishermen's quarter is in the picture postcard top
division and extremely agreeable. The Samà Park, on the outskirts, is a
pleasing garden (open: Sunday mornings).

Fiestas: Towards the end of May, on Ascension Day, the town hosts a very
popular agricultural fair. As befits its status as the gastronomic capital of the
Costa Dorada, Cambrils stages a fish cookery competition for top chefs in
July. An **International Chamber Music Festival** is held in July and August.

Local sights: SALOU, REUS, TARRAGONA and other towns along the **Costa
Dorada** are all local sights.

Sports: There is good fishing and underwater fishing here and ideal
conditions for sailing and windsurfing. The yacht club is the *Club Náutico de
Cambrils* ☎ 36 05 31. Tennis is played at *C.D. Vilafortuny* ☎ 36 06 59.

CARDONA **Barcelona** ☎ (93), pop. 6,714, *i* Pl de la Fira, 1 ☎ 869 10 00. Barcelona 99km, Lérida 127km, Madrid 596km.

The Roman geographer Strabonus was the first to make documentary reference to its nearby salt mountain, and you can find out virtually everything you ever wanted to know about salt at the Museo de la Sal, the Salt Museum, c/ Pompeu Fabra, 4. The 11C castle, now a parador, has a **collegiate church** attached to it which shows clear Italian influences. If you are interested in old rites, visit the town on the second Sunday of September, when the *Corre de Bou*, the oldest festivity involving bulls in Catalonia, is celebrated.

👁👁 ▦ ★★★★ *Parador Duques de Cardona*, Cardona Castle ☎ 869 12 75 ⇌ 65 🅿 ✦ 🎤 ⅏ ≪ $$$. This is a very peaceful parador in a medieval castle with lovely mountain and valley views.

CASTELLDEFELS **Barcelona** ☎ (93), pop. 27,646, *i* Pl Rosa dels Vents ☎ 664 23 01. Barcelona 24km, Tarragona 72km, Madrid 615km.

A fortified town between the 12C and the 15C, Castelldefels is now better known among Barcelona day trippers for its wide open **beaches**. Its restored medieval castle has a Romanesque chapel.

▦ ★★★★ *Gran Hotel Rey Don Jaime*, Av del Hotel, s/n, 2km from the town centre at Torre Barona ☎ 665 13 00 ⇌ 88 🅿 ✦ 🎤 ⅏ ⌁ ⚲ ⛾ AE, DC, V $$$$$. Very quiet.

▦ ★★★ *Mediterráneo*, Paseo Marítimo, 294 ☎ 665 21 00 ⇌ 47 ✕ ⅄ 🅿 ✦ ⚲ AE, DC, EC, V $$$.

▦ ★★★ *Neptuno*, Paseo Garbi, 74 ☎ 665 14 50 ⇌ 38 🅿 ✦ 🎤 ⚲ ⛾ 🎠 ⛾ AE, DC, EC, V $$$. Surrounded by pine woods.

🍴 *La Bonne Table* (closed: Mondays and November), Av Constitución, 390 ☎ 665 37 55 🅿 ✦ ❄ AE, DC, MC, V $$ to $$$. French cuisine in a small and agreeable restaurant.

🍴 *Las Botas*, Av Constitución, 326 ☎ 665 18 24 ✦ MC, V $$$. Traditional Catalan decor and cooking.

🍴 *Nàutic*, Paseo Marítimo, 374 ☎ 665 01 74 ❄ ≪ AE, DC, EC, V $$$. Fish and sea food in a nautical atmosphere.

🍴 *Sant Maximin* (closed: Sunday nights, Mondays and November), Av dels Banys, 41 ☎ 665 00 88 🅿 ✦ ❄ AE, DC, EC, V $$$.

CERVERA **Lérida** ☎ (973), pop. 6,437, *i* Paseo Balmes, 8 ☎ 53 13 50, ✚ 53 05 45. Lérida 57km, Madrid 532km.

This is an unspoilt small town that has preserved its medieval atmosphere. One of its curiosities is that it was the home of the sole university in Catalonia for a period during the 18C when the incoming Bourbon dynasty shut down all other centres of higher learning as a reprisal for Catalan opposition to the Bourbons during the War of Spanish Succession.

▦ ★★★ *Balneario* (closed: 1/11-20/5), Ctra Balneari, s/n, 2km from Vallfogona de Rincorp ☎ (977) 88 00 25 ⇌ 96 🅿 ✦ ⅏ ⚲ 🏞 ⛾ $$ to $$$. A quiet, relaxing hotel with lovely gardens.

Best buys: Hand-crafted baskets and wickerwork are made and sold at *A. Minguell*, c/ Sant Magín, 21.

Cultural highlights: The Baroque Church of San Antonio, the **Church of Santa María** in the Romanesque style, containing some fine tombs, and the 11C **Church of San Pere el Gros** on the town's outskirts are all worth visiting.

Fiestas: Cervera has preserved a number of ancient local customs including a series of **Passion Plays** which are acted by the townspeople during Lent.

Sports: Tennis is played at the *Club de Tenis Castelldefels* ☎ 665 12 85.

COSTA BRAVA (WILD COAST) Gerona ☎ (972).

Much like the Costa del Sol, the Costa Brava barely needs an introduction for it is known to millions of tourists who arrive from all over the world in ever increasing numbers for their summer holidays. Seen today with its hotels, apartments and camping sites, its discos and fast food takeaways, you have to make an effort of the imagination to believe that the Costa was at any stage anything other than a gigantic playground on the Mediterranean. In fact, in common with Spain's other key tourist centres, virtually all the facilities you see now are barely 30 years old and a great proportion has been built up over the last decade. Right up to the 1950s the Costa Brava was the quiet stretch of coastline, dotted with fishing villages, that it always had been. Development has been extremely rapid, and is an ongoing process. If you want to get the feel of the virginal beauty of the Costa, your best bet is to take a ride on the pleasure steamers that ply their way up and down the resorts. Seen from the sea you will understand the essential ingredients of the Costa's loveliness as you pass by the rocky **coves** with their tiny isolated beaches and pine-covered clifftops. This natural setting combined with the limpid waters and the all-round luminosity of the sun bouncing off the sea and the woods is what makes the Costa something special.

The really big tourist centres are between **BLANES** and **PALAMOS**. Resorts such as **LLORET DE MAR** and **PLAYA DE ARO** are the places that provide a value-for-money packaged holiday for the mass tourist market. They do it with an expertise that has been borne out of years of experience in dealing with the annual invasion of holidaymakers. Resorts such as **TOSSA DE MAR** and, in particular, **S'AGARO** have fared better in preserving their innate characteristics. In general the northern part of the Costa has been the more successful from the environmental point of view though there are exceptions such as **ROSAS** (see separate entry). Resorts such as **L'ESTARTIT**, **CADAQUES** and **EL PUERTO DE LA SELVA** have established, on the whole, a judicious balance between preserving their original character and meeting the demands of tourism, and although they offer sophisticated entertainment, it is still possible to get away from it all.

If it is sun and fun, sand, *sangría* and chips with everything that you are looking for on the Costa you will find it to your heart's content. The choice available is very considerable. There are, of course, many other possibilities. The Costa is very well equipped sportswise and, naturally, you can do whatever you want on, in and under the Mediterranean. Many visitors miss out on the timeless atmosphere of the old villages that stand just a few kilometres back from the concrete highrises of the Costa. Here and there you will find castles and churches set in a bucolic landscape and in **AMPURIAS** (see 'Rosas') there are very important archaeological remains. On the Costa you are by no means condemned to fast food. There are numerous restaurants that will satisfy the most demanding gourmet. And if you tire of beaches and the smell of suntan lotions you can stroll around the botanical gardens at **Cabo Roig** (see 'Palafrugell') and **Mar i Murtra** (see 'Blanes') and encounter other scents.

COSTA DORADA (GOLDEN COAST) Tarragona ☎ (977).

The Costa Dorada, or Golden Coast, is a 212km stretch of long sandy beaches interspersed with little coves nestling among cliffs against a backdrop of pine woods and the spectacular landscape of the Ebro Delta. Unsurprisingly, its resorts, mostly within a 40km radius of Tarragona, attract a lot of tourists.

CUNIT, once a little fishing port and now a tourist resort, has an interesting 13C Romanesque church and a very good restaurant, *L'Avi Pau* (closed: Tuesdays out of season), Av Diagonal, 20 ☎ 67 48 61 ♥ ✳ DC, EC, V $$$, serving fish and seafood. Heading down the coast you will come to lovely beaches like Calafell —one of the most popular on the Catalan coast— and Comarruga, around which complexes of tourist accommodation have sprung up. In **COMARRUGA**, try the ★★★★ *Gran Hotel Europe*, Vía Palfuriana, 107 ☎ 68 04 11 ⇋ 154 P ♥ ⚓ ≪ $$$$, with lovely views, and the ★★★ *Casa Martí* (closed 15/10-15/3), c/ Vilafranca, 8 ☎ 68 01 11 ⇋ 136 P ⚓ ≪ AE, DC, EC, V $$. **CALAFELL** has its own beach and a ruined hilltop castle —for accommodation here try the ★★★★ *Kursaal*, Av San Juan de Dios, 119 ☎ 69 23 00 ⇋ 39 Ⴑ TV P ♥ ⅋ ≪ AE, DC, EC, V $$$ to $$$$, a quiet hotel with good views, and for dinner go to *Da Giorgio*, c/ Angel Guimerá, 4 ☎ 69 11 59 (closed: lunchtime from May to October) $$ to $$$, serving Italian food.

EL VENDRELL, slightly inland, has remains of its Roman and medieval past and is famous for its *castellers*, who form human towers during the celebrations in honour of Santa Ana (July 26), and the carpets of flowers that decorate the streets at Corpus Christi. A greater claim to fame is the fact that it is the birthplace of virtuoso cellist Pablo Casals, in whose honour there is a museum —the **Casa-Museo Pau Casals**, c/ Palfuriana, 14 (open: 11.00-2.00 and 5.00-7.00; holidays: 5.00-8.00)— and a concert hall where the Casals Music Festival is held. Five kilometres away, the impressive 2C Roman arch, the **Arco de Bara**, spans the Via Augusta.

Approaching the local capital, **TARRAGONA** (see separate entry), the coast is lined with seaside tourist complexes and beaches like Rebasada's, stretching S of the city as far as Salou. **SALOU** itself is a seaside playground for the whole of Europe and attracts more visitors than anywhere else along this coast (it can accommodate 200,000), largely thanks to its beaches —La Canonja, La Pineda and El Racó. Nearby **CAMBRILS** is a little fishing village famous for its excellent restaurants (see separate entry).

Pine, hazel, almond and olive trees occupy long stretches of this coastal belt which sometimes has a distinctly N African look to it. The closer you get to the Ebro Delta, the less touristy it becomes. **HOSPITALET DEL INFANTE** has a good **beach**, a marina and a hotel, the ★★★ *Club Pino Alto*, Urb Pino Alto, in Montroig ☎ 81 08 51 ⇋ 137 ৬ P ♥ ♫ ⚓ ≪ ⊞ ⚞ ⚭ AE, DC, EC, V $$ to $$$, while **L'AMETLLA DE MAR** is pleasantly quiet, with pretty coves close at hand and good fishing possibilities —for accommodation, try ★ *Bon Repos* (closed: 1/10-31/5), Pl Cataluña, 49 ☎ 45 60 25 ⇋ 38 Ⴑ P ♥ ⚓ ⚞ ⚭ $$, with a pleasant garden. The landscape of the **Ebro Delta** is fascinating not only for its extensive rice paddies but also because its inland lakes and waterways constitute one of mainland Spain's major bird sanctuaries. **SAN CARLOS DE LA RAPITA**, on the S tip of the Ebro Delta (see 'Delta del Ebro'), was founded by Charles III and is an exemplary model of rationalist town planning. Las Casas de Alcanar, a few kilometres further S, is the latest fishing village along this *costa* to have developed into a fully-fledged tourist resort.

CUBELLAS-CUBELLES Barcelona ☎ (93), pop. 2,445. Tarragona 41km, Barcelona 54km, Lérida 127km, Madrid 584km.

This choice leisure spot on the Mediterranean, set against the Garraf mountains, comes complete with a marina, tennis clubs and other facilities.
▥ ★★★★ *Llicorella*, Ctra C-246, Camino Viejo de San Antonio, 101 ☎ 895 00 44 ⇋ 11 ✕ TV ♥ ♫ ⅋ ⚓ AE, DC, MC, V $$$$. A very quiet, small hotel attached to a very good **restaurant** $$$ to $$$$ (or vice versa) created for a discerning market. The hotel has interesting art exhibits and a lovely garden.

DELTA DEL EBRO (EBRO DELTA) **Tarragona** ☎ (977).

The mighty Ebro river has been silting its way into the Mediterranean down the centuries and created an extraordinarily unusual and large area of natural real estate in the process. The swampy alluvial fingers of the delta continue to advance into the sea at the rate of 10m a year and the appearance of new stretches of beach is an annual surprise. The whole place, with its lagoons and dunes, its alternating dry land and water, has a fantastic air about it. Parts of the delta resemble a desert, in other zones the vegetation is extremely exuberant and whole areas have been cleared for cultivation and criss-crossed with irrigation ditches to form rice paddies. Birds of many species arrive to nest in the delta and human visitors have also discovered the pleasures of its long, virgin beaches and its peaceful, warm waters. Eucalyptus beach, near Amposta, and the beaches at **Punta del Fangar** and the **Istmo del Trabucador** at the extremities of the delta belong to the unspoiled paradise category.

The whole delta was virtually uninhabited until the 19C and avoided by all save the odd fisherman and shepherd because its swamps were believed to induce fevers. Things changed fast with the introduction of **rice cultivation** for the area began to produce bumper crops. Farming has continued to expand and nowadays maize is also grown. Fishing is another local industry and the prize catch consists of the baby eels, *angulas*, which become a top Spanish delicacy when they are cooked in sizzling oil, garlic and chili peppers.

SAN CARLOS DE LA RAPITA is the most important town in the Delta after Amposta. It was founded by Spain's enlightened 18C monarch, Charles III, who in the rationalist manner of his age ordered detailed plans to be drawn up for the creation of a model port at the mouth of the Ebro. The port was never a very viable commercial proposition but San Carlos is an excellent spot for savouring the local giant prawns that are known as *langostinos*. If you plan to stay the night, try the ★★★ *Miami Park*, Av Constitución, 33 ☎ 74 03 51 ⊯ 80 TV P ♨ ≪ AE, DC, MC, V $$$, which is near the beach and has good sea views. For lunch or dinner, try *Fernandel* (closed: Mondays and 15/1-15/2), 2km on the Valencia-Barcelona road ☎ 74 03 58 P ≪ AE, DC, MC, V $$$, serving particularly good fish and vegetables, or *Miami Can Pons* (closed: 15/1-15/2), Av Constitución, 35 ☎ 74 05 51 ✳ AE, DC, EC, V $$$, specializing in fish-based regional cooking.

FIGUERAS-FIGUERES **Gerona** ☎ (972), pop. 32,122, *i* Pl del Sol ☎ 50 31 55, ✚ 50 56 01. Gerona 37km, Barcelona 137km, Madrid 744km.

As the birthplace and occasional residence of **Salvador Dalí** and the site of his astonishing Theatre-Museum, the town basks in the reflected glory of the Surrealist master. Followers of the Dalí cult descend in droves on this very agreeable and prosperous provincial small town where *avant garde* art and down-to-earth bourgeois virtues such as a splendid cuisine coexist contentedly together.

🏨 ★★★ *Ampurdán*, km763 on the road to France ☎ 50 05 62 ⊯ 42 ✕ TV P ✦ AE, DC, MC, V $$$ to $$$$. Its **restaurant**, $$$ to $$$$, which boasts a first class wine cellar, commands a large following.

🏨 ★★★ *Durán*, c/ Lasauca, 5 ☎ 50 12 50 ⊯ 67 ✕ P ♦ AE, DC, MC, V $$$. It also has a very popular **restaurant**, $$$, combining top quality regional cooking with good prices.

🏨 ★★ *El Molí* (closed: 15/10 to Holy Week), on the road to Les Escaules, in Port de Molins, 6km from Figueras ☎ 52 80 11 ⊯ 10 ✕ P ✦ ⚒ ℺ AE, DC,V $$. A quiet hotel in an old windmill, with a good **restaurant** serving mountain cuisine.

¶¶ ***Can Jeroni*** (closed: Sundays, holidays and 15/10-15/11), c/ Castelló, 36 ☎ 50 09 83 ❄ $$$. Simple cooking.

◐ ¶¶ ***Mas Pau*** (closed: Sunday nights and 10/1-28/2), in Aviñonet de Puigventós, 4km along the road to Olot ☎ 54 61 54 **P** ✦ **AE, DC, EC, V** $$$ to $$$$. Sophisticated, French influenced food with good game during the season. This old farmhouse also has **accommodation**.

Best buys: Antiques are sold at ***Quintana Novell***, c/ Pep Ventura, 27, while *Distribucions D'Art Surrealiste*, at Pl Gala i Dalí, sells all sorts of things related to Salvador Dalí. Local cakes and desserts such as custard-filled buns called *xuxos* are available at ***Pastelería Cubana***, Carrer Nou, 5.

◐ **Cultural highlights:** More a happening than a gallery, the **Teatro-Museo Dalí**, Pl Gala i Dalí (open: 10.00-12.30 and 3.30-7.00 ☎ 50 56 97), is a monument to the artist's fervid imagination. Giant eggs on the roof and huge totems created out of spent tyres and dead T.V. sets give you a fair impression of what to expect. The curators boast that it is the most visited museum in Spain after Madrid's Prado. There are two other museums in town: the Museo de Juguetes, or Toy Museum, c/ Rambla, 10 (open: 10.00-12.30 and 4.00-7.30; closed: Tuesdays in winter ☎ 50 45 85) and the Museo del Ampurdán, c/ Rambla, 1 (open: 11.00-1.00 and 4.00-8.00; weekends: 11.00-2.00 and 4.30-8.00; closed: Mondays ☎ 50 23 05).

Fiestas: The *Feria de la Santa Cruz*, May 3, is marked by a long established and popular exchange and barter second-hand fair. An International Music Festival is held in September at the Monasterio de Vilabertrán.

◐ GERONA-GIRONA **Gerona** ☎ (972), pop. 87,648, *i* c/ Ciutadans, 12 ☎ 20 16 94, *i* Pl del Vi, 1 ☎ 20 26 79, *i* Pl de España, 1 ☎ 21 62 96, ✝ c/ Bonastruch de Porta ☎ 20 04 15, ✈ 11km on the Barcelona road (Iberia, Pl Marqués de Camps, 8 ☎ 20 58 00), ⊶ RENFE, Pl Marquina, s/n ☎ 20 70 93. Perpignan 91km, Barcelona 100km, Madrid 708km.

Though pleasantly unpretentious and provincial, Gerona is steeped in history. Known as *Gerunda* by the Romans who turned it into an important stopping point on the Via Augusta which led into Provence and, like all such roads, to Rome, the town has known battles and sieges from the times of Charlemagne's skirmishes with the Saracen to those of Napoleon's invasion of the Iberian peninsula. To add to Gerona's troubles its river Onyar has periodically broken its banks and flooded the town.

Gerona's best feature is its old quarter and, within it, the Jewish quarter known as the ***call***. Its tortuous, narrow steeped streets have, on the whole, endured the passage of time fairly well and some buildings have been excellently restored thanks to contributions from Israel and the United States. The *call* is extremely atmospheric and, as a perfect example of a medieval Jewish quarter, rivals Prague's. The several bridges over the Onyar, linking old

◐ and new Gerona, offer **fine views** of the riverside houses and of the cathedral behind them.

▦ ★★★★ ***Novotel Gerona***, at Ruidellots de la Selva, 12km outside the town on the A-17 ☎ 47 71 00 ⊨ 82 ⅋ **P** ✦ ⬤ ⚓ ⛭ ℃ **AE, DC, V** $$$$.

▦ ★★★ ***Ultonia***, c/ Gran Vía Jaume I, 22 ☎ 20 38 50 ⊨ 45 **DC, EC, V** $$$ to $$$$.

¶¶ ***Cal Ros*** (closed: Wednesday nights and Thursdays in winter, and 20/12-20/1), c/ Cort Real, 9 ☎ 20 10 11 $$$. Catalan cuisine.

¶¶ ***Cipresaia*** (closed: September), c/ General Fournàs, 2 ☎ 20 30 38 **P** ❄ **AE, DC, EC, V** $$$ to $$$$.

¶¶ ***Rosaleda***, Paseo Dehesa, s/n ☎ 21 36 68 ✦ ≪ **AE, DC, EC, V** $$ to $$$. Next to the lovely Dehesa Park.

Best buys: Antiques can be bought at **D. García**, c/ Carmen, 145, and works of art at **Expoart Montjuïc**, c/ Abat Escarré, 8. The town also has plenty of boutiques, and shoes (**Patricia**, c/ Hortes, 11) and clothes are generally good value for money here.

Cultural highlights: The **Cathedral** is essentially Gothic but, as so often occurred to such buildings in Spain from the 17C onwards, a Baroque façade and, in Gerona as in Santiago de Compostela, a massive staircase were later added to the W front as a gesture towards changing architectural tastes. The **cloister**, in the Romanesque style, dates from the 11C and together with the cathedral's **Charlemagne Tower** is part of the original Romanesque church which stood on this site. The hugeness of the **nave** demonstrates how expert builders had become by the 15C at creating lofty and wide spaces. Once that has been digested, attention centres on the cathedral's twin Gothic showpieces, its **main altarpiece** and the sepulchre of Bishop Bernard de Pau. The cathedral's museum, the **Tesoro de la Seo** (open: 10.00-1.00 and 3.30-7.30; summer: 10.00-7.30; Saturdays and holidays: 10.00-1.00 ☎ 21 44 26), contains a unique 12C **tapestry** depicting the Creation and a priceless **Commentary on the Apocalypse** by that master of very early codices, the Beato de Liébana.

A leisurely stroll around Gerona brings pleasurable rewards. The old towers at the end of c/ Força used to guard a gateway in the medieval walls. The **Collegiate Church of San Felix** contains a bit of everything, from **Roman tombs** to a Renaissance altarpiece depicting the life of Saint Vincent. Nearby you will come across 12C **Arab Baths** and, in the 9-12C **Monastery of San Pedro de Galligans**, the **Archaeological Museum** (open: 10.00-1.00 and 4.00-7.00; holidays: 10.00-1.00; closed: Mondays ☎ 20 26 32). In a patio of the old university, there are remains of a wall that dates from the 5C BC. After a walk along the **Paseo Arqueológico**, in front of the Arab Baths, and a stroll in the agreeable **Dehesa Park** you could visit the town's **Art Museum**, housed in the Episcopal Palace (open: 9.00-1.00 and 4.30-7.00; holidays: 10.00-1.00; closed: Mondays ☎ 20 95 36), which contains a number of Romanesque wooden sculptures, some Catalan Gothic paintings and a collection of contemporary works by mostly local painters.

Fiestas and festivals: Gerona's **Corpus Christi** celebrations are interesting. The local *fiesta*, the *Ferias de San Narciso*, is celebrated in the Dehesa Park in late October. Gerona also organizes a number of cultural events including an

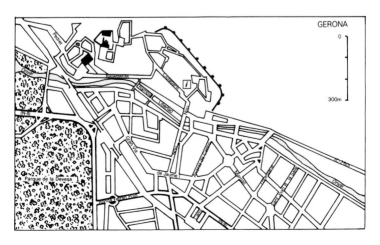

GERONA

0

300m

Parque de la Devesa

experimental theatre festival in May and a cycle of concerts and recitals in June and July.

Local sights: SANTA COLOMA DE FARNES, 30km on the N-141 to Anglés and then the C-152, is an ancient spa whose cure-all waters were appreciated by the Romans. The ★★ *Balneario Termas Orión* (closed: February), Av Termas Orión, s/n ☎ 84 00 65 ⇌ 50 ♿ ✦ ♨ ☕ 📺 🐎 ☾ $$$, is in its own park and is very quiet. The village has fine old buildings and a couple of Romanesque churches, San Pedro Cercada and Santa Victoria de Sauleda, on the outskirts. In **CALDAS DE MALAVELLA** (Airport-Costa Brava exit on the A-15) there are two further well established spas, the ★★★ *Balneario Vichy Catalán*, Av Doctor Furest, 32 ☎ 47 00 00 ⇌ 80 🅿 ✦ ♨ ☕ 📺 🐎 ☾ V $$ to $$$, and the ★★★ *Balneario Prats*, Pl Sant Esteve, 7 ☎ 47 00 51 ⇌ 76 🅿 ✦ ♫ ♨ ☕ 📺 AE, DC, EC, V $$.

On the town: In a place like Gerona the thing to do is to stroll up and down the Rambla, which is what half the town does every evening, but if you prefer to have a drink while listening to live music, head for the *Sala Boomerang*.

◑ **LERIDA-LLEIDA** **Lérida** ☎ (973), pop. 111,507, *i* Arc del Pont, s/n ☎ 24 81 20, ✛ 26 66 66, 🚃 RENFE ☎ 23 74 67. Tarragona 97km, Zaragoza 150km, Barcelona 169km, Madrid 470km.

Capital of the only landlocked province in Catalonia, Lérida stretches S from the snow-capped ridges of the Pyrenees to the arid tableland bordering Aragón. It was here, in this not overtly hospitable area, that the first known inhabitants of Spain created their earliest settlements. The twin heroes of the province are the semi-Barbarian local chieftains **Indíbil** and **Mandonius** who waged very successful hit and run attacks against the Carthaginians and the Romans. Later the Romans, specifically Caesar and Pompey, fought it out among themselves in Lérida before peace was finally restored and bridges, temples and walls built in what was known as *Ilerda*. The arrival of the Muslims here was entirely beneficial, for they put their engineering skills to work and built irrigation channels that are the basis of today's intensive fruit farming economy in the province. Lérida was a prosperous place with its own famous university in the 14C but began to decline sharply 200 years later due, in great part, to the expulsion from Spain of the highly productive population of Moriscos, the Moors who had lived on in Spain after the Christian reconquest of the Islamic kingdoms. The city itself was severely battered during the Peninsular War against Napoleon and again during the 1936-1939 Spanish Civil War.

🏨 ★★★★ *Condes de Urgel II*, Av de Barcelona, 17 ☎ 20 23 00 ⇌ 105 ✕ 🅿 ♫ AE, MC, DC, V $$$. The restaurant is good.

🏨 ★★★ *Sansi Park*, Av Alcalde Porqueres, 4 ☎ 24 40 00 ⇌ 94 📺 🅿 ♫ V $$$.

◑ ⅋ *Forn del Nastasi* (closed: Sunday nights, Mondays and 1/8-15/8), c/ Salmerón, 10 ☎ 23 45 10 ❋ AE, MC, DC, V $$$ to $$$$. Catalan cooking.

◑ ⅋ *Molí de la Nora* (closed: Sunday nights and Mondays in winter), km7 on the Puigcerdà-Andorra road, in Vilanova de la Barca ☎ 19 00 17 ✦ ❋ AE, DC, V $$$. Good fish and seafood.

⅋ *Sheyton Pub*, Av Prat de la Riba, 39 ☎ 23 81 97 ❋ AE, DC, MC, V $$$ to $$$$. Elegant decor.

Best buys: Most of the interesting shops are around the Seo Antigua. *Tasies*, Paseo de Ronda, on the corner of c/ Doctor Fleming, sells antiques, and a large selection of local gastronomic products and wine is available at *J. Sendra*, Av Blondel, 27. Shoes, always good buys in Spain, are sold at *Espuña*, c/ Mayor, 24.

<u>Cultural highlights:</u> The **Seo Antigua**, or Old Cathedral, and its vicinity illustrate the passing of civilizations through Lérida. The Seo itself began to be built in 1203 on a site which had been previously occupied by a Roman temple and a mosque. Bits of Roman masonry form the plinths of the huge thrones by the present day church's Anunciata door. The best feature of the Seo is its 14C **cloister** where the fine **capitals** and the view over the city compete for attention. The 13C **church** also has magnificent **capitals**. The ruins of the Moorish fortress, called the **Zuda**, are nearby and excavations have established that this castle was built over what used to be a Roman citadel. Descending the hill to modern Lérida, you pass by the town's old quarter called the **Canyeret**. The new cathedral was built by the 18C Italian Baroque designer Sabatini whose numerous projects in Spain include the gardens of the Royal Palace in Madrid. The nearby **Hospital de Santa María** is a good example of Catalan Gothic civic architecture and it now acts as the town's cultural centre for it is the home of the library and of a number of cultural organizations. The **Archaeological Museum** (open: 12.00-2.00 and 6.00-9.00 ☎ 27 15 00), with exhibits from local digs, is also housed in the Hospital. For an example of late Romanesque religious architecture you could visit the **Church of San Lorenzo**, which also contains valuable carved wooden statues and **altarpieces**.

<u>Fiestas:</u> Interesting processions take place at Corpus Christi. The ***Aplec del Caragol***, on or around May 11, is clearly not to everyone's taste but it is a must for serious gourmets: it consists of a collective feast, conducted with considerable ritual, of roast snails. The *Feria de San Miguel*, at the end of September, is a major agricultural and farm machinery show that attracts mostly locals.

<u>Local sights:</u> **COGULL**, 20km on the local road to Artesa de Lérida, is the site of arguably the best rupestrian art in all of Spain: in the cave known as the **Roca dels Moros** there is a painting of ritual dances being performed by a group of women around an obviously phallic symbol. The small town of **BALAGUER**, 27km along the C-1313, was the capital of the county of Urgel in the early Middle Ages and the centre of a number of baronial revolts against the local monarchy. Its highlights today include its castle, the Gothic Church of Santa María, the magnificent **cloister**, now a National Monument, in the Convent of Santo Domingo, and the very picturesque Pl del Pozo in the town centre. You can stay at ★★★★ *Conde Jaime de Urgel*, c/ Urgell, 2 ☎ 44 56 04 ⊨ 60 ♦ 🎤 ~ 🎵 MC, DC, V $$$, and *Cal Morell* (closed: Mondays and 1/9-9/9), Paseo de la Estación, 18 ☎ 48 80 09 ♦ ❄ AE, DC, MC, V $$$ to $$$$, can be recommended for its good local cooking and its wine list.

The walled village of **CASTELLO DE FARFANYA**, which contains one of the many palaces in Spain owned by the Duchy of Alba, is 10km from Balaguer. For a very rewarding drive, take the C-147 which runs parallel to the Segre river and, beyond the Camarasa reservoir, across the **Noguera Pallaresa valley**. Some 70km from Lérida are the utterly unspoilt villages of Tremp, Talarn, Aramunt and Salás on the shores of the Talarn reservoir.

<u>On the town:</u> *Assoc Celler*, c/ La Palma, 24, is popular for its elegance, drinks and live music. *Krakers*, c/ Sant Martí, 57, is a disco for the young, as is the out of town *Wonderful*, a huge place at km461 on the road to Zaragoza.

<u>Sports:</u> Tennis is played at the *Club de Tenis Urgell* ☎ 23 40 37, and squash at the *Squash Lérida*, c/ Humbert Torres, 9 ☎ 24 37 16. Pilots and skydiving enthusiasts should note the *Aero Club Alto de Urgell*, La Seo ☎ 35 23 00, and the *Aero Club Lérida*, Rambla Aragón, 31 ☎ 26 71 92. The Segre river is a favourite among anglers.

LLORET DE MAR Gerona ☎ (972), pop. 14,788, [*i*] Pl de la Vila, 1 ☎ 36 47 35, 🚌 on the Blanes road ☎ 36 57 88. Gerona 39km, Barcelona 67km, Madrid 695km.

Together with Benidorm and Torremolinos, Lloret stands for **mega mass tourism**. Make a supreme effort of imagination and picture it as it once was: a tiny little fishing village on a quiet bay that was moderately prosperous because it generated extra income from its cork trees and odd spinning loom. Then someone began building highrises and the rest is history. The off-season population of under 15,000 swells to more than 120,000 in the summer months.

★★★★ *Monterrey* (closed: 1/11-1/3), on the road to Tossa ☎ 36 40 50 🛏 229 🕭 ✦ 🎤 ⚓ 🐎 ९ AE, DC, EC, V $$$$$. Set in a large garden.

★★★★ *Rigat Park* (closed: 1/11-1/3), Fanals beach, 2km from Lloret ☎ 36 52 00 🛏 99 ✦ 🎤 🐠 ⚓ ⚲ ≪ ९ MC, V $$$$ to $$$$$. In its own wooded gardens, this is a quiet hotel with good views.

★★★★ *Roger de Flor* (closed: 1/1-14/3), Turó de L'Estelat, s/n ☎ 36 48 00 🛏 100 ✦ ❄ 🎤 🐠 ⚓ ⚲ ≪ 🐎 ९ AE, DC, MC, V $$$$. Quiet, with pleasant terraces overlooking the sea.

★★★★ *Santa Marta* (closed: 20/12-20/1), Santa Cristina beach, 3km from Lloret ☎ 36 49 04 🛏 78 ✕ ✦ 🎤 🐠 ⚓ ⚲ 🎵 🐎 ९ AE, DC, MC, V $$$$ to $$$$$. This quiet hotel, set in 6ha of parks and gardens, has a good **restaurant** $$$$ and a midday beach buffet.

★★★ *Surf Mar* (closed: 11/11-16/3), c/ Ramón Casas, 2, Fanals beach, 2km from Lloret ☎ 36 53 62 ✦ 🐠 ⚓ ⚲ 🐎 ९ $$ to $$$. Quiet, with a good swimming pool.

🍴 *El Trull*, Cala Canyelles (3km) ☎ 36 49 28 🅿 ✦ ⚓ ≪ ९ AE, DC, MC, V $$$ to $$$$. Rustic decor.

Beaches: Apart from the well equipped but rather small **local** one, there are beaches at Canyelles, Fanals and Santa Cristina.

Best buys: The best souvenirs are the local textiles and lace. *Fabregas*, Carrer de Villa, 4, is good for shoes.

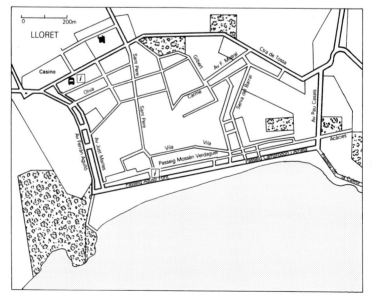

Cultural highlights: You don't go to Lloret to examine Iberian and Roman remains, but they are there if you want to see them on the road to Tossa. The Church of San Román is late Gothic and parts of the Sant Quirze shrine were built before the 11C.

Fiestas: On July 24, Lloret celebrates its main *fiestas* in honour of Saint Christine; they involve, among others, the *Dança de la Morratxa*.

Local sights: The clifftop drive along the corniche to **TOSSA DE MAR** and from there on to San Feliú de Guixols is very memorable. The views are magnificent and drivers are hard put to keep their eyes on the road. You will find yourself stopping repeatedly to take in the scenery at leisure.

On the town: Most people find their favourite pub, cafeteria and discotheque soon enough. *Cala Banys*, on the outskirts of town, is a terrace among the rocks and by the sea; *Hollywood*, on the road to Hostalrich, is a fairly frivolous disco while *Campmajó*, c/ Carmen, 61, is an agreeable tea room and completely different. The *Gran Palace*, on the road to Blanes, puts on big live shows and, in town, *Rosamar* is an old style cabaret and *Revolution* is a youth-orientated disco —both are open only in the summer. *Tropics*, c/ Ferrán Agulló, 34, is open all year round and is somewhat select, while *Moby's Fun Pub*, in the same building, is less so and has good music. The *Piano-Bar*, Paseo Marítimo, 29, has live jazz piano playing. Adults will find that the *Casino Lloret de Mar*, on the Tossa road ☏ 36 65 12, offers a range of gambling possibilities and has a restaurant, bars, a disco and other facilities for spending their winnings or drowning their sorrows; youngsters, on the other hand, will prefer to visit the local aquaparks —*Marineland* in Malgrat de Mar (a ten minute bus ride) and *Water World* on the road to Vidreres (free bus ride).

Sports: Water sports fans will have a great time in Lloret, especially fishermen ☏ 33 13 48, water skiers and windsurfers. Golfers can play at the 18-hole *Club de Golf Costa Brava*, in Santa Cristina de Aro ☏ 83 71 50.

MANRESA **Barcelona** ☏ (93), pop. 65,280 *i* Pl Mayor, 1 ☏ 872 53 78, ✛ 872 56 44. Barcelona 67km, Tarragona 115km, Lérida 122km, Madrid 591km.

This inland manufacturing and commercial town is representative of Catalonia's long established industrial energy but it holds more than a passing interest for some visitors for it was here, in the 16C, that **Saint Ignatius of Loyola** wrote what is known as his *Spiritual Exercises*, a series of rules and guidelines that to this day form the intellectual backbone of the Jesuit Order that he founded. To catch the spirit of Ignatius, however, it is better to go to the Abbey of Montserrat (see 'Montserrat, Sierra de') which is where he spent a night in vigil before the Virgin and vowed to dedicate his life to God.

❢❢ *Aligué* (closed: Sunday nights), on the Vic road, Barriada El Guix ☏ 873 79 33 **P** ✳ AE, V $$$. Good Catalan cooking.

MONASTERY OF POBLET **Tarragona** ☏ (977). Tarragona 46km, Lérida 51km, Barcelona 122km, Madrid 528km.

If you want an idea of the extent of the power of the church in medieval Spain you need look no further than the massive, fortified Monastery of Poblet. Founded to house a Cistercian community in 1150 by **Count Ramón Berenguer IV**, in thanksgiving for his victories over the Muslims, its history and that of Catalonia are intertwined. Poblet was the spiritual counterweight to Catalonia's temporal rulers in the Middle Ages and also their burial ground, for the abbey includes a royal pantheon. Poblet's story is long, often complicated, sometimes controversial and always central to the fortunes of

Catalonia. As it built up its reputation so it grew in splendour, adopting and adapting the different architectural and artistic styles that make for a fascinating cultural visit today. A period of decadence that set in by the 18C culminated in the sacking of the monastery in 1835 during one of Spain's periodic 19C civil wars, and the destruction of its 20,000 volume library. The monastery and its lands were subsequently sold off at a time when all church properties in the country were disentailed and it was not until 1940 that the buildings were restored and a monastic community re-established.

The guided tour of the monastery (tours: 10.00-12.30 and 3.00-6.00; winter: 10.00-12.30 and 3.00-5.30; closed: Good Friday afternoon and Christmas Day ☎ 87 00 89) starts at a 16C doorway that opens a route through the no fewer than three fortified walls and two doorways, the 15C **Puerta Dorada** and the **Puerta Real**, that protect the abbey and eventually leads into the monastic buildings, the church and its cloister, the 13C chapter house, the kitchen which dates from the same period and the refectory. These areas form the oldest part of the monastery and they belong, essentially, to the Romanesque age although there are numerous later renovating additions. The **cloister** is a large one measuring 40m by 35m. It was built between the 13-14C and its **capitals**, as is often the case, are very noteworthy features. The **church**, in its austere simplicity, is quite obviously a Cistercian house of prayer. The alabaster **retable behind the main altar** was sculpted by the Renaissance artist Damian Forment. The **Panteón Real**, or Royal Crypt, contains the tombs of the kings of Catalonia-Aragón from the end of the 12C. They are extremely artistic alabaster sepulchres deftly carved in the Gothic style. One of the most impressive rooms, on account of its length, is the one that used to be the monastic **dormitory**. It is 87m long and one is left wondering how crowded it was. A second dormitory, which was where the older monks slept, now houses a **Museum** which illustrates the step by step reconstruction of the abbey. The visit also includes a tour of the **Palace of King Martin the Humane** built towards the 14C with sumptuous rooms and elegant ogival windows.

MONASTERY OF SANTA CREUS-SANTES CREUS Tarragona ☎ (977). Tarragona 32km, Lérida 83km, Barcelona 95km, Madrid 555km.

This monastery is in many ways Poblet's twin and it is certainly no less impressive. It was also founded as a Cistercian house by the Berenguer dynasty in the 12C at the height of the medieval splendour of the Catalan-Aragonese crown. Like Poblet it was at one time a very rich monastery and an important cultural and political force, it was also a victim of the 19C civil wars, was disentailed and abandoned. Fortunately, Santa Creus too has been restored and is open to visitors (open: 10.00-1.00 and 3.00-7.00; winter: 10.00-1.00 and 3.00-5.00; closed: Christmas Day).

Again like Poblet, Santa Creus is in reality part monastery, part royal palace and part fortified camp, a mix that gives an immediate idea of the role that such abbeys played in the Middle Ages. Visitors pass through a Baroque gate into what is known as the **Plaza Mayor**. In the background stands the church's sober and austere W front (12-13C), and on the right the **Puerta Real** or Royal Gate which leads to the splendid 14C **cloister**, pure Gothic in style and containing a **Romanesque fountain**. The Romanesque **Chapter House** contains the tombs of the monastery's abbots. Construction of the **church** began in 1174 in the Cistercian Romanesque style, and continued long enough to allow Gothic elements to superimpose themselves. Its highpoints are the magnificent **rose window** illuminating the apse and the **royal tombs** in the side chapels of the transept where King Peter III, the Great, is buried. The small Romanesque cloister, called the **Claustro de la**

Enfermería, is peaceful, intimate and spiritual with its four cypress trees and fountain. The tour takes visitors through what used to be the monastic cellar, the kitchen and the refectory and on to the **Royal Apartments** which are graced by a lovely **patio** and an excellent 14C staircase.

MONTBLANCH-MONTBLANC **Tarragona** ☎ (977), pop. 5,640, *i* Pl Mayor, 1 ☎ 86 00 09. Tarragona 36km, Lérida 61km, Barcelona 112km, Madrid 518km.

This well preserved, picturesque walled village some 15km from the Monastery of Poblet (see separate entry) still retains its medieval atmosphere.
▥ ★★ *Coll de Lilla*, Ctra N-240, km29 ☎ 86 09 07 ⇔ 16 TV P ✦ ♨ ≪ ⚲ AE, DC, EC, V $$$.
▮ *Fonda Colom* (closed: Sunday nights), c/ Civadeira, 5 ☎ 86 01 53 $$$. Home style cooking.

Cultural highlights: The **walls** encircle a good number of churches and buildings that tell the tale of the town's grandeur 500 years ago. Among them is the 14C **Church of Santa María**, whose Baroque façade indicates how Montblanch bravely tried to keep up with changing fashions but it is its **interior**, real, original Gothic stuff, that is its most interesting feature. The older, 13C, Church of San Miguel doubled up on a number of occasions as an assembly hall for the medieval *Cortes*, or Parliament, of the Catalan Aragonese kingdom. Energetic and motivated visitors also look in on the old **Hospital of Santa Magdalena** which has a very pleasing patio, the Frederic Marès Museum of art and liturgical items that is housed in the Church of San Marcial (open: 11.00-2.00 and 4.00-8.00; holidays: 11.00-2.00), and spend some time in the **Museo Comarcal** in the Gothic Josa Mansion (open: 11.00-2.00 and 5.00-8.00; weekends and winter: 11.00-2.00). The town's **bridge** over the Francolí river dates from the 14C.

MONTSENY, SIERRA DE **Barcelona** ☎ (93).

A **Nature Park** stands in this attractive, thickly wooded range of hills that runs its course back from the coast between the Vic valley in the NW and the Vallés valley in the SE. There are a number of attractive villages set among the pine, fir and beech woods including the extremely peaceful **VILADRAU**, the lumberjack settlement of Espinelvas and the charming village of **BREDA** which has a long established ceramics tradition and a fine Romanesque bell tower atop its monastery of San Salvador. The village of **HOSTALRICH**, which has medieval walls encircling it and boasts the added protection of eight towers, is something of a showpiece in the sierra. The most popular scenic routes across these mountains are the 22km drive linking **Sant Celoní with Santa Fe de Montseny** and the **drive** from Sant Celoní to Tona.
▥ ★★★★ *Hostal La Cartoixa*, 4.5km SE from Montseny ☎ 847 30 00 ✗ P ✦ ♨ ≈ ♫ V $$$. A quiet inn with a very good **restaurant** $$ to $$$.
▥ ★★★ *San Bernat*, 8km from Montseny on the Tona road ☎ 847 30 11 ⇔ 20 P ♨ ⚘ ≪ AE, DC, V $$$. A very quiet hotel in an utterly scenic location.
▮ *El Racó de Can Fabrés* (closed: Sunday nights, Mondays and February), c/ Sant Joan, 6 ☎ 867 28 51 ✳ AE, DC, EC, V $$$. Imaginative cuisine served in an authentic stone mansion.

MONTSERRAT, SIERRA DE **Barcelona** ☎ (93). Barcelona 52km, Lérida 125km, Madrid 594km.

Montserrat takes its name from its extraordinary boulder formations which, like the teeth of a giant saw, turn this range of 1,200m high peaks into a serrated mountain looming over the central depression of inland

Catalonia. It is said that Wagner was inspired by this sierra for the decor of his *Parsifal* and seeing Montserrat one is perfectly willing to believe it. Mythical and sacred attributes are associated with certain mountains all over the world and this is very much the case of Montserrat for it is imbued with magical majesty. The sierra here has legend, symbolism and religion lurking behind every rock, stick and stone of its desolate slopes. For Catalans, Montserrat's ravines and peaks, created as they were by some incredible geological convulsion, form the cradle and the shrine of Catalonia's nationhood. The Virgin of Montserrat is a central element of this identification and the cult surrounding her has existed for more than a millennium.

🏨 ★★★ *Abat Cisneros*, Pl Monestir, s/n ☎ 835 02 01 ⊨ 41 🅿 🦻 🦪 ⚲ AE, DC, V $$$.

🍴 *Montserrat*, Pl Apostols ☎ 835 02 51 (ext. 165) ≪ AE, DC, EC, V $$$ to $$$$. Lunches only.

Cultural highlights: The **Monastery of Our Lady of Montserrat** is the focal point of the whole sierra and the home of the much venerated figure of the Virgin. The actual abbey one sees today dates mostly from last century and the main façade was completed in 1939. This was because the monastery was cruelly sacked by Napoleon's troops during the Peninsular War and subsequently suffered years of decay. The origins of the abbey, however, date back to 1025 when the first community of Benedictine monks came to live at the foot of the mountain. Well before then the upper reaches of the sierra had been settled by **hermits**, each occupying his cave and living in solitary contemplation. The monastery that Napoleon's soldiers did their level best to smash up was a Gothic-style edifice built in the 13C and its illustrious abbots included men of the calibre of Julius II, the pope who set Michelangelo to work on the Sistine Chapel. The abbey did manage to save its **library**, which now numbers some 250,000 volumes and more than 400 incunabula, and its **art collection** which includes works by Caravaggio, Luca Giordano, El Greco, Zurbarán and Brueghel among others (open: 10.00-2.30 and 3.30-6.00).

The church retains original Romanesque elements; the focal point of the nave is the **Virgin of Montserrat**, a small, blackened Romanesque statue carved in the 12C, who occupies the apse. Affectionately known as *La Moreneta* (the Dusky One) by every breathing Catalan, she is the unquestioned patron saint of Catalonia. Apart from venerating the Virgin, people come to the church from far and wide to attend its daily plain-chant

⏰ services and listen to its superbly trained boys' choir, the *escolanía* (Monastery of Montserrat ☎ 835 02 51).

The sierra offers considerable rock climbing and trekking possibilities and near the monastery there are facilities for those less energetically inclined

⏰⏰ who still want to get to the top and enjoy the **best views**. The San Jerónimo **cable car**, or *teleférico*, 3km from the abbey, takes visitors right up to the mountain's summit (departures: every half hour from 10.00-2.00 and 3.00-5.30); and the San Juan **funicular** right by the abbey offers magnificent **views** along its route (departures: every 20 minutes from 9.00-2.00 and 3.00-7.00).

Local sights: Igualada, 27km W, is an important leather goods and textiles manufacturing centre, and has two interesting museums largely devoted to these industries, the Museo de la Piel (Leather Museum) and the more

⏰ eclectic Museo de la Ciudad (City Museum). *El Jardí de la Granja Pla* (closed: 25/7-15/8), Rambla de Sant Isidre, 12 ☎ 803 18 64 🅿 ✦ ✳ AE, DC, MC, V $$$, serves good game and fish. Two nearby villages, Esparraguera (26km) and the scenically situated Olesa de montserrat (18km) stage famous **Passion Plays** every year during Lent and Holy Week.

OLOT **Gerona** ☎ (972), pop. 25,357, *i* c/ Mulleras, 33 ☎ 26 01 41, ✢ 26 23 18. Gerona 55km, Barcelona 130km, Madrid 700km.

Design conscious Catalonia is a byword in Spain for fervid creativity and industriousness and Olot fairly represents this enduring image. The town is the capital of the district known as La Garrotxa and it is a thriving cultural and manufacturing centre. It has earned a measure of distinction thanks to its Fine Arts School and its no fewer than 14 workshops that specialise in religious **imagery**.

🏨 **★★ *Montsacopa***, c/ Mulleras, s/n ☎ 26 07 62 ⏢ 70 **P** ♦ AE, DC, MC, V $$.

🍽 ***Purgatori*** (closed: Sunday nights, Mondays and 15/7-31/7), c/ Bisbe Serra, 58 ☎ 26 16 06 ✳ AE, DC, MC, V $$$..

Best buys: Religious sculptures are sold at *F. Cañados*, c/ Hostal del Sol, 25.

Cultural highlights: The 18C Church of San Esteban has an imposing Baroque main altarpiece and an El Greco Crucifixion in its museum (for visits ☎ 26 04 74). There are a number of Modernist houses such as the Casa de Solà Morales in the La Malagrida quarter which, in Catalonia, is a sure sign of a town's prosperity. The local museum, the Museo Comarcal de La Garrotxa, c/ Hospici, 4 (open: 11.00-2.00 and 4.00-7.00; closed: Tuesdays ☎ 26 64 57) proudly shares its exhibition space between the local manufacturers and their products and the local artists and their paintings.

Fiestas and festivals: The *Virgen del Carmen's* feast day is duly celebrated on July 16 with the *Drac i Conill* (Dragon and Rabbit) festivities. On October 18 the *Fires de Sant Lluc* take place.

Local sights: The **road** to San Juan de las Abadesas is picturesque, and **CASTELFOLLIT DE LA ROCA** is spectacularly **located** in a volcanic area that has been designated a national park.

PALAFRUGELL **Gerona** ☎ (972), pop. 16,019, *i* c/ Carrilet, 2 ☎ 30 02 28. Gerona 39km, Barcelona 123km, Madrid 736km.

Set back from the sea, the town's location illustrates the innate prudence of the inhabitants of the Costa Brava who centuries ago sought inland protection from pirate attacks on the coast. From running away from the buccaneers Palafrugell has now turned to welcoming the current invasion of tourists and its satellite resorts of **Calella, Llafranc** and **Tamariu** are top tourist centres on the Costa. What has not changed is Palafrugell's much admired tradition of excellent local **Ampurdán** food which can be savoured at establishments such as *Xarcutería Barris*, c/ Barris y Buixó, 4.

🏨 **★★★★ *Alga*** (closed: 21/10-18/3), c/ Costa Blanca, 43, in Calella ☎ 30 00 58 ⏢ 54 ♦ ♀ ⅏ ⚓ 🛎 250m 🐴 ℚ MC, V $$$ to $$$$. Set in its own gardens, 250m from the beach.

🏨 **★★★ *Garbi*** (closed: 15/10-31/3), c/ del Mirto, s/n, in Calella ☎ 30 01 00 ⏢ 30 **P** ♦ ⅏ ⚓ 🛎 🐴 EC, V $$ a $$$. Set in a quiet pine grove.

🏨 **★★★ *Hostalillo*** (closed: 25/9-26/5), c/ Bellavista, 22, in Tamariu ☎ 30 01 58 ⏢ 70 **P** ⅏ ⚓ ≪ $$$$. Peaceful and scenically located overlooking a cove.

🏨 **★★★ *Paraíso*** (closed: 15/10-1/5), Paraje Font d'en Xeco, s/n, in Llafranc ☎ 30 04 50 ⏢ 55 **P** ♦ ⚓ 🐴 ℚ AE, EC, V $$ to $$$.

🏨 **★★★ *Sant Roc*** (closed: 1/11-30/4), Pl Atlántic, 2, in Calella ☎ 30 05 00 ⏢ 41 **TV** ♦ ⅏ ⚓ ≪ AE, DC, EC, V $$ to $$$. Quiet and with good sea views.

🏨 **★★★ *Terramar*** (closed: 1/10-30/4), Paseo de Cypsele, 1, in Llafranc ☎ 30 02 00 ⏢ 56 **P** ♦ ⅏ ⚓ ≪ $$$. Quiet and very near the beach.

¶ *Hostal Cypsele*, c/ Ample, 30 ☎ 30 01 92 **P** ✦ AE, DC, EC, MC, V
$$$. Established at the turn of the century, its menu changes with the
seasons.

¶ *Reig* (closed: Sunday nights in winter), c/ Torres Jonama, 53 ☎
30 07 95 ✳ AE, DC, MC, V $$$.

¶ *San Sebastián*, next to the lighthouse on Cape San Sebastián ☎
30 05 86 **P** ≪ $$. Panoramic views of the countryside, coast and sea.

Beaches: Tamariu's beach, 4km, and the one at **Llafranc**, 5km, which is
separated from **Calella's** by a rocky promontory, are well equipped.

Cultural highlights: The medieval shrine of San Sebastián, next to the
lighthouse, has been well restored because it has an inn attached to it. The
local museum, the Museo Archivo Municipal, c/ Cervantes, 10 (open:
5.00-8.00 ☎ 30 11 12) is interesting because it traces the development of
the cork industry which was the mainstay of Palafrugell's moderately
prosperous economy before the Costa Brava became a European summer
playground.

Fiestas and festivals: A festival of sea shanties called the *Concurso de
Habaneras* is held on the first Saturday of July. The town's street partying
celebrations, the *Fiesta Mayor*, begin on July 20. Theatre productions are
staged during the summer months.

◐ **Local sights:** Tamariu, Llafranc and **Calella** are very popular **beach**
resorts but developers have, on the whole, shown exemplary restraint and
respected the environment, which makes a refreshing and welcome change.

◐◐ Near Calella there are some beautiful **Hanging Gardens** at Cabo Roig's

◐ Botanical Gardens. The town of **LA BISBAL**, 12km on the N-255, is the capital
of the district called the Bajo Ampurdán and it is an important **ceramics**
centre which makes distinctive green and caramel glazed pottery. The *Juan
Bertrán* pottery on the road linking Gerona and Palamós is a prominent
example of this well developed local industry. La Bisbal is an old town with a
13C **castle** which is used as an exhibition centre. In the l'Aigüeta district you
will find a concentration of shops selling the locally made ceramics.

On the town: There is no shortage of terrace cafeterias, bars and discos
around Palafrugell, particularly in Llafranc and Calella. Popular meeting places
include *Charlot*, c/ Barris y Buixó, and in Calella, the *Les Voltes* terrace at c/
Les Voltes, 7. Discos include *Xarai* (open: weekends only), c/ Barris y Buixó,
42, and *Sirtakis*, c/ Chopitea, 14, in Calella.

Sports: Llafranc's facilities include a marina and a yacht club, the *Club
Náutico Llafranc* ☎ 30 07 54, and the *Club de Tenis Llafranc* tennis club ☎
30 23 08. There is horseback riding at the *Club Hípico Baix Ampurdá* ☎

◐◐ 30 03 14, and golf 6km inland at the 18 hole *Club de Golf de Pals* ☎
62 30 06.

PALAMÓS **Gerona** ☎ (972), pop. 12,082, *i* Paseo del Mar, 8 ☎
31 43 90. Gerona 49km, Barcelona 109km, Madrid 726km.

◐ Palamós was a respectable trading and fishing port and a cork producing
centre before the **tourist** invasion. Its old quarter, with its narrow streets and
closely bunched houses has survived the highrises. Like Blanes, Lloret and
other such Costa Brava small towns, the population swells tenfold in the
summer season and its whole character changes.

▥ ★★★ *Trias* (closed: 10/10-23/3), Paseo del Mar, s/n ☎ 31 41 00 ⛵
81 ✗⛟ TV **P** ✦ ⚲ ≈ ⚲ ≪ MC, V $$$ to $$$$. A hotel with good views
and a pleasant **restaurant** with a terrace $$$.

▥ ★★ *Ancora* (closed: 15/11-15/1), c/ Josep Pla, s/n, in La Fosca, 2km
NE of Palamos ☎ 31 54 86 ⛵ 34 **P** ✦ ⚘ ≈ ⚲ ≪ ⚲ V $$. A quiet hotel
with good views.

¶| *La Cuineta* (closed: weekdays out of season), c/ Adrián Alvarez, 111 ☎
31 40 01 ✳ **AE, DC, EC, V** $$$ to $$$$.

¶| *La Gamba* (closed: Wednesdays out of season and 6/1-6/2), Pl Sant
Pere, 1 ☎ 31 46 33 ✦ ✳ ≪ **AE, DC, MC, V** $$$. A quayside restaurant
specializing in fish and seafood.

¶| *María de Cadaqués* (closed: Mondays and 15/12-15/1), c/ Notaries,
39 ☎ 31 40 09 ✳ **AE, DC, MC, V** $$$ to $$$$. Regional cuisine; always
busy.

Beaches: There is a large and pleasant local beach and, 2km N, **La Fosca**,
a lovely beach surrounded by apartment buildings. El Castell, S'Alguer and
Mallerida are beaches in tiny fishing villages near Palamós. Three kilometres
S along the C-253, the beach at San Antonio de Calonge is more tourist
oriented.

Best buys: Leather fashions and luggage are sold at *Majorpell* and *Modas
Francina*, both at c/ Mayor. Gourmets go to *Valles*, c/ Mayor 25, for wines,
and for pastries head for *Xidors*, on the Gerona road, which is also a tea
shop. There is a quayside daily fish auction in the port.

Cultural highlights: Palamós was prosperous enough to afford a Gothic
church, the Iglesia de Santa María del Mar, and important enough to have a
castle, the Castillo de Bell-lloc, which is now in ruins. There is an interesting
collection of shells in the local hotch-potch museum that also shows modern
paintings and exhibits archaeological remains, the Museo Cau de la Costa
Brava, Pl del Forn, 4 (open: 10.00-1.00 and 4.00-6.30 ☎ 31 43 50).

Fiestas and festivals: The two major *fiestas* are the *Fiesta Mayor*, on June
24, and the day of the *Virgen del Carmen*, on July 16, celebrated with a
picturesque sea-borne procession. August sees the *Aplec sardana* dancing
festival in La Arboleda, a Sea Shanty Festival and a Drama Festival. In
Calonge, 7km away, a Classical Music Festival is held from July to August.

Local sights: See 'Costa Brava'.

On the town: There are masses of bars, but drinks on the seafront terrace of
the *Club Náutico* or *tapas* at **Los Caracoles**, in the centre of town, are
particularly good. Disco enthusiasts will enjoy the centrally situated *Marinada*.

Sports: This is a good **sailing** and **windsurfing** part of the coast and a
winter regatta, the *Palamós Christmas Race*, based on the local marina, is
a popular annual event. Tennis players head for the *Club de Tenis Costa
Brava* ☎ 31 43 24, and the *Club de Tenis Palamós* ☎ 31 55 57.

PERATALLADA Gerona ☎ (972), pop. 502. Gerona 33km, Barcelona
133km, Madrid 752km.

This is a bijou, tiny **medieval walled village** which has its **castle** within
the battlements and, such was the value system of this locality, has its
church, the Romanesque Iglesia de San Esteban, outside them.

¶| *Can Bonay* (closed: Mondays and 2/11-30/11), Pl Les Voltes, 6 ☎
63 40 34 ▣ ✦ $$ to $$$. Catalan cooking.

¶| *La Riera* (closed: Mondays except in summer and 9/12-9/3), Pl Les
Voltes, 9 ☎ 63 41 42 ▣ ✦ $$$. Honest and unfrilled Catalan cuisine in a
restored medieval house.

Local sights: The nearby village of **ULLASTRET** has a similar timeless
atmosphere to it. The walls here are in ruins but the village's Romanesque
church is very much standing and several of its houses have fine Gothic
carved windows indicating that Ullastret was once a place of some
importance. Recent excavations have uncovered an ancient **Iberian
settlement** underneath the village and the archaeological finds are exhibited
in the local museum (open in winter: 10.00-2.00 and 4.00-6.00; summer:
10.30-1.00 and 4.00-8.00).

PERELADA-PERALADA **Gerona** ☎ (972), pop. 1,259. Gerona 42km, Barcelona 142km, Madrid 761km.

This is the home of a popular brand of champagne-style sparkling wines sold under the Perelada trademark.

Cultural highlights: Apart from the wineries, most people visit the 14-15C **Castle of Perelada** which was built in the Renaissance age and is now a bit of everything. The castle has an exceptional **library** which boasts a good collection of incunabula and also a Wine Museum and a Glass Museum (open: 10.00-12.00 and 4.30-6.30; weekends: 10.00-12.00). The castle is also home to a **casino**. Other village highlights include its 9C parish church, the pleasing Romanesque cloister of Santo Domingo, the Gothic convent founded by the Carmelite Order and the Iron Age caves outside the village, called the Cavas del Ampurdán.

Festivals: In summer an **International Music Festival** is staged in the fortress' grounds.

On the town: The castle is mostly known as home to a top *Casino* (open: 5.00 pm-3.00 am) ☎ 53 81 25 **AE, DC, MC, V**: it has French and American roulette, *chemin de fer*, baccarat and *boule* tables and many other facilities, including bars, restaurants and museums.

PIRINEOS CATALANES (THE CATALAN PYRENEES) **Gerona-Lérida**.

The Pyrenees are more than Catalonia's natural border in the N for their foothills drive down S in a series of mountain ranges or sierras such as those of Boumort, Cadí, Pedraforga, Montsec and Montroig which are known as the Prepyrenees and occupy large areas of the provinces of Lérida and Gerona. Virtually all Catalonia's rivers are born in the Pyrenees proper or the Prepyrenees and what you have, as a result, is a succession of deep **valleys** that run N-S between towering, lofty **peaks**. Communication between the valleys is difficult for the ridges rise to more than 2,500m and each valley, with its woods and meadows, is a little world of its own centred on picturesque little villages and **Romanesque** churches and monasteries.

Going W to E, the first big valley that scars its way through the Pyrenees is the deep, natural depression of the **Valle de Arán** (see separate entry) which is home to the **ski stations** of *Baqueira-Beret* and *Tuca-Betrén* (see 'Viella'). The C-147 enters the **Valley of the Noguera Pallaresa river** after crossing the Bonaigua mountain pass, and from here you can press on E to the **Aigües Tortes National Park** (see separate entry) and to the *Super-Espot* ski station. The valley's villages such as Isil, Esterri d'Aneu and Gerri la Val, which are all in the district known as **Pallars Sobirá**, have endearing Romanesque church buildings with their characteristic stumpy towers and their porches to protect congregations from the harsh winters. The valley S of Sort has the **Valle de Llesui** branching off from it. The chief river in the area is the fast flowing Segre which powers its way through the Alto Urgel heights and down through the valley of Cerdaña. The peaks over the Cerdaña valley rise to more than 3,000m and are the highest in the Catalan section of the Pyrenees. This is the location of a number of ski stations including *La Molina* (see 'Puigcerdá'), *Masella*, *Llés* and *Aranser*.

The Prepyrenees stretch S as far as Berga, embracing historic towns like the beautiful **CASTELLAR DE NUCH**, and buildings like the **Monastery of San Juan de las Abadesas** (see 'Ripoll'). La Pobla de Lillet, San Jaime de Frontanyá and the churches of Guardiola de Berguedá and Sant Quirze de Pedret are redolent of the events witnessed by these hills and valleys during the Middle Ages when **RIPOLL** (see separate entry) was the focal point of what would become the Kingdom of Catalonia. *Nuria* and *Vallter 2.000* are the top ski stations in this area of the Pyrenees. To the E lies **La Garrotxa**, a cattle-breeding area of woodlands set against a backdrop of mountain peaks. The foothills of the Pyrenees reach right down to the sea in the N of the **Ampurdán** in the deeply indented stretch of coastline dominated by the headland of **Cabo de Creus**.

PLAYA DE ARO-PLATJA D'ARO **Gerona** ☎ (972), pop. 4,219, *i* c/ Jacinto Verdaguer, 11 ☎ 81 71 79. Gerona 37km, Barcelona 102km, Madrid 715km.

Playa de Aro is a popular **beach resort** complemented by a cosmopolitan atmosphere and lifestyle: it has good shops, big hotels, plenty of terraces, bars and discos next to the sea, and a swinging night life. During the day, it is an ideal place to practise water sports, and its lovely 3km-long **beach**, even if crowded in summer, is perfect for getting a suntan.

- ★★★★ *Columbus*, Paseo del Mar, s/n ☎ 81 71 66 ⍾ 110 ✦ ⬥ ⬥ ⬥ ⬥ « ⬥ ⬥ AE, DC, EC, V $$$ to $$$$$. Quiet, with good sea views.
- ★★★★ *Park Hotel San Jorge* (closed: 5/10-28/5), 2km from Playa de Aro in Condado de San Jorge ☎ 65 23 11 ⍾ 117 ✦ ⬥ ⬥ « ⬥ AE, DC, EC, V $$$$ to $$$$$.
- ★★★ *Aromar* (closed: 1/10-31/3), Paseo del Mar, s/n ☎ 81 70 54 ⍾ 155 P ✦ ⬥ ⬥ ⬥ ⬥ « AE, DC, EC, V $$$ to $$$$. A quiet hotel with good views of the sea.
- ★★★ *Cosmopolita* (closed: 20/11-20/12), c/ Pinar del Mar, 1 ☎ 81 73 50 ⍾ 90 ✦ ⬥ « EC, V $$$ to $$$$.
- ★★★ *Costa Brava*, on the road from Palamós to Punta d'en Ramís ☎ 81 73 08 ⍾ 57 P ✦ ⬥ ⬥ « AE, DC, EC, V $$$. Good views.
- ★★ *Xaloc* (closed: 1/11-31/3), on the road to Palamós, Rovira beach ☎ 81 73 00 ⍾ 43 P ✦ ⬥ ⬥ « EC, V $$ to $$$$. Quiet.
- ¶¶ *Carles Camós-Big Rock* (closed: Mondays except in summer and 1/1-31/1), Barri de Fanals, 5, on the road to Mas Nou ☎ 81 80 12 P ✦ ❄ ⬥ AE, DC, EC, V $$$ to $$$$. Modern Catalan cuisine served in a sumptuously decorated *masía*. It also offers luxurious **accommodation** in its 5 suites ⬥ $$$$$$.
- ¶¶ *Mas Nou* (closed: Wednesdays out of season and 10/1-15/2), Urb Mas Nou, 4km from Playa de Aro ☎ 81 78 53 P ✦ ⬥ « ⬥ AE, DC, EC, V $$$ to $$$$. This restaurant has a lovely summer terrace and is one of the favourite meeting places in Playa de Aro..

Best buys: You will find that leatherwear is good value for money in any of the many shops along Ctra San Felíu: *Franc Fills* at No. 22, *Marvill* at No. 42, *Montserrat* at No. 48, *Marc Franc 7* at No. 52, and *Marc Franc 5*. In this same road, at No. 8, you will come across the Costa Brava's department store, *Magatzems Vall*. Innovative Spanish fashion is also available at *Adolfo Domínguez*, Carrillon shopping centre, Ctra Palamós, 353.

On the town: Playa de Aro comes into its own at night, teeming with discos and bars with live music —the **nightlife** here is packed with opportunities for excitement and adventure, and that is why the young in years, or spirit, love it. Favourite places to start out the night are *Kings* video-pub and the more romantic *Don Quijote*, c/ Esglesia, 13. From there, the action moves to the town's discos: *Palladium*, on the road to Palamós, is the craziest and most fashionable disco on the Costa Brava; the pyramidal-shaped *Kamel*, also on the road to Palamós, is exactly the opposite; in between, *Malibú*, in downtown Playa de Aro, is lots of fun; and then there is *Madox*, *Pachá*, *Tiffany's*...

Sports: This is an ideal place to practise water sports, especially **sailing** and **windsurfing**. There are tennis facilities at the *Club de Tenis de Aro* ☎ 81 74 00, and there is a golf course nearby at Santa Cristina de Aro.

PUIGCERDA **Gerona** ☎ (972), pop. 6,029, *i* c/ Querol, s/n ☎
88 05 42, ✚ Av Segre, 9 ☎ 88 05 47. Gerona 152km, Barcelona 169km,
Lérida 184km, Madrid 653km.

The capital of the highland Cerdaña, this is a bracing and pleasing town
well equipped for **winter sports** and climbing, and with a good number of
Romanesque and Gothic architectural gems for the art lover.

🌢 🏬 ★★★ *Adserá*, in La Molina ☎ 89 20 01 ⇌ 35 **P** ✦ ☒ ☒ ≪ ☒ DC, V
$$$. A very quiet hotel with lovely mountain views.

🏬 ★★★ *Alp Hotel* (closed: 1/10-14/12), Urb Masella, in Alp ☎ 89 01 51
⇌ 146 **P** ✦ ♫ ☒ ☒ ☒ ☒ $$$.

🌢🌢 🏬 ★★★ *Boix*, on the road from Lérida to Puigcerdá, km154 ☎ 51 50 50
⇌ 34 ✕ ☒ **TV** (**P** ✦ ☒ ☒ AE, DC, EC, V $$$$. A mountain hotel with a
good **restaurant** serving imaginative seasonal cuisine.

🏬 ★★★ *Chalet del Golf*, in Bolvir, 4.5km from Puigcerdá on the road to
Seo de Urgel and then taking a private path, Devesa del Golf ☎ 88 09 62
⇌ 16 ☒ **P** ✦ ♫ ☒ ≪ ⤴ $$$$. Very peaceful, with views of the golf
course.

🏬 ★★ *Del Lago*, Av Doctor Piguillén, s/n ☎ 88 04 00 ⇌ 16 **TV** **P** ✦ ☒ ☒
$$. A quiet hotel with pleasant gardens and a swimming pool.

🏬 ★★ *Del Prado*, Ctra Llivia, s/n, 1km NE of Puigcerdá ☎ 88 04 00 ⇌ 45
☒ ☖ **P** ✦ ☒ ☒ ☒ ☒ AE, EC, V $$.

🌢 🏬 ★★ *La Solana*, in the outskirts of La Molina ☎ 89 20 00 ⇌ 30 **P** ✦ ☒
☒ ≪ ☒ $$. A quiet hotel with beautiful mountain views.

🏬 ★★ *Sanillés* (closed: 1/10-30/4), 2km from town along the Llés road,
in Martinet ☎ 51 50 00 ⇌ 39 **P** ☒ ≪ EC, V $ to $$. Quiet, with good
views.

🌢 ¶¶ *Can Borell* (closed: Sunday nights and Mondays except in summer), c/
Regreso, 3, in Meranges ☎ 88 00 33 **P** ✦ ≪ AE, DC, EC, V $$$ to
$$$$. Good Ampurdán cuisine. It also has ★★ apartment accommodation
⇌ 8 ☒ $$$.

Cultural highlights: Puigcerdá has a well preserved old quarter with
picturesque streets and houses and a couple of good religious buildings.
The 14C Church of Santa María has an interesting tower and façade and the
13C Convent of Santo Domingo's W front received a marble facelift in the
Renaissance.

Local sights: There are ample possibilities for scenic touring in this area.
Local excursions include the route along the N-152 through the pleasant
villages of Caixáns, Urtq and Alp. The road also leads to the town of **LLIVIA**
which, by a quirk of medieval map-drawing and treaty-signing is a Spanish
enclave within French territory. Llivia is an agreeable small town to walk
around in. It has an interesting fortified church and a fascinating old
Pharmacy Museum (open in winter: 10.00-1.00 and 3.00-6.00; summer:
10.00-1.00 and 3.00-7.00), considered to be the oldest pharmacy in Spain.
Taking the C-1313 you pass through Isópol and the very scenic **BELLVER DE
CERDAÑA** that appears to cling from the crags as it looks down onto the
Segre river. Further on you reach **LLES** from where there are good **views** of 🌢
the Cadí peak and access to the sulphurous springs of Senillers and to the
lakes of Pera.

Sports: The **ski** resorts of *La Molina*, 15km on the N-152 ☎ 89 21 75, and
Nuria ☎ 73 03 26, are very popular. *Masella* ☎ 89 01 51, at Lles-Arànser
and Meranges-Guils, specializes in cross country skiing. The air club at the
Aeródromo Deportivo de Das ☎ 89 00 88, draws flying, gliding and
skydiving enthusiasts and there is a golf club at Bolvir, 3km, *Real Club de* 🌢🌢
Golf de la Cerdaña ☎ 88 13 38. Puigcerdá's sports centre has an ice
skating rink and an indoor swimming pool and the town also boasts a lake.

REUS **Tarragona** ☎ (977), pop. 83,251, *i* c/ Sant Joan, 36 ☎
31 00 61, ✈ Reus, 3km ☎ 30 35 04, 🚌 Pl de la Estación ☎ 31 11 34.
Tarragona 14km, Lérida 90km, Barcelona 118km, Madrid 547km.

Tarragona is the administrative capital of the province of the same name
and the site of very important archaeological remains. Reus, in contrast, is
Tarragona province's busy commercial capital and has a good number of
ostentatious Modernist buildings, a tell-tale sign of 19C Catalan prosperity. It
has more reason than most places for boasting such architecture for it was
the birthplace of the Modernist architect and genius, **Antonio Gaudí**.

🏨 ★★ *Antic Priorat*, km702 along the C-242, in Poboleda ☎ 82 70 06 🛏
18 **P** ✦ 🏊 ≈ ≪ 🔧 V $$. A very quiet hotel with good views.

🏨 ★★ *Francia*, c/ Vicaria, 8, on the Salou road ☎ 30 42 40 🛏 39 𝚼 (🎤
🏊 ≈ 📺 V $$$. Quiet.

🍴 *Masía Típica Crusells*, 1km on the Tarragona road ☎ 30 40 60 **P** ✳ AE,
DC, EC, V $$ to $$$. In an old *masía* or farmhouse.

Best buys: Antiques and works of art are sold at *Anquín*, c/ Sant Joan, s/n;
local cakes at *Poy*, c/ Arrabal de Jesús 8, and *Padreny*, c/ Sol y Ortega, 15,
and local wines at *Gili*, c/ Arrabal de Santa Ana, 42.

Cultural highlights: The town is proud of its **Cambrer Castle** and of the
remains of its **Jewish quarter**. The homes of the Reus merchant class, the
Bofarull Mansion, the Marc Mansion and the Espuny Mansion (c/ Abadía)
show off Reus' wealth as do the group of Modernist houses built by Gaudí's
contemporary Domènech i Montaner, which include the Navàs Mansion (*El
Mercadal*), the Rull Mansion and the Gasull Mansion. The town's museum,
the Museo Comarcal, Pl Llibertat, 13 (closed: Tuesdays ☎ 30 60 01) exhibits
archaeological finds, ceramics and 16-17C paintings, and there are more
archaeological exhibits at the Museo de Arqueología Salvador Vilaseca, c/
Raval Santa Ana, 59 (open: 11.00-1.00 and 5.00-7.00; holidays:
10.00-1.00) and the Museo Arxiu Prim Rull, c/ Sant Joan, 27 (open:
10.00-1.00 and 4.00-7.00) houses historical documents and assorted works
of art.

Fiestas: Saint Peter's Day, June 29, is marked in traditional Catalan style by
fireworks, parades of giant *papier-maché* figures and displays of the intricate
human tower balancing acts that are the speciality of the *castellers*. An older
event, celebrated for the past six centuries every July 25, is the *Feria de San
Jaime*.

RIPOLL **Gerona** ☎ (972), pop. 11,326, *i* Pl Abat Oliba, 3 ☎ 70 23 51
and 70 01 88, ✣ 70 06 01, **Civil Guard** ☎ 70 11 85. Gerona 86km,
Barcelona 104km, Madrid 675km.

This small Pyrenean town grew up in the shadow of its **monastery**, the
Abbey of Santa María, whose cultural reputation in the Middle Ages spread
throughout Christian Europe. The abbey was founded by the first Count of
Barcelona, **Wilfred the Hairy**, in the 9C and it became a particularly
important cultural centre under the guidance of the cultured and ambitious
Abbot Oliba, who was also Bishop of Vic, in the 11C. Students who came
from far and wide to study at the monastery's excellent library included a
monk named Gebert who in 999 was elected **Pope Sylvester II**.

🏨 ★★ *Solana del Ter* (closed: November), km104 on the N-152 ☎
70 10 62 🛏 28 ✕ **P** ✦ 🎤 ≈ 🔧 ♉ V $$$. It has a **restaurant** $$$.

Cultural highlights: The **Monasterio de Santa María** is one of the
highpoints of Romanesque architecture in Catalonia. Its **church**, innovative in
its time, has five naves and seven apsed transepts, a perfect **cloister** and a
beautifully sculptured 12C **W door**. There is an interesting **Folk Museum**
which traces local customs, industry and art in the Romanesque Church of

San Pedro, the Archivo-Museo Folklórico, Pl Abat Oliba (open: 9.00-1.00 and
3.00-7.00; Mondays: 9.00-1.00).

Fiestas: A series of very typical and genuine *fiestas* which reflect a jealously
preserved local folklore takes place in mid-May.

Local sights: The **Monastery of San Juan de las Abadesas**, which was
also founded by Wilfred in the 9C, lies just 10km from Ripoll along the
C-151. There are several highlights here but the abbey's Gothic **cloister** and
13C polychromed wood *Descent from the Cross*, the church's **capitals** and
the 14C alabaster **altarpiece**, and the beautiful Gothic **patio** of the **Abbot's
Palace** are the most outstanding. **CAMPRODON**, 24km on the N-151, is a
pretty Pyrenean village with an important Romanesque church in its 12C
Monastery of San Pedro. CASTELLAR DE NUCH (see 'Pirineos Catalanes'),
39km NW of Ripoll on the road to Pobla de Lillet, is no less picturesque and
is a mountain summer resort. There are pleasant waterfalls nearby at the
source of the Llobregat river —for accommodation, try the ★★ *Les Fonts*
(closed: 1/11-30/11), on the outskirts of town ☎ (93) 823 60 89 ⇌ 33 ⏍
P ✦ ⚲ ⚲ ⚲ « ⚲ EC, V $$. In **RIBAS DE FRESER**, you could try staying at
the ★★ *Balneario Montagut*, 3km S along the N-152 ☎ (972) 72 70 21
⇌ 100 **P** ✦ ⚲ $ to $$, set in a large park, or at the ★★ *Terralta*, 6km SW
along the Campellas road, in El Baiell ☎ (972) 72 73 50 ⇌ 22 **P** ✦ ⚲ ⚲
« $ to $$, a very peaceful hotel with scenic views of the valley and
mountains.

Sports: Ripoll is well placed for access to the ski stations of *Nuria*, 22km
along the N-152 to Ribas de Freser and then along a local road ☎ 73 03 16
and 73 02 01, and of *Vallter 2.000*, 35km along the C-151 to Campródon
and then along a local road to Setcasas ☎ 74 03 53. It is also the base
camp for numerous hikes through the Pyrenees and for the climb up Puigmal
(2,913m). There are good fishing and shooting reserves here ☎ 20 09 87,
like the **Freser and Setcasas National Reserve** just N of Ripoll.

ROSAS-ROSES Gerona ☎ (972), pop. 8,131, [i] Av de Rhode, s/n ☎
25 73 31, ✉ Av de Rhode, 77 ☎ 25 78 48, ✚ 25 68 28, P 25 66 32.
Gerona 56km, Barcelona 145km, Madrid 763km.

Originally founded by the Greeks in the 9C BC when it was known as
Rhode, today Rosas is a busy holiday resort with a well developed tourist
infrastructure around the very scenic Bay of Rosas. The **beach** is roomy, with
fine, pale sand, and there are numerous pretty coves nearby. Water sports are
ideally practised here.

▦ ★★★★ *Almadraba Park* (closed: 18/10-22/4), Almadraba beach, 4km
SE of Rosas ☎ 25 65 50 ⇌ 66 **P** ✦ ⚲ ⚲ ⚲ ▦ « ⚲ ⚲ AE, DC, EC,
V $$$ to $$$$. A quiet hotel with good views of the sea.

▦ ★★★ *Canyelles Platja* (closed: 1/10-31/3), Av Díaz Pacheco, 7,
Canyelles Petites beach, 2.5km SE of Rosas ☎ 25 65 00 ⇌ 99 ⚲ ✦ ⚲
⚲ « ⚲ AE, DC, EC, V $$$.

▦ ★★★ *Coral Playa* (closed: 1/11-31/3), Av Rhode, 28, Rastillo beach ☎
25 62 50 ⇌ 128 ⚲ **P** ✦ ⚲ « ⚲ AE, EC, V $$ to $$$. Good views.

▦ ★★★ *Goya Park* (closed: 1/10-30/4), Port de Reig, Urb Santa
Margarita, 2km W of Rosas ☎ 25 75 50 ⇌ 224 **P** ✦ ⚲ ⚲ « AE, DC,
EC, V $$ to $$$. Good views.

▦ ★★★ *La Terraza* (closed: 1/11-31/3), Passeig Marítim, 16 ☎ 25 61 54
⇌ 111 **P** ✦ ⚲ ⚲ « ⚲ DC, EC, V $$$$. Good views and facilities,
including an indoor swimming pool.

▦ ★★★ *Marian Platja* (closed: 15/10-30/4), Av de Salatá, s/n, Salatá
beach ☎ 25 61 08 ⇌ 145 **P** ⚲ ⚲ « ⚲ AE, DC, EC, V $$ to $$$.
Good views.

⊞ ★★★ *Monterrey* (closed: 1/11-28/2), Passeig Maritim, 106 ☎ 25 66 76 ⊨ 138 **P ✦ ❧ ⚲ «** AE, DC, EC, V $$$.

⊞ ★★★ *San Carlos* (closed: 1/10-30/4), Urb Mas Busca, 3.5km from Rosas on the road to Cadaqués ☎ 25 61 97 and 25 43 00 ⊨ 99 ⚹ **P ✦ ❧ ⚲ «** ⚲ AE, EC, V $$ to $$$. Good views.

⊞ ★★★ *Vistabella* (closed: 1/11-31/3), Canyelles Petites beach, 2.5km SE of Rosas ☎ 25 62 00 ⊨ 46 ⚺ **P ✦ ❧ ❧ ⚲ «** ❧ ⚲ AE, DC, EC, V $$$ to $$$$. Quiet, with good views of the bay and a pleasant terrace.

❢❢ *Hacienda El Bulli* (closed: lunchtime Mondays and Tuesdays except July-September and 15/1-15/3), Cala Montjoí, 7km SE of Rosas ☎ 25 76 51 **P ✦ ✳ «** AE, DC, MC, V $$$$$. A high temple of sophisticated cuisine.

❢❢ *La Llar* (closed: Thursdays except July-August, 15/11-30/11 and 1/2-28/2), 4km on the Figueras road in Castelló de Ampurias ☎ 25 53 68 **P ✳** AE, DC, MC, V $$$ to $$$$$. A restaurant that serves the regional food of the Ampurdán with more than a touch of French influence. It has a good wine list.

Cultural highlights: Historic buildings include the Castillo de la Trinidad, a 16C castle built on the mountain of Puig Rom for Charles V and demolished in the Peninsular War, after defending the coastline for centuries against the Turks. On Puig Rom you can also see the ruins of a Visigothic settlement. The Ciudadela wall (16-17C) surrounds the ruins of a former Benedictine monastery and of the Church of Santa María de Rosas, a Romanesque-Lombard structure with a watch tower.

Fiestas: The day of *Nuestra Señora de la Asunción*, patron saint of Rosas, is duly celebrated on August 15.

Local sights: CASTELLO DE AMPURIAS, 14km, originally a Greek colony and later a Roman one, is one of the most impressive **archaeological sites** in Spain. The Greeks arrived here in 55 BC from what is today Marseilles and founded first *Palaiapolis*, or the old city, and then *Neapolis*, the new city in the area of what is nowadays San Martín de Ampurias, then an island. The Roman conquest that followed the arrival in 218 of Cornelius Scipio led to the foundation of a third city, *Emporiae*. There is also evidence of a very early Christian basilica which suggests that this was also a bishopric toward the end of the Roman Empire. In the 3C, Barbarian invasions destroyed the basilica and all three cities. The tour of the **archaeological site** (open: 10.00-7.00; winter: 10.00-1.00 and 3.00-5.00) takes in the **sacred area** where the **temples** were located, a **watch tower** and the **agora**, or public square, and the market place of *Neapolis*, next to which are the remains of the early **Christian basilica**. Excavations of the Roman site (on the other side of the road) have unearthed the **forum**, two **villas** (one with mosaic floors) and the **amphitheatre**. The museum, the Museo Monográfico (open: same hours as the site), shows in well laid out models the different stages of development of Ampurias. A number of treasures discovered during the excavations, both on the Greek and the Roman sites, are exhibited here and one of the highpoints is a painstakingly reassembled Greek **mosaic**. The museum is at the entrance to the Roman site. In the village of Castelló itself, the 12C **Church of Santa María** is worth visiting for a look at its magnificent 15C **altarpiece**.

AMPURIA BRAVA, 3km E of Castelló, has a really big beach and is a highly developed tourist resort with every facility on hand. This lovely part of the Costa is particularly good for underwater fishing, other water sports —Ampuria Brava has a good **marina**— and **parachuting**.

Sports: Sailing and **windsurfing** are ideally practised at the marina, Av de Rhode, s/n ☎ 25 73 31.

❍❍ S'AGARÓ **Gerona** ☎ (972). Gerona 38km, Barcelona 103km, Madrid 717km.

S'Agaró is the Costa Brava's summer **showpiece**, with beautiful gardens and pine woods and not a scrap of litter anywhere. The promenade offers
❍ excellent **views** of the coastline and a close up look at the rows of millionaire villas.

❍❍❍ ▥ ★★★★★ *La Gavina* (closed: 1/11-31/3), Pl de la Rosaleda, s/n ☎ 32 11 00 ⇌ 74 ✕ TV P ✦ 🎤 🏊 ⚓ 🌳 ▦ ≪ ♒ AE, DC, MC, V $$$$$$. A really very grand hotel, the sort of place that makes you feel undressed if you are not wearing a tie and an expensive one at that. It has a good **restaurant $$$$**.

  ▥ ★★★ *Caleta Park* (closed: 25/10-25/3), San Pol beach, 2km from San Feliú de Guixols ☎ 32 00 12 ⇌ 105 Υ TV P 🎤 🏊 ⚓ 🌳 ≪ ♒ DC, EC, V $$$$ to $$$$$.

Festivals: There is a music festival in summer.
❍ **Sports:** Golfers go to the *Club de Golf Costa Brava*, Santa Cristina de Aro, 6km ☎ 83 71 50. The town is also a haven of water sports.

❍ SALOU-VILA SECA I SALOU **Tarragona** ☎ (977), pop. 20,468, [i] c/ Espigó del Moll ☎ 74 07 17, [i] c/ Levante, 2 ☎ 38 56 58. Tarragona 10km, Barcelona 108km, Madrid 556km.

❍❍ This is the top **resort** of Tarragona's Costa Dorada and tens of thousands
❍ of tourists crowd it out in the summer season, attracted by its lovely **beaches** and surroundings. The bay forms a natural harbour that was much used in the Middle Ages and served the Catalan-Aragonese fleet as the *rendez-vous* point before setting sail for the conquest of the Balearic Islands in 1229. Hundreds of yachts have now replaced the galleons and only a couple of medieval turrets on the outskirts of town indicate that Salou was ever anything other than a cosmopolitan beachside playground. A spectacularly illuminated grand **fountain** on the **promenade** is today's eyecatcher.

  ▥ ★★★★ *Salou Park*, c/ Amposta, s/n ☎ 38 02 08 ⇌ 108 TV P ✦ 🎤 ⚓ 🌳 ≪ AE, DC, V $$$ to $$$$. Good views.

  ▥ ★★★ *Cala Font* (closed: 1/11-30/4), Urb Cap de Salou, in Cala Font ☎ 37 04 54 ⇌ 318 (✦ ⚓ 🌳 ≪ AE, DC, V $$ to $$$. A fine hotel with wonderful views, facing onto a quiet cove.

  ▥ ★★★ *Carabela Roc* (closed: 1/10-1/3), Paseo Pau Casals, 108, in La Pineda beach ☎ 37 01 66 ⇌ 98 P ✦ 🌳 ≪ 🐴 EC, V $$$. Set among pines, it offers good views.

  ▥ ★★★ *Negresco* (closed: 1/11-31/3), Punta Dorada ☎ 37 03 92 ⇌ 299 Υ (⚓ 🐴 EC, MC, V $$$.

  ▥ ★★ *Planas* (closed: 15/10-31/3), Pl Bonet, 3 ☎ 38 01 08 ⇌ 100 Υ ✦ 🌳 $$. It has an agreeable terrace.

  ▯ *Casa Font* (closed: Sunday nights, Mondays and 8/1-15/2), c/ Colón, 17 ☎ 38 04 35 ✦ ❅ AE, DC, EC, V $$$. It has a pleasant open-air terrace in summer.

  ▯ *Casa Soler*, c/ Virgen del Carmen, s/n ☎ 38 04 63 P ✦ AE, DC, EC, V $$$ to $$$$. French cuisine.

  ▯ *La Goleta*, c/ Gavina, s/n, Capellans beach ☎ 38 35 66 P ✦ ❅ AE, DC, EC, V $$$. It has a pleasant summer terrace.

  ▯ *Macarrilla* (closed: 1/1-1/4), Paseo Jaime I, 24 ☎ 38 54 15 ✦ ❅ AE, V $$. Open-air dining in summer.

❍ **Beaches:** On either side of the **Cabo Salou** promontory there are in all
❍ 13km of beach. The actual town beaches are the ones known as **Levante**
❍ and **Poniente**. **La Pineda** beach, set in pinewoods outside the town, ❍ provides an alternative.

Best buys: Leather goods are good buys at the many shops around c/ Barcelona, c/ Zaragoza, c/ Principat d'Andorra and Av Carles Buigas. Crafts and works of art are sold at c/ Iglesia, c/ Ponent and c/ Valencia in the old quarter. Bargain hunters will also enjoy the street markets.

Fiestas and festivals: The town's red letter day, the *Fiesta Mayor de Vila-Seca i Salou* is on August 13, and there is a winter equivalent in February. This is a music loving town —an International Music Festival is held in May and the *Fiesta Mayor de Verano* in September includes concerts, theatre productions and firework displays. There is also *sardana* dancing at the Torre Vella on Saturdays, and the students of the music conservatory give choral concerts periodically.

Local sights: See 'Costa Dorada'.

On the town: The choice is almost limitless. For children, there is a fun fair by the yacht club and an *Aquapark*, a water amusement park, between Salou and La Pineda. Salou is the top entertainment centre of the Costa Dorada and there are numerous bars, pubs, cafeterias and discos, particularly around c/ Barcelona and c/ Zaragoza. A short list of where to go for a drink and to listen to music would include *Acantilados*, c/ Colón, 23, *Claqué*, Paseo Miramar, *Desliz*, c/ Aragón, and *Musgo* and *Paparazzi*, c/ Zaragoza. The two top discos, *Level-O* and *Mister Disc*, are in La Pineda. *Galas*, Av Vilaseca a Salou, is the town's first-class nightclub, famous throughout Spain, with seating for 1,500 spectators.

Sports: This is a good area for scuba diving, rod and underwater fishing, sailing and windsurfing. For water sports, go to the yacht club, the *Club Náutico de Salou* ☎ 38 21 66/67. There are tennis courts and horse riding facilities in the La Pineda area.

SAN FELIU DE GUIXOLS-SANT FELIU DE GUIXOLS Gerona ☎ (972), pop. 15,428, *i* Pl d'Espanya, 1 ☎ 32 03 80. Gerona 35km, Barcelona 100km, Madrid 713km.

This port town, turned **family resort**, rivals Palamós for the title of capital of the **Costa Brava**. San Feliú grew up in the 11C around a Benedictine abbey and then became, like its rival, moderately important thanks to the cork industry, its fishing fleet and coastal trading. The tourist revolution made the town an important urban centre almost overnight. It retains from its quieter days a fine promenade and a lovely balcony, the Mirador de Sant Elm, which gives fantastic views along the rocky coast all the way down to Tossa.

★★★ *Curhotel Hipócrates*, Ctra San Pol, 229 ☎ 32 06 62 ⊨ 87 Y ⅋ P ✦ ⬧ ⬧ ⬧ ⬧ ⬧ ⬧ ⬧ $$$. Therapeutic services are available in this quiet and scenically located establishment (see 'Health and Beauty').

★★★ *Eden Roc*, in Port Salvi ☎ 32 01 00 ⊨ 120 (P ⬧ ⬧ «. Quiet, with good views.

★★★ *Montjoi* (closed: 16/10-30/4), in Sant Elm ☎ 32 03 00 ⊨ 64 ✦ ⬧ ⬧ ⬧ « ⬧ AE, DC, V $$ to $$$. Good views, tree-shaded terraces and a swimming pool.

★★★ *Murlá Park Hotel*, Paseo dels Guixols, 21 ☎ 32 04 50 ⊨ 89 ✦ ⬧ ⬧ ⬧ « MC, V $$$. Sea views.

⁙ *Bahía*, Paseo del Mar, 17 ☎ 32 02 19 P ✦ ✳ AE, DC, MC, V $$$. Seafood.

⁙ *Can Toni* (closed: Tuesdays from October to April), c/ Garrofers, 54 ☎ 32 10 26 ✳ AE, DC, MC, V $$$$. Fish dishes cooked in authentic Catalan style.

⁙ *Eldorado Petit* (closed: Wednesdays from October to April and also November), Rambla Vidal, 23 ☎ 32 18 18 ✳ AE, DC, MC, V $$$$. Imaginative Catalan seafood cookery.

Beaches: The town's beach, **Santa Cristina**, satisfies most visitors for it is clean and has good facilities. Going N along the C-253, the beach at S'Agaró (2km) and, beyond it, the large one at **Playa de Aro** offer alternatives.

Best buys: Local pastries are sold at *La Vienesa*, Rambla Vidal, 33, and wine at *Casellas*, c/ Clavé, 9. Look out for bargains at the Sunday market held in the Plaza Mayor. A district fair showing off the products of the Bajo Ampurdán area is held in September. Spanish fashion is sold at *P. Cuello*, Galerías Metropol Sports, Paseo dels Guixols, 20, and leather goods at *Platero*, c/ Clavé, 14.

Cultural highlights: The Monastery of San Feliú, now in ruins, was built in the 11C and restored in the 14C. Its **main façade**, called the Porta Ferrada, shows an interesting interplay of the Romanesque and Mozarabic styles. The nearby San Benito Gate built in the 17C shows how important the town was beginning to feel 300 years ago and the Modernist *Nuevo Casino de la Constancia*, the main *rendez-vous* for the townspeople, underlines the fact that by the turn of the century San Feliú was a place of some substance. The town's museum, Pl del Monasterio (open: 11.00-1.00 and 5.00-8.00 ☎ 32 00 29), exhibits Iberian, Greek and Roman finds from local digs and some medieval panels.

Fiestas: San Feliú stages its Summer Festival of concerts and assorted shows during July and August but the town's real *fiestas* take place during the first week of August, when good **bullfights** are held. As in other fishing towns, July 16, the feast day of *La Virgen del Carmen*, is celebrated with maritime processions.

Local sights: The clifftop **coastal road** S to **TOSSA**, 22km away, is as twisty as it is beautiful.

Sports: Water skiing, sailing, scuba diving and fishing are widely practised here —go to the yacht club, the *Club Náutico de San Feliú de Guixols* ☎ 32 17 00 and 32 13 00. The nearest golf course, the *Club de Golf Costa Brava*, is at Santa Cristina de Aro, 4km ☎ 83 71 50.

SANTA CRISTINA DE ARO-SANTA CRISTINA D'ARO Gerona ☎ (972), pop. 1,500, *i* c/ Carrer Verdaguer, 11, Playa de Aro ☎ 81 71 79. Gerona 31km, Barcelona 87km, Madrid 709km.

If you want an instant respite from Playa de Aro's non-stop high-life, Santa Cristina ideally fits the bill. For total contrasts there is nothing quite like viewing Santa Cristina's Megalithic Terme Gross menhir, the rocking stone of Pedralba or the remains of the Les Pedres d'en Lloveres dolmen after you have spent the night under the strobes of Playa's freaky discos.

★★★★ *Golf Costa Brava* (closed: 12/10-19/3), Urb Club de Golf Costa Brava ☎ 83 70 52 ⇌ 91 **P** ✦ ♨ ♨ ☇ ≪ ♀ ↙ AE, DC, EC, V $$$$. Very quiet and well situated.

Les Panolles (closed: Wednesdays in winter and November), on the C-250 to Gerona, 2km outside the village ☎ 83 70 11 **P** ✦ ❊ AE, DC, MC, V $$$. A rustic old farmhouse serving innovative dishes and updated local cooking.

Sports: The village is home to the well established 18 hole, par 70 *Club de Golf Costa Brava* ☎ 83 71 50.

SEO DE URGEL-LA SEU D'URGELL Lérida ☎ (973), pop. 10,686, *i* Paseo José Antonio ☎ 35 09 91, ✚ 35 00 30, ✈ Seo de Urgel, 7km ☎ 35 23 08 (Iberia, c/ José Betriú Tàpies ☎ 35 15 74; Aviaco, Airport ☎ 35 18 26), 🚌 35 02 20. Andorra La Vella 20km, Lérida 133km, Barcelona 200km, Madrid 602km.

This is a splendidly located historical town in the verdant Segre river valley surrounded by the imposing peaks of the Cadí sierra and the Andorra mountains. One of the curiosities of this town is that its bishop holds the title of co-prince and head of state of neighbouring **Andorra** with the President of France. This is an oddity that dates back to the Middle Ages. Seo de Urgel is the natural entry to Andorra and a popular starting point for trips through the Pyrenees.

- ★★★★ *El Castell*, 1km out of town on the Lérida road, in Castellciutat ☎ 35 07 04 ⇌ 40 ✕ TV P ♦ ♦ ♨ ≈ ≪ AE, DC, MC, V $$$$ to $$$$$. A quiet hotel with lovely views of the city, valley and mountains. The **restaurant** (closed: 15/1-15/2) serves Catalan and international cuisine.
- ★★★ *Parador de La Seo de Urgel*, c/ Santo Domingo, s/n ☎ 35 20 00 ⇌ 84 P ♦ ≈ AE, DC, MC, V $$$.

Best buys: Local sausages and patés are the local specialities —you can buy them at the market in the old quarter every Tuesday and Friday.

Cultural highlights: The **Cathedral of Santa María** is very impressive. Built between the 11-12C, it shows clear Lombardy influences on its basic Romanesque design. Its best features are its **main façade** and its 13C **cloister**. If you want to see the frescoes that once decorated the Romanesque **Church of San Miguel** (11C), you will have to go to Barcelona's Museo de Arte de Cataluña which is where they are now displayed. The **Diocesan Museum** (open: 9.00-1.30 and 3.30-8.00; Sundays: 9.00-1.30; closed: 1/9-31/3 ☎ 35 11 77) has among its treasures one of the few existing 11C copies of a *Commentary on the Apocalypse* written in the 8C by the monk known as the Beato de Liébana. The picturesque c/ de los Canonges and c/ La Mayor are partly porticoed.

Fiestas: A medieval mystery play called the *Misterio del Retablo de San Ermengol* is acted out on Sundays from July 25 to September 24. There is folk dancing during the *fiestas* held on the last Sunday of August.

Local sights: Six kilometres on the C-1313 towards Lérida, you pass by the picturesque villages of **ORGAÑA** (22km) and Coll de Nargó (26km), both with beautiful Romanesque churches.

Sports: Sportsmen equipped with the proper licences can hunt at the **Cerdaña National Reserve**.

SITGES **Barcelona** ☎ (93), pop. 11,849, *i* Paseo Vilafranca, Centro Oasis ☎ 894 47 00 and 894 12 30, ✛ Pl Hospital, 5 ☎ 894 02 26, **P** Pl Ayuntamiento ☎ 894 07 68, ✈ El Prat, 35km ☎ 317 01 78 and 325 43 04 (Iberia ☎ 370 10 11), ⇞ Pl E. Maristany ☎ 894 18 89. Barcelona 43km, Tarragona 53km, Madrid 597km.

This is a rather special resort. It was made fashionable at the turn of the century by **Santiago Rusiñol**, a Catalan cultural pace-setter who was equally at home with the pen and with the paintbrush but was mostly admired for his originality as a conversationalist and for his wide circle of acquaintances. Sitges became the summer camp for the artists and litterati who formed a sort of Barcelona Bloomsbury group. Nowadays Sitges is distinctive because it is a gathering place for the European gay community. The tolerance that Rusiñol's crowd induced has stood the test of time.

The old quarter is certainly picturesque for Sitges was a well established fishing village before the arty crowd descended on it. The town's appearance was subsequently spruced up with the **Modernist villas** that architects such as Puig i Cadafalch, Domènech and Sunyer built for Barcelona's prosperous middle classes. Sitges was a forerunner of today's summer resorts. The well equipped beach, the lovely promenade and a host of cultural events serve to underline the fact that Sitges is a cut above the average seaside resort.

- ★★★★ *Aparthotel Mediterráneo*, Av Sofía, 3 ☎ 894 51 34 ⇌ 84 ♈ 🅿 ✦ ♨ ⚓ 🛴 « AE, DC, EC, MC, V $$$$ to $$$$$. Comfortable room or apartment accommodation in a modern building with a pleasant swimming pool and good sea views.

- ★★★★ *Calípolis* (closed: 1/11-30/11), Paseo Marítimo, s/n ☎ 894 15 00 ⇌ 163 (✦ ✳ ♨ 🛴 « AE, DC, MC, V $$$ to $$$$. Good views.

- ★★★★ *Terramar* (closed: 1/11-30/4), Paseo Marítimo, 30 ☎ 894 00 50 ⇌ 209 ✦ ♨ 🐟 ⚓ 🛴 🎵 « ☪ ✒ AE, DC, EC, V $$$$ to $$$$$. Somehow old-fashioned and quiet, it has a nice swimming pool in a garden terrace overlooking the sea.

- ★★★ *Antemare* (closed: Christmas), Av Verge de Montserrat, 48 ☎ 894 19 08 ⇌ 72 🅿 ✦ ♨ 🐟 ⚓ 🛴 70m ☪ DC, EC, V $$$ to $$$$. A quiet hotel.

- ★★★ *La Reserva* (closed: 20/9-30/4), Paseo Marítimo, 62 ☎ 894 18 33 ⇌ 24 ✕ 🅿 ✦ ⚓ 🛴 « EC, V $$$. Quiet, with a pleasant garden and swimming pool.

- ★★★ *Los Pinos* (closed: 1/11-1/3), Paseo Marítimo, s/n ☎ 894 15 50 ⇌ 42 🅿 🐟 ⚓ 🛴 « DC, EC, V $$ to $$$. Quiet with sea views and a good swimming pool.

- ★★ *Sitges Park* (closed: 15/10-15/4), c/ Jesús, 12 ☎ 894 02 50 ⌸ 🛏
  79 ✦ ⚲ ⚓ $$. A hidden jewel, that offers good value for money.
- ★ *Romantic* (closed: 15/10-15/4), c/ San Isidro, 33 ☎ 894 06 43 ⌸
  55 ⅄ ✦ AE, EC, V $$. Turn of the century and suitably romantic, it has a
  beautiful inner garden patio.
- ¶ *El Velero César* (closed: Sunday nights, Mondays and Christmas), Paseo
  de la Ribera, 38 ☎ 894 20 51 ✦ ≪ AE, DC, MC, V $$$. Imaginative
  Catalan cooking.
- ¶ *El Vivero* (closed: November and Tuesdays from December to May),
  Paseo Balmins, s/n ☎ 894 21 49 🅟 ✦ ❋ ≪ DC, EC, V $$$. Sea views
  and sea produce.
- ¶ *La Fragata* (closed: weekday nights), Paseo de la Ribera, 1 ☎ 894 10 86
  ✦ ❋ AE, DC, MC, V $$$ to $$$$. Fish and sea food served on a
  pleasant terrace.
- ¶ *La Masía*, Paseo Vilanova, 164 ☎ 894 10 76 🅟 ✦ AE, DC, MC, V $$ to
  $$$. Catalan cooking and regional decor.
- ¶ *Mare Nostrum* (closed: Wednesdays and 15/12-15/1), Paseo de la
  Ribera, 60 ☎ 894 33 93 ✦ AE, MC, V $$$. Summer terrace.

Beaches: There are numerous well-kept beaches but they do tend to get
crowded in the high season. The closest ones to the town centre are **San
Sebastián** and **La Ribera**. The beaches known as Home Mort, Roses,
Desenrocada, Raldiris and l'Ombra are used by nudists.

Best buys: Sitges is the sort of place you expect to find arts and crafts shops
(basketwork and pottery) and art galleries, and you won't be disappointed.
There is also a daily craft market by San Sebastián beach. Look out, too, for
shoes and leather goods in general. On Saturdays there is a fruit market by
the Pl de la Estación.

Cultural highlights: The old part of town is a pleasure to stroll around in. Its
focal point is the Baroque **Church of San Bartolomé and Santa Tecla**
which stands on a rocky promontory jutting out into the Mediterranean in the
area called the Cap de la Vila. There is an historic feel and the odd Gothic
hint to the tortuous maze made up by the c/ Devallada, c/ D'En Bosch, c/
San Juan and c/ La Vall. The **promenade** is a different scene altogether and
belongs to the age of modern tourist developments. For the Modernist
houses you have to return towards the Cap de la Vila where you will find
them on c/ San Bartolomé, c/ Isla de Cuba and c/ San Gaudencio. The
Museo Cau Ferrat (open in summer: 10.00-1.00 and 5.00-7.00; in winter:
10.00-1.00 and 4.00-6.00; Sundays: 10.00-3.00; closed: Mondays ☎
894 03 64) exhibits paintings by Rusiñol and objets d'art from his personal
collection. These range from a canvas attributed to El Greco to ornamental
wrought-iron work. An annexe houses the **Museo Maricel de Mar** (open:
same times as the Museo Cau Ferrat) which displays an extensive collection
of mostly Gothic religious objects. The **Museo Romántico**, c/ San
Gaudencio (open in summer: 10.00-1.30 and 5.00-7.00; winter: 10.00-1.30
and 4.00-6.00; Sundays: 10.00-2.00; closed: Mondays ☎ 894 29 69), is in
a fine Neoclassical building and has an amusing collection of mechanical
toys, music boxes and 17-19C dolls.

Fiestas and festivals: Carnival is celebrated in style in Sitges and is the
highpoint in the town's calendar. The town, rather than its people, disguises
itself to celebrate **Corpus Christi**: the streets in the old quarter are covered
with **blankets of flowers**, and tapestries and other decorations are hung out
of windows and from balconies. There is an **International Theatre Festival**
in spring ☎ 893 66 34, a cycle of concerts in summer —crowned by the
town's *Fiesta Mayor* in the last week of August, involving *sardana* and
moixiganga dancing and **firework displays**— and an **International Film**

Festival specializing in Sci-Fi cinema in early October. Early in the year there is an **International Vintage Car Rally** that starts in Barcelona and ends up along the town's promenade.

Local sights: **VILANOVA I LA GELTRU**, 6km SW, a centre of industrial activity since the 18C, is a typical Catalan town set on a gentle bay with its own little beach, a fishing port and a marina. It has an interesting museum, the **Museo Romántico** (open: 10.00-1.00 and 5.00-7.00; closed: Sunday afternoons and Mondays), and a collection of contemporary paintings in the 13C **Castle of La Geltrú**. The pleasant local park has fountains designed by Carlos Buigas. You can have a fine meal at *Peixerot*, Paseo Marítimo, 56 ☎ 815 06 25 ♣ AE, DC, EC, V $$$, serving fish and seafood, and *Chez Bernard et Marguerite*, c/ Ramón Llull, 4 ☎ 815 56 04 ♣ AE, DC, EC, V $$$, serving French cuisine. For accommodation, try the ★★★ *César*, c/ Isaac Peral, 4 ☎ 815 11 25 ⚏ 21 ✕ Υ ♣ ⚓ AE, DC, EC, V $$$ to $$$$.

On the town: At night, Sitges is a world of its own. There are a few very strange places for there are, indeed, some very strange people and there are, even, some fairly conventional places where normally stay-at-home people will feel at ease. A visitor will soon get his or her bearings and work out that different kinds of action are in separate zones. If there is only a limited time available the best bet is to head for the c/ Dos de Mayo which is known throughout the town as the *Calle del Pecado* or Sin Street. Temptation Street would be a better name, for it is just one long line of bars and discos, cheek by jowl, crammed full until the wee hours by doers and watchers. **Aiguadolç port** has a number of popular places such as *La Canasta*, *Ceferino*, *Chui* and, the latest mecca of the ultimate fads, *El Penúltimo*. The area around the Cap de la Vila, and especially c/ Parelladas and c/ Sant Francesc, has a number of crowded *tapa* bars including *Bar La Vinya* and *El Xatet*, which is said to be the oldest in the town. Top discos include *Pachá*, Paseo Vilafranca, and *Atlántida*, Les Coves beach, 3km. A short list of the *gay* community spots includes *Bourbon's* and *Top Kapi*, No. 3 and No. 13 of c/ Buenaventura respectively, *Lord's Club*, c/ Marqués de Montroig, 14, and *Trailer*, c/ Angel Vidal, 14. If the cliché Spanish scene is what you want, head for *Casa de Andalucía*, km42.5 on the road to Vilanova, where you can enjoy an Andalusian meal while watching the flamenco shows staged on Saturdays and Sundays after midnight. Opposite the road, the *Gran Casino de Barcelona* (see 'Barcelona') ☎ 893 20 43, is a magnificent place to flirt with Lady Luck or to have a buffet dinner on Fridays and Saturdays.

Sports: There are three marinas —*Aiguadolç*, Garraf and Ginesta— and a yacht club, the *Club Náutico de Sitges* ☎ 894 54 05. For golfers and tennis players, there is an 18-hole golf course and tennis courts at the *Club de Golf Terramar*, Paseo Marítimo, s/n ☎ 894 05 80 and 894 20 43, and there are more courts at the *Club de Tenis Levantina*, in the Levantina housing development. Horses may be hired at *Caballos el Vinyet*.

SOLSONA **Lérida** ☎ (973), pop. 6,114, *i* c/ Castell, 20 ☎ 811 00 50, ✛ 811 06 52. Lérida 108km, Barcelona 119km, Madrid 577km.

Solsona is a mostly unspoiled, old cathedral town on the banks of the River Nere. It is somewhat rundown, like its medieval walls, but agreeable enough.

▥ ★★★ *Gran Sol*, 1km on the Manresa road ☎ 48 10 00 ⚏ 55 🅿 ♣ ♙ ⚓ Q V $$.

Best buys: Sausages and such like are sold at *Can Tarallo*, c/ Castell, 14.

Cultural highlights: The essentially Gothic **Cathedral** houses the much venerated Romanesque figure of the *Virgen del Claustro* (12-13C). The **Diocesan Museum** in the Episcopal Palace (open in summer: 10.00-1.00

and 4.30-7.00; winter: 10.00-1.00 and 4.00-6.00; closed: Mondays ☎ 48 21 01) has an interesting collection of **Romanesque and Gothic paintings** of the Catalan school and some prehistoric **pottery**. There is a curious museum in an annexe dedicated to the subject of salt. The Town Hall has some rooms set aside as a local **Folk Museum**.

Fiestas: The town's **Carnival** celebrations have a long tradition behind them. The bands and the *papier-maché* giants do duty again during the town's September 8 *fiestas* and also on Corpus Christi.

Local sights: The well equipped ski station of ***Port del Comte*** ☎ 811 04 81, lies 60km N on a local road.

TARRAGONA **Tarragona** ☎ (977), pop. 109,557, [i] c/ Fortuny, 4 ☎ 23 34 15, [i] Paseo de las Palmeras, 1 ☎ 23 89 22, ☾ Rambla Nova, 74, ✉ Pl Corsini, s/n ☎ 21 01 49, ✚ Av María Cristina, 17 ☎ 23 65 11, **P** c/ Pau Casals, 23 ☎ 23 33 11, ✈ Reus Airport, 10km ☎ 30 35 04 (Iberia, Rambla Nova, 116 ☎ 23 05 12), ⛴ Trasmediterránea ferry, c/ Nueva San Olegario, 16 ☎ 22 55 06, 🚆 RENFE, Rambla Nova, 40 ☎ 23 25 34. Lérida 97km, Barcelona 109km, Castellón 184km, Madrid 555km.

Tarragona was a very important Roman city indeed and for a period shared imperial privileges with Rome itself. When it comes to antique name dropping the city can hold its own against virtually all comers for a succession of Emperors, including Augustus Caesar, sojourned within its walls, and its not-so-favourite sons included Pontius Pilate who was born here. Christianity got its own back, for tradition has it that none other than Saint Paul brought the faith to the city. The legions had first arrived much earlier, in 218 BC, under the command of Publius Scipio. Huge dykes were built out into the Mediterranean and Tarragona, or *Tarraco* as it was known to the Romans, was during the Punic Wars the depot for the most important fleet in the Mediterranean. The Romans certainly left giant footprints in Tarragona but one is left wondering about the even greater splendour that once was before the Franks in the 2C, the Visigoths in the 5C and the Muslims in the 8C successively reduced so much of Tarragona to rubble.

Modern Tarragona has the Rambla Nova boulevard as its main axis and its best feature is the wonderful view over the sea from the aptly named **Balcón del Mediterráneo** (Mediterranean Balcony) that looks out onto the sea that the Caesars sailed.

- ★★★★ *Imperial Tarraco*, Rambla Vella, 2 ☎ 23 30 40 🛏 170 **P** ✱ 🎙 ≈ ⚲ **AE, DC, MC, V** $$$$.
- ★★★ ***Astari*** (closed: 1/11-30/4), Vía Augusta, 95 ☎ 23 69 11 🛏 83 **P** ✱ ≈ « **AE, DC, V** $$ to $$$. The terrace has good views.
- ★★★ ***Lauria***, Rambla Nova, 20 ☎ 23 67 12 🛏 72 **P** 🎙 ≈ **AE, DC, EC, V** $$ to $$$. Central.
- 🍴 ***La Galería*** (closed: Sunday nights), Rambla Nova, 16 ☎ 23 61 43 ✱ ❄ **AE, DC, MC, V** $$ to $$$. Good fish dishes.
- 🍴 *Mesón del Mar*, Playa Larga, 4km from Tarragona ☎ 23 94 01 **P** ✱ ⛱ « **AE, MC, V** $$$. Fish cuisine. Open air eating by the beach in summer.
- 🍴 ***Sol Ric*** (closed: Sunday nights, Mondays and 15/12-15/1), Vía Augusta, 227 ☎ 23 20 32 **P** ✱ **AE, EC, MC, V** $$$ to $$$$. This rustic restaurant, with a fine terrace, specializes in fish.

Beaches: The best bet is to head down the coast to **La Pineda** (8km) and **Salou** (12km), because the town beach here is tragically contaminated. At a pinch you could try the beaches of La Rabasada and the Playa Larga on the outskirts.

Best buys: Antiques and works of art are sold at ***Gómez***, c/ Llano de la Catedral, 4, ***Arimany***, c/ Augusto, 10, ***L'Antiquari***, c/ Santa Ana, and

Poblet, c/ Mayor, 27. For typical local pastries, go to ***Cuadras***, Rambla Nova, 65, and ***Lemon***, Rambla Nova, 27, and for wine and cava to ***Los Alpes***, Av Ramón y Cajal, 43. Fashion boutiques are mainly centred around the Rambla Nova.

Cultural highlights: The first stop is, without a doubt, the **Paseo Arqueológico** where not much imagination is needed among such remains to reconstruct the temples and triumphal arches that once were. The **Museo Arqueológico**, the Archaeological Museum (open in summer: 10.00-1.00 and 4.30-8.00; winter: 10.00-1.30 and 4.00-7.00; closed: Mondays ☎

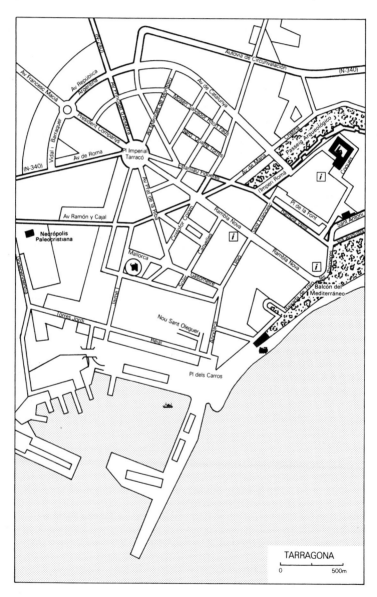

23 62 11), is a magnificently rich permanent exhibition of antiquity which boasts a **Medusa mosaic** as its star turn. The 1C BC **praetorium** nearby was reconstructed in the Middle Ages and is where Augustus lived and Pilate was born. You reach an early Christian cemetery along Av Ramón y Cajal where the so-called **sarcophagus of the Lions** is especially interesting.

The **Cathedral** was built on the site of a temple dedicated to Jupiter and it is the main building of the medieval quarter. Most of the Cathedral was built in the 12C and it shows the transition between the Romanesque and the Gothic styles. Later improvements heightened the Gothic elements and brought in new ones in accordance with the Plateresque tastes of the Spanish Renaissance and the Churrigueresque ornamentation of the Baroque age. Its highpoints include the **main altarpiece** which narrates the life of the early Christian martyr, Santa Tecla, who is the patroness of Tarragona and the **marble chapel**, the third on the right, which is dedicated to her. The **cloister** which is entered through a fine Romanesque sculpted door is also very pleasing. The **Diocesan Museum**, which is open when services are being conducted, exhibits Gothic altarpieces and some Renaissance tapestries.

Still in the medieval quarter, there are fine old town houses along c/ Mayor, c/ de Cavallers, c/ de la Mercería and c/ de la Civadería. The Museum of Modern Art, the Museo de Arte Moderno, c/ Santa Ana, 8 (open: 10.00-1.00 and 5.00-8.00; closed: Sunday afternoons and Mondays), exhibits paintings by local artists. The dual focal point of the modern part of the city is the **Roman amphitheatre** by the beach and the **Balcón del Mediterráneo** which looks out over it towards the horizons.

Fiestas and festivals: Santa Tecla's feastday on September 23 is celebrated with all the typically Catalan accessories of fireworks, parades featuring *papier-maché* giants and human towers constructed by the daring groups of *castellers* in the Pl de las Cols on the following day. A music, dance and theatre festival is held in the summer during the *Festivales de Verano* ☎ 23 48 12.

Local sights: Tarragona's antique remains are scattered around a fairly large area. There is a very well preserved **Roman aqueduct** 4km out of town on the N-240 and a 2C Roman arch, the **Arco de Bará**, astride a Roman road, 20km NE on the A-7. Taking a local road to Constantí, 5km, you come to an interesting 4C mausoleum, the **Mausoleo de Centcelles**, where fine mosaics in its interior may be viewed daily from 10.00-2.00 except Mondays. The **Scipio Tower**, or Torre de los Escipiones, is an earlier funeral monument, probably dating from the 1C, which lies 16km NE of the town on the N-340. Also see the 'Costa Dorada' entry.

On the town: People generally meet for drinks and *tapas* on the Rambla and in the upper part of the city at places like *Oliver* and *Motoclub*. *La Tasca* and *Mesón Andalucía* on Pons d'Icart are also popular places. *Poetes*, c/ Sant Llorenç, is a musical bar, and there are good cocktails to the sound of live music at *La Habana*, c/ Corraló de Sant Magí, 4. *Estudio 81* at Cala Romana (4km on the N-340) is a fashionable disco.

Sports: Water sports and fishing are practised at the yacht club, the *Club Náutico de Tarragona* ☎ 21 03 60. Golfers go to the 9-hole, par 72 *Club de Golf Costa Dorada*, 8km ☎ 23 29 31, and tennis players to the *C. D. Tenis Park* in Cala Romana, 4km on the Barcelona road ☎ 23 55 13.

TARRASA-TERRASA Barcelona ☎ (93), pop. 159,530, *i* Pl Eduardo Maristany ☎ 894 12 30, ✛ 788 89 04. Barcelona 28km, Lérida 156km, Madrid 613km.

Together with the neighbouring town of Sabadell, Tarrasa accounts for 75 per cent of Spain's **textile** production.

¶ *Burrull-Hostal del Fum* (closed: Sunday nights, Mondays and August), Ctra de Moncada, 19 ☎ 788 83 77 **P** ❋ AE, DC, EC, V $$$.

Cultural highlights: It comes as something of a surprise to discover that Tarrasa, a powerhouse in the Industrial Revolution, has three very old churches that have survived the onslaught of the dark satanic mills. The churches of **Santa María** (which has a magnificent 15C *Santos Abdón y Senén* altarpiece), **San Pedro** and **San Miguel** were built on the site known as **Ciudad de Egara** between the 4C and the 10C and could best be described as Visigothic-Romanesque. The local art museum, the Museo Municipal de Arte, c/ Salmerón, 17 (open: 10.00-1.30 and 3.00-7.00; Sundays: 10.00-2.00; closed: Mondays ☎ 785 71 44), housed in a former Charterhouse, has a varied collection of paintings, sculptures and archaeological exhibits with particular emphasis on 19C painting. The **Textile Museum**, the Museo Textil, is next door, at No. 19 (open: 10.00-1.00 and 3.00-8.00; Sundays: 10.00-2.00; closed: Mondays ☎ 785 72 98) and the Aymerich Factory, which was designed by one of Gaudí's pupils, houses the **Catalan Museum of Science and Technology**, the Museo de la Ciencia y de la Técnica de Cataluña, Rambla d'Egara, 27 (open: 4.00-7.00; Saturdays: 4.00-8.00; Sundays: 10.00-2.00; closed: Mondays ☎ 780 67 55).

Fiestas: The annual street parties take place on the first Sunday after June 29 and they include traditional dancing of the *ball de plaça*. A Jazz Festival is staged in March ☎ 231 89 59.

TORTOSA **Tarragona** ☎ (977), pop. 29,120, ✣ 44 07 71. Tarragona 83km, Barcelona 192km, Madrid 487km.

Tortosa is an old cathedral city, capital of the Bajo Ebro area, that was founded by the Romans, occupied by the Muslims and, in 1148, reconquered by the Christians under the command of Ramón Berenguer IV, the expansionist King of Aragón and Count of Barcelona. A great number of Muslims and Jews continued to live in the city after the Christian occupation and as a result the town has a tolerant air to it and a varied cultural background. Its historic old quarter is called *la zuda*.

▦ ★★★★ *Parador Castillo de la Zuda*, in the castle ☎ 44 44 50 ⊨ 82 **P** ❦ ⬩ ⍋ ⌇ « ⊭ AE, DC, MC V $$$ to $$$$. Quiet, with scenic views of the area.

Best buys: Wooden carvings are sold at *J. Guinovart*, c/ Larga de San Vicente, 84, and local pastries at *Pallares Bonet*, c/ San Blas, 19.

Cultural highlights: The 14-16C **Cathedral** has a Baroque façade and cloister. Its main features are the sumptuous 18C chapel dedicated to the *Virgen de la Cinta*, two massive 15C stone **pulpits** and a lovely 14C polychromed **triptych**. If you like graceful galleried patios, look in on the **Episcopal Palace**, a Gothic design restored in the 18C and on the **Colegio San Luis** (with a beautiful **patio**), a school founded by the Emperor Charles V in the 16C for the education of the sons of converted Muslims. Other places of interest include the former Jewish quarter which is known as the *call* and the old medieval market, which has been moved stone by stone to the municipal park.

Fiestas: At Easter there are a couple of *romerías*, or festive pilgrimages, to local shrines out of town, the Ermita de Mig-Camí and the Ermita de Coll de l'Alba. These events are a happy mix of religious celebrations, picnics and country dancing. The festivities in honour of the *Virgen de la Cinta* start on the first Sunday of September.

Local sights: SE along the C-235 is **AMPOSTA**, in the heart of the **Ebro Delta** (see 'Delta del Ebro'). The landscapes here are quite unexpected and the dunes form utterly unspoiled beaches.

TOSSA DE MAR Gerona ☎ (972), pop. 3,361, *i* Ctra de Lloret, Bus
Station ☎ 34 01 08. Gerona 39km, Barcelona 79km, Madrid 707km.

A well established Costa Brava resort, Tossa de Mar is similar to the
holiday centres of Lloret, San Feliú de Guixols and Palamós and is linked to
them both by pleasure steamers and by the clifftop coastal road. A number of
artists from all over Europe congregated here in the 1930s and Marc Chagall
donated one of the Tossa seascapes he painted to the local museum after his
stay. The old quarter, the Vila Vella, is walled for the town was a popular
pirate target.

▥ ★★★★ *Gran Hotel Reymar* (closed: 1/11-14/4), Mar Menuda beach
  ☎ 34 03 12 ⊨ 131 **P** ✦ ♨ ⅏ ⇌ ⚊ ≪ ⚘ $$$$. This quiet hotel is well
  located.

▥ ★★★ *Mar Menuda* (closed: 1/10-30/4), Mar Menuda beach ☎
  34 10 00 ⊨ 40 **P** ✦ ⅏ ⇌ ⚊ ≪ ⚘ ⚘ DC, MC, V $$ to $$$. Peaceful,
  with a pleasant terrace and good views.

▥ ★★ *Ancora* (closed: 15/9-31/5), Av de la Palma, 4 ☎ 34 02 99 ⊨ 58
  P ✦ ⚊ ⚘ ⚘ ⚘ $$$. It has a pleasant patio.

▥ ★ *Neptuno* (closed: 1/10-30/4), c/ La Guardia, 52 ☎ 34 01 43 ⊨ 49
  P ✦ ⅏ ⇌ $$ to $$$. Quiet.

▥ ★ *Sant March* (closed: 1/10-30/4), c/ Nueva, 9 ☎ 34 00 78 ⊨ 30 ✦
  ⅏ ⇌ $$. Quiet.

⑂ *Bahía* (closed: Mondays in autumn and winter and 1/11-18/1), c/
  Socorro, 4 ☎ 34 03 22 **P** ✦ ❄ ≪ AE, DC, MC, V $$$. Local seafood
  cuisine and game dishes in season.

⑂ *Castell Vell* (open: 15/5-15/10), Pl Roig y Soler ☎ 34 10 30 ✦ AE,
  DC, EC, V $$$. In the Vila Vella.

⑂ *Es Molí* (closed: Tuesdays and 15/10-31/3), c/ Tarull, 5 ☎ 34 14 14 ✦
  AE, DC, EC, V $$$. It has a pleasant patio.

Beaches: **Tossa's** own beach is well equipped, clean and popular. The
different coves outside the town, **Cala de Mar Menuda**, **Cala Bona**, **Cala
Giberola** and **Cala de Salions** are the alternatives. San Feliú's beach is less
than 10km away and the **Playa de Canyellas** is on the road to Lloret.

Cultural highlights: The chief features of the old quarter are its 12C
cylindrical towers, its **lighthouse** and the Governor's palace which is now a
museum, Pl Pintor Roig y Soler (open in summer: 10.00-1.00 and
3.00-8.00; winter: 10.00-1.00 and 3.00-5.00; Sundays 11.00-1.00 ☎
34 07 09), exhibiting paintings and sculptures and also some splendid
mosaics, the results of a dig at a nearby Roman villa.

Fiestas: Like so many other Spanish towns, Tossa has adopted Saint Peter's
Day, June 29, for its annual *fiestas*. A Theatre Festival is staged in the
summer months ☎ 34 01 00 and, on January 20 when the tourist invasion
is still months away, the townspeople keep up the tradition of a 15C votive
pilgrimage, the *Pelegrí de Tossa*, to Santa Coloma de Farnés.

Local sights: The **coastal drive** 22km N to San Feliú de Guixols and 12km
S to Lloret de Mar will have you reaching for your camera and wanting to
stop time and again. Also see the '**Costa Brava**' entry.

On the town: A short list of popular bars would include *La Tortuga*, c/ San
Raimundo de Peñafort, s/n, which has live jazz music, and *Lolita*, c/ Sant
Telm, 17, with Latin American music. There are a great number of discos and
popular ones include *Drink Club*, Av Plana, *Siba's*, c/ Iglesia, *Casbah*, on
the Tossa-Lloret road, and *Ely Club*, c/ Pola. *Tahití*, c/ San José, 30, offers
big floor shows and dancing.

Sports: Sailing, water skiing and scuba diving are all excellent here. There are
a number of tennis courts at many hotels and the nearest golf course is at
Santa Cristina de Aro, 16km away on the coastal road (see separate entry).

🔴🔴 `VALLE DE ARAN-LA VALL D'ARAN (ARAN VALLEY)` **Lérida** ☎ (973), [i] c/ Sarriulera, 6, in Viella ☎ 64 01 10, [i] c/ Librería Neus in Lés ☎ 64 82 79. Lérida 167km, Madrid 604km.

The valley is an odd mix of sophisticated ski-resorts where top people, including the Spanish Royal Family, are to be seen regularly on the slopes, and timeless villages and ancient customs, for the whole area was until recently extremely isolated. Unlike most Pyrenean valleys that run N to S, Aran's is E-W. It is surrounded by high peaks like Molieres (3,010m), Les Salenques (2,986m) and Montardo (2,830m) in the S which taper off towards the smaller valleys and meadowlands of the E.

The outside world began to discover Arán after a road was built in 1925 over the 2,072m Bonaigua pass and communications improved significantly after the **Viella tunnel** was built in 1948. The valley was so cut off that it evolved its own dialect, known as ***aranés***, and its own set of administrative laws. In all, there are 39 villages in the valley. Almost without exception the houses have slate roofs and are bunched around the tower of the local Romanesque parish church like chicks around a mother hen.

🔴🔴 **VIELLA** (see separate entry) is the valley's capital and the centre of its communications and *Baqueira-Beret*, which is where King Juan Carlos goes, is its most prestigious ski resort. The several picturesque villages in the area include **SALARDU**, which has a porched plaza and a Romanesque church and tower, **VILAMOS**, which is very high up and offers great **views**, and **BOSSOST**, which has arguably the valley's most attractive church. 🔴
Sports: In winter the whole valley is geared to **skiing** at *Baqueira-Beret* and *Tuca-Betrén* (see 'Viella'), while in summer rock climbing and hill trekking take over. There is also a fair amount of game (wild boar, roebuck and partridge) at the **Alto Pallars-Arán National Reserve**, and the rivers are well stocked with trout —for permits and further information ☎ 24 66 50.

🔴 `VALLE DE BOHI-LA VALL DE BOI (BOHI VALLEY)` **Lérida** ☎ (973), [i] Barruera Town Hall ☎ 69 60 29, **Civil Guard**, Pont de Suert ☎ 69 00 06.

Between Pont de Suert and Caldas de Bohí, this valley is dotted with one **Romanesque church** after another, like **San Clemente** and **Santa María** in 🔴 **TAHULL** (12C), San Juan in Bohí, Santa Eulalia in Erill-la-Vall, San Félix in Barruera and the one at Durro. The valley's attractions are enhanced by the 🔴🔴 proximity of the **Aigües Tortes National Park** (see separate entry) and by the spa at **Caldas de Bohí.**

🔴 🏨 ★★★★ *Balneario El Manantial* (closed: 1/10-23/6), Caldas de Bohí ☎ 69 01 91 🛏 119 🅿 ✦ 🕴 ≈ ≪ 🖼 ♀ $$$ to $$$$. Set in its own extensive grounds and extremely peaceful.

🏨 ★ *Caldas* (closed: 1/10-23/6), Caldas de Bohí ☎ 69 04 49 🛏 125 🅿 ✦ 🕴 ≈ 🖼 🐎 ♀ $$. Quiet and well situated within the same park.

🔴 `VICH-VIC` **Barcelona** ☎ (93), pop. 28,694, [i] c/ Ciutat, 1 ☎ 886 20 91. Barcelona 63km, Gerona 79km, Madrid 637km.

This very old cathedral town was a permanent settlement well before the arrival of the Romans. It is the commercial and cultural capital for a wide area and is famous for its salami-type *salchichón* sausages.

🏨 ★★★★ *Parador de Vic*, 14km out of town in the direction of Roda de Ter ☎ 888 72 11 🛏 36 🕭 🅿 ✦ 🕴 ≈ ≪ ♀ AE, DC, MC, V $$$ to $$$$. Very peaceful with good views of the mountains and of the Sau reservoir.

🏨 ★ *Montcel* (closed: 1/1-31/3), on the outskirts of San Baudilio de Llusanés ☎ 857 80 57 🛏 32 Ⅰ 🅿 ✦ 🕴 ≈ $$. Set in a pine grove.

🍴 *La Taula* (closed: Sunday nights, Mondays and 7/2-26/2), Pl Miguel de Clariana, 4 ☎ 886 32 29 ✸ $$$. Traditional fare imaginatively concocted.

Best buys: You cannot visit Vich and leave without a selection of its salami-style sausages —*llonganisses* and *fuets* are two highly rated varieties. An open air market is held on Tuesdays and Saturdays at the Pl del Mercadal.

Cultural highlights: The **Cathedral** was built in the Neoclassical style between 1781 and 1803 on the site of a Romanesque church building whose crypt and tower remain, but its most interesting feature was added during World War II when the Catalan artist **José María Sert** set to work decorating the cathedral's interior with a series of **murals**. The style that Sert developed during a very successful career involved massive forms and sombre colours and its originality is always very arresting. The **main altarpiece** in the apse —sculpted out of alabaster— dates from the 15C and merits closer attention as does the Gothic **tomb** of Canon Bernardo Despujol. The **Episcopal Museum**, Pl Bisbe Oliba, s/n (open: 10.00-1.00 and 4.00-7.00; holidays: 10.00-1.00; closed: afternoons from 1/11-30/4 ☎ 886 22 14), has a collection of medieval religious panels and sculptures.

Local sights: TONA, 8km along the N-152 to Granollers, has a fierce looking military tower and a couple of peaceful Romanesque churches. Continuing for 17km along the N-141 you reach the pleasant village of **MOYA**, which has a fine parish church and several good secular buildings to match. Eight kilometres from Vich on a local road, the 12C **Monastery of Santa María de l'Estany** has interesting narrative **capitals** in its cloister.

Sports: The Sau reservoir, 20km on the N-141, is well equipped for water sports.

▒▒▒ **VIELLA-VIELHA E MIG-ARAN** Lérida ☎ (973), pop. 3,039, *i* c/ Sarriulera, 6 ☎ 64 01 10, ✚ 64 00 06, **Civil Guard** 64 00 05. Lérida 163km, Madrid 595km.

Standing at the confluence of the Garonne and Negre rivers, Viella is the capital of the **Arán Valley**. In recent years housing developments for skiers and summer vacationers have encircled the old town.

▥ ★★★★ *Montarto* (closed: 1/9-30/11 and 17/4-25/7), 4km from Salardú on the road to the Bonaigua pass, in Baqueira Beret ☎ 64 50 75 ⊨ 166 ♠ 🎤 ⚓ ≪ ⚘ ℚ AE, MC, V $$$ to $$$$. Wonderful mountain views.

▥ ★★★★ *Parador Don Gaspar de Portolá*, in Artíes ☎ 64 08 01 ⊨ 40 **P** ♠ 🎤 ≪ ⚘ AE, DC, MC, V $$$$. Good views.

▥ ★★★★ *Tuca* (closed: 15/10-15/12), in Betrén, 1km from Viella on the Salardú road ☎ 64 07 00 ⊨ 118 **P** ♠ 🎤 ≪ ⚓ AE, DC, MC, V $$$ to $$$$$. Quiet.

▥ ★★★ *Parador del Valle de Arán*, Ctra del Túnel, s/n, 2.5km outside Viella ☎ 64 01 00 ⊨ 135 **P** ♠ 🎤 ♨ ⚓ ≪ ⚘ AE, DC, V $$$$. Peaceful, with panoramic views.

▥ ★★★ *Tuc Blanc* (closed: 30/4-1/7 and 31/8-1/12), at the Baqueira-Beret ski station ☎ 64 51 50 ⊨ 165 **P** 🎤 $$$ to $$$$$.

▥ ★★ *Val de Ruda* (closed: 17/4-1/8 and 1/9-10/12), on the Bonaigua road ☎ 64 58 11 ⊨ 34 **TV** (**P** ≪ AE, DC, EC, V $$$ to $$$$.

▯ *Can Turnay* (closed: 30/4-15/7 and 30/9-1/12), Pl Mayor, s/n, in Escuñau, 2km from Viella ☎ 64 02 92 **P** AE $$ to $$$. Simple regional cooking.

▯ *Casa Irene* (closed: Mondays in winter, 13/10-31/12 and 17/4-30/6), c/ Mayor, 3, in Artíes ☎ 64 09 00 **P** ✳ ♨ ≪ AE, DC, EC, V $$$. Caring cuisine. It also has peaceful **accommodation** $$.

▯ *Chalet Suizo* (closed: Mondays, Tuesdays lunchtime, 1/7-15/7 and 1/10-1/12), c/ Pas d'Arru, 48, in Viella ☎ 64 09 63 **P** AE, DC, MC, V $$$. Swiss food.

¶ *Era Mola* (open: 15/7-30/9 and 1/12-30/4), c/ Marrec, 8, Viella ☎ 64 08 68 $$$. Local cuisine.

¶ *Et Restillé* (closed: Mondays in summer, Sundays in winter, 3/5-15/6 and 12/10-30/10), Pl Carrera, 2, in Garós, 5km from Viella on the Salardú road ☎ 64 15 39 **V** $$$. Rustic decor and local cuisine.

¶ *La Borda Lobato* (closed: 1/5-1/12), at Baqueira-Beret ☎ 64 50 75 **MC, V** $$$. Catalan cooking.

¶ *Patxiku Quintana* (closed: Tuesdays and 1/5-15/12), c/ Remedios, s/n, in Artíes ☎ 64 16 13 **AE, DC, EC, V** $$$ to $$$$. Basque cuisine, particularly fish and seafood.

Cultural highlights: The Church of San Miguel is in a transitional architectural style, with a Romanesque tympanum and a solid 13C Gothic bell tower. Inside is a Romanesque figure of Christ, the *Cristo del Mig Arán*. The Museo del Valle de Arán, Casa Santesmasses (open: 5.00-8.00; Saturdays and holidays: 11.00-1.00 and 5.00-8.00; closed: Tuesdays), has interesting exhibits illustrating the valley's idiosyncracies and customs.

Local sights: The **valley's** *pueblos* are a delight to explore. You can start off on the N-230 to pass through Aubert, **VILAMOS**, Les Bordes, **BOSSOST** and **LES** or on the C-147 for Escuñau and, 9km on, the ruins of a Templar castle in the old village of **ARTIES**.

On the town: *Zacarías*, on the road to Salardú, has very good music. In Baqueira-Beret, the après-ski night life revolves around *Tiffany's* disco.

Sports: The *Baqueira-Beret* ski station, which slopes from 1,520m to 2,470m, is one of the best in Spain, with 12 ski lifts, eight ski tows and one telebaby which give access to 37 runs covering all levels. It has a cross country course, two slalom stadiums, a ski school and full hire facilities ☎ 64 50 25. For lodgings see above. *Tuca-Betrén* station has two ski lifts, two telebabies, 16 runs and hire facilities ☎ 64 08 55. Viella is the starting point for a number of exploratory trips into the Pyrenees. There are horses and four-wheel drive vehicles for hire and the area has a good network of mountain cabins for overnight stays.

VILLAFRANCA DEL PANADES-VILAFRANCA DEL PENEDES | Barcelona

☎ (93), pop. 26,412, [i] c/ Cort, 4 ☎ 892 03 58, ♱ 890 25 25. Barcelona 54km, Tarragona 51km, Madrid 572km.

The **Penedés** region grows some of Spain's better wines and almost all the **cava sparkling wines** that are made by the champagne method.

Best buys: Wine and cava are definite musts. Try to buy from the smaller wineries, particularly in San Sadurní de Noya —*Mestres, Recaredo, Gramona, Llopart, Nadal*...

Cultural highlights: A **Wine Museum** and an Archaeological Museum are housed in the Palace of the Kings of Aragón, Pl Jaume I, 1 (open: 10.00-2.00 and 4.00-7.00; weekends: 10.00-2.00 and 4.00-8.00; closed: Mondays ☎ 890 05 82), one of Villafranca's several fine Gothic buildings. The town also has its fair share of **Modernist buildings**, the locals having grown wealthy on bubbles.

Fiestas: The annual blow-out, the *Festa Major de Sant Felix*, is timed to coincide with the end of the grape harvest between August 29 and September 2. The *castellers* here build terrifying human towers.

Local sights: **OLERDOLA**, 3km, has remains of Iberian and Roman settlements, a medieval castle and a Romanesque church with a Mozarabic chapel. *Celler del Penedès* ☎ 890 20 01 **P** ♣ ❋ **AE, DC, MC, V** $$ to $$$ is a recommended restaurant. **SAN SADURNI DE NOYA**, 13km on the C-243, is the sparkling-wine capital. The *Codorniu winery*, built by the Modernist architect Puig i Cadafalch in the 19C, gives tours around the premises.

EXTREMADURA

With its mighty rivers, its wild and desolate mountain ranges and its rolling plains, Extremadura is one of the most unspoiled regions of Spain. This is another way of saying that the area is backward and primitive and in comparison to many other parts of the peninsula it is. But there is an ancestral dignity to underdevelopment in Spain, and Extremadura is welcoming and genuinely hospitable. The area is indisputably beautiful and there are times of the year, especially spring, when the landscapes are stunning. But there is much more to Extremadura than the sight of a golden eagle soaring in the early morning over hills of ilex and cork trees. The region has a great deal to be proud of. Its history is a very long one and its cultural legacy rivals that of any other part of Spain. The **'cradle of the conquistadors'** is a title that Extremadura carries with dignified aplomb.

Things were happening in Extremadura at the dawn of time as prehistoric tribes made their way west along the banks of the Tagus and Guadiana rivers. Some work has been done on these Paleolithic settlements and it has been more than sufficient to indicate that should there be more research and more excavations, the results would be scientifically spectacular. The Romans, for their part, left all too obvious traces of their passage through Extremadura. They built spectacular bridges, such as the ones at Mérida and Alcántara, over the rivers where their Stone Age forebears grunted and grovelled. **MÉRIDA**, where a magnificent museum of antiquity has recently been opened, is in the world's premier division as far as **Roman remains** are concerned. Caesar's legions were after the silver in the mines they discovered among the ravines of the Sierra de Gata which borders Extremadura in the north. The so-called Roman 'Silver Route', with its fine roads, bridges, aqueducts, temples and cities was the precious metal's artistic spin-off.

The traces of Islam's passage through Extremadura are less obvious but the persistent traveller will discern them soon enough in the popular *pueblo* architecture as he travels south through the daunting Sierra Morena that separates the region from Andalusia. The Christian footprints of those who combated the Moors and pushed them back southwards are, in contrast, very evident. The frontline troops were the **Military Orders** of Santiago and of Alcántara which were modelled on crusader organizations, part monk and part knight, such as the Templars. These two Spanish orders carved up Extremadura between them, speckled it with castles and, when they were not actually fighting, spent their time galloping around with their falcons. They certainly ignored the land where their serfs tilled for a subsistence living.

It was probably the warlike example of the few, and the desperate, grinding poverty of the many that shaped Extremadura's conquistador destiny. Wherever you see a substantial town house in Extremadura —and there are dozens in every one of the region's cities— you can be certain that it was built by a returning buccaneer who had discovered his personal El Dorado through guts, cunning and viciousness after years of sweating through the South American jungles. Men from Extremadura, like **Cortés** and **Pizarro**, are only the tip of the iceberg. **Valdivia, Orellana** and **Núñez de Balboa**, and dozens more, stretched human endurance to new limits as they explored, mapped and charted. In the process, their pillage and plunder created an enduring black legend.

The colossal monastery venerating the **Virgin of Guadalupe** is the acceptable side of the conquistadors' feats of arms. The civilizing cross went with the sword and the Guadalupe cult spread across the Atlantic to set down lasting roots in the New World. It was to Guadalupe that the conquistadors returned to offer thanks and to expiate their excesses. Guadalupe is the spiritual landmark of Extremadura among the scores of monasteries that the region boasts, but there is another that deserves special mention. Yuste lacks Guadalupe's grandeur but it was for a short time home to **Emperor Charles V**, the greatest of the Spanish monarchs, and it was the place where he elected to die when he made the grand gesture of abdicating all his very considerable possessions in favour of his son, Philip II. There is an endearing vanity and vulnerability to Charles' monastic sojourn. He divided his time in Yuste between rehearsing his funeral to make certain he would be remembered in this life and confessing his sins to ensure he would be welcomed into the next one.

After the conquistador excitement, Extremadura did not exactly slide backwards but it did more or less stand still. There is a certain poignancy about latter-day Pizarros who, in the last 30 years have been forced to emigrate to Spain's big cities and even abroad to the factories of northern Europe. The land still does not provide a living for all, but yesterday's Inca treasure house is today a place on the production line of a car plant. The timelessness of Extremadura is very apparent, and not least in the proud and dignified survival of **artisan crafts** such as ceramics, embroidery, filigree metal work, wicker basket weaving and a host of other items.

ALCÁNTARA **Cáceres** ☎ (927), pop. 2,172. Cáceres 63km, Madrid 350km.

The 2C **Roman bridge** over the Tagus river, 194m long and 70m high at its apex, is an astonishing engineering achievement. The Moors were so impressed by it that they immediately named the village *Al Qantara* (The Bridge) when they occupied it. The name was subsequently Christianized and was adopted by the **Military Order of Alcántara** that held jurisdiction over a wide area of northern Extremadura. The knights admired the village's strategic position near the Portuguese frontier and the valuable real estate that the bridge represented. They built an abbey, which still stands, in honour of Saint Benedict within the village's walls in 1218, and used it as their headquarters. **On the town**: Good bars for drinks and *tapas*.

BADAJOZ **Badajoz** ☎ (924), pop. 126,340, [*i*] Pasaje de San Juan, 1 ☎ 22 27 63, ✉ 22 02 04, ✚ Av Pardalera, s/n ☎ 23 50 00, **P** 22 33 66, ✈ 14km out of town on the Ctra Madrid ☎ 25 11 11, 🚂 23 71 70. Portuguese border 7km, Mérida 62km, Cáceres 91km, Seville 218km, Lisbon 240km, Córdoba 278km, Madrid 409km.

History, or rather marauding armies, are not usually kind to busy commercial centres that are close to frontiers and Badajoz is no exception to the rule. Little remains of what was once the capital of a small Moorish kingdom. Reconquering Christians, sallies by the Portuguese, Napoleon's troops, then Wellington's and, finally, Franco's during the Spanish Civil War, successively buffeted the town, plundering it and levelling it almost to the ground time and again. Only the area between the Alcazaba and the Pl de San José, with its labyrinthine alleyways, catches the flavour of the medieval city. Badajoz's most famous son mirrors the town's frequently dismal fortunes. He was **Manuel Godoy** (1767-1851), a junior officer of the palace guard, whose good looks endeared him to the incompetent Charles IV and to his ugly, scheming wife and helped him become Prime Minister of Spain at the age of 25. Godoy was too friendly to Napoleon for the liking of the Spanish patriots and they staged a successful uprising to run him out of Spain.

- ★★★★ *Gran Hotel Zurbarán*, Paseo de Castelar, s/n ☎ 22 37 41 ⋈ 215 ✦ ⚓ ♀ AE, DC, MC, V $$$ to $$$$.
- ★★★ *Lisboa*, Av de Elvas, 13 ☎ 23 82 00 ⋈ 176 V $$.
- ★★★ *Río*, Av Díaz Ambrona, s/n ☎ 23 76 00 ⋈ 90 ♿ P ✦ ⚓ ♀ AE, DC, MC, V $$.
- ⅋ *La Toja* (closed: Sunday evenings), Av Elvas, 21 ☎ 23 74 77 AE, DC, MC, V $$. Galician cooking.
- ⅋ *Los Gabrieles* (closed: Sundays), c/ Vicente Barrantes, 21 ☎ 22 42 75 AE, DC, MC, V $$$. Unfussy, regional cooking.
- ⅋ *Mesón Zacarías* (closed: Sunday evenings), c/ Miguel Saavedra, 9 ☎ 23 68 53 AE, DC, V $$$. A well-established classic.

Cultural highlights: The **Puente de las Palmas**, a 600m-long, granite bridge over the Guadiana river, entering the town from Cáceres, was designed by Juan de Herrera, Philip II's adored architect who built the Escorial and stamped his severe 16C counter-reformation style on Spanish taste for succeeding generations. The twin towers behind the bridge mark the **Puerta de las Palmas**, the fortified gate which was the entrance to the old walled town. The building of the **Cathedral** began in 1232 and it is now just about the only old building in what is the modern part of Badajoz. Its interior shows the transition from Romanesque to Gothic and incorporates many later Renaissance decorative elements. The **choir stalls** deserve a more prolonged examination as do the very fine 17C Flemish tapestries in the sacristy. Badajoz's Fine Arts Museum, the **Museo Provincial de Bellas Artes**, c/ Meléndez Valdés, 32 (open in winter: 10.00-2.00 and 4.00-6.00; summer: 9.30-2.00 and 5.00-7.00) exhibits the work of mostly local painters and sculptors, while finds made during excavations in the area are on show at the **Museo Arqueológico** (Archaeological Museum) (open in winter: 10.00-2.00 and 4.00-6.00; summer: until 7.00 pm; closed: Sunday and holiday afternoons, and Mondays). The museum building was once a mosque.

Local sights: The small town of **OLIVENZA**, 24km from Badajoz, has a very Portuguese air to it, which is not surprising for it was part of Portugal until 1801 when it was finally ceded to Spain. The **Church of Santa María Magdalena** is typical of the 16C late Gothic style in Portugal that came to be known as Manueline after King Manuel. The 13C **castle** has a very sturdy keep which was added in 1448 and the Town Hall has an ornate marble façade that also dates from the 15C. Olivenza's local sweet with the intriguing name of *técula-mécula* has a suitably secret recipe and is sold at *Casa Fuente*, c/ Moreno Romero, s/n.

On the town: The area around the Cathedral called the Campo de San Juan has dozens of *tapa* bars and is very popular in the evenings.

CACERES **Cáceres** ☎ (927), pop. 72,342, [i] Plaza Mayor, s/n ☎ 24 63 47, ✉ Av de Primo de Rivera, 2 ☎ 22 50 71, ☨ 24 78 62, 🚌 Ctra de Mérida, s/n ☎ 24 59 50, 🚂 Av de Alemania, s/n ☎ 24 50 61. Badajoz 91km, Salamanca 210km, Seville 265km, Coimbra 292km, Madrid 307km.

Even in a country like Spain where walled cities, castles, Gothic cathedrals and medieval convents often seem two-a-penny, Cáceres stands out as an exceptional town. Its old quarter is almost perfectly preserved. Two features are immediately striking about this area and they are almost paradoxical. There is its mix of styles which allows the visitor a first-hand appreciation of the development of Gothic tastes into those of the Renaissance. Yet there is also an absolute harmony about the quarter, almost as if each individual building had been erected with the express purpose of forming an aesthetic whole that would amaze people centuries later. In point of fact the succession of palaces that the local nobles built and the convents they endowed were the result of an intense rivalry among them. Cáceres had the medieval distinction of a thriving local nobility on account of the charter it obtained when it was reconquered by the Christians from the Moors in 1212. The charter gave the city freedom from feudal dues and, more importantly, from the omnipresent military orders that had staked out their claims in Extremadura. Civic architecture boomed as a result as each noble tried to outdo his neighbour. The splendid buildings even survived a 1477 royal decree, issued by Queen Isabella, that ordered the destruction of all fortified turrets on private mansions in an attempt to control inter-family fighting. Isabella, who with her husband King Ferdinand formed the unique partnership of the Catholic Monarchs, feared that the quarrelsome nobles were becoming too powerful. Finally, the conquistadors, returning in wealthy triumph, embellished the city still further, pitching it straight into the new styles of the 16C.

- ★★★ *Alcántara*, Av Virgen de Guadalupe, 14 ☎ 22 89 00 ⇌ 67 **AE, DC, MC, V** $$$.
- ★★★ *Extremadura*, Av Virgen de Guadalupe, 5 ☎ 22 16 00 ⇌ 68 ✦ ⚲ **AE, DC, MC, V** $$$.
- ❙❙ *El Figón de Eustaquio*, Pl de San Juan, 12 ☎ 24 81 94 **AE, DC, V** $$$. Always crowded.

Best buys: Cáceres, and Extremadura as a whole, is a good area to buy handicrafts. It is a good idea first to obtain an overview of the area's craft

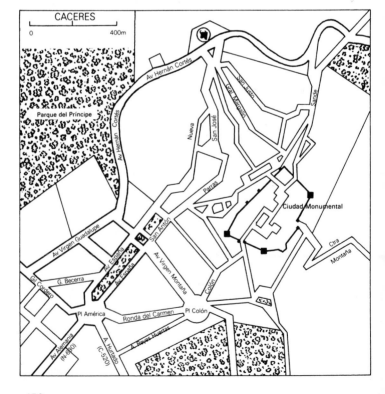

from the region's development agency, *Patronato de Promoción del Turismo y la Artesanía*, Palacio de Carvajal, Pl de Santa María, s/n ☎ 21 77 29. Most of the craft shops, selling ceramics, lace, embroidery, gold and silver filigree ornaments, leatherwork and other souvenirs are in and around the Plaza Mayor. The **Artespaña** store, c/ San Antón, 17, belongs to a prestigious chain of state-owned arts and craft shops and is well worth a browse. The region's cheeses, hams and sausages are excellent —*Mostazo*, c/ San Antón 6, stocks a good range.

Cultural highlights: You must first ensure you are wearing sensible shoes. Then you simply start strolling around **old Cáceres**. If you start with the walls keep in mind that stone has been piled on stone by succeeding civilizations. They were originally Roman, and the first **battlements** were erected in AD 35 when the city was called *Norba Caesarina*. The conquering Almohads renamed the city *Hizn Quazris* and rebuilt the walls. Certain towers along the walls, such as the **Bujaco tower** and the ones called Desmochada and Redonda, are much the same as the Arabs left them. The main part of the fortifications dates from the medieval Christian period. The most evocative points along the walls are the **Estrella archway** and the tower of Los Púlpitos.

Within the walls what you have is a maze of narrow streets that worm their way into plazas flanked by massive buildings. The centre of this medieval labyrinth is the cathedral square or the **Pl de Santa María**. Apart from the Cathedral itself, which is late Gothic and was completed in the 16C, the plaza has a number of palaces that set the tone for the whole medieval quarter. The building known as the **Palacio de los Golfines de Abajo** has a façade that is representative of the austere mix between the Gothic style and the Mudéjar, a style peculiar to Spain and developed by Muslim craftsmen who remained living and working under Christian rule. The other palace owned by this leading Cáceres family, the **Palacio de los Golfines de Arriba** is on higher ground by the walls. This second palace illustrates the shift towards new architectural tastes as it mixes Gothic and Renaissance styles. In the **cathedral**, in addition to a very fine high altarpiece, you will see the tombs of many of the once proud owners of the succession of fine buildings. Such families, the Ovandos, the Ulloas, the Aldanas and the rest, strove to impress each other with their opulence. Those not buried in the cathedral are mostly interred in the very fine **Church of San Mateo** where again the characteristic mix of styles is all too evident. Its main front is Plateresque, its nave Gothic and its curious 18C reredos is emphatically Rococo. The City Museum, the **Museo Provincial** (open: 10.00-2.00 and 5.00-8.00; winter: 10.00-2.00 and 4.00-6.00; closed: Sunday and holiday afternoons), has a good archaeology and ethnography collection. It is housed in yet another palace, the **Casa de las Veletas**, which was built over part of the old Moorish fortress and preserves its original **water cistern**.

Inevitably you walk around the awesome old quarter almost stealthily, speaking in hushed tones. The real heart of the city and the place where it hums is the **Plaza Mayor** which is pleasingly porticoed and irregular in shape. The 19C **Town Hall**, with its ostentatious balcony looking out over the square, serves as a reminder, however, that not every age has the ability to erect magnificent buildings.

Fiestas: Cáceres is one of several Spanish cities —Barcelona is another— that have adopted Saint George as their patron saint. His feast day on April 23 is celebrated in Cáceres with processions, which include one involving mock dragons, street parties, sports events and bullfights during the day, and bonfires at night. On the first Sunday of May there is a very popular *romería* to the shrine of the *Virgen de la Montaña*, outside the town.

Local sights: The 17C **shrine of the Virgen de la Montaña**, 3km E of the town, provides a good **view** of Cáceres and its surrounding plain. The village of **GARROVILLAS**, 36km along the N-630 is an extremely picturesque and authentic *pueblo* with a lovely colonnaded plaza. The church at **ARROYO DE LA LUZ**, 19km W, has an exceptionally fine reredos with **paintings** by Luis Morales, a 17C Spanish artist so admired in his lifetime that he was nicknamed *El Divino*, the Divine One. The village's ceramics can be bought at *V. Collado*, c/ Castañeda, 48.

On the town: The time honoured custom of *tapa* **bar hopping** centres around the Plaza Mayor and the Pl San Jorge; look out for *Manso*, Plaza Mayor, *Dallas*, c/ Obispo Segura Sáez, 9, and *Coimbra*, Av Alemania, 20. *Lennon*, c/ Doctor Fleming, and *New People*, c/ Profesor Hernández Pacheco, 14, are the town's most popular discos.

Sports: Cáceres is well served with sports complexes such as the *Ciudad Deportiva*, Av El Brocense, s/n ☎ 22 00 65, the *Club Deportivo Cacereño*, c/ Sergio Sánchez, 1 ☎ 24 81 98, the *Complejo Deportivo de la Diputación*, on the road to Trujillo, and the *Club de Tenis Cabeza Rubia*, c/ Sierrilla, s/n ☎ 24 12 74, with facilities for football, basketball, tennis and other sports. The hunting, shooting and fishing crowd are in their element in Extremadura and should obtain information about seasons and licences at the *Servicio de Conservación de la Naturaleza, Caza y Pesca* (Nature Conservancy, Hunting and Fishing Service), c/ García Plata de Osma, 1 ☎ 22 76 01 and 22 05 04. The *Aeroclub de Cáceres* flying club ☎ 24 34 31, has facilities for ultralight and gliding enthusiasts.

CORIA **Cáceres** ☎ (927), pop. 10,877, ✚ 50 00 72, **P** 50 00 22. Cáceres 69km, Salamanca 174km, Madrid 321km.

Very much off the beaten track and set in magnificent countryside, Coria is disarmingly unpretentious although it has **Roman walls** that were partially rebuilt in the Middle Ages, an above average cathedral and fine noble houses and minor palaces. The **Cathedral** dates from the 13C and had a lot more money spent on it 200 years later to give it a Renaissance feel and a fine Plateresque portico. The choir stalls, the wrought iron **grilles** and the 18C reredos are interesting. All that remains of the town's 15C castle is a fortified tower and that is impressive enough.

GUADALUPE, MONASTERY OF **Cáceres** ☎ (927), pop. 2,662. Cáceres 129km, Mérida 129km, Madrid 225km.

This is one of the most important Marian shrines in the whole Spanish-speaking world. The conquistadors revered this virgin and built shrines in her honour wherever they went. Columbus went as far as naming one of the islands he discovered after her. Guadalupe's fame and fortune pre-dated the conquest of the New World, however. The virgin's alleged miraculous intervention in a key battle against the Moors caused the 14C monarch **Alfonso XI** to endow the monastery handsomely and succeeding kings and queens followed his example. Such patronage turned Guadalupe into an artistic treasure-house and a community of Franciscan friars, who currently occupy the monastery, are its caretakers.

🏨 ★★★ *Parador Zurbarán*, c/ Marqués de la Romana, 10 ☎ 36 70 75 🛏 40 ✦ ⅏ ≈ « ୯ AE, DC, MC, V $$$ to $$$$. Set in a 16C hospital.

🏨 ★★ *Hospedería del Monasterio* (closed: 14/1-14/2), Pl Juan Carlos I, s/n ☎ 36 70 00 🛏 40 ✦ ⅏ MC, V $$. The monastery's guest house also has a restaurant.

🍽 *Mesón El Cordero* (closed: Mondays and February), c/ Convento, 11 ☎ 36 71 31 $$$. Home cooking.

Best buys: Traditional hand-made copper items like jars, boxes and jugs that are hard to find elsewhere in Spain are sold at ***Juan Poderoso***, Pl Mayor, 41 and c/ Convento, 1. Sticky local sweets called *muégados*, concocted from honey and almonds are sold at *Las Altamiras*, c/ Convento, s/n.

Cultural highlights: The **monastery** stands above the town's picturesque plaza and its general defensive and fortified air reflects the epoch of see-saw struggles between Christians and Muslims that characterized the period during which it was founded. The basic structure is Mudéjar, but successive extensions and improvements added Gothic, Renaissance and Baroque elements.

Built in the 14C and substantially altered later, the **church's** artistic focal points include the 16C Classical **reredos** created by Giraldo de Merlo with the help of one of El Greco's sons, the splendid 16C wrought iron **grille** forged by Fray Francisco de Salamanca and Juan de Avila, and the ornate choir stalls in the Churrigueresque style. The centre of attention is, of course, the 18C **chamber** which houses the Guadalupe Virgin's statue. Centuries of devotion have made this virgin one of the most richly endowed in the world. Her shrine is a staggering array of exotic woods, marble, gilded stucco and paintings by Luca Giordano. The statue itself seems mysterious, blackened and tiny. You can reflect for a long time before the Virgin of Guadalupe, pondering on how it must have projected some electric force that convinced men of her protection and propelled them into the unknown New World. The **artistic wealth** that surrounds the virgin spills out of her chamber and invades the whole monastery. The Hieronymite order, which was the first one to occupy Guadalupe, commissioned a succession of **canvases** from **Zurbarán** and, apart from the Prado Museum in Madrid, it is in this monastery that you gain the best insight into this strangely powerful and mystical Spanish painter who was so representative of his age. The **sacristy**, with its Zurbaráns and its other canvases by Luis Morales, José de Ribera and Juan Carreño de Miranda, will delight everyone who is fascinated by the Baroque age.

There is much to see in the monastery. The **Chapter House**, with yet more Zurbaráns and a collection of rare books, is a room that any museum in the world would be proud to possess. The 15C **cloister** is a very good example of Mudéjar tastes and ornamentation and there is a collection of superb **church vestments** dating from the 16C in what used to be the monastery's refectory. The guest house, which leads off from a Gothic cloister that was added later, is in a building that used to be a pharmacy run by the monks to supply four hospitals dependent on the monastery.

Fiestas: The Virgin of Guadalupe's day is September 8; October 12, Columbus Day, known in Spain as the *Fiesta Nacional*, is a second excuse to set off rockets and celebrate.

Local sights: The 40km drive to the mountain pass of San Vicente takes you through the mountainous area called Las Villuercas and across the valley of the Guadarranque. The road is not the best in Spain but the **views**, particularly when you catch sight of the plain of Castile, are among the country's finest.

HERVAS **Cáceres** ☎ (927), pop. 3,646. Cáceres 127km, Madrid 230km.

Standing in the midst of particularly beautiful countryside, this is a village that echoes the lament for Sepharad, the Hebrew name for Spain, and the anguish of the expulsion of the Jews from Spain in 1492. Its perfectly preserved medieval atmosphere speaks of the industrious and tightly-knit **Sephardic** community that once was before intolerance triggered off the Diaspora.

HURDES, LAS **Cáceres** ☎ (927). Access from Plasencia along the C-512, reached by local roads.

The area known as Las Hurdes in the N of Cáceres province is synonymous in Spanish with extreme underdevelopment and poverty. In the 1930s Luis Buñuel made a very strong protest film called *Tierra sin Pan* (*Land without Bread*) to shock the authorities into doing something for the area. Years earlier, King Alfonso XIII had made a celebrated tour of Las Hurdes on horseback to see conditions for himself. The lot of the region's sparse inhabitants has improved since, but the legend has remained. A drive through the area will take you through a peasant environment that has almost completely disappeared elsewhere in Spain. In its way this rocky, wild part of the province is intensely moving. The bar *La Chata* in Nuñomoral is a good place to stop for a glass of wine and a *tapa* and hearty stews are served at the *Mesón del Abuelo* in the charmingly named village of Caminomorisco, the Path of the Converted Muslims.

JEREZ DE LOS CABALLEROS **Badajoz** ☎ (924), pop. 9,081. Badajoz 72km, Madrid 444km.

Hidden away amid the rolling Sierra Morena, this is an old market town that has the distinction of being the birthplace of **Vasco Núñez de Balboa**, the first conquistador to set eyes on the Pacific Ocean. Its three proud Baroque **church towers** make a pleasing sight as you approach. The timeless air to Jerez de los Caballeros is compounded by the 16C houses that stand in its Plaza Mayor.

◐ MERIDA **Badajoz** ☎ (924), pop. 52,416, [i] c/ Puente, 9 ☎ 30 21 61 and 31 53 53, ✉ 31 24 58, ✚ 31 44 13, **P** 30 10 30, 🚗 31 39 55, 🚌 31 20 05. Badajoz 63km, Cáceres 71km, Seville 194km, Madrid 347km.

The town's name is a vulgarization of *Emerita Augusta* and refers to the fact that it once served as a retreat for Roman legionnaires retired from the service of Emperor Caesar Augustus. The emperor founded the settlement here in 25 BC for his weary and worthy soldiers, and gradually this old men's camp grew into a big city, the capital of the Roman province of Lusitania that stretched right across to what is modern day Portugal. Mérida owed its importance to its strategic position at the point where the Roman roads from Seville to Salamanca and from Toledo to Lisbon crossed each other. The all-important 'Silver Route' also passed through the city which must have been more of a thoroughfare in the 1C than it is today. Subsequently, Barbarian and then Muslim invasions reduced the city to rubble. Modern man finally did his bit to disfigure the city. Fortunately what lay outside Mérida, a sort of giant Roman amusement park, was left largely untouched and today it constitutes a staggering token of the genius and grandeur of the Roman conquerors of Spain.

🏨 ★★★★ *Las Lomas*, Ctra de Madrid, km340 ☎ 31 10 11 🛏 134 ふ ♣ ♒ 🐎 🖢, DC, V $$$$.

◐ 🏨 ★★★★ *Parador Vía de la Plata*, Pl de la Constitución, 3 ☎ 31 38 00 🛏 45 ♣ AE, DC, MC, V $$$$$. Set in an old convent. Restaurant $$$.

🏨 ★★★ *Emperatriz*, Pl de España, 19 ☎ 31 31 11 🛏 41 ♣ AE, V $$ to $$$.

🏨 ★★ *Nova Roma*, c/ Suárez Somonte, 42 ☎ 31 12 01 🛏 28 **P** V $$$.

🍴 *Bocao*, c/ Atarazanas, 4 ☎ 30 13 02 ✳ AE, DC, V $$$.

🍴 *Nicolás* (closed: Sunday nights), c/ Félix Valverde Lillo, 13 ☎ 31 96 10 ♣ ✳ AE, DC, V $$$.

Best buys: Santa Eulalia must be one of the very few religious martyrs in the world to have **sweets** named after her. They are manufactured and sold at

Confitería Gutiérrez, c/ Santa Eulalia, 70. *Zancada*, c/ Santa Eulalia, 38, sells local wines.

Cultural highlights: Approaching Mérida from Badajoz, the antique Roman scene is perfectly set by the awesome **1C BC bridge** over the Guadiana with its 60 massive granite arches. It is 792m long. Entering Mérida from Cáceres along the N-630 you will first see the remains of an aqueduct known as the **Acueducto de los Milagros**. The remains of what must have been the home of a very wealthy patrician are near the bullring. It is called the **Casa de Mithraeo** and extremely good **mosaics** have survived. Such landmarks are, however, mere appetizers to Mérida's Roman feast.

The best Roman remains in all Spain stand outside the city by a small hill in a complex known as the **Parque Arqueológico**. One imagines that the collection of buildings here represented a sort of Disneyland two millennia ago. This is where the Romans went to relax and be entertained. The **theatre**, for example, which was donated to the city by the Emperor Agrippa in 24 BC, was a perfect place to see plays. The stage is beautifully decorated with marble and the acoustics are quite superb. Every one of the 6,000 spectators who fit into the semicircular theatre could hear everything that was going on and they still can, for productions continue to be staged there. Modern-day actors hardly have to alter the pitch of their delivery when they perform in this classical setting. The **amphitheatre** nearby, built in 8 BC and with a capacity of 14,000, was the setting for prize fights between gladiators and wild animals. An intricate system of water channels could flood the amphitheatre if required so that naval battles could be staged. Just behind this building are the remains of a **Roman house** where excellent mural paintings and **mosaic**

pavements have been preserved. There were obviously several other such buildings around the theatres and stadiums, that served as taverns and guest houses for visitors to the games, for Mérida was certainly a top rate leisure and tourism resort. The main landmark of the whole complex must have been the **Trajan Triumphal Arch** which was clearly huge. What remains is a 15m-high minor part of it. The most popular of its facilities was undoubtedly the **circus** which held as many as 30,000 chariot racing fans. The entrance is at the end of c/ José Ramón Mélida ☎ 31 25 30. There is a recently inaugurated museum, the **Museo Nacional de Arte Romano** (open: 10.00-2.00 and 4.00-6.00; closed: Sunday and holiday afternoons, and Mondays), set in a very successfuly designed modern building at the exit to the complex. The exhibits, as one might expect, are very impressive.

The richness of the Roman legacy in Mérida is probably enough for most visitors. Culture and art enthusiasts should, however, pay a visit to the 11C Moorish **Alcazaba** or castle which was built on the banks of the Guadiana river to defend the all-important bridge. Much of the material used in the castle's construction came from Roman and Visigothic buildings that were destroyed during the Muslim occupation of the city. The castle's *aljibe*, or **water cistern**, is a good example of the Moorish cult of and ingenuity with water. The 13C Church of Santa Eulalia is a Romanesque building that also made use of Roman and Visigothic stone and rubble.

Fiestas and festivals: The city's annual blowout takes place in the first week of September. More merrymaking occurs during a **Gypsy Festival** that is held in the second week of October. A **Classical Theatre Festival** holds the stage of the Roman theatre during June, July and August ☎ 31 25 30.

Local sights: 5km out of town, taking the Cáceres exit and then the C-537, there is a pleasant reservoir, named after Persephone, the Embalse de Proserpina, which, suitably, is at its best in springtime. In Roman times its waters supplied Mérida via the Milagros aqueduct. The Cornalvo reservoir is less well known and is beautifully situated among cork trees. You reach it by taking the N-V in the direction of Madrid, turning off to the left 9km out of Mérida and continuing for another 6km along a local road.

PLASENCIA **Cáceres** ☎ (927), pop. 34,466, *i* c/ Trujillo, 17 ☎ 41 77 66, ✉ 41 23 77, ✠ 41 26 79, P 41 00 33, ⚕ 41 00 49. Cáceres 82km, Salamanca 132km, Madrid 257km.

This is an undeservedly forgotten town for it has its full share of architectural and artistic treasures. It also happens to be extremely well situated on the banks of the Jerte river just before the land starts climbing rapidly up to the Gredos sierra. Being off the beaten track, of course, has its compensations. Plasencia lacks pretension and tourist gimmicks and is a wholesomely genuine old town. It enjoyed a period of prosperity in the Middle Ages, during the boom years of the Castilian wool trade, when it was much favoured by shepherds who brought their flocks down to Plasencia from Gredos in winter. Since then it has been declining gracefully and has consequently never got round to completing its Gothic 'New' Cathedral.

🏨 ★★★ *Alfonso VIII*, c/ Alfonso VIII, 32 ☎ 41 02 50 🛏 57 & P AE, V $$$. The **restaurant** serves Extremaduran regional food $$$.

Cultural highlights: As in most towns, the cathedral square is in the middle of the **old quarter** and serves as the centre of the town's life. Plasencia, like Salamanca, is fortunate in being a two **cathedral** city. But unlike Salamanca, where one was built alongside the other, Plasencia's new cathedral was built as the old one was being knocked down. What occurred was that since the substitute cathedral was never finished, Plasencia ended up having both, back to back and communicating from within. This two for the price of one bonus means that you can admire a very fine Romanesque main façade and also a superb Gothic one in the Plateresque style. The combination of the two looks muddling until you get the hang of what was going on and then it makes for a delightful course in the development of architecture. The old cathedral has a particularly good 14C **cloister** and a worthy **Chapter House**. But Plasencia, in its heyday, thought this was not sufficiently impressive given its then booming status and ordered the new cathderal to be built midway through the 15C. It was a time of intense rivalry between cathedral cities and Plasencia commissioned the best architects, artists and craftsmen of the day to start work. Key people such as Diego de Siloé, Juan de Alava and Alonso Covarrubias, a trio that stamped its mark of excellence on religious and civic buildings all over central Spain, worked on the Plasencia project to create soaring Gothic vaults and to carve the intensely ornate stone filigree ornamentation that is so characteristic of the Plateresque style. Before the money finally ran out there was just enough to have Gregorio Fernández, the Baroque master of writhing realism, carve the **main altarpiece**.

The **Dean's House** next to the cathedral was built in the 16C and has an exceptional corner **balcony** that demonstrates how anxious the city's authorities were to show off taste and opulence at that time. The **Palacio de Mirabel** is in the Renaissance style and has a large patio with two tiers of arches. At the other end of the scale there are several magical old streets (c/ **Sancho Polo, Plaza Mayor**) with humble whitewashed houses near the city's walls.

Local sights: Excursions eastwards into the valleys of the Gredos sierra are made even more memorable from February onwards by the arrival of thousands of **storks** who very sensibly reckon that this particular corner of Spain is especially gratifying. The best trips are along the Tietar valley which is the area known as **La Vera** (see 'Vera, La') and along the **Valle del Jerte**, the Jerte river valley which runs along the N flank of the Gredos sierra. This route, taking the N-110 towards Avila, is spectacular at the start of spring when the cherry trees are in blossom. For eating, try *Mesón Rosario y Tomás*, 14km out of Plasencia.

On the town: Drinks and *tapas* are served at *Gaby*, c/ Pedro Isidro and *Media Luna*, c/ de las Moreras. Disco fans should head for *Psiquis*, c/ Vidrieros, 10 and *Carol's*, Plazuela Leal.

TRUJILLO **Cáceres** ☎ (927), pop. 9,476, *i* Plaza Mayor, 18 ☎ 32 06 53, ✠ 32 11 77, **P** 32 10 50. Cáceres 47km, Mérida 89km, Madrid 254km.

If Extremadura was the nursery of the **conquistadors**, Trujillo was their actual cradle. The town must have been virtually empty of able-bodied men in the mid-16C for as many as 600 *Trujillanos* were hard at work staking their claims to the New World. Trujillo's most famous son is **Francisco Pizarro** whose massive bronze statue is the centrepiece of the town's main square. With 14 men he crossed the Andes and conquered the Inca empire of Peru. Pizarro never returned (rival conquerors murdered him in Lima) but others did and by the 17C the once lowly Trujillo could boast as many solid town houses with coats of arms adorning their façades as any aristocratic city in Spain. Trujillo as a whole, but particularly the Plaza Mayor, has a flamboyant conquistador feel to it. The square, built later than the far more austere one in Cáceres, is positively boastful in its ornamentation.

Like other towns in Extremadura, Trujillo went into a genteel decline once the New World fizz ebbed away. In the last 30 years, however, it has managed to attract a select and cultured group of Spaniards and foreigners who have acquired properties in the town and done much to restore and preserve the decaying palaces and convents. The rescue of Trujillo has been carried out in an exemplary manner for though the town is fast becoming an architectural showcase it is also developing as a busy and lively regional centre.

🏨 ★★★★ *Parador de Trujillo*, Pl de Santa Clara ☎ 32 13 50 🛏 46 ✦ ⚓ ⚒ AE, DC, MC, V $$$$. Set in an old convent with a very fine 16C Renaissance cloister. The **restaurant** serves imaginative regional food.

🏨 ★★★ *Las Cigüeñas*, Ctra Madrid-Lisboa, km253 ☎ 32 12 50 🛏 78 ✦ ≪ AE, DC, V $$.

🏨 ★ *Hostal Pizarro*, Plaza Mayor, s/n ☎ 32 02 55 🛏 5 ✕ AE, V $$. Unfussy, hearty Extremaduran cooking.

Best buys: *Chanquet*, c/ San Francisco, sells filigree work from local workshops and *Maribel Vallar*, c/ Paredones de Santa Clara, stocks fabrics woven on traditional looms. There is also a considerable amount of local ceramic ware available in the town. Extremely good cured hams (the variety called *pata negra* is the best) are sold at *Pepe Mateos Correa*, c/ Sillería, and the cakes made by the nuns of the *Convento de Santa Clara*, Plazuela de Santa Clara, are deservedly popular.

Cultural highlights: The **Plaza Mayor** takes a bit of getting used to. One building after another distracts the eye and awakens the curiosity. Built up between the late 15C and the late 17C, there is a mix here of Plateresque façades and Renaissance galleries, hints of sober Mudéjar and examples of transitional Gothic. The inventiveness and flair of what was an exhilaratingly self-confident epoch are all too evident. Trujillo's main square is in sharp contrast to the uniformity of the Plaza Mayor of Salamanca or Madrid. Here it was a case of outdoing your neighbour.

As in Spain's other historic towns, the best idea is to put on comfortable walking shoes and stroll around the streets, dropping in to the nearest bar for a fortifying *tapa* and glass of wine when the spirits start to flag. In Trujillo's case you should head to the top of the town, by the **castle**, get a good view from the ramparts and then saunter downwards towards the Plaza Mayor at your leisure. You are unlikely to encounter anything built after the late 17C. Interesting buildings include the Plateresque **Palacio del Marqués de la Conquista**, the Gothic and Renaissance **Church of San Martín**, the **Old Town Hall**, the **Palacio de los Vargas Carvajal**, the Gothic **Palacio del Marqués de Piedras Albas**, the **House of Chains** and the Mudéjar **Pin Tower**. The 16C **Palacio de Orellana Pizarro**, the Gothic **Church of Santa María** and the **Church of Santiago**, with its Romanesque bell tower, are also noteworthy.

Fiestas: Easter Sunday is celebrated in style but the big event is the *fiesta* of the Virgin of Victory, celebrated with street parties, parades, bullfights and the rest, which takes place in September.

On the town: The best local discos are *Royal*, c/ Francisco Pizarro and, 1km away in La Huerta de las Animas, *Viñero*.

VERA, LA **Cáceres** ☎ (927). Access from Plasencia or from Arenas de San Pedro along the C-501.

Vera means a river bank and the river in question is the gurgling Tiétar that forms a bucolic valley along the southern flanks of the mighty Gredos sierra. Popularly known as the Andalusia of Castile because its microclimate recalls that of southern Spain and enables the cultivation of crops such as tobacco, la Vera starts 30km out of Plasencia and runs from Madrigal de la Vera to the village of Jaraiz. The 20-odd river bank villages are on the whole delightfully unspoilt and preserve characteristic elements of the area's popular architecture such as porticoed plazas and carved wooden balconies.

VILLANUEVA DE LA VERA and **VALVERDE DE LA VERA**, with their little cobbled streets and minuscule house patios adorned with geranium pots and strings of red peppers are particularly picturesque. **Fiestas:** Villanueva maintains old customs which include a religious procession on Maundy Thursday during which hooded penitents, known as ***empalaos***, have crosses strapped to their backs, and one on Shrove Tuesday called ***pero-palo***, in which a straw figure with a wooden head is carried around the village just before the start of Carnival, only to be decapitated and beaten to destruction on the last day of the *fiesta*.

JARANDILLA has a restored, picture postcard, 15C castle, the **Castillo de los Condes de Oropesa**, which is now a parador —★★★ *Parador Carlos V*, Ctra Plasencia, s/n ☎ 56 01 17 ⛺ 53 ✷ ⅗ ⚲ ⚞ ♋ AE, DC, MC, V $$$$. Emperor Charles V stayed here in 1556 while his retirement home was being prepared in the nearby monastery of Yuste. *Cueva de Puta Parió* and *Jardinera*, in the village, serve good regional *tapas*.

Nine kilometres from Jarandilla is the picturesque town of **CUACOS** where John of Austria, son of Charles V, spent his childhood. A little turn-off 2km away leads to the unpretentious **Monastery of Yuste** where Charles V's quarters are open to the public. It is a very atmospheric place.

ZAFRA Badajoz ☎ (924), pop. 13,511, *i* Pl de España ☎ 55 10 36, ✚ 55 02 97, **P** 55 07 93, ⛟ 55 02 15. Badajoz 76km, Mérida 58km, Seville 147km, Madrid 401km.

Zafra is a prosperous, solid old town that is the commercial centre of a fertile area called Tierra de Barros. In September it hosts an important regional cattle fair. The town owes its fortified look to the Military Orders of Alcántara and Santiago, which at different times had feudal jurisdiction over it, and its artistic legacy to the 15C Duke of Feria who was as wealthy as he was cultured.

🏨 ★★★ *Huerta Honda*, c/ López Asme, s/n ☎ 55 08 00 ⛺ 46 ⅖ **P** ✷ ⚲
    🖥 DC, MC, V $$$ to $$$$. An Andalusian-style building with an interesting restaurant.

🏨 ★★★ *Parador Hernán Cortés*, Pl Corazón de María ☎ 55 02 00 ⛺ 28
    ✷ ⅗ ⚲ AE, DC, MC, V $$$ to $$$$. Set in an elegant 15C castle.

Best buys: Tierra de Barros has a long-standing **ceramics** tradition and there are more than 40 potters in the village of **Salvatierra de los Barros**. A good selection is available in Zafra at *Cerámica Extremeña*, Pl Corazón de María.
Cultural highlights: The 15C **Castle of the Dukes of Feria**, now a parador named after the conquistador of México, Hernán Cortés, who was once the duke's house guest, looks intimidating because it has no fewer than nine fortified towers and inviting because it has an admirable Renaissance **patio** designed by Juan de Herrera. The 16C **Collegiate Church of la Candelaria** was well endowed: it has **altarpieces** by Zurbarán and Churriguera. The town's chief benefactor, Lorenzo Suárez de Figueroa, the Duke of Feria, is buried in the Convent of Santa Clara. For more popular architecture, see the appealing little 16C square called **La Plaza Chica** and a neighbouring larger one, built in the 18C, which is called **La Plaza Mayor**. Both are porticoed and were used in times gone by for fairs and bullfights.
Local sights: LLERENA, 42km SE on the N-342, was famed in the Middle Ages for being the seat of the Grand Masters of the Military Order of Santiago and in the 16C for being the home of the even more powerful Holy Inquisition. Its **Plaza Mayor** is pretty and its Gothic church, the Iglesia de la Granada, has an 18C Baroque tower built on to it. Like Zafra and scores of other towns in Spain, Llerena also has a Santa Clara convent and in this particular one the nuns make and sell delicious almond cakes.

GALICIA

Tucked away in the NW corner of Spain, Galicia is a self-contained unit. Its wet climate and its exuberantly green vegetation remind visitors of the west coast of Ireland. A closer acquaintance reveals common roots, for Galicia is first and foremost a **Celtic land**, misty, legend-packed, redolent with ancient myths and echoing with the sound of primitive bagpipes. Like Ireland, Galicia is also a 'goodbye land', many of whose inhabitants have been forced by local hardships to make a living far from home, in this case, more often than not, in South America. It is a sentimental country whose people speak the gentle-sounding Galician language —*gallego*— and whose writers and musicians are imbued with a sense of nostalgia. Its focal point is the magical city of **Santiago de Compostela**, site of the shrine of Saint James the Apostle and one of the holy cities of medieval Christendom. In the Middle Ages, pilgrims travelled to Santiago as they did to Rome and Jerusalem. The **Way of Saint James** was a route trod by hundreds of thousands every year and one is tempted to think that they, like today's visitors, were also refreshed after their arduous journey by the natural beauty of Galicia, by its artistic treasures and by its unassuming hospitality.

Galicia is divided into four provinces: Lugo and La Coruña occupy the northern seaboard, Pontevedra has the western coast while Orense is a stock-raising and agricultural inland province. The coastline is dramatically indented by long fjord-like estuaries called *rías*: the Rías Altas, the Upper Estuaries, stretch into the northern coastline of Lugo and La Coruña while the Rías Bajas, the Lower Estuaries, form long spindly inlets that fracture the Pontevedra shore. Inland Galicia is a succession of valleys and forest-covered hills connected by usually tortuous, winding roads. Its countryside is unspoiled, a land of homestead farming dotted with rustic villages and hamlets, noble mansions, called *pazos*, and parish churches and monasteries that bear the stamp of the **Romanesque** age.

The Romans established themselves here forming the province of *Gallaecia* which covered part of northern Portugal (the capital was the Portuguese town of Braga) and included what is the modern day Spanish region of Asturias. The Muslim invaders never set down strong roots in this area and instead of the see-saw struggle for reconquest between Christians and Moors which engulfed medieval Spain, Galicia during that period experienced a series of peasant revolts which pitched small farmers and landless labourers against feudal barons and powerful ecclesiastics. The Way of Saint James brought wealth to the region, particularly to the Archbishopric of Santiago, and it prompted the creation of military orders such as the **Knights of Santiago**, originally created to protect pilgrims along the route, which developed into powerful institutions. The opening up of the New World in the 16C brought new opportunities to Galicia, traditionally a land of skilled and courageous seamen, and the region's close links with Latin America persist to this day.

A world unto itself, for communications with the rest of Spain and within Galicia itself have always been difficult, the land has developed an ethnic culture of its own that is marked by a rich **folk dancing** and **musical tradition** and by a set of ancient beliefs and superstitions. In Galicia **witch-lore**, the presence of spirits and of the broomstick riding ladies that the Galicians call *meigas* lies close to the surface. ***Romerías*** to local shrines, events which are a mix of a pilgrimage, picnic and open air *fiesta* to the sound of bagpipes, are an integral part of village life. Strong cultural roots tend to be complemented by well-established **arts and crafts** industries and by specific culinary traditions and Galicia is no exception to these norms. Beaten copper, filigree work and ceramics will gladden the heart of the souvenir hunter and the region's rich stews, hand-made cheeses, superlative **fish and seafood** and fresh, slightly acidic white **wines** —the famous Ribeiro and Albariño— will intrigue and satisfy the most professional of gourmets.

BAYONA-BAIONA **Pontevedra** ☎ (986), pop. 10,066, 🚌 ALSA ☎ 35 53 30. Vigo 21km, Pontevedra 55km, Madrid 688km.

Bayona ranks as one of the most historic ports in Europe: Columbus' galleon *La Pinta* returned here in 1493 to tell the Old World that a new one had been discovered. A century later hit and run attacks by Sir Francis Drake and other English sea dogs were beaten back from the present day parador, the **Castle of Monterreal**. Situated at the entrance to the beautiful **Ría de Vigo** opposite the Islas Cíes nature reserve, this one-time strategic **port** is now a lively summer resort.

🏨 **★★★★ *Parador Conde de Gondomar***, in Monterreal castle ☎ 35 50 00 🛏 128 ♦ 👄 🏊 ≈ ≪ 🎾 ♉ AE, DC, EC, MC, V $$$$ to $$$$$. The hotel building reproduces a typical Galician *pazo* within the medieval walls. Very quiet and scenically located.

🏨 **★★ *Tres Carabelas***, c/ Ventura Misa, 61 ☎ 35 51 33 and 35 54 41 🛏 10 ⑁ TV ♉ V $$. In a pleasant Galician *pazo*.

🍴 ***O Moscón***, c/ Alférez Barreiro, 2 ☎ 35 50 08 AE, DC, EC, V $$ to $$$. Grilled fish and seafood.

Beaches: There are quiet stretches of sand between Ladeira and Riveira beaches.

Cultural highlights: Bayona's top building is its 12-13C collegiate church which mixes the Romanesque and the Gothic styles. The Town Hall is housed in an 18C *pazo* and there are several substantial residences of that period with the attractive glassed-in balconies so typical of Galicia. You can take an extremely agreeable and bracing **walk along the castle's battlements** overlooking the sea and there is a very fine view of the *ría* and the Islas Cíes from the vast religious monument, La Virgen de la Roca, 1km out of town.

Fiestas: On the second Sunday in August, a folk festival includes a ritual sword dance called the ***Danza de las Espadas***. In the Bayona-Oya area wild horse round-ups called *rapa das bestas* or ***curros*** (see 'Fiestas') are held on the second Sunday in May and on the first and second Sundays in June.

Local sights: The C-550 **coastal route** to the small fishing village of **LA GUARDIA** (see 'Tuy'), 30km, is very picturesque and from it you are likely to catch sight of the **wild horses** that are rounded up and branded in the *rapa das bestas* festivities. Just over half way, **OYA**, 19km, boasts a 13C Cistercian monastery, Santa María la Real, which had a fine Baroque façade added to it.

On the town: *El Mosquito*, c/ Ventura Misa, 32, and *O Pote*, c/ A. Barreiro, 17, are popular *tapa* bars.

Sports: The local yacht club, the ***Monte Real Club Internacional de Yates de Bayona*** ☎ 35 52 34, is reputed to be the best equipped in Galicia.

BETANZOS **La Coruña** ☎ (981), pop. 11,745, ✉ Pl Alfonso IX, 30 ☎ 77 18 88, ✚ 70 15 15, **P** 77 06 02. La Coruña 23km, El Ferrol 38km, Santiago de Compostela 64km, Madrid 578km.

Situated at the opening of the *ría* that bears its name and at the estuary of two rivers, Betanzos is an old historic town, the seat, for a period, of the ancient kings of Galicia and an important stopping place on the **Way of Saint James** to Compostela. Always a prosperous town, the medieval guilds played a large part in its development.

⫟ *Edreira* (open: lunch only; closed: Mondays and 10/9-30/9), c/ Linares Rivas, 8 ☎ 77 08 03 **P** $$$. A very good *tortilla* (potato omelette) features on its home cooking menu.

Best buys: Antiques and ceramics, local cheeses and wines can be bought at the town's market, the ***Feria de Betanzos***, which takes place on the 1 and 15 of every month. Galician *gaitas*, or bagpipes, are sold at c/ Cerca.

Cultural highlights: The Town Hall is a fine building by Ventura Rodríguez, one of the most prolific architects of 18C Spain, and the author of several Madrid landmarks. The **Church of Santiago** was built by the tailors' guild and, over its W door it has a fine image of Saint James in his Moor-slaying guise of *Santiago Matamoros*. The fishermen's guild funded the **Church of Santa María del Azogue** which has an interesting main façade dominated by a rose window and contains a fine 15C Flemish main altarpiece. The Gothic **Church of San Francisco**, 14C, houses the **tomb of Fernán Pérez de Andrade**, the head of one of the most powerful feudal families in medieval Galicia. Some towers and gateways to the town are all that remain of the walls that the Catholic Monarchs ordered built. The local folk museum, the Museo de las Mariñas, tracing the area's traditions and customs, is in the 16C Convent of Santo Domingo, c/ Linares Rivas, 1 (open: 5.00-8.00). Just outside the town there are the ruins of an oriental garden, a very romantic folly, that was built at the end of last century by a local *indiano*, which is the term applied to those who returned enriched from Latin America. The abandoned gardens are called the **Finca El Pasatiempo**.

Fiestas: The feastdays of San Roque and of Santa María del Azogue, August 14 and 25, are celebrated by ***romerías*** which take the form of rides up and down the Mandeo river in elaborately decorated boats.

Local sights: The agreeable little town of **PUENTEDEUME** is also on the Ría de Betanzos, to the N, and the *Brasilia* restaurant, on the N-VI ☎ 43 02 49, is one of its attractions. There are at least three interesting monasteries in the vicinity of Betanzos. Driving inland on the C-640, through the Sierra de Moscoso, you reach the 12C **Monasterio de Monfero**, 21km, with a beautiful Baroque **façade**, to which Juan de Herrera, the builder of the Escorial palace and monastery for Philip II, added a beautiful **cloister**. Also in the Eume river valley and 14km E, the **Monasterio de Caaveiro** is located in particularly **beautiful countryside** and has a splendid 12C Romanesque church. Taking the C-540 from Betanzos, you reach the welcoming community of monks in the **Monasterio de Sobrado de los Monjes**, founded in the 10C, though some of the present buildings date from as late as the 18C.

On the town: The Pl Hermanos García Naveira is a popular *tapa* bar area.

Sports: Salmon fishing in the Mandeo river is popular.

COSTA DE LA MUERTE (COAST OF DEATH) La Coruña ☎ (981). Access from La Coruña on the C-552 and then local roads; from Santiago de Compostela, on the C-545.

This lugubrious stretch of shoreline —the Coast of Death— has struck fear into the hearts of seamen down the ages, and still does. Its rocks and coves are littered with wrecks and in the village cemeteries there are tombstones to sailors of every nationality. The lashing ocean builds up to a crescendo as the coast rounds **Cape Finisterre** which, as its Latin name indicates, was the end of the world known to Antiquity. The Roman legions were left quaking at the sight, on a clear day, of the sun falling in the evening like a red fireball into a sea they dared not explore. The daunting Cape Finisterre, with its all-important lighthouse, is the furthest point in a 140km, three and a bit hours' round trip along the Costa de la Muerte that starts in La Coruña.

From La Coruña the coastal route starts properly at the picturesque fishing village of **MALPICA** and continues to Corme on the Roncudo promontory and on to Lage on the *ría* of the River Allones. Near here is the famous **dolmen of Dombate**. Passing over cliffs and alongside beaches, you reach the headland of Cabo Villano and, rounding it, the whitewashed village of **CAMARIÑAS** on the *ría* of the same name. The village women here are expert **lacemakers** (see 'Design') and their work can be bought at *Dolores Albores*, c/ Del Medio, 11. From here, continue to the lively port of **MUGIA** and skirt the *ría* southwards, leaving Cape Touriñana on your right, as far as **CORCUBION**. This village has a **Romanesque church** which contains a much revered figure of Christ. You are now within hailing distance of **Cape Finisterre**, where you have a wonderful **view**; in the afternoon you can watch the sun disappear and, if you are classically inclined, you can quote Horace —*The brilliant skylight of the sun drags behind it the black night over the fruitful breasts of the earth'*— for the Latin poet was clearly as impressed as the next man by end of the earth tales.

The Costa de la Muerte itinerary is one to be taken slowly and not just because of the state of the **roads**; you should take your time to savour all the manifold legends that surround this coast. One of its unexplained mysteries lies right on Finisterre's doorstep, for nobody is quite sure how the old village of Duyo came to sink beneath the waters here. Tales of ghost ships without crew and of caves haunted by the wailing of drowned mariners are, naturally, two a penny for Galicia is addicted to encounters of the third kind. To return to your starting point along the inland route, take the C-552 past Camariñas (not to be confused with the coastal village of the same name) to **VIMIANZO**, which lies in a very typical Galician valley and has, for good measure, a castle and a fortified prehistoric hill settlement called **Ougás**.

EL FERROL-O FERROL La Coruña ☎ (981), pop. 88,101, *i* Pl Marqués de Alborán ☎ 35 14 97, ✉ Pl Galicia, s/n ☎ 35 28 38 and 35 32 64, ✚ 32 48 04, P 32 14 25, 🚂 RENFE ☎ 31 46 55. La Coruña 66km, Santiago 94km, Madrid 661km.

This is one of the shipbuilding centres of Spain, situated on one of the loveliest of the **Rías Altas**, and it has been closely associated with the Spanish navy since the beginning of the 18C when its first dockyards were built.

🏨 ★★★ *Parador de El Ferrol*, Pl Eduardo Pondal, s/n ☎ 35 67 20 🛏 39 **P** ✚ ⚓ AE, DC, MC, V $$$$. Set in a comfortable building in the style of the region.

🏨 ★★★ *Almirante*, c/ María, 2 ☎ 32 84 49 🛏 121 **P** AE, DC, $$$.

🍴 *Casa Paco*, in Jubia ☎ 38 02 30 **P** AE, DC, V $$ to $$$. Good fish and seafood.

🍴 *Casa Tomás* (closed: Sunday nights), in Jubia-Neda ☎ 38 02 40 **P** DC, MC, EC, V $$. Particularly good grilled fish.

🍴 *Pataquiña* (closed: Sunday nights except in summer), c/ Dolores, 35 ☎ 35 23 11 AE, DC, EC, V $$$. Galician cuisine.

🍴 *Xantar*, c/ Real, 182 V $$$. *Nouvelle* cuisine.

Best buys: Galician arts and crafts are sold at *T. Cavelo*, c/ Iglesia, 96; cakes at *Ramos*, c/ Real, 144, and cheeses at *Amador*, c/ Carmen, 17.

Cultural highlights: The town has an old quarter with a medieval flavour to its winding, narrow streets, but its dominant architectural feature is the grid-pattern enlargement that the town underwent during the reign of the enlightened monarch Charles III, according to the rationalist principles of the late 18C. This quarter, known as the Ensanche, is where the cathedral is located and it has two symmetrical large squares that are linked by six broad parallel avenues. However, El Ferrol's heart and soul are down on the quayside, though much of this area is sadly run down as a result of the decline of the shipbuilding industry.

Local sights: The trip to **CEDEIRA** along the C-646 is a pleasant drive through green, undulating country. Sticking by El Ferrol's *ría* you reach the **shrine of San Andrés de Teixido** at the foot of the Sierra de Capelada mountains. This is the site, every September 8, of one of the most famed and popular *romerías* in all Galicia. These rural events, which are a mix of religious ceremonies and pagan celebrations with picnics and country dancing thrown in, are a particular *fiesta* feature of this NW corner of Spain. At the shrine you can acquire curious religious charms called *ex-votos* which are made out of bread and then hand painted. On the last Sunday in June there are *curros* (see 'Fiestas'), the rodeo-like roundups of wild horses for branding, in Capelada. There are a number of very picturesque coastal villages near El Ferrol such as **ORTIGUEIRA** (see 'Rias Altas') and **PUERTO DEL BARQUERO**. Lovers of untamed seascapes should make a point of visiting promontories such as Ortegal and Estaca de Bares, as well as the small seaside town of **BARES**.

On the town: The c/ del Sol area in the old quarter has a number of good *tapa* bars, such as *El Sol*, *La Jovita* and *Toldo*, where you can enjoy good seafood aperitifs washed down with local wine.

● ▊LA CORUÑA-A CORUÑA (CORUNNA)▊ La Coruña ☎ (981), pop. 241,808, *i* Dársena de la Marina ☎ 22 18 22, (c/ San Andrés, 101, ✉ Av de la Marina ☎ 22 19 56 and 22 20 00, ✚ 20 59 75, **P** 20 83 00, ✈ La Coruña-Alvedro, 10km ☎ 23 22 40 (Iberia ☎ 22 87 30/37), ⚓ Trasmediterránea, Pl San Cristóbal, s/n ☎ 22 85 00, 🚌 c/ Caballero, s/n ☎ 23 96 44, 🚢 Muelle del Este ☎ 23 03 09. Lugo 95km, Vigo 155km, Madrid 601km.

Although Santiago is Galicia's historic and administrative capital, busy, bustling La Coruña is the region's commercial and business focal point. Like Vigo, La Coruña is a big, assertive town that offers a dramatic contrast to the sleepy ruraldom of most of Galicia. Since the 18C it has grown steadily prosperous through its trade with Latin America and its highly developed canning industry. Set on a small peninsula, it has been a landmark for mariners since the earliest times and its lighthouse, the 104m high **Torre de Hércules** (Tower of Hercules), which was built by the Romans in the 2C, still guides ships and is the oldest working lighthouse in the world. La Coruña has a number of English links for the ill-fated **Spanish Armada** sailed from here in 1588, a fact that was not lost on that scourge of the Spanish Main, **Sir Francis Drake**, who attacked the port several times. The city's old cemetery is the final resting place of the romantic Peninsular War general **Sir John Moore** who died as his men embarked for home after a long and costly retreat from central Spain. Moore's burial at Corunna has been immortalized in the poem 'Not a drum was heard, not a funeral note...' that every British schoolchild learns.

🏛 ★★★★ *Atlántico*, Jardines de Méndez Núñez ☎ 22 65 00 🛏 200 ♦ 🎤 🖼 AE, DC, MC, V $$$ to $$$$.

● 🏛 ★★★★ *Finisterre*, Paseo del Parrote, s/n ☎ 20 54 00 🛏 127 ♦ 🎤 ♨ 🖼 « 🐎 ♀ AE, DC, MC, V $$$ to $$$$. Well situated for views of the bay.

▥ ★★★ *Ciudad de La Coruña*, Polígono de Adormideras ☎ 21 11 00
🛏131 ⅙ **P** ✦ 🔱 🐌 🛶 « 🐎 AE, DC, MC, V $$$. Quiet and scenic.

¶ *Casa Pardo* (closed: Sundays and May) c/ Novoa Santos, 15 ☎
28 71 78 ✳ AE, MC, V $$$. Simple, hearty fare.

¶ *Coral* (closed: Sundays except in July and August), c/ Estrella, 5 ☎
22 10 82 ✳ AE, DC, EC, V $$$. Fish and seafood.

¶ *El Gallo de Oro* (closed: Sunday nights, Mondays and Christmas), in
Arteijo ☎ 60 04 10 **P** ✦ ✳ AE, MC, V $$$$. Fish and seafood.

¶ *El Rápido* (closed: Monday nights), c/ Estrella, 7 ☎ 22 42 21 ✳ AE, DC, ◖
MC, V $$$ to $$$$. A vast choice of seafood.

¶ *La Viña* (closed: Sundays and Christmas), Av Pasaje, 5 ☎ 28 08 54 **P** ✳
AE, V $$$. Fish and seafood.

Beaches: There are two city beaches, Riazor beach in the N and Santa
Cristina in the S.

Best buys: Antiques are sold at *C. de la Peña*, c/ Orzán, 89, and *C. Vidal
Pan*, c/ Parrote, 2. Works of art by young Galician painters are available at
Arrancada, c/ Zapatería, 4, and *Gruporzán*, c/ Orzán, 139. Books on all
things Galician are found at *Couceiro*, Pl del Libro. Cakes and charcuterie are
available from *C. Blanco*, c/ Juan Flórez, 78, while marvellous fresh produce
and lots more are sold in La Coruña's covered markets at Pl de San Agustín,
Pl de Lugo and c/ Inés de Castro. Spanish fashion is sold at *Adolfo*　　　　◖
Domínguez, Av Finisterre, 3, *Bogar*, c/ Estrecha de San Andrés, 4, *La
Bambola*, c/ San Andrés, 67, and *Gloria Osset*, c/ Real, 32; accessories at
Romano, c/ Cantón Pequeño, 28; and footwear at *Candela*, c/ Rosalía de
Castro, 14, *Ovot*, c/ F. Mariño, 12, *Triay*, c/ Real, 15, and *Zorba*, c/ General
Mola, 22. *El Corte Inglés*, the town's large department store, is on Av Ramón
y Cajal, 57.

Cultural highlights: A bracing, sea-tangy city, La Coruña's landmarks are
the Hercules Tower lighthouse and the lovely glassed-in balconies of the
◖ houses that line the port's promenade, the Av de la Marina. The old
quarter, on the rocky peninsula N of the port, is delightful to explore on foot.
Visit, too, the aptly named Jardín Romántico (Romantic Garden) in the old
San Carlos fortress, or the Jardines de Méndez Núñez (Méndez Núñez
Gardens) next to the port and between the Cantones. The commercial centre
is the c/ Real and the main square is the porticoed and pleasantly
proportioned Pl de María Pita which is named after a local heroine who
rallied the townspeople during one of Drake's sallies against the port. The Pl
de Santa Barbara is also worth a visit. The city's best religious buildings are
the Collegiate Church of Santa María del Campo which has a finely
carved late 13C W door in a transitional Romanesque-Gothic style, and the
Church of Saint James, also Romanesque-Gothic in style. The town's
museums include the Museo Arqueológico, the Archaeological Museum
(open: 10.00-2.00 and 4.00-8.00 ☎ 20 59 94), the Casa-Museo de Emilia
Pardo Bazán, c/ Tabernas, 11 (open: 10.00-12.00) which houses
memorabilia of Spain's great 19C woman novelist whose home it was, and
the Museo de Bellas Artes, the Fine Arts Museum, Pl Pintor Soto Mayor
(open: 10.00-2.00 and 5.00-7.30; Saturdays: 10.00-2.00; closed: Mondays
☎ 20 56 30) which exhibits works by Velázquez and Goya as well as
Sargadelos ceramics. There is also a planetarium, the Casa de las Ciencias, in
Santa Margarita park.

Fiestas: The city's celebrations last through most of August and they include
an International Comic Cinema Festival, the *Festival Internacional de Cine de
Comedia* ☎ 22 54 67. In July there is a series of concerts, stage productions
and film shows on the general theme of the Way of Saint James, the
Encontros Europeos No Camiño de Santiago ☎ 22 77 00.

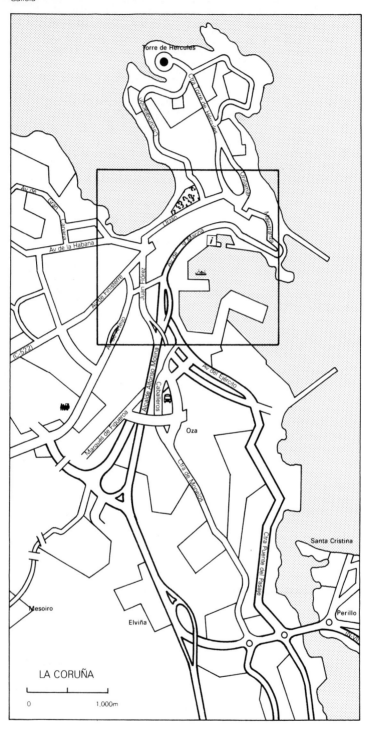

LA CORUÑA

Local sights: The **Tower of Hercules lighthouse**, 104m above sea level, is 2km out of town (open: 10.00-1.30 and 4.00-7.30). Possibly Phoenician in origin, it was reconstructed in the 2C during the reign of the Emperor Trajan and was strengthened in the 18C by Charles III. Taking the N-550 towards Betanzos, the village of **CAMBRE**, 11km, is distinguished by a wonderful Romanesque church, the **Iglesia de Santa María** which is one of the most unspoiled 12C buildings in Galicia. Nearby there is an interesting *cruceiro* monument, a typically Galician stone cross, erected in the 17C. Some places near La Coruña are especially worth visiting at particular times of year. This is the case of the resort of **SADA** which hosts a **sardine eating festival**, known as a *sardiñada*, in August.

On the town: The *tapa* bar scene is in the old quarter and around c/ Juan Flórez and c/ Orzán. Popular taverns include *María Illo* in c/ Juan Flórez, *Fornos*, c/ Olmos, 25, and *O Lionardo*, Av Fernández Latorre, 22 (specializes in octopus and Ribeiro wine). There is live music at *Don Pedro* in the old quarter and *Que Papá No Se Entere*, c/ Pontevedra, is a favourite final nightcap bar. Those wanting to flirt with Lady Luck should head for the *Casino del Atlántico* at the Hotel Atlántico, Jardines de Méndez Núñez ☎ 22 16 00.

Sports: The *Real Club Náutico de La Coruña*, Muelle de las Animas ☎ 20 79 10, is the local yacht club, and the *Club Casino La Coruña* ☎ 22 11 91, attracts speedboat racing enthusiasts. There is an 18-hole, par 72 golf course at Arteijo, the *Club de Golf de La Coruña* ☎ 28 52 00, and there are tennis courts at the *Club de Tenis La Coruña* ☎ 66 05 19.

LA TOJA, ISLAND OF A TOXA **Pontevedra** ☎ (986). Access across the bridge from El Grove which is on the C-550 to Pontevedra, ✉ Rúa de Castelao, 58, El Grove ☎ 73 14 22, 🚌 La Unión, Pl del Corgo, El Grove ☎ 73 00 55. Pontevedra 32km, Vigo 57km, Santiago de Compostela 75km, Madrid 640km.

A grand luxury hotel, a casino, a golf course and medicinal mud baths have turned this tiny, **scenic island** E of the El Grove peninsula into a very upmarket resort. It is situated on the **Ría de Arosa**, one of the gentlest and loveliest of the **Rías Bajas**. Legend has it that a sick and elderly donkey was left to die on the island when it was uninhabited early last century and that the beast reappeared weeks later absolutely restored to health and looking years younger. By 1842, humans were taking the mudbaths the donkey had discovered.

- 🏨 ★★★★★ *Gran Hotel de La Toja*, Isla de La Toja ☎ 73 00 25 🛏 201 ♦ 🎤 ⚊ ▦ « 🛋 ᛩ ᒫ AE, DC, MC, V $$$$ to $$$$$. A sumptuous turn of the century hotel, beautifully situated overlooking the estuary.
- 🏨 ★★★★ *Louxo*, Isla de La Toja ☎ 73 02 00 🛏 96 ♦ 🎤 ⚊ « ᛩ ᒫ AE, DC, MC, V $$$ to $$$$. Scenically located with excellent views.
- 🍴 *Crisol*, c/ Hospital, 10, El Grove ☎ 73 00 29 **MC, V** $$$ to $$$$. Excellent fish.

Beaches: La Lanzada, S, is semi-wild and 8km long.

Fiestas: The *Virgen del Carmen* feastday, July 16, is solemnly observed and there is a popular *romería* pilgrimage to **La Lanzada** on the last Sunday of August. On the second Sunday of October the *Fiesta del Marisco*, a seafood eating *fiesta*, is a real crowd-puller.

Local sights: The Ría de Arosa, with its picturesque villages and its oyster and mussel farms is well worth exploring. **CAMBADOS**, in the NE along the C-550 is famous for its superb **Albariño wine**, which can be sampled at bars such as *Piñeiro*, c/ Isabel II, s/n, and *O Castriño*, Av Pastora, s/n. The town has an impressive 18C mansion, the **Pazo de Fefiñanes**, and the ruins of the

Church of Santa Marina D'Ozo are interesting. Best buys in town include the local wine from ***Bodegas del Pazo de Fefiñanes*** ☎ 54 22 04, and fish from the *Lonja*, the quayside fish market, in the early morning —even if you don't buy, the spectacle of boxes of many varieties of fish being auctioned in Galician is marvellous. The village's *romería* pilgrimage on July 11 is genuinely folkloric. For accommodation in town, try ★★★ *Parador El Albariño*, Paseo Cervantes, s/n ☎ 54 22 50 ⇌ 63 🅿 ✦ 🔱 ⅏ AE, DC, EC, V $$$ to $$$$, a quiet and beautiful hotel set in a restored old *pazo*, and for

☻ eating, head for ***O Arco*** (closed: Sunday nights in winter and 15/9-30/9), c/ Real, 14 ☎ 54 23 12 V $$ to $$$, serving good fish and seafood.

Continuing N up the coast, the village of **VILAXOAN** is known to literature lovers as the birthplace of the eccentric Ramón María del Valle Inclán and to

☻☻ gourmets as the home of ***Chocolate*** (closed: Sundays, holiday nights and 20/12-20/1), Av Cambados, 151 ☎ 50 11 99 🅿 ✳ AE, DC, EC, V $$$ to $$$$, the restaurant against which all others in Galicia measure themselves. There is a particularly good beauty spot over the *ría*, the **Mirador de Lobeira**, 4km short of Villagarcía de Arosa. If you feel like spending the night here, the ★★★★ ***Pazo O Rial***, c/ El Rial, 1 ☎ 50 56 22 ⇌ 60 ✦ ⚭ ≪ AE, MC, V $$ to $$$, is a restored country mansion set in a quiet pine wood.

☻ **On the town:** The ***Casino de La Toja*** ☎ 73 10 00, has an array of gambling tables with all the usual games of chance. The nearest popular discotheque is ***Faro***, in El Grove, c/ González Besada, s/n.
Sports: The range of sports possibilities includes canoeing, fishing, riding and target shooting, as well as playing golf on the beautifully situated 9-hole,

☻ par 72 ***Golf La Toja*** course ☎ 73 07 26.

LUGO **Lugo** ☎ (982), pop. 77,728, *i* Pl de España, s/n ☎ 23 13 61, ℂ c/ Río Neira, s/n, ✉ c/ San Pedro, 5 ☎ 22 63 12, ✚ 21 22 99, **P** 22 56 52, 🚌 Pl de la Constitución, s/n ☎ 22 39 85, ⚎ Pl del Conde Fontau ☎ 22 21 41. Orense 96km, La Coruña 98km, Oviedo 255km, Madrid 506km.

Lugo is distinguished by the Miño river that flows through it and, above

☻☻ all, by its impressive **city walls**. The walls were built to protect the Roman city of *Lucus Augusti* in the 3C and they survived Christian attacks when the city was Muslim, Muslim attacks when it was taken by the Christians, and the Norman raids that plagued much of the Galician coast in the Middle Ages. Capital of the province of the same name, Lugo is the centre of an important agricultural and stock-raising area and it has long since outgrown its walled old quarter.

▦ ★★★★ ***Gran Hotel Lugo***, Av Ramón Ferreiro, s/n ☎ 22 41 52 ⇌ 168 ₺ 🔱 ⚭ ⚱ AE, DC, EC, V $$$ to $$$$.

▦ ★★★ ***Méndez Núñez***, c/ Reina, 1 ☎ 23 07 11 ⇌ 94 🔱 $$ to $$$.

▦ ★★ ***Portón do Recanto***, Ctra N-640 Vegadeo, km74, in La campiña ☎ 22 33 55 ⇌ 23 ✗ TV ℂ ≪ V $$.

🍴 ***Campos***, Rúa Nova, 4 ☎ 22 97 43 AE, DC, MC, V $$ to $$$. Updated Galician cuisine.

🍴 ***La Barra***, c/ San Marcos, 27 ☎ 24 24 29 ✳ AE, DC, EC, V $$ to $$$. Steaks and seafood.

🍴 ***La Coruñesa***, c/ Doctor Castro, 16 ☎ 22 10 87 AE, DC, EC, MC, V $$ to $$$. Galician cuisine.

☻ 🍴 ***Mesón de Alberto*** (closed: Sundays except in high season), c/ Cruz, 4 ☎ 22 83 10 AE, DC, MC, V $$$. A wide-ranging menu of Lugo specialities.

☻ 🍴 ***Verruga*** (closed: Mondays), c/ Cruz, 12 ☎ 22 98 55 AE, DC, EC, V $$$. Galician cooking.

Best buys: Typical Galician brass pots and pans are sold at *La Avilesina*, c/ Amor Meilán, 12, and more local arts and crafts, including musical instruments (made to order), at *Chacarela*, c/ San Froilán, 12 ☎ 24 21 96. Earthenware is sold at the open-air market, or *Rastro*, in the Pl de la Soledad; while pottery is available from the nearby villages like Bonge (10km), Cela and Mantela in the Otero de Rey district. Local artisan cheeses can be bought from *Victorina*, in the Pl de Abastos.

Cultural highlights: A walk around the **walls** starts at any one of the 10 gates that, like the Carmen gateway which was used by the Compostela pilgrims, lead into the city. Parts of the walls were strengthened in the Middle Ages and in all they extend for 2km. Fortified by a succession of semicircular towers, they are between 10-14m high and nearly 5m thick. A stroll along the battlements is the best introduction to Lugo for it will give you a good **overall picture** of the layout of the city.

The Santiago Gate, which was rebuilt in 1759, leads to the **Cathedral** which is an interesting mix of architectural styles. Building of the cathedral started in 1129 and it retains the Romanesque nave and apses from its earliest period. The main façade, the W door, was completely redesigned in 1769 by the Neoclassical architect Sánchez Bort but the **N door**, that opens onto the Pl de Santa María, retains its original set of 12C carvings dominated by a huge figure of *Christ*. One of the main features of the Cathedral is the Chapel of Nuestra Señora de los Ojos Grandes (Our Lady of the Big Eyes), that contains a Gothic alabaster statue of the Virgin which is highly revered throughout Galicia. The chapel was built in the 18C by Fernando Casas y Novoa who also designed the Baroque cloister. The former main altarpiece, by Cornelius of Holland (1531), has been divided into two parts which now adorn both wings of the transept.

Leaving the cathedral by the N door and entering the Pl de Santa María, you are standing opposite the **Episcopal Palace** which occupies a fine 18C mansion of the type that in Galicia are called *pazos*. This old quarter of Lugo with its cobblestones, colonnaded streets, pretty **squares** and well-appointed town houses is picturesque and pleasant. The Plaza Mayor is ostensibly dominated by the Town Hall, a Baroque pile, but it is the romantic turn of the century bandstand in its centre that steals the show. The **Provincial Museum**, Pl de la Soledad (open: 10.00-2.00 and 4.00-7.00; closed: Saturday afternoons and holidays ☎ 24 21 12) has an eclectic collection of exhibits that includes Roman engravings, Celtic artifacts, a series of sundials and 19C paintings.

Fiestas and festivals: The celebrations in honour of San Froilán (October 2-12), Carnival and Corpus Christi are the main events in Lugo's *fiesta* calendar. There is a Film Week in September ☎ 22 41 51.

Local sights: The town's **spa** is just 2km out of Lugo in wooded countryside on the banks of the Miño. The Romans took the waters here and remains of their thermal baths can still be seen. For accommodation at the baths, try ★★ *Balneario de Lugo*, Barrio del Puente, s/n ☎ 22 12 28 ⇌ 28 Ⴤ ᕯ ⊕ ✦ $$.

The pre-Romanesque church of **Santa Eulalia de Bóveda**, 15km, is one of the earliest Christian shrines in Galicia and is especially interesting for its frescoes showing birds and plants. You reach it by taking the N-640 towards Orense and turning right after 4km onto the local road to Friol.

The trip to the rugged mountainous area of **Ancares** puts you in touch with a Galician ruraldom that in places has hardly changed since the Stone Age. This is very wild countryside, a succession of narrow green valleys hidden among high peaks, and sparsely populated by shepherds. The houses in the isolated *pueblos* are what is known as *pallozas*, primitive thatched circular dwellings.

You reach the Ancares sierra by taking the N-VI towards Ponferrada, turning off at Becerreá for Puentes de Gatín. On this road, as you enter the sierra, you will pass the 16C Castle of Doiras and the villages of Cela, Cabanes, Degrada, Donís, Vilarello de Donís and Piornedo. From this last village you can continue on foot, through the thick woods of the **Donís forest**, to Suárbol which is in a part of the Ancares that lies within the province of León.

CEBRERO, which is on the N-VI, is particularly interesting: several of its ancient *pallozas* have been restored to house a folk museum. This village marked the beginning of the final stage of the Way of Saint James, and Cebreiro was well equipped to receive pilgrims as a monastery and hospital were built in the 9C to provide succour for the weary travellers (the Church of Santa María la Real and the now restored hostelry). From here the pilgrims moved on to the lovely Benedictine **Abbey of Samos**, which still offers accommodation to guests. It has had several facelifts since the Middle Ages and is now mostly Baroque Neoclassical. In the nearby town of **SARRIA**, the Hospital de la Magdalena was built in the 13C for the Compostela travellers. The pilgrim church in this town is the Romanesque Iglesia del Salvador. Samos and Sarriá can be reached from Lugo on the C-546.

The C-535 from Sarriá leads to the new village of **PUERTOMARIN** built to replace the old one which now lies under the waters of the reservoir. The chief feature here is the ancient **Iglesia de los Caballeros de San Juan** (Knight Hospitallers of Saint John), who were one of several such groups patrolling the pilgrim route. The church was lifted stone by stone to its present location before the valley below was flooded. Puertomarín is famed for its *empanadas de anguila* (traditional eel pies) and *aguardiente*, a potent distilled liquor. The town is also well known for its *fiestas*: Easter is celebrated with the *Día del Aguardiente*, a celebration in which *aguardiente* looms large. *Posada del Camino*, c/ Lugo, 1 ☎ 54 50 07 $$, is a good place to stop off for a bite to eat.

On the town: *Cinza* and *De Rua*, at the start of Rúa Nova, are popular *tapa* bars. **Pharmacia de Guardia**, c/ Clérigos, is Lugo's top disco.

Sports: Hunting and fishing are popular in the province. Flying facilities are available at the *Aero Club de Lugo* ☎ 22 67 52.

⦿ **MONDOÑEDO** Lugo ☎ (982), pop. 6,518, ✛ 52 11 84. Lugo 62km, Oviedo 205km, La Coruña 120km, Madrid 546km.

An ancient capital of the kingdom of Galicia, this is an extremely agreeable small cathedral town set in a typically verdant valley.

- ▦ **★★★ *Mirador de Mondoñedo***, 2km SW on the N-634 ☎ 52 17 00 ⭲ 19 ⚹ **P** ✦ 🕯 🐾 ⚞ $$. Very quiet, with excellent views of the town, the valley and the mountains.
- ▦ **★ *Montero II***, c/ Cándido Martínez, 8 ☎ 52 10 41 ⭲ 8 **MC, V** $$$. In an old house full of local colour, opposite the cathedral.

Best buys: Delicious cakes, particularly little sponges known as *magdalenas*, can be bought from *El Rey de las Tartas*, c/ Sarmiento, 2.

⦿ Cultural highlights: The **Cathedral** is of the type that some critics call pointed Romanesque and others transitional to Gothic. Its W door and towers, as is often the case in Galicia, are Baroque. Its chief interior features

⦿ are its 16C paintings and its 17C Neoclassical **cloister**. The **Diocesan Museum** (open in summer: 11.00-1.00 and 4.00-7.00; rest of the year: 12.00-1.00) has an extensive collection of paintings, altarpieces, statues and church ornaments. The town's **old quarter** has preserved its old whitewashed houses which show off fine wrought-iron balconies and, through the heraldic shields, the nobility of their original occupants. Stroll around the 16C **Plaza**

Mayor, the Rúa das Monxas and the Alameda on which stands the Church of Los Remedios (12C and rebuilt in the 18C) which has, over the years, acquired a strong collection of *ex-votos*. These are usually wax figurines placed in the church by members of the parish as an offering for hoped-for divine favours or as thanks for favours already received.

Fiestas: *As San Lucas* is celebrated on October 18-19.

ORENSE-OURENSE **Orense** ☎ (988), pop. 96,085 [*i*] Curros Enríquez, 1 ☎ 23 47 17, (Av Generalísimo Franco, 63, ✉ Av Generalísimo Franco, 63 ☎ 22 30 83 and 22 20 00, ✛ 22 14 62, P 22 94 11, ⚕ 21 10 64. Pontevedra 102km, Santiago de Compostela 111km, La Coruña 183km, Madrid 499km.

On the banks of the Miño river, Orense's chief feature is its old quarter which is built around the city's three warm springs, the *Burgas*. The Celts and the Romans were aware of these thermal waters though neither showed much interest in establishing a permanent settlement. Orense, now capital of one of Galicia's four provinces, did not come into its own until the early Middle Ages when it obtained a degree of prosperity thanks, in part, to the commercial enterprise of its Jewish population.

▦ ★★★★ *San Martín*, c/ Curros Enríquez, 1 ☎ 23 56 11 ⊨ 60 ⚭ AE, DC, EC, V $$$.

▦ ★★★ *Sila*, Av de la Habana, 61 ☎ 23 63 11 ⊨ 64 EC, V $$$.

▦ ★★ *Padre Feijoo*, Pl Eugenio Montes, 1 ☎ 22 31 00 ⊨ 71 DC, EC, V $$. A central hotel.

❙❙ *Carroleiro* (closed: Mondays), c/ San Miguel, 10 ☎ 22 05 66 AE, DC, MC, V $$ to $$$. Classic Galician cuisine.

❙❙ *Martín Fierro*, c/ Sáez Díez, 65 ☎ 23 48 20 P ✦ ✳ AE, DC, EC, V $$$ to $$$$. Excellent steaks and a good selection of Galician wines.

❙❙ *O Rupeiro* (closed: Sunday nights, Mondays and July), in Derrasa, km152 on the N-120 ☎ 21 63 40 P AE, MC, V $$ to $$$. Galician cuisine.

❙❙ *Sanmiguel* (closed: Tuesdays, except holidays), c/ San Miguel, 12 ☎ 22 12 45 P ✦ ✳ AE, DC, EC, V $$$ to $$$$. A mix of traditional and updated Galician cuisine. A good selection of local *aguardientes*, potent distilled liquors made from various fruits.

Best buys: Avant garde fashion designer Adolfo Domínguez, a local Orense boy who now has shops all over the world, opened his first shop here: *Adolfo Domínguez*, c/ Habana, 56. Antiques are sold at *Casa Ros*, Av de Zamora, 166, and *U. Ferreiro*, Av de Portugal, 121. Hand-woven fabrics are available from *A. Outeriño*, Av de Portugal, 59, while local, hand-made cheeses can be bought at the covered market, the *Mercado Municipal*.

Cultural highlights: Orense's **old quarter** is undeniably picturesque with its white houses, stepped, irregular streets, and small plazas such as the **Plazuela de la Magdalena**, with its 18C Church of Santa María, the **Pl del Trigo**, alongside the S door of the Cathedral and the **Pl del Hierro**. The **Cathedral**, built on the site of one which was destroyed by the Muslims in the 8C, incorporates a variety of styles from the Romanesque through to the Baroque. The W door, with its Romanesque-Gothic explosion of carvings, is called the **Pórtico del Paraíso** in reference to the astonishing and far better-known Pórtico de la Gloria of Santiago de Compostela's Cathedral. The chief features of the interior are the main altarpiece which is attributed to the 16C artist Cornelius of Holland who also produced the split altarpiece in Lugo cathedral; the 16C wrought-iron grilles and pulpits; the Baroque chapel called the **Capilla del Santo Cristo** and the **choir stalls** which again date from the 16C. The **Diocesan Museum**, which is in the unfinished 16C cloister, can be visited on request (☎ 22 09 92).

The cathedral stands on the Plaza Mayor, as do the Town Hall and the Archaeology Museum, or **Museo Arqueológico Provincial**, which is in the old Episcopal Palace (open: 10.00-1.00 and 5.00-8.00; Sundays: 11.00-1.00; closed: Mondays ☎ 22 38 84). The museum exhibits finds from Neolithic and Bronze Age digs and examples of Romanesque and Gothic art. The old bridge, or **Puente Viejo**, over the Miño was originally Roman and was rebuilt in the 13C and again in the 15-16C.

Fiestas: Around May 3 the *Dos Maios* celebrations are held (see 'Fiestas'). The canoeing race down the Miño between Peares and Orense is as much a sporting event as a giant party. The rail tracks skirt along the river bank so spectators crowd into trains for a good view of the scullers.

Local sights: In the bucolic valleys of Orense province you are going to run across spas and monasteries which respectively minister to the body and the soul. Nearby **spas** include the ones at Molgas (30km ☎ 46 32 11), Berán (40km) and Carballino (29km ☎ 27 09 26).

Twenty-nine kilometres S on the N-540, the impressive Benedictine **Monastery of San Salvador** occupies the main square of the village of **Celanova**. Founded in 936 by Saint Rosendo it now boasts a massive 17C Baroque **church** which has an excellent organ and a lovely **cloister** dating from the 16C. In its garden there is a 10C **Mozarabic shrine** honouring San Miguel. Nearby, to the W, the **Monastery of Mosteiro** was one of the scores of institutions founded in the early Middle Ages to cope with the arrival of hundreds of thousands of Compostela pilgrims. Heading S towards Bande, you reach the 7C **Church of Saint Comba**, one of the most important Visigothic survivals in Spain.

Allariz, an historic and picturesque old town, lies SE on the N-525. Travelling to it you pass by Santa Marina de Aguas Santas which is one of the most popular shrines in Galicia and the site of a very well attended *romería*, or festive religious picnic, in July. Nearby, 5km from Junquera de Ambía, there is an original 10C Visigothic church dedicated to **Santa Eufemia de Ambía**. Heading NW you reach **Osera** and the 12C **Monastery of Santa María la Real** which has been repeatedly pillaged down the ages. Behind its 17C Baroque façade, the **church** retains the pure lines of the austere Cistercian order that occupied it. The 15C **sacristy**, in particular, has very intricate vaulting and retains its original columns. The outstanding features of the monastery complex are its **cloister** and the **Patio de los Medallones** (Medallion Courtyard). Continuing on, you reach **Chantada**, in the province of Lugo, which is known for the lovely murals of its Benedictine monastery. The town is also famous for its exquisite locally hand-woven bedspreads, delicious local cheeses and Chantada bread which are sold at its open air market held on the 5 and 21 of every month.

If you drive NE on the C-546 you reach the extremely pleasant and beautiful town of **Monforte de Lemos** (Lugo) with its 10C Monastery of San Vicente del Pino and its castle, the seat of the counts of Lemos, which has a distinctive keep. This is a wine-growing area, so it is only natural while here to buy Amandi wine direct from the vineyards in the nearby village of Sober.

Sports: Skiing is practised at the *Manzaneda* ski station, 77km on the N-120 ☎ 31 08 75, 1,450-1,750m, with five ski lifts and ten pistes.

PONTEVEDRA **Pontevedra** ☎ (986), pop. 70,238, [i] General Mola, 1 ☎ 85 37 16, (c/ General Mola, 5, ✉ c/ Oliva, 21 ☎ 85 16 77, ✚ 85 20 77, P 85 19 72, ✈ Vigo, 40km ☎ 27 05 50 (Iberia ☎ 22 70 05, Aviaco ☎ 27 40 56), 🚃 Av de la Estación ☎ 85 24 08, 🚌 85 45 43. Vigo 31km, Santiago de Compostela 57km, Orense 105km, La Coruña 120km, Madrid 599km.

Tucked away nowadays on its *ría*, Pontevedra in the Middle Ages was a busy commercial port serving Santiago de Compostela and the home of some of the region's best seamen. By the 17C its role as Galicia's great foreign trading centre was drastically diminished when the harbour silted up so badly that it could no longer accommodate large vessels. Pontevedra therefore began to decline gracefully and gently, adjusting itself to becoming an agreeable and peaceful provincial capital, while nearby Vigo became the area's shipping and industrial hub.

▦ ★★★ *Parador Casa del Barón*, Pl Maceda, s/n ☎ 85 58 00 ⇌ 47 **P** ✦ ♨ ⚲ AE, MC, V $$$ to $$$$. Set in an old and beautifully restored *pazo*. The **restaurant** is classy.

▦ ★★★ *Rías Bajas*, c/ Daniel de la Sota, 7 ☎ 85 51 00 ⇌ 100 **P** ♨ AE, DC, MC, V $$ to $$$.

▦ ★★★ *Virgen del Camino*, c/ Virgen del Camino, 55 ☎ 85 59 00 ⇌ 53 ♨ MC, V $$ to $$$.

❚❙ *Casa Román* (closed: Sunday nights except in July and August), c/ Augusto García Sánchez, 12 ☎ 84 35 60 AE, DC, V $$ to $$$. Galician cooking.

❚❙ *Casa Solla* (closed: Thursday nights, Sunday nights and Christmas), Ctra El Grove-La Toja, km2, in Poyo ☎ 85 26 78 **P** ✦ ❋ AE, MC, V $$$. Famed for first rate seafood and fish, although it also serves good local meat.

❚❙ *Doña Antonia*, c/ Soportales de la Herrería, 9 ☎ 84 72 74 AE, V $$$. Elegant decor and an imaginative approach to local cuisine, serving excellent fish and seafood.

Beaches: A string of excellent sandy beaches stretches from Pontevedra to Bueu. The most popular beaches include Marín and Portocelo.

Best buys: Old and modern jewelry in silver and jet is sold at *Moreira*, c/ Peregrina, 8. Galicia is a pace-setter in contemporary Spanish fashion, and not only thanks to the Orense born and bred superstar Adolfo Domínguez; as far as fashion shops are concerned, head for *Teodoro*, in Nuevas Galerías de la Oliva, *Isaygon*, c/ Oliva, 12, and *Marga y Valenzuela*, c/ Sagasta, 11. Antiques can be bought from *Altamira*, c/ Charino, 14, and *Arte Moreira*, Pl de la Leña, 2. Bargains of one kind or another can be found at the open air market, or *mercadillo*, held on the 1, 8, 15, and 23 of every month.

Cultural highlights: Pontevedra's **old quarter** is as pleasant as any in Galicia for a stroll among the fading *pazos* and well-appointed town houses that tell of former grandeur. A succession of quiet plazas, **Pl de Teucro, Pl de la Leña, Pl de Mugártegui**, the streets by the river, like **c/ Real** and **c/ San Nicolás** together with the main shopping street, **c/ Sarmiento** lend the city a charm all its own and make the modern visitor feel thankful for the clogging sandbanks of the ría that arrested Pontevedra's development. The local museum, the **Museo Provincial**, is housed in two good looking 18C *pazos* on c/ Sarmiento, 51 (open: 11.00-1.00 and 5.00-8.00; closed: Mondays ☎ 85 14 55), and has the chaotic mix of exhibits and periods that one comes to expect of such institutions. There is some prehistoric bric-à-brac, examples of the jet craftsmanship typical of Compostela and of Sargadelos ceramics, some sketches attributed to Rubens and a rather good still life by Zurbarán. The **Church of Santa María la Mayor** was built in the 16C with funds provided by the local mariners' guild. Its apse is in the Isabelline style of the court of the Catholic Monarchs, and Cornelius of Holland and Juan Nobre were responsible for the carvings on the **W façade**. Pontevedra's two other notable churches are in sharply contrasting styles: the Rococo **Iglesia de la Peregrina** and the 14C Gothic **Church of San Francisco** in the Pl de la Ferreiría.

Fiestas: The *Dos Maios* celebrations are held at the beginning of May (see 'Fiestas'). Celebrations in honour of San Benitiño (July 11-25) include a *romería* or processional picnic which takes place on a small flotilla of vessels up and down the River Lérez. It is traditional on Santiago's Day, July 25, to offer up to the Apostle James the first bunch of grapes and the first sprig of corn.

Local sights: In order to get the lie of the land it is a good idea to take the N-550 for 6km in the direction of Vigo before turning off to the right in the direction of Lake Castiñeiras. This road climbs up amidst pines and eucalyptus trees to a high hilltop lookout called the **Mirador de Cotorredondo** which commands magnificent **views**. The coast formed by the **Rías Bajas** (see separate entry) is one of Galicia's greatest attractions. The 60km **drive** SE along the C-531 to **A CANIZA** makes for a fine outing which will take you up barren hill and down verdant dale, and will offer you good **views** of the area.

On the town: The old quarter is, as is usual in Spanish towns, the best *tapa* bar area. Popular taverns include *La Bombilla*, c/ San Martiño, 14, *La Chiruca*, c/ Figueroa, 17, and *Rianxo*, c/ Pasantería, 8. *Marrón Galcé*, Av Vigo, 25, is the town's disco and *Siroco*, Av Fernández Ladreda, s/n, its cabaret.

Sports: This is a sailing area and the local yacht club is the *Club de Mar de Aguete* ☎ 70 23 73. Salmon fishing is commonly practised along the Verdugo river —Puente Caldetas, 20km, is a good base.

◔ **RIAS ALTAS (UPPER ESTUARIES)** Lugo and La Coruña

One of Galicia's several singularities is the manner in which the sea burrows into it with long spindly fingers. What the world knows as a fjord in Galicia is called a *ría* and these long rocky inlets are here divided into the upper and the lower estuaries, the Rías Altas and the Rías Bajas. The division does not refer to one group being high because the inlets are ringed with cliffs but to their geographical situation. The Rías Altas lie in the N and run along the Cantabrian coastline of Lugo province continuing along what is the Atlantic coastline, proper, of the province of La Coruña. The boundaries of these upper *rías* are Ribadeo, on Lugo's border with the region of Asturias, and La Coruña. Between La Coruña and starting at Malpica, the gentle *rías* become a fast receding memory for there you enter and continue through to Cape Finisterre, the cruel stretch of sea that is known as the Coast of Death, **Costa de la Muerte** (see separate entry).

Starting on the NE, the **Ría de Ribadeo** is formed by the estuary of the river Eo that forms the frontier between Galicia's Lugo province and Asturias. **RIBADEO** (see separate entry) has been an active coastal trading port since the last century and is now joined to Asturias by a modern bridge. For the **best views** of the fjord and the port of Castropol on the Asturian side of the estuary, head S along the old N-640 to Vegadeo. Driving W from Ribadeo along the N-642 you reach the **Ría de Foz** passing, on the way, the interesting **Church of San Martín de Mondoñedo** which was an episcopal see until the 12C. **Foz** is a flourishing fishing village and a quiet summer resort with two fine **beaches** separated by a 15m high stretch of **cliff**. Recommended restaurants here include *Casa Palmira*, c/ Villaronte, s/n ☎ (982) 14 04 96 $$, which has earned a reputation for its *tortilla* (potato omelette), and *Xoiña* (closed: Mondays), 1km S on the C-642 ☎ (982) 14 09 44 ▣ ✦ V $$, which specializes in fish and seafood. Continuing W there are quite a few solitary beaches such as the one at Barreiros and also prosperous fishing villages such as **BURELA**. A detour inland here will take you to Cervo and the ceramic centre of *Sargadelos* whose products rank high on the shopping list of most visitors to Galicia (open: 8.30-1.00 and 4.30-6.00; closed: weekends) —see 'Design'. Returning to the C-642, driving through pines and eucalyptus trees and one good view after another, you reach the **Ría de Vivero**. The village of **VIVERO** has an historic, medieval air to it. It preserves part of its old walls and an old gate, the **Puerta de Carlos V**, which is nearly on the water's edge, and it has several fine old churches. In summer the village becomes a lively, cosmopolitan resort that makes the most of its good **Covas beach**. Most of the summer action in the town takes place in the *tapa* bars around the centre such as *Pepe*, c/ M. Cortiñas, 15, and at the *Seidamar* disco in the *Hostal Cociña* on Covas beach. Vivero revels in a very typical Galician pilgrimage *fiesta*, the *Romería del Naseiro* at the end of August and there are *curros* (see 'Fiestas') in the nearby village of San Andrés de Boimente on the first Sunday in July. For lunch, try *Nito*, on Playa de Area beach ☎ (982) 56 09 87 **P** « AE, EC, V $$ to $$$, which serves fish and seafood. For accommodation, try ★★ *Ego*, Playa de Area ☎ (982) 56 09 87 🛏 22 **P** ⚠ ⚓ « AE, EC, V $$, which is peaceful and has good views, or ★★★ *Las Sirenas*, Playa de Covas ☎ (982) 56 02 00 🛏 29 **P** ✦ ≈ ⚓ $$. Continuing a further 13km NW to Vicedo you will come across magnificent beaches (Aerealonga and Xillo), and great views over the estuary. The crops here, mostly maize, grow right down to the sea's edge and oxen form part of the scenery to make everything picture postcard pretty.

From here on the coast becomes rougher. Cape Estaca de Bares, the Ría de Ortigueira, Cape Ortegal and the Candelaria promontory are its most dramatic features, and the cultivated fields give way to gorse, oaks and pines. **ORTIGUEIRA** is an important fishing village at the start of the *ría* that bears its name and around here you will come upon completely unspoiled wild beaches such as Cabalar. Towards the end of August, an annual International Celtic Folk Festival is staged at Ortigueira. From here you return to civilization by way of **EL FERROL** (see separate entry), **PUENTEDEUME** (see 'Betanzos') and **BETANZOS** (see separate entry). Continuing W, you pass the 16C **Pazo de Meirás**, a palace where Countess Emilia de Pardo Bazán (see 'Literature') wrote the larger part of her opus and where General Franco spent most of his summer holidays. The Rías Altas wind up at the Ría de Betanzos and **LA CORUÑA** (see separate entry). The next stretch of coast is the mythical **Costa de la Muerte** (see separate entry) leading to 'World's End', or Cape Finisterre.

RIAS BAJAS (LOWER ESTUARIES) La Coruña and Pontevedra

Staring straight out across the Atlantic, the Rías Bajas are the long tongues of ocean that gently lap their way into western Galicia in the provinces of La Coruña and Pontevedra, providing one of the great scenic spectacles of the entire region. Looking N-S the main lower *rías* are **Muros y Noya, Arosa, ❧ Pontevedra** and **Vigo**. Like their sister fjords, the Rías Altas, these are resort areas that are excellently equipped for sailing and for beach-side holidays. The Rías Bajas are, in addition, the source of some of the best *mariscos*, or **seafood**, in Spain.

One of the pleasures of the *rías* is that although the fjord itself might be busy with boats, parts of its shore can be unspoiled and wild and this contrast is particularly true of the **N shore** of the Muros y Noya estuary. **MUROS** is a picturesque Galician fishing village and **NOYA**, reached by the C-550, is somewhat grander with well-appointed houses, an impressive market square looking out onto the ocean and a Gothic church, the **Iglesia de San Martín**. Galicians are not macabre but they are concerned with the spirits of the dead and their **cemeteries** usually provide rewarding insights into their cult of the afterlife. The tombs around the Church of Santa María a Nova here are a case in point for they consist of carvings representing the trades that the occupants of the graves practised during their lifetime. Noya stages a popular sardine eating festival (August 15-18) and at other times a recommended place to eat is *Ceboleiro* (closed: 20/12-20/1), c/ General Franco, 15 ☎ (981) 82 05 31 **AE, V** $ to $$, where you can also get accommodation.

Between the Ría de Muro y Noya to the N and the one in Arosa to the S there is a hilly block of land that is called the Barbanza peninsula. There are a number of quiet, solitary beaches here between Noya and Puerto del Son and at Baroña there are remains of an old Celtic camp or *castro*. Continuing S a further 12km, the village of Oleiros boasts a fine dolmen, known as the **dolmen de Areitos**, that has survived from Galicia's Megalithic age, and the nearby **Cabo de Corrubedo** headland provides great **ocean views** as well as underwater fishing possibilities off Ladeira beach.

In the **Ría de Arosa**, industry puts in an appearance for the town of **RIBEIRA** is an important canning centre as well as a fishing port. Going inland for 10km from Puebla del Caramiñal you reach a magnificent **panoramic viewing** area nearly 500m above sea level, called the **Mirador de Curota**. This particular beauty spot is graced by a monument to the 20C Galician man of letters Ramón María del Valle Inclán, and it provides what is certainly the best birdseye **view** of the Rías Bajas and possibly the best landscape panorama in all Galicia. The nearby Pazo de Mercede was the country house used by Valle Inclán as a retreat at which he wrote many of his controversial and extravagant plays and novels. The next village on the itinerary, **RIANJO**, also has literary associations for it was the home of Payo Gómez Chariño, a medieval seaman who achieved the rank of admiral and found time to write elegant chivalric ballads, and also of Alfonso Castelao, a polemical essayist and prolific artist who is honoured throughout Galicia as the founder of the region's modern nationalism.

PADRON, the next stopping place, is the spot where tradition has it that the body of Saint James the Apostle, the ubiquitous Santiago, arrived aboard a mysterious stone boat. This is the home town of the Romantic 19C poetess Rosalía de Castro whose mournful and skilful use of Galician put the vernacular language on the literary map and projected her as a sort of Spanish Emily Dickinson. Her house, the **Casa Museo de Rosalía de Castro** ☎ (981) 81 12 04, is open to the public.

> *Give me your perfumes, loveliest of roses.*
> *Oh, quench the burning of my thirst, clear fountains,*
> *For it is scorching me. Clouds made of gossamer*
> *Like veils of lightest lace now cover over*
> *The bright beams of the sun at its most burning.*
> *And you, you temperate and loving breezes,*
> *Make a beginning of mysterious concerts*
> *Among the oak trees of the shaded farmland*
> *Through which the Sar passes with a light murmur.*
>
> Rosalía de Castro   *On the Banks of the Sar*

Chef Rivera, c/ Enlace Parque, 7 ☎ (981) 81 04 13 ❋ **AE, DC, EC, V** $$ to $$$, is a recommended restaurant. If you visit in summer, be sure to try *pimientos de Padrón*, tiny green peppers served fried, the occasional one of which can be very piquant indeed. Continuing S on the C-550, **VILLAGARCIA DE AROSA** (Pontevedra) is a summer beach resort from where pleasure steamers depart on trips along the estuary and to the lovely island of Arosa. This is a good sailing and water sports area and enthusiasts should make contact with the local yacht club, the *Club de Mar Villagarcía de Arosa* ☎

(986) 50 01 23. As far as entertainment is concerned, *Illa d'Arosa*, Pl Independencia, 3, is a popular *tapa* bar, and the *Durán* piano-bar in Los Duranes is good for a nightcap. In early May, the famous *Maios* are celebrated. Villagarcía de Arosa is also known for its local produce, which can be bought at the **open-air market** held every Tuesday and Saturday. For dining and accommodation, see 'Vilaxoan' in 'La Toja'. In addition at Carril, 2km, *Loliña* (closed: Sunday nights and November), Pl del Muelle, 1 ☎ (986) 50 12 81 ♣ AE, DC, EC, V $$$ to $$$$, serves lobsters and a wide variety of other seafood. The next stops are **Cambados** (See 'La Toja'), El Grove and the dream-like **La Toja** (see separate entry).

The **Ría de Pontevedra** is smaller than the Arosa one but no less interesting. You will come across fine beaches, like Portonovo and the one at **Sangenjo** (see separate entry), and the picturesque fishing village of **Combarro** where the scenically located ★ *Stella Maris*, on the road to La Toja ☎ (986) 77 03 66 ⇐ 35 🅿 ≪ $$, can be recommended. **Pontevedra** (see separate entry) is next, followed by the important port of **Marin**, which is the headquarters of Spain's Naval Academy. Nearby in Mogor there are engraved stones called **petroglyphs** which are over 5,000 years old. The appealing village of **Bueu**, continuing SW, counts amongst its attractions the possibility of taking a boat ride to the **Isla de Ons**, an island that is all but uninhabited save for the odd bar where they serve first class octopus. Cape Udra is a good place for views and **Hio** has a superb *crucero* monument fashioned in the Baroque style by José Cerviño that ranks among the best in Galicia.

The islands at the entry to the **Ría de Vigo**, the **Islas Cíes**, have been designated a national park. This is a particularly beautiful inlet as well as a productive one for it is used for mussel breeding. There are numerous beaches, like the **Playa de América**, between **Cabo de Home** on the N shore and **Bayona** (see separate entry), as well as small fishing ports and, in the case of **Vigo** (see separate entry), important industrial areas.

RIBADAVIA **Orense** ☎ (988), pop. 6,612, ✚ 47 01 71. Orense 20km, Vigo 70km, Pontevedra 91km, Madrid 532km.

A prosperous old town with a well preserved *judería*, or Jewish quarter, Ribadavia is now the centre of the **wine growing** district of Ribeiro. There are several fine buildings in the town, a ruined castle and a wine museum for those who want to find out more about the delicate local white wine: El Museo del Ribeiro, c/ Santiago, s/n (☎ 47 18 43).

Best buys: Ribeiro wines can be purchased at the local winery, *Cosecheros de Vino del Ribeiro*, c/ Sampayo, s/n, and at the *Cooperativa Vinícola del Ribeiro*, which is in the neighbouring village of Valdepereira.

Fiestas and festivals: The *Fiesta del Vino de Ribeiro* in April is a good opportunity for tasting the new wine. The harvest is marked by more celebrations which begin on September 8, the feast day of *La Virgen del Portal*, Ribeiro's patron. An International Theatre Festival is staged in August.

Local sights: There are a number of country *pazos* in this area and the 8C church in **Francelos** is interesting.

RIBADEO **Lugo** ☎ (982), pop. 8,910, *i* Pl de España, s/n ☎ 11 06 89. Lugo 89km, Oviedo 169km, La Coruña 158km, Madrid 591km.

This pleasant coastal resort on the Galicia-Asturias border shares its small *ría* with the Asturian town of Castropol on the opposite bank of the Eo estuary. Ribadeo's Town Hall on the Plaza Mayor is a particularly fine 18C building which belonged to the Count of Sargadelos, an important figure in the Spanish Enlightenment.

🏨 ★★★ *Eo* (closed: 1/10-31/3), Av Asturias, 5 ☎ 11 07 50 ⇌ 20 🅿 🐎 ⚓ « AE, DC, EC, MC, V $$ to $$$. Peaceful atmosphere and good views over the fjord.

🏨 ★★★ *Parador de Ribadeo*, c/ Amador Fernández, s/n ☎ 11 08 25 ⇌ 47 🅿 ✦ 🐌 ♨ « AE, DC, EC, V $$$ to $$$$. Quiet and well located for views of the estuary and the mountains. The **restaurant** serves a good buffet breakfast.

🍽 *O Xardin* (closed: February), c/ Reinante, 20 ☎ 11 02 22 DC, EC, V $$ to $$$. Good fish and seafood.

Fiestas: A popular *romería*, or picnic-like pilgrimage, is held at the local shrine, the Ermita de Santa Cruz, on the first Sunday in August.

💮 **Local sights:** See 'Rías Altas'.

Sports: Salmon fishing and canoeing are very popular.

SANGENJO-SANXENXO **Pontevedra** ☎ (986), pop. 15,387, [i] Town Hall ☎ 72 00 75, ✉ c/ Progreso, 6 ☎ 72 10 87. Pontevedra 18km, Santiago de Compostela 75km, Orense 123km, Madrid 622km.

💮 Said to enjoy the best climate in Galicia, this resort on the **Ría de Pontevedra** becomes crowded in summer. The countryside is very beautiful here and is studded with *pazos*, or aristocratic country houses.

🏨 ★★★ *Rotilio*, Av do Porto, s/n ☎ 72 02 00 ⇌ 32 ♨ « AE, DC, EC, V $$$. Good views over Silgar beach.

🏨 ★★ *Maricielo* (closed: 15/10 to Holy Week), Av Generalísimo, 26 ☎ 72 00 50 ⇌ 40 ✦ ♨ « V $$.

🏨 ★★ *Minso*, Av do Porto, 1 ☎ 72 01 50 ⇌ 21 ♨ « AE, DC, MC, V $$ to $$$. Scenically set among the pine trees of Punta Vicaño which separates Sangenjo from Portonovo.

🍽 *Cachalote* (closed: 1/11-1/3), Av Marina, s/n, 1.5km W of Portonovo ☎ 72 08 52 EC, V $$ to $$$. Fish and seafood.

💮 🍽 *Taberna de Rotilio* (closed: Sunday nights and Mondays except in July and August), Av do Porto, s/n ☎ 72 02 00 ✳ AE, DC, MC, V $$$ to $$$$. Fish, seafood and classic Galician stews.

Beaches: The beach of La Lanzada, 9.5km N, is an alternative to the **local** one.

Best buys: Ceramics are sold at *Xaraiba*, c/ Primo de Rivera, and traditional Galician *empanada* pies at *Casa Teodoro*, c/ A. Domingo Delego, s/n. A **flea-market** is held on Mondays.

Cultural highlights: The Church of Santa María Adina has a 16C chapel and parts of the main church date back to the 12C. The 17C house named after the *Virrey*, or Viceroy, Miraflores was used by the novelist Emilia Pardo Bazán in the last century.

💮 **Local sights:** The fishing village of **COMBARRO**, with its granite *crucero* crosses and its *hórreos*, or raised rectangular granaries, is picturesque. See also separate entry for **Rías Bajas**. There are pleasant, scenic and quiet hotels by La Lanzada beach: ★★ **Marola** ☎ 74 36 36 ⇌ 25 🅿 🐌 ♨ « 🐎 🦮 $$, ★★ **La Lanzada** ☎ 74 32 32 ⇌ 26 🅿 ✦ 🐌 ♨ « DC $$, and ★ **Con de Arbón** (open: spring and summer) ☎ 74 36 37 ⇌ 25 🅿 ✦ 🐌 ♨ « 🦮 DC, EC, V $$ to $$$.

On the town: There are a number of popular bars and taverns in the Portonovo area such as the *Bar del Puerto* near the fish market on the quay. During the high summer season *D. Quijote*, c/ Primo de Rivera, s/n, *La Luna*, Pl José Antonio, s/n, and *Zoo* in Arenal (on the ring road from Sangenjo to Portonovo) are fashionable places among the young and lively.

Sports: The local yacht club, the *Club Náutico de Sangenjo* ☎ 72 00 59, organizes frequent regattas.

SANTIAGO DE COMPOSTELA **La Coruña** ☎ (981), pop. 104,045, [i] 🌢🌢🌢
Rúa del Villar, 43 ☎ 58 40 81, **(** c/ Franco, 4, ✉ Travesía de Fonseca, s/n
☎ 58 17 92 ✚ 58 69 69, **P** 58 16 78, ✈ Santiago de Compostela-Labacolla
☎ 59 75 50 (Iberia ☎ 59 41 00), 🚃 San Cayetano ☎ 58 77 00, 🚌 c/ del
Hórreo, s/n ☎ 59 60 50. La Coruña 65km, Vigo 85km, Madrid 613km.

This is one of Spain's great historical cities, in many ways the greatest for
during the Middle Ages it was, together with Jerusalem and Rome, one of the
three holy cities of Christendom. Santiago de Compostela is indissolubly
linked to Santiago, **Saint James the Apostle**, the patron saint of Spain. The
cult of Santiago, the son of Zebedee and the brother of John the Evangelist,
drew hundreds and thousands from all over medieval Europe to pay homage
here at his shrine. The **pilgrims** came with the seashell emblems of
Compostela pinned onto the broad brimmed hats they wore to protect them
from the fierce Castilian sun and onto their long capes that served as
blankets to ward off the cold at night. They carried long staffs to help them
pace the arduous route across northern Spain and kept their precious water .
supply in gourds attached to their waists. *'Give me my scallop shell of
quiet,/My staff of faith to walk upon,'* wrote Sir Walter Raleigh, *'My gown of
glory, hope's true gage;/And thus I'll take my pilgrimage.'*

Tradition has it that after Saint James was martyred by Herod in
Jerusalem, his body came to the coast of Galicia aboard a marble boat
guided by an angel and reached *Iria Flavia*, the capital of Roman Galicia,
which is modern day Padrón. In 813 a strong, supernatural light shone on a
wood turning it into a ***Campus Stellae*** or field of stars and the shrine which
was later to be today's cathedral was built. The discovery of Saint James'
body here came at a crucial time in the early days of the long saga of the
Christian Reconquest of Spain from the Muslims. They had the arm of the
prophet and from now on the Christian armies had no less a morale-boosting
relic in Saint James. At the battle of Clavijo in 844, Santiago put in a
personal appearance riding a white charger. This miraculous intervention
ensured the Christian victory and was the talk of half Europe, Christian and
Muslim. As well as in the scallop-shell robes of Santiago the pilgrim, Spain's
special saint is depicted as *Santiago Matamoros*, Saint James the Moor
Slayer, a valiant crusading knight lashing out at the infidel with his
broadsword. All this was incredibly exciting for the medieval world. Up went
the cathedral and a succession of monasteries and hospitals to house visitors
and to minister to them; out went the word of new and ever more wonderful
miracles; kings ensured protection for pilgrims, and popes granted
indulgences. As the Muslim threat receded, Santiago de Compostela turned
the pilgrimage tourist trade into an art form.

Santiago and his shrine remain the focal point of Compostela today for
this is very much a Cathedral city. It is also a university town whose 30,000
students keep it young and lively and it is, in addition, the political capital of
Galicia which ensures that its grand old buildings, filled as they are with
officials, are in generally good shape. Architecturally the old part of the city
stopped developing in the Baroque age and as a result it has a very special
feel to it.

🏢 ★★★★★ *Araguaney*, c/ Alfredo Brañas, 5 ☎ 59 59 00 🛏 57 ✦ 🎙 🌊
🖥 AE, DC, EC, V $$$$$.

🏢 ★★★★★ *Hotel Reyes Católicos*, Pl de España, 1 ☎ 58 22 00 🛏 157 🌢🌢🌢
✦ 🎙 ♨ ≪ AE, DC, EC, V $$$$$. The magnificent 16C Royal Hospital
on the Cathedral square now has luxurious facilities such as air
conditioning. A night here is an aesthetic experience.

🏢 ★★★★ *Compostela*, c/ Hórreo, 1 ☎ 58 57 00 🛏 99 🎙 AE, DC, EC,
V $$$.

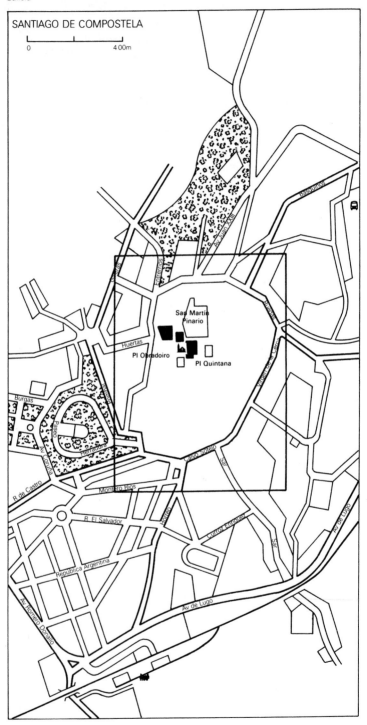

SANTIAGO DE COMPOSTELA

0   400m

San Martín Pinario

Pl Obradoiro

Pl Quintana

▦ ★★★★ *Los Tilos*, Ctra de la Estrada, km2, in Montouto ☎ 59 77 00 ⊨
84 ✦ 🎤 🐾 ➳ « AE, DC, EC, MC, V $$$ to $$$$. Quiet.

▦ ★★★★ *Peregrino*, Av Rosalía de Castro, s/n ☎ 59 18 50 ⊨ 148 ✦ 🎤
➳ « AE, DC, EC, V $$$ to $$$$.

▦ ★★★ *Gelmírez*, c/ Hórreo, 92 ☎ 56 11 00 ⊨ 138 🎤 AE, DC, EC,
MC, V $$ to $$$.

(For more economical accommodation in boarding houses and the like,
enquire at the Tourism Office.)

🍴 *Anexo Vilas* (closed: Mondays), Av Vilagarcía, 21 ☎ 59 83 87 ✳ AE, 🍷🍷
DC, EC, V $$$ to $$$$. Something of an institution, this restaurant has
been serving classic Galician food since the turn of the century.

🍴 *Camilo* (closed: Saturdays lunchtime), c/ A Raíña, 24 ☎ 58 11 66 V $$$.
Galician cuisine and good Ribeiro wines.

🍴 *Don Gaiferos* (closed: Sundays and Christmas), Rúa Nova, 23 ☎ 🍷
58 38 94 ✳ AE, DC, EC, V $$$ to $$$$. A relaxing atmosphere and a
menu which combines international and Galician cuisine.

🍴 *El Asesino* (closed: Saturdays lunchtime and Sundays), Pl Universidad,
16 ☎ 58 15 68 $$$. It has been popular with students for generations.

🍴 *Fornos* (closed: Sunday nights), c/ Hórreo, 24 ☎ 56 57 21 AE, DC, EC,
V $$$. A local classic.

🍴 *La Tacita de Oro*, c/ Hórreo, 31 ☎ 56 32 55 ✳ AE, DC, EC, V $$$.
Long-established.

🍴 *Las Huertas* (closed: Sundays), c/ Huertas, 16 ☎ 56 19 79 ✳ AE, DC,
EC, V $$$. Stylish French-Basque cuisine.

🍴 *Retablo* (closed: Sunday nights and Mondays), Rúa Nova, 13 ☎
56 59 50 ✳ AE, DC, EC, V $$$ to $$$$. Elegant setting for the expense
account client.

🍴 *Vilas* (closed: Sunday nights from May to October), Av Rosalía de Castro, 🍷🍷
88 ☎ 59 10 00 ✳ AE, DC, MC, V $$$ to $$$$. The founding restaurant
of *Anexo Vilas* (see above).

Best buys: Jet and silver jewelry and art objects are sold at *Malde
Aragonés*, Rúa del Villar, 38; *Sargadelos* ceramics at Rúa Nova, 16; antique 🍷
🍷 furniture and crafts at *Artespaña*, c/ General Pardiñas, 21, and at *Sánchez
Veres*, Av Rajoy, 13; works of art by young Galician painters at the *Trinta*
gallery, Rúa Nova, 30; Galician cakes and delicacies at *Confitería Mora*, Rúa
del Villar, 60; local cheese at *La Casa de los Quesos*, c/ Bautizados, 10, and
wines at *Carro*, c/ Cantón Toural, 6. Spanish fashion can be bought at *A.
Alzate*, c/ General Pardiñas, 8, *Bella Otero*, Rúa Nova, 4, and *Carpe Diem*,
c/ Dr. Teixeiro, 20.

🍷🍷 **Cultural highlights:** In the **old quarter**, the great Cathedral square, the **Pl
del Obradoiro**, is one the great squares of the world. It is flanked by 🍷🍷🍷
magnificent buildings, the **Royal Hospital** built by the Catholic Monarchs
🍷 and now a luxury hotel with a fine **façade**, the 18C **Rajoy Palace**, now the
seat of the Galician Regional Government and the Town Hall, the **Gelmírez
Palace** and the **Cathedral** itself, and the square and its buildings achieve a 🍷🍷🍷
rare grace, harmony and balance. The Cathedral's **Obradoiro façade** was 🍷🍷🍷
designed in 1738 by **Casas y Novoa**, and sets the tone for Santiago's
Baroque but the real jewel is right behind, as you enter the Cathedral, in the
form of the truly awesome Romanesque doorway, the **Pórtico de la Gloria**. 🍷🍷🍷

You can spend hours gazing at each and every one of the more than 200
figures carved on the portico for together they sum up the whole medieval
universe. As you drag yourself away, dig your fingers into the holes at the
foot of the tree of Jesse in the central column, which is what people have
been doing for nearly a thousand years, and then bump your forehead
against the self-portrait of the portico's 12C creator, **Master Mateo**, which is

on the other side of the column. The tradition is that some of Mateo's wisdom and artistry might rub off with a friendly bump. The S door, called the **Puerta de las Platerías**, also dates from the early Romanesque Cathedral and was completed at the beginning of the 12C. To the right stands the 17C **Torre del Reloj**. The **Azabachería façade** is Baroque, designed by Ferro Caaveiro though later modified by the ubiquitous Ventura Rodríguez. The door known as the **Puerta del Perdón** dates from 1611 and gives onto the **Pl de la Quintana** on which also stand the lovely 17C houses, the **Casa de la Parra** and **Casa de la Canónica**.

Entering the Cathedral, all attention is focused on the statue of Santiago, the *Señor Santiago* as he is known here, which looks out over the main nave from its vantage point behind the main altar. It is traditional to mount the small staircase behind the altar which brings you level with the 12C statue and to embrace Santiago with an Hispanic *abrazo*. You will find yourself drawn irresistibly to do so. The interior of the cathedral is dripping with Baroque riches and intricacies, ornamentation and finery beneath the medieval vaults. It is heady with the scent of incense and candlewax and at the side altars whispered confessions are heard in just about every language as befits a universal Catholic shrine. If you catch a major church service, such as the one on Saint James's feast day on July 25, you will see the church triumphant in full cry as the organ booms out and as a giant thurible, called the *botafumeiro*, which needs eight strong men to carry it, swings dramatically from a pulley fixed to the ceiling and careers up and down the crossing. It is theatre of the highest order. The **cloister**, entered by the N crossing is in a florid Gothic style built by Castilian Renaissance master masons Gil de Hontañón and Juan de Alava. The **Cathedral Museum** exhibits **archaeological finds** and excellent **tapestries**.

When you have 'done' the cathedral, get the feel of Santiago by strolling along the colonnaded **Rúa del Villar** and along the **c/ Franco** and the **Rúa Nova**. The old quarter is a succession of convents and monasteries (like the 16-18C **San Martín Pinario** on the Pl de la Inmaculada), palaces and **university** buildings (notice the Gothic-Renaissance **Colegio Fonseca**), porticoes and old houses that take you through an architectural course from the Romanesque to the Baroque by way of the Gothic style. To appreciate the sweep of this unique area take a walk along the **Paseo de la Herradura**, from where you get a lovely **view** of the cathedral and the city, and beyond the old quarter, along c/ Castrin d'Ouro, don't forget to visit the 12C Romanesque **Collegiate Church of Santa María del Sar**, outstanding for its originality.

Fiestas: Ascension Thursday, the sixth after Easter, and especially **Saint James's day** (patron saint of the city), July 25, are celebrated in style with spectacular fireworks.

Local sights: The **Monasterio de Santa María de Conxo**, 2km on the N-550 towards Pontevedra, was founded in the 9C and rebuilt in the 17C. Part of its Romanesque cloister still stands. Taking the N-525 to Orense, turn left after 12km onto a local road at Lestedo to reach the **Pico Sacro**, Galicia's sacred mountain. Continuing on the N-525, the **Pazo de Oca**, 25km away, is a fascinating Baroque country mansion with charmingly romantic **gardens** (open: 9.00-1.00 and 3.00-8.00).

On the town: The old quarter of the town is an ideal *tapa* bar hopping zone. The done thing is to drink the local wines and eat octopus Galician style. Popular bars and taverns include *Beadense*, c/ Entremurallas, 7, *Camilo*, c/ A Raíña, 29, *Submarino*, c/ Franco, 49, *Suso*, Rúa del Villar, 65, *Vilas*, c/ Rosalía de Castro, 88, and *Xachegou*, c/ Algalia de Abajo, 27. *Derby*, c/ Huérfanas, 29, is a classic coffee house that has been popular for more than a century. Night-time drinking among the student crowd goes on at *Modus Vivendi*, Pl de Feijóo, and *Tamboura*, c/ General Pardiñas, 22. C/ Alfredo Brañas had three discotheques on it at the last count: *Araguaney*, *Don Juan* and *Liberty*. Finally, those who rise very early or who won't sleep until after dawn meet at the cafés *Azul*, Rúa del Villar, 85, or at *Pereira*, c/ A Senra, 4.

Sports: Gliding, golf, squash and tennis can be practised at the *Aero Club de Santiago*, Labacolla airport ☎ 59 24 00. Tennis and squash can also be played at *G. Spargart*, c/ Fernando III el Santo, s/n, and on the university campus. For information on local salmon fishing and hunting licences, contact *La Venatoria de Santiago de Compostela*, c/ Hórreo, 108 ☎ 56 26 63 —*Galaico Caza*, Av R. de Padrón, 2 ☎ 58 18 55, and *Spain Safaris*, Apdo Correos 752 ☎ 58 41 78, also organize shoots. Horse lovers can go riding at the *Escuela de Equitación Barbacena* in Arines (7km).

TUY-TUI **Pontevedra** ☎ (986), pop. 15,950, [i] Av de Portugal ☎ 60 17 89, ✉ c/ Martínez Padín, 12 ☎ 60 02 20, ✛ 60 16 84, **P** 60 08 10, 🚍 Av La Concordia ☎ 60 08 13. Vigo 29km, Pontevedra 48km, Madrid 604km.

A cathedral town that stands on the River **Miño**, the natural border between Galicia and Portugal, Tuy was first settled by the Romans. The international bridge, built in 1884, turned the town into the main entry point from Galicia into Portugal.

- 🏨 ★★★ *Parador San Telmo*, Av Portugal, s/n ☎ 60 03 09 ⚏ 22 **P** ✦ ⚘ ⚲ ≪ ♪ 🅠 AE, DC, EC, MC, V $$$ to $$$$. An extremely quiet and scenically located parador built on the lines of the region's *pazos*. The **restaurant** is good.
- 🏨 ★★★ *Colón Tuy*, c/ Colón, 11 ☎ 60 02 23 ⚏ 45 ⵉ 🆃🆅 **P** ✦ ⚲ ≪ ♁ AE, DC, EC, V $$ to $$$.

Best buys: There are bargains of all sorts in this bustling border town, especially at the **open-air market** held on Thursdays. Antiques can be bought at *Anfora*, Av Portugal, 38.

Cultural highlights: The **Cathedral**, as was usual with border cities, was heavily fortified in the Middle Ages. Its N door is in the Romanesque style and its interior cloister, 13C with a 15C facelift, is very attractive. There are good **views** over the town from the battlements. The cathedral is set in the picturesque **old quarter** of the town where the heraldic shields on the buildings let you know that Tuy felt itself to be an important place down the ages. The **Church of San Bartolomé**, on the outskirts, is early Romanesque, though its Neoclassical façade was added in the 18C. The **Church of San Telmo** owes more to Portugal than to Spain in its Baroque ornamentation, and the **Church of Santo Domingo**, situated alongside the **Santo Domingo Park** with good views of the Miño and of the Cathedral, is essentially Gothic with Baroque additions.

Fiestas: The town's red letter day is the second Monday after Easter, the feast of San Telmo. There is a *romería* pilgrimage to the shrine of the *Virgen de las Angustias* in July, and in August the canoeing event down the Miño, the *Descenso del Miño*, is a gigantic party.

Local sights: The C-550 follows the Miño down to the ocean and passes through the splendid wine growing district called the Valle del Rosal. **LA GUARDIA** is a picturesque little fishing village that is made more delightful by the quality of its lobsters. There is a good **open-air market** on Tuesdays. Nearby, 3km S, the **Monte Santa Tecla** is a superb vantage point on a clear day for **views** of the Miño estuary and of the Portuguese and Galician coastlines.

VERÍN **Orense** ☎ (988), pop. 10,642, ✚ 41 16 00. Orense 79km, Madrid 430km.

This picturesque old castle town with its paved streets and noble homes was already an important market centre in the Middle Ages. It produces wines and also bottled mineral water (sold under the names of **Fontenova, Villaza, Sousas** and **Cabreiroa**) so its prosperity is suitably diversified and assured.

🅿🅿 ▦ ★★★ *Parador de Monterrey*, 4km out of town on the Orense road and next to the castle ☎ 41 00 75 ⊨ 23 🅿 ✚ ⚒ ⚓ ≪ AE, DC, EC, MC, V $$$ to $$$$. Very quiet with marvellous views and comfortably decorated in the regional style. The **restaurant** serves Galician cuisine.

🍴 *Gallego* (closed: Tuesdays except in summer), c/ Luis Espada, 24 ☎ 41 06 18 $$$. Regional cooking.

Best buys: Take a look at the bargains from the Wednesday and Friday markets. Antiques are sold at *M. Fernández García*, Pl García Bardón, 9.

🅿 **Cultural highlights:** The medieval **Castle of Monterrey** offers a fine **view** of the valley of Verín and the Portuguese border which is precisely why it was built here. The first line of walls dates from the 17C and the keep, built in the 15C, is the oldest part of the fortress. The village church (13C) has a good

🅿 W door.

Fiestas: A *romería* pilgrimage in honour of San Antón is held on January 17. **Local sights:** The nearby **Monastery of Santa María** at Mijós is a good example of 10C Mozarabic architecture. **GINZO DE LIMIA**, 33km on the N-525, which has a 16C castle, the Castillo de Sandías, is famed for its ancient and characteristic **carnival** celebrations. You can acquire the very extraordinary masks that are worn for the event at *J. Carreras*, c/ San Roque, 15. Similar carnivals, with very clear pagan associations, are held in the village of **LAZA**, 19km N of Verín, but be warned that you are not allowed to watch: you have to take part.

VIGO **Pontevedra** ☎ (986), pop. 263,998, 🛈 c/ Avenidas, s/n ☎ 43 05 77, ☎ Av José Antonio, s/n, ✉ Pl Compostela ☎ 43 81 44, ✚ 43 89 00, P 43 22 11, ✈ Vigo, 9km ☎ 27 05 50 (Iberia ☎ 22 70 05, Aviaco ☎ 27 40 56), ⚓ Trasmediterránea ☎ 43 03 11 🚌 ALSA, c/ Carral, 14 ☎ 21 60 21, 🚋 43 11 14. Pontevedra 27km, Orense 101km, La Coruña 156km, Madrid 600km.

Together with La Coruña and El Ferrol, Vigo is the industrial hub of Galicia as well as the most important **fishing port** in Spain. If most of Galicia is backward and rural, Vigo comes as a strong contrast. It is a self-confident, assertive town, a place that attracts people to work and live there rather than forcing them to emigrate, which is what tragically occurs in so much of the

🅿 region. As industrial hubs go it is also **scenic**, for the **Ría de Vigo** is very 🅿 lovely.

Originally *Vicus Spacorum*, a Roman settlement and an important stopping point on the Roman road linking Braga in Portugal with Astorga in the province of León, Vigo was destroyed by the 10C Muslim warlord Al-Mansur, a brilliant campaigner who was in the habit of reducing to rubble everything that stood in his path. Ferdinand II repopulated it in the 12C, making it a dependency of the archbishopric of Santiago de Compostela, and Philip II, in the 16C, built it up into a key trading port with Spanish America. Towards the end of the 18C, Vigo was 'discovered' by entrepreneurs from Catalonia who settled in the town and rapidly developed its fishing industry and its commerce. In the c/ Arenal there are a number of the Modernist houses which are two a penny in Barcelona and here is a sure sign that the Catalans set down roots and prospered.

▦ ★★★★ *Bahía de Vigo*, Av Cánovas del Castillo, 5 ☎ 22 67 00 ⬤ 110
  ⬤ ≪ AE, DC, MC, V $$$$ to $$$$$. The town's best hotel and matched
  by a good **restaurant**.

▦ ★★★★ *Ciudad de Vigo*, c/ Concepción Arenal, 5 ☎ 22 78 20 ⬤ 101
  ⬤ ⬤ AE, DC, EC, MC, V $$$$. Modern.

▦ ★★★★ *Coia*, c/ Sangenjo, 1 ☎ 20 18 20 ⬤ 126 ⬤ ⬤ AE, DC,
  MC, V $$$ to $$$$.

▦ ★★★★ *Gran Hotel Samil Playa*, on Samil beach, 6.5km from Vigo ☎
  20 52 11 ⬤ 127 ✦ ⬤ ⬟ ⌖ ▦ ≪ ⬤ ⋪ AE, DC, EC, MC, V $$$ to
  $$$$.

▦ ★★★ *Ensenada*, c/ Alfonso XIII, 35 ☎ 22 61 00 ⬤ 109 🅿 AE, EC, DC,
  MC, V $$ to $$$.

▦ ★★★ *Ipanema*, c/ Alcalde Vázquez Varela, 31 ☎ 47 13 44 ⬤ 60 🅿 ⬤
  DC, V $$$.

🍴 *Casa Simón* (closed: Mondays and 15/10-30/10), in Balea, near
  Cangas de Morrazo ☎ 30 00 16 🅿 AE, MC, V $$$. Very good seafood
  and classic fish stews with some imagination thrown in.

🍴 *Cíes*, Playa de Canido, 9km from Vigo ☎ 49 01 01 🅿 ≪ MC, V $$$.

🍴 *El Canario* (closed: Sunday nights, Mondays and November), in Chapela,
  7km ☎ 45 30 40 AE, DC, MC, V $$$. Seafood and fish stews.

🍴 *El Castillo* (closed: Mondays), Paseo Rosalía de Castro, s/n, in Monte del
  Castro ☎ 42 12 99 🅿 ✦ ❋ ≪ $$$. Grills, steaks, fish and seafood.

🍴 *El Mosquito* (closed: Sundays and 15/8-15/9), Pl de Juan Villavicencio,
  4 ☎ 43 35 70 ❋ V $$$. Classic Galician cooking.

🍴 *Puesto Piloto Alcabre* (closed: Sunday nights), Av Atlántida, 194 ☎
  29 79 75 🅿 ≪ AE, DC, MC, V $$$. Fish and seafood.

🍴 *Síbaris* (closed: Sundays and 1/10-15/10), Av García Barbón, 168 ☎
  22 15 26 ❋ AE, MC, V $$$ to $$$$. Delicious modern Galician cooking.

🍴 *Timón Playa* (closed: Sundays and November), c/ Carrasqueira, 12, in
  Corujo ☎ 49 08 15 🅿 ✦ ≪ AE, DC, EC, V $$$. Fish and seafood.

Beaches: The beaches of Alcabre, Canido and **Samil**, S of the city, are well
equipped and have a lovely promenade. Avoid bathing near the Lagares river
which is polluted.

Best buys: Bargains of all sorts can be obtained at the *Mercado de la
Piedra*, Pl de Villavicencio, which is great fun, and from the Wednesday and
Saturday **open-air market**. Fish and seafood can be bought at the *Mercado
del Berbés* by the port. Antiques, chiefly silver and porcelain, can be found at
Baptista, Gran Vía, 118, *C. Román*, c/ Paraguay, 15, and *Lepina*, Pl
Constitución, 6, while cut glass and hand-painted porcelain are best bought at
Artisán, c/ Marqués de Valladares, 34. Fashion, much of it Galician, is sold at
Charme, c/ Urzaiz, 117, *D'Aquino*, c/ López Neira, 8, *María Moreira*, c/
López de Neira, 16, and *Reverie*, c/ Velázquez Moreno, 25. The town's large
department store, *El Corte Inglés*, is on c/ Gran Vía, 25.

Cultural highlights: The **old quarter** around the very lovely Plaza Mayor,
the Pl Almeida and the c/ Real is a picturesque mix of steep bustling narrow
streets and old 15-18C stone town houses. It leads to the even older **barrio
de Berbés**, a quarter where the ancient colonnades have a salty tang to them
because originally this was the sea front. The Ensanche is the area built up at
the turn of the century as Vigo's prosperity increased and its main features
are the **Modernist houses** of the 19C new rich and the Neoclassical
collegiate church and co-cathedral (it shares cathedral status with Santiago),
the Colegiata Concatedral de Santa María. The church is alongside the
Mercado de la Piedra, a very agreeable market which is one of the liveliest
and most picturesque spots in Vigo. The **Municipal Museum** is in the 18C
Pazo Quiñones de León, Av de Castrelos (open: 9.00-7.00; Sundays:

10.00-2.00; closed: Mondays ☎ 47 10 66) and houses some archaeological finds as well as works by contemporary Galician painters.

Fiestas and festivals: The feast of the *Santísimo Cristo de los Afligidos*, on the third Sunday in July is celebrated in Bouzas with boat processions and sporting and cultural events. There is also a music festival during July.

Local sights: El Castro and La Guía are hills, 3km in the direction of Cangas de Morrazo, which offer panoramic **views** of the city and the Ría de Vigo. The **Islas Cíes** nature reserve can be reached by boat from the port of Vigo. Following the estuary inland, you reach the scenic village of **REDONDELA**, which has a fine Gothic church, the Iglesia de Santiago and, nearby **ARCADE**, famous for its excellent oysters. The A-9 motorway, crossing the *ría*, passes the village of **CANGAS DE MORRAZO**, which figures in Galicia's abundant witch lore for a celebrated coven was discovered here and its members were burnt at the stake. *Casa Simón* (see above) attracts food lovers from Vigo. The village of **PORRIÑO**, SE, is graced by the fine Pazo de Castrelos, and **MONDARIZ**, continuing along the N-120, is a spa town with a medieval castle, the ruins of an old monastery and the remains of a Celtic *castro* called Toaña. The C-550 leads to the little port village of **PANJON**, and to the **Playa América**, which is one of the busiest of Galicia's summer resorts. If you climb up the Monteferro, you will get lovely **views** of the area.

On the town: The best *tapa* bar areas are around the *Mercado de la Piedra* and in the Berbés quarter by the port. *Tapas* in Vigo are **seafood** orientated and oysters are very reasonably priced. Popular Galician wine bars include *Costa do Mariñeiro*, c/ Real, and *Chabolas*, c/ de los Cestos. Evening *rendez-vous* points include *La Goleta*, c/ Luis Taboada, 29, and *Lord Byron*, Don Rúa, s/n, and late night drinking (for Vigo is a late night town) goes on in places such as *Luada*, Gran Vía, the sophisticated *No Se Lo Digas a Mamá*, c/ Arenal, the rather avant garde *Ruralex*, c/ Lepanto, *Xip*, c/ Arenal, and the more conventional *Manco*, c/ Lepanto, and *Nova Olimpia*, c/ Uruguay, 3.

Sports: The local yacht club, the *Real Club Náutico de Vigo* ☎ 43 26 03, organizes a number of competitions and regattas and also has a sailing school. There is a 9-hole, par 72 golf course as well as flying facilities at the local flying club, the *Aeroclub de Vigo*, 8km ☎ 22 11 60. Squash players head for *Squash 79*, c/ Arenal, 148 ☎ 22 75 65, and tennis players for *Club de Campo* ☎ 49 01 11.

VILLALBA **Lugo** ☎ (982), pop. 16,225, ✚ 51 11 51, **P** 51 07 67. Lugo 39km, La Coruña 87km, Madrid 540km.

This old town was part of the fiefdom of a powerful medieval family called Andrade and the scene of much warlike activity. Nowadays it is famed and visited for pleasanter reasons such as its excellent **capons**, traditional Christmas fare, and its San Simón **cheeses**, arguably the best in Galicia.

★★★ *Parador Condes de Villalba*, c/ Valeriano Valdesuso, s/n ☎ 51 00 11 ☙ 6 **P** AE, DC, MC, V $$$$. Tiny and historic, this parador is set in the medieval tower where the Andrade family held out.

★★★ *Villamartín*, Av Tierra Llana, s/n, 1km E on the Meira road ☎ 51 12 15 ☙ 60 **P** ♦ ♪ ⚊ ♘ ♙ AE, DC, EC, V $$.

♜ *O Sardiña*, in Lanzós, 10km **P** $$. Set in a pretty farmhouse.

Fiestas: A capon fair is held on December 19, when people snap up the fattened birds for their Christmas dinner.

Local sights: **MONDOÑEDO** (see separate entry), 34km on the N-634, is interesting. Following this road, or taking the C-641 from Villalba and then the C-640, you can explore the beautiful Lugo coastline which is oddly off the normal tourist beat (see 'Rías Altas').

LEVANTE

Every nation has its market garden area whose people have industriously and for many generations produced fruit and vegetables for their fellow countrymen. The Levante region, which comprises the three provinces that make up the Valencian Autonomous Community, and the adjoining single province Community of Murcia are the market garden of Spain; the volume of their agricultural produce is such that they are also able to supply much of Europe. The two regions occupy the central stretch of Spain's Mediterranean coastline with the shore of Catalonia to the N and that of Andalusia to the S. They share, also, the excellent frost-free climate that permits intensive cultivation and their respective populations have in common a hardworking, mercantile approach to life that has prompted a wealth of local industries and high cultural standards. Although grouped together here for the sake of convenience, Levante and Murcia are distinct regions with a different historical and artistic heritage.

The **Autonomous Community of Valencia** extends along the Mediterranean, from Vinaroz in the N to Orihuela, on the border with Murcia, in the S. Flat and fertile along the coast, the land rises steeply inland. In the N of the Levante region the **Sistema Ibérico** mountain range that forms a barrier along northern Castile and southern Aragón finally tapers off as it meets the sea. In the S a different sierra formation, the **Sub-bético**, makes its appearance. Between the two ranges, Levante climbs upward to meet the high tableland plateau of southern Castile.

Some four million people live in Levante making it one of the more densely populated areas of Spain and in addition to Castilian Spanish they speak *valenciano*, a dialect of the Catalan language: the area was conquered from the Muslim invader by Catalonia and repopulated by Catalans. This prosperous region of theirs is a patchwork of **orchards**, **rice** growing paddy fields and **vineyards**. However, farm land has been giving way to industry, particularly from the 1960s onwards, for Levante is a key manufacturing centre for the textile, toy making and shoe sectors. Today's Valencians owe much to the early medieval **Muslims** who occupied Levante. The Arabs, skilled in these matters, introduced the complex irrigation system that ensures the region's fertility and also introduced the cultivation of oranges and rice that have remained the mainstay of Levante's agriculture. It was during this period of occupation that a silk industry grew up, paper manufacturing began in the Játiva area and distinctive ceramics began to be fashioned at Manises. The Levante region provided rich booty for the 13C Aragonese-Catalan monarch **James I, the Conqueror**, and he retook it for the Christians, creating the **Kingdom of Valencia**. After the war of Spanish Succession at the start of the 18C, the local, semi-autonomous, privileges of Valencia were abolished, as were those of Catalonia and Aragón, by the incoming Bourbon dynasty.

Levante has a well developed culture of its own and it can be traced way back to prehistoric cave paintings and to the extraordinary ancient Iberian sculpture called the *Dama de Elche* (the *Lady of Elche*). The Romans left their mark on this region, notably in Sagunto where a well preserved Roman theatre still survives, and the Arabs bequeathed their castles and their architectural tradition. To this day the mock battles between Moors and

Christians are a much loved *fiesta* ritual throughout the region. In Levante, *fiestas* are as colourful as anywhere in Spain, perhaps more so for the Valencians love music and gunpowder which means that they have unrivalled mass bands and state of the art fireworks. When it comes to celebrating, Valencians are joyful and showy to the point of ostentation which could explain why Baroque architecture struck such strong roots in the area. The cultivation of rice, of course, explains why Levante is the home of *paella*, the most travelled of all Spanish dishes.

Wedged between the Valencia region and Andalusia, **Murcia** was historically coveted by Castilians and Catalans alike but nevertheless managed to develop a strong personality of its own. Arid in some areas but more **fertile** than any other along the Segura river, Murcia was home to the Iberians, the Carthaginians and the Romans, to the Visigoths and Muslims. All found it a land of plenty and Murcia evolved as a synthesis of the different civilizations that passed through Spain. The potential of its 250km of coastline, which is not unlike the highly developed Alicante one in Levante, is only now being discovered and is leading to a different sort of invasion as **resorts** are built up along La Ribera and **La Manga** and by Mazarrón and Aguilas. The Murcia region receives 3,000 hours of **sunshine** a year and the **Mar Menor**, a virtual inland sea closed in by sand banks, provides magnificently warm waters.

Murcia's prime quality market garden produce makes it one of the best food centres of Spain and connoisseurs who visit the region for its cuisine soon find themselves attracted by other cultural aspects of the area's personality. These range from the moving folk music that evolved from the region's ancient mines and is called the *Cante de la Minas* to the odd traditional custom called *trovo* which consists of maintaining impromptu dialogues in rhyming verses. Art lovers should note that Murcia is famed for its **Baroque architecture**. As in the case of Levante, this ornate style suits the Murcian personality and its evolution in the 17C coincided with a time of prosperity in this generally affluent region.

ALCOY-ALCOI **Alicante** ☎ (96), pop. 65,435, ✚ 533 22 40, **P** 554 05 48. Alicante 55km, Valencia 110km, Murcia 136km, Madrid 403km.

Ringed by factories that produce paper, textiles and toys, Alcoy is representative of Levante's industrial energy. The town itself stands astride three rivers and as many ravines and its different districts are linked by a network of bridges. Its textile workers staged a revolutionary uprising in 1873 which was squashed, as was the Paris commune that had inspired it. Since then the town has been mostly prosperous and quiet.

🏨 ★★★ *Reconquista*, c/ Puente de San Jorge, 1 ☎ 533 09 00 ⛌ 77 **P** 🎤 🎵 ≪ AE, DC, EC, V $$ to $$$.

◐ 🍴 *Venta del Pilar* (closed: Sundays, August and Holy Week), Ctra de Valencia, km2.5, in Concentaina ☎ 559 23 25 **P** ♣ ❄ DC, EC, V $$$. A nice-looking 18C tavern serving regional cuisine.

◐ **Cultural highlights:** The town looks extremely **picturesque** if you view it from the Cristina bridge which is on the road to Callosa de Ensarría. The old Town Hall, a pleasing Renaissance building, now houses an archaeological museum, the Museo Arqueológico Camilo Visedo, c/ San Miguel, 29 (open: 8.00-1.00; closed: Sundays ☎ 554 03 02) and in the same street, at No. 60, the Museo de Fiestas del Casal de Sant Jordi (open: 10.00-1.30 and 5.30-8.00; closed: Saturdays and holiday afternoons) exhibits the costumes worn in the Christian and Moor battles fought during the town's *fiestas*.

◐ **Fiestas:** The *Moros y Cristianos* fiestas are held on Saint George's Day, April 23, or thereabouts.

`ALICANTE-ALACANT` **Alicante** ☎ (96), pop. 265,543, *i* Explanada de
España, 2 ☎ 521 22 85, ✛ 523 07 02, **P** 528 44 11, ✈ El Altet, 12km on
the N-332 ☎ 528 50 11 (Iberia ☎ 520 60 00), ⚓ Trasmediterránea ferries
☎ 520 60 11, 🚌 522 07 00, 🚆 522 68 40. Murcia 81km, Albacete 168km,
Valencia 174km, Madrid 417km.

Now the bustling capital of the busy **Costa Blanca** resort area, the
expanding town of Alicante handles, in addition to tourists, the export of the
agricultural produce of southern Levante and of the neighbouring region of
Murcia.

Founded originally by the Greeks, who called it *Akra Leuka*, the White
City, and then settled by the Romans who changed the name to *Lucentum*,
the City of Light, Alicante was ruled by the Muslims between 8-13C and
known as *Al-Lekant*. It received its town charter in 1490 from Ferdinand the
Catholic King as a reward for harrying the Muslims during the campaign to
take the Moorish kingdom of Granada. The expulsion from Spain of the
Moriscos, the converted Muslims, in the 17C severely undermined the
town's economy and it was not until 1778 that the town began to recover
thanks to a special royal privilege that allowed it to trade with Latin America.
In 1858 a railroad linking it to Madrid was inaugurated and gradually
Alicante became a favourite Mediterranean resort.

🏨 ★★★★★ *Sidi San Juan Palace*, Playa de San Juan, Partida Cabo la
Huerta (5km from Alicante) ☎ 516 13 00 🛏 176 TV ♦ 🎤 🏂 ⚓ 🏊 🖼 «
🐎 **DC, EC, V** $$$$ to $$$$$. A quiet hotel on the beach, with very good
views.

🏨 ★★★★ *Adoc*, La Albufereta beach, Finca Adoc, Edif Rocafel, bl 17-18
(4km from Alicante) ☎ 526 59 00 🛏 93 TV ♦ ⚓ 🏊 🖼 « 🐎 ♜ **AE, DC,
MC, V** $$ to $$$.

🏨 ★★★★ *Gran Sol*, Av Méndez Núñez, 3 ☎ 520 30 00 🛏 150 ⚷ TV 🎤 «
AE, DC, MC, V $$$$. Central, with lovely views from the bar.

🍴 *Auberge de France* (closed: Tuesdays and 13/10-31/10), La Albufereta
beach, Finca Las Palmeras ☎ 526 06 02 **P** ♦ ❋ **AE, EC, V** $$$. A
pleasantly situated restaurant serving French cuisine.

🍴 *Dársena* (closed: Sunday nights and Mondays), on the quayside ☎
520 75 89 ♦ ❋ « **AE, DC, EC, V** $$$. Regional cooking with modern
touches.

🍴 *El Delfín*, c/ Explanada de España, 12 ☎ 521 49 11 ♦ ❋ « **AE, DC,
MC, V** $$$ to $$$$. Good quality fresh food.

🍴 *Nou Manolín*, c/ Villegas, 3 ☎ 520 03 68 ❋ **AE, DC, MC, V** $$$$.
Valencian cooking. The bar is very popular.

Beaches: The local one, El Postiguet, is utterly crowded in summer but
pleasant enough at other times. The beaches of **San Juan** and Muchavista
are 10km-worth of fine sand, though there too you can find standing room
only at summer weekends.

Best buys: Shoes and bags are sold at *Arpel*, c/ Explanada de España, 7,
and leather goods at *Soriano*, c/ Castaños, 1. Jewelry can be bought at
Amaya, Pl Calvo Sotelo, 13, and costume jewelry at *Lipssy*, c/ A. Lozano, 8.
Spanish fashion is available at *Diseño Moda*, c/ General Goded, 20, *Esther
González*, Pl Montañela, 1, and *Stileto*, c/ San Francisco, 14. For art and
antiques go to *Sala Goya*, c/ Gadea, 11, and for books to *Librería
Internacional*, c/ Altamira, 6. Wines are good buys at *Campo Alto*, c/
Manero Molló, 13, and cakes at *La Murciana*, c/ Rafael Terol, 7. A flea
market called the *Mercadillo de Campoamor* operates on Thursday and
Saturday mornings by the bullring. The city's department stores are *El Corte
Inglés*, c/ Arquitecto Morell, 4 and c/ Tauro, 2, and *Galerías Preciados*, Av
Federico Soto, 1.

Cultural highlights: The **Castle of Santa Bárbara**, on the hill known as Monte Benacantil, is the city's main landmark. You can get there by road from the Plà district or by cable car from Postiguet beach, and it commands fine **views** of the city and port. The oldest, and the highest, part of the fort is believed to have been raised by the Carthaginian general Hamilcar Barca in 200 BC. The middle section was built in the 16C and the third, and most recent refurbishing was carried out by the Bourbon monarchs in the 18C. The **Church of Santa María** stands at the foot of the castle in the old quarter of the town. It was founded in 1265 on the site of a former mosque and it received many subsequent facelifts including a Baroque façade in

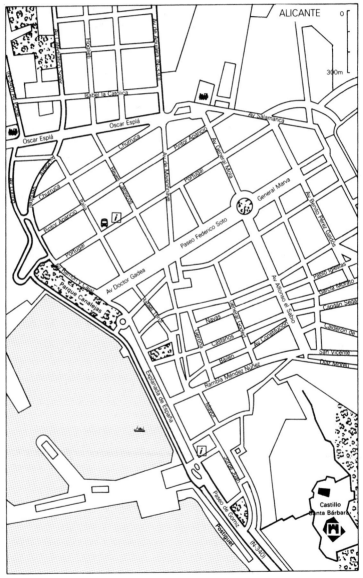

1721. The **Concatedral de San Nicolás** (it is a co-cathedral because it shares power with the older see of Orihuela), also built on the site of a former mosque, dates from the 16-17C period. The best civic buildings are the **Town Hall**, housed in an ornate 18C Churrigueresque palace, and the Casa de la Asegurada, a palace from the same period which currently houses a modern art museum, the **Museo de Arte Siglo XX**, c/ Villavieja (open: 10.00-1.00 and 5.00-8.00; closed: Sunday afternoons and Mondays ☎ 521 45 78), exhibiting works by Pablo Picasso, Salvador Dalí, Joan Miró and Juan Gris among others. The local archaeology museum, the Museo Arqueológico Provincial, is at c/ General Mola, 6 (open: 9.00-2.00; Sundays: 11.00-1.00; closed Mondays ☎ 512 12 14). The palm-tree lined promenade beside the Mediterranean known as the **Explanada de España** is one of the most agreeable in Spain.

Fiestas: Bonfires, fireworks and music mark the midsummer nights around Saint John's feastday, the *Hogueras de San Juan* (June 21-24).

Local sights: The Monastery of Santa Faz, 6km along the Valencia road, dates from the 17C. Its highpoint is an interesting Byzantine icon. Lovers of stalactites and stalagmites won't be disappointed by the **Cuevas de Canalobre** caves at Busot, 19km (open from 1/4-30/9: 10.30-8.30; rest of the year: 11.00-6.30). Taking the N-330 you reach the old town of VILLENA, 57km, which was the centre of a powerful medieval fiefdom that was dotted with **castles**, notably those of Chinchilla, Almansa, **Biar**, **Sax** and **La Mola**. Villena's own castle, the **Castillo de la Atalaya**, was occupied by men of the calibre of the Infante Juan Manuel (see 'Literature') and by the poet and occult dabbler, the Marquis of Villena. The archaeological museum, or **Museo Arqueológico**, in the Town Hall building, exhibits important Bronze Age artifacts, some made of solid gold, that are known as the **Treasure of Villena**. For a graceful late Gothic nave inspect the **Church of Santiago**; for fun visit the town during its famous **Christian versus Moors** *fiestas* at the beginning of August and for a good meal try *El Rinconcico de la Espuela*, c/ J. Zapater, 4 ☎ 580 71 34 $$, which serves local specialities.

On the town: Popular *tapa* bars include *Cervecería El Canto*, Av Alemania, 26, *El Marítimo*, c/ San Fernando, 42, *Manolín*, Pl España, 3, and *Nou Manolín*, c/ Villegas, 3. There are a number of disco pubs and music bars in the old quarter. *Peret*, on the Explanada promenade, is one of several winter sun trap terraces. In summer there is an endless choice of discotheques and bars along the beaches. Top discos include *Morasol Costa* and *Bugatti*, c/ San Fernando, 36, and *Le Palais* and *Va Bene*, on the Playa de San Juan beach. Late nightcap bars in this area include *Calígula* and *Voy Voy*.

Sports: The yacht club, the *Real Club de Regatas*, is at Paseo Conde de Vallellano, 30 ☎ 521 86 00. Tennis can be played at *C.T. Alicante*, Partida de Orgegia, s/n ☎ 526 46 11.

ALTEA **Alicante** ☎ (96), pop. 12,232, *i* Paseo Marítimo, s/n ☎ 584 23 01. Benidorm 11km, Alicante 57km, Gandía 60km, Madrid 475km.

Perched on a hill above its port, Altea is fighting hard against developers to maintain its picture postcard prettiness. There is something of an artists' colony here for the village has been a source of inspiration for a succession of painters.

🏨 ★★★ *Cap Negret*, km132 on the N-332 ☎ 584 12 00 🛏 250 P ♦ ♒ AE, V $$$ to $$$$.

🍴 *Bahía* (closed: Saturdays in winter and 24/1-1/2), Ctra de Alicante, s/n ☎ 584 00 11 P ♦ ❄ ≪ AE, DC, EC $$$. Alicante cooking.

🍴 *El Negro* (closed: Mondays), c/ Santa Bárbara, 4 ☎ 584 18 26 ♦ ❄ ≪ MC, V $$$. Excellent views from the terrace. Steaks and pasta.

🍴 ***Gullerías*** (closed: Sundays except in summer, November and December), c/ San Pedro, 1 ☎ 584 22 81 ♣ ❄ **AE, DC, EC, V** $$$.

🍴 ***La Costera*** (open: dinner only; closed: Wednesdays and August), Costera del Mestre de Música, 8 ☎ 584 02 30 ❄ **DC, V** $$ to $$$. Home cooking with a Swiss bias.

🍴 ***L'Obrador*** (closed: Sundays and February), c/ Concepción, 18 ☎ 584 09 06 ❄ **AE, EC** $$. Good pizzas.

Beaches: The local beach, El Albir, La Olla beach (with waterside bars) and the Playa de Levante (for nudists) are reasonably quiet.

Best buys: Hand-made jewelry and other crafts are sold at ***Marlyse Schmid***, c/ General Sanjurjo, 1, and ceramics at *Fina Llacer*, Travesía de San José, 5. Arts and crafts can also be bought from the flea market, the *Mercado de Artesanía*, held every afternoon by the church during July and August.

Cultural highlights: A walk up the old streets to the church and a spot of meditation there, on the high ground looking out to the Peñón de Ifach in the distance, will help you understand why sensitive, creative souls are drawn to this beauty spot.

Fiestas: Mock battles between Christians and Moors are staged on the third Sunday of April to the accompaniment of massed bands competitions to celebrate the town's patronal festival.

On the town: There are a number of fun *tapa* and music bars at the top of the town in the Pl de la Iglesia, such as the ***Bar dels Artistes***, down below near the beach, and along the high street, like the ***Bar Lledó*** and the ***Bodegón de Pepe***.

Sports: Water sports are practised at the yacht clubs, the *Club Náutico de Altea* ☎ 584 15 91 and the ***Puerto Deportivo Luis Campomanes*** ☎ 584 22 00. Golfers head for the 9-hole, par 72 course at the *Club de Golf Don Cayo*, 4km away by the Altea exit from the Autopista del Mediterráneo ☎ 584 07 16 and 584 09 50.

BENICASIM-BENICASSIM **Castellón** ☎ (964), pop. 5,257, [i] Town Hall ☎ 30 02 81. Castellón de la Plana 14km, Valencia 88km, Madrid 436km.

Benicasim was a traditional resort that was popular, thanks to its mild **microclimate**, long before the mass tourism frenzy built a concrete wall along so much of the coastline. There is a Jazz Festival in July and **Classical Guitar Concerts** are staged in August. The town features a well appointed promenade flanked by old villas and newer apartment blocks, a **beach** with **excellent facilities** and also an aquapark.

🏨 **★★★ *Azor*** (closed: 1/11-31/3), Paseo Marítimo, s/n ☎ 30 03 50 🛏 88 ✕ ♣ ≈ ⛱ « 🐴 🎾 🏌 **DC, EC, V** $$ to $$$. Good views.

🏨 **★★★ *Orange*** (closed: 1/11-31/3), Gran Avenida, s/n ☎ 30 06 00 🛏 415 ✕ ♣ 🎤 ≈ 🎾 **DC, EC, V** $$ to $$$. Pleasant swimming pools.

🏨 **★★★ *Trinimar*** (closed: 1/11-31/3), Av Ferrándis Salvador, s/n ☎ 30 08 50 🛏 170 ✕ P 🎤 ≈ ⛱ « $$$. Modern.

🏨 **★★★ *Voramar*** (closed: 13/10 to Holy Week), Paseo Marítimo, s/n, Playa de las Villas ☎ 30 01 50 🛏 55 Y ♣ ⛱ « 🐴 🎾 $$. It has a large terrace with good views.

🏨 **★★ *Bonaire*** (closed: 15/11-1/3), Paseo Marítimo, s/n ☎ 30 08 00 🛏 78 Y P ♣ ≈ ⛱ « 🎾 🏌 **DC, EC, V** $$. Set in a small pine grove.

🏨 ***Centro de Termalismo Helio-Marino y Recuperación Funcional***. A health centre —see 'Health and Beauty'.

🍴 ***Villa del Mar***, Paseo Coloma, 24 ☎ 30 28 52 P ♣ ❄ **DC, MC, V** $$$ to $$$$. A period villa set in its own gardens.

Best buys: Local liqueurs and sweet moscatel wine can be bought at ***Carmelitano***, Av Castellón, s/n.

BENIDORM **Alicante** ☎ (96), pop. 66,224, *i* Av Martínez Alejos, 16 ☎ 🖤
585 32 24 and Av de la Marina Española, s/n ☎ 585 30 75, ✉ c/
Herrerías, s/n ☎ 585 30 75 and in the *La Noria* shopping mall, c/ Lepanto,
s/n ☎ 585 07 73, ⛪ Av de la Marina Española, s/n ☎ 585 56 74, **P** c/ del
Forn, s/n ☎ 585 02 22, ✈ El Altet in Alicante, 55km ☎ 528 50 11, 🚌 c/
Portugal, 17 ☎ 522 07 00, 🚢 in Alicante ☎ 522 68 40. Alicante 44km,
Valencia 136km, Madrid 459km.

The symbol of Spain's tourist boom, Benidorm was a fishing hamlet 30
years ago. Today its population swells to more than 200,000 during the high
summer season when Britons, in particular, descend on the town to enjoy
their value for money package holidays. It is one of the biggest **beach and
leisure resorts** in the world and you either love it or leave it. The bay is
beautiful but if you want to get near the water's edge in August you will have
to get up early to book your space. Its **climate** is lovely all year round so
many plump for out-of-season Benidorm.

   ▦ ★★★★★ *Gran Hotel Delfín* (closed: 1/10-25/3), Poniente-La Cala
     beaches ☎ 585 34 00 ⇌ 87 ♿ TV ✦ ⌣ ⚓ ☂ « 🐎 AE, DC, EC, MC, V
     $$$$. Away from a lot of the town's noise.

   ▦ ★★★★ *Avenida*, c/ Gambo, s/n ☎ 585 41 08 ⇌ 150 TV ⚓ ☂ AE, DC,
     EC, MC, V $$$ to $$$$.

   ▦ ★★★★ *Belroy Palace*, Av Europa, 5 ☎ 585 02 03 ⇌ 102 ✦ ♨ ⚓ ☂
     AE, DC, EC, V $$$. Modern and functional.

   ▦ ★★★★ *Cimbel*, Av Europa, 1 ☎ 585 21 00 ⇌ 144 TV ✦ ⚓ ☂ « AE,
     DC, EC, MC, V $$$ to $$$$. Highly rated by some. Good views.

   ▦ ★★★★ *Costa Blanca-Sol* (closed: 1/11-31/3), Levante beach ☎
     585 54 50 ⇌ 190 ♿ TV ⚓ ☂ « AE, DC, EC, MC, V $$$ to $$$$.

   ▦ ★★★★ *Don Pancho*, Av del Mediterráneo, s/n ☎ 585 29 50 ⇌ 251 ✦
     ♨ ⚓ ☂ ▦ 🐎 ℚ AE, DC, EC, MC, V $$$ to $$$$. Good facilities.

   ▦ ★★★★ *Los Dálmatas Sol*, c/ Estocolmo, 4 ☎ 585 19 00 ⇌ 270 ♿ TV
     ♨ ⚓ ☂ 100m 🐎 AE, DC, EC, MC, V $$$ to $$$$. Comfortable.

   ▦ ★★★ *Las Garzas Sol* (closed: 1/11-31/3), Av de la Marina Española,
     s/n ☎ 585 48 50 ⇌ 306 TV ℙ ✦ ⌣ ⚓ ☂ 🐎 AE, DC, EC $$$. Quiet.

   ▦ ★★★ *Los Pelícanos Sol*, c/ Gerona, s/n ☎ 585 23 50 ⇌ 476 ✦ ⌣ ⚓
     ☂ ℚ AE, DC, EC, V $$$. Quiet.

   ❙❙ *Casa L'Esclau*, c/ Panaderos, s/n ☎ 585 64 15 ✦ ✳ AE, MC, V $$$.

   ❙❙ *Don Luis* (closed: January), c/ Doctor Orts Llorca, s/n ☎ 585 46 73 ✦
     ✳ AE, DC, MC, V $$$. Italian specialities.

   ❙❙ *I Fratelli* (closed: 2/11-3/12), c/ Doctor Orts Llorca, 21 ☎ 585 39 79
     ✦ ✳ AE, DC, MC, V $$$ to $$$$. Italian food.

   ❙❙ *La Barca* (closed: Mondays), Ctra Valencia, s/n ☎ 586 09 60 ℙ ✳ AE,
     DC, MC, V $$$ to $$$$. Fish and seafood.

   ❙❙ *La Caserola*, Av Bruselas, 7 ☎ 585 17 19 ✦ ✳ AE, EC, V $$ to $$$.

   ❙❙ *Tiffany's* (closed: 6/1-6/2), Av del Mediterráneo, 3 ☎ 585 44 68 ✳ AE,
     DC, EC, V $$$$. Dinners only.

Beaches: In addition to the 2km **Levante beach** and the 3km **Poniente** one,
there is **La Cala** at the entrance to the town with access from the ringroad
and the small **Mal Pas** beach at the foot of the castle. Nudists gather in a
small cove near the Alfaz del Pí lighthouse.

Best buys: The whole town is one great shopping emporium. Leather goods
are sold at *Arpel*, Rambla Méndez Núñez, 18, Av Gambo, 4 and Av
Mediterráneo, Edif Coblanca; Spanish fashion at *Betty-Boop*, Pl Triangular,
and teenage gear at *Don Algodón*, Av Europa, s/n. If you have a sweet tooth,
try the pastries at *Pastelería Moderna*, which is also a tea-shop.

Cultural highlights: Tips to avoid the highrises and the concrete jungle
include walking about the *Poble*, or old quarter, admiring the **sea views** from
the aptly named **Balcón del Mediterráneo** (Mediterranean Balcony) on the
promontory where the old fort once stood and heading 2km E along the Av
del Mediterráneo to reach the area known as the **Rincón de Loix** which has
views of orchards, mountains and the Mediterranean.

Fiestas: There are Valencian-style *fallas* (see 'Fiestas') with bonfires and
fireworks in mid-March and Benidorm's own patron saint celebrations are
staged from November 8-12.

Local sights: A good boat service makes the 3km trip to the huge rock
called **L'Illa**, beyond the bay. If you tire of Benidorm's unflagging energy,
seek peace and quiet exploring the orange and almond groves of the **Marina
Baja** area inland, or had 28km NW to the hilltop **Castell de Guadalest**, then
on to the picturesque villages of **Polop** and **Callosa de ensarria** where
local crafts like cheese making have not been forgotten. Visit the **Coll de
Rates** and the **Fuentes de Algar** fountains on your way. The neighbouring
whitewashed village of **Altea** (see separate entry) is also worth a visit.

On the town: In the high season, Benidorm is a 24 hour long activity. The centre of much of the **night life** action is the **Pl Triangular** and streets leading off it are a succession of discos, bars, fastfood places and the rest. The more typical *tapa* bars such as *La Rana*, c/ Santo Domingo, 12, and *Calpi*, Pl de la Constitución, 5, are in the old quarter of the town. The Playa de Levante area never goes to bed. Aside from the well established *Pachá* discotheque and the international shows put on at the *Benidorm Palace* in the Rincón de Loix, the two fashionable drinking and dancing spots are *Penélope* and *Star Garden* which are on the ring road and fairly wild. Daytime alternatives include the water slides, pools and gimmicks at *Aqualand*, in Sierra Helada ☎ 586 01 00 and the giant funfair at *Europa Park* ☎ 585 61 36. Gamblers go to the *Casino Costa Blanca* in Villajoyosa (see separate entry).

Sports: Water sports are practised at the yacht club, the *Club Náutico*, Paseo de Colón, s/n ☎ 585 30 67; scuba diving at the *Centro de Actividades Subacuáticas*, c/ Limones, s/n ☎ 585 44 22, and water skiing at *Cable Esquí* ☎ 585 13 86. If you prefer land sports, you can roller skate at the rink on c/ Mallorca, ice skate at *Disco-hielo Azahar*, Av Los Almendros, 3, or go bowling at the *Bowling Centre* on Av Mediterráneo. For an air expedition, you can hire ultralights ☎ 589 07 28.

CALPE-CALP **Alicante** ☎ (96), pop. 10,032, *i* Av Ejércitos Españoles, 40 ☎ 583 12 50, ✆ 583 16 16, **P** 528 44 11. Benidorm 22km, Alicante 63km, Madrid 464km.

This is a **picturesque** town whose landmark is the 332m high rock called the **Peñón de Ifach**, which is due to be turned into a nature park. You can follow a path up to the top (one hour's walk) and admire the view.

▦ **★★★ *Galetamar***, on the Moraira road, La Calalga, s/n ☎ 583 23 11 ⊨ 117 **P** ✦ ⌕ ⇌ ⌕ ≪ AE, DC, V $$$. A quiet hotel with good views.

❙❙ *Capri* (closed: Mondays from January to April and 15/11-15/12), Av Gabriel Miró, Arenal beach ☎ 583 06 14 **P** ✦ ✳ ≪ AE, DC, MC, V $$$.

❙❙ *Casita Suiza* (open: dinners only; closed: Sundays, Mondays, 18/12-15/1 and 25/6-13/7), c/ Jardín, s/n ☎ 583 06 06 ✳ AE, V $$$. Swiss cuisine.

❙❙ *El Girasol* (closed: Mondays except in summer), in Moraira ☎ 574 43 73 **P** ✦ ✳ AE, DC, EC, V $$$$. Central European cooking in an elegant villa.

Beaches: Alternatives to the port's beach are the quiet, pretty little beach at **Levante**, and Fustera on the N side of the Peñón rock.

Fiestas: There are religious processions on July 16 marking the day of the Virgin of Mount Carmel, and Moors and Christians battles are staged on October 22-23.

Local sights: The 14km drive to Moraira offers **fine views** of the sea.

Sports: Water sports are practised at the yacht club, the *Club Náutico de Calpe* ☎ 583 18 09. Golf players head for the 9-hole, par 60 course at the *Club de Golf Ifach* at Benisa, 13km from Calpe.

CARAVACA DE LA CRUZ **Murcia** ☎ (968), pop. 22,527, *i* Town Hall ☎ 70 20 00 ext 8, ✆ 70 27 12. Lorca 60km, Murcia 70km, Albacete 139km, Madrid 386km.

A hillside castle town, this was once an important wool producing centre. In the Middle Ages the town was a fiefdom of the Templar Knights and later of the Military Order of Santiago.

Best buys: Typical gold and silver crosses can be bought at *Comunidad de Bienes Chavo*, c/ Sor Evanista, 7, and sweet egg yolk candies called *yemas* at *Reina*, c/ Trafalgar, 3.

Cultural highlights: The 15C **Castle-Sanctuary of Santa Cruz** has a splendid Baroque façade. It houses a precious relic, a *Vera Cruz*, which legend says is part of the True Cross that was brought down from heaven by angels when a bullying Muslim chief called Abu-Zeid ordered a captive priest to say mass in his presence. The castle-sanctuary's History and Religious Art Museum is open from 8.00-7.00. The Convent of San José, one of the many founded by the reforming 16C mystic **Saint Teresa of Avila**, also houses a Religious Museum which is open during church services. There is an Archaeology Museum in the former Church of la Soledad (open: 10.00-1.30; closed: Sundays).

Fiestas: Moors and Christians celebrations are held from April 30 through May 5. On May 2 there is also a traditional competition involving harnessing horses and races, which is called the *Caballos del Vino*.

CARTAGENA **Murcia** ☎ (968), pop. 168,809, *i* Pl Castellini, 5 ☎ 50 75 49, ✉ Glorieta San Francisco, s/n ☎ 50 15 27, ✚ 50 27 50, **P** 10 00 00, ⚑ Av América, s/n ☎ 50 17 96. Murcia 49km, Alicante 110km, Almería 240km, Madrid 444km.

Built around a narrow, deep-water bay that is well protected by hills, Cartagena is the naval depot of Spain's Mediterranean fleet. It was already a military base in 223 BC when the Carthaginians established here what they called *Cartago Nova* or New Carthage. After the Punic Wars it became a prosperous Roman colony. The port was strongly fortified by Philip II at the time of the 16C naval wars against the Turks and the present day Arsenal dates from the 18C reign of Charles III.

🏨 **★★★** *Cartagonova*, c/ Marcos Redondo, 3 ☎ 50 42 00 ⚏ 126 ♿ **P** **AE, DC, EC, V $$$**.

🍴 *Chamonix* (closed: Sunday nights), Puerta de Murcia, 11 ☎ 50 74 00 ❇ **AE, DC, V $$$**.

🍴 *Los Habaneros* (closed: Sunday nights), c/ San Diego, 60 ☎ 50 52 50 ❇ **AE, MC, V $$$**. Fish and seafood. It is also a **★★** boarding house.

Beaches: Heading towards Mazarrón, El Portús beach has a nudist section, and beyond it lie the beaches of Cabo Tiñoso, Isla Plana and Azohía. In the Cabo de Palos direction, the coves of Reona, Calblanque, Las Cañas, Reventón and Cuervo are popular.

Cultural highlights: The town is not without its architectural interest. The Town Hall, or Ayuntamiento, built in 1907, is an example of the Modernist style; there are remains of a 13C Romanesque church, the Iglesia de Santa María, and an interesting 1C Roman monument, called the Torre Ciega, stands in the Pl de Alfonso XIII. There are works by Salzillo, the master carver of the Baroque period from Murcia, in the Iglesia de la Caridad and in the Iglesia de Santa María de Gracia. The latter church also houses a revered 13C Byzantine statue of the Virgin, the *Virgen de Rossel*. A walk around the 18C ramparts of the **Castillo de la Concepción**, rebuilt in the 13C, in the Torres park, offers good views of the port and the bay. The local archaeology museum, the Museo Arqueológico Municipal, c/ Ramón y Cajal, 45 (open: 9.00-1.00; weekends: 10.00-1.00 ☎ 51 21 37), stands on the site of a Roman burial ground and exhibits antiquities from the Iberian, Phoenician, Carthaginian and Roman eras.

Fiestas and festivals: Religious occasions such as **Holy Week** and Corpus Christi are solemnly celebrated. In November there is a Film Week dealing with nautical themes ☎ 51 20 99 and 52 05 05.

Sports: Water sports are practised at the yacht club, the *Real Club de Regatas de Cartagena*, Muelle Alfonso XII ☎ 50 46 85 and 50 69 05. Golfers head for the *La Manga Club de Golf*, 30km (see 'Costa Cálida').

CASTELLON DE LA PLANA-CASTELLO DE LA PLANA Castellón ☎
(964), pop. 129,813, *i* Pl María Agustina, 5 ☎ 22 77 03, (c/ Ruiz Zorrilla,
45, ✉ Pl Tetuán ☎ 21 47 53 and 22 20 00, ✚ 22 48 50, **P** 22 40 00, ⊞
20 32 40. Valencia 65km, Tarragona 186km, Madrid 417km.

This modern town, capital of the province of Castellón, is the market
centre for the fertile area of La Plana and lies 4km back from the sea. Its sea
port, **El Grao**, is a busy fishing and commercial harbour that handles La
Plana's orange exports and also the ceramics, furniture, shoes and textiles
produced by the area's industrial plants. A good 36 miles out to sea there is
an originally volcanic archipelago called the **Islas Columbretes** which used
to be a thriving pirate centre. Nowadays it is an important nesting ground and
plans are in motion to turn the islands into a nature reserve and bird
sanctuary. Between El Grao and Benicasim a considerable amount of tourist
resort development is going on.

🏨 ★★★★ *Mindoro*, c/ Moyano, 4 ☎ 22 23 00 ⇌ 114 [TV] ♦ AE, DC, MC,
V $$$$.

🏨 ★★★ *Del Golf*, Pinar beach, in El Grao ☎ 22 19 50 ⇌ 127 ✕ ♦ ♦ ☞
🏊 ▦ ♘ ♜ DC, MC, V $$$.

🏨 ★★★ *Myriam*, c/ Obispo Salinas, 1 ☎ 22 21 00 ⇌ 25 DC, V $$.

🍽 *Casa Juanito* (closed: Wednesdays except in summer, and November), c/
Buenavista, 11, in El Grao ☎ 22 20 66 ❋ AE, DC, EC, V $$$.

🍽 *Nina y Angelo* (closed: Mondays, 1/1-15/1 and 16/9-30/9), Paseo
Buenavista, 32, in El Grao ☎ 23 92 92 ♦ AE, DC, MC, V $$$. Innovative
cooking.

🍽 *Rafael* (closed: Sundays, 1/9-15/9 and 24/12-7/1), c/ Churruca, 26,
in El Grao ☎ 22 20 88 AE, DC, MC, V $$$. Excellent fish.

Beaches: El Grao beach is big, easy to get to and popular with families.
Going N, **Pinar** beach is also large and sandy and even more family
orientated.

Best buys: Spanish fashion is sold at *Chez Lovi*, c/ Mayor, 1, and leisure
wear at *Don Algodón*, c/ Escultor Viciano, 1.

Cultural highlights: The **Cathedral** of Santa María was badly damaged in
the 1936-1939 Spanish Civil War and has been totally reconstructed. It has
a very fine tower, originally built in the late 16C, that is popularly known as *El
Fadri*, the bachelor, because a second tower was never built. The early 18C
Town Hall has an interesting collection of paintings including works by
16-17C local painter **Ribalta** and there are paintings by Zurbarán in the 17C
Convento de las Capuchinas. The town's museum is the Museo Provincial de
Bellas Artes y Arqueología, c/ Caballeros, 25 (open: 10.00-2.00; closed:
Sundays).

Fiestas: The **Magdalena** *fiestas* head the calendar (see 'Spring Fiestas' in
'Fiestas').

Local sights: Heading inland on the C-232, you reach the picturesque
village of **LUCENA DEL CID**, which was founded by the Arabs. Folklore and
customs lie close to the surface here and in one local *fiesta*, on San Antón's
Day, January 17, local youths on horseback jump over blazing bonfires. A
detour on a local road before reaching Lucena takes you through the villages
of Alcora, Onda and Ribesalbes, famous for their ceramics and glazed tiles.
The first tile factory in **ALCORA** dates from the 18C and its products can be
bought at *La Muy Noble y Artística Cerámica de Alcora*, c/ Pintor Ferrer,
12. In **ONDA** there are remains of a medieval castle known as the Trescientas
Torres, or Three Hundred Towers, and there is also an interesting **Natural
Science Museum**. **VILLAREAL DE LOS INFANTES**, on the C-223, is famous for
its mandarin oranges and has an imposing 18C **church** that houses
paintings by 16C painter Juan de Juanes and Gothic church ornaments. The

trip to Segorbe, between the Espadán mountain range and the River Palancia, passes through fertile orchard country. **SEGORBE** itself is an important old town, originally an Iberian settlement and an episcopal see, known as *Segóbriga* during the Visigothic period. The cathedral was remodelled in the 18C and its showpiece is the collection, in the cloister, of more than fifty 15C religious panels, including several by **Juan de Juanes** and **Juan Vicente Macip**. The Town Hall has a particularly good 16C coffered ceiling, and parts of the old medieval town walls are still standing.

Sports: Water sports are practised at the yacht club, the *Club Náutico*, at El Grao ☎ 22 30 47 and 22 27 64; golf at the 9-hole, par 66 *Club de Golf Costa de Azahar*, in El Grao ☎ 22 70 64 and 23 61 23, and at the 18-hole, par 72 *Club de Campo del Mediterráneo*, in Borriol, Urb La Loma.

COSTA DEL AZAHAR (ORANGE BLOSSOM COAST) **Castellón** and **Valencia**.

The Costa Blanca, the Costa Brava and the Costa del Sol are household names among foreign visitors to Spain. The Costa del Azahar, which runs along the Levante coast from Vinaroz in the N to La Oliva in the S, is less familiar among non-Spaniards although it boasts a number of resorts that have long been firm favourites among the perhaps more discerning domestic tourist market. This stretch of Coast takes its name from the fragrant blooms of the area's extensive **orange groves** for *azahar*, one of the several gorgeously sounding Arabic words incorporated into the Spanish language, means orange blossom.

Valencia cuts the Costa del Azahar into two rather different sections. N of the big city the coastal strip is narrower and the coast itself is rockier and scored through by dry river beds, known as *ramblas*, of white shingle. Tourism here is less developed and the visitors who do spend their holidays between **Vinaroz and Valencia** tend to be Spanish. S of the big city, between **Valencia and La Oliva**, the Costa del Azahar is straighter, flatter, sandier and more populated.

VINAROZ (see separate entry) is an important fishing village which is deservedly famous for its scampi. Travelling S down the coast, **BENICARLO** (see 'Peñíscola') is nearby and beyond it lies the medieval town of **PEÑÍSCOLA**, which has an extremely picturesque castle on a peninsula that is joined by a thin isthmus to the mainland. The road then swings inland to the Sierra de Irta mountains and returns to the Mediterranean at the fishing village turned quiet and scenic resort of **ALCOCEBER**. It has four beaches and there is good, quiet accommodation at the ★★★★ *Las Fuentes*, Playa de las Fuentes, s/n ☎ (964) 41 03 25 ⇌ 50 ⵂ ♦ ⵂ ⚲ ⵂ ⵂ $$$ to $$$$, the ★ *Aparthotel Jeremías-Romana* (closed: 1/11-1/3), 1.5km outside the village ☎ (964) 41 02 60 ⇌ 38 ♦ ⵂ ⵂ ≪ ⵂ AE, DC, EC, V $ to $$, and at the ★ *Jeremías* (closed: 1/11-1/3), 1km outside the village ☎ (964) 41 08 31 ⇌ 38 P ⵂ ⵂ AE, DC, EC, V $$. Continuing S, **OROPESA** is another quiet spot that has lately caught up with tourism and the leisure industry. Its long, curved beach, now lined by apartment blocks, is protected by Cape Oropesa where a 16C **lookout tower** against pirates still stands. The local hotels include ★★ *Oropesa* (closed: 1/10-1/4), Av Madrid, 11, Ctra del Faro, 97 ☎ (964) 31 01 50 ⇌ 50 P ♦ ⵂ ⵂ $$, and the ★★ *Zapata* (closed: 1/10-1/4), Ctra del Faro, 91 ☎ (964) 31 04 25 ⇌ 65 P ♦ ⚲ ⵂ $$. *Luis Elvira*, c/ Ramón y Cajal, 1, is a good antique shop.

The coastal route continues past the agreeable resort of **BENICASIM** (see separate entry) and the provincial capital of **CASTELLON DE LA PLANA** (see separate entry). The next village, **VILA-REAL**, has a **parish church** which is big enough to be a cathedral and which contains some interesting pictures.

BURRIANA is an orange-exporting port and next to it lies the old and new city of **SAGUNTO** (see separate entry) which has Roman remains and modern industrial plants. Close by, **PUZOL** has a good hotel, absurdly decorated in kitsch Castilian style, but with good facilities and courteous service, the ★★★★★ *Monte Picayo*, Urb Monte Picayo ☎ (96) 142 01 00 ⇌ 83 P ✦ ≈ ▦ ≪ ♀ ♨ AE, DC, EC, MC, V $$$$$. Finally, **PUEBLA DE FARNALS**, just 14km from Valencia, is a built-up resort with a family-orientated beach and a marina. *Bergamonte* ☎ (96) 144 26 12 ≈ ♨ ♀ AE, V $$$, on the beach and with a swimming pool and tennis courts, serves good rice dishes and local stews.

The first stretch of the **Valencia-La Oliva** section of the Costa del Azahar is marked by the rice paddies of **La Albufera** (see 'Valencia'), by the long, semi-wild **beach** of **EL SALER** and by this resort's championship golf course, the 18-hole, par 72 *Golf El Saler* ☎ (96) 161 11 86. The greens form part of the grounds of the ★★★★★ *Parador Luis Vives*, Ctra El Saler, km16 ☎ (96) 161 11 86 ⇌ 58 ✦ ♩ ♨ ≈ ♀ ♪ AE, DC, MC, V $$$$, which is very peaceful and scenically located. There is also extremely comfortable accommodation at the ★★★★★ *Sidi Saler Palace-Sol*, in El Saler ☎ (96) 161 04 11 ⇌ 272 P ✦ ♨ ≈ ▦ ≪ ♀ ♪ AE, DC, MC, V $$$$$ to $$$$$$, with a highly rated restaurant, the *Grill Bendinat* $$$$.

EL PALMAR, a small hamlet in the centre of La Albufera (see 'Valencia'), comes next, followed by **EL PERELLO** and the long, sandy **beaches of LAS PALMERAS**. **CULLERA** (see separate entry) is a well developed resort and the town of **GANDIA** (see separate entry) is the key leisure centre of this stretch of coast. **OLIVA**, marking the southern boundary of the Costa de Azahar, is a rice and orange growing town set 3km back from its rather extensive sandy **beach**.

COSTA BLANCA (WHITE COAST) **Alicante** ☎ (96).

Called the White Coast because of its dazzling light, this is one of the best known of the Spanish coasts, the holiday playground for millions of foreign visitors and the retirement home for an increasingly large number of northern Europeans. Running between Denia and Torrevieja and with Benidorm as its undisputed capital, the *costa's* reputation rests on its dry winters, its year-round sunshine and its wealth of leisure facilities. Parts of it have certainly been blighted by speculators' greed.

The first section of the Coast, between **Denia and Altea**, is the more attractive thanks to the cliffs and secluded rocky coves that break the monotony of the beaches. It is fairly densely populated by villas and housing developments and it is well served by marinas and golf courses. Its villages nevertheless retain their pre-tourist boom rural and fishing port charm. **DENIA** (see separate entry) is a popular tourist resort and has a permanent expatriate colony, as do many urban centres in the area. The rocky promontory of **Cabo San Antonio**, set among pine woods and villas and graced by a lighthouse, is one of the local beauty spots. From here the **views** take in Jávea and the Cabo de la Nao to the S. From **JAVEA** (see separate entry) a road leads to the limits of the **Cabo de la Nao** promontory. The coast here is extremely rocky and is punctuated by intimate little pebbly coves, such as Cala Blanca and Cala de la Granadella, sea caves and grottoes. It is an excellent area for scuba diving but to take full advantage of the private inlets you will need a boat. The **view** from the La Nao headland stretches as far as the Peñón de Ifach. **MORAIRA** is a little fishing village surrounded by vineyards and by villas. It is a peaceful spot, a popular retirement area and arguably the classiest resort on this coast. The fishing port doubles up as a marina and its rocky coast is a favourite among underwater fishermen. As far as accommodation is concerned, there are a couple of quiet hotels —★★★★ *Swiss Hotel Moraira*, Club Moraira, s/n, in Teulada ☎ 574 44 54 🛏 13 ⅋ TV ✦ 🎤 🐾 ⚓ ⚐ $$$$$, which is quiet and has a good **restaurant**, and ★★ *Moradix* (closed: 1/10-31/3), Partida Moravit ☎ 574 40 56 🛏 55 P 🐾 « AE, DC, EC, V $$. Recommended restaurants include *El Corregidor* (closed: Sundays), km3.5 on the Moraira-Benitachell road ☎ 574 40 01 V $$, *El Girasol* (closed: Mondays in low season), in Moraira ☎ 574 43 73 P ✦ ❄ AE, DC, EC, V $$$$, serving modern, international cuisine in an elegant villa, and *Mesón Cap D'Or* (closed: Sundays and 5/1-20/2), c/ Castillo, 5 ☎ 574 41 09 AE, MC, V $$.

From Moraira, the narrow **road** winds its way along 14km, hugging the blue Mediterranean and passing lovely little coves, to **CALPE** (see separate entry) and its gigantic **Peñón de Ifach** landmark. The **route** continues to be **picturesque** as it crosses the Sierra de Bernia, to reach the pleasant fishing village turned artist colony of **ALTEA** (see separate entry).

BENIDORM (see separate entry) is the capital of the Costa Blanca and is something of a concrete jungle of apartments, hotels, discos and fast-food bars. Millions love it for its non-stop, pulsating **night-life** and its **beaches** are packed in summer. An increasing number of tourists are also using Benidorm for sunny winter holidays. From here on to **ALICANTE** (see separate entry) the coast tends to resemble a concrete wall for it has undergone frenzied speculative development. The biggest and best-equipped beaches in this area are Paraíso beach in **VILLAJOYOSA** (see separate entry), Muchavista in **CAMPELLO** and **San Juan** beach in Alicante itself. Continuing S from Alicante the coast is characterized by gentle bays, sand dunes and the white salt flats of **SANTA POLA** (see separate entry) and **TORREVIEJA** (see separate entry) and by the inevitable line of apartment blocks. **GUARDAMAR DE SEGURA**, which is famed for its *langostinos* (scampi), has remarkably long sandy **beaches** and extensive dunes whose advance inland had to be halted at the beginning of the century by the planting of pines and eucalyptus trees. ★★ *Meridional*, Urb Dunas de Guardamar ☎ 572 83 40 🛏 37 P « V $$ is a pleasant hotel to spend the night, as is ★ *Delta*, c/ Torrevieja, 43 ☎ 572 87 12 🛏 16 P ✦ ⚐ $$. For meals, try *Rincón de Pedro* (closed: Wednesdays), Urb Las Dunas ☎ 572 80 95 P V $$$.

LA ZENIA, 8km from Torrevieja, is a well-appointed development featuring a fine **beach**, a marina and a golf course, the 18-hole, par 72 *Club de Golf Villamartín* ☎ 532 03 50, among its facilities —★★★★ *La Zenia*, Urb La Zenia ☎ 532 02 00 🛏 220 ⅋ ✦ 🐾 ⚓ « 🏌 ⚐ AE, DC, V $$$$, is a quiet hotel with good views from its spacious terrace overlooking the sea.

S of Torrevieja, **DEHESA DE CAMPOAMOR**, 11km, is another well-equipped residential complex with two good **beaches** and a quiet hotel, the ★★★ *Montepiedra*, c/ Rosalía de Castro ☎ 532 03 00 🛏 64 ⅋ ✦ 🐾 ⚓ ⚐ V $$ to $$$, which has a pleasant garden with a swimming pool. Hungry visitors go to *Mesón las Villas* ☎ 532 00 05.

Nudist beaches on the Costa Blanca include a section of the Les Roquetes beach (Denia), La Torre de Ambolo (Jávea), Cumbres del Sol (Benitachel), the beach at **ALFAZ DEL PI**, and Racó Conill (Villajoyosa), Cabo de las Huertas (Alicante), and El Carabasí (Elche).

COSTA CALIDA (WARM COAST) ⚑Murcia ☎ (968).

The 250km of Murcia's coastline are aptly called the Costa Cálida, or Warm Coast. The water's temperature is several degrees above the normal because the sea is unusually shallow here. It is a safe coastline and ideal for underwater fishing and all nautical sports. This is particularly true of the virtual inland sea called the **Mar Menor** where the water is at most 7m deep.

This vast lagoon or salt water lake is separated from the Mediterranean by a long strip of land known as **La Manga**, essentially a sand bank which is about 1.5km at its widest and a mere 100m at its narrowest and which runs between San Pedro del Pinatar and Cabo de Palos. The inland waters join the Mediterranean through the creeks of Marchamelo and El Estacio and the small archipelago formed by the islands of Ventorrillo and Bienteveo. The whole area is tailor-made for sailing and waterskiing.

The villages around the Mar Menor have now become important tourist resorts such as **SAN PEDRO DEL PINATAR**, **SANTIAGO DE LA RIBERA**, **LOS ALCAZARES**, which has an attractive palm-tree lined promenade and the densely populated highrise town of **LA MANGA DEL MAR MENOR**. There are numerous apartments and hotels, restaurants and bars, marinas and yacht clubs and the lovely **beaches** here, at Los Alcázares and, particularly at **La Manga**, can become extremely crowded in summer. For accommodation, you could try ★★★★ *Doble Mar Casino* (closed: 1/11-25/2), Gran Vía, in La Manga del Mar Menor ☎ 56 39 10 ⇌ 485 🅿 ✦ ♨ �◻ ☲ ▦ « AE, DC, EC, V $$$, a popular hotel with good views of the area; ★★★★ *Galúa-Sol*, Hacienda Dos Mares, in La Manga del Mar Menor ☎ 56 32 00 ⇌ 170 🅿 ✦ ♨ ⌖ ☲ ☼ « ◁ AE, DC, EC, V $$$ to $$$$, a quiet hotel with good views; or ★★★★ *La Manga Club Hotel*, Los Belones ☎ 56 91 11 ✦ ⌖ ☲ ▦ ◁ ⅃ ⅂ $$$$ to $$$$$, something of an oasis with all sorts of water and land facilities, this is an extremely quiet hotel overlooking the golf course. For lunch or dinner in La Manga, try *Borsalino y Gran Borsalino* (closed: Tuesdays in winter and 15/11-15/12), Edif Babilonia ☎ 56 31 30 🅿 ✦ ❊ AE, DC, V $$$, serving French cuisine; *Dos Mares*, Pl Bohemia, s/n ☎ 56 30 93 🅿 ✦ ❊ AE, DC, MC, V $$$, specializing in fish; or the central *Tropical* (closed: 13/1-13/2), Edif La Martinique, Gran Vía ☎ 56 33 45 ✦ ❊ ☲ ◁ DC, EC, V $$$. *Fiestas* in the area take place in the second fortnight in August, when there is a festival devoted to the traditional songs of the local miners —this *Festival del Cante de las Minas* is held in the inland mining village of **LA UNION**. For everyday fun, the *Casino de La Manga* (open: 7.00 pm-4.00 am) has tables for roulette, black jack and other games of chance ☎ 56 38 50, the best *tapa* bars are around Cabo de Palos and the top disco is *Baccara* in the *Doble Mar* hotel. **Water sports** fans will be in their element here, since there are plenty of yacht clubs, including the *Puerto Deportivo Tomás Maestre*, in San Javier ☎ 56 31 88, the *Puerto Deportivo Islas Menores*, in La Manga del Mar Menor, the *Club Náutico Los Nietos*, in Los Nietos ☎ 56 07 37, the *Real Club de Regatas de Santiago de la Ribera*, in Santiago ☎ 57 02 50 and the *Club Náutico Dos Mares*, in La Manga del Mar Menor ☎ 56 31 17, which organizes a number of regattas. Golfers can head for the two lovely 18-hole, par 72 courses at the *La Manga Club de Golf* ☎ 56 91 11.

From Cabo de Palos to **CARTAGENA** (see separate entry) the shore is rocky and scored by inlets and then it smooths out towards **PUERTO DE MAZARRON**. The resort of **AGUILAS** was founded by the Count of Aranda, one of the most energetic reforming ministers of the enlightened 18C monarch Charles III; it was intended to be a centre for new local industries. Today it is a little fishing village whose population swells several-fold in summer when some 150,000 tourists arrive to spend their holidays. It has a 16C castle which is reached by steep paths and which offers good views once you get to the battlements. The beach is grey sand and the nearby rocky **coves** are ideal for underwater exploring. In the area, the ★★★ *Carlos III*, c/ Rey Carlos III, 22 ☎ 41 16 50 ⇌ 32 AE, DC, EC, V $$ to $$$ is a recommended boarding house, and *Las Brisas* (closed: Mondays), Explanada del Muelle, s/n ☎ 41 00 27 $$, a recommended restaurant.

CULLERA **Valencia** ☎ (96), pop. 19,196, *i* c/ Del Riu, 56 ☎ 152 09 74. Valencia 38km, Alicante 136km, Madrid 388km.

The tourist boom of the 1960s changed for evermore this once sleepy little village founded by the Muslims. Fishermen's cottages have given way to tall apartment buildings —if you want to see the change go to the shrine of Nuestra Señora del Castillo, on the outskirts, which has a **good view** of the old village and the new resort town. There is a marina with plenty of scope for water sports, and an aquapark. The **beach** is safe.

🏨 *Sicania* (closed: December), El Racó beach, 4km ☎ 152 01 43 ⇌ 117 P ♪ ⅋ ⚓ ☂ ≪ AE, DC, EC, V $$$. Well situated, overlooking the sea.

🍴 *Les Mouettes* (open: dinners only; closed: Sunday nights, Mondays from September to June and 15/12-15/2), Subida al Castillo, s/n ☎ 152 00 01 ✦ ❊ ⚓ DC, MC, V $$$ to $$$$. French cuisine.

DENIA **Alicante** ☎ (96), pop. 23,206, *i* c/ Patricio Ferrándiz, s/n ☎ 578 09 57, ⛴ Cía. Flebasa Lines (ferries to the Balearic Islands) ☎ 578 41 00. Alicante 92km, Valencia 93km, Madrid 447km.

Once a Greek colony called *Dianium* and much later the capital of a small Muslim kingdom, Denia is today a lively cosmopolitan summer resort and year round retirement area. It has a busy **port** with regular ferries to the Balearic Islands, a full range of facilities for nautical sports, a thriving arts and crafts industry and two very long beaches, **Les Marines** and **Les Rotes**, that have good facilities. Bathing is not encouraged in the port area.

🏨 ★★★ *Denia* (closed: 1/11-31/3), Partida Suertes del Mar, s/n ☎ 578 12 12 ⇌ 280 ✦ ♪ ⚓ ☂ ⚲ $$ to $$$. Modern and comfortable.

🍴 *Mesón Troya*, Ctra Les Rotes ☎ 578 14 31 ❊ $$$. Seafood cuisine.

Best buys: Local glazed tiles, called *socarrats*, and ceramics are sold at *Cerámicas Artísticas Españolas*, Ctra Denia, s/n, and model boats at *Boat Art*. Spanish fashion can be bought at *Gilten*, c/ Diana, 14, and *Pepe Cabrera*, Av Marqués de Campos, 2, and shoes at *D'Campos*, Av Marqués de Campos, 50.

Cultural highlights: Above the town, in the castle there is an interesting **Archaeological Museum**.

Fiestas: The local *fiestas*, on July 2, involve releasing bulls in the port area; spectators and beasts tend to end up in the water.

Sports: Water sports can be practised at the local marina, the *Club Náutico de Denia* ☎ 578 09 89.

ELCHE-ELX **Alicante** ☎ (96), pop. 73,392, *i* Parque Municipal ☎ 545 27 47, ✛ 545 29 89, P 542 25 44, ✈ Altet, 22km in Alicante ☎ 528 50 11, ▣ Av Llibertat, s/n ☎ 545 58 58 and 545 98 43, ▥ Estación Ferrocarril ☎ 545 62 54. Alicante 22km, Murcia 65km, Madrid 409km.

This industrious, agreeable town is famed for its **palm trees**, its annual religious **mystery play** and its **shoe industry**. Its origins go back to the Phoenicians, who were followed by the Carthaginians, the first to plant the palms and collect the dates, and the Romans who gave considerable importance to the town and called it *Illicis*. The medieval mystery play, traditionally performed in mid-August, is a unique event that fascinates academics and draws large crowds. Its content underlines the cultural switch that followed the Christian reconquest of the town from the Muslims. Shoes today have taken over from a long artisan tradition of working with hemp and esparto to supply most of Spain with rope-soled sandals.

🏨 ★★★★ *Huerto del Cura* (linked to the Parador network), c/ Federico García Sanchíz, 14 ☎ 545 80 40 ⇌ 70 TV ✦ ♪ ⅋ ⚓ ▦ ⚲ AE, DC, EC, V $$$$. Set among the palm trees, its **restaurant** is excellent.

¶ *Gran Mariscada*, c/ Martín de Torres, 11 ☎ 545 82 16 **DC, MC, V** $$$.
Hearty, fresh fare.

Cultural highlights: The two most important buildings in the town are the
17C **Basilica de Santa María**, which has an impressive W door, and the
15C Gothic palace that houses the Ayuntamiento, or Town Hall. The image of
the Virgin that dominates the basilica's main façade was sculpted by Nicolás
Busi, as was the image of San Agatángelo on the side door. The most
popular feature of the Town Hall is the ceremonious manner in which two
figurines on its clock clang out the hours as they have done for the past 200
years. Elche's show stopper is, however, its extraordinary 2,000 year old
palm grove, the only one of its kind in Europe. In the 18C there were said to 🐦🐦
be a million palm trees here and although there are obviously far fewer now
there are certainly more palms than you are likely to see in a lifetime of
visiting oases. The best palm tree, standing in the section called the **Huerto
del Cura**, is one that is more than 150 years old and is something of a freak 🐦🐦
for it has no fewer than seven trunks. In the **municipal park** which forms 🐦
part of the palm grove, there is a museum, the **Museo de la Artesanía de
la Palma** (open weekends: 11.00-1.30), dedicated to crafts connected with
palm leaves. The **Museo de Arte Contemporáneo**, or Museum of Modern
Art, Pl Raval, s/n (open: 11.00-1.00 and 5.00-8.00; closed: Mondays)
includes works by Juan Gris, Antonio Tàpies, Pablo Picasso and Joan Miró,
and 2km out of town, on the road to Dolores, there is a permanent exhibition
(closed: Mondays) of the Carthaginian, Iberian and Roman finds from a
famous dig in a local Iberian settlement called **La Alcudia**. The great treasure
discovered there was the ***Dama de Elche*** (*Lady of Elche*), a remarkable
polychromed stone bust of an enigmatic Iberian lady or goddess, but she is
exhibited at Madrid's National Archaeological Museum.

Fiestas: The mystery play, the ***Misteri d'Elx***, is performed on August 14 and 🐦
15 (see 'Fiestas'). After the performances there are spectacular firework
displays.

Sports: Tennis is played at the *Club de Tenis Elche* ☎ 545 45 16; for pigeon
shooting, contact the *Sociedad de Tiro de Pichón* ☎ 546 87 21.

GANDIA **Valencia** ☎ (96), pop. 51,522, *i* Pl de la Constitución, s/n ☎
287 16 00, ✚ 360 68 00, **P** 352 54 78, 🚌 351 36 12. Valencia 68km,
Albacete 170km, Madrid 416km.

The tourist boom and **speculators' greed** have done their worst to
destroy the historic aspects of this old town. Gandía was the seat of the
duchy of the same name, one of whose dukes was Saint Francis Borgia, one
of the very first Jesuits, who succeeded his close friend, the Jesuit founder
Saint Ignatius of Loyola, as leader of the Order. In the Middle Ages, Gandía
was a cultured town that produced, among other poets, writer and
humanist **Joanot Martorell**, who was the author of an important 15C
chivalric novel, *Tirant lo Blanch*. In time Gandía became a thriving
orange-growing area and its port, the **Grao de Gandía**, was the first to
specialize in exporting citrus fruit.

🏨 **★★★★** *Bayren I*, Paseo de Neptuno, s/n ☎ 284 03 00 🛏 164 ✚ ⚲ ≈
🎾 ♈ **DC, MC, V** $$$ to $$$$. On the promenade.

🏨 **★★★** *Bayren II* (closed: 1/10-30/5), c/ Mallorca, 19 ☎ 284 07 00 🛏
125 **P** ✚ ≈ 🎾 50m ♈ $$ to $$$.

¶ *El As de Oros* (closed: Mondays and 15/1-31/1), Paseo de Neptuno,
s/n ☎ 284 02 39 ✳ **AE, DC, MC, V** $$$ to $$$$. Seafood, rice dishes
and fresh salads.

¶ *Kayuko II* (closed: Mondays and November) c/ Cataluña, 14 ☎
284 01 37 ✚ ✳ **AE, DC, MC, V** $$$. Fish and seafood.

¶ *La Gamba* (closed: Mondays, evenings in winter and December), Ctra Nazaret-Oliva, s/n ☎ 284 13 10 **P ♦ ❋ ≈ AE, DC, MC, V $$$$**. Fish and seafood.

Beaches: There are 3km of fine sand and good facilities between the port and **Jaraco** beach.

Cultural highlights: The 18C Neoclassical Town Hall stands alongside the 14C Gothic Collegiate Church of Santa María which had a Baroque tower added to it in the 18C. Saint Francis was born in the **Palacio Ducal**, c/ Sant Duc, which has a pleasing Gothic patio and sumptuous **rooms** decorated with frescoes, marble and glazed tiles. The palace, now the property of the Jesuit Order, is open to the public (open in summer: 10.00-12.00 and 5.00-7.00; winter: 11.00-12.00 and 4.30-5.30; closed: Sunday afternoons). The building that used to house Gandía's University (founded in the 16C and closed down two centuries later when the Jesuits were temporarily expelled from Spain) is in the c/ Mayor.

Fiestas: Two weeks of celebrations mark the feast days of San Miguel, September 29, and San Francisco de Borja, October 3. There are Valencia-style *fallas* (see 'Fiestas') on March 19, and the Holy Week celebrations are also picturesque.

On the town: The promenade, the Paseo Marítimo Neptuno, is lined with bars and terraces where people gather in summer.

Sports: Water sports are practised at the yacht club, the *Club Náutico de Gandía* ☎ 284 10 50, and tennis at the *Club de Tenis Gandía* ☎ 284 00 96.

JATIVA-XATIVA **Valencia** ☎ (96), pop. 24,313, *i* Alameda Santa Jaume, 35 ☎ 288 25 61, ✚ 227 02 39, 🚍 227 16 64. Valencia 59km, Alicante 108km, Madrid 379km.

This is one of the most historic and picturesque walled towns of the Valencia region and is set in a fertile, scenic area of vineyards and orchards. Two rivers, the Cañoles and the Albaida, flow past it and it is protected from inclement weather by the Enguera and Grossa mountain ranges. The Iberians settled here, and it subsequently became a Roman town of some standing and, in the Visigothic era, an episcopal see. The Muslim occupation was wholly beneficial for agriculture flourished and one of the first paper manufacturing centres in Europe was established here. Two future popes, **Calixtus III** and **Alexander VI**, both members of the Valencia branch of the Borgia family, were born here as was the painter **José Ribera**, a contemporary and rival of Velázquez. The expulsion of the **Moriscos**, the Christianized Moors, at the start of the 17C pitched Játiva into a steady economic decline and its fall was completed a century later when it chose to oppose the Bourbon candidate in the War of Spanish Succession. The new Bourbon monarch, Philip V, sacked the town, exiled its inhabitants and, for good measure, renamed the place San Felipe. Játiva did not recover its proper name until 1811.

¶ *Casa la Abuela*, c/ Reina, 17 ☎ 227 05 25 **❋ DC, EC, V $$ to $$$**. Good rice dishes.

Cultural highlights: The **collegiate church** was built in the 16C but was restored in the 18C and again after the 1936-1939 Spanish Civil War. Opposite it, the old town hospital has a splendid Plateresque façade. The Gothic **Church of San Félix**, going up towards the castle, has an interesting

● collection of **early Valencian paintings**. From the upper part of the town, which is where the **castle** stood before Philip V destroyed it, there are good views of old and new Játiva.

Fiestas: Valencian-style *fallas* appear around Saint Joseph's Day, March 19, and local *fiestas* are celebrated on August 15-20.

JAVEA-XABIA **Alicante** ☎ (96), pop. 12,999, *i* Pl Almirante Bastarreche 🖝
☎ 579 05 00, ✆ 579 07 36, **P** 579 00 81. Alicante 87km, Valencia 109km,
Madrid 457km.

This choice residential resort, between the capes of San Antonio and San
Martín, stands in a typically Mediterranean setting of vines and orchards. The
old town is set back from the sea on a hillside and is clustered around the
Gothic fortified Church of San Bartolomé. New buildings, mostly detached
villas, have sprung up around the port.

🏨 ★★★★ *Parador Costa Blanca*, Playa del Arenal, 2 ☎ 579 02 00 🛏 65 ✦
🍴 🏊 ⚓ 🎾 🖼 « ✦ AE, DC, EC, V $$$$. A quiet hotel with good views.

🏨 ★★★ *Bahía Vista*, km7.5 at Portichol ☎ 577 04 61 🛏 17 **P** ✦ 🏊 ⚓ 🎾
EC, V $$$ to $$$$. A quiet hotel with a good swimming pool.

🍴 *La Estrella* (closed: Sunday evenings and Mondays except in summer, and
24/12-28/2), Av El Arenal, bl 4 ☎ 579 08 02 **P** ✦ ❄ V $$$.

🍴 *Lázaro*, Partida Capsaes, 19, on the road to Benitachel ☎ 579 01 74 **P**
✦ $$$. In a pretty villa.

🍴 *Tossalet Casino Club*, c/ Algarrobos, s/n, Urb El Tossalet ☎ 577 09 58
P ✦ ❄ ⚓ AE, DC, MC, V $$$. International cuisine.

Beaches: The alternatives to the local **Arenal** beach are the small coves that
dot the coast between Cabo de San Martín and Cabo de la Nao. **Granadella**
is one of the nicest.

Best buys: Spanish fashion is sold at *Pepa*, Pl Almirante Bastarreche, 21,
and shoes at *La Rulla*, c/ Cristo del Mar, 22.

Fiestas: Midsummer bonfires, the *Hogueras de San Juan* (see 'Fiestas'), light
up the town on June 19-24.

Local sights: **GATA DE GORGOS**, 8km E, has a well developed basket
weaving and bamboo furniture industry. Its products can be bought at
Artesanía Tere, Av del Caudillo, 172. For lunch, try *El Corral del Pato*,
Partida Trosets, 31 $$, which serves unfussy, regional home cooking.

Sports: Water sports are practised at the marina, the *Club Náutico de Jávea*,
Embarcadero, s/n ☎ 579 10 25 and 579 06 52. Golfers head for the
9-hole, par 72 course at the *Club de Golf Jávea*, km4.5 on the road to
Benitachel.

JUMILLA **Murcia** ☎ (968), pop. 21,296. Murcia 74km, Alicante 94km,
Madrid 364km.

Jumilla is a wine producing town under the shadow of an Arab castle.

Best Buys: Jumilla's robust red wine can be bought at *J. García Carrión*, c/
Barón de Solar, 10.

Cultural Highlights: There are archaeological exhibits at the Museo
Jerónimo Molina (☎ 78 00 36), and the 15C Church of Santiago and the
16C Monastery of Santa Ana are interesting.

Fiestas: Holy Week is celebrated solemnly and the August wine harvest
festival joyously.

LORCA **Murcia** ☎ (968), pop. 66,880, *i* c/ López Gisbert, 12 ☎
46 61 57, ✆ 46 60 62. Murcia 64km, Cartagena 83km, Almería 157km,
Madrid 459km.

Set in an oasis of fertility in the midst of a fairly arid area, Lorca was an
important Roman and Arab town. It was partially destroyed by an earthquake
in the 17C and fine Baroque buildings were erected when the town was
rebuilt.

🏨 ★★★ *Alameda*, c/ Musso Valiente, 8 ☎ 46 75 00 🛏 43 AE, DC, EC,
V $$.

🍴 *Los Naranjos*, c/ Jerónimo Santa Fé, 43 ☎ 46 93 22 **P** ✦ ❄ DC, V $$$.

Best buys: Lorca's famous rugs, bedspreads and embroidery can be bought at *A. Díaz*, c/ Los Guiraos, 9; ceramics at *I. Lario*, Ctra de Murcia, 47; and local cakes and sweets at *Confitería Gil*, c/ Corredera, 11.

Cultural highlights: The **Plaza Mayor** is flanked by the Baroque façades of the Town Hall, the Collegiate Church of San Patricio and the local **court**. The Palace of the Guevara family, the **Palacio de los Guevara**, has a splendidly ostentatious Baroque façade dating from 1694 and a good patio. The **castle**, built in the 13C, used to have 35 towers but only two, the Torre Alfonsina and the remains of the Torre del Espolón, are visible today.

Fiestas: Holy **Week** (see 'Fiestas') is an important component of the town's calendar, and there is more lighthearted merrymaking at the *romerías*, traditional picnic-pilgrimages, to the Monastery of Our Lady of Huertas (September 8) and to the castle (November 23).

MORELLA **Castellón** ☎ (964), pop. 3,337, *i* Torres de San Miguel (see 'Maestrazgo' in 'Aragón').

Morella is the most important town in the wild historic Maestrazgo area. Its highlights are its 14C walls, its 19C **castle** and the 12-14C **Iglesia Arcipestral de Santa María** which has a very fine organ.

Best buys: Fabrics made to traditional Maestrazgo designs, and some modern ones, are sold at *Artesanía Textil Artística*, Pl San Francisco, s/n.

MURCIA **Murcia** ☎ (968), pop. 309,504, *i* c/ Alejandro Séiguer, 3 ☎ 21 37 16, ✚ 21 88 93, P 26 02 46, ✈ Murcia-San Javier, 50km on the C-3319 ☎ 57 05 54 (Iberia, Av Alfonso X el Sabio ☎ 24 00 50) ▣ c/ Barrionuevo, 4 ☎ 25 21 54. Cartagena 49km, Alicante 81km, Valencia 256km, Madrid 395km.

Murcia, the *Medina Mursiya* founded by **Abd ar-Rahman II** in 831, was one of the richest cities of Muslim Spain and it has continued to be prosperous down the centuries. On the banks of the Segura, the city is the centre of the river's extremely fertile *vega* or valley and has solidly established fruit and vegetable growing and processing industries. The Arab occupation, which lasted until the late 13C, bequeathed a well developed linen and silk industry in addition to a complex irrigation system and an advanced approach to agriculture. Murcia was the home of **Francisco Salzillo**, a master of religious sculpture, who established a solid reputation throughout 17C Spain although he never left the city. The **Count of Floridablanca**, one of the most enlightened of a batch of intelligent and reform-minded ministers during the reign of Charles III in the late 18C, was also born in Murcia.

▦ ★★★★ *Siete Coronas Meliá*, Paseo de Garay, 5 ☎ 21 77 71 ⇌ 122 TV ✦ ♮ AE, DC, MC, V $$$$. It has a good terrace.

▦ ★★★ *Conde de Floridablanca*, c/ Corbalán, 7 ☎ 21 46 26 ⇌ 60 TV P ♮ AE, DC, MC, V $$$ to $$$$.

▦ ★★★ *Hispano II*, c/ Radio Murcia, 3 ☎ 21 61 52 ⇌ 35 TV ♮ AE, DC, MC, V $$$ to $$$$.

❙❙ *Barlovento* (closed: Sundays in July and August, Mondays in winter and 1/10-15/10), Av Libertad, 6 ☎ 24 45 22 ✳ AE, DC, EC, V $$$. Fresh fish and seafood.

❙❙ *Hispano*, c/ Lucas, 7 ☎ 21 61 52 ✦ ✳ AE, DC, EC, V $$$. Very popular for its Murcian cuisine.

❙❙ *Rincón de Pepe* (closed: Sundays in summer and Sunday evenings in winter), c/ Apóstoles, 34 ☎ 21 22 39 P ✳ AE, DC, MC, V $$$ to $$$$. Also a ★★★ boarding house $$$ to $$$$. One of the best restaurants in Spain serving inspired cooking based on magnificent local produce and delicious desserts.

Best buys: Typical Spanish nativity scenes called ***belenes*** which are full of little figurines and have pride of place in the house at Christmas can be bought at *J. Cuenca*, km1 on the Fuensanta road, *J. Fernández*, c/ José Castaño, 6, and ***P. Serrano***, Ctra de Churrua ☎ 23 45 48. Toys are available at *Bazar Murciano*, c/ Platería 44. Gifts, antiques and furniture are sold at ***Artespaña***, Travesía Marcos Redondo, 5, and art and antiques at *Ahora*, c/ Jaime I, 7, and *C. Llopis*, c/ Vinadel, 8. For local gourmet delicacies, go to *Bonache*, Pl de las Flores, 8, and *Barba*, c/ Serrano Alcázar, 5, and for a wider assortment of goods, visit the **open-air markets** —*Alkila*, specializing in shirts, and the one held on Thursdays. Spanish fashion is available at ***Adolfo Domínguez***, Pl de Santo Domingo, 12, ***F. Medina***, Gran Vía, 16, ***J. Messeguer***, c/ Maestro Alonso, 5, and ***J. Barquero***, c/ Alfonso X el Sabio, 5; shoes at ***Farrutx***, Pl Cetina, 6. The city's large department stores are *El Corte Inglés*, Av de la Libertad, and *Galerías Preciados*, Gran Vía, 42.

Cultural highlights: The city's **Cathedral**, whose construction began in 1394, is immediately intriguing for its superb, 95m-high bell tower. Its base and first floors were built in the Renaissance style by Francisco and Jacobo Florentino and Jerónimo Quijano. The Baroque style came in with a vengeance in the third floor and developed, or degenerated, into the Rococo style by the time Juan de Gea started designing the actual belfry. Ventura Rodríguez capped it all with a cupola built according to his Neoclassical principles. Jaime Bort designed the Baroque **main façade**. Within, the cathedral has three naves, a transept and an ambulatory and its highpoints are the flamboyant Gothic style of the **Vélez Chapel** and the Plateresque **Junterones Chapel**. The choir stalls date from the 16C and were brought to

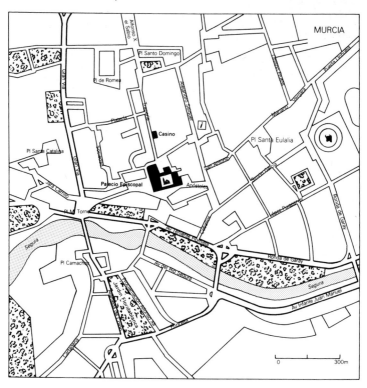

the cathedral from a Castilian monastery. The **Diocesan Museum** has a rich collection of liturgical articles, several Salzillo sculptures and a Roman sarcophagus. The **view** from the top of the bell tower is panoramic over the whole city and its fertile outskirts. The heart of Murcia's old quarter is the **Trapería** district where one of the landmarks is the late 19C *Casino*, a place which is not to be confused with a gambling den. The *Casino* here, as in other Spanish provincial towns, was the private club and meeting place of the local bigwigs and, in Murcia's case, it is an exceptionally well-appointed building. Murcia's traditional economic muscle can be appreciated by the number of grand ornate buildings, mostly in the Baroque style such as the Episcopal Palace. The **Museo Salzillo**, in the Iglesia de Jesús (open in winter: 9.30-1.30 and 3.00-6.00; summer: 9.30-1.00 and 4.00-7.00; Sundays: 10.00-1.00), exhibits fine examples of the master sculptor's realistic religious imagery. There are eight processional floats illustrating scenes of Christ's life and Passion, which are carried through the streets during Holy Week and there is also a Nativity scene with no fewer than 500 figures. The city's museum, the Museo de Murcia, c/ Obispo Frutos, 12 (open: 9.00-2.00; Wednesdays: 9.00-2.00 and 5.00-9.00; closed: Mondays) has a Fine Arts section which contains works by Ribera, Bassano and painters of Murcian life, and an Archaeology section, c/ Alfonso X el Sabio, 7 (open: same times as above) which has a very good collection of **ceramics** from the 12-18C.

Fiestas: The Salzillo images make the **Holy Week** processions very special. In spring, after Easter, there is a *Fiesta de Primavera* which is celebrated in a carnival atmosphere and includes flower battles.

Local sights: The 16C **shrine of Nuestra Señora de la Fuensanta**, 5km, and the hill called the **Cuesta del Gallo** alongside are local beauty spots which provide good **views** of the city and of the fertile valley. **ALCANTARILLA**, 9.5km, is in the centre of the intensely cultivated *huerta* and it has an interesting museum, the **Museo de la Huerta**, that traces the agricultural tradition of the area. **ARCHENA**, NW, is a deservedly famous spa whose curative properties have been recognized for centuries. **MULA**, E along the C-415 from Murcia, is a picturesque castle town where Holy Week is marked by marathon drumming sessions.

On the town: In summer people meet on the **terraces** of the Av Alfonso X el Sabio. *Pepico El del Tío Ginés*, c/ Mulas, 4, is an authentic Murcian tavern and there are good *tapas* at *Los Zagales*, by the Pl Belluga, *La Tapa*, Pl Flores, and *El Fénix*, Pl Santa Catalina, 1. *La Granja*, Ctra de Sangonera, is somewhat different; it serves sweet wines and fruit juices in an atmosphere compounded of religious music and decorative flowers and fruit.

Sports: Riders go to the *Club de Jinetes Chúcaro*, Av Constitución, 11 ☎ 21 69 00 and *El Carrascoy*, at Sangonera la Verde ☎ 86 81 36. For tennis, go to the *Murcia Club de Tenis* ☎ 24 30 45, for clay pigeon shooting to the *Real Sociedad de Tiro de Pichón* ☎ 84 10 20, and for gliding and ultralight flying to the *Aero Club Murcia* ☎ 80 03 00.

ORIHUELA **Alicante** ☎ (96), pop. 52,400, *i* c/ Francisco Díez, 25 ☎ 530 12 85, ✛ 530 51 51, P 530 16 40, ⚐ 530 02 84. Murcia 25km, Alicante 59km, Madrid 415km.

This agreeable old town, set in the fertile Segura valley, was known as *Orcelis* by the Romans and as *Aurariola*, meaning 'pot of gold', by the Visigoths. It was reconquered from the Muslims in 1264 and became an important medieval town with its own bishop and university. It was the birthplace of **Miguel Hernández**, a powerful lyric poet of the 1930s who died in Franco's prison after the Civil War, his promise tragically cut short.

Although Orihuela is administratively part of the Levante province of Alicante, it is culturally and linguistically part of Murcia and was, under the Visigoths and the Arabs, capital of the Murcia region.

🍴 *Casa Corro* (closed: Monday nights), Palmeral de San Antón ☎ 530 29 63 🅿 ✦ V $$$.

Cultural highlights: Approaching the town on the N-340 you pass by the palm grove, or **Palmeral**. The **Colegio Santo Domingo** used to be the university, built in the 16C and closed down in the 19C. It has an austere Renaissance façade, two cloisters and an interesting Baroque church containing frescoes. A museum honouring the poet Miguel Hernández, the Casa-Museo de Miguel Hernández, stands opposite. Highpoints of the 14-15C **Cathedral**, the Gothic **Concatedral de El Salvador**, include the 18C carved choir stalls and the Diocesan Museum (open: 10.30-12.30; closed: holidays) which boasts a **Velázquez**, a Ribera and a Morales. The **Iglesia de Santiago** was built during the reign of the Catholic Monarchs and is a good example of the Isabelline style of that period. It contains a number of sculptures attributed to Salzillo. Other main buildings include the 18C Episcopal Palace and the Béjar Palace. The former has a fine collection of pictures and the latter houses a library and a Holy Week float called *La Diablesa* which was carved by Nicolás de Busi.

Fiestas: The Holy Week processions featuring sculptures by Salzillo are interesting. There are also Christians versus Moors battles from July 8-17.

PEÑISCOLA **Castellón** ☎ (964), pop. 3,605, *i* Paseo Marítimo ☎ 48 02 08, P 48 01 21. Castellón de la Plana 76km, Tarragona 124km, Madrid 494km.

The showpiece of this walled, seaside village of white and ochre cubist houses, set on a rocky peninsula, is the fortress that became the last redoubt of Pedro de Luna who in the 15C was elected pope and took the name of Benedict XIII. Dethroned in Rome he took refuge here where he was known as **Papa Luna** and continued to press his claims to the papacy. Peñíscola's two sandy beaches, in combination with its innate picturesque qualities, make it a popular summer holiday resort.

🏨 ★★★★ *Hostería del Mar* (linked to the Parador chain), km6 on the Benicarló-Peñíscola road ☎ 48 06 00 🛏 85 📺 🅿 ✦ 🍴 ⚶ ≈ ⌕ 25m ≪ 🐎 ℚ AE, DC, EC, V $$$ to $$$$. Its **restaurant** stages medieval banquets on Saturdays.

🏨 ★★★ *Cartago* (closed: 1/10-31/5), Av Papa Luna, 34 ☎ 47 33 11 🛏 26 🅿 ✦ ≈ ⌕ 25m ≪ 🐎 ℚ AE, DC, EC, V $$ to $$$.

🏨 ★★★ *Papa Luna* (closed: 1/11-14/3), km6.6 on the Benicarló-Peñíscola road ☎ 48 07 60 🛏 250 ✦ 🍴 ≈ ⌕ 25m ≪ 🐎 DC, EC, V $$ to $$$.

🍴 *Casa Severino* (closed: Wednesdays except in summer, and November), Urb Las Atalayas ☎ 48 07 03 🅿 ✳ MC, V $$$. Regional cuisine.

Beaches: The **Playa Norte**, nearly 7km long, is bordered by a promenade.

Best buys: Locally made alabaster trinkets and general bargains in the flea market held on Mondays between the two beaches make for good buys.

Cultural highlights: The **castle** was built by the Templar Knights on the site of an existing Arab fortification and was reformed by Papa Luna who added the basilica and his own palace. There are wonderful **views** to be had from the battlements of the town and the Mediterranean. Peñíscola's **old quarter** has maintained its medieval atmosphere with a distinctly Moorish flavour amidst the hotels and apartments of the tourist boom, which have sprouted up along its beaches. The shrine of La Ermitana, next to the castle, is decorated with 18C glazed tiles manufactured in the village of Alcora.

Fiestas: Traditional folk dancing is the highpoint of the September 8 *fiestas*.

Local sights: BENICARLO, 7km, is a busy tourist resort set around a fishing port. Its local history museum, the Museo de Historia de la Ciudad, c/ Rayón (open: 7.00-9.00 pm; closed Sundays) exhibits finds excavated at a nearby Iberian settlement. For accommodation, the ★★★ *Parador Costa de Azahar*, Av Papa Luna, 5 ☎ 47 01 00 ⬚ 108 🅿 ♦ ✳ ⌕ ⚓ ≪ ⌕ AE, DC, EC, V $$$$ is recommended.

REQUENA **Valencia** ☎ (96), pop. 17,622, ⊕ 230 08 38, **P** 230 13 25. Valencia 69km, Madrid 279km.

Set in stark countryside reminiscent of Castile, this is a wine producing village which has an old quarter, walled and unspoiled, with narrow streets lined with fine old houses. The churches of **Santa María** and **El Salvador** date from the late 15C and have glazed tiles, a typically Valencian touch, decorating their interiors. There is a Wine Museum and an Art Museum in the village's Arab castle.

🍴 *Mesón del Vino* (closed: Tuesdays and September) c/ General Valera, 13
☎ 230 00 01 **EC, V** $$$.

❧ **SAGUNTO-SAGUNT** **Valencia** ☎ (96), pop. 54,876, *i* La Autonomía, 2 ☎ 246 12 30, ⊕ 246 29 99, **P** 246 12 60. Valencia 27km, Castellón de la Plana 56km, Madrid 375km.

Every Spanish school child knows about Sagunto, a landmark town in Spain's history. The battle between the Romans and the Carthaginians for possession of strategic Sagunto sparked off the second Punic War in 218 BC. Hannibal's troops besieged the city for eight months and when he finally breached its defences, the desperate defenders burned down the town and committed collective suicide. Five years later the town was rebuilt by Scipio and became, once more, a flourishing Roman colony.

The Romans and the Carthaginians coveted Sagunto on account of its mines and its port. The town's industrial energy has continued to this day and although recession has forced the closure of its steel works it remains an important engineering and manufacturing centre.

Cultural highlights: The **Roman theatre**, built in the 2C, can seat 8,000 spectators and has extraordinarily good acoustics. The antique remains excavated at Sagunto are exhibited at the Museo Arqueológico (open: 10.00-2.00 and 4.00-6.00). Old Sagunto has a *judería*, or Jewish quarter, a Romanesque church, the 13C Iglesia de El Salvador, and a 16C Gothic one, the Iglesia Arciprestal de Santa María.

Fiestas and festivals: The Roman theatre hosts an International Choral Singing Festival and, in August, a Fortnight of Classical Theatre, the *Sagunt a Escena* ☎ 351 00 51.

On the town: The promenade by the port is the town's liveliest area for cafeterias, bars, pubs and discos.

SANTA POLA **Alicante** ☎ (96), pop. 13,604, *i* Pl de la Diputación ☎ 541 49 84. Alicante 19km, Murcia 75km, Cartagena 91km, Madrid 423km.

Renowned for its excellent seafood, particularly for its *langostinos* (king prawns) and *salmonetes* (red mullet), Santa Pola's picturesque bay was well known to the Romans who founded the harbour of *Portus Illicitanus* here to serve the town of Elche. The harbour remains busy (Santa Pola's is one of the most important fishing fleets on Spain's Mediterranean coast) as does the local salt industry, and in recent years the town has become an important tourist resort.

🏨 ★★★ *Pola-Mar*, Playa de Levante, 6 ☎ 541 32 00 ⬚ 76 📺 🅿 ♦ ⚓ ≪ AE, EC, V $$$.

🏨 ★★ *Rocas-Blancas*, km17 on the Alicante-Cartagena road ☎ 541 13 12 🛏 100 🅿 ✦ 🎤 ⚓ ≪ 🐎 $$ to $$$.

🍴 *Batiste*, Playa de Poniente ☎ 541 14 85 🅿 ❊ ≪ AE, DC, EC, V $$$. Seafood cuisine.

🍴 *Galerna* (closed: Sunday nights and 12/10-27/10), c/ Poeta Miguel Hernández, 15 ☎ 541 52 82 AE, V $$$. Basque cuisine.

🍴 *María Picola* (closed: October, Mondays midday in summer, and Sunday evenings and Mondays in winter), km24 on the Santa Pola-Elche road ☎ 541 35 13 🅿 ✦ AE, EC, V $$$. Alicante cooking in a pleasant villa.

🍴 *Miramar*, Playa de Poniente ☎ 541 38 96 🅿 ❊ AE, DC, EC, V $$$. Rice dishes and seafood.

Beaches: There are five beaches in all, and they are all crowded in the high season. **Lisa** beach, between the harbour and the Pinet salt flats, is safe.

Best buys: You can buy fresh fish and seafood from the market on the quay.

Cultural highlights: The 16C castle houses a Museum of Archaeology, Marine Life and the Fishing Industry (open in summer: 11.00-2.00 and 6.00-10.00; winter: 11.30-1.30 and 4.00-7.00).

Local sights: There are regular boats from Santa Pola and Alicante which make the three-mile trip to the islands called **Isla de Tabarca** and **L'Illa Plana** which have Roman remains.

Sports: Sailing, fishing and scuba diving are all local sports —contact the port ☎ 541 24 03.

TORREVIEJA Alicante ☎ (96), pop. 18,454, 🛈 Pl Catepón, s/n ☎ 571 07 22, ✚ 571 18 18, P 571 01 50. Murcia 45km, Alicante 50km, Cartagena 60km, Madrid 435km.

This town grew up in the 18C around the local salt industry and it has now boomed thanks to tourism.

🏨 ★★★ *Fontana*, Rambla Juan Mateo, 19 ☎ 571 41 11 🛏 156 🅿 🎤 ⚓ AE, DC, EC, V $$$.

🏨 ★★ *Berlín*, c/ Torre del Moro, s/n ☎ 571 15 37 🛏 27 ✦ 🐸 ⚓ ≪ $$$. Good sea views.

🍴 *Cap Roig*, km8 on the Cartagena road, Urb Cabo Roig ☎ 532 02 90 🅿 ✦ ≪ AE, DC, MC, V $$$. Good views and even better fish and seafood.

🍴 *El Tamarindo* (closed: Wednesdays in the low season and 1/12-7/1), c/ La Sal, 27 ☎ 571 51 37 ✦ DC, MC, V $$$. Regional and French cooking.

🍴 *La Tortuga*, c/ María Pasodí, 3 ☎ 571 09 60 V $$$.

🍴 *Miramar*, Paseo Vista Alegre, 6 ☎ 571 07 65 🅿 ❊ ≪ AE, DC, EC, MC, V $$$. An elegant restaurant serving fish-based rice dishes and *caldereta de langosta* (lobster stew) by the sea shore.

Beaches: El Cura beach is a good one.

Best buys: Clothing bargains are available at the Friday flea market.

Cultural highlights: The **salt flats** are attractive and scenic. The watchtowers on the Cervera and La Mata headlands were an early warning insurance against pirate raids.

Fiestas: As in most seaport towns and villages, the feastday of the *Virgen del Carmen*, July 16, is celebrated with processions of decorated boats. Caribbean folk songs called *habaneras*, which originated in Cuba, are popular here and they are the subject of a song festival, the **Certamen Nacional de Habaneras y Polifonía**, on August 12-15.

Sports: Golf can be played at the 18-hole, par 72 **Campo de Golf Villamartín**, 7.5km on the N-332 to Cartagena ☎ 532 03 50. The *Puerto Deportivo Torrevieja* and the *Puerto Deportivo Cabo Roig*, 15km, are the local marinas.

🐾🐾 VALENCIA **Valencia** ☎ (96), pop. 738,575, *i* Pl País Valenciano, 1 ☎ 351 04 17, at the airport ☎ 370 95 00, and c/ La Paz, 46 ☎ 332 40 96, ⊂ Pl Ayuntamiento, ✉ Pl del Caudillo, 24 ☎ 351 67 50, ✚ 360 68 00, **P** 352 14 78, ✈ at Manises, 9.5km on the N-III ☎ 370 34 08 (Iberia, c/ Paz, 14 ☎ 352 05 00) ⚓ Trasmediterránea (Canaries and Balearics), Av Ingeniero Manuel Soto, 15 ☎ 367 65 12, 🚍 Av Menéndez Pidal, 13 ☎ 349 72 22, 🚃 Pl Alfonso el Magnánimo, 2 ☎ 231 06 34. Castellón de la Plana 69km, Alicante 185km, Madrid 350km, Barcelona 354km.

A busy and bustling city, the largest in Spain after Madrid and Barcelona, Valencia has forever been associated with oranges and also with rice in general and *paella* in particular. Valencia's rich agriculture is the magnificent legacy of its more than five centuries of Muslim occupation. The Arabs introduced crops and, far more importantly, evolved a complex irrigation system that ensured the fertility of the area's alluvial plain. To this day a 'Water Tribunal', the *Tribunal de las Aguas*, meets every Thursday at midday on the steps of the cathedral, just as it has done for more than a thousand years, to resolve disputes over the distribution of water. Noise, fireworks and brass bands are also characteristic of Valencia. This is a place of non-stop liveliness, commercially keyed up, ambitious and eager, and yet, because it is first and foremost a Mediterranean city, content with itself, relaxed and more than aware of the better things in life.

Settled sporadically by Greeks, Phoenicians and Carthaginians, Valencia properly came into being under the Romans in the 2C. Its name *Valentia* is said to refer to the valour that the Roman legionaries had to demonstrate in order to obtain some real estate in the potential-packed area. Valencia did well out of the Romans and it did even better following the 8C Muslim invasion which brought the city under the aegis of the **Al-Andalus** civilization of Arab Spain. Christian Spain's top hero, **El Cid**, conquered the city in 1094 but the Muslims recovered it following his death six years later and remained in control until Valencia's definitive takeover in 1238 by the expansionist monarch of Aragón and Catalonia, **James I, the Conqueror**. Catalans, who implanted their language, today's Valencian dialect, and Aragonese repopulated the city so successfully that in the 15C Valencia was one of the biggest urban centres in all Europe and exerted influence throughout the Mediterranean. The city's best buildings, the Cathedral, the gateways in its walls, the Exchange and grand palaces all date from this flourishing period. Artists such as **Luis Dalmau, Rodrigo de Osuna** and **Juan Reixach** formed part of a **Valencian School of Painting** and the city had a growing artisan class whose output included **ceramics** (Paterna and Manises), embroidery, tapestries, gold and silver-work and wrought iron. The expulsion of the **Moriscos**, the Christianized Moors, in 1609, meant a serious setback for Valencia's development for this industrious sector of the community made an important contribution to the region's economy. Worse was to follow during the War of Spanish Succession at the end of the century when Valencia backed the losing candidate to the throne, Archduke Charles of Austria. The eventual new monarch, French-born Philip V who initiated Spain's Bourbon dynasty, punished his disloyal Valencian subjects by stripping the area of the self-governing privileges it had enjoyed since the 13C and even banning the use of the Valencian dialect. But Valencia is nothing if not irrepressible and soon prosperity returned with the development of agriculture, silk and ceramics industries and the introduction of the railway. The city grew fast and at the turn of the century, when a keynote regional fair was organized on the left bank of the River Turia, Valencia was rich and confident enough to experiment with the new Modernist architecture.

Valencia's expansion has drifted into its fertile agricultural surroundings, the so-called **huerta**. The now dried-up river bed of the Turia delimits the old quarter of the city and the railway, entering from the S, forms the main axis of the *ensanche*, or expansion area, which was built up in the past century. The Ronda de Tránsitos, c/ Guillén de Castro, c/ Colón and c/ Játiva follow the lines of the old medieval walls and separate the old city from the new one.

- ★★★★ *Astoria Palace*, Pl Rodrigo Botet, 5 ☎ 352 67 37 ⌨ 208 TV ♪ AE, DC, MC, V $$$$$. Central.
- ★★★★ *Azafata Sol*, in Manises, 9km ☎ 154 61 00 ⌨ 130 ✦ ♪ ≈ AE, DC, MC, V $$$$$. Modern.
- ★★★★ *Dimar*, Gran Vía Marqués del Turia, 80 ☎ 334 18 07 ⌨ 95 TV ♪ AE, DC, MC, V $$$$$. Central.
- ★★★★ *Reina Victoria*, c/ Barcas, 4 ☎ 352 04 87 ⌨ 92 TV ♪ AE, DC, MC, V $$$$$.
- ★★★★ *Rey Don Jaime Sol*, Av Baleares, 2 ☎ 360 73 00 ⌨ 314 TV ♪ ≈ AE, DC, MC, V $$$$$ to $$$$$$. Modern.
- ★★★ *Excelsior*, c/ Barcelonina, 5 ☎ 351 46 12 ⌨ 65 TV P AE, DC, MC, V $$$.
- ★★★ *Expo Hotel*, Av Pío XII, 4 ☎ 347 09 09 ⌨ 396 TV P ♪ ≈ AE, DC, MC, V $$$$ to $$$$$. Modern.
- ★★★ *Feria Sol*, Av Feria, 2 ☎ 364 44 11 ⌨ 136 TV P ♪ DC, MC, V $$$$ to $$$$$. Near the Feria de Muestras exhibition centre.
- ★★★ *Inglés*, c/ Marqués de Dos Aguas, 6 ☎ 351 64 26 ⌨ 62 TV ♪ AE, DC, MC, V $$$ to $$$$.

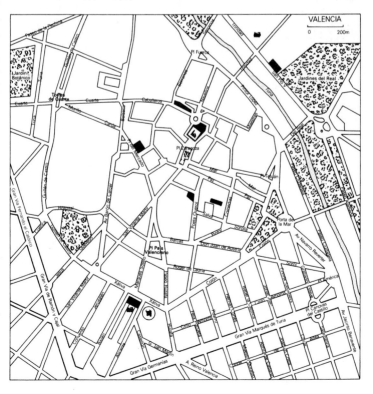

VALENCIA
0   200m

- ★★★ *Lehos*, c/ General Urrutia, s/n ☎ 334 78 00 🛏 104 TV (P ✚ ⚞ ⚘ ⚘ AE, DC, EC, V $$$.
- ★★★ *Mediterráneo*, Av Barón de Carcer, 45 ☎ 351 01 42 🛏 30 Y (A central boarding house.
- ¶¶ *Civera* (closed: Mondays and August), c/ Lérida, 11 ☎ 347 59 11 ✳ AE, DC, EC, V $$$$. Seafood.
- ¶¶ *Comodoro* (closed: Sundays), c/ Transits, 3 ☎ 321 38 15 ✳ AE, DC, V $$$ to $$$$.
- ¶¶ *Eguzki* (closed: Sundays and August), Av Baleares, 1 ☎ 369 90 60 ✳ $$$. Basque cuisine.
- ¶¶ *El Cachirulo* (closed: Saturdays midday, Sunday evenings and August), c/ Cronista Almela y Vives, 3 ☎ 360 10 84 ✳ AE, DC, MC, V $$$.
- ¶¶ *El Condestable* (closed: Sundays), c/ Artes Gráficas, 15 ☎ 369 92 50 AE, DC, MC, V $$$$. International cuisine.
- ¶¶ *El Estimat* (closed: Tuesdays and September), Av Neptuno, 16 ☎ 371 10 18 ✳ MC, V $$$. Fish and seafood.
- ¶¶ *El Gourmet* (closed: Sundays and 15/8-15/9), c/ Taquígrafo Martí, 3 ☎ 374 50 71 ✳ AE, DC, MC, $$$.
- ¶¶ *El Plat* (closed: Sunday nights and Mondays), c/ Conde de Altea, 41 ☎ 334 96 38 ✳ V $$$. Good rice dishes.
- ¶¶ *Eladio* (closed: Sundays and August), c/ Chiva, 40 ☎ 326 22 44 ✳ AE, DC, MC, V $$$. Good fish.
- ◔ ¶¶ *La Hacienda* (closed: Saturdays midday and Sundays), c/ Navarro Reverter, 12 ☎ 373 18 59 ✳ AE, DC, MC, V $$$ to $$$$. Smart food for expense account clients.
- ¶¶ *Lionel* (closed: Sunday nights), c/ Pizarro, 9 ☎ 351 65 66 ✳ AE, DC, MC, EC, V $$$. French cuisine.
- ◔ ¶¶ *Ma Cuina* (closed: Sundays), Gran Vía Germanías, 49 ☎ 341 77 99 ✳ AE, DC, MC, V $$$ to $$$$. Wide-ranging menu which changes with the seasons.

Best buys: The best shopping area is in the city centre around Colón, Cirilo Amorós, Sorní, Poeta Querol and Salva streets. Spanish fashion boutiques
◔ include **Adolfo Domínguez**, c/ Sorní, 13, **20 años**, c/ Barcas, 9, **Buque**, Pl Alfonso el Magnánimo, 11, *Don Carlos*, c/ Marqués de Sotelo, 4, **Hollywood**, c/ Correos, 6, and **Thai-Look** and **Zion**, c/ Sorní, 21 and 6. Shoe stores also abound, among them *A. Parriego*, c/ Poeta Querol, 10, **Austria 36**, c/ Juan de Austria, 36, **Farrutx**, c/ Sorní, 6, **Scorpetto**, c/ C. Amorós, 44, and **Zappa**, c/ Juan de Austria, 34. Leather goods can be
◔◔ bought at **Loewe**, c/ Poeta Querol, 7, and at *Saco*, c/ Cirilo Amorós, 72. Imaginative gifts are sold at **Agua de Limón**, c/ Jorge Juan, 22, and **Bañón**,
◔ Pl País Valenciano, 12; gifts and crafts at **Artespaña**, c/ de la Paz, 7. Artistic
◔ glassware is sold at **Pertegaz y Hernández**, Pl Honduras, 29, and porcelain at **Lladró**, Av Menéndez Pidal, in the *Nuevo Centro* shopping mall. Antiques hunters head for **Sambuca**, c/ Grabador Esteve, 21, and **S. Ribes**, c/ Vilaragut, 7, and jewelry lovers for **Giménez**, Pl País Valenciano, 16, and **Gracia** and **R. Torres**, c/ Paz, 24 and 5. Valencian **fans** (see 'Design') are ◔ sold at **Nela**, c/ San Vicente, 2, and at the **V. Mallol** workshop, Pl Rojas Clemente, 16. Wines are sold at *Bodegas La Sangre*, c/ Sangre, 4, and cakes at *Lerma*, c/ Paz, 18. There is a daily **flea market** at the Pl Alfonso el Magnánimo and a very typical and popular Sunday one in the Pl Redonda. Finally, the **Nuevo Centro**, on the corner of Av Menéndez Pidal and Pío XII, is a shopping mall with 300 shops, banks, a hotel and many facilities, and the city's large department stores are at c/ Colón, 29 and at c/ Pintor Sorolla.
Cultural highlights: The railway station, the Estación del Norte is a good starting point for a tour of the city since it sets the tone for what Valencia

likes to think of itself. The station itself reflects in its Modernism the self-assurance and prosperity of Valencia at the turn of the century and the station's cafeteria is decorated with tiled murals of rural scenes and flowers, illustrating a rural idyll. The buildings in the **Pl del País Valencià**, a city focal point, date from the 1920s and 1930s. The Ayuntamiento, or Town Hall, is an 18C mansion which acquired a new façade in 1905. It houses the History Museum, or Museo Histórico (open: 9.00-1.00; closed: weekends), which exhibits 14C documents dealing with the city's early medieval privileges.

The Gothic **Iglesia de San Martín** has an interesting façade added in the 18C and a Flemish bronze sculpture, attributed to Becker, of Saint Martin opting for the path of holiness by sharing his cape with a beggar. The earliest parts of the **Cathedral** date from 1262 and, as is often the case with such buildings, it was erected on the site of what had been, in turn, a Roman temple, a Visigothic church and a mosque. Most of the church was built in the 14C and the 15C, though the main façade was not executed until 1703. Towards the end of the 18C, Gothic pointed arches and columns were modified to conform with the new fashion which demanded rounded arches, Corinthian pillars and lots of gold plate. This sort of facelift went on all over Valencia, with varying degrees of taste and success, and is evident in a number of the region's churches. The intricately carved **Puerta de los Apóstoles** was created by the Gothic master sculptor Nicolás Autun. The octagonal Gothic **bell tower**, known familiarly in the city as the *Micalet*, was initiated in 1381 and finally completed in the 18C. From the top of the tower you can get your bearings about the city as well as have an excellent view of Valencia's characteristic domes of glazed tiles and ceramic. The **Cathedral Museum** (open: 10.00-1.00 and 4.00-6.00; closed: Sundays, holidays and December to February) contains early Valencian altarpieces, a Zurbarán, a Juan de Juanes, two Goyas and many valuable liturgical objects. The 17C **Real Basílica de Nuestra Señora de los Desamparados** houses the image of the much venerated *Maredeueta* (Little Mother), as the *Virgen de los Desamaparados*, patroness of Valencia, is popularly known.

The **Palacio de la Generalidad** is a fine 15C Gothic building with towers added in the 18C and in the present century. This was where Valencia's parliament used to meet until the institution was abolished in 1707 along with the region's other self governing privileges. The 18C tower has excellent **panelling** (open: weekdays 9.00-2.00 by prior arrangement). Further examples of Valencia's 14-15C Gothic architecture are the **Convento de Santo Domingo**, Pl de Tetuán, which has a particularly attractive Royal Chapel, the 15C **Capilla de los Reyes**, the **Torres de Cuarte**, which were damaged by Peninsular War cannonballs, the **Serranos** towers, which were once gateways into the city and, best of all, the 15C **Lonja** building which was the old silk market, with lovely **coffered ceilings** in the Consulado del Mar hall. The main market, the Mercado Central, which stands opposite the Lonja is, in contrast, a Modernist cast-iron structure.

Renaissance period architecture in Valencia includes the **Colegio del Corpus Christi** which has a **museum** (open: weekends and holidays 11.00-1.00) exhibiting works by Juan de Juanes, Caravaggio, Francisco Ribalta, El Greco, and Luis de Morales. The church is fairly exotic with green jasper columns, a glazed tile dado and Flemish tapestries, and a lovely cloister. Three of the bridges over the Turia —La Mar, Serranos and San José— were built in the 16C.

Turning to the Baroque period, one that suits Valencia particularly well, the impressive S door of the **Iglesia de los Santos Juanes** should not be missed. But the city's Baroque highpoint is undoubtedly the 18C alabaster **Palacio del Marqués de Dos Aguas**. The palace's splendid **façade** was sculpted by Ignacio Vergara to a design by the engraver Hipólito Rovira. The building houses the **National Ceramics Museum**, or Museo Nacional de Cerámica (open: 10.00-2.00 and 4.00-6.00; holidays: 10.00-2.00; closed: Mondays ☎ 351 63 92), which has a vast collection of more than 5,000 pieces dating from the early Iberian period to the present day. The collection includes Chinese and Japanese porcelain and local work produced in Paterna during the 13C and in Manises between the 15C and the 18C. The **Fine Arts Museum**, or Museo de Bellas Artes (open: 10.00-2.00 and 4.00-6.00; Sundays: 10.00-2.00; closed: Mondays ☎ 331 26 93), exhibits works by Juan de Juanes, El Greco, Bosch, Van Dyck, Velázquez, Ribalta, Ribera and Goya as well as canvases by Joaquín Sorolla, the much admired turn-of-the-century Valencian painter of luminous Mediterranean scenes. The former 14C granary known as the **Almudín** now contains an Art and Geological Museum, the Museo Paleontológico (open: 10.00-1.00 and 4.00-6.00; weekends: 10.00-1.00; closed: Mondays, July and August ☎ 331 85 62) and there is a **Prehistorical Museum**, the Museo de la Prehistoria (open: 10.00-1.00 and 4.00-6.00; Sundays: 10.00-1.00), at c/ Corona, 36. The **Jardines del Real** is the city's biggest park.

Fiestas: March 12-19 sees the annual *Fallas* fireworks and bonfire extravaganza (see 'Fiestas'). **Corpus Christi** is marked by processions that are solemn, colourful and very traditional. There is good **bullfighting** during July, the *Feria de Julio*, a competition for brass bands, the *Certamen Internacional de Bandas de Música Ciudad de Valencia*, and in October there is a cinema festival, the *Mostra de Valencia de Cinema Mediterrani*.

Local sights: La Albufera, 10km S, is a fresh water lake separated from the Mediterranean by a strip of land that was called the *Albuhaira* or 'little sea' by the Arabs. Farmers and builders reclaiming land, pesticides and industrial waste threaten this lovely natural setting. There are a number of tree-shaded open-air restaurants and bars between the sea shore and the lagoon in the area called La Dehesa de El Saler.

The island of **EL PALMAR**, S of La Albufera, has a cluster of fishermen's cottages, among them some traditional thatched *barracas*. Boats leaving from the quay take visitors on trips around the lake.

MANISES, 8km W, is a famous ceramics centre and you can visit potteries still working in the centuries' old traditional craft like *Sucesores de J. Jimeno* at c/ Huerto, 1, and buy local ware at *La Sart*, c/ Maestro Guillén, s/n. The other great trademark of Valencian ceramics is **PATERNA**, a village 6km N of the city centre. *Alfarería Giner*, Cueva de Albarchi, s/n, is a modern workshop that specializes in reproductions of old designs.

On the town: Valencia is an extremely lively city, full of bars and terraces that are open till all hours, crowded and fun. Its night life rivals that of Madrid and Barcelona. Action areas include the **Pl Cánovas del Castillo** and, by the Playa de Malvarrosa, **c/ Eugenia Viñes**, as well as the University area around c/ Ramón Gordillo where there are disco pubs such as *Mamá Ya Lo Sabe*, *Veo, Veo, Delirio* and *La Bola*. Alternatives are the Pl Xúquer zone for *Café Maravillas* and *Pan de Azúcar* and the Barrio del Carmen district for *Negrito, Malvarrosa, Café San Jaime, Madrid, Metrópolis, La Barraca, Spook Factor* and *Dreams Village*. **Belle Epoque**, c/ Cuba, 8, stages big shows and there is jazz at *Hoyo 19*, c/ Cronista Carretes, 3. *Distrito 10*, c/ General Elio, 10, is an ultra-modern disco and *Pachá*, c/ Emilio Baro, 71, stages live rock and pop concerts. *Barrachina*, Pl País Valenciano, is a coffee shop, bar and delicatessen all in one, and is something of an institution: it is the first place to open and the last to close. Adults will enjoy the *Casino Monte Picayo*, in Puzol, 14km ☎ 142 12 11, with all the usual game tables, while youngsters will prefer the **zoo** at the Jardines del Real.

Sports: Golfers head for the 9-hole *Campo de Golf de Manises*, 12km ☎ 379 08 50, the 18-hole, par 72 *Campo de Golf El Saler*, 18km ☎ 161 11 86, the 18-hole *Club de Campo El Bosque*, 4km ☎ 326 38 00, or the 18-hole, par 72 *Club de Golf Escorpión*, at Bétera ☎ 160 12 11. Water sports are practised at the yacht club, the *Real Club Náutico de Valencia*, at the commercial port ☎ 323 39 83, and fishing is a popular sport in the rivers Túria and Júcar. Tennis is played at the *Club de Tenis Valencia* ☎ 369 06 58, and the *Club Español de Tenis*, in Rocafort ☎ 131 00 00. Ultra light flying and gliding can be practised at the *Aero Club Valencia*, Manises airport ☎ 370 95 00.

VILLAJOYOSA-LA VILA JOIOSA Alicante ☎ (96), pop. 21,411, [*i*] Pl Castelar, 2 ☎ 589 30 43, ✚ 589 14 00, P 589 00 50, 🚍 Pl Generalitat ☎ 589 00 25. Benidorm 6km, Alicante 32km, Gandía 79km, Madrid 451km.

Villajoyosa is a very agreeable little village under threat of being swallowed up by Benidorm's gargantuan growth. The **brightly painted houses** along the promenade are very picturesque and the locals make their living out of fishing, making nets and manufacturing chocolates.

🏨 **★★★★** *Montíboli*, 3km on the N-337 to Alicante ☎ 589 02 50 🛏 49 ✦ 🎤 🏊 ⚓ ⚘ ≪ ⚰ AE, DC, EC, V $$$$ to $$$$$. Modern and quiet with a semi-private beach (where a buffet is served in summer) and a good **restaurant** $$$ to $$$$.

🍴 *El Brasero*, Av del Puerto, s/n ☎ 589 03 33 ✦ AE, EC, MC, V $$$. Fish and seafood.

Beaches: The local beach is the one at **Torres.**

Cultural highlights: The **Torre de Hércules**, on the main road to Benidorm, is the most important **Roman monument** in Alicante province.

Fiestas: Moors and Christians battle it out on land and sea from dawn onwards between July 24-31.

On the town: The *Casino Costa Blanca*, with a full range of gambling alternatives, is at km115 of the N-332 ☎ 589 07 00 AE, DC, V (open: 8.00 pm-4.00 am). Try the local orange-blossomy drink called *nardo* at bars such as *Mercantil*, in the port, *Náutica*, c/ Pizarro, and *Policeta*, c/ Colón.

VINAROZ-VINARÒS Castellón ☎ (964), pop. 17,467, [*i*] Pl Jovellar ☎ 45 02 00, ✚ 45 08 56, P 45 02 00, 🚌 45 19 44. Castellón de la Plana 76km, Tarragona 109km, Madrid 498km.

A prosperous small town with local industries in addition to its farming and fishing tradition, Vinaroz is famed for its *langostinos* (king prawns).

🏨 **★★★** *Miramar*, Paseo de Blasco Ibáñez, 12 ☎ 45 14 00 🛏 17 ✦ ≪ V $$.

🍴 *Casa Pocho* (closed: Sunday nights, Mondays and December), c/ San Gregorio, 53 ☎ 45 10 95 V $$$$. Seafood.

🍴 *El Langostino de Oro* (closed: Mondays), c/ San Francisco, 31 ☎ 45 12 04 DC, MC, V $$$. Fish and seafood.

Beaches: The local beach has been improved with imported sand and there are rocky **coves** nearby.

Best buys: Local fresh produce is sold at a Thursday open-air market in the Av Jaime I.

Cultural highlights: The 17C Iglesia Arciprestal de la Asunción has an impressive Baroque façade. The 16C Convento de San Agustín has been restored and now serves as a municipal auditorium.

Fiestas: Top celebrating dates are San Sebastián, January 20; the *Virgen de la Misericordia*, on the Sunday before Corpus Christi; and Saint John and Saint Peter's Days, June 24 and 29.

MADRID AND
CASTILE-LA MANCHA

As you travel around the vast expanse of **tableland** that stretches S from Madrid to the mountains of the Sierra Morena and the frontier with Andalusia, the Knight of the Mournful Countenance, the Man of La Mancha, keeps putting in an appearance. This is just as well because but for **Don Quixote** these plains could be just a huge, dull flat expanse of arid land. Don Quixote turned it into a land of fantasy. Thanks to him, when the shadows lengthen and the sky grows pink, every rocky crag becomes a fortress, every flock of sheep a threatening army and every group of windmills a band of hostile giants that has to be charged and subdued. Guided by the fantastic character that Cervantes conjured up you will never be lost for an idea or a sensation in Castile-La Mancha for this is a land of castles and cathedrals, of chivalry and heroism, mysticism and romance.

Distant horizons and a huge, wide open sky are the essential elements that define the area. It is scored through by two great rivers, the **Tagus** and the **Guadiana** that meander towards the Atlantic and by the smaller **Júcar** which battles eastward to the Mediterranean. The wild hills of the Toledo mountains and Cuenca's sierra are mere interruptions to the rolling flatness and seem only to accentuate it. With your eye trained to fantasy by the endearing Quixote you begin to grasp the colours of the tableland and to appreciate the golden hues of the corn, the silver sparkle of the olives and the mix of deep green and deeper red that the vine produces. Were you to glide lazily over the steppes like one of the storks that nest in anything from church towers to abandoned electric pylons, you would note, also, how the fields form geometric patterns and how the lonely villages, miles from anywhere, look like wheels, their narrow streets acting like spokes that converge on that hub of *pueblo* life, the **Plaza Mayor**.

In contemporary Spain, Castile-La Mancha and Madrid form two distinct administrative regions. Historically both were known as New Castile while the prolongation of the area N of Madrid, beyond the Guadarrama mountain range, used to be termed Old Castile, today's region of Castile and León. The two Castiles, the Old and the New, were the chief components that moulded the Spanish nation for they were in the front line of the long, 800 year march S against the Muslims that formed the backbone of Spanish history and is known as the *Reconquista*, or Reconquest. For a long period the steppes of La Mancha were a frontier land between the Christian and the Muslim armies. For a while the splendid city of **TOLEDO** was a magnificent multi-cultured oasis of tolerance where **Christians, Muslims** and **Jews** lived at peace with each other. As the reconquest gathered pace and forged its way deep into Muslim Andalusia, Castile-La Mancha became the feudal preserve of the Spanish **Military Orders**, the Knights of Santiago, of Calatrava, of Montesa and of San Juan, which were modelled on institutions, such as the Templar Knights, that were born out of the crusades. It was the military orders, with their **castles**, fortified churches and monasteries, that gave La Mancha its warlike aspect.

In the 16C reign of **Philip II MADRID** was designated the capital of the Kingdom of Spain. Geographically it had been the centre of the Peninsula since the dawn of creation but was little more than a straggly little village, totally unimportant when compared to Barcelona or Burgos, Salamanca or

Seville, when it became the **seat of political power** at the height of Spain's imperial glory. Madrid has always had an instinctive belief in its ability to cope and muddle through and it rose to the challenge with alacrity. Today it is a fascinating city of more than three million inhabitants and it is the melting pot of the several Spains that make up the nation. Madrid is a place of enormous vitality, throbbing with pace. Castile-La Mancha has changed much less —in places hardly at all. It must look much the same as it did in the days when Don Quixote and his faithful, down-to-earth Sancho Panza criss-crossed its dusty paths.

ALARCON **Cuenca** ☎ (966), pop. 273. Cuenca 85km, Madrid 189km.

Little more than a walled-in cluster of houses grouped around a castle, Alarcón is grandly **situated** on the crest of a hill. The castle belonged to the remarkable Infante Don Juan Manuel, a grandson of Ferdinand III, the Saint, who conquered Seville. The prince owned a string of castles that stretched all the way from Peñafiel in Valladolid province to Alicante on the Mediterranean which were each a day's ride from each other. He is held to have been the greatest prose writer of 14C Spain and is best known for his treatise on morals, *Count Lucanor*. The village **Church of Santa María** has a good Renaissance portico and an interesting 16C altarpiece within.

▦ ★★★ *Parador Marqués de Villena*, Av Amigos del Castillo, s/n ☎ 33 13 50 ⇥ 13 ✕ �Y ▣ ♣ ⅋ ≪ ⅙ AE, DC, MC, V $$$$. A quiet hotel in the lovely setting of a medieval castle.

ALBACETE **Albacete** ☎ (967), pop. 116,500. *i* c/ Virrey Morcillo, 1 ☎ 21 56 11, ✉ c/ Dionisio Guardiola, s/n ☎ 23 06 13, ✚ 21 90 12, **P** 21 60 45, 🚌 c/ Federico García Lorca, s/n ☎ 21 60 12, ⛟ Av de la Estación, s/n ☎ 21 20 96. Cuenca 142km, Alicante 165km, Madrid 245km.

Albacete's origins go back to the early days of the Iberians and it was also a Roman town of some importance. It became wealthier under the Arabs (they called it *Al Basite*, the Plain) who introduced a knife-making industry that has survived in the city to present times. Little of Albacete's long past remains to be seen nowadays in what is essentially a modern town that serves as a crossroads on the Madrid-Alicante highway and is the capital of the agricultural province of the same name.

▦ ★★★★ *Los Llanos*, Av España, 9 ☎ 22 37 50 ⇥ 102 ✕ TV ♠ AE, DC, EC, MC, V $$$.

▦ ★★★ *Gran Hotel*, c/ Marqués de Molina, 1 ☎ 21 37 87 ⇥ 69 ✕ TV ▣ ♠ AE, DC, EC, MC, V $$$.

▦ ★★★ *Parador de La Mancha*, km260 on the N-301, 5km from the centre ☎ 22 94 50 ⇥ 70 ✕ Y ▣ ♣ ⅋ ≈ ≪ ⵕ AE, DC, EC, MC, V $$$. A very quiet hotel (note the typical local architecture) with good views and a pleasant **restaurant**.

▦ ★★ *Albar*, c/ Isaac Peral, 3 ☎ 21 68 61 ⇥ 51 V $$ to $$$. Unpretentious.

⑂ *Mesón Las Rejas* (closed: Sunday nights and Mondays), c/ Dionisio Guardiola, 7 ☎ 22 72 42 ▣ ✳ AE, EC, V $$ to $$$. A typical old-fashioned Castilian inn.

⑂ *Nuestro Bar* (closed: Sunday nights, holidays and July), c/ Alcalde Conangla, 102 ☎ 22 72 15 ▣ ♣ ✳ AE, DC, EC, MC, V $$ to $$$. Regional cooking.

Best Buys: Knives of all sorts are sold at *Arcos*, c/ La Feria, 30, *Gómez*, c/ La Feria, 12, and *Mañas*, c/ Mayor, 6; cheese at *La Tienda*, c/ Concepción, s/n, and fashion at the *Pipol* shopping mall, c/ Tesifonte Gallego, s/n, and *Maratas*, c/ Virgen de Belén, 17.

Cultural highlights: Albacete's strong points are its 16C Cathedral and the Church of the Asunción which dates from the same period. There are some good examples of 18C popular architecture in c/ Feria and c/ Mayor and the city museum, the **Museo de Albacete**, Parque de Abelardo Sánchez (open: 10.00-2.00 and 4.00-7.00; closed: Sunday afternoons and Mondays ☎ 22 83 07) exhibits an interesting collection of finds from digs at Iberian and Roman sites in the province.

Fiestas and festivals: The big local annual event is the *Feria*, which lasts from September 7 to 17, with a livestock fair and bullfighting serving as an excuse for general merrymaking.

Local sights: CHINCHILLA DE MONTEARAGON, 12km out of Albacete on the N-430, is a very agreeable little walled town with a 15C castle that belonged to the extremely powerful Marquis of Villena who was the Grand Master of the Military Order of Santiago. Like most historic Castilian towns, Chinchilla has a nice-looking **Plaza Mayor** on which stands the Neoclassical **Town Hall**. Note, too, the 15C **Church of San Salvador** and the old **Lonja**, or Corn Exchange. Traditional local pottery is still made at workshops like *A. Tortosa*, c/ San Antón, 4.

The extraordinarily **situated ALCALA DEL JUCAR**, to the NE, is a troglodyte town in so far as many of its admittedly few inhabitants live in caves carved into the rock. Further away and heading S, you can explore the **Sierra de Alcaraz** and the village of **ALCARAZ** which has past grandeur written all over it —it has a splendid **c/ Mayor**, a 16C **Church of La Trinidad** and a **Plaza Mayor** with a number of fine buildings such as the 16C **Town Hall** and the 18C **Corn Exchange**. Alcaraz was the birthplace of the Renaissance architect Andrés de Vandelvira who designed several buildings in his native town and found fame and fortune during the reigns of Charles V and Philip II.

On the Town: Pl del Altozano is the focal point of the young scene, with lots of bars, pubs and summer *terrazas*. For good *tapas* and seafood, head for *Cantábrico*, c/ Marqués de Villores, 22, and *Cruz Blanca*, c/ Gaona, 18. The liveliest discos are *Extasis*, c/ Dionisio Guardiola, 7, *Triángulo*, c/ Teodoro Camino, 13, *Zodial*, Av España, 9, and *Café Bécquer*, c/ Carnicerías, 17.

Sports: Flying at the *Aeroclub Albacete*, Av España, 10 ☎ 33 88 11, and small-game hunting are the local sports.

ALCALA DE HENARES **Madrid** ☎ (91), pop. 151,221, [i] Callejón de Santa María, 1 ☎ 889 26 94. Guadalajara 27km, Madrid 31km.

Try not to notice the apartment blocks of modern, dormitory town Alcalá and head straight for the old quarter that was the site of Spain's premier university in the 16C. It was here, under the patronage of Cardinal Cisneros who was the Catholic Monarchs' favourite churchman, that Europe's first **polyglot bible** was produced comparing the Greek, Hebrew and Latin texts. Alcalá was the birthplace of **Miguel de Cervantes**, author of *Don Quixote*, and also of **Catherine of Aragón**, the first of Henry VIII's six wives and the eldest daughter of the Catholic Monarchs.

▦ ★★★ *El Bedel*, Pl San Diego, 6 ☎ 889 37 00 ⇥ 51 Ⴤ ℙ AE, DC, EC, V $$$.

❚❘ *Hostería del Estudiante*, c/ Colegios, 3 ☎ 888 03 30 ✳ AE, DC, EC, V $$$. Castilian decor and a lovely 15C cloister.

Cultural highlights: The Plateresque façade of the **University** was created in 1543 by Rodrigo Gil de Hontañón who had learnt the architectural and sculptural design trade at the elbow of his father as they worked on major projects that included the cathedrals of Salamanca and Segovia. The young Rodrigo here in Alcalá produced one of the greatest buildings of the

Spanish Renaissance and firmly established his reputation as the supreme master builder of his age. The second showpiece of this academic complex is the **Paraninfo**, or University Senate House, Pl San Diego, s/n (open: weekends 11.00-1.00 and 4.00-6.00 ☎ 888 22 00) which has a splendid Plateresque stuccoed gallery and a fine coffered ceiling. The tour of the university also takes in the **Patio Trilingüe**, built in 1557 to honour the famous bible, and the later **Patio Mayor** which is in Baroque style. The wise old Cardinal Cisneros who founded the university in 1498 is buried in a

○ Carrara marble **tomb** in the **Capilla de San Ildefonso**. This building, in a possible tribute to the polyglot bible's benefactor, provides a multicultural delight with its marvellous synthesis of the Gothic and the Mudéjar styles. If you want to remember Cervantes you should visit the chapel called the **Capilla del Oidor** which is where he was baptized in 1547 and the **Casa de Cervantes**, c/ Mayor, 48 (open: 10.00-12.00 and 4.00-8.00) which stands on what was probably the site of the house where he was born and which looks very much like the sort of building he might have grown up in but which was in fact built in 1955. A number of rare editions of *Don Quixote* are on show here together with other memorabilia.

Fiestas and festivals: The *Jornadas Musicales Cervantinas* music festival is held in April.

Local sights: Nuevo baztan, 20km SE, is a curious village for it has hardly changed since the 18C when it was built from scratch to house Navarrese farmers from the Baztán valley in the Pyrenees. The northerners arrived here as part of a scheme typical of that enlightened period which sought to introduce proper farming to the area.

Sports: Golfers can play at the 9-hole *Club Valdeláguila* course ☎ 885 96 59, 8km out of town.

ALMAGRO **Ciudad Real** ☎ (926), pop. 8,751, [*i*] c/ Carnicería, 11 ☎ ○
86 07 17. Ciudad Real 24km, Madrid 190km.
  This picturesque and unspoilt town was the seat of the powerful Military Order of Calatrava in the Middle Ages. In the 16C it was home also to Charles V's German bankers, the Fuggar family, known in Spain as *los Fúcares*.

▥ ★★★★ *Parador de Almagro*, c/ Ronda de San Francisco, s/n ☎ ○○
86 01 00 ⇌ 55 ✕ ⅄ ✦ � ⵛ ⵛ AE, DC, EC, V $$$$. A quiet hotel in the historic setting of the 16C Santa Catalina convent. The restaurant serves good Manchegan cuisine.

⑂ *Calatrava* (closed: Monday nights), c/ Egido Calatrava, 7 ☎ 86 01 85 V $$. Typical Manchegan cuisine.

Best buys: Traditional bobbin lace, still made by local women, is sold at *C. Manzano*, c/ Dominicas, 24. If you are interested in *avant garde* art, head for the *Fúcares* centre, c/ San Francisco, 2. Gastronomes will find preserved aubergines, the local speciality, at *Conservas La Plaza*, Pl de Toros, 2.

Cultural highlights: The elongated **Plaza Mayor** is very pleasing and its ○ showpiece is a small building on its S side that is Spain's answer to the Shakespearian Globe Theatre: the **Corral de Comedias**, a playhouse where ○ Golden Age drama was actually staged during Lope de Vega's lifetime (open: 10.00-2.00 and 4.00-7.00). The town has several good period mansions and the **Convento de Calatrava** has an outstanding staircase and a cloister in ○ the Plateresque style.

Fiestas and festivals: A festival of classical drama, the *Festival de Teatro Clásico*, is held in the Corral de Comedias playhouse in September.

Local sights: Aldea del rey is the seat of the 12C monastic fortress of the Calatrava Knights, the **Sacro Convento de Calatrava la Nueva**.

ALMANSA **Albacete** ☎ (967), pop. 21,568, ✚ 34 11 90, ⛑ 34 16 72. Albacete 77km, Madrid 322km.

The **castle** here is another link in the chain of fortresses that the literary prince, the Infante Don Juan Manuel, had built for himself across Spain (see 'Alarcón'). For a time Almansa was on the front line of the Reconquest and it was put in the safekeeping of the Templar Knights when it was captured from the Muslims. A decisive battle was fought here in 1707 during the War of Spanish Succession between the Austrian claimant, the Archduke Charles, and his rival Philippe of Anjou who was to reign as Philip V and found the Bourbon dynasty in Spain.

🍴 *Los Rosales* (closed: Tuesdays from November to February), Ctra de Circunvalación, s/n ☎ 34 07 50 $$. Good *tapas* in the bar (you can also buy local cheese here) and home-cooking in the restaurant.

🍴 *Mesón Pincelín* (closed: Mondays and 20/7-10/8), c/ Las Norias, 10 ☎ 34 00 07 **AE, DC, MC, V** $$$. Home-cooking.

Best buys: Local specialities include hand-made cow-bells from *M. Sánchez*, c/ Manuel de Falla, 13, and local wine from *Bodegas Piqueras*, c/ Juan Ramón Jiménez, 1.

Cultural highlights: The **castle** was built in the 14C and was reinforced with massive walls in the 15C. The **Iglesia de la Asunción** was built in the Isabelline-Gothic style in the 16C and had a Renaissance portal added to it later.

Local sights: The village of **CAUDETE**, to the SE, re-enacts episodes of the medieval battles between Christians and Moors during its September *fiestas*. If you are interested in reproductions of muskets, duelling pistols and other weapons, there is a good range at *Trabucos el Rojo*, c/ Corona de Aragón, 1.

● ARANJUEZ **Madrid** ☎ (91), pop. 37,265, [*i*] Pl Santiago Rusiñol, s/n ☎ 891 04 27. Toledo 44km, Madrid 46km.

This is Madrid's version of Versailles, a purpose-built 18C leisure town of royal palaces and gardens along the lush banks of the River Tagus which offered cool relief from the heat and dust of the capital. The Catholic Monarchs saw its potential and designated it a **Real Sitio** or Royal Estate and Philip II actually commissioned Juan de Herrera, the architect who built the Escorial for him, to build a palace here which later burned down. It was the first of the Bourbon kings, Philip V, with his Versailles background, who began to build up Aranjuez in earnest and his enthusiasm for the town was matched by that of his successors, Ferdinand VI, Charles III and Charles IV.

🍴 *Casa Pablo* (closed: 1/8-25/8), c/ Almíbar, 20 ☎ 891 14 51 ✳ $$$. Home-cooking.

🍴 *Chirón* (closed: 3/8-28/8), c/ Real, 10 ☎ 891 09 41 ✳ **AE, DC, V** $$$. Local regional dishes.

Best buys: Fresh local asparagus and strawberries are the town's specialities.

● **Cultural highlights:** The reconstruction of the **Royal Palace** began in 1727, during the reign of Philip V, on the site of the Hapsburg buildings which had been badly damaged by fire; it was completed between 1775-1778 by Charles III's architect Francisco Sabatini, designer of much of Madrid's Royal Palace, the Palacio de Oriente. Like all royal buildings in Spain, the Aranjuez palace is run by the *Patrimonio Nacional*, the National Trust, and its guides take conducted tours of visitors through the areas open to the public (open: 10.00-1.00 and 3.00-6.00; gardens: 10.00-sunset; closed: Tuesdays ☎ 891 03 05). The high points of the tour are the **Salón**
●● de Porcelana, a hall which serves as a showcase for the porcelain created in

Madrid's Real Fábrica del Buen Retiro; a Chinese Salon displaying a large collection of rice paper drawings that were presented last century to Isabella II by the Emperor of China, and the **Museo de Trajes Reales** which is a museum of court costumes and military uniforms dating from the 16C to the turn of this century.

The best sections of the royal gardens are the 16C **Jardín de la Isla** and the **Jardín del Príncipe**, named in honour of the future Charles IV, which features a number of species brought from America. Charles and his wife María Luisa of Parma (a couple painted time and again and not altogether favourably by Goya) also had a pleasure house built here that is quaintly called the **Casa del Labrador**, or Peasant's House, although there is nothing rustic or cottage-like about it for it is a proper little palace with marble floors, silk tapestries and chandeliers and reflects the classically-inspired romantic style that was then the rage. There is a boathouse in the gardens, the **Casa de los Marinos**, that contains a number of gondolas that were used by the Spanish royals for boating trips along the Tagus.

Local sights: OCAÑA, 17km beyond Aranjuez on the N-II, stages **Passion Plays** during Holy Week. Its Plaza Mayor acquired its present form in the 18C and its main buildings are the 15C Palace of the Dukes of Frias and the Carmelite convent that was built in the severe style that Juan de Herrera made popular during Philip II's reign. If you feel peckish, you can buy hand-made sweets at the *Convento de Santa Catalina de Siena*.

On the town: You can enjoy the Spanish equivalent of sedate afternoon tea at the *Cafetería Italiana*, c/ San Antonio, 17, ice creams at *Reno*, c/ Stuart, 20, and coffee and aperitifs at *La Rana Verde* near the bridge over the Tagus.

BELMONTE **Cuenca** ☎ (967), pop. 2,652. Cuenca 99km, Madrid 158km.

Belmonte is a little medieval town that in the 15C belonged to the Marquis of Villena, the all-powerful favourite of the dithering Henry IV of Castile. Villena built its collegiate church and also the castle which is where Henry's alleged daughter, Juana la Beltraneja, took refuge when she was disputing the succession to the crown of Castile with her aunt Isabella, the future Catholic Queen. Belmonte was the birthplace of Fray Luis de León who as a poet and as the chief theologian of Salamanca University was to make a singular mark on 16C Spanish society. The town is also linked with Eugenia de Montijo, better known as the Empress Eugénie, wife of Napoleon III of France, who owned the castle in the last century and carried out extensive alterations that included bricking up the patio's galleries, presumably to keep out draughts.

Cultural highlights: The **castle** is an impressive example of what a late Gothic fortress ought to look like and some of its rooms have excellent **coffered ceilings** that bear the geometric pattern trademark of Mudéjar craftsmen. The **Colegiata de San Bartolomé** includes the sepulchre of Villena among its collection of alabaster tombs and has interesting 15C **choir stalls** and **altarpieces** that were sculpted between the 15-17C. Luis de León was baptized at the church's font.

Local sights: The parish church of **VILLAESCUSA DE HARO**, 6km away on the N-420, has an early 16C chapel, the **Capilla de la Asunción**, which is an excellent example of the late Gothic in Spain.

CHINCHÓN **Madrid** ☎ (91), pop. 4,090. Madrid 52km, Cuenca 131km.

Chinchón is a pretty *pueblo* built around an undeniably attractive **Plaza Mayor** where bullfights have been staged since the 16C. The village is a favourite with weekend day-trippers from Madrid who come here to eat at the numerous taverns that have sprung up around the plaza.

◎◐ ▣ ★★★★ *Parador de Chinchón*, Av Generalísimo, 1 ☎ 894 08 36 🛏 38 ✕ ♈ TV ♦ 🎤 ⚓ AE, DC, EC, MC, V $$$$. In a beautifully restored 17C Augustine monastery, with secluded gardens and a very good **restaurant** serving local dishes.

¶¶ *Café de la Iberia* (closed: 1/9-15/9 and Wednesdays in winter), Pl Mayor, 17 ☎ 894 09 98 ♦ ❋ ≪ AE, EC, V $$ to $$$. An old café with a patio and tables on the balconies overlooking the square.

¶¶ *Mesón Cuevas del Vino*, c/ Benito Hortelano, 13 ☎ 894 02 06 **AE, DC, EC, V** $$$. In an old oil mill.

Best buys: The local anisette liqueur is a must.

Cultural highlights: The houses around the **Plaza Mayor** with their wooden balconies and porticoes, are a good example of Castilian popular architecture. The Church of the Asunción contains a Goya painting of the Virgin.

Fiestas: A picturesque **Passion Play** is staged in the Plaza Mayor on the Saturday of Holy Week.

Local sights: The village of **COLMENAR DE OREJA**, 6km away on a local road, has a fine old porticoed Plaza Mayor and several wineries such as *J. Díaz e Hijos*, c/ Convento, 30, selling local red and white wines.

CIUDAD REAL **Ciudad Real** ☎ (926), pop. 55,295, [*i*] Av Alarcos, 31 ☎ 21 29 25, (Pl del Caudillo, 20, ✉ c/ Toledo, 26 ☎ 22 34 00, ✛ 22 33 22, **P** 21 10 44, 🚗 c/ Larache, s/n ☎ 22 13 42, 🚍 c/ Ferrocarril, s/n ☎ 22 12 13. Jaén 170km, Madrid 198km, Córdoba 264km.

Ciudad Real today is an undistinguished town, capital of the province of the same name, and a bare shadow of the time when it was a walled Christian bastion in the battle against the Muslims and then a royalist stronghold in the fight to subdue the feudal power of the Calatrava military order. It was founded in 1225 by Alfonso X, the Wise, Spain's greatest medieval king.

▣ ★★★ *Castillos*, Av del Rey Santo, 8 ☎ 21 36 40 🛏 131 **P** 🎤 **AE, DC, MC, V** $$$.

▣ ★★★ *El Molino*, km242 on the N-420 ☎ 22 30 50 🛏 18 **P** 🎤 V $$$. Unpretentious.

▣ ★★ *Almanzor*, c/ Bernardo Valbuena, s/n 🛏 66 ♿ TV **P** AE, DC, EC, V $$$.

¶¶ *Casablanca* (closed: Sunday nights), Ronda de Granada, 23 ☎ 22 59 98 **P** ❋ AE, DC, EC, V $$$. Good fish dishes.

¶¶ *Miami Park* (closed: Sunday nights), c/ Ronda Ciruela, 48 ☎ 22 72 39 ❋ AE, DC, MC, V $$$. Seasonal cuisine.

Best buys: Cheese and charcuterie from *Salchichería Martón García*, c/ Real, 1, wine from *E. Vigón*, Ctra de la Atalaya, s/n, and confectionery from *Pastelería Cruz*, Plaza Mayor, 33, are the city's best buys.

Cultural highlights: The **Cathedral** is in the third division class and is barely saved by a couple of Gothic doorways and an attempt to beautify the main façade with Renaissance touches. It was finally completed last century more than 300 years after it was begun. The **Iglesia de San Pedro** is 14C Gothic and the Toledo gateway, the **Puerta de Toledo**, is all that remains of the 14C city walls. The Provincial Museum is at c/ Prado, 4 (open: 10.00-2.00 and 5.00-8.00; closed: Sunday afternoons and Mondays ☎ 22 68 96).

On the town: Good *tapas* are served in *Casablanca*, Av Rey Santo, 3, and *El Doblón*, Av Torreón, 11, near the Plaza Mayor. *Cueva 2*, c/ Antonio Blázquez, 2, is the 'in' disco.

Sports: There is good hunting throughout the province.

CUENCA **Cuenca** ☎ (966), pop. 43,139, *i* c/ Dalmacio García Izcara, 8 ☎
☎ 22 22 31, (c/ Cervantes, 2, ✉ c/ Parque de San Julián, 18 ☎
22 40 16, ✛ 22 22 00, **P** 22 48 59, 🚌 22 07 20. Albacete 145km, Madrid
164km, Toledo 185km.

The old part of Cuenca is on a wedge of high ground that towers above
the deep gorges created by the Huécar and the Júcar rivers and it is a town
that appears to revel in its utterly **spectacular location**. The so-called ☎☎
hanging houses that seem suspended above the gorge and impervious to
the law of gravity are alone worth the trip. Capital of a sparsely populated
province which embraces great tracts of wild sierra country, Cuenca is an
extremely agreeable town that is unexpectedly full of artistic sentiment; it has
become something of a cultural showpiece.

- 🏨 ★★★★ *Torremangana*, c/ San Ignacio de Loyola, 9 ☎ 22 33 51 🛏
  115 ⅊ TV ✦ ♀ AE, DC, MC, V $$$ to $$$$.
- 🏨 ★★★ *Alfonso VIII*, Parque de San Julián, 3 ☎ 21 43 25 🛏 48 **P** ✦ ♀
  AE, EC, V $$ to $$$.
- 🏨 ★★★ *Cueva del Fraile* (closed: 8/1-1/3), km7 on the Buenache road
  ☎ 21 15 71 🛏 54 ⅊ **P** ✦ ♀ ⅊ ⅊ ⅊ ⅊ AE, DC, EC, MC, V $$$. A
  relaxing atmosphere in a 16C mansion.
- 🏨 ★★ *Posada de San José*, c/ Julián Romero, 4 ☎ 21 13 00 🛏 25 ✦
  « DC, EC, V $$. The only hotel in the old quarter, it is set in a former
  convent which still retains its atmosphere of tranquillity.
- 🍴 *Figón de Pedro* (closed: Sunday nights), c/ Cervantes, 13 ☎ 22 68 21 ☎
  ❀ AE, DC, MC, V $$$ to $$$$. Also a ★★ hotel. Regional cuisine.
- 🍴 *Los Claveles* (closed: Thursdays and September), c/ 18 de Julio, 32 ☎
  21 38 24 ❀ V $$. Home-cooking.

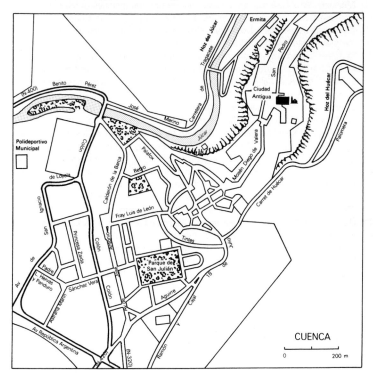

CUENCA

0   200 m

○ ¶ ***Mesón Casas Colgadas*** (closed: Monday nights), c/ Canónigos, s/n ☎ 22 35 09 ✳ « **AE, DC, MC, V** $$$. An absolute must on any visitor's itinerary, this restaurant is in one of the houses hanging over the Huécar gorge and serves very good local food.

Best buys: Handicrafts, including hand-made paper, are sold at the shops and workshops around the Plaza Mayor, like ***Segundo Santos***. Traditional Cuenca pottery can be bought from ***A. Fernández Cruz***, km2 on the Madrid road, and local sweets like the clearly Moorish *alajú* from ***Ruiz***, c/ José Antonio, 12, and ***Martínez Romero***, Plaza Mayor de Pío XII, 10.

Cultural highlights: You enter the Plaza Mayor through an archway which
○ is part of the Town Hall and emerge into the shadow of the **Cathedral** which is an early construction dating from the 12-13C and is Norman-Gothic, though altered during the Renaissance. One of its towers collapsed at the beginning of the century and the old style has been adhered to in the reconstruction of the building. The ubiquitous 18C Neoclassicist architect Ventura Rodríguez designed the main altarpiece, which is technically skilful
○ but not very exciting, and other focal points of the interior are the **grilles** of the chancel and of the **Capilla de los Caballeros**. The **Diocesan Museum**, c/ Obispo Valero, 11 (open: 11.00-2.00 and 4.00-6.00; closed: Sunday afternoons and Mondays ☎ 21 20 11) has recently been renovated and is an extremely good example of what such ecclesiastical collections in Spain ought to be.

○ The extraordinary 14C **hanging houses**, or ***casas colgantes***, c/ Canónigos, s/n, are now the home of a fascinating modern art museum, the
○ **Museo de Arte Abstracto Español** (open: 11.00-2.00 and 4.00-6.00; Saturdays: 11.00-2.00 and 4.00-8.00; Sundays: 11.00-2.30; closed: Mondays ☎ 21 29 83), which was founded on the initiative of leading Spanish artists in the 1960s, many of whom had studios in Cuenca. Spaniards in general have a great visual awareness and once you have seen the Old Masters in the Prado Museum and elsewhere it is as well to come here and reflect on how the tradition continues alive and well in the second half of the 20C. Aside from the intrinsic merit of the works exhibited (Zóbel, Chillida, Tàpies...) it is a daringly designed museum in a magnificent setting. To appreciate the wonder of the hanging houses you will have to cross to the other side of the Huécar gorge which you can do across a footbridge if you have a head for heights or by the roundabout route if you haven't.

○ Like the Diocesan Museum, the **Museo de Cuenca**, c/ Obispo Valero, 2 (open: 10.00-2.00 and 4.00-7.00; closed: Sunday afternoons and Mondays ☎ 21 30 69), which exhibits antique remains, is an excellent example of how art treasures should be shown to the public and one is tempted to think that the real contribution of the Abstract Museum artists was to stimulate the authorities into renovating their own exhibitions. After visiting the Cathedral and the museums you should move up hill through the extremely unspoilt
○○ **old town**, with its splendid **Pl de los Descalzos** and **c/ Julián Romero**, to view the astonishing gorges that girdle it.

Fiestas: Saint Matthew's Day, **San Mateo**, on September 21, is the big local celebration, when young bulls are let loose in the streets of the old
○ quarter. The town also stages lovely traditional **Holy Week processions**, the most moving being the one held in the early hours of Good Friday morning.
○ A festival of sacred music, the week-long ***Semana de Música Religiosa***, starts a few days before with performances in several of the town's churches (☎ 21 16 00).

Local sights: There are good scenic excursions along the **Júcar** and **Huécar gorges** (see 'Wide Open Spaces'). The **Ciudad Encantada**, or Enchanted City, 29km away, is a fairy-tale name given to an area of mountain parkland where a series of rocks have been eroded into fantastic formations. The marked out routes through the 'city' are a fun walk for adults and children alike and a great opportunity for camera enthusiasts. **PRIEGO**, 74km away on the N-320, is a fine-looking mountain village producing traditional pottery and wickerwork which are on show at *J. Barrio*, c/ El Remedio, 34. Nearby there is a **spectacularly situated** old convent, the **Convento de San Miguel de las Victorias**. Driving on the C-202, you will reach the impressive **Beteta Canyon** 6km beyond Cañizares. In the opposite direction from Cuenca, 77km on the N-400 as far as Carrascosa del Campo and then taking the local road to Saelices, you can tour the extensive **Roman ruins** of the city of Segóbriga which are in a generally good state and are all the more remarkable because they are little visited. Nearby, and again suprisingly off the beaten track, is the Renaissance and Baroque **monastery** of **UCLES** which was the headquarters of the Military Order of Santiago. Its proportions are astonishing and it was evidently built both as a fortress and a place of prayer.

On the town: *La Ponderosa*, c/ San Francisco, 20, serves excellent *tapas*.

Sports: There is good fishing in the Júcar river and the Toba reservoir, and hunting throughout the province.

GUADALAJARA **Guadalajara** ☎ (911), pop. 59,657, *i* Travesía de Beladiez, 1 ☎ 22 06 98, ✉ c/ Teniente Figueroa, 5 ☎ 21 14 93, ✚ 22 17 88, P 21 24 40, ☷ Paseo de la Estación, s/n ☎ 21 13 42. Madrid 55km, Cuenca 156km.

Capital of the province of the same name and fast becoming industrialized, Guadalajara is associated with the powerful late medieval Mendoza family one of whose members, **Cardinal Pedro González de Mendoza**, was Archbishop of Toledo (where he is buried in a sumptuous tomb beside the cathedral's high altar) and Primate of Spain during the reign of the Catholic Monarchs. The Mendoza family was linked to the Dukes of Infantado who were important patrons of the arts during the Spanish Renaissance. Guadalajara takes its name from *Wad-al-Hayara*, Arabic for 'Rocky River' which was the name given by the city's Muslim occupants to the Henares river that flows through it.

▦ ★★★ *Pax Hotel*, km57 on the N-II ☎ 22 18 00 ⊨ 61 🅿 ✚ ⚡ ⅏ ⚓ ≪ ♀ AE, DC, EC, MC, V $$$. A quiet, scenically situated hotel.

❙❙ *El Ventorrero*, c/ Alonso López de Haro, 4 ☎ 21 22 51 ✳ DC, EC, V $$ to $$$. A typical old-fashioned inn.

❙❙ *Mesón Hernando* (closed: Mondays and 20/12-7/1), km52 on the N-II ☎ 22 27 67 🅿 ✚ ⚓ EC, MC, V $$ to $$$. Castilian cooking .

Best buys: Traditional sweets are sold at *Hernando*, c/ Mayor, 32, and *Villalba*, c/ Mayor 29. General bargains (and local colour) can be had at the street market held on Tuesdays and Saturdays in the Pl del Mercado.

Cultural highlights: The town's showpiece is the **Palacio del Infantado** which is an outstanding example of the ornamentation that the Renaissance brought to Spain. It was built in 1480 by the Flemish master-builder Juan Guas, architect of many major buildings of the period such as the Church of San Juan de los Reyes in Toledo and the Colegio de San Gregorio which houses the sculpture museum in Valladolid. In this palace Philip II married the French princess Elizabeth of Valois, the third of his four wives, after the death of Mary Tudor. The palace is currently home to the Guadalajara Provincial Museum (open: 10.00-2.00 and 4.00-7.00; closed: Sunday afternoons and Mondays ☎ 21 33 01). Members of the Mendoza and the Infantado families are buried in Gothic splendour in the Church of San Ginés and in the Convent of San Francisco.

Fiestas: The town has patronal celebrations in September and an Autumn Fair during which bullfights are held.

Local sights: Continuing on the N-II towards Zaragoza and Barcelona you reach the walled town of **HITA** where a **Medieval Theatre Festival** is staged toward the end of June. N on the C-101 is **JADRAQUE**, which was a disputed village during the Reconquest. It has a fine **castle** built by Cardinal Mendoza. For Castilian fare try *El Castillo*, km47 on the Soria road $$$.

Sports: Flying at the *Aeroclub Guadalajara*, in Robledillo ☎ 80 01 52, and good hunting and fishing throughout the province are the local sports.

● ▮ GUADARRAMA, SIERRA DE ▮ **Madrid** ☎ (91). Access from Madrid on the N-VI, N-I and the N-601; from Segovia, on the N-601, N-603 and the N-110.

One of Madrid's great privileges is to have this granite, pine-coated mountain range almost on its doorstep. Its E limit is the Puerto (mountain pass) de Somosierra which you cross on the N-I. Moving W the other passes are the Puerto de la Morcuera, which you approach from the resort village of Miraflores de la Sierra and which leads into the valley of Lozoya in the very heart of the mountain range; the Puerto de Navacerrada, the road which passes through the ski resorts and which leads to Segovia; the Puerto de la Fuenfría which is crossed by forestry tracks and a Roman road (no vehicles) and links Cercedilla with Segovia; the Alto de los Leones pass, approached on the N-VI from Guadarrama and the Puerto de Malagón, in the province of Avila which is the mountain range's W limit. This is magnificent hiking and picnicking country, used by Ernest Hemingway as the backdrop for his Spanish Civil War novel *For Whom the Bell Tolls*. There is skiing at Navacerrada and at Cotos and there is challenging rock climbing in the area called La Pedriza near Manzanares el Real. The highest mountain is the Pico de Peñalara (2,429m) which has lakes of glacial origin near its summit. To approach Peñalara turn off onto the N-604 at the Puerto de Navacerrada and continue to the *Cotos* ski-station where ski lifts bring you close to the lakes. The C-604 winds down into the valley of Lozoya where the showpiece is the

● 14C **Monastery of Santa María del Paular**, part of which is a luxury hotel although the monks can also put you up in simpler quarters (see 'Where to Stay'.) The church here has a stunning and very unusual late 15C alabaster

●● **altarpiece** which is variously attributed to Juan Guas and to anonymous Italian craftsmen, and a fine Plateresque **grille**. The buildings have features, like the monastery's Plateresque **façade**, by the Gil de Hontañón father and son team, Rodrigo and Juan, builders of the Salamanca and Segovia cathedrals, who hailed from the neighbouring village of **RASCAFRIA**. Here you

● can stay at the ★★★★ *Santa María del Paular*, El Paular ☎ 869 10 11 ⊨ 58 ✕ TV ✦ ⬦ ⅄ ≈ ♨ ⛳ ⚓ AE, DC, MC, V $$$$$, which is in an idyllically quiet setting and has very good facilities. The scenic little village of **ALAMEDA DEL VALLE** also has a good little inn where you can stay overnight or just eat in its restaurant which is furnished with antiques —the *Hostal del Marqués* (closed: Mondays and Christmas), km21 on the Loyozuela-Navacerrada road ☎ 869 12 64 ✕ P ❊ $$$.

The road continues parallel to the Lozoya river and its reservoir to cross the N-I by **BUITRAGO DEL LOZOYA** where there is a small Picasso **museum** that was a donation to the village by a local man who used to be the artist's personal hairdresser. On the other side of the N-I the mountain range is wilder. The high points here are the fabulous beech tree forest called the **Hayedo de Montejo** and a semi-abandoned, little village called **PATONES DE ARRIBA** which, because of its isolated situation, was never conquered by the Muslims, nor indeed by Napoleon's Peninsular War troops, and which was the capital of a tiny little kingdom until the 18C.

Alternatively you can turn S along a local road from Rascafría and cross over the **Puerto de la Morcuera** pass (1,796m) to descend SE into **MIRAFLORES DE LA SIERRA**, where many Madrid residents keep summer homes. On the Sunday after San Blas' Day, February 3, a traditional festive pilgrimage, or *romería*, is held here. ***Mesón Maito***, c/ Calvo Sotelo, 5 ☎ 844 35 67 ❋ V $$, is a recommended restaurant, and there is accommodation at the scenically situated ★★ *Refugio*, Ctra Madrid-Miraflores, 50 ☎ 844 42 11 ⛭ 48 P ✦ ⬥ ⅍ ⚓ « V $$. The road then continues SW along the sierra's S flank to **MANZANARES EL REAL**, which is by the **La Pedriza** rock climbing area and the **La Cuenca del Manzanares Nature Park**. This village's show-stopper is its 15C **castle** which is everyone's idea of a castle in Spain. Juan Guas had a hand in its design and it was the home of the Marquis of Santillana, a Renaissance soldier-poet who was a member of Guadalajara's Dukes of Infantado family. After visiting the castle you can stop for a bite to eat at ***Parra***, c/ Panaderos, 15 ☎ 853 03 99 V $$, which serves particularly good meat. For accommodation in nearby **NAVACERRADA**, try the ★★★ *Arcipreste de Hita*, Praderas de San Sebastián ☎ 856 01 25 ⛭ 25 TV P ✦ ⬥ ⚓ « 🐎 ⚲ AE, V $$, or the ★★★ *La Barranca*, Valle de La Barranca ☎ 856 00 00 ⛭ 56 P ✦ ⬥ ⅍ ⚓ 📷 « 🐎 ⚲ AE, EC, V $$$, both set in spectacular mountain surroundings. For meals, try *Venta Arias* (closed: Tuesdays and October), Puerto de Navacerrada ☎ 852 14 34 P ✦ ❋ « V $$$ and, 8km away, the ***Fonda Real***, km52 on the Madrid-Segovia road ☎ 856 03 05 P ✦ AE, EC, V $$$ to $$$$, with pleasant 18C Castilian decor, good food and attentive service.

The N-601 now continues N to the **Puerto de Navacerrada** (1,860m), the frontier between Old and New Castile, with marvellous **views**. Its *Navacerrada* ski station has 12 runs, seven lifts and full facilities ☎ 230 55 72 and 852 14 35. Nearby are the ski stations of ***Valcotos***, near the Cotos pass (1,830m), with 11 runs and eight lifts ☎ 852 08 57 and 239 75 03, and of ***Valdesquí***, with six runs and 11 lifts ☎ 215 59 29 and 852 04 16, which also have good facilities.

Instead of climbing up to the Navacerrada pass you can continue on the C-607 or a local road along the flank of the mountain range S in the direction of **GUADARRAMA** past the summer resort villages of **LOS MOLINOS** and **CERCEDILLA**. Cercedilla has a very good little restaurant, the *Mirasierra*, Ctra Los Molinos, 11 ✦ AE, DC, MC, V $$$, and the very picturesque Los Molinos has an excellent restaurant for roasts, the *Asador Paco* near the parish church. Guadarrama is on the N-VI and from there you can climb up the sierra again taking the **scenic route** to the Alto de los Leones pass (there is also a tunnel through the mountains) or you can continue on the C-600 to El Escorial and the **Valle de los Caídos** (see 'San Lorenzo de El Escorial').

LA MANCHA **Albacete, Ciudad Real, Cuenca** and **Toledo**.

The Man of La Mancha's land is unrelentingly flat and dry. Olive trees, corn fields and especially vines —for La Mancha is Europe's biggest **wine producing** area— stretch as far as the eye can see. Here, where **Don Quixote** dreamt his impossible dreams, there is an extraordinary sense of space. The villages, large and gleamingly white-washed, are spread out from each other, protected here and there by a castle and on occasions made picturesque by the windmills that are the region's chief emblem. As you trace the steps of the demented knight and Sancho Panza, his salt-of-the-earth retainer, towards La Mancha's horizons you are at the very core of Spain and accompanying those two magnificent literary creations who together exemplify the Spanish character.

For **VALDEPEÑAS**, the most important town of La Mancha and its wine producing centre, see separate entry. **ALCAZAR DE SAN JUAN** is the main railway junction for trains travelling S from Madrid and it has its points as a La Mancha town. There are windmills and there is also a museum dedicated to heraldry and to contemporary paintings in the tower called the Torreón de Don Juan de Austria. Local cakes are sold at *Espinosa*, c/ Doctor Bernadell, 5; La Mancha's cheeses, the ubiquitous Manchegos, can be bought at *G. Díaz Miguel*, Ctra Quintanar, and local wines are sold at *J. Mendieta*, Av Cervera, 73. For accommodation you could try the ★★ *Don Quijote*, Av Criptana, 5 ☎ (926) 54 38 00 ⇌ 44 ✕ **P** ♣ AE, DC, EC, V $$$, which also has a restaurant, and for eating only *Casa Paco* (closed: Mondays), Av Alvarez Guerra, 5 ☎ (926) 54 10 15 ✳ V $$ to $$$, which serves wholesome home cooking. A third important urban centre is **DAIMIEL**, the focal point of a prosperous wine-producing district —you can buy local wines at the *Cooperativa La Daimieleña*. The marshes of the **Parque Nacional de las Tablas de Daimiel** (see 'Wide Open Spaces') lie 11km from the town.

The places particularly associated with Don Quixote include **ARGAMASILLA DE ALBA**, where Cervantes spent a spell in prison in what is called the Cueva de Medrano, and the windmill and castle town of **CONSUEGRA** which has changed little since Cervantes' day. The district called the **Campo de Montiel** was the backdrop to several Quixotic episodes and notably to the knight's hallucinatory experiences in the Cave of Montesinos. Here, in the area called **Las Lagunas de Ruidera**, La Mancha's stark plain is interrupted by lagoons which are the source of the Guadiana river and are set in a natural park of woodland, hills and small lakes; it is totally at odds with the surrounding plains. There is accommodation at the *Aparthotel Albamanjón* ☎ (926) 52 80 88 **TV** **P** ⚲ «. **PUERTO LAPICE** claims for itself the location of the inn where Don Quixote donned his knightly arms. Just about every *pueblo* in La Mancha understandably seeks to establish some connection with Cervantes' hero but of all the Manchegan villages the one with the strongest links is **EL TOBOSO** which was the home of Don Quixote's beloved Dulcinea, whose house you can visit. The Ayuntamiento, or Town Hall, has a collection of editions of *Don Quixote* in dozens of languages. Photographers looking out for a classical Quixotic scene will find it in nearby **CAMPO DE CRIPTANA**, where the group of windmills on the crest above the village are just waiting for you to tilt at them with your lens. An old-style forge here at *J. Torres Escribano*, c/ Gran Capitán, 19, produces excellent wrought iron pieces.

MADRID **Madrid** ☎ (91), pop. 3,123,713, *i* Plaza Mayor, 3 ☎ 266 54 77 and 266 48 74, *i* c/ Señores de Luzón, 10 ☎ 242 55 12 and 248 74 26, *i* Barajas airport ☎ 205 86 56, *i* Chamartín railway station ☎ 215 99 76, *i* Pl España, Edif Torre de Madrid ☎ 241 23 25, *i* c/ Duque de Medinaceli, 2 ☎ 429 49 51, ℂ c/ Recoletos, 37 and Gran Vía, 30, ✉ c/ Alcalá, 54 ☎ 521 81 95, 521 40 04 and 522 20 00, ✚ 233 77 77, P 092, ✈ Barajas, km12 on the N-II ☎ 205 43 72 and 231 44 36 (Iberia ☎ 261 91 00), 🚌 Estación Sur de Autobuses (bus station), c/ Canarias, 17 ☎ 468 42 00, 🚆 Estación de Chamartín ☎ 315 99 76, 🚆 Estación de Atocha ☎ 228 52 37, 🚆 Estación de Príncipe Pío ☎ 248 87 16, **Radio-Taxi** ☎ 247 82 00 and 247 86 00.

More than the nation's capital and its largest city, Madrid is Spain's melting pot. **Philip II** decided in 1561 that it should be the administrative centre of his empire for the essential reason that it was right in the middle of his peninsular domains. Since then the city has been the *rendezvous* for the various peoples that make up Spain and, indeed, all Spanish roads lead to

Madrid where kilometre zero lies in the capital's grandiosely named Puerta del Sol, the Gateway of the Sun. From Madrid the Spanish highways fan out like the spokes of a wheel and wherever you are on a main road in Spain you will know by the roadside markers just how many kilometres you are from Madrid.

It is perhaps precisely because Madrid is a synthesis of all things, customs, traditions and peoples in Spain that the city is wide open, hospitable, and always attuned to new fads and fashions. Yet Madrid has a very specific character of its own. Basically the people of Madrid are street smart for the city has seen it all and done it all for nearly 500 years. Madrid saw a Hapsburg dynasty come and go and then a Bourbon one arrive, leave and return. It has been monarchist and republican, it resisted Napoleon, surrendered to him and then revolted against him and it held out against General Franco until the end of the Spanish Civil War, enduring a bitter bombing in the process. It then became the powerhouse of his regime. A Madrilenian is as warm-hearted, spontaneous and sentimental as the next man in Spain but he has the cynical wit of the world-weary about him and an inner core that is fundamentally sceptical.

Publicly, the Madrilenian will make extraordinary claims for his city and bumper stickers affirm that Madrid is the threshold of heaven. To give Madrid its due, despite the traffic jams, the pollution and the hustle you suddenly become reconciled to the place for its astonishing **light**, sharp in the early morning and touched with gold and warmth at sunset. The sky is something special in Madrid and one learns to understand the bumper sticker boast. **Velázquez**, for one, painted Madrid's heavens to his heart's content. Though huge now, Madrid has never quite lost the quality of the little La Mancha village it once was, almost a mountain town that stood high up on the plateau and within a day's ride of the peaks of the Guadarrama mountain range.

Like all big urban centres, Madrid is a series of communities held together within the city limits. The La Mancha village is still discernible in the old neighbourhood grouped around the **Plaza Mayor**, a fine square by any standards. Thanks to the presence of the court since Philip's days, Madrid has more than its fair share of old palaces and convents. In the 19C the city was booming and the legacy of those halcyon days was the extended residential quarter, built on a grid pattern, that occupies the downtown E side Madrid. The city has been growing by leaps and bounds since the 1960s and its business centre has shifted uptown and N where highrises now reign supreme. The central axis of the city is the wide **Castellana** boulevard that slices through it from N-S. The rule of thumb is that the N end of the Castellana is modern, new Madrid while the S end has always been around. The E side of the boulevard was the area of bourgeois expansion during the last century while the W side remained more popular.

Madrid is, if nothing else, a place of astonishing **vitality** that leaves many visitors prostrate with exhaustion until they get used to its pace. It is the nation's **political and business capital** and it also calls the tune in its **cultural** life. Madrid is where reputations are made and broken in Spain and its artistic life is as strong as that of any major city in the world. This is where Spain's great dramatists wrote and where the great painters established studios and found patrons. The **Prado Museum** is Madrid's great treasure house but there are dozens of other museums and galleries, a thriving theatre and cinema circuit and a non-stop cultural round. The city is always moving and visitors wonder when any Madrilenian gets to bed. In the summer months the city virtually lives out of doors and *terrazas* are packed with people chatting long after the rest of Europe has gone to sleep.

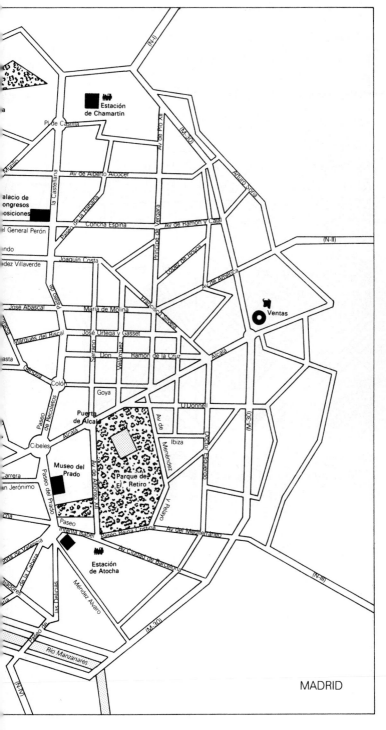

MADRID

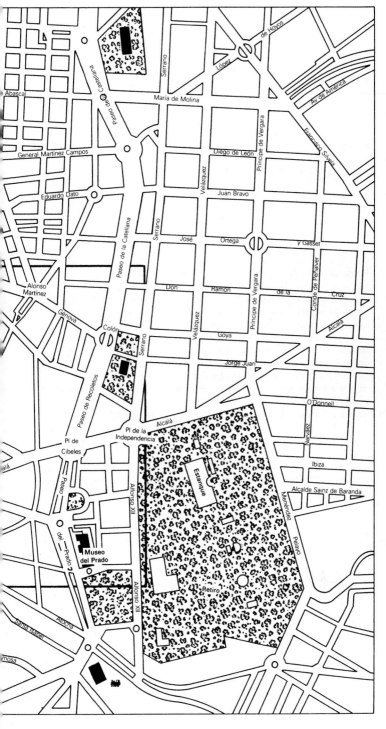

Madrid owes its name to the Muslim Emir **Muhammad I** who established a stronghold, known as *Magerit*, on the site of what is today's Royal Palace, the Palacio de Oriente. Secure in their Alcázar dominating the **Manzanares** river, the Muslims were able to head off Christian attacks from Castile and León until 1083 when the town finally fell to the troops of Alfonso VI as they surged across the Guadarrama mountains in pursuit of the greater conquest of Toledo. Throughout the Middle Ages Madrid led an amiable life, quietly building up its trade and crafts as the mobile court of the Castilian monarchs moved about the country, from Seville to Barcelona by way of Toledo, Valladolid and Burgos. **Philip II** changed all that with his decision to establish his capital in the town that was the crossroads to everywhere.

The next important stimulus to Madrid came 200 years later in the 18C reign of the Bourbon **Charles III**, Spain's enlightened despot. Historic landmarks of today's Madrid such as the Alcalá Arch, the Prado Museum buildings, the Retiro Park gardens and the Palacio de Oriente itself all bear the Neoclassical stamp of this period. Charles himself spent most of his time hunting in the forests of El Pardo, W of the city, and his portraits in the Prado Museum depict him musket in hand and looking as weather-beaten as the most veteran of his gamekeepers.

Madrid is fortunate in that it had a powerful chronicler of city life in **Francisco Goya** whose canvases in the Prado capture the city at play and at war when it rose up against the Napoleonic invader. Last century it was above all the novelist **Benito Pérez Galdós** who mirrored the life of Madrid with a Dickensian sweep of genius. In their different ways and different periods the two artists depicted a city that was aristocratic and revolutionary, traditional and innovative, tender and tough at the same time. Above all they reflected the intrigues that are part and parcel of Madrid's café-society effervescence. That has not changed, for to this day Madrid continues to ensnare visitors and to involve them in its day to day details.

- ★★★★★ *Barajas*, Av de Logroño, 305 ☎ 747 77 00 ⊨ 230 ✕ ⅄ TV ✦ ♨ ♪ 🖪 ≪ AE, DC, EC, V $$$$$$. Near the airport.
- ★★★★★ *Eurobuilding*, c/ Padre Damián, 23 ☎ 457 17 00 ⊨ 420 ✕ TV ✦ ♪ ♨ 🎵 🖪 ≪ AE, DC, EC, V $$$$$$. Comfortable rooms and good service. Pleasant swimming pool in summer.
- ★★★★★ *Meliá Castilla*, c/ Capitán Haya, 43 ☎ 571 22 11 ⊨ 1,000 ✕ ⅄ ♿ TV ✦ ♪ ♨ 🖪 ≪ AE, DC, EC, V $$$$$$. A huge hotel in Madrid's new commercial centre. It has two restaurants worth trying: *La Albufera* ($$$$) serving good Valencian rice dishes, and *La Fragata* ($$$$), for seafood, fish and meat.
- ★★★★★ *Meliá Madrid*, c/ Princesa, 27 ☎ 241 82 00 ⊨ 266 ✕ ⅄ TV 🖪 ≪ AE, DC, EC, V $$$$$$. Modern and centrally situated.
- ★★★★★ *Miguel Angel*, c/ Miguel Angel, 31 ☎ 442 81 99 ⊨ 304 ✕ ⅄ ♿ TV ✦ ♪ 🏊 ♨ 🖪 ≪ AE, DC, EC, V $$$$$$. A classic hotel in a modern area of Madrid.
- ★★★★★ *Mindanao*, c/ San Francisco de Sales, 15 ☎ 449 55 00 ⊨ 289 ✕ TV ✦ ♪ ♨ 🖪 AE, DC, EC, V $$$$$. Good service.
- ★★★★★ *Monte Real*, c/ Arroyo del Fresno, 17, in Puerta de Hierro ☎ 216 21 40 ⊨ 77 ✕ ⅄ ♿ TV ✦ ♪ 🏊 ♨ 🖪 ≪ AE, DC, EC, V $$$$$$. Set in a residential area, 10 minutes from the city centre.
- ★★★★★ *Palace*, Pl de las Cortes, 7 ☎ 429 75 51 ⊨ 518 ✕ ⅄ ♿ TV ♪ ≪ AE, DC, EC, V $$$$$$. A long-standing favourite, established 75 years ago. Its restaurant, the *Grill Neptuno* ($$$$) can be recommended, and light dinners are served until very late in *El Ambigú* ($$$).
- ★★★★★ *Princesa Plaza*, c/ Serrano Jover, 3 ☎ 242 35 00 ⊨ 406 ✕ ⅄ TV ♪ 🖪 ≪ AE, DC, EC, V $$$$$$. In the student quarter of Argüelles.

▦ ★★★★★ GL *Ritz*, Pl de la Lealtad, 5 ☎ 521 28 57 🛏 156 ✕ ੲ ੬ TV ✦ ⬤⬤⬤
 🎤 🐾 ≪ AE, DC, EC, V $$$$$$. The most sophisticated and elegant
 hotel in Madrid, it has a good **restaurant** and a pretty garden for dining
 out in summer, though the quality of the food there is less good. There is
 also an excellent Sunday **brunch** served from 11.00-1.00 ($$$).

▦ ★★★★★ *Tryp Palacio*, Paseo de la Castellana, 57 ☎ 442 51 00 🛏 182
 ✕ ੲ TV 🎤 🖼 ≪ AE, DC, EC, V $$$$$$. Modern, with good service.

▦ ★★★★★ GL *Villamagna*, Paseo de la Castellana, 22 ☎ 261 49 00 🛏 ⬤⬤
 194 ✕ ੲ ੬ TV P ✦ 🎤 🖼 ≪ AE, DC, EC, V $$$$$$. One of Spain's most
 luxurious hotels.

▦ ★★★★★ *Wellington*, c/ Velázquez, 8 ☎ 275 44 00 🛏 260 ✕ ੲ TV ✦ 🎤
 ⇌ 🖼 ≪ AE, DC, EC, V $$$$$$. Prestigious and pleasant. A favourite
 with the bullfighting fraternity.

▦ ★★★★ *Agumar*, Paseo Reina Cristina, 9 ☎ 552 69 00 🛏 252 TV AE, DC,
 EC, V $$$$. Near Atocha Station.

▦ ★★★★ *Aitana*, Paseo de la Castellana, 152 ☎ 250 71 07 🛏 111 ✕ ੲ TV
 🐾 AE, DC, EC, V $$$$. A pleasant hotel frequented by executives.

▦ ★★★★ *Alameda*, Av de Logroño, 100 ☎ 747 48 00 🛏 145 ✕ ੲ TV 🎤
 ⇌ 🖼 AE, DC, EC, V $$$$$. Convenient for the airport.

▦ ★★★★ *Alcalá*, c/ Alcalá, 66 ☎ 435 10 60 🛏 153 ✕ ੲ TV 🖼 ≪ AE,
 DC, EC, V $$$$$. Near the smart Barrio de Salamanca, it has a good
 restaurant.

▦ ★★★★ *Castellana Intercontinental*, Paseo de la Castellana, 49 ☎
 410 02 00 🛏 313 ✕ ੲ TV ✦ 🎤 🖼 ≪ AE, DC, EC, V $$$$$$. Haunt of
 politicians and journalists.

▦ ★★★★ *Cuzco*, Paseo de la Castellana, 133 ☎ 456 06 00 🛏 330 ✕ ੲ
 ੬ TV P 🎤 🖼 ≪ AE, DC, EC, V $$$$. Well located in Madrid's new
 business centre.

▦ ★★★★ *Emperador*, Gran Vía, 53 ☎ 247 28 00 🛏 231 ੲ TV 🎤 ⇌ ≪
 AE, DC, EC, V $$$$$. Traditional.

▦ ★★★★ *Emperatriz*, c/ López de Hoyos, 4 ☎ 413 65 11 🛏 170 ੲ TV 🎤
 AE, DC, EC, V $$$$. Good service.

▦ ★★★★ *Escultor*, c/ Miguel Angel, 3 ☎ 410 42 03 🛏 82 ੲ TV ✦ 🎤 ≪
 AE, DC, EC, V $$$$$. Apartments, well situated but with unreliable
 service.

▦ ★★★★ *Eurobuilding 2*, c/ Orense, 69 ☎ 279 22 00 🛏 154 ✕ TV ✦ 🎤 ⬤
 🐾 ⇌ 🖼 AE, DC, V $$$$. A luxurious aparthotel in N Madrid.

▦ ★★★★ *Holiday Inn Madrid*, c/ Orense, 22 ☎ 597 01 02 🛏 344 ✕ ੲ TV
 ✦ 🎤 ⇌ 🖼 ≪ AE, DC, EC, V $$$$$$. Right in the AZCA centre, it serves
 brunch on Sundays ($$$)

▦ ★★★★ *Los Galgos-Sol*, c/ Claudio Coello, 139 ☎ 262 42 27 🛏 358
 ੲ ੬ TV 🎤 AE, DC, EC, V $$$$. A modern hotel in the Barrio de
 Salamanca, used by executives.

▦ ★★★★ *Pintor*, c/ Goya, 79 ☎ 435 75 45 🛏 176 TV 🎤 🎵 AE, V $$$$.
 Functional.

▦ ★★★★ *Plaza*, Gran Vía, 84 ☎ 247 12 00 🛏 306 ੲ TV ✦ 🎤 ⇌ ≪ AE,
 DC, EC, V $$$$$. Used by American package-tourists, it has excellent
 views from the rooms and its roof-top terrace.

▦ ★★★★ *Sanvy*, c/ Goya, 3 ☎ 276 08 00 🛏 141 ✕ ੲ TV ✦ 🎤 ⇌ AE,
 DC, EC, V $$$$$. Recently modernized, its restaurant, the *Belagua*
 ($$$$), is recommendable.

▦ ★★★★ *Suecia*, c/ Marqués de Casa Riera, 4 ☎ 231 69 00 🛏 67 ✕ ੲ
 TV AE, DC, EC, V $$$$ to $$$$$. Near the Círculo de Bellas Artes cultural
 centre, it has a good *smorgasbord* in the *Bellman* restaurant ($$$). It is
 frequented by the intellectual set.

🏨 ★★★★ *Tryp Menfis*, Gran Vía, 74 ☎ 247 09 00 🛏 122 ✗ Ⴤ ≪ **AE, DC, V** $$$$.

🏨 ★★★★ *Tryp Velázquez*, c/ Velázquez, 62 ☎ 275 28 00 🛏 130 ✗ Ⴤ 📺 ♨ $$$$. A classic, well-situated hotel in the Barrio de Salamanca.

🏨 ★★★ *Conde Duque*, Pl Conde del Valle Suchil, 5 ☎ 447 70 00 🛏 138 ♨ **AE, DC, EC, V** $$$$. Central.

🏨 ★★★ *Foxá 32*, c/ Agustín de Foxá, 32 ☎ 733 10 60 🛏 161 Ⴤ 📺 **P** ♨ **AE, DC, MC, V** $$$$. An elegant aparthotel near the Chamartín railway station.

🏨 ★★★ *Gran Vía*, Gran Vía, 25 ☎ 522 11 21 🛏 163 Ⴤ 📺 **AE, DC, EC, V** $$$. A classic, its guests are mostly visiting Americans.

🏨 ★★★ *Inglés*, c/ Echegaray, 8 ☎ 429 65 51 🛏 58 Ⴤ **P** 🎦 **AE, DC, EC, V** $$$.

🏨 ★★★ *Las Alondras Sol*, c/ José Abascal, 8 ☎ 447 40 00 🛏 72 Ⴤ 📺 **AE, DC, EC, V** $$$$$. Conveniently situated.

🏨 ★★★ *Opera*, c/ Cuesta de Santo Domingo, 2 ☎ 241 28 00 🛏 81 $$$.

🏨 ★★★ *Orense 38*, c/ Pedro Teixeira, 5 ☎ 571 22 19 🛏 140 ✗ Ⴤ 📺 (**P** ♨ 🎦 **AE, DC, EC, MC, V** $$$$$. Modern aparthotel in the heart of Madrid's new business centre.

🏨 ★★★ *Príncipe Pío*, c/ Cuesta de San Vicente, 14 ☎ 247 80 00 🛏 157 Ⴤ **P** ♨ ≪ **AE, DC, EC, MC, V** $$$. Good views.

🏨 ★★★ *Puerta de Toledo*, Glorieta Puerta de Toledo, 4 ☎ 474 71 00 🛏 152 Ⴤ **P AE, DC, MC, V** $$$. A modern hotel in a busy, traditional part of town.

🏨 ★★★ *Tirol*, c/ Marqués de Urquijo, 4 ☎ 248 19 00 🛏 93 ✗ Ⴤ **P** ≪ **MC, V** $$$. Best known for the good cocktails served in the bar.

🏨 ★★★ *Tryp Osuna*, c/ Luis de la Mata, 18 ☎ 741 81 00 🛏 169 ✗ Ⴤ **P** ♦ ♨ 🐎 ⚓ ≪ 🐎 **AE, DC, V** $$$. Near the airport.

🏨 ★★★ *Zurbano*, c/ Zurbano, 79 ☎ 441 45 00 🛏 261 Ⴤ 📺 **P** ♨ **AE, EC, MC, V** $$$$. Near the Paseo de la Castellana.

🏨 ★★ *Alcázar Regis*, Gran Vía, 61 ☎ 247 93 17 🛏 12 $$.

🏨 ★★ *Alexandra*, c/ San Bernardo, 29 ☎ 242 04 00 🛏 69 📺 ≪ **V** $$$. Central.

🏨 ★★ *Hostal Delfina*, Gran Vía, 12 ☎ 522 21 51 🛏 18 $$.

🏨 ★★ *París*, c/ Alcalá, 2 ☎ 521 64 96 🛏 114 $$$.

🏨 ★★ *Tryp Asturias*, c/ Sevilla, 2 ☎ 429 66 76 🛏 175 ≪ **AE, V** $$$.

🍴 *Al-Mounia* (closed: Sundays, Mondays and August), c/ Recoletos, 5 ☎ 275 01 73 ✳ **AE, DC, EC, V** $$$ to $$$$. North African food.

🍴 *Aroca* (closed: Sundays and August), Pl de los Carros, 3 ☎ 265 11 14 ✳ **V** $$$. Good, simple cooking.

🍴 *Asador Frontón* (closed: Sundays and August), Pl Tirso de Molina, 7 ☎ 468 16 17 **P** ✳ **AE, DC, EC, V** $$$. Unpretentious traditional Basque cooking.

🔴 🍴 *Balzac* (closed: Saturdays lunchtime and Sundays), c/ Moreto, 7 ☎ 239 19 22 **P** ✳ **AE, DC, V** $$$$ to $$$$$. Imaginative Basque cuisine in an attractive setting.

🔴🔴 🍴 *Cabo Mayor* (closed: Sundays, 15/8-31/8, Christmas and Holy Week), c/ Juan Ramón Jiménez, 37 ☎ 250 87 76 **P** ✳ **AE, DC, EC, V** $$$ to $$$$. Excellent fish dishes, prepared with a light touch.

🔴 🍴 *Café de Oriente* (closed: Saturdays lunchtime, Sundays and August), Pl de Oriente, 2 ☎ 241 39 74 ♦ ✳ **AE, DC, V** $$$$ to $$$$$. French cuisine in a lovely old café.

🔴 🍴 *Casa Botín*, c/ Cuchilleros, 17 ☎ 266 42 17 ✳ **AE, DC, EC, V** $$$ to $$$$. According to the *Guinness Book of Records*, this is the oldest restaurant in the world. It serves classic Castilian roasts.

¶¶ *Casa Ciriaco* (closed: Wednesdays and August), c/ Mayor, 84 ☎ 248 06 20 **AE** $$$. A traditional Madrid *tasca.*

¶¶ *Casa d'a Troya* (closed: Sundays, holidays and 15/7-1/9), c/ Virgen del Portillo, 3, Ciudad Lineal ☎ 404 64 53 ✳ $$$. Good Galician food.

¶¶ *Casa Lucio* (closed: Sundays lunchtime and August), c/ Cava Baja, 35 ☎ 265 32 52 ✳ **AE, DC, V** $$$. A cut above the usual traditional *tasca* in terms of comfort, it serves good Spanish food.

¶¶ *Casa Paco* (closed: Sundays and August), c/ Puerta Cerrada, 11 ☎ 266 31 66 ✳ **DC, EC, V** $$$. A famous old restaurant.

¶¶ *Casa Portal* (closed: Sundays and holidays), c/ Doctor Castelo, 26 ☎ 274 20 26 ✳ $$$. Asturian food.

¶¶ *Casa Puebla* (closed: Sundays and holidays, and Saturdays too in summer), c/ Príncipe de Vergara, 6 ☎ 435 12 02 $$$. An unpretentious *tasca.*

¶¶ *Club 31* (closed: August), c/ Alcalá, 58 ☎ 231 00 92 **P** ✳ **AE, DC, EC, V** $$$$ to $$$$$. Traditional Spanish and French-influenced cuisine.

¶¶ *Combarro* (closed: Sunday nights and August), c/ Reina Mercedes, 12 ☎ 254 77 84 **P** ✳ **AE, DC, EC, V** $$$ to $$$$. A luxurious seafood restaurant.

¶¶ *Currito*, Pabellón de Vizcaya, in the Trade Fair Area of the Casa de Campo ☎ 464 57 04 **P** ♣ ✳ **AE, DC, V** $$$ to $$$$. Traditional Basque cooking.

¶¶ *De la Riva* (closed: Sunday nights and August), c/ Cochabamba, 13, on the corner with Paseo de la Habana, 84 ☎ 250 77 57 ✳ $$$. Good home cooking.

¶¶ *Don Víctor* (closed: Saturdays lunchtime, Sundays and August), c/ Emilio Vargas, 18, on the corner of c/ Arturo Soria, 99 ☎ 415 47 47 ✳ **AE, DC, V** $$$$. Galician cuisine.

¶¶ *Doñana* (closed: Saturdays lunchtime, Sundays and August), c/ Fernando el Santo, 17 ☎ 410 31 25 **V** $$$. Seasonal cuisine.

¶¶ *Edelweiss* (closed: Sundays and August), c/ Jovellanos, 7 ☎ 221 03 26 **AE, DC, EC, V** $$$. German food in hearty helpings.

¶¶ *El Amparo* (closed: Saturdays lunchtime, Sundays, Holy Week and August), Callejón de Puigcerdá, 8, on the corner of c/ Jorge Juan ☎ 431 64 56 ✳ **AE, V** $$$$ to $$$$$. Imaginative cuisine.

¶¶ *El Bodegón* (closed: Saturdays lunchtime, Sundays, holidays and August), c/ Pinar, 15 ☎ 262 31 37 **P** ✳ **AE, DC, EC, V** $$$$. Basque *nouvelle cuisine* in a very stylish restaurant. Already a firm favourite.

¶¶ *El Buey* (closed: Sundays and holiday evenings), c/ General Pardiñas, 10 ☎ 431 44 92, and Pl de la Marina Española, 1 ☎ 241 30 41 ✳ $$$. Good for grills.

¶¶ *El Cenador del Prado* (closed: Saturdays lunchtime and Sundays), c/ Prado, 4 ☎ 429 15 61 ✳ **AE, DC, EC, V** $$$$. Imaginative cooking.

¶¶ *El Chiscón de Castelló* (closed: Sundays and August), c/ Castelló, 3 ☎ 275 56 62 ✳ $$$. Traditional Basque cuisine and imaginative new dishes.

¶¶ *El Landó* (closed: Sundays and August), Pl Gabriel Miró, 8 ☎ 266 76 81 **P** ✳ **AE, DC, EC, V** $$$ to $$$$. Unpretentious cooking.

¶¶ *El Mentidero de la Villa* (closed: Saturdays lunchtime, Sundays and 15/8-31/8), c/ Santo Tomé, 6 ☎ 419 55 06 ✳ **AE, DC, EC, V** $$$ to $$$$. *Avant garde* decor and an imaginative menu.

¶¶ *El Pescador* (closed: Sundays and 10/8-15/9), c/ Ortega y Gasset, 75 ☎ 402 12 90 **P** ✳ $$$ to $$$$. Fish and seafood dishes.

¶¶ *El Viejo 1* (closed: Sunday nights, Mondays and September), c/ Ribera del Manzanares, 123 ☎ 241 06 19 **P** ♣ ✳ **AE, DC, V** $$$. Polish dishes and good game in season.

Esteban (closed: Sundays and July), c/ Cava Baja, 36 ☎ 265 90 91 ✳ AE, DC, V $$$. A typical *tasca* in the heart of Old Madrid.

Fass, c/ Rodríguez Marín, 84, on the corner of c/ Concha Espina ☎ 457 22 02 ♣ ✳ AE, DC, EC, V $$$. German food.

🕭 **Fortuny** (closed: Saturdays lunchtime, Sundays and holidays), c/ Fortuny, 34 ☎ 410 77 07 🅿 ♣ ✳ AE, DC, EC, V $$$$ to $$$$$. International cuisine in the luxurious setting of a 19C mansion, with a pleasant summer terrace.

🕭 **Gure-Etxea** (closed: Sundays and August), Pl de la Paja, 12 ☎ 265 61 49 ✳ AE, DC, V $$$ to $$$$. Traditional Basque cuisine.

Guría (closed: Sundays and 1/7-15/9), c/ Huertas, 12 ☎ 429 09 85 ✳ V $$$. One of Madrid's longest established Basque restaurants.

🕭 **Handicap 2** (closed: Sundays, holidays and August), c/ General Oraa, 56 ☎ 262 21 59 DC, EC, V $$$. French-influenced food during the day and more innovative dishes at night.

🕭🕭 **Horcher** (closed: Sundays), c/ Alfonso XII, 6 ☎ 522 07 31 🅿 ✳ AE, DC, V $$$$$. A distinguished Madrid classic serving elegant central European food with some innovative touches, and excellent game dishes in season.

Horno de Santa Teresa (closed: Saturdays, Sundays and August), c/ Santa Teresa, 12 ☎ 419 02 45 ✳ AE, DC, EC, V $$$ to $$$$. An imaginative interpretation of Asturian cuisine.

🕭 **Irízar-Jatetxea** (closed: Saturdays lunchtime, Sundays, holiday nights, Holy Week and 22/12-27/12), c/ Jovellanos, 3 ☎ 231 45 69 ✳ AE, DC, V $$$ to $$$$. Basque *nouvelle cuisine*.

Jaun de Alzate, c/ Princesa, 18 ☎ 247 00 10 🅿 ✳ AE, DC, EC, V $$$$$. Inspired cooking and delicious desserts.

🕭🕭 **Jockey** (closed: Sundays, holidays and August), c/ Amador de los Ríos, 6 ☎ 419 10 03 🅿 ✳ AE, DC, EC, V $$$$$. Classic Spanish dishes as well as excellent international cuisine.

La Ancha (closed: Sundays), c/ Príncipe de Vergara, 204 ☎ 457 03 23 ♣ ✳ AE, DC, EC, V $$$. Simple Spanish food. The clientele includes the film and newspaper set.

La Barraca, c/ Reina, 29 ☎ 232 71 54 ✳ AE, DC, EC, V $$$. A classic for *paella* and Valencian rice dishes.

🕭 **La Dorada** (closed: Sundays and August), c/ Orense, 64 ☎ 270 20 04 🅿 ✳ AE, MC, V $$$$$. Andalusian cuisine, with good seafood and fried fish dishes.

🕭 **La Fuencisla** (closed: Sundays and August), c/ San Mateo, 4 ☎ 221 61 86 ✳ AE, DC, EC $$$. A favourite among serious gastronomes.

La Gamella (closed: Sundays and Mondays lunchtime), c/ Alfonso XII, 4 ☎ 532 45 09 ✳ AE, DC, EC, V $$$. Imaginative cuisine by an American chef.

La Gran Tasca (closed: Sundays, July and August), c/ Ballesta, 1 ☎ 231 00 44 $$$, and c/ Santa Engracia, 22 (closed: Sunday nights) ☎ 448 77 79 🅿 ✳ AE, DC, EC, V $$$ to $$$$. One of Madrid's longest established *tascas*.

La Parra (closed: Saturdays lunchtime and Sundays), c/ Monte Esquinza, 34 ☎ 419 54 98 ✳ AE, DC, EC, V $$$ to $$$$. Haunt of the famous.

La Taberna del Alabardero, c/ Felipe V, 6 ☎ 247 25 77 ✳ AE, DC, V $$$ to $$$$. Homely, mainly Basque, food.

🕭🕭 **La Trainera** (closed: Sundays and August), c/ Lagasca, 60 ☎ 276 80 35 🅿 ✳ V $$$$. Excellent fish and seafood dishes.

🕭 **Las Cuatro Estaciones** (closed: Sundays and August), c/ General Ibáñez Ibero, 5 ☎ 253 63 05 🅿 ✳ AE, DC, V $$$$. International cuisine with innovative touches.

¶ *Lola* (evenings only), c/ Costanilla de San Pedro, 11 ☎ 265 88 01 ▣ ✳
$$$$$. A nightclub restaurant serving good food.

¶ *Los Remos* (closed: evenings on Sundays and holidays and 15/8-31/8),
km12.7 on the N-VI, the La Coruña motorway, in El Plantío ☎ 207 72 30
▣ ♦ ✳ AE, DC, EC, V $$$ to $$$$. Fish and seafood.

¶ *Luarqués* (closed: Sunday nights, Mondays and 20/7-1/9), c/ Ventura
de la Vega, 16 ☎ 429 61 74 ✳ $$$. Asturian home cooking.

¶ *Lucca*, c/ Ortega y Gasset, 29 ☎ 276 01 44 ✳ AE, DC, EC, V $$$. One
of Madrid's favourite Italian restaurants.

¶ *Lúculo* (closed: Saturdays lunchtime, Sundays, holidays and 15/8-15/9),
c/ Génova, 19 ☎ 419 40 29 ▣ ♦ ✳ AE, DC, V $$$$$. Imaginative
cuisine.

¶ *Lur Maitea* (closed: Saturdays lunchtime, Sundays, holidays and August),
c/ Fernando el Santo, 4 ☎ 419 09 38 ✳ AE, DC, EC, V $$$. Basque
cuisine.

¶ *Nicolasa* (closed: Sundays, Holy Week and August), c/ Velázquez, 150
☎ 261 99 85 ▣ ✳ AE, DC, EC, V $$$ to $$$$. Traditional Basque
cooking.

¶ *O'Pazo* (closed: Sundays and August), c/ Reina Mercedes, 20 ☎
253 23 33 ▣ ✳ $$$$$. Seafood and fish dishes.

¶ *Or-dago* (closed: Saturdays, Sundays, August and 1/9-7/9), c/ Sancho
Dávila, 15 ☎ 246 71 85 ✳ $$$. A family restaurant serving Basque food.

¶ *Peñas Arriba* (closed: Sundays, Holy Week, Christmas and August), c/
Francisco Gervás, 15 ☎ 279 29 66 ▣ ✳ DC, V $$$. Imaginative home
cooking.

¶ *Príncipe de Viana* (closed: Saturdays lunchtime, Sundays, August and
Holy Week), c/ Manuel de Falla, 5 ☎ 259 14 48 ▣ ✳ AE, DC, V $$$$$.
Very creative seasonal cuisine.

¶ *Rugantino*, c/ Velázquez, 136 ☎ 261 02 22 ✳ AE, DC, EC, V $$$.
Italian food.

¶ *Sacha* (closed: Sundays, holidays, Holy Week and August), c/ Juan
Hurtado de Mendoza, 11, entrance through the garden behind ☎
457 59 52 ▣ ♦ ✳ AE, V $$$. A pleasant restaurant with a limited but
excellent range of seasonal dishes. Open-air eating in summer.

¶ *Saint-James* (closed: Sundays), c/ Juan Bravo, 26 ☎ 275 00 69 ✳ AE,
DC, EC, V $$$ to $$$$. One of the best places in Madrid for *paella*.

¶ *Salvador* (closed: Sundays and August), c/ Barbieri, 12 ☎ 521 45 24 ▣
✳ AE, DC, V $$$. Good home cooking.

¶ *Semon* (closed: Sundays and evenings after 9.00), c/ Capitán Haya, 23
☎ 455 46 90 ▣ ✳ AE, V $$$. Good food in a sophisticated restaurant
which also has a delicatessen.

¶ *Señorío de Bertiz* (closed: Sundays), c/ Comandante Zorita, 6 ☎
234 45 90 ▣ ✳ AE, DC, EC, V $$$. Basque-Navarrese cuisine.

¶ *Serramar* (closed: Sundays), c/ Rosario Pino, 12 ☎ 270 05 37 ▣ ✳ AE,
DC, EC, V $$$ to $$$$. Andalusian cuisine.

¶ *Solchaga* (closed: Saturdays lunchtime and Sundays), Pl Alonso Martínez,
2 ☎ 447 14 96 ✳ AE, DC, EC, V $$$ to $$$$. Basque-Navarrese
cuisine.

¶ *Tattaglia*, Paseo de la Habana, 17 ☎ 262 85 90 ✳ AE, DC, EC, V $$$.
Dependable Italian food.

¶ *Valentín*, c/ San Alberto, 3 ☎ 521 16 38 ✳ AE, DC, EC, V $$$ to
$$$$. A long-established restaurant serving simple, good food with
old-fashioned courteous service.

¶ *Viridiana* (closed: Sundays and August), c/ Fundadores, 23 ☎
256 77 73 ✳ $$$ to $$$$. Original, imaginative cuisine.

🍲🍲🍲 ¶ *Zalacaín* (closed: Saturdays lunchtime, Sundays, holidays, Holy Week and August), c/ Alvarez de Baena, 4 ☎ 261 10 79 🅿 ✳ AE, DC, V $$$$$. One of the best restaurants in the world, serving *haute cuisine* which varies with the seasons.

Best buys: Arts, crafts, antiques, jewelry, fashion, shoes and leather goods, wine... these are a few highlights from among Madrid's 54,000 shops.

🍲🍲   The area of Madrid known as the **Barrio de Salamanca**, whose main axis is the smart **c/ Serrano**, is where the most chic and exclusive shops are concentrated. The contrasting quarter around the Puerta del Sol and c/ Preciados is full of more traditional shops, often selling the most unlikely things, at much lower prices. Argüelles, centred on c/ Princesa, is the

🍲 student part of town, and its shops reflect the fact, while **c/ Almirante** and adjacent streets (c/ Conde de Xiquena and c/ Piamonte) is the shopping territory of the chic *avant garde*. On c/ Orense and the Paseo de la Castellana you will find mostly chain-stores, fashion shops and shoe shops.

    If you are looking for **antiques**, take note of the several shops along c/ del Prado and c/ Claudio Coello, as well as of the **Centro de Arte y Antigüedades**, c/ Serrano, 5, and, for bargain-hunters, the stalls of the

🍲 *Rastro*, the Sunday morning flea-market, and the antique shops in adjacent streets like c/ Ribera de Curtidores. Works of art are sold at Madrid's 100 or so **commercial art galleries** (see the daily papers for current exhibitions),

🍲 among them Goya prints from the **Calcografía Nacional**, c/ Alcalá, 13. You
🍲🍲 can also visit two of the best auction houses for art and antiques, **Durán**, c/
🍲🍲 Serrano, 12, and **Sotheby's**, Pl de la Independencia, 8. But if you prefer high quality crafts, interior decor pieces and fabrics, then your best bet is to head

🍲 for **Artespaña**, with branches at Gran Vía, 32, Pl de las Cortes, 3, c/ Don Ramón de la Cruz, 33, c/ Hermosilla, 14, and the Vaguada shopping centre.

🍲🍲🍲 Guitars are good buys at **F. Manzanero**, Pl Santa Ana, 12, and **Ramírez**, c/   🍲 Concepción Jerónima, 2; tapestries are best bought at the **Real Fábrica de**
🍲🍲 *Tapices*, c/ Fuenterrabía, 2, founded in the 18C; and typical Spanish
🍲 ceramics are sold at **Sargadelos**, c/ Zurbano, 46, and **La Tierra**, c/ Almirante, 28.

    You will find stylish modern **design** in furniture and decorative items at **Atico**, c/ Cea Bermúdez, 70, **B.D. Ediciones de Diseño**, c/ Villanueva, 5,   🍲 **La Compañía de la China y del Oriente**, c/ Conde Aranda, 14, **La Continental**, c/ Príncipe de Vergara, 48, and **Musgo**, with branches at c/ Hermosilla, 36, c/ O'Donnell, 15, and Paseo de la Habana, 34.

    Fashion fans will find **shoes, leather garments** and **accessories** at **Camper**, with shops at c/ Ayala, 13, the Vaguada shopping centre and Paseo de la Habana, 50, **Casus Belli**, c/ Padre Damián, 33, **Excrupulus Net**, c/ Almirante, 7, 🍲 **Farrutx**, c/ Serrano, 5, **Maud Frizon**, c/ Claudio Coello, 83, **Walter Steiger**, c/ Zurbarán, 16, **Loewe**, with branches at Gran   🍲 Vía, 8 and c/ Serrano, 26 (women) and 34 (men), **Paco Lobo**, with shops at c/ Serrano, 88 (at the Multicentro shopping mall), c/ Princesa, 67 (at the

🍲 Multicentro shopping mall), and c/ Lagasca, 67, **Patricia**, c/ Lagasca, 45, **Peñalba**, c/ Almirante, 22, **Prada**, c/ Goya, 4, and **Willy Van Rooy**, c/ Piamonte, 19...

    For a wide selection of everything, try any of Madrid's several **shopping malls** —the *Vaguada Shopping Centre*, officially known as *Madrid 2*, in the Barrio del Pilar on the outskirts of Madrid, has up-to-date shops of all sorts which keep very late hours; the *Mercado Puerta de Toledo*, c/ Ronda de Toledo, 1 (to be opened in late 1988) will centre on art, crafts and fashion; while the **Multicentro** group —**Multicentro Serrano**, c/ Serrano, 88, *Multicentro Orense*, c/ Orense 6, and **Multicentro Princesa**, c/ Princesa,

47— specializes in young fashion and accessories. Madrid's department stores include *Celso García*, c/ Serrano, 52 and Paseo de la Castellana, 83, *Galerías Preciados*, with shops at c/ Arapiles, 10, c/ Goya, 87, Pl del Callao, 1, c/ Serrano, 47, and the La Vaguada shopping centre, and the prestigious *El Corte Inglés*, with branches at c/ Princesa, 56, c/ Goya, 76, c/ Preciados, 3, and c/ Raimundo Fernández Villaverde, 79, the latter with a good delicatessen section called the *Club del Gourmet*.

Gourmets looking for edible delicacies in general make a note of the following places: *Embassy*, Paseo de la Castellana, 12, sells good cakes, paté, smoked fish and English tea; *Mallorca*, with branches at c/ Pérez Zúñiga, 24, c/ Velázquez, 59, c/ Bravo Murillo, 7, c/ Comandante Zorita, 39, and c/ Alberto Alcocer, 48 (open on Sunday mornings), is an excellent delicatessen, with a wide assortment of cakes and take-away dishes; *La Pajarita*, c/ Villanueva, 13 and Puerta del Sol, 6, is a sweetshop established in 1881; *Pecastaing*, c/ Príncipe, 11, has been a supplier to the Royal Family since 1868; *El Riojano*, c/ Mayor, 10, is a good confectionery; *Santa*, c/ Serrano, 56, is good for elegant sweets and chocolates; *Semon*, c/ Capitán Haya, 23, is a lovely delicatessen with a good wine and spirits selection; *Vázquez*, c/ Ayala, 11, specializes in excellent, and often exotic, fruit and vegetables, and *Santa Cecilia*, c/ Blasco de Garay, 74, is good for reasonably priced wines.

Sporting equipment is sold at *Arte Caza*, Paseo de la Habana, 26, and *Diana-Turba*, c/ Serrano, 68, both specializing in hunting; *Equus*, c/ Hilarión Eslava, 32, for riding kit, and *Caribbean*, c/ Columela, 5, for water sports. Well-known jewellers', both traditional and more adventurous, include *Carrera y Carrera*, c/ Serrano, 27, *Durán*, c/ Serrano, 30, *Grassy*, c/ Gran Vía, 1, *Joaquín Berao*, c/ Conde de Xiquena, 13, *Meneses*, c/ Serrano, 31, *Plata Viva*, c/ Argensola, 2 (selling work by young designers), *Suárez*, c/ Serrano, 63, and *Yanes*, c/ Goya, 27. Books in general are sold at the permanent stalls along the **c/ Cuesta de Moyano**, a good hunting-ground for second-hand books, rare editions and so on, and the *Casa del Libro*, Gran Vía, 29, with a stock of some 300,000 titles; English novels and textbooks, on the other hand, are best bought at *Turner*, c/ Génova, 3, and *Booksellers*, c/ José Abascal, 48.

The centuries-old *Rastro* is more than just a flea-market. It is a 'happening' which takes place every Sunday morning (and to a lesser degree on Saturdays and some holidays as well) and is a marvellous chance to observe a slice of Madrid life, even if you don't want to buy anything. Possible bargains include antiques, all sorts of second-hand things and crafts made by young designers. Be on the lookout for pickpockets and remember that haggling over prices is expected. If you are interested in stamps, you had better head for the *Mercado Filatélico* open-air market held in the Plaza Mayor on Sundays and holidays from 9.00-2.00.

Spanish **fashion** is in fashion. Some of the most outstanding stores include *Adolfo Domínguez*, with stores at c/ Ayala, 24, c/ Serrano, 96, and c/ Ortega y Gasset, 4, *Agatha Ruiz de la Prada*, c/ Marqués de Riscal, 8, *Antonio Alvarado*, c/ Caballero de Gracia, 22, *Ararat*, c/ Almirante, 12 (women) and c/ Conde de Xiquena, 13 (men), *Ascot*, c/ Serrano, 88, *Azero*, c/ Castelló, 9 (men), *Berlín*, c/ Almirante, 10 (women), *Cabasse*, c/ Serrano, 8 (women) and c/ Conde de Aranda, 2 (women), *Coal*, c/ Valenzuela, 9 (women), *Dafnis*, Paseo de la Habana, 174 (women), *Emporio Armani*, c/ Claudio Coello, 77 (men and women), *Enrique P*, c/ Almirante, 6 and c/ Gaztambide, 24 (men and women), *Fancy Men*, c/ Serrano, 93 (men), *Francis Montesinos*, c/ Argensola, 8, *Giorgio Armani*, c/ Ortega y Gasset, 15 (women), *Irene Prada*, c/ Columela, 3 (women), *Jesús del Pozo*,

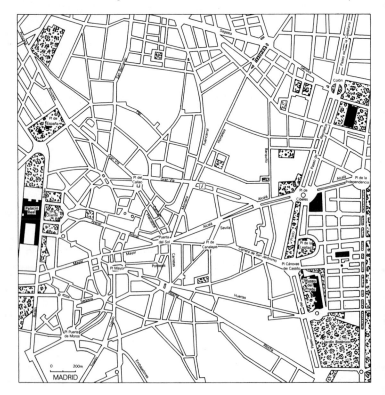 c/ Almirante, 28 (men), *Loewe*, c/ Gran Vía, 8 and c/ Serrano, 26 (women) and 34 (men), *Pedro Morago*, c/ Almirante, 20 (men), *Purificación García*, 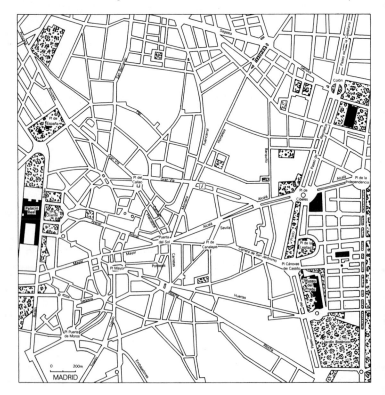 c/ Velázquez, 55 (women), *Robert Max*, c/ Columela, 2 and c/ San Francisco de Sales, 21 (men and women) and c/ Milaneses, 3 (men), *Sybilla*, c/ Jorge Juan, 12 (women), *Teresa Ramallal*, c/ Almirante, 5 (women), and *Tres Zetas*, c/ Ortega y Gasset, 17 (women). Accessories are sold at *Pendiente de Ti*, c/ Travesía de Belén, 4, *Spleen*, c/ Almirante, 8, and *Tokio*, c/ Almirante, 8 and c/ Claudio Coello, 66. For furs, turn to *Arturo Barrios*, c/ Juan Bravo, 1, *Elena Benarroch*, c/ Monte Esquinza, 24 and 18, *José Luis*, c/ Génova, 19...

Cultural highlights: Old Madrid is also known as the *Madrid de los Austrias* after the Austrian Hapsburg dynasty that inherited the throne of Spain with the Emperor Charles V and held it for nearly 200 years until the end of the 17C. The centre of this area is the Plaza Mayor and it extends W to the Royal Palace, the Palacio Real, which is also called the Palacio de Oriente, and to the old artisan districts of Lavapiés, Embajadores and La Latina in the S.

The **Plaza Mayor** was designed early in the 17C by **Gómez de Mora** and is a perfectly symmetrical, rectangular and colonnaded square that is quintessentially Castilian. In its centre there is a **statue** of Philip III, son of Philip II and Gómez de la Mora's chief employer, riding astride his royal charger. In the 18C Juan de Villanueva, Madrid's other great architect, remodelled the square somewhat and gave it a less rustic and more classical air. Gómez de Mora was reponsible for the two main civic buildings in the Plaza's immediate neighbourhood, the **Palacio de Santa Cruz** which today houses the foreign ministry, and the **Casa de la Villa** which is the Town Hall. Opposite the latter, in the small square called the **Pl de la Villa**, there is a 15C tower, the **Torre de los Lujanes**, and a Mudéjar building which houses the public records library, the **Hemeroteca Nacional**. Also in the vicinity stands the 17C **Catedral de San Isidro** which is not impressive as Spanish cathedrals go but is in the pleasantest of the city's old quarters. In this area you should simply stroll around —follow c/ del Sacramento, c/ del Rollo, c/ del Nuncio and c/ Puñónrrostro and visit the Pl de San Pedro, Pl de San Andrés, Pl de la Cruz Verde, Pl del Alamillo and **Pl del Cordón**...— marvelling at how old buildings and atmospheric streets and medieval plazas have escaped the property speculator's greed. Mercifully a lot of good restoration work is being conducted in this area and much of it is now pedestrian only. In the Pl de la Paja the Gothic **Capilla del Obispo** has an interesting altarpiece and on the corner of c/ Nuncio, the **Church of San Pedro** has a fine 14C Mudéjar **tower**.

The **Palacio Real**, c/ Bailén, 2 (open in summer: 10.00-1.00 and 4.00-6.15; winter: 9.30-12.45 and 3.30-5.15; Sundays: 10.00-1.00), is very big and impressive. It gives onto the large Pl de Oriente and looks every bit as grand as a royal palace should. Building started during the reign of Philip V, the first of the new Bourbon dynasty kings, in 1737, and continued for the rest of the century. Like all royal palaces in Spain it is run by the *Patrimonio Nacional*, the National Trust, and its guides take visitors on an extended trip of the rooms and collections that are open to the public. High points of the tour are the State Room, the **Salón de Embajadores**, with a ceiling by Mengs, and its antechamber which is decorated with royal portraits by Goya, the sumptuous **Throne Room**, the **Art Collection** with canvases by Rubens, El Greco, Watteau, Zurbarán and Goya and the **Music Museum** which includes Stradivarius violins among its exhibits. The Royal Armoury, or **Real Armería**, with a large collection of suits of armour and weapons, is in an annexe, and an outbuilding in the Palace's gardens (the **Campo del Moro**) houses the **Museo de Carruajes**, a collection of carriages and coaches.

The centrepiece of the **Pl de Oriente**, the palace square, is an **equestrian statue** of Philip IV, the monarch who employed Velázquez as court painter. Opposite the palace stands the **Teatro Real** concert hall which is due to be extensively redesigned and re-converted into the opera house it was originally intended to be. The N side of the square is occupied by a 17C convent, the **Real Monasterio de la Encarnación**, Pl Encarnación, 1 (open: 10.00-1.00 and 4.00-6.00), which was founded by Queen Margarita, wife of the third King Philip and mother of the fourth, and built by the constantly busy Gómez de Mora. The monastery's church is deceptively austere seen from the outside for it is richly ornate within. A second convent in the neighbourhood, the **Descalzas Reales**, Pl Descalzas Reales (open Mondays to Thursdays: 10.30-12.45 and 4.00-5.15; Fridays and Saturdays: 10.30-1.30 ☎ 522 06 87), is in reality a first-class **museum** housing an impressive art collection and particularly fine furniture. This convent was founded by Juana de Austria, a daughter of the Emperor Charles V. Proceeding now towards the **Puerta del Sol**, you will find the famed kilometre zero on the pavement in front of the square's main building, an 18C mansion that was originally the city's post office and is now a government department. The c/ de Alcalá, one of Madrid's main thoroughfares that slices E-W through the city, starts in this square and at No. 8 stands the Fine Arts Academy, the **Real Academia de Bellas Artes de San Fernando** (open: 9.00-7.00; Sundays and Mondays: 9.00-2.00), with a collection of old masters that, in Madrid, is second only to the Prado's. The academy has a particularly good collection of Goyas.

The S side of the old Madrid of the Austrias is occupied by the districts of La Latina, Embajadores and Lavapiés which are a world away from modern highrise Madrid. These are neighbourhoods that few tourists tread and those who do venture into them find that the artisan workshops and the taverns of yesteryear are still in business. The architectural interest here focuses on the authentic old tenements called **corralas** such as the ones on c/ Mesón de Paredes between c/ Sombrerete and c/ Tribulete. Nearby the gateway called the **Puerta de Toledo** marked the city's W limits when it was built in 1827 to commemorate the victory over France in what Spaniards call the War of Independence and Anglo-Saxons know as the Peninsular War. Doubling back from here along c/ Bailén and past the Royal Palace you reach the 18C **Basílica de San Francisco el Grande** with its huge dome and a Neoclassical façade designed by Francisco Sabatini, one of the rationalist group of architects that was fully employed during Charles III's enlightened reign. Inside there are frescoes by Goya and by his father-in-law Francisco Bayeau.

Taking now a different itinerary which has the Prado Museum as its focal point and the Castellana boulevard as its main axis, you can start at the Glorieta de Carlos V and the cast iron structure of the Atocha railway station. Recently restored and also looking on to the square is the cultural centre called the **Centro de Arte Reina Sofía**, c/ Santa Isabel, 52 (open: 10.00-9.00; closed: Tuesdays). The itinerary now continues up the leafy **Paseo del Prado** boulevard, with its classical statues and **fountains**. On the right are the gardens of the 18C **Jardín Botánico** which has some 30,000 different species in a romantic, shaded setting enclosed by fine wrought iron railings and with an interesting pavilion which houses a nursery and a library.

The **Prado Museum** (open Tuesdays to Saturdays: 9.00-7.00; Sundays: 9.00-1.45; closed: Mondays ☎ 230 34 39) needs no introduction. If you are visiting it for the first time, do as you would in any other of the world's top half dozen art galleries: arm yourself with a plan of the museum and take it slowly. Remember that the Prado is a royal collection put together by the kings of the Hapsburg and the Bourbon dynasties between the 16-18C and that as such it reflects the personal tastes of the monarchs and the areas of Spanish influence of the time. The Flemish School is well represented as much because **Rubens** was liked and **Hieronymus Bosch** admired as because the Netherlands was then a Spanish stronghold. The same can be said, for example, of **Titian** and **Mantegna** of Italy. The real strength of the Prado is, naturally, the Spanish School and the trinity of greats, **El Greco, Velázquez** and **Goya**, is represented with stunning, magnificent richness. To cap it the Prado now also houses Picasso's *Guernica* in an annexe called the **Casón del Bueno Retiro**, a five minutes walk from the main museum on c/ Alfonso XII, the street that borders the Retiro Park. The rest of the Casón annexe exhibits 19C Spanish paintings. There is a second Prado annexe, the **Palacio de Villahermosa**, on the other side of the Castellana boulevard. Currently this good-looking Neoclassical mansion exhibits Baroque religious painting but it is soon to be the home of the fabulous Thyssen art collection which has been lent to Spain for an initial 10-year period. A word of warning about visiting the main Prado Museum and the Guernica canvas: if you want to see the exhibits in relative comfort go early to avoid the crowds.

The residential district around the Prado Museum is the stateliest in Madrid. At one time this whole area was a complex of palaces and leisure gardens that was built by Philip IV but nowadays only the building containing the Army Museum, the **Museo del Ejército**, c/ Méndez Núñez, s/n (open: 10.00-2.00; closed: Mondays ☎ 231 46 24) remains from the original royal residence. Just behind the Prado stands the originally Gothic and heavily restored **Church of San Jerónimo el Real** which is again all that remains of a large monastic institution that existed when this neighbourhood lay outside the city's limits. In front of the museum, the Paseo del Prado leads into the **Pl de Neptuno** and the boulevard (under the guise now of Paseo de Recoletos) continues on to Neptune's partner statue, the monument to **Cibeles**, the queen of the sea, which is Madrid's main landmark. As you move up the Paseo del Prado and Paseo de Recoletos and their continuation, the Paseo de la Castellana, you will pass a succession of plazas that stretch N to the city's uptown modern districts.

The Neptune and Cibeles squares are in keeping with the classical vogue of Charles III's enlightened reign. Looking on to the Neptune plaza and across the road from the *Ritz* hotel, there is a second monument that honours the Spanish patriots who rose up against Napoleon and whose execution was so terrifyingly depicted by Goya in a giant canvas that hangs in the Prado. An eternal flame, commemorating those who gave their lives for Spain, burns by this monument. The Cibeles plaza, which is the busy intersection of the Castellana and the c/ de Alcalá, is flanked by large public buildings including the 19C Bank of Spain, the Army Headquarters (set in its own gardens) and the Post Office headquarters. The latter building was completed in 1919 and looks more like a cathedral built by an eccentric than a clearing house for parcels and letters. Just up from Cibeles on the c/ de Alcalá stands the **Alcalá Arch** which was built by Sabatini in 1778 and used to mark the city's E limits. This well proportioned archway stands now by the entrance to the **Retiro Park**, Madrid's main city park and, by any standards, a very beautiful and extensive stretch of gardens. At weekends it becomes extremely lively

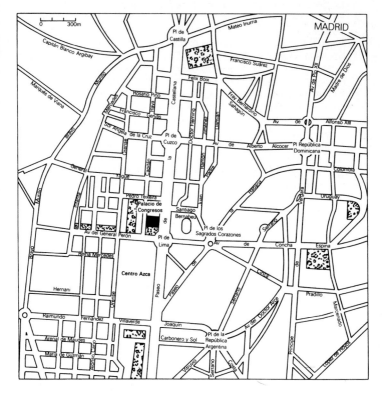

and it is a favourite haunt of street musicians and mime artists. The park has two exhibition halls —one of them being a delightful **Crystal Palace**—, a boating lake, a rose garden, jogging courses, *terrazas* and bars, carriages for hire, an outdoor cinema in summer and just about everything that a good city park should have. Among its many monuments there is one statue that is perfectly unusual: near the rose garden a monument honours the *Angel Caído* or the Fallen Angel, also known as the Devil.

Doubling back to the main boulevard and going N, the next square after Cibeles is the very spacious Pl del Descubrimiento. This marks the end of the Paseo de Recoletos and from here on the avenue is called the Paseo de la Castellana. The plaza honours the discoverer Christopher Columbus, depicted in a 19C statue in one corner of the square, and commemorates his voyages of exploration with four great concrete blocks at the rear of the square which list the names of all who sailed with him and feature a selection of contemporary texts dealing with his discoveries. Underneath the square there is a bus station linking the city with Barajas airport and the city's arts centre, the **Centro Cultural de la Villa de Madrid**, which has a packed year-round programme of exhibitions, lectures, stage productions and concerts.

The very large severe-looking building that flanks the plaza on the S is the National Library or **Biblioteca Nacional**. The library's reading rooms, housing some three million volumes, are only open to bona fide researchers and there is usually a literary exhibition in one of its salons. Part of the building serves as the National Archaeological Museum, the **Museo Arqueológico Nacional**, entered by c/ Serrano, 13 (open: 9.30-1.30 ☎ 403 66 07). The star of the show here is the extraordinarily lifelike 4C BC bust of that totally enigmatic Iberian lady who is known as the *Dama de Elche*. Another highlight is the re-creation of the Altamira caves and their prehistoric murals. The museum has several collections and though mainly devoted to prehistory and antiquity it also includes galleries of medieval and Renaissance art and of art and fashions of the 18C and 19C.

Continuing N from the Pl del Descubrimiento you are now entering an 11km stretch of boulevard that leads to the city's limits. This first stretch of it, up to the Pl del Doctor Marañón, still retains the odd town mansion of a more graceful epoch now rubbing shoulders with modern office blocks. Some of the contemporary architecture, notably the **Bankinter** building at No. 29, which was designed by Rafael Moneo, the **Bankunión** at No. 46, the Adriática building at No. 47, and the Catalana de Occidente one which stands opposite the latter and was styled by De la Hoz, are very worthwhile examples of contemporary architecture. In summer the boulevard here turns into a succession of *terrazas* where people drink, chat and table hop until dawn. Just off the Castellana on this stretch there are a couple of museums worth visiting. The **Museo Lázaro Galdiano**, c/ Serrano, 122 (open: 10.00-2.00; closed: Mondays and August ☎ 261 49 79), is the result of a lifetime's collecting by the discerning art lover after whom the museum is named. It contains old masters of the Italian and Spanish schools and good jewelry, **enamelwork and ivory exhibits**. The **Museo Sorolla**, c/ Martínez Campos, 37 (open: 10.00-2.00; closed: Mondays ☎ 410 15 84), is a delightful little mansion that was home to the very successful painter Joaquín Sorolla (1863-1923). The museum is a good introduction to a Sorolla world that mixed 'anyone for tennis' pre-first World War society portraits with skilfully excecuted observations of everyday life. His mastery of light is what leaves the most enduring impression.

Beyond the fountains that follow the Pl del Doctor Marañón, the **Paseo de la Castellana** straightens up and acquires a very uptown feel to it. The grim-looking buildings to the W of the first stretch house a series of government ministries and beyond them a whole new business area has sprouted up among the skyscrapers. The highrises include the Torre de Picasso which towers up 157m and is claimed to be the highest office block in Europe, and the **Banco de Bilbao's** striking 107m-high slab of ochre steel and glass designed by Sainz de Oíza. Just behind the squatter circular block known as the Torre Europa, a low-slung building, the Palacio de Congresos, which serves as the city's main convention centre, has a large ceramic mural designed by Joan Miró adorning its façade.

To complete the list of Madrid's **museums and exhibition centres** you should take note of the following: in downtown Madrid the city museum, the **Museo Municipal**, c/ Fuencarral, 78 (open: 10.00-2.00 and 5.00-7.00; closed: Mondays ☎ 521 66 56), traces the capital's history in its rich collection of documents. The building used to be a hospice and it has a superbly ostentatious Baroque façade. For another extraordinary 18C façade you should examine the portal of the **Cuartel Conde Duque**, c/ Conde Duque, 9, which used to be a military barracks and is now an arts centre run by the Madrid city council, housing temporary exhibitions on a wide range of subjects. The **Museo Romántico**, c/ San Mateo, 13 (open: 10.00-6.00; Sundays: 10.00-2.00; closed: Mondays), is a charming collection of 19C furniture, paintings and bric-à-brac that has a suitably nostalgic air to it. The **Palacio de Liria** (open to the public Saturday mornings by prior appointment ☎ 247 53 02), in contrast, is very grand indeed for it is the residence of the Duchess of Alba, Spain's premier aristocrat, and it has an extremely valuable art collection. There are more old masters **paintings** in the **Museo Cerralbo**, c/ Ventura Rodríguez, 17, there is a 16C atmosphere in the **Casa Museo de Lope de Vega**, c/ Cervantes, 11, and there is a whole world of tapestry and carpet making in the 18C **Real Fábrica de Tapices** (see 'Best buys').

Slightly out of town lie the Amerindian and Latin American exhibits of the **Museo de América**, Av Reyes Católicos, 6 (open: 10.00-2.00; closed: Mondays ☎ 243 94 37) and the Modern Art Museum, the **Museo Español de Arte Contemporáneo** (open: 9.00-2.00 and 4.00-7.00; closed: Sunday afternoons and Mondays) which is on the University campus. S of the Parque del Oeste (see below), the **Ermita de San Antonio de la Florida**, Glorieta de San Antonio de la Florida, s/n (open Mondays to Thursdays: 11.00-1.00 and 3.00-7.00; Sundays and holidays: 11.00-1.30; closed: Fridays), with interesting Goya **frescoes**, is the burial place of the headless body of the painter Goya —the whereabouts of his head is a continuing mystery.

For **open spaces**, in addition to the Retiro Park Madrid has exceptionally pleasant gardens in the **Parque del Oeste** on the W side of town. They slope down from the c/ Rosales, which has very agreeable terraces from which to watch the sunset. This park is linked by a cable car to Madrid's vast parkland area, the **Casa de Campo** which used to be a royal hunting reserve. This very extensive park is home to Madrid's **Trade Exhibition Zone**, its **Zoo** and its **Amusement Park**, or *Parque de Atracciones*, and facilities include a boating lake and enough jogging space to run a marathon.

Fiestas and festivals: You will soon discover that Madrid is a year-round *fiesta*. At Christmas, fairy-lights, Christmas trees and nativity scenes appear all over town and stalls selling elaborate nativity figures and other decorations are set up in the Plaza Mayor. Crowds gather to see in the New Year in the Puerta del Sol, popping a grape into their mouths with each of the 12 strokes of midnight. In January, the *Fiesta de San Antón* features a traditional procession of animals around the Church of San Antonio Abad. **Carnival time** strikes in February and is the occasion for general fun and disguises. On May 2, in the Pl Dos de Mayo in the Malasaña area of Madrid, the events depicted in Goya's famous painting are commemorated with processions. The day of **San Isidro** (May 15), patron saint of Madrid, is celebrated with a **bullfighting season** and countless concerts, shows and a traditional festive pilgrimage, or ***romería***. On June 13, a traditional open-air celebration with singing and dancing, the ***Verbena de San Antonio***, is held in San Antonio de la Florida. Two months later, the feast-day of San Cayetano, August 3, is celebrated with an age-old *fiesta* which links up neatly with San Lorenzo on August 5 and the ***Verbena de la Paloma***, featuring old-style dancing to the typical accompaniment of a barrel organ, on August 15. Finally, on November 9, the day of the ***Virgen de la Almudena***, patroness of Madrid, also has its own traditional *fiesta* events.

Festivals of a different sort are also held all year round: the **Madrid International Theatre Festival**, staged in March, and the ***Encuentro Internacional de Teatro de Madrid***, in May, are for serious theatre lovers; the ***Festival Internacional de Cine Imaginario y de Ciencia Ficción*** (International Festival of Fantasy and Science Fiction Films) takes place in April; the ***Cumbre Flamenca***, also in April, is a week-long flamenco festival that attracts the best performers from all over Spain; the ***Festival de Rock*** is held in May-June; the *Semana del Erotismo*, held in July, combines serious with the frivolous, the ***Veranos de la Villa***, from July to September, is a continuous calendar of activities including folk performances from all over the world, rock and pop concerts, theatre and so on; the **Madrid Jazz Festival**, one of the best in Europe, is held in late October-early November; and the ***Festival de Otoño*** (Autumn Festival) spans the months of October to December and presents productions by major companies from all over the world in various theatres and concert halls throughout Madrid.

The Casa de Campo has an area of pavilions for **trade fairs** and the like, some thirty of which are held a year (*IFEMA*, Madrid Trade Fair Organization ☎ 470 10 14). One of the outstanding events held here is the international contemporary art fair ***ARCO*** in February.

Local sights: Ten kilometres away, taking the N-VI out of Madrid and turning off onto the C-601, **EL PARDO**, surrounded by parkland, was a royal residence and hunting preserve of the Castilian monarchs in the 15C. The park is heavily wooded and full of game, including deer. The **palace**, whose present appearance is the result of adaptations made by Sabatini during the reign of Charles III, was the summer residence and retreat of General Franco up to the time of his death. Nearby are the little summer house known as the **Casita del Príncipe**, built in 1772 and altered by Villanueva in 1784, and the **Quinta del Pardo**, a museum with a fascinating collection of 19C handpainted wallpapers (open: 10.00-12.30 and 3.30-5.30; closed: Sunday afternoons and Mondays ☎ 216 48 45). On the outskirts is the **Convento de los Capuchinos**, a monastery whose prize work of art is a masterpiece of Baroque sculpture, a recumbent figure of ***Christ***, by Gregorio Fernández (1605). The Palacio de la Zarzuela, residence of the Spanish Royal Family, is also in El Pardo. Recommended restaurants in the area include ***Pedro's***, Av de la Guardia, s/n ☎ 736 08 83 **P ✦ ✳ AE, V $$$**, with a rather pleasant open-air terrace in summer, and ***La Marquesita***, Av de la Guardia, 4 ☎ 736 03 77 **✦ ✳ AE, DC, EC, V $$$ to $$$$**, also with open-air eating in summer.

On the town: The Spanish like to live life to the full and have a natural talent for having a good time at all times of day and night. Madrid is an excellent place to discover the typically Spanish phenomenon of ***el tapeo***, going from bar to bar eating *tapas* (see 'Cuisine') as you go. The area around the **c/ de la Victoria**, from c/ Cruz to c/ Carrera de San Jerónimo, is traditional *tapeo* territory and is densely packed with old-fashioned bars, often with bullfighting as the predominant theme of both decor and conversation

—**Los Gabrieles**, c/ Echegaray, 17, is a genuine old *taberna*, *Casa Labra*, c/ Tetuán, 12, and *El Portugués*, c/ Cruz, 3, are both well known for their excellent *bacalao* (salt cod) *tapas*, and *Vista Alegre*, c/ Pozo, 2, also has a good selection. *Casa Paco* in Pl del Humilladero, 8, is a long-standing favourite, and nearby, in **c/ Cava Baja** and around the Plaza Mayor, are Madrid's famous *mesones*, traditional inns which have now become tourist haunts. Almost opposite the Palacio Real, the **Anciano Rey de los Vinos**, c/ Bailén, 19, an old *taberna*, is worth a visit. **La Bilbaína**, c/ Marqués de Urquijo, 27, serves good seafood; **Cervecería Alemana**, Pl Santa Ana, 6, and **La Cervecería Internacional**, c/ Regueros, 8, are good beer halls; and **Cervecería Santa Bárbara**, Pl de Santa Bárbara, 8 and c/ José Castán, 1, and **La Cruz Blanca**, c/ Alcalá, 149, both serve good beer and excellent seafood snacks. For a trip back to the turn of the century, try **Lhardy**, c/ Carrera de San Jerónimo, 8, which serves good *tapas* (hot broth and chicken croquettes are a traditional snack here) and also has a delightful restaurant on the first floor. **Santander**, c/ Augusto Figueroa, 25, is another favourite for *tapas*.

More upmarket and **late-night haunts** include **Balmoral**, c/ Hermosilla, 10, where the cocktails are among the best in the world, according to *Newsweek;* **El Balneario**, c/ Juan Ramón Jiménez, 37, stylish and pleasant; the bar of the **Palace Hotel**, Pl de las Cortes, 7, frequented by intellectuals and politicians; *Boccacio*, Pl Marqués de la Ensenada, 16, haunt of actors and journalists; **Cock**, c/ Reina, 16, a favourite among the chic *avant garde* set; **Hispano**, Paseo de la Castellana, 78, generally packed with top executives, journalists and the like; **La Pecera**, c/ Alcalá, 42, the bar of the Círculo de Bellas Artes cultural centre which attracts the young intellectual and theatrical crowd; **El Sur**, c/ Alberto Bosch, 14, a tropical setting for beautiful people; **Viva Madrid**, c/ Manuel Fernández y González, 7, near the Pl de Santa Ana, a lovely old turn of the century café, and **Zénith**, c/ Conde de Xiquena, 12, for *avant garde* trendies.

Traditional Madrid cafés include the *Café Comercial*, Glorieta de Bilbao, 10, which still has much of its original decor intact but now attracts a young, lively clientele; the **Café Gijón**, Paseo de Recoletos, 21, now, as always, favoured by the literati; the **Café Latino**, c/ Augusto Figueroa, 47, a good place for a late dinner; the teetotal **Café de Ruiz**, c/ Ruiz, 11; the **Café Universal**, c/ Fernando VI, 13, and the **Café Viena**, c/ Luisa Fernanda, 23, where you can dine to the sound of classical music. In a category all its own is the salon of the **Hotel Ritz** where you can enjoy the timeless experience of afternoon tea with sedate musical accompaniment.

Archy, c/ Marqués de Riscal on the corner of c/ Fortuny, is quite a place —set in a lovely old mansion, its bar is open from midday on, its restaurant from 1.00 pm to 3.00 am, and its disco from 11.00 pm to 4.00 am. *Vip's* (with branches at c/ Velázquez 84 and 136, c/ Princesa, 5, Paseo de la Habana, 17, c/ Orense 16 and 79, c/ Julián Romea, 4, c/ O'Donnell, 17, Gran Vía, 43 and Paseo de la Castellana, 83) and *Bob's* (c/ Serrano, 42) are based on the American drugstores idea and combine a restaurant and cafeteria with a shopping section selling books, records, gifts, and even foodstuffs in some of them. They can be very useful for the disorganized since they keep very long hours, especially at weekends.

Night-owls have more than 250 **discos** to choose from. A full listing is given in the *Guía del Ocio* (available at all news-stands), but among the best known are **Amnesia**, Paseo de la Castellana, 93, open from 3.00 am to 7.00 am; **Four Roses**, c/ Osa Mayor, Aravaca, at km9.2 on the N-VI, the La Coruña motorway, certainly one of the best summer discos; **Joy Eslava**, c/ Arenal, 11, in an old theatre; **Keeper**, c/ Juan Bravo, 39, frequented by well-heeled youngsters; *Mau Mau*, c/ José Lázaro Galdiano, 3 (in the Eurobuilding hotel), haunt of the *crème de la crème*; *Oh! Madrid*, km8.7 on the N-VI, the La Coruña motorway, famous for its summertime parties; *Pachá*, c/ Barceló, 11, crowded with beautiful people, actresses, pop personalities and young executives, and *Piña's*, c/ Alberto Alcocer, 33, an elegant disco aimed at the 30-40 age-group.

For **flamenco**, make for the *Café de Chinitas*, c/ Torija, 7 ☎ 248 51 35; the *Corral de la Pacheca*, c/ Juan Ramón Jiménez, 26 ☎ 458 11 13; the *Venta del Gato*, Av de Burgos, 214, at km7.7 on the N-I motorway ☎ 202 34 37; *Zambra*, c/ Velázquez, 8, and for a particularly ebullient flamenco atmosphere, to *La Peña Flamenca La Carcelera*, c/ Monteleón, 10, basement, Saturdays only from 10.00 pm on.

The *Casino de Madrid*, in Torrelodones, at km28.3 on the N-VI, the La Coruña motorway ☎ 859 03 12, is something of a gambler's mecca, being the biggest in Europe both in terms of customers and money —it has 52 gaming-tables with French and American roulette, black-jack, *punto y banca*, baccarat, one-armed bandits, a night-club and three restaurants (open: 4.00 pm-4.00 am, except for baccarat which lasts until 9.00; jackets obligatory in winter).

For **live music and shows**, see the local press and the *Guía del Ocio*, making special note of the *Café Central*, Pl del Angel, 10, which plays live jazz; *Café Manuela*, c/ San Vicente Ferrer, 29, a café with kitsch decor and live concerts; *Elígeme*, c/ San Vicente Ferrer, 23, which features folk music, salsa and so on in a young, rather tough atmosphere; *La Fídula*, c/ Huertas, 57, with live classical music; *Café de Maravillas*, c/ San Vicente Ferrer, 33, where cabaret is enjoying a revival; *Lola*, c/ Costanilla de San Pedro, 11 ☎ 265 88 01, with live performances and good food; *Noches del Cuplé*, c/ de la Palma, 51, which stages performances of *cuplés* by Olga Ramos, one of the few remaining exponents of this old-fashioned genre of popular song, and *Scala Meliá*, c/ Capitán Haya, 43 ☎ 450 44 00, a restaurant with large-scale shows in the international vein.

Music and dance of all sorts go on all year round: see 'Fiestas' above for special festivals and the local press and the *Guía del Ocio* for programme details of pop and rock concerts. The **classical music season** lasts from October to April, and as well as performances by major Spanish and foreign orchestras there are **Chamber Music** and **Polyphony** cycles. Concerts are held in the **Teatro Real**, Pl de Oriente ☎ 248 14 05. The **opera**, **zarzuela** and **ballet** season is from October to June and performances are given in the **Teatro de La Zarzuela**, c/ Jovellanos, 4 ☎ 429 82 25. There are also chamber music cycles and lunch-time concerts in the **Fundación Juan March**, c/ Castelló, 77 ☎ 435 42 40. *Radio Nacional* holds Monday concerts in the Círculo de Bellas Artes, and the Municipal Band plays on Sundays, weather permitting, in the Retiro Park. The **theatre** is alive and well: some 30 theatres stage regular performances, not counting fringe activity, ranging in scope from the **Centro Nacional de Nuevas Tendencias Escénicas** (Centre for New Trends in the Theatre), the **María Guerrero National Theatre** and the **National Classical Theatre Company** to small local theatrical companies: see the local press for programme information.

Summer in Madrid produces the *terraza* phenomenon. From May to October, more than 30 open-air bars spring up along the **Paseo del Prado**, **Paseo de Recoletos** and the **Paseo de la Castellana**, hives of fashionable activity until the early hours of the morning, and often qualifying as street theatre in themselves. There are some 4,000 summer *terrazas* all over town: the one in **Las Vistillas**, c/ Bailén on the corner of the Viaduct, is a traditional meeting place with a quiet atmosphere and marvellous views; the

Paseo del Pintor Rosales has more of a family atmosphere, while in the smart Barrio de Salamanca the *terrazas* along **c/ Juan Bravo** attract the conservative, well-off younger set. The *terraza* of the **Café de Oriente**, Pl de Oriente, 2, is outstanding for its lovely setting, while the most chic is at the **Hotel Ritz**. The ones beside the lake in the extensive Casa de Campo park are deliciously relaxing on weekdays though very crowded at weekends.

Bullfighting takes place at the *Plaza de Toros Monumental*, c/ Alcalá, 231, one of the top bullrings in Spain. The season lasts from April to October.

For the young, take note of the **fun-fairs, aquaparks** and other such places in or near Madrid —*Aquapark*, Ctra de Andalucía, km44, in Aranjuez ☎ 891 06 41; *Aquópolis*, km25 on the El Escorial road, in Villanueva de la Cañada (open: 10.00-8.00, free bus service from the Pl de España ☎ 815 69 11 and 815 69 86); **Casa de Campo Fun-Fair** ☎ 463 29 00; **Museo Colón de Figuras de Cera**, a waxworks museum in the Pl de Colón ☎ 419 22 82 (open: 10.30-1.30 and 4.00-8.30); **Planetario de Madrid**, Enrique Tierno Galván Park ☎ 467 34 61 (tours of the planetarium in the afternoons from Tuesday to Friday, mornings and afternoons on Saturday and Sunday; closed: Monday); *Safari Madrid-Reserva El Rincón* safari park, km22 on the Navalcarnero to Villa del Prado road taking the N-V out of Madrid, in Aldea del Fresno ☎ 862 06 57, where animals wander around freely (open: 10.00-6.00; closed: Mondays); and the Casa de Campo **Zoo** ☎ 711 99 50, one of the best in Europe, which includes a pair of giant pandas and a Dolphinarium among its main attractions (open in spring and summer: 10.00-9.00; winter: 10.00-7.30).

<u>Sports:</u> Madrid has facilities for just about every sport imaginable, both spectator and participatory (see the press and the *Guía del Ocio* for sporting event programmes). Here is just a brief selection:

Car and Motorcycle Racing. At the motor-racing track, the **Circuito del Jarama**, km27 on the N-I to Burgos, major racing events like the **Formula 1 Grand Prix** in both car and motorcycle racing count as preliminaries to their respective World Championships.

Equestrian Events. An **International Show-Jumping Competition** is held to coincide with the San Isidro celebrations (see 'Fiestas' above). In autumn there is the **Príncipe de Asturias Trophy**, and around Christmas, the *Torneo de Campeones* ☎ 419 02 33. At the city race-track, the **Hipódromo de la Zarzuela**, there is racing on Saturdays, Sundays and holidays during the spring and autumn seasons ☎ 207 01 40.

Golf. The city has 11 golf courses, including the excellent **Club de Campo Villa de Madrid**, Ctra de Castilla, km2 ☎ 207 03 95 and 449 07 26, with one 18-hole, par 72 course and another 9-hole one, the **Club de Golf La Moraleja**, Urb La Moraleja, Alcobendas ☎ 650 07 00, with an 18-hole, par 72 course designed by Jack Nicklaus, and the **Real Club de Golf Puerta de Hierro**, Av Miraflores, s/n ☎ 216 17 45, with two 18-hole courses, one par 72 and the other par 67, founded in 1904, and designed by Harris and Simpson.

Horseback Riding. Stables and pony clubs include the **Club de Campo**, Ctra de Castilla, s/n ☎ 207 03 95, the **Escuela Española de Equitación**, Av de la Iglesia, 9, in Pozuelo de Alarcón ☎ 212 12 47, which has horses for hire and gives riding classes, and the **Poney Club-Escuela de Equitación**, in La Moraleja ☎ 650 02 71, which specializes in riding crash courses.

Indoor Sports. Martial arts are practised at the **Gimnasio Argüelles**, c/ Andrés Mellado, 21 ☎ 449 00 40; top-level **basketball** games (the *Real Madrid* have been European champions several times) are held at the *Palacio de los Deportes*, c/ Jorge Juan, 99 ☎ 401 91 00; bowling is played at the

AMF Bowling Center, Paseo Castellana, 77, in the AZCA centre, and at **Bowling Chamartín**, in the Chamartín railway station; and there are indoor jogging, body-building, sauna, swimming and squash facilities at **Paladium Sport Center**, c/ Carlos Maurrás, 5 ☎ 250 88 05.

🏐🏐🏐   **Squash and Tennis**. The **Castellana Squash Club**, at the Chamartín railway station ☎ 733 88 98, is outstandingly good. Other squash clubs include the **Paladium Sport Center**, c/ Carlos Maurrás, 5 ☎ 250 88 05, the **Palestra** centre, c/ Bravo Murillo, 5 ☎ 448 98 22, and the **Squash Abascal** centre, c/ José Abascal, 46 ☎ 442 79 00. As far as tennis is concerned, Madrid holds its own professional Grand Prix, the **Gran Premio de Madrid**. The best tennis clubs are the **Club de Campo**, Ctra de Castilla, s/n ☎ 207 03 95, the **Real Club Puerta de Hierro**, Ciudad Puerta de Hierro ☎ 216 17 45, and the **Club de Tenis Chamartín**, c/ Federico Salmón, 2 ☎ 250 59 65, although many municipal sports centres also have their own courts ☎ 463 55 63 and 464 90 50.

   Swimming Pools. Try the heated pool at the **Club de Natación Canoe**, c/ Pez Volador, 30 ☎ 273 59 77 and those at the various municipal sports centres, where there are facilities for many other sports as well ☎ 463 55 63 and 464 90 50. There are also several pools in the city's top hotels.

MOLINA DE ARAGON   Guadalajara ☎ (911), pop. 3,894. Guadalajara 141km, Zaragoza 144km, Madrid 197km.

   Parts of the **walls** of this old warrior town survive and so do four of the original eight towers of its impressive **castle**. Molina was on the frontier of the old kingdoms of Castile and Aragón and was for a period disputed by the monarchies. The churches of San Martín and San Francisco date from the Romanesque period and the houses down by the river formed the old Jewish quarter, the *judería*.

🏛 ★ *Rosanz*, Paseo de los Adarves, 12 ☎ 83 08 36 🛏 33 $ to $$.

MONTES DE TOLEDO   Toledo ☎ (952).

   This low slung range of hills in the S of Toledo province is one of Spain's best hunting areas. Elaborately organized shoots are staged here for deer, wild boar and for the fast-flying Spanish partridge. The hills are fairly wild and the thickets of holm oak offer good cover for game. Outside the hunting season the only sign of human existence that you are likely to see are spent cartridge cases. The villages in the area are unpretentious mountain *pueblos* that are well off the beaten track. There are some Muslim ruins known as the **Ciudad de Vascos** in **NAVALMORALEJO**, and ancestral folk dances are performed at **ALCAUDETE DE LA JARA**, to mark the feast of Candlemass on February 2. **VILLAREJO DE MONTALBAN** in the W boasts a Roman bridge, a medieval castle and the site of a prehistoric settlement. There is another castle at **HONTANAR**, the 12C fortress of Malmoneda, as well as a 16C church. One of the traditions of this village is its annual festive and religious procession on the third Sunday in May which meets up with a similar exodus from the neighbouring *pueblo* of **NAVAHERMOSA** at a typical country *romería*, a picnic-cum-religious ceremony called the **Romería de la Milagra**. The joint *romería* is unusual for towns are normally jealous about these events and each stages its own, disparaging the rival one of the neighbouring village. The *fiesta* called La Encamisada on February 1 in the village of **MENASALBAS** is another one with long traditions behind it. The best-equipped *pueblo* in the whole Montes de Toledo area is **LAS VENTAS CON PEÑA AGUILERA**, a favourite meeting place for huntsmen not least because it has an excellent store selling shooting equipment called **A. Gutiérrez Serrano** , c/ Arroyo 9, which includes an extensive range of leather boots, chaps, bags and belts. The

Hostal Joaquín, c/ Victoria, 45 ☎ 41 80 23 $$ specializes, as you would expect, in game dishes.

ORGAZ, 34km from Toledo, is notable for its **castle** and its Baroque church and **LOS YEBENES**, much like Las Ventas, is a *rendez-vous* for some of the best guns in Spain. The local equipment store here is *M. Sánchez Garrido*, Pl del Caudillo, s/n.

PASTRANA **Guadalajara** ☎ (911), pop. 1,303. Guadalajara 47km, Madrid 105km.

This historic and extremely unspoilt and agreeable village is linked to the one-eyed **Princess of Eboli**, one of the most fascinating celebrities at the court of Philip II. This intriguing, ambitious lady, who loved and lived to the hilt, ended her days under house arrest in the austere palace, the **Palacio de los Duques de Pastrana** which occupies a whole façade of the village square.

¶ *Hostería Princesa de Eboli* (closed: weekend evenings), c/ Monjas, s/n $$. Home cooking.

Cultural highlights: The **Colegiata**, the 16C collegiate church (open: 1.00-2.30 and 3.30-6.00), has an absolute treasure in its collection of four large **tapestries** that were woven in Brussels between 1471 and 1476 to celebrate the exploits in N Africa of King Alfonso V of Portugal. The craftsmanship is outstanding and the Flemish vision of a campaign against the Moors is touchingly amusing.

Local sights: A nearby network of reservoirs, flooding the deep gorges of Guadalajara's sierras, has created an inland sea that has come to be known as the *Mar de Castilla*. The main reservoirs are those of **Bolarque**, **Entrepeñas** and **Buendía**, which are used for water sports and fishing. It is a very **scenic** area and has become popular as a summer resort.

SAN LORENZO DE EL ESCORIAL **Madrid** ☎ (91), pop. 6,153, [i] c/ Floridablanca, 10 ☎ 890 15 54. Segovia 50km, Madrid 55km, Avila 65km.

Overshadowed by the **Real Monasterio de El Escorial** that Philip II built, San Lorenzo is the little satellite town that grew up around the huge royal edifice. The monastery-palace is one of Spain's major tourist draws. Philip II had it raised on a grand scale, intending it to symbolize the scope, solidity and eternity of his empire. He achieved his objective. To understand what Spain was all about in its 16C Golden Age, you have to visit this enormous, brooding building that was the powerhouse of Philip's might. The town, lying in the cool of the Guadarrama Sierra, is a very popular weekend and summer resort.

▦ ★★★★ *Victoria Palace*, c/ Juan de Toledo, 4 ☎ 890 15 11 ▭ 87 ✕ ￥ ⊤⊽ ✦ ♨ ⇌ AE, DC, MC, V $$$ to $$$$. Very close to the monastery.

▦ ★★ *Miranda Suizo*, c/ Floridablanca, 20 ☎ 890 47 11 ▭ 47 ✦ AE, DC, V $$. A classic.

¶ *Charolés*, c/ Floridablanca, 24 ☎ 890 59 75 ✦ ✳ AE, DC, MC, V $$$ to $$$$. Aimed at the gourmet.

¶ *Mesón la Cueva*, c/ San Antón, 4 ☎ 890 15 16 AE, DC, EC, V $$ to $$$. An old staging post tavern serving straight Spanish food.

Cultural highlights: The **Monasterio de San Lorenzo del Escorial** (open: 10.00-1.30 and 3.30-6.00; closed: Mondays ☎ 890 59 03) is immediately striking in its proportions: the official guides who take visitors round it reel off figures about its 1,200 doors and 2,600 windows. It is arresting, also, in its use of the granite stone from the Guadarrama mountains —the monastery looks as indestructible as the surrounding mountain range. Astonishingly, it was built in just 25 years (1563-1584). Philip wanted it to serve as a pantheon for his father, the Emperor Charles V, and he also wanted to offer thanksgiving for the Spanish conquest of the French town of Saint Quentin in 1557. The battle was fought on Saint Lawrence's day and it so happened that Philip's troops destroyed a church dedicated to the saint when they took the town. The king accordingly had the monastery dedicated to Saint Lawrence, *San Lorenzo*, and had it specifically built on a pattern of interlinking courtyards and patios that makes it look, from the air, like the grid-iron on which Saint Lawrence was martyred. The design was entrusted to **Juan de Herrera** who perfectly captured Philip's sombre, austere and yet grandiose character, and its impact was so great that the Herrera style of building was reproduced everywhere in Spain, providing a counterpoint to the bounce and extravagance of the Baroque period.

The **Basilica** is entered across the massive courtyard called the **Patio de los Reyes** and its façade is adorned with sculptures of Spain's royalty. Built on the original plan of Saint Peter's in Rome, the church is extremely impressive in its richness: the bare walls of the interior contrast with the Baroque frescoes of the vaults, painted by **Luca Giordano** and Lucas Cambiaso. The **altarpiece**, designed by Herrera, is the natural focal point. Its gilded bronze figures were carved by the brothers León and Pompeo Leoni and the paintings by Zuccaro and Tibaldi. It is flanked by the kneeling groups of Charles V's family and of Philip II's (Philip is accompanied by three of his four wives, Mary Tudor being the absent one) which were also created by the Leoni brothers.

From the church you enter the **Royal Pantheon**, an octagonal chamber of black marble and gold trimming which is directly underneath the Basilica's high altar. This main chamber has the remains of virtually all the Spanish kings from Charles V's day in caskets set in niches around the sides and it leads to other chambers where queens and princes are buried. The effect leads to comparisons with the burial chamber of a pyramid. Returning to the Patio de los Reyes, you can visit the monastery's magnificent **Chapter Houses** and the imposing **Library**, which has codices, illustrated manuscripts and other treasures in its display cases and wonderful frescoes by Pellegrino Tibaldi on the ceilings depicting Grammar, Dialectic, Arithmetic, Music and other liberal arts of the 16C.

Walk round the monastery to enter the **Palace** part of it on the N side. Guides here take parties round the chambers that were built by the Bourbon kings, Charles III and Charles IV, and to the more interesting section containing the **Royal Apartments** used by **Philip II** and his daughter Isabel Clara Eugenia. Philip's chambers are extremely small and austere considering the size both of the edifice and of his empire. The tour carries on into a basement area called the **Nuevos Museos** which serve to exhibit the Monastery's **Art Collection**. The star of the show here is El Greco but the Italians Titian, Tintoretto, Veronese and others are well represented as are the Spaniards Velázquez, Zurbarán and Alonso Cano. Part of the museum, the **Museo de la Arquitectura**, traces the process of the building of the monastery.

The final part of the tour takes in the monastery's gardens and outbuildings. The latter include pavilions built by Villanueva in Charles III's reign, such as the delightful **Casita del Principe** which was used by the future Charles IV.

Fiestas and festivals: A **Baroque and Rococo Music Festival** is held in summer ☎ 890 15 54.

Local sights: For a Philip II eye **view** of the monastery take the road to El Robledo, crossing to the other side of the valley, and clamber up to what is called **La Silla de Felipe II** (the path is well marked). Here the monarch had a seat carved out for himself among the rocks from where he watched the progress of his monumental project. Just 4km away is the **Casita de Arriba**, a little summer house built by Villanueva in the 18C for Prince Gabriel, brother of Charles IV.

For more monumentalism take the road to Guadarrama and turn off into the **Valle de los Caídos**, the Valley of the Fallen, where a 125m high **cross**, visible for miles around, stands atop a craggy peak that has had a 262m basilica tunelled into its granite. This is the monument commemorating the 1936-1939 Spanish Civil War and the burial place of General Franco who ordered it built by prisoners of the defeated Republican band. The place evokes all sorts of emotions among different people but its setting is indisputably beautiful (open: 10.00-6.00 ☎ 890 56 11).

On the town: *Crochet*, c/ Floridablanca, 24, is the 'in' place to meet for drinks.

Sports: Golfers can play at the 18-hole, par 72 course in the shadow of the monastery at the *Herrería Club de Golf*, Ctra de Robledo ☎ 890 51 11.

SAN MARTIN DE VALDEIGLESIAS Madrid ☎ (91), pop. 5,040. Avila 58km, Madrid 73km, Toledo 81km.

This is a very agreeable little town in the lush valley of the Alberche river. El Escorial builder Juan de Herrera designed its parish church, dedicated to Saint Martin, and the castle was owned by the 15C strongman Alvaro de Luna and served as a refuge for Isabella the Catholic in the civil war that followed her proclamation as Queen of Castile.

¶ *Los Arcos* (closed: November), Pl Generalísimo, 1 ☎ 861 04 34 ✦ ❊ **AE, DC, EC, V** $$$ to $$$$. Regional cooking.

Local sights: The nearby reservoirs called the **Pantano de San Juan** and the **Embalse de Burguillo** are well equipped for watersports and are popular summer resort areas. Taking the Avila road for 16km you reach the extremely old and totally mysterious stone sculptures known as the **Toros de Guisando**, although they look more like hippopotami than bulls. They have been standing in their field for thousands of years and there are several conflicting theories as to who put them there (see also 'Gredos, Sierra of').

SIGUENZA Guadalajara ☎ (911), pop. 5,266, [i] c/ Obispo Don Bernardo, s/n ☎ 39 08 50, ⬛ 39 14 94. Guadalajara 85km, Madrid 121km.

This is an extremely pleasant cathedral and castle town that has been a stopping point on the road to Zaragoza and to Barcelona since Roman times and has mercifully preserved its medieval charm by standing back from the modern day N-II highway. It was richly endowed by its long line of bishops, among them the illustrious and powerful Cardinal Mendoza in the Middle Ages (see 'Guadalajara' and 'Toledo'). Conquered in 713 by the Muslims, Sigüenza was retaken by the Christians in 1124.

▦ ★★★★ *Parador Castillo de Sigüenza*, Pl del Castillo, s/n ☎ 39 01 00 ⬅ 77 ✕ ☿ ⬥ ⬥ **AE, DC, EC, MC, V** $$$$. Quiet, luxurious and historic, with a good restaurant.

▦ ★★ *El Motor*, Ctra de Madrid, 2 ☎ 39 08 27 ⬅ 10 ☿ ✕ **P MC, V** $$. In the agreeable setting of an old, restored house, with a homely restaurant serving Castilian fare.

¶ *El Moderno* (closed: 6/6-9/7 and Sundays except in summer), c/ General Mola, 1 ☎ 39 00 01 ❊ $$ to $$$. Home cooking.

Best buys: Hand-crafted carpets are sold at *Aurita*, km12 on the Madrid road, and leather wineskins are good buys at *J. Blasco*, c/ Cruz Dorada, s/n.

Cultural highlights: Unlike so many of the cathedrals you come across in
🐚🐚 Spain, Sigüenza's **Cathedral** is uncluttered by surrounding buildings and
allows you to admire it in its entirety and make sense of its proportions. Built
between the 12C and the 15C, its twin W towers give it a sturdy, castle-like
air. **Inside** there are several eye-catching features such as the 15C tomb of
Cardinal Carrillo de Albornoz on the S side of the main altar, the alabaster
pulpits, the flamboyant Gothic choir stalls which were donated to the
cathedral by Cardinal Mendoza after he had been elevated to the
archbishopric of Toledo, and the work by the masterful Renaissance
stonemason Alonso de Covarrubias in the Plateresque **altarpiece** on the N
🐚🐚 transept that is dedicated to Sigüenza's patron Saint Librada. But the show is
utterly stolen by the 15C tomb of Martín Vázquez de Arce who was killed in
action aged 25 in 1486 during the long campaign to take Granada. The
🐚🐚 young knight is universally, although incorrectly, known as the ***Doncel de
Sigüenza***, or pageboy, because of his haircut and boyish looks. His attitude
of unconcern as he lies reclining and relaxed is extraordinarily contemporary
and intensely moving. The exhibits in the **Diocesan Museum** (open:
11.30-2.00 and 5.00-7.30; Sundays: 4.00-6.00 ☎ 39 14 40) include a
sculptural group attributed to Pompeo Leoni, an *Annunciation* by El Greco
and canvases by Zurbarán and Morales. Sigüenza is a delightful little town to
stroll around in. It has a fair crop of Romanesque churches, an appealing
porticoed Plaza Mayor, a fine 16C **Town Hall**, a stately 15C mansion called
the **Casa del Doncel** in the Jewish quarter and, looming over it all, a castle
built by the Moors, now excellently restored to serve as a parador.
Local sights: The village of **ATIENZA** has everything you would expect from
a medieval stronghold: a castle protecting it, stout walls surrounding it,
gateways into it and old churches and plazas inside it. To cap it all there is a
lingering memory of El Cid, the Christian superman of the reconquest saga,
who took the village from the Muslims. On Pentecost Sunday the village
horsemen parade around on their steeds during the ***Caballada***, a *fiesta* that
commemorates their ancestors who rode out to rescue Alfonso VII in 1162
when he had fallen captive to the Moors. The *Fonda Molinero*, c/ Héctor
Vázquez, 11 ☎ 39 90 17 $$, serves unfussy food.

TALAVERA DE LA REINA **Toledo** ☎ (925), pop. 66,659, ✚ 80 32 29, **P**
80 00 37, 🚌 80 13 88. Toledo 75km, Madrid 113km.
   Now a prosperous, and pretty ugly, industrial town, its name is the
trademark for a highly successful and centuries-old **ceramics** industry.
   🏨 ★★★ ***Beatriz***, Av Madrid, 1 ☎ 80 76 00 🛏 161 TV P ✦ 🍴 AE, MC, V
   $$$. Its restaurant, the ***Anticuario*** ($$$), serves seasonal cuisine.
   🍴 *El Arcipreste*, c/ Banderas de Castilla, 14 ☎ 80 40 92 ✳ V $$$. A
   Castilian inn.
Best buys: Ceramics are sold at ***Artesanía Talavera***, Av Portugal, 32,
🐚 hand-made saddles at *L. Vázquez*, and hand-made shoes at ***Mazuecos***,
opposite the Town Hall.
Cultural highlights: The chapel known as the **Ermita de la Virgen del
Prado**, standing in a park at the entrance to the town from the Madrid end, is
a perfect place for appreciating Talavera ceramics in their natural state. The
yellow-based geometrical ones in the sacristy date from the 14-15C and the
blue-based ones on the portico and interior walls from the 16-18C. The
Museo de Cerámica Ruiz de Luna (☎ 80 01 49) has a very complete
collection that traces the development of the town's ceramics industry. The
14-15C collegiate church, the Colegiata de Santa María, is Gothic.
Fiestas: Traditional celebrations known as *Las Mondas* are held on Easter
Tuesday.

Local sights: Continuing W along the N-V for 32km, you reach the town of **OROPESA** which has a fine 16-17C parish church that was built to plans by Juan de Herrera and has a fine Plateresque W door. The town's showpiece is its **castle**, now a parador, the **★★★★ *Parador Virrey de Toledo***, Pl del Palacio, 1 ☎ 43 00 00 ⬌ 44 ✕ ⵦ ✦ ⬥ ⅋ ≪ AE, DC, EC, MC, V $$$$. The views from the castle-parador's battlements, looking out over the plain towards the distant peaks of the Gredos mountain range, are very good indeed.

Just 4km on from Oropesa, the village of **LAGARTERA** maintains a charming **embroidery** tradition that has a well established reputation throughout Spain —you can appreciate it at ***Pepa Alia Chico***, c/ Ramón y Cajal, 10. The village of **PUENTE DEL ARZOBISPO**, 34km SW of Talavera, produces excellent traditional **ceramics**, less well known than Talavera's but nowadays unquestionably more genuine. Potteries and showrooms include ***F. Fernández Robles***, Av Generalísimo, 140, and ***G. de la Cal***, c/ Comandante Castejón, 15 ☎ 43 61 57.

On the town: *Green's*, in the *Beatriz* hotel, is the fashionable disco.

TOLEDO Toledo ☎ (925), pop. 62,831, *i* Pl de Zocodover, 11 ☎ 22 14 00, *i* Puerta de Bisagra ☎ 22 08 43, ☏ c/ de la Plata, 18, ✉ c/ de la Plata, 1 ☎ 22 20 00, ✛ 22 29 00, P 22 34 07, 🚍 Ctra Circunvalación, s/n ☎ 21 58 50, 🚂 Paseo de la Rosa, s/n ☎ 22 12 72. Madrid 70km, Ciudad Real 120km, Avila 137km.

Of all Spain's historic cities Toledo is the most visited, the most written about and the most painted. Nobody forgets his first impression of the city, compact on its hill, old, fortress-like and full of churches, closed in on itself and girded by the River Tagus. It would take a lifetime of subsequent stays within Toledo's walls to unravel its treasures and its secrets. Virtually all that is truly grand about Spain lies within Toledo. Most important of all, here the three great cultures that intertwine in the fabric of the Spanish heritage, the Hebrew, the Arab and the Christian, mingled and enriched each other. Toledo had Spain's largest Jewish population, it was a Visigothic and a Muslim capital, it was home to Spain's most learned king, **Alfonso X, the Wise**, and to its most European one, **Charles V**, the Holy Roman Emperor. Symbols of Toledo's cross culture are the Mudéjar sensibility which developed in the city into a genuine art form and the **School of Translators**, established in Toledo by the wise Alfonso X, which brought together the brightest and best of the three cultures. It is fitting that Toledo's painter should have been a wandering Cretan, Domenico Theotocopouli, better known as **El Greco**. This strange man of the Byzantine, Mediterranean world arrived in Toledo in 1577. He found in the city the perfect complement to his mystical vision of humanity and he remained in it until his death in 1614.

Titus Livy makes the earliest references to *Toletum*, a Roman town that was to be the capital of the province of *Carpetania*. In 554 the Visigoths had established a royal court in the city and Hispano-Romans, Goths and Jews apparently lived peacefully together. Toledo was also set to become the religious powerhouse of Spain for it was here that the Visigothic chieftain Recared became a Christian. The arrival of the Moors in 712 did little to alter the tolerant atmosphere and much the same occurred when Alfonso VI finally recaptured the city for the Christians in 1085. Toledo now became the capital of the kingdom of León and Castile and here Alfonso VII, the conqueror's son, had himself crowned Emperor of Spain and King of both the Christian and the Muslim religions. The period that followed, especially the 13C reigns of Ferdinand III, the Saint, and his son Alfonso X, the Wise, was Toledo's Golden Age.

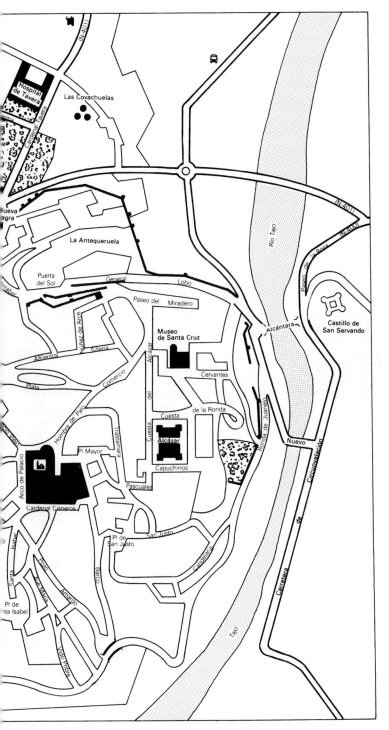

The Reconquest saga had by this time penetrated as far S as Córdoba and Seville, and Toledo was the big Castilian city in the rearguard, a hive of officialdom, commerce, religious decisions and cultural activity. By virtue of the see of Toledo, the most powerful archbishopric in the land, the city always had political clout. The **Catholic Monarchs**, whose court was a wandering one that constantly criss-crossed Spain, were frequent visitors to the city and ensured that their trusted officials held all its influential positions. When their grandson, **Charles V**, arrived from the Netherlands to claim the throne of Spain he made Toledo his permanent capital although he too was constantly on the move and spent most of his time politicking and fighting throughout Europe. From Charles, Toledo gained its emblem of the double-headed Hapsburg eagle and more power than ever before as artisans and merchants of every kind poured into the city.

The subsequent reign of Philip II stopped Toledo's development in its tracks for the monarch, who apparently disliked the pretensions of the city's clergy, made Madrid his capital and El Escorial his home. Toledo remains to this day a city frozen in the 16-17C. What is immediately striking is the harmony and unity of the place and this is best appreciated by seeing it from the other side of the River Tagus as El Greco did when he painted it. Once in the city you soon lose yourself among the narrow streets and you rapidly become aware that you are in a **living museum** and walking back through history —indeed UNESCO has declared it part of the **Heritage of Mankind**.

Two fairly obvious pieces of advice to first time visitors. Try to avoid the day trip and spend at least one night in the city for Toledo deserves to be savoured leisurely. If you can visit it during the week you will avoid the crowds. Secondly, wear sensible shoes. A lot of Toledo is pedestrian only and, in any case, you would be tempting fate if you tried to drive through it. Toledo demands a considerable amount of walking and it can be tiring: the city has steep little hills and sharp little cobblestones.

🖭 ▦ ★★★★ *Parador Conde de Orgaz*, Cerro del Emperador ☎ 22 18 50 🛏 77 ✕ ⅋ TV ✦ 🎤 ⅏ ⚓ ≪ AE, DC, MC, V $$$$$. A beautifully situated hotel in the local architectural style with unbeatable views of Toledo. The restaurant serves good local fare.

▦ ★★★ *Alfonso VI*, c/ General Moscardó, 2 ☎ 22 26 00 🛏 88 ⅋ TV 🎤 AE, DC, EC, MC, V $$$.

▦ ★★★ *Cardenal*, Paseo de Recaredo, 24 ☎ 22 49 00 🛏 27 ✕ ⅋ ✦ ⅏ ≪ AE, DC $$$. This quiet hotel, in a 17C palace with a tree-shaded garden, has a good **restaurant** ($$$) serving Spanish cooking and with an outside terrace in summer.

▦ ★★★ *Carlos V*, Pl Horno Magdalena, 1 ☎ 22 21 00 🛏 55 ✕ ⅋ AE, DC, EC, V $$ to $$$. Family atmosphere.

🖭 ▦ ★★★ *María Cristina*, c/ Marqués de Mendigorría, 1 ☎ 21 32 02 🛏 43 ✕ ⅋ TV ⅏ AE, DC, EC, MC, V $$$. In the old Hospital of San Lázaro, it has a very good restaurant, *El Abside*, set in a Mudéjar apse.

▦ ★★ *La Almazara* (closed: 3/11-14/3), km3.4 on the road to Cuerva ☎ 22 38 66 🛏 21 ⅋ P ⅏ EC, V $$.

🍴 *Asador Adolfo*, c/ La Granada, 6 ☎ 22 73 21 ✳ AE, DC, MC, V $$$. In a 14C house with a beautiful coffered ceiling.

🖭 🍴 *El Abside*, c/ Marqués de Mendigorría, 1 ☎ 21 26 50 ✳ AE, DC, EC, MC, V $$$ to $$$$. Arabic and Jewish food in the restaurant of the *María Cristina* hotel.

🍴 *Hierbabuena* (closed: Sunday nights), c/ Cristo de la Luz, 9 ☎ 22 34 63 ✦ ✳ AE, EC, MC, V $$$. Elegant and romantic.

🍴 *La Botica*, Pl de Zocodover, 13 ☎ 22 55 57 ✦ ✳ AE, DC, MC, V $$$ to $$$$. Regional food with original touches.

¶ *Venta de Aires*, c/ Circo Romano, 35 ☎ 22 05 45 ♣ ✳ AE, DC, EC, MC, V \$\$\$. A typical Toledan inn dating from the 19C, with a spacious, tree-shaded terrace.

Best buys: Typical craftsman-made traditional Toledo weapons are sold at the ***Real Fábrica de Armas***, c/ Núñez de Arce, s/n, and at *Fábrica Garrido*, near the bullring, where other crafts typical of Toledo are also sold.

Embroidery and lace from Lagartera and nearby places can be bought at the *Tienda de Artesanía Española*, opposite El Greco's house, while locally made marzipan is sold at ***Santo Tomé***, c/ Santo Tomé, 5 and Pl de Zocodover, 11, and ***Casa Telésforo***, Pl de Zocodover, 17.

Cultural highlights: Toledo's **walls** have been kept up since Roman times with the Visigoths and the Arabs adding to them to protect the city. The most 'modern' of the nine gateways into the city is the one called the **Puerta Nueva de Bisagra**, erected by Alonso de Covarrubias in 1550 in honour of Charles V. This gate is a good example of Renaissance military architecture and underlines the awe with which the city viewed its emperor. The older gate, the **Puerta Vieja de Bisagra**, is in the Mudéjar style and was the one used by Alfonso VI when he entered the city in 1085. The most beautiful one is the **Puerta del Sol** which is also Mudéjar in origin, though rebuilt in the 14C.

The city's focal point is the **Cathedral** (open: 10.30-1.00; Sundays: 11.00-1.30 and 3.30-6.00 ☎ 22 22 41). The first stone was laid in 1226 and Enrique Egas and Juan Guas were among the master builders employed on the project. It was essentially completed by 1492, that action-packed year in Spain's history when Granada was conquered, Columbus reached the New World and the Jewish population was expelled. Mudéjar elements are clearly present in the basic Gothic structure and outline of the building and later the Baroque and even the Neoclassical tastes left their mark. It is difficult to fully appreciate the size of the Cathedral from the oustide (it has the longest nave in Spain after the one in Seville's cathedral) for it is cluttered by the narrow streets and tightly packed buildings around it. The best door is the flamboyant Gothic S portal called the **Puerta de los Leones**, and the oldest is the N, originally 13C **Puerta del Reloj**. The tower, built in the 14C, is as impressive as you could wish for and towers majestically over the city. You enter the Cathedral by a side door, which also gives onto the sober Gothic **cloister**, and suddenly you are within gloom and grandeur, beneath massive vaulting and peering into the distance trying to get your bearings. You should make your way to the **chancel** which is almost nose to nose with the choir, a placement which lets you know just how important the cathedral's clergy and canons are. Philippe de Vigarni and Juan de Borgoña, or John of Burgundy, employed their skills on the magnificent flamboyant **altarpiece** just as they did in Burgos, Valladolid and elsewhere and the huge Renaissance **grille** is by Francisco de Villalpando. On the S side of the altar you will find the great **sepulchre** of the all-powerful Cardinal Mendoza, the mentor of the Catholic Monarchs, who died in 1495, and on the opposite side there are the tombs of a number of medieval kings including that of Alfonso VII. The 15C **choir** which faces the altar is exceptional for its **stalls** which were brilliantly sculpted by Rodrigo Alemán to show a blow by blow account of the 1483-1492 campaign that culminated in the conquest of Granada. If you now walk round to the back of the high altar you come to the amazing Baroque showpiece of the Cathedral known as the **Transparente**. The effect of the light, colour and exuberance of this Rococo masterpiece put together by Narciso Tomé in 1732 is all the more staggering since you are coming from the Gothic tenebrae of the long aisles. Among the 22 side chapels, the most outstanding are the **Mozarabic Chapel**, which can be visited during the

Mozarabic mass celebrated on Sunday mornings, the 15C **Chapel of San Ildefonso**, with fascinating noble tombs, and the **Chapel of Santiago**. As you would expect in a Cathedral of this size and history, the dependencies are well worth visiting. The **Chapter House**, or *Sala Capitular*, has a magnificent Mudéjar **coffered ceiling** and the **Sacristy** has an **art collection** —which includes a memorable *Expolio* by El Greco, one of his real masterpieces— that is worthy of the finest museum in the world. Pride of place among the liturgical ornaments in the Cathedral's collection, the **Tesoro**, goes to the processional **monstrance** which is wheeled out on the feast of Corpus Christi.

The 15C **Church of San Juan de los Reyes** is Toledo's second most important religious building and is probably the most architecturally pleasing. Certainly it is the greatest of Juan Guas' creations and he quite properly put all his energies into it for it was intended to be the pantheon of the Catholic Monarchs (they were eventually buried in Granada cathedral instead). Guas concentrated here on **filigree stone work**, the Plateresque trademark, that creates in this large building an effect of extraordinary lightness and grace. The church's **cloister** (open: 10.00-1.45 and 3.30-6.00) is stunningly lovely. Very near to the church are Toledo's two **synagogues**, the one called **El Tránsito** (open: 10.00-2.00 and 4.00-6.00; closed: Sunday afternoons and Mondays) and the synagogue of **Santa María la Blanca** (open: 10.00-2.00 and 3.30-6.00). Fortunately these twin, but very different, showpieces of Toledo's medieval Jewish legacy survived later periods of intolerance to become key monuments on the city's artistic itinerary.

The spirit of **El Greco** permeates all of Toledo but you can recreate his life and times by visiting what is called the **Casa del Greco** (open: 10.00-2.00 and 4.00-6.00; closed: Sunday afternoons and Mondays ☎ 22 40 46). He never lived in this restored 16C building but the one he did inhabit must have been very like it, had more or less the same furniture and comforts and was in the same area. To realize what El Greco was fully about, to get close to his very personal ideas about man and divinity, you must visit the Mudéjar **Church of Santo Tomé** (open: 10.00-1.45 and 3.30-6.00), which is where one of the master's greatest works hangs, the vast canvas called *The Burial of the Count of Orgaz*.

The highlights of a tour of Toledo are really very numerous. They must certainly include the former charitable institution called the **Hospital de Tavera** (open: 10.30-1.30 and 3.30-6.00) which was founded by Cardinal Juan de Tavera in the 16C. The building, which is at the entrance to Toledo on the Madrid road and outside the city walls, is now a **museum** housing works by El Greco, Zurbarán and Ribera and, of course, the founder's **tomb**, an impressive alabaster sepulchre sculpted by no less an artist than Alonso Berruguete. The city's two old **bridges** over the River Tagus, the 13C **Alcántara bridge** and the 14C **San Martín bridge**, deserve special mention if only because until quite recently they carried a full flow of heavy traffic. Down by the river bank, below the San Martín bridge, the chapel called the **Ermita del Cristo de la Vega** has a lovely Mudéjar apse that survived an 18C reconstruction and a famous crucifixion beside its altar whose Christ has one arm loosened from the cross. Tradition has it that the arm came loose when a young girl dragged her errant boyfriend who had decided not to marry her before the same crucifix. The pair were so dumbstruck by the miracle that she became a nun and he a priest.

A short list of the scores of churches and convents of Toledo must include the 12C **Santiago del Arrabal**, in the Toledo Mudéjar style; **San Clemente el Real**, which has a very good Plateresque façade by Covarrubias; **Santo Domingo El Antiguo**, which was possibly founded by

Alfonso VI and has three El Greco canvases; **Santa Eulalia**, dating from pre-Muslim days, with Visigothic capitals and later Moorish columns; **San Román**, a very good example of the Mudéjar style in Toledo, with **Romanesque paintings** and Moorish columns topped with Visigothic, Mozarabic and Byzantine capitals (open: 10.00-2.00 and 4.00-7.00; closed: Sunday afternoons and Mondays) and the very beautiful **Mezquita del Cristo de la Luz**, a 10C mosque which became a Christian place of worship in the 12C.

Toledo's main square, the **Pl de Zocodover**, was designed by Juan de Herrera, the builder of El Escorial, and is the usually bustling centre point of a provincial town's activity although it is in fact on the edge of the city. The **Alcázar**, the great big fortress that together with the cathedral's spire looms over Toledo, is nearby and a visit to it ranks high on every city itinerary. The building dates from the very early days of Alfonso VI's conquest but it was knocked down and rebuilt on a variety of occasions such as during the War of Spanish Succession, the Peninsular War and, most recently, the 1936-1939 Spanish Civil War. Between July and September 1936 the Alcázar was held by General Franco's supporters who endured constant shelling from besieging Republican forces until they were eventually relieved by Francoist troops. The commandant of the fortress went down in history when he refused to surrender in exchange for the life of his son who had been captured by the attacking forces. The commandant's office, riddled with shrapnel, remains exactly as it was during the siege and the telephone conversation between the father and the captive son is printed up in several languages on the walls.

Near the Alcázar stands the noble Plateresque building called the **Hospital de Santa Cruz**, a former charity home which was designed by Enrique Egas and endowed by Cardinal Mendoza. The **patio** is one of the building's best features and looking on to it nowadays are the **Museo de Bellas Artes**, which has no fewer than 22 El Grecos in its collection, and the archaeology and folk museums, the **Museo Provincial de Arqueología** and the **Museo de Artes Aplicadas y Populares**, c/ Miguel de Cervantes, 3 (open: 10.00-6.00; Sundays: 10.00-2.00; closed: Mondays ☎ 22 14 02). For Mudéjar art you shoud visit the *Taller del Moro* which houses the **Museo Mudéjar**, c/ Taller del Moro, 4 (open: 10.00-2.00 and 4.00-7.00; closed: Sunday afternoons and Mondays ☎ 22 71 15). In the **Palacio de los Condes de Fuensalida**, which is close to Santo Tomé Church with its massive El Greco canvas, you can visit the private apartments used by Charles V and his family. The 16C palace is now a government building.

Fiestas and festivals: **Corpus Christi** is celebrated with a famous procession through streets carpeted with flowers and aromatic herbs, bullfights, open-air concerts and so on which last throughout the week. The outstanding Holy Week event is the procession known as the *Procesión del Silencio*. A music festival, the *Semana de Música*, takes place in October.

Local sights: Taking the C-502, after 33km you will reach the pleasant village of **LA PUEBLA DE MONTALBAN**, which has a picturesque Plaza Mayor. Heading S for 14km you will come across a very impressive Templar castle built in the 12C. An earlier turn-off leads to the lovely 9C Mozarabic Church of Santa María de Melque whose horseshoe arches have, more or less, stood the test of time. If you leave Toledo on the C-401 to Navahermosa, after 15km you will reach the dreamlike Gothic 15C **castle** of **GUADAMUR**. What makes this castle special is that it is not only fit for human habitation (most of the castles in Spain are not) but that it also has magnificent genuinely old Spanish furniture (again something you find less often than you would expect).

For more castles you can leave Toledo on the N-403 and head for **TORRIJOS**, 27km, and continue to see a second fortress 12km further on at **MAQUEDA**. From here you can press on for yet another **castle** at **ESCALONA**, a village which is set in gorgeous countryside by the Alberche river and which boasts a pretty Plaza Mayor and a 16C Franciscan convent. For a really picturesque **Plaza Mayor** you should drive to **TEMBLEQUE** (57km from Toledo taking first the C-400 to Mora and then turning off on the C-402). Finally, returning to Madrid on the N-401, **ILLESCAS**, at the halfway point, has five El Grecos in the former charitable institution called the Hospital de la Caridad and a parish church with a pleasing 14C Mudéjar tower.

On the town: The Pl de Zocodover is the focal point around which most of Toledo's bars, inns and cafés are concentrated. Nearby, you can sample excellent *tapas* in **Ludeña**, Pl de la Magdalena. The best discos are *Shiton's*, c/ Lucio, 4, and *Agualoca*, Ctra Polán, which is in the open-air in summer. *La Marina*, in the *María Cristina* hotel, is pleasant for a quiet late-night drink.

Sports: Hunting in organized parties for deer, wild boar and other smaller game and **fishing** (contact the office at Pl San Vicente, 6 ☎ 22 21 66 and 22 21 62 for further information) are the local sports.

VALDEPEÑAS Ciudad Real ☎ (926), pop. 25,154, *i* km199 on the N-IV ☎ 32 02 61, ✚ 32 02 61, P 32 28 04, ⇌ 32 34 50. Ciudad Real 59km, Jaén 135km, Madrid 203km.

Home of the prosperous Valdepeñas wine industry which produces millions of bottles of mostly light unpretentious and extremely drinkable red *vino*, the town used to belong, like most of the surrounding area, to the powerful medieval Military Order of Calatrava.

▥ ★★★ *Meliá El Hidalgo*, km194 on the N-IV ☎ 32 32 54 ⇌ 54 ✕ Ⴤ TV P ✦ ⬤ ♿ ⇌ ⚘ AE, DC, MC, V $$$. A quiet roadside motel.

Best buys: The town's best buys include local wine from, for example, *Viña Albali*, Ctra Madrid-Cádiz, 199, and *Luis Mejía*, c/ Salida del Peral, 1; Manchego cheese from *Quesería Hispano-Finlandesa*, km202 on the N-IV; and traditional confectionery from *La Flor de La Mancha* c/ Seis de Junio, 51.

Cultural highlights: The main square, called the Pl de España, is a pleasant porticoed affair flanked by the 15C **Church of la Asunción**, which has a Plateresque gallery, a 17C altarpiece and, its best feature, a fine tower. Real culture in a place like this, however, involves visiting the local **wineries** like the *Cooperativa La Invencible*, c/ Raimundo Caro-Patón, 102.

Local sights: Pushing on S along the N-IV highway to Andalusia you reach **MANZANARES**, 27km away, which is another important wine producing town. There is a castle here and a handy parador, the ★★★ *Parador de Manzanares*, km175 on the N-IV ☎ 61 04 00 ⇌ 50 ✕ Ⴤ P ✦ ⬤ ⚘ AE, DC, EC, V $$$, which is modern and comfortable and has a good restaurant and a swimming pool. There is alternative accommodation at the ★★★ *El Cruce*, km173 on the N-IV ☎ 61 19 00 ⇌ 37 ✕ Ⴤ P ✦ ⬤ ⚘ DC, V $$, which has also got a decent **restaurant**. Pressing on S for a further 14km you reach **SANTA CRUZ DE MUDELA** which is famed for having the oldest **bullring** still in use in Spain. It was built in 1641 and is in fact square so that 'bullring' is a misnomer. From here you can continue to **VISO DEL MARQUES**, where the Renaissance castle of Don Alvaro de Bazán, one of Spain's greatest admirals and the man who would have led the Spanish Armada had he not died just before it set off, houses the archives of the Spanish Navy. Returning to Valdepeñas and taking a local road you reach **SAN CARLOS DEL VALLE**, 22km away, which has a delightful 18C brick **Plaza Mayor** graced by a Baroque church.

NAVARRE
AND LA RIOJA

Navarre is an astonishingly varied part of Spain. You will be travelling through the most luxuriously verdant valleys deep down among the craggy overhangs of the Pyrenees. The ravines gradually bottom out and the pine forests give way to acres of vines and cornfields. You pass from imposing peaks to rolling hills and to farm land. Such is the variety of the vegetation that in a corner of the province, known as Las Bárdenas, there is even a mini desert. The essential bearings are that the N of Navarre is mountainous (the Pyrenees at this point reach a height of 2,504m) and that the S is flat and heavily cultivated. The diversity of the land is complemented by equally amazing contrasts in the region's varied traditions. The Pyrenean N is the home of strange ancestral dances and of hard, matured Roncal cheeses. The S is the wide valley of the Ebro river, known simply as La Ribera (the Valley), and here the cheeses, known as *cuajada*, are fresh and soft and are more like yoghurt and people dance the lively, high leaping *jota*. Life is hard on the barren mountains while in the Ribera flat lands, where fine wine is made and magnificent vegetables grown, the locals have made **eating well** into an art form.

You soon realize that although small, Navarre has a history all its own that is worthy of a continent. The Romans were fully stretched to subdue the local Vascons (the Basques and Gascons) who peopled Navarre, and Charlemagne, after his defeat at Roncesvalles (Roncevaux), thought it better to cut his losses and establish his imperial frontier at the point where it met this fiercely independent land. Nor were the Arabs able to set down roots in Navarre, and the region was able to maintain its own **kingdom** and to preserve its identity, with occasional help from French alliances, for a full 600 years. Attempted encroachments by the neighbouring states of Castile and Aragón were sturdily resisted. The creation of the modern, unified Spanish state is usually said to date from 1492 when Isabella and Ferdinand, the Catholic Monarchs, conquered Granada and expelled the Arabs. But, as the Navarrese like to point out, their homeland remained independent and separate from the rest of Spain until 1512. Even after Navarre formed part of the new Spanish nation state, it retained its local codes of law, its sacrosanct *Fueros*.

As you would expect, Navarre's rich history has left its imprint. The towns and villages are old and the region is dotted with palaces and mansions, cathedrals and monasteries. In Navarre there are many ways in which you can walk back through history but none is finer or more clearly marked than that great pilgrimage route to Santiago de Compostela, the **Way of Saint James**. From all over medieval Europe, pilgrims arrived in Navarre where their different routes converged to form one tidal wave of humanity making its way to the Apostle's great shrine in Galicia, in NW Spain. The pilgrim route enriched Navarre with **Romanesque churches** and chapels and with hospitals and inns for those who walked the Way. It is a magnificent religious, cultural and artistic legacy. It is also safe to assume that the singular phenomenon of the pilgrim route added openness and hospitality to strangers and visitors to the ancient Navarrese characteristics of tenacity and independence. Today's tourist magnet is the world famous festival of **San Fermín**, when bulls are set loose in the streets and for a few heady moments locals and foreigners alike taste the thrills of the bullring.

Bordering Navarre, and S of the Ebro river, lies **La Rioja**. If the name means anything to you it will bring to mind excellent red wine. But there is more to it than just that. It has a distinct personality of its own owing, in part, to the fact that it is a frontier zone and was disputed between the powerful kingdoms of Castile and Navarre. It is an area that is very much associated with the Way of Saint James which passes through it. A local man who came to be known as **Santo Domingo de la Calzada**, Saint Dominic of the Highway, was a charming medieval holy man who lived humbly in a hermitage and built a bridge on the route to Compostela to keep watch at night for pilgrims who had lost their way. You will learn more about him if you visit Santo Domingo de la Calzada, the town near which he lived and which took his name after he died. It is an area that also produced the first important literary figure writing in Castilian Spanish; it was the home of **Gonzalo de Berceo**. La Rioja is also varied: it is made up of the Rioja Alta (Upper Rioja), a wet upland zone where the terrain is more abrupt and whose **wine** is the best in the area, and the Rioja Baja (Lower Rioja), a rich fruit and vegetable growing area alongside the Ebro river. A third, well-defined zone in the interior, back from the river, is characterized by its fine mountains and lush valleys which produce the excellent fruit the locals are so expert at preserving. In inland Rioja, the old and the new live side by side: you will come across ancient buildings, very odd customs such as the **stilt walkers' dance**, which is the classic attraction of the medieval village of **ANGUIANO**, within easy reach of modern, well-equipped **ski stations** where you can spend a winter holiday.

ALSASUA **Navarre** ☎ (948), pop. 7,250. Vitoria 46km, Pamplona 50km, San Sebastián 71km, Madrid 402km.

Set among magnificent mountain landscape in the far NW of Navarre and surrounded by small Basque-speaking towns and villages, this is an important commercial crossroads.

■ ★★★ *Alaska*, Ctra N-I, km403, 6km from Alsasua ☎ 56 28 02 ⇨ 29 **P**
♦ ♪ ☞ ☜ DC, MC, V $$. A lovely garden with oak trees and a large lawn.

‖ *Oyarbide* (closed: Mondays and 15/9-30/9), Pl Fueros, 4 ☎ 56 23 74 $$$.

Best buys: Aralar and Urbasa cheeses.

● **Fiestas:** The local celebration is the traditional ***romería*** to San Pedro.
Local sights: The Sierra de Urbasa and Sierra de Aralar are interesting. As you approach Izurzun take the road leading to Echarri and Lecumberri. This route takes you through the splendid beech tree forest of the **Sierra de Aralar** and to a fascinating chapel, the shrine dedicated to **San Miguel in**
● **Excelsis** or Saint Michael in Heaven. Local legend has it that this same spot was the lair of what is known as an ***erensugue***, a frightful serpent beloved of Basque mythology and that it was dedicated to the Archangel Michael when the area was christianized. Another legend claims that a local knight called Teodoro de Goñi, doing penance in this very area, was attacked here by a dragon and saved by Saint Michael. What you have at this legend-steeped shrine is a Romanesque church with three naves containing a magnificent
● ● gilded and enamelled **altarpiece** believed to have been made in Limoges in the late 12C. It is well worth the detour to this dragon and serpent's lair to see this jewel of a medieval retable.

● **BAZTAN, VALLEY OF** **Navarre** ☎ (948), pop. 2,516. San Sebastián 34km, Pamplona 57km.

You reach this pastoral maize-growing and cattle-rearing valley by

574

following the Ctra N-121 N of Pamplona. The valley, along the upper reaches of the Bidasoa river, is dotted with scattered villages and lonely farmhouses called *caseríos* that are the typical Basque homestead. The main centre of population in this Brigadoon-like valley is **ELIZONDO** which has numerous noble stone houses with heraldic shields on their façades. They were built by the younger sons of the *caseríos* who went to Latin America to seek their fortunes, made a packet and returned home to live like country gentlemen.

🏨 ★★★ *Baztán*, Ctra N-121, km52 ☎ 58 00 50 ⊨ 84 ♣ ♨ ⚓ ≪ ♞ DC, MC, V $$$. A mountain resort hotel that offers organized tours of the valley and nearby areas.

🍴 *Santxotena*, c/ Pedro Axular, s/n ☎ 58 02 97 V $$$.

Local sights: If you have a penchant for old ladies flying on broomsticks read on and continue the trip. Driving up and past the green fields that clothe the mountainside towards Otsonso pass, you will reach the crossroads to **ZUGARRAMUNDI**, the centre of Navarre's highly documented witch-lore. On the outskirts of the village is the so-called *Cueva de Brujas* (Witches' Cave) where the Inquistion claimed a Black Sabbath was held every Friday. Down river, among the initial foothills of the western Pyrenees, you enter a district known as the **Cinco Villas**, or Five Towns, so called because they once formed a confederate alliance to defend their joint interests. They also share fine examples of popular architecture adapted to the local climate, with porches, hay lofts on the upper floor to avoid the damp and balconies specially built to dry out certain crops. In each of the five towns there are striking dovecotes and in one of them, **ECHALAR**, pigeon trapping with nets is a very popular pastime during an open season which lasts from 20/9-15/11. The other towns in the five-strong confederation are **ARANAZ**, **LESACA**, **VERA DE BIDASOA** and **YANCI** —*Hita*, Ctra Pamplona-Irún, km68 ☎ 63 78 02, is a good place to stop for lunch.

Heading S on Ctra C-133, you can visit a **botanical garden** created at the turn of the century by a romantic Navarrese horticulturalist in Oronoz Mugaire. It is called **El Señorío de Bértiz**, and is, in fact, a natural park to be explored on foot.

Sports: Salmon fishing on the Bidasoa river. Deer stalking in the Quinto Real game reserve.

CALAHORRA **La Rioja** ☎ (941), pop. 17,695. Logroño 55km, Zaragoza 128km, Madrid 320km.

Originally an Iberian settlement, Calahorra became a prosperous Roman city known as *Calagurris Nassica*. It was the birthplace of the rhetorician **Quintilian** and of the poet Prudentius. Pompey at one stage laid siege to it during his civil war against Sertorius and the city's desperately hungry population was forced to eat human flesh.

🏨 ★★★ *Parador Marco Fabio Quintiliano*, c/ Era Alta, s/n ☎ 13 03 58 ⊨ 63 🅿 ♨ AE, DC, MC, V $$$ to $$$$. This comfortable hotel has a restaurant serving typical Rioja cuisine.

🍴 *Casa Mateo* (closed: Sundays and September) c/ Quintiliano, 15 ☎ 13 00 09 $$. Good vegetable dishes.

🍴 *Chef Nino* (closed: Thursdays), c/ Basconia, 1 ☎ 13 20 29 AE $$$. Good fish.

🍴 *La Taberna de la Cuarta Esquina* (closed: Tuesdays and June), c/ Cuatro Esquinas, 16 ☎ 13 43 55 DC, MC, V $$$.

🍴 *Montserrat-2* (closed: Mondays), c/ Manuel de Falla, 7 ☎ 13 00 17 AE, DC, MC, V $$$. Seafood.

Best buys: Antiques from *A. Jiménez*, c/ Antonio Machado, 8.

Cultural highlights: The Gothic (13-15C) **Cathedral** has a façade that dates from the 18C. In the interior it has a magnificent sacristy, a choir, chapels, Renaissance wrought-iron grilles, and a Diocesan Museum which is only open on Sundays and on religious holidays. The 14C Gothic **Iglesia de San Andrés** (Church of Saint Andrew) in the town centre is worth visiting, as is the Carmelite Convent which has a magnificent crucifix by 16-17C sculptor Gregorio Fernández. The remains of the Roman walls and the 18C Episcopal Palace are also interesting.

Local sights: The town of **ARNEDO**, 20km to the SW, is the capital of the Rioja Baja. Visit the ruins of the Moorish castle, the **Gothic churches** of Santo Tomás and of Santa Eulalia and, out of the town and on the road to Prejano, the Monastery of Vico. **Best buys** in Vico include porcelain, in Arnedo, espadrilles and shoes.

- 🏨 ★★★ *Victoria*, c/ Constitución, 97, in Arnedo ☎ 38 01 00 🛏 48 ♣ 🎙 ⚭ ◵ DC, MC, V $$$. It has an interesting **restaurant**.
- 🍽 *Picabea*, c/ Virrey Lizana, 4, in Arnedo ☎ 38 13 58 **MC, V** $$.
- 🍽 *Sopitas* (closed: Sundays and 15/6-30/6), c/ Carrera, 4, in Arnedo ☎ 38 02 66 **AE, DC, MC, V** $$. Set in an old cellar, it serves good mushrooms and roast meats.

🌑 [ESTELLA] **Navarre** ☎ (948), pop. 13,086. Pamplona 41km, Vitoria 70km, Madrid 380km.

This charming, self-contained little town was the capital of the Kingdom of Navarre in the 12C and was the stronghold and capital of the Carlist faction during last century's civil wars. In the Middle Ages, it was an important stopping place along the **Way of Saint James** and as such has a number of inns and hospices, including San Lázaro, especially built for lepers.

- 🏨 ★★★ *Irache*, Ctra Logroño, km43, 3km from Estella in Ayegui ☎ 55 11 50 🛏 74 🅿 ⚭ ≪ ◵ **DC, EC** $$$. A nice place to relax and enjoy good views of the area.
- 🍽 *Navarra* (closed: Sunday nights except in July and August), c/ Gustavo de Maeztu, 16 (Los Llanos) ☎ 55 00 40 ♣ **V** $$. A pretty house in a pleasant garden. The roast meat is recommended.

Best buys: Leather wineskins from *La Estellica*, Paseo la Inmaculada, 44, and wood carvings from *C. Boneta*, c/ Rúa, 20.

Cultural highlights: Within the pilgrim, or Jacobean, quarter of the town is the 12-13C **Church of San Pedro de la Rúa**. Its **portal** contains Moorish 🌑 elements, its triple apse is Romanesque and it has a Baroque chapel which contains relics of Saint Andrew (13C). The church's best feature is its 🌑 Romanesque **cloister** which has magnificent capitals depicting biblical and mythological scenes.

The 14C **Iglesia del Santo Sepulcro** (Church of the Holy Sepulchre) on the street known as the Rúa, which was the main thoroughfare for pilgrims, has an interesting Gothic façade, but the **Church of San Miguel**, on the other side of the river Ega in a medieval quarter known as the *Navarrería*, is 🌑 architecturally more interesting. Its **façade** is a Romanesque masterpiece. Note, too, the depiction of the Pantocrator (All-powerful Christ) of the **tympanum**, the decoration of the **archivolts** and **capitals** and, above all, the 🌑🌑 splendid **high reliefs** on the lower part of the wall. In the **Pl de San Martín** stands a splendid and very rare example of Romanesque civic architecture: the **Palace of the Kings of Navarre**, built in the 12C by Sancho the Wise. The former **Town Hall** building, which has heraldic shields on its façade, stands on the same square.

Festivals: The **Estella Festival of Ancient Music** takes place in July.

🌑 **Local sights:** Three kilometres S is the **Monasterio de Irache**, a one-time Benedictine abbey that provided shelter for pilgrims in the 10C. Its 12-13C

church has a fine Romanesque apse and vault and a choir and cloister
dating from the Renaissance period. The main façade of the church and the
monastery buildings date from the 17C. The abbey stands at the foot of a
peak called **Montejurra** which is hallowed ground for the Carlist faction that
opposed the liberals during the 19C civil wars. Carlist supporters continue to
gather here on the first Sunday in May to commemorate a notable Carlist
victory in 1873.

In **LOS ARCOS**, 20km away on the N-111, the 16C **Iglesia de la
Asunción** has a beautiful Gothic cloister and a Baroque interior. Taking the
C-121, you reach **SORLADA**, the site of an outstanding Baroque building, the
18C **Basílica de San Gregorio Ostiense**. Every year, on May 9, crowds
gather here for a *romería*, a pilgrimage, country fair and communal picnic.
There are excellent views from here of the surrounding countryside. Returning
to Los Arcos and continuing along the N-111 for 7km, you will come to the
medieval village of **TORRES DEL RIO** where there is an early 13C Romanesque
church, the **Iglesia del Santo Sepulcro**, something of a curiosity with its
magnificent Mudéjar **dome** and a cylindrical tower.

A turn-off to the NW will take you to the **Santuario de Nuestra Señora
de Codés**, containing a 13C Gothic figure of the Virgin. This shrine is one of
the most venerated in all Navarre, which is saying a lot, for this is a very
religious area. Back on the N-111, head for **VIANA**, a walled town founded by
Sancho the Strong in the 13C. Its outstanding building is the 14-15C Gothic
Church of Santa María which has a Plateresque façade. For lunch or dinner,
try *Viana* (closed: Sundays), c/ S. Urra, 1 ☎ 64 57 81 **AE, DC, V $$$$**.

Back in Estella, head N on the N-111 to the **Monasterio de Iranzu**, a
12C Cistercian abbey which has been much restored but still preserves rustic
fan-vaulting in its church. The monastery is situated in an extraordinary **gorge**
which is one of the most stunning features of the Andía mountains.
Continuing up the road, you will come to the **Puerto de Lizarraga**, a
1,090m high mountain pass from which there are fabulous **views** of the lush
Ergoyena valley below.

FITERO **Navarre** ☎ (948), pop. 2,021. Soria 82km, Pamplona 93km,
Zaragoza 105km, Madrid 308km.

This historic town provides succour for soul and body: it has a Cistercian
monastery (celebrated by Spain's often gloomy Romantic poet, Gustavo
Adolfo Bécquer) and a spa for taking the waters.

🏨 ★ *Balneario Bécquer* (open: 1/5-31/10), Baños de Fitero ☎ 77 61 00
🛏 212 ⊻ (🅿 ♦ ⅋ ⚭ 🎬 ⚐ ⚲ V $$$. Thermal waters in a peaceful
    setting.
🏨 ★ *Virrey Palafox* (open: 1/5-31/10), Baños de Fitero ☎ 77 62 75 🛏
    60 ⊻ ⅋ 🅿 ♦ ⅋ ⚭ 🎬 V $$$. Thermal waters in a quiet and relaxing
    atmosphere.

Cultural highlights: The **Monasterio de Santa María la Real** is a 12C
Cistercian foundation. Its Gothic church, incorporating some Romanesque
elements, is typically Cistercian in its austerity. The 13C **Chapter House**, 14C
cloister and the monastery's art collection are particularly interesting.

Local sights: Wine lovers should visit **CINTRUENIGO**, where the **best buys**
are young and vintage wines from the *bodegas* or wineries. At *Montpiel*, c/
Ligues, 30, the leather and furs are good value for money.

HARO **La Rioja** ☎ (941), pop. 9,144. Vitoria 43km, Logroño 49km,
Madrid 330km.

This is the capital of the Rioja Alta wine growing district and, as you
would expect, it is a prosperous town with many fine old houses.

▣ **★★ *Iturrimurri***, 1km out of town on the Ctra N-232 ☎ 31 12 13 🛏 24 ✕ ✦ ❋ 🎤 ～ ≪ 🏌 V $$$. Fine views.

🍴 ***Beethoven*** (closed: Monday nights, Tuesdays and 10/12-10/1), c/ Santo Tomás, 3 and 6 ☎ 31 11 81 $$$. Regional Rioja cuisine.

🍴 ***La Kika*** (open: lunch only), c/ Santo Tomás, 9 ☎ 31 14 47. Home cooking.

🍴 ***Terete*** (closed: Mondays, Sunday evenings and October), c/ Lucrecia Arana, 17 ☎ 31 00 23 $$. It has been serving roast meats since 1867.

Best buys: Wine, canned asparagus and peppers from *J. González Muga*, Pl de la Paz, 5, and *La Catedral de los Vinos*, c/ Santo Tomás, 4. Wineskins from *Arnaez*, c/ La Ventilla, 11. Antiques from *D. Contreras*, c/ Vega, 32.

Cultural highlights: The old quarter, especially the Gothic period **mansions** on c/ del Castillo, are interesting. The 16C **Iglesia de Santo Tomás** has a magnificently decorative S front carved by master mason Vigarni and a spacious Gothic interior. The 18C **Town Hall**, the *Casa Consistorial*, is Neo-classical and was designed by Villanueva, architect of a number of Madrid landmarks, including the Prado Art Museum. Many big wine names have their ***bodegas*** in Haro.

Fiestas: On June 25 there is a *romería*, or pilgrimage, involving feasting and dancing, to the nearby shrine of Biblio. A central element in the merrymaking is a **Wine Battle** in which combatants drench each other in wine, so don't wear your Sunday best if you plan to attend.

Local sights: The nearby village of **SAN VICENTE DE LA SONSIERRA** is famed for its dramatic and age-old Holy Week celebrations during which penitents, the *picaos*, publicly flagellate themselves. An altogether less disturbing excursion involves taking the N-232 towards Logroño and stopping at the ◐ Herrera mountain pass: the aptly named **Balcón de la Rioja** (Rioja Balcony) has **good views** of the region.

On the town: There are plenty of excellent *tapa* bars in the town centre.

LOGROÑO **La Rioja** ☎ (941), pop. 118,770, *i* c/ Miguel Villanueva, 10 ☎ 25 54 97, 🛎 c/ Portales, 77, ✉ Pl de San Agustín, s/n ☎ 22 00 66 and 22 89 06, **P** c/ Doctor Castroviejo, 9 ☎ 25 60 60 and 25 62 22, 🚍 c/ Calvo Sotelo, 13 ☎ 25 88 55. Pamplona 92km, Vitoria 93km, Burgos 144km, Madrid 331km.

This city has a prosperous and satisfied air to it. It has always been that way. Situated on the Ebro River, it was a river port in Roman times and later became an important stopping point for the medieval pilgrims heading ◐◐◐ towards Compostela on **The Way of Saint James**. Its Arab occupiers were ousted by the Kingdom of Navarre in 755, but it decoupled from Navarre in 1076 and joined the Kingdom of Castile. It owes its present day fame and prosperity to the juice of the vines that were first planted alongside the River Oja. The wine came to be known as Rioja (an elision of *Río Oja*) and so did the self-administering region, or Autonomous Community, of which Logroño is the capital.

▣ **★★★★ *Carlton Rioja***, Gran Vía del Rey Juan Carlos I, 5 ☎ 24 21 00 🛏 120 🎤 AE, DC, EC, V $$$$.

▣ **★★★★ *Los Bracos Sol***, c/ Bretón de los Herreros, 29 ☎ 22 66 08 🛏 72 🎤 AE, DC, EC, V $$$$.

▣ **★★★ *Gran Hotel***, c/ General Vara del Rey, 5 ☎ 25 21 00 🛏 69 **P** ✦ 🎤 $$.

▣ **★★★ *Murrieta***, c/ Marqués de Murrieta, 1 ☎ 22 41 50 🛏 113 **P** 🎤 $$$.

🍴 ***Asador La Chata*** (closed: Sunday nights and November), c/ Carnicerías, 3 ☎ 25 12 96 $$$. It has been serving roast meat for over 100 years.

¶ *Avenida 21* (closed: Sundays in summer), Av Portugal, 21 ☎ 22 86 02 **AE, DC, V** $$$. Decorated to look like an old wine cellar. Regional dishes.

¶ *Carabanchel* (closed: Mondays, June and September), c/ San Agustín, 2 ☎ 22 38 83 $$$. Very long established.

¶ *El Cachetero* (closed: Wednesday nights, Sundays and 15/7-15/9), c/ Laurel, 3 ☎ 22 84 63 $$. Home cooking in the most popular restaurant in La Rioja.

¶ *La Merced* (closed: Sundays and August), c/ Marqués de San Nicolás, 109 ☎ 22 11 66 ♣ **AE, DC, EC, MC, V** $$$. This stylish restaurant in an **18C palace** has a magnificent wine cellar (amazing variety of Riojas).

¶ *Las Cubanas* (closed: Saturday nights, Sundays and September), c/ San Agustín, 17 ☎ 22 00 50 $$. Simple regional cooking.

¶ *Machado* (closed: Sundays and two weeks in August), c/ Portales, 49, 1º ☎ 24 84 56 ♣ **AE, DC, V** $$$. Elegant.

¶ *Mesón Lorenzo* (closed: Sunday nights, Mondays and July), c/ Marqués de San Nicolás, 136 ☎ 25 81 40 ❋ **AE, DC, MC, V** $$. Regional cooking and a first-rate wine list.

Best buys: Leather wineskins from *F. Barbero*, c/ Sagasta, 8; antiques from *F. Martínez/N. Eguizabal*, Pl Mercado, 24, and *M. Rodríguez*, Rúa Vieja, 17; wines and preserves from *Rioja Selección*, c/ República Argentina, 12, *Palacio del Vino*, Av Burgos, 136, and *Aragón*, Pl San Agustín, s/n; fashion from shops at c/ Doctores Castroviejo, 32, c/ Jorge Vigón, 10, c/ Juan XXIII, 19 and c/ Portales. Espadrilles from *Hijos de G. Gil*, Pl Mercado, 15. Leather and furs are good value for money at *Extrapiel*, c/ Cabo Noval, 6, and Spanish fashion at *Adolfo Domínguez*, c/ Drs. Castroviejo, 3.

Cultural highlights: In the **Cathedral of Santa María de la Redonda**, the twin towers, the chancel end and the façade were built in the 18C but the nave and vaults date from the 15C. Among the chapels inside the cathedral two are especially interesting: the 18C, Rococo **Capilla de Nuestra Señora de los Angeles**, and the **Capilla de los Reyes** which has a Plateresque altarpiece. The choir stalls, the wrought-iron grille and the altarpiece of the **Capilla de Santa María de San Ildefonso** are worth closer examination.

You will come across an unusual pyramid-shaped **windowed turret** built in the 13C in the roof of the **Iglesia de Santa María del Palacio**, a church so called because it used to belong to the palace of King Alfonso VII. Parts of the church date from the 11C and 12C though it was extensively restored in the 16C and 17C. The Gothic cloister is interesting. Another of Logroño's noteworthy churches, the **Iglesia de San Bartolomé** is small and has a beautifully sober 13-14C interior; the Gothic main entrance shows scenes from the life of its patron saint, Bartholomew. In the local museum, the Museo Provincial (Palacio de Espartero, Pl San Agustín, 23. Open: 10.00-2.00 and 4.00-7.00; closed: Mondays) you will find a mixture of art and anthropological exhibits. Logroño also has remains of its ancient **walls**.

Fiestas and festivals: The Rioja Wine Harvest Festival in September is deservedly famous for its general merrymaking and its bullfights (there is also some Pamplona-style bull-running). That month, the city also stages an **International Music Festival** and an **International Theatre Festival** ☎ 24 32 21 and 24 32 22.

Local sights: TORRES DEL RIO (see the 'Estella' entry) is 21km NE. CLAVIJO, 17km S, is the site of a famous Christian victory over the Moors in 844. The scales were tipped for the Christians by the dramatic appearance on the battlefield of Saint James the Apostle, atop a white charger and wielding a sword. Santiago Matamoros, or Saint James the Moor-slayer, became an enduring Christian myth and a battle slogan from then on. There is a castle on the site. Travelling S for 41km on the N-111, you can make a pleasant country excursion to the **Iregua Valley** and the highlands of the **Sierra de Camero**. Well cultivated and fertile land gives way to a narrow canyon formed by red-hued rocks. The mountain villages in the area —such as **VILLANUEVA DE CAMEROS**— still maintain their local popular architecture more or less intact. **Best buys**: handmade textiles from the crafts school run by *Lola Barásoain* in the village of Villoslada de Cameros. **Sports**: hunting in the Coto Villanueva de Cameros reserve.

On the town: *Tapa* bar hopping on c/ Laurel, c/ San Juan and adjacent streets. Night life revolves around c/ Duquesa de la Victoria (*Area 7, Yo Qué Sé, La Taberna del Mere*...) and Gran Vía (*Café Turina* and the discotheque *Robinson*). At Pl Alferez Provisional, 1, *No se lo Digas a Papá* is both a fashionable disco and a good place to have a quiet drink.

NAJERA **La Rioja** ☎ (941), pop. 6,609. Logroño 26km, Madrid 332km.
Reconquered from the Moors by the Christians in 920, this town was for a period the seat of the kings of Navarre. In 1076 it became part of the Kingdom of Castile and one of the key medieval kings, Ferdinand III, The Saint, was crowned here. It was also an important **Way of Saint James** stopping point.

▦ ★★ *San Fernando*, Paseo A. Martín Gamero, 1 ☎ 36 07 00 ⌦ 40 🅿 $$.
🍴 *Los Parrales*, c/ Mayor, s/n. A small bar with a summer terrace overlooking the river. It serves Rioja regional food and excellent aperitifs.
🍴 *Mesón Duque Forte* (closed: Tuesday nights and 20/8-10/9), c/ Paseo, 11 ☎ 36 15 20 🅿 $$$.

Cultural highlights: The **Monasterio de Santa María la Real** (open: 9.30-12.30 and 4.30-7.30) was built on the site of a grotto where an 11C king of Navarre found a statue of the Virgin Mary. Completely restored in the 15C, this monastery is the **royal burial place** of more than 30 kings, queens and princes of the crowns of Castile, Navarre and León. It has a beautiful **cloister** with flamboyant Gothic tracery and a sober Gothic **church** with an interesting gallery. The 12C Romanesque **tomb of Queen Blanca of Navarre** in the crypt is particularly outstanding. Note, too, the flamboyant Gothic **choir stalls**, curiously carved with rather irreverent scenes which have led to suggestions that they were the work of a somewhat lukewarm convert. **Fiestas:** In the second half of July a *son et lumière* based on local history is staged at the monastery.

Local sights: Taking the N-120 towards Logroño, you will pass through **NAVARRETE**, a fine old town that is worth stopping at for closer inspection. It has arcaded streets and houses decorated with heraldic shields (a key battle was fought here in 1367 in which Peter the Cruel defeated Henry of Trastámara, the head of a rival medieval dynasty), and the church has a good Flemish triptych and 16-17C altarpieces. **Best buys**: traditional pottery. Return now to Nájera and take the C-113 S, following the course of the River Najerilla, to the mountainous area of the Sierra de Camero Nuevo, stopping at the village of **ANGUIANO**. Besides being one of the prettiest of the highland villages, Anguiano stages a very curious *fiesta* on July 21-23 and on the last Saturday of September in which men on stilts, wearing old, traditional costumes perform a strange ancestral dance, propelling themselves through the village's extremely steep streets. If you press on for a further 17km to the **Santuario de Nuestra Señora de Valvanera**, a shrine dedicated to the patron saint of La Rioja, you will be rewarded by stunning mountain views; inside the monastery complex, ★★ *Valvanera* ☎ 37 70 44 🕭 provides simple lodging for hunters or for anybody wishing to relax in this setting. **Sports:** Trout fishing in the river Najerilla and hunting in the Coto de Anguiano reserve.

OLITE **Navarre** ☎ (948), pop. 3,010. Pamplona 43km, Zaragoza 140km, Madrid 310km.

The kings of Navarre moved their courts here in the 15C and you can understand why once you have caught sight of its breathtaking castle.

🏛 ★★★ *Parador Príncipe de Viana*, Pl de los Teobaldos, 2 ☎ 74 00 00
  🛏 39 ♣ ⚲ $$$ to $$$$. Magnificently located within the castle. Peaceful atmosphere.

Best buys: *Clarete* wines from *Cosecheros Reunidos*, Ctra Biere, 1.

Cultural highlights: Castles in Spain are two-a-penny, but the **Castle of the Kings of Navarre** (open May-August: 11.00-1.00 and 4.00-7.00; September-April: 11.00-1.00 and 3.00-5.00), with its courtly air, is extremely unusual. It was built by Charles III of Navarre, known as Charles the Noble, in 1406 and it owes its refinement to the French architects who worked on the project. The walls, which are reinforced by 15 towers, once had magnificent hanging gardens and the interior state rooms are richly decorated with stucco, polychrome carvings and glazed tiles. As you pass the main entrance, the sight of the Cistern Tower and the one known as Las Tres Coronas (the Three Crowns) is extremely impressive. The castle's chapel is now the **Church of Santa María la Real**, whose 14C **portal** is a fine example of Navarrese Gothic. The **Church of San Pedro** in the village is Romanesque; it has a pleasant cloister, a fine main door and a Gothic tower built in the late 13C.

Festivals: The **Festival of Navarre** —a varied programme of dance, theatre and concerts— is held in the Castle at weekends during August.

PAMPLONA-IRUÑA **Navarre** ☎ (948), pop. 183,703, *i* c/ Duque de Ahumada, 3 ☎ 22 07 41, ℂ c/ Amaya, 4, ✉ Paseo de Sarasate, 9 ☎ 21 12 26 and 22 72 20, P 25 51 50, ✈ Noaín, 5km from the city centre ☎ 31 72 02 (Aviaco ☎ 31 71 82), 🚂 Rochapea ☎ 11 15 31. San Sebastián 88km, Bilbao 159km, Zaragoza 176km, Madrid 411km.

It is thought that Pamplona is so called because it was founded by the Roman general Pompey who named it *Pompeiopolis* (City of Pompey). Whatever its origins, the indigenous population built up a fine city that was coveted by the Moors, the French and the Castilians. In the 8C the Moors conquered it but they were soon expelled by Charlemagne. The great emperor made the mistake of knocking down Pamplona's walls in the process and the indignant Navarrese in revenge attacked his rearguard at Roncevaux. In the following century, the Count of Navarre, a man called García, crowned himself King of Navarre and installed his court in the city. As Pamplona grew in importance so did its attraction for outsiders. Al-Mansur, the great Moorish military chieftain, briefly reconquered it for Islam in the 10C. More troubles came when a 13C king, Sancho VII, the Strong, died without a direct heir and left his throne to his nephew, the Count of Champagne, who reigned as Thibaud I. The presence of a Frenchman on the throne of Navarre divided the population into supporters of a union with Castile and the backers of the Champagne dynasty. For nearly two centuries there were civil wars on and off until in 1512 the Duke of Alba finally took the city for the **Catholic Monarchs**, Isabella of Castile and Ferdinand of Aragón. That last siege of Pamplona signalled the final reunification of Spain and established the national frontiers that we know today. The battle was also an important event in the life of a young nobleman, Iñigo López de Recalde, who was badly wounded in the assault. Recovering from his wounds, the youth decided to change his dissolute and warlike ways; he is known to history as **Saint Ignatius of Loyola**, the founder of the Jesuit Order.

Pamplona today has a bit of everything. The medieval world of narrow streets lives on around the Cathedral, while other parts of the city, such as the **Pl del Castillo**, have a graceful 19C air to them and still others are extremely modern. Contrasts are everywhere. You have the annual blow out of complete licentiousness in the San Fermín **bull-running** festival and you have in the city's **University**, which is privately run, a quiet seat of learning with high academic standards.

- ★★★★ *Tres Reyes*, Jardines de la Taconera, s/n ☎ 22 66 00 🛏 168 ✦ 🎤 ☁ AE, DC, EC, V $$$$$. Well located.
- ★★★ *Ciudad de Pamplona*, c/ Iturrana, 21 ☎ 26 60 11 🛏 117 **P** 🎤 ▦ $$$ to $$$$. Next to the University.
- ★★★ *Nuevo Hotel Maisonnave*, c/ Nueva, 20 ☎ 22 26 00 🛏 160 **P** ✦ 🎤 AE, DC, MC, V $$$ to $$$$. In the old quarter.
- ★★★ *Orhi*, c/ Leyre, 7 ☎ 22 85 00 🛏 55 **P** AE, DC, V $$$ to $$$$. Next to the bullring.
- ★★★ *Sancho Ramírez*, c/ Sancho Ramírez, 11 ☎ 27 17 12 🛏 82 **P** 🎤 AE, DC, MC, V $$$ to $$$$. In the new part of the city. It has an interesting **restaurant**.
- ★★★ *Yoldi*, Av de San Ignacio, 11 ☎ 22 48 00 🛏 48 🎤 DC, MC, V $$$ to $$$$. Centrally located.

(Accommodation prices increase during the *Sanfermines* festivities.)

- 🍴 *Alhambra* (closed: Sundays), c/ Bergamín, 7 ☎ 24 50 07 ❋ AE, DC, MC $$$$. Excellent food.
- 🍴 *Casa Luis* (closed: Tuesdays and 10/8-25/8), Paseo Calatayud, 11 ☎ 23 36 75 AE, V $$$.
- 🍴 *Don Pablo* (closed: Sunday nights and August), c/ Navas de Tolosa, 19 ☎ 22 52 99 AE, DC, V $$$. A simple and welcoming steakhouse.

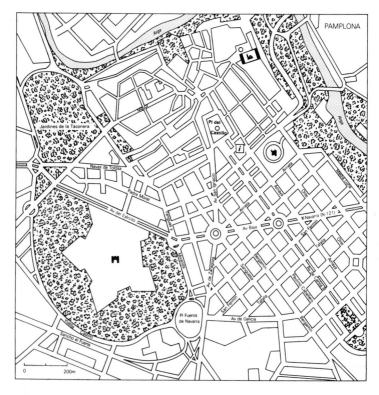

¶¶ *El Mosquito* (closed: Sundays and August), Travesía de San Alberto Magno, 3 ☎ 25 50 26 ❋ **DC, EC, V** $$$. The best fish and seafood in Pamplona.

¶¶ *Europa* (closed: Sundays and 15/7-22/7), c/ Espoz y Mina, 11 ☎ 22 18 00 **AE, DC, EC, V** $$$$. Serves good fish in generous portions.

¶¶ *Hartza* (closed: Mondays, Christmas and 15/7-3/8), c/ Juan de Labrit, 19 ☎ 22 45 68 ❋ **AE, MC, V** $$$. *Haute cuisine*, both traditional and seasonal.

¶¶ *Josetxo* (closed: August and Sundays except in May and June), Pl Príncipe de Viana, 1 ☎ 22 20 97 ❋ **AE, V** $$$. Navarrese cuisine.

¶¶ *Las Pocholas* (closed: Sundays and August), Paseo de Sarasate, 6 ☎ 21 17 29 ❋ **AE, DC, EC, V** $$$$. A Pamplona classic.

¶¶ *Maitena* (closed: Sunday nights and 15/7-24/7), Av Guipúzcoa, km4 ☎ 30 10 50 **AE, DC, MC, V** $$$$. Good fish, especially the *ajoarriero* (cod in garlic sauce).

¶¶ *Rodero* (closed: Sundays and 1/7-31/8), c/ Arrieta, 3 ☎ 24 93 42 ❋ **AE, DC, EC, V** $$$. Basque-Navarrese and French cuisine.

¶¶ *Sarasate* (closed: Sunday nights, Mondays, Holy Week and 10/8-24/8), c/ García Castaños, 12 ☎ 22 51 02 **V** $$$. Modern cuisine.

¶¶ *Shanti* (closed: Sunday and Monday nights, July, and Sundays in August and September), c/ Castillo de Maya, 39 ☎ 23 10 04 **V** $$$. Home cooking.

Best buys: Gourmets should look out for the local spicy *chistorra* sausages (available from *Azagra*, c/ San Juan de la Cadena, 4), the young red wines of Navarre and an excellent local liqueur, not unlike sloe-gin, called *pacharán Las Tres Z*, c/ Comedias 7, has been selling leather wineskins since 1873. Hand-made glassware is sold at *J. del Río*, c/ Eslava 28, and bargain hunters will enjoy the weekend flea markets at the Pl de San Nicolás and the Pl del Cine (not in July and August). Most of the good *boutiques* are in and around Av Carlos III, which has a shopping centre at No. 13 for good measure —another shopping centre is at c/ Tudela, 18. Good Spanish fashion is available from *María Alonso*, c/ Felipe Gorriti, 22bis; *Philippe*, c/ F. Bergamín, 2, and *Saboya*, Av Zaragoza, 7. Furs are a good buy at *Rome*, Pl del Castillo, 38. For antiques, visit *Carlos III*, c/ Mayor, 67; *F. Echaurri*, c/ Navas de Tolosa, 13, and *Migueleiz*, Av Roncesvalles, 11. *Avelina*, Av Roncesvalles, 10, specializes in embroideries. Typical coffee and milk sweets can be bought from *Hijas de Lozano*, c/ Zapatería, 11, and wines and *pacharán* are available from *La Vinoteca*, Av Carlos III, 71.

Cultural highlights: All that remains of the original 12C **Cathedral** are some Romanesque capitals which are in the Museum of Navarre. It was rebuilt entirely in the Gothic style in the 14C and 15C, and in the 18C Ventura Rodríguez, a key architect of the Spanish Enlightenment, added a Neo-classical façade. The ground plan is in the form of the Latin cross, with three naves, and there are several side chapels with altarpieces of different styles (the 15C *Altar de Caparroso* in the ambulatory is probably the best). The **alabaster tomb** of Charles III, the Noble, and his wife, in front of the main altar is a fine Gothic piece created in 1416 by the Frenchman Lomme. The **cloister** is elegantly Gothic; it houses several interesting tombs and its S entrance, the so-called **Puerta de la Sala Preciosa**, is decorated with outstanding 14C carvings. The **Diocesan Museum** (open: 9.30-12.30 and 4.00-7.00; closed: Mondays) is housed in what used to be the original cathedral's refectory and kitchens. The rich collection of exhibits includes a number of Gothic figures (13-16C) and several relics, among them a *Lignum Crucis* (a piece of the True Cross) and a relic of the Holy Sepulchre that was donated to the Cathedral in 1258 by Saint Louis, King Louis IX of France.

You reach the best of the **old city walls** if you walk down c/ Redín. In the old quarter two churches are worth inspecting. The **Iglesia de San Saturnino** has Romanesque towers and 13C Gothic façade and vaults. The Neo-classical Church of San Lorenzo (c/ Mayor) has to be visited because it houses the Chapel of **San Fermín** dedicated to Pamplona's much loved patron saint in whose honour the bull-running *fiesta* is held. The **Ciudadela** fortress (Av del Ejercito, s/n) was built during the 16C reign of Philip II and is now an exhibition and concert hall.

Several of Pamplona's civic buildings are fine examples of different architectural styles and together they underline the city's importance down the ages. The old mint of the Kingdom of Navarre, **Cámara de Comptos Reales** (c/ Ansoleaga 10), is a fabulous 14C Gothic, the Ayuntamiento, or Town Hall, is a harmonious edifice with a fine 18C Baroque façade, and next to the Palacio de la Diputación Foral, seat of the regional government (c/ Carlos III, 2), the Archivo Real y General de Navarra, or central regional archive, is a fine Neo-classical building which houses an extremely rich and valuable collection of medieval manuscripts.

Fiestas and festivals: Pamplona's **bull-running festival**, known as *Sanfermines* after San Fermín, the local patron saint, is extremely well known thanks to Mr Ernest Hemingway among others. Suffice it to say that the festival lasts from July 6-14, that the bulls are let loose at 8.00 am, that there is a bullfight every afternoon and that there is round-the-clock non-stop drinking, eating and dancing every day of the *fiestas*. If you plan to attend the festival remember that tens of thousands from all over the world will also be there and book yourself somewhere quiet and restful for a post-*fiesta* dry-out. The **Festivals of Navarre** are quite different. They are a series of cultural events —music, dance and theatre— held in August and September.

> '*I have this crazy thing. All year long, when I'm working in Paris, I keep thinking of Pamplona. San Fermín. To run, to touch, to feel the horn tips edging closer.'*
>
> '*Is it something mystical?'* I asked.
>
> Matt (Carney) looked at me as if I were out of my mind. '*Christ, you miss the whole flaming point. It's fun! It's joy! … I run the bulls for joy, which is the chief ingredient in generosity. In this way I prove that I have the capacity to give myself whole hog to some activity.'*
>
> '*Do you run to prove your bravery?'* I asked, for in recent years the most courageous acts at Pamplona had been Matt's.
>
> '*To stand in the street before the run begins… to visualize the bulls coming at you… to sense what might happen… yes, that takes courage. But when those rockets go off and the black shapes come tumbling at you… Hell, you've already made your commitment and all it takes now is a sense of joy… to be part of the stampede.'*
>
> James A. Michener   *Iberia*

On the town: Drinking and *tapa* nibbling is an art form in Pamplona, and pub crawling and bar hopping *aficionados* should follow the crowd in the morning as it moves around the old quarter. They shouldn't miss the most famous bar in the city, the *Cafe Iruña* on Pl del Castillo, opened in 1888. Around Pl del Castillo, and especially along c/ San Nicolás and c/ Estafeta, there are over 20 *tascas*. At night the scene moves over to places like the *Casino Eslava* on c/ Nicolás and the bars, discotheques and pubs —**Conocerte Es Amarte, Baby** and **El Molino**— in the San Juan district, on either side of Av Bayona. The disco *By By*, c/ Abejeras, 11, has good music.

Sports: There is a nine-hole, par 71 golf club, the *Club de Golf de Ulzama*, 21km out of town ☎ 31 31 62. Championship level jai-alai or *pelota*, the traditional Basque game, is played at the ***Frontón Euskal-Jai Berri*** ☎ 33 11 59, in Huarte, 6km from Pamplona, on Thursdays, Saturdays, Sundays and public holidays from 4.00 pm onwards. Pamplona also boasts a first division football club.

PUENTE LA REINA **Navarre** ☎ (948), pop. 2,035. Pamplona 24km, Madrid 403km.

This was a key point on the **Way of Saint James** for it was here that the two main pilgrim routes into Spain, the Navarre route over the Roncesvalles pass and the Aragón route over the Somport pass, converged and formed one single way to Compostela. An 11C queen, called Doña Mayor, had a bridge built for the pilgrims over the River Agra and so gave the village its name —Queen Bridge.

★★ ***Mesón del Peregrino***, Ctra N-111, km23 ☎ 34 00 75 ⊨ 15 ♣ ♦ ⚬ ⚒ **EC, MC, V** $$. A rustic, comfortable hotel and **restaurant** that serves good food.

Cultural highlights: The 12C **Iglesia del Crucifijo** is a church which used to be joined on to a pilgrim's hospice. A nave added in the 14C contains a very expressive wooden carving of *Christ*. You reach the excellently preserved **medieval bridge** along the c/ Mayor. The 16C **Iglesia de Santiago** has a fine Romanesque **portico** and several interesting altarpieces.
Local sights: **Eunate**, 5km E, is a Romanesque chapel which is oddly octagonal in shape and could therefore be connected to the Templar Knights. The village of **OBAÑOS** is very medieval in character and in August, its locals perform a medieval mystery play which depicts an obscure incident that occurred on the pilgrim route when a French prince passed by doing penance for having knifed his sister. She came to be known as Saint Felicia and he as Saint Guillén. In **CIRAUQUI**, 6km away, the Church of San Román has a good 13C **portico**.

PYRENEES, THE NAVARRE **Navarre** ☎ (948). Access by Ctra N-240 (Huesca-Pamplona), from which a number of local roads branch off into the mountains. Ctra N-121 (Pamplona-France) passes through the entire **Baztán Valley** (see the 'Baztán' entry).

The area of the Pyrenees which falls within Navarre extends from the Anie peak (2,504m), on the border with France and the Aragonese province of Huesca, to the Basque coast and the province of Guipuzcoa. The western end is typically Basque with its meadows, maize fields and lonely homesteads, while the eastern end is similar to the Huescan Pyrenees, rocky and menacingly barren.

The numerous **valleys** of Navarre's Pyrenees constitute the most striking feature of the area. There are many witch-lore tales associated with them and they were the scene of witch-hunts and trials during the 15C and later. The valleys are isolated even today and they have maintained their ancestral customs and their traditional lifestyle to a remarkable degree. The main ones are the valleys of Roncal, Salazar, Aézcoa, Arce, Irati, Roncesvalles (see the 'Roncesvalles' entry), Ulzama and Baztán (see the 'Baztán' entry).

The **Valle de Roncal** is the easternmost valley and is a good example of the timeless traditions that all the valleys share —every year on July 13, the people of Baretous valley still pay the inhabitants of Roncal the **Tribute of the Three Cows**, following a judgment dating from 1375. **Best buys** include the extremely good **cheeses** made here called Roncal. Snow sports lovers take note that there is a small ski station at Isaba —accommodation is available at ★★ *Isaba* (closed: 4/11-4/12), Ctra Pamplona, s/n ☎ 89 30 00 ⇌ 50 ✕ ⅏ ⚭ ≪ V $$ to $$$.

The **Valle de Salazar** boasts a very fine 12C shrine, the sanctuary of the Virgin of Musquilda, in the village of **OCHAGAVIA**. In September, religious celebrations are held here that include a strange and ancient dance in front of the statue of the Virgin in which the eight dancers are led by a masked 'fool'. The **Valle de Irati** is particularly beautiful for it has one of Europe's largest **beech woods** and the **Valle de Arce** has a lovely 12C church that is perfectly Romanesque.

Best buys: *Kaikus*, the typical wooden bowls for cheese and *cuajada*.

RONCESVALLES **Navarre** ☎ (948), pop. 31.

This is certainly one of the most beautiful mountain passes and valleys in the Pyrenees, deeply steeped in legend and history. It was here that Roland blew his horn in a desperate attempt to call the Emperor Charlemagne to his aid when the rearguard of the Christian troops were being slaughtered by Saracen and Vascon attacks. Roland's plight and Charlemagne's defeat at Roncesvalles, or Roncevaux, in 778 had the medieval world in awe as troubadours recounted the story in great epic poems such as the *Chanson de Roland*. About that time, in the 12C, the pass and the valley into Spain along the Urobi river became one of the great highways of the Middle Ages. For literally tens of thousands of pilgrims, this was part of the **Way of Saint James** to Santiago de Compostela. If you have a minimum of historical imagination you can recreate here in your mind's eye this human tidal wave of an earlier age of faith surging along the rocky mountain paths, each pilgrim with his staff, cockleshell and gourd.

A monastery was built here in the 12C to help the pilgrims on their way by providing material shelter and spiritual succour and the pilgrims returned the favours by endowing the abbey with precious relics. The **Colegiata Real**, as the monastery's church is known, built in the French Gothic style was consecrated in 1219. The Virgin of Roncesvalles, found, according to legend, by local shepherds in the 9C, stands on the high altar and is a much revered image. The monastery's founder, Sancho VII, the Strong, who reigned in Navarre from 1154-1234, is buried in the church's **Chapter House**. There is a **museum** here which exhibits a rich collection of carvings, ornaments, religious paintings and precious stones.

▥ ★★ *La Posada*, set in the old medieval inn inside the monastery's walls ☎ 76 02 25 ⇌ 11 ✕ ⅏ EC, V $$.

▥ ★ *Casa Sabina*, Ctra N-111 ☎ 76 00 12 ⇌ 6 ✕ $. Its restaurant serves good, fresh trout.

SAN MILLAN DE LA COGOLLA **La Rioja** ☎ (941).

This is the spiritual heart of La Rioja and one of the most beautiful spots in the whole region. But it also has an honoured place in Spanish culture for it was here that the language as it is now spoken was first written down. As such it is known as the 'Cradle of Castilian'.

The place was already famous in the 6C when a venerable hermit, **San Millán**, gathered about him a small community of faithful followers. In the 10C a Mozarabic monastery was built on the mountain and it came to be known as the Monasterio de Suso (Upper Monastery). The following century, the monks came down the mountain and built the Monasterio de Yuso (Lower Monastery) in the valley. Here, the *Glosas Emilianenses*, written commentaries on Latin religious texts constituting the first known examples of written Castilian Spanish, were later found, presumably the work of the monks of this monastery. In the 13C, a priest called **Gonzalo de Berceo** was to write here the Spanish language's first sophisticated poetry. The monastery was rebuilt in the 18C but abandoned in the 19C when church lands were expropriated. Now restored, it is occupied by Benedictine monks.

¶ *San Lorenzo*, Ctra San Millán **☎** 37 30 08 $$. Castilian cooking.

Cultural highlights: The **Monasterio de Suso** (open: 10.00-2.00 and 4.00-7.00; closed: Mondays) was partly excavated from the rock and built in the Mozarabic style of the 11C with two naves separated by horseshoe arches. Its cave-like interior contains the **tomb of San Millán**, and in the atrium are the **tombs of the Siete Infantes de Lara**, seven murdered young noblemen who were the subject of a medieval epic poem. Among the rocks is the **cemetery** of the members of the ancient community and a cave where Saint Oria barricaded herself for life in what was an extraordinary gesture even for that age of mystical hermits.

The **Monasterio de Yuso** (guided visits: 10.30-12.30 and 4.00-6.00; summer 4.00-7.00; closed: Mondays) was built in the 11C by the kings of Navarre, García IV and Sancho IV, who had the remains of Saint Millán transferred to it from their resting place up the hill. It was rebuilt in grandiose style in the 16C and 17C and what we have today is an extremely beautiful Gothic **cloister**, a Renaissance **church** with fine porticoes in the style made famous by Herrera, and rich Baroque altarpieces. The Baroque sacristy houses some good paintings. There are more paintings, and also church ornaments, in the museum in the upper part of the monastery but the most interesting exhibits are a collection of 11C **ivory bas-reliefs** that used to serve as plaques covering the reliquary urns of Saint Felices and Saint Millán. The museum also contains a copy of the *Glosas Emilianenses* (see above) and a number of medieval codices and illustrated manuscripts.

SANGÜESA Navarre **☎** (948), pop. 4,528, [*i*] c/ Mercado, 2 **☎** 87 03 29. Pamplona 46km, Huesca 128km, Zaragoza 140km, Madrid 408km.

This village is a favourite among students of **Romanesque** art and architecture for it contains more than 30 buildings dating from this pre-Gothic period. However, Sangüesa's origins as a settlement stretch much further back in time, for prehistoric and Roman remains have been found in the area. In the early Middle Ages, **Rocaforte** hill was a natural refuge against Moorish incursions and was a lookout post for the surrounding region. The village came into its own with the **Way of Saint James** pilgrim route to Compostela: grand mansions, hospices and **shrines** were built to accommodate the great medieval tourist trade moving towards NW Spain. In this way Sangüesa became a sort of museum of the Romanesque art form.

Cultural highlights: The **Iglesia de Santa María la Real** is a triple-apsed church known as *la Real* because it received royal patronage. Built in the 12-13C, it is an oustanding example of Romanesque architecture. The **S façade** has wonderful examples of Romanesque sculpture —note particularly the representation of the Last Judgement in the **tympanum**. The **Iglesia de Santiago** (13C), dedicated to the Apostle James, the object of the whole pilgrimage, and the church of **San Salvador** with its Gothic nave are no less impressive. The importance that Sangüesa acquired as a halt on the pilgrim route can be gauged by the numerous small **shrines**, or *ermitas*, in the village such as San Pedro de Añués, San Miguel de Rocaforte (Gothic), San Adrián en la Magdalena (12C Romanesque), and San Babil, which is associated with a number of miracles. Its civic buildings are also interesting. The **Rúa Mayor**, the village high street along which the pilgrims tramped, is flanked by old brick houses with wooden galleries. Among the more important buildings, the present day **Town Hall** was once the palace of the local feudal Viana family, and the **Palacio de Vallesantoro** was built much later in the Baroque period.

Local sights: 7km to the E, the **Castillo de Javier** is hallowed ground for the Jesuits for it was the birthplace of **Saint Francis Xavier**, who helped Saint Ignatius of Loyola found the order and then went on to evangelize the Far East. The castle was in fact destroyed in the 16C and rebuilt from scratch in the present century (guided visits: 9.00-1.00 and 4.00-7.00, with *son et lumière* on Saturdays, Sundays and public holidays from June to September).

NE of Sangüesa lies the very fine and well maintained old monastery of **San Salvador de Leyre** in the foothills of the Sierra de Leyre mountain range. In the 11C it was a very important institution: its monks had jurisdiction over some 60 villages and it was a burial place for the kings of Navarre. Its importance later declined, and in the 13C it was taken over by the contemplative Cistercian order. Nowadays it is run by Benedictine monks.

Architecturally, the most interesting part of the monastery is its 11C **crypt** which has high vaults supported by wide, roughly-hewn capitals with geometric designs that stand on stumpy columns of uneven height. The orginal Romanesque **church** was updated by the Cistercians, who roofed it with Gothic vaults. The so-called **Porta Speciosa**, the 12C W door, is richly sculptured and is a good illustration of narrative carvings of figures and symbols that were as instantly understandable to a largely illiterate medieval audience as a newspaper is to us today. A charming legend associated with Leyre concerns an abbot who fell into an ecstasy listening to birdsong and returned to the monastery 300 years later. If you don't manage to hear a blackbird in full song here, you will nevertheless be moved to near ecstasy by the magnificent **views** from the road approaching the monastery over the Yesa reservoir and the mountains looming to the north. The ★★ *Hospedería de Leyre* (closed: 15/1-1/3), in the monastery ☎ 88 41 00 ⇌ 29 ✦ ✗ ⚓ **AE, DC, MC, V** $$, is a splendid place to rest in this lovely setting; its restaurant serves rather good food $$.

The Leyre mountains provide **spectacular scenery** and good walking country. Near the village of **LUMBIER**, the Irati river has carved a dramatic **gorge**, and there is another magnificent mini-canyon, the **Hoz de Arbayun**, which you can reach on foot by following the fast-flowing river Salazar upstream.

SANTO DOMINGO DE LA CALZADA La Rioja ☎ (941), pop. 5,737. Burgos 67km, Logroño 47km, Vitoria 65km, Madrid 310km.

This town was founded expressly for the Compostela pilgrims in 1044 by the energetic **Saint Domingo** who built a properly paved road, a bridge, an inn, and a hospital for them. It was here that one of the most important miracles of the **Way of Saint James** occurred. The story, circulated throughout medieval Europe, concerned a young pilgrim who, unjustly accused of robbery by the local innkeeper's daughter whose advances he had chastely resisted, was hanged just outside the town. When the lad's parents discovered that he was still miraculously alive on the gibbet they rushed to inform the judge who, since he happened to be about to start his dinner, declared that the young man was as dead as the chickens he was about to eat. What had medievaldom agog was that the roast fowls instantly flew up into the air, very much alive. Since that time, in what must be one of the most unusual ecclesiastical ornaments of the Catholic Church, a live cock and a hen have been kept in a coop set into a wall inside the cathedral.

▦ ★★★ *Parador Santo Domingo de la Calzada*, Pl del Santo, 3 ☎ 34 03 00 ⇌ 27 **AE, DC, EC, V** $$$$. A medieval pilgrim hospital now turned into an hotel with all the latest in comfort.

🍴 *El Rincón de Emilio* (closed: February and Tuesday nights from October to March), Pl Bonifacio Gil, 7 ☎ 34 09 90 🅿 ✦ $$.

🍴 *Mesón El Peregrino* (closed: 22/12-7/1) c/ Zumalacárregui, 18 ☎ 34 02 02 🅿 ✦ MC, V $$. Simple regional cuisine.

Cultural highlights: The **Cathedral** mixes the primitive Romanesque style of the apse and ambulatory chapels with the Gothic of the 16C main body of the building and the Baroque of the elegant tower that was added in the 18C. In the right wing of the transept is the 12C **tomb of Santo Domingo**, opposite the Gothic **coop** where the cock and hen are kept behind artistic wrought iron railings. The **high altarpiece** was the last work sculpted by the talented Damian Forment before he died in 1538, and is just a step away from the Baroque exuberance that was to take the artistic world by storm. The 15C **altarpiece** in the Chapel of Saint John the Baptist is particularly rich. Other places of interest include the town's recently restored 14C **walls**, the porticoed Pl del Ayuntamiento in front of the Town Hall, the convents of **San Francisco** and **Las Bernadas**, and the several mansions that have heraldic shields on their façades.

Fiestas: May 12 is the day of Santo Domingo and is the excuse for several days of general merrymaking. These are authentically popular fun *fiestas*.

Local sights: The village of **EZCARAY**, 14km S, has very old spinning looms (c/ González Gallarza, 4) and fine old stone houses —★ *Echaurren*, c/ General Mola, 2 ☎ 35 40 47 ⇌ 29 ⅄ 🅿 ✦ AE, DC, MC, V $, is an old inn that serves traditional Rioja cuisine. **Sports:** in winter, skiing at **Valdezcaray**, 1,550-1,857m, with 11 ski-lifts ☎ 35 42 91/2; in summer, hunting (deer and wild boar) and fishing.

On the town: *Tapa* tasting in the *Mumm* tavern, c/ Madrid, 5. Coffee and late night drinks in *Equus*, c/ Beato Hermosilla, 30.

TAFALLA **Navarre** ☎ (948), pop. 10,172. Pamplona 38km, Logroño 86km, Zaragoza 135km, Madrid 365km.

A solid market town on the edge of the fertile Ribera region of Navarre protected by a medieval castle, Tafalla has for centuries been a trading centre for the area's grain, horticultural produce and wines.

🏨 ★★ *Hostal Tafalla* (closed: Fridays and Christmas) Ctra N-121, km38 ☎ 70 03 00 ⇌ 28 AE, DC, MC, V $$. This hotel has comfortable rooms and a rather good restaurant.

🍴 *Tubal* (closed: Mondays and 21/8-9/9), Pl de Navarra, 2 ☎ 70 08 52 AE, DC, V $$$. Regional cuisine.

Cultural highlights: The **Iglesia de Santa María**, in the very heart of the town's old neighbourhood, has an interesting 16C **altarpiece**. Note, too, the 16C stone cross in the church's square and the Convento de la Concepción, c/ Recoletos, 15, which has a good 16C Flemish altarpiece.

Local sights: The fortified village of **ARTAJONA**, 11km NW, was a base for the Templar Knights in the 12C. The **walls**, with 12 watchtowers, are impressive as are the Gothic **Iglesia de San Saturnino** and several sturdy yellow sandstone houses with family shields and crests on their façades, once occupied by local nobles.

The medieval village of **UJUE**, 19km E on the Ctra C-132, perched on a peak in the Ujué mountain range, has fine views of the Pyrenees to the N and of the Ribera region to the S. Its church, the **Iglesia de Santa María**, combines the 11C Romanesque of the original building with 14C Gothic.

Fiestas: On the evening of April 30 there is a well-attended religious celebration —the **Pilgrimage of the Twelve Apostles to the Virgin of Ujué**— in which locals dressed in black tunics, lantern in hand, walk the 17km from Ujué to Tafalla.

The Cistercian **Monasterio de la Oliva** was one of the first monasteries built by this contemplative order in Spain and is worth a detour. You reach it by taking the Ctra N-121 (or the A-15 motorway) to Caparroso, and then branching off onto the C-124 for Carcastillo and the monastery. The **church** was built in the 12C in accordance with the sober and pure lines of this strict religious order. The extremely beautiful Gothic **cloister** was added in the 15C although some of its capitals date from the earlier Romanesque period.

TUDELA **Navarre** ☎ (948), pop. 25,576, *i* Pl de los Fueros, s/n ☎ 82 15 39. Zaragoza 81km, Pamplona 84km, Madrid 316km.

Tudela is a town noted for its good local wines, **vegetables** and fruit. This is only to be expected for it lies alongside the Ebro river and is the chief centre of the fertile Ribera area of Navarre. Just as the local produce is varied and of an outstanding quality so was Tudela a racial and ethnic mix of a town, and some fine buildings showing different cultural influences survive to this day. Founded by the Moors, Tudela was conquered by the Christians in 1114 but it remained for a time an open and tolerant town. There was a large Morisco, or converted Muslim, population and the traces of its Mudéjar architecture are still evident. There was also a significant Jewish population, one of whose members, **Benjamín de Tudela**, was a noted 12C rabbi and geographer who travelled extensively in the Near and Middle East and visited more than 300 places.

🏨 ★★★ *Hostal de Tudela*, Av de Zaragoza, 56 ☎ 82 05 58 ⇌ 16 🅿 ♦ DC, MC, V $$.

🏨 ★★★ *Morase*, Paseo de Invierno, 2 ☎ 82 17 00 ⇌ 7 ♦ $$$ to $$$$. It has a good **restaurant** serving local regional cuisine on the first floor.

🍴 *Beethoven* (closed: Sunday nights, Mondays and 1/8-15/8), Ctra N-232, km3, Enfotellas ☎ 82 52 60 🅿 ✻ AE, DC, EC, V $$$. Fresh fish and vegetables.

🍴 *El Choko* (closed: Mondays and 1/10-15/10), Pl de los Fueros, 5 ☎ 82 28 19 ✻ MC, V $$$. Serves dishes featuring fresh local vegetables.

Cultural highlights: The **Cathedral** (open: 9.00-1.00 and 4.30-8.00) was built in the 12-13C over the remains of an old mosque in the austere Cistercian style of the transitional period between the Romanesque and Gothic. The splendid **portico** represents the Last Judgement and spares no details in its realistic depiction of the horrors of hell. Inside, you will find that the building starts off in the Romanesque manner and develops into the style of the later period with the characteristic Gothic vaults. The **high altarpiece**, completed in 1493, and the 16C choir stalls are both very good and the **Nuestra Señora de la Esperanza** side chapel contains two 15C masterpieces, a tomb with fine 15C Gothic sculptures and a first-class altarpiece that likewise dates from the 15C. In the small, intimate 12C **cloister** the capitals are expertly carved with biblical scenes. As you walk around it you will come across a doorway that has been preserved from the original mosque.

The 12C **Iglesia de San Nicolás** in the town's old quarter was restored in the 18C but the delicate Romanesque ornamentation of its tympanum remained untouched. In c/ Sainz, several houses are decorated with old family shields.

Fiestas: Easter Sunday is celebrated in great style in Tudela with the *Bajadica del Angel*, an act that simulates the descent of an angel, country dancing and street parties. Not to be outdone by Pamplona, the town celebrates its bull-running saga of thrills and spills, along with processions of 'giants', starting on **Saint Anne's** day, July 26, a fortnight after the end of the Pamplona *fiesta*.

Alphabetical
Index